the apocryphal shakespeare

Being a collection of fourteen plays which have been ascribed to Shakespeare

EDITED, WITH INTRODUCTION, NOTES, AND BIBLIOGRAPHY

BY

C.F. TUCKER BROOKE

the apocryphile press
BERKELEY, CA
www.apocryphile.org

apocryphile press
BERKELEY, CA

Apocryphile Press
1700 Shattuck Ave #81
Berkeley, CA 94709
www.apocryphile.org

First published in 1908 as *The Shakespeare Apocrypha* by the Clarendon Press, Oxford, UK. Apocryphile Press Edition, 2004.

Reprinted by permission of Oxford University Press, London.
For sale in the USA only. Sales prohibited in the UK.
Printed in the United States of America
ISBN 0-9747623-2-6

PREFACE

THIS volume is designed to satisfy a need which during the past two generations has been variously and often expressed. The ambition of the editor has been to provide an accurate and complete text, with adequate critical and supplementary matter, of all those plays which can, without entire absurdity, be included in the 'doubtfully Shakespearian' class. A similar work —to comprise the first thirteen dramas in this book, in addition to *The Arraignment of Paris*, *The Death of Stucley*, and *The Siege of Antwerp*—appears, indeed, on the list of suggested publications of the New Shakspere Society (*Transactions*, 1874, p. 4), but it did not get beyond the stage of projection.

Since the days of Malone, only three of the works before us—*Arden of Feversham*, *The Two Noble Kinsmen*, and *Sir Thomas More*—have appeared in English-speaking countries in what can at all justly be termed independently edited texts. Tolerable versions of four others have been published by Germans in editions now practically unprocurable. As regards the other seven plays, no real attempt at purification of the text or collation of the early editions has been made, if made at all, for more than two centuries, and in the case of *Sir John Oldcastle*, it has remained for this book to give the very first reprint of what is most unmistakably the only reliable and uncorrupted version. Thus considerable and important passages appear here for the first time since 1600.

In the preparation of the body of the text, the main object has been to give a faithful reproduction of the most authoritative edition of each play; that is, of the earliest, except in the rare instances where a later edition is demonstrably truer to the author's manuscript. Supplementary passages are printed, within brackets, from the earliest edition which contains them. Where a variant or an emendation has appeared inevitable, it has been adopted, but the reading of the *editio princeps* has invariably been given in the footnotes. Great pains have been taken—it is hoped with a fair measure of success—to register in the footnotes all variants in accessible sixteenth and seventeenth-century editions which are not purely orthographic, and all such later emendations and conjectures as possess any degree of usefulness or probability.

Silent alteration of the original has been tolerated only in such purely mechanical matters as the abandonment of the long 's'; the correction of obviously unintentional mis-spacing; the rectifying of the most transparent typographical errors, such as *Flaundsrs* for *Flaunders* (*Edward III*, I. i. 151) and *thinekst* for *thinkest* (Ibid. II. i. 98); and the introduction of modern punctuation where the sense would otherwise be unintelligible to the ordinary reader. The old punctuation is, however, retained where possible, and all misprints which can conceivably have interest or significance are recorded in the footnotes. The numeration of lines is, of course, new, and it should be noted that the parts of divided metrical lines are often separately numbered for convenience of reference and in order to preserve the appearance of the original page.

It is believed that the text will be found as free from inaccuracy as a reprint can well be made. Except for the few additional passages from the third quarto of *Mucedorus*, personally copied by the editor, transcription has in no case been trusted. The texts of the six plays contained in the third Shakespeare folio and that of the first edition of *Mucedorus* have been based on photographic facsimiles of the original quartos; the other plays are printed from the best modern old-spelling editions very carefully corrected by the originals. The collation of the early editions has been done twice to ensure accuracy, and the proof sheets revised by the original quartos. Particular care has been taken to verify readings which are in opposition to those recorded by other modern editors.

The general notes are to be considered in connexion with the footnotes. They have been kept within modest compass, and their *raison d'être*—the explanation or defence of the readings of the text—has perhaps not often been lost sight of. If more general comments have here and there intruded themselves, it is trusted that they will be found always to serve some more legitimate purpose than the mere display of 'all such reading as was never read'.

Like so many students of Elizabethan literature, I have to acknowledge a large debt of gratitude to Mr. P. A. Daniel. My obligations to him for textual comments and conjectures, particularly relating to *The Merry Devil of Edmonton* and *The Two Noble Kinsmen*, will, I hope, be sufficiently evident from the notes to those plays; but for a great deal of other trouble willingly undertaken on my behalf I have only this opportunity of rendering my sincere thanks. I am equally indebted to Dr. Furnivall for unfailing interest and sympathy as well as for a number of valuable suggestions for my Introduction; and I gladly take this occasion of expressing also my recognition of Dr. W. Aldis Wright's courtesy to me while reading in the Library of Trinity College, Cambridge, and since.

Finally, it is with especial pleasure that I acknowledge my many obligations to Professor Raleigh, to whom are due both the original inspiration for this book and continued helpful encouragement during its preparation. It is my sincere hope that the volume may be regarded as a testimony and a small tribute to the force of his influence and example.

C. F. T. B

January, 1908.

CONTENTS

INTRODUCTION

The *Shakespeare Apocrypha* are indisputably the work of many hands, varying to the extreme of possibility in strength, in skill, and in manner. Not even the amateur Tieck, insatiable in his quest of literary curios, has had the bardihood to ascribe the entire number to the greatest of the Elizabethans. Yet unequal as they are in literary merit, these plays diverge still more, if possible, in subject-matter, style, and general tone. Between certain individuals of the group, indeed, a few similarities may be noted and a few comparisons drawn; but to attempt to treat the collection comprehensively and as a generic whole would be like undertaking a family history of Falstaff's motley company. The pseudo-Shakespearian plays are waifs and strays of the Elizabethan drama, brought together adventitiously from here, there, and everywhere, and with no common bond but that mighty name, beneath whose broad influence they all seek shelter.

Disconcerting though it is to the commentator, this infinite variety yet lends a special zest to the consideration of the pseudo-Shakespearian cycle. The plays are almost without exception interesting, but for very different reasons. Two of them, *Arden of Feversham* and *The Two Noble Kinsmen*, and probably they alone, can rest their case boldly on their character as artistic wholes and claim a position, when judged thus in their entirety, in the very first rank of the extra-Shakespearian drama. Three others—*Edward III*, *A Yorkshire Tragedy*, and *Sir Thomas More*—failing either in dignity or in unity of outline, rise in parts to an equal height of poetry, a height where the question becomes less whether they are good enough for Shakespeare than whether they are like him.

The remaining members of the group belong distinctly to a lower order, that is, except on the theory of apprentice work or the hastiest of retouching, modern criticism can hardly admit their claim of Shakespearian origin to be even plausible. Yet there is scarcely any other dramatist of the period, save Marlowe and Ben Jonson, whose reputation would suffer by the fathering of plays like *The London Prodigal*, *The Merry Devil of Edmonton*, or *The Puritan*.

As there is no difficulty in selecting the five best pseudo-Shakespearian dramas, so there need be little hesitation in pointing out the worst. Literary and dramaturgical considerations would pretty certainly assign the position of discredit to *Fair Em* and *Mucedorus*, productions that bear the mark of vagabondage on every feature. Yet, for the reader of to-day, these plays, distinctly the weaklings of the flock, possess an attractiveness of their own by very virtue of their dull impersonality, because they display so little of the individual author and so much of the vulgar dramatic taste. Such literary phenomena evolve themselves, they are not created; the writer does no more than drift down the current of theatrical convention, and is doubtless as undiscoverable—certainly as little worth discovering—as the author of a political election song or a low melodrama of a generation ago.

There is a curious dramatic irony in the fact that *Mucedorus* and *Fair Em* have been attributed by serious and respectable critics to the pen of Shakespeare. Composed in utter disregard of probability and reason, with little poetry and less psychology—with no particular merit, indeed, but the freshness that comes of complete unintelligent conventionality—these performances made their appeal frankly to the groundlings. In the case of *Mucedorus*, at least, we know that the appeal was enormously successful. This absurd play, with the merits and defects of a nursery tale, was acted by strolling companies everywhere till long after the Commonwealth, and passed through seventeen editions between 1598 and 1700 a record unequalled in the history of the pre-Restoration drama. The only play of the pseudo-Shakespearian class, which can at all compare with *Mucedorus* in popularity with the early book-publishers, is a considerably better comedy of similar kind, *The Merry Devil of Edmonton.* Six quarto editions of the latter are recorded between 1608 and 1655. It may be added, as a commentary on Shakespeare knowledge after the Restoration, that *Mucedorus, Fair Em,* and *The Merry Devil of Edmonton,* were bound together into a volume for the library of King Charles II with the label, ' Shakespeare. Vol. I.'

The *Shakespeare Apocrypha* have been accumulating during three centuries. Each generation has attributed to the poet, in good faith or in fraud, tentatively or with conviction, the authorship of plays with which his name had not previously been connected. At the same time, certain plays once ascribed to Shakespeare have gradually disappeared from the list, as the actual authors have been discovered or the absurdity of the ascription has made itself generally felt. In the present state of the case, the preparation of an adequate and practical catalogue of pseudo-Shakespearian plays is a matter of some difficulty. The epithet ' pseudo-Shakespearian ' no longer carries with it any presumption as to Shakespeare's authorship. Certain plays, a baker's dozen in all, have acquired a prescriptive right to the title, and must be mentioned in every list ; twenty or thirty others have at various times been proposed, with greater or less diffidence, but are still far from having established their position in the category. In regard to these last, each writer on the subject must decide for himself which may be admitted into the ' doubtfully Shakespearian ' class without offence to the rules of critical seemliness. The catalogue of a seventeenth-century bookseller, for instance, gives to Shakespeare three histories : *Edward II*, *Edward III*, and *Edward IV*. The second of these is universally regarded as one of the doubtful plays, but to admit into the group either of the others, known to be by Marlowe and Heywood respectively, would show an absurdly uncritical deference to the blunder or deceit of the bookseller, the only mortal who has ever hinted at the connexion.

The long critical history of the *Shakespeare Apocrypha* divides itself into three pretty well defined epochs. The first, which lasted from the close of the sixteenth century till well into the eighteenth, was the age of purely unliterary attribution. Plays were stated on title-pages, on the Stationers' Registers, or in book-lists to be by William Shakespeare, and there, for a time, the matter ended. No evidence, internal or external, was adduced in support of the attribution, and in few cases or none could the attributors by any stretch of the imagination be called literary critics. Such ascriptions are either the most authoritative of all, or they are utterly valueless; they may rest on personal knowledge or general contemporary report; they may, on the other hand, be no more than the fabrication of an ignorant or fraudulent bookseller. It requires a considerable amount of boldness to deny the *possibility* of Shakespeare's concern in *The Two Noble Kinsmen*, in the face of the title-page of the first edition,[1] which declares it to be 'written by the memorable Worthies of their time; Mr. John Fletcher, and Mr. William Shakespeare, Gentlemen'; and the evidence of the Stationers' Registers [2] and first edition [2] of *A Yorkshire Tragedy* in favour of Shakespeare's authorship of that play is perhaps even stronger, because dating from the poet's lifetime. Yet an edition of *Sir John Oldcastle* in 1600 likewise bears the words, 'Written by William Shakespeare,' and this boast, absurd on the face of it, is proved mendacious beyond the shadow of a doubt, by the record in Henslowe's Diary of the actual authors: Munday, Drayton, Wilson, and Hathway. To sum up, we have in the seventeenth century practically no evidence to indicate that Shakespeare's dramatic activities extended beyond the list of canonical plays, save that of printers, publishers, and stationers. This evidence is worthy of serious consideration in case, and only in case, there is no *prima facie* cause to believe the witnesses grossly ignorant of the matter, or dishonestly intent on palming off their spurious wares as the works of Shakespeare.

The generation of Capell, Steevens, and Malone, ushered in the second epoch in the criticism of the doubtful plays. They and their followers took a purely literary point of view, judging the dramas on catholic lines and, in general, with accuracy and fairness, though they suffered from inadequate comprehension of the peculiarly distinguishing features of Shakespeare's art and placed a mischievous amount of confidence in such vanities as parallel passages and identical archaisms. This tendency of criticism—to which the apocryphal plays owe as much perhaps, after all, as to any that has so far succeeded it—vanished in a burst of midsummer madness with the wild attributions of Tieck and his romantic satellites.

For these last, Germans all, and incapable of appreciating the delicacies of English style, Shakespeare appears to have meant rather a poetic principle than a poet. Dazed by the newly discovered and ill-understood brilliance of the Shakespearian drama, they tended to appropriate to the individual poet qualities of freshness and freedom which, in truth, were the common property of the age. To this misconception and to the desire, so characteristic of later German

[1] 1634. [2] Both in 1608.

criticism, to outstrip Shakespeare's countrymen in magnifying his name, is due without doubt Tieck's championship of the genuineness of plays like *Mucedorus* and *George a Greene.*

Many of the utterances of Tieck and Schlegel concerning the doubtful plays form a crushing though unconscious parody of the general impressionist method inaugurated by Capell and Malone. The generation that followed Tieck saw the rise in England of the third tendency in the criticism of the *Shakespeare Apocrypha.* Here, as elsewhere, the trend of the time was towards more exact knowledge, towards the careful consideration and classification of minutiae; for the first time an attempt was made, and with a good measure of success, to establish definite criteria for style and spirit, whereby the work of one dramatist might be distinguished from that of another. The most tangible, but surely not the sole result of this effort is the development of the 'metrical tests'. The new system, however, is at least as liable to abuse as that which it superseded; at its best, exact knowledge of metrical and dramatic details shows itself chastened and directed by broad literary appreciation, as in Professor Spalding's essay on the authorship of *The Two Noble Kinsmen;* at its worst, as in some of Mr. Fleay's radical pronunciamentoes, the ultimately all-important considerations of tone and spirit are either slighted or forced into unwilling compliance with the results of statistical tabulation.

The following is a list, as complete as seems practicable, of the uncanonical plays which have been ascribed to Shakespeare—arranged roughly according to the date of attribution:—

1. *The First Part of Sir John Oldcastle,* 1600. In this year appeared two editions, one anonymous, the other bearing the words: 'Written by William Shakespeare.'

2. *The London Prodigal,* 1605.

3. *A Yorkshire Tragedy,* 1608.

4, 5. *The Troublesome Reign of King John,* in two parts. The title-page of the edition of 1611 says: 'Written by W. Sh.' The earlier edition of 1591 was anonymous. There can be little doubt that the public was meant to interpret 'W. Sh.' as 'William Shakespeare', and these words indeed appeared in full on the title-page of the third edition (1622).

6, 7. *The First Part of the Contention betwixt the Two Famous Houses of Yorke and Lancaster* and *The True Tragedy of Richard, Duke of Yorke.* These old plays were reprinted in 1619 for T. P⟨avier⟩, the title-page asserting them to be 'written by William Shakespeare, Gent.'

8. *The Taming of a Shrew.* Ascribed to Shakespeare in Smetwick's reprint, 1631. The first edition [1] is anonymous.

9. *The Two Noble Kinsmen.* Attributed to Fletcher and Shakespeare on title-page of the first edition, 1634.

10. *The Merry Devil of Edmonton.* Entered by H. Moseley in 1653 as by Shakespeare. All the early editions are anonymous.

11, 12. *Henry I* and *Henry II,* 'by Wm. Shakespeare and Robert Davenport,' so entered Sept. 9, 1653.

13. *The History of Cardenio,* 'A Play by Mr. Fletcher and Shakespeare;'

[1] 1594.

entered Sept. 9, 1653. It has been suggested that this play is identical with *Double Falsehood* (No. 25).

14. *The Second Maiden's Tragedy.* Entered Sept. 9, 1653, but read in MS. and approved by Sir George Buc as early as Oct. 31, 1611; printed 1824.[1] This is one of the three survivors of Warburton's famous collection of fifty-three manuscript plays, the rest of which were sacrificed by his cook to make pie-covers; in this way perished the only known copies of Nos. 11, 12, 13, 15, 16, 17, which were likewise in Warburton's possession. *The Second Maiden's Tragedy* was labelled by Warburton 'A Play by William Shakespeare', but has been attributed also to Th. Goff and to Chapman.

15, 16, 17. *The History of King Stephen; Duke Humphrey, a Tragedy; Iphis and Ianthe, or a Marriage without a Man.* All these were entered on June 29, 1660, under Shakespeare's name. No. 16 may be a version of *Henry VI, Part* 2.

18. *The Arraignment of Paris,*[2] by Peele; ascribed to Shakespeare in the catalogues of the booksellers Kirkman, Winstanley, and others, 1656–70.

19. *The Birth of Merlin.* The first edition, 1662, claims William Shakespeare and William Rowley as joint authors.

20, 21. *Fair Em* and *Mucedorus.* A volume in Charles the Second's library, which contained these two plays and *The Merry Devil of Edmonton,* bore on the outside the title, 'Shakespeare. Vol. I.'

22, 23, 24. *The Puritan, Thomas Lord Cromwell, Locrine.* The first edition of each of these plays gives the author merely as 'W. S.' The earliest definite connexion with Shakespeare is their inclusion—together with *Oldcastle, The London Prodigal, A Yorkshire Tragedy,* and *Pericles*—in the third Shakespeare folio, 1664.

25. *Double Falsehood, or The Distrest Lovers.* Assigned to Shakespeare, perhaps fraudulently, by Theobald in the preface to the first edition, 1728.

26, 27, 28. *Edward II* (1594), *Edward III, Edward IV* (1600). Casually listed as Shakespeare's in an early bookseller's catalogue. *Edward III* was first seriously ascribed to Shakespeare by Capell in 1760.

29. *Arden of Feversham.* Shakespearian authorship was first suggested by Edward Jacob in 1770.

30, 31. *King Leir and his Daughters* (1605) and *George a Greene, the Pinner of Wakefield* (1599). First attributed by Tieck;[3] 31 is now accepted as Robert Greene's.

32, 33, 34. *Wily Beguiled* (1606), *Satiro-Mastix* (1602), *A Warning for Fair Women* (1599). Ascribed to Shakespeare by W. Bernhardi[4] in 1856; 33 is probably by Dekker.

35. *Sir Thomas More.* First printed, 1844; Shakespeare's part authorship suggested by Simpson in 1871.

From Mr. Simpson's list of doubtful plays[5] may be added for the sake of completeness:

36. The *Merry Wives* of 1602.

37, 38. *The Prodigal Son* and *Titus and Vespasia⟨n⟩*;[6] both preserved only in worthless old German translations.

[1] In vol. i of *The Old English Drama,* London.

[2] 1st ed., 1584.

[3] *Altenglisches Theater. oder Supplemente zum Shakespeare.* Berlin, 1811.

[4] *Hamburger Litteraturblatt,* No. 79.

[5] *Transactions,* New Shakspere Society, 1875–6, p. 155 ff.

[6] Mentioned by Henslowe. An early version of *Titus Andronicus,* printed in Cohn's *Shakespeare in Germany.* London, 1865.

39. The lost *Hamlet* of 1589 and '*Corambis*' *Hamlet* of 1603.
40. *The True Tragedy of Richard III.* First edition, 1594.
41. *A Larum for London, or the Siege of Antwerp,* 1602.[1]
42. *Albumazar ;* generally accepted as the work of Tomkis. First edition in 1615.

From this catalogue[2] *Pericles* and *Titus Andronicus* are designedly omitted because they have established their position in practice, if not in universal opinion, among the genuine works. It is hardly necessary to call attention to the further omission of such transparent and confessed forgeries as *Vortigern*[3] and *Henry the Second,*[4] by W. H. Ireland, and *The Fifth of November ; or The Gunpowder Plot,*[5] by George Ambrose Rhodes.

Of the forty-two 'doubtful plays' just enumerated, only thirteen can be regarded as having acquired a real claim to the title ; to these thirteen is added in the present volume *Sir Thomas More,* a play discovered less than a century ago and destitute, therefore, of prescriptive right of membership. Yet the evidence, internal and external, which can be submitted in defence of the pleasing idea that Shakespeare had a reviser's part in the authorship of *Sir Thomas More* is of so interesting and plausible a nature that no apology seems necessary for its inclusion. The following, then, are the names and earliest dates of publication of the fourteen dramas here reprinted, which alone appear entitled, on grounds either of reason or of custom, to a place among the *Shakespeare Apocrypha* :

I. *Arden of Feversham,* 1592.
II. *Locrine,* 1595.
III. *Edward III,* 1596.
IV. *Mucedorus,* 1598.
V. *The First Part of Sir John Oldcastle,*[6] 1600.
VI. *Thomas Lord Cromwell,* 1602.
VII. *The London Prodigal,* 1605.
VIII. *The Puritan,* 1607.
IX. *A Yorkshire Tragedy,* 1608.
X. *The Merry Devil of Edmonton,* 1608.
XI. *Fair Em.* First edition not dated ; second edition, 1631.
XII. *The Two Noble Kinsmen,* 1634.
XIII. *The Birth of Merlin,* 1662.
XIV. *Sir Thomas More,*[7] 1840.

The exact likelihood of Shakespeare's connexion with any member of this various group must be determined by careful individual examination. On the whole, it may be said, the reader will be impressed more with the unlikeness of the doubtful to the authentic plays than with their likeness.

There can, indeed, be no stronger vindication of the honesty and intelligence of the editors of the first Shakespeare Folio, Hemings and Condell, than careful study of the works which they excluded. As all attempts to deprive the poet of

[1] Reprinted, 1872, by R. Simpson, *School of Shakespeare,* No. 1.
[2] For several other utterly absurd attributions cf. the catalogue of 1656 mentioned in my Bibliography, V. (b) 1 (p. 454).
[3] 1799. Reprinted 1832. [4] 1799. [5] 1830.
[6] The second part of this play is not extant. [7] Date of composition *circa* 1590.

a large interest in any of the thirty-six plays published by them have so far failed, so it seems in the highest degree improbable that their list will ever be augmented by more than the genuine act or two of *Pericles* and a few broken fragments which Shakespeare would doubtless have been the last of all men to include among his works.

As regards the fundamental matters of plot and dramatic structure, there is no member of the *Shakespeare Apocrypha*, with the exception possibly of *The Two Noble Kinsmen*, which displays special kinship with any genuine play. There is not, for instance, a single French or Italian plot to be found in the doubtful group and, except in the case of *Mucedorus* and *The Two Noble Kinsmen*, the leading characters are invariably English. In the Shakespeare canon the matter is entirely different; if we leave out of account the ten English histories, we find that fourteen out of twenty-seven genuine works have French or Italian plots, derived usually directly or indirectly from novels, while (with the necessary exception again of the ten histories, the closely associated *Merry Wives of Windsor*, and the three mythical British dramas) not a single authentic play is avowedly English either in scene or characters.

Moreover, seven of the apocryphal dramas belong to well-defined dramatic species, of which there is not a single instance among Shakespeare's accepted works, and which there is inherent reason for supposing he would have avoided. These species are:—

1. What may be termed the 'biographical history', represented by *Sir John Oldcastle*, *Thomas Lord Cromwell*, and *Sir Thomas More*. Such dramas depict in loosely cohering scenes disconnected passages from the life of the hero; structural chaos is the prerequisite of their existence. To this group belong also the first two acts of *Pericles*—which are certainly un-Shakespearian.

2. The dramatic record of contemporary crime. *Arden of Feversham* and *A Yorkshire Tragedy* are remarkably fine instances of a class which, because it concerns itself primarily with actual physical horror, can scarcely rise to the level of high art.

3. Comedy of contemporary London manners, of which *The London Prodigal* and *The Puritan* are examples. This type of drama, superlatively interesting to our age for its richness of topical allusion, is opposed to the method of Shakespeare, who sets his realistic sketches against a romantic background and never condescends, like Ben Jonson and the author of these plays, to copy the life before his door in all its uninspiring mediocrity.

It seems improbable, then, for many reasons, that Shakespeare had an interest in the original construction of any of the doubtful plays. When we consider the possibility, however, of his co-operation in the capacity of reviser or elaborator, there is less cause for disbelief. During his long and many-sided connexion with the stage, the poet-manager would doubtless have had occasion to retouch and refine much of the inferior work which came to his company. Several of the canonical plays bear witness that Shakespeare did, indeed, follow this usual

Elizabethan practice, but his acknowledged works would not naturally, and do not, include his slight or casual revisionary labours. It is at present a thoroughly permissible belief, though one which can hardly be strengthened into certainty, that some of the splendid passages in the best apocryphal plays are thus the hasty and fragmentary creation of the master's hand. More exact knowledge as to this and other points of interest can be acquired only, if at all, from the study of the individual plays, to the separate discussion of which we may now proceed.

I. *Arden of Feversham* was entered on the Stationers' Register on April 3, 1592.[1] The same year appeared the first edition, in quarto (Q. 1), with the following title-page: '*The Lamentable and True Tragedie of M. Arden of Feversham in Kent. Who was most wickedlye murdered, by the meanes of his disloyall and wanton wyfe, who for the loue she bare to one Mosbie, hyred two desperat ruffins Blackwill and Shakbag, to kill him. Wherin is shewed the great mallice and discimulation of a wicked woman, the vnsatiable desire of filthie lust and the shamefull end of all murderers. Jmprinted at London for Edward White, dwelling at the lyttle North dore of Paules Church at the signe of the Gun.* 1592.'

This edition, of which copies are preserved in the Bodleian and in the Dyce Collection, South Kensington, is in black letter; it gives a remarkably good text and appears to have been closely followed by the second edition (Q. 2), of 1599. The only copy of Q. 2 known to exist is in the library of the Duke of Devonshire. In 1633 a third quarto (Q. 3) was published; this poor edition, which is to be found both in the Bodleian and in the British Museum, has a different pagination from Q. 1, and is especially remarkable for the number of words it omits.

The murder which *Arden of Feversham* represents took place on February 15, 1550–1—considerably more than a generation, therefore, before the publication of the first edition, or the earliest date (1590) to which the actual writing of the play can easily be referred. Yet there can be no doubt that popular interest in the event was still lively and widespread. Holinshed's Chronicle contains a detailed account, which many common inaccuracies and embellishments show to have been followed closely by the author of the tragedy. Stow's Chronicle gives a brief narrative of the crime and its punishment, while the actual facts are recorded in the Wardmote Book of Faversham.

To the dramatic talent of Holinshed we seem to owe the story of the repeated unsuccessful attempts on Arden's life, and the merging of the two colourless individuals of the Wardmote Book into the single effective figure of Susan. Finally the Roxburghe Collection preserves a long ballad of forty-eight stanzas—probably inspired by the play—with the following title: '*Complaint and lamentation of Mistresse Arden of Feversham in Kent, who for the love of one Mosbie, hired certaine Ruffians and Villaines most cruelly to murder her Husband; with the fatall end of her and her Associats. To the tune of* Fortune my Foe.'

Not till nearly two centuries after the first appearance of *Arden of Feversham,*

[1] '3 Aprilis ⟨1592⟩. Edward white, Entred for his copie vnder th⟨e h⟩andes of the Lord Bishop of London and the wardens The tragedie of Arden of Feuersham and Blackwall ⟨i.e. Black Will⟩. vjd A.'

was the play coupled with the name of Shakespeare. This service—and, right or wrong, it should be deemed a service—we owe to a loyal but somewhat uncritical citizen of Faversham, Edward Jacob, who in 1770 published a reprint of the first edition with the title: '*The Lamentable and True Tragedie of M. Arden, of Feversham in Kent. . . . With a Preface; in which some Reasons are offered in favour of its being the earliest dramatic Work of Shakespeare now remaining . . .*' The only reasons which Jacob actually offers are embraced in a scant half-page of parallel phrases between *Arden* and various genuine plays, and the similarity thus indicated is of so general a character as to prove nothing at all, beyond the obvious fact that *Arden of Feversham* and Shakespeare both belong to the Elizabethan period.[1]

Around few plays has so large a mass of able criticism accumulated during the last century with so little definite result as around *Arden of Feversham.* Those readers who feel impelled to assign this fine tragedy to the pen of the youthful Shakespeare have on their side the great authority of Mr. Swinburne and the more hesitating testimony of Charles Knight, Delius, and the Dutch translator Kuitert. But the balance of critical opinion, it may safely be said, is turning slowly to the side of respectful incredulity, the side represented by Tyrrell, Ulrici, Ward, Professor Saintsbury, Symonds, and the editors of the three modern texts: Mr. Bullen, Warnke and Proescholdt, and the Reverend Ronald Bayne.[2]

In considering the claim to authenticity of the work before us and others of its class, it is but fair to recognize that the reader's sympathies will ordinarily incline him strongly toward their acceptance. Besides the pleasure involved in the fancied recognition of a real personality, and that the greatest, behind the frigid mask of anonymity, allowance must be made, particularly on first perusal, for the intoxicating effect of the poetry. In the five doubtful plays in which the question of Shakespeare's authorship lends itself to rational discussion, there are gorgeous poetic passages that grip the imagination and overwhelm the reason. If, however (as is the case with regard to *Arden of Feversham* and its companions), our enthusiasm dies away when we consider the work in its dramatic entirety, or fit the words to the speaker, then surely we should pause long ere we venture on anything approaching a general attribution to Shakespeare. There is nothing fitful or transitory about the true Shakespearian quality; his creations gain, instead of losing, by repeated and various examination, and the very sign-manual of his work is the subordination of the expression to the idea, the complete amalgamation of the parts in the whole.

Arden of Feversham fails in all of these great tests, and a full century of the

[1] The following is the list of phrases and words for which Jacob cites Shakespearian parallels: 'such a taunting letter,' 'painted cloth,' 'Mermaid's song,' 'Basiliske,' 'lean faced knave,' 'white livered,' 'buy his merriment as dear,' 'Precisian,' 'a Raven for a Dove,' 'wild cat,' 'swear me on the interrogatories,' 'horned beast,' 'Endimion,' 'death makes amends for sin.'

[2] For more exact details as to works referred to here and elsewhere, readers are requested to consult the Bibliography.

most searching inquiry has not been able to add one iota to the probability of its authenticity. In such cases, not to advance is to recede hopelessly; were there enough of Shakespeare in *Arden of Feversham* to make up more than two or three purple patches at the most, its presence would long ago have made itself perceptible to the dullest vision, as it has done in the less intrinsically interesting play of *Pericles*.

Mr. Fleay and Mr. Charles Crawford [1] have argued with a considerable amount of plausibility that *Arden of Feversham* was written by Thomas Kyd, who is known to be the author of a prose work on a very similar subject, the murder of John Brewen. It seems likely that there are indeed more parallels in feeling and expression between our play and the tragedies of Kyd than coincidences will account for, but they presume imitation, as Sarrazin [2] and Mr. Boas [3] have pointed out, rather than identity of authorship. Whether the unknown author of *Arden of Feversham* was debtor or creditor to Kyd, must for the present be left in uncertainty.

There is but one character of the first magnitude in *Arden of Feversham:* Alice, Arden's wife and murderess. It is her demoniacal persistence in the execution of her horrible purpose, while her confederates fail or fall away, that gives the tragedy—otherwise hopelessly disjointed and ineffective—an ultimate unity and a really dramatic spirit. To her, too, belong much of the finest poetry and the two most dramatic speeches,[4] probably, in the play. Yet this gigantic figure is vulgarized and degraded by the two vices, which are most distinctively un-Shakespearian, and which, perhaps, it is hardest of all to pardon in a tragic heroine: purposeless revolting deceit and coarseness of feeling. Through all the dialogues between Alice and her husband, the reader is shocked by the moral obtuseness—the love of clever lying and hypocrisy for its own sake, even where there is no dramatic need for it—which is so entirely absent from Shakespeare's works and so unpleasantly conspicuous in many of his contemporaries'. So, too, Alice has little of the sustained delicacy of tragic feeling; from the heights of lofty passion she descends into the deepest mire of criminal brutality with such words as those she speaks concerning the news of her husband's intended assassination:

'They be so good that I must laugh for ioy,
Before I can begin to tell my tale.'[5]

For a truly rounded poet, sensible of the dignity and delicacy of tragedy, such lines would be as impossible as the undisguised doggerel of Black Will's leave-taking, which comes like a dash of cold water at the most breathless moment of the play:

'We haue our gould; mistris Ales, adew;
Mosbie, farewell, and Michaell, farewell too.'[6]

II. The first and only early edition of *Locrine* dates from 1595. The title-

[1] Jahrbüch der deutsch. Shakespeare-Gesellschaft 39, p. 74 ff.
[2] *Th. Kyd u. sein Kreis*, pp. 73–4. [3] Introduction to Kyd's Works, lxxxix.
[4] I. 186–205; III. v 106–134. [5] I. 553–4. [6] V. i. 261–2.

page reads: '*The Lamentable Tragedie of Locrine, the eldest sonne of King Brutus, discoursing the warres of the Britaines, and Hunnes, with their discomfiture: The Britaines victorie with their Accidents, and the death of Albanact. No lesse pleasant then profitable. Newly set foorth, ouerseene and corrected, By W. S. London. Printed by Thomas Creede.* 1595.'

During the previous year, on July 20, 1594, the play had been entered on the Stationers' Register.[1] The first definite suggestion of Shakespearian authorship belongs to 1664, when *Locrine* was reprinted, for the first time since its original appearance, as the last of the seven new plays in the third folio of Shakespeare. The fourth folio, printed in 1685, retained these supplementary dramas, *Locrine* among the number, but, of the seven, only *Pericles* has succeeded in establishing its claim to a place in modern editions. The mythical story on which the tragedy of *Locrine* is founded was current at the end of the sixteenth century in several forms. Herr Theodor Erbe, who has written a dissertation[2] on the subject, believes the dramatist to have followed Geoffrey of Monmouth's Chronicle in the main, with occasional borrowings from the versions of Caxton and of Holinshed.

The inquiry into the authorship of *Locrine* begins naturally with the consideration of the initials 'W. S.' on the title-page. And here our play connects itself at once with two other apocryphal works, *Thomas Lord Cromwell* and *The Puritan*, the first editions of which, in 1602 and 1607 respectively, bear the identical words, 'by W. S.' Now it is pretty clear, from the evidence of style, spirit, and method alike, that these three dramas are not by the same author—whether the William Smith suggested by Malone and Knight, or another—and we do not know of any two or three competent dramatists of the time, leaving Shakespeare out of the question, each of whom had the initials 'W. S.' In 1611, moreover, the early play of *The Troublesome Reign of King John* was republished with the new claim: 'Written by W. Sh.', where it seems certain that a dishonest but cautious bookseller meant the public to construe 'W. Sh.' as 'William Shakespeare'. From all this we may conclude with tolerable assurance: First, that the initials 'W. S.' on the title-pages of *Locrine, Cromwell,* and *The Puritan,* may well stand for 'William Shakespeare'.[3] Second, that such doubtful and suspicious evidence, though it apparently impressed the editors of the third folio, has almost no weight in deciding the question of Shakespeare's authorship of the plays under discussion.

Tieck accepts *Locrine* as the earliest of Shakespeare's dramatic works, and Schlegel registers his belief that this tragedy and *Titus Andronicus* must stand or fall together on their claim to authenticity. Few succeeding critics have been

[1] 'xx° die Julij. Thomas Creede, Entred for his Copie vnder th⟨e h⟩andes of the Wardens, The lamentable Tragedie of Locrine, the eldest sonne of Kinge Brutus. discoursinge the warres of the Brittans, &c. . . . vjd.'

[2] *Die Locrinesage und die Quellen des Pseudo-Shakespeareschen Locrine.* Halle a. S. 1904.

[3] In the case of *Locrine,* however, the probability of a reference to Shakespeare is much less than in the case of the other two later plays, both by reason of the former's early date and because of the wording of the title-page. Cf. p. xx.

willing to admit the possibility of Shakespeare's concern in the serious part of *Locrine*, which is indeed composed in the most exaggerated manner of the 'university wits'. The comic scenes, however, which centre around the figure of Strumbo, are more successful and more in the early style of Shakespeare. Accordingly Hopkinson and Ulrici agree in pronouncing the Strumbo scenes Shakespearian, while Hopkinson gives the rest of the play to George Peele. The distinction in tone between the tragic and the comic elements appears, however, to rest, not on duality of authorship, but on the change from a very affected type of poetry and a mythical age to prose and what is, to all intents and purposes, contemporary life. The dove-tailing of comedy and tragedy in such scenes as II, iii, iv, v, and IV, ii, is much too perfect to be explained on any hypothesis of double authorship; and these four scenes, unquestionably the work of a single man, represent all the peculiarities of the play, which I feel a large degree of confidence in attributing as a whole to the pen of Robert Greene. Before, however, entering specifically upon the vexed, and vexing, problem of the author's identity, it will be well to summarize the more obvious general features of the style.

Locrine is possibly as characteristic an example as can be found of the type of drama developed by Greene and Peele. The usual faults of their school are in this play exaggerated into vices, but the special lyric beauty, the imaginative fervour, and the delicate feeling for natural loveliness are equally prominent; and both in its defects and its merits *Locrine* manifests a close consanguinity with the acknowledged plays of the 'university wits'. No reader can well fail to note the infinity of classical allusion,[1] the craze for mouth-filling but meaningless adjectival epithets,[2] the ranting bombast of the heroic figures,[3] the wearisome lyrical repetition of high-sounding words and phrases,[4] or the childish delight in such freaks of verbiage as 'agnominated' and 'contentation'. No less striking, however, and no less indicative of its authorship are the poetic beauties of *Locrine*, detached, for the most part, and scattered like living springs in the dreary waste of rhetoric and affectation. There are few touches of purer pastoral feeling even in *Friar Bacon and Friar Bungay*, or in *The Arraignment of Paris*, than Estrild's description of England:

> The aierie hills enclosd with shadie groues,
> The groues replenisht with sweet chirping birds,
> The birds resounding heauenly melodie, &c.'[5]

or the allusion to

> the fields of martiall *Cambria*,
> Close by the boystrous *Iscans* siluer streames,
> Where lightfoote faires skip from banke to banke.[6]

The enthusiasm for external life and action, bound up so closely with the reflective tendencies of the 'university wits', is worthily expressed in Hubba's martial speech,[7] and in the splendid outburst of national feeling in IV. i. 28–37.

[1] e.g. I. i. 235–56.
[2] Ibid. and III. i. 43–4.
[3] e.g. Humber's raving in III. 6.
[4] e g. II. i. 102–5.
[5] II. i. 36 ff.
[6] III. i. 71–3.
[7] III. ii. 36 ff.

Malone has put it on record as his 'creed', that this play 'was written by Christopher Marlowe, whose style it appears to me to resemble more than that of any other known dramatick author of that age'. It is to be hoped that Mr. Malone's creed contained other saving articles; else his hopes of salvation must be reckoned to be small, for with the exception of a few of the generic qualities just mentioned, which Marlowe also shared, there is not a jot of resemblance between the two styles. Indeed, it is perhaps a degree less possible to imagine Marlowe the author of the flatter and feebler parts of *Locrine* than to believe them the output of the youthful Shakespeare himself.

The various-minded Mr. Fleay has several times decided upon Peele [1] as the author of our play, and Hopkinson is of the same opinion as regards the tragic portion of the piece. Peele's authorship—at least in the present state of our knowledge of that poet—is no such self-evident impossibility as that of Shakespeare or Marlowe, but it seems for many reasons improbable. The importance, character, and success of the comic element,[2] the excessive richness of mythological allusion—far greater than in any play of Peele's and differently employed, the extreme rarity of run-on lines, and the general appearance of over-decoration all indicate that the author of *Locrine* is not Peele, and that he is Peele's more humorous, but weaker and more florid companion, Robert Greene.

In the discussion of Greene's special claims to the play of *Locrine* is involved the consideration of another play closely and curiously linked to ours—the first part,[3] that is, of *The Tragical raigne of Selimus, sometime Emperour of the Turkes*, published anonymously in 1594 by the same Thomas Creede who brought out *Locrine, Alphonsus, The Looking Glass*, and *James IV*. Mr. P. A. Daniel first called attention to the connexion between *Selimus* and *Locrine*, a connexion so close as to prove indisputably either common authorship or conscious plagiarism. The one comic passage in *Selimus* (ll. 1873 ff.) is appropriated bodily from *Locrine*, IV. ii, and the two works have more identical or similar lines than could easily be enumerated; sometimes considerable passages in one play are repeated in the other with the change of only a word or two.[4] For an imposing but by no means exhaustive array of parallel passages and a discussion of the relationship of the two dramas, the reader may be referred to Mr. Churton Collins's Introduction to Greene's Works.[5] Mr. Charles Crawford has further shown that some of the more elaborate parallel passages in *Locrine* and *Selimus* are imitations of lines

[1] In his *History of the Stage* he gives the play wholly to Peele; in the *Shakspere Manual* (286) he assigns it to Charles Tilney, but believes that it was revised by Peele. There is nothing to support either theory. The two parallels from Peele's *Farewell to Norris and Drake*, 1589, noted by Dyce and alluded to impressively by Fleay are these: 'To arms, to arms, to honourable arms,' and 'Take helm and targe'! Tilney's only claim to this or any other play rests upon an unauthenticated statement of Collier's that the former is mentioned as the author in a manuscript note written in a copy of the first quarto. Cf. Tilney in *Dict. Nat. Biog.*

[2] Cf. p. xxiii.

[3] No second part exists.

[4] e.g. *Locrine* II. v. 7–11, and *Selimus*, 2434–8 (Temple edition).

[5] Oxford, 1905, pp. 64–7.

in Spenser's *Ruins of Rome*, which was probably known in MS. some years before its publication in 1591.

Dr. Grosart has claimed *Selimus* for Greene, and on the whole with a greater show of probability than Mr. Collins is willing to allow. The fact that two selections [1] from this drama are quoted in *England's Parnassus*, 1600, over the name of R. Greene ought surely to be given very considerable weight when there is no contradictory external evidence and when the internal evidence must be agreed to point in the same direction. In the variety and amount of mythological reference, in general dramatic structure, in the number and kind of borrowings from Spenser, Marlowe, and Greene himself, there is little doubt that *Selimus* bears more likeness to *Orlando Furioso* and *Alphonsus, King of Arragon* than to any work of any other contemporary writer. As for Mr. Crawford's fine-spun theory that *Selimus*, with its multiplex heroes, disjointed plot, frequent rhyme, and total absence of any strikingly original situation or poetry, is the production of Christopher Marlowe, it is assuredly not unjust to pronounce the suggestion worthy of keeping company in the limbo of rash and unbalanced criticism with Mr. Simpson's arguments in defence of Shakespeare's authorship of *Fair Em*, and with that egregious sentence of Schlegel which declares that *Cromwell* and *Oldcastle* deserve to be classed among his best and maturest works.

Robert Greene's early dramatic method is marked by two features, which especially distinguish *Locrine*. The first is his constant borrowing of lines and phrases from other poets and from himself ; the second is his tendency to beautify himself with borrowed feathers in greater matters—to copy the plot and general structure of the most fashionable work of the hour. How continually in *Locrine* we find Greene's favourite epithets, phrases, and classical divinities forcing themselves uncalled for into the lines will not escape the notice of any one who will, for example, make a cursory catalogue, as I have done, of the mythological references in *Locrine* and compare it with *Selimus*, *Alphonsus*, *Orlando*, and the *Looking Glass*.

Crawford has pointed out—truly, I think—that *Locrine* is less influenced by Marlowe than *Selimus*, and that the former play, unlike the latter, does not borrow from the *Faery Queene*. I differ from Mr. Daniel in regarding *Locrine* as the earlier play, and I believe it to have been written before Greene fell under the spell of *Tamburlaine* and while he was taking as his models for tragedy the species of drama represented by *Gorboduc* and *The Misfortunes of Arthur*. The choice of subject, the dumb shows, and the presence of lyrical speeches arranged in stanzas,[2] all mark *Locrine* as belonging to this class as surely as *Alphonsus* belongs to the class of *Tamburlaine*. The true, if not very powerful or original poetic gifts of Greene raise *Locrine*, however, as far above the barely respectable work of Norton and Sackville and the unmitigated rubbish of Hughes as all Greene's early plays are themselves transcended by the first achievement of the mighty Marlowe.

Selimus I would take as marking the transition from *Locrine* to *Alphonsus*.

[1] 503–9, 853–7.

[2] The last feature is found also, more rarely, in *Selimus*.

The trumpet blast of *Tamburlaine* reverberates through many of its speeches, but the cramping walls of Senecan dramaturgy are tottering rather than fallen. Lyrical stanzas and couplets occur here and there, and the action goes a-straying, as in *Locrine,* from one principal character to another. The sequence I have indicated is borne out by examination of the style, which is most artificial and hyper-classical in *Locrine* and grows very gradually but steadily less so in *Selimus, Orlando Furioso,* and *Alphonsus,* till the culmination is reached in the excellent simplicity of *James IV.*

Locrine is a tragedy of the type of about 1585; that it could have been composed—with all its dumb show machinery and so forth—immediately before 1595 is practically impossible. Yet the reference in the epilogue to the thirty-eighth year of Elizabeth's reign points clearly to 1595–6, and these lines must therefore be considerably later than the play as a whole. There is, indeed, no shadow of a reason why we should not accept as absolute truth the statement of the title-page that the drama was in 1595 'newly set foorth, ouerseene, and corrected by W. S.' This W. S. *may* have been William Shakespeare or William Smith, or any one else possessed of these initials. His identity will probably never be known, and there is no question connected with *Locrine* which is less worth the settling, for the whole character of the play shows that, but for the addition of the twelve-line epilogue,[1] the activities of W. S. can hardly have extended beyond the crossing of an occasional 't' or the dotting of an 'i'.

III. *Edward III,* in some ways the most extraordinary of all the doubtful plays, is first heard of in the Stationers' Register for Dec. 1, 1595[2]; three other entries are recorded between this date and Feb. 23, 1625. The earliest edition (Q. 1) has the following title-page: '*The Raigne of King Edward the third: As it hath bin sundrie times plaied about the Citie of London. London, Printed for Cuthbert Burby.* 1596.' The play must have been temporarily popular, for in 1599 there appeared a second quarto (Q. 2), printed likewise for Cuthbert Burby. From this time, however, *Edward III* seems to have been very largely neglected during more than a century and a half, till it was permanently rescued from oblivion by the scholarly editing of Capell in 1760.

Scene 2 of the first act, and the second act of *Edward III* are based in part on Holinshed's Chronicle of Scotland and in part on a novel by Bandello, as translated in Painter's Palace of Pleasure.[3] The only source of the rest of the drama, according to Warnke and Proescholdt, is Holinshed's Chronicle of England; but Knight may be correct in recognizing through the last three acts the influence of Froissart as well. The Villiers-Salisbury episode[4] is not found either in Holinshed or Froissart and is of uncertain derivation. The two editions of the play were anonymous; however, in 'An exact and perfect Catalogue of all

[1] v. iv. 261–72.

[2] 'primo die decembris ⟨1595⟩. Cuthbert Burby Entred for his copie vnder the handes of the wardens A book Intitled Edward the Third and the Blacke Prince their warres with kinge John of Fraunce . . . vjd.'

[3] Novel XLVI.

[4] IV. i. 19–43; iii. 1–56; v. 56–126.

Playes that are Printed', prefixed to T. G⟨off⟩'s *Careless Shepherdess*, 1654, the three plays of *Edward II*, *Edward III*, and *Edward IV*, are assigned to Shakespeare. Such an attribution is uncritical and untrustworthy on the face of it and appears to have been ignored in the case of *Edward III*, as, of course, it was in the case of the other two histories, till Capell's introduction to our play in his volume of 'Prolusions, or Select Pieces of Ancient Poetry,'[1] put the arguments for its authenticity boldly and persuasively before the popular mind.

The first two acts of *Edward III* concern themselves mainly with a love intrigue. The beginning of the third act brings with it a complete change of plot and a considerable diminution in dramatic force. Since Capell, only Tieck, Collier, Teetgen, and Hopkinson—untrustworthy critics all—have assigned the entire play to Shakespeare; but the number of those who regard the main portion of the first episode as Shakespearian, includes at least three high authorities: Tennyson, Ward, and Fleay, while Halliwell-Phillips, Tyrrell, and Freiherr von Vincke recognize the authenticity of these scenes as at least possible. In the criticism of *Edward III*, however, as in that of *Arden of Feversham*, the trend of modern opinion inclines strongly to the negative side. The long list of those who deny the presence in the play of more than, conceivably, a few brief insertions by Shakespeare, includes: Mr. Swinburne, Dr. Furnivall, Saintsbury, Knight, Symonds, G. C. Moore Smith, Ulrici, Delius, Warnke and Proescholdt, H. von Friesen, and Liebau.

It will doubtless be generally agreed by readers of the play that the last acts, dealing with the French wars, though full of fine dramatic poetry, are, as a whole, not by Shakespeare; and there seems good reason to believe that the earlier 'countess scenes', so much more Shakespearian at first sight, are in reality by the same author as the rest of the drama. Whether the scenes in which the countess appears, and possibly other passages, were later revised by a second hand, Shakespeare's or another's, is a question that must be left open.

The supporters of the authenticity of the love episode explain it usually as a relatively late addition, written by Shakespeare to eke out the insufficiently long military scenes; at all events, it is certain that, if there is any difference in date of composition, the military scenes represent the original dramatic conception, to which the love episode is subsequent. But there are two passages in Act III, which belong apparently to the very first draft and which refer directly to the love episode. In the third scene[2] King John says:

> 'For whats this Edward but a belly god,
> A tender and lasciuious wantonnes,
> That *thother daie* was almost dead for loue?

And in Scene 5,[3] King Edward likewise reminds the audience of the events of the first two acts:

> 'Now, Iohn of Fraunce, I hope,
> Thou knowest King Edward for no wantonesse
> No loue sicke cockney.'

[1] 1760. [2] ll. 155–7. [3] ll. 100–2.

The author of Act III, must, therefore, have had the contents of Acts I and II distinctly before his mind.

A more definite indication of singleness of authorship is the fact that, wherever in the last three acts the necessity of portraying actual events disappears, there we find, as in IV. iii, a return to the tone and style of the earlier unhistoric scenes. Indeed, it is not too much to assert that the true lover and student of this play will be likely to turn with most pleasure not to the brilliant intrigue scenes of the first acts, which have, I think, a rather cloying sweetness, but to the freshness and perfect sincerity of some of the later passages, uneven and sometimes uncouth though they are. There is a verve and exhilaration about the scene in which the Black Prince receives his arms [1] and that [2] in which he returns to his father triumphant from the shadow of death, or in the brief eighth scene of Act IV, where Audley passes wounded and dying across the stage, which are nowhere to be found in the countess episode. The latter is certainly a much finer entity than any other division of the play, but there is probably not a passage in it which does more credit to the poetic ability of the author than this single line of Audley's: [3]

> 'Good friends, conuey me to the princely Edward,
> *That in the crimson brauerie of my bloud*
> I may become him with saluting him.'

or the four spoken by the second citizen of Calais: [4]

> 'The Sun, dread Lord, that in the western fall
> Beholds vs now low brought through miserie,
> Did in the Orient purple of the morne
> Salute our comming forth, when we were knowne.'

Mr. Symonds has remarked that, in case *Edward III* was written as a whole by some imitator of Shakespeare's Marlowesque manner, the unknown author would naturally have succeeded better in his treatment of the love story which Bandello had shaped ready to his hand, than when he came in the later acts to deal with the refractory material of actual history. The nature of the play, from beginning to end, lends special weight to this criticism; throughout we recognize the writer's love of noble situations and his sympathy with high-minded characters, but the continual inferiority of his hand to his heart is equally obvious. The inability to grasp strongly the realities of life produces in the historical scenes a woodenness and restraint, which mark these portions of the play as distinctly un-Shakespearian, despite several bursts of magnificent poetry. In the greater part of the first two acts, however, and occasionally elsewhere, the demands of realistic sanity are less obvious, and the author has been able to rise to a very great height by his fine poetic sense and delicacy of feeling.

Yet the central fault is present here as elsewhere. Notwithstanding their figurative richness of style, their melody and forcefulness of expression, and their real likeness in many outward features to Shakespeare, the scenes between the countess and the king will hardly bear frequent re-reading. Tried by the test

[1] III. iii. [2] III. v. [3] IV. viii. 7. [4] V. 27–30.

of what they say, not how they say it, these passages sound hollow and insincere; the sophistry of nearly all the arguments becomes more objectionable as one knows the play better, as one comes to feel—once the bewildering effect of the declamation has abated—how much the characters guide their actions by the dictates of complex academic reasoning and how little by the inner voice of nature.

Yet after declaring Shakespeare utterly incapable, at the mature period presumed by the artistic finish of *Edward III*, of the quibbling mawkishness of Warwick and the Countess, the conscientious critic will pause long before he undertakes to name the actual author—one of the truest poets and most ardent patriots, certainly, of his generation.

I should like to see this fine though very imperfect play recognized as the crown and conclusion of the work of George Peele, a poet who has perhaps received scant justice in recent times, but who in the fire and melody of his poetry rises high above all but the two greatest of his contemporaries. *David and Bethsabe* is only just inferior in its best parts to *Edward III* and the two works bear a very marked resemblance in all essential particulars. In both there is the basal lack of unity arising from the juxtaposition of a love episode conceived in a vein of rare lyrical beauty and a military-political plot for which the author's hand shows itself less well adapted. Both are characterized by nearly total abstinence from the mythological jargon of Greene, by the peculiar liquid beauty of Peele's best poetry, and by a verse movement which is almost identical.[1]

As in *David and Bethsabe* and *The Battle of Alcazar*, so in *Edward III*, there is not a vestige of comedy—a fact which would surprise us in the work of almost any writer of the time, except two. For it is a curious truth that Peele, with his immense reputation as a jester and social buffoon, has left us less comedy, and that little of a feebler sort, than any of his contemporaries save Christopher Marlowe. For the type of ardent but rather undiscriminating patriotism which pervades *Edward III* any number of parallels will be found in *The Arraignment of Paris*, *Edward I*, and *The Battle of Alcazar*.

It must be conceded that *Edward III* is a finer production than any with which Peele is at present accredited. Yet I believe that the majority of persons who will compare the first act of *David and Bethsabe* with the first two acts of *Edward III*, will recognize not only that the general characteristics—merits and defects—are the same, but furthermore that there is nothing in the latter play which was not potentially within the grasp of the poet who could write the former. A few years more of practice, a free hand,[2] and the change from the dry threshed husks of Biblical narrative to the full and stimulating garners of native history might have performed a far greater transfiguration.

IV. *Mucedorus* appears first in an edition of 1598, with the title-page:

[1] The proportion of run-on lines in *David and Bethsabe* is about one in five; in *Edward III* it is slightly less than one in six. There is absolutely no appreciable difference in this regard—though Mr. Fleay rather insinuates that there is—between the three King-Countess scenes and the rest of *Edward III*.

[2] At least in the non-historical scenes.

'*A Most pleasant Comedie of Mucedorus the kings sonne of Valentia and Amadine the kings daughter of Arragon, with the merie conceites of Mouse. Newly set foorth as it hath bin sundrie times plaide in the honorable Cittie of London. Very delectable and full of mirth. London. Printed for William Jones, dwelling at Holborne conduit, at the signe of the Gunne.* 1598.' There is no mention of the play in the extant Stationers' Registers till September 17, 1618.[1]

Of all pre-Restoration plays *Mucedorus* passed through the greatest number of early editions. Seventeen have been enumerated by Mr. W. W. Greg,[2] the dates in order of publication being as follows: 1598 (Q. 1), 1606 (Q. 2), 1610 (Q. 3), 1611 (Q. 4), 1613 (Q. 5), 1615 (Q. 6), 1618 (Q. 7), 1619 (Q. 8), 1621 (Q. 9), 1626 (Q. 10), 1631 (Q. 11), 1634 (Q. 12), 1639 (Q. 13), 1663 (Q. 14), 1668 (Q. 15), an undated edition (Q. 16), and an edition of which the only extant copy[3] lacks the title-page (Q. 17). Collier has mentioned yet another quarto, dated 1609, upon which he professed to base his text of the play, but it is highly probable that this edition, known to nobody but Collier, is entirely imaginary. Nine of the existing quartos are to be found in the British Museum;[4] to these the Bodleian,[5] Trinity College, Cambridge,[6] and the Dyce Collection[7] add two others each. Q. 7 and Q. 9, neither of which is important, are the only ones not easily accessible, the former being in Mr. Huth's private library, the latter in the Municipal Library of Dantzig. Collation of all the British Museum quartos and careful consideration of the rest show that it is possible to divide the early texts of *Mucedorus* into the following three groups:—

Group A, including only Q. 1 and Q. 2, is characterized by the absence of certain scenes and passages found in all the others.

Group B embraces Q. 3–6; all the editions of this group as well as Q. 1 and Q. 2 were published by William Jones.

Group C includes Q. 7–17; the first seven of these editions (Q. 7–13) were published by John Wright, Q. 14–16, and probably Q. 17, by Francis Coles. In this group the text has been superficially edited, the spelling modernized to some extent, and grammatical irregularities normalized. The divergences within the various groups appear quite unintentional and are confined as a rule to mere misprints and variant spellings.

The title-page of Q. 3 runs: '*A Most pleasant Comedie of Mucedorus ... Amplified with new additions, as it was acted before the king's Maiestie at White-hall on Shroue-*

[1] This notice is of interest as explaining the change of publisher after the sixth edition (1615). It runs as follows: '17 Septembris 1618. John Wright Assigned ouer vnto him by Mistris Sara Jones widowe late wife of william Jones Deceased and by Direction from Master warden Adames by a note vnder his hand theis two bookes following xijd.

vizt.
The schoole of good manners
The Comedy Called Mucedorus.'

[2] *Jahrbuch* XL., 95 ff.

[3] In Library of Trin. Coll., Camb.

[4] Q. q. 1, 3, 5, 6, 8, 11, 12, 15, 16.

[5] Q. 4, Q. 14.

[6] Q. 13, Q. 17.

[7] Q. 2, Q. 10.

Sunday night. By his Highnes Seruants usually playing at the Globe. Very delectable, and full of conceited Mirth...' The title-pages of the subsequent quartos are as nearly as possible the same. Most of the critical interest attaching to *Mucedorus* concerns the 'new additions' found in the texts of groups B and C and the definite statement in these editions that the play was acted by the King's men 'usually playing at the Globe'. The additions are certainly not by the original author and are superior to the rest of the comedy; they include the Prologue, Scenes 1 and 2 of the first Act, Scene 1 of the fourth Act, a revision and amplification of Act V, Scene 2, from line 91, and of the Epilogue from line 14.

The source of the comedy has not been discovered; Schlegel, who had not read the play, conjectured wrongly that it was founded on the story of Valentine and Orson,[1] the subject of a Spanish drama by Lope de Vega. Among the Roxburghe Ballads [2] there is a poem, which, though hardly older in its present form than the seventeenth century, differs from our play in several particulars and may be based in part on an earlier version of the story. The heading of the ballad reads: 'The wandring Prince and Princess or Musidorus and Amadine, both of Royal Progeny, who being unfortunately seperated by means of their parents disagreeing; as fortunately met in a Desert, while both resolved never to cease from searching, till they had found out each other.

In shady Deserts there was none
  but Beasts to hear these Lovers moan,
There these faithful Lovers met,
  Their marriage day was quickly set.

Tune, *Young Phaon.*'

Besides the conclusive testimony of the large number of early editions and the circulation of a ballad on the subject, we have several other evidences of the special popularity of *Mucedorus* with vulgar audiences in the seventeenth century. The Citizen's Wife in *The Knight of the Burning Pestle* says [3] of an apprentice: 'Nay, gentlemen, he hath played before, my husband says, *Mucedorus*, before the wardens of our company.' To the same effect is the following interesting record of the comedy's vogue in the provinces during the Commonwealth: 'The comedy of *Mucedorus* was revived by some strollers in 1652, and privately exhibited in the villages of Moore, Standlake, Southleigh and Cumner in Oxfordshire, till in the following February, they ventured to represent it publicly at Witney. The use of the Town-hall being denied them, they were obliged to perform it at the White-hart inn, where a numerous audience assembled on the evening of the 3d.' [4] On this occasion several persons were killed by the giving way of the floor, and the town lecturer Rowe profited by the catastrophe to deliver a series of sermons against theatrical performances.

The only external evidence which in any degree sanctions the attribution of *Mucedorus* to Shakespeare consists in the statement on the title-pages of

[1] A play with this title, by Hathway and Munday, is mentioned by Henslowe under date of July 19, 1597. [2] Vol. ii, pp. 490–1. [3] Induction.

[4] Quoted from a clipping pasted in the British Museum copy of Q. 8.

1610 and after, that the play belonged to the repertoire of the Globe Company, and the fact of its inclusion, with *Fair Em* and *The Merry Devil of Edmonton*, in the famous 'Shakespeare' volume prepared for Charles the Second's library. Tieck alone has ascribed the whole of *Mucedorus* to Shakespeare, and modern criticism will no longer tolerate so absurd an attribution. There can be little doubt that the comedy in its original form was the work of some member of the school of 'university wits'. Malone attempted, on the most dubious of external testimony, to establish Greene's authorship, and Mr. Hopkinson holds the same view, which, however, has recently been discredited by Mr. Churton Collins;[1] Mr. Fleay prefers to give to Lodge such credit as the composition of these crude early scenes carries with it, while H. von Friesen supposes Peele to have written them. The spirit of the school is everywhere visible, especially so, perhaps, in such a pastoral bit as iv. 3, but there is little to identify the individual poet. If he be one of the three or four famous members of the group, then much of the play must represent hasty or slovenly work, but it is more likely that these old scenes were written by an obscure and only moderately gifted disciple.

The additional scenes, written apparently between the publication of the second edition in 1606 and the third in 1610, are of greater poetic merit than the rest of the comedy and somewhat more in Shakespeare's manner. It is agreed that they fall far short of what one would expect from Shakespeare at this period; yet Collier, Hopkinson, and Simpson accept them, with reservations, as hurried and careless patch-work, done by the master in his capacity of theatre manager. Against this, and in support of the negative position occupied by Fleay, Ward, Tyrrell, Knight, Warnke and Proescholdt, and Soffé, it may be mentioned:—

First. That, though the single authorship of the additions is pretty evident, only one of the new scenes (iv. 1) shows anything which can possibly be regarded as the imperfect work of genius, while the others display merely workmanlike mediocrity.

Second. That all the new scenes indicate the very reverse of haste and carelessness; their great fault is that they impress the reader as laboured.

Third. That the style, even in the finest scene of all, is sometimes so strained and artificial as not conceivably to be Shakespeare's in 1606–10. Take, for instance, this couplet in IV. i.[2]:—

> 'No, no; till Mucedorus I shall see againe,
> All ioy is comfortlesse, all pleasure paine.'

Mr. Fleay suggests Wilkins as the author of the additions, but the matter is not likely soon to be settled. So much seems certain: that the additions to *Mucedorus* were written by a person of true, but neither great nor mature poetic gifts who stood somewhat under the influence of Shakespeare.

V. Two quarto editions of the *First Part of Sir John Oldcastle* were published in 1600. One, which we may call Q. 1, bears the title: '*The first part Of the true*

[1] Introduction to Greene's Works, pp. 60–1. [2] ll. 15–16.

and honorable historie, of the life of Sir John Old-castle, the good Lord Cobham. As it hath been lately acted by the right honorable the Earle of Notingham Lord high Admirall of England his seruants. London. Printed by V. S. for Thomas Pauier, and are to be solde at his shop at the signe of the Catte and Parrots neere the Exchange. 1600.' The other quarto (Q. 2) inserts the words 'Written by William Shakespeare' and replaces the full particulars as to the publisher's name and address by the non-committal sentence: 'London printed for T. P. 1600.' This dishonest and defective text has been followed by the editors of the third and fourth Shakespeare folios (F. 1, F. 2) and by all modern publishers.[1] There can be no doubt, though, that the anonymous quarto (Q. 1) is infinitely superior; it contains many fine passages which Q. 2 has either omitted entirely or hopelessly corrupted. The play was registered by Pavier, August 11, 1600.[2]

Sir John Oldcastle has many pleasant and a few really good scenes, but there is perhaps no member of the pseudo-Shakespearian group more totally destitute of a single passage which might imaginably have been written by Shakespeare. Only Tieck and Schlegel have championed its genuineness; and the question of authorship has now been settled with a most agreeable definiteness by the unearthing of the following entries in Henslowe's Diary: [3] 'This 16 of october ⟨15⟩99. Receved by me, Thomas Downton, of phillip Henslow, to pay *Mr. Monday, Mr. Drayton,* and *Mr. Wilson* and *Hathway,* for the first pte of the lyfe of Sr. Jhon Ouldcasstell and in earnest of the second pte., for the use of the compayny, ten pound, I say receved . . . 10^{li}.'

'Receved of Mr. Hinchloe, for Mr. Mundaye and the Reste of the poets, at the playnge of Sr. John Oldcastell, the ferste tyme. As a gefte . . . x^{s}.'

From other entries it appears that the *Second Part of Sir John Oldcastle,* now lost, was written by Drayton alone.

The first part of *Oldcastle* was beyond question composed for the Lord Admiral's Company as a reply to the successful Falstaff plays [4] which the Lord Chamberlain's Servants had been acting. The character of Falstaff, originally called Oldcastle, is certainly aimed at in the slur of the prologue: [5]

'It is no pamperd glutton we present,
Nor aged Councellor to youthfull sinne.'

The gambling scene between the disguised king and Sir John of Wrotham suggests *Henry V*, IV, i; while the reference to the thieving exploits of the king's youth

[1] It may well be that Q.2 is the earlier of the two quartos and that it was hastily printed from a shorthand version several months before Pavier secured the accurate version from which he published Q.1. It is noteworthy that both editions have the curious transposition of Scenes 2–8 of the last act.

[2] '11 Augusti. Thomas pavier Entred for his copies vnder the handes of master Vicars and the wardens. These iij copies, viz.
The first parte of the history of the life of Sir John Oldcastell lord Cobham.
Item the second and last parte of the history of Sir John Oldcastell lord Cobham with his martyrdom.
Item ye history of the life and Deathe of Captaine Thomas Stucley . . .'

[3] Edition of 1845, p. 158.

[4] The two parts of *Henry IV*, 1597–8; *Henry V*, 1599.

[5] ll. 6, 7.

is a clear allusion to the first part of *Henry IV*, and the two mentions [1] of Falstaff by name are reminiscences of the same play:

> '*King*. . . . Where the diuel are all my old theeues, that were wont to keepe this walke ? Falstaffe, the villaine, is so fat, he cannot get on 's horse, but me thinkes Poines and Peto should be stirring here abouts ; '

and

> '*sir Iohn*. . . . Because he ⟨i.e. the King⟩ once robde me before I fell to the trade my selfe ; when that foule villainous guts, that led him to all that rogery, was in's company there, that Falstaffe.'

VI. *Thomas Lord Cromwell* was entered on the Stationers' Register by William Cotton, Aug. 11, 1602.[2] In the same year appeared the first edition (Q. 1) with the title : '*The True Chronicle Historie of the whole life and death of Thomas Lord Cromwell. As it hath beene sundrie times publikely Acted by the Right Honorable the Lord Chamberlaine his Seruants. Written by W. S. Imprinted at London for William Iones, and are to be solde at his house neere Holburne conduict, at the signe of the Gunne.* 1602.'

A second quarto (Q. 2) was printed by Thomas Snodham in 1613. The only important variation from Q. 1 on the title-page of this edition consists in the necessary change of the name of Shakespeare's company : 'As it hath beene sundry times publikely Acted by the King's Maiesties Seruants. Written by W. S.' The play was included in the third and fourth Shakespeare folios (F. 1, F. 2), and was reprinted by Rowe, Pope, and again separately by R. Walker in 1734, as 'A Tragedy. By Shakespear.' Q. 2, the later quarto, was, as usual, followed by the editors of the folios, as well as by Malone, who was not acquainted with Q. 1, and has thus served as basis for all modern texts. Q. 1 is certainly to be preferred ; the variations of Q. 2 are for the most part due merely to the conventionalizing of syntax and spelling, but there are several cases where the original reading has been falsified by the insertion or substitution of new words. The later editions have no critical importance.

Thomas Lord Cromwell exceeds *Sir John Oldcastle* in all the particular defects of that defective though interesting play, and it has fewer merits. The scenes of *Cromwell* are disconnected and undramatic to such a degree that the real plot cannot be said to begin before the close of the third act, and there is hardly a passage in the work, with the exception of III. iii, which excites special attention. Tieck and Schlegel, to their lasting discredit, have defended the genuineness of this play, and Ulrici also is inclined, against his better judgement, to accept it as a very early work of Shakespeare, anterior to 1592. Hopkinson assigns the main part of the performance to Greene,[3] but he—alone of English critics—would like

[1] III. iv. 61–5, 102–5.

[2] '11° Augustj ⟨1602⟩. William Cotton Entred for his Copie vnder th⟨e h⟩andes of master Jackson and master waterson warden A booke called "the lyfe and Deathe of the Lord Cromwell" as yt was lately Acted by the Lord Chamberleyn his servantes, vjd.'

[3] It is possibly worth remarking—though not as an indication of Greene's authorship, than which few things are more unlikely—that the episode of Seely and his cow

to establish Shakespeare's connexion as reviser of the greater part of the comic scenes and of III. ii and iii; IV. i and v; and V.

Other writers have suggested the authorship of Wentworth Smith, William Sly, Heywood, and Drayton respectively, but there is strong reason against ascribing the play to any of these, while it appears as absolutely certain as so undemonstrable a matter well can be, that William Shakespeare was never concerned with a single line of it. On this point it is pleasant to find the first and the last of the critics of *Cromwell* in complete and emphatic agreement. Malone says:[1] 'To vindicate Shakespeare from having written a single line of this piece would be a waste of time. The poverty of language, the barrenness of incident and the inartificial conduct of every part of the performance, place it rather perhaps below the compositions of even the second-rate dramatick authors of the age in which it was produced.' And Mr. Swinburne writes in the same strain, but with even greater and rather excessive disapproval: '*Thomas Lord Cromwell* is a piece of such utterly shapeless, spiritless, bodiless, soulless, senseless, helpless, worthless rubbish, that there is no known writer of Shakespeare's age to whom it could be ascribed without the infliction of an unwarrantable insult on that writer's memory.'[2]

The source of the play is 'The History concerning the Life, Acts, and Death of the famous and worthy Councillor, Lord Thomas Cromwell, Earl of Essex' in Fox's Book of Martyrs.[3] The story of Frescobald, which Fox[4] has incorporated, comes, as Malone has remarked, from one of Bandello's novels (Part II, No. 27).

VII. *The London Prodigal* appears not to have been entered on the Stationers' Books.[5] The only early quarto (Q. 1) was published in 1605 with the title: '*The London Prodigall. As it was plaide by the Kings Maiesties seruants. By William Shakespeare, London. Printed by T. C. for Nathaniel Butter, and are to be sold neere S. Austins gate, at the signe of the pyde Bull.* 1605.'

It was next published in the third and fourth Shakespeare folios (F. 1, F. 2), in supplements to Rowe's and to Pope's Shakespeare, and in careless separate reprints by Walker and Tonson.[6]

All these editions ascribe the comedy unreservedly to Shakespeare, and their

may have been inspired by the speeches of Alcon in *A Looking Glasse for London and England* (I. iii, II. ii).

[1] About 1780. [2] *A Study of Shakespeare*, 3rd ed., p. 232.

[3] Cf. Streit's dissertation on the subject. [4] Ed. 1684, II. 429–30.

[5] I have found the following entry, which is of slight interest, though it is not very probable that the work mentioned had much to do with our play:—'27 Novembris ⟨1598⟩. Nicholas linge Entred for his copie vnder the handes of master Sonibanke and the wardens A booke called The Portraiture of the prodigall sonne. vjd.'

[6] In 1734 both these publishers brought out worthless editions of *Locrine*, *Oldcastle*, *The London Prodigal*, and *The Puritan*, while Walker printed *Cromwell* in the same year, and Tonson *A Yorkshire Tragedy* in 1735, in which last year appeared also another reprint of *Oldcastle*, this time with no publisher's name. All these editions claim Shakespeare unreservedly as the author, and they are all quite worthless save as curiosities. Naturally the rival publishers were foes, and Tonson has denounced Walker in unmeasured terms as a pirate.

unanimous testimony gains weight from the facts that *The London Prodigal* was performed by Shakespeare's Company, and that the quarto was printed during the poet's lifetime for Butter, the publisher of *King Lear*. Yet in spite of this evidence and the acceptance of its genuineness by Tieck, Schlegel, and Hopkinson, any theory which supports the play's authenticity may safely be branded as utterly untenable.

The London Prodigal deals entirely with humours and manners. Like *The Puritan*, which it resembles in many points,[1] it depends for its value and effect on the bare plot and the really admirable delineation of the externalities of contemporary life. Shakespeare's catholicity and psychological insight are conspicuously absent, and every principle of his dramatic morality is outraged in the treatment of the prodigal's career. The only supposition on which the attribution can at all be justified is that put forward by Mr. Fleay; namely, that Shakespeare 'plotted' the comedy roughly and then left his vague design to be very imperfectly executed by another.

Mr. Fleay feels certain that *The London Prodigal* and *Thomas Lord Cromwell* are by the same author, and Ulrici ascribes our play to one of the writers of *Sir John Oldcastle*. There seems no reason for either belief. Considered with regard to general spirit, *The London Prodigal*, so full of the intimate details of domestic life, shows as much affinity perhaps to the early works of Dekker or to those of Marston as to the writings of any other well-known dramatist of the period; but in Dekker's case such a theory of authorship would become plausible only if he could be shown to have written for the King's Players just before 1605.[2] We know that Marston's *Malcontent*, 1607, was acted by the King's Majesty's Servants.

VIII. *The Puritan* was entered at Stationers' Hall on Aug. 6, 1607, by G. Eld,[3] and published in quarto (Q.) immediately after. The title-page runs: '*The Puritaine or the Widdow of Watling-streete. Acted by the Children of Paules. Written by W. S. Imprinted at London by G. Eld.* 1607.' The next editions were those of the third and fourth Shakespeare folios (F. 1, F. 2), of Rowe and Pope, and the separate reprints of Walker and Tonson in 1734.[4]

The first definite recognition of this comedy as the work of Shakespeare appears in a bookseller's catalogue of plays[5] published in 1656. The authority of the folios doubtless established the belief in its authenticity for a time, and we find Gildon in 1702[6] alluding to it as one of the genuine plays. Since the time

[1] There is good reason for believing that *The London Prodigal* and *The Puritan* are by the same author, or that the same author had a hand in both. See the discussion of the authorship of *The Puritan*, p. xxxi. f. It may be mentioned, though not as a fact of much significance in itself, that there is a close resemblance between Luce's Dutch-English in our play and that of Franchesina in Marston's *Dutch Courtesan*.

[2] He appears to have written ordinarily for Henslowe's Company.

[3] '6 Augusti ⟨1607⟩. George Elde Entred for his copie vnder th⟨e h⟩andes of Sir George Bucke knight and the wardens a book called the comedie of "the Puritan Widowe". vjd.' [4] See p. xxix, note 6. [5] Appended to an edition of *The Old Law*.

[6] Also listed as one of the genuine plays in Gildon's revision of Langbain's *Lives*

of Malone, however, no English critic seems to have doubted its spuriousness, and of the Germans, perhaps, only Tieck and Schlegel have attempted to enroll it among the works of Shakespeare.

Crude and farcical as *The Puritan* is, it contains some good bourgeois scenes, of a thoroughly un-Shakespearian kind, and has, moreover, the not very usual merit of making the reader laugh with genuine amusement. The spirit of the piece is light-hearted and pleasing, but it has small claim to consideration as serious art.

On the strength of the initials ' W. S.', and for no other reason, *The Puritan* has been attributed to each of the two forgotten dramatists, William and Wentworth Smith. There is slightly better cause possibly, from internal evidence,[1] to accept the theory of Middleton's authorship, favoured by Fleay, Bullen, Hopkinson, and Ward ; but this attribution, besides being entirely problematical, is not in accord with the certainty, first pointed out by Dr. Farmer, that the second scene of Act I, with its college cant and reminiscence, is the work of an Oxford man.[2]

So far, it must be generally allowed, rather less than no progress at all has been made towards the solution of the mystery of this play's authorship ; nor can the present editor presume to offer more than a very diffident and tentative answer to the question. Yet there are, I think, several facts, hitherto overlooked, which appear incontrovertible, and which, if they do not justify a final decision, should at least offer to future inquiry that definite *terminus a quo* so conspicuously lacking in the contradictory and unsupported theories previously advanced.

The most obvious of these facts is the extremely close affinity between *The Puritan* and the comedy of *Eastward Hoe*, published just two years earlier (1605) and authoritatively assigned to Chapman, Jonson, and Marston. It will be impossible, perhaps, for any one to read the two plays consecutively without being struck by their likeness in all the more significant and less easily imitated characteristics. The outward details of plot are for the most part different, but in general tone and dramatic method, as well as in a number of mannerisms and personal touches, there is a similarity which approaches near to absolute identity, and which makes it very hard to resist the conviction that the pen of one of the authors of *Eastward Hoe* has been employed in the other play.

It is not unlikely that in the later drama, as in the earlier, we have to do with a case of collaboration. The connexion of *The Puritan* with *Bartholomew Fair* would be explained if we could prove Ben Jonson to have been concerned in the former, but I feel much more sure of the authorship of John Marston, who, like

and Characters of the English Dramatick Poets, 1698, p. 128, where he adds : ' This was accounted a very diverting Play.'

[1] Reference to Mr. Bullen's valuable Index at the end of his edition of Middleton will show that a great number of passages in *The Puritan* and *The London Prodigal* may be illustrated by similar allusions in Middleton's works, but the parallels are by no means such as to suggest, even remotely and afar off, the idea of common authorship.

[2] Note, for example, the references to ' quadrangles ', ' batteling,' and to the Welsh at Jesus College.

the creator of Pye-board, was a member of Oxford University, and whose special traits—as known from his independent works and partly distinguishable in the tangled mesh of *Eastward Hoe*—are conspicuous in *The Puritan.*

The outlook upon London life in the last two dramas is practically identical. Both are realistic in the coarsest sense, and the types are the same, representing and satirizing, in the one play as in the other, the two hostile classes of court and city. Touchstone and Sir Godfrey, Quicksilver and Master Edmund, have little to distinguish them. Sir Petronel is but a composite of Pye-board and Penny-dub, with the villainy of the first and the inanity of the second. But the greatest resemblance appears in the female characters: Gertrude and Moll, one hopes and believes, can have but one creator. Both are revolting to the finger-tips, twin embodiments of middle-class vulgarity without a shade of difference. With their craving for coaches and ladyship, their loud expressed dread of 'leading apes in hell', and their continued mouthing of obscenities, they illustrate what, in one of the few pregnant phrases to be found in German dissertational literature, has been called [1] the *schmutzige Spur* which Marston's hand leaves ever behind it.

How often minor allusions in *The Puritan* answer to similar references in *Eastward Hoe* may be seen to a small extent from the notes to the former play. Both presume an encyclopaedic knowledge on the author's part of the Counter prison, with its manners and customs, its denizens and apartments. In both also we find sarcastic references to King James's new-made knights, though the allusions in *The Puritan* [2] are somewhat milder than the bold satire of *Eastward Hoe,*[3] which assisted in drawing down upon Marston's innocent associates the wrath of the sovereign. The two plays likewise were acted by what was practically the same company, though in the three years that separated them, its name and personnel had suffered alteration.[4]

In both the dramas before us there are frequent parodies and imitations of Shakespeare—humorous often, but not unkindly. In the one we have the changes rung on Pistol's rants about the welkin, and see 'Hamlet, a footeman', 'entering in haste' for the purpose of being asked, 'Hamlet, are you madde?' to the delectation probably of an audience already beginning to addle its brains and lose its temper over this infinitely discussed question. In the other play—that which immediately concerns us—Puttock and Ravenshaw serve Pye-board as Falstaff has been served by their colleagues Fang and Snare; while Corporal Oath is made to sit, instead of Banquo's spectre, as 'the ghost ith white sheete at vpper end a'th Table', and the mighty tragedy of the fifth act of Othello is burlesqued by the imitation of Pye-board, Skirmish, and Oath.

A further characteristic of *The Puritan,* which can hardly fail to impress the

[1] Emil Koeppel: *Quellen Studien zu den Dramen B. Jonson's, J. Marston's u. Beaumont's u. Fletcher's.* Erlangen-Leipzig, 1895.

[2] I. i. 85 ff; IV. i. 4.

[3] *Belles Lettres* ed., IV. i. 213–18.

[4] *The Children of her Maiesties Reuels,* mentioned on the title-page of *Eastward Hoe,* were replaced in 1606 by *The Children of Paules,* who acted *The Puritan.* Cf. Fleay: *History of the Stage,* pp. 184, 185.

careful reader is the especial bitterness of the author against his Puttocks and Ravenshaws. It is obvious that he looks upon himself as belonging to the poor scholar class, and that, if he does not regard Pye-board as a friend and a brother, he at least resents in a very personal way the insults and indignities to which the latter is subjected by the minions of the law.[1] It seems certain that there must have gone into the vivid portraiture of the poltroonery, brutality, and rapacity of Yeoman Dogson and his confederates, and into the realistic delineation of conditions in the Counter, a very considerable amount of unpleasant personal experience.

The general similarity of *The Puritan* to *Bartholomew Fair* is, of course, obvious, and has been alluded to repeatedly. For the most part the likeness is one of subject rather than treatment, and has no great significance, but in the case of a few details it merits more serious consideration. I cannot but think that the rough sketch of Master Ful-bellie the Minister—who is an excellent feeder and will be horribly drunk upon occasion, though he rails against players mightily because they once brought him drunk upon the stage—stood clear before the memory of Ben Jonson, when he came in 1614 to immortalize the race of Ful-bellies in Zeal-of-the-Land Busy.

The name of the central figure in *The Puritan*, George Pye-board, is probably a punning allusion to George Peele,[2] who was the perpetrator, according to contemporary story, of two of the tricks described in the comedy.[3] For any more definite information as to the source and authorship of the play, we must be content to await the discovery of further facts.[4]

IX. *A Yorkshire Tragedy* has from its first appearance been coupled with the name of Shakespeare. On May 2, 1608, it was entered on the Stationers' Register by the notorious Thomas Pavier (the publisher of *Oldcastle*) as a play ' by Wylliam Shakespere '.[5] A quarto (Q. 1) followed at once, with the title: '*A Yorkshire Tragedy. Not so New as Lamentable and true. Acted by his Maiesties Players at the Globe. Written by W. Shakspeare. At London. Printed by R. B. for Thomas Pauier, and are to bee sold at his shop on Cornhill, neere to the exchange.* 1608.' At the top of the first page of the text is the heading, ' All's One, or, One of the foure Plaies in one, called a York-shire Tragedy: as it was

[1] See, for example, the feeling behind Pye-board's and Puttock's colloquy on the gentlemanliness of scholars, III. iii. 62–72.

[2] '*Peel.* A baker's shovel . . . for thrusting loaves, pies, &c., into the oven and withdrawing them from it.' *New Eng. Dict.*

[3] Cf. the second and the eleventh of *The Merrie conceited Jests of George Peele, Gent.*, 1607. Licensed Dec. 14, 1605.

[4] The Stationers' Register has the following entry under date of Aug. 15, 1597, but it is by no means certain that the works referred to have any bearing upon our play: ' Richard Jones. Entred for his Copie by warraunt from master Warden man ij ballades beinge the ffirste and Second partes of the wydowe of Watling streete. xijd. Provided that noe Drapers name be set to them.' See *Shirburn Ballads*, I.

[5] ' 2do die maij ⟨1608⟩. Master Pavyer Entered for his Copie vnder the handes of master Wilson and master Warden Seton A booke Called A Yorkshire Tragedy written by Wylliam Shakespere. vjd.'

plaid by the Kings Maiesties Plaiers.' Eleven years later a second quarto (Q. 2) was issued with the imprint, 'Written by W. Shakespeare. Printed for T. P. 1619.' The text of this latter edition, though inferior to that of Q. 1 in the few points of difference, was followed by the editors of the third and fourth Shakespeare folios (F. 1, F. 2), Rowe, Pope, and Tonson.

The murders represented in *A Yorkshire Tragedy* occurred in 1605, and are thus recorded in Stow's Chronicle: 'Walter Callverly of Calverly in Yorkshire Esquier, murdred 2 of his young children, stabbed his wife into the bodie with full purpose to have murdred her, and instantly went from his house to have slaine his youngest child at nurse, but was prevented. For which fact at his triall in Yorke hee stood mute and was judged to be prest to death, according to which judgment he was executed at the castell of Yorke the 5th of August ⟨1605⟩.'

This sensational crime, as might be supposed, attracted no less attention than the earlier murder of Arden. At least three narrative accounts of it were licensed within a couple of months of its occurrence. On June 12 (1605) a pamphlet was entered [1] with the title: 'A booke called Twoo vnnaturall Murthers, the one practised by master Coverley a Yorkshire gent. vppon his wife and happened on his children the 23 of Aprilis 1605 . . .' [2] In July we have notice of 'A ballad of Lamentable Murther Done in Yorkeshire by a gent. vppon 2 of his owne Children sore woundinge his Wyfe and Nurse,' [3] and on August 24 we hear already of 'The Araignement Condempnacon and Execucon of Master Caverly at Yorke in Auguste 1605'.

The authenticity of the *Yorkshire Tragedy* has been allowed by Steevens, Ulrici, Hopkinson, Ward [5], and others; but the case which has been made out for the negative by Malone, Tyrrell, Knight, Halliwell-Phillips, Symonds, and Swinburne seems much the stronger. The barbaric force of the play and the splendour of some of the prose it contains cannot fail to impress the reader; but the late date (1605–8) is in itself an almost conclusive argument against the possibility of Shakespeare's authorship.

Neither in characterization, nor in plot, nor in metrical peculiarities have the most ardent defenders of the *Yorkshire Tragedy's* authenticity pretended that there is any approach to Shakespeare's manner subsequent to 1605. There are only two really considerable characters in the tragedy, the husband and the wife, and they are represented in a quite un-Shakespearian fashion. Each is

[1] By Nathaniel Butter, 'vnder th⟨e h⟩andes of master Hartwell and master norton warden.'

[2] The entry continues: 'The other ⟨murder⟩ practised by Mistress Browne and performed by her servant vpon her husband who in lent last were executed at Berry in Suffolk.' This last crime forms the subject of *A Warning for Fair Women.*

[3] 'Tertio Julii ⟨1605⟩. Thomas Pavyer Entred for his Copie vnder the handes of the wardens A ballad,' &c.

[4] '24 Augustj ⟨1605⟩. Nathanael Butter Entred for his Copie vnder the hand of Master ffeild The Araignement,' &c.

[5] Ward accepts only the best prose passages.

a mere type, not even invested with a name, and quite without the definite personality that Shakespeare in his maturity gives even to subordinate figures. The husband is a brilliant incarnation of wild fury and misdirected remorse. An unreasoning hatred of the world in which he has played so ignoble a rôle, and the ever-present consciousness of personal and family disgrace, drive him to seek momentary relief in brutish violence. The wife typifies the opposite extreme of rather unattractive docility. When this is said, there is little more to say; few or none of the individualizing and humanizing touches that Shakespeare gives his characters are here to be found.

The plot itself, in its nature narrow, sensational, and quite devoid of the morality of all Shakespeare's later work, speaks loud against the possibility of his authorship. To admit all this, as has been done, and explain *A Yorkshire Tragedy* as a sudden excursion by Shakespeare, during the last decade of his life, into a new and essentially lower field of literature, is to join the critical school of the famous friend of Schlegel,[1] who defended the authenticity of *The Puritan* on the ground that it was a successful attempt of Shakespeare to forsake his own style and write for once in that of Ben Jonson.

Finally, the verse of the *Yorkshire Tragedy* has few, if any, of the characteristics of Shakespeare's later verse. The end-stopped lines amount to about 88 per cent., an exceedingly high proportion for late work, while as many as 20 per cent. of the verse lines—two in every ten—are in rhyme. This large number of rhyming lines is not to be found in any but the earliest of the genuine plays, and the rhymes, moreover, are frequently obtained by means of a distortion in the word order, such as Shakespeare was not reduced to even in his apprentice work. The following six lines exemplify the quality of verse to be found in the duller parts of *A Yorkshire Tragedy*:

'Oh that I might my wishes now attaine,
I should then wish you liuing were againe,
Though I did begge with you, which thing I feard:
Oh, twas the enemy my eyes so bleard.
Oh, would you could pray heauen me to forgiue,
That will vnto my end repentant liue.'[2]

If Shakespeare's hand is to be traced anywhere in this play, we must look for it solely in the two hundred lines of prose scattered through the first four scenes. Some of this prose is, indeed, very fine, particularly the opening scene between the servants, and the splendid monologue of the husband in Scene 4. The latter passage of twenty-five lines, to the beginning of the feeble verse appendage, is certainly the poetic climax of the play, and perhaps not unworthy of Shakespeare. Yet it may be denied most emphatically that there is, here or elsewhere, anything either in thought or in expression which bears credible witness to the presence of the true Shakespearian touch.

As the heading of the first page of the quartos indicates,[3] the brief *Yorkshire Tragedy*, which runs to little over 700 lines, was performed in connexion with

[1] Cf. Schlegel's Lectures, ii. p. 266. [2] x. 45–50. [3] Cf. p. xxxiii.

three other dramatic fragments. It is probable that these last were of yet cruder workmanship than our play, and that no effort was made to preserve them from oblivion once they had served their turn upon the stage. Their connexion with *A Yorkshire Tragedy* may have been solely a matter of theatrical convenience, but it is at least possible that some or all of them concerned the earlier history of Calverley, and presented much the same incidents which Wilkins has used in *The Miseries of Enforced Marriage.*[1]

X. *The Merry Devil of Edmonton* was entered on the Stationers' Register, Oct. 22, 1607, the author's name being omitted.[2] A second entry [3] on April 5, 1608, referring to a 'booke called the lyfe and deathe of the merry Devill of Edmonton. . . . By T. B.', alludes certainly to a prose work by Tony Brewer, which has only the remotest connexion with our comedy. The latter, however, is again mentioned on the books of the Stationers' Company, and for the first time coupled with Shakespeare's name, in a re-entry by H. Moseley, the book-publisher, on Sept. 9, 1653.

There are six seventeenth-century editions of *The Merry Devil of Edmonton,* all in quarto and all anonymous. The first (Q. 1), dated 1608, is to be found in the library of Trinity College, Cambridge, and bears the following title-page: '*The Merry Deuill of Edmonton. As it hath beene sundry times Acted, by his Maiesties Seruants, at the Globe on the bank-side. London, Printed by Henry Ballard for Arthur Iohnson, dwelling at the signe of the white-horse in Paules Churchyard, ouer against the great North doore of Paules,* 1608.' Other quartos followed in 1612 (Q. 2), 1617 (Q. 3), 1626 (Q. 4), 1631 (Q. 5), 1655 (Q. 6).[4]

The text of this play abounds in difficulties, and a few passages seem hopelessly corrupt. The later editions sometimes correct misprints and insert emendations, but they throw little light on the real obscurities and have no independent authority. Altogether, though none of the quartos can perhaps be regarded as decidedly the best intrinsically, Q. 1, which gives as good sense as any, and stands nearest the original, appears to offer the best basis for modern editions, and has here regularly been followed.

The Merry Devil of Edmonton was as popular in the theatres as it appears to have been with the reading public. Reed first quoted [5] what is probably the

[1] Registered and published, 1607. This drama deals largely with the fate of the 'young mistress' alluded to in the first line of *A Yorkshire Tragedy*; it has a happy ending. Cf. Hazlitt's Dodsley, vol. ix, for the text of the *Miseries*. Its connexion with our play was first pointed out by Mr. P. A. Daniel, *Athenaeum*, Oct. 4, 1879.

[2] '22 Octobris ⟨1607⟩. Arthur Johnson Entred for his copie vnder th⟨e h⟩andes of Sir George Buck knight and Th⟨e⟩ Wardens. A Plaie called the Merry Devill of Edmonton. vjd.'

[3] '5to Aprilis ⟨1608⟩. Joseph Hunt, Thomas Archer Entred for their copie. Vnder the hand of master Seton Warden a booke called the lyfe and deathe of the merry Devill of Edmonton with the pleasant prankes of Smugge the Smythe. Sir John. and myne Hoste of the "George" about their stealynge of Venson, by T. B. vjd.'

[4] Q. 2 is not in any public library, but has been carefully collated by Warnke and Proescholdt from Mr. A. H. Huth's copy. Qq. 3–6 are in the British Museum; Q. 3, Q. 5, also in the Bodleian.

[5] Dodsley's Select Plays, 2nd ed., 1780. Vol. v, p. 247.

first extant mention from the *Blacke Booke* by T. M. (1604): 'Giue him leaue to see the Merry Devil of Edmunton or A Woman kill'd with kindness.' [1] From this we see that the play had attained a general reputation on the stage at least three years before it was registered for publication. Its vogue must, indeed, soon have become proverbial, for Ben Jonson asks in the Prologue to *The Devil is an Ass*: [2]

'And show this but the same face you have done
Your dear delight, the Devil of Edmonton.'

In Cunningham's *Revels Accounts* [3] there is the following mention of a performance before the King: 'To the said John Heminges upon a Warrant dated 15 May 1618 for presenting before his Ma^ty the thirde of May the Merry Divell of Edmonton . . . x^li.' It is not unimportant to note, if this extract can be relied on—and there seems no cause to suspect a forgery—that the presentation here referred to took place only two years after Shakespeare's death, and five before the publication of the first folio. If, then, Hemings later failed to include *The Merry Devil of Edmonton* in his edition of Shakespeare's works, it could not be because the play had not been brought conspicuously before his attention.

The external evidence which has been collected to prove Shakespeare's authorship of *The Merry Devil of Edmonton* is of the most dubious kind. It consists merely in the unsupported statements of the booksellers Moseley and Kirkman [4] about the middle of the seventeenth century, and in the play's presence in the 'Shakespeare volume' [5] of Charles the Second's library. Internal evidence there is none, unless we accept as such the not very significant likeness of Host Blague to the host in *The Merry Wives of Windsor*—a likeness which, as far as it shows anything, shows that the one writer has imitated the other, or that both have found dramatic use for a very common stock type.

Tieck was the first 'critic' who ascribed *The Merry Devil of Edmonton* to Shakespeare. He offered no serious evidence in favour of his theory, but has been followed by two other German writers, Franz Horn and H. von Friesen. No English reader, except Hopkinson, has been able to detect in this comedy the slightest approach to Shakespeare's manner, and the more trustworthy Elizabethan scholars in Germany—Bodenstedt,[6] Ulrici, Warnke and Proescholdt—are equally incredulous. Two eighteenth-century antiquaries, Coxeter and Oldys,[7] assigned the play to Michael Drayton, for no very apparent reason except that the country in which the scene is laid is described in *Polyolbion*. Charles

[1] Middleton's Works, ed. Bullen, vol. viii, p. 36. [2] 1616. [3] p. xlv.

[4] The editor of the first edition of Dodsley's *Select Collection of Old Plays* has the following prefatory note, which is both sound and candid: 'One Kirkman, a bookseller, who, about fourscore years ago, made diligent enquiry after old plays, and collated and published a great number, affirms this play to have been wrote by Shakespear; but I cannot help thinking he must be mistaken. When it was wrote I cannot say, or who was the author of it.'

[5] Cf. p. vii. [6] Note appended to Friesen's article: *Jahrbuch* I, p. 165.

[7] Cf. Reed's note on the play in the second edition of Dodsley's Collection, vol. v, p. 247, 1780.

Lamb and Mr. Fleay slightly favour this attribution, while Hazlitt and Ulrici ascribe the comedy to Thomas Heywood instead.

There seems no adequate reason to accept either Shakespeare, Drayton, or Heywood as the author of this fine play, and it will probably be long before we can venture with safety beyond the statement of Knight, that it is 'the performance of a true poet, whoever he be'. Certainly the vitality of the scenes, the heartiness of the humour, and the unsurpassed delicacy in the portrayal of true love and true friendship, make *The Merry Devil of Edmonton* one of the most delightful of all the pseudo-Shakespearian plays to read and to re-read.

XI. *Fair Em* does not appear to have been registered at Stationers' Hall, though at least two early quarto editions were published. One of these, which we shall refer to as Q. 1, is undated, and has the title: '*A Pleasant Commodie, of faire Em the Millers daughter of Manchester: With the loue of William the Conqueror: As it was sundrietimes publiquely acted in the honourable citie of London, by the right honourable the Lord Strange his seruaunts. Imprinted at London for T. N. and I. W. and are to be solde in S. Dunstones Church-yarde in Fleete-streete.*'

The only known copy of this edition is in the Bodleian; the other, somewhat commoner, quarto has a practically identical title-page, except as regards the imprint, which reads: 'Printed for John Wright, and are to be sold at his shop at the signe of the Bible in Guilt-spur street without Newgate. 1631.' The textual differences between the two editions are for the most part merely orthographic or accidental, but it seems likely that Q. 1, with its archaic spelling and grammar, is the older by perhaps a generation or more. The play is pretty definitely dated by the statement that it was acted by Lord Strange's servants, for this name was applied to one of the London companies [1] only from 1589 to 1593, and it seems probable that Q. 1 was published while the memory of 'the right honourable the Lord Strange his seruaunts' was still fairly fresh in the mind of the publisher and the public to whose tastes he was catering. Q. 2 is hardly more than a reprint of Q. 1, occasionally correcting an obvious mistake but never venturing on the real elucidation which some passages greatly require.

W. R. Chetwood, an eighteenth-century editor of *Fair Em*, enumerates three early editions of the play, assigning to one the date 1619. It was this 1619 quarto which Chetwood claimed to follow, but as the alterations which he introduced into the text are certainly not Elizabethan,[2] and as no one else has alluded to the edition of 1619, there is reason to believe it a mere figment of Chetwood's imagination, devised to give authority to his departure from the text of the two genuine quartos.

Regarding the authorship of *Fair Em* we have not a shred of evidence previous

Originally the Earl of Leicester's; later successively the Earl of Derby's, Lord Hunsdon's, the Lord Chamberlain's, &c., cf. Fleay's *History of the Stage*, pp. 82 ff., 133, &c.

[2] For a fuller discussion of this question, cf. Introduction to Warnke and Proescholdt's edition of *Fair Em*, pp. viii, ix.

to the Restoration. The only seventeenth-century hint of Shakespeare's connexion with the play is the label 'Shakespeare. Vol. I' on the back of the book which contained *Fair Em*, *Mucedorus*, and *The Merry Devil of Edmonton*, in the library of Charles II. Such small weight as this doubtful testimony may have is quite balanced by the assertion of Edward Phillips in his *Theatrum Poetarum* [1] that *Fair Em* was written by Robert Greene. Both these ascriptions have found defenders, but it is at present almost certain that neither of the poets suggested was ever in the least degree connected with the writing of our comedy.

The theory of Greene's authorship, advanced by Phillips and accepted by Dyce, has been discredited by R. Simpson, who shows that two lines in the last scene [2] are ridiculed, and the unknown author violently attacked, in Greene's *Farewell to Folly*, published in 1591. Tieck, Horn, Hopkinson, and Simpson have imagined that they saw in *Fair Em* indications of Shakespeare's handiwork, but only the last has produced arguments which to-day deserve even casual consideration. Simpson's idea, which he has elaborated with rather excessive ingenuity, is that Shakespeare wrote *Fair Em* as an allegorical attack on Greene and his school. William the Conqueror represents William Kempe, who had recently led a theatrical company to Denmark; Mountney typifies Marlowe, Manvile Greene, and the successful Valingford, Shakespeare himself, while Fair Em symbolizes the prize of the dramatic contest, the Manchester public. This interpretation is accepted in general by Mr. Fleay, who, however, ascribes the play to R. Wilson instead of Shakespeare, and explains Valingford as George Peele, while Fair Em, in his judgement, means the company of Queen's Players, not the Manchester audience.

In regard to the possible allegorical significance of *Fair Em*, the sanest conclusion is doubtless that to which Warnke and Proescholdt have come: there may be a substratum of allegory beneath the structure of the comedy, but it is only vaguely discernible, if it exists, and fails entirely to support the elaborate edifice of theory which both Mr. Simpson and Mr. Fleay have attempted to erect upon it. Mr. Simpson appears to have proved two facts: first, that *Fair Em* was not written by Greene; and, secondly, that it antedates Greene's *Farewell to Folly*.[3] It is doubtless equally certain that he has not succeeded in establishing, from external evidence, even the slightest probability of the play's Shakespearian origin, while, as he practically admits himself, the dramatic character and style of the work tend strongly to negative his arguments. In *Fair Em*, as Charles Knight says, 'we look in vain for all that sets Shakespeare so high above his contemporaries; his wit, his humour, his poetry, his philosophy, his intimate knowledge of man, his exquisite method.'

Fair Em is a thoroughly childish and inartistic production. Its only charm rests in the fact that it exhibits, with much of the crudity, also something of the heartiness and freshness of childish performances. Regarded as a serious essay

[1] 1675. [2] v. 121 and 157.
[3] 1591. For another indication of date, cf. p. xxxviii.

in dramatic art, it is full of impossibilities and absurdities both in the conception of the characters and in the incidents by which the action is carried along. Yet for the reader who can overlook its puerilities and occasional flatnesses, this indifferent play will probably justify the claim of the title-page, that it is 'a pleasant commodie'.

Fair Em might well have been defined in terms dear to the Elizabethan playwrights as 'Two Comedies in One'. Only in the fifth act is there any sort of real connexion between the two plots which make up the drama. The source of the story that gives the work its title is so far undiscovered; the other plot—that of William the Conqueror and the Danish Court—has been shown by Professor Schick, in his scholarly Preface to *The Spanish Tragedy*,[1] to come from Henry Wotton's *Courtlie controuersie of Cupids Cautels* (1578), which is itself a translation of Jaques Yver's *Prin-Temps d'Yver*. The novel which concerns us is the fourth in the collection; it ends tragically with the execution of Lubeck and the suicide of William.

XII. Of all the doubtful plays, *The Two Noble Kinsmen* is the one which has inspired the greatest amount of criticism and conjecture; yet there is perhaps no other member of the class that has so thoroughly maintained the mystery of its authorship, or has so often obliged candid investigators to retract their theories and confess themselves at a loss. This brilliant and puzzling drama was registered April 8, 1634,[2] and appeared first in quarto (Q.) with the interesting title-page: '*The Two Noble Kinsmen: Presented at the Blackfriers by the Kings Maiesties servants, with great applause: Written by the memorable Worthies of their time;*

Mr. John Fletcher, and }
Mr. William Shakespeare. } *Gent.*

Printed at London by Tho. Cotes, for Iohn Waterson: and are to be sold at the signe of the Crowne in Pauls Church-yard. 1634.'

The only other seventeenth-century edition is that (F.) which was published in 1679, with no mention of Shakespeare's name, in the second Beaumont-Fletcher folio. That this text is only a reprint of Q. with revised spelling, is made clear both from collation and from the express indication at the beginning of the folio that *The Two Noble Kinsmen* is one of the seventeen plays omitted in the first folio of Beaumont and Fletcher, and printed 'out of 4to'. The play has maintained its position in subsequent editions of Beaumont and Fletcher, and has been frequently published of late years, either separately or in collections. The standard edition is that prepared in 1876 for the New Shakspere Society by Harold Littledale.

We first hear of a drama on the subject of Chaucer's *Knightes Tale* in the

[1] *Temple Dramatists* edition, p. xxvi.

[2] '8° Aprilis ⟨1634⟩. Master John Waterson Entred for his Copy vnder the hands of Sir Henry Herbert and master Aspley warden a TragiComedy called *the two noble kinsmen* by John ffletcher and William Shakespeare. vjd.'

accounts of Queen Elizabeth's entertainment at Oxford in 1566. Stow's Chronicle for August 31, 1566, contains the following allusion: 'Comedies also and Tragedies were played in Christs Church, where the Queene's Highnesse lodged. Among the which, the Comedie entituled *Palemon and Arcet*, made by Master Edwards of the Queenes Chappell, had such tragicall successe as was lamentable; for at that time, by the fall of a wall, and a paire of staires, and great presse of the multitude, three men were slaine.' [1]

In Henslowe's Diary for the months of September–November, 1594, occur four notices of receipts from the presentation of a play with the same name, 'palamon and arsett.' The letters 'ne', affixed to the earliest entry, that of Sept. 17, show that the drama was on that day acted for the first time.[2] Collier's theory is that the work here mentioned is a revision of Edwards's old play, prepared by Shakespeare for joint performance by the Lord Chamberlain's and Lord Admiral's companies at the Newington Theatre, and that the Shakespearian portions were later elaborated by Fletcher in *The Two Noble Kinsmen.* Skeat and Littledale, however, base our play directly on Chaucer, and deny with probable justice that it has any connexion with either of the earlier dramas just mentioned, both of which are now lost.

Modern criticism is unanimous on two points: First, that *The Two Noble Kinsmen* was written by two poets, very different in style, genius, and character. Second, that the longer and weaker portion is mainly or exclusively the work of Fletcher. The separation is thus made by Littledale:

(*a*) The non-Fletcher part: I. i (except ll. 1–40), part of ii, iii, iv; II. i; III. i, ii; nearly all of IV. iii; V. i (except ll. 1–19), part of iii, iv (except ll. 99–113).

(*b*) The Fletcher part: All the rest.

The 'metrical tests' have been applied to this play with striking effect. The results of Littledale's reckoning as to the comparative proportion of double endings and run-on lines in the two divisions of the work may be tabulated thus:

	Double endings.	*Run-on lines.*
Part not by Fletcher	1 to 3·49	1 to 1·78
Part by Fletcher	1 to 1·89	1 to 4·06

The utter dissimilarity is obvious at a glance. In fact there is not the least difficulty in distinguishing the parts, except in one or two prose scenes belonging to the underplot, and in several passages which appear to combine the work of both hands. It is of importance to note that the style of the un-Fletcherian part of *The Two Noble Kinsmen,* as represented by the metrical tests, approaches very near to that of *The Winter's Tale* and *The Tempest,* and that it almost

[1] Littledale (Introduction 10*, 11*) quotes a fuller account of this catastrophe from Nicholls, *Progr. of Eliz.*, 1823, pp. 210–13. The authority is Anthony Wood.

[2] The following allusion in *Bartholomew Fair*, 1614 (IV. ii, *Mermaid* ed., pp. 103–4), is probably to this play: '*Quar.* . . Well, my word is out of the *Arcadia*, then; *Argalus.*—*Winw.* And mine out of the play; *Palemon.*' From the reference to the *Arcadia*, we may infer that the work coupled with it was not a recent one. Though it is possible, it seems to me excessively improbable that *The Two Noble Kinsmen* was acted as early as 1614, or indeed for some years after.

coincides with that of the un-Fletcherian part of *Henry VIII*, ascribed usually to Shakespeare, but by some recent critics to Massinger.

The answer to the long-mooted question as to Shakespeare's part-authorship of *The Two Noble Kinsmen* has always depended, and still depends, on the balancing of the undeniably Shakespearian tone of the style against the quite un-Shakespearian characterization. There are great names in abundance on each side.

The authenticity of the so-called Shakespeare parts has been defended by Lamb, Coleridge, De Quincey, Tyrrell, Spalding, Hallam, Hickson, Skeat, Furness, Littledale, Hopkinson, and Swinburne. The number of the sceptics is equally large and no less distinguished, including, strange to say, the usually over-credulous German writers. The case for the negative has been put boldly and trenchantly by Shelley in a letter to his wife:[1] 'I have been reading the "Noble Kinsmen", in which, with the exception of that lovely scene, to which you added so much grace in reading to me, I have been disappointed. The Jailor's Daughter is a poor imitation, and deformed. The whole story wants moral discrimination and modesty. I do not believe Shakespeare wrote a word of it.' The same disbelief has been expressed by Steevens, Hazlitt, Knight, Ulrici, Delius, von Friesen, Halliwell-Phillips, Boyle, Bierfreund, Furnivall, and Fleay.

In all that pertains to verse form and poetic expression the un-Fletcherian scenes of *The Two Noble Kinsmen* must probably impress the majority of readers as more overwhelmingly Shakespearian than any considerable passage in *Edward III*, *Arden of Feversham*, or *A Yorkshire Tragedy*. Yet in the case of this play no less certainly than in the case of the others it seems to be the tendency of good criticism to discredit the idea of Shakespeare's authorship. As Professor Ward says,[2] 'The ordinary results of a prolonged reflexion on the problem of the authorship of the doubtful portions of *The Two Noble Kinsmen* seems to be either an increased unwillingness, or at least a diminished willingness, to decide it in favour of the only specious claim—that which has been advanced on behalf of Shakespeare.'

An interesting case in point is that of Mr. Spalding, who in 1833 defended the genuineness of the 'Shakespearian' scenes in his classic *Letter on Shakespeare's Authorship of the Two Noble Kinsmen*. Seven years later his opinion was 'not now so decided as it once was'; and in 1847 he had become so doubtful as to declare: 'The question of Shakespeare's share in this play is really insoluble.'[3] Similarly, Mr. Fleay and Dr. Furnivall, who at first accepted the authenticity of the doubtful scenes, came, on maturer consideration, to pronounce them certainly spurious.

It is highly improbable that any critical reader of this play has met with a single scene which, after judging it on its own merits, he has been able to

[1] Prose Works (ed. 1888), ii. 235. [2] *Eng. Dram. Lit.* ii. 243.

[3] Cf. the reprint of the *Letter* with 'Forewords' by Furnivall in Publications of New. Sh. Soc., 1876.

pronounce candidly and with absolute confidence to be the work of Shakespeare. It would scarcely be too much to say that there is not even one speech which has ever seemed thoroughly and completely convincing to any conscientious student —no speech, that is, on which he would have been willing to rest the whole question, declaring that just here, if nowhere else, the fingers of the greatest poet of the world have infallibly left their mark. On the contrary, when we consider individually the parts of *The Two Noble Kinsmen* which have been ascribed to Shakespeare, we find invariably that each act, scene, or verse falls just short of what it should be. Always there is the strong Shakespearian reminiscence, but nowhere quite the full and perfect reality that we could swear to.

The advocates of the play's authenticity are, therefore, driven upon one or the other of two entirely illegitimate courses: either they argue from vague generalities of impression, without venturing upon the examination of details, whether of method, characterization, or technique; or they go on the hypothesis—perfectly unjustifiable and illogical—that we have before us not, indeed, Shakespeare's work as we all know it, but the same work degraded and weakened by the mischievous revision of Fletcher. On this last assumption there is no depth of critical absurdity which may not be reached. Admitting once that we are to judge of the work of Shakespeare not by what we know it to be, but by what we imagine that it might have been after alteration and debasement at the hands of a Fletcher or a Rowley, we may prove Shakespeare's concern in any wretched play of his age—in *Fair Em* itself, if we like—by merely assuming a sufficiently small amount of the Shakespearian gold and a relatively large amount of the alloy.

That portion of *The Two Noble Kinsmen* which is obviously not Fletcher's contains some of the most brilliant of Jacobean poetry. It is not less certain, I think, that it contains no spark of psychological insight or philosophy of life which can in sober moments be thought either worthy of the mature Shakespeare or even suggestive of him.

On the utter absurdity of associating Emilia, as she appears in any scene of the play, with Imogen or Miranda, or indeed with any other reputable dramatic heroine, Dr. Furnivall appears to have spoken the final word. Nor can her coarseness be explained, as critics have attempted to explain the spinelessness of Palamon and Arcite, by the theory that Fletcher has marred the promise of Shakespeare's plan. In the most distinctly un-Fletcherian scenes of all she is what Dr. Furnivall has called her, 'a silly lady's-maid or shop girl, not knowing her own mind, up and down like a bucket in a well.' [1]

On the dramatic character of the scenes not Fletcher's, few words require to be said, but they must be strong ones. There are two portions of the play which probably dwell so vividly in every reader's mind as to obscure the recollection of all the rest. They are the first scene of the first act and the first scene of the fifth. Both, it need hardly be said, are by another than Fletcher, and

[1] Note, for instance, her really revolting wishy-washiness and ingrained sensuality in what are perhaps her best scenes, IV. ii (the portrait scene) and V. iii.

neither has much to do with the action of the play. They are, as De Quincey has remarked,[1] examples of the most gorgeous rhetoric, and there is little reason, I think, for adding De Quincey's qualification that they are anything much better.

Had the first scene of *The Two Noble Kinsmen* come in the middle, the play's claim to authenticity would probably have found far fewer supporters. As it is, we are gripped at the very start by the grand operatic opening, the music of the verse, the spectacular effect of the marriage procession met by the sombre and hysterical widows, by the swaying of the opposing groups to and fro across the stage, by the co-operative supplication and bending of knees—not singly and individually, but in symmetrical groups, and, as it were, to the sound of music—by all the specious clap-trap, in fact, which seems to be dramatic action, and is really mere verbiage and ballet-dancing. That Shakespeare wrote a syllable of this scene will hardly be believed by any diligent reader who will take the trouble to ask himself what it all means and what is its connexion with the rest of the play.

The other memorable scene is that in which Arcite, Palamon, and Emilia offer their prayers before the altars of their patron deities. Here again we have an entire lack of dramatic utility or propriety cloaking itself behind spectacular brilliance and fine but unmeaning poetry. The whole incident is, of course, transported bodily from Chaucer's tale, where it is in keeping, to the closing act of the drama, where it most emphatically is not. Two of the speeches—those of Arcite and Emilia—are in De Quincey's words, 'gorgeous rhetoric'; the third is hardly that. They would make a fine though somewhat tedious division of an epic poem, but to suppose that they were foisted in by Shakespeare himself at the very climax of his play, and were meant by him for representation before an audience uninterested in mythical rites or divinities, but craving immediate and realistic action, this surely is to strain credulity to the breaking-point.

In conclusion we may thus sum up the matter: metrical and external evidence agree in proving that, if Shakespeare wrote any part of *The Two Noble Kinsmen*, in its present form, he must have done so during the very last period of his career. But, rich as the language and verse are in Shakespearian reminiscence, there is practically nothing in characterization or dramatic structure which points to the author of *The Tempest*; while such defects as the ambiguous personality of Emilia, the failure properly to distinguish between Palamon and Arcite, and the low dramatic pitch of the doubtful scenes render their ascription to the mature Shakespeare all but unpardonable. The only hypothesis, indeed, on which present-day criticism can even consider the idea of Shakespeare's connexion with *The Two Noble Kinsmen* is that laid down, not very probably, by Mr. Herford; namely, that the play consists of very late 'poetic'[2] fragments by Shakespeare, subsequently connected and completed by Fletcher.

If we put aside for the present the theory of Shakespeare's authorship as

[1] Works, ed. 1862, x. 49.

[2] Fragments, that is, in which the requirements of practical stagecraft were neglected to a much greater extent than in *The Tempest*.

being at the very least quite undemonstrable, there remain for consideration the claims of three other poets. George Chapman was suggested by Knight [1] many years ago, but no other writer has accepted the idea as even conceivable, and it need be mentioned only to be rejected. An acute Danish scholar, Dr. Bierfreund, maintains in his dissertation on 'Palamon og Arcite' [2] that Beaumont was Fletcher's sole collaborator in *The Two Noble Kinsmen*,[3] which he believes to be their first joint work. This attribution is favoured by the well-known fact of the literary partnership between Beaumont and Fletcher, and by the metrical similarity of Beaumont's verse to that of Shakespeare's last period and of the 'Shakespearian' part of *The Two Noble Kinsmen*. Beyond this, however, there seems to be nothing to support Dr. Bierfreund's theory, which, till it is further substantiated, can hardly be regarded as more than an ingenious guess.

Undoubtedly the most serious claimant to the honour, besides Shakespeare, is Philip Massinger, whose cause has been championed with a good deal of ability by Boyle and Fleay. In poetic technique, Massinger has been shown to approach nearest of all the Elizabethans to Shakespeare, and the metrical tests give him an even better title than his master to the doubtful part of our play. Moreover, the structural and psychological imperfections of the work, the tendency to unnecessary coarseness of language, the feeble imitation of Shakespeare, the frequent similarity to Massinger's acknowledged writings, all tell as strongly for Massinger's authorship as against that of Shakespeare.

There appears, indeed, to be but one serious objection to the assumption, otherwise very probable, that *The Two Noble Kinsmen* was written by Fletcher and Massinger, and that is the magnificent poetry of the un-Fletcherian part, with which hardly anything in Massinger's accepted work can compare. Prudent criticism will leave the whole question in doubt, till more evidence can be obtained. Yet, if a tentative decision is to be made from the facts at present before us, it appears both a more logical and a more pleasant course to assume that Massinger should, for once, have risen to the lofty poetry of *The Two Noble Kinsmen*, than to assume that the ripened Shakespeare should have stooped to its low level of character and morality.

XIII. *The Birth of Merlin* survives in a late seventeenth-century quarto (Q.) with the following title: '*The Birth of Merlin: or The Childe hath found his Father. As it hath been several times Acted with great Applause. Written by William Shakespear, and William Rowley. Placere cupio. London: Printed by Tho. Johnson for Francis Kirkman, and Henry Marsh, and are to be sold at the Princes Arms in Chancery-Lane.* 1662.'

There seems to have been no second edition till the publication of Tyrrell's 'Doubtful Plays of Shakspere' in 1851. The spelling of Q, as might be expected, is of the usual Restoration character, and the metre has been corrupted, in many

[1] Pictorial Shakespeare, vii. p. 182 ff. [2] p. 77.

[3] The same view has been expressed more casually by Colman (*Beaumont and Fletcher's Works*, 1778) and Hazlitt (*Elizabethan Literature*).

cases irretrievably, by the printing of the entire play in long prose lines—apparently to save space. From the language and grammar, however, as well as from the general tone, it is clear that *The Birth of Merlin* was not composed later than the reign of James I; nor is it at all likely that it antedates James's accession. Mr. Fleay assigns it, in its present form, to the year 1622.

There is no external evidence of Shakespeare's partial authorship except that of the publisher, Kirkman, repeated in his catalogues of 1661 and 1671, where we read: 'Shakespear and Rowley . . Birth of Merlin . . T⟨ragi⟩ C⟨omedy⟩.' This attribution, made so long after Shakespeare's death, and by a particularly untrustworthy authority, has met with scant respect in modern times save from the early German critics, Tieck and Horn. There is not a single poetic passage in *The Birth of Merlin*, which will justify for an instant the hypothesis of Shakespeare's authorship. The disjointed nature of the plot, moreover, the foolish and immature morality of the Modestia scenes, and the repeated appeals to the cheap make-shifts of sorcery and divination, stamp it as distinctively un-Shakespearian.

Yet the reader of this play will perceive, as no modern reader of *Cromwell* or *The London Prodigal* easily can, what was in the minds of those critics who have defended its genuineness. One meets with occasional bits of poetry and characterization which have certainly a remote kinship to Shakespeare and were probably written under his influence. In passages like the speeches of Prince Uter in II. iii[1], we recognize dimly and afar off the syntactic rush, the ease of verse flow, the figurative power, and sincerity of emotion, which we know in Shakespeare. The strength and naturalness of the lines given to Edoll in II. ii, show that the author could portray deep passion in lucid, simple verse.

But in other places we find what seems to be intentional and rather disastrous imitation of Shakespeare's broken syntax and bold use of words. In these cases we acknowledge ourselves in the presence of a poet of rather more than respectable endowments, yet we must often feel that the actual value of the thought is hardly sufficient recompense for untwisting the convolutions of a sentence such as this:

> 'Or like to Marius soldiers, who, o'retook,
> The eyesight killing Gorgon at one look
> Made everlasting stand: so fear'd my power,
> Whose cloud aspir'd the Sun, dissolv'd a shower.' [2]

No commentator has seen particular reason to deny William Rowley's concern in *The Birth of Merlin*, since this Rowley was too obscure a dramatist to be credited with a play, without at least hearsay evidence in his favour. Hopkinson assigns the entire performance to Rowley, while Fleay, on the other hand, believes his part to consist solely or mainly in the revision of another man's work. Mr. P. A. Daniel (1884) suggested Middleton as the author of the play, and Mr. Fleay at one time accepted this attribution with conviction, at least as regards the serious

[1] ll. 162-9, 183-205.

[2] II. i, ll. 95-8.

parts.[1] Till the matter has been much more thoroughly investigated, however, the connexion of Middleton with *The Birth of Merlin* must remain quite problematical. It is perhaps an indication in his favour that the detailed legal allusions [2] prove the author to have been one well versed in the law,[3] and the fact of his frequent collaboration [4] with William Rowley adds a little more to the weight of confirmatory evidence.

XIV. Until 1844, the fine play of *Sir Thomas More* existed only in a confused, mutilated, and generally unknown manuscript belonging to the British Museum.[5] In that year it was transcribed by Dyce, with admirable fidelity, and printed for the Shakespeare Society. The only other edition, with modernized spelling, was published in 1902 by A. F. Hopkinson for private circulation. As Mr. Hopkinson did not consult the MS., his variations from Dyce have no claim to consideration except as pure conjecture.

The text of Dyce contains a few unintentional deviations from the MS., such as the difficult and varied handwriting of the latter rendered practically unavoidable. These trifling inaccuracies, so far as careful collation has revealed them, have been set right in the present edition. For certain parts of the play, however, Dyce's version must remain the ultimate authority, since a number of words and lines, intelligible to him, have by the subsequent deterioration of the MS. become quite indecipherable or have entirely crumbled away. The manuscript consists of twenty sheets, written in five [6] different hands. The paper is not of the same kind throughout, and some of the scenes are obviously misplaced. In several cases we get two drafts of the same scene, while small portions of other scenes have been entirely lost. Altogether the confusion is extreme ; yet Dyce has succeeded in effecting what appears to be certainly the proper arrangement, and the lacunae are nowhere so great as to obscure the plot.

Leaves 3–5, 10, 11, 14, 15, 17–22, of the MS.,[7] comprising about two-thirds of the whole, are undoubtedly older than the rest. These thirteen leaves, written closely on both sides of the paper, with a certain amount of neatness and only the usual copyist's errors, belong, without doubt, to the draft of the play which was submitted to Sir Edmund Tilney, the Master of the Revels, for licence to act. On the margins of these pages we meet, from time to time, with Tilney's comments, called forth by what he regarded as the seditious nature of various passages. Thus, at the top of the very first page he has written : 'Leaue out ye insurrection wholy and the cause thereoff, and begin with Sir Tho. Moore at ye mayors sessions, with a reportt afterwardes off his good seruice don, being shriue off London,

[1] *Life of Shakespeare*, 1889, pp. 289–90. Withdrawn *Biog. Chron. Eng. Dr.*, 1891, II. 105, where he regards the *Birth of Merlin* as a refashioning by Rowley of an older play, possibly the *Uter Pendragon*, acted by the Admiral's Company in 1597.

[2] e.g. II. iii. 20–2 ; III. i. 89–91 ; III. ii. 38–44.

[3] Middleton *may* have been a member of Gray's Inn.

[4] Cf. Fleay, *Biograph. Chron.* on 'Middleton'.

[5] Harleian 7368.

[6] Possibly only four; cf. p. xlviii. According to Dr. Furnivall, there are clearly six, and perhaps seven.

[7] That is, leaves 1–3, &c., of the play, which begins on the third leaf of the MS.

vppon a mutiny agaynst ye Lumbardes, only by a shortt reportt, and nott otherwise, att your own perrilles. E. Tyllney.'

The insurrection scene, however, and the other parts to which the Master of the Revels took exception were not left out, but merely recast. There appears, indeed, to have been no difference of plot between the original version of *Sir Thomas More,* as submitted to Tilney, and the elaborated form in which the MS. preserves it. The new scenes are revisions of the old ones, indescribably finer in several instances as poetry and drama, but adding no fresh element to the general design.

In one or two cases a page of the original matter has been almost totally hidden by having a new passage pasted bodily over it. The thirteen legible leaves of the original draft give us the following scenes. Act I, Scene i, ii, iii; II. i, iv (ll. 173–end); III. i; IV. i (ll. 1–309), ii, iii, iv, v (except new draft of ll. 68–104); V. i, ii, iii, iv. Scraps of other important scenes, such as II. ii and III. ii, are also occasionally discernible, but the old versions of these parts of the play have generally been deleted or pasted over to prevent confusion with the new, improved readings.

The original draft of the play, as submitted to Tilney, is in a single hand and runs on almost without a blot or correction; it is a clean copy, made perhaps not by the author himself, but by a professional scribe. The later insertions, however,—leaves 6–9, 12, 13, 16—are for the most part preserved exactly as they were composed. They are full of deletions and alterations, and are written on paper of varying sorts and sizes, in certainly three, probably four, different hands, none of which resembles that of the original thirteen sheets. If, then, we call the handwriting of the first draft Hand A, we may thus indicate the various sorts which appear on the seven new leaves:—

Hand B. Found only on leaf 6, which contains a revision [1] of the scene between More and his wife (IV. v, ll. 68–104). This passage of seventy lines was never properly fitted into the play, so that the old version in Hand A has been left standing in its proper place, while the improved, lengthened version in Hand B was negligently inserted between II. i and II. ii.

Hand C. Occurring on the first page of leaf 7 (II. ii) and on leaf 16 (IV. i. 309, S. D. 'Enter a Servingman,' to end of scene).

Hand D. This is the handwriting which Mr. Simpson and Mr. Spedding have united in assigning to Shakespeare upon evidence of a most interesting character. The only difficulty connected with the discrimination between the various handwritings of the MS. concerns itself with this Hand D. Mr. Simpson [2] believed that all the passages in the play, which are not in the easily recognizable A, B, and C hands, are written in Hand D and by Shakespeare. This would make the latter the author or reviser of the following scenes: II. iii, iv (ll. 1–172); III. ii and iii.

Mr. Spedding,[3] on the contrary, recognizes a fifth hand, to which he assigns:

[1] Printed in the Appendix to the play, pp. 419, 420.
[2] 4 *Notes and Queries,* viii. 1 ff. [3] 4 *Notes and Queries,* x. 227 ff.

II. iii ; III. ii, ll. 1–282 ; III. iii ; and perhaps the remaining part of III. ii. Thus Spedding leaves to Shakespeare only the magnificent insurrection scene [1] to the end of line 172, and a very doubtful title to the end of III. ii from line 283. The best judgement on this difficult question seems that kindly given me by Mr. Herbert, of the British Museum,[2] who considers all the scenes ascribed by Simpson to Shakespeare to be in one handwriting, with the exception of III. ii, ll. 283–end. In agreement with this opinion we divide as follows :—

Hand D : II. iii, iv (ll. 1–172) ; III. ii (ll. 1–282), iii.

Hand E : III. ii (ll. 283-end).

The manuscript of *Sir Thomas More* contains no direct statement in regard to the play's origin. The questions of authorship, date, and stage production are all left dark, except for such doubtful light as a few casual allusions in the body of the text may shed. That the drama belongs to the end of the sixteenth century, and probably not to the extreme end, is indicated by several considerations. In Act IV, Scene 1,[3] there occur two anachronistic references to Ogle, a theatrical wig-maker mentioned in Cunningham's *Revels Accounts* for 1573, and again under date of 1584. As one of the players is represented as leaving More's house to get from Ogle a false beard, with which he later appears, the realistic effect of the allusion would have been lost, had not Ogle's shop been in actual existence when the drama was produced.

Dyce suggested 1590, or just before, as the date of the play, and Simpson, who regarded the insurrection scenes as inspired by a similar outbreak in 1586, decided positively for that year or the next. Mr. Fleay, on the other hand, supported by Hopkinson, pronounced 1595–6 the earliest probable date, and refers to a rising in June, 1595, which might well have given appositeness to the insurrection scenes and rendered them particularly distasteful to the Master of the Revels. The two dates proposed by Simpson and Fleay respectively may safely be accepted as determining the period within which *Sir Thomas More* was written.

The additions were most likely composed soon after the body of the play. This is almost certainly true of More's magnificent speech in defence of order and humanity in II. iv, intended obviously as a balance to the revolutionary scenes which so displeased Tilney. Without such a makeweight on the side of law, no theatre manager, however bold, could well have ventured to perform the first part of the play, in the face of the tremendous prohibition : 'Leaue out ye insurrection wholy and the cause thereoff . . . att your own perrilles.' The most probable explanation of the number of hands concerned in the work

[1] II. iv.

[2] Through the kindness of Dr. Furnivall I am able to give also the careful opinion of Mr. Warner, the Keeper of the MSS. at the British Museum. His belief is that ff. 8, 9—the leaves containing the insurrection scene (II. iv. 1–172)—are in a different hand from the rest, but he is not sure of the matter. This view would make the problem much simpler, but I have thought it safer to accept the decision which is less favourable to the idea of Shakespeare's authorship.

[3] ll. 126, 292

and the extraordinary disorder of the MS. seems to be that the manager, anxious to act the play with the least possible loss of time, but afraid to run directly counter to authority, turned the original draft over to several writers, each of whom hastily revised what seemed to him most glaringly in need of alteration.

There is reason for believing that *Sir Thomas More* was acted by the Lord Chamberlain's Servants. Before the speech of the Messenger in III. iii, the MS. writes: Mess. T. Goedal, } which, of course, means that the messenger's part was to be taken by T. Goedal. Thomas Goodale, who is here indicated, is known [1] to have been in 1592 a subordinate member of the Lord Strange's Company, later called the Lord Chamberlain's.

Such discussion as this play has received hitherto has concerned itself chiefly with the interesting possibility that the scenes in Hand D, or some part of them, may be directly from the pen and brain of Shakespeare. The theory of Shakespearian part-authorship was evolved by Richard Simpson in 1871, and supported in the following year by James Spedding, with the differences as to detail already specified. Mr. Hopkinson has accepted their general conclusions, and Professor Ward, declaring his inability to judge concerning the genuineness of the so-called Shakespearian handwriting, goes on to say: [2] 'As to the style and manner of the passages in question, not only may the speeches of More, in particular that addressed to the insurgents, which may have been specially elaborated to suit the requirements of the licenser, be said without hesitation to have the true Shakespearean manner, besides being genuinely Shakespearean in feeling, but it is with difficulty they can be conceived to have been written by any other contemporary author.' Dr. Furnivall, on the other hand, doubts that the text of the insurrection scene, &c., in the MS., is in Shakespeare's writing, and says of this portion of the play that there is 'nothing necessarily Shaksperean in it, though part of it ⟨is⟩ worthy of him'.[3] Mr. Fleay appears likewise to be incredulous.[4]

The difficult question raised by these dissimilar opinions would be much easier of solution if we could, with Spedding, dismiss all but the supreme passage in the play, the culminating insurrection scene and speech of More,[5] as written in a different hand, and therefore not belonging to the Shakespearian matter. This, it must be said in candour, we are perhaps hardly justified in doing.[6] All the scenes enumerated on p. xlix as belonging to Hand D—including the relatively weak Randall-Erasmus-More passages in III. ii, and the even more commonplace II. iii—may very probably be in the same handwriting. Moreover, it is practically certain, from the appearance of the MS. of the 'insurrection scene' (as will be indicated later) that the handwriting is that of the author. If, therefore, we

[1] Cf. Fleay, *Hist. of the Stage*, p. 84.
[2] *Eng. Dram. Lit.*, ii, 214.
[3] *Royal Shakspere*, i, cxv. His opinion has not altered materially since.
[4] *Life of Shakespeare*, 292 ff.
[5] II. iv, ll. 1-172.
[6] At least for the present, though we should have Mr. Warner's great authority for doing so. Cf. p. xlix, note 2.

decide that II. iv, ll. 1–172, is written and composed by Shakespeare, then we should be prepared to accept II. iii; III. ii, ll. 1–282; III. iii, as at least transcribed in Shakespeare's hand. It is quite possible to do this, and the necessity of doing so detracts little perhaps from the strength of the case which may be founded on the 'insurrection scene' alone.

The first 172 lines of the 'insurrection scene' appear to me more thoroughly in the tone of Shakespeare than any other passage in the doubtful plays. There is possibly more striking poetry in *Edward III* and *The Two Noble Kinsmen*, and greater intensity of feeling in parts of *Arden of Feversham*, but it would be difficult or impossible to find, outside the plays of the ordinary canon, any extract of similar length which reminds the reader so strongly and lastingly of the special peculiarities of Shakespeare's genius. We get something of the familiar ring in the very first sentence, Lincoln's appeal to the unruly mob he has gathered about him.

'*Lincolne.* Peace, heare me: he that will not see a red hearing [1] at a Herry grote, butter at alevenpence a pounde, meale at nyne shillings a bushell, and beeff at fower nobles a stone, lyst to me.

Geo. Bett. Yt will come to that passe, yf straingers be sufferd. Mark him.'

This, and the speeches that follow inevitably suggest Jack Cade and his company in 2 *Henry VI.*[2] The perception of the individual Shakespearian touch grows stronger in the mob's clamorous debate as to whether Shrewsbury, Surrey, or More, is to address them—a debate decided finally for More with the true mob logic of Shakespeare.—

'*Doll.* Letts heare him: a keepes a plentyfull shrevaltry, and a made my brother Arther Watchins Seriant Safes yeoman: lets heare Shreeve Moore.

All. Shreiue Moor, Moor, More, Shreue Moore!' [3]

The speech of More, which follows, is praised on all hands both for its splendid poetry and for its likeness to Shakespeare, but it, as well as the earlier part of the scene, must be read in its entirety to be appreciated. The numerous parallels of word and phrase with the acknowledged works will not escape the notice of any reader. Equally apparent and generally recognized is the similarity to Shakespeare's early style in all matters of technique. The bold figurative use of words,[5] the rich smoothness of verse, and the total absence of strain or affectation at the height of poetic intensity, mark these lines as not less Shakespearian in metrical quality than any part of *The Two Noble Kinsmen* or *Edward III.*

The top scene of *Sir Thomas More*, however, exhibits the surest indications of Shakespearian authorship just where the claim of all the other doubtful plays breaks down; that is, when we judge it dramatically rather than poetically, giving less regard to the manner and more to the matter. The 172 lines in question say precisely what we should expect Shakespeare, the man and dramatist,

[1] herring. [2] IV. ii. [3] ll. 58–63. ll. 80–172.

[5] e.g. 'And you in *ruff* of your opynions clothd,' l. 99.
'Your noyce
Hath *chidd* downe all the maiestie of Ingland.' 92–3, &c.

to say; we have here the same attitude toward the mob—half good-natured laughter, half scorn and distrust—and the same eloquent championship of law and order against anarchic tendencies, which appear so consistently throughout the genuine works.

Moreover, the 'insurrection scene' satisfies fully the almost decisive test ot utility. Whereas the so-called Shakespearian portion of *Edward III* splits the play into two irreconcilable halves, and the analogous scenes in *The Two Noble Kinsmen* seldom touch at all the dramatic crises, which are regularly left to the pen of Fletcher, the author of the 'insurrection scene' in *Sir Thomas More* has turned his attention to the crucial point in the drama, and has revised it in just the way which best answers the requirements both of stage effect and of managerial prudence. It is not too much to say of this scene, by way of summary, that it is exactly the sort of scene we should expect Shakespeare to write, had he been called upon to revise the play, full of his well-known sentiments, and expressed in a style which is very remarkably like his own during the period 1590–5.

If these lines are really by Shakespeare, we have a most interesting illustration of the method of composition during his early maturity. The frequent interlineations and substitutions of one phrase for another show how the work took form as it proceeded, and make it evident that the sheet of paper on which this scene is written in the Harleian MS. contains the author's first draft, set down line by line as the passage evolved itself in his brain. In the final version, ll. 132 ff. read as follows:

'Wash your foule mynds with teares, and those same handes,
That you lyke rebells lyft against the peace,
Lift vp for peace, and your vnreuerent knees, 134
Make them your feet to kneele to be forgyven! 135
Tell me but this; what rebell captaine,
As mutynies ar incident, by his name
Can still the rout?' &c.

These fine lines were not arrived at without difficulty. In their first form there was a pause after 'feet' in 135, after which the poet wrote:

'To kneele to be forgyven
Is safer warrs then euer you can make
Whose discipline is ryot, why euen your warrs 3
Cannot proceed but by obedience; what rebell captaine,' &c.

This failed to satisfy him and caused him an obvious struggle, before it could be remodelled to his taste. First he deleted 'warrs' at the end of the third line and wrote instead 'hurly', apparently because of the presence of 'warrs' in the preceding line. Then, as a substitute for 'why . . . hurly' he has written above 'in in to yr obedience', which in turn is lined out with all the rest, to be replaced by the single half-line, 'Tell me but this.' At the same time, apparently, the pause in 123 was shifted from the middle to the end of the line.

Of the other scenes, possibly written in Hand D, only the soliloquy of More [1]

[1] III. ii, ll. 1–21.

and the comic Faulkner passages [1] seem at all worthy of Shakespeare. They, however, may doubtless be attributed to him, without excessive temerity, as careless revisionary work, fundamentally similar in style and tone to his genuine performances, but naturally more hasty and somewhat less spirited. II. iii, the Erasmus part of III. ii, and the whole of III. iii, must be allowed to be decidedly un-Shakespearian ; but of the last two of these passages it is quite certain, and it is extremely probable of the first, that the person who transcribed them in Hand D (?) was not in any real sense their author. The two Erasmus bits of III. ii (ll. 22–47, and 142–240), and the two Faulkner bits (ll. 48–141 and 241–end), alternate with each other and are not easily separated. From the scraps of the old version of the scene in Hand A, which are still legible, it appears that the Erasmus part was largely copied with only casual embellishments by the reviser, while the Faulkner part is remodelled and immensely improved. Thus the Erasmus passages are basically the work of the original author of the play and have been rewritten in Hand D, with merely incidental improvements, because they are wedged into the same scene with the Faulkner episode to which the reviser gave serious attention.

The brief and tame Scene 3 of the third act is copied in Hand D (?) verbatim, except for the insertion of the single word 'hether', from the original draft written in Hand C just after IV. i. It is clear that scribe C, having added to IV. i the final lines 310–68, used the remaining half-sheet of paper for the sketch of a much-needed connecting scene between the third act and the fourth. The deletions prove the priority of this copy of the scene to that in Hand D (?). Line 5, for instance, was first written : 'As sent to tell your lordship of his cominge.' Then the first two words were deleted, and the last three replaced by 'that they ar at hand', which later was also scratched out in favour of the final reading : 'of ther neer aproche.' Scribe D has merely copied this scene in its final form, inserting 'hether' in line 3 for the sake of the metre, and has pasted his copy where the scene obviously belongs—at the end of Act III. What is certainly true of the Erasmus parts in III. ii, and of III. iii, is in the highest degree likely of II. iii, the only other mediocre scene in Hand D (?). Here, too, the scribe seems to have been not the author, but merely the theatrical arranger, though, from the incomplete state of the MS., it is not possible in this case to compare the revised version with the original.

Setting these scenes aside, then, we are left with the first 172 lines of II. iv, and three passages from III. ii (ll. 1–21, 48–141, 241–282), all of which are written in Hand D (?) and are in large measure composed by the writer. Through these three hundred lines we meet the same general characteristics, though they display themselves in greater freedom and grandeur in the completely new-cast 'insurrection scene' than in the merely revised and elaborated passages of III. ii.

When we consider this part of *Sir Thomas More* in its poetic, and particularly in its dramatic and personal aspects, taking into account the play's probable

[1] III. ii, ll. 48–141, 241–282.

date and the probable company by which it was acted, it is hardly possible to withstand the conviction that if Shakespeare was ever concerned with any of the apocryphal plays, then surely it was with this.

Of the body of the play little need be said, though *Sir Thomas More* ranks high among the productions of its decade. Lack of unity is a defect inherent in its style of composition, but the absence of anything like a consecutive plot is to some extent atoned for by the effectiveness of More's genial character. The really attractive personality of the central figure, and the genuine spirit of light-heartedness which inspires even the tragic scenes, are two merits covering a multitude of imperfections, and raising *Sir Thomas More* far above the flatness of *Oldcastle* and *Cromwell*. In no work of the period do we get a more vivid portrayal of the management of an aristocratic household. The dinner to the Lord Mayor, the picture of More in the midst of his family circle, and the glimpse behind the scenes of a Tudor morality [1] are charming bits of domesticity which it would not be easy to parallel in the range of Elizabethan dramatic literature.

The main source of the drama is doubtless Hall's Chronicle, from which Dyce quotes illustrative excerpts; however, the story of More's life and death was such common property in the reign of Elizabeth that it is unsafe perhaps to fix upon any one authority. I have found an account of the fight in Pannier Alley, and of the episode of the long-haired Faulkner (III. ii) in Fox's Book of Martyrs (ed. 1684, II, 431), where both incidents are related in connexion with Thomas Cromwell. The stock account of More's execution, very much as it appears in the play, will be found in the same work (II, 294). The authorship of *Sir Thomas More* in its first form has been assigned to Lodge, whose doubtful claim is favoured by Fleay and Hopkinson.[2]

A few words remain to be said regarding the editorial history of the *Shakespeare Apocrypha*. Of the fourteen plays here printed, all but the recently discovered *Sir Thomas More* have suffered at the hands of late sixteenth and seventeenth-century editors. During the period which began with Kirkman [3] and culminated with Malone, Capell, and Steevens, critical energies were engaged here as elsewhere, in the well-meant but mischievous task of levelling out grammatical archaisms, and normalizing the frequently rough or irregular flow of the lines.

[1] It may be remarked that the play here presented (IV. i) has only its name in common with the *Marriage of Wit and Wisdom*, edited for the Shakespeare Society by Halliwell in 1846. The morality of Luggins and his companions is, as Mr. Fleay and others have pointed out, a medley of *Lusty Juventus* and *The Disobedient Child*. The real *Mariage of wyt and wisdome* appears on the Stationers' Register as the first of a list of books transferred from Th. Marshe, deceased, to Th. Orwyn, June 23, 1591. Cf. Arber's *Transcript*, ii, 275*b*.

[2] Mr. Fleay (*Life of Sh.*, 292-3; *Biog. Chr. Eng. Dr.*, ii. 312, 313) identifies Sir *Thomas More* with the play called *Abuses*, which, we are told, contained a comedy and a tragedy, and which was acted by the Children of Paul's before James I and the King of Denmark on July 30, 1606. This is a guess pure and simple.

[3] *Circa* 1660.

Under this régime, which shows itself almost at its worst in the emendations of the modern German critics Delius, Moltke, and Elze, the present plurals in -s, for example, and such expressions as 'thou was'[1] disappeared, while 'the *hugie* monsters' of *Locrine*[2] reappeared as 'the *hugest* monsters'. At the same time, the frequent nine-syllable lines of the originals, and the lines in which words like 'grace,' 'fear,' 'lord,' were pronounced in two syllables, were made arithmetically orthodox by the insertion of some colourless monosyllable. Thus in *Cromwell*,[3] instead of the correct old reading,

> 'Well hath your Grace said, my Lord of *Norffolke;*
> Therefore let vs presently to *Lambeth*.'

we find in Malone's and every succeeding text:

> 'Well hath your grace said, my *good* lord of Norfolk:
> Therefore let us *go* presently to Lambeth.'

In the last two acts of this one play thirty-four words have been thus unwarrantably inserted, and the number of omissions is almost as great.

Only within the last few decades has any attempt been made to purge the text of the apocryphal plays of the impurities which all had accumulated during the long period of careless or ill-advised editing. Even since the beginning of the nineteenth century, edition after edition has reprinted the insipid texts of the later quartos and Malone, or has differed only in the incorporation of yet other unnecessary emendations. For two hundred years there has not appeared a reliable version of *Locrine, Mucedorus, Sir John Oldcastle, Thomas Lord Cromwell, The London Prodigal, The Puritan*, or *A Yorkshire Tragedy*—and that, too, notwithstanding the fact that all these plays, except *Mucedorus*, are included in the third and fourth Shakespeare folios, and that all of them in their garbled form have been many times reprinted.

The other seven plays have in recent times been edited from the original quarto texts, with varying accuracy. Undoubtedly the most valuable of these editions are the standard texts of *The Two Noble Kinsmen* and *Sir Thomas More*, by Littledale and Dyce respectively. *Arden of Feversham* has been carefully edited by Mr. Bullen, and, independently, by the indefatigable German scholars, Warnke and Proescholdt, to whom we owe also editions of *Edward III, The Merry Devil of Edmonton, The Birth of Merlin, Fair Em*, and *Mucedorus*.

The value of the texts by Warnke and Proescholdt differs considerably. The earliest, that of *Mucedorus*, cannot be accepted as a critical edition at all, though well provided with *apparatus criticus* and laboriously prepared. Of the many quartos only the eighth has been consulted at first hand, and the editors have made the fatal mistake of adopting, as the readings of the first and third quartos respectively, what are in reality the silent emendations of Hazlitt and Collier.[4]

Fair Em, the second of the plays edited by Warnke and Proescholdt, is better

[1] *Edward III*, I. i. 106. [2] I. i. 238. [3] IV. v. 115–16.
[4] This so-called third quarto of Collier's probably never existed; cf. p. xxiv.

done. The spelling is not modernized, as in their text of *Mucedorus*, and the two old quartos have really been collated. Yet numberless small corrections are required to render this edition at all authoritative. In some way, which it would be difficult to explain, the orthography and variant readings of the two quartos have been so mixed that the resultant text gives no faithful representation of either. The editors appear to have profited by experience, for they have had much more success with the other four plays published by them ; namely, *The Merry Devil of Edmonton, Edward III, The Birth of Merlin,* and *Arden of Feversham.* In these editions the text of the earliest quarto is in each case pretty faithfully preserved, while the list of variant readings is full and, on the whole, exact. As might be expected, in transcribing from the originals a good many unintentional deviations in spelling have been made, and occasional errors in more important matters require correction. It is to be regretted that conjectural emendations by Professor Elze and other modern critics have so frequently been admitted into the text without absolute necessity. On the whole, however, these editions deserve the favourable opinions they have received on many hands.

ADDENDA

To No. IV of the Bibliography should be added the following:

44* (p. 451) GAUD, W. S., *The Authorship of Locrine,* Modern Philology, vol. i, pp. 409–22.

Peele's authorship defended.

63* (p. 452) NEUBNER, ALFRED, *Missachtete Shakespeare-Dramen. Eine literarhistorisch-kritische Untersuchung,* Berlin, 1907.

General discussion of the doubtful plays and of others.

THE LAMENTA=
BLE AND TRVE TRA-
GEDIE OF M. AR-
DEN OF FEVERSHAM
IN KENT.

Who was most wickedlye murdered, by
the meanes of his disloyall and wanton
wyfe, who for the loue she bare to one
Mosbie, hyred two desperat ruf-
fins Blackwill and Shakbag,
to kill him.

**Wherin is shewed the great mal-
lice and discimulation of a wicked wom
man, the vnsatiable desire of filthie lust
and the shamefull end of all
murderers.**

Imprinted at London for Edward
White, dwelling at the lyttle North
dore of Paules Church at
the signe of the
Gun. 1592.

*

Q 1	=	Quarto of 1592
Q 2	=	,, ,, 1599
Q 3	=	,, ,, 1633
J	=	Jacob, 1770
T	=	Tyrrell, 1851
D	=	Delius, 1855
Bull.	=	Bullen, 1887
WP	=	Warnke and Proescholdt, 1888
Bayne	=	Temple Dramatists edition, 1897
pr. ed.	=	present editor

THE TRAGEDY OF
M. ARDEN OF FEVE⟨R⟩SHAME

⟨Persons represented.

Mr. Arden, *of Feversham.*
Francklin, *his friend.*
Mosbie.
Clarke, *a Painter.*
Adam Fowle, *Landlord of the Flower-de-Luce.*
Bradshaw, *a Goldsmith.*
Michaell, Arden's *Servant.*
Greene.
Richard Reede, *a Sailor.*

Black Will } *Murderers*
Shakbag }
A Prentice.
A Ferryman.
Lord Cheiny, *and his Men.*
Mayor of Feversham, and Watch.

Alice, *Arden's Wife.*
Susan, *Mosbie's Sister.*

The Scene: Feversham, London, *and there between.*⟩

⟨ACT I.

A Room in Arden's House.⟩

Enter Arden, and Francklin.

Franklin. Arden, cheere vp thy spirits and droup no more:
My gratious Lord, the Duke of Sommerset,
Hath frely giuen to thee and to thy heyres,
By letters patents from his Maiesty,
All the lands of the Abby of Feuershame.
Heer are the deedes,
Sealed and subscribed with his name and the kings:
Read them, and leaue this melancholy moode.

Arden. Francklin, thy loue prolongs my weary lyfe;
And but for thee how odious were this lyfe,
That showes me nothing but torments my soule,
And those foule obiects that offend myne eies!
Which makes me wish that for this vale of Heauen
The earth hung ouer my heede and couerd mee.
Loue letters past twixt Mosbie and my Wyfe,
And they haue preuie meetings in the Towne:
Nay, on his finger did I spy the Ring
Which at our Marriage day the Preest put on.
Can any greefe be halfe so great as this?

Fran. Comfort thy selfe, sweete freend: it is not strange
That women will be false and wauering.

Arden. I, but to doat on such a one as hee
Is monstrous, Francklin, and intollerable.

Dram. Personae first in T   Act I. . . House *add. T*   6, 7 *One line Qq*   15 past *Qq*: pass *Bull.*   18 day *om. Q3*

Francklin. Why, what is he?

Arden. A Botcher, and no better at the first;
Who, by base brocage getting some small stock,
Crept into seruice of a noble man,
And by his seruile flattery and fawning
Is now become the steward of his house,
And brauely iets it in his silken gowne.

Fran. No noble man will countnaunce such a pesant.

Arden. Yes, the Lord Clifford, he that loues not mee.
But through his fauour let not him grow proude;
For were he by the Lord Protector backt,
He should not make me to be pointed at.
I am by birth a gentle man of bloode,
And that iniurious riball, that attempts
To vyolate my deare wyues chastitie,
(For deare I holde hir loue, as deare as heauen
Shall on the bed which he thinks to defile
See his disseuered ioints and sinewes torne,
Whylst on the planchers pants his weary body,
Smeard in the channels of his lustfull bloode.

Fran. Be patient, gentle freend, and learne of me
To ease thy griefe and saue her chastitye:
Intreat her faire; sweete words are fittest engines
To race the flint walles of a womans breast.
In any case be not too Jelyouse,
Nor make no question of her loue to thee;
But, as securely, presently take horse,
And ly with me at London all this tearme;

40 no] a *D*

For women, when they may, will not,
But, beeing kept back, straight grow outragious.
Arden. Though this abhorres from reason, yet ile try it,
And call her foorth and presently take leaue.
How! Ales!

Heere ente⟨r⟩s ales.

Ales. Husband, what meane you to get vp so earely?
Sommer nights are short, and yet you ryse ere day.
Had I beene wake, you had not risen so soone.
Ard. Sweet loue, thou knowst that we two, Ouidlike,
Haue often chid the morning when it gan to peepe,
And often wisht that darke nights purblind steedes
Would pull her by the purple mantle back,
And cast her in the Ocean to her loue.
But this night, sweete Ales, thou hast kild my hart:
I heard thee cal on Mosbie in thy sleepe.
Ales. Tis lyke I was asleepe when I nam'd him,
For beeing awake he comes not in my thoughts.
Arden. I, but you started vp and suddenly,
In steede of him, caught me about the necke.
Ales. In steede of him? why, who was there but you?
And where but one is, how can I mistake?
Fran. Arden, leaue to urdge her ouerfarre.
Arden. Nay, loue, there is no credit in a dreame;
Let it suffice I know thou louest me well.
Ales. Now I remember where vpon it came:
Had we no talke of Mosbie yesternight?
Fra. Mistres Ales, I hard you name him once or twice.
Ales. And thereof came it, and therefore blame not me.
Arden. I know it did, and therefore let it passe.
I must to London, sweete Ales, presently.
Ales. But tell me, do you meane to stay there long?
Arden. No longer there till my affaires be done.
Fran. He will not stay aboue a month at most.
Ales. A moneth? aye me! Sweete Arden, come againe
Within a day or two, or els I die.
Arden. I cannot long be from thee, gentle Ales.
Whilest Michel fetch our horses from the field,
Franklin and I will down vnto the key;
For I haue certaine goods there to vnload.
Meanewhile prepare our breakfast, gentle Ales;
For yet ere noone wele take horse and away.
[*Exeunt* Arden *&* Francklin.
Ales. Ere noone he meanes to take horse and away!
Sweete newes is this. Oh that some ayrie spirit
Would in the shape and liknes of a horse
Gallope with Arden crosse the Ocean,
And throw him from his backe into the waues!
Sweete Mosbie is the man that hath my hart:
And he vsurpes it, having nought but this,
That I am tyed to him by marriage.
Loue is a God, and mariage is but words;
And therefore Mosbies title is the best.
Tushe! whether it be or no, he shall be mine,
In spight of him, of Hymen, and of rytes.

Here enters Adam *of the Flourdeluce.*

And here comes Adam of the flourdeluce:
I hope he brings me tydings of my loue.
—How now, Adam, what is the newes with you?
Be not affraid: my husband is now from home.
Adam. He whome you wot of, Mosbie, Mistres Ales,
Is come to towne, and sends you word by mee
In any case you may not visit him.
Ales. Not visit him?
Adam. No, nor take no knowledge of his beeing heere.
Ales. But tell me, is he angree or displeased?
Adam. Should seeme so, for he is wondrous sad.
Ales. Were he as mad as rauing Hercules,
Ile see him, I, and were thy house of force,
These hands of mine should race it to the ground,
Vnles that thou wouldst bring me to my loue.
Adam. Nay, and you be so impatient, Ile be gone.
Ales. Stay, Adam, stay; thou wert wont to be my frend.
Aske Mosbie how I haue incurred his wrath;
Beare him from me these paire of siluer dice,
With which we plaid for kisses many a tyme,
And when I lost, I wan, and so did hee
(Such winning and such losing Joue send me);

55–6 *One line Qq* 57 get vp] rise *Q 3* 59 rise *Qq* 61 Haue chid *Bull.* 67 when nam'd *Q 3* 68 in] to *Q 3*

And bid him, if his loue doo not decline,
⟨To⟩ come this morning but along my dore,
And as a stranger but salute me there:
This may he doo without suspect or feare.
Adam. Ile tell him what you say, and so farewell. [*Exit* Adam.
Ales. Doo, and one day Ile make amends for all.—
I know he loues me well, but dares not come,
Because my husband is so Jelious,
And these my narrow prying neighbours blab
Hinder our meetings when we would conferre.
But, if I liue, that block shall be remoued,
And, Mosbie, thou that comes to me by stelth,
Shalt neither feare the biting speach of men
Nor Ardens lookes: as surely shall he die
As I abhorre him and loue onely thee.

Here enters Michaell.

How now, Michaell, whether are you going?
Michael. To fetch my masters nagge.
I hope youle thinke on mee.
Ales. I; but, Michaell, see you keepe your oath,
And be as secret as you are resolute.
Michaell. Ile see he shall not liue aboue a weeke.
Ales. On that condition, Michaell, here is my hand:
None shall haue Mosbies sister but thy selfe.
Michaell. I vnderstand, the Painter heere hard by
Hath made reporte that he and Sue is sure.
Ales. There's no such matter, Michaell; beleeue it not.
Michael. But he hath sent a dagger sticking in a hart,
With a verse or two stollen from a painted cloath,
The which I heere the wench keepes in her chest.
Well, let her kepe it: I shall finde a fellow
That can both write and read and make rime too.
And if I doo — well, I say no more:
Ile send from London such a taunting letter
As ⟨she⟩ shall eat the hart he sent with salt
And fling the dagger at the Painters head.
Ales. What needes all this? I say that Susan's thine.
Michaell. Why, then I say that I will kill my master,
Or anything that you will haue me doo.
Ales. But, Michaell, see you doo it cunningly.
Michaell. Why, say I should be tooke, ile nere confesse
That you know any thing; and Susan, being a Maide,
May begge me from the gallous of the Shriefe.
Ales. Truste not to that, Michaell.
Michaell. You can not tell me, I haue seene it, I.
But, mistres, tell her, whether I liue or die,
Ile make her more woorth then twenty Painters can;
For I will rid myne elder brother away,
And then the farme of Bolton is mine owne.
Who would not venture vpon house and land,
When he may haue it for a right downe blowe?

Here enters Mosbie.

Ales. Yonder comes Mosbie. Michaell, get thee gone,
And let not him nor any knowe thy drifts. [*Exit* Michaell.
Mosbie, my loue!
Mosbie. Away, I say, and talke not to me now.
Ales. A word or two, sweete hart, and then I will.
Tis yet but early daies, thou needest not feare.
Mosbie. Where is your husband?
Ales. Tis now high water, and he is at the key.
Mos. There let him be; hence forward know me not.
Ales. Is this the end of all thy solemne oathes?
Is this the frute thy reconcilement buds?
Haue I for this giuen thee so many fauours,
Incurd my husbands hate, and, out alas,
Made shipwrack of myne honour for thy sake,
And doest thou say 'hence forward know me not'?
Remember, when I lockt the in my closet,
What were thy words and mine; did we not both
Decree to murder Arden in the night?
The heauens can witnes, and the world can tell,
Before I saw that falshoode looke of thine,
Fore I was tangled with thy tysing speach,
Arden to me was dearer then my soule, —
And shall be still: base pesant, get thee gone,
And boast not of thy conquest ouer me,
Gotten by witch-craft and meere sorcery!
For what hast thou to countenaunce my loue,
Beeing discended of a noble house,
And matcht already with a gentleman

128 To *add.* *Q 3* 135 narrow] marrow *Q 1* 141 onely] none but *Q 2* 160 she *add.* *D*

174 Bocton *J* 187 this *om.* *Q 3*

Whose seruant thou maist be? — and so farewell.
Mos. Vngentle and vnkinde Ales, now I see
That which I euer feard, and finde too trew:
A womans loue is as the lightning flame,
Which euen in bursting forth consumes it selfe.
To trye thy constancie haue I beene strange:
Would I had neuer tryed, but liued in hope!
Ales. What needs thou try me whom thou neuer found false?
Mos. Yet pardon me, for loue is Jelious.
Ales. So list the Sailer to the Marmaids song,
So lookes the trauellour to the Basiliske:
I am content for to be reconcilde,
And that, I know, will be mine ouerthrow.
Mos. Thine ouerthrow? first let the world dissolue.
Ales. Nay, Mosbie, let me still inioye thy loue,
And happen what will, I am resolute.
My sauing husband hoordes vp bagges of gould
To make our children rich, and now is hee
Gone to vnload the goods that shall be thine,
And he and Francklin will to London straight.
Mos. To London, Ales? if thoult de rulde by mee,
Weele make him sure enough for comming there.
Ales. Ah, would we could.
Mos. I happend on a Painter yesternight,
The onely cunning man of Christendoome;
For he can temper poyson with his oyle,
That who so lookes vpon the worke he drawes
Shall, with the beames that issue from his sight,
Suck vennome to his breast and slay him selfe.
Sweete Ales, he shall draw thy counterfet,
That Arden may by gaizing on it perish.
Ales. I, but, Mosbie, that is dangerous,
For thou, or I, or any other els,
Comming into the Chamber where it hangs,
May die.
Mos. I, but weele haue it couered with a cloath
And hung vp in the studie for himselfe.
Ales. It may not be, for when the pictur's drawne,
Arden, I know, will come and shew it me.
Mos. Feare not; weele haue that shall serve the turne.
This is the painters house: Ile call him foorth.
Ales. But, Mosbie, Ile haue no such picture, I.
Mos. I pray thee leaue it to my discretion.
How! Clarke!

Here enters Clarke.

O, you are an honest man of your word! you serud me wel.
Clark. Why, sir, ile do it for you at any time,
Prouided, as you haue giuen your worde,
I may haue Susan Mosbie to my wife.
For, as sharpe witted Poets, whose sweete verse
Make heauenly gods break of their Nector draughts
And lay their eares down to the lowly earth,
Vse humble promise to their sacred Muse,
So we that are the Poets fauorits
Must haue a loue; I, Loue is the Painters Muse,
That makes him frame a speaking countenaunce,
A weeping eye that witnesses hartes griefe.
Then tell me, Master Mosbie, shall I haue hir?
Ales. Tis pittie but he should; heele vse her well.
Mosbie. Clarke, heers my hand: my sister shall be thine.
Cla. Then, brother, to requite this curtesie,
You shall command my lyfe, my skill, and all.
Ales. Ah, that thou couldst be secret.
Mosbie. Feare him not; leaue, I haue talkt sufficient.
Cla. You know not me that ask such questions.
Let it suffice I know you loue him well,
And faine would haue your husband made away:
Wherein, trust me, you shew a noble minde,
That rather then youle liue with him you hate
Youle venture lyfe, and die with him you loue.
The like will I do for my Susans sake.
Ales. Yet nothing could inforce me to the deed
But Mosbies loue. Might I without controll
Inioy thee still, then Arden should not die:
But seeing I cannot, therefore let him die.
Mos. Enough, sweete Ales; thy kinde words makes me melt.
Your tricke of poysoned pictures we dislyke;
Some other poyson would do better farre.
Ales. I, such as might be put into his broth,
And yet in taste not to be found at all.
Clarke. I know your minde, and here I haue it for you.
Put but a dram of this into his drinke,
Or any kinde of broth that he shall eat,
And he shall die within an houre after.

214 lists *Q 3* 219 me] him *Q 3* 238-9 *One line in edd.*

247-8 *One line Qq* 252 to] for *Q 3* 271 shew] beare *Q 3* 284 it *om. Q 3*

Ales. As I am a gentle-woman, Clarke, next day
Thou and Susan shall be maried.
Mos. And ile mak her dowry more then ile talk of, Clark.
Clarke. Yonder's your husband. Mosbie, ile be gone.

Here enters Arden *and* Francklin.

Ales. In good time see where my husband comes.
Maister Mosbie, aske him the question your selfe. [*Exit* Clarke.
Mos. Maister Arden, being at London yester night,
The Abby lands, whereof you are now possest,
Were offred me, on some occasion,
By Greene, one of sir Antony Agers men:
I pray you, sir, tell me, are not the lands yours?
Hath any other interest herein?
Arden. Mosby, that question wele decyde anon.
Ales, make ready my brekfast, I must hence. [*Exit* Ales.
As for the lands, mosbie, they are mine
By letters patents from his Maiesty.
But I must haue a Mandat for my wyfe;
They say you seeke to robbe me of her loue:
Villaine, what makes thou in her company?
Shees no companion for so base a groome.
Mosbie. Arden, I thought not on her, I came to thee;
But rather then I pocket vp this wrong —
Francklin. What will you doo, sir?
Mos. Reuenge it on the proudest of you both.
[*Then* Arden *drawes forth* Mosbies *sword.*
Arden. So, sirha; you may not weare a sword,
The statute makes against artificers;
I warrand that I doo. Now vse your bodkin,
Your spanish needle, and your pressing Iron,
For this shall go with me; and marke my words,
You goodman botcher, tis to you I speake:
The next time that I take thee neare my house,
In steede of Legs Ile make thee crall on stumps.
Mos. Ah, maister Arden, you have iniurde mee:
I doo appeale to God and to the world.
Fran. Why, canst thou deny thou wert a botcher once?
Mos. Measure me what I am, not what I was.
Ar. Why, what art thou now but a Veluet drudge,
A cheating steward, and base minded pesant?
Mos. Arden, now thou hast belcht and vomited
The rancorous venome of thy mis-swolne hart,
Heare me but speake: as I intend to liue
With God and his elected saints in heauen,
I neuer meant more to solicit her;
And that she knowes, and all the world shall see.
I loued her once, sweete Arden, pardon me,
I could not chuse, her beauty fyred my hearte;
But time hath quench't these ouerraging coles:
And, Arden, though I now frequent thy house,
Tis for my sisters sake, her waiting maid,
And not for hers. Maiest thou enioy her long:
Hell fyre and wrathfull vengeance light on me,
If I dishonor her or iniure thee.
Ard. Mosbie, with these thy protestations
The deadly hatred of my hart is appeased,
And thou and Ile be freends, if this proue trew.
As for the base tearmes I gaue thee late,
Forget them, Mosbie: I had cause to speake,
When all the Knights and gentlemen of Kent
Make common table talke of her and thee.
Mos. Who liues that is not toucht with slaunderous tongues?
Fra. Then, Mosbie, to eschew the speache of men,
Upon whose generall brute all honor hangs,
Forbeare his house.
Ard. Forbeare it! nay, rather frequent it more:
The worlde shall see that I distrust her not.
To warne him on the sudden from my house
Were too confirme the rumour that is growne.
Mos. By my faith, sir, you say trew,
And therefore will I soiourne here a while,
Untill our enemies haue talkt their fill;
And then, I hope, theile cease, and at last confesse
How causeles they haue iniurde her and me.
Ard. And I will ly at London all this tearme
To let them see how light I wey their words.

Here enters Ales.

Ales. Husband, sit down; your brekfast will be could.
Ard. Come, M⟨aister⟩ Mosbie, will you sit with vs?
Mos. I can not eat, but ile sit for company.
Ard. Sirra Michaell, see our horse be ready.
Ales. Husband, why pause ye? why eat you not?

299 therein *Q 3* 303 from] of *Q 3* 309 I put *Q 3* 314 doo, now *Q 1* 335 now *om. Q 3* 337 hers, maiest *Q 1* 355 By faith my sir *Qq* *S. D. new scene T* 365 our] your *Q 2, 3* 366 you] ye *Q 3*

Ard. I am not well; thers something in this broth
That is not holesome: didst thou make it, Ales?
Ales. I did, and thats the cause it likes not you.
Then she throwes down the broth on the grounde.
Thers nothing that I do can please your taste:
You were best to say I would haue poysoned you.
I cannot speak or cast aside my eye,
But he Imagines I haue stept awry.
Heres he that you cast in my teeth so oft:
Now will I be conuinced or purge my selfe.
I charge thee speake to this mistrustfull man,
Thou that wouldst see me hange, thou, Mosbye, thou:
What fauour hast thou had more then a kisse
At comming or departing from the Towne?
Mos. You wrong your selfe and me to cast these douts:
Your louing husband is not Jelious.
Ard. Why, gentle mistres Ales, cannot I
Be ill, but youle accuse your selfe?
Franckline, thou, haste! a boxe of Methridate:
Ile take a lytle to preuent the worst.
Fran. Do so, and let vs presently take horse:
My lyfe for yours, ye shall do well enough.
Ales. Giue me a spoone, Ile eat of it my selfe:
Would it were full of poyson to the brim,
Then should my cares and troubles haue an end.
Was euer silly woman so tormented?
Arden. Be patient, sweete loue; I mistrust not thee.
Ales. God will reuenge it, Arden, if thou doest;
For neuer woman lou'd her husband better
Then I do thee.
Ard. I know it, sweete Ales; cease to complaine,
Least that in teares I answer thee againe.
Fran. Come, leaue this dallying, and let vs away.
Ales. Forbeare to wound me with that bitter word;
Arden shall go to London in my armes.
Arden. Loth am I to depart, yet I must go.
Ales. Wilt thou to London, then, and leaue me here?
Ah, if thou loue me, gentle Arden, stay:
Yet, if thy busines be of great Import,
Go if thou wilt, Ile beare it as I may;
But write from London to me euery weeke,
Nay, euery day, and stay no longer there
Then thou must nedes, least that I die for sorrow.
Arden. Ile write vnto thee euery other tide:
And so farewell, sweete Ales, till we meete next.
Ales. Farewell, Husband, seeing youle haue it so;
And, M⟨aister⟩ Francklin, seeing you take him hence,
In hope youle hasten him home, Ile giue you this.
and then she kisseth him.
Fran. And if he stay, the fault shall not be mine.
Mosbie, farewell, and see you keepe your oath.
Mosbie. I hope he is not Jelious of me now.
Arden. No, Mosbie, no: hereafter thinke of me
As of your dearest frend, and so farewell.
[*Exeunt* Arden, Franklin, & Michaell.
Ales. I am glad he is gone; he was about to stay,
But did you marke me then how I brake of?
Mosbie. I, Ales, and it was cunningly performed.
But what a villaine is this painter Clarke!
Ales. Was it not a goodly poyson that he gaue?
Why, he's as well now as he was before.
It should haue bene some fine confection
That might haue giuen the broth some daintie taste:
This powder was to grosse and populos.
Mosbie. But had he eaten but three spoonefulles more,
Then had he died and our loue continued.
Ales. Why, so it shall, Mosbie, albeit he liue.
Mosbie. It is vnpossible, for I haue sworne
Neuer hereafter to solicite thee,
Or, whylest he liues, once more importune thee.
Ales. Thou shalt not neede, I will importune thee.
What? shall an oath make thee forsake my loue?
As if I haue not sworne as much my selfe
And giuen my hand vnto him in the church!
Tush, Mosbie; oathes are wordes, and words is winde,
And winde is mutable: then, I conclude,
Tis childishnes to stand vpon an oath.

382 *ends* ill *edd.* 394–5 *One line Qq* 400 mine *Q3*

409 other *om. Q3* 417 of] on *Q3* 418 of *om. Q3* 427 populos] palpable *D, later retracted* 430 so . . shall *om. Q3*

Mos. Well, proued, Mistres Ales; yet by your leaue
Ile keepe mine vnbroken whilest he liues.
Ales. I, doo, and spare not, his time is but short;
For if thou beest as resolute as I,
Weele haue him murdered as he walkes the streets.
In London many alehouse Ruffins keepe,
Which, as I heare, will murther men for gould.
They shall be soundly feed to pay him home.

Here enters Greene.

Mos. Ales, whats he that comes yonder? knowest thou him?
Ales. Mosbie, be gone: I hope tis one that comes
To put in practise our intended drifts.
[*Exit* Mosbie.
Gre. Mistres Arden, you are well met.
I am sorry that your husband is from home,
When as my purposed iourney was to him:
Yet all my labour is not spent in vaine,
For I suppose that you can full discourse
And flat resolue me of the thing I seeke.
Ales. What is it, maister Greene? If that I may
Or can with safety, I will answer you.
Greene. I heard your husband hath the grant of late,
Confirmed by letters patents from the king,
Of all the lands of the Abby of Feuershame,
Generally intitled, so that all former grants
Are cut of; whereof I my selfe had one,
But now my interest by that is void.
This is all, mistres Arden; is it trew or no?
Ales. Trew, maister Greene; the lands are his in state,
And whatsoeuer leases were before
Are void for tearme of Maister Ardens lyfe;
He hath the grant vnder the Chancery seale.
Gre. Pardon me, mistres Arden, I must speake,
For I am toucht. Your husband doth me wrong
To wring me from the little land I haue:
My liuing is my lyfe, onely that
Resteth remainder of my portion.
Desyre of welth is endles in his minde,
And he is gredy gaping still for gaine,
Nor cares he though young gentlemen do begge,
So he may scrape and hoorde vp in his poutche.
But, seeing he hath taken my lands, Ile value lyfe
As careles as he is carefull for to get:
And tell him this from me, Ile be reuenged,
And so as he shall wishe the Abby lands
Had rested still within their former state.
Ales. Alas, poore gentleman, I pittie you,
And wo is me that any man should want;
God knowes tis not my fault: but wonder not
Though he be harde to others, when to me, —
Ah, maister Greene, God knowes how I am vsde.
Gre. Why, mistres Arden, can the crabbed churle
Vse you vnkindely? respects he not your birth,
Your honorable freends, nor what you brought?
Why, all Kent knowes your parentage and what you are.
Ales. Ah, M⟨aister⟩ Greene, be it spoken in secret heere,
I neuer liue good day with him alone:
When hee is at home, then haue I froward lookes,
Hard words and blowes, to mend the match withall;
And though I might content as good a man,
Yet doth he keepe in euery corner trulles;
And, weary with his trugges at home,
Then rydes he straight to London; there, for sooth,
He reuelles it among such filthie ones
As counsels him to make away his wyfe.
Thus liue I dayly in continuall feare,
In sorrow, so dispairing of redres
As euery day I wish with harty prayer
That he or I were taken forth the worlde.
Gre. Now trust me, mistres Ales, it greeueth me
So faire a creature should be so abused.
Why, who would haue thought the ciuill sir so sollen?
He lookes so smoothly: now, fye vpon him, Churle!
And if he liue a day, he liues too long.
But frolick, woman, I shall be the man
Shall set you free from all this discontent;
And if the Churle deny my intereste
And will not yelde my lease into my hand,
Ile paye him home, what euer hap to me.
Ales. But speake you as you thinke?
Gre. I, Gods my witnes, I meane plaine dealing,
For I had rather die then lose my land.
Ales. Then, maister Greene, be counsailed by me:
Indaunger not your selfe for such a Churle,
But hyre some Cutter for to cut him short,
And heer's ten pound to wager them withall;

448 fed *Qq* 449 him *om. Q 3* 460 had *Qq 2, 3* 466 or] nor *Q 1* 468 were *om. Q 3*

503 counsell *Q 3*

When he is dead, you shall haue twenty more,
And the lands whereof my husband is possest
Shall be intytled as they were before.
Gre. Will you keepe promise with me?
Ales. Or count me false and periurde whilst I liue.
Gre. Then heeres my hand, Ile haue him so dispatcht.
Ile vp to London straight, Ile thether poast,
And neuer rest til I haue compast it:
Till then farewell.
Ales. Good Fortune follow all your forward thoughts, [*Exit* Grene.
And whosoeuer doth attempt the deede,
A happie hand I wish, and so farewell. —
All this goes well: Mosbie, I long for thee
To let thee know all that I haue contriued.

Here enters Mosbie *&* Clarke.

Mos. How now, Ales, whats the newes?
Ales. Such as will content thee well, sweete hart.
Mos. Well, let them passe a while, and tell me, Ales,
How haue you dealt and tempered with my sister?
What, will she haue my neighbour Clarke, or no?
Ales. What, M⟨aister⟩ Mosbie! let him wooe him self:
Thinke you that maides looke not for faire wordes?
Go to her, Clarke; shees all alone within;
Michaell my man is cleane out of her bookes.
Clarke. I thanke you, mistres Arden, I will in;
And if faire Susan and I can make a gree,
You shall command me to the vttermost,
As farre as either goods or lyfe may streatch. [*Exit* Clark.
Mos. Now, Ales, lets heare thy newes.
Ales. They be so good that I must laugh for ioy,
Before I can begin to tell my tale.
Mos. Lets heare them, that I may laugh for company.
Ales. This morning, M⟨aister⟩ Greene, dick greene I meane,
From whome my husband had the Abby land,
Came hether, railing, for to know the trueth
Whether my husband had the lands by grant.
I tould him all, where at he stormd amaine
And swore he would cry quittance with the Churle,
And, if he did denye his enterest,
Stabbe him, whatsoeuer did befall him selfe.
When as I sawe his choller thus to rise,
I whetted on the gentleman with words;
And, to conclude, Mosbie, at last we grew
To composition for my husbands death.
I gaue him ten pound to hire knaues,
By some deuise to make away the Churle;
When he is dead, he should haue twenty more
And repossesse his former lands againe.
On this we greed, and he is ridden straight
To London, to bring his death about.
Mos. But call you this good newes?
Ales. I, sweete hart, be they not?
Mos. Twere cherefull newes to hear the churle wer dead;
But trust me, Ales, I take it passing ill
You would be so forgetfull of our state
To make recount of it to euery groome.
What? to acquaint each stranger with our drifts,
Cheefely in case of murther, why, tis the way
To make it open vnto Ardens selfe
And bring thy selfe and me to ruine both.
Forewarnde, forearmde: who threats his enemye,
Lends him a sword to guarde himselfe with all.
Ales. I did it for the best.
Mos. Well, seing tis don, cherely let it pas.
You know this Greene: is he not religious,
A man, I gesse, of great deuotion?
Ales. He is.
Mos. Then, sweete Ales, let it pas: I haue a dryft
Will quyet all, what euer is amis.

Here enters Clarke *and* Susan.

Ales. How now, Clarke? haue you found me false?
Did I not plead the matter hard for you?
Clarke. You did.
Mos. And what? Wilt be a match?
Clarke. A match, I faith, sir: I, the day is mine.
The Painter layes his cullours to the lyfe,
His pensel draws no shadowes in his loue.
Susan is mine.
Ales. You make her blushe.
Mos. What, sister, is it Clarke must be the man?
Su. It resteth in your graunt; some words are past,
And happely we be growne vnto a match,
If you be willing that it shall be so.
Mos. Ah, maister Clarke, it resteth at my grant:
You see my sister's yet at my dispose.
But, so youle graunt me one thing I shall aske,

549 make agree *Q 3*

587 cheerefully *Q 3* 591 sweete Ales *om.* *Q 3*

I am content my sister shall be yours.
Clark. What is it, M⟨aister⟩ Mosbie?
Mos. I doo remember once in secret talke
You tould me how you could compound by Arte
A crucifix impoysoned,
That who so looke vpon it should waxe blinde
And with the sent be stifeled, that ere long
He should dye poysond that did view it wel.
I would haue you make me such a crucifix,
And then Ile grant my sister shall be yours.
Cla. Though I am loath, because it toucheth lyfe,
Yet, rather or Ile leaue sweete Susans loue,
Ile do it, and with all the haste I may.
But for whome is it?
Ales. Leaue that to vs. Why, Clarke, is it possible
That you should paint and draw it out your selfe,
The cullours beeing balefull and impoysoned,
And no waies preiudice your selfe with all?
Mos. Well questioned, Ales: Clarke, how answer you that?
Clarke. Very easily: Ile tell you straight
How I doo worke of these Impoysoned drugs.
I fasten on my spectacles so close
As nothing can any way offend my sight;
Then, as I put a leafe within my nose,
So put I rubarbe to auoid the smell,
And softly as another worke I paint.
Mos. Tis very well; but against when shall I haue it?
Cla. Within this ten dayes.
Mos. Twill serue the turne.
Now, Ales, lets in and see what cheere you keepe.
I hope, now M⟨aister⟩ Arden is from home,
Youle giue me leaue to play your husbands part.
Ales. Mosbie, you know, whose maister of my hart,
He well may be the master of the house.
[*E*⟨*x*⟩*eunt.*

⟨ACT II.

SCENE I.

Country between Feversham and London.⟩

Here enters Greene *and* Bradshaw.

Brad. See you them that coms yonder, M⟨aister⟩ Greene?
Gren. I, very well: doo you know them?

Here enters Blacke Will *and* Shakebagge.

Brad. The one I knowe not, but he seemes a knaue
Cheefly for bearing the other company;
For such a slaue, so vile a roge as he,
Lyues not againe vppon the earth.
Black-will is his name. I tell you, M⟨aister⟩ Greene,
At Bulloine he and I were fellow souldiers,
Where he plaid such prankes,
As all the Campe feard him for his villany:
I warrant you he beares so bad a minde
That for a croune heele murther any man.
Gre. The fitter is he for my purpose, mary.
Will. How now, fellow Bradshaw? Whether away so earely?
Brad. O Will, times are changed: no fellows now,
Though we were once together in the field;
Yet thy freend to doo thee any good I can.

Will. Why, Bradshawe, was not thou and I Fellow-souldiers at Bulloine, wher I was a corporall and thou but a base mercenarye groome? No fellowes now! because you are a gouldsmith and haue a lytle plate in your shoppe! You were gladde to call me 'fellow Will', and with a cursy to the earth 'One snatch, good corporall', when I stole the halfe Oxe from John the vitler, and domineer'd with it amongst good fellowes in one night.

Brad. I, Will, those dayes are past with me.

Will. I, but they be not past with me, for I kepe that same honorable mind still. Good neighbour Bradshaw, you are too proude to be my fellow; but were it not that I see more company comming down the hill, I would be fellowes with you once more, and share Crownes with you to. But let that pas, and tell me whether you goe.

Brad. To London, Will, about a peece of seruice,
Wherein happely thou maist pleasure me.
Will. What is it?
Brad. Of late Lord Cheiny lost some plate,
Which one did bring and soulde it at my shoppe,
Saying he serued sir Antony Cooke.
A search was made, the plate was found with me,
And I am bound to answer at the syse.
Now, Lord Cheiny solemnly vowes,
If law will serue him, hele hang me for his plate.
Now I am going to London vpon hope
To finde the fellow. Now, Will, I know
Thou art acquainted with such companions.

620 Ile] I *Q3* 625 *Two lines Qq, div. after* Ales 636 *Two lines Qq* Act II. *etc. add. T*

14 *Two lines Qq* 18–27 *Verse Qq, corr. WP* 29–36 *Verse Qq*

Will. What manner of man was he?
Brad. A leane faced writhen knaue,
Hauke nosde and verye hollow eied,
With mightye furrowes in his stormye browes;
Long haire down his shoulders curled;
His Chinne was bare, but on his vpper lippe
A mutchado, which he wound about his eare.
Will. What apparell had he?
Brad. A watchet sattin doublet all to torne,
The inner side did beare the greater show;
A paire of threed-bare Veluet hose, seame rent,
A wosted stockin rent aboue the shoe,
A liuery cloake, but all the lace was of;
Twas bad, but yet it serued to hide the plate.

Will. Sirra Shakebagge, canst thou remember since we trould the boule at Sittingburgh, where I broke the Tapsters head of the Lyon with a Cudgill-sticke?

Shak. I, very well, Will.

Will. Why, it was with the money that the plate was sould for. Sirra Bradshaw, what wilt thou giue him that can telle thee who soulde thy plate?

Brad. Who, I pray thee, good Will?

Will. Why, twas one Jacke Fitten. He's now in Newgate for stealing a horse, and shall be arrainde the next sise.

Brad. Why, then let Lord Cheiny seek Jack Fitten forth,
For Ile backe and tell him who robbed him of his plate.
This cheeres my hart; M⟨aister⟩ Greene, Ile leaue you,
For I must to the Ile of Sheppy with speede.
Greene. Before you go, let me intreat you
To carry this letter to mistres Arden of Feuershame
And humbly recommend me to her selfe.
Brad. That will I, M⟨aister⟩ Grene, and so farewell.
Heere, Will, theres a Crowne for thy good newes. [*Exit* Bradshawe.

Will. Farewell, Bradshaw; Ile drinke no water for thy sake whilest this lasts.—Now, gentleman, shall we haue your company to London?

Gre. Nay, stay, sirs:
A lytle more I needs muste vse your helpe,
And in a matter of great consequence,
Wherein if youle be secret and profound,
Ile giue you twenty Angels for your paines.

Will. How? twenty Angells? giue my fellow George shakbag and me twenty Angels? And if thoult haue thy owne father slaine, that thou mayst inherit his land, weele kill him.

Shak. I, thy Mother, thy sister, thy brother, or all thy kin.

Gre. Well, this it is: Arden of Feuershame
Hath highly wrongd me about the Abby land,
That no reuendge but death will serue the turne.
Will you two kill him? heeres the Angels downe,
And I will lay the platforme of his death.

Will. Plat me no platformes; giue me the money, and ile stab him as he stands pissing against a wall but Ile kill him.

Sha. Where is he?

Greene. He is now at London, in Aldersgate streete.

Shak. He's dead as if he had beene condemned by an act of parliament, if once Black Will and I sweare his death.

Gre. Here is ten pound, and when he is dead,
Ye shall haue twenty more.

Will. My fingers itches to be at the pesant. Ah, that I might be set a worke thus through the yeere, and that murther would grow to an occupation, that a man might without daunger of law —: zounds, I warrant I should be warden of the company. Come, let vs be going, and wele bate at Rochester, where Ile giue thee a gallon of Sack to hansell the match with all. [*Exeunt.*

⟨SCENE II.

London. A Street near St. Paul's.⟩

Here enters Michael.

Mich. I haue gotten suche a letter as will touche the Painter: and thus it is:

Here enters Arden *and* Francklin *and heares* Michaell *read this letter.*

'*My duetye remembred, Mistres Susan, hoping in God you be in good health, as I Michaell was at the making heereof. This is to certifie you that as the Turtle true, when she hath lost her mate, sitteth alone, so I, mourning for your absence, do walk vp and down Poules til one day I fell a sleepe and lost my maisters Pantophelles. Ah, mistres Susan, abbolishe that paltry Painter, cut him off by the shinnes with a frowning looke of your crabed countenance, & think vpon Michaell, who, druncke with the dregges of your fauour, wil cleaue as fast to*

53 his *om.* *Q 3* 54 his] to his *Q 3* 64–7, 69–72, 74–6, 86–9, 95–9 *Verse Qq* 65 Sittingburne *Q 3 etc.* 66 of] at *Q 3* 78 Ile] Ile goe *Q 3* 90–1 *One line Qq*

106–8, 111–13, 116–24 *Verse Qq* 117 a] at *Q 3* Scene II. *etc. add. T* 1, 2 *Verse Qq*

your loue as a plaster of Pitch to a gald horse back. Thus hoping you will let my passions penetrate, or rather impetrate mercy of your meeke hands, I end.

Yours, Michaell, *or els not* Michaell.

Ard. Why, you paltrie knaue,
Stand you here loytering, knowing my affaires,
What haste my busines craues to send to Kent?

Fran. Faith, frend Michaell, this is very ill,
Knowing your maister hath no more but you,
And do ye slacke his busines for your owne?

Ard. Where is the letter, sirra? let me see it.

Then he giues him the letter.

See, maister Francklin, heres proper stuffe:
Susan my maid, the Painter, and my man,
A crue of harlots, all in loue, forsooth;
Sirra, let me heare no more of this.
Now for thy lyfe once write to her a worde!

Here enters Grene, Will, *and* Shakebag.

Wilt thou be married to so base a trull?
Tis Mosbies sister: come I once at home,
Ile rouse her from remaining in my house.
Now, M(aister) Francklin, let vs go walke in Paules;
Come but a turne or two, and then away.

[*Exeunt.*

Gre. The first is Arden, and thats his man,
The other is Francklin, Ardens dearest freend.

Will. Zounds, Ile kill them all three.

Gre. Nay, sirs, touch not his man in any case;
But stand close, and take you fittest standing,
And at his comming foorth speede him:
To the Nages head, ther' is this cowards haunt.
But now Ile leaue you till the deed be don.

[*Exit* Greene.

Sha. If he be not paid his owne, nere trust shakebagge.

Wil. Sirra Shakbag, at his comming foorth
Ile runne him through, and then to the black-freers,
And there take water and away.

Sha. Why, thats the best; but see thou misse him not.

Wil. How can I misse him, when I thinke on the fortye Angels I must haue more?

Here enters a prentise.

Prentise. Tis very late; I were best shute vp my stall,
For heere will be ould filching, when the presse
Comes foorth of Paules.

Then lettes he downe his window, and it breaks Black Wils *head.*

Wil. Zounds, draw, Shakbag, draw, I am almost kild.

Pren. Wele tame you, I warrant.

Wil. Zounds, I am tame enough already.

Here enters Arden, Fran., *&* Michael.

Ard. What trublesome fray or mutany is this?

Fran. 'Tis nothing but some brabling paltry fray,
Deuised to pick mens pockets in the throng.

Ard. Ist nothing els? come, Franklin, let vs away. [*Exeunt.*

Wil. What mends shal I haue for my broken head?

Pren. Mary, this mends, that if you get you not away all the sooner, you shall be well beaten and sent to the counter.

[*Exit* prentise.

Wil. Well, Ile be gone, but looke to your signes, for Ile pull them down all. Shakbag, my broken head greeues me not so much as by this meanes Arden hath escaped.

Here enters Greene.

I had a glimse of him and his companion.

Gre. Why, sirs, Arden's as wel as I; I met him and Francklin going merrilly to the ordinary. What, dare you not do it?

Wil. Yes, sir, we dare do it; but, were my consent to giue againe, we would not do it vnder ten pound more. I value euery drop of my blood at a french Crowne. I haue had ten pound to steale a dogge, and we have no more heere to kill a man; but that a bargane is a bargane, and so foorth, you should do it your selfe.

Gre. I pray thee, how came thy head broke?

Will. Why, thou seest it is broke, dost thou not?

Sha. Standing against a staule, watching Ardens comming, a boy let down his shop-window and broke his head; wherevpon arose a braul, and in the tumult Arden escapt vs and past by vnthought on. But forberance is no acquittance; another time wele do it, I warrant thee.

Gre. I pray thee, will, make cleane thy bloodie brow,
And let vs bethink vs on some other place
Where Arden may be met with handsomly.
Remember how deuoutly thou hast sworne
To kill the villaine; thinke vpon thyne oath.

25 for *om. Q 3* 31 Now *Qq*: Nor *J etc.* 34 from] for *Q 3* 41 you] your *Q 3* 43 this *om. Q 3*

55 draw, I] I *Q 3* 63-91 *Verse Qq* . 74 Yes, sir, sir *Q 3*

Will. Tush, I haue broken fiue hundred oathes!
But wouldst thou charmè me to effect this dede,
Tell me of gould, my resolutions fee;
Say thou seest Mosbie kneeling at my knees,
Offring me seruice for my high attempt,
And sweete Ales Arden, with a lap of crownes,
Comes with a lowly cursy to the earth,
Saying 'take this but for thy quarterige,
Such yeerely tribute will I answer thee.'
Why, this would steale soft metled cowardice,
With which black Will was neuer tainted with.
I tell thee, Greene, the forlorne trauailer,
Whose lips are glewed with sommers parching heat,
Nere longd so much to see a running brooke
As I to finish Ardens Tragedy.
Seest thou this goare that cleaueth to my face?
From hence nere will I wash this bloody staine,
Til Ardens hart be panting in my hand.
Gre. Why, thats wel said; but what saith shakbag?
Shak. I cannot paint my valour out with words:
But, giue me place and opportunitie,
Such mercy as the staruen Lyones,
When she is dry suckt of her eager young,
Showes to the pray that next encounters her,
On Arden so much pitty would I take.
Gre. So should it faire with men of firme resolue.
And now, sirs, seeing this accident
Of meeting him in Paules hath no successe,
Let vs bethinke vs on some other place
Whose earth may swallow vp this Ardens bloode.

Here enters Michaell.

Se, yonder comes his man: and wat you what?
The foolish knaue is in loue with Mosbies sister,
And for her sake, whose loue he cannot get
Unlesse Mosbie solicit his sute,
The villaine hath sworne the slaughter of his maister.
Weele question him, for he may stead vs muche. —
How now, Michael, whether are you going?
Mic. My maister hath new supt,
And I am going to prepare his chamber.
Gre. Where supt M⟨aister⟩ Arden?
Mic. At the Nages head, at the 18 pence ordinarye. How now, M⟨aister⟩ Shakbag? what, Black Wil! Gods deere lady, how chaunce your face is so bloody?
Wil. Go too, sirra, there is a chaunce in it:
This sawcines in you wil make you be knockt.
Mic. Nay, and you be offended, ile be gone.
Gre. Stay, michael, you may not scape vs so.
Michael, I knowe you loue your M⟨aister⟩ wel.
Mic. Why, so I do; but wherefore vrdge you that?
Gre. Because I thinke you loue your mistres better.
⟨*Mic.*⟩ So think not I; but say, yfaith, what, if I should?
Shak. Come to the purpose, Michael; we heare
You haue a pretty loue in Feuershame.
Mic. Why, haue I two or three, whats that to thee?
Wil. You deale to mildely with the pesant. Thus it is:
Tis knowne to vs you loue mosbies sister;
We know besides that you haue tane your oath
To further Mosbie to your mistres bed,
And kill your M⟨aister⟩ for his sisters sake.
Now, sir, a poorer coward then your selfe
Was neuer fostered in the coast of Kent:
How comes it then that such a knaue as you
Dare sweare a matter of such consequence?
Gre. Ah, will —
Will. Tush, giue me leaue, thers no more but this:
Sith thou hast sworne, we dare discouer all;
And hadst thou or shouldst thou vtter it,
We haue deuised a complat vnder hand,
What euer shall betide to any of vs,
To send thee roundly to the diuell of hell.
And therefore thus: I am the very man,
Markt in my birth howre by the destynies,
To giue an end to Ardens lyfe on earth;
Thou but a member but to whet the knife
Whose edge must search the closet of his breast:
Thy office is but to appoint the place
And traine thy M⟨aister⟩ to his tragedy;
Myne to performe it when occasion serues.
Then be not nice, but here deuise with vs
How and what way we may conclude his death.
Sha. So shalt thou purchase Mosbie for thy frend,
And by his frendship gaine his sisters loue.
Gre. So shal thy mistres be thy fauorer,
And thou disburdned of the oath thou made.
Mic. Wel, gentlemen, I cannot but confesse,
Sith you haue vrdged me so aparantly,

107 tainted with *Qq*: tainted yet *J etc.* 119 her *om. Q3* 125 on *Qq*: of *WP*

142 be *om. Q2, 3* 148 *Given to Greene in Q1* 153 kowne *Q1* 159 then *om. Q3*

That I haue vowed my M⟨aister⟩ Ardens death ;
And he whose kindly loue and liberall hand
Doth challenge naught but good deserts of me,
I wil delyuer ouer to your hands.
This night come to his house at Aldersgate:
The dores Ile leaue vnlockt against you come.
No sooner shall ye enter through the latch,
Ouer the thresholde to the inner court,
But on your left hand shall you see the staires
That leads directly to my M⟨aisters⟩ chamber :
There take him and dispose him as ye please.
Now it were good we parted company;
What I haue promised, I will performe.

Wil. Should you deceiue vs, twould go wrong with you.

Mic. I will accomplish al I haue reuealde.

Wil. Come, let's go drinke: choller makes me as drye as a dog.

Exeunt Will, Gre., *and* Shak. *Manet* Michaell.

Mic. Thus feedes the Lambe securely on the downe,
Whilst through the thicket of an arber brake
The hunger bitten Woulfe orepryes his hant
And takes aduantage to eat him vp.
Ah, harmeles Arden, how, how hast thou misdone,
That thus thy gentle lyfe is leueld at?
The many good turnes that thou hast don to me,
Now must I quitance with betraying thee.
I that should take the weapon in my hand
And buckler thee from ill intending foes,
Do lead thee with a wicked fraudfull smile,
As vnsuspected, to the slaughterhouse.
So haue I sworne to Mosby and my mistres,
So haue I promised to the slaughtermen;
And should I not deale currently with them,
Their lawles rage would take reuenge on me.
Tush, I will spurne at mercy for this once:
Let pittie lodge where feeble women ly,
I am resolued, and Arden needs must die.
[*Exit* Michaell.

⟨ACT III.

Scene I.

A Room in Francklin's *House, at Aldersgate.*⟩

Here enters Arden *&* Fran.

Arden. No, Francklin, no: if feare or stormy threts,
If loue of me or care of womanhoode,
If feare of God or common speach of men,
Who mangle credit with their wounding words,
And cooch dishonor as dishonor buds,
Might ioyne repentaunce in her wanton thoughts,
No question then but she would turn the leafe
And sorrow for her desolution;
But she is rooted in her wickednes,
Peruerse and stobburne, not to be reclaimde;
Good counsell is to her as raine to weedes,
And reprehension makes her vice to grow
As Hydraes head that flourisht by decay.
Her faults, me thinks, are painted in my face,
For euery searching eye to ouerreede;
And Mosbies name, a scandale vnto myne,
Is deeply trenched in my blushing brow.
Ah, Francklin, Francklin, when I think on this,
My harts greefe rends my other powers
Worse then the conflict at the houre of death.

Fran. Gentle Arden, leaue this sad lament:
She will amend, and so your greefes will cease;
Or els shele die, and so your sorrows end.
If neither of these two do happely fall,
Yet let your comfort be that others beare
Your woes, twice doubled all, with patience.

Ard. My house is irksome, there I cannot rest.

Fra. Then stay with me in London, go not home.

Ard. Then that base Mosbie doth vsurpe my roome
And makes his triumphe of my beeing thence.
At home or not at home, where ere I be,
Heere, heere it lyes, ah Francklin, here it lyes
That wil not out till wretched Arden dies.

Here enters Michaell.

Fra. Forget your greefes a while; heer coms your man.

Ard. What a Clock ist, sirra?

Mic. Almost ten.

Ard. See, see, how runnes away the weary time!
Come, M⟨aister⟩ Franklin, shal we go to bed?
[*Exeunt* Arden *&* Michaell.
[*Manet* Francklin.

Fran. I pray you, go before: Ile follow you.
— Ah, what a hell is fretfull Jelousie!
What pitty mouing words, what deepe fetcht sighes,
What greeuous grones and ouerlading woes
Accompanies this gentle gentleman!
Now will he shake his care oppressed head,
Then fix his sad eis on the sollen earth,
Ashamed to gaze vpon the open world;

204 to] for to *T*   207 that *om. Q 3*   211 wicked *om. Q 3*   Act III. *etc. add. T*

5 couch *Q 3* : crop *D*   13 flourisht *conj. D* : perisht *Qq* : plenisht *WP*   14 think *Q 1* : thinke *Q 3*   41 moning *Q 1*

Now will he cast his eyes vp towards the heauens,
Looking that waies for redresse of wrong:
Some times he seeketh to beguile his griefe
And tels a story with his carefull tongue;
Then comes his wiues dishonor in his thoughts
And in the middle cutteth of his tale,
Powring fresh sorrow on his weary lims.
So woe begone, so inlye charged with woe,
Was neuer any lyued and bare it so.

Here enters Michaell.

Mic. My M⟨aister⟩ would desire you come to bed.
Fra. Is he himselfe already in his bed?
[*Exit* Fran. *Manet* Mic.
Mic. He is, and faine would haue the light away.
— Conflicting thoughts, incamped in my brest,
Awake me with the Echo of their strokes,
And I, a iudge to censure either side,
Can giue to neither wished victory.
My masters kindnes pleads to me for lyfe
With iust demaund, and I must grant it him:
My mistres she hath forced me with an oath,
For Susans sake, the which I may not breake,
For that is nearer then a masters loue:
That grim faced fellow, pittiles black Will,
And Shakebag, stearne in bloody stratageme,
Two Ruffer Ruffins neuer liued in Kent,
Haue sworne my death, if I infrindge my vow,
A dreadfull thing to be considred of.
Me thinks I see them with their bolstred haire
Staring and grinning in thy gentle face,
And in their ruthles hands their dagers drawne,
Insulting ore thee with a peck of oathes,
Whilest thou submissiue, pleading for releefe,
Art mangled by their irefull instruments.
Me thinks I heare them aske where Michaell is,
And pittiles black Will cryes: 'Stab the slaue!
The Pesant will detect the Tragedy!'
The wrincles in his fowle death threatning face
Gapes open wide, lyke graues to swallow men.
My death to him is but a merryment,
And he will murther me to make him sport.
He comes, he comes! ah, M⟨aister⟩ Francklin, helpe!
Call vp the neighbors, or we are but dead!

Here enters Fran. & Arden.

Fran. What dismall outcry cals me from my rest?
Ard. What hath occasiond such a fearefull crye?
Speake, Michaell: hath any iniurde thee?
Mic. Nothing, sir; but as I fell asleepe,
Vpon the thresholde leaning to the staires,
I had a fearefull dreame that troubled me,
And in my slumber thought I was beset
With murtherer theeues that came to rifle me.
My trembling ioints witnes my inward feare:
I craue your pardons for disturbing you.
Ard. So great a cry for nothing I nere heard.
What? are the doores fast lockt and al things safe?
Mic. I cannot tel; I think I lockt the doores.
Ard. I like not this, but Ile go see my selfe. —
Nere trust me but the dores were all vnlockt:
This negligence not halfe contenteth me.
Get you to bed, and, if you loue my fauour,
Let me haue no more such prancks as these.
Come, M⟨aister⟩ Francklin, let vs go to bed.
Fran. I, by my faith; the aire is very colde.
Michaell, farewell; I pray thee dreame no more. [*Exeunt.*

⟨SCENE II.

Outside Francklin's *House.*⟩

Here enters Will, Gre., & Shak.

Shakebag. Black night hath hid the pleasurs of ye day,
And sheting darknesse ouerhangs the earth
And with the black folde of her cloudy robe
Obscures vs from the eiesight of the worlde,
In which swete silence such as we triumph.
The laysie minuts linger on their time,
Loth to giue due audit to the howre,
Til in the watch our purpose be complete
And Arden sent to euerlasting night.
Greene, get you gone and linger here about,
And at some houre hence come to vs againe,
Where we will giue you instance of his death.
Gre. Speede to my wish, whose wil so ere sayes no;
And so ile leaue you for an howre or two.
[*Exit* Gre.
Will. I tel thee, Shakebag, would this thing wer don:
I am so heauy that I can scarse go;
This drowsines in me bods little good.
Shake. How now, Will? become a precissian?
Nay, then lets go sleepe, when buges and feares
Shall kill our courages with their fancies worke.
Will. Why, Shakbagge, thou mistakes me much,

76 thee *Q 3*: there *Q 1, 2* 86 ah *om. Q 3*

92 leading *D* 102 were *Q 1*: are *Q 2, 3* 107 by *Q 3*, be *Q 1* Scene II. *etc. add. T* *S. D.* Here..Shak. *follows line* 1 *in Q 1* 4 Obscures *Q 3*: Obscure *Q 1, 2*

And wrongs me to in telling me of feare.
Wert not a serious thing we go about,
It should be slipt til I had fought with thee,
To let thee know I am no coward, I.
I tel thee, Shakbag, thou abusest me.
Sha. Why, thy speach bewraied an inlye kind of feare,
And sauourd of a weak relenting spirit.
Go forward now in that we haue begonne,
And afterwards attempt me when thou darest.
Wil. And if I do not, heauen cut me of!
But let that passe, and show me to this house,
Where thou shalt see Ile do as much as Shakbag.
Sha. This is the doore; but soft, me thinks tis shut.
The villaine Michaell hath deceiued vs.
Wil. Soft, let me see; shakbag, tis shut indeed.
Knock with thy sword, perhaps the slaue will heare.
Sha. It wil not be; the white liuerd pesant
Is gon to bed, and laughs vs both to scorne.
Wil. And he shall by his mirriment as deare
As euer coistrell bought so little sport:
Nere let this sworde assist me when I neede,
But rust and canker after I haue sworne,
If I, the next time that I mete the hind,
Loppe not away his leg, his arme, or both.
Sha. And let me neuer draw a sword againe,
Nor prosper in the twilight, cockshut light,
When I would fleece the welthie passenger,
But ly and languish in a loathsome den,
Hated and spit at by the goers by,
And in that death may die vnpittied,
If I, the next time that I meete the slaue,
Cut not the nose from of the cowards face
And trample on it for this villany.
Wil. Come, lets go seeke out Green; I know hele swear.
Sha. He were a villane, and he would not sweare.
Twould make a pesant sweare amongst his boyes,
That nere durst say before but yea and no,
To be thus flouted of a coysterel.
Will. Shakbag, lets seeke out Green, & in the morning
At the Alehouse butting Ardens house
Watch thee out comming of that prick eard cur,
And then let me alone to handle him.
[*Exeunt.*

⟨Scene III.

Room in Francklin's *House as before.*⟩

Here enters Ard., Fra., & Michaell.

Ard. Sirra, get you back to billensgate
And learne what time the tide will serue our turne;
Come to vs in Paules. First go make the bed,
And afterwards go harken for the floude.
[*Exit* Michaell.
Come, M⟨aister⟩ Francklin, you shall go with me.
This night I dreamd that, beeing in a parke,
A toyle was picht to ouerthrow the deare,
And I vppon a little rysing hill
Stoode whistely watching for the herds approch.
Euen there, me thought, a gentle slumber tooke me,
And sommond all my parts to sweete repose;
But in the pleasure of this golden rest
An ill thewd foster had remoued the toyle,
And rounded me with that beguyling home
Which late, me thought, was pitcht to cast the deare.
With that he blew an euill sounding horne,
And at the noise an other heardman came,
With Fauchon drawn, and bent it at my brest,
Crying aloud 'Thou art the game we seeke!'
With this I wakt and trembled euery ioynt,
Lyke one oscured in a lytle bushe,
That sees a lyon foraging about,
And, when the dreadfull forest King is gone,
He pryes about with timerous suspect
Throughout the thorny casements of the brake,
And will not think his person daungerles,
But quakes and shewers, though the cause be gone:
So, trust me, Francklin, when I did awake,
I stoode in doubt whether I waked or no:
Such great impression tooke this fond surprise.
God graunt this vision bedeeme me any good.
Fran. This fantassie doeth rise from Michaels feare,
Who being awaked with the noyse he made,
His troubled sences yet could take no rest;
And this, I warant you, procured your dreame.
Ard. It may be so, God frame it to the best:
But often times my dreames presage to trew.
Fran. To such as note their nightly fantasies,
Some one in twenty may incurre beliefe;
But vse it not, tis but a mockery.

38 *Line ends* bed *Qq* 53 of *om.* *Q 3* 54 this] his *Q 2, 3* 62 thee *Q 1* : the *Q 3*

Scene III. *etc. add. T* 10 thoughts *Q 1, 2* 27 sheuers *Q 2* : shiuers *Q 3*

Ard. Come, M⟨aister⟩ Francklin; wele now walke in Paules
And dyne togeather at the ordinary,
And by my mans direction draw to the key,
And with the tyde go down to Feuershame.
Say, M⟨aister⟩ Francklin, shall it not be so?
Francklin. At your good pleasure, sir; Ile beare you companye.
[*Exeunt.*

⟨SCENE IV.

Aldersgate.⟩

Here enters Michaell *at one doore*

Here enters Grene, Will, *and* Shakebag *at another doore.*

Wil. Draw, Shakbag, for heers that villaine Michael.
Gre. First, Will, lets heare what he can say.
Wil. Speak, milkesope slaue, & neuer after speake.
Mic. For Gods sake, sirs, let me excuse my selfe:
For heare I sweare, by heauen and earth and all,
I did performe the outmost of my task,
And left the doores vnbolted and vnlockt.
But see the chaunce: Francklin and my master
Were very late conferring in the porch,
And Francklin left his napkin where he sat
With certain gould knit in it, as he said.
Being in bed, he did bethinke himselfe,
And comming down he found the dores vnshut:
He lockt the gates, and brought away the keyes,
For which offence my master rated me.
But now I am going to see what floode it is,
For with the tyde my M⟨aister⟩ will away;
Where you may frons him well on Raynum downe,
A place well fitting such a stratageme.
Wil. Your excuse hath somewhat molyfied my choller.
Why now, Greene, tis better now nor ere it was.
Gre. But Michaell, is this trew?
Mic. As trew as I report it to be trew.
Shak. Then, Michaell, this shall be your pennance,
To feast vs all at the Salutation,
Where we wil plat our purpose throughly.
Gre. And, Michael, you shal bear no newes of this tide,
Because they two may be in Raynum down
Before your M⟨aister⟩.
Mic. Why, Ile agree to any thing youle haue me,
So you will accept of my company. [*Exeunt.*

⟨SCENE V.

Arden's *House at Feversham.*⟩

Here enters Mosby.

Mos. Disturbed thoughts dryues me from company
And dryes my marrow with their watchfulnes;
Continuall trouble of my moody braine
Feebles my body by excesse of drinke,
And nippes me as the bitter Northeast wind
Doeth check the tender blosoms in the spring.
Well fares the man, how ere his cates do taste,
That tables not with foule suspition;
And he but pines amongst his delicats,
Whose troubled minde is stuft with discontent.
My goulden time was when I had no gould;
Though then I wanted, yet I slept secure;
My dayly toyle begat me nights repose,
My nights repose made daylight fresh to me.
But since I climbd the toppe bough of the tree
And sought to build my nest among the clouds,
Each gentle stary gaile doth shake my bed,
And makes me dread my downfall to the earth.
But whether doeth contemplation carry me?
The way I seeke to finde, where pleasure dwels,
Is hedged behinde me that I cannot back,
But needs must on, although to dangers gate.
Then, Arden, perish thou by that decre;
For Greene doth erre the land and weede thee vp
To make my haruest nothing but pure corne.
And for his paines Ile heaue him vp a while,
And after smother him to haue his waxe:
Such bees as Greene must neuer liue to sting.
Then is there Michael and the Painter to,
Cheefe actors to Ardens ouerthrow;
Who when they shall see me sit in Ardens seat,
They wil insult vpon me for my mede,
Or fright me by detecting of his end.
Ile none of that, for I can cast a bone
To make these curres pluck out each others throat,
And then am I sole ruler of mine owne.
Yet mistres Arden liues; but she's my selfe,
And holy Church rites makes vs two but one.
But what for that? I may not trust you, Ales:
You haue supplanted Arden for my sake,
You will extirpen me to plant another.

46 *Two lines Qq, div. after* sir   Scene IV. *etc. add. T*   2 Will *om. Q 3*   18 frons *Q 1, 2*: front *Q 3*   22 this] it *Q 3*

28–9 *One line Qq*   31 accept *Q 3*: except *Q 1*   Scene V. *WP*: *New act T*   *S. D.* Arden's *etc. add. T*   12 Thought *Q 1*   24 erre] heyre *Q 3*   26 hive *D*   31 shall *om. Q 3*

Tis feareful sleeping in a serpents bed,
And I wil cleanely rid my hands of her.

Here enters A⟨l⟩es.

But here she comes and I must flatter her.
— How now, Ales? what, sad and passionat?
Make me pertaker of thy pensiuenes:
Fyre deuided burnes with lesser force.
Ales. But I will damne that fire in my breast
Till by the force therof my part consume.
Ah, Mosbie!
Mos. Such depe pathaires lyke to a cannons burst
Dischargde against a ruinated wall,
Breakes my relenting hart in thousand pieces.
Vngentle Ales, thy sorrow is my sore;
Thou knowst it wel, and tis thy pollicy
To forge distressefull looks to wound a breast
Where lyes a hart that dies when thou art sad.
It is not loue that loues to anger loue.
Ales. It is not loue that loues to murther loue.
Mos. How meane you that?
Ales. Thou knowest how dearly Arden loued me.
Mos. And then?
Ales. And then — conceale the rest, for tis too bad,
Least that my words be carried with the wind,
And publisht in the world to both our shames.
I pray thee, Mosbye, let our springtime wither;
Our haruest els will yeald but lothsome weedes.
Forget, I pray thee, what hath past betwix vs,
For now I blushe and tremble at the thoughts.
Mos. What? are you changde?
Ales. I, to my former happy lyfe againe,
From tytle of an odious strumpets name
To honest Ardens wife, not Ardens honest wife.
Ha, Mosbye, tis thou hast rifled me of that
And made me slaundrous to all my kin;
Euen in my forehead is thy name ingrauen,
A meane Artifiecer, that lowe borne name.
I was bewitched: woe worth the haples howre
And all the causes that inchaunted me!
Mos. Nay, if thou ban, let me breath curses forth,
And if you stand so nicely at your fame,
Let me repent the credit I haue lost.
I haue neglected matters of import
That would haue stated me aboue thy state,
Forslowde aduantages, and spurnd at time:
I, Fortunes right hand Mosbie hath forsooke
To take a wanton giglote by the left.
I left the Mariage of an honest maid,
Whose dowry would haue weyed down all thy wealth,
Whose beauty and demianor farre exceeded thee:
This certaine good I lost for changing bad,
And wrapt my credit in thy company.
I was bewitcht,—that is no theame of thine,—
And thou vnhallowed hast enchaunted me.
But I will breake thy spels and excirsi⟨s⟩mes
And put another sight vpon these eyes
That shewed my hart a rauen for a doue.
Thou art not faire, I vieud thee not till now;
Thou art not kinde, till now I knew the not;
And now the raine hath beaten of thy gilt,
Thy worthles copper showes thee counterfet.
It grieues me not to see how foull thou art,
But maddes me that euer I thought thee faire.
Go, get thee gone, a copesmate for thy hyndes;
I am too good to be thy fauorite.
Ales. I, now I see, and too soone find it trew,
Which often hath beene tould me by my freends,
That Mosbie loues me not but for my wealth,
Which too incredulus I nere beleeued.
Nay, heare me speake, Mosbie, a word or two;
Ile byte my tongue if it speake bitterly.
Looke on me, Mosby, or Ile kill my selfe:
Nothing shall hide me from thy stormy looke.
If thou cry warre, there is no peace for me;
I will do pennance for offending thee,
And burne this prayer booke, where I here vse
The holy word that had conuerted me.
See, Mosbie, I will teare away the leaues,
And al the leaues, and in this golden couer
Shall thy sweete phrases and thy letters dwell;
And thereon will I chiefly meditate,
And hould no other sect but such deuotion.
Wilt thou not looke? is all thy loue ouer-whelmde?
Wilt thou not heare? what malice stopes thine eares?
Why speaks thou not ? what silence ties thy tongue?
Thou hast bene sighted as the eagle is,
And heard as quickly as the fearefull hare,
And spoke as smoothly as an orator,
When I haue bid thee heare or see or speak,

49–50 *One line Qq* 51 depe pathaires] deep-fet airs *D*: depe-fet sighs *WP* 69 now *Q 1*: Now *WP* 74 has *WP* 80 thou] you *WP*

94 hast *Q 1, 3*: has *WP* 95 excirsimes *Q 1*: exorcismes *Q 3* 97 dowe *Q 1*: Dove *Q 3* 99 the *Q 1*: thee *Q 3* 107 me *om. Q 3* 112 or] or else *Q 3*

And art thou sensible in none of these?
Waigh all thy good turns with this little fault,
And I deserue not Mosbies muddy lookes.
A fence of trouble is not thickned still:
Be cleare againe, Ile nere more trouble thee.

Mos. O no, I am a base artificer;
My winges are feathred for a lowly flight.
Mosby? fy! no, not for a thousand pound.
Make loue to you? why, 'tis vnpardonable;
We beggers must not breath where gentiles are.

Ales. Swete Mosbie is as gentle as a King,
And I too blinde to iudge him otherwise.
Flowres do some times spring in fallow lands,
Weedes in gardens, Roses grow on thornes;
So, what so ere my Mosbies father was,
Himselfe ⟨is⟩ valued gentle by his worth.

Mos. Ah, how you women can insinuate,
And cleare a trespasse with your sweete set tongue!
I will forget this quarrel, gentle Ales,
Prouided Ile be tempted so no more.

Here enters Bradshaw.

Al. Then with thy lips seale vp this new made match.

Mos. Soft, Ales, for here comes some body.

Ales. How now, Bradshaw, whats the news with you?

Brad. I haue little news, but heres a letter
That M⟨aister⟩ Greene importuned me to giue you.

Ales. Go in, Bradshaw; call for a cuppe of beare;
Tis almost suppertime, thou shalt stay with vs.
[*Exit* ⟨Bradshaw.⟩

Then she reades the Letter.

'We haue mist of our purpose at London, but shall perform it by the waye. We thanke our neighbour Bradshaw.
Yours, Richard Greene.'

How lykes my loue the tennor of this letter?

Mos. Well, were his date compleat and expired.

Ales. Ah, would it were! Then comes my happy howre:
Till then my blisse is mixt with bitter gall.
Come, let vs in to shun suspition.

Mosb. I, to the gates of death to follow thee.
[*Exeunt.*

⟨SCENE VI.

Country near Rochester.⟩

Here enters Greene, Will, & Shakbag.

Shak. Come, Will, see thy tooles be in a redynes:
Is not thy Powder dancke, or will thy flint stryke fyre?

Will. Then aske me if my nose be on my face,
Or whether my toung be frosen in my mouth.
Zounds, heres a coyle!
You were best sweare me on the intergatories
How many pistols I haue tooke in hand,
Or whether I loue the smell of gunne powder,
Or dare abide the noise the dagge will make,
Or will not wincke at flashing of the fire.
I pray thee, shackbag, let this answer thee,
That I haue tooke more purses in this down
Then ere thou handledst pistols in thy life.

Sha. I, happely thou hast pickt more in a throng:
But, should I bragge what booties I haue tooke,
I think the ouerplus thats more then thine
Would mount to a greater somme of money
Then either thou or all thy kinne are worth.
Zounds, I hate them as I hate a toade
That cary a muscado in their tongue,
And scarce a hurting weapon in their hand.

Wil. O Greene, intollerable!
It is not for mine honor to beare this.
Why, shakbag, I did serue the King at Bulloyne,
And thou canst bragge of nothing that thou hast done.

Shak. Why, so can Jack of Feuershame,
That sounded for a phillope on the nose,
When he that gaue it him hollowed in his eare,
And he supposed a Cannon bullet hit him.

Then they fight.

Grene. I pray you, sirs, list to Esops talk:
Whilest two stout dogs were striuing for a bone,
There comes a cur and stole it from them both;
So, while you stand striuing on these termes of manhoode,
Arden escapes vs, and deceaue⟨s⟩ vs al.

Shake. Why, he begun.

Will. And thou shalt finde Ile end;
I doo but slip it vntil better time:
But, if I do forget —

Then hee kneeles downe and houldes vp his hands to heauen.

Grene. Wel, take your fittest standings, & once more

131 thy] my *J* 135 O] O, fie *Q 3* 136 flght *Q 1* 142 do *om. Q 3* 145 is *add. J* 151 for *om. WP* *S. D.* exit *after 155 Q 1* 162 *Two lines Qq div.* were 165 *Prefix* Mosb *Q 3* : Ales *Q 1*

Scene VI. *etc. add. T* 2 *Two lines, Qq div.* dancke 5–7 *Prose Q 1* 25 that *om. Q 3* 34 escape *Q 3* : deceaue *Q 1* : deceive *Q 3*

Lime your twigs to catch this wary bird.
Ile leaue you, and at your dags discharge
Make towards, lyke the longing water dog
That coucheth til the fowling peece be of,
Then ceazeth on the pray with eager moode.
Ah, might I see him stretching foorth his limmes,
As I haue seene them beat their wings ere now!
Shak. Why, that thou shalt see, if he come this way.
Gre. Yes, that he doth, shakbag, I warrant thee:
But braul not when I am gone in any case.
But, sirs, be sure to speede him when he comes,
And in that hope Ile leaue you for an houre.
[*Exit* Gre.

Here enters Arden, Fran., & Mic.

Mic. Twere best that I went back to Rochester:
The horse halts downright; it were not good
He trauailed in such paine to feuershame;
Remouing of a shoe may happely help it.
Ard. Well, get you back to Rochester; but, sirra, see
Ye ouertake vs ere we come to Raynum down,
For it will be very late ere we get home.
Mic. — I, God he knowes, & so doth Will and shakebagge,
That thou shalt neuer go further then that downe;
And therefore haue I prickt the horse on purpose,
Because I would not view the massacar.
[*Exit* Michaell.
Arden. Come, M⟨aister⟩ Francklin, onwards with your tale.
Fran. I assure you, sir, you taske me much:
A heauy bloode is gathered at my hart,
And on the sudden is my winde so short
As hindereth the passage of my speach;
So ferse a qualme yet neere assayled me.
Ard. Come, M⟨aister⟩ Francklin, let vs go on softly:
The anoyance of the dust or els some meat
You eat at dinner cannot brooke with you.
I haue bene often so, and soone amended.
Fra. Do you remember where my tale did leaue?
Ard. I, where the gentleman did chek his wife.
Fran. She being reprehended for the fact,
Witnes produced that tooke her with the deed,
Her gloue broght in which there she left behind,
And many other assured Arguments,
Her husband askt her whether it were not so.
Ard. Her answer then? I wonder how she lookt,
Hauing forsworne it with such vehement oathes,
And at the instant so approued vppon her.
Fra. First did she cast her eyes down to the earth,
Watching the drops that fell amaine from thence;
Then softly drawes she foorth her handkercher,
And modestly she wypes her teare staind face;
Then hemd she out, to cleare her voice, should seeme,
And with a maiesty addrest her selfe
To encounter all their accusations.—
Pardon me, M⟨aister⟩ Arden, I can no more;
This fighting at my hart makes shorte my wynde.
Ard. Come, we are almost now at Raynum downe:
Your pretty tale beguiles the weary way;
I would you were in state to tell it out.
Shak. Stand close, Will, I heare them cumming.

Here enters Lord Cheiny *with his men.*

Wil. Stand to it, Shakbag, and be resolute.
Lord Che. Is it so neere night as it seemes
Or wil this black faced euening haue a showre?
— What, M⟨aister⟩ Arden? you are well met,
I haue longd this fortnights day to speake with you:
You are a stranger, man, in the ile of Sheppy.
Ard. Your honors alwayes: bound to do you seruice.
Lord Che. Come you from London, & nere a man with you?
Ard. My man's comming after, but her's
My honest freend that came along with me.
Lord Che. My Lord protectors man I take you to bee.
Fran. I, my good Lord, and highly bound to you.
Lord Che. You & your frend come home & sup with me.
Ard. I beseech your honor pardon me;
I haue made a promise to a gentleman,
My honest freend, to meete him at my house;
The occasion is great, or els would I wait on you.
Lord C. Will you come to morrow & dyne with me,
And bring your honest frend along with you?
I haue dyuers matters to talke with you about.

39 wary *J*: weary *Qq* 55–6 *Prose Q 1* 67 ferse] fierce *Q 3* 70 with *add. Q 3*

100 Shepny *Q 1* 103–4 *Div.* after *Q q'*

Arden. To morrow wele waite vpon your honor.
Lord C. One of you staye my horse at the top of the hil.
—What! black Will? for whose purse wait you?
Thou wilt be hanged in Kent, when all is done.
Wil. Not hanged, God saue your honor;
I am your bedesman, bound to pray for you.
Lord C. I think thou nere saidest prayer in all thy lyfe. —
One of you giue him a crowne: —
And, sirra, leaue this kinde of lyfe;
If thou beest tainted for a penny matter,
And come in question, surely, thou wilt trusse.
— Come, M⟨aister⟩ Arden, let vs be going;
Youre way and mine lyes foure myle togeather.
[*Exeunt. Manet* Black Wil & Shakbag.
Wil. The Deuill break all your necks at 4 myles end!
Zounds, I could kill my selfe for very anger!
His Lordship chops me in, euen when
My dagge was leaueld at his hart.
I would his crowne were molten down his throat.
Sha. Arden, thou hast wondrous holye luck.
Did euer man escape as thou hast done?
Well, Ile discharge my pistoll at the skye,
For by this bullet Arden might not die.

Here enters Greene.

Gre. What, is he down? is he dispatcht?
Sha. I, in health towards Feuershame, to shame vs all.
Gre. The Deuill he is! why, sirs, how escapt he?
shak. When we were ready to shoote,
Comes my Lord Cheiny to preuent his death.
Grene. The Lord of heauen hath preserued him.
Will. Preserued a figge! The L⟨ord⟩ Cheiny hath perserued him,
And bids him to a feast to his house at shorlow.
But by the way once more Ile meete with him,
And, if all the Cheinies in the world say no,
Ile haue a bullet in his breast to morrow.
Therefore come, Greene, and let vs to Feuershame.
Gre. I, and excuse our selues to mistres Arden:
O, how shele chafe when she heares of this!
sha. Why, ile warrant you shel think we dare not do it.
Wil. Why, then let vs go, & tell her all the matter,
And plat the newes to cut him of to morrow.
[*Exeunt.*

124 a] one *Q 3* 130–1 *Div.* in *WP*

⟨ACT IV.

SCENE I.

Arden's *House at Feversham.*⟩

Here enters Arden *and his wife,* Francklin, *and* Michaell.

Ard. See how the howrs, the gardeant of heauens gate,
Haue by their toyle remoued the darksome cloudes,
That Soll may wel deserne the trampled pace
Wherein he wount to guide his golden car:
The season fits; come, Francklin, let's away.
Ales. I thought you did pretend some speciall hunt,
That made you thus cut shorte the time of rest.
Ard. It was no chase that made me rise so early,
But, as I tould thee yesternight, to go
To the Ile of Sheppy, there to dine with my Lord Cheiny;
For so his honor late commanded me.
Ales. I, such kinde husbands seldome want excuses;
Home is a wilde Cat to a wandring wit.
The time hath bene,—would God it were not past,—
That honors tytle nor a Lords command
Could once haue drawne you from these armes of mine.
But my deserts or your desires decay,
Or both; yet if trew loue may seeme desert,
I merite stil to haue thy company.
Fran. Why, I pray you, sir, let her go along with vs;
I am sure his honor wil welcome her
And vs the more for bringing her along.
Ard. Content; sirra, saddle your mistres nagge.
Ales. No, begde fauor merits little thankes;
If I should go, our house would runne away,
Or els be stolne; therefore Ile stay behind.
Ard. Nay, see how mistaking you are!
I pray thee, goe.
Ales. No, no, not now.
Ard. Then let me leaue thee satisfied in this,
That time nor place nor persons alter me,
But that I hould thee dearer then my life.
Ales. That will be seene by your quick returne.

Act IV. *etc. add. T* 1 gardeant] guard at *Q 3* 3 deserne *WP*: deserue *Q 1*: discerne *Q 3* pace] path *WP, but cf. N. E. D.* 9–10 *Div.* Sheppy *Qq* 17 desires *WP*: deserues *Qq*

Ard. And that shall be ere night, and if I liue.
Farewell, sweete Ales, we mind to sup with thee. [*Exit* Al.

Fra. Come, Michaell, are our horses ready?

Michaell. I, your horse are ready, but I am not ready, for I haue lost my purse, with six and thirtie shillinges in it, with taking vp of my M⟨aisters⟩ Nagge.

Fra. Why, I pray you, let vs go before,
Whilest he stayes behind to seeke his purse.

Ard. Go too, sirra, see you follow vs to the ile of sheppye
To my Lord Cheynyes, where we meane to dine.

[*Exeunt* Arden *&* Francklin.
[*Manet* Michaell.

Mic. So, faire weather after you, for before you lyes black Will and shakebag in the broome close, to close for you: theyle be your ferrymen to long home.

Here enters the Painter.

But who is this? the Painter, my corriual, that would nedes winne M⟨istris⟩ Susan.

Clark. How now, Michael? how doth my Mistresse and all at home?

Mic. Who? susan Mosbye? she is your Mistres, too?

Cla. I, how doth she and all the rest?

Mic. Al's well but susan; she is sicke.

Cla. Sick? Of what disease?

Mic. Of a great feare.

Cla. A feare of what?

Mic. A great feuer.

Cla. A feuer? God forbidde!

Mic. Yes, faith, and of a lordaine too, as bigge as your selfe.

Cla. O, Michael, the spleane prickles you. Go too, you carry an eye ouer mistres susan.

Mic. I, faith, to keepe her from the Painter.

Cla. Why more from a Painter then from a seruing creature like your selfe?

Mic. Because you Painters make but a painting table of a pretty wench, and spoile her beauty with blotting.

Cla. What meane you by that?

Mic. Why, that you Painters paint lambes in the lyning of wenches peticots, and we seruingmen put hornes to them to make them become sheepe.

Cla. Such another word wil cost you a cuffe or a knock.

Mic. What, with a dagger made of a pensell? Faith, tis too weake, and therefore thou to weak to winne susan.

Cla. Would susans loue lay vppon this stroke.

Then he breakes Michaels *head.*

Here enters Mosby, Greene, *&* Ales.

Ales. Ile lay my lyfe, this is for susans loue.
Stayd you behinde your M⟨aister⟩ to this end?
Haue you no other time to brable in
But now when serious matters are in hand?—
Say, Clarke, hast thou done the thing thou promised?

Cla. I, heare it is; the very touch is death.

Ales. Then this, I hope, if all the rest do faile,
Wil catch M⟨aister⟩ Arden,
And make him wise in death that liued a foole.
Why should he thrust his sickle in our corne,
Or what hath he to do with thee, my loue,
Or gouerne me that am to rule my selfe?
Forsooth, for credit sake, I must leaue thee:
Nay, he must leaue to liue that we may loue,
May liue, may loue; for what is lyfe but loue?
And loue shall last as long as lyfe remaines,
And lyfe shall end before my loue depart.

Mos. Why, whats loue without true constancy?
Lyke to a piller built of many stones,
Yet neither with good morter well compact
Nor cement to fasten it in the ioynts,
But that it shakes with euery blast of winde,
And, being toucht, straight falles vnto the earth,
And buries all his haughty pride in dust.
No, let our loue be rockes of Addamant,
Which time nor place nor tempest can asunder.

Gre. Mosbie, leaue protestations now,
And let vs bethinke vs what we haue to doo.
Black Will and shakebag I haue placed
In the broome close, watching Ardens comming;
Lets to them, and see what they haue done.

[*Exeunt.*

⟨Scene II.

The Kentish Coast opposite the Isle of Sheppey.⟩

Here enters Ard. *&* Fra.

Ard. Oh, ferryman, where art thou?

Here enters the Ferriman.

Fer. Here, here, goe before to the boat, and I will follow you.

33 be *om. Q 3* 36 horses *Q 3* 36–9 *Verse Qq : corr. D* 38 of *om. Q 3* 39 M. *Q 1* : mistris *Q 3* 42 see] see that *Q 3* 44 weather] whether *Q 1* 44–9, 61–4 *Verse Qq* 49 M. *Q 1* : mistris *Q 3* 57 feuer *D* 72–5 *Two verse lines Qq*

78–80 *Three verse lines Qq* 103 cement *Q 3* : semell *Q 1, 2* 112 broom, close *J etc.* Scene II. *etc. add. T* 2–3 *Verse Qq*

Ard. We haue great haste; I pray thee, come away.

Fer. Fy, what a mist is here!

Ard. This mist, my frend, is misticall,
Lyke to a good companions smoaky braine,
That was halfe dround with new ale ouer night.

Fer. Twere pitty but his scull were opened to make more Chimny roome.

Fran. Freend, whats thy opinion of this mist?

Fer. I think tis lyke to a curst wife in a lytle house, that neuer leaues her husband till she haue driuen him out at doores with a wet paire of eyes; then lookes he as if his house were a fire, or some of his freends dead.

Ard. Speaks thou this of thine owne experience?

Fer. Perhaps, I; perhaps, no: For my wyfe is as other women are, that is to say, gouerned by the Moone.

Fran. By the Moone? how, I pray thee?

Fer. Na, thereby lyes a bargane, and you shall not haue it fresh and fasting.

Ard. Yes, I pray thee, good ferryman.

Fer. Then for this once; let it be midsommer Moone, but yet my wyfe has another moone.

Fran. Another Moone?

Fer. I, and it hath influences and Eclipses.

Ard. Why, then, by this reconing you somtimes play the man in the Moone?

Fer. I, but you had not best to meddle with that moone, least I scratch you by the face with my bramble bush.

Ard. I am almost stifled with this fog; come, lets away.

Fran. And, sirra, as we go, let vs haue som more of your bolde yeomandry.

Fer. Nay, by my troth, sir, but flat knauery.
[*Exeunt.*

⟨Scene III.

Another place on the Coast.⟩

Here enters Will *at one doore, and* Shakbag *at another.*

Sha. Oh, Will, where art thou?

Wil. Here, shakbag, almost in hels mouth, where I can not see my way for smoake.

Sha. I pray thee speake still that we may mete by the sound, for I shall fall into some ditche or other, vnles my feete see better then my eies.

Wil. Didest thou euer see better weather to runne away with another mans wife, or play with a wenche at potfinger?

shak. No; this were a fine world for chandlers, if this weather would last; for then a man should neuer dyne nor sup without candle light. But, sirra Will, what horses are those that past?

Wil. Why, didst thou heare any?

Sha. I, that I did.

Will. My life for thine, twas Arden, and his companion, and then all our labour's lost.

Sha. Nay, say not so, for if it be they, they may happely loose their way as we haue done, and then we may chaunce meete with them.

Wil. Come, let vs go on lyke a couple of blind pilgrims.

Then Shakebag *falles into a ditch.*

Sha. Helpe, Will, help! I am almost drownd.

Here enters the ferryman.

Fer. Whose that that calles for help?

Wil. Twas none heere, twas thou thy selfe.

Fer. I came to help him that cald for help.
Why, how now? who is this thats in the ditch?
You are well enough serued to goe without a guyde such weather as this.

Wil. Sirra, what companyes hath past your ferry this morning?

Fer. None but a cupple of gentlemen, that went to dyne at my Lord cheyneis.

Wil. Shakbag, did not I tell thee as much?

Fer. Why, sir, will you haue any letters caried to them?

Wil. No, sir; get you gone.

Fer. Did you euer see such a mist as this?

Wil. No, nor such a foole as will rather be hought then get his way.

Fer. Why, sir, this is no hough munday; you ar deceiud.—Whats his name, I pray you, sir?

Sha. His name is black will.

Fer. I hope to see him one day hangd vpon a hill. [*Exit Ferriman.*

Sha. See how the Sunne hath cleard the foggy mist,
Now we haue mist the marke of our intent.

Here enters Grene, Mosbye, *and* Ales.

Mos. Black Will and Shakbag, what make you heer?
What, is the deed don? is Arden dead?

Wil. What could a blynded man performe in armes?
Saw you not how till now the sky was darke,
That neither horse nor man could be decerned?

9–10, 12–16, 22–3, 25–7, 30–4 *Verse Qq* 26 has *Q 3*: as *Q 1, 2* 32 not best] best not *WP* Scene III. *etc. add. WP* 2–3 *Verse Qq* 5 for] or *Q 3*

11–15, 18–9, 28–31 *Verse Qq* 16 thou *om. Q 3* 20 thats] that lies *Q 3* 43 though Munday *Q 3*

Yet did we heare their horses as they past.
Gre. Haue they escapt you, then, and past the ferry?
Sha. I, for a while; but here we two will stay,
And at their comming back meete with them once more.
Zounds, I was nere so toylde in all my lyfe
In following so slight a taske as this.
Mos. How camst thou so beraide?
Wil. With making false footing in the dark;
He needs would follow them without a guide.
Ales. Here's to pay for a fire and good cheere:
Get you to Feuershame to the flowre de luce,
And rest your selues vntil some other time.
Gre. Let me alone; it most concernes my state.
Will. I, mistres Arden, this wil serue the turne,
In case we fal into a second fog.
[*Exeunt* Grene, Will, *and* Shak.
Mos. These knaues wil neuer do it, let vs giue it ouer.
Ales. First tell me how you like my new deuice:
Soone, when my husband is roturning back,
You and I both marching arme in arme,
Lyke louing frends, wele meete him on the way,
And boldly beard and braue him to his teeth.
When words grow hot and blowes beginne to ryse,
Ile call those cutters foorth your tenement,
Who, in a manner to take vp the fray,
Shall wound my husband hornesbie to the death.
Mos. Ah, fine deuise! why, this deserues a kisse. [*Exeunt.*

⟨Scene IV.

The Open Country.⟩

Here enters Dicke Reede *and a Sailer.*

Sayler. Faith, Dick Rede, it is to lytle end:
His conscience is too liberall, and he too nigardly
To parte from any thing may doo thee good.
Rede. He is coming from Shorlow as I vnderstand;
Here ile intercept him, for at his house
He neuer will vouchafe to speake with me.
If prayers and faire intreaties will not serue,
Or make no battry in his flintye breast,

Here enters Fra., Ard., *and* Michaell.

Ile cursse the carle, and see what that wil doo.
Se where he comes to further my intent!—
M⟨aister⟩ Arden, I am now bound to the sea;
My comming to you was about the plat
Of ground which wrongfully you detaine from me:
Although the rent of it be very small,
Yet will it helpe my wife and children,
Which here I leaue in Feuershame, God knowes,
Needy and bare: for Christs sake, let them haue it!
Ard. Francklin, hearest thou this fellow speake?
That which he craues I dearely bought of him,
Although the rent of it was euer mine.—
Sirra, you that aske these questions,
If with thy clamarous impeaching tongue
Thou raile on me, as I haue heard thou dost,
Ile lay thee vp so close a twelue months day,
As thou shalt neither see the Sonne nor Moone.
Looke to it, for, as surely as I liue,
Ile banish pittie if thou vse me thus.
Rede. What, wilt thou do me wrong & threat me, too?
Nay, then, Ile tempt thee, Arden, doo thy worst.
God, I beseech thee, show some miracle
On thee or thine, in plaguing thee for this.
That plot of ground which thou detaines from me,
I speake it in an agony of spirite,
Be ruinous and fatall vnto thee!
Either there be butcherd by thy dearest freends,
Or els be brought for men to wonder at,
Or thou or thine miscary in that place,
Or there runne mad and end thy cursed dayes!
Fra. Fy, bitter knaue, brydle thine enuious tongue;
For curses are like arrowes shot vpright,
Which falling doun light on the s⟨h⟩uters head.
Rede. Light where they will! Were I vppon the sea,
As oft I haue in many a bitter storme,
And saw a dreadfull suthern flaw at hand,
The Pylate quaking at the doubtfull storme,
And all the saylers praying on their knees,
Euen in that fearefull time would I fall down,
And aske of God, what ere betide of me,
Vengeance on Arden or some misevent
To shewe the world what wrong the carle hath done.

76 blowes] words *Q 3* 79 Hornbeast *WP* 80 Ah] A *WP* Scene IV. *etc. add. T* 3 thee] him *Q 3*

12 *ends* ground *Qq* 27 thou] you *Q 3* 31 plauging *Q 1* 41 sutors *Q 1, 2*: shooters *Q 3*

This charge Ile leaue with my distresfull wife,
My children shall be taught such praiers as these:
And thus I go, but leaue my cursse with thee.
[*Exeunt* Rede *& Sayler.*

Ard. It is the raylingest knaue in christendome,
And oftentimes the villaine will be mad;
It greatly matters not what he sayes,
But I assure you I nere did him wrong.

Fra. I think so, M⟨aister⟩ Arden.

Ard. Now that our horses are gone home before,
My wife may hapely mete me on the way.
For God knowes she is growne passing kinde of late,
And greatly chaunged from the oulde
Humor of her wounted frowardnes,
And seekes by faire meanes to redeeme ould faults.

Fra. Happy the change that alters for the best!
But see in any case you make no speache
Of the cheare we had at my Lord Cheineis,
Although most bounteous and liberall,
For that will make her think her selfe more wrongd,
In that we did not carry her along;
For sure she greeued that she was left behinde.

Ard. Come, Francklin, let vs strain to mend our pace,
And take her vnawares playing the cooke;

Here enters Ales *and* Mosbie.

For I beleeue sheele stryue to mend our cheere.

Fran. Why, thers no better creaturs in the world,
Then women are when they are in good humors.

Ard. Who is that? Mosbie? what, so familiare?
Iniurious strumpet, and thou ribald knaue,
Vntwyne those armes.

Ales. I, with a sugred kisse let them vntwine.

Ard. Ah, Mosbie! periurde beast! beare this and all!

Mos. And yet no horned beast; the hornes are thine.

Fran. O monstrous! Nay, then tis time to draw.

Ales. Helpe, helpe! they murther my husband.

Here enters Will *and* Shak.

Sha. Zounds, who iniures M⟨aister⟩ Mosbie?—
Help, Wil! I am hurt.

Mos. I may thank you, Mistres arden, for this wound.
[*Exeunt* Mosby, Will, *and* Shakbag.

Ales. Ah, Arden, what folly blinded thee?
Ah, Jelious harebraine man, what hast thou don!
When we, to welcome thy intended sport,
Came louingly to mete thee on thy way,
Thou drewst thy sword, inraged with Jelousy,
And hurte thy freende whose thoughts were free from harme;
All for a woorthles kisse and ioyning armes,
Both don but mirrely to try thy patience.
And me vnhappy that deuysed the Jest,
Which, though begonne in sporte, yet ends in bloode!

Fran. Mary, God defend me from such a Jeast!

Ales. Couldst thou not see vs frendly smyle on thee,
When we ioynd armes, and when I kist his cheeke?
Hast thou not lately found me ouer kinde?
Didst thou not heare me cry, they murther thee?
Cald I not helpe to set my husband free?
No, eares and all were witcht; ah me accurst
To lincke in lyking with a frantick man!
Hence foorth Ile be thy slaue, no more thy wife,
For with that name I neuer shall content thee.
If I be merry, thou straight waies thinks me light;
If sad, thou saiest the sullens trouble me;
If well attyred, thou thinks I will be gadding;
If homely, I seeme sluttish in thine eye:
Thus am I still, and shall be till I die,
Poore wench, abused by thy misgouernment!

Ard. But is it for trueth that neither thou nor he
Entendedst malice in your misdemeanor?

Ales. The heauens can witnes of our harmles thoghts.

Ard. Then pardon me, sweete Ales, and forgiue this faulte:
Forget but this and neuer see the lyke.
Impose me pennance, and I will performe it,
For in thy discontent I finde a death,—
A death tormenting more then death it selfe.

Ales. Nay, hadst thou loued me as thou doest pretend,

51 my] wy *Q 1* 60 me *om. Q 3* 62 *ends* humor *Qq*: from *D* 73 her *om. Q 3* to play *Q 3* 75 creature *3* 82 horne-beast *Q 3* *two lines Q 1, 2, div.* beast 90 thy] thee with *WP* 93 *Two lines Qq, div.* freende 112 till] whill *Q 1*: while *Q 3, etc.* 117 *Two lines Qq, div.* Ales

Thou wouldst haue markt the speaches of thy frend,
Who going wounded from the place, he said
His skinne was peirst only through my deuise ;
And if sad sorrow taint thee for this falt,
Thou wouldst haue followed him, and sene him drest,
And cryde him mercy whome thou hast misdone:
Nere shall my hart be eased till this be done.

Arden. Content thee, sweete Ales, thou shalt haue thy wil,
What ere it be. For that I iniurde thee,
And wrongd my frend, shame scourgeth my offence;
Come thou thy selfe, and go along with me,
And be a mediator twixt vs two.

Fran. Why, M⟨aister⟩ Arden! know you what you do?
Will you follow him that hath dishonourd you?

Ales. Why, canst thou proue I haue bene disloyall?

Fran. Why, Mosbie taunts your husband with the horn.

Ales. I, after he had reuyled him
By the iniuryous name of periurde beast:
He knew no wrong could spyte an Jelious man
More then the hatefull naming of the horne.

Fran. Suppose tis trew; yet is it dangerous
To follow him whome he hath lately hurt.

Ales. A fault confessed is more then halfe amends;
But men of such ill spirite as your selfe
Worke crosses and debates twixt man and wife.

Ard. I pray the, gentle Francklin, holde thy peace:
I know my wife counsels me for the best.
Ile seeke out mosby where his wound is drest,
And salue his haples quarrell if I may.

[*Exeunt* Arden *&* Ales.

Fran. He whome the diuel driues must go perforce.
Poore gentleman, how sone he is bewitcht!
And yet, because his wife is the instrument,
His frends must not be lauish in their speach.

[*Exit* Fran.

⟨ACT V.

Scene I.

A street in Feversham.⟩

Here enters Will, shakabage, *&* Greene.

Wil. Sirra Greene, when was I so long in killing a man?

Gre. I think we shall neuer do it; let vs giue it ouer.

Sha. Nay, Zounds! wele kill him, though we be hangd at his dore for our labour.

Wil. Thou knowest, Greene, that I haue liued in London this twelue yeers, where I haue made some go vppon wodden legges for taking the wall on me; dyuers with siluer noses for saying 'There goes black will!' I haue crackt as many blades as thou hast done Nutes.

Gre. O monstrous lye!

Will. Faith, in a maner I haue. The bawdie houses haue paid me tribute there durst not a whore set vp, vnlesse she haue aggreed with me first for opning her shoppe windowes. For a crosse worde of a Tapster I haue pearced one barrell after another with my dager, and held him by the eares till all his beare hath run out. In Temes streete a brewers carte was lyke to haue runne ouer me: I made no more ado, but went to the clark and cut all the natches of his tales and beat them about his head. I and my companye haue taken the Constable from his watch, and carried him about the fields on a coltstaffe. I haue broken a Sariants head with his owne mace, and baild whome I list with my sword and buckler. All the tenpenny alehouses would stand euery morning with a quart pot in their hand, saying, 'will it please your worship drinke?' He that had not doone so, had beene sure to haue had his Signe puld down & his latice borne away the next night. To conclude, what haue I not done? yet cannot do this; doubtles, he is preserued by Miracle.

Here enters Ales *and* Michaell.

Gre. Hence, Will! here comes M⟨istris⟩ Arden.

Ales. Ah, gentle michaell, art thou sure thei'r frends?

Mic. Why, I saw them when they both shoke hands.
When Mosbie bled, he euen wept for sorrow,
And raild on Francklin that was cause of all.
No sooner came the Surgen in at doores,
But my M⟨aister⟩ tooke to his purse and gaue him money,
And, to conclude, sent me to bring you word
That Mosbie, Francklin, Bradshaw, Adam fowle,
With diuers of his neighbors and his frends,

138 taunts your *Q 3* : traunt you *Q 1* : taunted your *D* 141 an] a *Q 3* 149 me *om. Q 3* 150 *Prefix* Ard. *repeated before this line Q 1* 151 his] this *D* Act V. *etc. add. T*

3–37 *Verse Qq* 10 of me *Q 2, 3* 12 done *om. WP* 20 by *Q 3* : be *Q 1* 24 all] off *Q 3* 27 him *om. Q 3* 30 men *add. J* 32 their] his *Q 1* 34 Singne *Q 1* 38 M. *Q 1* : mistris *Q 3* 44 to *om. Q 3*

Will come and sup with you at our house this night.

Ales. Ah, gentle Michaell, runne thou bak againe,
And, when my husband walkes into the faire,
Bid Mosbie steale from him and come to me;
And this night shal thou and Susan be made sure.

Mic. Ile go tell him.

Ales. And as thou goest, tell John cooke of our guests,
And bid him lay it on, spare for no coast.

[*Exit* Michaell.

Wil. Nay, and there be such cheere, we wil bid our selues.—
Mistres Arden, Dick Greene & I do meane to sup with you.

Ales. And welcome shall you be. Ah, gentlemen,
How mist you of your purpose yesternight?

Gre. Twas long of shakebag, that vnluckye villaine.

Sha. Thou doest me wrong; I did as much as any.

Wil. Nay then, M⟨istris⟩ Ales, Ile tell you how it was:
When he should haue lockt with both his hilts,
He in a brauery florisht ouer his head;
With that comes Francklin at him lustely,
And hurts the slaue; with that he slinks away.

Now his way had bene to haue come hand and feete, one and two round, at his costerd: he lyke a foole beares his sword point halfe a yarde out of danger. I lye here for my lyfe; if the deuill come, and he haue no more strength then fence, he shall neuer beat me from this warde.

Ile stand to it, a buckler in a skilfull hand
Is as good as a castell; nay,
Tis better then a sconce, for I haue tryde it.
Mosbie, perceiuing this, began to faint:
With that comes Arden with his arming sword,
And thrust him through the shoulder in a tryce.

Ales. I, but I wonder why you both stoode still.

Wil. Faith, I was so amazed, I could not strike.

Ales. Ah, sirs, had he yesternight bene slaine,
For euery drop of his detested bloode
I would haue cram'd in Angels in thy fist,
And kist thee, too, and hugd thee in my armes.

Wil. Patient your selfe, we can not help it now.
Greene and we two will dogge him through the faire,
And stab him in the croud, and steale away.

Here enters Mosbye.

Ales. It is vnpossible; but here comes he
That will, I hope, inuent some surer meanes.
Swete Mosbie, hide thy arme, it kils my hart.

Mos. I, mistres Arden, this is your fauour.

Ales. Ah, say not so; for when I sawe thee hurt,
I could haue toke the weapon thou letst fall,
And runne at Arden; for I haue sworne
That these mine eyes, offended with his sight,
Shall neuer close till Ardens be shut vp.
This night I rose and walkt about the chamber,
And twise or thrise I thought to haue murthred him.

Mos. What, in the night? then had we bene vndone.

Ales. Why, how long shall he liue?

Mos. Faith, Ales, no longer then this night.—
Black Will and shakbag, will you two performe
The complot that I haue laid?

Will. I, or els think me a villaine.

Gre. And rather then you shall want, Ile helpe my selfe.

Mos. You, M⟨aister⟩ Greene, shal single Francklin foorth,
And hould him with a long tale of strange newes,
That he may not come home till suppertime.
Ile fetch M⟨aister⟩ Arden home, & we like frends
Will play a game or two at tables here.

Ales. But what of all this? how shall he be slaine?

Mosbie. Why, black Wil and shakebag lockt within the countinghouse
Shall at a certaine watchword giuen rush foorth.

Wil. What shall the watch word be?

Mos. 'Now I take you' that shall be the word:
But come not forth before in any case.

Wil. I warrant you. But who shall lock me in?

Ales. That will I do; thou'st kepe the key thy selfe.

Mos. Come, M⟨aister⟩ Greene, go you along with me.

62 mistris Alice *Q 3* : M. Arden *WP* 67 haue *om. Q 3* 67–73 *Verse Qq* : *corr. D* 72 then] than I haue *WP* 84 have cram'd *Q 3* : cramme *Q 1* 85 mine *Q 2, 3*

103 *ends* two *Qq* : *corr. WP* 105 a] as a *Q 1* 106 *Two lines Qq, div.* want 112 *Two lines Qq, div.* this 119 do *om. Q 3* thou'st] thou'lt *Q 3*

See all things ready, Ales, against we come.
Ales. Take no care for that; send you him home, [*Exeunt* Mosbie *and* Greene.
And if he ere go forth againe, blame me.
Come, blacke Will, that in mine eies art faire;
Next vnto Mosbie doe I honour thee;
Instead of faire wordes and large promises
My hands shall play you goulden harmonie :
How like you this? say, will you doe it, sirs?
Will. I, and that brauely too. Marke my deuice:
Place Mosbie, being a stranger, in a chaire,
And let your husband sit vpon a stoole,
That I may come behind him cunninglie,
And with a towell pull him to the ground,
Then stab him till his flesh be as a siue;
That doone, beare him behind the Abby,
That those that finde him murthered may suppose
Some slaue or other kild him for his golde.
Ales. A fine deuice: you shall haue twenty pound,
And when he is dead, you shal haue forty more.
And, least you might be suspected staying heere,
Michaell shall saddle you two lusty geldings;
Ryde whether you will, to Scotland, or to Wales,
Ile see you shall not lacke, where ere you be.
Wil. Such wordes would make one kill 1000. men.
Giue me the key: which is the counting house?
Ales. Here would I stay and still encourage you,
But that I know how resolute you are.
Sha. Tush, you are too faint harted; we must do it.
Ales. But Mosbie will be there, whose very lookes
Will ad vnwounted courage to my thought,
And make me the first that shall aduenture on him.
Wil. Tush, get you gone; tis we must do the deede.
When this doore oppens next, looke for his death. ⟨*Exeunt* Will *and* Shakebag.⟩
Ales. Ah, would he now were here that it might oppen!
I shall no more be closed in Ardens armes,
That lyke the snakes of blacke Tisiphone
Sting me with their embraceings: mosbies Armes
Shal compasse me, and, were I made a starre,
I would haue none other spheres but those.
There is no nector but in Mosbies lypes!
Had chast Diana kist him, she like me
Would grow loue sicke and from her watrie bower
Fling down Endimion and snatch him vp:
Then blame not me that slay a silly man
Not halfe so louely as Endimion.

Here enters Michaell.

Mic. Mistres, my maister is comming hard by.
Ales. Who comes with him?
Michaell. Nobody but mosbye.
Ales. Thats well, michaell. Fetch in the tables,
And when thou hast done, stand before the countinghouse doore.
Mic. Why so?
Ales. Black will is lockt within to do the deede.
Mic. What? shall he die to night?
Ales. I, michaell.
Mic. But shall not susan know it?
Ales. Yes, for shele be as secreete as our selues.
Mic. Thats braue. Ile go fetch the tables.
Ales. But, michaell, hearke to me a word or two:
When my husband is come in, lock the streete doore;
He shall be murthred, or the guests come in. [*Exit* mic.

Here enters Arden *&* Mosbie.

Husband, what meane you to bring mosby home?
Although I wisht you to be reconciled,
Twas more for feare of you then loue of him.
Black Will and Greene are his companions,
And they are cutters, and may cut you shorte:
Therefore I thought it good to make you frends.
But wherefore do you bring him hether now?
You haue giuen me my supper with his sight.
Mos. M⟨aister⟩ Arden, me thinks your wife would haue me gone.
Arden. No, good M⟨aister⟩ Mosbie; women will be prating.
Ales, bid him welcome; he and I are frends.
Ales. You may inforce me to it, if you will;
But I had rather die then bid him welcome.
His company hath purchest me ill frends,
And therefore wil I nere frequent it more.
Mos. — Oh, how cunningly she can dissemble!
Ard. Now he is here, you wil not serue me so.

124 my *Q 3* 134 siue *Q 3* : sine *Q 1* 153 *S. D.* *add. WP*

163 snath *Q 1* 180 or *Q 1*: ere *Q 3* : or e'er *J* 182 Althought *Q* 1 190 prattling *Q 3*

Ales. I pray you be not angree or dis-pleased;
Ile bid him welcome, seing youle haue it so.
You are welcome, M⟨aister⟩ Mosbie; will you sit down?
Mos. I know I am welcome to your louing husband;
But for your selfe, you speake not from your hart.
Ales. And if I do not, sir, think I haue cause.
Mos. Pardon me, M⟨aister⟩ Arden; Ile away.
Ard. No, good M⟨aister⟩ Mosbie.
Ales. We shal haue guests enough, thogh you go hence.
Mos. I pray you, M⟨aister⟩ Arden, let me go.
Ard. I pray thee, Mosbie, let her prate her fill.
Ale. The dores are open, sir, you may be gone.
Mic. — Nay, thats a lye, for I haue lockt the dores.
Ard. Sirra, fetch me a cup of Wine, Ile make them freends.
And, gentle M⟨istris⟩ Ales, seeing you are so stout,
You shal beginne: frowne not, Ile haue it so.
Ales. I pray you meddle with that you haue to do.
Ard. Why, Ales! how can I do too much for him
Whose lyfe I haue endaungered without cause?
Ale. Tis true; & seeing twas partly through my means,
I am content to drinke to him for this once.
Here, M⟨aister⟩ Mosbie! and I pray you, henceforth
Be you as straunge to me as I to you.
Your company hath purchased me ill freends,
And I for you, God knowes, haue vndeserued
Beene ill spoken of in euery place;
Therefore hencefoorth frequent my house no more.
Mos. Ile see your husband in dispight of you.
Yet, Arden, I protest to thee by heauen,
Thou nere shalt see me more after this night.
Ile go to Roome rather then be forsworne.
Ar. Tush, Ile haue no such vowes made in my house.
Ales. Yes, I pray you, husband, let him sweare;
And, on that condition, Mosbie, pledge me here.
Mos. I, as willingly as I meane to liue.
Ard. Come, Ales, is our supper ready yet?
Ales. It wil by then you haue plaid a game at tables.
Ard. Come, M⟨aister⟩ Mosbie, what shall we play for?
Mos. Three games for a french crowne, sir, and please you.
Ard. Content.

Then they play at the Tables. ⟨*Enter* Will *and* Shakebag⟩.

Wil. — Can he not take him yet? what a spight is that?
Ales. — Not yet, Will; take hede he see thee not.
Wil. — I feare he will spy me as I am coming.
Mic. — To preuent that, creepe betwixt my legs.
Mos. One ace, or els I lose the game.
Ard. Mary, sir, theres two for fayling.
Mos. Ah, M⟨aister⟩ Arden, 'now I can take you.'

Then Will pulles him down with a towell.

Ard. Mosbie! Michaell! Ales! what will you do?
Will. Nothing but take you vp, sir, nothing els.
Mos. Thers for the pressing Iron you tould me of. ⟨*Stabs him.*⟩
Sha. And ther's for the ten pound in my sleeue. ⟨*Stabs him.*⟩
Ales. What! grones thou? nay, then giue me the weapon!
Take this for hindring Mosbies loue and mine. ⟨*She stabs him.*⟩
Michaell. O, Mistres!
Will. Ah, that villaine wil betray vs all.
Mos. Tush, feare him not; he will be secrete.
Mic. Why, dost thou think I will betray my selfe?
Sha. In Southwarke dwels a bonnie northerne lasse,
The widow Chambley; ile to her house now,
And if she will not giue me harborough,
Ile make bootie of the queane euen to her smocke.
Will. Shift for your selues; we two will leaue you now.
Ales. First lay the bodie in the counting-house.

Then they lay the body in the Countinghouse.

211 *Two lines Qq, div.* Wine 220 you as] as *Q 3* 231 Mosbie *om. Q 3* 236 *Two lines Qq, div.* sir 237 *S. D. Bracketed words add. WP* 238 yet *om. Q 3* 247–50 *S. D. D. add. T* 257 And] Ind *Q 1*

Will. We haue our gould; mistris Ales, adew;
Mosbie, farewell, and Michaell, farewell too. [*Exeunt.*

Enter Susan.

Susan. Mistres, the guests are at the doores.
Hearken, they knocke: what, shall I let them in?
Ales. Mosbie, go thou & beare them companie. [*Exit* M.
And, susan, fetch water and wash away this bloode.
Susan. The bloode cleaueth to the ground & will not out.
Ales. But with my nailes ile scrape away the blood;—
The more I striue, the more the blood appeares!
Susan. Whats the reason, M⟨istris⟩, can you tell?
Ales. Because I blush not at my husbands death.

Here enters Mosbie.

Mos. How now? whats the matter? is all well?
Ales. I, wel, if Arden were aliue againe.
In vaine we striue, for here his blood remains.
Mos. Why, strew rushes on it, can you not?
This wench doth nothing: fall vnto the worke.
Ales. Twas thou that made me murther him.
Mos. What of that?
Ales. Nay, nothing, Mosbie, so it be not known.
Mos. Keepe thou it close, and tis vnpossible.
Ales. Ah, but I can not! was he not slaine by me?
My husbands death torments me at the hart.
Mos. It shall not long torment thee, gentle Ales;
I am thy husband, thinke no more of him.

Here enters Adam fowle *and* Brad.

Brad. How now, M⟨istris⟩ Arden? what ayle you weepe?
Mos. Because her husband is abroad so late.
A cupple of Ruffins threatned him yesternight,
And she, poore soule, is affraid he should be hurt.
Adam. Ist nothing els? tush, hele be here anone.

Here enters Greene.

Gre. Now, M⟨istris⟩ Arden, lacke you any guests?
Ales. Ah, M⟨aister⟩ Greene, did you se my husband lately?
Gre. I saw him walking behinde the Abby euen now.

Here enters Francklin.

Ales. I do not like this being out so late.—
M⟨aister⟩ Francklin, where did you leaue my husband?
Fra. Beleeue me I saw him not since Morning.
Feare you not, hele come anone; meane time
You may do well to bid his guests sit down.
Ales. I, so they shall; M⟨aister⟩ Bradshaw, sit you there;
I pray you, be content, Ile haue my will.
M⟨aister⟩ Mosbie, sit you in my husbands seat.
Michaell. — Susan, shall thou and I wait on them?
Or, and thou saist the word, let vs sit down too.
Su. — Peace, we haue other matters now in hand.
I feare me, Michael, al wilbe bewraied.
Mic. — Tush, so it be knowne that I shal
marry thee in the morning, I care not though
I be hangde ere night.
But to preuent the worst, Ile by some rats bane.
Su. — Why, Michael, wilt thou poyson thy selfe?
Mic. — No, but my mistres, for I feare shele tell.
Su. — Tush, Michel; feare not her, she's wise enough.
Mos. — Sirra Michell, giues a cup of beare.—
M⟨istris⟩ Arden, heers to your husband.
Ales. My husband!
Fra. What ailes you, woman, to crie so suddenly?
Ales. Ah, neighbors, a sudden qualm came ouer my hart;
My husbands being foorth torments my mynde.
I know some thing's amisse, he is not well;
Or els I should haue heard of him ere now.
Mo. — She will vndo vs through her foolishnes.
Gre. Feare not, M⟨istris⟩ Arden, he's well enough.
Ales. Tell not me; I know he is not well:
He was not wount for to stay thus late.
Good M⟨aister⟩ Francklin, go and seeke him foorth,
And if you finde him, send him home to mee,

267 *Prefix* Alice *Q 3*

305–7 *Verse Qq, div.* tho   317 deing *Q 1*

And tell him what a feare he hath put me in.
Fra. —I lyke not this; I pray God all be well.
Ile seeke him out, and find him if I can.
[*Exeunt* Fra., Mos., *&* Gre.

Ales. —Michaell, how shall I doo to rid the rest away?

Mic. —Leaue that to my charge, let me alone.—
Tis very late, M⟨aister⟩ Bradshaw,
And there are many false knaues abroad,
And you haue many narrow lanes to pas.

Brad. Faith, frend Michaell, and thou saiest trew.
Therefore I pray thee lights foorth and lends a linck.
[*Exeunt* Brad., Adam, *&* Michael.

Ales. Michael, bring them to the dores, but doo not stay;
You know I do not loue to be alone.
—Go, Susan, and bid thy brother come:
But wherefore should he come? Heere is nought but feare;
Stay, Susan, stay, and helpe to counsell me.

Susan. Alas, I counsell! feare frights away my wits.

Then they open the countinghouse doore and looke vppon Arden.

Ales. See, Susan, where thy quandam Maister lyes,
Sweete Arden, smeard in bloode and filthy gore.

Susan. My brother, you, and I shall rue this deede.

Ales. Come, susan, help to lift his body forth,
And let our salt teares be his obsequies.

Here enters Mosbie *and* Greene.

Mos. How now, Ales, whether will you beare him?

Ales. Sweete Mosbie, art thou come? Then weepe that will:
I haue my wishe in that I ioy thy sight.

Gre. Well, it houes vs to be circumspect.

Mos. I, for Francklin thinks that we haue murthred him.

Ales. I, but he can not proue it for his lyfe.
Wele spend this night in daliance and in sport.

Here enters Michaell.

Mic. O mistres, the Maior and all the watch
Are comming towards our house with glaues & billes.

Ales. Make the dore fast; let them not come in.

Mos. Tell me, swete Ales, how shal I escape?

Ales. Out at the back dore, ouer the pyle of woode,
And for one night ly at the floure de luce.

Mos. That is the next way to betray my selfe.

Gre. Alas, M⟨istris⟩ Arden, the watch will take me here,
And cause suspition, where els would be none.

Ales. Why, take that way that M⟨aister⟩ Mosbie doeth;
But first conuey the body to the fields.

Then they beare the body into the fields.

Mos. Vntil to morrow, sweete Ales, now farewel:
And see you confesse nothing in any case.

Gre. Be resolute, M⟨istris⟩ Ales, betray vs not,
But cleaue to vs as we wil stick to you.
[*Exeunt* Mosbie *&* Grene.

Ales. Now, let the iudge and iuries do their worst:
My house is cleare, and now I feare them not.

Susan. As we went, it snowed al the way,
Which makes me feare our footesteps will be spyed.

Ales. Peace, foole, the snow wil couer them againe.

Susan. But it had done before we came back againe.

Ales. Hearke, hearke, they knocke! go, Michaell, let them in.

Here enters the Maior *and the* Watch.

How now, M⟨aister⟩ Maior, haue you brought my husband home?

Maior. I sawe him come into your house an hour agoe.

Ales. You are deceiued; it was a Londoner.

Maior. Mistres Arden, know you not one that is called blacke Will?

Ales. I know none such: what meane these questions?

Maior. I haue the counsels warrand to aprehend him.

Ales. —I am glad it is no worse.
Why, M⟨aister⟩ maior, thinke you I harbour any such?

Ma. We are informd that here he is;
And therefore pardon vs, for we must search.

Ales. I, search, and spare you not, through euery roome:
Were my husband at home, you would not offer this.

S. D. follows 327 *Qq*   333 narrow *om. Q 3*   335 light's .. lend's *Q 3*   343 filthy *om. Q 2, 3*   348 *Two lines Qq, div.* come   354 all *om. Q 3*

375 *Two lines Qq, div.* knocke

Here enters Francklin.

M⟨aister⟩ Francklin, what meane you come so sad?
Fra. Arden, thy husband and my freend, is slaine.
Ales. Ah! by whome? M⟨aister⟩ Francklin, can you tell?
Fra. I know not; but behind the abby
There he lyes murthred in most pittious case.
Mai. But, M⟨aister⟩ Francklin, are you sure tis he?
Fra. I am too sure; would God I were deceiued.
Ales. Finde out the Murthrers, let them be knowne.
Fran. I, so they shall; come you along with vs.
Ales. Wherefore?
Fran. Know you this handtowel and this knyfe?
Su. — Ah, michael, through this thy negligence
Thou hast betraied and vndone vs all.
Mic. — I was so affraide I knew not what I did:
I thought I had throwne them both into the well.
Ales. It is the pigs bloode we had to supper.
But wherfore stay you? finde out the murthrers.
Ma. I feare me youle proue one of them your selfe.
Ales. I one of them? what meane such questions?
Fra. I feare me he was murthred in this house
And carried to the fields; for from that place
Backwards and forwards may you see
The print of many feete within the snow.
And looke about this chamber where we are,
And you shall finde part of his giltles bloode;
For in his slipshoe did I finde some rushes,
Which argueth he was murthred in this roome.
Ma. Looke in the place where he was wont to sit.
See, see! his blood! it is too manifest.
Ales. It is a cup of Wine that michaell shed.
Mic. I, truely.
Fran. It is his bloode, which, strumpet, thou hast shed.
But if I liue, thou and thy complices
Which haue conspired and wrought his death shall rue it.
Ales. Ah, M⟨aister⟩ Francklin, God and heauen can tell
I loued him more than all the world beside.
But bring me to him, let me see his body.
Fra. Bring that villaine and mosbies sister too;
And one of you go to the flowre de luce,
And seeke for mosbie, and apprehend him to.
[*Exeunt.*

⟨Scene II.

An obscure street in London.⟩

Here enters shakebag *solus.*

Sh. The widdow chambly, in her husbands dayes,
I kept; and now he's dead, she is growne so stout
She will not know her ould companions.
I came thither, thinking to haue had
Harbour as I was wount,
And she was ready to thrust me out at doores;
But whether she would or no, I got me vp,
And as she followed me, I spurnd her down the staires,
And broke her neck, and cut her tapsters throat,
And now I am going to fling them in the Temes.
I haue the gould; what care I though it be knowne!
Ile crosse the water and take sanctuary.
[*Exit* shakbag.

⟨Scene III.

Arden's House at Feversham.⟩

Here enters the Maior, Mosbie, Ales, Francklin, Michaell, *and* Susan.

Maior. See, M⟨istris⟩ Arden, where your husband lyes;
Confesse this foule fault and be penitent.
Ales. Arden, sweete husband, what shall I say?
The more I sound his name, the more he bleedes;
This bloode condemnes me, and in gushing foorth
Speakes as it falles, and askes me why I did it.
Forgiue me, Arden: I repent me nowe,
And, would my death saue thine, thou shouldst not dye.
Ryse vp, swete Arden, and enioy thy loue,
And frowne not on me when we mete in heauen:

393 you *om. Q 3* 421 *Two lines Qq, div.* death

Scene II. *etc. add. T* 1 *ends* kept *Qq* 7 got] goe *Q 3* Scene III. *etc. add. T*

In heauen I loue thee, though on earth I did not.

Maior. Say, Mosby, what made thee murther him?

Fra. Study not for an answer; looke not down:
His pursse and girdle found at thy beds head
Witnes sufficiently thou didst the deede;
It bootles is to sweare thou didst it not.

Mos. I hyred black Will and Shakebagge, Ruffynes both,
And they and I haue done this murthrous deed.
But wherefore stay we? Come and beare me hence.

Fran. Those Ruffins shall not escape; I will vp to London,
And get the counsels warrand to apprehend them. [*Exeunt.*

⟨SCENE IV.

The Kentish Coast.⟩

Here enters Will.

Will. Shakebag, I heare, hath taken sanctuary,
But I am so pursued with hues and cryes
For petty robberies that I haue done,
That I can come vnto no Sanctuary.
Therefore must I in some Oyster bote
At last be faine to go a boord some Hoye,
And so to Flushing. There is no staying here.
At Sittinburgh the watch was like to take me,
And had I not with my buckler couerd my head,
And run full blanck at all aduentures,
I am sure I had nere gone further then that place;
For the Constable had 20 warrands to apprehend me;
Besides that, I robbed him and his Man once at Gades hill.
Farewell, England; Ile to Flushing now. [*Exit* Will.

⟨SCENE V.

Justice-Room at Feversham.⟩

Here enters the Maior, Mosbye, Ales, Michaell, Susan, *and* Bradshaw.

Maior. Come, make haste & bring away the prisoners.

Brad. M⟨istris⟩ Arden, you are now going to God,
And I am by the law condemned to die
About a letter I brought from M⟨aister⟩ Greene.
I pray you, M⟨istris⟩ Arden, speak the trueth:
Was I euer priuie to your intent or no.

Ales. What should I say? You brought me such a letter,
But I dare sweare thou knewest not the contents.
Leaue now to trouble me with worldly things,
And let me meditate vpon my sauiour Christ,
Whose bloode must saue me for the bloode I shed.

Mos. How long shall I liue in this hell of griefe?
Conuey me from the presence of that strumpet.

Ales. Ah, but for thee I had neuer beene ⟨a⟩ strumpet.
What can not oathes and protestations doe,
When men haue opportunity to woe?
I was too young to sound thy villanies,
But now I finde it and repent too late.

Su. Ah, gentle brother, wherefore should I die?
I knew not of it till the deed was don.

Mos. For thee I mourne more then for my selfe;
But let it suffice, I can not saue thee now.

Mic. And if your brother and my Mistres
Had not promised me you in marriage,
I had nere giuen consent to this foule deede.

Maior. Leaue to accuse each other now
And listen to the sentence I shall giue:
Beare Mosbie and his sister to London straight,
Where they in smithfield must be executed;
Beare M⟨istris⟩ Arden vnto Canterburye,
Where her sentence is she must be burnt;
Michaell and Bradshaw in Feuershame
Must suffer death.

Ales. Let my death make amends for all my sinnes.

Mos. Fy vpon women! this shall be my song;
But beare me hence, for I haue liued to long.

Susan. Seing no hope on earth, in heauen is my hope.

Mic. Faith, I care not, seeing I die with Susan.

Bradshaw. My bloode be on his head that gaue the sentence.

Maior. To speedy execution with them all! [*Exeunt.*

11 I] I'll *T*   17 *Two lines Qq*   19 *Two lines Qq*   20 *ends* escape *Qq*   Scene IV. *etc. add. T*   8 Sittingburn *J*   9 I not] not I *Q 3, etc.*   Scene V. *etc. add. T*   2 M. *Q 1*: Master *Q 3*

7 *Two lines Qq*   14 a *add. J*   22 But *om. J*   32–3 *Two lines Q 3*: *one line Q 1*   34 sinne *Q 3*

⟨Epilogue.⟩

Heere enters Francklin.

Fran. Thus haue you seene the trueth of Ardens death.
As for the Ruffins, Shakbag and blacke Will,
The one tooke Sanctuary, and, being sent for out,
Was murthred in Southwark as he past
To Greenewitch, where the Lord Protector lay.
Black Will was burnt in Flushing on a stage;
Greene was hanged at Osbridge in Kent;
The Painter fled & how he dyed we know not.
But this aboue the rest is to be noted:
Arden lay murthred in that plot of ground
Which he by force and violence held from Rede;
And in the grasse his bodyes print was seene
Two yeeres and more after the deede was doone.
Gentlemen, we hope youle pardon this naked Tragedy,
Wherin no filed points are foisted in
To make it gratious to the eare or eye;
For simple trueth is gratious enough,
And needes no other points of glosing stuffe.

Finis.

Epilogue : Scene VI *WP* 6 at a stake *J* 7 Osbringe *J*

THE

Lamentable Tragedie of

Locrine, the eldest sonne of King *Brutus*, discoursing the warres of the *Britaines*, and *Hunnes*, with their discomfiture:

The Britaines *victorie with their Accidents, and the death of* Albanact. *No lesse pleasant then profitable.*

Newly set foorth, ouerseene and corrected, By *VV. S.*

LONDON
Printed by Thomas Creede.
1595.

Q = Quarto of 1595
F 1 = (Third) Folio Shakespeare, 1664
F 2 = (Fourth) ,, ,, 1685
R = Rowe, 1709
Pope = Supplement to Pope's Shakespeare, 1728
M = Malone, 1780
St. = Steevens, ibid.
Th. = Theobald, ibid.
S = Simms, 1848
T = Tyrrell, 1851
Haz. = Hazlitt, 1852
Molt. = Moltke, 1869
pr. ed. = present editor

THE LAMENTABLE TRAGEDIE OF LOCRINE,

THE ELDEST SONNE OF KING BRVTVS, DISCOVRSING THE WARRES OF THE BRITAINES AND HVNNES, WITH THEIR DISCOMFITVRE, THE BRITAINES VICTORY WITH THEIR ACCIDENTS, AND THE DEATH OF ALBANACT

⟨DRAMATIS PERSONAE.

BRUTUS, *King of* Britain.
LOCRINE, CAMBER, ALBANACT, *his Sons.*
CORINEIUS, ASSARACHUS, *Brothers to* Brutus.
THRASIMACHUS, Corineius *his Son.*
DEBON, *an old Officer.*
HUMBER, *King of the* Scythians.
HUBBA, *his Son.*
THRASSIER, *a* Scythian *Commander.*
STRUMBO, TRUMPART, OLIVER, WILLIAM, *Clowns.*

GUENDOLINE, Corineius *his Daughter, married to* Locrine.
ESTRILD, Humber's *Wife.*
ATE, *the Goddess of Revenge.*

Ghosts of Albanact, *and* Corineius.⟩

The first Act. Prologue.

Enter Atey *with thunder and lightning all in black, with a burning torch in one hand, and a bloodie swoord in the other hand, and presently let there come foorth a Lion running after a Beare or any other beast; then come foorth an Archer who must kill the Lion in a dumbe show, and then depart. Remaine* Atey.

Atey. In pœnam sectatur & Vmbra.
A Mightie Lion, ruler of the woods,
Of wondrous strength and great proportion,
With hideous noyse scarring the trembling trees,
With yelling clamors shaking all the earth,
Trauerst the groues, and chast the wandring beasts.
Long did he raunge amid the shadie trees,
And draue the silly beasts before his face,
When suddeinly from out a thornie bush,
A dreadfull Archer with his bow ybent,
Wounded the Lion with a dismall shaft.
So he him stroke that it drew forth the blood,
And fild his furious heart with fretting yre;
But all in vaine he threatneth teeth and pawes,
And sparkleth fire from forth his flaming eies,
For the sharpe shaft gaue him a mortall wound.
So valiant *Brute*, the terror of the world,
Whose only lookes did scarre his enemies,
The Archer death brought to his latest end.
Oh what may long abide aboue this ground,
In state of blisse and healthfull happinesse.
[*Exit.*

The first Act. Scene 1.

Enter Brutus *carried in a chaire,* Locrine, Camber, Albanact, Corineius, Guendelin, Assaracus, Debon, Thrasimachus.

Brutus. Most loyall Lords and faithful followers,
That haue with me, vnworthie Generall,
Passed the greedie gulfe of *Ocean,*
Leauing the confines of faire *Italie,*
Behold, your *Brutus* draweth nigh his end,
And I must leaue you, though against my will.
My sinewes shrunke, my numbed sences faile,
A chilling cold possesseth all my bones;
Blacke vgly death, with visage pale and wanne,
Presents himselfe before my dazeled eies,
And with his dart prepared is to strike.
These armes my Lords, these neuer daunted armes,

Dramatis Personae add. Rowe   *S. D.* Prologue] Scene 1 *Q*   11 strook *Ff*

S. D. Scene 1] Scene 2 *Q*   7 shrink *M*

That oft haue queld the courage of my foes,
And eke dismayd my neighbours arrogancie,
Now yeeld to death, orelaid with crooked age,
Deuoyd of strength and of their proper force,
Euen as the lustie cedar worne with yeares,
That farre abroad her daintie odore throwes,
Mongst all the daughters of proud Lebanon.
This heart, my Lords, this neare appalled heart,
That was a terror to the bordring lands,
A dolefull scourge vnto my neighbor Kings,
Now by the weapons of vnpartiall death,
Is cloue asunder and bereft of life,
As when the sacred oake with thunderbolts,
Sent from the fiery circuit of the heauens,
Sliding along the aires celestiall valts,
Is rent and clouen to the verie rootes.
In vaine, therefore, I strangle with this foe;
Then welcome death, since God will haue it so.

Assar. Alasse, my Lord, we sorrow at your case,
And greeue to see your person vexed thus;
But what so ere the fates determind haue,
It lieth not in vs to disanull,
And he that would annihillate his minde,
Soaring with *Icarus* too neare the Sunne,
May catch a fall with yoong *Bellerophon.*
For when the fatall sisters haue decreed
To seperate vs from this earthly mould,
No mortall force can countermaund their minds:
Then, worthie Lord, since ther's no way but one,
Cease your laments, and leaue your grieuous mone.

Corin. Your highnesse knows how many victories,
How many trophees I erected haue
Tryumphantly in euery place we came.
The Grecian Monarke, warlike *Pandrassus,*
And all the crew of the Molossians;
Goffarius, the arme strong King of *Gaules,*
And all the borders of great *Aquitane,*
Haue felt the force of our victorious armes,
And to their cost beheld our chiualrie.
Where ere *Aurora,* handmayd of the Sunne,
Where ere the Sun, bright gardiant of the day,
Where ere the ioyfull day with chearfull light,
Where ere the light illuminates the world,
The Troyans glorie flies with golden wings,
Wings that do soare beyond fell enuies flight.
The fame of *Brutus* and his followers
Pearceth the skies, and with the skies the throne
Of mightie *Ioue,* Commaunder of the world.
Then worthie *Brutus,* leaue these sad laments;
Comfort your selfe with this your great renowne,
And feare not death though he seeme terrible.

Brutus. Nay, *Corin⟨e⟩us,* you mistake my mynd
In construing wrong the cause of my complaints.
I feard to yeeld my selfe to fatall death!
God knowes it was the least of all my thought⟨s⟩;
A greater care torments my verie bones,
And makes me tremble at the thought of it,
And in you, Lordings, doth the substance lie.

Thrasi. Most noble Lord, if ought your loyall peers
Accomplish may, to ease your lingring grief,
I, in the name of all, protest to you,
That we will boldly enterprise the same,
Were it to enter to black *Tartarus,*
Where triple *Cerberus* with his venomous throte,
Scarreth the ghoasts with high resounding noyse.
Wele either rent the bowels of the earth,
Searching the entrailes of the brutish earth,
Or, with his Ixions ouerdaring sonne,
Be bound in chaines of euerduring steele.

Bru. Then harken to your soueraigns latest words,
In which I will vnto you all vnfold
Our royall mind and resolute intent:—
When golden *Hebe,* daughter to great *Ioue,*
Couered my manly cheeks with youthful downe,
Th' vnhappie slaughter of my lucklesse sire,
Droue me and old *Assarachus,* mine eame,
As exiles from the bounds of *Italy;*
So that perforce we were constraind to flie
To *Græcias* Monarke noble *Pandrassus.*
There I alone did vndertake your cause,
There I restord your antique libertie,
Though *Grecia* fround, and all *Mollossia* stormd,
Though braue *Antigonus,* with martiall band,
In pitched field encountred me and mine,
Though *Pandrassus* and his contributories,
With all the rout of their confederates,
Sought to deface our glorious memorie
And wipe the name of *Troians* from the earth.
Him did I captiuate with this mine arme,
And by compulsion forcst him to agree

29 strangle *Q*: struggle *Ff*, *etc.* 35 their minds *M* 49 *om. Ff*, *etc.* 52 Ancora *Q* 53 Sunbright *Q* 55 world] word *Q* 57 enuious *Q*, *Ff*

67 thorght *all edd.* 80 son *M*: soone *Q*: soon *Ff* 91 Graecians *Q*, *Ff*

To certain artickles which there we did propound.
From *Græcia* through the boisterous *Hellespont,*
We came vnto the fields of *Lestrigon,*
Whereas our brother *Corineius* was.
Since when we passed the *Cicillian* gulfe,
And so transfretting the *Illirian* sea,
Arriued on the coasts of *Aquitane,*
Where with an armie of his barbarous *Gaules*
Goffarius and his brother *Gathelus*
Encountring with our hoast, sustaind the foile.
And for your sakes my *Turnus* there I lost,
Turnus that slew six hundreth men at armes
All in an houre, with his sharpe battle-axe.
From thence vpon the strons of *Albion*
To *Corus* hauen happily we came,
And queld the giants, comme of *Albions* race,
With *Gogmagog* sonne to *Samotheus,*
The cursed Captaine of that damned crew.
And in that Ile at length I placed you.
Now let me see if my laborious toiles,
If all my care, if all my greeuous wounds,
If all my diligence were well imploid.
Corin. When first I followed thee & thine, braue king,
I hazarded my life and dearest blood,
To purchace fauour at your princely hands,
And for the same in daungerous attempts
In sundry conflicts and in diuers broiles,
I shewd the courage of my manly mind.
For this I combated with *Gathelus,*
The brother to *Goffarius* of *Gaule*;
For this I fought with furious *Gogmagog,*
A sauage captaine of a sauage crew;
And for these deeds braue *Cornwale* I receiu'd,
A gratefull gift giuen by a gratious King;
And for this gift, this life and dearest blood,
Will *Corineus* spend for *Brutus* good.
Deb. And what my frend, braue prince, hath voud to you,
The same wil *Debon* do vnto his end.
Bru. Then, loyall peeres, since you are all agreed,
And resolute to follow *Brutus* hoasts,
Fauour my sonnes, fauour these *Orphans,* Lords,
And shield them from the daungers of their foes.
Locrine, the columne of my familie,
And onely piller of my weakned age,
Locrine, draw neare, draw neare vnto thy sire,
And take thy latest blessings at his hands:
And for thou art the eldest of my sonnes,
Be thou a captaine to thy bretheren,
And imitate thy aged fathers steps,
Which will conduct thee to true honors gate;
For if thou follow sacred vertues lore,
Thou shalt be crowned with a lawrell braunch,
And weare a wreath of sempiternall fame,
Sorted amongst the glorious happie ones.
Locrin. If *Locrine* do not follow your aduise,
And beare himselfe in all things like a prince
That seekes to amplifie the great renowne
Left vnto him for an inheritage
By those that were his ancestors,
Let me be flung into the Ocean,
And swallowed in the bowels of the earth,
Or let the ruddie lightning of great *Ioue*
Descend vpon this my deuoted head.
Brutus (*taking* Guendoline *by the hand*).
But for I see you all to be in doubt,
Who shall be matched with our royall sonne,
Locrine, receiue this present at my hand,
A gift more rich then are the wealthie mines
Found in the bowels of *America.*
Thou shalt be spoused to faire *Guendoline*;
Loue her, and take her, for she is thine owne,
If so thy vnckle and her selfe do please.
Corin. And herein how your highnes honors me
It cannot ⟨now⟩ be in my speech exprest;
For carefull parents glorie not so much
At their honour and promotion,
As for to see the issue of their blood
Seated in honor and prosperitie.
Guend. And far be it from any maydens thoughts
To contradict her aged fathers will.
Therefore, since he to whom I must obey
Hath giuen me now vnto your royall selfe,
I will not stand aloofe from off the lure,
Like craftie dames that most of all deny
That which they most desire to possesse.
Brutus (*turning to* Locrine. Locrine *kneeling*). Then now, my sonne, thy part is on the stage,
For thou must beare the person of a King.
[*Puts the Crowne on his head.*
Locrine, stand vp, and weare the regall Crowne,
And thinke vpon the state of Maiestie,
That thou with honor well maist weare the crown.
And if thou tendrest these my latest words,

103 which there *om. M*   107 Since *M*: Which *Q, Ff*   Cilician *M*   108 transfreighting *Molt.*   Illician *Q, Ff*   116 stronds *Ff*   118 comne *Q*   142 hests *M*

161 his] his glorious *M*   165 deuolted *Q*   175 now *add. Ff*   177 their] their own *M*   180 any *conj. Th*: my *Q*: my pure *Ff*   Maiden *Ff*

As thou requirst my soule to be at rest,
As thou desirest thine owne securitie,
Cherish and loue thy new betrothed wife.
Locrin. No longer let me wel enioy the crowne,
Then I do ⟨honour⟩ peerlesse *Guendoline.*
Brut. *Camber.*
Cam. My Lord.
Brut. The glorie of mine age,
And darling of thy mother *Innogen,*
Take thou the South for thy dominion.
From thee there shall proseed a royall race,
That shall maintaine the honor of this land,
And sway the regall scepter with their hands.
[*Turning to* Albanact.
And *Albanact,* thy fathers onely ioy,
Yoongst in yeares, but not the yoongst in mind,
A perfect patterne of all chiualrie,
Take thou the North for thy dominion,
A country full of hills and ragged rockes,
Replenished with fearce vntamed beasts,
As correspondent to thy martiall thoughts.
Liue long, my sonnes, with endlesse happinesse,
And beare firme concordance amongst your selues.
Obey the counsels of these fathers graue,
That you may better beare out violence.—
But suddeinly, through weaknesse of my age,
And the defect of youthfull puissance,
My maladie increaseth more and more,
And cruell death hastneth his quickned pace,
To dispossesse me of my earthly shape.
Mine eies wax dimme, ouercast with clouds of age,
The pangs of death compasse my crazed bones;
Thus to you all my blessings I bequeath,
And with my blessings, this my fleeting soule.
My glasse is runne, and all my miseries
Do end with life; death closeth vp mine eies,
My soule in haste flies to the Elisian fields.
[*He dieth.*
Loc. Accursed starres, damd and accursed starres,
To abreuiate my noble fathers life!
Hard-harted gods, and too enuious fates,
Thus to cut off my fathers fatall thred!
Brutus, that was a glorie to vs all,
Brutus, that was a terror to his foes,
Alasse, too soone, by *Demagorgons* knife,
The martiall *Brutus* is bereft of life!
Corin. No sad complaints may moue iust *Aeacus,*
No dreadfull threats can feare iudge *Rhodomanth.*
Wert thou as strong as mightie *Hercules,*
That tamde the hugie monsters of the world,
Plaidst thou as sweet, on the sweet sounding lute,
As did the spouse of faire *Euridise,*
That did enchant the waters with his noise,
And made stones, birds, and beasts, to lead a dance,
Constraind the hillie trees to follow him,
Thou couldst not moue the iudge of *Erebus,*
Nor moue compassion in grimme *Plutos* heart;
For fatall *Mors* expecteth all the world,
And euerie man must tread the way of death.
Braue *Tantalus,* the valiant *Pelops* sire,
Guest to the gods, suffred vntimely death,
And old *Tithonus,* husband to the morne,
And eke grim *Minos,* whom iust *Iupiter*
Deigned to admit vnto his sacrifice.
The thundring trumpets of blood-thirstie *Mars,*
The fearfull rage of fell *Tisiphone,*
The boistrous waues of humid Ocean,
Are instruments and tooles of dismall death.
Then, noble cousin, cease to mourne his chaunce,
Whose age & yeares were signes that he shuld die.
It resteth now that we interre his bones,
That was a terror to his enemies.
Take vp the coarse, and, princes, hold him dead,
Who while he liu'd, vpheld the *Troyan* state.
Sound drums and trumpets; march to *Troinouant,*
There to prouide our chieftaines funerall.
⟨*Exeunt.*⟩

The first Act. Scene 2.

⟨*The house of* Strumbo.⟩

Enter Strumbo *aboue in a gowne, with inke and paper in his hand, saying:—*

Strum. Either the foure elements, the seuen planets, and all the particuler starres of the pole Antastick, are aduersatiue against me, or else I was begotten and borne in the wane of the Moone, when euerie thing as *Lactantius* in his fourth booke of Constultations dooth say, goeth asward. I, maisters, I, you may laugh, but I must weepe; you may ioy, but I

197 do honour peerlesse *M*: do peerlesse *Q, Ff*: do honour *Haz.* 199 Iunoger *Q, Ff*: *corr. Th* 203 And] That *Q, Ff* 204 onely] other *conj. S* 212 concordance firm among *S* 229 and ye too *S*

235 *Prefix* Corin. *precedes 236 in Q* Iacus *Q, Ff* 236 just *Haz.* 238 hugest *S* 240 Enridies *Q* 244 Crebus *Q, Ff* *S. D.* Scene 2] Scene 3 *Q* *Bracketed words add. T* 3 Antarctic *T* 5 as] as saith *Q*

must sorrow; sheading salt teares from the watrie fountaines of my moste daintie faire eies, along my comely and smooth cheeks, in as great plentie as the water runneth from the buckingtubbes, or red wine out of the hogs heads: for trust me, gentlemen and my verie good friends, and so foorth, the little god, nay the desperate god *Cuprit*, with one of his vengible birdbolts, hath shot me vnto the heele: so not onlie, but also, oh fine phrase, I burne, I burne, and I burne a, in loue, in loue, and in loue a. Ah, *Strumbo*, what hast thou seen? not *Dina* with the Asse *Tom*? Yea, with these eies thou hast seene her, and therefore pull them out, for they will worke thy bale. Ah, *Strumbo*, hast thou heard? not the voice of the Nightingale, but a voice sweeter then hers. Yea, with these eares hast thou heard it, and therefore cut them off, for they haue causde thy sorrow. Nay, *Strumbo*, kill thy selfe, drowne thy selfe, hang thy selfe, sterue thy selfe. Oh, but then I shall leaue my sweet heart. Oh my heart! Now, pate, for thy maister! I will dite an aliquant loue-pistle to her, and then she hearing the grand verbositie of my scripture, will loue me presently.

[*Let him write a litle and then read.*

My penne is naught; gentlemen, lend me a knife. I thinke the more haste the worst speed.

[*Then write againe, and after read.*

So it is, mistresse Dorothie, *and the sole essence of my soule, that the little sparkles of affection kindled in me towards your sweet selfe hath now increased to a great flame, and will ere it be long consume my poore heart, except you, with the pleasant water of your secret fountaine, quench the furious heate of the same. Alasse, I am a gentleman of good fame and name, maiesticall, in parrell comely, in gate portlie. Let not therefore your gentle heart be so hard as to despise a proper tall, yoong man of a handsome life, and by despising him, not onlie, but also to kill him. Thus expecting time and tide, I bid you farewell. Your seruant,* Signior Strumbo.

Oh wit! Oh pate! O memorie! O hand! O incke! O paper! Well, now I will send it away. *Trompart, Trompart!* what a villaine is this? Why, sirra, come when your maister calls you. *Trompart!*

Trompart, *entring, saith;*

Anon, sir.

Strumbo. Thou knowest, my prettie boy, what a good maister I haue bene to thee euer since I tooke thee into my seruice.

Trom. I, sir.

Strum. And how I haue cherished thee alwaies, as if you had bene the fruit of my loines, flesh of my flesh, and bone of my bone.

Trom. I, sir.

Strum. Then shew thy selfe herein a trustie seruant, and carrie this letter to mistresse *Dorothie*, and tell her—

[*Speaking in his eare. Exit* Trompart.

Strum. Nay, maisters, you shall see a marriage by and by. But here she comes. Now must I frame my amorous passions.

Enter Dorothie *and* Trompart.

Doro. Signior Strumbo, well met. I receiued your letters by your man here, who told mee a pittifull storie of your anguish, and so vnderstanding your passions were so great, I came hither speedily.

Strum. Oh my sweet and pigsney, the fecunditie of my ingenie is not so great, that may declare vnto you the sorrowful sobs and broken sleeps, that I suffred for your sake; and therefore I desire you to receiue me into your familiaritie.

For your loue doth lie,
As neare and as nigh
Vnto my heart within,
As mine eye to my nose,
My legge vnto my hose,
And my flesh vnto my skin.

Dor. Truly, M⟨aister⟩ *Strumbo*, you speake too learnedly for mee to vnderstand the drift of your mind, and therfore tell your tale in plaine termes, and leaue off your darke ridles.

Strum. Alasse, mistresse *Dorothie*, this is my lucke, that when I most would, I cannot be vnderstood; so that my great learning is an inconuenience vnto me. But to speake in plaine termes, I loue you, mistresse *Dorothie*, if you like to accept me into your familiaritie.

Dor. If this be all, I am content.

Strum. Saist thou so, sweet wench; let me lick thy toes. Farwell, mistresse.

[*Turning to the people.*]

If any of you be in loue, prouide ye a capcase full of new coined wordes, and then shall you soone haue the *succado de labres*, and something else. [*Exeunt.*

16 Cuprit *om. Haz., Molt.* 24 hast] what hast *M* 26 it *M*: them *Q, Ff* 36 worse *M* 64 you had] thou hadst *Ff* 104 *S. D. after 102 Q*

The first Act. Scene 3.

⟨An apartment in the palace.⟩

Enter Locrine, Guendoline, Camber, Albanact, Corineus, Assaracus, Debon, Thrasimachus.

Locrine. Vncle, and princes of braue *Britany*,
Since that our noble father is intombd,
As best beseemd so braue a prince as he,
If so you please, this day my loue and I,
Within the temple of *Concordia*,
Will solemnize our roiall marriage.

Thra. Right noble Lord, your subiects euery one,
Must needs obey your highnesse at commaund;
Especially in such a cause as this,
That much concerns your highnesse great content.

Locr. Then frolick, lordings, to fair *Concords* wals,
Where we will passe the day in knightly sports,
The night in dauncing and in figured maskes,
And offer to God *Risus* all our sports. [*Exeunt.*

The 2. Act. Prologue.

Enter Atey *as before. After a litle lightning and thundring, let there come forth this show:*—Perseus *and* Andromeda, *hand in hand, and* Cepheus *also, with swords and targets. Then let there come out of an other doore,* Phineus, *all blacke in armour, with Aethiopians after him, driuing in* Perseus, *and hauing taken away* Andromeda, *let them depart,* Ate *remaining, saying:*

Ate. Regit omnia numen.
When *Perseus* married faire *Andromeda*,
The onlie daughter of king *Cepheus*,
He thought he had establisht well his Crowne,
And that his kingdome should for aie endure.
But, loe, proud *Phineus* with a band of men,
Contriu'd of sun-burnt *Aethiopians*,
By force of armes the bride he tooke from him,
And turnd their ioy into a floud of teares.
So fares it with yoong *Locrine* and his loue,
He thinkes this marriage tendeth to his weale;
But this foule day, this foule accursed day,
Is the beginning of his miseries.
Behold where *Humber* and his *Scithians*
Approcheth nigh with all his warlike traine.
I need not, I, the sequel shall declare,
What tragicke chances fall out in this warre.

S. D. Scene 3] Scene 4 *Q* *Bracketed words add. T* 9 cause] case *M* 14 sports] tasks *conj. M* *S. D.* Prologue] Scene 1 *Q* 7 Composed *S* 16 shall] should *M*

The 1. Scene.

Enter Humber, Hubba, Estrild, Segar, *and their souldiers.*

Hum. At length the snaile doth clime the highest tops,
Ascending vp the stately castle walls;
At length the water with continuall drops,
Doth penetrate the hardest marble stone;
At length we are arriued in *Albion.*
Nor could the barbarous *Dacian* soueraigne,
Nor yet the ruler of braue *Belgia*,
Staie vs from cutting ouer to this Ile,
Whereas I heare a troope of *Phrigians*
Vnder the conduct of *Postumius* sonne,
Haue pitched vp lordly pauillions,
And hope to prosper in this louely Ile.
But I will frustrate all their foolish hope,
And teach them that the *Scithian* Emperour
Leades fortune tied in a chaine of gold,
Constraining her to yeeld vnto his will,
And grace him with their regall diademe,
Which I will haue maugre their treble hoasts,
And all the power their pettie kings can make.

Hubba. If she that rules faire *Rhamnis* golden gate
Graunt vs the honour of the victorie,
As hitherto she alwaies fauourd vs,
Right noble father, we will rule the land,
Enthronized in seates of *Topace* stones,
That *Locrine* and his brethren all may know,
None must be king but *Humber* and his sonne.

Hum. Courage, my sonne, fortune shall fauour vs,
And yeeld to vs the coronet of bay,
That decketh none but noble conquerours.
But what saith *Estrild* to these regions?
How liketh she the temperature thereof?
Are they not pleasant in her gratious eies?

Estr. The plaines, my Lord, garnisht with *Floras* welth,
And ouerspred with party colored flowers,
Do yeeld sweet contentation to my mind.
The aierie hills enclosd with shadie groues,
The groues replenisht with sweet chirping birds,
The birds resounding heauenly melodie,
Are equall to the groues of *Thessaly*,
Where *Phœbus* with the learned Ladies nine,
Delight themselues with musicke harmonie,
And from the moisture of the mountaine tops,
The silent springs daunce downe with murmuring streams,
And water al the ground with cristal waues.
The gentle blasts of *Eurus*, modest winde,

The 2. Scene *Q* 13 hopes *S* 33 *Prefix* Astr. *Q* 41 musick's *M*

Mouing the pittering leaues of *Siluanes* woods,
Do equall it with *Tempes* paradice;
And thus consorted all to one effect,
Do make me thinke these are the happie Iles,
Most fortunate, if *Humber* may them winne.
Hubba. Madam, where resolution leads the way,
And courage followes with imboldened pace,
Fortune can neuer vse her tyrannie;
For valiantnesse is like vnto a rocke
That standeth in the waues of Ocean,
Which though the billowes beat on euery side,
And *Boreas* fell with his tempestuous stormes
Bloweth vpon it with a hideous clamour,
Yet it remaineth still vnmooueable.
Hum. Kingly resolu'd, thou glorie of thy sire.
But, worthie *Segar,* what vncoth nouelties
Bringst thou vnto our royall maiestie?
Seg. My Lord, the yoongest of all *Brutus* sonnes,
Stout *Albanact,* with millions of men,
Approcheth nigh, and meaneth, ere the morne,
To trie your force by dint of fatall sword.
Hum. Tut, let him come with millions of hostes;
He shall find entertainment good inough,
Yea, fit for those that are our enemies:
For weell receiue them at the launces points,
And massaker their bodies with our blades:
Yea, though they were in number infinit,
More then the mightie Babilonian queene,
Semiramis the ruler of the West,
Brought gainst the Emperour of the Scithians;
Yet would we not start back one foote from them:
That they might know we are inuincible.
Hub. Now, by great *Ioue,* the supreme king of heauen,
And the immortall gods that liue therein,
When as the morning shewes his chearfull face,
And Lucifer, mounted vpon his steed,
Brings in the chariot of the golden sunne,
Ile meet yoong *Albanact* in the open field,
And crack my launce vpon his burganet,
To trie the valour of his boyish strength.
There will I shew such ruthfull spectacles
And cause so great effusion of blood,
That all his boyes shall wonder at my strength:
As when the warlike queene of *Amazon,*
Penthisilea, armed with her launce,
Girt with a corslet of bright shining steele,
Coupt vp the fainthart Græcians in the campe.
Hum. Spoke like a warlike knight, my noble son;
Nay, like a prince that seekes his fathers ioy.
Therefore, to morrow, ere faire *Titan* shine,
And bashfull *Eos,* messenger of light,
Expells the liquid sleep from out mens eyes,
Thou shalt conduct the right wing of the hoste;
The left wing shall be vnder *Segars* charge,
The rearеward shall be vnder me my selfe.
And louely *Estrild,* faire and gratious,
If fortune fauour me in mine attempts,
Thou shalt be queene of louely *Albion.*
Fortune shall fauour me in mine attempts,
And make the Queene of louely *Albion.*
Come, let vs in and muster vp our traine,
And furnish vp our lustie souldiers,
That they may be a bullwarke to our state,
And bring our wished ioyes to perfect end.

The 2. Scene.

Enter Strumbo, Dorothie, Trompart, *cobling shooes and singing.* ⟨*To them enter Captain.*⟩

Trum. We Coblers lead a merie life:
All. Dan, dan, dan, dan:
Strum. Void of all enuie and of strife:
All. Dan diddle dan.
Dor. Our ease is great, our labour small:
All. Dan, dan, dan, dan.
Strum. And yet our gaines be much withall:
All. Dan diddle dan.
Dor. With this art so fine and faire:
All. Dan, dan, dan, dan.
Trum. No occupation may compare:
All. Dan diddle dan.
Dor. For merie pastime and ioyfull glee:
Dan, dan, dan, dan.
Strum. Most happie men we Coblers bee:
Dan diddle dan.
Trum. The can stands full of nappie ale:
Dan, dan, dan, dan:
Strum. In our shop still withouten faile:
Dan diddle dan.
Dor. This is our meate, this is our foode:
Dan, dan, dan, dan:
Trum. This brings vs to a mery mood:
Dan didle dan.
Strum. This makes vs worke for companie:
Dan, dan, dan, dan:
Dor. To pull the tankards cheerfully:
Dan didle dan.
Trum. Drinke to thy husband, *Dorothie,*
Dan, dan, dan, dan:

46 pattering *T* 48 consorted *R*: comforted *Q, Ff* 57 Borras *Q* 83 the *om. T* 89 Amazons *M*

3 ennie *Q* 13 *Prefix* Strum. *before 13,* Dor. *before 15 Q, Ff*: *corr. M*

Dor. Why, then, my *Strumbo,* ther's to thee:
Dan didle dan:
Strum. Drinke thou the rest, *Trumpart,* amaine:
Dan, dan, dan, dan.
Dor. When that is gone, weell filt againe:
Dan didle dan.
Cap. The poorest state is farthest from annoy.
How merily he sitteth on his stoole!
But when he sees that needs he must be prest,
Heele turne his note and sing another tune.
Ho, by your leaue, maister Cobler.

Stru. You are welcom, gentleman. What wil you? any olde shooes or buskins? or will you haue your shooes clouted? I will do them as well as any Cobler in *Cathnes* whatsoeuer.

Captaine, shewing him presse mony. O maister Cobler, you are farre deceiued in mee, for don you see this? I come not to buy any shooes, but to buy your selfe; come, sir, you must be a souldier in the kings cause.

Strum. Why, but heare you, sir; has your king any commission to take any man against his will. I promise you, I can scant beleeue it; or did hee giue you commission?

Cap. O sir, ye neede not care for that; I neede no commission. Hold, here: I command you, in the name of our king *Albanact,* to appeare to morrow in the towne-house of *Cathnes.*

Strum. King Nactaball! I crie God mercy! what haue we to doo with him, or he with vs? But you, sir master capontaile, draw your pastebourd, or else I promise you, Ile giue you a canuasado with a bastinado ouer your shoulders, and teach you to come hither with your implements.

Cap. I pray thee, good fellow, be content; I do the kings commaund.

Strum. Put me out of your booke, then.

Cap. I may not.

Strumbo, snatching vp a staffe. No! Well, come, sir, will your stomacke serue you? by gogs blew hood and halidom, I will haue a bout with you.

Fight both.

Enter Thrasimachus.

How now, what noyse, what sodain clamors this?
How now, my captain and the cobler so hard at it?
Sirs, what is your quarrell?

Cap. Nothing, sir, but that he will not take presse mony.

Thra. Here, good fellow; take it at my command,
Vnlesse you meane to be stretcht.

Strum. Truly, master gentleman, I lacke no mony; if you please, I will resigne it to one of these poore fellowes.

Thrasi. No such matter,
Looke you be at the common house to morrow.

[*Exit* Thrasimachus *and the captaine.*

Strum. O, wife, I haue spunne a faire thredde! If I had bene quiet, I had not bene prest, and therefore well may I wayment. But come, sirrha, shut vp, for we must to the warres. [*Exeunt.*

The 3. *Scene.*

⟨*The camp of* Albanact.⟩

Enter Albanact, Debon, Thrasimachus, *and the Lords.*

Alba. Braue cauileres, princes of *Albany,*
Whose trenchant blades with our deceased sire,
Passing the frontiers of braue *Græcia,*
Were bathed in our enemies lukewarme blood,
Now is the time to manifest your wills,
Your hautie mindes and resolutions.
Now opportunitie is offred
To trie your courage and your earnest zeale,
Which you alwaies protest to *Albanact*;
For at this time, yea, at this present time,
Stout fugitiues, come from the Scithians bounds,
Haue pestred euerie place with mutinies.
But trust me, Lordings, I will neuer cease
To persecute the rascall runnagates,
Till all the riuers, stained with their blood,
Shall fully shew their fatall ouerthrow.

Deb. So shal your highnes merit great renowne,
And imitate your aged fathers steppes.

Alba. But tell me, cousin, camst thou through the plaines?
And sawst thou there the faint heart fugitiues
Mustring their weather-beaten souldiers?
What order keep they in their marshalling?

Thra. After we past the groues of *Caledone,*
Where murmuring riuers slide with silent streames,
We did behold the stragling Scithians campe,
Repleat with men, storde with munition;
There might we see the valiant minded knights
Fetching carreers along the spatious plaines.

31 here's *Molt.* 48 don't *M* 60 Nactabell *Q, Ff* 62 capoutaile *Q* 64 bastinano *Q* 71 Well] will *Q* 74 about *Q, F1* 76 *Two lines, div. after* now *M*

S. D. The 4. Scene *Q* *Bracketed words add. T* 28 carriers *Q, Ff*: *corr. in ed. of 1728 and independently by M*

Humber and *Hubba* arm'd in azure blew,
Mounted vpon their coursers white as snow,
Went to behold the pleasant flowring fields;
Hector and *Troialus, Priamus* louely sonnes,
Chasing the Græcians ouer *Simoeis,*
Were not to be compared to these two knights.

Alba. Well hast thou painted out in eloquence
The portraiture of *Humber* and his sonne,
As fortunate as was *Policrates*;
Yet should they not escape our conquering swords,
Or boast of ought but of our clemencie.

Enter Strumbo *and* Trompart, *crying often; Wilde fire and pitch, wilde fire and pitch, &c.*

Thra. What, sirs! what mean you by these clamors made,
Those outcries raised in our stately court?

Strum. Wilde fire and pitch, wilde fire and pitch.

Thra. Villaines, I say, tell vs the cause hereof?

Strum. Wilde fire and pitch, &c.

Thra. Tell me, you villaines, why you make this noise,
Or with my launce I will prick your bowels out.

Al. Where are your houses, wher's your dwelling place?

Strum. Place? Ha, ha, ha! laugh a moneth and a day at him. Place! I cry God mercy: why, doo you think that such poore honest men as we be, hold our habitacles in kings pallaces? Ha, ha, ha! But because you seeme to be an abhominable chieftaine, I wil tel you our state.

From the top to the toe,
From the head to the shoe;
From the beginning to the ending,
From the building to the burning.

This honest fellow and I had our mansion cottage in the suburbes of this citie, hard by the temple of *Mercury.* And by the common souldiers of the Shitens, the Scithians—what do you call them?—with all the suburbes were burnt to the ground, and the ashes are left there, for the countrie wiues to wash buckes withall.

And that which greeues me most,
My louing wife,
(O cruell strife!)
The wicked flames did roast.
And therefore, captaine crust,
We will continuallie crie,
Except you seeke a remedie
Our houses to reedifie
Which now are burnt to dust.

Both cry: Wild fire and pitch, wild fire and pitch.

Alba. Well, we must remedie these outrages,
And throw reuenge vpon their hatefull heads.
And you, good fellowes, for your houses burnt,
We will remunerate you store of gold,
And build your houses by our pallace gate.

Strumbo. Gate! O pettie treason to my person! nowhere else but by your backside? Gate! Oh how I am vexed in my coller! Gate! I crie God mercie! Doo you hear, master king? If you mean to gratifie such poore men as we bee, you must build our houses by the Tauerne.

Alba. It shall be done, sir.

Strum. Neare the Tauerne, I! by ladie, sir, it was spoken like a good fellow. Do you heare, sir? when our house is builded, if you do chance to passe or repasse that way, we will bestowe a quart of the best wine vpon you. [*Exit.*

Alb. It greeues me, lordings, that my subiects goods
Should thus be spoiled by the Scithians,
Who, as you see, with lightfoote forragers
Depopulate the places where they come.
But cursed *Humber* thou shalt rue the day
That ere thou camst vnto *Cathnesia.* [*Exeunt.*

The 2. *Act. Scene* 4.

⟨*The camp of* Humber.⟩

Enter Humber, Hubba, Segar, Trussier, *and their souldiers.*

Hum. *Hubba,* go take a coronet of our horse,
As many launciers, and light armed knights
As may suffice for such an enterprise,
And place them in the groue of *Caledon.*
With these, when as the skirmish doth encrease,
Retire thou from the sheltiers of the wood,
And set vpon the weakened Troians backs,
For pollicie ioyned with chiualrie
Can neuer be put back from victorie. [*Exit.*

Albanact *enter and say (clownes with him).*

⟨*Alb.*⟩ Thou base borne *Hunne,* how durst thou be so bold

37 *M thinks a line has been lost before this and suggests*: But were they brave as Phthia's arm-strong chief   38 shall *T*   58 brenning *conj. Th*: brending *T*   67–70 *Prose in Q, Ff*: *corr. M*   74 redifie *Q*   90 by our lady *M*   *S. D.* Scene 5 *Q*   *Bracketed words add. T*   6 shelters *Ff*   *S. D.* Enter Albanact, Clownes with him *Ff*

As once to menace warlike *Albanact,*
The great commander of these regions?
But thou shalt buy thy rashnesse with thy death,
And rue too late thy ouer bold attempts;
For with this sword, this instrument of death,
That hath bene drenched in my foe-mens blood,
Ile separate thy bodie from thy head,
And set that coward blood of thine abroach.

Strum. Nay, with this staffe, great *Strumbos* instrument,
Ile crack thy cockscome, paltry Scithian.

Hum. Nor wreake I of thy threats, thou princox boy,
Nor do I feare thy foolish insolencie;
And but thou better vse thy bragging blade,
Then thou doest rule thy ouerflowing toong,
Superbious Brittaine, thou shalt know too soone
The force of *Humber* and his Scithians.

Let them fight.

Humber *and his souldiers runne in.*

Strum. O horrible, terrible.

⟨*Exit.*⟩

The 5. *Scene.*

⟨*Another part of the field of battle.*⟩

Sound the alarme.

Enter Humber *and his souldiers.*

Hum. How brauely this yoong Brittain, *Albanact,*
Darteth abroad the thunderbolts of warre,
Beating downe millions with his furious moode,
And in his glorie triumphs ouer all,
Mouing the massie squadrants of the ground;
Heape⟨s⟩ hills on hills, to scale the starrie skie,
As when *Briareus,* armed with an hundreth hands,
Floong forth an hundreth mountains at great *Ioue,*
And when the monstrous giant *Monichus*
Hurld mount *Olimpus* at great *Mars* his targe,
And shot huge cædars at *Mineruas* shield.
How doth he ouerlooke with hautie front
My fleeting hostes, and lifts his loftie face
Against vs all that now do feare his force,
Like as we see the wrathfull sea from farre,
In a great mountaine heapt, with hideous noise,
With thousand billowes beat against the ships,
And tosse them in the waues like tennis balls.

Sound the alarme.

Humb. Ay me, I feare my *Hubba* is surprisde.

Sound againe; Enter Albanact.

Alba. Follow me, souldiers, follow *Albanact;*
Pursue the Scithians flying through the field:
Let none of them escape with victorie;
That they may know the Brittains force is more
Then al the power of the trembling *Hunnes.*

Thra. Forward, braue souldiers, forward! keep the chase.
He that takes captiue *Humber* or his sonne
Shall be rewarded with a crowne of gold.

Sound alarme, then let them fight, Humber *giue backe,* Hubba *enter at their backs, and kill* Debon, *let* Strumbo *fall downe,* Albanact *run in, and afterwards enter wounded.*

Alba. Iniurious fortune, hast thou crost me thus?
Thus, in the morning of my victories,
Thus, in the prime of my felicitie,
To cut me off by such hard ouerthrow!
Hadst thou no time thy rancor to declare,
But in the spring of all my dignities?
Hadst thou no place to spit thy venome out,
But on the person of yoong *Albanact?*
I, that ere while did scare mine enemies,
And droue them almost to a shamefull flight,
I, that ere while full lion-like did fare
Amongst the dangers of the thick throngd pikes,
Must now depart most lamentably slaine
By *Humbers* trecheries and fortunes spights.
Curst be her charms, damned be her cursed charms
That doth delude the waiward harts of men,
Of men that trust vnto her fickle wheele,
Which neuer leaueth turning vpside downe.
O gods, O heauens, allot me but the place
Where I may finde her hatefull mansion!
Ile passe the Alpes to watry *Meroe,*
Where fierie *Phœbus* in his charriot,
The wheels wherof are dect with Emeraldes,
Casts such a heate, yea such a scorching heate,
And spoileth *Flora* of her checquered grasse;
Ile ouerrun the mountaine *Caucusus,*
Where fell *Chimæra* in her triple shape
Rolleth hot flames from out her monstrous panch,
Scaring the beasts with issue of her gorge;
Ile passe the frozen Zone where ysie flakes,

21 reck *M* S. D. Exit *add. M* S. D. The sixt Act *Q*: Scena Sexta *Ff* *Bracketed words add. T* 5 squadrons off *M* 6 Heaps *M* 7 As *om. Q* 9 And] As *M*

42 her charms *R*: their charms *Q, Ff* 49 Fhoebus *Q* 51 Casts *R*: Cast *Q, Ff* 52 And] As *S* 53 overturn *Ff, etc.*

Stopping the passage of the fleeting shippes,
Do lie like mountaines in the congeald sea:
Where if I finde that hatefull house of hers,
Ile pull the fickle wheele from out her hands,
And tie her selfe in euerlasting bands.
But all in vaine I breath these threatnings;
The day is lost, the *Hunnes* are conquerors,
Debon is slaine, my men are done to death,
The currents swift swimme violently with blood,
And last, O that this last might so long last,
My selfe with woundes past all recouery
Must leaue my crowne for *Humber* to possesse.

Strum. Lord haue mercy vpon vs, masters, I think this is a holie day; euerie man lies sleeping in the fields, but, God knowes, full sore against their wills.

Thra. Flie, noble *Albanact*, and saue thy selfe.
The Scithians follow with great celeritie,
And ther's no way but flight, or speedie death;
Flie, noble *Albanact*, and saue thy selfe.

⟨*Exit* Thra.⟩

Sound the alarme.

Alba. Nay, let them flie that feare to die the death,
That tremble at the name of fatall mors.
Neu'r shall proud *Humber* boast or brag himselfe
That he hath put yoong *Albanact* to flight;
And least he should triumph at my decay,
This sword shall reaue his maister of his life,
That oft hath sau'd his maisters doubtfull life:
But, oh, my brethren, if you care for me,
Reuenge my death vpon his traiterous head.

Et vos queis domus est nigrantis regia ditis,
Qui regitis rigido stigios moderamine lucos:
Nox cœci regina poli, furialis Erinnis,
Diique deœque omnes, Albanum tollite regem,
Tollite flumineis vndis rigidaque palude.
Nunc me fata vocant, hoc condam pectore ferrum.

[*Thrust himselfe through.*

Enter Trompart.

⟨*Tr.*⟩ O, what hath he don? his nose bleeds.
But, oh, I smel a foxe:
Looke where my maister lies. Master, master.

Strum. Let me alone, I tell thee, for I am dead.

Trum. Yet one word, good master.

Strum. I will not speake, for I am dead, I tel thee.

Trum. And is my master dead?
O sticks and stones, brickbats and bones,
and is my master dead?
O you cockatrices and you bablatrices,
that in the woods dwell:
You briers and brambles, you cookes shoppes and shambles,
come howle and yell.
With howling & screeking, with wailing and weeping,
come you to lament,
O Colliers of *Croyden*, and rusticks of *Royden*,
and fishers of *Kent*;
For *Strumbo* the cobler, the fine mery cobler
of *Cathnes* towne:
At this same stoure, at this very houre,
lies dead on the ground.
O maister, theeues, theeues, theeues.

Strum. Where be they? cox me tunny, bobekin! let me be rising. Be gone; we shall be robde by and by. [*Exeunt.*

The 6. *Scene.*

⟨*The camp of the* Huns.⟩

Enter Humber, Hubba, Segar, Thrassier, Estrild, *and the souldiers.*

Hum. Thus from the dreadful shocks of furious *Mars,*
Thundring alarmes, and *Rhamnusias* drum,
We are retyred with ioyfull victorie.
The slaughtered Troians, squeltring in their blood,
Infect the aire with their carcasses,
And are a praie for euerie rauenous bird.

Estrild. So perish they that are our enemies!
So perish they that loue not *Humbers* weale,
And mightie *Ioue,* commander of the world,
Protect my loue from all false trecheries.

Hum. Thanks, louely *Estrild*, solace to my soule.
But, valiant *Hubba,* for thy chiualrie,
Declarde against the men of *Albany*,
Loe, here a flowring garland wreath'd of bay,
As a reward for thy forward minde.

Set it on his head.

Hub. This vnexpected honor, noble sire,
Will prick my courage vnto brauer deeds,
And cause me to attempt such hard exploits,
That all the world shall sound of *Hubbaes* name.

Hum. And now, braue souldiers, for this good successe,
Carouse whole cups of *Amazonian* wine,

67 might *conj. M*: night *Q, Ff* 76 flight *R*: fight *Q, Ff* *S. D.* Exit Thra. *add. M* 96 word *M*: good *Q, Ff*

S. D. The 8. Act *Q*: Scena Octava *Ff* *Bracketed words add. T*

Sweeter then Nectar or Ambrosia,
And cast away the clods of cursed care,
With goblets crownd with *Semeleius* gifts.
Now let vs martch to *Abis* siluer streames,
That clearly glide along the *Champane* fields,
And moist the grassie meades with humid drops.
Sound drummes & trumpets, sound vp cheerfully,
Sith we returne with ioy and victorie.
⟨*Exeunt.*⟩

The 3. *Act. Prologue.*

Enter Ate *as before. The dumb show. A Crocadile sitting on a riuers banke, and a little Snake stinging it. Then let both of them fall into the water.*

Ate. Scelera in authorem cadunt.
High on a banke by *Nilus* boystrous streames,
Fearfully sat the Aegiptian Crocodile,
Dreadfully grinding in her sharpe long teethe
The broken bowels of a silly fish.
His back was armde against the dint of speare,
With shields of brasse that shind like burnisht gold;
And as he stretched forth his cruell pawes,
A subtill Adder, creeping closely neare,
Thrusting his forked sting into his clawes,
Priuily shead his poison through his bones;
Which made him swel, that there his bowels burst,
That did so much in his owne greatnesse trust.
So *Humber*, hauing conquered *Albanact*,
Doth yeeld his glorie vnto *Locrines* sword.
Marke what ensues and you may easily see,
That all our life is but a Tragedie.

The 1. *Scene.*

⟨*Troynovant. An apartment in the Royal Palace.*⟩

Enter Locrine, Guendoline, Corineus, Assaracus, Thrasimachus, Camber.

Locrine. And is this true? Is *Albanactus* slaine?
Hath cursed *Humber*, with his stragling hoste,
With that his armie made of mungrell curres,
Brought our redoubted brother to his end?
O that I had the Thracian *Orpheus* harpe,
For to awake out of the infernall shade
Those ougly diuels of black *Erebus*,
That might torment the damned traitors soule!
O that I had *Amphions* instrument,
To quicken with his vitall notes and tunes
The flintie ioynts of euerie stonie rocke,
By which the Scithians might be punished!
For, by the lightening of almightie *Ioue*,
The *Hunne* shall die, had he ten thousand liues:
And would to God he had ten thousand liues,
That I might with the arme-strong *Hercules*
Crop off so vile an *Hidras* hissing heads!
But say me, cousen, for I long to heare,
How *Albanact* came by vntimely death.

Thrasi. After the traitrous hoast of Scithians
Entred the field with martiall equipage,
Yoong *Albanact*, impatient of delaie,
Ledde forth his armie gainst the stragling mates,
Whose multitude did daunt our souldiers mindes.
Yet nothing could dismay the forward prince,
But with a courage most heroicall,
Like to a lion mongst a flock of lambes,
Made hauocke of the faintheart fugitiues,
Hewing a passage through them with his sword.
Yea, we had almost giuen them the repulse,
When suddeinly, from out the silent wood,
Hubba, with twentie thousand souldiers,
Cowardly came vpon our weakened backes,
And murthered all with fatall massacre.
Amongst the which old *Debon*, martiall knight,
With many wounds was brought vnto the death,
And *Albanact*, opprest with multitude,
Whilst valiantly he feld his enemies,
Yeelded his life and honour to the dust.
He being dead, the souldiers fled amaine,
And I alone escaped them by flight,
To bring you tidings of these accidents.

Locr. Not aged *Priam*, King of stately *Troy*,
Graund Emperour of barbarous *Asia*,
When he beheld his noble minded sonnes
Slaine traiterously by all the *Mermidons*,
Lamented more then I for *Albanact*.

Guen. Not *Hecuba*, the queene of *Ilium*,
When she beheld the towne of *Pergamus*,
Her pallace, burnt with all deuouring flames,
Her fiftie sonnes and daughters fresh of hue
Murthred by wicked *Pirrhus* bloodie sword,
Shed such sad teares as I for *Albanact*.

Cam. The griefe of *Niobe*, faire *Athens* queene,
For her seuen sonnes, magnanimious in field,
For her seuen daughters, fairer then the fairest,
Is not to be comparde with my laments.

Cor. In vain you sorow for the slaughtred prince,
In vain you sorrow for his ouerthrow;

23 clouds *S* *S. D.* Exeunt *add. R* *S. D.* Prologue] Scene 1 *Q* *S. D.* The 2. Scene *Q* *Bracketed words add. T*

18 my cousin *M* 26 But] He *M*: Who *S* 54 Athens] Amphion's *conj. M*

He loues not most that doth lament the most,
But he that seekes to venge the iniurie.
Thinke you to quell the enemies warlike traine
With childish sobs and womannish laments?
Vnsheath your swords, vnsheath your conquering swords,
And seek reuenge, the comfort for this sore.
In *Cornwall,* where I hold my regiment,
Euen iust tenne thousand valiant men at armes
Hath *Corineus* readie at commaund:
All these and more, if need shall more require,
Hath *Corrineus* readie at commaund.
Cam. And in the fields of martiall *Cambria,*
Close by the boystrous *Iscans* siluer streames,
Where lightfoote faires skip from banke to banke,
Full twentie thousand braue couragious knights,
Well exercisde in feates of chiualrie,
In manly maner most inuincible,
Yoong *Camber* hath with gold and victuall:
All these and more, if need shall more require,
I offer vp to venge my brothers death.
Loc. Thanks, louing vncle, and good brother, too;
For this reuenge, for this sweete word, reuenge
Must ease and cease my wrongfull iniuries.
And by the sword of bloodie *Mars,* I sweare,
Nere shall sweete quiet enter this my front,
Till I be venged on his traiterous head
That slew my noble brother *Albanact.*
Sound drummes and trumpets; muster vp the camp,
For we will straight march to *Albania.*
[*Exeunt.*

The 2. *Scene.*

⟨*The banks of the river, afterward the Humber.*⟩

Enter Humber, Estrild, Hubba, Trussier, *and the souldiers.*

Hum. Thus are we come, victorious conquerors,
Vnto the flowing currents siluer streames,
Which, in memoriall of our victorie,
Shall be agnominated by our name,
And talked of by our posteritie:
For sure I hope before the golden sunne
Posteth his horses to faire *Thetis* plaines,
To see the water turned into blood,
And chaunge his blewish hue to rufull red,
By reason of the fatall massacre
Which shall be made vpon the virent plaines.

Enter the ghoast of Albanact.

⟨*Ghost.*⟩ See how the traitor doth presage his harme,
See how he glories at his owne decay,
See how he triumphs at his proper losse;
O fortune vilde, vnstable, fickle, fraile!
Hum. Me thinkes I see both armies in the field:
The broken launces clime the cristall skies;
Some headlesse lie, some breathlesse on the ground,
And euery place is straw'd with carcasses.
Behold! the grasse hath lost his pleasant greene,
The sweetest sight that euer might be seene.
Ghost. I, traiterous *Humber,* thou shalt find it so.
Yea, to thy cost thou shalt the same behold,
With anguish, sorrow, and with sad laments.
The grassie plaines, that now do please thine eies,
Shall ere the night be coloured all with blood:
The shadie groues which now inclose thy campe
And yeeld sweet sauours to thy damned corps,
Shall ere the night be figured all with blood:
The profound streame, that passeth by thy tents,
And with his moisture serueth all thy campe,
Shall ere the night conuerted be to blood,—
Yea, with the blood of those thy stragling boyes;
For now reuenge shall ease my lingring griefe,
And now reuenge shall glut my longing soule.
Hub. Let come what wil, I meane to beare it out,
And either liue with glorious victorie,
Or die with fame renowmed for chiualrie.
He is not worthie of the honie combe,
That shuns the hiues because the bees haue stings:
That likes me best that is not got with ease,
Which thousand daungers do accompany;
For nothing can dismay our regall minde,
Which aimes at nothing but a golden crowne,
The only vpshot of mine enterprises.
Were they inchanted in grimme *Plutos* court,
And kept for treasure mongst his hellish crue,
I would either quell the triple *Cerberus*
And all the armie of his hatefull hags,
Or roll the stone with wretched *Sisiphos.*

64 conquering sword *Q, Ff*: *corr. R* 72 Isca's *Haz.* 82 my] thy *Q* *S. D.* The 3. Scene *Q* *Bracketed words add. T* 8 water *M*: waters *Q, Ff* 9 chaunge] ? chaunged *pr. ed.*

S. D. Almanact *Q* 12 *Prefix add. R* 19 Anb *Q* 20 his] its *T* 38 renown'd *Ff, etc.* 46 *M suggests that a line has been lost after 45* inchanted] enchained *conj. M* 50 Sisiphon *Q*

Hum. Right martiall be thy thoughts my noble sonne,
And all thy words sauour of chiualrie.—

⟨*Enter* Segar.⟩

But warlike *Segar,* what strange accidents
Makes you to leaue the warding of the campe.
Segar. To armes, my Lord, to honourable armes!
Take helme and targe in hand; the Brittaines come,
With greater multitude then erst the Greekes
Brought to the ports of Phrigian *Tenidos.*
Hum. But what saith *Segar* to these accidents?
What counsell giues he in extremities?
Seg. Why this, my Lord, experience teacheth vs:
That resolution is a sole helpe at need.
And this, my Lord, our honour teacheth vs:
That we be bold in euerie enterprise.
Then since there is no way but fight or die,
Be resolute, my Lord, for victorie.
Hum. And resolute, *Segar,* I meane to be.
Perhaps some blisfull starre will fauour vs,
And comfort bring to our perplexed state.
Come, let vs in and fortifie our campe,
So to withstand their strong inuasion. [*Exeunt.*

The 3. *Scene.*

⟨*Before the hut of a peasant.*⟩

Enter Strumbo, Trumpart, Oliuer, *and his sonne* William *following them.*

Strum. Nay, neighbour *Oliuer,* if you be so whot, come, prepare your selfe. You shall finde two as stout fellowes of vs, as any in all the North.

Oliu. No, by my dorth, neighbor *Strumbo.* Ich zee dat you are a man of small zideration, dat wil zeek to iniure your olde vreendes, one of your vamiliar guests; and derefore, zeeing your pinion is to deale withouten reazon, iche and my zonne *William* will take dat course, dat shall be fardest vrom reason. How zay you, will you haue my daughter or no?

Strum. A verie hard question, neighbour, but I will solue it as I may. What reason haue you to demaund it of me?

Wil. Marry, sir, what reason had you, when my sister was in the barne, to tumble her vpon the haie, and to fish her belly.

Strum. Mas, thou saist true. Well, but would you haue me marry her therefore? No, I scorne her, and you, and you. I, I scorne you all.

Oliu. You will not haue her then?

Strum. No, as I am a true gentleman.

Wil. Then wil we schoole you, ere you and we part hence.

⟨*They fight.*⟩

Enter Margerie *and snatch the staffe out of her brothers hand, as he is fighting.*

Strum. I, you come in pudding time, or else I had drest them.

Mar. You, master sausebox, lobcock, cockscomb, you slopsauce, lickfingers, will you not heare?

Strum. Who speake you too? me?

Mar. I, sir, to you, *Iohn* lackhonestie, little wit. Is it you that will haue none of me?

Strum. No, by my troth, mistresse nicebice. How fine you can nickname me. I think you were broght vp in the vniuersitie of bridewell; you haue your rhetorick so ready at your toongs end, as if you were neuer well warned when your were yoong.

Mar. Why then, goodman cods-head, if you wil haue none of me, farewell.

Strum. If you be so plaine, mistresse drigle dragle, fare you well.

Mar. Nay, master *Strumbo,* ere you go from hence, we must haue more words. You will haue none of me?

They both fight.

Strum. Oh my head, my head! leaue, leaue, leaue! I will, I will, I will!

Mar. Vpon that condition I let thee alone.

Oliu. How now, master *Strumbo*? hath my daughter taught you a new lesson?

Strum. I, but heare you, goodman *Oliuer*: it will not bee for my ease to haue my head broken euerie day; therefore remedie this and we shall agree.

Oli. Well, zonne, well—for you are my zonne now—all shall be remedied. Daughter, be friends with him. [*Shake hands.*

⟨*Exeunt* Oliver, William, *and* Margery.⟩

Strum. You are a sweet nut! The diuel crack you. Maisters, I thinke it be my lucke: my first wife was a louing quiet wench, but this, I thinke, would weary the diuell. I would she might be burnt as my other wife was. If not, I must runne to the halter for help. O codpeece, thou hast done thy maister! this it is to be medling with warme plackets. [*Exeunt.*

S. D. add. R 62 a *om. S* *S. D.* The 4. Scene *Q* *Bracketed words add. T*

26 *S. D. add. M* 59 *S. D. Bracketed words add. M* 66 done *Q, M* : undone *Ff, R, etc.*

The 4. Scene.

⟨*The camp of* Locrine.⟩

Enter Locrine, Camber, Corineus, Thrasimachus, Assarachus.

Loc. Now am I garded with an hoste of men,
Whose hautie courage is inuincible:
Now am I hembde with troupes of souldiers,
Such as might force *Bellona* to retire,
And make her tremble at their puissance:
Now sit I like the mightie god of warre,
When, armed with his coat of Adament,
Mounted his charriot drawne with mighty bulls,
He droue the Argiues ouer *Xanthus* streames:
Now, cursed *Humber*, doth thy end draw nie.
Downe goes the glorie of thy victories,
And all thy fame, and all thy high renowne
Shall in a moment yeeld to *Locrines* sword.
Thy bragging banners crost with argent streames,
The ornaments of thy pauillions,
Shall all be captiuated with this hand,
And thou thy selfe, at *Albanactus* tombe,
Shalt offred be in satisfaction
Of all the wrongs thou didst him when he liu'd.—
But canst thou tell me, braue *Thrasimachus*,
How farre we are distant from *Humbers* campe?

Thra. My Lord, within yon foule accursed groue,
That beares the tokens of our ouerthrow,
This *Humber* hath intrencht his damned campe.
March on, my Lord, because I long to see
The trecherous Scithians squeltring in their gore.

Locri. Sweet fortune, fauour *Locrine* with a smile,
That I may venge my noble brothers death;
And in the midst of stately *Troinouant*,
Ile build a temple to thy deitie
Of perfect marble and of *Iacinthe* stones,
That it shall passe the high *Pyramides*,
Which with their top surmount the firmament.

Cam. The armestrong offspring of the doubled night,
Stout *Hercules*, *Alcmenas* mightie sonne,
That tamde the monsters of the threefold world,
And rid the oppressed from the tyrants yokes,
Did neuer shew such valiantnesse in fight,
As I will now for noble *Albanact*.

Cori. Full foure score yeares hath *Corineus* liu'd,
Sometime in warre, sometime in quiet peace,
And yet I feele my selfe to be as strong
As erst I was in sommer of mine age,
Able to tosse this great vnwildie club
Which hath bin painted with my foemens brains;
And with this club ile breake the strong arraie
Of *Humber* and his stragling souldiers,
Or loose my life amongst the thickest prease,
And die with honour in my latest daies.
Yet ere I die they all shall vnderstand
What force lies in stout *Corineus* hand.

Thra. And if *Thrasimachus* detract the fight,
Either for weaknesse or for cowardise,
Let him not boast that *Brutus* was his eame,
Or that braue *Corineus* was his sire.

Loc. Then courage, souldiers, first for your safetie,
Next for your peace, last for your victory.
[*Exeunt.*

⟨*Scene V. The field of battle.*⟩

Sound the alarme.

Enter Hubba *and* Segar *at one doore, and* Corineus *at the other.*

Cori. Art thou that *Humber*, prince of fugitiues,
That by thy treason slewst yoong *Albanact*?

Hub. I am his sonne that slew yoong *Albanact*,
And if thou take not heed, proud *Phrigian*,
Ile send thy soule vnto the Stigian lake,
There to complaine of *Humbers* iniuries.

Cori. You triumph, sir, before the victorie,
For *Corineus* is not so soone slaine.
But, cursed Scithians, you shall rue the day
That ere you came into *Albania*.
So perish they that enuie Brittaines wealth,
So let them die with endlesse infamie;
And he that seekes his soueraignes ouerthrow,
Would this my club might aggrauate his woe.
[*Strikes them both downe with his club.*

⟨*Scene VI. Another part of the field.*⟩

Enter Humber.

⟨*Hum.*⟩ Where may I finde some desart wildernesse,
Where I may breath out curses as I would,
And scare the earth with my condemning voice;

S. D. The 5. Scene *Q* *Bracketed words add. T* 8 his] in's *T* 11 his *T*: thy *old edd.* 12 his . . his *T*: thy . . thy *old edd.* 21 we distant are *Haz.* 22 yon *R*: your *Q, Ff* 29 Troinonant *Q* 34 doubled night *St.*: doubted knight *Q, Ff*: 'doubted night *T*

S. D. Scene V. *add. M*: *place first indicated T* 11 they that] that they *Q* *S. D.* Scene VI. *add. M*: *place first indicated T*

Where euerie ecchoes repercussion
May helpe me to bewaile mine ouerthrow,
And aide me in my sorrowfull laments?
Where may I finde some hollow vncoth rocke,
Where I may damne, condemne, and ban my fill
The heauens, the hell, the earth, the aire, the fire,
And vtter curses to the concaue skie,
Which may infect the aiery regions,
And light vpon the Brittain *Locrines* head?
You vgly sprites that in *Cocitus* mourne,
And gnash your teeth with dolorous laments:
You fearfull dogs that in black *Læthe* howle,
And scare the ghoasts with your wide open throats:
You vgly ghoasts that, flying from these dogs,
Do plunge your selues in *Puryflegiton*:
Come, all of you, and with your shriking notes
Accompanie the Brittaines conquering hoast.
Come, fierce *Erinnis,* horrible with snakes;
Come, vgly Furies, armed with your whippes;
You threefold iudges of black *Tartarus,*
And all the armie of you hellish fiends,
With new found torments rack proud *Locrins* bones!
O gods, and starres! damned be the gods & starres
That did not drowne me in faire *Thetis* plaines!
Curst be the sea, that with outragious waues,
With surging billowes did not riue my shippes
Against the rocks of high *Cerannia,*
Or swallow me into her watrie gulfe!
Would God we had arriu'd vpon the shore
Where *Poliphemus* and the *Cyclops* dwell,
Or where the bloodie *Anthropophagie*
With greedie iawes deuours the wandring wights!

Enter the ghoast of Albanact.

But why comes *Albanacts* bloodie ghoast,
To bring a corsiue to our miseries?
Ist not inough to suffer shamefull flight,
But we must be tormented now with ghoasts,
With apparitions fearfull to behold?

Ghoast. Reuenge! reuenge for blood!

Hum. So nought wil satisfie your wandring ghost
But dire reuenge, nothing but *Humbers* fall,
Because he conquerd you in *Albany.*
Now, by my soule, *Humber* would be condemn'd
To *Tantals* hunger or *Ixions* wheele,
Or to the vultur of *Prometheus,*
Rather then that this murther were vndone.
When as I die ile dragge thy cursed ghoast
Through all the riuers of foule *Erebus,*
Through burning sulphur of the Limbo-lake,
To allaie the burning furie of that heate
That rageth in mine euerlasting soule.

Alba. ghost. Vindicta, vindicta. [*Exeunt.*

The 4. Act. Prologue.

Enter Ate *as before. Then let their follow* Omphale, *daughter to the king of* Lydia, *hauing a club in her hand, and a lions skinne on her back,* Hercules *following with a distaffe. Then let* Omphale *turn about, and taking off her pantofle, strike* Hercules *on the head; then let them depart,* Ate *remaining, saying:*

Quem non Argolici mandata seuera Tyranni,
Non potuit Iuno vincere, vicit amor.

Stout *Hercules,* the mirrour of the world,
Sonne to *Alcmena* and great *Iupiter,*
After so many conquests wonne in field,
After so many monsters queld by force,
Yeelded his valiant heart to *Omphale,*
A fearfull woman voyd of manly strength.
She tooke the club, and ware the lions skinne;
He tooke the wheele, and maidenly gan spinne.
So martiall *Locrine,* cheerd with victorie,
Falleth in loue with *Humbers* concubine,
And so forgetteth peerlesse *Guendoline.*
His vncle *Corineus* stormes at this,
And forceth *Locrine* for his grace to sue.
Loe here the summe, the processe doth ensue. [*Exit.*

The 1. Scene.

⟨*The camp of* Locrine.⟩

Enter Locrine, Camber, Corineus, Assaracus, Thrasimachus, *and the souldiers.*

Loc. Thus from the fury of *Bellonas* broiles,
With sound of drumme and trumpets melodie,
The Brittaine king returnes triumphantly.
The Scithians slaine with great occision
Do æqualize the grasse in multitude,
And with their blood haue staind the streaming brookes,
Offering their bodies and their dearest blood
As sacrifice to *Albanactus* ghoast.
Now, cursed *Humber,* hast thou payd thy due,
For thy deceits and craftie trecheries,
For all thy guiles and damned stratagems,
With losse of life, and euerduring shame.

15 You] Yea *Q* 20 Accompaie *Q* 24 your *F2* 30 Ceraunia *M* 31 swallow *M*: swallowed *Q, Ff* 33 Poliphlemus *Q* 34 Anthropomphagic *Q*: Anthropophagites *Pope* 42 you *S*

Prologue] Scene 1 *Q* 9 wore *Ff* *S. D.* The 2. Scene *Q* *Bracketed words add. T*

Where are thy horses trapt with burnisht gold,
Thy trampling coursers rulde with foming bits?
Where are thy souldiers, strong and numberlesse,
Thy valiant captains and thy noble peeres?
Euen as the countrie clownes with sharpest sithes
Do mowe the withered grasse from off the earth,
Or as the ploughman with his piercing share
Renteth the bowels of the fertile fields,
And rippeth vp the rootes with razours keene:
So *Locrine* with his mightie curtleaxe
Hath cropped off the heads of all thy *Hunnes*;
So *Locrines* peeres haue daunted all thy peeres,
And droue thine hoast vnto confusion,
That thou maist suffer penance for thy fault,
And die for murdring valiant *Albanact*.

Cori. And thus, yea thus, shall all the rest be seru'd
That seeke to enter *Albion* gainst our willes.
If the braue nation of the *Troglodites*,
If all the coleblacke *Aethiopians*,
If all the forces of the *Amazons*,
If all the hostes of the Barbarian lands,
Should dare to enter this our little world,
Soone should they rue their ouerbold attempts,
That after vs our progenie may say,
There lie the beasts that sought to vsurp our land.

Loc. I, they are beasts that seeke to vsurp our land,
And like to brutish beasts they shall be seru'd.
For mightie *Ioue*, the supreame king of heauen,
That guides the concourse of the *Metiors*,
And rules the motion of the azure skie,
Fights alwaies for the Brittaines safetie.—
But staie! mee thinkes I heare some shriking noise,
That draweth neare to our pauillion.

Enter the souldiers leading in Estrild.

Estrild. What prince so ere, adornd with golden ⟨crowne,⟩
Doth sway the regall scepter in his hand,
And thinks no chance can euer throw him downe,
Or that his state shall euerlasting stand:
Let him behold poore *Estrild* in this plight,
The perfect platforme of a troubled wight.
Once was I guarded with mauortiall bands,
Compast with princes of the noble blood;
Now am I fallen into my foemens hands,
And with my death must pacifie their mood.
O life, the harbour of calamities!
O death, the hauen of all miseries!
I could compare my sorrowes to thy woe,
Thou wretched queen of wretched *Pergamus*,
But that thou viewdst thy enemies ouerthrow.
Nigh to the rocke of high *Caphareus*,
Thou sawst their death, and then departedst thence;
I must abide the victors insolence.
The gods that pittied thy continuall griefe
Transformd thy corps, and with thy corps thy care;
Poore *Estrild* liues dispairing of reliefe,
For friends in trouble are but fewe and rare.
What, said I fewe? I! fewe or none at all,
For cruell death made hauock of them all.
Thrice happie they whose fortune was so good,
To end their liues, and with their liues their woes!
Thrice haplesse I, whome fortune so withstood,
That cruelly she gaue me to my foes!
Oh, souldiers, is there any miserie,
To be comparde to fortunes trecherie.

Loc. *Camber*, this same shuld be the Scithian queen.

Cam. So may we iudge by her lamenting words.

Loc. So faire a dame mine eies did neuer see;
With floods of woes she seems orewhelmed to bee.

Cam. O *Locrine*, hath she not a cause for to be sad?

Locrine (at one side of the stage).

If she haue cause to weepe for *Humbers* death,
And shead sault teares for her ouerthrow,
Locrine may well bewaile his proper griefe,
Locrine may moue his owne peculiar woe.
He, being conquerd, died a speedie death,
And felt not long his lamentable smart;
I, being conqueror, liue a lingring life,
And feele the force of *Cupids* suddaine stroke.
I gaue him cause to die a speedie death,
He left me cause to wish a speedie death.
Oh that sweete face painted with natures dye,
Those roseall cheeks mixt with a snowy white,
That decent necke surpassing yuorie,
Those comely brests which *Venus* well might spite,
Are like to snares which wylie fowlers wrought,
Wherein my yeelding heart is prisoner cought.
The golden tresses of her daintie haire,

46 crowne *om. Q*: *supplied Ff* 47 sceptler *Q* 52 manortiall *Q* 53 noblest *T*

80 Locrine *om. M* 82 her] his dread *S*: her own *Molt.* 85 He] Humber *S* 88 stroke] dart *conj. Th. for sake of rhyme* 92 mizt *Q*

Which shine like rubies glittering with the sunne,
Haue so entrapt poore *Locrines* louesick heart,
That from the same no way it can be wonne.
How true is that which oft I heard declard,
One dramme of ioy, must haue a pound of care.

Estr. Hard is their fall who, from a golden crown,
Are cast into a sea of wretchednesse.

Loc. Hard is their thrall who by *Cupids* frowne
Are wrapt in waues of endlesse carefulnesse.

Estr. Oh kingdome, obiect to all miseries.

Loc. Oh loue, the extreemst of all extremities.

Let him go into his chaire.

A sold. My Lord, in ransacking the Scithian tents,
I found this Ladie, and to manifest
That earnest zeale I beare vnto your grace,
I here present her to your maiestie.

Another sold. He lies, my Lord; I found the Ladie first,
And here present her to your maiestie.

1. *Sold.* Presumptuous villaine, wilt thou take my prize?

2. *Sold.* Nay, rather thou depriuest me of my right.

1. *Sol.* Resigne thy title, catiue, vnto me,
Or with my sword ile pearce thy cowards loines.

2. *Sol.* Soft words, good sir, tis not inogh to speak;
A barking dog doth sildome strangers bite.

Loc. Vnreuerent villains, striue you in our sight?
Take them hence, Iaylor, to the dungeon;
There let them lie and trie their quarrell out.
But thou, faire princesse, be no whit dismayd,
But rather ioy that *Locrine* fauours thee.

Estr. How can he fauor me that slew my spouse?

Loc. The chance of war, my loue, tooke him from thee.

Est. But *Locrine* was the causer of his death.

Loc. He was an enemy to *Locrines* state,
And slue my noble brother *Albanact.*

Estr. But he was linckt to me in marriage bond,
And would you haue me loue his slaughterer?

Loc. Better to liue, then not to liue at all.

Estrild. Better to die renownd for chastitie,
Then liue with shame and endlesse infamie.
What would the common sort report of me,
If I forget my loue, and cleaue to thee?

Loc. Kings need not feare the vulgar sentences.

Estr. But Ladies must regard their honest name.

Loc. Is it a shame to liue in marriage bonds?

Estr. No, but to be a strumpet to a king.

Loc. If thou wilt yeeld to *Locrines* burning loue,
Thou shalt be queene of faire *Albania.*

Estr. But *Guendoline* will vndermine my state.

Lo. Vpon mine honor, thou shalt haue no harme.

Est. Then lo, braue *Locrine, Estrild* yeelds to thee;
And by the gods whom thou doest inuocate,
By the dead ghoast of thy deceased sire,
By thy right hand and by thy burning loue,
Take pitie on poore *Estrilds* wretched thrall.

Cori. Hath *Locrine* then forgot his *Guendoline,*
That thus he courts the Scithians paramore?
What, are the words of *Brute* so soone forgot?
Are my deserts so quickly out of minde?
Haue I bene faithfull to thy sire now dead,
Haue I protected thee from *Humbers* hands,
And doest thou quite me with vngratitude?
Is this the guerdon for my greeuous wounds,
Is this the honour for my labors past?
Now, by my sword, *Locrine,* I sweare to thee,
This iniury of thine shall be repaide.

Loc. Vncle, scorne you your royall soueraigne,
As if we stood for cyphers in the court?
Vpbraid you me with those your benefits?
Why, it was a subiects dutie so to do.
What you haue done for our deceased sire,
We know, and all know you haue your reward.

Cori. Auaunt, proud princoxe; brau'st thou me withall?
Assure thy self, though thou be Emperor,
Thou nere shalt carry this vnpunished.

Cam. Pardon my brother, noble *Corineus;*
Pardon this once and it shall be amended.

Assar. Cousin, remember *Brutus* latest words,
How he desired you to cherish them;
Let not this fault so much incense your minde,
Which is not yet passed all remedie.

Cori. Then, *Locrine,* loe, I reconcile my selfe;
But as thou lou'st thy life, so loue thy wife.

101 declare *S* 105 by Cupido's *M*: still by Cupid's *T* 107 object] subject *S* 133 Better to love *conj. St.*: Better to loue and liue *conj. pr. ed.*

156 hand *F2, etc.* 157 quit *Ff, etc.* ingratitude *M*

But if thou violate those promises,
Blood and reuenge shall light vpon thy head.
Come, let vs backe to stately *Troinouant,*
Where all these matters shall be setteled.

Locrine (*to himselfe*). Millions of diuels wayt vpon thy soule!
Legions of spirits vexe thy impious ghoast!
Ten thousand torments rack thy cursed bones!
Let euerie thing that hath the vse of breath
Be instruments and workers of thy death!

[*Exeunt.*

The 2. *Scene.*

⟨*A forest.*⟩

Enter Humber *alone, his haire hanging ouer his shoulders, his armes all bloodie, and a dart in one hand.*

Hum. What basiliskt was hatched in this place,
Where euerie thing consumed is to nought?
What fearefull Furie haunts these cursed groues,
Where not a roote is left for *Humbers* meate?
Hath fell *Alecto,* with inuenomed blasts,
Breathed forth poyson in these tender plaines?
Hath triple *Cerberus,* with contagious fome,
Sowde *Aconitum* mongst these withered hearbes?
Hath dreadfull *Fames* with her charming rods
Brought barreinnesse on euery fruitfull tree?
What, not a roote, no frute, no beast, no bird,
To nourish *Humber* in this wildernesse?
What would you more, you fiends of *Erebus*?
My verie intralls burne for want of drinke,
My bowels crie, *Humber, giue vs some meate.*
But wretched *Humber* can giue you no meate;
These foule accursed groues affoord no meat.
This fruitles soyle, this ground, brings forth no meat.
The gods, hard harted gods, yeeld me no meat.
Then how can *Humber* giue you any meat?

Enter Strumbo *with a pitchforke, and a scotch-cap, saying:*

How do you, maisters, how do you? how haue you scaped hanging this long time? Yfaith, I haue scapt many a scouring this yeare; but I thanke God I haue past them all with a good *couragio, couragio,* & my wife & I are in great loue and charitie now, I thank my manhood & my strength. For I wil tell you, maisters: vpon a certain day at night I came home, to say the verie truth, with my stomacke full of wine, and ran vp into the chamber where my wife soberly sate rocking my little babie, leaning her back against the bed, singing lullabie. Now, when she saw me come with my nose formost, thinking that I ⟨had⟩ bin drunk, as I was indeed, ⟨she⟩ snatcht vp a fagot stick in her hand, and came furiously marching towards me with a bigge face, as though shee would haue eaten mee at a bit; thundering out these words vnto me: *Thou drunken knaue, where hast thou bin so long? I shall teach thee how to benight mee an other time;* and so shee began to play knaues trumps. Now, althogh I trembled, fearing she would set her ten commandements in my face, ⟨I⟩ ran within her, and taking her lustily by the midle, I carried her valiantly to the bed, and flinging her vpon it, flung my selfe vpon her; and there I delighted her so with the sport I made, that euer after she wold call me sweet husband, and so banisht brawling for euer. And to see the good will of the wench! she bought with her portion a yard of land, and by that I am now become one of the richest men in our parish. Well, masters, whats a clocke? it is now breakfast time; you shall see what meat I haue here for my breakfast.

[*Let him sit down and pull out his vittailes.*

Hum. Was euer land so fruitlesse as this land?
Was euer groue so gracelesse as this groue?
Was euer soyle so barrein as this soyle?
Oh no: the land where hungry *Fames* dwelt
May no wise æqualize this cursed land;
No, euen the climat of the torrid zone
Brings forth more fruit then this accursed groue.
Nere came sweet *Ceres,* nere came *Venus* here;
Triptolemus, the god of husbandmen,
Nere sowd his seed in this foule wildernesse.
The hunger-bitten dogs of *Acheron,*
Chast from the ninefold *Puriflegiton,*
Haue set their footesteps in this damned ground.
The yron harted Furies, arm'd with snakes,
Scattered huge *Hidras* ouer all the plaines,
Which haue consum'd the grasse, the herbes, the trees;
Which haue drunke vp the flowing water springs.

Strumbo, *hearing his voice, shall start vp and put meat in his pocket, seeking to hide himselfe.*

Hum. Thou great commander of the starry skie,

S. D. The 3. Scene *Q* *Bracketed words add. S* 6 in] on *S* 11 nor fruit, nor beast, nor bird *S* 24 good coraggio, and *M*

34 had *om. Q* 35 she *add. M* 45 I *add. M*

That guidst the life of euerie mortall wight,
From the inclosures of the fleeting clouds
Raine downe some foode, or else I faint and die:
Powre downe some drinke, or else I faint and die.
O *Iupiter,* hast thou sent *Mercury*
In clownish shape to minister some foode?
Some meate! some meate! some meate!

Strum. O, alasse, sir, ye are deceiued. I am not *Mercury*; I am *Strumbo.*

Hum. Giue me som meat, vilain; giue me som meat,
Or gainst this rock Ile dash thy cursed braines,
And rent thy bowels with my bloodie hands.
Giue me some meat, villaine; giue me some meat!

Strum. By the faith of my bodie, good fellow, I had rather giue an whole oxe then that thou shuldst serue me in that sort. Dash out my braines? O horrible! terrible! I thinke I haue a quarry of stones in my pocket.

Let him make as though hee would giue him some, and as he putteth out his hand, enter the ghoast of Albanact, *and strike him on the hand; and so* Strumbo *runnes out,* Humber *following him.* [*Exit.*

Alba. ghost. Loe, here the gift of fell ambition,
Of vsurpation and of trecherie!
Loe, here the harmes that wait vpon all those
That do intrude themselues in others lands,
Which are not vnder their dominion. [*Exit.*

The 3. *Scene.*

⟨*A chamber in the Royal Palace.*⟩

Enter Locrine *alone.*

Loc. Seuen yeares hath aged *Corineus* liu'd,
To *Locrines* griefe, and faire *Estrildas* woe,
And seuen yeares more he hopeth yet to liue.
Oh supreme *Ioue,* annihilate this thought!
Should he enioy the aires fruition?
Should he enioy the benefit of life?
Should he contemplate the radiant sunne,
That makes my life equall to dreadfull death?
Venus, conuay this monster fro the earth,
That disobeieth thus thy sacred hests!
Cupid, conuay this monster to darke hell,
That disanulls thy mothers sugred lawes!
Mars, with thy target all beset with flames,
With murthering blade bereaue him of his life,
That hindreth *Locrine* in his sweetest ioyes!
And yet, for all his diligent aspect,
His wrathfull eies, piercing like *Linces* eies,
Well haue I ouermatcht his subtiltie.
Nigh *Deurolitum,* by the pleasant Lee,
Where brackish *Thamis* slides with siluer streames,
Making a breach into the grassie downes,
A curious arch, of costly marble fraught,
Hath *Locrine* framed vnderneath the ground;
The walls whereof, garnisht with diamonds,
With ophirs, rubies, glistering emeralds,
And interlast with sun-bright carbuncles,
Lighten the roome with artificiall day:
And from the Lee with water-flowing pipes
The moisture is deriu'd into this arch,
Where I haue placed faire *Estrild* secretly.
Thither eftsoones, accompanied with my page,
I couertly visit my harts desire,
Without suspition of the meanest eie;
For loue aboundeth still with pollicie:
And thither still meanes *Locrine* to repaire,
Till *Atropos* cut off mine vncles life. [*Exit.*

The 4. *Scene.*

⟨*The entrance of a cave, near which runs the river, afterward the Humber.*⟩

Enter Humber *alone, saying:*

Hum. *O vita misero longa, fœlici breuis,*
Eheu! malorum fames extremum malum.
Long haue I liued in this desart caue,
With eating hawes and miserable rootes,
Deuouring leaues and beastly excrements.
Caues were my beds, and stones my pillow-beares,
Feare was my sleep, and horror was my dreame,
For still me thought, at euery boisterous blast,
Now Locrine *comes, now,* Humber, *thou must die:*
So that for feare and hunger, *Humbers* minde
Can neuer rest, but alwaies trembling stands,
O, what *Danubius* now may quench my thirst?
What *Euphrates,* what lightfoot *Euripus,*
May now allaie the furie of that heat,
Which, raging in my entralls, eates me vp?
You gastly diuels of the ninefold *Stickes,*
You damned ghoasts of ioylesse *Acheron,*
You mournfull soules, vext in *Abissus* vaults,
You coleblack diuels of *Auernus* pond,
Come, with your fleshhooks rent my famisht arms,
These armes that haue sustaind their maisters life.

82 you *M* *S. D.* The 4. Scene *Q* *Bracketed words add. S* 7 sonne *Q*: sun *Ff* 9 from *F 2*

19 Durolitum *M*: Deucolitum *Q, Ff* 22 wrought *conj. St.* 24 garnish *Q* *S. D.* The 5. Scene *Q* *Bracketed words add. S* 2 Ehen malorem *Q*

Come, with your raisours rippe my bowels vp,
With your sharp fireforks crack my sterued bones:
Vse me as you will, so *Humber* may not liue.
Accursed gods, that rule the starry poles,
Accursed *Ioue,* king of the cursed gods,
Cast downe your lightning on poore *Humbers* head,
That I may leaue this deathlike life of mine!
What, heare you not? and shall not *Humber* die?
Nay, I will die, though all the gods say nay!
And, gentle *Aby,* take my troubled corps,
Take it and keep it from all mortall eies,
That none may say, when I haue lost my breath,
The very flouds conspirde gainst *Humbers* death.
[*Fling himselfe into the riuer.*

Enter the ghoast of Albanact.

En cædem sequitur cædes, in cæde quiesco.
Humber is dead! ioy heauens! leap earth! dance trees!
Now maist thou reach thy apples, *Tantalus,*
And with them feed thy hunger-bitten limmes!
Now, *Sisiphus,* leaue tumbling of thy rock,
And rest thy restlesse bones vpon the same!
Vnbind *Ixion,* cruell *Rhadamanth,*
And laie proud *Humber* on the whirling wheele.
Backe will I post to hell mouth *Tænarus,*
And passe *Cocitus,* to the Elysian fields,
And tell my father *Brutus* of these newes.
[*Exit.*

The 5. *Act. Prologue.*

Enter Ate *as before.* Iason, *leading* Creons *daughter.* Medea, *following, hath a garland in her hand, and putting it on* Creons *daughters head, setteth it on fire, and then, killing* Iason *and her, departeth.*

Ate. Non tam Tinacriis exaestuat Aetna cauernis,
Læsæ furtiuo quam cor mulieris amore.

Medea, seeing *Iason* leaue her loue,
And choose the daughter of the *Thebane* king,
Went to her diuellish charmes to worke reuenge;
And raising vp the triple *Hecate,*
With all the rout of the condemned fiends,
Framed a garland by her magick skill,
With which she wrought *Iason* and *Creons* ill.
So *Guendoline,* seeing her selfe misvs'd,
And *Humbers* paramour possesse her place,
Flies to the dukedome of *Cornubia,*
And with her brother, stout *Thrasimachus,*
Gathering a power of Cornish souldiers,
Giues battaile to her husband and his hoste,
Nigh to the riuer of great *Mertia.*
The chances of this dismall massacre
That which insueth shortly will vnfold. [*Exit*

The 1. *Scene.*

⟨*A chamber in the Royal Palace.*⟩

Enter Locrine, Camber, Assarachus, Thrasimachus.

Assa. But tell me, cousin, died my brother so?
Now who is left to helplesse *Albion,*
That as a piller might vphold our state,
That might strike terror to our daring foes?
Now who is left to haplesse *Brittanie,*
That might defend her from the barbarous hands
Of those that still desire her ruinous fall,
And seeke to worke her downfall and decaie?

Cam. I, vncle, death is our common enemie,
And none but death can match our matchles power:
Witnesse the fall of *Albioneus* crewe,
Witnesse the fall of *Humber* and his *Hunnes.*
And this foule death hath now increast our woe,
By taking *Corineus* from this life,
And in his roome leauing vs worlds of care.

Thra. But none may more bewaile his mournful hearse,
Then I that am the issue of his loines.
Now foule befall that cursed *Humbers* throat,
That was the causer of his lingring wound.

Lo. Teares cannot raise him from the dead again.
But wher's my Ladie, mistresse *Guendoline*?

Thra. In Cornwall, *Locrine,* is my sister now,
Prouiding for my fathers funerall.

Lo. And let her ther prouide her mourning weeds
And mourne for euer her owne widdow-hood.
Ner shall she come within our pallace gate,
To countercheck braue *Locrine* in his loue.
Go, boy, to *Deurolitum,* downe the Lee,
Vnto the arch where louely *Estrild* lies.
Bring her and *Sabren* strait vnto the court;
She shall be queene in *Guendolinas* roome.
Let others waile for *Corineus* death;
I meane not so to macerate my minde
For him that bard me from my hearts desire.

31 Abus *Haz.* Prologue] Scene 1 *Q* 1 Tincriis excestuat *Q* : *corr. Ff*

S. D. The 2. Scene *Q* *Bracketed words add. S* 1 my] by *Q* 28 Deucolitum *Q, Ff* : Durolitum *M*

Thra. Hath *Locrine*, then, forsooke his *Guendoline?*
Is *Corineus* death so soone forgot?
If there be gods in heauen, as sure there be,
If there be fiends in hell, as needs there must,
They will reuenge this thy notorious wrong,
And powre their plagues vpon thy cursed head.

Loc. What! prat'st thou, pesant, to thy soueraigne?
Or art thou strooken in some extasie?
Doest thou not tremble at our royall lookes?
Dost thou not quake, when mighty *Locrine* frowns?
Thou beardlesse boy, wer't not that *Locrine* scornes
To vexe his mind with such a hartlesse childe,
With the sharpe point of this my battale-axe,
I would send thy soule to *Puriflegiton.*

Thra. Though I be yoong and of a tender age,
Yet will I cope with *Locrine* when he dares.
My noble father with his conquering sword,
Slew the two giants, kings of *Aquitaine.*
Thrasimachus is not so degenerate
That he should feare and tremble at the lookes
Or taunting words of a venerian squire.

Loc. Menacest thou thy roiall soueraigne,
Vnciuill, not beseeming such as you?
Iniurious traitor (for he is no lesse
That at defiance standeth with his king)
Leaue these thy tauntes, leaue these thy bragging words,
Vnlesse thou meane to leaue thy wretched life.

Thra. If princes staine their glorious dignitie
With ougly spots of monstrous infamie,
They leese their former estimation,
And throw themselues into a hell of hate.

Loc. Wilt thou abuse my gentle patience,
As though thou didst our high displeasure scorne?
Proud boy, that thou maist know thy prince is mou'd,
Yea, greatly mou'd at this thy swelling pride,
We banish thee for euer from our court.

Thra. Then, losell *Locrine*, looke vnto thy selfe,
Thrasimachus will venge this iniurie. [*Exit.*

Lo. Farwel, proud boy, and learn to vse thy toong.

Assa. Alas, my Lord, you shuld haue cald to mind
The latest words that *Brutus* spake to you:
How he desirde you, by the obedience
That children ought to beare vnto their sire,
To loue and fauour Ladie *Guendoline.*
Consider this, that if the iniurie
Do mooue her mind, as certainly it will,
Warre and dissention followes speedely.
What though her power be not so great as yours?
Haue you not seene a mightie elephant
Slaine by the biting of a silly mouse?
Euen so the chance of warre inconstant is.

Loc. Peace, vncle, peace, and cease to talke hereof;
For he that seekes, by whispering this or that,
To trouble *Locrine* in his sweetest life,
Let him perswade himselfe to die the death.

Enter the Page, with Estrild *and* Sabren.

Estr. O, say me, Page, tell me, where is the king?
Wherefore doth he send for me to the court?
Is it to die? is it to end my life?
Say me, sweete boy, tell me and do not faine!

Page. No, trust me, madame; if you will credit the litle honestie that is yet left me, there is no such danger as you feare. But prepare your selfe; yonders the king.

Estr. Then, *Estrild*, lift thy dazled spirits vp,
And blesse that blessed time, that day, that houre,
That warlike *Locrine* first did fauour thee.
Peace to the king of *Brittany*, my loue!
Peace to all those that loue and fauour him!

Locrine (*taking her vp*). Doth *Estrild* fall with such submission
Before her seruant, king of *Albion?*
Arise, faire Ladie; leaue this lowly cheare.
Lift vp those lookes that cherish *Locrines* heart,
That I may freely view that roseall face,
Which so intangled hath my louesick brest.
Now to the court, where we will court it out,
And passe the night and day in *Venus* sports.
Frollick, braue peeres; be ioyfull with your king. [*Exeunt.*

The 2. *Scene.*

⟨*The camp of Guendolen.*⟩

Enter Guendoline, Thrasimachus, Madan, *and the souldiers*

Guen. You gentle winds, that with your modest blasts
Passe through the circuit of the heauenly vault,
Enter the clouds vnto the throne of *Ioue*,
And beare my praiers to his all hearing eares,
For *Locrine* hath forsaken *Guendoline*,

45 wert *Q* 52 giant kings *S* 57 thou *S* 61 mean'st *Ff*

S. D. The 3. Scene *Q*: *corr. M* *Bracketed words add. S*

And learnt to loue proud *Humbers* concubine.
You happie sprites, that in the concaue skie
With pleasant ioy enioy your sweetest loue,
Shead foorth those teares with me, which then you shed,
When first you wood your ladies to your wils.
Those teares are fittest for my wofull case,
Since *Locrine* shunnes my nothing pleasant face.
Blush heauens, blush sunne, and hide thy shining beams;
Shadow thy radiant locks in gloomy clouds;
Denie thy cheerfull light vnto the world,
Where nothing raigns but falshood and deceit.
What said I? falshood? I, that filthie crime,
For *Locrine* hath forsaken *Guendoline.*
Behold the heauens do waile for *Guendoline.*
The shining sunne doth blush for *Guendoline.*
The liquid aire doth weep for *Guendoline.*
The verie ground doth grone for *Guendoline.*
I, they are milder then the Brittaine king,
For he reiecteth lucklesse *Guendoline.*

Thra. Sister, complaints are bootlesse in this cause;
This open wrong must haue an open plague,
This plague must be repaid with grieuous warre,
This warre must finish with *Locrinus* death;
His death will soone extinguish our complaints.

Guen. O no, his death wil more augment my woes.
He was my husband, braue *Thrasimachus,*
More deare to me then the apple of mine eie,
Nor can I finde in heart to worke his scathe.

Thra. Madame, if not your proper iniuries,
Nor my exile, can moue you to reuenge,
Thinke on our father *Corineus* words;
His words to vs stands alwaies for a lawe.
Should *Locrine* liue that caus'd my fathers death?
Should *Locrine* liue that now diuorceth you?
The heauens, the earth, the aire, the fire reclaimes,
And then why should all we denie the same?

Guen. Then henceforth, farwel womanish complaints!
All childish pitie henceforth, then, farwel!
But, cursed *Locrine,* looke vnto thy selfe,
For *Nemesis,* the mistresse of reuenge,
Sits arm'd at all points on our dismall blades;
And cursed *Estrild,* that inflamed his heart,
Shall, if I liue, die a reproachfull death.

Madan. Mother, though nature makes me to lament
My lucklesse fathers froward lecherie,
Yet, for he wrongs my Ladie mother thus,
I, if I could, my selfe would worke his death.

Thra. See, madame, see, the desire of reuenge
Is in the children of a tender age!
Forward, braue souldiers, into *Mertia,*
Where we shall braue the coward to his face. [*Exeunt.*

The 3. *Scene.*

(The camp of Locrine.)

Enter Locrine, Estrild, Sabren, Assarachus, *and the souldiers.*

Loc. Tell me, *Assarachus,* are the Cornish chuffes
In such great number come to *Mertia?*
And haue they pitched there their pettie hoste,
So close vnto our royall mansion?

Assa. They are, my Lord, and meane incontinent
To bid defiance to your maiestie.

Loc. It makes me laugh, to thinke that *Guendoline*
Should haue the hart to come in armes gainst me.

Estr. Alas, my Lord, the horse wil runne amaine,
When as the spurre doth gall him to the bone.
Iealousie, *Locrine,* hath a wicked sting.

Loc. Saist thou so, *Estrild,* beauties paragon?
Well, we will trie her chollor to the proofe,
And make her know, *Locrine* can brooke no braues.
March on, *Assarachus;* thou must lead the way,
And bring vs to their proud pauillion. [*Exeunt.*

The 4. *Scene.*

(The field of battle.)

Enter the ghost of Corineus, *with thunder & lightening.*

Ghost. Behold, the circuit of the azure sky
Throwes forth sad throbs and grieuous suspirs,
Preiudicating *Locrines* ouerthrow.
The fire casteth forth sharpe dartes of flames,
The great foundation of the triple world
Trembleth and quaketh with a mightie noise,
Presaging bloodie massacres at hand.
The wandring birds that flutter in the darke,
When hellish night, in cloudie charriot seated,
Casteth her mists on shadie *Tellus* face,

6 learne *Q*: *corr. Ff*

S. D. The 4. Scene *Q*: *corr. M* *Bracketed words add. S* Habren *Q, Ff* 8 against *F 2, etc.* *S. D.* The 5. Scene *Q*: *corr. M* *Bracketed words add. S* 2 grievously *S*

With sable mantels couering all the earth,
Now flies abroad amid the cheerfull day,
Foretelling some vnwonted miserie.
The snarling curres of darkened *Tartarus,*
Sent from *Auernus* ponds by *Radamanth,*
With howling ditties pester euerie wood.
The watrie ladies and the lightfoote fawnes,
And all the rabble of the wooddie Nymphs,
All trembling hide themselues in shadie groues,
And shrowd themselues in hideous hollow pitts.
The boysterous *Boreas* thundreth forth reuenge;
The stonie rocks crie out on sharpe reuenge;
The thornie bush pronounceth dire reuenge.

Sound the alarme.

Now, *Corineus,* staie and see reuenge,
And feede thy soule with *Locrines* ouerthrow.
Behold, they come; the trumpets call them foorth;
The roaring drummes summon the souldiers.
Loe, where their army glistereth on the plaines!
Throw forth thy lightning, mightie *Iupiter,*
And powre thy plagues on cursed *Locrines* head.

[*Stand aside.*

Enter Locrine, Estrild, Assaracus, Sabren *and their soldiers at one doore;* Thrasimachus, Guendolin, Madan *and their followers at an other.*

Loc. What, is the tigre started from his caue?
Is *Guendoline* come from *Cornubia,*
That thus she braueth *Locrine* to the teeth?
And hast thou found thine armour, prettie boy,
Accompanied with these thy stragling mates?
Beleeue me, but this enterprise was bold,
And well deserueth commendation.

Guen. I, *Locrine,* traiterous *Locrine!* we are come,
With full pretence to seeke thine ouerthrow.
What haue I don, that thou shouldst scorn me thus?
What haue I said, that thou shouldst me reiect?
Haue I beno disobedient to thy words?
Haue I bewrayd thy Arcane secrecie?
Haue I dishonoured thy marriage bed
With filthie crimes, or with lasciuious lusts?
Nay, it is thou that hast dishonoured it;
Thy filthie minde, orecome with filthie lusts,
Yeeldeth vnto affections filthie darts.
Vnkind, thou wrongst thy first and truest feer;
Vnkind, thou wrongst thy best and dearest friend;
Vnkind, thou scornst all skilfull *Brutus* lawes,
Forgetting father, vncle, and thy selfe.

Estr. Beleeue me, *Locrine,* but the girle is wise,
And well would seeme to make a vestall Nunne.
How finely frames she her oration!

Thra. *Locrin,* we came not here to fight with words,
Words that can neuer winne the victorie;
But for you are so merie in your frumpes,
Vnsheath your swords, and trie it out by force,
That we may see who hath the better hand.

Loc. Thinkst thou to dare me, bold *Thrasimachus?*
Thinkst thou to feare me with thy taunting braues,
Or do we seeme too weake to cope with thee?
Soone shall I shew thee my fine cutting blade,
And with my sword, the messenger of death,
Seal thee an acquitance for thy bold attempts.

[*Exeunt.*

Sound the alarme. Enter Locrine, Assaracus, *and a souldier at one doore;* Guendoline, Thrasimachus, *at an other;* Locrine *and his followers driuen back. Then let* Locrine & Estrild *enter again in a maze.*

Loc. O faire *Estrilda,* we haue lost the field;
Thrasimachus hath wonne the victorie,
And we are left to be a laughing stocke,
Scoft at by those that are our enemies.
Ten thousand souldiers, armd with sword & shield,
Preuaile against an hundreth thousand men;
Thrasimachus, incenst with fuming ire,
Rageth amongst the faintheart souldiers
Like to grim *Mars,* when couered with his targe
He fought with *Diomedes* in the field,
Close by the bankes of siluer *Simois.*

[*Sound the alarme.*

O louely *Estrild,* now the chase begins:
Ner shall we see the stately *Troynouant,*
Mounted on the coursers garnisht all with pearles;
Ner shall we view the faire *Concordia,*
Vnlesse as captiues we be thither brought.
Shall *Locrine* then be taken prisoner
By such a yoongling as *Thrasimachus?*
Shall *Guendolina* captiuate my loue?
Ner shall mine eies behold that dismall houre;
Ner will I view that ruthfull spectacle,
For with my sword, this sharpe curtleaxe,
Ile cut in sunder my accursed heart.
But O! you iudges of the ninefold *Stix,*

S. D. Habren *Q, Ff*

54 vastall *Q* 66 a quittance *S* *S. D. New scene in S, Molt.* 80 with coursers *Ff, R* : on coursers *M* 88 this] or this *R* : this sharpest *S* : this my *Molt.*

Which with incessant torments racke the ghoasts
Within the bottomlesse *Abissus* pits,
You gods, commanders of the heauenly spheres,
Whose will and lawes irreuocable stands,
Forgiue, forgiue, this foule accursed sinne!
Forget, O gods, this foule condemned fault!
And now, my sword, that in so many fights
[*kisse his sword.*
Hast sau'd the life of *Brutus* and his sonne,
End now his life that wisheth still for death;
Worke now his death that wisheth still for death;
Worke now his death that hateth still his life.
Farwell, faire *Estrild,* beauties paragon,
Fram'd in the front of forlorne miseries!
Ner shall mine eies behold thy sunshine eies,
But when we meet in the Elysian fields;
Thither I go before with hastened pace.
Farwell, vaine world, and thy inticing snares!
Farwell, foule sinne, and thy inticing pleasures!
And welcome, death, the end of mortall smart,
Welcome to *Locrines* ouerburthened hart!
[*Thrust himselfe through with his sword.*

Estr. Break, hart, with sobs and greeuous suspirs!
Streame forth, you teares, from forth my watry eies;
Helpe me to mourne for warlike *Locrines* death!
Powre downe your teares, you watry regions,
For mightie *Locrine* is bereft of life!
O fickle fortune! O vnstable world!
What else are all things that this globe containes,
But a confused chaos of mishaps,
Wherein, as in a glasse, we plainly see,
That all our life is but as a Tragedie?
Since mightie kings are subiect to mishap—
I, mightie kings are subiect to mishap!—
Since martiall *Locrine* is bereft of life,
Shall *Estrild* liue, then, after *Locrines* death?
Shall loue of life barre her from *Locrines* sword?
O no, this sword, that hath bereft his life,
Shall now depriue me of my fleeting soule:
Strengthen these hands, O mightie *Iupiter,*
That I may end my wofull miserie.
Locrine, I come; *Locrine,* I follow thee.
[*Kill her selfe.*

Sound the alarme. Enter Sabren.

Sab. What dolefull sight, what ruthful spectacle
Hath fortune offred to my haplesse hart?
My father slaine with such a fatall sword,
My mother murthred by a mortall wound?
What *Thracian* dog, what barbarous *Mirmidon,*
Would not relent at such a ruthfull case?
What fierce *Achilles,* what hard stonie flint,
Would not bemone this mournfull Tragedie?
Locrine, the map of magnanimitie,
Lies slaughtered in this foule accursed caue,
Estrild, the perfect patterne of renowne,
Natures sole wonder, in whose bewteous brests
All heauenly grace and vertue was inshrinde:
Both massacred are dead within this caue,
And with them dies faire *Pallas* and sweet loue.
Here lies a sword, and *Sabren* hath a heart;
This blessed sword shall cut my cursed heart,
And bring my soule vnto my parents ghoasts,
That they that liue and view our Tragedie
May mourne our case with mournfull plaudities.
[*Let her offer to kill her selfe.*
Ay me, my virgins hands are too too weake,
To penetrate the bullwarke of my brest;
My fingers, vsde to tune the amorous lute,
Are not of force to hold this steely glaiue.
So I am left to waile my parents death,
Not able for to worke my proper death.
Ah, *Locrine,* honord for thy noblenesse!
Ah, *Estrild,* famous for thy constancie!
Il may they fare that wrought your mortall ends!

Enter Guendoline, Thrasimachus, Madan, *and the souldiers.*

Guen. Search, souldiers, search, find *Locrin* and his loue;
Find the proud strumpet, *Humbers* concubine,
That I may change those her so pleasing lookes
To pale and ignominious aspect.
Find me the issue of their cursed loue,
Find me yoong *Sabren, Locrines* only ioy,
That I may glut my mind with lukewarme blood,
Swiftly distilling from the bastards brest.
My fathers ghoast stil haunts me for reuenge,
Crying, *Reuenge my ouerhastened death.*
My brothers exile and mine owne diuorce
Banish remorse cleane from my brazen heart,
All mercie from mine adamintine brests.

Thra. Nor doth thy husband, louely *Guendoline,*

106 hastenened *Q*   120 as *om. Ff, etc.*   122 *om. S, Haz., Molt.*

150 plaudites *F2*: plaudite *M*: plaudits *Haz.*   151 virgin *M*   154 glaine *Q* : glain *F1*   155 lieft *Q*   172 adamantiue *Q* : *corr. R*

That wonted was to guide our stailesse steps,
Enioy this light; see where he murdred lies
By lucklesse lot and froward frowning fate;
And by him lies his louely paramour,
Faire *Estrild,* goared with a dismall sword;—
And as it seemes, both murdred by themselues,
Clasping each other in their feebled armes,
With louing zeale, as if for companie
Their vncontented corpes were yet content
To passe foule *Stix* in *Charons* ferry-boat.

Guen. And hath proud *Estrild* then preuented me?
Hath she escaped *Guendolinas* wrath
Violently, by cutting off her life?
Would God she had the monstrous *Hidras* liues,
That euery houre she might haue died a death
Worse then the swing of old *Ixions* wheele;
And euery houre reuiue to die againe,
As *Titius,* bound to housles *Caucason,*
Doth feed the substance of his owne mishap,
And euery day for want of foode doth die,
And euery night doth liue, againe to die.
But staie! meethinks I heare some fainting voice,
Mournfully weeping for their lucklesse death.

Sa. You mountain nimphs, which in these desarts raign,
Cease off your hastie-chase of sauadge beasts;
Prepare to see a heart opprest with care;
Addresse your eares to heare a mournfull stile!
No humane strength, no work can work my weale,
Care in my hart so tyrant like doth deale.
You *Driades* and lightfoote *Satiri,*
You gracious Faries which, at euening tide,
Your closets leaue with heauenly beautie storde,
And on your shoulders spread your golden locks;
You sauadge beares in caues and darkened dennes,
Come waile with me the martiall *Locrines'* death;
Come mourn with me for beauteous *Estrilds* deth.
Ah! louing parents, little do you know
What sorrow *Sabren* suffers for your thrall.

Guen. But may this be, and is it possible?
Liues *Sabren* yet to expiat my wrath?
Fortune, I thanke thee for this curtesie;
And let me neuer see one prosperous houre,
If *Sabren* die not a reproachfull death.

Sab. . Hard harted death, that, when the wretched call,
Art furthest off, and sildom heerst at all;
But, in the midst of fortunes good successe,
Vncalled comes, and sheeres our life in twaine:
When wil that houre, that blessed houre, draw nie,
When poore distressed *Sabren* may be gone?
Sweet *Atropos,* cut off my fatall thred!
What art thou death? shall not poore *Sabren* die?

Guendoline (*taking her by the chin shall say thus*).

Guen. Yes, damsell, yes; *Sabren* shall surely die,
Though all the world should seeke to saue her life;
And not a common death shall *Sabren* die,
But after strange and greeuous punishments
Shortly inflicted vpon thy bastards head,
Thou shalt be cast into the cursed streames,
And feede the fishes with thy tender flesh.

Sab. And thinkst thou then, thou cruell homicid,
That these thy deeds shall be vnpunished?
No, traitor, no; the gods will venge these wrongs,
The fiends of hell will marke these iniuries.
Neuer shall these blood-sucking mastie curres,
Bring wretched *Sabren* to her latest home;
For I my selfe, in spite of thee and thine,
Meane to abridge my former destenies,
And that which *Locrines* sword could not perform,
This pleasant streame shall present bring to passe.

[*She drowneth her selfe.*

Guen. One mischiefe followes ⟨on⟩ anothers necke.
Who would haue thought so yoong a mayd as she
With such a courage wold haue sought her death?
And for because this Riuer was the place
Where little *Sabren* resolutely died,
Sabren for euer shall this same be call'd.
And as for *Locrine,* our deceased spouse,
Because he was the sonne of mightie *Brute,*
To whom we owe our country, liues and goods,
He shall be buried in a stately tombe,
Close by his aged father *Brutus* bones,
With such great pomp and great solemnitie,
As well beseemes so braue a prince as he.
Let *Estrild* lie without the shallow vaults,

186 By violently *R* 191 Tityus . . Caucasus *M* 201 no words *S* 204 You . . which] Ye . . who *S* even-tide *M* 220 com'st . . sheer'st *M* 232 thinst *Q* 236 mastiff *M, etc.* 241 This present *Ff, etc.* 242 on *add. R* 247 same] stream *conj. S* 255 vauts *Q*

Without the honour due vnto the dead,
Because she was the author of this warre.
Retire, braue followers, vnto *Troynouant,*
Where we will celebrate these exequies,
And place yoong *Locrine* in his fathers tombe.
[*Exeunt omnes.*

⟨*Enter* Ate.⟩

Ate. Lo here the end of lawlesse trecherie,
Of vsurpation and ambitious pride;
And they that for their priuate amours dare
Turmoile our land, and set their broiles abroach,
Let them be warned by these premisses.
And as a woman was the onely cause
That ciuill discord was then stirred vp,
So let vs pray for that renowned mayd,
That eight and thirtie yeares the scepter swayd,
In quiet peace and sweet felicitie;
And euery wight that seekes her graces smart,
Wold that this sword wer pierced in his hart!
[*Exit.*

FINIS.

260 yoong] your *conj. S*: king *Molt.* *S. D. add. M*

264 sce *Q*

THE

RAIGNE OF KING EDVVARD the third:

As it hath bin sundrie times plaied about the Citie of London.

LONDON,
Printed for Cuthbert Burby.
1596.

Q 1 = Quarto of 1596.
Q 2 = „ 1599
C = Capell, 1760
T = Tyrrell, 1851
D = Delius, 1854
Molt. = Moltke, 1869
Col. = Collier, 1878
WP = Warnke and Proescholdt, 1886
pr. ed. = present editor

THE RAIGNE OF K. EDWARD THE THIRD

⟨PERSONS REPRESENTED.

Edward *the third, King of* England.
Edward, *Prince of* Wales, *his Son.*
Earl of Warwick.
Earl of Derby.
Earl of Salisbury.
Lord Audley.
Lord Percy.
Lodowick, Edward's *Confident.*
Sir William Mountague.
Sir John Copland.
Two Esquires, and a Herald, English.
Robert, *stiling himself Earl, of* Artois.
Earl of Montfort, *and*
Gobin de Grey.
John, *King of France.*
Charles, *and* Philip, *his Sons.*
Duke of Lorrain.
Villiers, *a* French *Lord.*
King of Bohemia *and* / *A* Polish *Captain* } *Aids to King* John.
Six[2] *Citizens of* Calais.
A Captain, and
A poor Inhabitant, of the same.
Another Captain.
A Mariner.
Three Heralds; and
Four other Frenchmen.
David, *King of* Scotland.
Earl Douglas; *and*
Two Messengers, Scotch.

Philippa, Edward's *Queen.*
Countess of Salisbury.
A French *Woman.*

Lords, and divers other Attendants; Heralds, Officers, Soldiers, &c.

Scene, dispers'd; in England, Flanders, *and* France.⟩[1]

⟨ACT I.

SCENE I.

London. A Room of State in the Palace. Flourish.⟩

Enter King Edward, Derby, Prince Edward, Audely, *and* Artoys.

King. Robert of Artoys, banisht though thou be
From Fraunce, thy natiue Country, yet with vs
Thou shalt retayne as great a Seigniorie:
For we create thee Earle of Richmond heere.
And now goe forwards with our pedegree:
Who next succeeded Phillip le Bew?

Ar. Three sonnes of his, which all successefully
Did sit vpon their fathers regall Throne,
Yet dyed, and left no issue of their loynes.

King. But was my mother sister vnto those?

Art. Shee was, my Lord; and onely Issabel
Was all the daughters that this Phillip had,
Whome afterward your father tooke to wife;
And from the fragrant garden of her wombe
Your gratious selfe, the flower of Europes hope,
Deriued is inheritor to Fraunce.
But note the rancor of rebellious mindes:
When thus the lynage of ⟨le⟩ Bew was out,
The French obscurd your mothers Priuiledge,
And, though she were the next of blood, proclaymed
Iohn, of the house of Valoys, now their king:
The reason was, they say, the Realme of Fraunce,
Repleat with Princes of great parentage,
Ought not admit a gouernor to rule,
Except he be discended of the male;
And thats the speciall ground of their contempt,
Wherewith they study to exclude your grace:
But they shall finde that forged ground of theirs
To be but dusty heapes of brittile sande.
Perhaps it will be thought a heynous thing,
That I, a French man, should discouer this;
But heauen I call to recorde of my vowes:
It is not hate nor any priuat wronge,
But loue vnto my country and the right,
Prouokes my tongue, thus lauish in report.
You are the lyneal watchman of our peace,
And Iohn of Valoys indirectly climbes:
What then should subiects but imbrace their King?
Ah, where in may our duety more be seene,
Then stryuing to rebate a tyrants pride

[1] *Add. C* [2] Two *C* Act I. *etc. add. C* 6 le *C*: of *Qq* 7 successively *C* 17 note *Q 2*: not *Q 1* 18 of Bew *Qq*: of le beau *C* 30 Art (*Ital.*) Perhaps *Q 1*: Perhaps *Q 2, etc.* 36 watchman *C*: watch men *Qq* 39 Ah] And *conj. C*

And place the true shepheard of our comonwealth?
King. This counsayle, Artoyes, like to fruictfull shewers,
Hath added growth vnto my dignitye;
And, by the fiery vigor of thy words,
Hot courage is engendred in my brest,
Which heretofore was rakt in ignorance,
But nowe doth mount with golden winges of fame,
And will approue faire Issabells discent,
Able to yoak their stubburne necks with steele,
That spurne against my souereignety in France. [*sound a horne.*
A messenger?—Lord Awdley, know from whence.
⟨*Exit* Audley, *and returns.*⟩
Aud. The Duke of Lorrayne, hauing crost the seas,
Intreates he may haue conference with your highnes.
King. Admit him, Lords, that we may heare the newes.
⟨*Exeunt Lords. King takes his State. Re-enter Lords; with* Lorrain, *attended.*⟩
Say, Duke of Lorrayne, wherefore art thou come?
Lor. The most renowned prince, K⟨ing⟩ Iohn of France,
Doth greete thee, Edward, and by me commandes,
That, for so much as by his liberall gift
The Guyen Dukedome is entayld to thee,
Thou do him lowly homage for the same.
And, for that purpose, here I somon thee,
Repaire to France within these forty daies,
That there, according as the coustome is,
Thou mayst be sworne true liegeman to our King;
Or else thy title in that prouince dyes,
And hee him self will repossesse the place.
K. Ed. See, how occasion laughes me in the face!
No sooner minded to prepare for France,
But straight I am inuited,—nay, with threats,
Vppon a penaltie, inioynd to come:
Twere but a childish part to say him nay.—
Lorrayne, returne this answere to thy Lord:
I meane to visit him as he requests;
But how? not seruilely disposd to bend,
But like a conquerer to make him bowe.
His lame vnpolisht shifts are come to light;
And trueth hath puld the visard from his face,
That sett a glosse vpon his arrogannce.
Dare he commaund a fealty in mee?
Tell him, the Crowne that hee vsurpes, is myne,
And where he sets his foote, he ought to knele.
Tis not a petty Dukedome that I claime,
But all the whole Dominions of the Realme;
Which if with grudging he refuse to yeld,
Ile take away those borrowed plumes of his,
And send him naked to the wildernes.
Lor. Then, Edward, here, in spight of all thy Lords,
I doe pronounce defyaunce to thy face.
Pri. Defiance, French man? we rebound it backe,
Euen to the bottom of thy masters throat.
And, be it spoke with reuerence of the King,
My gratious father, and these other Lordes,
I hold thy message but as scurrylous,
And him that sent thee, like the lazy droane,
Crept vp by stelth vnto the Eagles nest;
From whence wele shake him with so rough a storme,
As others shalbe warned by his harme.
War. Byd him leaue of the Lyons case he weares,
Least, meeting with the Lyon in the feeld,
He chaunce to teare him peecemeale for his pride.
Art. The soundest counsell I can giue his grace,
Is to surrender ere he be constraynd.
A voluntarie mischiefe hath lesse scorne,
Then when reproch with violence is borne.
Lor. Degenerate Traytor, viper to the place
Where thou was fostred in thine infancy,
Bearest thou a part in this conspiracy?
[*He drawes his Sword.*
K. Ed. Lorraine, behold the sharpnes of this steele: ⟨*Drawing his.*⟩
Feruent desire that sits against my heart,
Is farre more thornie pricking than this blade;
That, with the nightingale, I shall be scard,
As oft as I dispose my selfe to rest,
Vntill my collours be displaide in Fraunce:
This is thy finall Answere; so be gone.
Lor. It is not that, nor any English braue,
Afflicts me so, as doth his poysoned view,
That is most false, should most of all be true.
⟨*Exeunt* Lorrain, *and Train.*⟩
K. Ed. Now, Lord, our fleeting Barke is vnder sayle;

S. D. Exit *etc. C*: Enter a messenger Lorragne *Qq* 54 *S. D. add. C* 64 our] the *Q 2* 71 childish] foolish *Q 2*

78 glasse *Q 1* 87 spight] sight *conj. C* 105 Degenerate *T*: Regenerate *Qq* 106 wast *Q 2* 108 *S. D. add. D* 117 *S. D. add. C* 118 lords *C*

Our gage is throwne, and warre is soone begun,
But not so quickely brought vnto an end.

Enter Mountague.

But wherefore comes Sir william Mountague?
How stands the league betweene the Scot and vs?
Mo. Crackt and disseuered, my renowned Lord.
The treacherous King no sooner was informde
Of your with drawing of your army backe,
But straight, forgetting of his former othe,
He made inuasion on the bordering Townes:
Barwicke is woon, Newcastle spoyld and lost,
And now the tyrant hath beguirt with seege
The Castle of Rocksborough, where inclosd
The Countes Salsbury is like to perish.
King. That is thy daughter, Warwicke, is it not?
Whose husband hath in Brittayne serud so long
About the planting of Lord Mouneford there?
War. It is, my Lord.
Ki. Ignoble Dauid! hast thou none to greeue
But silly Ladies with thy threatning armes?
But I will make you shrinke your snailie hornes!
First, therefore, Audley, this shalbe thy charge,
Go leuie footemen for our warres in Fraunce;
And, Ned, take muster of our men at armes:
In euery shire elect a seuerall band.
Let them be Souldiers of a lustie spirite,
Such as dread nothing but dishonors blot;
Be warie, therefore, since we do comence
A famous Warre, and with so mighty a nation.
Derby, be thou Embassador for vs
Vnto our Father in Law, the Earle of Henalt:
Make him acquainted with our enterprise,
And likewise will him, with our owne allies
That are in Flaunders, to solicite to
The Emperour of Almaigne in our name.
My selfe, whilst you are ioyntly thus employd,
Will, with these forces that I haue at hand,
March, and once more repulse the trayterous Scot.
But, Sirs, be resolute; we shal haue warres
On euery side; and, Ned, thou must begin
Now to forget thy study and thy bookes,
And vre thy shoulders to an Armors weight.
Pr. As cheereful sounding to my youthfull spleene
This tumult is of warres increasing broyles,
As, at the Coronation of a king,
The ioyfull clamours of the people are,
When *Aue, Cæsar!* they pronounce alowd.
Within this schoole of honor I shal learne
Either to sacrifice my foes to death,
Or in a rightfull quarrel spend my breath.
Then cheerefully forward, ech a seuerall way;
In great affaires tis nought to vse delay.
[*Ex*⟨*e*⟩*unt*.

⟨Scene II.

Roxborough. *Before the Castle.*⟩

Enter the Countesse.

⟨*Countesse.*⟩ Alas, how much in vaine my poore eyes gaze
For souccour that my soueraigne should send!
Ah, cosin Mountague, I feare thou wants
The liuely spirit, sharpely to solicit
With vehement sute the king in my behalfe:
Thou dost not tell him, what a griefe it is
To be the scornefull captiue to a Scot,
Either to be wooed with broad vntuned othes,
Or forst by rough insulting barbarisme:
Thou doest not tell him, if he heere preuaile,
How much they will deride vs in the North,
And, in their vild, vnseuill, skipping giggs,
Bray foorth their Conquest and our ouerthrow
Euen in the barraine, bleake, and fruitlesse aire.

Enter Dauid *and* Douglas, Lorraine.

I must withdraw, the euerlasting foe
Comes to the wall; Ile closely step aside,
And list their babble, blunt and full of pride.
K. Da. My Lord of Lorrayne, to our brother of Fraunce
Commend vs, as the man in Christendome
That we most reuerence and intirely loue.
Touching your embassage, returne and say,
That we with England will not enter parlie,
Nor neuer make faire wether, or take truce;
But burne their neighbor townes, and so persist
With eager Rods beyond their Citie Yorke.
And neuer shall our bonny riders rest,
Nor rusting canker haue the time to eate
Their light borne snaffles nor their nimble spurres,
Nor lay aside their Iacks of Gymould mayle,
Nor hang their staues of grayned Scottish ash
In peacefull wise vpon their Citie wals,
Nor from their buttoned tawny leatherne belts
Dismisse their byting whinyards, till your King

121 *Preceded by prefix* Moun. *Q 1*   125 our armie *Q 2*   146 mighty nation *C*   155 Scots *C*

Scene II. *etc. add. C*   1 *No prefix Q 1*   3 Ah] A *Q 1*   want'st *Q 2*   17 rabble *Q 2*   20 must *Q 1*   25 roads *C*   27 rusting *C*: rust in *Qq*   28 spurre *Q 1* (*B.M. copy. The Bodl. copy has only* spu)

Cry out: *Enough, spare England now for pittie!*
Farewell, and tell him that you leaue vs heare
Before this Castle; say, you came from vs,
Euen when we had that yeelded to our hands.
Lor. I take my leaue, and fayrely will returne
Your acceptable greeting to my king. [*Exit Lor.*
K. D. Now, Duglas, to our former taske again,
For the deuision of this certayne spoyle.
Dou. My liege, I craue the Ladie, and no more.
King. Nay, soft ye, sir; first I must make my choyse,
And first I do bespeake her for my selfe.
Du. Why then, my liege, let me enioy her iewels.
King. Those are her owne, still liable to her,
And who inherits her, hath those with all.

Enter a Scot in hast.

Mes. My liege, as we were pricking on the hils,
To fetch in booty, marching hitherward,
We might discry a mighty host of men;
The Sunne, reflicting on the armour, shewed
A field of plate, a wood of pickes aduanced.
Bethinke your highnes speedely herein:
An easie march within foure howres will bring
The hindmost rancke vnto this place, my liege.
King. Dislodge, dislodge! it is the king of England.
Dug. Iemmy, my man, saddle my bonny blacke.
King. Meanst thou to fight, Duglas? we are to weake.
Du. I know it well, my liege, and therefore flie.
Cou. My Lords of Scotland, will ye stay and drinke?
King. She mocks at vs, Duglas; I cannot endure it.
Count. Say, good my Lord, which is he must haue the Ladie,
And which her iewels? I am sure, my Lords,
Ye will not hence, till you haue shard the spoyles.
King. Shee heard the messenger, and heard our talke;
And now that comfort makes her scorne at vs.

Annother messenger.

Mes. Arme, my good Lord! O, we are all surprisde!
⟨*Coun.*⟩ After the French embassador, my liege,
And tell him, that you dare not ride to Yorke;
Excuse it that your bonnie horse is lame.
K. She heard that to; intollerable griefe!
Woman, farewell! Although I do not stay . . . [*Ex⟨e⟩unt Scots.*
Count. Tis not for feare, and yet you run away.—
O happie comfort, welcome to our house!
The confident and boystrous boasting Scot,
That swore before my walls they would not backe
For all the armed power of this land,
With facelesse feare that euer turnes his backe,
Turnd hence against the blasting North-east winde
Vpon the bare report and name of Armes.

Enter Mountague.

O Sommers day! See where my Cosin comes!
Mo. How fares my Aunt? We are not Scots;
Why do you shut your gates against your friends?
Co. Well may I giue a welcome, Cosin, to thee,
For thou comst well to chase my foes from hence.
Mo. The king himselfe is come in person hither;
Deare Aunt, discend, and gratulate his highnes.
Co. How may I entertayne his Maiestie,
To shew my duety and his dignitie?
⟨*Exit, from above.*⟩

Enter king Edward, Warwike, Artoyes, *with others.*

K. Ed. What, are the stealing Foxes fled and gone,
Before we could vncupple at their heeles?
War. They are, my liege; but, with a cheereful cry,
Hot hounds and hardie chase them at the heeles.

Enter Countesse.

K. Ed. This is the Countesse, Warwike, is it not?
War. Euen shee, my liege; whose beauty tyrants feare,

38 I *om.* *Q 1* 43 ye *om.* *Q 2* 45 *Prefix* Da. *Q 1* 52 pikes *Q 2, etc.* 59 flee *Q 2* 62 good *om.* *C*

68 *Prefix om.* *Qq* 71 She *C*: He *Qq* 76 they] he *conj.* *C* 79 against *conj.* *C*: againe *Qq* 80 names *Q 2* 82 *Prefix precedes* 81 *Qq* 82 we *Qq*: Why, aunt, we *C, etc.* 89 *S. D. add.* *C* 93 hunds *Q 1* 95 my *om.* *Q 1* · tyrant *D*

As a May blossome with pernitious winds,
Hath sullied, withered, ouercast, and donne.
K. Ed. Hath she been fairer, Warwike, then she is?
War. My gratious King, faire is she not at all,
If that her selfe were by to staine her selfe,
As I haue seene her when she was her selfe.
K. Ed. What strange enchantment lurkt in those her eyes,
When they exceld this excellence they haue,
That now her dym declyne hath power to draw
My subiect eyes from persing maiestie,
To gaze on her with doting admiration?
Count. In duetie lower then the ground I kneele,
And for my dul knees bow my feeling heart,
To witnes my obedience to your highnes,
With many millions of a subiects thanks
For this your Royall presence, whose approch
Hath driuen war and danger from my gate.
K. Lady, stand vp; I come to bring thee peace,
How euer thereby I haue purchast war.
Co. No war to you, my liege; the Scots are gone,
And gallop home toward Scotland with their hate.
⟨*King.*⟩ Least, yeelding heere, I pyne in shamefull loue,
Come, wole persue the Scots;—Artoyes, away!
Co. A little while, my gratious soueraigne, stay,
And let the power of a mighty king
Honor our roofe; my husband in the warres,
When he shall heare it, will triumph for ioy;
Then, deare my liege, now niggard not thy state:
Being at the wall, enter our homely gate.
King. Pardon me, countesse, I will come no neare;
I dreamde to night of treason, and I feare.
Co. Far from this place let vgly treason ly!
K. No farther off, then her conspyring eye,
Which shoots infected poyson in my heart,
Beyond repulse of wit or cure of Art.
Now, in the Sunne alone it doth not lye,
With light to take light from a mortall eye;
For here two day stars that myne eies would see
More then the Sunne steales myne owne light from mee.
Contemplatiue desire, desire to be
In contemplation, that may master thee!
Warwike, Artoys, to horse and lets away!
Co. What might I speake to make my soueraigne stay?
King. What needs a tongue to such a speaking eie,
That more perswads then winning Oratorie?
Co. Let not thy presence, like the Aprill sunne,
Flatter our earth and sodenly be done.
More happie do not make our outward wall
Then thou wilt grace our inner house withall.
Our house, my liege, is like a Country swaine,
Whose habit rude and manners blunt and playne
Presageth nought, yet inly beautified
With bounties, riches and faire hidden pride.
For where the golden Ore doth buried lie,
The ground, vndect with natures tapestrie,
Seemes barrayne, sere, vnfertill, fructles, dry;
And where the vpper turfe of earth doth boast
His pide perfumes and party colloured cost,
Delue there, and find this issue and their pride
To spring from ordure and corruptions side.
But, to make vp my all to long compare,
These ragged walles no testimonie are,
What is within; but, like a cloake, doth hide
From weathers Waste the vnder garnisht pride.
More gratious then my tearmes can let thee be,
Intreat thy selfe to stay a while with mee.
Kin. As wise, as faire; what fond fit can be heard,
When wisedome keepes the gate as beuties gard?—
Countesse, albeit my busines vrgeth me,
Yt shall attend, while I attend on thee:
Come on, my Lords; heere will I host to night.
[*Exeunt.*

⟨ACT II.

Scene I.

The Same. Gardens of the Castle.

Enter Lodowick.⟩

Lod. I might perceiue his eye in her eye lost,
His eare to drinke her sweet tongues vtterance,
And changing passion, like inconstant clouds
That racke vpon the carriage of the windes,
Increase and die in his disturbed cheekes.
Loe, when shee blusht, euen then did he looke pale,
As if her cheekes by some inchaunted power

102 lurke *Q 1* 104 her] their *conj. C* 116 hate] haste *C* 117 *Prefix om. Q 1* 133 two] to *Q 1* 153 pide *conj. C*: pride *Qq*: proud *C* presumes *Q 2* 157 testomie *Q 1* 159 waste *D*: West *Qq* Act II. *etc. add. C* 1 *Prefix* Lor. *Q 1* 4 rackt *Q 2, etc.*

Attracted had the cherie blood from his:
Anone, with reuerent feare when she grew pale,
His cheekes put on their scarlet ornaments;
But no more like her oryentall red,
Then Bricke to Corrall or liue things to dead.
Why did he then thus counterfeit her lookes?
If she did blush, twas tender modest shame,
Being in the sacred presence of a King;
If he did blush, twas red immodest shame,
To vaile his eyes amisse, being a king:
If she lookt pale, twas silly womans feare,
To beare her selfe in presence of a king;
If he lookt pale, it was with guiltie feare,
To dote amisse, being a mighty king.
Then, Scottish warres, farewell; I feare twill prooue
A lingring English seege of peeuish loue.
Here comes his highnes, walking all alone.

Enter King Edward.

King. Shee is growne more fairer far since I came hither,
Her voice more siluer euery word then other,
Her wit more fluent. What a strange discourse
Vnfolded she of Dauid and his Scots!
'Euen thus', quoth she, 'he spake', and then spoke broad,
With epithites and accents of the Scot,
But somewhat better then the Scot could speake:
'And thus', quoth she, and answered then her selfe—
For who could speake like her but she her selfe—
Breathes from the wall an Angels note from Heauen
Of sweete defiance to her barbarous foes.
When she would talke of peace, me thinkes, her tong
Commanded war to prison; when of war,
It wakened Cæsar from his Romane graue,
To heare warre beautified by her discourse.
Wisedome is foolishnes but in her tongue,
Beauty a slander but in her faire face,
There is no summer but in her cheerefull lookes,
Nor frosty winter but in her disdayne.
I cannot blame the Scots that did besiege her,
For she is all the Treasure of our land;
But call them cowards, that they ran away,
Hauing so rich and faire a cause to stay.—
Art thou there, Lodwicke? Giue me incke and paper.

Lo. I will, my liege.

K. And bid the Lords hold on their play at Chesse,
For wee will walke and meditate alone.

Lo. I will, my soueraigne. ⟨*Exit* Lodowick.⟩

Ki. This fellow is well read in poetrie,
And hath a lustie and perswasiue spirite:
I will acquaint him with my passion,
Which he shall shadow with a vaile of lawne,
Through which the Queene of beauties Queene shall see
Her selfe the ground of my infirmitie.

Enter Lodwike.

Ki. Hast thou pen, inke, and paper ready, Lodowike?

Lo. Ready, my liege.

Ki. Then in the sommer arber sit by me,
Make it our counsel house or cabynet:
Since greene our thoughts, greene be the conuenticle,
Where we will ease vs by disburdning them.
Now, Lodwike, inuocate some golden Muse,
To bring thee hither an inchanted pen,
That may for sighes set downe true sighes indeed,
Talking of griefe, to make thee ready grone;
And when thou writest of teares, encouch the word
Before and after with such sweete laments,
That it may rayse drops in a Tarters eye,
And make a flyntheart Sythian pytifull;
For so much moouing hath a Poets pen:
Then, if thou be a Poet, moue thou so,
And be enriched by thy soueraignes loue.
For, if the touch of sweet concordant strings
Could force attendance in the eares of hel,
How much more shall the straines of poets wit
Beguile and rauish soft and humane myndes?

Lod. To whome, my Lord, shal I direct my stile?

King. To one that shames the faire and sots the wise;
Whose bodie is an abstract or a breefe,
Containes ech generall vertue in the worlde.
Better then bewtifull thou must begin,
Deuise for faire a fairer word then faire,
And euery ornament that thou wouldest praise,
Fly it a pitch aboue the soare of praise.
For flattery feare thou not to be conuicted;
For, were thy admiration ten tymes more,
Ten tymes ten thousand more the worth exceeds

10 cheeke *Qq* 11 oryent all *Q 1* 15 present *Q 1* 17 vail *C*: waile *Qq* 25 thither *Q 1* 29 spoke] spake *Q 2*

49 soueraigne *Q 2* 52 liege *Q 2* *S. D. add. C* 53 well *om. Q 2* 57 beauties Queenes *WP* 71 Torters *Qq* 75 soueraigne *Q 1* 78 straine *Q 2* 79 beguild *Q 1* 80 *Prefix* Lor. *Q 1* 82 is] as *C, etc.* 90 the] thy *Q 1*

Of that thou art to praise, thy praises worth.
Beginne; I will to contemplat the while:
Forget not to set downe, how passionat,
How hart sicke, and how full of languishment,
Her beautie makes mee.
Lod. Write I to a woman?
King. What bewtie els could triumph ouer me,
Or who but women doe our loue layes greet?
What, thinkest thou I did bid thee praise a horse?
Lod. Of what condicion or estate she is,
Twere requisit that I should know, my Lord.
King. Of such estate, that hers is as a throane,
And my estate the footstoole where shee treads:
Then maist thou iudge what her condition is
By the proportion of her mightines.
Write on, while I peruse her in my thoughts.—
Her voice to musicke or the nightingale—
To musicke euery sommer leaping swaine
Compares his sunburnt louer when shee speakes;
And why should I speake of the nightingale?
The nightingale singes of adulterate wrong,
And that, compared, is to satyrical;
For sinne, though synne, would not be so esteemd,
But, rather, vertue sin, synne vertue deemd.
Her hair, far softor then the silke wormes twist,
Like to a flattering glas, doth make more faire
The yelow Amber:—*like a flattering glas*
Comes in to soone; for, writing of her eies,
Ile say that like a glas they catch the sunne,
And thence the hot reflection doth rebounde
Against my brest, and burnes my hart within.
Ah, what a world of descant makes my soule
Vpon this voluntarie ground of loue!—
Come, Lodwick, hast thou turnd thy inke to golde?
If not, write but in letters Capitall
My mistres name, and it wil guild thy paper:
Read, Lorde, reade;
Fill thou the emptie hollowes of mine eares
With the sweete hearing of thy poetrie.
Lo. I haue not to a period brought her praise.
King. Her praise is as my loue, both infinit,
Which apprehend such violent extremes,
That they disdaine an ending period.
Her bewtie hath no match but my affection;
Hers more then most, myne most and more then more:
Hers more to praise then tell the sea by drops,
Nay, more then drop the massie earth by sands,
And sand by sand print them in memorie:
Then wherefore talkest thou of a period
To that which craues vnended admiration?
Read, let vs heare.
Lo. 'More faire and chast then is the queen of shades,'—
King. That line hath two falts, grosse and palpable:
Comparest thou her to the pale queene of night,
Who, being set in darke, seemes therefore light?
What is she, when the sunne lifts vp his head,
But like a fading taper, dym and dead?
My loue shall braue the ey of heauen at noon,
And, being vnmaskt, outshine the golden sun.
Lo. What is the other faulte, my soueraigne Lord?
King. Reade ore the line againe.
Lo. 'More faire and chast'—
King. I did not bid thee talke of chastitie,
To ransack so the treasure of her minde;
For I had rather haue her chased then chast.
Out with the moone line, I wil none of it;
And let me haue hir likened to the sun:
Say shee hath thrice more splendour then the sun,
That her perfections emulats the sunne,
That shee breeds sweets as plenteous as the sunne,
That shee doth thaw cold winter like the sunne,
That she doth cheere fresh sommer like the sunne,
That shee doth dazle gazers like the sunne;
And, in this application to the sunne,
Bid her be free and generall as the sunne,
Who smiles vpon the basest weed that growes
As louinglie as on the fragrant rose.
Lets see what followes that same moonelight line.
Lo. 'More faire and chast then is the queen of shades,
More bould in constancie'—
King. In constancie! then who?
Lo. 'Then Iudith was.'
King. O monstrous line! Put in the next a sword,

91 thy *C*: their *Qq* 95 *Prefix* Lor. *Q 1* Writ *Q 1* a *om. Q 2* 96 ouer *Q 2*: on *Q 1* 99 *Prefix* Lor. *Q 1* 106 *A line may have been lost after* 105 111 ? that compare is 115 to] as *Q 2* 124–6 *Two lines Qq, div. after* name: *C ends* capital, name, read

137 And said, by said *Qq*: *corr. C* 142 line] loue *Q 1* 152 treasure *C*: treason *Qq* 167 queen *C*: louer *Qq*

And I shall woo her to cut of my head.
Blot, blot, good Lodwicke! Let vs heare the next.
Lo. Theres all that yet is donne.
King. I thancke thee then; thou hast don litle ill,
But what is don, is passing, passing ill.
No, let the Captaine talke of boystrous warr,
The prisoner of emured darke constraint,
The sick man best sets downe the pangs of death,
The man that starues the sweetnes of a feast,
The frozen soule the benefite of fire,
And euery griefe his happie opposite:
Loue cannot sound well but in louers toungs;
Giue me the pen and paper, I will write.

Enter Countes.

But soft, here comes the treasurer of my spirit.—
Lodwick, thou knowst not how to drawe a battell;
These wings, these flankars, and these squadrons
Argue in thee defectiue discipline:
Thou shouldest haue placed this here, this other here.
Co. Pardon my boldnes, my thrice gracious Lords;
Let my intrusion here be cald my duetie,
That comes to see my soueraigne how he fares.
Kin. Go, draw the same, I tell thee in what forme.
Lod. I go. ⟨*Exit* Lodowick.⟩
Cou. Sorry I am to see my liege so sad:
What may thy subiect do to driue from thee
Thy gloomy consort, sullome melancholie?
King. Ah, Lady, I am blunt and cannot strawe
The flowers of solace in a ground of shame:—
Since I came hither, Countes, I am wronged.
Cont. Now God forbid that anie in my howse
Should thinck my soueraigne wrong! Thrice gentle King,
Acquaint me with your cause of discontent.
King. How neere then shall I be to remedie?
Cont. As nere, my Liege, as all my womans power
Can pawne it selfe to buy thy remedy.
King. Yf thou speakst true, then haue I my redresse:
Ingage thy power to redeeme my Ioyes,
And I am ioyfull, Countes; els I die.
Coun. I will, my Liege.
King. Sweare, Counties, that thou wilt.
Coun. By heauen, I will.
King. Then take thy selfe a litel waie a side,
And tell thy self, a King doth dote on thee:
Say that within thy power ⟨it⟩ doth lie
To make him happy, and that thou hast sworne
To giue him all the Ioy within thy power:
Do this, and tell me when I shall be happie.
Coun. All this is done, my thrice dread soueraigne:
That power of loue, that I haue power to giue,
Thou hast with all deuout obedience;
Inploy me how thou wilt in profe therof.
King. Thou hearst me saye that I do dote on thee.
Coun. Yf on my beauty, take yt if thou canst;
Though litle, I do prise it ten tymes lesse:
If on my vertue, take it if thou canst,
For vertues store by giuing doth augment:
Be it on what it will, that I can giue
And thou canst take awaie, inherit it.
King. It is thy beautie that I woulde enioy.
Count. O, were it painted, I would wipe it of
And dispossesse my selfe, to giue it thee.
But, souereigne, it is souldered to my life:
Take one and both; for, like an humble shaddow,
Yt hauntes the sunshine of my summers life.
⟨*King.*⟩ But thou maist lend it me to sport with all.
Count. As easie may my intellectual soule
Be lent awaie, and yet my bodie liue,
As lend my bodie, pallace to my soule,
Awaie from her, and yet retaine my soule.
My bodie is her bower, her Court, her abey,
And shee an Angell, pure, deuine, vnspotted:
If I should leaue her house, my Lord, to thee,
I kill my poore soule and my poore soule me.
King. Didst thou not swere to giue me what I would?
Count. I did, my liege, so what you would I could.
King. I wish no more of thee then thou maist giue:—

177 immured *C* 184 treasure *Q 2* 186 squadrons here *C* 189 lord *C* 193 *Prefix* Lor. *Q 1* *S. D. add. C* 196 Thy] This *Q 2* 202 your] theyr *Q 1* 203 *Prefix* King *precedes* 202 *in Q 1*

213 it *add. C* 214 that *om. Q 2* 215 him] me *C* 228 beauie *Q 1* 230 disposse *Q 1* 234 *Prefix add. Q 2* lend *Q 2*: leue *Q 1* 241 leaue *Q 1*: lend *Q 2*

Nor beg I do not, but I rather buie—
That is, thy loue; and for that loue of thine
In rich exchaunge I tender to thee myne.
Count. But that your lippes were sacred, my Lord,
You would prophane the holie name of loue.
That loue you offer me you cannot giue,
For Cæsar owes that tribut to his Queene;
That loue you beg of me I cannot giue,
For Sara owes that duetie to her Lord.
He that doth clip or counterfeit your stamp
Shall die, my Lord; and will your sacred selfe
Comit high treason against the King of heauen,
To stamp his Image in forbidden mettel,
Forgetting your alleageance and your othe?
In violating mariage sacred law,
You breake a greater honor then your selfe:
To be a King is of a yonger house
Then to be maried; your progenitour,
Sole ragning Adam on the vniuerse,
By God was honored for a married man,
But not by him annointed for a king.
It is a pennalty to breake your statutes,
Though not enacted with your highnes hand:
How much more, to infringe the holy act,
Made by the mouth of God, seald with his hand?
I know, my souereigne, in my husbands loue,
Who now doth loyall seruice in his warrs,
Doth but so try the wife of Salisbury,
Whither shee will heare a wantons tale or no,
Lest being therein giulty by my stay,
From that, not from my leige, I tourne awaie. [*Exit.*
King. Whether is her bewtie by her words dyuine,
Or are her words sweet chaplaines to her bewtie?
Like as the wind doth beautifie a saile,
And as a saile becomes the vnseene winde,
So doe her words her bewties, bewties wordes.
O, that I were a honie gathering bee,
To beare the combe of vertue from this flower,
And not a poison sucking enuious spider,
To turne the iuce I take to deadlie venom!
Religion is austere and bewty gentle;
To strict a gardion for so faire a ward!
O, that shee were, as is the aire, to mee!
Why, so she is, for when I would embrace her,
This do I, and catch nothing but my selfe.
I must enioy her; for I cannot beate
With reason and reproofe fond loue a waie.

Enter Warwicke.

Here comes her father: I will worke with him,
To beare my collours in this feild of loue.
War. How is it that my souereigne is so sad?
May I with pardon know your highnes griefe;
And that my old endeuor will remoue it,
It shall not comber long your maiestie.
King. A kind and voluntary gift thou proferest,
That I was forwarde to haue begd of thee.
But, O thou world, great nurse of flatterie,
Whie dost thou tip mens tongues with golden words,
And peise their deedes with weight of heauie leade,
That faire performance cannot follow promise?
O, that a man might hold the hartes close booke
And choke the lauish tongue, when it doth vtter
The breath of falshood not carectred there!
War. Far be it from the honor of my age,
That I should owe bright gould and render lead;
Age is a cynicke, not a flatterer.
I saye againe, that if I knew your griefe,
And that by me it may be lesned,
My proper harme should buy your highnes good.
Kin. These are the vulger tenders of false men,
That neuer pay the duetie of their words.
Thou wilt not sticke to sweare what thou hast said;
But, when thou knowest my greifes condition,
This rash disgorged vomit of thy word
Thou wilt eate vp againe, and leaue me helples.
War. By heauen, I will not, though your maiestie
Did byd me run vpon your sworde and die.
⟨*Kin.*⟩ Say that my greefe is no way medicinable
But by the losse and bruising of thine honour.
War. Yf nothing but that losse may vantage you,
I would accompt that losse my vauntage to.
King. Thinkst that thou canst unswere thy oth againe?
War. I cannot; nor I would not, if I could.
King. But, if thou dost, what shal I say to thee?

249 my] O my *C* 260 secred *Q 1* 268 with] by *C* 273 so *pr. ed.*: to *Qq, etc.* 281 bewties, bewtie *Q 1*: beauty, beauty *C* 283 this *C*: his *Qq* 285 iuce *Col.*: vice *Qq, C* 287 Too strict *Q 2*: To stricke *Q 1* ward *C*: weed *Qq*

299 offerest *Q 2* 310 cyncke *Q 1* 311 if I] I if *Q 1* 314 *Prefix* Kin. *precedes* 316 *Qq* 322 *Prefix om. Q 1* 325 account *Q 2*: accomplish *Q 1* 326 unswere *WP*: unswear *C*: answere *Qq*

War. What may be said to anie periurd villane,
That breake⟨s⟩ the sacred warrant of an oath.
King. What wilt thou say to one that breaks an othe?
War. That hee hath broke his faith with God and man,
And from them both standes excommunicat.
King. What office were it, to suggest a man
To breake a lawfull and religious vowe?
War. An office for the deuill, not for man.
Ki. That deuilles office must thou do for me,
Or breake thy oth, or cancell all the bondes
Of loue and duetie twixt thy self and mee;
And therefore, Warwike, if thou art thy selfe,
The Lord and master of thy word and othe,
Go to thy daughter; and in my behalfe
Comaund her, woo her, win her anie waies,
To be my mistres and my secret loue.
I will not stand to heare thee make reply:
Thy oth breake hers, or let thy souereigne dye. [*Exit.*
War. O doting King! O detestable office!
Well may I tempt my self to wrong my self,
When he hath sworne me by the name of God
To breake a vowe made by the name of God.
What, if I sweare by this right hand of mine
To cut this right hande of? The better waie
Were to prophaine the Idoll then confound it:
But neither will I do; Ile keepe myne oath,
And to my daughter make a recantation
Of all the vertue I haue preacht to her:
Ile say, she must forget her husband Salisbury,
If she remember to embrace the king;
Ile say, an othe may easily be broken,
But not so easily pardoned, being broken;
Ile say, it is true charitie to loue,
But not true loue to be so charitable;
Ile say, his greatnes may beare out the shame,
But not his kingdome can buy out the sinne;
Ile say, it is my duety to perswade,
But not her honestie to giue consent.

Enter Countesse.

See where she comes; was neuer father had
Against his child an embassage so bad!
Co. My Lord and father, I haue sought for you:
My mother and the Peeres importune you
To keepe in presence of his maiestie,
And do your best to make his highnes merrie.
War. ⟨*Aside.*⟩ How shall I enter in this gracelesse arrant?
I must not call her child, for wheres the father
That will in such a sute seduce his child?
Then, 'wife of Salisbury'; shall I so begin?
No, hees my friend, and where is found the friend
That will doe friendship such indammagement?
⟨*To the Count.*⟩ Neither my daughter nor my deare friends wife,
I am not Warwike, as thou thinkst I am,
But an atturnie from the Court of hell,
That thus haue housd my spirite in his forme,
To do a message to thee from the king.
The mighty king of England dotes on thee:
He that hath power to take away thy life,
Hath power to take thy honor; then consent
To pawne thine honor rather then thy life:
Honor is often lost and got againe,
But life, once gon, hath no recouerie.
The Sunne, that withers heye, doth nourish grasse;
The king, that would distaine thee, will aduance thee.
The Poets write that great Achilles speare
Could heale the wound it made: the morrall is,
What mighty men misdoo, they can amend.
The Lyon doth become his bloody iawes,
And grace his forragement by being milde,
When vassell feare lies trembling at his feete.
The king will in his glory hide thy shame;
And those that gaze on him to finde out thee,
Will loose their eie-sight, looking in the Sunne.
What can one drop of poyson harme the Sea,
Whose hugie vastures can digest the ill
And make it loose his operation?
The kings great name will temper thy misdeeds,
And giue the bitter potion of reproch
A sugred, sweet and most delitious tast.
Besides, it is no harme to do the thing
Which without shame could not be left vndone.
Thus haue I in his maiesties behalfe
Apparaled sin in vertuous sentences,
And dwel vpon thy answere in his sute.
Cou. Vnnaturall beseege! woe me vnhappie,
To haue escapt the danger of my foes,
And to be ten times worse inuierd by friends!
Hath he no meanes to stayne my honest blood,
But to corrupt the author of my blood
To be his scandalous and vile soliciter?
No maruell though the braunches be then infected,
When poyson hath encompassed the roote:
No maruell though the leprous infant dye,

330 breaks *Q 2*: breake *Q 1* 338 and cancell *WP* 347 *Prefix* War. *Q 2*: King *Q 1* King, or *Qq* 371 presence *Q 2*: promise *Q 1* 373 *S. D. add. WP* 379 *S. D. add. WP* 390 doth] goth *Q 1* 404 thy *C*: their *Qq* 405 portion *Q 1* 414 iniured *WP*: inwir'd *D*

When the sterne dame inuennometh the Dug.
Why then, giue sinne a pasport to offend,
And youth the dangerous reigne of liberty:
Blot out the strict forbidding of the law,
And cancell euery cannon that prescribes
A shame for shame or pennance for offence.
No, let me die, if his too boystrous will
Will haue it so, before I will consent
To be an actor in his gracelesse lust.

Wa. Why, now thou speakst as I would haue thee speake:
And marke how I vnsaie my words againe.
An honorable graue is more esteemd
Then the polluted closet of a king:
The greater man, the greater is the thing,
Be it good or bad, that he shall vndertake:
An vnreputed mote, flying in the Sunne,
Presents a greater substaunce then it is:
The freshest summers day doth soonest taint
The lothed carrion that it seemes to kisse:
Deepe are the blowes made with a mightie Axe:
That sinne doth ten times agreuate it selfe,
That is committed in a holie place:
An euill deed, done by authoritie,
Is sin and subbornation: Decke an Ape
In tissue, and the beautie of the robe
Adds but the greater scorne vnto the beast.
A spatious field of reasons could I vrge
Betweene his glorie, daughter, and thy shame:
That poyson shewes worst in a golden cup;
Darke night seemes darker by the lightning flash;
Lillies that fester smel far worse then weeds;
And euery glory that inclynes to sin,
The shame is treble by the opposite.
So leaue I with my blessing in thy bosome,
Which then conuert to a most heauie curse,
When thou conuertest from honors golden name
To the blacke faction of bed blotting shame.

Coun. Ile follow thee; and when my minde turnes so,
My body sinke my soule in endles woo!
[*Exeunt.*

⟨Scene II.

The Same. A Room in the Castle.⟩

Enter at one doore Derby *from Fraunce, At an other doore* Audley *with a Drum.*

Der. Thrice noble Audley, well incountred heere!
How is it with our soueraigne and his peeres?

Aud. Tis full a fortnight, since I saw his highnes,
What time he sent me forth to muster men;
Which I accordingly haue done, and bring them hither
In faire aray before his maiestie.
What newes, my Lord of Derby, from the Emperor?

Der. As good as we desire: the Emperor
Hath yeelded to his highnes friendly ayd,
And makes our king leiuetenant generall
In all his lands and large dominions:
Then *via* for the spatious bounds of Fraunce!

Aud. What, doth his highnes leap to heare these newes?

Der. I haue not yet found time to open them;
The king is in his closet, malcontent;
For what, I know not, but he gaue in charge,
Till after dinner none should interrupt him:
The Countesse Salisbury and her father Warwike,
Artoyes and all looke vnderneath the browes.

Aud. Vndoubtedly, then, some thing is a misse. ⟨*Trumpet within.*⟩

Dar. The Trumpets sound, the king is now abroad.

Enter the King.

Aud. Here comes his highnes.

Der. Befall my soueraigne all my soueraignes wish!

King. Ah, that thou wert a Witch to make it so!

Der. The Emperour greeteth you. ⟨*presenting Letters.*⟩

Kin. —Would it were the Countesse!

Der. And hath accorded to your highnes suite.

King. —Thou lyest, she hath not; but I would she had.

Au. All loue and duety to my Lord the King!

Kin. Well, all but one is none.—What newes with you?

Au. I haue, my liege, leuied those horse and foote
According to your charge, and brought them hither.

Kin. Then let those foote trudge hence vpon those horse
According too our discharge, and be gonne.—
Darby, Ile looke vpon the Countesse minde anone.

Dar. The Countesse minde, my liege?

Kin. I meane the Emperour:—leaue me alone.

448 glory *C*: gloomie *Q 1* 458 Ils *Q 1* Scene II. *etc. add. C*

5 hither *om. C* 7 *Prefix* King *before this line in Q 1* 13 these] this *Q 2* 20, 25 *S. DD. add. C* 21 *S. D. follows* 20 *in Qq* 22 Ar. (*Ital.*) Hhere *Q 1* 32 to *Q 2*: as *Q 1*

Au. What is his mind?
Dar. Lets leaue him to his humor. [*Ex⟨e⟩unt.*
Ki. Thus from the harts aboundance speakes the tongue;
Countesse for Emperour: and indeed, why not?
She is as imperator ouer me
And I to her
Am as a kneeling vassaile, that obserues
The pleasure or displeasure of her eye.

Enter Lodwike.

Ki. What saies the more then Cleopatras match
To Cæsar now?
Lo. That yet, my liege, ere night
She will resolue your maiestie. ⟨*Drum within.*⟩
Ki. What drum is this that thunders forth this march,
To start the tender Cupid in my bosome?
Poore shipskin, how it braules with him that beateth it!
Go, breake the thundring parchment bottome out,
And I will teach it to conduct sweete lynes
Vnto the bosome of a heauenly Nymph;
For I will vse it as my writing paper,
And so reduce him from a scoulding drum
To be the herald and deare counsaile bearer
Betwixt a goddesse and a mighty king.
Go, bid the drummer learne to touch the Lute,
Or hang him in the braces of his drum,
For now we thinke it an vnciuill thing,
To trouble heauen with such harsh resounds:
Away! [*Exit.*
The quarrell that I haue requires no armes
But these of myne: and these shall meete my foe
In a deepe march of penytrable grones;
My eyes shall be my arrowes, and my sighes
Shall serue me as the vantage of the winde,
To wherle away my sweetest artyllerie.
Ah, but, alas, she winnes the sunne of me,
For that is she her selfe, and thence it comes
That Poets tearme the wanton warriour blinde;
But loue hath eyes as iudgement to his steps,
Till too much loued glory dazles them.—

Enter. Lodwike.

How now?
Lo. My liege, the drum that stroke the lusty march,
Stands with Prince Edward, your thrice valiant sonne.

Enter Prince Edward.

King. I see the boy; oh, how his mothers face,
Modeld in his, corrects my straid desire,
And rates my heart, and chides my theeuish eie,
Who, being rich ennough in seeing her,
Yet seekes elsewhere: and basest theft is that
Which cannot cloke it selfe on pouertie.—
Now, boy, what newes?
Pr. E. I haue assembled, my deare Lord and father,
The choysest buds of all our English blood
For our affaires in Fraunce; and heere we come
To take direction from your maiestie.
Kin. Still do I see in him deliniate
His mothers visage; those his eies are hers,
Who, looking wistely on me, make me blush:
For faults against themselues giue euidence;
Lust is a fire, and men like lanthornes show
Light lust within them selues, euen through them selues.
Away, loose silkes of wauering vanitie!
Shall the large limmit of faire Brittaynė
By me be ouerthrowne, and shall I not
Master this little mansion of my selfe?
Giue me an Armor of eternall steele!
I go to conquer kings; and shall I not then
Subdue my selfe? and be my enimies friend?
It must not be.—Come, boy, forward, aduaunce!
Lets with our coullours sweete the Aire of Fraunce.

Enter Lodwike.

Lo. My liege, the Countesse with a smiling cheere
Desires accesse vnto your Maiestie.
King. Why, there it goes! That verie smile of hers
Hath ransomed captiue Fraunce, and set the King,
The Dolphin, and the Peeres at liberty.—
Goe, leaue me, Ned, and reuell with thy friends. [*Exit* Pr.
Thy mother is but blacke, and thou, like her,
Dost put it in my minde how foule she is.—
Goe, fetch the Countesse hether in thy hand,
And let her chase away these winter clouds,

38 is *Q 1*: is in *Q 2, etc.* 39 abundance *Col.*: aboundant *Qq* 41, 42 *One line in Qq* 47 *S. D. add. C* 56 counsaiie *Q 1* 61 wrth *Q 1* *Line ends* Away *Qq* 73 too *Q 2*: two *Q 1* *S. D. after* 74 *Qq*

78 Molded *Q 2* 82 cloke] check *C* 86 in *Q 2*: to *Q 1* 90 made *Q 2* 92 is *C*: as *Qq* men *C*: me *Qq* lanthorne *Qq* 94 of *Q 2*: or *Q 1* 95 Britany *Q 2* 99 not *om. C, etc.* 102 sweep *C*: beat *D* 112 those *Q 2*

For shee giues beautie both to heauen and earth. [*Exit* Lod.
The sin is more to hacke and hew poore men,
Then to embrace in an vnlawfull bed
The register of all rarieties
Since Letherne Adam till this youngest howre.
Enter Countesse ⟨*escorted by* Lodwike⟩.
King. Goe, Lodwike, put thy hand into my purse,
Play, spend, giue, ryot, wast, do what thou wilt,
So thou wilt hence awhile and leaue me heere.
⟨*Exit* Lodowick.⟩
Now, my soules plaiefellow, art thou come
To speake the more then heauenly word of yea
To my obiection in thy beautious loue?
Count. My father on his blessing hath commanded—
King. That thou shalt yeeld to me?
Coun. I, deare my liege, your due.
King. And that, my dearest loue, can be no lesse
Then right for right and tender loue for loue.
Count. Then wrong for wrong and endles hate for hate.—
But,—sith I see your maiestie so bent,
That my vnwillingnes, my husbands loue,
Your high estate, nor no respect respected
Can be my helpe, but that your mightines
Will ouerbeare and awe these deare regards—
I bynd my discontent to my content,
And what I would not Ile compell I will,
Prouided that your selfe remoue those lets
That stand betweene your highnes loue and mine.
King. Name them, faire Countesse, and, by heauen, I will.
Co. It is their liues that stand betweene our loue,
That I would haue chokt vp, my soueraigne.
Ki. Whose liues, my Lady?
Co. My thrice louing liege,
Your Queene and Salisbury, my wedded husband,
Who liuing haue that tytle in our loue,
That we cannot bestow but by their death.
Ki. Thy opposition is beyond our Law.
Co. So is your desire: if the law
Can hinder you to execute the one,
Let it forbid you to attempt the other.
I Cannot thinke you loue me as you say,
Vnlesse you do make good what you haue sworne.
⟨*King.*⟩ No more; thy husband and the Queene shall dye.
Fairer thou art by farre then Hero was,
Beardles Leander not so strong as I:
He swome an easie curraunt for his loue,
But I will through a Hellespont of bloud,
To arryue at Cestus where my Hero lyes.
Co. Nay, youle do more; youle make the Ryuer to
With their hart bloods that keepe our loue asunder,
Of which my husband and your wife are twayne.
Ki. Thy beauty makes them guilty of their death
And giues in euidence that they shall dye;
Vpon which verdict I, their Iudge, condemne them.
Co. ⟨*Aside.*⟩ O periurde beautie, more corrupted Iudge!
When to the great Starre-chamber ore our heads
The vniuersell Sessions cals to count
This packing euill, we both shall tremble for it.
Ki. What saies my faire loue? is she resolute?
Co. Resolute to be dissolude; and, therefore, this:
Keepe but thy word, great king, and I am thine.
Stand where thou dost, ile part a little from thee,
And see how I will yeeld me to thy hands.
⟨*turning suddenly upon him, and shewing two Daggers.*⟩
Here by my side doth hang my wedding knifes:
Take thou the one, and with it kill thy Queene,
And learne by me to finde her where she lies;
And with this other Ile dispatch my loue,
Which now lies fast a sleepe within my hart:
When they are gone, then Ile consent to loue.
Stir not, lasciuious king, to hinder me;
My resolution is more nimbler far,
Then thy preuention can be in my rescue,
And if thou stir, I strike; therefore, stand still,
And heare the choyce that I will put thee to:
Either sweare to leaue thy most vnholie sute
And neuer hence forth to solicit me;
Or else, by heauen, this sharpe poynted knyfe

113 *S. D. after* 111 *Qq* 116 varieties *Col.* 118 my *C*: thy *Qq* 120 *S. D. add. C* 121 art] and art *C* 123 subjection *D* 128 tender *C*: render *Qq* 139 them *C*: then *Qq* 142 loning *Q 1* 147 And so *C*

152 *Prefix om. Q 1* 156 through *Q 2*: throng *Q 1* Hellespont *conj. T*: hellie spout *Qq* 157 To *om. C.* at] that *C* 164 *S. D. add. WP* 168 resolude *WP* 169 Resolv'd *conj. C*: Resolude *WP* *S. D. add. C* 176 this] the *Q 2*

Shall staine thy earth with that which thou would staine,
My poore chast blood. Sweare, Edward, sweare,
Or I will strike and die before thee heere.
King. Euen by that power I sweare, that giues me now
The power to be ashamed of my selfe,
I neuer meane to part my lips againe
In any words that tends to such a sute.
Arise, true English Ladie, whom our Ile
May better boast of then euer Romaine might
Of her, whose ransackt treasurie hath taskt
The vaine indeuor of so many pens:
Arise; and be my fault thy honors fame,
Which after ages shall enrich thee with.
I am awaked from this idle dreame.—
Warwike, my Sonne, Darby, Artoys, and Audley!
Braue warriours all, where are you all this while?

Enter all.

Warwike, I make thee Warden of the North:
Thou, Prince of Wales, and Audley, straight to Sea;
Scoure to New-hauen; some there staie for me:
My selfe, Artoys, and Darby will through Flaunders,
To greete our friends there and to craue their aide.
This night will scarce suffice me to discouer
My follies seege against a faithfull louer;
For, ere the Sunne shal guilde the esterne skie,
Wele wake him with our Marshall harmonie.
[*Exeunt.*

⟨ACT III.

SCENE I.

Flanders. *The* French *Camp.*⟩

Enter King Iohn of Fraunce, *his two sonnes,* Charles of Normandie, *and* Phillip, *and the* Duke of Lorraine.

King Iohn. Heere, till our Nauie of a thousand saile
Haue made a breakfast to our foe by Sea,
Let vs incampe, to wait their happie speede.—
Lorraine, what readines is Edward in?
How hast thou heard that he prouided is
Of marshiall furniture for this exployt?
Lo. To lay aside vnnecessary soothing,
And not to spend the time in circumstaunce,
Tis bruted for a certenty, my Lord,
That hees exceeding strongly fortified;
His subiects flocke as willingly to warre,
As if vnto a tryumph they were led.
Ch. England was wont to harbour malcontents,
Blood thirsty and seditious Catelynes,
Spend thrifts, and such as gape for nothing else
But changing and alteration of the state;
And is it possible
That they are now so loyall in them selues?
Lo. All but the Scot, who sollemnly protests,
As heeretofore I haue enformd his grace,
Neuer to sheath his Sword or take a truce.
Io. Ah, thats the anchredge of some better hope!
But, on the other side, to thinke what friends
King Edward hath retaynd in Netherland,
Among those euer-bibbing Epicures,
Those frothy Dutch men, puft with double beere,
That drinke and swill in euery place they come,
Doth not a little aggrauate mine ire;
Besides, we heare, the Emperor conioynes,
And stalls him in his owne authoritie:
But, all the mightier that their number is,
The greater glory reapes the victory.
Some friends haue we beside domesticke power;
The sterne Polonian, and the warlike Dane,
The king of Bohemia, and of Cycelie,
Are all become confederates with vs,
And, as I thinke, are marching hither apace.
⟨*Drum within.*⟩
But soft, I heare the musicke of their drums,
By which I gesse that their approch is neare.

Enter the King of Bohemia, *with* Danes, *and a Polonian Captaine, with other soldiers, another way.*

King of Boheme. King Iohn of Fraunce, as league and neighborhood
Requires, when friends are any way distrest,
I come to aide thee with my countries force.
Pol. Cap. And from great Musco, fearefull to the Turke,
And lofty Poland, nurse of hardie men,
I bring these seruitors to fight for thee,
Who willingly will venture in thy cause.
K. Io. Welcome, Bohemian king, and welcome all:
This your great kindnesse I will not forget.
Besides your plentiful rewards in Crownes,
That from our Treasory ye shall receiue,
There comes a hare braind Nation, deckt in pride,

187 wouldst *Q 2, etc.*   204 Thou] You *C*   210 gild *C*: guide *Qq*   Act III. *etc. add. C*   2 to] of *conj. pr. ed.*

17, 18 *One line Q 2*   33 domestick *C*: drum stricke *Q 1*: drumsticke *Q 2*   37 *S. D. add. C*

The spoyle of whome will be a trebble gaine.
And now my hope is full, my ioy complete:
At Sea, we are as puissant as the force
Of Agamemnon in the Hauen of Troy;
By land, with Zerxes we compare of strength,
Whose souldiers drancke vp riuers in their thirst:
Then, Bayardlike, blinde, ouerweaning Ned,
To reach at our imperiall dyadem
Is either to be swallowed of the waues,
Or hackt a peeces when thou comest ashore.

Enter ⟨*Marriner*⟩.

Mar. Neere to the cost I haue discride, my Lord,
As I was busie in my watchfull charge,
The proud Armado of king Edwards ships:
Which, at the first, far off when I did ken,
Seemd as it were a groue of withered pines;
But, drawing neere, their glorious bright aspect,
Their streaming Ensignes, wrought of coulloured silke,
Like to a meddow full of sundry flowers,
Adornes the naked bosome of the earth:
Maiesticall the order of their course,
Figuring the horned Circle of the Moone:
And on the top gallant of the Admirall
And likewise all the handmaides of his trayne
The Armes of England and of Fraunce vnite
Are quartred equally by Heralds art:
Thus, titely carried with a merrie gale,
They plough the Ocean hitherward amayne.
⟨*K. Iohn.*⟩ Dare he already crop the Flewer de Luce?
I hope, the hony being gathered thence,
He, with the spider, afterward approcht,
Shall sucke forth deadly venom from the leaues.—
But wheres our Nauy? how are they prepared
To wing them selues against this flight of Rauens?
Ma. They, hauing knowledge, brought them by the scouts,
Did breake from Anchor straight, and, puft with rage
No otherwise then were their sailes with winde,
Made forth, as when the empty Eagle flies,
To satisfie his hungrie griping mawe.
Io. Theres for thy newes. Returne vnto thy barke;
And if thou scape the bloody strooke of warre
And do suruiue the conflict, come againe,
And let vs heare the manner of the fight.
[*Exit* ⟨Marriner⟩.
Meane space, my Lords, tis best we be disperst
To seuerall places, least they chaunce to land:
First you, my Lord, with your Bohemian Troupes,
Shall pitch your battailes on the lower hand;
My eldest sonne, the Duke of Normandie,
Togeither with this aide of Muscouites,
Shall clyme the higher ground another waye;
Heere in the middle cost, betwixt you both,
Phillip, my yongest boy, and I will lodge.
So, Lords, be gon, and looke vnto your charge:
You stand for Fraunce, an Empire faire and large. [*Ex*⟨*e*⟩*unt*.
Now tell me, Phillip, what is thy concept,
Touching the challenge that the English make?
Ph. I say, my Lord, clayme Edward what he can,
And bring he nere so playne a pedegree,
Tis you are in possession of the Crowne,
And thats the surest poynt of all the Law:
But, were it not, yet ere he should preuaile,
Ile make a Conduit of my dearest blood,
Or chase those stragling vpstarts home againe.
King. Well said, young Phillip! Call for bread and Wine,
That we may cheere our stomacks with repast,
To looke our foes more sternely in the face.

⟨*A Table and Provisions brought in.*⟩ *The battell hard a farre off.*

Now is begun the heauie day at Sea:
Fight, Frenchmen, fight; be like the fielde of Beares,
When they defend their younglings in their Caues!
Stir, angry Nemesis, the happie helme,
That, with the sulphur battels of your rage,
The English Fleete may be disperst and sunke.
[*Shot.*
Ph. O Father, how this eckoing Cannon shot,
Like sweete hermonie, disgests my cates!
K. Io. Now, boy, thou hearest what thundring terror tis,
To buckle for a kingdomes souerentie:
The earth, with giddie trembling when it shakes,
Or when the exalations of the aire
Breakes in extremitie of lightning flash,
Affrights not more then kings, when they dispose

52 gaine *Q 2* : game *Q 1* 61 *S. D.* Marriner *add. Q 2* 62 discride *Q 2* : discribde *Q 1* 73 And *om. C* 79 *Prefix om. Q 1* 84 fleete *Q 2* 89 satifie *Q 1* 90 Thees *Q 1*

93 *S. D.* Marriner *om. Q 1* 104 *S. D. after* 103 *in Qq* 105 thy conceite *Q 2* : their concept *Q 1* 116 *S. D. Bracketed words add. C* 120 Stir *Qq* : Steer *C* 124 sweetest *C, etc.* 125 *ends* thundring *Q 2*

To shew the rancor of their high swolne harts. [*Retreate.*
Retrea⟨t⟩e is sounded; one side hath the worse:
O, if it be the French, sweete fortune, turne;
And, in thy turning, change the forward winds,
That, with aduantage of a fauoring skie,
Our men may vanquish, and the other flie!

Enter Marriner.

My hart misgiues:—say, mirror of pale death,
To whome belongs the honor of this day?
Relate, I pray thee, if thy breath will serue,
The sad discourse of this discomfiture.
Mar. I will, my Lord.
My gratious soueraigne, Fraunce hath tane the foyle,
And boasting Edward triumphs with successe.
These Iron harted Nauies,
When last I was reporter to your grace,
Both full of angry spleene, of hope, and feare,
Hasting to meete each other in the face,
At last conioynd; and by their Admirall
Our Admirall encountred manie shot:
By this, the other, that beheld these twaine
Giue earnest peny of a further wracke,
Like fiery Dragons tooke their haughty flight;
And, likewise meeting, from their smoky wombes
Sent many grym Embassadors of death.
Then gan the day to turne to gloomy night,
And darkenes did as wel inclose the quicke
As those that were but newly reft of life.
No leasure serud for friends to bid farewell;
And, if it had, the hideous noise was such,
As ech to other seemed deafe and dombe.
Purple the Sea, whose channel fild as fast
With streaming gore, that from the maymed fell,
As did her gushing moysture breake into
The crannied cleftures of the through shot planks.
Heere flew a head, disseuered from the tronke,
There mangled armes and legs were tost aloft,
As when a wherle winde takes the Summer dust
And scatters it in middle of the aire.
Then might ye see the reeling vessels split,
And tottering sink into the ruthlesse floud,
Vntill their lofty tops were seene no more.
All shifts were tried, both for defence and hurt:
And now the effect of vallor and of force,
Of resolution and of cowardize,
We liuely pictured; how the one for fame,
The other by compulsion laid about:
Much did the *Nonpareille*, that braue ship;
So did the blacke snake of Bullen, then which
A bonnier vessel neuer yet spred sayle.
But all in vaine; both Sunne, the Win⟨d⟩e and tyde,
Reuolted all vnto our foe mens side,
That we perforce were fayne to giue them way,
And they are landed.—Thus my tale is donne:
We haue vntimly lost, and they haue woone.
K. Io. Then rests there nothing, but with present speede
To ioyne our seueral forces al in one,
And bid them battaile, ere they rainge to farre.
Come, gentle Phillip, let vs hence depart;
This souldiers words haue perst thy fathers hart. [*Exeunt.*

⟨SCENE II.

Picardy. *Fields near* Cressi.⟩

Enter two French men; a woman and two little Children meet them, and other Citizens.

One. Wel met, my masters: how now? whats the newes?
And wherefore are ye laden thus with stuffe?
What, is it quarter daie that you remoue,
And carrie bag and baggage too?
Two. Quarter day? I, and quartering day, I feare:
Haue ye not heard the newes that flies abroad?
One. What newes?
Three. How the French Nauy is destroyd at Sea,
And that the English Armie is arriued.
One. What then?
Two. What then, quoth you? why, ist not time to flie,
When enuie and destruction is so nigh?
One. Content thee, man; they are farre enough from hence,
And will be met, I warrant ye, to their cost,
Before they breake so far into the Realme.
Two. I, so the Grashopper doth spend the time
In mirthfull iollitie, till Winter come;
And then too late he would redeeme his time,
When frozen cold hath nipt his carelesse head.
He, that no sooner will prouide a Cloake,
Then when he sees it doth begin to raigne,
May, peraduenture, for his negligence,
Be throughly washed, when he suspects it not.

131 *S. D. after* 132 *Qq* 134 froward *Q 2* 135 sauoring *Q 1* 136 the other *C*: thither *Q 1*: th' other *Q 2* 164 crannied *WP*: cranny'd *C*: cranny *Qq* 165 dissuuered *Q 1* 173 force] fear *C, etc.* 174 of] of a *Q 1* 175 We] Were *C*

177 Nonpareille *C*: Nom per illa *Qq* 180 Wine *Q 1*: winde *Q 2* Scene II. *etc. add. C* *S. D.* and other *Q 2*: another *Q 1* 5 quartering pay *Q 1* 6 ye] we *Q 1* 22 negilgence *Q 1*

We that haue charge and such a trayne as this,
Must looke in time to looke for them and vs,
Least, when we would, we cannot be relieued.

One. Belike, you then dispaire of all successe,
And thinke your Country will be subiugate.

Three. We cannot tell; tis good to feare the worst.

One. Yet rather fight, then, like vnnaturall sonnes,
Forsake your louing parents in distresse.

Two. Tush, they that haue already taken armes
Are manie fearefull millions in respect
Of that small handfull of our enimies:
But tis a rightfull quarrell must preuaile;
Edward is sonne vnto our late kings sister,
Where Iohn Valoys is three degrees remoued.

Wo. Besides, there goes a Prophesie abroad,
Published by one that was a Fryer once,
Whose Oracles haue many times prooued true;
And now he sayes, the tyme will shortly come,
When as a Lyon, rowsed in the west,
Shall carie hence the fluerdeluce of France:
These, I can tell yee, and such like surmises
Strike many french men cold vnto the heart.

Enter a French man.

⟨*Four.*⟩ Flie, cuntry men and cytizens of France!
Sweete flowring peace, the roote of happie life,
Is quite abandoned and expulst the lande;
In sted of whome ransackt constraining warre
Syts like to Rauens vppon your houses topps;
Slaughter and mischiefe walke within your streets,
And, vnrestrained, make hauock as they passe;
The forme whereof euen now my selfe beheld
Vpon this faire mountaine whence I came.
For so far of as I directed mine eies,
I might perceaue fiue Cities all on fire,
Corne fieldes and vineyards, burning like an ouen;
And, as the reaking vapour in the wind
Tourned but aside, I like wise might disserne
The poore inhabitants, escapt the flame,
Fall numberles vpon the souldiers pikes.
Three waies these dredfull ministers of wrath
Do tread the measuers of their tragicke march:
Vpon the right hand comes the conquering King,
Vpon the lefte his hot vnbridled sonne,
And in the midst our nations glittering hoast;
All which, though distant yet, conspire in one,
To leaue a desolation where they come.
Flie therefore, Citizens, if you be wise,
Seeke out som habitation further of:
Here if you staie, your wiues will be abused,
Your treasure sharde before your weeping eies;
Shelter you your selues, for now the storme doth rise.
Away, away; me thinks I heare their drums:—
Ah, wreched France, I greatly feare thy fal;
Thy glory shaketh like a tottering wall.
⟨*Exeunt.*⟩

⟨Scene III.

The same. Drums.⟩

Enter King Edward, *and the* Erle of Darby, *With Souldiors, and* Gobin de Graie.

Kin. Wheres the French man by whose cunning guide
We found the shalow of this Riuer Some,
And had direction how to passe the sea?

Go. Here, my good Lord.

Kin. How art thou calde? tell me thy name.

Go. Gobin de Graie, if please your excellence.

Kin. Then, Gobin, for the seruice thou hast done,
We here inlarge and giue thee liberty;
And, for recompenc⟨e⟩ beside this good,
Thou shalt receiue fiue hundred markes in golde.—
I know not how, we should haue met our sonne,
Whom now in heart I wish I might behold.

Enter Artoyes.

⟨*Art.*⟩ Good newes, my Lord; the prince is hard at hand,
And with him comes Lord Awdley and the rest,
Whome since our landing we could neuer meet.

Enter Prince Edward, Lord Awdley, *and Souldiers.*

K. E. Welcome, faire Prince! How hast thou sped, my sonne,
Since thy arriuall on the coaste of Fraunce?

Pr. Ed. Succesfullie, I thanke the gratious heauens:
Some of their strongest Cities we haue wonne,
As Harflew, Lo, Crotay, and Carentigne,
And others wasted, leauing at our heeles
A wide apparant feild and beaten path

27 all *C*: ill *Qq* 46 *No prefix in Qq* 58 reeking *conj. C*: leaking *Qq* 59 I tourned but *Qq*: Turned *C* 65 his] is *Q 1* 73 you *om. C, etc.* 76 *S. D. om. Q 1* Scene III. *etc. add. C* 1 guide *Qq*: guidance *C, etc.* 2 Some *WP*: Sone *Qq* 9 for] for a *C* 13 *Prefix om. Q 1* 20 Harslen, Lie, Crotag *Qq*: Harfleur, Lo, Crotage *C*

For sollitarines to progresse in:
Yet those that would submit we kindly pardned,
But who in scorne refused our proffered peace,
Indurde the penaltie of sharpe reuenge.

Ki. Ed. Ah, Fraunce, why shouldest thou be thus obstinate
Agaynst the kind imbracement of thy friends?
How gently had we thought to touch thy brest
And set our foot vpon thy tender mould,
But that, in froward and disdainfull pride,
Thou, like a skittish and vntamed coult,
Dost start aside and strike vs with thy heeles!
But tel me, Ned, in all thy warlike course,
Hast thou not seene the vsurping King of Fraunce?

Pri. Yes, my good Lord, and not two owers ago,
With full a hundred thousand fighting men—
Vppon the one side of the riuers banke
And on the other both, his multitudes.
I feard he would haue cropt our smaller power:
But happily, perceiuing your approch,
He hath with drawen himselfe to Cressey plaines;
Where, as it seemeth by his good araie,
He meanes to byd vs battaile presently.

Kin. Ed. He shall be welcome; thats the thing we craue.

Enter King Iohn, Dukes of Normanndy *and* Lorraine, King of Boheme, *yong* Phillip, *and Souldiers.*

Iohn. Edward, know that Iohn, the true king of Fraunce,
Musing thou shouldst incroach vppon his land,
And in thy tyranous proceeding slay
His faithfull subiects and subuert his Townes,
Spits in thy face; and in this manner folowing
Obraids thee with thine arrogant intrusion:
First, I condeme thee for a fugitiue,
A theeuish pyrate, and a needie mate,
One that hath either no abyding place,
Or else, inhabiting some barraine soile,
Where neither hearb or frutfull graine is had,
Doest altogether liue by pilfering:
Next, insomuch thou hast infringed thy faith,
Broke leage and solemne couenant made with mee,
I hould thee for a false pernitious wretch:
And, last of all, although I scorne to cope
With one so much inferior to my selfe,
Yet, in respect thy thirst is all for golde,
Thy labour rather to be feared then loued,
To satisfie thy lust in either parte,
Heere am I come, and with me haue I brought
Exceding store of treasure, perle, and coyne.
Leaue, therfore, now to persecute the weake,
And, armed entring conflict with the armd,
Let it be seene, mongest other pettie thefts,
How thou canst win this pillage manfully.

K. Ed. If gall or wormwood haue a pleasant tast,
Then is thy sallutation hony sweete;
But as the one hath no such propertie,
So is the other most satiricall.
Yet wot how I regarde thy worthles tants:
If thou haue vttred them to foile my fame
Or dym the reputation of my birth,
Know that thy woluish barking cannot hurt;
If slylie to insinuate with the worlde,
And with a strumpets artifitiall line
To painte thy vitious and deformed cause,
Bee well assured, the counterfeit will fade,
And in the end thy fowle defects be seene;
But if thou didst it to prouoke me on,
As who should saie I were but timerous,
Or, coldly negligent, did need a spurre,
Bethinke thy selfe howe slacke I was at sea,
How since my landing I haue wonn no townes,
Entered no further but vpon the coast,
And there haue euer since securelie slept.
But if I haue bin other wise imployd,
Imagin, Valoys, whether I intende
To skirmish, not for pillage, but for the Crowne
Which thou dost weare; and that I vowe to haue,
Or one of vs shall fall into his graue.

Pri. Ed. Looke not for crosse inuectiues at our hands,
Or rayling execrations of despight:
Let creeping serpents, hid in hollow banckes,
Sting with theyr tongues; we haue remorseles swordes,
And they shall pleade for vs and our affaires.
Yet thus much, breefly, by my fathers leaue:
As all the immodest poyson of thy throat
Is scandalous and most notorious lyes,
And our pretended quarell is truly iust,
So end the battaile when we meet to daie:
May eyther of vs prosper and preuaile,
Or, luckles curst, receue eternall shame!

Kin. Ed. That needs no further question; and I knowe,

25 But *conj. C*: For *Qq* poffered *Q 1* 27 thus *Q 2*: this *Q 1* 37 an *Q 2* 38 of] with *Qq*: o' *C* 39 I on the other; with *C. etc.* 60 false] most *Q 2* 62 so much *C*: such *Qq*: such an *D*

64 Thy] They *Q 1* 66 I haue *Q 2* 77 soil *conj. C* 81 line] hue *conj. Col.* 89 How *C*: Now *Qq* 90 the] thy *Q 2* 92 otherwayes *Q 2* 94 for the] the *C* 96 his] this *Q 1* 99 hide *Q 1* 105 is *om. C*

His conscience witnesseth, it is my right.—
Therfore, Valoys, say, wilt thou yet resigne,
Before the sickles thrust into the Corne,
Or that inkindled fury turne to flame?
Ioh. Edward, I know what right thou hast in France;
And ere I basely will resigne my Crowne,
This Champion field shallbe a poole of bloode,
And all our prospect as a slaughter house.
Pr. Ed. I, that approues thee, tyrant, what thou art:
No father, king, or shepheard of thy realme,
But one, that teares her entrailes with thy handes,
And, like a thirstie tyger, suckst her bloud.
Aud. You peeres of France, why do you follow him
That is so prodigall to spend your liues?
Ch. Whom should they follow, aged impotent,
But he that is their true borne soueraigne?
Kin. Obraidst thou him, because within his face
Time hath ingraud deep caracters of age?
Know, these graue schollers of experience,
Like stiffe growen oakes, will stand immouable,
When whirle wind quickly turnes vp yonger trese.
Dar. Was euer anie of thy fathers house
King but thyselfe, before this present time?
Edwards great linage, by the mothers side,
Fiue hundred yeeres hath helde the scepter vp:
Iudge then, conspiratours, by this descent,
Which is the true borne soueraigne, this or that.
Philip. Father, range your battailes, prate no more;
These English faine would spend the time in words,
That, night approching, they might escape vnfought.
K. Ioh. Lords and my louing Subiects, nowes the time,
That your intended force must bide the touch.
Therfore, my frinds, consider this in breefe:
He that you fight for is your naturall King;
He against whom you fight, a forrener:
He that you fight for, rules in clemencie,
And raines you with a mild and gentle byt;
He against whome you fight, if hee preuaile,
Will straight inthrone himselfe in tyrranie,
Make slaues of you, and with a heauie hand
Curtall and courb your swetest libertie.
Then, to protect your Country and your King,
Let but the haughty Courrage of your hartes
Answere the number of your able handes,
And we shall quicklie chase theis fugitiues.
For whats this Edward but a belly god,
A tender and lasciuious wantonnes,
That thother daie was almost dead for loue?
And what, I praie you, is his goodly gard?
Such as, but scant them of their chines of beefe
And take awaie their downie featherbedes,
And presently they are as resty stiffe,
As twere a many ouer ridden iades.
Then, French men, scorne that such should be your Lords,
And rather bind ye them in captiue bands.
All Fra. Viue le Roy! God saue King Iohn of France!
Io. Now on this plaine of Cressie spred your selues,—
And, Edward, when thou darest, begin the fight.
⟨*Exeunt* King Iohn, Cha., Phi., Lor., Boh. *and Forces.*⟩
Ki. Ed. We presently wil meet thee, Iohn of Fraunce:—
And, English Lordes, let vs resolue this daie,
Either to cleere vs of that scandalous cryme,
Or be intombed in our innocence.
And, Ned, because this battell is the first
That euer yet thou foughtest in pitched field,
As ancient custome is of Martialists,
To dub thee with the tipe of chiualrie,
In solemne manner wee will giue thee armes.
Come, therefore, Heralds, orderly bring forth
A strong attirement for the prince my sonne.

Enter foure Heraldes, bringing in a coate armour, a helmet, a lance, and a shield.

Kin. Edward Plantagenet, in the name of God,
As with this armour I impall thy breast,
So be thy noble vnrelenting heart
Wald in with flint of matchlesse fortitude,
That neuer base affections enter there:
Fight and be valiant, conquere where thou comst!
Now follow, Lords, and do him honor to.
Dar. Edward Plantagenet, prince of Wales,
As I do set this helmet on thy head,
Wherewith the chamber of thy braine is fenst,

113 turned *Q 2* 116 champain *Col.* 120 tearst *conj. C* 128 Know that these *Qq* 131 *Line ends* king *Qq* 134 helde] kept *Q 2* 137 *Prefix* Philip *Q 2* : Pri. *Q 1* 138 wodrs *Q 1* 140 nowes] knowes *Qq* 144 you] ye *Q 2*

167 *S. D. add. C* 169 this *C* : the *Qq* 171 innocencie *Q 2* 188 thy *C* : this *Qq*

So may thy temples, with Bellonas hand,
Be still adornd with lawrell victorie:
Fight and be valiant, conquer where thou comst!
Aud. Edward Plantagenet, prince of Wales,
Receiue this lance into thy manly hand;
Vse it in fashion of a brasen pen,
To drawe forth bloudie stratagems in France,
And print thy valiant deeds in honors booke:
Fight and be valiant, vanquish where thou comst!
Art. Edward Plantagenet, prince of Wales,
Hold, take this target, weare it on thy arme;
And may the view thereof, like Perseus shield,
Astonish and transforme thy gazing foes
To senselesse images of meger death:
Fight and be valiant, conquer where thou comst!
Ki. Now wants there nought but knighthood, which deferd
Wee leaue, till thou hast won it in the fielde.
⟨*P. Ed.*⟩ My gratious father and yee forwarde peeres,
This honor you haue done me, animates
And chears my greene, yet scarse appearing strength
With comfortable good presaging signes,
No other wise then did ould Iacobes wordes,
When as he breathed his blessings on his sonnes.
These hallowed giftes of yours when I prophane,
Or vse them not to glory of my God,
To patronage the fatherles and poore,
Or for the benefite of Englands peace,
Be numbe my ioynts, waxe feeble both mine armes,
Wither my hart, that, like a saples tree,
I may remayne the map of infamy.
K. Ed. Then thus our steelde Battailes shall be rainged:
The leading of the vawarde, Ned, is thyne;
To dignifie whose lusty spirit the more,
We temper it with Audlys grauitie,
That, courage and experience ioynd in one,
Your manage may be second vnto none:
For the mayne battells, I will guide my selfe;
And, Darby, in the rereward march behind.
That orderly disposd and set in ray,
Let vs to horse; and God graunt vs the daye!
[*Exeunt.*

193 manly] manlike *Q 2* 197 vanquish] conquer *Q 2, etc.* 206 *Prefix om. Q 1* 209 persaging *Q 1* 219 thus] this *Q 1* 220 vowarde *Q 1*

⟨SCENE IV.
The Same.⟩

Alarum. Enter a many French men flying. After them Prince Edward, *run⟨n⟩ing. Then enter* King Iohn *and* Duke of Loraine.

Iohn. Oh, Lorrain, say, what meane our men to fly?
Our nomber is far greater then our foes.
Lor. The garrison of Genoaes, my Lorde,
That cam from Paris weary with their march,
Grudging to be ⟨so⟩ soddenly imployd,
No sooner in the forefront tooke their place,
But, straite retyring, so dismaide the rest,
As likewise they betook themselues to flight,
In which, for hast to make a safe escape,
More in the clustering throng are prest to death,
Then by the ennimie, a thousand fold.
K. Io. O haplesse fortune! Let vs yet assay,
If we can counsell some of them to stay.
⟨*Exeunt.*⟩

⟨SCENE V.
The Same.⟩

Enter King Edward *and* Audley.

Ki. E. Lord Audley, whiles our sonne is in the chase,
With draw our powers vnto this little hill,
And heere a season let vs breath our selues.
Au. I will, my Lord. [*Exit. Sound Retreat.*
K. Ed. Iust dooming heauen, whose secret prouidence
To our grosse iudgement is inscrutable,
How are we bound to praise thy wondrous works,
That hast this day giuen way vnto the right,
And made the wicked stumble at them selues!

Enter Artoys.

⟨*Art.*⟩ Rescue, king Edward! rescue for thy sonne!
Kin. Rescue, Artoys? what, is he prisoner,
Or by violence fell beside his horse?
Ar. Neither, my Lord; but narrowly beset
With turning Frenchmen, whom he did persue,
As tis impossible that he should scape,
Except your highnes presently descend.
Kin. Tut, let him fight; we gaue him armes to day,
And he is laboring for a knighthood, man.

Scene IV. *etc. add. C* 5 so *add. C* 10 throng] through *Q 2* 13 *S. D. om. Q 1* Scene V. *etc. add. C* 2 our] your *Q 2, etc.* 10 *Prefix om. Q 1* 12 Or] Or else *C*

Enter Derby.

Da. The Prince, my Lord, the Prince! oh, succour him!
Hees close incompast with a world of odds!
Ki. Then will he win a world of honor to,
If he by vallour can redeeme him thence;
If not, what remedy? we haue more sonnes
Then one, to comfort our declyning age.

Enter Audley.

Au. Renowned Edward, giue me leaue, I pray,
To lead my souldiers where I may releeue
Your Graces sonne, in danger to be slayne.
The snares of French, like Emmets on a banke,
Muster about him; whilest he, Lion like,
Intangled in the net of their assaults,
Frantiquely wrends, and byt⟨e⟩s the wouen toyle:
But all in vaine, he cannot free him selfe.
K. Ed. Audley, content; I will not haue a man,
On paine of death, sent forth to succour him:
This is the day, ordaynd by desteny,
To season his courage with those greeuous thoughts,
That, if he breaketh out, Nestors yeares on earth
Will make him sauor still of this exployt.
Dar. Ah, but he shall not liue to see those dayes.
Ki. Why, then his Epitaph is lasting prayse.
Au. Yet, good my Lord, tis too much wilfulnes,
To let his blood be spilt, that may be saude.
Kin. Exclayme no more; for none of you can tell
Whether a borrowed aid will serue, or no;
Perhapps he is already slayne or tane.
And dare a Falcon when shees in her flight,
And euer after sheele be haggard like:
Let Edward be deliuered by our hands,
And still, in danger, hele expect the like;
But if himselfe himselfe redeeme from thence,
He wil haue vanquisht cheerefull death and feare,
And euer after dread their force no more
Then if they were but babes or Captiue slaues.
Aud. O cruell Father! Farewell, Edward, then!
Da. Farewell, sweete Prince, the hope of chiualry!
Art. O, would my life might ransome him from death!
K. Ed. But soft, me thinkes I heare ⟨*Retreat sounded.*⟩
The dismall charge of Trumpets loud retreat.
All are not slayne, I hope, that went with him;
Some will returne with tidings, good or bad.

Enter Prince Edward *in tryumph, bearing in his hande his shiuered Launce, and the* King of Boheme, *borne before, wrapt in the Coullours. They runne and imbrace him.*

Aud. O ioyfull sight! victorious Edward liues!
Der. Welcome, braue Prince!
Ki. Welcome, Plantagenet!
Pr. (*kneele and kisse his fathers hand*). First hauing donne my duety as beseemed,
Lords, I regreet you all with harty thanks.
And now, behold, after my winters toyle,
My paynefull voyage on the boystrous sea
Of warres deuouring gulphes and steely rocks,
I bring my fraught vnto the wished port,
My Summers hope, my trauels sweet reward:
And heere, with humble duety, I present
This sacrifice, this first fruit of my sword,
Cropt and cut downe euen at the gate of death,
The king of Boheme, father, whome I slue;
Whose thousands had intrencht me round about,
And laye as thicke vpon my battered crest,
As on an Anuell, with their ponderous glaues:
Yet marble courage still did vnderprop;
And when my weary armes, with often blowes,
Like the continuall laboring Wood-mans Axe
That is enioynd to fell a load of Oakes,
Began to faulter, straight I would recorde
My gifts you gaue me, and my zealous vow,
And then new courage made me fresh againe,
That, in despight, I carud my passage forth,
And put the multitude to speedy flyght.
Lo, thus hath Edwards hand fild your request,
And done, I hope, the duety of a Knight.
Ki. I, well thou hast deserud a knighthood, Ned!
And, therefore, with thy sword, yet reaking warme
[*His Sword borne by a Soldier.*
With blood of those that fought to be thy bane,
Arise, Prince Edward, trusty knight at armes:
This day thou hast confounded me with ioy,
And proude thy selfe fit heire vnto a king.
Pr. Heere is a note, my gratious Lord, of those

36 his green courage with those thoughts *C* 37 breathe out *conj. C* 47 huggard *Q 1*

57 *S. D. add. C* 75 Whose thousands *C*: Whom you sayd *Qq* 82 recorde *pr. ed.*: recouer *Qq*: remember *C* 85 caru'd *Q 2*: craud *Q 1* 87 thus *Q 2* this *Q 1* 90 *S. D. after* 86 *in Q 1* 91 sought *T*

That in this conflict of our foes were slaine:
Eleuen Princes of esteeme, Foure score Barons,
A hundred and twenty knights, and thirty thousand
Common souldiers; and, of our men, a thousand.
⟨*K. Ed.*⟩ Our God be praised! Now, Iohn of Fraunce, I hope,
Thou knowest King Edward for no wantonesse,
No loue sicke cockney, nor his souldiers iades.
But which way is the fearefull king escapt?
Pr. Towards Poyctiers, noble father, and his sonnes.
King. Ned, thou and Audley shall pursue them still;
My selfe and Derby will to Calice streight,
And there begyrt that Hauen towne with seege.
Now lies it on an vpshot; therefore strike,
And wistlie follow, whiles the games on foote.
What Pictures this?
Pr. A Pellican, my Lord,
Wounding her bosome with her crooked beak,
That so her nest of young ones may be fed
With drops of blood that issue from her hart;
The motto *Sic & vos,* 'and so should you'.
[*Exeunt.*

⟨ACT IV.

SCENE I.

Bretagne. Camp of the English.⟩

Enter Lord Mountford *with a Coronet in his hande; with him the* Earle of Salisbury.

Mo. My Lord of Salisbury, since by your aide
Mine ennemie Sir Charles of Bloys is slaine,
And I againe am quietly possest
In Brittaines Dukedome, knowe that I resolue,
For this kind furtherance of your king and you,
To sweare allegeance to his maiesty:
In signe whereof receiue this Coronet,
Beare it vnto him, and, withall, mine othe,
Neuer to be but Edwards faithful friend.
Sa. I take it, Mountfort. Thus, I hope, eare long
The whole Dominions of the Realme of Fraunce
Wilbe surrendred to his conquering hand.
[*Exit* ⟨Mountford.⟩
Now, if I knew but safely how to passe,
I would at Calice gladly meete his Grace,
Whether I am by letters certified
That he intends to haue his host remooude.
It shal be so, this pollicy will serue:—
Ho, whose within? Bring Villiers to me.

Enter Villeirs.

Villiers, thou knowest, thou art my prisoner,
And that I might for ransome, if I would,
Require of thee a hundred thousand Francks,
Or else retayne and keepe thee captiue still:
But so it is, that for a smaller charge
Thou maist be quit, and if thou wilt thy selfe.
And this it is: Procure me but a pasport
Of Charles, the Duke of Normandy, that I
Without restraint may haue recourse to Callis
Through all the Countries where he hath to doe;
Which thou maist easely obtayne, I thinke,
By reason I haue often heard thee say,
He and thou were students once together:
And then thou shalt be set at libertie.
How saiest thou? wilt thou vndertake to do it?
Vil. I will, my Lord; but I must speake with him.
Sa. Why, so thou shalt; take Horse, and post from hence:
Onely before thou goest, sweare by thy faith,
That, if thou canst not compasse my desire,
Thou wilt returne my prisoner backe againe;
And that shalbe sufficient warrant for mee.
Vil. To that condition I agree, my Lord,
And will vnfaynedly performe the same. [*Exit.*
Sal. Farewell, Villiers.—
Thus once I meane to trie a French mans faith.
[*Exit.*

⟨SCENE II.

Picardy. The English Camp before Calais.⟩

Enter King Edward *and* Derby, *with Souldiers.*

Kin. Since they refuse our profered league, my Lord,
And will not ope their gates, and let vs in,
We will intrench our selues on euery side,
That neither vituals nor supply of men
May come to succour this accursed towne:
Famine shall combate where our swords are stopt.

Enter sixe poore Frenchmen.

Der. The promised aid, that made them stand aloofe,
Is now retirdc and gone an other way:
It will repent them of their stubborne will.
But what are these poore ragged slaues, my Lord?

97–9 *Four lines in C, etc.* 99 Common] Priuate *Q 2* 100 *Prefix add. Q 2* 110 *Prefix* Ki. *repeated before* What *in Q 1* 112 may] might *Q 1* Act IV. *etc. add. C* 1 your *Q 2*: our *Q 1* 4 Btittaines *Q 1* 8 my *Q 2* 12 *S. D. om. Q 2* 14 at *C*: to *Qq* 16 That *C*: Yet *Qq*

31 thou] thyself *C* wert *Q 2* 39 mee] thee *C* 43 This *conj. C* Scene II. *etc. add. C* 2 their] the *Q 2* 6 *S. D. after* 9 *in C* sixe] some *C*

Ki. Edw. Aske what they are; it seemes, they come from Callis.
Der. You wretched patterns of dispayre and woe,
What are you, liuing men or glyding ghosts,
Crept from your graues to walke vpon the earth?
Poore. No ghosts, my Lord, but men that breath a life
Farre worse then is the quiet sleepe of death:
Wee are distressed poore inhabitants,
That long haue been deseased, sicke, and lame;
And now, because we are not fit to serue,
The Captayne of the towne hath thrust vs foorth,
That so expence of victuals may be saued,
K. Ed. A charitable deed, no doubt, and worthy praise!
But how do you imagine then to speed?
We are your enemies; in such a case
We can no lesse but put ye to the sword,
Since, when we proffered truce, it was refusde.
Poore. And if your grace no otherwise vouchsafe,
As welcome death is vnto vs as life.
Ki. Poore silly men, much wrongd and more distrest!
Go, Derby, go, and see they be relieud;
Command that victuals be appoynted them,
And giue to euery one fiue Crownes a peece:
⟨*Exeunt* Derby *and* Frenchmen.⟩
The Lion scornes to touch the yeelding pray,
And Edwards sword must flesh it selfe in such
As wilfull stubbornnes hath made peruerse.

Enter Lord Pearsie.

Ki. Lord Persie! welcome: whats the newes in England?
Per. The Queene, my Lord, comes heere to your Grace,
And from hir highnesse and the Lord vicegerent
I bring this happie tidings of successe:
Dauid of Scotland, lately vp in armes,
Thinking, belike, he soonest should preuaile,
Your highnes being absent from the Realme,
Is, by the fruitfull seruice of your peeres
And painefull trauell of the Queene her selfe,
That, big with child, was euery day in armes,
Vanquisht, subdude, and taken prisoner.
Ki. Thanks, Persie, for thy newes, with all my hart!
What was he tooke him prisoner in the field?
Per. A Esquire, my Lord; Iohn Copland is his name:
Who since, intreated by her Maiestie,
Denies to make surrender of his prize
To anie but vnto your grace alone;
Whereat the Queene is greouously displeasd.
Ki. Well, then wele haue a Pursiuaunt dispatcht,
To summon Copland hither out of hand,
And with him he shall bring his prisoner king.
Per. The Queene's, my Lord, her selfe by this at Sea,
And purposeth, as soone as winde will serue,
To land at Callis, and to visit you.
Ki. She shall be welcome; and, to wait her comming,
Ile pitch my tent neere to the sandy shore.

Enter a ⟨*French*⟩ *Captayne.*

⟨*Captaine.*⟩ The Burgesses of Callis, mighty king,
Haue by a counsell willingly decreed
To yeeld the towne and Castle to your hands,
Vpon condition it will please your grace
To graunt them benefite of life and goods.
K. Ed. They wil so! Then, belike, they may command,
Dispose, elect, and gouerne as they list.
No, sirra, tell them, since they did refuse
Our princely clemencie at first proclaymed,
They shall not haue it now, although they would;
⟨I⟩ will accept of nought but fire and sword,
Except, within these two daies, sixe of them,
That are the welthiest marchaunts in the towne,
Come naked, all but for their linnen shirts,
With each a halter hangd about his necke,
And prostrate yeeld themselues, vpon their knees,
To be afflicted, hanged, or what I please;
And so you may informe their masterships.
[*Exeunt* ⟨Edward *and* Percy⟩.
Cap. Why, this it is to trust a broken staffe:
Had we not been perswaded, Iohn our King
Would with his armie haue releeud the towne,
We had not stood vpon defiance so:
But now tis past that no man can recall,
And better some do go to wrack then all. [*Exit.*

⟨Scene III.

Poitou. Fields near Poitiers. The French camp; Tent of the Duke of Normandy.⟩

Enter Charles of Normandy *and* Villiers.

Ch. I wounder, Villiers, thou shouldest importune me

12 partners *Q 2* 13 ye *Q 2* or] er *Q 1* 22 no doubt *om. C* 25 ye] you *Q 2* 27 *Prefix* Poore *Q 2*: So. *Q 1* 32 *S. D. add. C* 34 flesh *Col.*: fresh *Qq* 37 comes heere] commends her *C* 43 fruitfull] faithfull *Q 2* 49 squire *Q 2*

54 dispatch *Q 1* 57 Queene *Q 1* 61 *S. D.* French *add. C* 62 *Prefix add. Q 2* 72 I will] Will *Q 1* 73 these] this *Q 2* 79 *S. D. Bracketed words add. C* Scene III. *etc. add. C*

For one that is our deadly ennemie.
Vil. Not for his sake, my gratious Lord, so much
Am I become an earnest aduocate,
As that thereby my ransome will be quit.
Ch. Thy ransome, man? why needest thou talke of that?
Art thou not free? and are not all occasions,
That happen for aduantage of our foes,
To be accepted of, and stood vpon?
Vil. No, good my Lord, except the same be iust;
For profit must with honor be comixt,
Or else our actions are but scandalous.
But, letting passe these intricate obiections,
Wilt please your highnes to subscribe, or no?
Ch. Villiers, I will not, nor I cannot do it;
Salisbury shall not haue his will so much,
To clayme a pasport how it pleaseth himselfe.
Vil. Why, then I know the extremitie, my Lord;
I must returne to prison whence I came.
Ch. Returne? I hope thou wilt not;
What bird that hath escapt the fowlers gin,
Will not beware how shees insnard againe?
Or, what is he, so senceles and secure,
That, hauing hardely past a dangerous gulfe,
Will put him selfe in perill there againe?
Vil. Ah, but it is mine othe, my gratious Lord,
Which I in conscience may not violate,
Or else a kingdome should not draw me hence.
Ch. Thine othe? why, that doth bind thee to abide:
Hast thou not sworne obedience to thy Prince?
Vil. In all things that vprightly he commands:
But either to perswade or threaten me,
Not to performe the couenant of my word,
Is lawlesse, and I need not to obey.
Ch. Why, is it lawfull for a man to kill,
And not, to breake a promise with his foe?
Vil. To kill, my Lord, when warre is once proclaymd,
So that our quarrel be for wrongs receaude,
No doubt, is lawfully permitted vs:
But in an othe we must be well aduisd,
How we do sweare, and, when we once haue sworne,
Not to infringe it, though we die therefore:
Therefore, my Lord, as willing I returne,
As if I were to flie to paradise.
Ch. Stay, my Villeirs; thine honorable minde
Deserues to be eternally admirde.
Thy sute shalbe no longer thus deferd:
Giue me the paper, Ile subscribe to it;
And, wheretofore I loued thee as Villeirs,
Heereafter Ile embrace thee as my selfe.
Stay, and be still in fauour with thy Lord.
Vil. I humbly thanke your grace; I must dispatch,
And send this pasport first vnto the Earle,
And then I will attend your highnes pleasure.
Ch. Do so, Villeirs;—and Charles, when he hath neede,
Be such his souldiers, howsoeuer he speede!
[*Exit* Villeirs.

Enter King Iohn.

K. Io. Come, Charles, and arme thee; Edward is intrapt,
The Prince of Wales is falne into our hands,
And we haue compast him; he cannot scape.
Ch. But will your highnes fight to day?
Io. What else, my son? hees scarse eight thousand strong,
And we are threescore thousand at the least.
Ch. I haue a prophecy, my gratious Lord,
Wherein is written what successe is like
To happen vs in this outragious warre;
It was deliuered me at Cresses field
By one that is an aged Hermyt there.

⟨*Reads*⟩ 'When fethered foul shal make thine army tremble,
And flint stones rise and breake the battell ray,
Then thinke on him that doth not now dissemble;
For that shalbe the haples dreadfull day:
Yet, in the end, thy foot thou shalt aduance
As farre in England as thy foe in Fraunce.':

Io. By this it seemes we shalbe fortunate:
For as it is impossible that stones
Should euer rise and breake the battaile ray,
Or airie foule make men in armes to quake,
So is it like, we shall not be subdude:
Or say this might be true, yet in the end,
Since he doth promise we shall driue him hence
And forrage their Countrie as they haue don ours,
By this reuenge that losse will seeme the lesse.
But all are fryuolous fancies, toyes, and dreames:
Once we are sure we haue insnard the sonne,
Catch we the father after how we can.
[*Exeunt.*

8 of] on *conj. C*   of our] over *conj. Col.*

68 *S. D. add. C*

⟨Scene IV.

The same. The English Camp.⟩

Enter Prince Edward, Audley, *and others.*

Pr. Audley, the armes of death embrace vs round,
And comfort haue we none, saue that to die
We pay sower earnest for a sweeter life.
At Cressey field our Clouds of Warlike smoke
Chokt vp those French mouths & disseuered them:
But now their multitudes of millions hide,
Masking as twere, the beautious burning Sunne,
Leauing no hope to vs, but sullen darke
And eielesse terror of all ending night.

Au. This suddaine, mightie, and expedient head
That they haue made, faire Prince, is wonderfull.
Before vs in the vallie lies the king,
Vantagd with all that heauen and earth can yeeld;
His partie stronger battaild then our whole:
His sonne, the brauing Duke of Normandie,
Hath trimd the Mountaine on our right hand vp
In shining plate, that now the aspiring hill
Shewes like a siluer quarrie or an orbe,
Aloft the which the Banners, bannarets,
And new replenisht pendants cuff the aire
And beat the windes, that for their gaudinesse
Struggles to kisse them: on our left hand lies
Phillip, the younger issue of the king,
Coting the other hill in such arraie,
That all his guilded vpright pikes do seeme
Streight trees of gold, the pendants leaues;
And their deuice of Antique heraldry,
Quartred in collours, seeming sundry fruits,
Makes it the Orchard of the Hesperides:
Behinde vs too the hill doth beare his height,
For like a halfe Moone, opening but one way,
It rounds vs in; there at our backs are lodgd
The fatall Crosbowes, and the battaile there
Is gouernd by the rough Chattillion.
Then thus it stands: the valleie for our flight
The king binds in; the hils on either hand
Are proudly royalized by his sonnes;
And on the Hill behind stands certaine death
In pay and seruice with Chattillion.

Pr. Deathes name is much more mightie then his deeds;
Thy parcelling this power hath made it more.
As many sands as these my hands can hold,
Are but my handful of so many sands;
Then, all the world, and call it but a power,
Easely tane vp, and quickly throwne away:
But if I stand to count them sand by sand,
The number would confound my memorie,
And make a thousand millions of a taske,
Which briefelie is no more, indeed, then one.
These quarters, squadrons, and these regements,
Before, behinde vs, and on either hand,
Are but a power. When we name a man,
His hand, his foote, his head hath seuerall strengthes;
And being al but one selfe instant strength,
Why, all this many, Audely, is but one,
And we can call it all but one mans strength.
He that hath farre to goe, tels it by miles;
If he should tell the steps, it kills his hart:
The drops are infinite, that make a floud,
And yet, thou knowest, we call it but a Raine.
There is but one Fraunce, one king of Fraunce,
That Fraunce hath no more kings; and that same king
Hath but the puissant legion of one king,
And we haue one: then apprehend no ods,
For one to one is faire equalitie.

Enter an Herald from king Iohn.

Pr. What tidings, messenger? be playne and briefe.

He. The king of Fraunce, my soueraigne Lord and master,
Greets by me his fo, the Prince of Wals:
If thou call forth a hundred men of name,
Of Lords, Knights, Squires, and English gentlemen,
And with thy selfe and those kneele at his feete,
He straight will fold his bloody collours vp,
And ransome shall redeeme liues forfeited;
If not, this day shall drinke more English blood,
Then ere was buried in our Bryttish earth.
What is the answere to his profered mercy?

Pr. This heauen, that couers Fraunce, containes the mercy
That drawes from me submissiue orizons;
That such base breath should vanish from my lips,
To vrge the plea of mercie to a man,
The Lord forbid! Returne, and tell the king,
My tongue is made of steele, and it shall beg
My mercie on his coward burgonet;
Tell him, my colours are as red as his,
My men as bold, our English armes as strong:

Scene IV. *etc. add. C*   3 To pay *C*   5 moths *D*   26 pendants *WP*: pendant *Qq*: pendant streamers *C*   28 sundy *Q 1*   30 two *Qq*

45 Is easily *C*   50 quarter'd squadrons *C*   61 and one king *C*   68 Greets thus *C*: Greeteth *Col.*   70 Squires *Q 2*: Esquires *Q 1*   75 our *Qq*: your *conj. Col.*   81 the] thy *Q 2*

Returne him my defiance in his face.
He. I go. ⟨*Exit.*⟩

Enter another ⟨*Herald*⟩.

Pr. What newes with thee?
He. The Duke of Normandie, my Lord & master,
Pittying thy youth is so ingirt with perill,
By me hath sent a nimble ioynted iennet,
As swift as euer yet thou didst bestride,
And therewithall he counsels thee to flie;
Els death himself hath sworne that thou shalt die.
P. Back with the beast vnto the beast that sent him!
Tell him I cannot sit a cowards horse;
Bid him to daie bestride the iade himselfe,
For I will staine my horse quite ore with bloud,
And double guild my spurs, but I will catch him;
So tell the carping boy, and get thee gone. ⟨*Exit Her.*⟩

Enter another ⟨*Herald*⟩.

He. Edward of Wales, Phillip, the second sonne
To the most mightie christian king of France,
Seeing thy bodies liuing date expird,
All full of charitie and christian loue,
Commends this booke, full fraught with prayers,
To thy faire hand and for thy houre of lyfe
Intreats thee that thou meditate therein,
And arme thy soule for hir long iourney towards—
Thus haue I done his bidding, and returne.
Pr. Herald of Phillip, greet thy Lord from me:
All good that he can send, I can receiue;
But thinkst thou not, the vnaduised boy
Hath wrongd himselfe in thus far tendering me?
Happily he cannot praie without the booke—
I thinke him no diuine extemporall—,
Then render backe this common place of prayer,
To do himselfe good in aduersitie;
Besides he knows not my sinnes qualitie,
And therefore knowes no praiers for my auaile;
Ere night his praier may be to praie to God,
To put it in my heart to heare his praier.
So tell the courtly wanton, and be gone.
He. I go. ⟨*Exit.*⟩

Pr. How confident their strength and number makes them!—
Now, Audley, sound those siluer winges of thine,
And let those milke white messengers of time
Shew thy times learning in this dangerous time.
Thy selfe art bruis'd and bit with many broiles,
And stratagems forepast with yron pens
Are texted in thine honorable face;
Thou art a married man in this distresse,
But danger wooes me as a blushing maide:
Teach me an answere to this perillous time.
Aud. To die is all as common as to liue:
The one inch-wise, the other holds in chase;
For, from the instant we begin to liue,
We do pursue and hunt the time to die:
First bud we, then we blow, and after seed,
Then, presently, we fall; and, as a shade
Followes the bodie, so we follow death.
If, then, we hunt for death, why do we feare it?
If we feare it, why do we follow it?
If we do feare, how can we shun it?
If we do feare, with feare we do but aide
The thing we feare to seize on vs the sooner:
If wee feare not, then no resolued proffer
Can ouerthrow the limit of our fate;
For, whether ripe or rotten, drop we shall,
As we do drawe the lotterie of our doome.
Pri. Ah, good olde man, a thousand thousand armors
These wordes of thine haue buckled on my backe:
Ah, what an idiot hast thou made of lyfe,
To seeke the thing it feares! and how disgrast
The imperiall victorie of murdring death,
Since all the liues his conquering arrowes strike
Seeke him, and he not them, to shame his glorie!
I will not giue a pennie for a lyfe,
Nor halfe a halfepenie to shun grim death,
Since for to liue is but to seeke to die,
And dying but beginning of new lyfe.
Let come the houre when he that rules it will!
To liue or die I hold indifferent. [*Exeunt.*

⟨Scene V.

The same. The French Camp.⟩

Enter king Iohn *and* Charles.

Ioh. A sodaine darknes hath defast the skie,
The windes are crept into their caues for feare,

87 *S. D.* Exit *add. Q 2* Herald *add. C* 99 capring *Q 1* *S. D. Bracketed words add. C* 104 with holy prayers *C* 112 thus] this *Q 1* 122 *S. D. add. Q 2*

124 winges] strings *D* 127 bruis'd *C*: busie *Qq* 129 texed *Q 2* 134 inch-wise *pr. ed.*: in choice *Qq, etc.* 142 *om. C* Scene V. *etc. add. C*

The leaues moue not, the world is husht and still,
The birds cease singing, and the wandring brookes
Murmure no wonted greeting to their shores;
Silence attends some wonder and expecteth
That heauen should pronounce some prophesie:
Where, or from whome, proceeds this silence, Charles?
Ch. Our men, with open mouthes and staring eyes,
Looke on each other, as they did attend
Each others wordes, and yet no creature speakes;
A tongue-tied feare hath made a midnight houre,
And speeches sleepe through all the waking regions.
Ioh. But now the pompeous Sunne, in all his pride,
Lookt through his golden coach vpon the worlde,
And, on a sodaine, hath he hid himselfe,
That now the vnder earth is as a graue,
Darke, deadly, silent, and vncomfortable.
[*A clamor of rauens.*
Harke, what a deadly outcrie do I heare?
Ch. Here comes my brother Phillip.
Ioh. All dismaid:

(*Enter* Philip.)

What fearefull words are those thy lookes presage?
Ph. A flight, a flight!
Ioh. Coward, what flight? thou liest, there needs no flight.
Ph. A flight.
Kin. Awake thy crauen powers, and tell on
The substance of that verie feare in deed,
Which is so gastly printed in thy face:
What is the matter?
Ph. A flight of vgly rauens
Do croke and houer ore our souldiers heads,
And keepe in triangles and cornerd squares,
Right as our forces are imbatteled;
With their approach there came this sodain fog,
Which now hath hid the airie floor of heauen
And made at noone a night vnnaturall
Vpon the quaking and dismaied world:
In briefe, our souldiers haue let fall their armes,
And stand like metamorphosd images,
Bloudlesse and pale, one gazing on another.
Io. I, now I call to mind the prophesie,
But I must giue no enterance to a feare.—
Returne, and harten vp these yeelding soules:
Tell them, the rauens, seeing them in armes,
So many faire against a famisht few,
Come but to dine vpon their handie worke
And praie vpon the carrion that they kill:
For when we see a horse laid downe to die,
Although (he be) not dead, the rauenous birds
Sit watching the departure of his life;
Euen so these rauens for the carcases
Of those poore English, that are markt to die,
Houer about, and, if they crie to vs,
Tis but for meate that we must kill for them.
Awaie, and comfort vp my souldiers,
And sound the trumpets, and at once dispatch
This litle busines of a silly fraude. [*Exit* Ph.

Another noise. Salisbury *brought in by a French Captaine.*

Cap. Behold, my liege, this knight and fortie mo,
Of whom the better part are slaine and fled,
With all indeuor sought to breake our rankes,
And make their waie to the incompast prince:
Dispose of him as please your maiestie.
Io. Go, & the next bough, souldier, that thou seest,
Disgrace it with his bodie presently;
For I doo hold a tree in France too good
To be the gallowes of an English theefe.
Sa. My Lord of Normandie, I haue your passe
And warrant for my safetie through this land.
Ch. Villiers procurd it for thee, did he not?
Sal. He did.
Ch. And it is currant; thou shalt freely passe.
K. Io. I, freely to the gallows to be hangd,
Without deniall or impediment.
Awaie with him!
Charles. I hope your highnes will not so disgrace me,
And dash the vertue of my seale at armes:
He hath my neuer broken name to shew,
Carectred with this princely hande of mine;
And rather let me leaue to be a prince
Than break the stable verdict of a prince:
I doo beseech you, let him passe in quiet.
Ki. Thou and thy word lie both in my command;
What canst thou promise that I cannot breake?

3 wood *conj. C* 20, 21 All .. presage *one line Q 1 S. D. add. C* 22, 24, 28 *Prefix* Pr. *Q 1* 33 floor *C*: flower *Qq* 41 those *Q 2, C* 47 he be *add. C* 55 *S. D.* Exit Pr. *Q 1* 63 Eor *Q 1* *The rest of the play is lacking in the Bodleian copy of Q 1: the text from* 64 *on is based on the copy in Trin. Coll. Camb.* 70 *Prefix* En: Io *Q 1* 73 *Prefix* Charles *Q 2*: Vil. *Q 1*

Which of these twaine is greater infamie,
To disobey thy father or thy selfe?
Thy word, nor no mans, may exceed his power;
Nor that same man doth neuer breake his worde,
That keepes it to the vtmost of his power.
The breach of faith dwels in the soules consent:
Which if thy selfe without consent doo breake,
Thou art not charged with the breach of faith
Go, hang him: for thy lisence lies in mee,
And my constraint stands the excuse for thee.

Ch. What, am I not a soldier in my word?
Then, armes, adieu, and let them fight that list!
Shall I not giue my girdle from my wast,
But with a gardion I shall be controld,
To saie I may not giue my things awaie?
Vpon my soule, had Edward, prince of Wales,
Ingagde his word, writ downe his noble hand
For all your knights to passe his fathers land,
The roiall king, to grace his warlike sonne,
Would not alone safe conduct giue to them,
But with all bountie feasted them and theirs.

Kin. Dwelst thou on presidents? Then be it so!
Say, Englishman, of what degree thou art.

Sa. An Earle in England, though a prisoner here,
And those that knowe me, call me Salisburie.

Kin. Then, Salisburie, say whether thou art bound.

Sa. To Callice, where my liege, king Edward, is.

Kin. To Callice, Salisburie? Then to Callice packe,
And bid the king prepare a noble graue,
To put his princely sonne, blacke Edward, in.
And as thou trauelst westward from this place,
Some two leagues hence there is a loftie hill,
Whose top seemes toplesse, for the imbracing skie
Doth hide his high head in her azure bosome;
Vpon whose tall top when thy foot attaines,
Looke backe vpon the humble vale beneath—
Humble of late, but now made proud with armes—
And thence behold the wretched prince of Wales,
Hoopt with a bond of yron round about.
After which sight, to Callice spurre amaine,
And saie, the prince was smoothered and not slaine:
And tell the king this is not all his ill;
For I will greet him, ere he thinkes I will.
Awaie, be gone; the smoake but of our shot
Will choake our foes, though bullets hit them not. [*Exit.*

⟨SCENE VI.

The same. A Part of the Field of Battle.⟩

Allarum. Enter prince Edward *and* Artoys.

Art. How fares your grace? are you not shot, my Lord?

Pri. No, deare Artoys; but choakt with dust and smoake,
And stept aside for breath and fresher aire.

Art. Breath, then, and too it againe: the amazed French
Are quite distract with gazing on the crowes;
And, were our quiuers full of shafts againe,
Your grace should see a glorious day of this:—
O, for more arrowes, Lord; thats our want.

Pri. Courage, Artoys! a fig for feathered shafts,
When feathered foules doo bandie on our side!
What need we fight, and sweate, and keepe a coile,
When railing crowes outscolde our aduersaries?
Vp, vp, Artoys! the ground it selfe is armd
⟨With⟩ Fire containing flint; command our bowes
To hurle awaie their pretie colored Ew,
And to it with stones: awaie, Artoys, awaie!
My soule doth prophesie we win the daie. [*Exeunt.*

⟨SCENE VII.

The same. Another Part of the Field of Battle.⟩

Allarum. Enter king Iohn.

⟨*K. Iohn.*⟩ Our multitudes are in themselues confounded,
Dismayed, and distraught; swift starting feare
Hath buzd a cold dismaie through all our armie,
And euerie pettie disaduantage promptes
The feare possessed abiect soul to flie.
My selfe, whose spirit is steele to their dull lead,
What with recalling of the prophesie,
And that our natiue stones from English armes
Rebell against vs, finde myselfe attainted
With strong surprise of weake and yeelding feare.

Enter Charles.

⟨*Charles.*⟩ Fly, father, flie! the French do kill the French,

102 bounty'd *conj. Elze* 116 Vpon] Unto *conj. C* 117 below *C* 120 bond *Q 1*: band *Q 2, etc.*

Scene VI. *etc. add. C* 14 With *add. C* Scene VII. *etc. add. WP* 1, 11 *Prefix add. Q 2*

Some that would stand let driue at some that flie;
Our drums strike nothing but discouragement,
Our trumpets sound dishonor and retire;
The spirit of feare, that feareth nought but death,
Cowardly workes confusion on it selfe.

Enter Phillip.

⟨*Phil.*⟩ Plucke out your eies, and see not this daies shame!
An arme hath beate an armie; one poore Dauid
Hath with a stone foild twentie stout Goliahs;
Some twentie naked staruelings with small flints,
Hath driuen backe a puisant host of men,
Araid and fenst in all accomplements.

Ioh. Mordiu, they quait at vs, and kill vs vp;
No lesse than fortie thousand wicked elders
Haue fortie leane slaues this daie stoned to death.

Ch. O, that I were some other countryman!
This daie hath set derision on the French,
And all the world will blurt and scorne at vs.

Kin. What, is there no hope left?

Phil. No hope, but death, to burie vp our shame.

Ki. Make vp once more with me; the twentith part
Of those that liue, are men inow to quaile
The feeble handfull on the aduerse part.

Ch. Then charge againe: if heauen be not opposd,
We cannot loose the daie.

Kin. On, awaie! [*Exeunt.*

⟨Scene VIII.

The same. Another Part of the Field of Battle.⟩

Enter Audley, *wounded, & rescued by two squirs.*

Esq. How fares my Lord?

Aud. Euen as a man may do,
That dines at such a bloudie feast as this.

Esq. I hope, my Lord, that is no mortall scarre.

Aud. No matter, if it be; the count is cast,
And, in the worst, ends but a mortall man.
Good friends, conuey me to the princely Edward,
That in the crimson brauerie of my bloud
I may become him with saluting him.
Ile smile, and tell him, that this open scarre
Doth end the haruest of his Audleys warre. [*Ex.*

⟨Scene IX.

The same. The English Camp.⟩

Enter prince Edward, king Iohn, Charles, *and all, with Ensignes spred.*

Retreat sounded.

Pri. Now, Iohn in France, & lately Iohn of France,
Thy bloudie Ensignes are my captiue colours;
And you, high vanting Charles of Normandie,
That once to daie sent me a horse to flie,
Are now the subiects of my clemencie.
Fie, Lords, is it not a shame that English boies,
Whose early daies are yet not worth a beard,
Should in the bosome of your kingdome thus,
One against twentie, beate you vp together?

Kin. Thy fortune, not thy force, hath conquerd vs.

Pri. An argument that heauen aides the right.

⟨*Enter* Artoys *with* Phillip.⟩

See, see, Artoys doth bring with him along
The late good counsell giuer to my soule.
Welcome, Artoys; and welcome, Phillip, to:
Who now of you or I haue need to praie?
Now is the prouerbe verefied in you,
'Too bright a morning breeds a louring daie.'

Sound Trumpets. Enter Audley.

But say, what grym discoragement comes heere!
Alas, what thousand armed men of Fraunce
Haue writ that note of death in Audleys face?
Speake, thou that wooest death with thy careles smile,
And lookst so merrily vpon thy graue,
As if thou wert enamored on thyne end:
What hungry sword hath so bereaud thy face,
And lopt a true friend from my louing soule?

Au. O Prince, thy sweet bemoning speech to me
Is as a morneful knell to one dead sicke.

Pr. Deare Audley, if my tongue ring out thy end,
My armes shalbe thy graue: what may I do
To win thy life, or to reuenge thy death?
If thou wilt drinke the blood of captyue kings,
Or that it were restoritiue, command

17 Phil. *add.* *Q 2* 21 Haue *Q 2, etc.* 22 accoutrements *WP* 23 quoit *C* 28 wilt *Q 1* 30 Phil. *Q 2, etc.* : Pr. *Q 1* Scene VIII. *etc. add.* *WP* *S. D.* squirs *Q 1* : Esquires *Q 2*

Scene IX. *WP* : Scene VII. *C* The . . Camp *add.* *C* 5 (?) subiect 11 *S. D. add.* *C* 23 thyne *Q 1* : thy *Q 2* 24 bewreath'd *Col.* 29 thy *Q 2* : the *Q 1*

A Health of kings blood, and Ile drinke to thee;
If honor may dispence for thee with death,
The neuer dying honor of this daie
Share wholie, Audley, to thy selfe, and liue.

Aud. Victorious Prince,—that thou art so, behold
A Cæsars fame in kings captiuitie—
If I could hold dym death but at a bay,
Till I did see my liege thy royall father,
My soule should yeeld this Castle of my flesh,
This mangled tribute, with all willingnes,
To darkenes, consummation, dust, and Wormes.

Pr. Cheerely, bold man, thy soule is all to proud
To yeeld her Citie for one little breach;
Should be diuorced from her earthly spouse
By the soft temper of a French mans sword?
Lo, to repaire thy life, I giue to thee
Three thousand Marks a yeere in English land.

Au. I take thy gift, to pay the debts I owe:
These two poore Esquires redeemd me from the French
With lusty & deer hazzard of their liues:
What thou hast giuen me, I giue to them;
And, as thou louest me, Prince, lay thy consent
To this bequeath in my last testament.

Pr. Renowned Audley, liue, and haue from mee
This gift twise doubled to these Esquires and thee:
But liue or die, what thou hast giuen away
To these and theirs shall lasting freedome stay.
Come, gentlemen, I will see my friend bestowed
With in an easie Litter; then wele martch
Proudly toward Callis, with tryumphant pace,
Vnto my royall father, and there bring
The tribut of my wars, faire Fraunce his king. [*Ex.*

⟨ACT V.

Picardy. The English Camp before Calais.⟩

Enter King Edward, Queen Phillip, Derby, *soldiers.*

Ed. No more, Queene Phillip, pacifie your selfe;
Copland, except he can excuse his fault,
Shall finde displeasure written in our lookes.
And now vnto this proud resisting towne!
Souldiers, assault; I will no longer stay,
To be deluded by their false delaies;
Put all to sword, and make the spoyle your owne.

Enter sixe Citizens in their Shirts, bare foote, with halters about their necks.

All. Mercy, king Edward, mercie, gratious Lord!

Ki. Contemptuous villaines, call ye now for truce?
Mine eares are stopt against your bootelesse cryes:—
Sound, drums allarum; draw threatning swords!

1. *Cit.* Ah, noble Prince, take pittie on this towne,
And heare vs, mightie king:
We claime the promise that your highnes made;
The two daies respit is not yet expirde,
And we are come with willingnes to beare
What tortering death or punishment you please,
So that the trembling multitude be saued.

Ki. My promise? Well, I do confesse as much:
But I require the cheefest Citizens
And men of most account that should submit;
You, peraduenture, are but seruile groomes,
Or some fellonious robbers on the Sea,
Whome, apprehended, law would execute,
Albeit seuerity lay dead in vs:
No, no, ye cannot ouerreach vs thus.

Two. The Sun, dread Lord, that in the western fall
Beholds vs now low brought through miserie,
Did in the Orient purple of the morne
Salute our comming forth, when we were knowne;
Or may our portion be with damned fiends.

Ki. If it be so, then let our couenant stand:
We take possession of the towne in peace,
But, for your selues, looke you for no remorse;
But, as imperiall iustice hath decreed,
Your bodies shalbe dragd about these wals,
And after feele the stroake of quartering steele:
This is your dome;—go, souldiers, see it done.

Qu. Ah, be more milde vnto these yeelding men!
It is a glorious thing to stablish peace,
And kings approch the nearest vnto God
By giuing life and safety vnto men:
As thou intendest to be king of Fraunce,
So let her people liue to call thee king;

33 Heath *Qq* 40 royal *C*: loyall *Qq* 46 She'ld *D* 51, 57 Esquires *Qq*: Squires *C, etc.* Act V. *etc. add. C*

7 *S. D. precedes* Enter King Edward, *etc. Q 1*: *corr. Q 2* 11 allarum *printed as S. D. by C, etc.* 12 1. Cit. *WP*: All *Qq* 20 requir'd *conj. C* 31 friends *C* 44 her *Q 1*: thy *Q 2*

For what the sword cuts down or fire hath spoyld,
Is held in reputation none of ours.
Ki. Although experience teach vs this is true,
That peacefull quietnes brings most delight,
When most of all abuses are controld;
Yet, insomuch it shalbe knowne that we
As well can master our affections
As conquer other by the dynt of sword,
Phillip, preuaile; we yeeld to thy request:
These men shall liue to boast of clemencie,
And, tyrannie, strike terror to thy selfe.
Two. Long liue your highnes! happy be your reigne!
Ki. Go, get you hence, returne vnto the towne,
And if this kindnes hath deserud your loue,
Learne then to reuerence Edward as your king.— [*Ex.* ⟨*Citizens*⟩.
Now, might we heare of our affaires abroad,
We would, till glomy Winter were ore spent,
Dispose our men in garrison a while.
But who comes heere?

Enter Copland *and* King Dauid.

De⟨r⟩. Copland, my Lord, and Dauid, King of Scots.
Ki. Is this the proud presumtious Esquire of the North,
That would not yeeld his prisoner to my Queen?
Cop. I am, my liege, a Northen Esquire indeed,
But neither proud nor insolent, I trust.
Ki. What moude thee, then, to be so obstinate
To contradict our royall Queenes desire?
Co. No wilfull disobedience, mightie Lord,
But my desert and publike law at armes:
I tooke the king my selfe in single fight,
And, like a souldier, would be loath to loose
The least preheminence that I had won.
And Copland straight vpon your highnes charge
Is come to Fraunce, and with a lowly minde
Doth vale the bonnet of his victory:
Receiue, dread Lorde, the custome of my fraught,
The wealthie tribute of my laboring hands,
Which should long since haue been surrendred vp,
Had but your gratious selfe bin there in place.
Q. But, Copland, thou didst scorne the kings command,
Neglecting our commission in his name.
Cop. His name I reuerence, but his person more;
His name shall keepe me in alleagaunce still,
But to his person I will bend my knee.
King. I praie thee, Phillip, let displeasure passe;
This man doth please mee, and I like his words:
For what is he that will attempt great deeds,
And loose the glory that ensues the same?
All riuers haue recourse vnto the Sea,
And Coplands faith relation to his king.
Kneele, therefore, downe: now rise, king Edwards knight;
And, to maintayne thy state, I freely giue
Fiue hundred marks a yeere to thee and thine.

Enter Salsbury.

Welcome, Lord Salisburie: what news from Brittaine?
Sa. This, mightie king: the Country we haue won,
And Iohn de Mountford, regent of that place,
Presents your highnes with this Coronet,
Protesting true allegeaunce to your Grace.
Ki. We thanke thee for thy seruice, valient Earle;
Challenge our fauour, for we owe it thee.
Sa. But now, my Lord, as this is ioyful newes,
So must my voice be tragicall againe,
And I must sing of dolefull accidents.
Ki. What, haue our men the ouerthrow at Poitiers?
Or is our sonne beset with too much odds?
Sa. He was, my Lord: and as my worthlesse selfe
With fortie other seruiceable knights,
Vnder safe conduct of the Dolphins seale,
Did trauaile that way, finding him distrest,
A troupe of Launces met vs on the way,
Surprisd, and brought vs prisoners to the king,
Who, proud of this, and eager of reuenge,
Commanded straight to cut of all our heads:
And surely we had died, but that the Duke,
More full of honor then his angry syre,
Procurd our quicke deliuerance from thence;
But, ere we went, 'Salute your king', quoth hee,
'Bid him prouide a funerall for his sonne:
To day our sword shall cut his thred of life;
And, sooner then he thinkes, wele be with him,
To quittance those displeasures he hath done.'
This said, we past, not daring to reply;

59 Edward *Q 2*: Edw. *Q 1*   64 Sots *Q 2*   65 Esq *Q 2*: Squire *C*   67 Northren *Q 2*   Squire *C*   72 at *Q 1*: of *Q 2*, *etc.*

90 great *Qq*: high *C*   *S. D. after* 97 *Q 1*   99 John *C*: Charles *Qq*   108 our *Qq*: my *C*

Our harts were dead, our lookes diffusd and wan.
Wandring, at last we clymd vnto a hill,
From whence, although our griefe were much before,
Yet now to see the occasion with our eies
Did thrice so much increase our heauines:
For there, my Lord, oh, there we did descry
Downe in a vallie how both armies laie.
The French had cast their trenches like a ring,
And euery Barricados open front
Was thicke imbost with brasen ordynaunce;
Heere stood a battaile of ten thousand horse,
There twise as many pikes in quadrant wise,
Here Crosbowes, and deadly wounding darts:
And in the midst, like to a slender poynt
Within the compasse of the horison,
As twere a rising bubble in the sea,
A Hasle wand amidst a wood of Pynes,
Or as a beare fast chaind vnto a stake,
Stood famous Edward, still expecting when
Those doggs of Fraunce would fasten on his flesh.
Anon the death procuring knell begins:
Off goe the Cannons, that with trembling noyse
Did shake the very Mountayne where they stood;
Then sound the Trumpets clangor in the aire,
The battailes ioyne: and, when we could no more
Discerne the difference twixt the friend and fo,
So intricate the darke confusion was,
Away we turnd our watrie eies with sighs,
As blacke as pouder fuming into smoke.
And thus, I feare, vnhappie haue I told
The most vntimely tale of Edwards fall.

Qu. Ah me, is this my welcome into Fraunce?
Is this the comfort that I lookt to haue,
When I should meete with my belooued sonne?
Sweete Ned, I would thy mother in the sea
Had been preuented of this mortall griefe!

Ki. Content thee, Phillip; tis not teares will serue
To call him backe, if he be taken hence:
Comfort thy selfe, as I do, gentle Queene,
With hope of sharpe, vnheard of, dyre reuenge.—
He bids me to prouide his funerall,
And so I will; but all the Peeres in Fraunce
Shall mourners be, and weepe out bloody teares,
Vntill their emptie vaines be drie and sere:
The pillers of his hearse shall be his bones;
The mould that couers him, their Citie ashes;
His knell, the groning cryes of dying men;
And, in the stead of tapers on his tombe,
An hundred fiftie towers shall burning blaze,
While we bewaile our valiant sonnes decease.

After a flourish, sounded within, enter an herald.

He. Reioyce, my Lord; ascend the imperial throne!
The mightie and redoubted prince of Wales,
Great seruitor to bloudie Mars in armes,
The French mans terror, and his countries fame,
Triumphant rideth like a Romane peere,
And, lowly at his stirop, comes afoot
King Iohn of France, together with his sonne,
In captiue bonds; whose diadem he brings
To crowne thee with, and to proclaime thee king.

Ki. Away with mourning, Phillip, wipe thine eies;—
Sound, Trumpets, welcome in Plantaginet!

Enter Prince Edward, king Iohn, Phillip, Audley, Artoys.

Ki. As things long lost, when they are found again,
So doth my sonne reioyce his fathers heart,
For whom euen now my soule was much perplext.

Q. Be this a token to expresse my ioy, [*kisse him.*
For inward passions will not let me speake.

Pr. My gracious father, here receiue the gift,
⟨*Presenting him with K. Iohn's crown.*⟩
This wreath of conquest and reward of warre,
Got with as mickle perill of our liues,
As ere was thing of price before this daie;
Install your highnes in your proper right:
And, heerewithall, I render to your hands
These prisoners, chiefe occasion of our strife.

Kin. So, Iohn of France, I see you keepe your word;
You promist to be sooner with our selfe
Then we did thinke for, and tis so in deed:
But, had you done at first as now you do,
How many ciuill townes had stoode vntoucht,
That now are turnd to ragged heaps of stones!
How many peoples liues mightst thou haue saud,
That are vntimely sunke into their graues!

138 and *Qq* : arm'd with *C* 148 they] we *conj.* *C* 149 clangors *C*

170 his bones (*K. John's*) *Qq* : their bones *D* 171 city's *Col.* 174 fiftie] lofty *Col.* *S. D. Printed as part of preceding speech Q 1* 192 *S. D. add. D* 202 you . . you *Q 1* : ye . . ye *Q 2* 205 might you *Q 2*

Io. Edward, recount not things irreuocable;
Tell me what ransome thou requirest to haue.
Kin. Thy ransome, Iohn, hereafter shall be known:
But first to England thou must crosse the seas,
To see what intertainment it affords;
How ere it fals, it cannot be so bad,
As ours hath bin since we ariude in France.
Ioh. Accursed man! of this I was fortolde,
But did misconster what the prophet told.
Pri. Now, father, this petition Edward makes
To thee, whose grace hath bin his strongest shield,
That, as thy pleasure chose me for the man
To be the instrument to shew thy power,
So thou wilt grant that many princes more,
Bred and brought vp within that little Isle,
May still be famous for lyke victories!
And, for my part, the bloudie scars I beare,
The wearie nights that I haue watcht in field,
The dangerous conflicts I haue often had,
The fearefull menaces were proffered me,
The heate and cold and what else might displease:
I wish were now redoubled twentie fold,
So that hereafter ages, when they reade
The painfull traffike of my tender youth,
Might thereby be inflamd with such resolue,
As not the territories of France alone,
But likewise Spain, Turkie, and what countries els
That iustly would prouoke faire Englands ire,
Might, at their presence, tremble and retire.
Kin. Here, English Lordes, we do proclaime a rest,
An intercession of our painfull armes:
Sheath vp your swords, refresh your weary lims,
Peruse your spoiles; and, after we haue breathd
A daie or two within this hauen towne,
God willing, then for England wele be shipt;
Where, in a happie houre, I trust, we shall
Ariue, three kings, two princes, and a queene.

FINIS.

237 An] And *D* interceasing *Q 2*, *etc.*

Moſt pleaſant Comedie of *Mucedorus* the kings ſonne of *Valentia* and *Amadine* the Kings daughter of *Arragon*, with the merie conceites of *Mouſe*.

Newly ſet foorth, as it hath bin *ſundrie times plaide in the honorable Cittie of London.*

Very delectable and full of mirth.

LONDON
Printed for *William Iones*, dwelling at Holborne conduit, at the ſigne of the Gunne.
1598.

Q 1	=	Quarto of 1598
Q 2	=	,, ,, 1606
Q 3	=	,, ,, 1610
Q 4	=	,, ,, 1611
Q 5	=	,, ,, 1613
Q 6	=	,, ,, 1615
Q 7	=	,, ,, 1618
Q 8	=	,, ,, 1619
Q 9	=	,, ,, 1621
Q 10	=	,, ,, 1626
Q 11	=	,, ,, 1631
Q 12	=	,, ,, 1634
Q 13	=	,, ,, 1639
Q 14	=	,, ,, 1663
Q 15	=	,, ,, 1668
Q 16	=	undated quarto
Q 17	=	Quarto with missing title page
Col.	=	Collier, 1824
T	=	Tyrrell, 1851
Haz.	=	Hazlitt's Dodsley 1874-6
D	=	Delius, 1874
WP	=	Warnke and Proescholdt, 1878
Wag.	=	Wagner: textual conjectures in Jahrbuch XI. and XIV.
Elze	=	Elze in Jahrbuch XV. and Notes on Eliz. Dramatists.
pr. ed.	=	present editor

A MOST PLEASANT COMEDIE OF

MVCEDORVS THE KINGS SONNE OF VALENTIA,

AND AMADINE, THE KINGS DAVGHTER OF ARRAGON

[THE PROLOGVE.

Most sacred Maiestie, whose great desertes
Thy Subiect England, nay, the World, admires:
Which Heauen graunt still increase: O may your Prayse,
Multiplying with your houres, your Fame still rayse;
Embrace your Counsell; Loue, with Fayth, them guide,
That both, as one, bench by each others side.
So may your life passe on and runne so euen,
That your firme zeale plant you a Throne in Heauen,
Where smiling Angels shall your guardians bee
From blemisht Traytors, stayn'd with Periurie:
And as the night 's inferiour to the day,
So be all earthly Regions to your sway.
Be as the Sunne to Day, the Day to Night;
For, from your Beames, Europe shall borrow light.
Mirth drowne your boosome, faire Delight your minde,
And may our Pastime your Contentment finde
Exit]

⟨DRAMATIS PERSONAE.⟩

Eight persons[1] may easily play it.

The King and Rombelo. } for one.
⟨*King Valencia,* } *for one.*⟩[2]
Mucedorus the prince of Valensia. } *for one.*
⟨*Anselmo,* } *for one.*⟩[2]
Amadine the Kinges daughter of Arragon. } *for one.*
Segasto a Noble man. } *for one.*
Enuie: Tremelio a Captaine: Bremo a wilde man. } *for one.*
Comedy, a boy, an ould woman, Ariena Amadines maide. } *for one.*
Collen a Counseller, A messenger. } *for one.*
Mouse the Clowne. } *for one.*

⟨INDUCTION.⟩

Enter Comedie ioyfull with a garland of baies on her head.

WHY so! thus doe I hope to please:
Musicke reuiues, and mirth is tollerable,
Comedie, play thy part and please,
Mak merry them that coms to ioy with thee:
Ioy, then, good gentilles; I hope to make you laugh.
Sound foorth *Bellonas* siluer tuned strings.
Time fits vs well, the daie and place is ours.

Enter Enuie, his armes naked, besmearde with bloud.

En. Nay, staie, minion, there lies a block.
What, al on mirth! Ile interrupt your tale
And mixe your musicke with a tragick end.
Co. What monstrous vgly hagge is this,
That dares comtrowle the pleasures of our will?
Vaunt, churlish curre, besmearde with gorie bloud,
That seemst to check the blossoms of delight,
And stifle the sound of sweete *Bellonas* breath:
Blush, monster, blush, and post away with shame,
That seekest disturbance of a goddesse deedes.
En. Post hence thy selfe, thou counter-checking trul;
I will possesse this habite, spite of thee,
And gaine the glorie of thy wished porte:
Ile thunder musicke shall appale the nimphes,
And make them sheuer their clattering strings:
Flying for succour to their dankish caues.
Sound drumes within and crie, 'stab! stab!'
Hearken, thou shalt hear a noise
Shall fill the aire with a shrilling sound,
And thunder musicke to the gods aboue:

Prologue add. Q 3 6 as *Q 3* : at *Haz.* [1] Ten persons *Q 3* [2] *Add. Q 3* Induction *add. WP* *S. D.* ioyfull *Q 1* : ioyfully *Q 3, etc.* 8 stay, minion, stay *Q 8, etc.* . 15 stifle *Q 1* : stiffe *Q 3* : still *Q 11* bearth *Q 3* 17 deedes *Q 1–5* : name *Q 6, etc.* : fame *conj. Wag.* 20 thy *Q 1–6* : this *Q 8, etc.* 22 shiuer *Q 3, etc.* 23 dankish *Col., Elze* : danes *Q 1* : Danish *Q 3, etc.* : darkest *conj. pr. ed.* 24 a *om. Q 8, etc.* 26 the *om. Q 4*

Mars shall himselfe breathe downe
A peerelesse crowne vpon braue enuies head,
And raise his chiuall with a lasting fame.
In this braue musicke *Enuie* takes delight,
Where I may see them wallow in there blood,
To spurne at armes and legges quite shiuered off,
And heare the cries of many thousand slaine.
How likst thou this, my trull? this sport alone for mee!

Co. Vaunt, bloodie curre, nurst vp with tygers sapp,
That so dost seeke to quaile a womans minde.
Comedie is mild, gentle, willing for to please,
And seekes to gaine the loue of all estates:
Delighting in mirth, mixt all with louely tales,
And bringeth things with treble ioy to passe.
Thou, bloodie, Enuious, disdainer of mens ioye,
Whose name is fraught with bloodie stratagemes,
Delights in nothing but in spoyle and death,
Where thou maist trample in their luke warme blood,
And graspe their hearts within thy cursed pawes:
Yet vaile thy mind, reuenge thou not on mee;
A silly woman begs it at thy hands:
Giue me the leaue to vtter out my play,
Forbeare this place, I humblie craue thee: hence,
And mixe not death amongst pleasing comedies,
That treats naught els but pleasure and delight.
If any sparke of humaine rests in thee,
Forbeare, be gon, tender the suite of mee.

En. Why so I wil; forbearance shall be such
As treble death shall crosse thee with despight,
And make thee mourne where most thou ioiest,
Turning thy mirth into a deadly dole,
Whirling thy pleasures with a peale of death,
And drench thy methodes in a sea of bloud:
This will I doe, thus shall I beare with thee;
And more to vex thee with a deeper spite,
I will with threates of bloud begin thy play,
Fauoring thee with enuie and with hate.

Co. Then, vglie monster, doe thy woorst,
I will defend them in despite of thee:
And though thou thinkst with tragick fumes
To braue my play vnto my deepe disgrace,
I force it not, I scorne what thou canst doe;
Ile grace it so, thy selfe shall it confesse
From tragick stuffe to be a pleasant comedie.

En. Why then, *Comedie,* send thy actors forth
And I will crosse the first steps of their tread:
Making them feare the verie dart of death.

Co. And Ile defend them maugre all thy spite:
So, vgly fiend, farewell, till time shall serue,
That we may meete to parle for the best.

En. Content, *Comedie*; ile goe spread my branch,
And scattered blossomes from mine enuious tree
Shall proue to monsters, spoiling of their ioyes.
Exit.

[⟨ACT I.

SCENE I.

Valentia. The Court.⟩

Sound. Enter Mucedorus and Anselmo his friend.

Muced. Anselmo.

Ansel. My Lord and friend.

Muc. True, my Anselmo, both thy Lord and friend
Whose deare affections boosome with my heart,
And keepe their domination in one orbe.

Ans. Whence neare disloyaltie shall roote it foorth,
But fayth plant firmer in your choyse respect.

Muc. Much blame were mine, if I should other deeme,
Nor can coy Fortune contrary allow:
But, my Anselmo, loth I am to say
I must estrange that frendship—
Misconsture not, tis from the Realme, not thee:
Though Landes part Bodies, Heartes keepe companie.
Thou knowst that I imparted often haue
Priuate relations with my royall Sire,
Had as concerning beautious Amadine,
Rich Aragons bright Iewell, whose face (some say)
That blooming Lillies neuer shone so gay,
Excelling, not exceld: yet least Report
Does mangle Veritie, boasting of what is not,
Wing'd with Desire, thither Ile straight repaire,

27 breathe] reach *conj. Way.* 28 crowene *Q 1* 29 chiuall *Qq* : rival *conj. Way.* 34 tis sport *Q 8, etc.* 46 thou *Q 1–3* : thee *Q 4, etc.* 58 pleasures] measures *Elze* 59 methodes] metres *Elze* 66 though] thought *Q 1* 67 braue *Q 1* : praue *Q 3–6* : lıroue *Q 8, etc.*

71 thy] the *Q 11* : now thy *WP* 72 tread *Q 1* : trade *Q 3, etc.* 75 farewell, till *Q 3, etc.* : frewell, tell *Q 1* 79 to *Q 1* : two *Q 3, etc.* their *Qq* : thy *D* *Act. I, Sc. I–II add. Q 3* *S. D.* Act I, Scene I *Acts and scenes first indicated WP ; indications of place add. pr. ed.* 3 *om. Q 5–16* 10, 11 *One line Q 3, etc.* 11 estrange *Q 3* : enlarge *Q 14–16* that] thy *Q 16* 20 Veritie] virtue *Col.*

And be my Fortunes, as my Thoughts are, faire.
Ans. Will you forsake Valencia, leaue the Court,
Absent you from the eye of Soueraigntie?
Do not, sweete Prince, aduenture on that taske,
Since danger lurkes each where: be wonne from it.
Mu. Desist disswasion,
My resolution brookes no batterie;
Therefore, if thou retaine thy wonted forme,
Assist what I intend.
Ans. Your misse will breed a blemish in the Court,
And throw a frostie deaw vpon that Beard,
Whose front Valencia stoopes to.
Mu. If thou my welfare tender, then no more;
Let Loues strong Magicke charme thy triuiail phrase,
Wasted as vainely as to gripe the Sunne:
Augment not then more answers; locke thy lippes,
Vnlesse thy wisedome suite me with disguise,
According to my purpose.
Ans. That action craues no counsell,
Since what you rightly are will more commaund,
Then best vsurped shape.
Mu. Thou still art opposite in disposition:
A more obscure seruile habillament
Beseemes this enterprise.
Ans. Then like a Florentine or Mountebancke?
Mu. Tis much too tedious; I dislike thy iudgement:
My minde is grafted on an humbler stocke.
Ans. Within my Closet does there hang a Cassocke,
Though base the weede is; t'was a Shepheards,
Which I presented in Lord Iulios Maske.
Mu. That, my Anselmo, and none else but that,
Maske Mucedorus from the vulgar view!
That habite suites my minde; fetch me that weede.
[*Exit Anselmo.*
Better then Kinges haue not disdaind that state,
And much inferiour, to obtaine their mate.

Enter Anselmo with a Shepheards coate.

So!
Let our respect commaund thy secrecie.
At once a briefe farewell:
Delay to louers is a second hell.
[*Exit Mucedorus.*
Ans. Prosperitie forerunne thee; Aucward chance
Neuer be neighbour to thy wishes venture:
Content and Fame aduance thee; euer thriue,
And Glory thy mortalitie suruiue. [*Exit.*

⟨Scene II.
A Forest in Arragon.⟩

Enter Mouse with a bottle of Hay.

Mous. O horrible, terrible! Was euer poore Gentleman so scard out of his seauen Senses? A Beare? nay, sure it cannot be a Beare, but some Diuell in a Beares Doublet: for a Beare could neuer haue had that agilitie to haue frighted me. Well, Ile see my Father hang'd, before Ile serue his Horse any more: Well, Ile carry home my Bottle of Hay, and for once make my Fathers Horse turne Puritane and obserue Fasting dayes, for he gets not a bit. But soft! this way she followed me, therefore Ile take the other Path; and because Ile be sure to haue an eye on him, I will take handes with some foolish Creditor, and make euery step backward.

As he goes backwards the Beare comes in, and he tumbles ouer her, and runnes away and leaues his bottle of Hay behind him.]

⟨Scene III. *The same.*⟩

Enter Segasto runing and Amadine after him, being persued with a beare.

Se. Oh fly, Madam, fly or els we are but dead.
Ama. Help, *Segasto,* help! help, swet *Segasto,* or els I die.
⟨*Seg.*⟩ Alas, madam, there is no way but flight;
Then hast and saue your selfe.
Segasto runnes away.
Ama. Why then I die; ah helpe me in distresse!

Enter Mucedorus like a shepheard with a sworde drawne and a beares head in his hande.

Mu. Stay, Lady, stay, and be no more dismaide.
That cruell beast most mercelesse and fell,
Which hath bereaued thousands of their liues,
Affrighted many with his hard pursues,

50 shepherd's once *Wag.* 57, 58 *One line Q 3, etc.*

Scene II. *WP* A Forest, *etc. add. pr. ed.* 13 on him *Q 3–4*: to him *Q 5–6*: to her *Q 8, etc.*: on her *Col.* take *Q 3–8*: shake *Q 11, etc.* Scene III. *WP* 1 are] art *Q 1* 2 ele *Q 1* 4 *S. D. after* 2 *Qq* 8 Which] That *Q 8* hath *Q 3, etc.*: haue *Q 1* 9 pursuits *WP*

Prying from place to place to find his praie,
Prolonging thus his life by others death,
His carcasse now lies headlesse, void of breth.
Ama. That fowle deformed monster, is he dead?
Mu. Assure your selfe thereof, behould his head:
Which if it please you, Lady, to accept,
With willing heart I yeeld it to your maiestie.
Ama. Thankes, worthy shepheard, thanks a thousand times.
This gift, assure thy selfe, contents me more
Then greatest bountie of a mighty prince,
Although he were the monarch of the world.
Mu. Most gracious goddesse, more then mortal wight,
Your heauenly hewe of right imports no lesse,
Most glad am I in that it was my chance
To vndertake this enterprise in hand,
Which doth so greatly glad your princely minde.
Ama. No goddesse, shepheard, but a mortall wight,
A mortall wight destressed as thou seest:
My father heere is king of Arragon.
I *Amadine* his only daughter am,
And after him sole heire vnto the crowne.
Now, where as it is my fathers will
To mary me vnto *Segasto*, on⟨e⟩,
Whose welth through fathers former vsury
Is knowen to be no lesse then woonderfull,
We both of custome oftentimes did vse,
Leauing the court, to walke within the fieldes
For recreation, especially ⟨in⟩ the spring,
In that it yelds greate store of rare delights:
And passing further then our wonted walkes,
Scarse were entred within these lucklesse woods,
But right before vs downe a steepe fall hil
A monstrous vgly beare did hie him fast,
To meete vs both. I faint to tell the rest,
Good shepherd, but suppose the gastly lookes,
The hiddious feares, the thousant hunderd woes,
Which at this instant *Amadine* susteind.
Mu. Yet, worthy princes, let thy sorrow cease,
And let this sight your former ioyes reuiue.
Ama. Beleeue me, shepheard, so it doth no lesse.
Mu. Long may they last vnto your hearts content.
But tell me, Ladie, what is become of him,
Segasto calld, what is become of him?
Ama. I knowe not, I; that knowe the powers diuine,
But God graunt this: that sweet *Segasto* liue.
Mu. Yet heard harted he in such a case,
So cowardly to saue himselfe by flight:
And leaue so braue a princesse to the spoyle.
Ama. Well, shephearde, for thy worthy valour tried,
Endangering thy selfe to set me free,
Vnrecompensed, sure, thou shalt not be.
In court thy courage shalbe plainely knowne:
Throughout the Kingdome will I spread thy name,
To thy renowne and neuer dying fame:
And that thy courage may be better knowne,
Beare thou the head of this most monstrous beast
In open sight to euerie courtiers viewe:
So will the king my father thee rewarde.
Come, lets away, and guard me to the court.
Mu. With all my heart. [*Exeunt.*

⟨SCENE IV. *Outskirts of the Forest.*⟩

Enter Segasto solus.

Se. When heapes of harmes do houer ouer head,
Tis time as then, some say, to looke about,
And of ensuing harmes to choose the least:
But hard, yea haplesse, is that wretchesse chaunce,
Lucklesse his lot and caytiffe like acourste,
At whose proceedings fortune euer frownes.
My selfe I meane, most subiect vnto thrall,
For I, the more I seeke to shun the worst,
The more by proofe I find my selfe accurst:
Ere whiles assaulted with an vgly beare,
Fayre *Amadine* in company all alone,
Forthwith by flight I thought to saue my selfe,
Leauing my *Amadine* vnto her shiftes:
For death it was for to resist the beare,
And death no lesse of *Amadines* harmes to heare.
Accursed I in lingring life thus long!
In liuing thus, each minute of an hower
Doth pierce my hart with dartes of thousand deathes:
If she by flight her fury doe escape,
What will she thinke?
Will she not say—yea, flatly to my face,
Accusing me of meere disloyaltie—

32 *Ends* Segasto *Qq* On *Q 1–5* : One *Q 6 ff.* 37 esecially *Q 1* in *add. Haz.* specially in spring *WP* 39 farther *Haz.* 40 entred were *Q 3, etc.* 45 hundred thousand *Q 5 ff.* 55 heard *Q 1* : hard *Q 3, etc.* 69 *Wrongly bracketed by Haz.* Scene IV. *WP* 3 of *Q 5, etc.* : so *Q 1–4* 4 wretches *Q 3 ff.* 11 Fayre *Qq* : With *WP* 17 liuing *Q 3, etc.* : leeuing *Q 1* 19 her] his *Col.*

A trustie friend is tride ⟨in⟩ time of neede,
But I, when she in danger was of death
And needed me, and cried, *Segasto, helpe:*
I turned my backe and quickly ran away.
Vnworthy I to beare this vitall breath!
But what! what needes these plaintes?
If *Amadine* do liue, then happie I;
Shee will in time forgiue and so forget:
Amadine is mercifull, not *Iuno* like,
In harmful hart to harbor hatred long.

Enter Mouse, the Clowne, running, crying: clubs.

Mouse. Clubs, prongs, pitchforks, billes! O helpe! a beare, a beare, a beare!

Se. Still beares, and nothing else but beares. Tell me, sirra, wher she is.

Clo. O sir, she is runne downe the woods: I see her white head and her white belly.

Se. Thou talkest of wonders, to tell me of white bears. But, sirra, didst thou euer see any such?

Clo. No, faith, I neuer sawe any such, but I remember my fathers woordes: hee bad mee take heede I was not caught with a white beare.

Se. A lamentable tale, no dout.

Clo. I tell you what, sir, as I was going a fielde to serue my fathers greate horse, & caried a bottle of hay vpon my head—now doe you see, sir—I, fast hudwinckt, that I could see nothing, perceiuing the beare comming, I threw my hay into the hedge and ran away.

Se. What, from nothing?

Clo. I warrant you, yes, I saw something, for there was two loade of thornes besides my bottle of hay, and that made three.

Se. But tell me, sirra, the beare that thou didst see,
Did she not beare a bucket on her arme?

Clo. Ha, ha, ha! I neuer saw beare goe a milking in all my life. But hark you, sir, I did not looke so hie as her arme: I saw nothing but her whit head, and her whit belly.

Se. But tell me, sirra, where doost thou dwell?

Clo. Why, doe you not knowe mee?

Se. Why no, how should I know thee?

Clo. Why, then, you know no bodie, and you knowe not mee. I tell you, sir, I am the goodman rats son of the next parish ouer the hill.

Se. Goodman rats son: why, whats thy name?

Clo. Why, I am very neere kin vnto him.

Se. I thinke so, but whats thy name?

Clo. My name? I haue ⟨a⟩ very pretie name; Ile tel you what my name is: my name is *Mouse.*

Se. What, plaine *Mouse*?

Clo. I, plaine mouse with out either welt or garde. But doe you heare, sir, I am but a very young mouse, for my taile is scarce growne out yet; looke you here els.

Se. But, I pray thee, who gaue thee that name?

Clo. Fayth, sir, I know not that, but if you would faine know, aske my fathers greate horse, for he hath bin halfe a yeare longer with my father then I haue.

Se. This seemes to be a merrie fellow;
I care not if I take him home with me.
Mirth is a comfort to a troubled minde,
A merrie man a merrie master makes.
How saist thou, sirra, wilt thou dwell with me?

Clo. Nay, soft, sir, two words to a bargaine: praie you, what occupation are you?

Se. No occupation, I liue vpon my landes.

Clo. Your lands! away, you are no maister for me: why, doe you thinke that I am so mad, to go seke my liuing in the lands amongst the stones, briars, and bushes, and teare my holy day apparell? not I, by your leaue.

Se. Why, I do not meane thou shalt.

Clo. How then?

Se. Why, thou shalt be my man, and waite vpon me at the court.

Clo. Whats that?

Se. Where the King lies.

Clo. Whats that same King, a man or woman?

Se. A man as thou arte.

Clo. As I am? harke you, sir; pray you, what kin is he to good man king of our parish, the church warden?

Se. No kin to him; he is the King of the whole land.

Clo. King of the land! I neuer see him.

Se. If thou wilt dwel with me, thou shallt see him euerie day.

Clo. Shal I go home againe to be torne in peces with beares? no, not I. I wil go home & put on a cleane shirt, and then goe drowne my selfe.

Se. Thou shallt not need; if thou wilt dwell with me, thou shalt want nothing.

Clo. Shal I not? then heares my hand; ile

23 in *om. Q 1* 28 need *Q 8 ff.* 35 else *om. Q 8 ff* 38 see *Q 1*: saw *Q 3, etc.* wite head *Q 1* 49 bottly *Q 1* 55 two] tow *Q 1* 68 am the *Q 1*; am *Q 8* 75 a *om. Q 1* 80 am but *Q 1–4*: am *Q 5 ff.* 94 two] tow *Q 1* 108 or *Q 1*: or a *Q 3 ff.* 116 see *Q 1–6*: saw *Q 8 ff.*

dwel with you. And harke you, sir, now you haue entertained me, I wil tell you what I can doe: I can keepe my tongue from picking and stealing, and my handes from lying and slaundering, I warrant you, as wel as euer you had man in all your life.

Se. Now will I to court with sorrowfull hart, rownded with doubts.
If *Amadine* doe liue, then happy I:
Yea, happie I, if *Amadine* doe liue.
[*Exeunt.*

⟨ACT II.

SCENE I. *The Camp of the King of Arragon.*⟩

Enter the King with a young prince prisoner, Amadine, ⟨Tremelio,⟩ with Collen and counsellers.

King. Now, braue Lords, our wars are brought to end,
Our foes ⟨to⟩ the foile, and we in safetie rest:
It vs behoues to vse such clemencie
In peace as valour in the warre
It is as great honor to be bountifull
At home as to be conquerers in the field.
Therefore, my Lords, the more to my content,
Your liking, and your countries safegarde,
We are disposde in marriage for to giue
Our daughter to Lord *Segasto* heare,
Who shall succeede the diadem after me,
And raigne heereafter as I tofore haue done,
Your sole and lawfull King of Arragon:
What say you, Lordings, like you of my aduise?

Col. And please your Maiesty, we doe not onely alowe of your highnesse pleasure, but also vow fathfully in what we may to further it.

King. Thankes, good my Lords, if long *Adrostus* liue,
Hee will at full requite your curtesies.
Tremelio,
In recompence of thy late valour done,
Take vnto thee the Catalonea prince,
Latelie our prisoner taken in the warres.
Be thou his keeper, his ransome shallbe thine;
Weele thinke of it when leasure shall afforde:
Meane while, doe vse him well; his father is a King.

Tre. Thankes to your Maiestie: his vsage shalbe such,
As he therat shall thinke no cause to grutce.
[*Exeunt ⟨Tremelio and Prince⟩.*

King. Then march we on to court, and rest our wearied limmes.
But, *Collen*, I haue a tale in secret kept for thee:
When thou shalt heare a watch woord from thy king,
Thinke then some waightie matter is at hand
That highlie shall concerne our state,
Then, *Collen*, looke thou be not farre from me:
And for thy seruice thou to fore hast done,
Thy trueth and valour proude in euerie point,
I shall with bounties thee enlarge therefore:
So guard vs to the courte.

Col. What so my soueraigne doth commaund me doe,
With willing mind I gladly yeeld consent.
[*Exeunt.*

⟨SCENE II. *The same.*⟩

Enter Segasto, and the Clowne with weapons about him.

Se. Tel me, sirra, how doe you like your weapons?

Clo. O verie wel, verie wel, they keep my sides warme.

Se. They keep the dogs from your shins very well, doe they not?

Clo. How, keep the dogs from my shins? I would scorne but my shins should keep the dogs from them.

Se. Well, sirra, leauing idle talke, tell me: Dost thou know captaine *Tremelioes* chamber?

Clo. I, verie well; it hath a doore.

Se. I thinke so, for so hath euery chamber. But dost thou know the man?

Clo. I, forsooth, he hath a nose on his face.

Se Why so hath euery on⟨e⟩.

Clo. Thats more then I know.

Se. But doest thou remember the captaine, that was heere with the king euen now, that brought the yong prince prisoner?

Clo. O, verie well.

Se. Go vnto him and bid him come to me. Tell him I haue a matter in secret to impart to him.

Clo. I wil, master:—master, whats his name?

Se. Why, captaine *Tremelio*.

Clo. O, the meale man. I knowe him verie well. He brings meale euery satturday. But harke you, master, must I bid him come to you or must you come to him?

Act II. Scene I. *WP* The Camp, *etc. pr. ed.* *S. D.* Tremelio *add. Q 3* 1 our *Qq*: that our *Haz.* 2 the foile *Qq*: haue had the foil *Haz.*: to foil *Wag.* 4 warres *Q 3 ff.* 3, 5 *End* peace, home *Qq* 6 to be *om. Q 8 ff.* 10 to *Q 1*: vnto *Q 8 ff.*: to the *Col.* 14 What *Qq*: How *WP* 15 And *Q 1*: An't *Q 3 ff.* 21, 22 *One line Qq* 23 Catalone aprince *Q 1*: Catalone, a Prince *Q 3 ff.*: Catalonian prince *Haz.* 26 thinke *Q 1-8*: haue *Q 11 ff.*

S. D. Tremelio, *etc. add. Haz.* 32 kept *Q 1-6* fit *Q 8 ff.* Scene II. *D* 6 very *om. Q 8*: very well *om. Q 14* 8 could *Q 3* 26 Tremelio, man *Elze*

Se. No, sir, he must come to me.

Clo. Harke you, master, how if he be not at home? What shall I doe then?

Se. Why, then ⟨thou⟩ leaust worde with some of his folkes.

Clo. Oh, maister, if there be no bodie within, I will leaue word with his dog.

Se. Why, can his dog speake?

Clo. I cannot tell; wherefore doth he keep his chamber els?

Se. To keepe out such knaues as thou art.

Clo. Nay, be ladie, then go your selfe.

Se. You will go, sir, wil ye not?

Clo. Yes, marrie, will I. O tis come to my head:
And a be not within, Ile bring his chamber to you.

Se. What, wilt thou plucke down the Kings house?

Clo. Nay, be ladie, ile knowe the price of it first. Master, it is such a hard name, I haue forgotten it againe. I praie you, tell me his name.

Se. I tell thee, captaine *Tremelio*.

Clo. Oh, captaine treble knaue, captaine treble knaue.

Enter Tremelio.

Tre. How now, sirra, doost thou call mee?

Clo. You must come to my maister, captain treble knaue.

Tre. My Lord *Segasto,* did you send for mee?

Se. I did, *Tremelio*. Sirra, about your businesse.

Clo. I, marry: whats that, can you tell?

Se. No, not well.

Clo. Marrie, then, I can: straight to the kitchen dresser, to Iohn the cooke, and get me a good peece of beefe and brewis, and then to the buttery hatch to Thomas the butler for a iacke of beare, and there for an houre ile so be labour my selfe! therefore, I pray you, cal me not till you thinke I haue done, I pray you, good mayster.

Se. Well, sir, away. ⟨*Exit Mouse.*⟩
Tremelio, this it is: thou knowest the valour of *Segasto* spred through all the kingdome of Arragon, and such as hath found triumph and fauours, neuer daunted at any tyme; but now a shepherd ⟨is⟩ admired at in court for worthynesse, and *Segastoes* honour layd a side. My wil, therefore, is this, that thou dost find som meanes to worke the shepheardes death. I know thy strength sufficient to performe my desire, & thy loue no other wise then to reuenge my iniuries.

Tre. It is not the frownes of a shepheard that *Tremelio* feares. Therefore, account it accomplished, what I take in hand.

Se. Thankes, good *Tremelio,* and assure thy selfe,
What I promise that will I performe.

Tre. Thankes, my good Lord, and in good time see where
He commeth: stand by a while, and you shall see
Me put in practise your intended driftes.
Haue at thee, swaine, if that I hit thee right.

Enter Mucedorus.

Mu. Vild coward, so without cause to strike a man.
Turne, coward, turne; now strike and doe thy woorst.

Mucedorus killeth him.

Se. Hould, shepheard, hould; spare him, kill him not!
Accursed villaine, tell me, what hast thou done?
Ah, *Tremelio,* trustie *Tremelio!*
I sorrow for thy death, and since that thou,
Liuing, didst prooue faithfull to *Segasto,*
So *Segasto* now, liuing, shall honoure
The dead corpes of *Trem*⟨*e*⟩*lio* with reuenge.
Bloudthirsty villaine,
Borne and bredde to mercilesse murther,
Tell me, how durst thou be so bold as once
To lay thy hands vpon the least of mine?
Assure thy selfe,
Thou shalt be vsd according to the law.

Mu. *Segasto*, cease, these threats are needlesse.
Accuse not me of murther, that haue done
Nothing but in mine owne defence.

Se. Nay, shepheard, reason not with me.
Ile manifest thy fact vnto the King,
Whose doome will be thy death, as thou deserust.
What hoe, Mouse, come away!

31 sir *Q 1*: sirra *Q 3, etc.* 32 how *om. Q 8* 34 thou *add. pr. ed.* leaust *Q 1* : leaue *Q 3, etc.* 36 Oh *Qq* : How *Haz.* 42, 48 by Lady *Q 3 ff.*: by'r Lady *Haz.* 43 ye *Q 1* : you *Q 3, etc.* 48 Nay *Q 1-6* : No *Q 8* 52 Tremelio, knave *Elze* 69 and therefore *Q 3, etc.* 72 *S. D. add. Haz.* 73-8 *Verse Qq, div.* Segasto, Arragon, fauours, shepherd, worthynesse, a side. *The speech may have been written in verse, but, if so, is hopelessly corrupt. Cf. ll.* 97-107, 131-4.

77 is *add. Haz.* at *om. Q 5 ff.* 89-91 *Div.* time, while *Qq* : *corr. Haz.* 91 intented *Q 1* drift *Q 3 ff.* 97-107 *Lines end* death, to, dead, reuenge, murther, bold, mine, law, *Qq* : *corr. pr. ed.* 102 Bloudthristy *Q 1* 109 *Ends* nothing *Qq*

⟨*Enter Mouse.*⟩

Clo. Why how now, whats the matter? I thougt you would be calling before I had done.

Se. Come, helpe; away with my friend.

Clo. Why, is he drunke? cannot he stand on his feet?

Se. No, he is not drunke, he is slaine.

Clo. Flaine? no, by Ladie, he is not flaine.

Se. Hees kild, I tell thee.

Clo. What, doe you vse to kil your friends? I will serue you no longer.

Se. I tell thee, the shepheard kild him.

Clo. O, did a so? but, master, I will haue al his apparel if I carry him away.

Se. Why, so thou shalt.

Clo. Come, then, I will healpe; mas, master, I thinke his mother song looby to him, he is so heauie. [*Exeunt* ⟨*Segasto and Mouse*⟩.

Mu. Behold the fickle state of man, alwaies mutable,
Neuer at one. Somtimes we feed on fancies
With the sweete of our desires; somtimes againe
We feele the heat of extreame miserie.
Now am I in fauour about the court and countrie.
To morrow those fauours will turne to frownes:
To daie I liue reuenged on my foe,
To morrow I die, my foe reuenged on me. [*Exit.*

⟨SCENE III. *The Forest.*⟩

Enter Bremo, a wild man.

Bre. No passengers this morning? what, not one?
A chance that seldome doth befall.
What, not one? then lie thou there,
And rest thyselfe til I haue further neede,
Now, Bremo, sith thy leasure so affords,—
An endlesse thing. Who knowes not Bremoes strength,
Who like a king commandes within these woods?
The beare, the boare, dares not abide my sight,
But hastes away to saue themselues by flight:
The christall waters in the bubbling brookes,
When I come by, doth swiftly slide away,
And claps themselues in closets vnder bankes,
Afraide to looke bold *Bremo* in the face:
The aged okes at *Bremoes* breath doe bowe,
And all things els are still at my commaund.
Els What would I ?
Rent them in peeces and plucke them from the earth,
And each waie els I would reuenge my selfe.
Why who comes heere with whome I dare not fight?
Who fights with me & doth not die the death?
Not on⟨e⟩ : What fauour shewes this sturdie sticke to those,
That heere within these woods are combatantes with me?
Why, death, and nothing else but present death.
With restlesse rage I wander through these woods,
No creature heere but feareth *Bremoes* force,
Man, woman, child, beast and bird,
And euery thing that doth approch my sight,
Are forst to fall if *Bremo* once but frowne.
Come, cudgel, come, my partner in my spoiles,
For heere I see this daie it will not be;
But when it falles that I encounter anie,
One pat suffiseth for to worke my wil.
What, comes not one? then lets begon;
A time will serue when we shal better speed. [*Exit.*

⟨SCENE IV. *Arragon. A Room of State in the Court.*⟩

Enter the King, Segasto, the Shepheard and the Clowne, with others.

King. Shephard, thou hast heard thine accusers;
Murther is laid to thy charge.
What canst thou say? thou hast deserued death.

Mu. Dread soueraigne, I must needes confesse,
I slewe this captaine in mine owne defence,
Not of any malice, but by chance;
But mine accuser hath a further meaning.

Se. Woords will not heere preuaile,
I seek for iustice, & iustice craues his death.

King. Shepheard, thine owne confession hath condemned thee.
Sirra, take him away, & doe him to execution straight.

Clo. So hee shall, I warrant him; but doe you heare, maister King, he is kin to a monkie, his necke is bigger then ⟨h⟩is head.

Se. Com, sirra, away with him, and hang him about the middle.

S. D. add. Q 3 121 by *Qq* : by'r *Haz.* 130 song *Q 1* : sung *Q 3, etc.* *S. D.* Segasto, *etc. add. pr. ed.* 132-5 *Three lines Qq., div.* one, desires, miserie : *corr. pr. ed.* 135 miserie *Q 1* : miseries *Q 3. etc.* *S. D.* Exit *Q 3, etc.*: Exeunt *Q 1* Scene III. *WP* 1 passenger *Q 3, etc.* 5 sith *Qq* : sit *Elze* 6 endlesse *Qq* : needless *Elze* : aimless *Wag.* 7 commander *Q 1-5* 9 haste *Q 3, etc.* 11 doe *Q 6 ff.*

17 Rent *Q 1* : Rend *Q 3 ff.* and *om. WP* 22 combatatines *Q 1* 26 child *Qq* : child and *Elze* 32 suffiezth *Q 3* : suffised *Q 1* Scene IV. *WP* Arragon, *etc. add. T* 11 *Two lines WP, div.* away straight to execution *WP* 13 hee *Qq* : I *WP* 16 Com *om. Haz.*

Clo. Yes, forsooth, I warrant you: come on, sir. A, so like a sheepe biter a lookes!

Enter Amadine and a boie with a beares head.

Ama. Dread soueraigne and welbeloued sire,
On bended knees I craue the life of this
Condemned shepheard, which heertofore preserued
The life of thy sometime distressed daughter.
K. Preserued the life of my somtime distressed daughter?
How can that be? I neuer knew the time
Wh⟨e⟩rein thou wast distrest; I neuer knew the daie
But that I haue maintained thy state,
As best beseemd the daughter of a king.
I neuer saw the shepheard vntil now.
How comes it, then, that he preserud thy life?
Ama. Once walkeing with *Segasto* in the woods,
Further then our accustomed maner was,
Right before vs, downe a steepe fal hill,
A monstrous vgly beare doth hie him fast
To meete vs both: now whether this bee trewe,
I referre it to the credit of *Segasto.*
Se. Most trew, and like your maiestie.
King. How then?
Ama. The beare, being eager to obtaine his praie,
Made forward to vs with an open mouth,
As if he meant to swallow vs both at once;
The sight whereof did make vs both to dread,
But speciallie your daughter *Amadine,*
Who, for I saw no succour incident
But in *Segastoes* valour, I grew desperate,
And he most cowardlike began to fly—
Left me distrest to be deuourd of him.
How say you, *Segasto,* is it not true?
K. His silence verifies it to be true. What then?
Ama. Then I amasde, distressed, all alone,
Did hie me fast to scape that vglie beare,
But all in vaine, for, why, he reached after me,
And hardly I did oft escape his pawes,
Till at the length this shepheard came,
And brought to me his head.
Come hither boy: loe, heere it is,
Which I present vnto your maiestie.
Ki. The slaughter of this beare deserues great fame.
Se. The slaughter of a man deserues greate blame.
King. Indeed occasion oftentimes so falles out.
Se. *Tremelio* in the wars, *O King,* preserued thee.
Ama. The shepheard in the woods, o king, preserued me.
S. Tremelio fought when many men did yeeld.
Ama. So would the shepheard, had he bin in field.
Clo. So would my maister, had he not run away.
Se. *Tremelioes* force saued thousands from the foe.
Ama. The shepheards force ⟨would⟩ haue saued thousands more.
Clo. Aye, shipstickes, nothing else.
King. *Segasto,* cease to accuse the shepheard,
His woorthynesse deserues a recompence,
All we are bound to doe the shepheard good:
Shepheard, whereas it was my sentence, thou shouldst die,
So shall my sentence stand, for thou shalt die.
Se. Thankes to your maiestie.
King. But soft, *Segasto,* not for this offence.—
Long maist thou liue, and when the sisters shal decree
To cut in twaine the twisted thread of life,
Then let him die: for this I set thee free:
And for thy valour I will honour thee.
Mu. Thankes to your maiestie.
King. Come, daughter, let vs now departe, to honour the worthy valour of the shepheard with our rewards. [*Exeunt.*

Clo. O mayster, heare you, you haue made a freshe hand now you would be slowe, you; why, what will you doe nowe? you haue lost me a good occupation by the meanes. Faith, maister, now I cannot hang the shepheard, I pray you, let me take the paines to hang you: it is but halfe an houres exercise.

Se. You are still in your knauery, but sith I cannot haue his life I will procure his banishment for euer. Come on, sirra.

Clo. Yes, forsooth, I come.—Laugh at him, I pray you. [*Exeunt.*

⟨ACT III.

Scene I. *Grove near the Court.*⟩

Enter Mucedorus solus.

Mu. From *Amadine* and from her fathers court,

21–3 *Prose Qq* 21 benden *Haz.* kees *Q 1*: knee *Q 3 ff.* 22 which tofore *WP* 34 doth *Q 1*: did *Q 3 ff.* 54–7 *Div.* brought, it is *WP* 56, 57 *One line Qq*: *corr. Haz.* 60 ofttimes *Elze* 67 haue *Q 1*: hath *Q 3, etc.*: would haue *pr. ed.* thousand *Q 1* 68 A ye *Q 3 ff.* 74 maistie *Q 1* 78 him free *Q 3 ff.* 85 you would be slowe you *Q 1–6*: I thought you would beshrow you *Q 8 ff.* 87 this means *Haz.* Act III, Scene I, *WP*

With gold and siluer and with rich rewardes,
Flowing from the bankes of golden tresuries,—
More may I boast and say: but I,
Was neuer shepheard in such dignitie.

Enter the messenger and the clowne.

Mess. All hayle, worthy shepheard.

Clo. All rayne, lowsie shepheard.

Mu. Welcome, my frindes; from whence come you?

Mess. The *King* and *Amadine* greetes thee well, and after greetings done, bids thee depart the court: shepheard, begon.

Clo. Shepheard, take lawe legs; flye away, shepheard.

Mu. Whose woordes are these? came these from *Amadine*?

Mess. Aye, from *Amadine.*

Clo. Aye, from *Amladine.*

Mu. Ah, luckelesse fortune, worse then *Phaetons* tale,
My former blisse is now become my bale.

Clo. What, wilt thou poyson thy selfe?

Mu. My former heauen is now become my hell.

Clo. The worst ale house that I euer came in, in al my life.

Mu. What shall I doe?

Clo. Euen goe hang thy selfe halfe an hower.

Mu. Can *Amadine* so churelishly commaund,
To banish the shepheard from her Fathers court?

Mess. What should shepheardes doe in the court?

Clo. What should shepherdes doe amongst vs? haue we not Lordes inough on vs in the courte?

Mu. Why, shepheardes are men, and kinges are no more.

Mess. Shepheardes are men and maisters ouer their flocke.

Clo. Thats a lie: who payes them their wages then?

Mes. Well, you are alwayes interrupting of me, but you are best looke to him, least you hang for him when he is gone. [*Exit.*

The Clowne sings.

Clo. And you shall hang for companie,
For leauing me alone.
Shepheard, stand foorth and heare thy sentence:
Shepheard, begone within three dayes in payne of
My displeasure: shepheard, begon; shepheard, begon; begon, begon, begon, shepheard, shepheard, shepheard. [*Exit.*

Mu. And must I goe, and must I needs depart?
Ye goodly groues, partakers of my songes
In tyme tofore when fortune did not frowne,
Powre foorth your plaints and waile a while with me;
And thou bright sunne, my comfort in the cold,
Hide, hide thy face and leaue me comfortlesse;
Ye holsome hearbes, and sweete smelling fauours,
Ye each thing els prolonging life of man,
Change, change your wonted course, that I,
Wanting your aide, in woefull sort may die.

Enter Amadine ⟨*and Ariena her maide*⟩.

Ama. *Ariena,* if any body aske for mee,
Make some excuse till I returne.

Ari. What and *Segasto* call?

Ama. Do thou the like to him; I mean not to stay long. ⟨*Exit Ariena.*⟩

Mu. This voyce so sweet my pining spirites reuiues.

Ama. Shepheard, wel met; tel me how thou doest.

Mu. I linger life, yet wish for speedy death.

Ama. Shepheard, although thy banishment already
Be decreed, and all agaynst my will,
Yet *Amadine*—

Mu. Ah, *Amadine,* to heare of banishment
Is death, I, double death to me,
But since I must depart, one thing I craue.

Ama. Say on with all my heart.

Mu. That in absence, either farre or neere,
You honor me, as seruant, with your name.

Ama. Not so.

Mu. And why?

Ama. I honour thee, as soueraigne, with my heart.

Mu. A shepheard and a soueraigne? nothing like.

Ama. Yet like enough where there is no dislike.

Mu. Yet great dislike, or els no banishment.

Ama. Shepheard, it is onely

3 golden *Q 1–6*: gold and *Q 8 ff.* tresuries *Q 1*: treasures *Q 3 ff.* *S. D.* messenger *Q 3*: messengers *Q 1* 11 greeting *Q 3 ff.* 15 Come *Haz.* 20 blesse *Q 1* 33 on *Qq*: o'er *Haz.* 42 were best to looke *Q 8 ff.*

46 thy *Q 1*: my *Q 3, etc.* 59 *Ends* course *Qq* *S. D.* and . . maide *add. Q 3 D,* *WP begins* Scene II. *here* 65 *S. D.* Exit *after* 63 *Q 3 ff.* 69 *Ends* be *Q 1* 70 my *Q 3, etc.*: thy *Q 1* 76 in my absence *WP* 77 with *Q 1–6*: to *Q 8 ff.* 80 Soueraigne of *Q 3, etc.* 84, 85 *One line Qq*

Segasto that procures thy banishment.
Mu. Vnworthy wightes are most in ielosie.
Ama. Would God they would free the from banishment,
Or likewise bannish mee.
Mu. Amen, say I, to haue your companie.
Ama. Well, shepheard, sith thou sufferest this for my sake,
With thee in exile also let me liue—
On this condition, shepheard, thou canst loue.
Mu. No longer loue, no longer let me liue!
Ama. Of lat I loued one indeed, now loue I none but onely thee.
Mu. Thankes, worthie princes; I borne likewise,
Yet smother vp the blast,
I dare not promise what I may performe.
Ama. Well, shepheard, harke what I shall say:
I will returne vnto my Fathers court,
There for to prouide me of such nescessaries,
As for our iourney I shall thinke most fit;
This being done, I will returne to thee.
Doe thou, therefore, appoint the place where we may meete.
Mu. Downe in the valley where I slue the beare:
And there doth grow a faire broade branched beach,
That ouershades a well; so who comes first
Let them abid the happie meeting of vs both.
How like you this?
Ama. I like it very wel.
Mu. Now, if you please, you may appoint the time.
Ama. Full three hours hence, God willing, I will returne.
Mu. The thankes that *paris* gaue the grecian queene
The like doth Mucedorus yeeld.
Ama. Then, *Mucedorus,* for three howres farewell. [*Exit.*
Mu. Your departure, ladie, breedes a priuie paine. [*Exit.*

⟨Scene II. *The Court.*⟩

Enter Segasto solus.

Se. Tis well, *Segasto,* that thou hast thy will;
Should such a shephard, such a simple swaine
As he, eclips thy credite famous through
The court? No, ply, *Segasto,* ply:
Let it not in Arragon be saide,
A shephard hath *Segastoes* honour wonne.

Enter Mouse the clowne calling his maister.

Clo. What hoe, maister, will you come away?

Se. Will you come hither? I pray you, whats the matter?

Clo. Why, is it not past aleauen a clock?

Se. How then, sir?

Clo. I pray you, com away to dinner.

Se. I pray you, come hither.

Clo. Heres such a doe with you! wil you neuer come?

Se. I pray you, sir, what newes of the message I sente you about?

Clo. I tell you all the messes be on the table alreadie. There wants not so much as a messe of mustard halfe an hower agoe.

Se. Come, sir, your minde is all vpon your belly;
You haue forgotten what I did bid you doe.

Clo. Faith, I knowe nothing, but you bad me goe to breakefast.

Se. Was that all?

Clo. Faith, I haue forgotten it; the verie sent of the meate hath made me forget it quite.

Se. You haue forgotten the arrant I bid you doe?

Clo. What arrant? an arrant knaue, or arrant whore?

Se. Why, thou knaue, did I not bid thee banish the shepheard?

Clo. O, the shephards bastard.

Se. I tell thee, the shepheardes banishment.

Clo. I tel you the shepheards bastard shalbe wel kept: ile looke to it myselfe else; but I pray you, come away to dinner.

Se. Then you wil not tell me whether you haue banished him or noe?

Clo. Why, I cannot say banishment, and you would giue me a thousand pounds to say so.

Se. Why, you horson slaue, haue you forgotten that I sent you and another to driue away the shephard.

Clo. What an asse are you; heers a sturre indeede: heeres 'message,' 'arrant,' 'banishment,' and I cannot tell what.

Se. I pray you, sir, shall I know whether you haue droue him away?

87, 88 *One line Q 1–3* : *corr. Q 6* 88 bamish *Q 1* 90, 91 *Prose Q 1* : *corr. Q 3* 96 burne *Q 3, etc.* 98 mayn't *conj. Wag.* 101 There for *Q 3, etc.*: Therefore *Q 1* 102 our *Q 1* : my *Q 3, etc.* Scene II] Scene III *WP* 3–5 *Div.* court, saide *Qq* 3 As he *om. WP*

4 ply . . ply *Qq, etc.* : ? fye . . fye 24 did *om. Q 3 ff.* 29 made me hath *Q 1–6* forgot *Q 3–6* 40 else *om. Q 3, etc.*

Clo. Faith, I thinke I haue; and you will not beleeue me, aske my stafe.

Se. Why, can thy staffe tell?

⟨*Clo.*⟩ Why, he was with me to.

Se. Then happie I that haue obtaind my will.

Clo. And happier I, if you would goe to dinner.

Se. Come, sirra, follow me.

Clo. I warrant you, I will not loose an inch of you, now you are going to dinner.—I promise you, I thought seauen yeare before I could get him away.

[*Exeunt.*

⟨SCENE III. *The Forest.*⟩

Enter Amadine sola.

Ama. God grant my long delaie procures no harme
Nor this my tarrying frustrate my pretence.
My *Mucedorus* surelie staies for me,
And thinks me ouer long: at length I come
My present promise to performe.
Ah, what a thing is firme vnfained loue!
What is it which true loue dares not tempt?
My father he may make, but I must match;
Segasto loues, but *Amadine* must like,
Where likes her best; compulsion is a thrall:
No, no, the heartie choise is all in all,
The shephards vertue *Amadine* esteemes.
But, what, me thinks myshephard is not come.
I muse at that, the hower is sure at hande:
Well here ile rest till *Mucedorus* come.

Shee sits her downe.

Enter Bremo looking about, hastily taketh hould of her.

Bremo. A hapie pray! now, *Bremo*, feede on flesh.
Dainties, *Bremo*, dainties, thy hungry panch to fill!
Now glut thy greedie guts with luke warme blood!
Come, fight with me, I long to see thee dead.

Ama. How can she fight that weapons cannot weeld?

Bre. What, canst not fight? then lie thou downe and die.

Ama. What, must I die?

Bre. What needes these words? I thirst to sucke thy bloud.

Ama. Yet pittie me and let me liue a while.

Bre. No pittie I, ile feed vpon thy flesh,
Ile teare thy bodie peecemeale ioynt from ioynt.

Ama. Ah, now I want my shephards company.

Bre. Ile crush thy bones betwixt two oken trees.

Ama. Hast, shephard, hast, or else thou comst to lat.

Bre. Ile sucke the sweetnes from thy marie bones.

Ama. Ah spare, ah spare to shed my guiltlesse blood!

Bre. With this my bat will I beate out thy braines.
Down, down, I say, prostrate thy selfe vpon the ground.

Ama. Then, *Mucedorus*, farewel; my hoped ioies, farewel.
Yea, farewell life, and welcome present death!

Shee kneeles.

To thee, O God, I yeeld my dying ghost.

Bre. Now, *Bremo*, play thy part.—
How now, what sudden chaunce is this?
My limmes do tremble and my sinewes shake,
My vnweakned armes haue lost their former force:
Ah *Bremo, Bremo*, what a foyle hast thou,
That yet at no time euer wast afraide
To dare the greatest gods to fight with thee,

he strikes.

And now want strength for one downe driuing blow!
Ah, how my courage failes when I should strike:
Some newe come spirit, abiding in my breast,
Sayth 'spare her, *Bremo*, spare her, do not kill.'
Shall I spare her which neuer spared any?
To it, *Bremo*, to it, say againe.—
I cannot weeld my weapons in my hand;
Me thinkes I should not strik so faire a one:
I thinke her beawtie hath bewitcht my force
Or else with in me altered natures course.
Ay, woman, wilt thou liue in woods with me?

Ama. Faine would I liue, yet loth to liue in woodes.

Bre. Thou shalt not chuse, it shalbe as I say, & therefore, follow me.

[*Exit.*

58 *Prefix* Clo. *add.* *Q 3* 66 thought *Qq* : thought it *Haz.* Scene III] Scene IV *WP* 2 tarring *Q 1* 7 attempt *Q 3, etc.* 14 sure *om.* *Q 3 ff.* 23 needs *Q 8 ff.* 25 I, ile *Qq* : I will *WP* 26 Ile *Q 1–6* : And *Q 8 ff.* 27 now *Qq* : how *Haz.* 28 two] tow *Q 1* 30 Marrow-bones *Q 3, etc.* 38 change *Elze* 40 weakened *Col.* 44 wants *Q 3 ff.* 47 Saith *Q 8, etc.* : Shall I *Q 1–6* 48 Shall I *Q 8, etc.* : Sayth *Q 1–6* 49 say *Qq* : essay *Haz.* 50 weapon *WP* 55–6 *Prose Q 1*

⟨Scene IV. *The same.*⟩

Enter Mucedorus solus.

Mu. It was my wil an hower a goe and more,
As was my promise, for to make returne,
But other busines hindred my pretence.
It is a world to see when man appoints,
And purposelie one certaine thing decrees,
How manie things may hinder his intent.
What one would wish, the same is farthest off:
But yet thappoynted time cannot be past,
Nor hath her presence yet preuented mee.
Well, heere ile staie, and expect her comming.

They crie within, 'hould him, staie him, holde!'

Mu. Some one or other is pursued, no doubt;
Perhaps some search for me: tis good
To doubt the worst, therefore ile be gone. [*Exit.*

⟨Scene V. *The same.*⟩

Crie within 'hold him, hold him.' Enter Mouse the Clowne with a pot.

Clo. Hold him, hold him, hold him! heers a stur in deed. Heere came hewe after the crier: and I was set close at mother Nips house, and there I calde for three pots of ale, as tis the manner of vs courtiers. Now, sirra, I had taken the maiden head of two of them. Now, as I was lifting vp the third to my mouth, there came: hold him, hold him! now I coulde not tell whome to catch hold on, but I am sure I caught one: perchance a maie be in this pot. Well, ile see: mas, I cannot see him yet; well, ile looke a little further. Mas, he is a little slaue, if a be heere. Why, heers no bodie. Al this goes well yet: but if the olde trot shoulde come for her pot—I, marrie, theres the matter, but I care not; ile face her out, and cal her ould rustie, dustie, mustie, fustie, crustie fire-bran, and worse then al that, and so face her out of her pot: but softe, heere she comes.

Enter the ould woman.

Old wo. Come on, you knaue: wheres my pot, you knaue?

Clo. Goe looke your pot; come not to me for your pot twere good for you.

Old. Thou liest, thou knaue; thou hast my pot.

Clo. You lie, and you say it. I your pot! I know what ile say.

Old. Why, what wilt thou say?

Clo. But say I haue him, and thou darste.

Olde. Why, thou knaue, thou hast not onelie my pot but my drinke vnpaide for.

Clo. You lie like an old—I will not say whore.

Old. Dost thou cal me whore? ile cap thee for my pot.

Clo. Cap me & thou darest, search me whether I haue it or no.

Shee searcheth him, and he drinketh ouer her head and casts downe the pot; she stumbleth at it; then they fal together by the eares; she takes her pot and goes out. [*Exit.*

Enter Segasto.

Se. How now, sirra, whats the matter?

Clo. Oh, flies, maister, flies.

Se. Flies? where are they?

Clo. Oh heere, maister, all about your face.

Se. Why, thou liest; I think thou art mad.

Clo. Why, maister, I haue kild a duncart ful at the least.

Se. Go to, sirra! leauing this idel talke, giue eare to me.

Clo. How? giue you one of my eares? not & you were ten maisters.

Se. Why, sir, I bid you giue eare to my wordes.

Clo. I tell you I will not be made a curtall for no mans pleasure.

Se. I tell thee, attend what I say: goe thy waies straight and reare the whole towne.

Clo. How? reare the towne? euen goe your selfe; it is more then I can doe: why, doe you thinke I can reare a towne, that can scarse reare a pot of ale to my heade? I should reare a towne, should I not?

Se. Go to the cunstable and make a priuie search, for the shephard is runne away with the Kings daughter.

Clo. How? is the shepheard run away with the kings daughter? or is the kings daughter runne away with the shepheard?

Se. I cannot tell, but they are both gon together.

Clo. What a foole is she to runne away with the shepheard! why, I thinke I am a litle hansomer man then the shepheard my selfe; but tel me, maister, must I make a priuie search, or search in the priuie?

Se. Why, dost thou thinke they will be there?

Clo. I cannot tell.

Se. Well, then, search euerie where; leaue no place vnsearched for them. [*Exit.*

Scene IV] Scene V *WP* 7 one *Q 3, etc.* : once *Q 1* 9 me *Q 3, etc.* : wee *Q 1* 12, 13 *Prose Q 1* : *div.* worst *Q 3 ff.* : *corr. Haz.* Scene V] Scene VI *WP* 6 tow *Q 1* 17 crustkie *Q 1* 22 look for your *WP*

35 my for *Q 1* 36 scarce *Q 1* 51 not] no *Q 1* 68 she is *Haz.*

Clo. Oh now am I in office; now wil I to that old firbrands house & wil not leaue one place vnsearched: nay, ile to her ale stand & drink as long as I can stand, & when I haue done, ile let out al the rest, to se if he be not hid in the barrel. & I find him not there, ile to the cubord; ile not leaue one corner of her house vnsearched: y' faith, ye old crust, I wilbe with you now. [*Exit.*

[⟨ACT IV.

SCENE I. *Valentia. The Court.*⟩

Sound Musicke.

Enter the King of Valentia, Anselmo, Roderigo, Lord Borachius, with others.

King Va. Enough of Musicke, it but ads to torment;
Delights to vexed spirits are as Dates
Set to a sickly man, which rather cloy then comfort:
Let mee intreate you to intreat no more.

Rod. Let your strings sleepe; haue done there.

Let the musicke cease.

Kin. V. Mirth to a soule disturb'd are embers turn'd,
Which sudden gleame with molestation,
But sooner loose their sight fort;
Tis Gold bestowd vpon a Ryotor,
Which not relieues, but murders him: Tis a Drugge
Giuen to the healthfull, Which infects, not cures.
How can a Father that hath lost his Sonne,
A Prince both wise, vertuous, and valiant,
Take pleasure in the idle actes of Time?
No, no; till Mucedorus I shall see againe,
All ioy is comfortlesse, all pleasure paine.

Ans. Your Sonne (my Lord) is well.

Ki. V. I pre-thee, speake that thrise.

Ans. The Prince, your Sonne, is safe.

K. V. O where, Anselmo? surfet me with that.

Ans. In Aragon, my Liege;
And at his parture, Bound my secrecie,
By his affectious loue, not to disclose it:
But care of him, and pittie of your age,
Makes my tongue blab what my breast vow'd concealment.

K. V. Thou not deceiu'st me?
I euer thought thee What I find thee now,
An vpright, loyall man. But what desire,
Or young-fed humour Nurst within the braine,
Drew him so priuatly to Aragon?

Ans. A forcing Adamant:
Loue, mixt with feare and doubtfull ielousie,
Whether report guilded a worthlesse truncke,
Or Amadine deserued her high extolment.

K. V. See our prouision be in readinesse;
Collect vs followers of the comliest hue
For our chiefe guardions, we will thither wend:
The christall eye of Heauen shall not thrise wincke,
Nor the greene Flood sixe times his shoulders turne,
Till we salute the Aragonian King.
Musicke speake loudly now, the season's apt,
For former dolours are in pleasure wrapt.
Exeunt omnes.]

⟨SCENE II. *The Forest.*⟩

Enter Mucedorus to disguise himselfe.

Mu. Now, *Mucedorus*, whither wilt thou goe?
Home to thy father, to thy natiue soile,
Or trie some long abode within these woods?
Well, I will hence depart and hie me home.—
What, hie me home, said I? that may not be;
In *Amadine* rests my felicitie.
Then, *Mucedorus*, do as thou didst decree:
Attire thee hermite like within these groues,
Walke often to the beach and view the well,
Make settles there and seate thy selfe thereon,
And when thou feelest thy selfe to be a thirst,
Then drinke a heartie draught to *Amadine*.
No doubt she thinkes on thee,
And wil one day come pleg thee at this well.
Come, habit, thou art fit for me:
he disguiseth himselfe:
No shepheard now, a hermit I must be.
Me thinkes this fits me verie well;
Now must I learne to beare a walking staffe.
And exercise some grauitie withall.

Enter the Clowne.

Clo. Heers throw the wods, and throw the wods, to looke out a shepheard & a stray kings daugter: but softe, who haue we heere? what art thou?

Mu. I am an hermit.

Clo. An emmet? I neuer saw such ⟨a⟩ big emmet in all my life before.

85 y' fayth *Q 3, etc.* : ye faith *Q 1* *Act IV, Sc. I. add. Q 3* Act IV, Scene I. *WP* 4 to repeat *conj. Col.* 5 your] yon *Haz.* 6 are *Qq* : is *Haz.* 8 sight *Qq* : light *Col.* 10, 11 *Three lines Qq, div.* him, healthfull. 10 Tis *om. Elze* 18 twice *Col.* 21 *Ends* parture *Qq* 22 parture *Q 3–6* : parting *Q 8 ff.* 23 affectious *Q 3–11* : affections *Q 12 ff.* loue *Qq* : loss *Elze*

26–9 *Div.* thought thee, man, humour *Qq* : *corr. pr. ed.* 29 the] his *Q 8 ff.* 38 eyes *Haz.* Scene II. *WP* 8 grouees *Q 1* 14 pledge *Q 3, etc.* 16 a *Q 1–6* : an *Q 8 ff.* must I *Q 3, etc.* 25 a *add. Q 3*

Mu. I tel you, sir, I am an hermit, one that leads a solitarie life within these woods.

Clo. O, I know the now, thou art hee that eates vp al the hips and hawes; we could not haue one peece of fat bacon for thee al this yeare.

Mu. Thou dost mistake me; but I pray thee, tell mee what dost thou seeke in these woods?

Clo. What doe I seeke? for a stray Kings daughter runne away with a shephard.

Mu. A stray Kings daughter runne away with a shephearde.
Wherefore? canst thou tell?

Clo. Yes, that I can; tis this: my maister and *Amadine*, walking one day abrod, nearer to these woods then they were vsed—about what I can not tell—but towarde them comes running a greate beare. Now my maister, he plaide the man and runne away, & *Amadine* crying after him: now, sir, comes me a shepheard & strikes off the beares head. Now whether the bear were dead before or no I cannot tell, for bring twentie bears before me and binde their hands & feete and ile kil them al:—now euer since *Amadine* hath bin in loue with the shepheard, and for good wil shees euen runne away with the shepheard.

Mu. What manner of man was a? canst describe him vnto mee?

Clo. Scrib him? aye, I warrant you, that I can: a was a littel, low, broad, tall, narrow, big, wel fauoured fellow, a ierkin of whit cloath, and buttons of the same cloath.

Mu. Thou discribest him wel, but if I chaunce to se any such, pray you, wher shal I find you, or whats your name?

Clo. My name is called maister mouse,

Mu. Oh, maister mouse, I pray you what office might you beare in the court?

Clo. Marry, sir, I am a rusher of the stable.

Mu. O, vsher of the table.

Clo. Nay, I say rusher and ile prooue mine office good; for looke, sir, when any coms from vnder the sea or so, and a dog chance to blow his nose backewarde, then with a whip I giue him the good time of the day, and strawe rushes presently: therefore, I am a rusher, a hie office, I promise ye.

Mu. But where shall I find you in the Courte?

Clo. Why, where it is best being, either in the kitching a eating or in the butterie drinking: but if you come, I will prouide for thee a peece of beefe & brewis knockle deepe in fat; pray you, take paines, remember maister mouse. [*Exit.*

Mu. Ay, sir, *I* warrant *I* will not forget you.
Ah, *Amadine,* what should become of the?
Whither shouldst thou go so long vnknowne?
With watch and warde eche passage is beset,
So that she cannot long escape vnknowne.
Doubtlesse she hath lost her selfe within these woods
And wandring too and fro she seekes the well,
Which yet she cannot finde; therefore will I seek her out. [*Exit.*

⟨Scene III. *The same.*⟩

Enter Bremo and Amadine.

Bre. *Amadine,* how like you *Bremo* & his woodes?

Ama. As like the woods of *Bremoes* crueltie:
Though I were dombe and could not answer him,
The beastes themselues would with relenting teares
Bewaile thy sauage and vnhumaine deedes.

Bre. My loue, why dost thou murmur to thy selfe?
Speake lowder, for thy *Bremo* heares thee not.

Ama. My *Bremo?* no, the shepheard is my loue.

Bre. Haue I not saued thee from sudden death,
Giuing thee leaue to liue that thou mightst loue?
And dost thou whet me on to crueltie?
Come kisse me, swete, for all my fauours past.

Am. I may not, *Bremo,* and therefore pardon me.

Bre. See how shee flings away from me; I will follow
And giue a rend to her. Denie my loue!
Ah, worme of beautie, I wil chastice the:
Com, com, prepare thy head vpon the block.

Ama. Oh, spare me, *Bremo,* loue should limit life,
Not to be made a murderer of him selfe.
If thou wilt glut thy louing heart with blood,
Encounter with the lion or the beare,
And like a wolfe pray not vpon a lambe.

Bre. Why then dost thou repine at me?
If thou wilt loue me thou shalt be my queene:
I will crowne thee with a chaplet made of Iuie,
And make the rose and lilly wait on thee:
Ile rend the burley braunches from the oke,

29 hee *Q 4, etc.*: her *Q 1, 3* 34 seeke *Qq*: seek for *Elze* 35 seek for? *WP* 45 and hee strikes *Q 3, etc.* 47 were] where *Q 1* 53 canst thou *WP* 67 mine *Qq*: my *Haz.* 77 a *om. Q 5 ff.*

83 the *Q 1*: thee *Q 3–6*: her *Q 8 ff.* 86 *om. Haz.* 89 her *Q 3, etc.*: hers *Q 1* Scene III. *WP* 14–17 *Div.* me, her, beautie *Q 1* 14 flings *Q 1–6*: flies *Q 8 ff.* 15 a rend *Q 1*: attend *Q 3 ff.*: attent *WP* 22 like a] a like *Q 1* 25 complet *Q 1–4* Ivy *D*: Iuorie *Qq*

To shadow thee from burning sunne.
The trees shall spred themselues where thou dost go,
And as they spread, ile trace along with thee,
Ama. You may, for who but you? ⟨*Aside.*⟩
Bre. Thou shalt bee fed with quailes and partridges,
With blacke birds, larkes, thrushes and nightingales.
Thy drinke shall bee goates milke and christal water,
Distilled from the fountaines & the clearest springs.
And all the dainties that the woods afforde.
Ile freely giue thee to obtaine thy loue.
Ama. You may, for who but you? ⟨*Aside.*⟩
Bre. The day ile spend to recreate my loue
With all the pleasures that I can deuise,
And in the night ile be thy bedfellow,
And louingly embrace thee in mine armes.
Ama. One may, so may not you. ⟨*Aside.*⟩
Bre. The satyres & the woodnimphs shal attend on the
And lull thee a sleepe with musickes sounde,
And in the morning when thou dost awake,
The lark shall sing good morne to my queene,
And whilst he singes, ile kisse my *Amadine*.
Ama. You may, for who but you? ⟨*Aside.*⟩
Br. When thou art vp, the wood lanes shalbe strawed
With violets, cowslips, and swete marigolds
For thee to trampel and to trace vpon,
And I will teach thee how to kill the deare,
To chase the hart and how to rowse the roe,
If thou wilt liue to loue and honour mee.
Ama. You may, for who but you? ⟨*Aside.*⟩

Enter Mucedorus.

Bre. Welcome, sir,
An howre ago I lookt for such a gest.
Be merrie, wench, weele haue a frollike feast:
Heeres flesh inough for to suffise vs both.
Staie, sirra, wilt thou fight or dost thou yeel to die?
Mu. I want a weapon; how can I fight?
Bre. Thou wants a weapon? why then thou yeelst to die.
Mu. I say not so; I doe not yeeld to die.
Bre. Thou shalt not choose. I long to see thee dead.
Ama. Yet spare him, *Bremo,* spare him.
Bre. Away, I say, I will not spare him.
Mu. Yet giue me leaue to speake.
Bre. Thou shalt not speake.
Ama. Yet giue him leaue to speake for my sake.
Bre. Speake on, but be not ouer long.
Mu. In time of yore, when men like brutish beasts
Did lead their liues in loathsom celles and woodes
And wholy gaue themselues to witlesse will,
A rude vnruly rout, then man to man
Became a present praie, then might preuailed,
The weak⟨e⟩st went to walles:
Right was vnknowen, for wrong was all in all.
As men thus liued in this great outrage,
Behould one *Orpheus* came, as poets tell,
And them from rudenes vnto reason brought,
Who led by reason soone forsooke the woods.
Insteade of caues they built them castles strong;
Citties and townes were founded by them then:
Glad were they, they found such ease,
And in the end they grew to perfect amitie;
Waying their former wickednesse,
They tearmd the time wherein they liued then
A golden age, a goodly golden age.
Now, Bremo, for so I heare thee called,
If men which liued tofore as thou dost now,
Wilie in wood, addicted all to spoile,
Returned were by worthy *Orpheus* meanes,
Let me like *Orpheus* cause thee to returne
From murder, bloudshed and like crueltie.
What, should we fight befor we haue a cause?
No, lets liue and loue together faithfully.
Ile fight for thee.
Bre. Fight for me or die: or fight or els thou diest.
Ama. Hold, *Bremo*, hold!
Bre. Away, I say, thou troublest mee.
Ama. You promised me to make me your queenne.
Bre. I did, I meane no less.
Ama. You promised that I should haue my wil.
Bre. I did, I meane no lesse.
Ama. Then saue this hermits life, for he may saue vs both.

B. At thy request ile spare him, but neuer any after him. Say, hermit, what canst thou doe?

Mu. Ile waite on thee, somtime vpon the queene. Such seruice shalt thou shortly haue as Bremo neuer had. [*Ex⟨e⟩unt.*

31, 38, 43, 49 Aside *add. Haz.* 47 good-morrow *Q 3, etc.* 52 trace *Qq* : tread *Col.* 56 Aside *add. WP* 57 Welcomd *Q 1* 62 how *Qq* : why, how *Elze* 63 why then *Qq* : then *Elze* 75 *Ends* became *Qq* 77 wall *Haz.* 79 this *pr. ed.* : his *Q 1* : their *Q 3, etc.* 82 Reason, soone *Q 6, etc.* : reasonson some *Q 1* : Reason, some *Q 3–5* 85 they, that they *Haz.* 92 Wilie *Q 1* : Wilde *Q 3 ff.* : Wildly *Haz.* 95 cruelties *Q 6 ff.* 102 your *om. Q 5 ff.* 110 the *Q 1* : thy *Q 3, etc.*

⟨Scene IV. *The Court.*⟩

Enter Segasto, the Clowne and Rumbelo.

Se. Come, sirs; what, shall I neuer haue you finde out *Amadine* and the shepheard?

Clo. And I haue bin through the woods, and through the woods, and could see nothing but an emet.

R. Why, I see thousand emets; thou meanest a little one?

Clo. Nay, that emet that I saw was bigger then thou art.

R. Bigger then I? what a foole haue you to your man: I pray you, maister, turne him away.

Se But dost thou heare? was he not a man?

Clo. ⟨I⟩ thinke he was, for he saide he did lead a saltseller life about the woods.

Se. Thou wouldest say a solitarie life about the woods.

Clo. I thinke it was so, indeed.

R. I thought what a foole thou art.

Clo. Thou art a wise man! why, he did nothing but sleepe since he went.

Se. But tell me, Mouse, how did he goe?

Clo. In a whit gowne and a whit hat on his head, and a staffe in his hande.

Se. I thought so: it was a hermit that walked a solitarie life in the woods. Well, get you to dinner, and after neuer leaue seeking til you bring some newes of them, or ile hang you both. [*Exit.*

Clo. How now, Rombelo? what shall we do now?

R. Faith, ile home to dinner, and afterwarde to sleep.

Clo. Why, then, thou wilt be hanged.

R. Faith, I care not, for I know I shal neuer find them: wel, ile once more abroad, & if I cannot find them, ile neuer come home againe.

Clo. I tel thee what, Rombelo, thou shalt go in at one end of the wood and I at the other, and wee wil meete both together at the midst.

R. Content! lets awaie to dinner. [*Exeunt.*

⟨ACT V.

Scene I. *The Forest.*⟩

Enter Mucedorus solus.

Mu. Vnknowne to any heere within these woods
With bloodie Bremo do I lead my life.
The monster, he doth murther all he meets,
He spareth none and none doth him escape.
Who would continue, who but onely I,
In such a cruell cutthroates company?
Yet *Amadine* is there; how can I choose?
Ah, sillie soule, how often times she sits
And sighes, and cals: 'come, shepheard, come,
Sweete *Mucedorus*, come and set me free;'
When *Mucedorus* present standes her by:
But here she comes.

Enter Amadine.

What newes, faire Ladie, as you walke these woods.

Ama. Ah, hermit, none but bad & such as thou knowest.

Mu. How doe you like your *Bremo* and his woods?

Ama. Not my *Bremo* nor Bremo his woods.

Mu. And why not yours? me thinks he loues you wel.

Ama. I like him not, his loue to me is nothing worth.

Mu. Ladie, in this me thinkes you offer wrong,
To hate the man that euer loues you best.

Ama. Ah hermit, I take no pleasure in his loue;
Neither yet doth *Bremo* like me best.

Mu. Pardon my boldnes, faire ladie: sith we both
May safely talke now out of *Bremos* sight,
Vnfould to me, if so you please, the full discourse
How, when, and why you came into these woods,
And fell into this blodie butchers hands.

Ama. Hermit, I wil;
Of late a worthie shepheard I did loue.

Mu. A shephard, lady? sure a man vnfit
To match with you.

Ama. Hermit, this is true, and when we had—

Mu. Staie there, the wild man comes.
Referre the rest vntill another time.

Enter Bremo.

⟨*Bre.*⟩ What secret tale is this? what whispering haue wee heere?
Villaine, I charge the tell thy tale againe.

Mu. If needes I must, loe, here it is againe:
When as we both had lost the sight of thee,
It greeud vs both, but specially thy queene,
Who in thy absence euer feares the worst,

Scene IV. *Preceding Scene continued T* 3 And *om. Q 8 ff.* 6 a thousand *Q 3, etc.* thou . . one *add. to Clown's speech WP* 13 I *add. Q 8* 14 Saltsellers *Q 3, etc.* 17 so it was *Q 6 ff.* 25 *Prefix Se. repeated before* Well *Q 1* 39 at *Q 1* : in *Q 3, etc.* Act V, Scene I. *pr. ed.*: Scene V. *WP*

11 present *Haz.* : pesent *Q 1* : Peasant *Q 3 ff.* *S. D. after* 13 *Q 1* 14 as *om. WP* 16 Bremo his *pr. ed.* : his Bremo *Qq* : my Bremo's *Elze* : Bremo's *Haz.* 18 wroth *Q 1* 33 men *Q 1* 34 Defer *Wag.* 35 Bre. *add. Q 3* 37 If *Q 3, etc.* : I *Q 1*

Least some mischance befal your royall grace.
'Shall my sweete *Bremo* wander through the woods?
Toile to and fro for to redresse my want,
Hazard his life; and all to cherishe me?
I like not this,' quoth she,
And thereupon craude to know of me
If I coulde teach her handle weapons well.
My aunswer was I had small skill therein,
But glad, most mightie king, to learne of thee.
And this was all.

Bre. Wast so? none can dislike of this. Ile teach
You both to fight: but first, my queene, begin.
Here, take this weapon; see how thou canst vse it.

Ama. This is to big, I cannot weeld it in my arme.

Bre. Ist so? weele haue a knotty crabtree staffe
For thee.—But, sirra, tell me, what saist thou?

Mu. With all my heart I willing am to learne.

Bre. Then take my stafe & see how canst weeld it.

Mu. First teach me how to hold it in my hand.

Bre. Thou houldest it well.
Looke how he doth; thou maist the sooner learne.

Mu. Next tell me how and when tis best to strike.

Bre. Tis best to strike when time doth serue,
Tis best to loose no time.

Mu. Then now or neuer is my time to strike. ⟨*Aside.*⟩

Bre. And when thou strikest, be sure thou hit the head.

Mu. The head?

Bre. The verie heade.

Mu. Then haue at thine! [*he striks him downe deade.*] So, lie there and die,
A death no dout acording to desert,
Or else a worse as thou deseruest a worse.

Ama. It glads my heart this tirants death to see.

Mu. Now, ladie, it remaines in you
To end the tale you latelie had begunne,
Being enterrupted by this wicked wight.
You said you loued a shepheard.

Ama. I, so I doe, and none but only him,
And will do stil as long as life shall last.

Mu. But tell me, ladie; sith I set you free,
What course of life do you intend to take?

Ama. I wil disguised wander through the world,
Til I haue found him out.

Mu. How if you find your shephard in these woods?

Ama. Ah, none so happie then as *Amadine.*
He discloseth himselfe.

Mu. In tract of time a man may alter much;
Say, Ladie, doe you know your shepheard well?

Ama. My *Mucedorus!* hath he set me free?

⟨*Mu.*⟩ *Mucedorus* he hath set thee free.

Ama. And liued so long vnknowne to *Amadine!*

Mu. Ay thats a question where of you may not be resolued.
You know that I am banisht from the court;
I know likewise each passage is beset,
So that we cannot long escape vnknowne:
There fore my will is this, that we returne
Right through the thickets to the wild mans caue,
And there a while liue on his prouision,
Vntil the search and narrow watch be past.
This is my counsel, and I thinke it best.

Ama. I thinke the verie same.

Mu. Come, lets begone.

[⟨*Enter*⟩ *The Clowne* ⟨*who*⟩ *searches and falsouer the wild man and so carry him away.*

Clo. Nay, soft, sir; are you heere? a bots on you! I was like to be hanged for not finding you. We would borrow a certaine stray kings daughter of you: a wench, a wench, sir, we would haue.

Mu. A wench of me! ile make the eate my sword.

Clo. Oh Lord! nay, and you are so lustie, Ile cal a cooling card for you. Ho, maister, maister, come away quicklie.

Enter Segasto.

Se. Whats the matter?

Cl. Looke, maister, *Amadine* & the shepheard: oh, braue!

Se. What, minion, haue I found you out?

Clo. Nay, thats a lie, I found her out myselfe.

Se. Thou gadding huswife,
What cause hadst thou to gad abroade,
When as thou knowest our wedding day so nie?

Ama. Not so, *Segasto,* no such thing in hand;
Shew your assurance, then ile answere you.

43 wants *Haz.* 46 she crav'd *Haz.* 51 Whast *Q 1* *Line ends* this *Qq* 55 *Line ends* thee *Qq* 65 is my *Q 1 ff.* : it is *Q 8 ff.* 66 thou hit *Q 1* : to hit *Q 3, 8 ff.* : to hid *Q 4* : to hide *Q 5, 6* 73–5 *Prose Q 1*

84 *S. D.* discloseth *Q 6, etc.* : disguiseth *Q 1–5* 88 Mu. *add. pr. ed.* Mucedorus he *Q 1* : Muc. He *Q 3 ff.* 101 *S. D.* Enter, who *add. Haz.*

Se. Thy fathers promise my assurance is.

Ama. But what he promist he hath not performde.

Se. It rests in thee for to performe the same.

Ama. Not I.

Se. And why?

Ama. So is my will, and therefore euen so.

Clo. Maister, with a nonie, nonie, noe!

Se. A, wicked villane, art thou here?

Mu. What needes these wordes? we way them not.

Se. We way them not, proud shepheard! I skorne thy companie.

Clo. Weele not haue a corner of thy companie.

Mu. I scorne not thee, nor yet the least of thine.

Clo. Thats a lie, a would haue kild me with his pugsnondo.

Se. This stoutnesse, *Amadine,* contents me not.

Ama. Then seeke an other that may you better please.

Mu. Well, *Amadine,* it onelie rests in thee
Without delay to make thy choice of three:
There stands *Segasto,* here a shepheard stands,
There stands the third; now make thy choise.

Clo. A Lord at the least I am.

Am. My choise is made, for I will none but thee.

Se. A worthy mate, no doubt, for such a wife.

Mu. And, *Amadine,* why wilt thou none but me?
I cannot keepe thee as thy father did;
I haue no landes for to maintaine thy state.
Moreouer, if thou meane to be my wife,
Commonly this must be thy vse:
To bed at midnight, vp at fowre,
Drudge all daie and trudge from place to place,
Whereby our dailie vittel for to winne;
And last of al, which is the worst of all,
No princes then but plaine a shepheards wife.

Clo. Then, god ge you god morrow, goody shepheard!

Ama. It shall not neede; if *Amadine* do liue,
Thou shalt be crowned king of *Arragon.*

Clo. Oh, maister, laugh! when hees King, then ile be a queene.

Mu. Then know that which nere tofore was known:
I am no shepheard, no Arragonian I,
But borne of Royall blood—my fathers of
Valentia King, my mother queene—who for
Thy secret sake tooke this hard task in hand.

Ama. Ah how I ioy my fortune is so good.

Se. Well now I see, *Segasto* shall not speede;
But, *Mucedorus,* I as much do ioy,
To see thee here within our Court of Arragon,
As if a kingdome had befalne me. This time
I with my heart surrender it to thee,
He giueth her vnto him.
And loose what right to Amadine I haue.

Clo. What ⟨a⟩ barnes doore, and borne where my father
Was cunstable! a bots on thee, how dost thee?

Mu. Thanks, *Segasto;* but yet you leueld at the crowne.

Clo. Maister, beare this and beare all.

Se. Why so, sir?

Clo. He saies you take a goose by the crowne.

Se. Go to, sir: away, post you to the king,
Whose hart is fraught with carefull doubts,
Glad him vp and tell him these good newes,
And we will follow as fast as we may.

Clo. I goe, maister; I runne, maister. [*Exeunt.*

⟨SCENE II. *Open Place near the Court of the King of Arragon.*⟩

Enter the King and Collen.

K. Break, heart, and end my paled woes,
My Amadine, the comfort of my life,
How can I ioy except she were in sight?
Her absence breedes sorrow to my soule
And with a thunder breakes my heart in twaine.

Col. Forbeare those passions, gentle King,
And you shall see twill turne vnto the best,
And bring your soule to quiet and to ioie.

K. Such ioie as death, I do assure me that,
And naught but death, vnlesse of her I heare,
And that with speede; I cannot sigh thus long—
But what a tumult doe I heare within?
The crie within, 'ioie and happinesse!'

Col. I heare a noyse of ouer-passing ioie
Within the court; my Lord, be of good comfort—
And heere comes one in hast.

128 nonny, nonny, no *Haz.* : none, none, noe *Q 1–4* : none, none so *Q 5 ff.* 129 villant *Q 1* 134 with his] with's *Q 14, 15* 140 here . . stands *Q 1–6* : a second here *Q 8 ff.* 151 all the day *WP* 154 plaine a *Q 1–5* : a plaine *Q 6 ff.*

162–3 *End* Valentia, sake *Q 1* : King, sake *Q 3 ff.* : *corr. pr. ed.* 169 me this *Q 1, etc.* 170 it *Q 1* : her *Q 3 ff.* 171 loose *Haz.* : looke *Qq* 172 a *add. Haz.* 173 thee *Q 1–6* : thou *Q 8 ff.* 177 saies] sees sees *Q 1* : sees *Q 3–6* : sayes *Q 8, etc.* Scene II. *pr. ed.*: Act V, Scene I. *WP* 3 in my sight *Q 14, 15* 4 breedes *Q 1–6* : breeds great *Q 8 ff.* : breedeth *WP* 6, 13 *Prefix* Clo. *Q 1* *S. D.* The *Q 1, 8* : They *Q 3 ff.* happinesse] gladness *Q 14, 15*

Enter the Clowne running.

Clo. A King! a King! a King!
Col. Why, how now, sirra? whats the matter?
Clo. O, tis newes for a king, 'tis woorth money.
K. Why, sirra, thou shalt haue siluer and gold if it bee good.
Clo. O, tis good, tis good. *Amadine*—
K. Oh, what of her? tell me, & I will make thee a knight.
Clo. How a spright? no, by ladie, I will not be a spright. Maisters, get ye away; if I be a spright, I shall be so leane I shall make you all afraide.
Col. Thou sot, the King meanes to make thee a gentleman.
Clo. Why, I shall want parrell.
King. Thou shalt want for nothing.
Clo. Then stand away, trick vp thy selfe: heere they come.

Enter Segasto, Mucedorus, and Amadine.

Ama. My gratious father, pardon thy disloyal daughter.
K. What do mine eies be hould? my daughter *Amadine*?
Rise vp, dere daughter & let these, my embrasing armes,
Shew some token of thy fathers ioie,
Which euer since thy departure hath languished in sorrow.
Ama. Deare father, neuer were your sorrows
Greater then my griefes,
Neuer you so desolate as I comfortlesse;
Yet, neuerthelesse, acknowledging my selfe
To be the cause of both, on bended knees
I humblie craue your pardon.
King. Ile pardon thee, deare daughter: but as for him—
Ama. Ah, father, what of him?
King. As sure as I am a king, and weare the crowne,
I will reuenge on that accursed wretch.
Mu. Yet, worthy prince, worke not thy will in wrath;
Shew fauour.
K. I, such fauour as thou deseruest.
Mu. I do deserue the daughter of a king.
K. Oh, impudent! a shepheard and so insolent!
Mu. No shepheard I, but a worthy prince.
King. In farre conceit, not princelie borne.
Mu. Yes, princely borne: my father is a king,
My mother Queene, and of Valentia both.
K. What, *Mucedorus!* welcome to our court.
What cause hadst thou to come to me disguisde?
Mu. No cause to feare; I caused no offence
But this:
Desiring thy daughters vertues for to see
Disguised my selfe from out my fathers court.
Vnknowen to any, in secret I did rest,
And passed many troubles neere to death;
So hath your daughter my partaker bin,
As you shall know heereafter more at large,
Desiring you, you will giue her to mee,
Euen as mine owne and soueraigne of my life;
Then shall I thinke my trauels are wel spent.
King. With all my heart, but this—
Segasto claimes my promise made to fore,
That he should haue her as his onely wife,
Before my counsel when we came from war.
Segasto, may I craue thee let it passe,
And giue *Amadine* as wife to *Mucedorus*?
Se. With all my heart, were it far a greater thing,
And what I may to furnish vp there rites
With pleasing sports and pastimes you shall see.
King. Thankes, good *Segasto,* I will thinke of this.
Mu. Thankes, good my Lord, & while I liue
Account of me in what I can or maie.
Ama. And, good *Segasto,* these great curtesies
Shall not be forgot.
Clo. Why, harke you, maister: bones, what haue you done? What, giuen away the wench you made me take such paines for? you are wise indeed! mas, and I had knowne of that I would haue had her my selfe! faith, master, now wee maie goe to breakefast with a woodcoke pie.
Se. Goe, sir, you were best leaue this knauerie.
K. Come on, my Lordes, lets now to court,
Where we may finish vp the ioyfullest daie
That euer hapt to a distressed King,
[Were but thy Father, the Valencia Lord,
Present in view of this combining knot.

23, 24 spright *Q 3 ff.*: spirit (spirrit) *Q 1* 32 dere *om. Q 8 ff.* my *om. Q 4 ff.* 33 father *Q 1* 35 *Prefix* Mu. *Q 1* 38 acknowledging *Q 1 ff.*: knowing *Q 8 ff.* 43 a *om. Q 3, etc.* 47 as *om. WP* 50 am I *Haz.* but am a *Col.*

51 farre *Q 1*: faire *Q 3, etc.* 66 are *Q 1–6*: all *Q 8 ff.* 73 far a *Q 1*: a far *Q 3, etc.* 92, *etc. add. Q 3* *For the concluding lines of the scene in Q 1 cf. Appendix, p.* 126 93 combined *Q 4 ff.*

A shout within. Enter a Messenger.

What shout was that?
Mes. My Lord, the great Valencia King,
Newly arriued, intreates your presence.
Mu. My Father?
King A. Prepared welcomes giue him entertainement:
A happier Planet neuer raigned then that,
Which gouernes at this houre. [*Sound.*

Enter the King of Valencia, Anselmo, Rodrigo, Borachius, with others; the King runnes and imbraces his Sonne.

King V. Rise, honour of my age, food to my rest:
Condemne not (mightie King of Aragon)
My rude behauiour, so compeld by Nature,
That manners stood vnknowledged.
King A. What we haue to recite would tedious prooue
By declaration; therefore, in, and feast:
To morrow the performance shall explaine,
What Words conceale; till then, Drummes speake, Belles ring,
Giue plausiue welcomes to our brother King.
Sound Drummes and Trumpets. Exeunt omnes.]

⟨EPILOGUE.⟩

Enter Comedie and Enuie.

Comedie. How now, *Enuie*? what, blushest thou all readie?
Peepe forth, hide not thy head with shame,
But with a courage praise a womans deeds.
Thy threates were vaine, thou couldst doe me no hurt.
Although thou seemdst to crosse me with despite,
I ouerwhelmde, and turnde vpside downe thy blocke
And made thy selfe to stumble at the same.
En. Though stumbled, yet not ouerthrowne.
Thou canst not draw my heart to mildenesse;
Yet must I needes confesse thou hast don well,
And plaide thy part with merth and pleasant glee:
Saie all this, yet canst thou not conquer mee;
Although this time thou hast got—yet not the conquest neither—
A double reuenge another time ile haue.
[*Com.* Enuie, spit thy gall;
Plot, worke, contriue; create new fallacies,
Teame from thy Wombe each minute a blacke Traytor,
Whose blood and thoughts haue twins conception:
Studie to act deedes yet vnchronicled,
Cast natiue Monsters in the moldes of Men,
Case vicious Diuels vnder sancted Rochets,
Vnhaspe the Wicket where all perinreds roost,
And swarme this Ball with treasons: doe thy worst;
Thou canst not (hel-hound) crosse my steare to night,
Nor blind that glorie, where I wish delight.
Enu. I can, I will.
Com. Neffarious Hagge, begin,
And let vs tugge, till one the mastrie winne.
Enu. Comedie, thou art a shallow Goose;
Ile ouerthrow thee in thine owne intent,
And make thy fall my Comick merriment.
Com. Thy pollicie wants grauitie; thou art
Too weake. Speake, Fiend, as how?
Enu. Why, thus:
From my foule Studie will I hoyst a Wretch,
A leane and hungry Meager Canniball,
Whose iawes swell to his eyes with chawing Malice:
And him Ile make a Poet.
Com. What's that to th' purpose?
Enu. This scrambling Rauen, with his needie Beard,
Will I whet on to write a Comedie,
Wherein shall be compos'd darke sentences,
Pleasing to factious braines:
And euery other where place me a Iest,
Whose high abuse shall more torment then blowes:
Then I my selfe (quicker then Lightning)
Will flie me to a puisant Magistrate,
And waighting with a Trencher at his backe,
In midst of iollitie, rehearse those gaules,
(With some additions)
So lately vented in your Theator.
He, vpon this, cannot but make complaint,
To your great danger, or at least restraint.
Com. Ha, ha, ha! I laugh to heare thy folly;
This is a trap for Boyes, not Men, nor such,

98 Prepare a welcome *Elze* welcomes : giue *Q 3* : *corr. Q 8* *S. D.* Barchius *Q 3–6*: Barachius *Q 8–12* : Brachius *Q 15* 104 unacknowledged *Col.*, *WP* 109 plausiue *Qq* : pleasant *Col.* Epilogue *WP* 5 seemest *Q 1–8*

15–end *add. Q 3. For the conclusion of the play in Q 1 cf. Appendix, p.* 126 18 twin *Haz.* 21 sainted *Wag.* Rochets *Q 3–6* : robes *Q 8 ff.* 22 Unclasp *Col.* wicked *WP* periureds *Q 3–6* : periures *Q 8* : periuries *Q 9 ff.* 31 Comict *Q 3* 32 *Ends* weake *Qq* : *corr. WP* 36 Meager *Q 5 ff.*: Neager *Q 3, 4* : negro *Haz.* 50–1 *One line Qq, etc.* 51 So lately *an interpolation according to Simpson* 53 your *Q 3–6* : our *Q 8 ff.*

Especially desertfull in their doinges,
Whose stay'd discretion rules their purposes.
I and my faction doe eschew those vices.
But see, O see! the weary Sunne for rest
Hath laine his golden compasse to the West,
Where he perpetuall bide and euer shine,
As Dauids of-spring, in his happy Clime.
Stoope, Enuie, stoope, bow to the Earth with mee,
Lets begge our Pardons on our bended knee.
They kneele.

Enu. My Power has lost her Might; Enuies date's expired.
Yon splendant Maiestie hath feld my sting,
And I amazed am. *Fall downe and quake.*

60 to *Qq* : in *Col.* 62 his *Qq* : this *Col.* 64 pardon *Q 9 ff.* 65 and Envy's *WP* 66 *om. Q 4 ff.*

Com. Glorious and wise Arch-Cæsar on this earth,
At whose appearance, Enuie's stroken dumbe,
And all bad thinges cease operation:
Vouchsafe to pardon our vnwilling errour,
So late presented to your Gracious view,
And weele endeuour with excesse of paine,
To please your senses in a choyser straine.
Thus we commit you to the armes of Night,
Whose spangled carkasse would, for your delight,
Striue to excell the Day; be blessed, then:
Who other wishes, let him neuer speake.

Enu. Amen.
To Fame and Honour we commend your rest;
Liue still more happie, euery houre more blest.

FINIS.]

76 carkasse *Qq* : darkness *Col.*

APPENDIX TO MVCEDORVS

In Act V, Scene I, and the Epilogue, Q 1 has different endings, given below.

After line 91 *of Act V, Scene I.*

With mirth and ioy and greate solemnitie,
Weele finish vp these hymens rightes most pleasantlie.

Clo. Hoe, Lordes, at the first, I am one to; but heare, maister King, by your leaue, a cast: now you haue done with them, I praie you begin with me.

K. Why, what wouldest thou haue?

Clo. O you forgot! now, a little apparrell to makes handsome: what, should Lordes goe so beggerlie as I doe?

K. What I did promise thee, I will performe; attende on mee. Come, lets depart.

They all speake.
Weele waite on you with all our hearts.

Clo. And with a peece of my liuer to.
[*Exeunt omnes.*

After line 14 *of the Epilogue.*

Co. Then, caitife cursed, stoope vpon thy knee,
Yeelde to a woman, though not to mee,
And pray we both togither with our hearts,
That she thrice Nestors yeares may with vs rest,
And from her foes high God defend her still,
That they against her may neuer worke thir will.

En. *Enuie,* were he neuer so stoute,
Would becke and bowe vnto her maiestie.
Indeede, *Comedie,* thou hast ouerrunne me now.
And forst me stoope vnto a womans swaie.
God grant her grace amongest vs long may raigne,
And those that would not haue it soe,
Would that by enuie soone their heartes they might forgoe.

Co. The Counsell, Nobles, and this Realme,
Lord guide it stil with thy most holy hand;
The Commons and the subiectes grant them grace,
Their prince to serue, her to obey, & treason to deface:
Long maie she raine, in ioy and greate felicitie!
Each Christian heart do saie amen with me.
[*Exeunt.*

FINIS.

20 wooke *Q 1* 28 Noble *Q 1*

The firſt part
Of the true and hono-
rable hiſtorie, of the life of Sir
Iohn Old-caſtle, the good
Lord Cobham.

As it hath been lately acted by the right honorable the Earle of Notingham Lord high Admirall of England his ſeruants.

LONDON
Printed by V.S. for Thomas Pauier, and are to be ſolde at his ſhop at the ſigne of the Catte and Parrots neere the Exchange.
1600.

Q 1	=	**Anonymous quarto of 1600**
Q 2	=	**Quarto bearing Shakespeare's name, 1600**
F 1	=	**(Third) Shakespeare Folio, 1664**
F 2	=	**(Fourth) ,, ,, 1685**
R	=	**Rowe, 1709**
M	=	**Malone, 1780**
Th.	=	**Theobald, ibid.**
St.	=	**Steevens, ibid.**
S	=	**Simms, 1848**
T	=	**Tyrrell, 1851**
Haz.	=	**Hazlitt, 1852**
pr. ed.	=	**present editor**

THE TRVE AND HONORABLE HISTORIE OF THE LIFE OF

SIR IOHN OLDCASTLE,

THE GOOD LORD COBHAM

⟨The Actors Names in the History of Sir *Iohn Oldcastle.*

King Henry the fifth.
Sir John Oldcastle, *Lord* Cobham.
Harpool, *Servant to the Lord* Cobham.
Lord Herbert, *with* Gough *his man.*
Lord Powis, *with* Owen *and* Davy *his men.*
The Mayor of Hereford, and Sheriff of Herefordshire, with Bayliffs and Servants.
Two Judges of Assize.
The Bishop of Rochester and Clun *his Sumner.*
Sir John *the Parson of Wrotham, and* Doll *his Concubine.*
The Duke of Suffolk.
The Earl of Huntington.
The Earl of Cambridge.
Lord Scroop *and Lord* Grey.
Chartres *the French Agent.*
Sir Roger Acton.
Sir Richard Lee.
M. Bourn, M. Beverly, *and* Murley *the Brewer of Dunstable, rebels.*
M. Butler, *Gentleman of the Privy Chamber.*
Lady Cobham *and Lady* Powis.
Cromer, *Sheriff of Kent.*
Lord Warden *of the Cinque Ports.*
Lieutenant of the Tower.
The Mayor, Constable, and Goaler of S. Albans.
A Kentish Constable and an Ale-man.
Soldiers and old men begging.
Dick *and* Tom, *servants to* Murley.
An Irishman.
An Host, Hostler, a Carrier and Kate.⟩

The Prologue.

The doubtful Title (Gentlemen) prefixt
Vpon the Argument we haue in hand,
May breede suspence, and wrongfully disturbe
The peacefull quiet of your setled thoughts.
To stop which scruple, let this briefe suffise:
It is no pamperd glutton we present,
Nor aged Councellor to youthfull sinne,
But one, whose vertue shone aboue the rest,
A valiant Martyr and a vertuous peere;
In whose true faith and loyaltie exprest
Vnto his soueraigne, and his countries weale,
We striue to pay that tribute of our Loue,
Your fauours merite. Let faire Truth be grac'te,
Since forg'de inuention former time defac'te.

⟨ACT I.

Scene I. *Hereford. A street.*

Enter lord Herbert, *lord* Powis, Owen, Gough, Davy, *and several other followers of the lords* Herbert *and* Powis; *they fight.*⟩ *In the fight, enter the Sheriffe and two of his men.*

Sheriffe. My Lords, I charge ye in his Highnesse name,
To keepe the peace, you, and your followers.

Herb. Good M⟨aister⟩ Sheriffe, look vnto your self.

Pow. Do so, for we haue other businesse.

Proffer to fight againe.

Sher. Will ye disturbe the Iudges, and the Assise?
Heare the Kings proclamation, ye were best.

Pow. Hold then, lets heare it.

Herb. But be briefe, ye were best.

Bayl. Oyes!

Dauy. Cossone, make shorter O, or shall marre your Yes.

Bay. Oyes!

Owen. What, has her nothing to say but O yes?

Bay. Oyes!

Da. O nay! pye Cosse plut downe with her, down with her! A Pawesse! a Pawesse!

Gough. A Herbert! a Herbert! and downe with Powesse!

Helter skelter againe.

Sher. Hold, in the Kings name, hold.

Owen. Downe i' tha knaues name, downe.

In this fight, the Bailiffe is knocked downe, and the Sheriffe and the other runne away.

Herb. Powesse, I thinke thy Welsh and thou do smart.

Pow. Herbert, I thinke my sword came neere thy heart.

The Actors Names, *etc. add. F1*   Act I. *etc. add. M*

18 e tha ka. naues *Q1* : with a kanaues *Q2*

Herb. Thy hearts best bloud shall pay the losse of mine.
Gough. A Herbert! a Herbert!
Dauy. A Pawesse! a Pawesse!

As they are lifting their weapons, enter the Maior of Hereford, and his Officers and Townes-men with clubbes.

Maior. My Lords, as you are liege men to the Crowne,
True noblemen, and subiects to the King,
Attend his Highnesse proclamation,
Commaunded by the Iudges of Assise,
For keeping peace at this assemblie.
Herb. Good M⟨aister⟩ Maior of Hereford be briefe.
Mai. Serieant, without the ceremonie of Oyes,
Pronounce alowd the proclamation.

Ser. The Kings Iustices, perceiuing what publique mischiefe may ensue this priuate quarrel, in his maiesties name do straightly charge and commaund all persons, of what degree soeuer, to depart this cittie of Hereford, except such as are bound to giue attendance at this Assise, and that no man presume to weare any weapon, especially welsh-hookes, forrest billes—

Owen. Haw, no pill nor wells hoog? ha?
Ma. Peace, and heare the proclamation.

Ser. And that the Lord Powesse do presently disperse and discharge his retinue, and depart the cittie in the Kings peace, he and his followers, on paine of imprisonment.

Dauy. Haw? pud her Lord Pawesse in prison! A Pawes!
A Pawesse! cossone liue and tie with her Lord.
Gough. A Herbert! a Herbert!

In this fight the Lord Herbert is wounded, and fals to the ground; the Maior and his company goe away, crying clubbes; Powesse runnes away; Gough and other of Herberts faction busie themselues about Herbert: enters the two Iudges in their roabes, the Sheriffe and his Bailiffes afore them, &c.

1. *Iud.* Where's the Lord Herbert? is he hurt or slaine?
Sher. Hee's here, my Lord.
2. *Iud.* How fares his Lordshippe, friends?
Gough. Mortally wounded, speechlesse; he cannot liue.
1. *Iud.* Conuay him hence; let not his wounds take ayre,
And get him dress'd with expedition.
[*Ex. Herb. & Gough.*
M⟨aister⟩ Maior of Hereford, M⟨aister⟩ Shriue o' th shire,
Commit Lord Powesse to safe custodie,
To answer the disturbance of the peace,
Lord Herberts perill, and his high contempt
Of vs, and you the Kings commissioners.
See it be done with care and diligence.
Sher. Please it your Lordship, my Lord Powesse is gone
Past all recouery.
2. *Iud.* Yet let search be made,
To apprehend his followers that are left.
Sher. There are some of them. Sirs, lay hold of them.
Owen. Of vs? and why? what has her done, I pray you?
Sher. Disarme them, Bailiffes.
Ma. Officers, assist.
Dauy. Heare you, Lor shudge, what resson is for this?
Owen. Cosson pe puse for fighting for our Lord?
1. *Iudge.* Away with them.
Dauy. Harg you, my Lord.
Owen. Gough my Lorde Herberts man's a shitten kanaue,
Dauy. Ise liue and tie in good quarrell.
Owen. Pray you do shustice; let awl be preson.
Dauy. Prison! no.
Both at once al this.
Lord shudge, I wooll giue you pale, good suerty.
2. *Iudge.* What Bale? what suerties?

Dauy. Her coozin ap Ries, ap Euan, ap Morrice, ap Morgan, ap Lluellyn, ap Madoc, ap Meredith, ap Griffen, ap Dauy, ap Owen, ap Shinken Shones.

2 *Iudge.* Two of the most sufficient are ynow.
Sher. And 't please your Lordship, these are al but one.
1. *Iudge.* To Iayle with them, and the Lord Herberts men;
Weele talke with them, when the Assise is done.
[*Exeunt.*
Riotous, audacious, and vnruly Groomes,
Must we be forced to come from the Bench,
To quiet brawles, which euery Constable
In other ciuill places can suppresse?
2. *Iudge.* What was the quarrel that causde all this stirre?

S. D. lifting their weapons] fighting *Q 2, etc.* 48 cossone] cossoon her will *Q 2, etc.*

66 of *Q 2, etc.*: on *Q 1* 74 shotten *Haz.* 83 ap Skinken, ap Shones *M*

Sher. About religion, as I heard, my Lord.
Lord Powesse detracted from the power of Rome,
Affirming Wickliffes doctrine to be true,
And Romes erroneous. Hot reply was made
By the lord Herbert, they were traytors all
That would maintaine it: Powesse answered,
They were as true, as noble, and as wise
As he, that would defend it with their liues;
He namde for instance sir Iohn Old-castle
The Lord Cobham: Herbert replide againe,
"He, thou, and all are traitors that so hold."
The lie was giuen, the seuerall factions drawne,
And so enragde, that we could not appease it.
1. *Iudge.* This case concernes the Kings prerogatiue,
And's dangerous to the State and common wealth.
Gentlemen, Iustices, master Maior, and master Shrieue,
It doth behoue vs all, and each of vs
In generall and particular, to haue care
For the suppressing of all mutinies,
And all assemblies, except souldiers musters
For the Kings preparation into France.
We heare of secret conuenticles made,
And there is doubt of some conspiracies,
Which may breake out into rebellious armes
When the King's gone, perchance before he go:
Note as an instance, this one perillous fray;
What factions might haue growne on either part,
To the destruction of the King and Realme.
Yet, in my conscience, sir Iohn Old-castle,
Innocent of it, onely his name was vsde.
We, therefore, from his Highnesse giue this charge:
You, maister Maior, looke to your citizens;
You, maister Sherife, vnto your shire; and you
As Iustices, in euery ones precinct,
There be no meetings. When the vulgar sort
Sit on their Ale-bench, with their cups and kannes,
Matters of state be not their common talke,
Nor pure religion by their lips prophande.
Let vs returne vnto the Bench againe,
And there examine further of this fray.

Enter a Baily and a Serieant.

Sher. Sirs, haue ye taken the lord Powesse yet?
Ba. No, nor heard of him.
Ser. No, hee's gone farre enough.
2. *Iu.* They that are left behind shall answer all. [*Exeunt.*

100 that] they *M* 107 And 'tis *Q 2, etc.* 121 Oldcastle's *Ff*

⟨Scene II. *Eltham. An antechamber in the palace.*⟩

Enter Suffolke, Bishop of Rochester, Butler, parson of Wrotham.

Suffolke. Now, my lord Bishop, take free liberty
To speake your minde: what is your sute to vs?
Bishop. My noble Lord, no more than what you know,
And haue bin oftentimes inuested with:
Grieuous complaints haue past betweene the lippes
Of enuious persons to vpbraide the Cleargy,
Some carping at the liuings which we haue,
And others spurning at the ceremonies
That are of auncient custome in the church.
Amongst the which, Lord Cobham is a chiefe:
What inconuenience may proceede hereof,
Both to the King and to the common wealth,
May easily be discernd, when like a frensie
This innouation shall possesse their mindes.
These vpstarts will haue followers, to vphold
Their damnd opinion, more than Harry shall
To vndergoe his quarrell gainst the French.
Suffolke. What proofe is there against them to be had,
That what you say the law may iustifie?
Bishop. They giue themselues the name of Protestants,
And meete in fields and solitary groues.
Sir Iohn. Was euer heard, my Lord, the like til now?
That theeues and rebells—s bloud, heretikes,
Playne heretikes, Ile stand toote to their teeth—
Should haue, to colour their vile practises,
A title of such worth as Protestant?

Enter one wyth a letter.

Suf. O, but you must not sweare; it ill becomes
One of your coate to rappe out bloudy oathes.
Bish. Pardon him, good my Lord, it is his zeale;
An honest country prelate, who laments
To see such foule disorder in the church.
Sir Iohn. Theres one—they call him Sir Iohn Old-castle—
He has not his name for naught: for like a castle
Doth he encompasse them within his walls;
But till that castle be subuerted quite,
We ne're shall be at quiet in the realme.
Bish. That is our sute, my Lord, that he be tane,

Scene II. *etc. add. M* 23 s bloud] s'blood, my lord *M*

And brought in question for his heresie.
Beside, two letters brought me out of Wales,
Wherin my Lord Herford writes to me,
What tumult and sedition was begun,
About the Lord Cobham at thè Sises there,
(For they had much ado the calme the rage),
And that the valiant Herbert is there slaine.

Suf. A fire that must be quencht. Wel, say no more,
The King anon goes to the counsell chamber,
There to debate of matters touching France:
As he doth passe by, Ile informe his grace
Concerning your petition: Master Butler,
If I forget, do you remember me.

But. I will, my Lord. [*Offer him a purse.*

Bish. Not for a recompence,
But as a token of our loue to you,
By me my Lords of the cleargie do present
This purse, and in it full a thousand Angells,
Praying your Lordship to accept their gift.

Suf. I thanke them, my Lord Bishop, for their loue,
But will not take their mony; if you please
To giue it to this gentleman, you may.

Bish. Sir, then we craue your furtherance herein.

But. The best I can, my Lord of Rochester.

Bish. Nay, pray ye take it; trust me but you shal.

Sir Iohn.—Were ye all three vpon NewMarket heath,
You should not neede straine curtsie who should ha'te;
Sir Iohn would quickely rid ye of that care.

Suf. The King is comming. Feare ye not, my Lord;
The very first thing I will breake with him
Shal be about your matter.

Enter K. Harry and Huntington in talke.

Har. My Lord of Suffolke,
Was it not saide the Cleargy did refuse
To lend vs mony toward our warres in France?

Suf. It was, my Lord, but very wrongfully.

Har. I know it was, for Huntington here tells me,
They haue bin very bountifull of late.

Suf. And still they vow, my gracious Lord, to be so,
Hoping your maiestie will thinke of them
As of your louing subiects, and suppresse
All such malitious errors as begin
To spot their calling, and disturb the church.

Har. God else forbid: why, Suffolke, is there
Any new rupture to disquiet them?

Suf. No new, my Lord; the old is great enough,
And so increasing as, if not cut downe,
Will breede a scandale to your royall state,
And set your Kingdome quickely in an vproare.
The Kentish knight, Lord Cobham, in despight
Of any law, or spirituall discipline,
Maintaines this vpstart new religion still,
And diuers great assemblies by his meanes
And priuate quarrells are commenst abroad,
As by this letter more at large, my liege,
Is made apparant.

Har. We do find it here:
There was in Wales a certaine fray of late,
Betweene two noblemen, but what of this?
Followes it straight, Lord Cobham must be he
Did cause the same? I dare be sworne, good knight,
He neuer dreampt of any such contention.

Bish. But in his name the quarrell did begin,
About the opinion which he held, my liege.

Har. How if it did? was either he in place,
To take part with them, or abette them in it?
If brabling fellowes, whose inkindled bloud,
Seethes in their fiery vaines, will needes go fight,
Making their quarrells of some words that passt
Either of you, or you, amongst their cuppes,
Is the fault yours, or are they guiltie of it?

Suffolke With pardon of your Highnesse, my dread lord,
Such little sparkes, neglected, may in time
Grow to a mighty flame: but thats not all;
He doth, beside, maintaine a strange religion,
And will not be compelld to come to masse.

Bish. We do beseech you, therefore, gracious prince,
Without offence vnto your maiesty,
We may be bold to vse authoritie.

Harry As how?

Bishop To summon him vnto the Arches,
Where such offences haue their punishment.

Harry To answere personally? is that your meaning?

Bishop It is, my lord.

Harry How, if he appeale?

Bishop He cannot, my Lord, in such a case as this.

Suffolke Not where Religion is the plea, my lord.

40 Herford] Hertford *Q2, Ff*: of Hereford *conj. M* 54 (my Lords) the Clergy doth *Q2, etc.* 62 pray take it, trust me you *Q2, Ff*: pray you take it, trust me sir, you *M*

91-2 *One line in Q2, Ff* 101 How] What *Q2, etc.* 122 My Lord, he cannot *Q2, etc.*

Harry I tooke it alwayes, that our selfe stoode out,
As a sufficient refuge, vnto whome
Not any but might lawfully appeale.
But weele not argue now vpon that poynt.
For sir Iohn Old-castle, whom you accuse,
Let me intreate you to dispence awhile
With your high title of preheminence.
[*in scorne.*
Report did neuer yet condemne him so,
But he hath alwayes beene reputed loyall:
And in my knowledge I can say thus much,
That he is vertuous, wise, and honourable.
If any way his conscience be seduc'de,
To wauer in his faith, Ile send for him,
And schoole him priuately; if that serue not,
Then afterward you may proceede against him.
Butler, be you the messenger for vs,
And will him presently repaire to court. [*exeunt.*

sir Iohn How now, my lord, why stand you discontent?
In sooth, me thinkes the King hath well decreed.

Bishop Yea, yea, sir Iohn, if he would keepe his word;
But I perceiue he fauours him so much,
As this will be to small effect, I feare.

sir Iohn Why, then, Ile tell you what y'are best to do:
If you suspect the King will be but cold
In reprehending him, send you a processe too
To serue vpon him: so you may be sure
To make him answer't, howsoere it fall.

Bishop And well remembred! I will haue it so.
A Sumner shall be sent about it strait. [*Exit.*

sir Iohn Yea, doe so. In the meane space this remaines
For kinde sir Iohn of *Wrotham,* honest Iacke.
Me thinkes the purse of gold the Bishop gaue
Made a good shew; it had a tempting looke.
Beshrew me, but my fingers ends do itch
To be vpon those rudduks. Well, tis thus:
I am not as the worlde does take me for;
If euer woolfe were cloathed in sheepes coate,
Then I am he,—olde huddle and twang, yfaith,
A priest in shew, but in plaine termes a theefe.
Yet, let me tell you too, an honest theefe,
One that will take it where it may be sparde,
And spend it freely in good fellowship.
I haue as many shapes as *Proteus* had,
That still, when any villany is done,
There may be none suspect it was sir Iohn.
Besides, to comfort me,—for whats this life,
Except the crabbed bitternes thereof
Be sweetened now and then with lechery?—
I haue my Doll, my concubine, as t'were,
To frollicke with, a lusty bounsing gerle.
But whilst I loyter here, the gold may scape,
And that must not be so. It is mine owne;
Therefore, Ile meete him on his way to court,
And shriue him of it: there will be the sport.
[*Exit.*

⟨Scene III. *Kent. An outer court before lord Cobham's house.*⟩

Enter three or foure poore people: somesouldiers, some old men.

1. God help! God help! there's law for punishing,
But theres no law for our necessity:
There be more stockes to set poore soldiers in,
Than there be houses to releeue them at.

Old man. Faith, housekeeping decayes in euery place,
Euen as Saint *Peter* writ, still worse and worse.

4. Maister maior of Rochester has giuen commaundement, that none shall goe abroade out of the parish; and they haue set an order downe forsooth, what euery poore housholder must giue towards our reliefe: where there be some ceased, I may say to you, had almost as much neede to beg as we.

1. It is a hard world the while.

Old man. If a poore man come to a doore to aske for Gods sake, they aske him for a licence, or a certificate from a Iustice.

2. Faith we haue none but what we beare vppon our bodies, our maimed limbs, God help vs.

4. And yet, as lame as I am, Ile with the king into France, if I can crawle but a shipboorde. I hadde rather be slaine in France, than starue in England.

Olde man. Ha, were I but as lusty as I was at the battell of Shrewsbury, I would not doe as I do: but we are now come to the good lord Cobhams, to the best man to the poore that is in all Kent.

4. God blesse him! there be but few such.

Enter Lord Cobham with Harpoole.

Cob. Thou peeuish, froward man, what wouldst thou haue?

Harp. This pride, this pride, brings all to beggarie.

124 out *Haz.*: ont *Q 1*: on't *Q 2, Ff* 143 Yea, yea] I, I *Q 2, Ff* 149 you] ye *Q 2, Ff* 158 those golden ruddocks *Ff, etc.*

Scene III. *etc. add. M* *S. D.* Enter foure *Q 2, Ff* 5 Faith] I *Q 2, Ff*: Ay *R, etc.* 8 command *Q 2, etc.* 9 and has set down an order *Q 2, etc.* 15 man aske at doore for *Q 2, etc.* 22 but crawle *Q 2, etc.* 26 at Shrewsbury battel *Q 2, etc.* 28 Cobhams, the *Q 2, etc.* that is *om. Q 2, etc.*

I seru'de your father, and your grandfather;
Shew me such two men now!
No! No! Your backes, your backes, the diuell and pride,
Has cut the throate of all good housekeeping.—
They were the best Yeomens masters,
That euer were in England.

Cob. Yea, except thou haue a crue of seely knaues
And sturdy rogues still feeding at my gate,
There is no hospitalitie with thee.

Harp. They may sit at the gate well enough, but the diuell of any thing you giue them, except they will eate stones.

Cob. Tis long, then, of such hungry knaues as you. [*pointing to the beggars.*
Yea, sir, heres your retinue; your guests be come.
They know their howers, I warrant you.

Old ⟨man⟩. God blesse your honour! God saue the good Lord Cobham
And all his house!

Soul. Good your honour, bestow your blessed almes
Vpon poore men.

Cob. Now, sir, here be your Almes knights. Now are you
As safe as the Emperour.

Harp. My Almes knights! nay, th'are yours.
It is a shame for you, and Ile stand too't;
Your foolish almes maintaines more vagabonds,
Then all the noblemen in Kent beside.
Out, you rogues, you knaues! worke for your liuings!—
Alas, poore men! O Lord, they may beg their hearts out;
Theres no more charitie amongst men then amongst
So many mastiffe dogges!—What make you here,
You needy knaues? Away, away, you villaines.

2. soul. I beseech you, sir, be good to vs.

Cobham Nay, nay, they know thee well enough. I thinke that all the beggars in this land are thy acquaintance. Goe bestowe your almes; none will controule you, sir.

Harp. What should I giue them? you are growne so beggarly, you haue scarce a bitte of breade to giue at your doore. You talke of your religion so long, that you haue banished charitie from amongst you; a man may make a flaxe shop in your kitchin chimnies, for any fire there is stirring.

Cobham If thou wilt giue them nothing, send them hence: let them not stand here staruing in the colde.

Harp. Who! I driue them hence? If I driue poore men from your doore, Ile be hangd; I know not what I may come to my selfe. Yea, God help you, poore knaues; ye see the world, yfaith! Well, you had a mother: well, God be with thee, good Lady; thy soule's at rest. She gaue more in shirts and smocks to poore children, then you spend in your house, & yet you liue a beggar too.

Cobham Euen the worst deede that ere my mother did was in releeuing such a foole as thou.

Harpoole Yea, yea, I am a foole still. With all your wit you will die a beggar; go too.

Cobham Go, you olde foole; giue the poore people something. Go in, poore men, into the inner court, and take such alms as there is to be had.

Souldier God blesse your honor.

Harpoole Hang you, roags, hang you; theres nothing but misery amongst you; you feare no law, you. [*Exit.*

Olde man God blesse you, good maister Rafe, God saue your life; you are good to the poore still.

Enter the Lord Powes disguised, and shrowde himselfe.

Cobham What fellow's yonder comes along the groue?
Few passengers there be that know this way:
Me thinkes he stops as though he stayd for me,
And meant to shrowd himselfe amongst the bushes.
I know the Cleargie hate me to the death,
And my religion gets me many foes:
And this may be some desperate rogue, subornd
To worke me mischiefe.—As it pleaseth God!
If he come toward me, sure Ile stay his comming—
Be he but one man—what soere he be.

The Lord Powis comes on.

I haue beene well acquainted with that face.

Powis Well met, my honorable lord and friend.

34 *Line ends* no, no *Qq, Ff* 34–8 *Four lines M, etc., ending* no, no, your backs; throat; best; England 37 *Line ends* that *Qq, Ff* 39 seely] filthy *Q 2, etc.* 45 you] (?) yon 48–9 *Prose all edd.* 52 *Ends* knights *Qq, Ff*: *corr. M* 54–62 *Prose M* 59 O Lord *om. Q 2, etc.* 60–2 *Four lines in Qq, Ff, ending* men; dogges; knaues; villaines 60 amongst: *pronounce* 'mongst 69, 70 that you can scarse giue a bit *Q 2, etc.*

72 amongst *om. Q 2, etc.* 80, 82 yea, yfaith *om. Q 2, etc.* 81 help ye *Q 2, etc.* 82 well, God] O God *Q 2, etc.* 90 Yea, yea] I *Q 2* 107 hates *Q 2, etc.* 109–12 *Lines end in Q 1* rogue; it; sure; man, be: *corr. M*

Cobham You are welcome, sir, what ere you be;
But of this sodaine, sir, I do not know you.

Powis I am one that wisheth well vnto your honor;
My name is Powes, an olde friend of yours.

Cobham My honorable lord, and worthy friend,
What makes your lordship thus alone in Kent,
And thus disguised in this strange attire?

Powis My Lord, an vnexpected accident
Hath at this time inforc'de me to these parts;
And thus it hapt:—Not yet ful fiue dayes since,
Now at the last Assise at Hereford,
It chanst that the lord Herbert and my selfe,
Mongst other things, discoursing at the table,
Did fall in speech about some certaine points
Of *Wickcliffes* doctrine gainst the papacie
And the religion catholique, maintaind
Through the most part of Europe at this day.
This wilfull teasty lord stucke not to say
That *Wickcliffe* was a knaue, a schismatike,
His doctrine diuelish and hereticall,
And what soere he was maintaind the same,
Was traitor both to God and to his country.
Being moued at his peremptory speech,
I told him some maintained those opinions,
Men, and truer subiects then lord Herbert was:
And he replying in comparisons,
Your name was vrgde, my lord, gainst his chalenge,
To be a perfect fauourer of the trueth.
And to be short, from words we fell to blowes,
Our seruants and our tenants taking parts—
Many on both sides hurt—and for an houre
The broyle by no meanes could be pacified,
Vntill the Iudges, rising from the bench,
Were in their persons forc'de to part the fray.

Cobham I hope no man was violently slaine.

Powis Faith, none, I trust, but the lord Herberts selfe,
Who is in truth so dangerously hurt,
As it is doubted he can hardly scape.

Cobham I am sory, my good lord, of these ill newes.

Powis This is the cause that driues me into Kent,
To shrowd my selfe with you, so good a friend,
Vntill I heare how things do speed at home.

Cobham Your lordship is most welcome vnto Cobham;
But I am very sory, my good lord,
My name was brought in question in this matter,
Considering I haue many enemies,
That threaten malice, and do lie in waite
To take aduantage of the smallest thing.
But you are welcome: and repose your lordship,
And keepe your selfe here secret in my house,
Vntill we heare how the lord Herbert speedes.
Here comes my man. [*Enter Harpoole.*
Sirra, what newes?

Harpoole Yonders one maister Butler of the priuie chamber, is sent vnto you from the King.

Powis I pray God the lord Herbert be not dead,
And the King, hearing whither I am gone,
Hath sent for me.

Cob. Comfort your selfe my lord, I warrant you.

Harpoole Fellow, what ailes thee? doost thou quake? dost thou shake? dost thou tremble? ha?

Cob. Peace, you old foole! Sirra, conuey this gentleman in the backe way, and bring the other into the walke.

Harpoole Come, sir; you are welcome, if you loue my lorde.

Powis God haue mercy, gentle friend. [*exeunt.*

Cob. I thought as much: that it would not be long,
Before I heard of something from the King
About this matter.

Enter Harpoole with Maister Butler.

Harpoole Sir, yonder my lord walkes, you see him;
Ile haue your men into the Celler the while.

Cobh. Welcome, good maister Butler.

Butler Thankes, my good lord: his Maiestie dooth commend
His loue vnto your lordship,
And wils you to repaire vnto the court.

Cobh. God blesse his Highnesse, and confound his ennemies!
I hope his Maiestie is well.

Butler In health, my lord.

Cobh. God long continue it! Mee thinkes you looke
As though you were not well: what ailes you, sir?

Butler Faith, I haue had a foolish odde mischance,

115 very welcome *M* 128 Did *M*: To *Qq*, *Ff* 139 (?) Truer men and subjects 141 his] this *Ff* 162 advantage *Qq*: the vantage *Ff*, *etc.* 171 I *om. Q 2*, *etc.* the] that the *M* 171–3 *Prose Qq*, *Ff*: *corr. M* 182 God haue mercy] Gramercy *Q 2*, *etc.* 183–5 *Prose Qq*, *Ff*: *corr. R* 186–7 *Prose M* 189–91 *Prose in all edd.* 192–3 *Prose Qq*, *Ff*: *corr. M* 194 In good health *Ff*, *etc.* 196 ailes you] ayle ye *Q 2*, *etc.* 197–206 *Prose Qq*, *Ff*: *corr. M*

That angers mee: comming ouer Shooters hill,
There came a fellow to me like a Sailer,
And asked me money; and whilst I staide my horse
To draw my purse, he takes th' aduantage of
A little banck and leapes behind me, whippes
My purse away, and with a sodaine ierke,
I know not how, threw me at least three yards
Out of my saddle. I neuer was so robbed
In all my life.

Cobh. I am very sorie, sir, for your mischance. Wee will send our warrant foorth, to stay such suspitious persons as shal be found. Then, maister Butler, we wil attend you.

Butler I humbly thanke your lordship, I will attend you.

⟨ACT II.

SCENE I. *The same.*⟩

Enter the Sumner.

Sum. I haue the law to warrant what I do; and though the Lord Cobham be a noble man, that dispenses not with law: I dare serue processe were a fiue noble men. Though we Sumners make sometimes a mad slip in a corner with a prettie wench, a Sumner must not goe alwayes by seeing: a manne may be content to hide his eies, where he may feele his profit. Well, this is my Lord Cobhams house if I can deuise to speake with him; if not, Ile clap my citation vpon's doore: so my lord of Rochester bid me. But me thinkes here comes one of his men.

Enter Harpoole.

Harp. Welcome, good fellow, welcome; who wouldst thou speake with?

Sum. With my lord Cobham I would speake, if thou be one of his men.

Harp. Yes, I am one of his men, but thou canst not speake with my lord.

Sum. May I send to him then?

Harp. Ile tel thee that, when I know thy errand.

Sum. I will not tel my errand to thee.

Harp. Then keepe it to thy selfe, and walke like a knaue as thou camest.

Sum. I tell thee, my lord keepes no knaues, sirra.

Harp. Then thou seruest him not, I beleeue: what lord is thy master?

Sum. My lord of Rochester.

Harp. In good time! And what wouldst thou haue with my lord Cobham?

Sum. I come, by vertue of a processe, to ascite him to appeare before my lord in the court at Rochester.

Harp. (*aside*). Wel, God grant me patience! I could eate this conger. My lord is not at home; therefore it were good, Sumner, you caried your processe backe.

Sum. Why, if he will not be spoken withall, then will I leaue it here; and see you that he take knowledge of it.

Harp. Swounds, you slaue, do you set vp your bills here! go to; take it downe againe. Doest thou know what thou dost? Dost thou know on whom thou seruest processe?

Sum. Yes, marry, doe I; Sir Iohn Old-castle, Lord Cobham.

Harp. I am glad thou knowest him yet; and, sirra, dost not thou know, that the lord Cobham is a braue lord, that keepes good beefe and beere in his house, and euery day feedes a hundred poore people at's gate, and keepes a hundred tall fellowes?

Sum. Whats that to my processe?

Harp. Mary, this, sir! is this processe parchment?

Sum. Yes, mary.

Harp. And this seale waxe?

Sum. It is so.

Harp. If this be parchment, & this wax, eate you this parchment and this waxe, or I will make parchment of your skinne, and beate your brains into waxe: Sirra Sumner, dispatch; deuoure, sirra, deuoure.

Sum. I am my lord of Rochesters Sumner; I came to do my office, and thou shalt answere it.

Harp. Sirra, no railing, but betake you to your teeth. Thou shalt eate no worse then thou bringst with thee: thou bringst it for my lord, and wilt thou bring my lord worse then thou wilt eate thy selfe?

Sum. Sir, I brought it not my lord to eate.

Harp. O, do you sir me now? all's one for that: but ile make you eate it, for bringing it.

Sum. I cannot eate it.

Harp. Can you not? sbloud ile beate you vntil you haue a stomacke. [*he beates him.*

Sum. O hold, hold, good master seruingman! I will eate it.

199 a fellow] one *Q 2, etc.* 200 ask'd my *M* 207-10 *Verse M* 208 stay all such *M* 210 we'll attend on you *M* Act II. *etc. add. M* 3-4 serue a processe were he *Q 2, etc.* 9 my *om. Q 2, etc.* 10 house; if I cannot speak with him, Ile *Q 2, etc.* 12 bad *Q 2, etc.*

34 scite *Q 2*: cite *R* 41 you *om. Q 2, Ff* 45 Dost thou] dost thee *Q 1* 46 a processe *Ff, etc.* 47 on Sir Iohn *Q 2, etc.* 50 thou *om. Ff, R* dost thou not *M* 58 marry is it *Ff, etc.* 62 this waxe] wax *Q 2* 69 you] your self *Ff, etc.* 76 but *om. Q 2, etc.* 79 till *Q 2, etc.*

Harp. Be champping, be chawing, sir; or Ile chaw you, you rogue! the purest of the hony! Tough waxe is the purest of the hony.

Sum. O Lord, sir! oh! oh! [*he eates.*

Harp. Feed, feed! wholsome, rogue, wholsome!
Cannot you, like an honest Sumner, walke with the diuell your brother, to fetch in your Bailiffes rents, but you must come to a noble mans house with processe? Sbloud! if thy seale were as broad as the lead that couers Rochester church, thou shouldst eate it.

Sum. O, I am almost choaked! I am almost choaked!

Harp. Who's within there? wil you shame my Lord? is there no beere in the house? Butler! I say.

Enter Butler.

But. Heere, here.

Harp. Giue him Beere. [*he drinkes.*
There; tough old sheepskins bare, drie meate.

Sum. O sir, let me go no further; Ile eate my word.

Harp. Yea, mary, sir! so I meane: you shall eate more then your own word, for ile make you eate all the words in the processe. Why, you drab monger, cannot the secrets of al the wenches in a sheire serue your turne, but you must come hither with a citation? with a poxe! Ile cite you. [*He has then done.*] A cup of sacke for the Sumner.

But. Here, sir, here.

Harp. Here, slaue, I drinke to thee.

Sum. I thanke you, sir.

Harp. Now if thou findst thy stomacke well—because thou shalt see my Lord keep's meate in's house—if thou wilt go in, thou shalt haue a peece of beefe to thy break fast.

Sum. No, I am very well, good M⟨aister⟩ seruing-man, I thanke you; very well sir.

Harp. I am glad on't. Then be walking towards Rochester to keepe your stomack warme: and Sumner, if I may know you disturb a good wench within this Diocesse; if I do not make thee eate her peticote, if there were four yards of Kentish cloth in't, I am a villaine.

Sum. God be with you, M⟨aister⟩ seruing-maan. ⟨*Exit.*⟩

Harp. Farewell, Sumner.

Enter Constable.

Con. God saue you M⟨aister⟩ Harpoole.

Harp. Welcome, Constable, welcom, Constable; what news with thee?

Con. And't please you, M⟨aister⟩ Harpoole, I am to make hue and crie, for a fellow with one eie that has rob'd two Clothiers, and am to craue your hindrance, for to search all suspected places; and they say there was a woman in the company.

Harp. Hast thou bin at the Alehouse? hast thou sought there?

Con. I durst not search, sir, in my Lord Cobhams libertie, except I had some of his seruants, which are for my warrant.

Harp. An honest Constable! an honest Constable! Cal forth him that keepes the Alehouse there.

Con. Ho! who's within there?

⟨*Enter Ale-man*⟩

Ale man Who calls there? come neere a Gods name! Oh, is't you, M⟨aister⟩ Constable and M⟨aister⟩ Harpoole? you are welcome with all my heart. What make you here so earely this morning?

Harp. Sirra, what strangers do you lodge? there is a robbery done this morning, and we are to search for all suspected persons.

Aleman. Gods bores! I am sory for't: yfaith, sir, I lodge no body but a good honest mery priest,—they call him sir Iohn a Wrootham—and a handsome woman that is his neece, that he saies he has some sute in law for; and as they go vp & down to London, sometimes they lie at my house.

Harp. What, is he here in thy house now?

Ale-m. She is, sir. I promise you, sir, he is a quiet man; and because he will not trouble too many roomes, he makes the woman lie euery night at his beds feete.

Harp. Bring her forth! Constable, bring her forth! let's see her, let's see her.

Ale-m. Dorothy, you must come downe to M⟨aister⟩ Constable.

Dol. Anon, forsooth. [*she enters.*

Harp. Welcome, sweete lasse, welcome.

Dol. I thank you, good M⟨aister⟩ seruing-man, and master Constable also.

Harp. A plump girle by the mas, a plump

84 Tough . . hony *given to* Sum. *Qq, Ff*: of the *om. Q 2, etc.* 83–4 Tough wax is the purest honey. Sum. The purest of the honey! *M* 85 O . . oh! *given to* Harp. *Qq, Ff* 86 tis wholsome Rogue *Q 2, etc.* 90 Sbloud *om. Q 2, etc.* 100 bare] but *conj. M* 102 so *om. Q 2, etc.* 121 may] do *Q 2, etc.* 126 with you] w'ye *Q 2, etc.* *S. D. add. Q 2* 128 God *om. Q 2, etc.* 132 hue to crie *Q 1* 134 for *om. Q 2, etc.* 139 sir *om. Ff, etc.* 141 which are *om. Q 2, etc.* 142 An honest Constable *once in Q 2, etc.* *S. D. add. M* 146–7 come . . name *om. Q 2, etc.* 156 mery *om. Ff, etc.* cal'd sir Iohn *Q 2, etc.* 161 he] she *Q 2, etc.* 162, 168 *Prefix* Con. *Qq*: *corr. Ff*

girle! Ha, Dol, ha! Wilt thou forsake the priest, and go with me?

Con. A! well said, M⟨aister⟩ Harpoole; you are a merrie old man, yfaith. Yfaith, you wil neuer be old. Now, by the macke, a prettie wench indeed!

Harp. Ye old mad mery Constable, art thou aduis'de of that. Ha, well said, Dol! fill some ale here.

Dol. (*aside*). Oh, if I wist this old priest would not sticke to me, by Ioue, I would ingle this old seruing-man.

Harp. Oh you old mad colt! yfaith, Ile feak you! fil all the pots in the house there.

Con. Oh, wel said, M⟨aister⟩ Harpoole! you are heart of oake when all's done.

Harp. Ha, Dol, thou hast a sweete paire of lippes, by the masse.

Doll Truely you are a most sweet olde man, as euer I sawe; by my troth, you haue a face, able to make any woman in loue with you.

Harp. Fill, sweete Doll; Ile drinke to thee.

Doll 'I' pledge you, sir, and thanke you therefore,
And I pray you let it come.'

Harp. (*imbracing her*). Doll, canst thou loue me? A mad merry lasse! would to God I had neuer seene thee!

Doll I warrant you, you will not out of my thoughts this tweluemonth; truely you are as full of fauour, as a man may be. Ah, these sweete grey lockes! by my troth, they are most louely.

Constable Gods boores, maister Harpoole, I will haue one busse too.

Harp. No licking for you, Constable! hand off, hand off!

Constable Bur lady, I loue kissing as wel as you.

Doll Oh, you are an od boie; you haue a wanton eie of your owne! ah, you sweet sugar lipt wanton, you will winne as many womens hearts as come in your company.

Enter Priest.

Wroth. Doll, come hither.

Harp. Priest, she shal not.

Doll Ile come anone, sweete loue.

Wroth. Hand off, old fornicator.

Harp. Vicar, Ile sit here in spight of thee. Is this fitte stuffe for a priest to carry vp and downe with him?

Wrotham Ah, sirra, dost thou not know, that a good fellow parson may haue a chappel of ease, where his parish Church is farre off?

Harp. You whooreson ston'd Vicar!

Wroth. You olde stale ruffin! you lion of Cotswold!

Harp. Swounds, Vicar, Ile geld you! [*flies upon him.*

Constable Keepe the Kings peace!

Doll Murder! murder! murder!

Ale man Holde! as you are men, holde! for Gods sake be quiet! Put vp your weapons; you drawe not in my house.

Harp. You whooreson bawdy priest!

Wroth. You old mutton monger!

Constable Hold, sir Iohn, hold!

Doll (*to the Priest*) I pray thee, sweet heart, be quiet. I was but sitting to drinke a pot of ale with him, euen as kinde a man as euer I met with.

Harp. Thou art a theefe, I warrant thee.

Wroth. Then I am but as thou hast beene in thy dayes. Lets not be ashamed of our trade; the King has beene a theefe himselfe.

Doll Come, be quiet. Hast thou sped?

Wroth. I haue, wench: here be crownes, ifaith.

Doll Come, lets be all friends then.

Constable Well said, mistris Dorothy, ifaith.

Harp. Thou art the madst priest that euer I met with.

Wroth. Giue me thy hand, thou art as good a fellow. I am a singer, a drinker, a bencher, a wencher! I can say a masse, and kisse a lasse! Faith, I haue a parsonage, and bicause I would not be at too much charges, this wench serues me for a sexton.

Harp. Well said, mad priest, weele in and be friends. [*exeunt.*

⟨Scene II. *London. A room in the Axe Inn, without Bishop-gate.*⟩

Enter sir Roger Acton, master Bourne, master Beuerley, and William Murley the brewer of Dunstable.

Acton Now, maister Murley, I am well assurde
You know our arrant, and do like the cause,
Being a man affected as we are.

Mu. Mary, God dild ye, daintie my deere! no master, good sir Roger Acton Knight, maister Bourne, and maister Beuerley esquires, gentlemen, and iustices of the peace—no maister I, but plaine William Murly, the brewer of Dunstable, your honest neighbour,

176 with mee, Doll *Q 2, etc.* 178 yfaith *once Q 2, etc.* 188 feak *Q 1*: ferke *Q 2, etc.* 197–8 *Prose Qq, Ff: corr. M. Part of an old ballad conj. M* 207 Gods] Cuds *Q 2, etc.* 209–10 hands . . hands *M* 213 o l] old *M* 220 hands *M* 224 Ah *om. Q 2, etc.*

251 ifaith *om. Q 2, etc.* *S. D.* Scene II. *etc. add. M* 5 Knight *om. Q 2, etc.* 6 esquires *om. Q 2, etc.*

and your friend, if ye be men of my profession.

Beuerley Professed friends to Wickliffe, foes to Rome.

Murl. Hold by me, lad; leane vpon that staffe, good maister Beuerley: all of a house. Say your mind, say your mind.

Acton You know our faction now is growne so great,
Throughout the realme, that it beginnes to smoake
Into the Cleargies eies, and the Kings eares.
High time it is that we were drawne to head,
Our generall and officers appoynted;
And warres, ye wot, will aske great store of coine.
Able to strength our action with your purse,
You are elected for a colonell
Ouer a regiment of fifteene bands.

Murley Fue, paltrie, paltrie! in and out, to and fro! be it more or lesse, vppon occasion. Lorde haue mercie vppon vs, what a world is this! Sir Roger Acton, I am but a Dunstable man, a plaine brewer, ye know: will lusty Caualiering captaines, gentlemen, come at my calling, goe at my bidding? Daintie my deere, theile doe a dogge of waxe, a horse of cheese, a pricke and a pudding. No, no, ye must appoint some lord, or knight at least, to that place.

Bourne Why, master Murley, you shall be a Knight:
Were you not in election to be shrieue?
Haue ye not past all offices but that?
Haue ye not wealth to make your wife a lady?
I warrant you, my lord, our Generall
Bestowes that honor on you at first sight.

Murley Mary, God dild ye, daintie my deare!
But tell me, who shalbe our Generall?
Wheres the lord Cobham, sir Iohn Old-castle,
That noble almes-giuer, housekeeper, vertuous,
Religious gentleman? Come to me there, boies,
Come to me there!

Acton Why, who but he shall be our Generall?

Murley And shall he knight me, and make me colonell?

Acton My word for that: sir William Murley, knight.

Murley Fellow sir Roger Acton, knight, all fellowes—I meane in armes—how strong are we? how many partners? Our enemies beside the King are mightie; be it more or lesse vpon occasion, reckon our force.

Acton There are of vs, our friends, and followers,
Three thousand and three hundred at the least;
Of northerne lads foure thousand, beside horse;
From Kent there comes with sir Iohn Oldcastle
Seauen thousand; then from London issue out,
Of maisters, seruants, strangers, prentices,
Fortie odde thousands into Ficket field,
Where we appoynt our speciall randeuous.

Murley Fue, paltry, paltry, in and out, to and fro! Lord haue mercie vpon vs, what a world is this! Wheres that Ficket fielde, sir Roger?

Acton Behinde saint Giles in the field neere Holborne.

Murley Newgate, vp Holborne, S. Giles in the field, and to Tiborne: an old saw. For the day, for the day?

Acton On friday next, the foureteenth day of Ianuary.

Murley Tyllie vallie, trust me neuer if I haue any liking of that day! fue, paltry, paltry! friday, quoth a! Dismall day! Childermasse day this yeare was friday.

Beuerley Nay, maister Murley, if you obserue such daies,
We make some question of your constancie.
All daies are like to men resolu'de in right.

Murley Say Amen, and say no more; but say, and hold, master Beuerley: friday next, and Ficket field, and William Murley, and his merry men shalbe al one. I haue halfe a score iades that draw my beere cartes,
And euery iade shall beare a knaue,
And euery knaue shall weare a iacke,
And euery iacke shal haue a scull,
And euery scull shal shew a speare,
And euery speare shal kill a foe
At Ficket field, at Ficket field.
Iohn and Tom, and Dicke and Hodge,
And Rafe and Robin, William & George,
And all my knaues shall fight like men,
At Ficket field on friday next.

Bourne What summe of money meane you to disburse?

Murley It may be modestly, decently, soberly, and handsomely I may bring fiue hundreth pound.

Acton Fiue hundreth, man! fiue thousand's not enough!
A hundreth thousand will not pay our men
Two months together. Either come preparde
Like a braue Knight, and martiall Colonell,
In glittering golde, and gallant furniture,
Bringing in coyne a cart loade at the least,
And all your followers mounted on good horse,
Or neuer come disgracefull to vs all.

77 quoth-a, a dismal *M* 87-90 *Prose all edd.* 93-4 Tom, Dicke and Hodge, Rafe *Q 2, etc.*

Beuerley Perchance you may be chosen Treasurer.
Tenne thousand pound's the least that you can bring.

Murley Paltry, paltry! in and out, to and fro, vpon occasion I haue ten thousand pound to spend, and tenne too. And rather than the Bishop shall haue his will of mee for my conscience, it shall out all. Flame and flaxe, flame and flaxe! it was gotte with water and mault, and it shal flie with fire and gunne powder. Sir Roger, a cart loade of mony til the axetree cracke, my selfe and my men in Ficket field on friday next: remember my Knighthoode, and my place. There's my hand; Ile bee there. [*Exit.*

Acton See what Ambition may perswade men to,
In hope of honor he will spend himselfe.

Bourne I neuer thought a Brewer halfe so rich.

Beuerley Was neuer bankerout Brewer yet but one,
With vsing too much mault, too little water.

Acton Thats no fault in Brewers now-adayes.
Come, away, about our businesse. [*exeunt.*

⟨SCENE III. *An audience-chamber in the palace at Eltham.*⟩

Enter K. Harry, Suffolke, Butler, and Oldcastle kneeling to the King.

Harry Tis not enough, Lord Cobham, to submit;
You must forsake your grosse opinion.
The Bishops find themselues much iniured,
And though, for some good seruice you haue done,
We for our part are pleasde to pardon you,
Yet they will not so soone be satisfied.

Cobham My gracious Lord, vnto your Maiestie,
Next vnto my God, I owe my life;
And what is mine, either by natures gift,
Or fortunes bountie, al is at your seruice.
But, for obedience to the Pope of Rome,
I owe him none, nor shall his shaueling priests
That are in England alter my beliefe.
If out of holy Scripture they can proue,
That I am in an errour I will yeeld,
And gladly take instruction at their hands;
But otherwise, I do beseech your grace,
My conscience may not be incroacht vpon.

Har. We would be loath to presse our subiects bodies,
Much lesse their soules, the deere redeemed part
Of him that is the ruler of vs all;
Yet let me counsell ye, that might command:
Do not presume to tempt them with ill words,
Nor suffer any meetings to be had
Within your house, but to the vttermost,
Disperse the flockes of this new gathering sect.

Cobham My liege, if any breathe, that dares come forth,
And say my life in any of these points
Deserues th'attaindor of ignoble thoughts,
Here stand I, crauing no remorce at all,
But euen the vtmost rigor may be showne.

Har. Let it suffice; we know your loyaltie.
What haue you there?

Cob. A deed of clemencie;
Your Highnesse pardon for Lord Powesse life,
Which I did beg, and you, my noble Lord,
Of gracious fauour did vouchsafe to grant.

Har. But yet it is not signed with our hand.

Cob. Not yet, my Liege.
[*one ready with pen and incke.*

Har. The fact, you say, was done,
Not of prepensed malice, but by chance.

Cob. Vpon mine honor so, no otherwise.

Har. There is his pardon; bid him make amends, [*writes.*
And cleanse his soule to God for his offence.
What we remit, is but the bodies scourge—

Enter Bishop.

How now, Lord Bishop?

Bishop Iustice, dread Soueraigne!
As thou art King, so graunt I may haue iustice.

Har. What meanes this exclamation? let vs know.

Bish. Ah, my good Lord, the state's abusde,
And our decrees most shamefully prophande.

Har. How? or by whom?

Bish. Euen by this heretike,
This Iew, this Traitor to your maiestie.

Cob. Prelate, thou liest, euen in thy greasie maw,
Or whosoeuer twits me with the name
Of either traitor, or of heretike.

Har. Forbeare, I say; and, Bishop, shew the cause
From whence this late abuse hath bin deriu'de.

Bish. Thus, mightie King:—By generall consent,
A messenger was sent to cite this Lord,
To make appearance in the consistorie;

115 out *om. Q 2, etc.* shall all go *F 2, etc.* Flame and flaxe, flaxe and flame *Q 2, etc.* 118 axletree *Q 2, etc.* 128 Come, let's away *M* *S. D.* Scene III. *etc. add. M* 8 do owe *M*

22 ye] you *Q 2, etc.* 41 pretensed *Q 2, Ff, M*: propensed *R, Pope* 50 is much abus'd *M*

And comming to his house, a ruffian slaue,
One of his daily followers, met the man,
Who, knowing him to be a parator,
Assaults him first and after, in contempt
Of vs and our proceedings, makes him eate
The written processe, parchment, seale and all:
Whereby his maister neither was brought forth,
Nor we but scornd for our authoritie.
Har. When was this done?
Bish. At sixe a clocke this morning.
Har. And when came you to court?
Cob. Last night, my Lord.
Har. By this it seemes, he is not guilty of it,
And you haue done him wrong t'accuse him so.
Bish. But it was done, my lord, by his appointment,
Or else his man durst ne're haue bin so bold.
Har. Or else you durst be bold to interrupt,
And fill our eares with friuolous complaints.
Is this the duetie you do beare to vs?
Was't not sufficient we did passe our word
To send for him, but you, misdoubting it,
Or—which is worse—intending to forestall
Our regall power, must likewise summon him?
This sauours of Ambition, not of zeale,
And rather proues you malice his estate,
Than any way that he offends the law.
Go to, we like it not; and he your officer,
That was imployde so much amisse herein,
Had his desert for being insolent.

Enter Huntington.

So, Cobham, when you please you may depart.
Cob. I humbly bid farewell vnto my liege. [*Exit.*
Har. Farewell.—What's the newes by Huntington?
Hunt. Sir Roger Acton and a crue, my Lord,
Of bold seditious rebels are in Armes,
Intending reformation of Religion.
And with their Army they intend to pitch
In Ficket field, vnlesse they be repulst.
Har. So nere our presence? Dare they be so bold?
And will prowd warre, and eager thirst of bloud,
Whom we had thought to entertaine farre off,
Presse forth vpon vs in our natiue boundes?
Must wee be forc't to hansell our sharp blades
In England here, which we prepar'd for France?
Well, a Gods name be it! What's their number, say,
Or who's the chiefe commander of this rowt?
Hunt. Their number is not knowne, as yet, my Lord,
But tis reported Sir Iohn Old-castle
Is the chiefe man on whom they do depend.
Har. How, the Lord Cobham?
Hunt. Yes, my gracious Lord.
Bish. I could haue told your maiestie as much
Before he went, but that I saw your Grace
Was too much blinded by his flaterie.
Suf. Send poast, my Lord, to fetch him backe againe.
But. Traitor vnto his country, how he smooth'de,
And seemde as innocent as Truth it selfe!
Har. I cannot thinke it yet he would be false;
But if he be, no matter; let him go.
Weele meet both him and them vnto their wo.
Exeunt ⟨*all but Bishop*⟩.
Bish. This falls out well, and at the last I hope
To see this heretike die in a rope.

⟨ACT III.

SCENE I. *An avenue leading to lord Cobham's house in Kent.*⟩

Enter Earle of Cambridge, Lord Scroope, Gray, and Chartres the French factor.

Scroop. Once more, my Lord of Cambridge, make rehersal,
How you do stand intiteled to the Crowne.
The deeper shall we print it in our mindes,
And euery man the better be resolu'de,
When he perceiues his quarrell to be iust.
Cam. Then thus, Lord Scroope, sir Thomas Gray, & you,
Mounsieur de Chartres, agent for the French:—
This Lionell, Duke of Clarence, as I said,
Third sonne of Edward (Englands King) the third,
Had issue Phillip, his sole daughter and heyre;
Which Phillip afterward was giuen in marriage
To Edmund Mortimer, the Earle of March,
And by him had a son cald Roger Mortimer;
Which Roger, likewise, had of his discent
Edmund, Roger, Anne, and Elianor—
Two daughters and two sonnes—but those three
Dide without issue. Anne, that did suruiue,
And now was left her fathers onely heyre,
My fortune was to marry, being too
By my grandfather of King Edwardes line:

78 ne're] not *Q 2, etc.* 79 durst not be *M* *Lines* 90 *and* 91 *transposed Q 2, etc.*

121 *S. D.* Exeunt *follows next line in Q 1: at end of scene Q 2, etc.* Act III. *etc. add. M* 16 but of those, three *Ff, etc.* 19 My] By *Q 2, Ff*

So of his sirname, I am calde, you know,
Richard Plantagenet. My father was
Edward, the Duke of Yorke, and son and heyre
To Edmund Langley, Edward the third's fifth sonne.

Scroop So that it seemes your claime comes by your wife,
As lawfull heyre to Roger Mortimer,
The son of Edmund, which did marry Phillip,
Daughter and heyre to Lyonell, Duke of Clarence.

Cam. True, for this Harry and his father both,
Harry the first, as plainely doth appeare,
Are false intruders and vsurp the Crowne.
For when yong Richard was at Pomfret slaine,
In him the title of prince Edward dide,
That was the eldest of king Edwards sonnes:
William, of Hatfield, and their second brother,
Death in his nonage had before bereft:
So that my wife, deriu'd from Lionell,
Third sonne vnto king Edward, ought proceede,
And také possession of the Diademe
Before this Harry, or his father king,
Who fetcht their title but from Lancaster,
Forth of that royall line. And being thus,
What reason ist but she should haue her right?

Scroope I am resolu'de our enterprise is iust.

Gray Harry shall die, or else resigne his crowne.

Chart. Performe but that, and Charles, the king of France,
Shall ayde you, lordes, not onely with his men,
But send you money to maintaine your warres.
Fiue hundred thousand crownes he bade me proffer,
If you can stop but Harries voyage for France.

Scrope We neuer had a fitter time than now,
The realme in such diuision as it is.

Camb. Besides, you must perswade ye, there is due
Vengeance for Richards murder, which, although
It be deferrde, yet will it fall at last,
And now as likely as another time.
Sinne hath had many yeeres to ripen in,
And now the haruest cannot be farre off,
Wherein the weedes of vsurpation
Are to be cropt, and cast into the fire.

Scroope No more, earle Cambridge; here I plight my faith,
To set vp thee and thy renowned wife.

Gray. Gray will performe the same, as he is knight.

Chart. And to assist ye, as I said before,
Charters doth gage the honor of his king.

Scroope We lacke but now Lord Cobhams fellowship,
And then our plot were absolute indeede.

Camb. Doubt not of him, my lord; his life's pursu'de
By th'incensed Cleargy, and of late,
Brought in displeasure with the king, assures
He may be quickly wonne vnto our faction.
Who hath the articles were drawne at large
Of our whole purpose?

Gray That haue I, my Lord.

Camb. We should not now be farre off from his house;
Our serious conference hath beguild the way.
See where his castle stands. Giue me the writing.
When we are come vnto the speech of him,
Because we will not stand to make recount,
Of that which hath beene saide, here he shall reade [*enter Cob.*
Our mindes at large, and what we craue of him.

Scroope A ready way. Here comes the man himselfe,
Booted and spurrd; it seemes he hath beene riding.

Camb. Well met, lord Cobham.

Cobh. My lord of Cambridge?
Your honor is most welcome into Kent,
And all the rest of this faire company.
I am new come from London, gentle Lordes:
But will ye not take Cowling for your host,
And see what entertainement it affordes?

Camb. We were intended to haue beene your guests:
But now this lucky meeting shall suffise
To end our businesse, and deferre that kind-nesse.

Cobh. Businesse, my lord? what businesse should you haue
But to be mery? We haue no delicates,
But this Ile promise you: a peece of venison,
A cup of wine, and so forth—hunters fare;
And if you please, weele strike the stagge our selues
Shall fill our dishes with his wel-fed flesh.

Scroope That is, indeede, the thing we all desire.

Cobh. My lordes and you shall haue your choice with me.

Camb. Nay, but the stagge which we desire to strike
Liues not in Cowling: if you will consent,
And goe with vs, weele bring you to a forrest,

24 fifth] first *Qq, Ff*: *corr. Percy in M* 30 Harry the fourth *M* 53 ye] you *Q 2, etc.*

68 life *M* 94–5 should Let you to be *Q 2, etc.*

Where runnes a lusty hierd; amongst the which
There is a stagge superior to the rest,
A stately beast that, when his fellows runne,
He leades the race, and beates the sullen earth,
As though he scornd it, with his trampling hoofes.
Aloft he beares his head, and with his breast,
Like a huge bulwarke, counter-checkes the wind:
And when he standeth still, he stretcheth forth
His prowd ambitious necke, as if he meant
To wound the firmament with forked hornes.
Cobh. Tis pitty such a goodly beast should die.
Camb. Not so, sir Iohn, for he is tyrannous,
And gores the other deere, and will not keep
Within the limites are appointed him.
Of late hees broke into a seueral,
Which doth belong to me, and there he spoiles
Both corne and pasture. Two of his wilde race,
Alike for stealth and couetous incroatching,
Already are remou'd; if he were dead,
I should not onely be secure from hurt,
But with his body make a royall feast.
Scroope How say you, then; will you first hunt with vs?
Cobh. Faith, Lords, I like the pastime; where's the place?
Camb. Peruse this writing; it will shew you all,
And what occasion we haue for the sport.
[*he reades*
Cobh. Call ye this hunting, my lords? Is this the stag
You faine would chase—Harry our dread king?
So we may make a banquet for the diuell,
And in the steede of wholsome meate, prepare
A dish of poison to confound our selues.
Camb. Why so, lord Cobham? See you not our claime?
And how imperiously he holdes the crowne?
Scroope Besides, you know your selfe is in disgrace,
Held as a recreant, and pursude to death.
This will defend you from your enemies,
And stablish your religion through the land.
Cobh. Notorious treason! yet I will conceale
[*aside*
My secret thoughts, to sound the depth of it.
My lord of Cambridge, I doe see your claime,
And what good may redound vnto the land
By prosecuting of this enterprise.
But where are men? where's power and furniture
To order such an action? We are weake;
Harry, you know's a mighty potentate.
Camb. Tut, we are strong enough: you are belou'de,
And many will be glad to follow you;
We are the like, and some will follow vs.
Besides, there is hope from France: heres an embassador
That promiseth both men and money too.
The commons likewise (as we heare) pretend
A sodaine tumult; we wil ioyne with them.
Cobh. Some likelihoode, I must confesse, to speede:
But how shall I beleeue this is plaine truth?
You are, my lords, such men as liue in Court,
And highly haue beene fauour'd of the king,
Especially lord Scroope, whome oftentimes
He maketh choice of for his bedfellow;
And you, lord Gray, are of his priuy councell:
Is not this a traine to intrappe my life?
Camb. Then perish may my soule! What, thinke you so?
Scroope Weele sweare to you.
Gray Or take the sacrament.
Cobh. Nay, you are noble men, and I imagine,
As you are honorable by birth and bloud,
So you will be in heart, in thought, in word.
I craue no other testimony but this:
That you would all subscribe, and set your hands
Vnto this writing which you gaue to me.
Camb. With all our hearts. Who hath any pen and inke?
Scroope My pocket should haue one: yea, heere it is.
Camb. Giue it me, lord Scroope.—There is my name.
Scroope And there is my name.
Gray And mine.
Cobh. Sir, let me craue,
That you would likewise write your name with theirs,
For confirmation of your maisters word,
The king of Fraunce.
Char. That will I, noble Lord.
Cobh. So now this action is well knit together,
And I am for you. Where's our meeting, lords?
Camb. Here, if you please, the tenth of Iuly next.
Cobh. In Kent? agreed: now let vs in to supper.
I hope your honors will not away to night.

105 among *Q 2, etc.* 131 our most dread *M*

151 like *F 1*: light *Qq* 157 is] in *Q 2, etc.* 163 traine laide to *Q 2, etc.* 174 yea] O *Q 2, etc.* 178–81 *Prose Q 2, Ff*

Camb. Yes, presently; for I haue farre to ride,
About solliciting of other friends.
Scroope And we would not be absent from the court,
Lest thereby grow suspition in the king.
Cobh. Yet taste a cup of wine before ye go.
Camb. Not now, my lord, we thanke you: so farewell. ⟨*Exeunt all but* Cobham.⟩
Cob. Farewell, my noble lordes.—My noble lords?
My noble villaines, base conspirators.
How can they looke his Highnesse in the face,
Whome they so closly study to betray?
But ile not sleepe vntill I make it knowne.
This head shall not be burdned with such thoughts,
Nor in this heart will I conceale a deede
Of such impietie against my king.
Madam, how now?

Enter Harpoole and the rest.

Lady Cobh. You are welcome home, my Lord.
Why seeme ye so disquiet in your lookes?
What hath befalne you that disquiets your minde?
Lady Po. Bad newes, I am afraide, touching my husband.
Cobh. Madam, not so: there is your husbands pardon.
Long may ye liue, each ioy vnto the other.
Powesse So great a kindnesse as I knowe not howe
To make reply; my sense is quite confounded.
Cobh. Let that alone: and madam, stay me not,
For I must backe vnto the court againe
With all the speede I can. Harpoole, my horse.
Lady Cob. So soone, my Lord? what, will you ride all night?
Cobham All night or day; it must be so, sweete wife.
Vrge me not why or what my businesse is,
But get you in. Lord Powesse, beare with me,
And madam, thinke your welcome nere the worse:
My house is at your vse. Harpoole, away.
Harp. Shall I attend your lordship to the court?
Cobh. Yea, sir; your gelding! mount you presently. *exe⟨unt⟩.*
Lady Cobh. I prythee, Harpoole, looke vnto thy Lord.
I do not like this sodaine posting backe.
Powes Some earnest businesse is a foote belike;
Whate're it be, pray God be his good guide.
Lady Po. Amen! that hath so highly vs bested.
Lady Co. Come, madam, and my lord, weele hope the best;
You shall not into Wales till he returne.
Powesse Though great occasion be we should departe,
Yet madam will we stay to be resolude
Of this vnlookt for, doubtful accident. [*Exeunt.*

⟨Scene II. *A road near Highgate.*⟩

Enter Murley and his men, prepared in some filthy order for warre.

Murly. Come, my hearts of flint, modestly, decently, soberly, and handsomly, no man afore his Leader; follow your master, your Captaine, your Knight that shal be, for the honor of Meale-men, Millers, and Mault-men. Dunne is the mowse. Dicke and Tom, for the credite of Dunstable, ding downe the enemie to morrow; ye shall not come into the field like beggars. Where be Leonard and Laurence, my two loaders? Lord haue mercie vpon vs, what a world is this? I would giue a couple of shillings for a dozen of good fethers for ye, and forty pence for as many skarffes to set ye out withall. Frost and snow! a man has no heart to fight till he be braue.

Dicke Master, I hope we be no babes. For our manhood, our bucklers and our towne foote-balls can beare witnesse: and this lite parrell we haue shall off, and weel fight naked afore we runne away.

Tom. Nay, I am of Laurence mind for that, for he meanes to leaue his life behind him; he and Leonard, your two loaders, are making their wills because they haue wiues. Now we Bachellers bid our friends scramble for our goods if we die: but, master, pray ye, let me ride vpon Cutte.

Murly Meale and salt, wheat and mault, fire and tow, frost and snow! why, Tom, thou shalt. Let me see: here are you, William and George are with my cart, and Robin and Hodge holding my owne two horses; proper men, handsom men, tall men, true men.

Dicke But, master, master, me thinkes you are a mad man to hazard your owne person and a cart load of money too.

193 *S. D. add. R*: Exit *Q 2, Ff* 204 ye] you *M* unquiet *Ff, etc.* 205 disturbes your minde *Q 2, etc.* 209–10 *Prose in Qq, Ff*: *corr. M* 210 make om. *Ff*

229–31 *Prose Qq, Ff*: *corr. R* Scene II. *etc. add. M* 16 I hope *om. Q 2, etc.* be] are *Q 2, etc.* 16–17 For .. bucklers and *om. Q 2, etc.* 18 lite] little *Q 2, etc.* 20 before *Q 2, etc.* 24 Now] and *M* 35 a mad man] mad *Ff, etc.*

Tom. Yea, and, maister, theres a worse matter in't. If it be as I heard say, we go to fight against all the learned Bishops, that should giue vs their blessing; and if they curse vs, we shall speede nere the better.

Dicke Nay, bir lady, some say the King takes their part; and, master, dare you fight against the King?

Murly Fie, paltry, paltry! in and out, to and fro, vpon occasion; if the King be so vnwise to come there, weele fight with him too.

Tom. What, if ye should kill the King?

Mur. Then weele make another.

Dicke Is that all? do ye not speake treason?

Mur. If we do, who dare trippe vs? we come to fight for our conscience, and for honor. Little know you what is in my bosome; looke here, madde knaues, a paire of guilt spurres.

Tom. A paire of golden spurres? Why do you not put them on your heeles? Your bosome's no place for spurres.

Mur. Bee't more or lesse vpon occasion, Lord haue mercy ⟨vpon⟩ vs, Tom, th'art a foole, and thou speakest treason to knighthood. Dare any weare golden or siluer spurs til he be a knight? No, I shall be knighted to morrow, and then they shall on. Sirs, was it euer read in the church booke of Dunstable, that euer mault man was made knight?

Tom. No, but you are more: you are mealman, maultman, miller, corne-master and all.

Dicke Yea, and halfe a brewer too, and the diuell and all for wealth. You bring more money with you, than all the rest.

Mur. The more's my honor. I shal be a knight to morow! Let me spose my men: Tom vpon cutte, Dicke vpon hobbe, Hodge vpon Ball, Raph vpon Sorell, and Robin vpon the forehorse.

Enter Acton, Bourne, and Beuerley.

Tom. Stand, who comes there?

Act. Al friends, good fellow.

Murl. Friends and fellowes, indeede, sir Roger.

Act. Why, thus you shew your selfe a Gentleman,
To keepe your day, and come so well preparde.
Your cart stands yonder, guarded by your men,
Who tell me it is loaden well with coine.
What summe is there?

Mur. Ten thousand pound, sir Roger; and modestly, decently, soberly, and handsomely, see what I haue here against I be knighted.

Act. Gilt spurs? tis well.

Mur. But where's our armie, sir?

Act. Disperst in sundry villages about:
Some here with vs in Hygate, some at Finchley,
Totnam, Enfield, Edmunton, Newington,
Islington, Hogsdon, Pancredge, Kenzington;
Some neerer Thames, Ratcliffe, Blackwall and Bow;
But our chiefe strength must be the Londoners,
Which, ere the Sunne to morrow shine,
Will be nere fiftie thousand in the field.

Mur. Mary, God dild ye, daintie my deere! but vpon occasion, sir Roger Acton, doth not the King know of it, and gather his power against vs?

Act. No, hee's secure at Eltham.

Mur. What do the Cleargie?

Act. Feare extreamly, yet prepare no force.

Mur. In and out, to and fro, Bullie my boikin, we shall carry the world afore vs! I vow by my worshippe, when I am knighted, weele take the King napping, if he stand on their part.

Act. This night we few in Higate will repose.
With the first cocke weele rise and arme our selues,
To be in Ficket fielde by breake of day,
And there expect our Generall.

Mur. Sir Iohn Old-castle? what if he come not?

Bourne Yet our action stands.
Sir Roger Acton may supply his place.

Mur. True, M⟨aister⟩ Bourne, but who shall make me knight?

Beuer. He that hath power to be our Generall.

Act. Talke not of trifles; come, let's away.
Our friends of London long till it be day.
[*exeunt.*

⟨Scene III. *A high road in Kent.*⟩

Enter sir Iohn of Wrootham and Doll.

Doll. By my troth, thou art as ielous a man as liues.

Priest Canst thou blame me, Doll? thou art my lands, my goods, my iewels, my wealth, my purse. None walks within xl. miles of London, but a plies thee as truely as the parish does the poore mans boxe.

Doll. I am as true to thee as the stone is in the wal; and thou knowest well enough, sir Iohn, I was in as good doing, when I came to thee, as any wench neede to be; and therefore

48 ye] you *M* 50 ye] you *M* 59 mercy vs *Q 1*: *corr. Q 2* 61 gold *Q 2, etc.*

89 But *om. Q 2, etc.* 104 They fear *M* 114 Sir Iohn Oldcastle *add. to Acton's speech, M* Scene III. *etc. add. M* *S. D.* Enter Priest and *Q 2, Ff* 9–10 sir Iohn *om. Q 2, etc.*

thou hast tried me, that thou hast: by Gods body, I wil not be kept as I haue bin, that I will not.

Priest Doll, if this blade holde, theres not a pedler walkes with a pack, but thou shalt as boldly chuse of his wares, as with thy ready mony in a Marchants shop. Weele haue as good siluer as the King coynes any.

Doll What, is al the gold spent you tooke the last day from the Courtier?

Priest Tis gone, Doll, tis flown; merely come, merely gon: he comes a horse backe that must pay for all. Weele haue as good meate as mony can get, and as good gownes as can be bought for gold. Be mery, wench, the mault-man comes on munday.

Doll You might haue left me at Cobham, vntil you had bin better prouided for.

Priest. No, sweet Dol, no; I do not like that. Yond old ruffian is not for the priest: I do not like a new cleark should come in the old belfrie.

Doll Ah, thou art a mad priest, yfaith.

Priest Come, Doll; Ile see thee safe at some alehouse here at Cray, and the next sheepe that comes shall leaue his fleece.

[*exeunt.*

⟨Scene IV. *Blackheath.*⟩

Enter the King, Suffolke and Butler.

King (*in great hast*). My lord of Suffolk, poste away for life,
And let our forces of such horse and foote,
As can be gathered vp by any meanes,
Make speedy randeuow in Tuttle fields.
It must be done this euening, my Lord;
This night the rebells meane to draw to head
Neere Islington, which if your speede preuent not,
If once they should vnite their seuerall forces,
Their power is almost thought inuincible.
Away, my Lord; I will be with you soone.

Suf. I go, my Soueraigne, with all happie speede. [*exit.*

King Make haste, my lord of Suffolke, as you loue vs.
Butler, poste you to London with all speede;
Commaund the Maior and shrieues, on their alegiance,
The cittie gates be presently shut vp
And guarded with a strong sufficient watch,
And not a man be suffered to passe
Without a speciall warrant from our selfe.
Command the Posterne by the Tower be kept,
And proclamation, on the paine of death,
That not a citizen stirre from his doores,
Except such as the Maior and Shrieues shall chuse
For their owne guarde and safety of their persons.
Butler, away; haue care vnto my charge.

But. I goe, my Soueraigne.

King Butler!

But. My Lord.

King Goe downe by Greenewich, and command a boate
At the Friers bridge attend my comming downe.

But. I will, my Lord. [*exit.*

King It's time, I thinke, to looke vnto rebellion,
When Acton doth expect vnto his ayd
No lesse then fiftie thousand Londoners.
Well, Ile to Westminster in this disguise,
To heare what newes is stirring in these brawles.

Enter sir Iohn ⟨*and Doll*⟩.

Sir Iohn Stand, true-man! saies a thiefe.

King Stand, thiefe! saies a true man. How if a thiefe?

Sir Iohn Stand, thiefe, too.

King Then, thiefe or true-man, I see I must stand. I see, how soeuer the world wagges, the trade of theeuing yet will neuer downe. What art thou?

sir Iohn A good fellow.

King So am I too. I see thou dost know me.

sir Iohn. If thou be a good fellow, play the good fellowes part: deliuer thy purse without more adoe.

King I haue no mony.

sir Iohn I must make you find some before we part. If you haue no mony, you shal haue ware: as many sound drie blows as your skin can carrie.

King Is that the plaine truth?

sir Iohn Sirra, no more adoe; come, come, giue me the mony you haue. Dispatch, I cannot stand all day.

King. Wel, if thou wilt needs haue it, there tis: iust the prouerb, one thiefe robs another. Where the diuel are all my old theeues, that were wont to keepe this walke? Falstaffe, the villaine, is so fat, he cannot get on's horse, but me thinkes Poines and Peto should be stirring here abouts.

12–13 by Gods body] and *Q 2, etc.* 30 I like not that *Q 2, etc.* 34 Ah *om. Q 2, etc.* 37 leaue behind his *Q 2, etc.* Scene IV. *etc. add. M*

S. D. Enter Priest *Q 2, Ff* and Doll *add. M* 40 true-man, I must *Q 2, etc.* 53 drie *om. Q 2, etc.* 61–2 that . . walke *om. Q 2, etc.* 62 the] that *Q 2, etc.*

sir Iohn How much is there on't, of thy word?

King A hundred pound in Angels, on my word.
The time has beene I would haue done as much
For thee, if thou hadst past this way, as I haue now.

sir Iohn Sirra, what art thou? thou seem'st a gentleman.

King I am no lesse; yet a poore one now, for thou hast all my mony.

sir Iohn From whence cam'st thou?

King From the court at Eltham.

sir Iohn Art thou one of the Kings seruants?

King Yes, that I am, and one of his chamber.

sir Iohn I am glad thou art no worse; thou maist the better spare thy mony: & thinkst thou thou mightst get a poor thiefe his pardon, if he should haue neede.

King. Yes, that I can.

sir Iohn Wilt thou do so much for me, when I shall haue occasion?

King Yes, faith will I, so it be for no murther.

sir Iohn Nay, I am a pittifull thiefe; all the hurt I do a man, I take but his purse; Ile kill no man.

King Then, of my word, Ile do it.

sir Iohn Giue me thy hand of the same.

King There tis.

sir Iohn Me thinks the King should be good to theeues, because he has bin a thiefe himselfe, though I thinke now he be turned true-man.

King Faith, I haue heard indeed he has had an il name that way in his youth; but how canst thou tell he has beene a thiefe?

sir Iohn How? Because he once robde me before I fell to the trade my selfe; when that foule villainous guts, that led him to all that rogery, was in's company there, that Falstaffe.

King (*aside*). Well, if he did rob thee then, thou art but euen with him now, Ile be sworne. —Thou knowest not the king now, I thinke, if thou sawest him?

sir Iohn Not I, yfaith.

King (*aside*). So it should seeme.

sir Iohn Well, if old King Henry had liu'de, this King that is now had made theeuing the best trade in England.

King Why so?

sir Iohn Because he was the chiefe warden of our company. It's pittie that ere he should haue bin a King; he was so braue a thiefe. But, sirra, wilt remember my pardon if neede be?

King Yes, faith, will I.

sir Iohn Wilt thou? well then, because thou shalt go safe—for thou mayest hap (being so earely) be met with againe before thou come to Southwarke—if any man, when he should bid thee good morrow, bid thee stand, say thou but *sir Iohn*, and he will let thee passe.

King Is that the word? well, then, let me alone.

sir Iohn Nay, sirra, because I thinke indeede I shall haue some occasion to vse thee, & as thou comst oft this way, I may light on thee another time not knowing thee, here! ile breake this Angell. Take thou halfe of it; this is a token betwixt thee and me.

King. God haue mercy; farewell. [*exit.*

sir Iohn O my fine golden slaues! heres for thee, wench, yfaith. Now, Dol, we wil reuel in our bouer! this is a tyth pigge of my vicaridge. God haue mercy, neighbour Shooters hill; you paid your tyth honestly. Wel, I heare there is a company of rebelles vp against the King, got together in Ficket field neere Holborne, and as it is thought here in Kent, the King will be there to night in's owne person; well, ile to the Kings camp, and it shall go hard, but, if there be any doings, Ile make some good boote amongst them. [*exit.*

⟨ACT IV.

Scene I. *A field near London. King Henry's camp.*⟩

Enter King Henry, Suffolke, Huntington, and two with lights.

K. Hen. My Lords of Suffolke and of Huntington,
Who skouts it now? or who stands Sentinells?
What men of worth? what Lords do walke the round?

Suff. May it please your Highnesse—

K. Hen. Peace, no more of that.
The King's asleepe; wake not his maiestie
With termes nor titles; hee's at rest in bed.
Kings do not vse to watch themselues; they sleepe,
And let rebellion and conspiracie
Reuel and hauocke in the common wealth.—
Is London lookt vnto?

70 *Two lines M, div. after* I 92 of] on *M* 93 of] on *M* 97 although *Ff, etc.* 101 tell that he *Q 2, etc.* 112 olde King Harry *Q 2, etc.*

128 well *om. Ff, etc.* 136 God a mercy *Q 2, etc.* 139 bower *conj. M* : beuer *Qq* 140 God a mercy *Q 2, etc.* 141 paid] ha paide *Q 2, etc.* 148 boote] booty *conj. M* Act IV. *etc. add. M*

Hunt. It is, my Lord:
Your noble Vncle Exceter is there,
Your brother Gloucester and my Lord of Warwicke,
Who, with the maior and the Aldermen,
Do guard the gates, and keepe good rule within;
The Earle of Cambridge and sir Thomas Gray
Do walke the Round; Lord Scroope and Butler skout.
So, though it please your maiestie to iest,
Were you in bed, well might you take your rest.

K. Hen. I thank ye, Lords, but you do know of old,
That I haue bin a perfect night-walker.
London, you say, is safely lookt vnto—
Alas, poore rebels, there your ayd must faile—
And the Lord Cobham, sir Iohn Old-castle,
Hee's quiet in Kent. Acton, ye are deceiu'd;
Reckon againe, you count without your host;
To morrow you shall giue account to vs.
Til when, my friends, this long cold winters night
How can we spend? King Harry is a sleepe
And al his Lords, these garments tel vs so;
Al friends at footebal, fellowes all in field,
Harry, and Dicke, and George. Bring vs a drumme;
Giue vs square dice, weele keepe this court of guard
For al good fellowes companies that come.
Wheres that mad priest ye told me was in Armes,
To fight, as well as pray, if neede required?

Suff. Hees in the Camp, and if he know of this,
I vndertake he would not be long hence.

Har. Trippe, Dicke; Trippe, George. [*they trippe.*

Hunt. I must haue the dice.
What do we play at? [*the⟨y⟩ play at dice.*

Suff. Passage, if ye please.

Hunt. Set round then: so; at all.

Har. George, you are out.
Giue me the dice. I passe for twentie pound.
Heres to our luckie passage into France.

Hunt. Harry, you passe indeede, for you sweepe all.

Suff. A signe king Harry shal sweep al in France.

ent⟨er⟩ sir Iohn.

sir Iohn Edge ye, good fellowes; take a fresh gamster in.

Har. Master Parson? We play nothing but gold.

sir Iohn. And, fellow, I tel thee that the priest hath gold. Gold? sbloud, ye are but beggerly souldiers to me. I thinke I haue more gold than all you three.

Hunt. It may be so, but we beleeue it not.

Har. Set, priest, set. I passe for all that gold.

sir Iohn Ye passe, indeede.

Harry Priest, hast thou any more ?

sir Iohn Zounds, what a question's that?
I tell thee I haue more then all you three.
At these ten Angells!

Harry. I wonder how thou comst by all this gold;
How many benefices hast thou, priest?

sir Iohn Yfaith, but one. Dost wonder how I come by gold? I wonder rather how poore souldiers should haue gold; for Ile tell thee, good fellow: we haue euery day tythes, offerings, christnings, weddings, burialls; and you poore snakes come seldome to a bootie. Ile speake a prowd word: I haue but one parsonage, Wrootham; tis better than the Bishopprick of Rochester. Theres nere a hill, heath, nor downe in all Kent, but tis in my parish: Barrham downe, Chobham downe, Gads hill, Wrootham hill, Blacke heath, Cockes heath, Birchen wood, all pay me tythe. Gold, quoth a? ye passe not for that.

Suff. Harry, ye are out; now, parson, shake the dice.

sir Iohn. Set, set; Ile couer ye at al. A plague on't, I am out: the diuell, and dice, and a wench, who will trust them?

Suff. Saist thou so, priest? Set faire; at all for once.

Har. Out, sir; pay all.

sir Iohn Sbloud, pay me angel gold.
Ile none of your crackt French crownes nor pistolets.
Pay me faire angel gold, as I pay you.

Har. No crackt french crownes? I hope to see more crackt french crownes ere long.

sir Iohn Thou meanest of French mens crownes, when the King is in France.

Hunt. Set round, at all.

sir Iohn Pay all: this is some lucke.

Har. Giue me the dice, tis I must shread the priest:
At all, sir Iohn.

26 Hee's *om. Q 2, etc.* 49 *S. D.* Enter Priest *Q 2, Ff*

55 sbloud] what *Q 2, etc.* 61 thou *om. Q 2, etc.* 62 Zounds] more *Q 2, etc.* 67 Faith *Q 2, etc.* 81 ye] you *M* 89 Sbloud] Sir *Q 2, etc.* 98 shread] shrieve *conj. M*

sir Iohn The diuell and all is yours. At that! Sdeath, what casting is this?

Suff. Well throwne, Harry, yfaith.

Har. Ile cast better yet.

sir Iohn Then Ile be hangd. Sirra, hast thou not giuen thy soule to the diuell for casting?

Har. I passe for all.

sir Iohn Thou passest all that ere I playde withall.
Sirra, dost thou not cogge, nor foist, nor slurre?

Har. Set, parson, set; the dice die in my hand:
When parson, when? what, can ye finde no more?
Alreadie drie? wast you bragd of your store?

sir Iohn Alls gone but that.

Hunt. What? halfe a broken angell?

sir Iohn Why sir, tis gold.

Har. Yea, and Ile couer it.

sir Iohn. The diuell do ye good on't, I am blinde, yee haue blowne me vp.

Har. Nay, tarry, priest; ye shall not leaue vs yet.
Do not these peeces fit each other well?

sir Iohn What if they do?

Har. Thereby beginnes a tale:
There was a thiefe, in face much like sir Iohn—
But t'was not hee, that thiefe was all in greene—
Met me last day at Blacke Heath, neere the parke,
With him a woman. I was al alone
And weaponlesse, my boy had al my tooles,
And was before prouiding me a boate.
Short tale to make, sir Iohn—the thiefe, I meane—
Tooke a iust hundreth pound in gold from me.
I storm'd at it, and swore to be reueng'de
If ere we met. He, like a lusty thiefe,
Brake with his teeth this Angel iust in two,
To be a token at our meeting next,
Prouided I should charge no Officer
To apprehend him, but at weapons point
Recouer that and what he had beside.
Well met, sir Iohn; betake ye to your tooles
By torch light, for, master parson, you are he
That had my gold.

sir Iohn Zounds, I won't in play, in faire square play, of the keeper of Eltham parke; and that I will maintaine with this poore whinyard, be you two honest men to stand and looke vpon's, and let's alone, and take neither part.

Har. Agreede! I charge ye do not boudge a foot.
Sir Iohn, haue at ye.

sir Iohn Souldier, ware your skonce.

[*Here, as they are ready to strike, enter Butler and drawes his weapon and steps betwixt them.*

But. Hold, villaines, hold! my Lords, what do you meane,
To see a traitor draw against the King?

sir Iohn The King! Gods wil, I am in a proper pickle.

Har. Butler, what newes? why dost thou trouble vs?

But. Please it your Highnesse, it is breake of day,
And as I skouted neere to Islington,
The gray ey'd morning gaue me glimmering
Of armed men comming downe Hygate hill,
Who by their course are coasting hitherward.

Har. Let vs withdraw, my Lords. Prepare our troopes
To charge the rebels, if there be such cause.
For this lewd priest, this diuellish hypocrite,
That is a thiefe, a gamster, and what not,
Let him be hang'd vp for example sake.

sir Iohn Not so my gracious soueraigne. I confesse I am a frayle man, flesh and bloud as other are: but, set my imperfections aside, by this light, ye haue not a taller man, nor a truer subiect to the Crowne and State, than sir Iohn of Wrootham.

Har. Wil a true subiect robbe his King?

sir Iohn Alas, twas ignorance and want, my gracious liege.

Har. Twas want of grace. Why, you should be as salt
To season others with good document,
Your liues as lampes to giue the people light,
As shepheards, not as wolues to spoile the flock.
Go hang him, Butler.

But. Didst thou not rob me?

sir Iohn I must confesse I saw some of your gold. But, my dread Lord, I am in no humor for death; therefore, saue my life. God will that sinners liue; do not you cause me die. Once in their liues the best may goe astray, and if the world say true, your selfe (my liege) haue bin a thiefe.

Har. I confesse I haue,
But I repent and haue reclaimd my selfe.

117 do] giue *Q2, etc.* 118 yee] you *Q2, etc.* 119 ye] you *Ff, etc.* 138 ye] you *M* 145 take *om. Ff, R, Pope*

150 villaine *Q2, etc.* what d'ye *Q2, Ff* 154 Please your Maiesty *Q2, etc.* 166 others *M* 167 by this light *om. Q2, etc.* ye] you *M* 169 Wrotham is *Q2, etc.* 177 *This speech added to the previous one Haz.* 180 therefore . . life *om. Q2, etc.* 181 wills *M* me to dye *Q2, etc.*

sir Iohn So will I do, if you will giue me time.
Har. Wilt thou? My lords, will you be his suerties?
Hunt. That when he robs againe, he shall be hang'd.
sir Iohn I aske no more.
Har. And we will grant thee that.
Liue and repent, and proue an honest man,
Which when I heare, and safe returne from France,
Ile giue thee liuing: till when take thy gold;
But spend it better then at cards or wine,
For better vertues fit that coate of thine.

sir Iohn *Viuat Rex & currat lex!* My liege, if ye haue cause of battell, ye shal see sir Iohn of Wrootham bestirre himself in your quarrel. [*exeunt.*

⟨Scene II. *A field of Battle near London.*⟩

After an alarum enter Harry, Suffolk, Huntington, sir Iohn, bringing forth Acton, Beuerly, and Murley prisoners.

Har. Bring in those traitors, whose aspiring minds
Thought to haue triumpht in our ouerthrow.
But now ye see, base villaines, what successe
Attends ill actions wrongfully attempted.
Sir Roger Acton, thou retainst the name
Of knight, and shouldst be more discreetly temperd,
Than ioyne with peasants: gentry is diuine,
But thou hast made it more then popular.
Act. Pardon, my Lord; my conscience vrg'd me to it.
Har. Thy conscience? then thy conscience is corrupt,
For in thy conscience thou art bound to vs,
And in thy conscience thou shouldst loue thy country;
Else what's the difference twixt a Christian
And the vnciuil manners of the Turke?
Beuer. We meant no hurt vnto your maiesty,
But reformation of Religion.
Har. Reforme Religion? was it that ye sought?
I pray who gaue you that authority?
Belike, then, we do hold the scepter vp
And sit within the throne but for a cipher.
Time was, good subiects would make knowne their griefe
And pray amendment, not inforce the same,
Vnlesse their King were tyrant, which I hope
You cannot iustly say that Harry is.
What is that other?
Suff. A mault-man, my Lord,
And dwelling in Dunstable as he saies.
Har. Sirra, what made you leaue your barly broth,
To come in armour thus against your King?

Mur. Fie, paltry, paltry; to and fro, in and out vpon occasion; what a worlde's this! Knight-hood (my liege) twas knight-hood brought me hither. They told me I had wealth enough to make my wife a lady.

Har. And so you brought those horses which we saw,
Trapt all in costly furniture, and meant
To weare these spurs when you were knighted once?
Mur. In and out vpon occasion, I did.
Har. In and out vppon occasion, therefore,
You shall be hang'd, and in the sted of wearing
These spurres vpon your heeles, about your necke
They shall bewray your folly to the world.

sir Iohn In and out vpon ocasion, that goes hard.

Mur. Fie, paltry, paltry, to and fro; good my liege, a pardon. I am sory for my fault.

Har. That comes too late: but tell me, went there none
Beside sir Roger Acton, vpon whom
You did depend to be your gouernour?
Mur. None, none, my Lord, but sir Iohn Old-castle.
Har. Beares he part in this conspiracie?

enter Bishop.

Act. We lookt, my Lord, that he would meet vs here.
Har. But did he promise you that he would come?
Act. Such letters we receiued forth of Kent.
Bish. Where is my Lord the King?—Health to your grace.
Examining, my Lord, some of these caitiue rebels,
It is a generall voyce amongst them all,
That they had neuer come vnto this place,
But to haue met their valiant general,
The good Lord Cobham, as they title him;
Whereby, my Lord, your grace may now perceiue,
His treason is apparant, which before
He sought to colour by his flattery.
Har. Now, by my roialtie, I would haue sworne,

190 of Wrootham *om. Q 2, etc.* Scene II. *etc. add. M* 17 ye] you *Q 2, etc.*

39–42 *Prose in Qq, Ff: corr. M* 49 None *once Qq, Ff*: None, my good lord *M* 50 a part *Q 2, etc.* 55 caitiue *om. Q 2, etc.* 56 among *Q 2, etc.* 57 into *Q 2, etc.*

But for his conscience, which I beare withall,
There had not liude a more true hearted subiect.
Bish. It is but counterfeit, my gracious lord,
And therefore, may it please your maiestie
To set your hand vnto this precept here,
By which weel cause him forthwith to appeare,
And answer this by order of the law.
Har. Bishop, not only that, but take commission
To search, attach, imprison, and condemne
This most notorious traitor as you please.
Bish. It shall be done, my Lord, without delay.—
So now I hold, Lord Cobham, in my hand,
That which shall finish thy disdained life.
Har. I thinke the yron age begins but now,
(Which learned poets haue so often taught)
Wherein there is no credit to be giuen,
To either wordes, or lookes, or solemne oathes.
For if there were, how often hath he sworne,
How gently tun'de the musicke of his tongue,
And with what amiable face beheld he me,
When all, God knowes, was but hypocrisie.

enter Cobham.

Cob. Long life and prosperous raigne vnto my Lord.
Har. Ah, villaine, canst thou wish prosperitie,
Whose heart includeth naught but treacherie?
I do arrest thee here my selfe, false knight,
Of treason capitall against the state.
Cob. Of treason, mightie prince? your grace mistakes.
I hope it is but in the way of mirth.
Har. Thy necke shall feele it is in earnest shortly.
Darst thou intrude into our presence, knowing
How haynously thou hast offended vs?
But this is thy accustomed deceit;
Now thou perceiust thy purpose is in vaine,
With some excuse or other thou wilt come,
To cleere thy selfe of this rebellion.
Cob. Rebellion, good my Lord? I know of none.
Har. If you deny it, here is euidence.
See you these men? you neuer councelled,
Nor offerd them assistance in their warres?
Cob. Speake, sirs. Not one but all; I craue no fauour.
Haue euer I beene conuersant with you,
Or written letters to incourage you,
Or kindled but the least or smallest part
Of this your late vnnaturall rebellion?
Speake, for I dare the vttermost you can.
Mur In and out vpon occasion, I know you not.
Har. No? didst not say that sir Iohn Oldcastle
Was one with whom you purposde to haue met?
Mur. True, I did say so, but in what respect?
Because I heard it was reported so.
Har. Was there no other argument but that?
Act. To cleere my conscience ere I die, my lord,
I must confesse, we haue no other ground
But only Rumor, to accuse this lord,
Which now I see was merely fabulous.
Har. The more pernitious you to taint him then,
Whome you knew not was faulty, yea or no.
Cobh. Let this, my Lord, which I present your grace,
Speake for my loyalty: reade these articles,
And then giue sentence of my life or death.
Har. Earle Cambridge, Scroope, and Gray corrupted
With bribes from Charles of France, either to winne
My Crowne from me, or secretly contriue
My death by treason? Is this possible?
Cobh. There is the platforme, and their hands, my lord,
Each seuerally subscribed to the same.
Har Oh neuer heard of, base ingratitude!
Euen those I hugge within my bosome most
Are readiest euermore to sting my heart.
Pardon me, Cobham, I haue done thee wrong;
Heereafter I will liue to make amends.
Is, then, their time of meeting so neere hand?
Weele meete with them, but little for their ease,
If God permit. Goe, take these rebells hence;
Let them haue martiall law: but as for thee,
Friend to thy king and country, still be free.
[*Exeunt.*
Murl. Be it more or lesse, what a world is this?
Would I had continued still of the order of knaues,
And neuer sought knighthood, since it costes so deere.
Sir Roger, I may thanke you for all.
Acton Now tis too late to haue it remedied,
I prithee, Murley, doe not vrge me with it.

66 lords *Q 1*   71 Bishop *om. Q 2, etc.*   81 there] he *Q 2, Ff*   85 vnto *Q 1*   110 didst thou not *Q 2, etc.*   120 know was not *Q 2, etc.*   127 Is this] Ist *Q 2, Ff*: Is it *M*   142 *Ends* costes *Qq, Ff*: *corr. M*

Hunt. Will you away, and make no more to do?
Murl. Fy, paltry, paltry! to and fro, as occasion serues;
If you be so hasty, take my place.
Hunt. No, good sir knight, you shall begin in your hand.
Murl. I could be glad to giue my betters place. [*Exeunt.*

⟨Scene III. *Kent. Court before lord Cobham's house.*⟩

Enter Bishop, lord Warden, Croamer the Shrieue, Lady Cob. and attendants.

Bishop I tell ye, Lady, its not possible
But you should know where he conueies himselfe,
And you haue hid him in some secret place.
Lady My Lord, beleeue me, as I haue a soule,
I know not where my lord my husband is.
Bishop Go to, go to, ye are an heretike,
And will be forc'de by torture to confesse,
If faire meanes will not serue to make ye tell.
Lady My husband is a noble gentleman,
And neede not hide himselfe for anie fact
That ere I heard of; therefore wrong him not.
Bishop Your husband is a dangerous schismaticke,
Traitor to God, the King, and common wealth:
And therefore, master Croamer, shrieue of Kent,
I charge you take her to your custodie,
And ceaze the goods of Sir Iohn Old-castle
To the Kings vse. Let her go in no more,
To fetch so much as her apparell out.
There is your warrant from his maiestie.
L. War. Good my Lord Bishop, pacifie your wrath
Against the Lady.
Bish. Then let her confesse
Where Old-castle her husband is conceald.
L. War. I dare engage mine honor and my life,
Poore gentlewoman, she is ignorant
And innocent of all his practises,
If any euill by him be practised.
Bish. If, my Lord Warden? nay, then I charge you,
That all the cinque Ports, whereof you are chiefe,
Be laid forthwith, that he escape vs not.
Shew him his highnesse warrant, M⟨aister⟩ Shrieue.
L. War. I am sorie for the noble gentleman—

Enter Old-castle & Harp.

Bish. Peace, he comes here; now do your office.
Old-castle Harpoole, what businesse haue we here in hand?
What makes the Bishop and the Shiriffe here?
⟨I⟩ feare my comming home is dangerous,
⟨I⟩ would I hadnot madesuch haste to Cobham.

Harp. Be of good cheere, my Lord: if they be foes, weele scramble shrewdly with them; if they be friends, they are welcome. One of them (my Lord Warden) is your friend; but me thinkes my ladie weepes; I like not that.

Croo. Sir Iohn Old-çastle, Lord Cobham, in the Kings maiesties name, I arrest ye of high treason.

Oldca. Treason, M⟨aister⟩ Croomer?
Harp. Treason, M⟨aister⟩ Shrieue? sbloud, what treason?
Oldca. Harpoole, I charge thee, stirre not, but be quiet still.
Do ye arrest me, M⟨aister⟩ Shrieue, for treason?
Bish. Yea, of high treason, traitor, heretike.
Oldca. Defiance in his face that calls me so.
I am as true a loyall gentleman
Vnto his highnesse, as my prowdest enemie.
The King shall witnesse my late faithfull seruice,
For safety of his sacred maiestie.
Bish. What thou art the kings hand shall testifie:
Shewt him, Lord Warden.
Old. Iesu defend me!
Is't possible your cunning could so temper
The princely disposition of his mind,
To signe the damage of a loyall subiect?
Well, the best is, it beares an antedate,
Procured by my absence, and your malice,
But I, since that, haue shewd my selfe as true
As any churchman that dare challenge me.
Let me be brought before his maiestie;
If he acquite me not, then do your worst.
Bish. We are not bound to do kind offices
For any traitor, schismatike, nor heretike.
The kings hand is our warrant for our worke,
Who is departed on his way for France,

149 you .. hand] eene tak't your selfe *Q 2, etc.* *S. D.* Exeunt] *Between Scene II. and Scene III. S inserts V., I.* Scene III. *etc. add. M* 6 Go too, go ye *Q 2, Ff*: *corr. R* ye] you *M* 8 ye] you *Q 2, etc.*

36 feare *Q 1*: I feare *Q 2, etc.* 37 would *Q 1*: I would *Q 2, etc.* 40-2 One .. like not that *om. Q 2, etc.* 44 maiesties *om. Q 2, etc.* ye] you *M* 46 Croomes *Qq*: *corr. Ff* 47 sbloud *om. Q 2, etc.* 48 still *om. Q 2, etc.* 49 ye] you *M* of Treason M. Sheriffe *Q 2, etc.* 57 Shewt] Shew *Q 2, etc.* 61 royall *Qq, Ff*: *corr. R*

And at Southhampton doth repose this night.
Harp. O that it were the blessed will of God, that thou and I were within twenty mile of it, on Salisbury plaine! I would lose my head if euer thou broughtst thy head hither againe. [*aside.*
. *Oldca.* My Lord Warden o'th cinque Ports, & my Lord of Rochester, ye are ioynt Commissioners: fauor me so much,
On my expence to bring me to the king.
Bish. What, to Southhampton?
Oldca. Thither, my go⟨o⟩d Lord,
And if he do not cleere me of al guilt,
And all suspition of conspiracie,
Pawning his princely warrant for my truth:
I aske no fauour, but extreamest torture.
Bring me, or send me to him, good my Lord:
Good my Lord Warden, M⟨aister⟩ Shrieue, entreate.
[*Here the Lord Warden, and Cromer vncouer to the Bishop, and secretly whispers with him.*
Come hither, lady—nay, sweet wife, forbeare
To heape one sorrow on anothers necke:
Tis griefe enough falsly to be accusde,
And not permitted to acquite my selfe;
Do not thou with thy kind respectiue teares,
Torment thy husbands heart that bleedes for thee,
But be of comfort. God hath help in store
For those that put assured trust in him.
Deere wife, if they commit me to the Tower,
Come vp to London to your sisters house:
That being neere me, you may comfort me.
One solace find I setled in my soule,
That I am free from treasons very thought:
Only my conscience for the Gospels sake
Is cause of all the troubles I sustaine.
Lady. O my deere Lord, what shall betide of vs?
You to the Tower, and I turnd out of doores,
Our substance ceaz'd vnto his highnesse vse,
Euen to the garments longing to our backes.
Harp. Patience, good madame, things at worst will mend,
And if they doe not, yet our liues may end.
Bish. Vrge it no more, for if an Angell spake,
I sweare by sweet saint Peters blessed keyes,
First goes he to the Tower, then to the stake.
Crom. But by your leaue, this warrant doth not stretch
To imprison her.
Bishop No, turne her out of doores,
[*L. Warden and Oldcastle whisper.*
Euen as she is, and leade him to the Tower,
With guard enough for feare of rescuing.
Lady O, God requite thee, thou bloudthirsty man.
Oldca. May it not be, my Lord of Rochester?
Wherein haue I incurd your hate so farre,
That my appeale vnto the King's denide?
Bish. No hate of mine, but power of holy church,
Forbids all fauor to false heretikes.
Oldca. Your priuate malice, more than publike power,
Strikes most at me, but with my life it ends.
Harp. O that I had the Bishop in that feare, [*aside.*
That once I had his Sumner by our selues!
Crom. My Lord, yet graunt one sute vnto vs all,
That this same auncient seruing man may waite
Vpon my lord his master in the Tower.
Bish. This old iniquitie, this heretike?
That, in contempt of our church discipline,
Compeld my Sumner to deuoure his processe!
Old Ruffian past-grace, vpstart schismatike,
Had not the King prayd vs to pardon ye,
Ye had fryed for it, ye grizild heretike.
Harp. Sbloud, my lord Bishop, ye do me wrong. I am neither heretike nor puritane, but of the old church: ile sweare, drinke ale, kisse a wench, go to masse, eate fish all Lent, and fast fridaies with cakes and wine, fruite and spicerie, shriue me of my old sinnes afore Easter, and beginne new afore whitsontide.
Crom. A merie, mad, conceited knaue, my lord.
Harp. That knaue was simply put vpon the Bishop.
Bish. Wel, God forgiue him and I pardon him.
Let him attend his master in the Tower,
For I in charity wish his soule no hurt.
Oldca. God blesse my soule from such cold charitie!
Bish. Too'th Tower with him, and when my leisure serues,
I will examine him of Articles.
Looke, my lord Warden, as you haue in charge,
The Shriue performe his office.
L. Ward. Yes, my lord.

73 that . . God *om.* *Q 2, etc.* 74 miles *Q 2, etc.* 76 euer *om.* *Q 2, etc.* 78 my *om.* *Q 2, etc.* *S. D.* They both entreat for him *Q 2, etc.* 115 *S. D. om.* *Q 2, etc.* 136 You . . you *M* 137–8 ye wrong me *Q 2, etc.* 137 ye] you *M* 154 Yes] I *Q 2, Ff*: Ay *R, etc.*

Enter the Sumner with bookes.

Bish. Whatbringst thou there? what, bookes of heresie?

Som. Yea, my lord, heres not a latine booke, no, not so much as our ladies Psalter. Heres the Bible, the testament, the Psalmes in meter, the sickemans salue, the treasure of gladnesse, and al in English, not so much but the Almanack's English.

Bish. Away with them, to'th fire with them, Clun!
Now fie vpon these vpstart heretikes.
Al English! burne them, burne them quickly, Clun!

Harp. But doe not, Sumner, as youle answere it, for I haue there English bookes, my lord, that ile not part with for your Bishopp-ricke: Beuis of Hampton, Owleglasse, the Frier and the Boy, Ellenor Rumming, Robin hood, and other such godly stories, which if ye burne, by this flesh, ile make ye drink their ashes in S⟨aint⟩ Margets ale. [*exeunt.*

⟨Scene IV. *The entrance of the Tower.*⟩

Enter the Bishop of Rochester with his men in liuerie coates.

1. *Ser.* Is it your honors pleasure we shal stay,
Or come backe in the afternoone to fetch you?

Bish. Now you haue brought me heere into the Tower,
You may go backe vnto the Porters Lodge,
And send for drinke or such things as you want,
Where if I haue occasion to imploy you,
Ile send some officer to cal you to me.
Into the cittie go not, I commaund you:
Perhaps I may haue present neede to vse you.

2 We will attend your worship here without.

Bish. Do so, I pray you.

3 Come, we may haue a quart of wine at the Rose at Barking, I warrant you, and come backe an hower before he be ready to go.

1 We must hie vs then.

3 Let's away. [*exeunt.*

Bish. Ho, M⟨aister⟩ Lieftenant.

Lieften. Who calls there?

Bish. A friend of yours.

Lieften. My lord of Rochester! your honor's welcome.

Bish. Sir, heres my warrant from the Counsell,
For conference with sir Iohn Old-castle,
Vpon some matter of great consequence.

Lieften. Ho, sir Iohn!

Harp. Who calls there?

Lieften. Harpoole, tel Sir Iohn, that my lord of Rochester
Comes from the counsell to conferre with him.

Harp. I will, sir.

Lief. I thinke you may as safe without suspition,
As any man in England, as I heare,
For it was you most labor'd his commitment.

Bish. I did, sir, and nothing repent it, I assure you.

Enter sir Iohn Old-castle ⟨and Harpool⟩.

M⟨aister⟩ Lieftenant, I pray you giue vs leaue,
I must conferre here with sir Iohn a little.

Lief. With all my heart, my lord.

Harp (*aside*). My lord, be rulde by me: take this occasion while tis offered, and on my life your lordship shal escape.

Old-ca. No more, I say; peace, lest he should suspect it.

Bish. Sir Iohn, I am come vnto you from the lords of his highnesse most honorable counsell, to know if yet you do recant your errors, conforming you vnto the holy church.

Old-ca. My lord of Rochester, on good aduise,
I see my error, but yet, vnderstand me,
I meane not error in the faith I hold,
But error in submitting to your pleasure;
Therefore, your lordship, without more to do,
Must be a meanes to help me to escape.

Bish. What meanes, thou heretike?
Darst thou but lift thy hand against my calling?

sir Iohn No, not to hurt you for a thousand pound.

Harp. Nothing but to borrow your vpper garments a little; not a word more, for if you do, you die: peace, for waking the children. There; put them on; dispatch, my lord. The window that goes out into the leads is sure enough, I told you that before: there, make

156–61 *Verse Qq* 160 and *om. Q 2, etc.* All English, no not *Q 2, etc.* 167 with] withal *Q 2, etc.* 169 Ellen of *Qq, Ff*: *corr. M* Scene IV. *etc. add. M* *Act V begins here in S* 5 *om. Q 2, etc.* 10 worship] honor *Q 2, etc.* 11 *om. Q 2, etc.* 13 I warrant you *om. Q 2, etc.* 14 before he'l go *Q 2, etc.*

28 *om. Q 2, etc.* *S. D.* and Harpool *add. R* 36–8 *Verse M* 38 shal] wil *Q 2, etc.* 40 vnto] to *Q 2, etc.* 41–2 of the Counsell *Q 2, etc.* 42 yet *om. Q 2, etc.* 43 conforming . . church *om. Q 2, etc.* 54–5 for if . . die *om. Q 2, etc.* 58–60 I told you . . roome] and as for you, Ile bind you surely in the inner roome *Q 2*: as for you, *etc. Ff, M, etc.*: but for you, *etc. R, Pope*

you ready; ile conuay him after, and bind him surely in the inner roome.

⟨Carries the bishop into the Tower, and returns.⟩

Old-ca. This is wel begun; God send vs happie speed,
Hard shift you see men make in time of need.
Harpoole.

⟨Puts on the bishop's cloak.⟩

Harp. Heere my Lord; come, come away.

Enter seruing men againe.

1 I maruell that my lord should stay so long.

2 He hath sent to seeke vs, I dare lay my life.

3 We come in good time; see, where he is comming.

Harp. I beseech you, good my lord of Rochester, be fauorable to my lord and maister.

Old-ca. The inner roomes be very hot and close,
I do not like this ayre here in the Tower.

Harp. His case is hard my lord.—You shall safely get out of the Tower; but I will downe vpon them, in which time get you away.

Old-ca. Fellow, thou troublest me.

Harp. Heare me, my Lord!—Hard vnder Islington wait you my comming; I will bring my Lady, ready with horses to conuay you hence.

Old-ca. Fellow, go back againe vnto thy Lord and counsell him.

Harp. Nay, my good lord of Rochester, ile bring you to S⟨aint⟩ Albons through the woods, I warrant you.

Old-ca. Villaine, away.

Harp. Nay, since I am past the Towers libertie, thou part'st not so. [*he drawes.*

Old-ca. Clubbes, clubs, clubs!

1 Murther, murther, murther!

2 Downe with him! [*they fight.*

3 A villaine traitor!

Harp. You cowardly rogues!

[*sir Iohn escapes.*

Enter Lieftenant and his men.

Lieft. Who is so bold as dare to draw a sword,
So neare vnto the entrance of the Tower?

1 This ruffian, seruant to sir Iohn Oldcastle,
Was like to haue slaine my Lord.

Lieft. Lay hold on him.

Harp. Stand off if you loue your puddings.

Rochester calls within.

Roch (*within*). Help, help, help! M⟨aister⟩
Lieftenant, help!

Lief. Who's that within? some treason in the Tower
Vpon my life. Looke in; who's that which calls?

enter Roch. bound.

Lief. Without your cloke, my lord of Rochester?

Harp. There, now it workes, then let me speed, for now
Is the fittest time for me to scape away. [*exit.*

Lief. Why do you looke so ghastly and affrighted?

Roch. Old-castle, that traitor, and his man,
When you had left me to conferre with him,
Tooke, bound, and stript me, as you see,
And left me lying in his inner chamber,
And so departed, and I—

Lief. And you? ne're say that the Lord Cobhams man
Did here set vpon you like to murther you.

1 And so he did.

Roch. It was vpon his master then he did,
That in the brawle the traitor might escape.

Lief. Where is this Harpoole?

2 Here he was euen now.

Lief. Where? can you tell?

⟨2⟩ They are both escap'd.

⟨*Lief.*⟩ Since it so happens that he is escap'de,
I am glad you are a witnesse of the same,
It might haue else beene laid vnto my charge,
That I had beene consenting to the fact.

Roch. Come, search shal be made for him with expedition,
The hauens laid that he shall not escape,
And hue and crie continue thorough England,
To find this damned, dangerous heretike.

[*exeunt.*

60, 62 *S. D. D. add. M* 62–3 Harpoole . . come away *om. Q 2, etc.* 72 safely] scarcely *M* 74–5 Old-ca. . . my Lord *om. Q 2, etc.* 77 to get hence *Q 2, etc.* 85 you part *Q 2, etc.* 86 *Prefix* Bish. *Qq, Ff*: Cob. *R* 89 *om. Q 2, etc.* 90 You] Out you *Q 2, etc.* 91 as to dare *Ff*: to dare *R, etc.* 93–4 *Prose Qq, Ff*: *corr. M*

99–100 *Prose Qq, Ff*: *corr. M* 100 Vpon] on *Q 2 Ff* 102–3 *Prose Q 1* 102 now I see it *M* 103 for me *om. Q 2, etc.* 108 his] this *Ff* 109 and I *given to* 1 Ser. *M* 110 you? ne're] you now *M* 111 vpon] on *Q 2, etc.* 117 Where fled, can *M* 118 They . . escap'd *given to* Lief. *Qq, Ff*: *alteration conj. S'.* 123–6 *Prose Qq, Ff*: *corr. R* 124 Haven's *Ff, etc.* 125 through *Q 2, Ff*: throughout *M, etc.*

⟨ACT V.

Scene I. *A room in lord Cobham's house in Kent.*⟩

Enter Cambridge, Scroope, and Gray, as in a chamber, and set downe at a table, consulting about their treason: King Harry and Suffolke listning at the doore.

Camb. In mine opinion, Scroope hath well aduisde,
Poison will be the only aptest meane,
And fittest for our purpose to dispatch him.
Gray But yet there may be doubt in their deliuery.
Harry is wise; therefore, Earle of Cambridge,
I Iudge that way not so conuenient.
Scroop What thinke ye then of this? I am his bedfellow,
And vnsuspected nightly sleepe with him.
What if I venture in those silent houres,
When sleepe hath sealed vp all mortall eies,
To murder him in bed? how like ye that?
Camb. Herein consistes no safetie for your selfe,
And, you disclosde, what shall become of vs?
But this day (as ye know) he will aboord—
The winds so faire—and set away for France.
If, as he goes, or entring in the ship,
It might be done, then it were excellent.
Gray Why any of these, or, if you will, Ile cause
A present sitting of the Councell, wherein
I will pretend some matter of such weight,
As needes must haue his royall company,
And so dispatch him in the Councell chamber.
Camb. Tush, yet I heare not any thing to purpose.
I wonder that lord Cobham staies so long;
His counsell in this case would much auaile vs.
[*They rise from the table, and the King steps in to them, with his Lordes.*
Scroop What, shal we rise thus, and determine nothing?
Har. That were a shame indeede; no, sit againe,
And you shall haue my counsell in this case.
If you can find no way to kill this King,
Then you shall see how I can further ye:
Scroopes way by poison was indifferent,
But yet, being bed-fellow vnto the King,
And vnsuspected sleeping in his bosome,
In mine opinion, that's the likelier way,
For such false friends are able to do much,
And silent night is Treason's fittest friend.
Now, Cambridge, in his setting hence for France,
Or by the way, or as he goes aboord,
To do the deed, that was indifferent too,
Yet somewhat doubtful, might I speake my mind,
For many reasons needelesse now to vrge.
Mary, Lord Gray came something neare the point:
To haue the King at councell, and there murder him,
As Cæsar was, amongst his dearest friends:
None like to that, if all were of his mind.
Tell me, oh tel me, you, bright honors staines,
For which of all my kindnesses to you,
Are ye become thus traitors to your king,
And France must haue the spoile of Harries life?
All. Oh pardon vs, dread lord. [*all kneeling.*
Har. How, pardon ye? that were a sinne indeed.
Drag them to death, which iustly they deserue,
[*they leade them away.*
And France shall dearely buy this villany,
So soone as we set footing on her breast.
God haue the praise for our deliuerance;
And next, our thankes, Lord Cobham, is to thee,
True perfect mirror of nobilitie. [*exeunt.*

⟨Scene II. *A high road near St. Albans.*⟩

Enter Priest and Doll.

sir Iohn Come, Dol, come; be mery, wench.
Farewell, Kent, we are not for thee.
Be lusty, my lasse, come, for Lancashire,
We must nip the Boung for these crownes.

Doll Why, is all the gold spent already that you had the other day?

sir Iohn Gone, Doll, gone; flowne, spent, vanished: the diuel, drinke and the dice has deuoured all.

Doll You might haue left me in Kent, that you might, vntil you had bin better prouided, I could haue staied at Cobham.

sir Iohn No, Dol, no, ile none of that; Kent's too hot, Doll, Kent's too hot. The weathercocke of Wrotham will crow no longer:

Act V. *etc. add. M*   *Act V, Sc. I follows IV. II S*   4 their] the *M*   5 and therefore *R*   15 wind *Q 1*   17 then were it *Q 2, etc.*   18, 19 *Lines end* will, Councell *Qq, Ff*: *corr. M*   22 so *Q 2, etc.*: to *Q 1*   the] his *Q 2, etc.*   29 this] the *Q 2, etc.*   30 further] furnish *Ff, etc.*   ye] you *M*   32 vnto] to *Q 2, etc.*

40 Yet] But *Q 2, etc.*   40–1 might I . . vrge *om. Q 2, etc.*   42 something] verie *Q 2, etc.*   45 *om. Q 2, etc.*   57 *S. D.* exeunt] *The following scenes have been misplaced in Qq, Ff, the order being: 4–7, 2, 3, 8: corr. R*   Scene II. *etc. add. M*   10–11 Kent till *Q 2, etc.*   12 I . . Cobham *om. Q 2, etc.*   13 ile . . that *om. Q 2, etc.*

we haue pluckt him, he has lost his feathers; I haue prunde him bare, left him thrice; is moulted, is moulted, wench.

Doll Faith, sir Iohn, I might haue gone to seruice againe; old maister Harpoole told me he would prouide me a mistris.

sir Iohn Peace, Doll, peace. Come, mad wench, Ile make thee an honest woman; weele into Lancashire to our friends: the troth is, Ile marry thee. We want but a little mony to buy vs a horse, and to spend by the way; the next sheep that comes shal loose his fleece, weele haue these crownes, wench, I warrant thee.

enter the Irish man with his master slaine.

Stay, who comes here? some Irish villaine, me thinkes, that has slaine a man, and drawes him out of the way to rifle him. Stand close, Doll, weele see the end.

[*The Irish man falls to rifle his master.*

⟨*Irishman.*⟩ Alas, poe mester, S⟨ir⟩ Rishard Lee, be saint Patricke is rob and cut thy trote for dee shaine, and dy money, and dee gold ring be me truly: is loue thee wel, but now dow be kil, thee bee shitten kanaue.

sir Iohn. Stand, sirra; what art thou?

Irishman. Be saint Patricke, mester, is pore Irisman, is a leufter.

sir Iohn Sirra, sirra, you are a damned rogue; you haue killed a man here, and rifled him of all that he has. Sbloud, you rogue, deliuer, or ile not leaue you so much as an Irish haire aboue your shoulders, you whorson Irish dogge. Sirra, vntrusse presently; come, off and dispatch, or by this crosse ile fetch your head off as cleane as a barke.

Irishman. Wees me, saint Patricke! Ise kill me mester for chaine and his ring, and nows be rob of all: mees vndoo.

[*Priest robs him.*

sir Iohn Auant, you rascal! Go, sirra, be walking. Come, Doll, the diuel laughes, when one theefe robs another: come, madde wench, weele to saint Albons, and reuel in our bower; hey, my braue girle.

Doll. O thou art old sir Iohn when all's done, yfaith. ⟨*Exeunt.*⟩

17 prun'd him, left him bare thrice *conj. St.* 17–18 is . . is] he is . . he is *M* 19 Faith, sir Iohn *om. Q 2, etc.* 25–7 to buy . . fleece *om. Q 2, etc.* 28 weele . . wench] & money we will haue *Q 2, etc.* 31–2 and drawes . . rifle him] and nowe is rifling on him *Q 2*: and now he is, *etc. Ff* 36 dee gold] dy golde *Q 2, etc.* 37 dee well *Q 2, etc.* 38 kil dee *Q 2, Ff*: kill, dow *M* 46 Irish *om. Q 2, etc.* 47–9 Sirra . . barke *om. Q 2, etc.* 50 by saint *M* 51 for his shain *M* 52 now I se *M* 57 hey *om. Q 2, etc.* *S. D. add. R*

⟨Scene III. *St. Albans. The entrance of a carrier's inn.*⟩

Enter the hoste of the Bell with the Irish man.

Irishman Be me tro, mester, is pore Irisman, is want ludging, is haue no mony, is starue and cold: good mester, giue her some meate; is famise and tie.

Host Yfaith, my fellow, I haue no lodging, but what I keep for my guesse, that I may not disapoint; as for meate thou shalt haue such as there is, & if thou wilt lie in the barne, theres faire straw, and roome enough.

Irishman Is thanke my mester hartily, de straw is good bed for me.

Host Ho, Robin!

Robin Who calls?

Host Shew this poore Irishman into the barne; go, sirra. [*exeunt.*

Enter carrier and Kate.

Club. Ho, who's within here? who lookes to the horses? Gods hatte! heres fine worke: the hens in the manger, and the hogs in the litter. A bots found you all; heres a house well lookt too, yvaith.

Kate Mas, goffe Club, Ise very cawd.

Club. Get in, Kate, get in to fier and warme thee.

Club Ho! Iohn Hostler.

⟨*Enter Hostler.*⟩

Hostler What, gaffer Club? welcome to saint Albons. How does all our friends in Lancashire?

Club Well, God haue mercie, Iohn; how does Tom; wheres he?

Hostler O, Tom is gone from hence; hees at the three horse-loues at Stony-stratford. How does old Dick Dunne?

Club Gods hatte, old Dunne has bin moyerd in a slough in Brickhil-lane, a plague found it; yonder is such abhomination weather as neuer was seene.

Hostler. Gods hat, thiefe, haue one half pecke of pease and oates more for that: as I am Iohn Ostler, hee has been euer as good a iade as euer traueld.

Club Faith, well said, old Iacke; thou art the old lad stil.

Scene III. *etc. add. M* 5 Faith fellow *Q 2, etc.* 6 Guests *F 2, etc.* 6–7 that . . disapoint *om. Q 2, etc.* 7 such] as much *Q 2, etc.* 10–11 de straw . . me *om. Q 2, etc.* 14 into] to *Q 2, etc.* 16 Ho *om. Q 2, etc.* 17 Vds hat *Q 2, Ff*: Uds heart *M* 24 Ho *om. Q 2, etc.* 28 God a mercy *Q 2, etc.* 30 O *om. Q 2, etc.* 33, 37 Vds hat *Q 2, Ff*: Uds heart *M* 35 as was neuer *Q 2, etc.*

Hostler Come, Gaffer Club, vnlode, vnlode, and get to supper, and Ile rub dunne the while. Come. [*exeunt.*

⟨SCENE IV. *The same. A room in the carrier's inn.*⟩

Enter the hoste, sir Iohn Old-castle, and Harpoole.

Hoste Sir, you are welcome to this house, to such as heere is with all my heart, but, by the masse, I feare your lodging wilbe the woorst. I haue but two beds, and they are both in a chamber, and the carier and his daughter lies in the one, and you and your wife must lie in the other.

L. Cobh. In faith, sir, for my selfe I doe not greatly passe.
My wife is weary, and would be at rest,
For we haue traueld very far to day;
We must be content with such as you haue.

Hoste But I cannot tell how to doe with your man.

Harpoole What, hast thou neuer an empty roome in thy house for me?

Hoste Not a bedde, by my troth: there came a poore Irish man, and I lodgde him in the barne, where he has faire straw, though he haue nothing else.

Harp. Well, mine hoste, I pray thee helpe mee to a payre of faire sheetes, and Ile go lodge with him.

Hoste By the masse, that thou shalt; a good payre of hempen sheetes, were neuer laine in: Come. [*exeunt.*

⟨SCENE V. *The same. A street.*⟩

Enter Constable, Maior, and Watch.

Maior What? haue you searcht the towne?

Const. All the towne, sir; we haue not left a house vnsearcht that vses to lodge.

Maior Surely, my lord of Rochester was then deceiude,
Or ill informde of sir Iohn Old-castle,
Or if he came this way hees past the towne.
He could not else haue scapt you in the search.

Const. The priuy watch hath beene abroad all night,
And not a stranger lodgeth in the towne
But he is knowne: onely a lusty priest
We found in bed with a pretty wench,
That sayes she is his wife—yonder at the *sheeres*:
But we haue chargde the hoste with his forth comming
To morow morning.

Maior What thinke you best to do?

Const. Faith, maister maior, heeres a few stragling houses beyond the bridge, and a little Inne where cariers vse to lodge, though I thinke surely he would nere lodge there: but weele go search, & the rather, because there came notice to the towne the last night of an Irish man, that had done a murder, whome we are to make search for.

Maior Come, I pray you, and be circumspect. [*exeunt.*

⟨SCENE VI. *The same. Before the Carrier's inn. Enter Watch.*⟩

1 *Watch.* First beset the house, before you begin the search.

2 *Watch.* Content; euery man take a seuerall place. [*heere is heard a great noyse within.*

Keepe, keepe, strike him downe there, downe with him.

Enter Constable with the Irish man in Harpooles apparell.

Con. Come, you villainous heretique, confesse where your maister is.

Irish man Vat mester?

Maior Vat mester, you counterfeit rebell? this shall not serue your turne.

Irish man Be sent Patrike I ha no mester.

Con. Wheres the lord Cobham, sir Iohn Old-castle, that lately is escaped out of the Tower.

Irish man. Vat lort Cobham?

Maior You counterfeit, this shal not serue you; weele torture you, weele make you to confesse where that arch-heretique, Lord Cobham, is: come, binde him fast.

Irish man Ahone, ahone, ahone, a Cree!

Con. Ahone, you crafty rascall! [*exeunt.*

⟨SCENE VII. *The same. The yard of the Inn.*⟩

Lord Cobham comes out in his gowne stealing.

Cobh. Harpoole, Harpoole, I heare a maruelous noyse about the house; God warant vs, I feare wee are pursued: what, Harpoole.

44–5 and Ile . . Come *om. Q 2, etc.* Scene IV. *etc. add. M* 1 Sir, y'are *Q 2, Ff* 2 is heere *Q 2, etc.* 2–3 by the masse *om. Q 2, etc.* 8 Faith *Q 2, etc.* 12 how] what *M* 16 in troth *Q 2, etc.* 18 although *Q 2, etc.* 20 prethee *Q 2*: prythee *Ff, etc.* 21 faire] cleane *Q 2, etc.* Scene V. *etc. add. M* 11 a young pretty *M* 18 although *Q 2, etc.* 24 Come] Come, then *M* Scene VI. *etc. add. M* 1 *Prefix* Const. *Qq, Ff*: *altered M* 3 *Prefix* Officer *Qq, Ff*: *altered M* 6–7 confesse] tell vs, *Q 2, etc.* 13 is *om. Q 2, etc.* 18–19 Lord Cobham *om. Q 2, etc.* Scene VII. *etc. add. M* 1–3 *Verse M, div. after* noise, feare

Harp. within. Who calles there?

Cobh. Tis I; dost thou not heare a noyse about the house? 6

Harp. Yes, mary, doe I:—zwounds, I can not finde my hose; this Irish rascall that was lodgde with me all night hath stolne my apparell, and has left me nothing but a lowsie mantle, and a paire of broags. Get vp, get vp, and if the carier and his wench be asleep, change you with them as he hath done with me, and see if we can escape. ⟨*Exit lord Cobham.*⟩

[*A noyse againe heard about the house, a pretty while; then enter the Constable, meeting Harpoole in the Irish mans apparrell.*

Con. Stand close, heere comes the Irish man that didde the murther; by all tokens, this is he. 17

Maior And perceiuing the house beset, would get away. Stand, sirra.

Harp. What art thou that bidst me stand?

Con. I am the Officer, and am come to search for an Irish man, such a villaine as thy selfe, that hast murthered a man this last night by the hie way. 24

Harp. Sbloud, Constable, art thou madde? am I an Irish man?

Maior Sirra, weele finde you an Irish man before we part: lay hold vpon him.

Con. Make him fast. O thou bloudy rogue!

Enter Lord Cobham and his lady in the carrier and wenches apparrell.

Cobham What, will these Ostlers sleepe all day? 30
Good morow, good morow. Come, wench, come.
Saddle! saddle! Now afore God too fair dayes, ha?

Con. Who comes there?

Maior Oh, tis Lankashire carier; let him passe. 35

Cobham What, will no body open the gates here?
Come, lets int stable to looke to our capons.
⟨*Exeunt* Cobham *and his Lady.*⟩

The carrier calling.

Club (*calling*) Hoste! why ostler! zwookes, heres such a bomination company of boies. A pox of this pigstie at the house end; it filles all the house full of fleas. Ostler! ostler! 41

⟨*Enter Ostler.*⟩

Ostler Who calles there? what would you haue?

Club Zwookes, do you robbe your ghests? doe you lodge rogues and slaues, and scoundrels, ha? they ha stolne our cloths here: why, ostler! 47

Ostler A murrein choake you, what a bawling you keepe.

⟨*Enter Host.*⟩

Hoste How now, what woulde the carrier haue? looke vp there. 51

Ostler They say that the man and woman that lay by them haue stolne their clothes.

Hoste What, are the strange folkes vp yet that came in yester night?

Const. What, mine hoste, vp so early? 56

Hoste What, maister Maior, and maister Constable!

Maior We are come to seeke for some suspected persons,
And such as heere we found, haue apprehended. 60

Enter the Carrier and Kate in lord Cobham and ladies apparell.

Con. Who comes heere?

Club Who comes here? a plague found ome! you bawle, quoth a! ods hat, Ile forzweare your house: you lodgde a fellow and his wife by vs that ha runne away with our parrel, and left vs such gew-gawes here!—Come Kate, come to mee, thowse dizeard, yfaith. 67

Maior Mine hoste, know you this man?

Hoste Yes, maister Maior, Ile giue my word for him. Why, neibor Club, how comes this geare about? 71

Kate Now, a fowle ont, I can not make this gew-gaw stand on my head: now the lads and the lasses won flowt me too too—

Const. How came this man and woman thus attired? 76

Hoste Here came a man and woman hither this last night, which I did take for substantiall people, and lodgde all in one chamber by these folkes, mee thinkes, haue beene so bolde to change apparell, and gone away this morning ere they rose. 82

Maior That was that villaine traitour, Oldcastle, that thus escaped vs: make out huy and cry yet after him, keepe fast that traiterous

7–14 *Verse M, div. after* find, me, and, mantle, and if, asleep, me 14 *S. D. add. M* Scene VIII. The same *add. M* 32 foord-dayes *Q 1* : farre-dayes *Q 2* : *corr. Ff* 33 comes] goes *Q 2, etc.* 34 him] them *Ff, etc.* 36 ope *Q 2, etc.* 37 capuls *conj. Percy* *S. D. add. R*

41, 49 *S. D. D. add. M* 44–7 *Verse Q 2, etc., div. after* guests, ha 52 that *om. Ff* and the woman *Q 2, etc.* 54 yet *om. M* 63 foreweare *Q 2, Ff* 73–4 now . . too too *om. Q 2, etc.* 77–92 *Verse M* 80 haue] they have *M* 83 villaine *om. Q 2, etc.* 84 out *om. Q 2, etc.*

rebell, his seruant, there: farewell, mine hoste.

Carier Come, Kate Owdham, thou and Ise trimly dizard.

Kate Ifaith, neame Club, Ise wot nere what to do, Ise be so flowted and so showted at: but byth messe Ise cry. [*exeunt.*

⟨Scene VIII. *A wood near St. Albans.*⟩

Enter sir Iohn Old-castle, and his Lady disguisde.

Oldca. Come, Madam, happily escapt; here let vs sit.
This place is farre remote from any path,
And here awhile our weary limbs may rest,
To take refreshing, free from the pursuite
Of enuious Rochester.

Lady But where, my Lord,
Shall we find rest for our disquiet minds?
There dwell vntamed thoughts that hardly stoupe,
To such abasement of disdained rags.
We were not wont to trauell thus by night,
Especially on foote.

Oldca. No matter, loue;
Extremities admit no better choice,
And were it not for thee, say froward time
Imposde a greater taske, I would esteeme it
As lightly as the wind that blowes vpon vs;
But in thy sufferance I am doubly taskt.
Thou wast not wont to haue the earth thy stoole,
Nor the moist dewy grasse thy pillow, nor
Thy chamber to be the wide horrison.

Lady How can it seeme a trouble, hauing you
A partner with me in the worst I feele?
No, gentle Lord, your presence would giue ease
To death it selfe, should he now seaze vpon me.
Behold what my foresight hath vndertane
[*heres bread and cheese & a bottle.*
For feare we faint; they are but homely cates,
Yet saucde with hunger, they may seeme as sweete
As greater dainties we were wont to taste.

Oldca. Praise be to him whose plentie sends both this
And all things else our mortall bodies need;
Nor scorne we this poore feeding, nor the state
We now are in, for what is it on earth,
Nay, vnder heauen, continues at a stay?
Ebbes not the sea, when it hath ouerflowne?
Followes not darknes when the day is gone?
And see we not sometime the eie of heauen
Dimmd with ouerflying clowdes: theres not that worke
Of carefull nature, or of cunning art,
(How strong, how beauteous, or how rich it be)
But falls in time to ruine. Here, gentle Madame,
In this one draught I wash my sorrow downe.
[*drinkes.*

Lady And I, incoragde with your cheerefull speech,
Wil do the like.

Oldca. Pray God poore Harpoole come.
If he should fall into the Bishops hands,
Or not remember where we bade him meete vs,
It were the thing of all things else, that now
Could breede reuolt in this new peace of mind.

Lady Feare not, my Lord, hees witty to deuise,
And strong to execute a present shift.

Oldca. That power be stil his guide hath guided vs!
My drowsie eies waxe heauy: earely rising,
Together with the trauell we haue had,
Make me that I could gladly take a nap,
Were I perswaded we might be secure.

Lady Let that depend on me: whilst you do sleepe,
Ile watch that no misfortune happen vs.
Lay then your head vpon my lap, sweete Lord,
And boldly take your rest.

Oldca. I shal, deare wife,
Be too much trouble to thee.

Lady Vrge not that;
My duty binds me, and your loue commands.
I would I had the skil with tuned voyce
To draw on sleep with some sweet melodie,
But imperfection, and vnaptnesse too,
Are both repugnant: feare inserts the one,
The other nature hath denied me vse.
But what talke I of meanes to purchase that,
Is freely hapned? sleepe with gentle hand
Hath shut his eie-liddes. Oh victorious labour,
How soone thy power can charme the bodies sense?
And now thou likewise climbst vnto my braine,
Making my heauy temples stoupe to thee.
Great God of heauen from danger keepe vs free. [*both sleepes.*

Enter sir Richard Lee, and his men.

Lee. A murder closely done, and in my ground?
Search carefully, if any where it were,

Scene VIII. *etc.*] Scene IX. *etc.* *M* Q1 5 Winchester 35 Flowes *Q1*: *corr.* *Q2* 36 sometimes *F2, etc.* 54 Makes *Q2, etc.* 58-9 Lay . . rest *om.* *Q2, etc.* 66 imperfectoin *Q1*

This obscure thicket is the likeliest place.
seruant. Sir, I haue found the body stiffe with cold,
And mangled cruelly with many wounds.
Lee Looke if thou knowest him, turne his body vp.—
Alacke, it is my son, my sonne and heire,
Whom two yeares since I sent to Ireland,
To practise there the discipline of warre,
And comming home (for so he wrote to me)
Some sauage hart, some bloudy diuellish hand,
Either in hate, or thirsting for his coyne,
Hath here slucde out his bloud. Vnhappy houre,
Accursed place, but most inconstant fate,
That hadst reserude him from the bullets fire,
And suffered him to scape the wood-karnes fury,
Didst here ordaine the treasure of his life,
(Euen here within the armes of tender peace,
And where security gaue greatest hope)
To be consumde by treasons wastefull hand!
And what is most afflicting to my soule,
That this his death and murther should be wrought
Without the knowledge by whose meanes twas done.
2 seru. Not so, sir; I haue found the authors of it.
See where they sit, and in their bloudy fistes,
The fatall instruments of death and sinne.
Lee Iust iudgement of that power, whose gracious eie,
Loathing the sight of such a hainous fact,
Dazeled their senses with benumming sleepe,
Till their vnhallowed treachery were knowne!
Awake, ye monsters; murderers, awake;
Tremble for horror; blush, you cannot chuse,
Beholding this inhumane deed of yours.
Old. What meane you, sir, to trouble weary soules,
And interrupt vs of our quiet sleepe?
Lee Oh diuellish! can you boast vnto your selues
Of quiet sleepe, hauing within your hearts
The guilt of murder waking, that with cries
Deafes the lowd thunder, and sollicites heauen
With more than Mandrakes shreekes for your offence?
Lady Old. What murder? you vpbraid vs wrongfully.
Lee Can you deny the fact? see you not heere
The body of my sonne by you mis-done?
Looke on his wounds, looke on his purple hew:
Do we not finde you where the deede was done?
Were notyour kniuesfast closed in your hands?
Is not this cloth an argument beside,
Thus staind and spotted with his innocent blood?
These speaking characters, were nothing else
To pleade against ye, would conuict you both.
Bring them away, bereauers of my ioy.
At Hartford, where the Sises now are kept,
Their liues shall answere for my sonnes lost life.
Old-castle As we are innocent, so may we speede.
Lee As I am wrongd, so may the law proceede. [*exeunt.*

⟨Scene IX. *St. Albans.*⟩

Enter bishop of Rochester, constable of S. Albons, with sir Iohn of Wrotham, Doll his wench, and the Irishman in Harpooles apparell.

Bishop What intricate confusion haue we heere?
Not two houres since we apprehended one,
In habite Irish, but in speech not so:
And now you bring another, that in speech
Is altogether Irish, but in habite
Seemes to be English: yea and more than so,
The seruant of that heretike Lord Cobham.
Irishman Fait, me be no seruant of the lord Cobhams,
Me be Mack Chane of Vlster.
Bishop Otherwise calld Harpoole of Kent; go to, sir,
You cannot blinde vs with your broken Irish.
sir Iohn Trust me, my Lord Bishop, whether Irish,
Or English, Harpoole or not Harpoole, that
I leaue to be decided by the triall:
But sure I am this man by face and speech
Is he that murdred yong sir Richard Lee—
I met him presently vpon the fact—
And that he slew his maister for that gold;
Those iewells, and that chaine I tooke from him.
Bishop Well, our affaires doe call vs backe to London,
So that we cannot prosecute the cause,

78 *M adds S. D.* Exit a servant.—Re-enter Servant bearing a dead body 94 *om. Q 2, etc.* gaue *pr. ed.*: gate *Q 1* 105 were] was *Q 2, etc.*

124 were] were there *Q 2, etc.* 125 against you *M* 126 *om. Q 2, etc.* 127 To Hartford with them, where *Q 2, etc.* Scene IX. *etc.*] Scene X. *etc. M* 4–6 *Two lines Q 2, Ff, div. after* Irish 5 altogether *om. Q 2, etc.* 6 Seemes to be *om. Q 2, etc.* 8 be me *Q 2* 12 my *om. Q 2, etc.* Lord] said *F 2, R, Pope* 12–14 *Two lines Q 2, etc., div. after* English 14 be decided by *om. Q 2, etc.* 20 faires *Q 2*

As we desire to do; therefore we leaue
The charge with you, to see they be conuaide
To Hartford Sise: both this counterfaite
And you, sir Iohn of Wrotham, and your wench,
For you are culpable as well as they,
Though not for murder, yet for felony.
But since you are the meanes to bring to light
This gracelesse murder, you shall beare with you
Our letters to the Iudges of the bench,
To be your friendes in what they lawfull may.
sir Iohn I thanke your Lordship.
Bish. So, away with them. [*exeunt.*

⟨SCENE X. *Hertford. A Hall of Justice.*⟩

Enter Gaoler and his man, bringing forth Old castle.

Gaoler Bring forth the prisoners, see the court preparde;
The Iustices are comming to the bench.
So, let him stand; away, and fetch the rest. [*exeunt.*
Old. Oh, giue me patience to indure this scourge,
Thou that art fountaine of that vertuous streame,
And though contempt, false witnes, and reproch
Hang on these yron gyues, to presse my life
As low as earth, yet strengthen me with faith,
That I may mount in spirite aboue the cloudes.

Enter Gaoler, bringing in Lady Old-castle and Harpoole.

Here comes my lady: sorow, tis for her
Thy wound is greeuous; else I scoffe at thee.
What, and poore Harpoole! art thou ith bryars too?
Harp. Ifaith, my Lord, I am in, get out how I can.
Lady Say, gentle Lord, for now we are alone,
And may conferre, shall we confesse in briefe,
Of whence, and what we are, and so preuent
The accusation is commencde against vs?
Old. What will that helpe vs? being knowne, sweete loue,
We shall for heresie be put to death,
For so they tearme the religion we professe.
No, if it be ordained we must die,
And at this instant, this our comfort be,
That of the guilt imposde, our soules are free.
Harp. Yea, yea, my lord, Harpcole is so resolude.
I wreake of death the lesse, in that I die
Not by the sentence of that enuious priest
The Bishop of Rochester: oh, were it he,
Or by his meanes that I should suffer here,
It would be double torment to my soule.
Lady Well, be it then according as heauen please.

Enter lord Iudge, two Iustices, Maior of Saint Albons, lord Powesse and his lady, and old sir Richard Lee: the Iudge and Iustices take their places.

Iudge Now, M⟨aister⟩ Maior, what gentleman is that,
You bring with you before vs and the bench?
Maior The Lord Powes, if it like your honor,
And this his Lady, trauelling toward Wales,
Who, for they lodgde last night within my house,
And my Lord Bishop did lay search for such,
Were very willing to come on with me,
Lest for their sakes suspition me might wrong.
Iudge We crie your honor mercy, good my Lord,
Wilt please ye take your place. Madame, your ladyship
May here or where you will repose your selfe,
Vntill this businesse now in hand be past.
Lady Po. I will withdraw into some other roome,
So that your Lordship and the rest be pleasde.
Iudge With all our hearts: attend the Lady there.
Lord Po. Wife, I haue eyde yond prisoners all this while,
And my conceit doth tel me, tis our friend,
The noble Cobham, and his vertuous Lady.
Lady Po. I thinke no lesse: are they suspected, trow ye,
For doing of this murder?
Lord Po. What it meanes
I cannot tell, but we shall know anon.
Meane space as you passe by them, ask the question,
But do it secretly, you be not seene,
And make some signe that I may know your mind.
Lady Po. My Lord Cobham? madam?
[*as she passeth ouer the stage by them.*

24 'sizes *M* 29 we shall *Q 2*: ye shall *Ff* 33 *om. Q 2, etc.* Scene X. *etc.*] Scene XI. *etc. M* 5 of this *M* 21-2 if.. instant] if we dye let *Q 2, etc.*

24 I, I my Lord *Q 2, etc.* 27-9 *om. Q 2, etc.* 32 and] to *Q 2, etc.* 33 if] an if *M* 36 search] waite *Q 2, etc.* 38 me *pr. ed.*: we *Qq, etc.* 40 ye] you *Q 2, etc.* 46 yon *Q 2, etc.* 49 trow ye *om. Q 2, etc.* 50 doing of *om. Q 2, etc.* 53 space] time *Q 2, etc.* 54 that you *M*

Old. No Cobham now, nor madam, as you loue vs,
But Iohn of Lancashire, and Ione his wife.
Lady Po. Oh tel, what is it that our loue can do,
To pleasure you? for we are bound to you.
Oldca. Nothing but this, that you conceale our names;
So, gentle lady, passe for being spied.
Lady Po. My heart I leaue, to beare part of your griefe. [*exit.*
Iudge Call the prisoners to the barre. Sir Richard Lee,
What euidence can you bring against these people,
To proue them guiltie of the murder done?
Lee. This bloudy towell and these naked kniues,
Beside we found them sitting by the place,
Where the dead body lay, within a bush.
Iudge What answer you why law should not proceed,
According to this euidence giuen in,
To taxe ye with the penalty of death?
Old. That we are free from murders very thought,
And know not how the gentleman was slaine.
1 *Iust.* How came this linnen cloth so bloudy then?
Lady Cob. My husband hot with trauelling, my lord,
His nose gusht out a bleeding, that was it.
2 *Iust.* But wherefore were your sharpe edgde kniues vnsheathde?
Lady Cob. To cut such simple victuall as we had.
Iudge Say we admit this answer to those articles,
What made ye in so priuate a darke nooke,
So far remote from any common path,
As was the thicke where the dead corpes was throwne?
Old. Iournying, my lord, from London from the terme,
Downe into Lancashire where we do dwell,
And what with age and trauell being faint,
We gladly sought a place where we might rest,
Free from resort of other passengers,
And so we strayed into that secret corner.
Iudge These are but ambages to driue of time,
And linger Iustice from her purposde end.
But who are these?

Enter the Constable, bringing in the Irishman, sir Iohn of Wrotham, and Doll.

Const. Stay Iudgement, and release those innocents,
For here is hee, whose hand hath done the deed,
For which they stand indited at the barre,—
This sauage villaine, this rude Irish slaue.
His tongue already hath confest the fact,
And here is witnes to confirme as much.
sir Iohn Yes, my good Lords, no sooner had he slaine
His louing master for the wealth he had,
But I vpon the instant met with him,
And what he purchacde with the losse of bloud:
With strokes I presently bereau'de him of;
Some of the which is spent, the rest remaining
I willingly surrender to the hands
Of old sir Richard Lee, as being his.
Beside, my Lord Iudge, I greet your honor
With letters from my Lord of Rochester. [*deliuers a letter.*
Lee Is this the wolfe whose thirsty throate did drinke
My deare sonnes bloud? art thou the snake
He cherisht, yet with enuious piercing sting
Assaildst him mortally? foule stigmatike,
Thou venome of the country where thou liuedst,
And pestilence of this: were it not that law
Stands ready to reuenge thy crueltie,
Traitor to God, thy master, and to me,
These hands should be thy executioner.
Iudge Patience, sir Richard Lee, you shall haue iustice,
And he the guerdon of his base desert.
The fact is odious; therefore, take him hence,
And being hangde vntil the wretch be dead,
His body after shall be hangd in chaines
Neare to the place where he did act the murder.
Irish. Prethee, Lord shudge, let me haue mine own clothes, my strouces there, and let me be hangd in a with after my cuntry—the Irish—fashion. [*exit.*
Iudge Go to; away with him. And now, sir Iohn,
Although by you this murther came to light,
And therein you haue well deseru'd, yet vpright law,
So will not haue you be excusde and quit,

72 ye] you *M* 75 boudy *Q 1* 78 wherefore were] how came *Q 2, etc.* 81 ye] you *Q 2, etc.*

107 I do greet *M* 108 Winchester *Q 1* : *corr. Q 2* 110 the cursed snake *M* 112–14 foule .. of this *om. Q 2, etc.* 119 *om. Q 2, etc.* 130 And .. deseru'd *om. Q 2, etc.* 130–1 *One line Q 2, etc.* 131 So .. quit] will not hold you excusde *Q 2, etc.*

For you did rob the Irishman, by which
You stand attainted here of felony.
Beside, you haue bin lewd, and many yeares
Led a lasciuious, vnbeseeming life.
sir Iohn Oh but, my Lord, he repents, sir Iohn repents, and he will mend.
Iudge In hope thereof, together with the fauour,
My Lord of Rochester intreates for you,
We are content you shall be proued.
sir Iohn I thanke your good Lordship.
Iudge These other falsly here accusde, and brought
In perill wrongfully, we in like sort
Do set at liberty, paying their fees.
Lord Po. That office, if it please ye, I will do,
For countries sake, because I know them well.
They are my neighbours, therefore of my cost
Their charges shall be paide.
Lee. And for amends,
Touching the wrong vnwittingly I haue done,
There are a few crownes more for them to drinke. [*giues them a purse.*

133 attained *Q 1* 136 he repents *om. Q 2, etc.* 139 Winchester *Q 1* 140 contented that you *M* 141 good *om. R* 142-4 *Two lines Q 2, Ff, div. after* brought: *wrongly rearranged in three lines M* 144 paying . . fees *om. Q 2, etc.* 145-8 *om. Q 2, etc.* 151 There . . drinke] I giue these few Crownes *Q 2, etc.*

Iudge. Your kindnes merites praise, sir Richard Lee:
So let vs hence.
[*exeunt all but Lord Powesse and Oldcastle.*
Lord Po. But Powesse still must stay.
There yet remaines a part of that true loue
He owes his noble friend vnsatisfide,
And vnperformd, which first of all doth bind me
To gratulate your lordships safe deliuery,
And then intreat, that since vnlookt for thus
We here are met, your honor would vouchsafe,
To ride with me to Wales, where to my power,
(Though not to quittance those great benefites,
I haue receiud of you) yet both my house,
My purse, my seruants, and what else I haue,
Are all at your command. Deny me not;
I know the Bishops hate pursues ye so,
As theres no safety in abiding here.
Old. Tis true, my Lord, and God forgiue him for it.
Lord Po. Then, let vs hence: you shall be straight prouided
Of lusty geldings, and once entred Wales,
Well may the Bishop hunt, but, spight his face,
He neuer more shall haue the game in chace.
[*exeunt.*

FINIS.

161 to my *M*: though my *Qq, Ff*: through my *conj. Percy* 162 May not acquittance *conj. M* 166 ye] you *M*

THE
True Chronicle Hi-
ſtorie of the whole life and death of *Thomas* Lord *Cromwell.*

As it hath beene ſundrie times pub-
likely Acted by the Right Hono-
rable the Lord Chamberlaine
his Seruants.

Written by W. S.

Imprinted at London for *William Iones*, and are
to be ſolde at his houſe neere Holburne con-
duict, at the ſigne of the Gunne.
1602.

Q 1	=	Quarto of 1602
Q 2	=	,, ,, 1613
F 1	=	the (third) Folio Shakespeare, 1664
F 2	=	,, (fourth) ,, ,, 1685
R	=	Rowe's Shakespeare, 1709
Pope	=	supplementary volume to Pope's Shakespeare, 1728
M	=	Malone, 1780
St.	=	Steevens, ibid.
Th.	=	Theobald, ibid.
S	=	Simms, 1848
T	=	Tyrrell, 1851
Haz.	=	Hazlitt, 1852
Molt.	=	Moltke, 1869
pr. ed.	=	present editor

THE LIFE AND DEATH OF THE LORD CROMWELL

⟨The Actors Names.

Old Cromwell, *a Black-smith of Putney.*
Yong Thomas Cromwell *his son.*
Hodge, Will *and* Tom, *old* Cromwell's *servants.*
Earle of Bedford *and his Host.*
Dukes of Norfolk *and* Suffolk.
Sir Christopher Hales.
Cardinal Wolsey.
Sir Thomas Moor.
Gardiner *Bishop of Winchester.*
Sir Ralph Sadler.
M. Bouser *a Merchant.*
Banister, *a broken Merchant and his wife.*
Bagot, *a cruel covetous Broker.*
Friskiball *a Florentine Merchant.*
The Governours of the English *house at* Antwerp.
States and Officers of Bononia.
Good-man Seely *and his wife* Joan.
Chorus.
A Post.
Messengers.
Ushers and servants.
Lieutenant of the Tower.
Two Citizens.
Two Merchants.⟩ [1]

⟨Act I. Scene I. *Putney. The entrance of a smith's shop.*⟩

Enter three Smithes, Hodge *and two other, old* Cromwels *men.*

Hodge. Come, masters, I thinke it be past fiue a clock; is it not time we were at worke: my old Master heele be stirring anon.

1. I cannot tell whether my old master will be stirring or no: but I am sure I can hardly take my afternoones nap, for my young Maister *Thomas,* he keepes such a quile in his studie, with the Sunne, and the Moone, and the seauen starres, that I do verily thinke heele read out his wits.

Hodge. He skill of the starres! theres goodman *Car* of *Fulhum,* he that carryed vs to the strong Ale, where goodie *Trundell* had her maide got with childe: O he knowes the Starres. Heele tickle you *Charles Waine* in nine degrees. That same man will tell you goodie *Trundell* when her Ale shall miscarie, onely by the starres.

2. I, thats a great vertue; indeed I thinke *Thomas* be no body in comparison to him.

1. Well, maisters, come, shall we to our hammers?

Hodge. I, content; first lets take our mornings draught, and then to worke roundly.

2. I, agreed; goe in, *Hodge.* [*Exit omnes.*

⟨Scene II. *The same.*⟩

Enter young Cromwell.

Crom. Good morrow, morne, I doe salute thy brightnesse.
The night seemes tedious to my troubled soule,
Whose black obscuritie binds in my minde
A thousand sundry cogitations:
And now *Aurora,* with a liuely dye,
Addes comfort to my spirit that mountes on high—
Too high indeede, my state being so meane.
My study, like a minerall of golde,
Makes my hart proude, wherein my hopes inrowld:
My bookes is all the wealth I do possesse,
[*Here within they must beate with their hammers.*
And vnto them I haue ingaged my hart.
O learning, how deuine thou seemes to me:
Within whose armes is all felicity.
Peace with your hammers! leaue your knocking there:
You doe disturbe my study and my rest.
Leaue off, I say, you madde me with the noyse.

Enter Hodge *and the two Men.*

Hodge. Why, how now, Maister *Thomas,* how now? Will you not let vs worke for you?

Crom. You fret my hart, with making of this noise.

Hod. How, fret your hart? I, but *Thomas,*

[1] *Add. F1* Act I. *etc. add. M* 1–3 *Verse Qq, F1, div. after* clock, worke 4 1.] Will *M: so l.* 21 7–25 *Verse Qq* 16 you *om. Q 2, etc.* 19, 25 2.] Tom *M*

Scene II. *etc. add. M* 3 binds] breeds *S* 6 on *om. S* 17–27 *Verse Qq, Ff: corr. M*

youle fret your fathers purse if you let vs from working.

2. I, this tis for him to make him a gentleman. Shal we leaue worke for your musing? thats well, I faith; But here comes my olde maister now.

Enter olde Cromwell.

Old. Cro. You idle knaues, what, are you loytring now?
No hammers walking and my worke to do!
What, not a heate among your worke to day?

Hod. Marrie, sir, your sonne *Thomas* will not let vs worke at all.

Old. Cro. Why, knaue, I say, haue I thus carkde & car'd
And all to keepe thee like a gentleman;
And dost thou let my seruants at their worke,
That sweat for thee, knaue, labour thus for thee?

Cro. Father, their hammers doe offend my studie.

Old. Cro. Out of my doores, knaue, if thou likest it not.
I crie you mercie! is your eares so fine?
I tell thee, knaue, these get when I doe sleepe;
I will not haue my Anuill stand for thee.

Crom. Theres monie, father, I will pay your men. [*He throwes money among them.*

Old. Cro. Haue I thus brought thee vp vnto my cost,
In hope that one day thou wouldst releeue my age,
And art thou now so lauish of thy coine,
To scatter it among these idle knaues.

Cro. Father, be patient, and content your selfe.
The time will come I shall hold golde as trash:
And here I speake with a presaging soule,
To build a pallace where now this cottage standes,
As fine as is King *Henries* house at Sheene.

Old Cro. You build a house! you knaue, youle be a begger.
Now, afore God, all is but cast away,
That is bestowed vpon this thriftlesse lad.
Well, had I bound him to some honest trade,
This had not beene, but it was his mothers doing,
To send him to the Vniuersitie.
How? build a house where now this cottage standes,
As faire as that at Sheene!—⟨*aside*⟩ He shall not here me.
A good boy Tom! I con thee thanke Tom!
Well said Tom! gramarcies Tom!—
Into your worke, knaues; hence, you sausie boy. [*Exit all but young* Cromwell.

Cro. Why should my birth keepe downe my mounting spirit?
Are not all creatures subiect vnto time:
To time, who doth abuse the world,
And filles it full of hodge-podge bastardie?
Theres legions now of beggars on the earth,
That their originall did spring from Kings:
And manie Monarkes now whose fathers were
The riffe-raffe of their age: for Time and Fortune
Weares out a noble traine to beggerie,
And from the dunghill minions doe aduance
To state and marke in this admiring world.
This is but course, which in the name of Fate
Is seene as often as it whirles about:
The Riuer *Thames,* that by our doore doth passe,
His first beginning is but small and shallow:
Yet keeping on his course, growes to a sea.
And likewise *Wolsey,* the wonder of our age,
His birth as meane as mine, a Butchers sonne,
Now who within this land a greater man?
Then, *Cromwell,* cheere thee vp, and tell thy soule,
That thou maist liue to flourish and controule.

Enter olde Cromwell.

Old Crom. *Tom Cromwell!* what, *Tom,* I say!

Crom. Do you call, sir.

Old Crom. Here is maister *Bowser* come to know if you haue dispatched his petition for the Lords of the counsell or no.

Crom. Father, I haue; please you to call him in.

Old Crom. Thats well said, *Tom*; a good lad, *Tom.*

Enter Maister Bowser.

Bow. Now, Maister *Cromwell,* haue you dispatched this petition?

Crom. I haue, sir; here it is: please you peruse it.

Bow. It shall not need; weele read it as we go by water:
And, Maister *Cromwell,* I haue made a motion
May do you good, and if you like of it.
Our Secretarie at *Antwarpe,* sir, is dead,
And the Marchants there hath sent to me,
For to prouide a man fit for the place:
Now I do know none fitter then your selfe,
If with your liking it stand, maister *Cromwell.*

24 *Prefix* Tom *M* 29 working *conj. M*: talking *conj. M* 45 thou] thee *Q2* 50 I'll build *Haz.* now *om. M*

65 the cheated world *M* 100 an if *M* 105 If it stand with your liking *S*

Crom. With all my hart, sir, and I much am bound,
In loue and dutie for your kindnesse showne.

Old Cro. Body of me, *Tom*, make hast, least some body get betweene thee and home, *Tom.* I thanke you, good maister *Bowser*, I thanke you for my boy; I thanke you alwayes, I thanke you most hartely, sir. Hoe, a cup of Beere there for maister *Bowser.*

Bow. It shall not need, sir. Maister *Cromwell,* will you go?

Crom. I will attend you, sir.

Old Crom. Farewell, *Tom*; God blesse thee, *Tom*; God speed thee, good *Tom.*

[*Exit omnes.*

⟨SCENE III. *London. A street before Frescobald's house.*⟩

Enter Bagot, *a Broker, solus.*

Bag. I hope this day is fatall vnto some,
And by their losse must *Bagot* seeke to gaine.
This is the lodging of maister *Fryskiball,*
A liberall Marchant, and a *Florentine,*
To whom *Banister* owes a thousand pound,
A Marchant Banckrout, whose Father was my maister.
What do I care for pitie or regarde?
He once was wealthy, but he now is falne,
And this morning haue I got him arested,
At the sute of maister *Friskiball,*
And by this meanes shall I be sure of coyne,
For dooing this same good to him vnknowne:
And in good time, see where the marchant comes.

Enter Fryskiball.

Bag. Go⟨o⟩d morrow to kind maister *Friskiball.*

Fri. Go⟨o⟩d morrow to your selfe, good maister *Bagot,*
And whats the newes, you are so early stirring:
It is for gaine, I make no doubt of that.

Bag. It is for the loue, sir, that I beare to you.
When did you see your debter *Banister*?

Fri. I promise you, I haue not seene the man
This two moneths day; his pouertie is such,
As I do thinke he shames to see his friends.

Bag. Why, then, assure your selfe to see him straight,
For at your sute I haue arrested him,
And here they will be with him presently.

Fry. Arrest him at my sute? you were to blame.
I know the mans misfortunes to be such,
As hees not able for to pay the debt,
And were it knowne to some he were vndone.

Bag. This is your pittifull hart to thinke it so,
But you are much deceaued in *Banister.*
Why such as he will breake for fashion sake,
And vnto those they owe a thousand pound,
Pay scarce a hundred. O, sir, beware of him.
The man is lewdly giuen to Dyce and Drabs,
Spends all he hath in harlots companies;
It is no mercy for to pitie him.
I speake the truth of him, for nothing els,
But for the kindnesse that I beare to you.

Fry. If it be so, he hath deceiued me much,
And to deale strictly with such a one as he—
Better seuere then too much lenitie.
But here is Maister *Banister* himselfe,
And with him, as I take, the officers.

Enter Banister, *his wife, and two officers.*

Ban. O maister *Friskiball*, you haue vndone me.
My state was well nigh ouerthrowne before,
Now altogether downe-cast by your meanes.

Mist. Ba. O maister *Friskiball,* pity my husbands case.
He is a man hath liued as well as any,
Till enuious fortune and the rauenous sea
Did rob, disrobe, and spoile vs of our owne.

Fri. Mistrisse *Banister,* I enuie not your husband,
Nor willingly would I haue vsed him thus,
But that I here he is so lewdly giuen,
Haunts wicked company, and hath enough
To pay his debts, yet will not be knowne thereof.

Ban. This is that damned Broker, that same *Bagot,*
Whom I haue often from my Trencher fed.
Ingratefull Villaine for to vse me thus!

Bag. What I haue said to him is naught but truth.

Mi. Ban. What thou hast said springs from an enuious hart.
A Canniball that doth eate men aliue!
But here vpon my knee, beleeue me, sir,
And what I speake, so helpe me God, is true:
We scarse haue meate to feed our little babes.
Most of our Plate is in that Brokers hand,
Which, had we mony to dephray our debt,
O thinke, we would not bide that penurie.

108–13 *Verse Qq, Ff* 109 home] honour *S* Scene III. *etc. add. M* 3 lodging] lodge *S* 9 I this morning have *M* 10 At suit of this same *M*

42 *M suggests that a preceding line has been lost.* Better seuere] Is better sure *conj. St.* 44 as I take't *Ff, etc.* 56 be knowne] own *S* 59 Ungrateful *M* 62 Λ] O *S* 67 debts *Q 2, etc.*

Be mercifull, kinde maister *Friskiball*.
My husband, children, and my selfe will eate
But one meale a day, the other will
We keepe and sell
As part to pay the debt we owe to you:
If euer teares did pierce a tender minde,
Be pittifull, let me some fauour finde.

Bag. Be not you so mad, sir, to beleeue hir teares.

Fri. Go to, I see thou art an enuious man.
Good misteris *Banister*, kneele not to me;
I pray rise vp, you shall haue your desire.
Holde; officers, be gone, theres for your paines.—
You know you owe to me a thousand pound:
Here, take my hand; if eare God make you able,
And place you in your former state againe,
Pay me: but if still your fortune frowne,
Vpon my faith Ile neuer aske you crowne:
I neuer yet did wrong to men in thrall,
For God doth know what to my selfe may fall.

Ban. This vnexpected fauour, vndeserued,
Doth make my hart bleed inwardly with ioy.
Nere may ought prosper with me is my owne,
If I forget this kindnesse you haue showne.

Mi. Ba. My children in their prayers, both night and day,
For your good fortune and successe shall pray.

Fri. I thanke you both; I pray, goe dine with me.
Within these three dayes, if God giue me leaue,
I will to *Florence,* to my natiue home.
Bagot, holde; theres a Portague to drinke,
Although you ill deserued it by your merit.
Giue not such cruell scope vnto your hart;
Be sure the ill you do will be requited.
Remember what I say, *Bagot*; farewell.
Come, Maister *Banister*; you shall with me.
My fare is but simple, but welcome hartily.
[*Exit all but* Bagot.

Bag. A plague goe with you; would you had eate your last!
Is this the thankes I haue for all my paines?
Confusion light vpon you all for me.
Where he had wont to giue a score of crownes,
Doth he now foyst me with a Portague?
Well, I will be reuenged vpon this *Banister*.
Ile to his creditors, buie all the debts he owes,
As seeming that I do it for good will.
I am sure to haue them at an easie rate,
And when tis done, in christendome he staies not,
But ile make his hart to ake with sorrow:
And if that *Banister* become my debter,
By heauen and earth ile make his plague the greater. [*Exit* Bagot.

⟨ACT II.⟩

Enter Chorus.

Cho. Now, gentlemen, imagine that young *Cromwell* ⟨is⟩
In *Antwarpe* Ledger for the English Marchantes:
And *Banister*, to shunne this *Bagots* hate,
Hearing that he hath got some of his debts,
Is fled to *Antwarpe*, with his wife and children;
Which *Bagot* hearing is gone after them:
And thether sendes his billes of debt before,
To be reuenged on wretched *Banister*.
What doth fall out, with patience sit and see,
A iust requitall of false trecherie. [*Exit.*

⟨SCENE I. *Antwerp.*⟩

Cromwell *in his study with bagges of money before him casting of account.*

Cro. Thus farre my reckoning doth go straight & euen,
But, *Cromwell,* this same ploying fits not thee:
Thy minde is altogether set on trauell,
And not to liue thus cloystered like a Nunne.
It is not this same trash that I regard,
Experience is the iewell of my hart.

Enter a Post.

Post. I praie, sir, are you readie to dispatch me?

Cro. Yes; heres those summes of monie you must carie;
You goe so farre as Frankford, do you not?

Post. I doe, sir.

Cro. Well, prethie make all the hast thou canst,
For there be certaine English gentlemen
Are bound for Venice, and may hapilie want,
And if that you should linger by the way:
But in hope that youle make good speed,
Theres two Angels to buie you spurres and wandes.

Po. I thank you, sir; this will ad winges indeede. ⟨*Exit Post.*⟩

Cro. Golde is of power would make an Eagles speed.

71–2 *One line Qq, Ff* 71–3 *Two lines, div. after* keep *M, etc.* 73 to you] you *M* 73–5 *om. Ff, R, Pope* 76 *om. Ff, etc.* 84 but yet if *M* 85 you] a *M* 90 is] as *S* 97 Hold, Bagot *R, etc.* 97, 108 Portague] cardecue *conj. M* 110 debt *Q 1*

Act II. *add. M* 1 is *add. Q 2* Scene I. *etc. M* 2 plodding *Q 2, etc.* 11 make then all *M* 15 in the hope *M* *S. D. add. M* 18 would] to *Q 2, etc.*

Enter Mistris Banister.

What gentlewoman is this that greeues so much?
It seemes she doth adresse her selfe to me.
Mi. Ba. God saue you, sir; praie, is your name maister *Cromwell*?
Cro. My name is *Thomas Cromwell,* gentlewoman.
Mi. Ba. Know you not one *Bagot*, sir, thats come to *Antwarpe*?
Cro. No, trust me, I neuer saw the man,
But here are billes of debt I haue receiued,
Against one *Banister*, a Marchant fallen into decaie.
Mi. Ba. Into decaie, indeede, long of that wretch.
I am the wife to wofull *Banister*:
And by that bloudie villaine am persu'de
From London here to *Antwarpe.*
My husband he is in the gouernours handes,
And God of heauen knowes how heele deale with him.
Now, sir, your hart is framed of milder temper;
Be mercifull to a distressed soule,
And God no doubt will trebell blesse your gaine.
Cro. Good mistris *Banister*, what I can, I will,
In any thing that lies within my power.
Mi. Ba. O speake to *Bagot,* that same wicked wretch,
An Angells voyce may mooue a damned diuell.
Cro. Why, is he come to *Antwarpe*, as you here?
Mi. Ba. I hard he landed some two houres since.
Cro. Well, mistris *Banister*, assure your selfe.
Ile speake to *Bagot* in your owne behalfe,
And winne him to all the pittie that I can.
Meane time, to comfort you in your distresse,
Receiue these Angells to releeue your neede,
And be assured that what I can effect
To do you good, no way I will neglect.
Mi. Ba. That mighty God, that knowes each mortalles hart,
Keepe you from trouble, sorrow, griefe, and smart.
[*Exit Mistris Banister.*
Crom. Thankes, courteous woman, for thy hartie praier.
It greeues my soule to see her miserie,
But we that liue vnder the worke of fate,
Maie hope the best, yet knowes not to what state
Our starres and destinies hath vs asignde.
Fickle is fortune and her face is blinde. ⟨*Exit.*⟩

⟨SCENE II. *A street in Antwerp.*⟩
Enter Bagot *solus.*

Ba. So all goes well; it is as I would haue it.
Banister he is with the Gouernour
And shortlie shall haue guiues vpon his heeles.
It glads my hart to thinke vpon the slaue;
I hope to haue his bodie rot in prison,
And after here his wife to hang her selfe,
And all his children die for want of foode.
The Iewels that I haue brought to Antwarpe
Are recond to be worth fiue thousand pound,
Which scarcelie stoode me in three hundreth pound.
I bought them at an easie kinde of rate;
I care not which way they came by them
That sould them me, it comes not neare my hart:
And least they should be stolne—as sure they are—
I thought it meete to sell them here in Antwarpe,
And so haue left them in the Gouernours hand,
Who offers me within two hundreth pound
Of all my price. But now no more of that:
I must go see and if my billes be safe,
The which I sent to maister *Cromwell,*
That if the winde should keepe me on the sea,
He might arest him here before I came:

⟨*Enter* Cromwell.⟩

And in good time, see where he is. God saue you sir.
Cro. And you: pray pardon me, I know you not.
Bag. It may be so, sir, but my name is *Bagot,*
The man that sent to you the billes of debt.
Cro. O, the man that persues *Banister*.
Here are the billes of debt you sent to me:
As for the man, you know best where he is.
It is reported you haue a flintie hart,
A minde that will not stoope to anie pittie,
An eye that knowes not how to shed a teare,
A hand thats alwaies open for reward;
But, maister *Bagot*, would you be ruled by me,
You should turne all these to the contrarie.
Your hart should still haue feeling of remorse,

25, 26 *Begin* Are, One *M* 26 into] to *M* 31–2 *Begin* He, Of *M* 30–2 Antwerp, where my husband Lies in the governor's hands; the God of Heaven He only knows how he will *etc. S, followed by Molt. with change* and God 43 I will to Bagot speak *S* owne *om. S, Molt.*

54 know *F2, etc.* 55 have *F2, etc.* *S. D.* Exit *add. R* Scene II. *etc. add. M* 8 that *om. Q2, etc.* have with me brought *M* 12 not much which *M* 20 sent before to *M* *S. D. add. R* 27 O, you're the *M*

Your minde according to your state be liberall
To those that stand in neede and in distresse;
Your hand to helpe them that do stand in want,
Rather then with your poyse to holde them downe;
For euerie ill turne show your selfe more kinde:
Thus should I doe; pardon, I speake my minde.

Bag. I, sir, you speake to here what I would say,
But you must liue, I know, as well as I:
I know this place to be extortion,
And tis not for a man to keepe him,
But he must lie, cog with his dearest friend,
And as for pittie, scorne it, hate all conscience.
But yet I doe commend your wit in this,
To make a show of what I hope you are not;
But I commend you and tis well done:
This is the onelie way to bring your gaine.

Cro. My gaine! I had rather chaine me to an ore,
And like a slaue there toile out all my life,
Before ide liue so base a slaue as thou:
I, like an hipocrite, to make a show
Of seeming vertue and a diuell within!
No, *Bagot*, would thy conscience were as cleare:
Poore *Banister* nere had beene troubled here.

Bag. Nay, good maister *Cromwell*; be not angrie, sir.
I know full well you are no such man;
But if your conscience were as white as Snow,
It will be thought that you are other wise.

Cro. Will it be thought that I am other wise?
Let them that thinke so know they are deceiu'de.
Shall *Cromwell* liue to haue his faith misconstered?
Antwarpe, for all the wealth within thy Towne,
I will not stay here not two houres longer.
As good lucke serues, my accountes are all made euen;
Therefore ile straight vnto the treasurer.
Bagot, I know youle to the gouernour;
Commend me to him, say I am bound to trauaile,
To see the fruitefull partes of Italie,
And as you euer bore a Christian minde,
Let *Banister* some fauour of you finde.

Bag. For your sake, sir, ile helpe him all I can—
To starue his hart out eare he gets a groate. ⟨*Aside.*⟩
So, maister *Cromwell*, doe I take my leaue,
For I must straight vnto the gouernour. [*Exit* Bagot.

Cro. Farewell, sir; pray you remember what I said.—
No, *Cromwell*, no; thy hart was nere so bace,
To liue by falshoode or by brokerie!
But 't falles out well, I little it repent;
Hereafter, time in trauell shalbe spent.

Enter Hodge, *his fathers man.*

Hod. Your sonne *Thomas*, quoth you: I haue beene *Thomast!* I had thought it had beene no such matter to a gone by water: for at Putnaie ile go you to Parish-garden for two pence, sitte as still as may be, without any wagging or ioulting in my guttes, in a little boate too: heere wee were scarce foure mile in the great greene water, but I—thinking to goe to my afternoones vnchines, as twas my manner at home—but I felt a kinde of rising in my guttes. At last one a the Sailers spying of me, *be a good cheere,* sayes hee, *set downe thy victualles, and vppe with it, thou hast nothing but an Eele in thy belly.* Well toote went I, to my victtualles went the Sailers, and thinking me to bee a man of better experience then any in the shippe, asked mee what Woode the shippe was made of: they all swore I tould them as right as if I had beene acquainted with the Carpenter that made it. At last wee grewe neere lande, and I grewe villanous hungrie, went to my bagge: the diuell a bitte there was. The Sailers had tickled mee; yet I cannot blame them: it was a parte of kindnesse, for I in kindnesse toulde them what Woode the shippe was made of, and they in kindnesse eate vp my victualles, as indeede one good turne asketh another. Well, would I could finde my maister *Thomas* in this Dutch Towne; he might put some English Beare into my bellie.

Cro. What, *Hodge,* my fathers man? by my hand, welcome!
How doth my father? whats the newes at home?

Hod. Maister *Thomas,* O God, maister *Thomas,* your hand, gloue and all. This is to giue you to vnderstanding that your father is in health, and *Alice Downing* here hath sent you a Nutmeg, & *Besse Makewater* a race of Ginger; my fellow *Will & Tom* hath between

39 stand] sink *S* 45 extortious *conj. M*: extortionous *Molt.* 46 keep safe here *Q 2, etc.* 52 your] you *T* 53 My *om. S* 58 would] if *Q 2, etc.* 60 good *om. S* 61 well that you *Q 2, etc.* 68 here full two *Q 2, etc.* S. D. Aside *add. M*

80 you *om. S* I] I've *S* 83 But falles *Q 1* 91 scarce some four *Ff* miles *R, etc.* 93 vnchines] Lunchines *R*: nuncheon *M* 94 but I *om. M* 100 me *Q 2, etc.*: I *Q 1* 106 and went *M* 112 would I, could I *Qq, Ff*: *corr. M* 123 Fellows *R*

them sent you a dozen of pointes, & good man *Tolle* of the Goate a paire of mittons; my selfe came in person: and this is all the newes.

Cro. Gramarsie, good *Hodge*, and thou art welcome to me,
But in as ill a time thou comest as may be:
For I am traueling into Italie.
What saist thou, *Hodge*? wilt thou beare me companie?

Hodge. Will I beare thee companie, *Tom*? What tell'st me of Italie? were it to the furthest part of Flaunders, I would goe with thee, *Tom*. I am thine in all weale and woe, thy owne to commaund. What, *Tom*! I haue passed the rigorous waues of *Neptunes* blastes; I tell you, *Thomas*, I haue beene in the danger of the flouds; and when I haue seene *Boreas* beginne to plaie the Ruffin with vs, then would I downe of my knees and call vppon *Vulcan*.

Cro. And why vpon him?

Hod. Because, as this same fellow *Neptune* is God of the Seas, so *Vulcan* is Lord ouer the Smithes, and therefore, I, being a Smith, thought his Godhead would haue some care yet of me.

Crom. A good conceit, but tell ⟨me⟩, hast thou dined yet?

Hod. *Thomas*, to speake the truth, not a bit yet I.

Crom. Come, go with me; thou shalt haue cheere good store.
And farewell, *Antwarpe*, if I come no more.

Hodg. I follow thee, sweet *Tom*, I follow thee. [*Exit omnes.*

⟨Scene III. *Another street in the same.*⟩

Enter the Gouernour of the English house, Bagot, Banister, *his wife, and two officers.*

Gouer. Is *Cromwell* gone then, say you, maister *Bagot*?
What dislike, I pray? what was the cause?

Bag. To tell you true, a wilde braine of his owne;
Such youth as they cannot see when they are well:
He is all bent to trauaile, thats his reason,
And doth not loue to eate his bread at home.

Gou. Well, good fortune with him, if the man be gone.
We hardly shall finde such a one as he,
To fit our turnes; his dealings were so honest.
But now, sir, for your Iewels that I haue,
What do you say? will you take my prise?

Bag. O, sir, you offer too much vnderfoote.

Gou. Tis but two hundred pound betweene vs, man.
Whats that in paiment of fiue thousand pound?

Bag. Two hundred pound! birladie, sir, tis great:
Before I got so much, it made me sweat.

Gou. Well, Maister *Bagot*, Ile proffer you fairelie.
You see this Marchant, maister *Banister*,
Is going now to prison at your sute.
His substance all is gone; what would you haue?
Yet in regarde I knew the man of wealth—
Neuer dishonest dealing, but such mishaps
Hath falne on him, may light on me or you—
There is two hundred pound betweene vs;
We will deuide the same: Ile giue you one,
On that condition you will set him free:
His state is nothing, that you see your selfe,
And where naught is, the King must lose his right.

Bag. Sir, sir, you speake out of your loue,
Tis foolish loue, sir, sure, to pittie him:
Therefore, content your selfe; this is my minde:
To do him good I will not bate a penie,

Ban. This is my comfort: though thou doost no good,
A mighty ebbe followes a mighty floud.

Mi. Ba. O thou base wretch, whom we haue fostered
Euen as a Serpent for to poyson vs,
If God did euer right a womans wrong,
To that same God I bend and bow my heart,
To let his heauy wrath fall on thy head,
By whome my hopes and ioyes are butchered.

Bag. Alas, fond woman, I praie thee, praie thy worst;
The Fox fares better still when he is curst.

Enter Maister Bowser, *a Marchant.*

Go. Maister *Bowser*! your welcome, sir, from England.
Whats the best newes? how doth all our friendes?

Bow. They are all well and do commend them to you;
Theres letters from your brother and your sonne:
So faire you well, sir; I must take my leaue.
My hast and businesse doth require such.

137 in danger *Ff, etc.* 140 of] a *Q 2, etc.* 147 tell me *Q 2, etc.*: tell *Q 1* Scene III. *etc. add. M* 2 In what dislike, I pray you *M* 4 as he can't *M* 8 such a man *Ff, R* 11 say? what, will *Q 2, etc.* 24 us two *M* 29 Sir, sir, I know you *M* O Sir.. love, but know *S* 39 heany *Qq* 41 I prethee *Q 2, etc.* 43 your *Qq*: you're *F 2* 44 and how *M* 47 faire *Q 1* 48 such] so *Q 2, Ff, M*: it so *S*

Go. Before you dine, sir? What, go you out of towne?
Bow. I, faith, vnlesse I here some newes in towne,
I must away; there is no remedie.
Gou. Maister *Bowser,* what is your busines? may I know it?
Bow. You may, sir, and so shall all the Cittie.
The King of late hath had his treasurie rob'd,
And of the choysest iewelles that he had:
The value of them was some seauen thousand pound.
The fellow that did steale these iewels, he is hanged,
And did confesse that for three hundred pound
He sould them to one *Bagot* dwelling in London:
Now *Bagots* fled, and, as we here, to Antwarpe,
And hether am I come to seeke him out;
And they that first can tell me of his newes
Shall haue a hundred pound for their reward.
Ba⟨n⟩. How iust is God to right the innocent.
Gou. Maister *Bowser,* you come in happie time:
Here is the villaine *Bagot* that you seeke,
And all those iewels haue I in my handes.
Officers, looke to him, hould him fast.
Bag. The diuell ought me a shame, and now hath paide it.
Bow. Is this that *Bagot*? fellowes, beare him hence.
We will not now stand for his replie.
Lade him with Yrons; we will haue him tride
In England, where his villanies are knowne.
Bag. Mischiefe, confusion, light vpon you all!
O hang me, drowne me, let me kill my selfe!
Let go my armes; let me run quick to hell.
Bow. Away, beare him away; stop the slaues mouth. [*They carry him away.*
Mi. Ba. Thy workes are infinite, great God of heauen.
Gou. I hard this *Bagot* was a wealthie fellow.
Bow. He was indeed, for when his goods were zeased,
Of Iewels, coine, and Plate within his house,
Was found the value of fiue thousand pound;
His furniture fullie worth halfe so much,
Which being all strainde for, for the King,
He francklie gaue it to the *Antwarpe* marchants,
And they againe, out of their bountious minde,
Hath to a brother of their companie,
A man decaide by fortune of the Seas,
Giuen *Bagots* wealth, to set him vp againe,
And keepe it for him: his name is *Banister.*
Gou. Maister *Bowser,* with this happie newes
You haue reuiued two from the gates of death:
This is that *Banister,* and this his wife.
Bow. Sir, I am glad my fortune is so good,
To bring such tidings as may comfort you.
Ban. You haue giuen life vnto a man deemed dead,
For by these newes, my life is newlie bred.
Mi. Ba. Thankes to my God, next to my Soueraigne King,
And last to you that these good hopes doth bring.
Gou. The hundred pound I must receiue as due
For finding *Bagot,* I freelie giue to you.
Bow. And, Maister *Banister,* if so you please,
Ile beare you companie, when you crosse the Seas.
Ban. If it please you, sir; my companie is but meane.
Stands with your liking, Ile waite on you.
Gou. I am glad that all things do accorde so well:
Come, Maister *Bowser,* let vs in to dinner:
And, Misterisse *Banister,* be mery, woman!
Come, after sorrow now lets cheere your spirit;
Knaues haue their due, and you but what you merit. [*Exit omnes.*

⟨ACT III. SCENE I. *The principal bridge at Florence.*⟩

Enter Cromwell *and* Hodge *in their shirtes, and without Hattes.*

Hod. Call yee this seeing of fashions? Marrie, would I had staide at *Putnaie* still. O, Maister *Thomas,* we are spoiled, we are gone.

Crom. Content thee, man, this is but fortune.

Hodg. Fortune; a plague of this Fortune makes me go wetshod; the roagues would not leaue me a shooe to my feete. For my hoase, they scorned them with their heeles; but for my Dublet and Hatte, O Lord, they imbrased me, and vnlased me, and tooke away my cloathes, and so disgraced me.

53 *Prefix* Bow. *before* 54 *Qq* may so, sir *M* 56 some *om. Q 2, etc.* 57 he *om. Q 2, etc.* 68 Here, officers *M* 69 now he hath *Ff, R* 71 stand here for *M* 83 worth fully *S* 84 strainde for the *Q 2, Ff*: distrained for the *M* 87 Have *Ff, etc.*

91 Good Master *S* this most happy *M* 99 hopes doth] newes doe *Q 2, etc.* Act III. Scene I. *etc. add. M* 1–4 *Verse Qq, Ff, div.* fashions, still 7 Fortune, it makes *Ff, etc.* 9–13 For my .. disgraced me] *Doggerel M, div.* hose, heels, hat, me, me, cloaths, me

Crom. Well, *Hodge,* what remedie? What shift shall we make now?

Hodge. Naie, I know not. For begging I am naught, for stealing worse: by my troth, I must euen fall to my olde trade, to the Hammer and the Horse heeles againe: but now the worst is; I am not acquainted with the humor of the horses in this countrie, whether they are not coultish, giuen much to kicking, or no; for when I haue one legge in my hand, if he should vp and laie tother on my chops, I were gone: there laie I, there laie *Hodge.*

Crom. *Hodge,* I beleeue thou must worke for vs both.

Hodge. O, Maister *Thomas,* haue not I tolde you of this? haue not I manie a time and often said, *Tom,* or *Maister Thomas, learne to make a Horse-shooe, it will be your owne another day:* this was not regarded. Harke you, *Thomas,* what doe you call the fellowes that robd vs?

Crom. The Bandetti.

Hod. The Bandetti, doe you call them? I know not what they are called here, but I am sure wee call them plaine theeues in England. O *Thomas,* that we were now at Putnay, at the ale there.

Cro. Content thee, man; here set vp these two billes,
And let vs keepe our standing on the bridge:
The fashion of this countrie is such,
If any stranger be oppressed with want,
To write the maner of his miserie,
And such as are disposed to succour him,
Will doe it. What, hast thou set them vp?

Hod. I, their vp; God send some to reade them, and not onelie to reade them, but also to looke on vs; and not altogether to looke on vs,

[*One standes at one end, and one at tother.*

But to releeue vs. O colde, colde, colde.

Enter Friskiball, *the Marchant, and reades the billes.*

Fris. Whats here? two Englishmen rob'd by the Bandetti!
One of them seemes to be a gentleman.
Tis pittie that his fortune was so hard,
To fall into the desperate handes of theeues.
Ile question him of what estate he is.
God saue you, sir; are you an Englishman?

Cro. I am, sir, a distressed Englishman.

Fri. And what are you, my friend?

Hod. Who? I, sir? by my troth, I do not know my self what I am now, but, sir, I was a smith, sir, a poore Farrier of Putnay. Thats my maister, sir, yonder. I was robbed for his sake, sir.

Fri. I see you haue beene met by the Bandetti,
And therefore neede not aske how you came thus.
But, *Friskiball,* why doost thou question them
Of their estate and not releeue their neede?
Sir, the coine I haue about me is not much:
Theres sixteene Duckets for to cloath your selues,
Theres sixteene more to buie your diet with,
And thers sixteene to paie for your horse hire:
Tis all the wealth, you see, my purse possesses,
But if you please for to enquire me out,
You shall not want for ought that I can doe.
My name is *Friskiball,* a *Florence* Marchant,
A man that alwayes loued your nation.

Crom. This vnexpected fauour at your hands,
Which God doth know if euer I shall requite it—
Necessitie makes me to take your bountie,
And for your gold can yeeld you naught but thankes.
Your charitie hath helpt me from dispaire;
Your name shall still be in my hartie praier.

Fri. It is not worth such thankes. Come to my house;
Your want shall better be releeu'd then thus.

Crom. I pray, excuse me; this shall well suffice
To beare my charges to *Bononia,*
Whereas a noble Earle is much distressed:
An Englishman, *Russell,* the Earle of *Bedford,*
Is by the French King solde vnto his death:
It may fall out, that I may doe him good;
To saue his life, Ile hazard my hart blood.
Therefore, kinde sir, thankes for your liberall gift;
I must be gone to aide him; ther's no shift.

Fri. Ile be no hinderer to so good an acte.
Heauen prosper you in that you goe about!
If Fortune bring you this way backe againe,
Pray let me see you: so I take my leaue;
All good a man can wish, I doe bequeath.

[*Exit* Friskiball.

Crom. All good that God doth send light on your head;
Theres few such men within our climate bred.
How say you now, *Hodge*? is not this good fortune?

24 on] of *Q 1* 35, 36 Bandetto *Qq* 39 Tom *Ff, etc.* 47 What, Hodge, hast *M* 48–51 *Verse Qq, Ff: corr. M* 50 to *om. Ff, etc.* 53 and robb'd *M* Bandetto *Qq*

66 Bandetto *Qq* 80 it *om. M* 103 now *om. M*

Hod. How say you? Ile tell you what, maister *Thomas*; if all men be of this Gentlemans minde, lets keepe our standings vpon this Bridge: we shall get more here with begging in one day, then I shall with making Horshoes in a whole yeare.

Crom. No *Hodge*, we must begone vnto *Bononia*,
There to releeue the noble Earle of *Bedford*:
Where, if I faile not in my policie,
I shall deceiue their subtile treacherie.

Hodge. Naye, Ile follow you. God blesse vs from the theeuing Bandettoes againe. [*Exit omnes.*

⟨Scene II. *Bononia. A room in an hotel.*⟩

Enter Bedforde *and his Hoast.*

Bed. Am I betraide? was *Bedforde* borne to die
By such base slaues in such a place as this?
Haue I escaped so many times in *France*,
So many battailes haue I ouer passed,
And made the French stirre when they hard my name;
And am I now betraide vnto my death?
Some of their harts bloud first shall pay for it.

Hoa. They do desire, my Lord, to speake with you.

Bed. The traitors doe desire to haue my bloud,
But by my birth, my honour, and my name,
By all my hopes, my life shall cost them deare.
Open the door; ile venter out vpon them,
And if I must die, then ile die with honour.

Hoa. Alas, my Lord, that is a desperate course;
They haue begirt you round about the house:
Their meaning is to take you prisoner,
And so to send your bodie vnto *France*.

Bed. First shall the Ocean be as drie as sand,
Before aliue they send me vnto *France*:
Ile haue my bodie first bored like a Siue,
And die as *Hector*, gainst the *Mirmidons*,
Eare *France* shall boast *Bedfordes* their prisoner.
Trecherous *France*, that, gainst the law of armes,
Hath here betraide thy enemie to death.
But be assured, my bloud shalbe reuenged
Vpon the best liues that remaines in *France*.—

Enter a Seruant.

Stand backe, or els thou run'st vpon thy death.

Mes. Pardon, my Lord; I come to tell your honour,
That they haue hired a *Neopolitan*,
Who by his Oratorie hath promised them,
Without the shedding of one drop of bloud,
Into their handes safe to deliuer you,
And therefore craues none but himselfe may enter
And a poore swaine that attendes on him. [*Exit seruant.*

Bed. A *Neopolitan*? bid him come in.
Were he as cunning in his Eloquence
As *Cicero*, the famous man of *Rome*,
His wordes would be as chaffe against the winde.
Sweete tong'd *Vlisses* that made *Aiaxe* mad,
Were he and his toung in this speakers head,
Aliue he winnes me not; then, tis no conquest dead.

Enter Cromwell *like a* Neopolitan, *and* Hodge *with him.*

Cro. Sir, are you the maister of the house?

Hoa. I am, sir.

Cro. By this same token you must leaue this place,
And leaue none but the Earle and I together,
And this my Pessant here to tend on vs.

Hoa. With al my hart. God grant, you doe some good.
[*Exit Hoast.* Cromwell *shuts the dore.*

Bed. Now, sir, whats your will with me?

Cro. Intends your honour not to yeeld your selfe?

Bed. No, good man goose, not while my sword doth last.
Is this your eloquence for to perswade me?

Cro. My Lord, my eloquence is for to saue you.
I am not, as you iudge, a *Neopolitan*,
But *Cromwell*, your seruant, and an Englishman.

Bed. How? *Cromwel*? not my Farriers sonne?

Cro. The same, sir, and am come to succour you.

Hod. Yes, faith, sir; and I am *Hodge*, your poore Smith. Many a time and oft haue I shooed your Dapper Gray.

Bed. And what auailes it me that thou art here?

Cro. It may auaile, if youle be rul'd by me.
My Lord, you know the men of *Mantua*

104–9 *Verse Qq, Ff: corr. M* 115 Bandetti *Ff* Scene II. *etc. add. M* 5 skir *conj. St.* 26 *S. D. after* 27 *Qq, Ff: corr. M* 57–9 *Verse Qq, Ff, div.* Smith 59 dapple-grey *M*

And these *Bononians* are at deadlie strife,
And they, my Lord, both loue and honour you.
Could you but get out of the *Mantua* port,
Then were you safe dispite of all their force.

Bed. Tut, man, thou talkest of thinges impossible.
Dost thou not see that we are round beset?
How, then, is it possible we should escape?

Crom. By force we cannot, but by pollicie.
Put on the apparell here that *Hodge* doth weare,
And giue him yours—the States, they know you not,
For, as I thinke, they neuer saw your face—
And at a watch-word must I call them in,
And will desire, that we safe may passe
To *Mantua,* where Ile say my businesse lies.
How doth your Honor like of this deuise?

Bed. O wondrous good! But wilt thou venter, *Hodge*?

Hod. Will I?—
O noble Lord, I do accorde,
In anything I can,
And do agree, to set thee free,
Do fortune what she can.

Bed. Come, then, lets change our apparrell straight.

Crom. Goe, *Hodge*; make hast, least they chance to call.

Hod. I warrant you ile fit him with a sute.

[*Exit* Earle *&* Hodge.

Crom. Heauens graunt this pollicie doth take successe,
And that the Earle may safelie scape away.
And yet it greeues me for this simple wretch,
For feare they should offer him violence:
But of two euils, tis best to shun the greatest,
And better is it that he liues in thrall,
Then such a Noble Earle as he should fall.
Their stubborne harts, it may be, will relent,
Since he is gone to whom their hate is bent.—
My Lord, haue you dispatched?

Enter Bedford *like the Clowne, and* Hodge *in his cloake and his Hat.*

Bed. How doost thou like vs, *Cromwell*? is it well?

Crom. O, my Lord, excellent; *Hodge*, how doost feele thy selfe?

Hodg. How do I feele my selfe? why, as a Noble man should do. O, how I feele honor come creeping on! My Nobilitie is wonderfull melancholie: Is it not most Gentleman like to be melancholie?

Crom. Yes, *Hodge*; now goe sitte downe in his studie, and take state vpon thee.

Hodge. I warrant you, my Lord; let me alone to take state vpon me: but harke you, my Lord, do you feele nothing bite about you?

Bed. No, trust me, *Hodge.*

Hod. I, they know they want their pasture; its a strange thing of this vermine, they dare not meddle with Nobilitie.

Crom. Go, take thy place, *Hodge*; Ile call them in.—

[Hodge *sits in the study, and* Cromwell *calles in the States.*

All is done, enter and if you please.

Enter the States and Officers, with Halberts.

Gou. What, haue you wone him? will he yeelde himselfe?

Crom. I haue, an't please you, and the quiet Earle
Doth yeeld himselfe to be disposed by you.

Gou. Giue him the monie that we promised him;
So let him go, whether it please himselfe.

Crom. My businesse, sir, lies vnto *Mantua,*
Please you to giue me safe conduct thether.

Gou. Goe and conduct him to the *Mantua* Port,
And see him safe deliuered presently.

[*Exit* Cromwell *and* Bedford.

Goe draw the curtaines, let vs see the Earle.—
O, he is writing; stand apart awhile.

Hodge. Fellow William, I am not as I haue beene: I went from you a Smith, I write to you as a Lord. I am, at this present writing, among the Polonyan Sasiges. I do commend my Lordship to Raphe & to Roger, to Bridget & to Doritie, & so to all the youth of Putnay.

Gou. Sure, these are the names of English Noblemen,
Some of his speciall friends, to whom he writes:
But stay, he doth adresse himselfe to sing.

[*Here he sings a song.*

My Lord, I am glad you are so frolick and so blithe:
Beleeue me, noble Lord, if you knew all,
Youde change your merrie vaine to sudden sorrow.

Hodg. I change my merrie vaine? no, thou *Bononian,* no.
I am a Lord—and therefore let me goe—

75 we two safe *Q 2, etc.* 79-83 *Two lines Qq, Ff, dir. after* I can 84 and change we our *S* 85 should chance *M* 90 fear lest they *M* 92 liue *Q 2, etc.* 93 he] this *S* 99 my good Lord, *Ff, etc.* 101-7 *Verse Qq, Ff*

106 go and sit *S* 107 his] the *Q 2, F 1, M*: thy *F 2, R, Pope* 112 their old pasture *Q 2, etc.* 116 Now all *M* 118 an't *Q 2*: ante *Q 1* 121 it] he *Ff* 123 a safe *M* 131 sausages *M*: Casiges *Qq, Ff*: cossacks *conj. Percy*

And doe defie thee and thy Sasigis;
Therefore stand off, and come not neere my honor.
Gou. My Lord, this iesting cannot serue your turne.
Hod. Doost thinke, thou blacke *Bononyan* beast,
That I doe floute, doe gibe, or iest,
No, no, thou Beare-pot, know that I,
A noble Earle, a Lord pardie—
A Trumpet soundes.
Gou. What meanes this Trumpets sound?

Enter a Messenger.

Cit. One come from the States of *Mantua.*
Gou. What would you with vs? speake, thou man of *Mantua.*
Mes. Men of *Bononia,* this my message is:
To let you know the Noble Earle of *Bedford*
Is safe within the towne of *Mantua,*
And willes you send the pessant that you haue,
Who hath deceiued your expectation;
Or els the States of *Mantua* haue vowed
They will recall the truce that they haue made,
And not a man shall stirre from forth your towne,
That shall returne, vnlesse you send him backe.
Go. O this misfortune, how it mads my hart!
The *Neopolitan* hath beguiled vs all.
Hence with this foole! what shall we do with him,
The Earle being gone? a plague vpon it all.
Hod. No, ile assure you, I am no Earle, but a smith, sir;
One *Hodge,* a smith at Putnay, sir;
One that hath gulled you, that hath bored you, sir.
Gou. Away with him! take hence the foole you came for.
Hod. I, sir, and ile leaue the greater foole with you.
Mes. Farewell, *Bononians.* Come, friend, a long with me.
Hod. My friend, afore; my Lordship will follow thee. [*Exit.*
Gou. Well, *Mantua,* since by thee the Earle is lost,
Within few dayes I hope to see thee crosd. [*Exit omnes.*

Enter Chorus.

Cho. Thus farre you see how *Cromwelles* fortune passed.
The Earle of *Bedford,* being safe in *Mantua,*
Desires *Cromwells* companie into France,
To make requitall for his courtesie:
But *Cromwell* doth denie the Earle his sute,
And telles him that those partes he meant to see,
He had not yet set footing on the land,
And so directlie takes his way to Spaine:
The Earle to France, and so they both do part.
Now let your thoughtes, as swift as is the winde,
Skip some few yeares, that *Cromwell* spent in trauell,
And now imagine him to be in England,
Seruant vnto the maister of the Roules,
Where in short time he there beganne to florish.
An houre shall show you what few yeares did cherish. [*Exit.*

⟨SCENE III. *London. A room in Sir Christopher Hales's house.*⟩

The Musick playes, they bring out the banquet. Enter Sir Christopher Hales, *and* Cromwell, *and two seruants.*

Hales. Come, sirs, be carefull of your maisters credit,
And as our bountie now exceedes the figure
Of common entertainment: so do you
With lookes as free as is your maisters soule,
Giue formall welcome to the thronged tables,
That shall receiue the Cardinals followers
And the attendants of the Lord Chancellor.
But all my care, *Cromwell,* depends on thee.
Thou art a man differing from vulgar forme,
And by how much thy spirit is ranckt boue these
In rules of Arte, by so much it shines brighter
By trauell whose obseruance pleades his merit,
In a most learned, yet vnaffecting spirit.
Good *Cromwell,* cast an eye of faire regarde
Bout all my house, and what this ruder flesh,
Through ignorance, or wine, do miscreate,
Salue thou with curtesie: if welcome want,
Full bowles and ample banquets will seeme scant.
Crom. Sir, what soeuer lies in me,
Assure ⟨you⟩, I will shew my vtmost dutie. [*Exit* Crom.
Hales. About it, then; the Lords will straight be here.—
Cromwell, thou hast those parts would rather sute
The seruice of the state, then of my house.

142 I do *M* Casiges *Ff* 147–8 *One line Qq* : *corr. Ff* *S. D. after* 149 *Qq, Ff* : *corr. M* 150 is come *M* 165–7 *Prose M*

187 he there *Q 2, etc.*: where he *Q 1* 188 nourish *conj. St.* Scene III. *etc. add. M* 5 former *Q 1* 7 the great Lord *Q 2, etc.* 11 *Ends* trauell *Qq, Ff* : *corr. M* 12 his] thy *S* 13 unaffected *S* 19 Sir, as to *M* 20 you *add. Q 2* 21 striaght *Q 1*

I looke vpon thee with a louing eye,
That one day will prefer thy destinie.

Enter Messenger.

Mess. Sir, the Lords be at hand.
Hales. They are welcome; bid *Cromwell* straight attend vs,
And looke you all things be in perfect readinesse.

The Musicke layes. Enter Cardinall Wolsay, *Sir* Thomas Moore *and* Gardiner.

Wol. O, sir *Christopher*,
You are too liberall. What, a banket to?
Hal. My Lordes, if wordes could show the ample welcome,
That my free hart affordes you, I could then
Become a prater, but I now must deale
Like a feast *Polititian* with your Lordshippes:
Deferre your welcome till the banket end,
That it may then salue our defect of faire:
Yet Welcome now and all that tend on you.
Wol. Thankes to the kinde maister of the Roules.
Come and sit downe; sit downe, sir *Thomas Moore.*
Tis strange, how that we and the Spaniard differ.
Their dinner is our banquet after dinner,
And they are men of actiue disposition.
This I gather: that by their sparing meate
Their bodie is more fitter for the warres,
And if that famine chance to pinch their mawes,
Being vsde to fast it breedes lesse paine.
Hal. Fill me some Wine: Ile answere Cardinall *Wolsay.*
My Lord, we English are of more freer soules
Then hungerstarued and ill complexioned spaniardes.
They that are rich in Spaine spare bellie foode,
To deck their backes with an Italian hoode,
And Silkes of Ciuill: And the poorest Snake,
That feedes on Lemmons, Pilchers, and neare heated
His pallet with sweete flesh, will beare a case
More fat and gallant then his starued face.
Pride, the Inquisition, and this bellie euill,
Are, in my iudgement, Spaines three headed diuell.
Mo. Indeede it is a plague vnto their nation,
Who stager after in blinde imitation.
Hal. My Lords, with welcome, I present your Lordships
A sollemne health.
Mo. I loue health well, but when ⟨as⟩ healthes doe bring
Paine to the head and bodies surfeting,
Then cease I healthes.—
Nay, spill not, friend, for though the drops be small,
Yet haue they force, to force men to the wall.
Wol. Sir *Christopher,* is that your man?
Hal. And like your grace; he is a Scholler and
A *Lingest,* one that hath trauelled manie partes
Of Christendome, my Lorde.
Wol. My friend, come nearer; haue you beene a traueller?
Cro. My Lord, I haue added to my knowledge the loe Countries,
France, Spaine, Germanie, and *Italie*:
And though small gaine of profit I did finde,
Yet did it please my eye, content my minde.
Wol. What doe you thinke of the seuerall states
And princes Courtes as you haue trauelled?
Cro. My Lord, no Court with England may compare,
Neither for state nor ciuill gouernement:
Lust dwelles in *France*, in *Italie,* and *Spaine,*
From the poore pesant to the Princes traine,
In *Germanie* and *Holland* riot serues,
And he that most can drinke, most he deserues:
England I praise not, for I here was borne,
But that she laugheth the others vnto scorne.
Wol. My Lord, there dwelles within that spirite
More then can be discerned by outwarde eye.
Sir *Cristopher,* will you part with your man?
Hal. I haue sought to proffer him to your Lordship,
And now I see he hath preferred himselfe.
Wol. What is thy name?
Crom. *Cromwell,* my Lorde.
Wol. Then, *Cromwell,* here we make thee
Solliciter of our causes, and nearest next our
selfe. Gardiner giue you kinde welcome to the
man.

Gardiner *imbraces him.*

Mo. My Lorde, you are a royall Winer,
Haue got a man besides your bountious dinner.
Well, Knight, praie we come no more:

28 perfect *om. S* 29–30 *One line Qq* : *corr. M* 32–5 *Three lines, div. after* prater, Polititian *Qq, F1* : *Prose F2, R* : *corr. M* 38 Our thanks *M* 43 By this *Molt.* 44 is *om. Q2* : bodies are *Ff, etc.* 46 breeds in them less *M* 48 English *M* : Spaniardes *Q1* : Englishmen *Q2, Ff* 59 Who] And *Q1*

62 love healths *M* as *add. Q2* 64 *Ends* friend *Qq, Ff* 68–70 *Two lines Qq, Ff, div. after* Lingest 73 With France *M* 76 think then of *M* 85 that she laughs *M* : sure she laughs *Haz.* 86 *Ends* more *M* 87 by] by the *M* 89 to your] unto your *M* 93–5 *Verse edd.* : *div.* causes *Qq, Ff* : *div.* solicitor *M* 93–6 *Verse Qq* 97 My lord cardinal *M* 98 Have *M* : Hath *Qq* 99 Well, my good knight *M* pray that we *M*

If we come often, thou maist shut thy doore.
Wol. Sir *Christopher*, hadst thou giuen me halfe thy landes,
Thou couldest not haue pleased me so much as with
This man of thine. My infant thoughtes do spell:
Shortlie his fortune shall be lifted higher;
True industrie doth kindle honours fier.
And so, kinde maister of the Roules, farewell.
Hal. *Cromwell*, farewell.
Cro. *Cromwell* takes his leaue of you,
That neare will leaue to loue and honour you.
[*Exit omnes. The Musicke playes, as they go in.*

⟨ACT IV.⟩

Enter Chorus.

Cho. Now *Cromwells* highest fortunes doth begin.
Wolsay, that loued him as he did his life,
Committed all his treasure to his hands.
Wolsay is dead, and *Gardiner*, his man,
Is now created Bishop of *Winchester*:
Pardon if we omit all *Wolsayes* life,
Because our play dependes on *Cromwelles* death.
Now sit and see his highest state of all;
His haight of rysing and his sodaine fall.
Pardon the errors is all readie past,
And liue in hope the best doth come at last:
My hope vpon your fauour doth depend,
And looke to haue your liking ere the end.
[*Exit.*

⟨SCENE I. *The same. A publick walk.*⟩

Enter Gardiner *Bishop of* Winchester, *The Dukes of* Norffolke, *and of* Suffolke, *Sir* Thomas Moore, *Sir* Christopher Halles, *and* Cromwell.

Nor. Maister *Cromwell*, since Cardinall *Wolsayes* death,
His maiestie is giuen to vnderstand
Theres certaine billes and writings in your hand,
That much concernes the state of England.
My Lord of *Winchester*, is it not so?
Gar. My Lord of *Norfolke*, we two weare whilom fellowes;
And, maister *Cromwell*, though our maisters loue
Did binde vs, while his loue was to the King,
It is no boote now to denie these things,
Which may be preiuditiall to the state:
And though that God hath raisde my fortune hyer
Then any way I lookt for or deseru'de,
Yet my life no longer with me dwell,
Then I prooue true vnto my Soueraigne:
What say you, maister *Cromwell*? haue you those writings?
I, or no?
Crom. Here are the writings, and vpon my knees,
I giue them vp vnto the worthy Dukes
Of Suffolke and of Norffolke: he was my Maister,
And each vertuous part,
That liued in him, I tenderd with my hart;
But what his head complotted gainst the state
My countries loue commands me that to hate.
His sudden death I greeue for, not his fall,
Because he sought to worke my countries thrall.
Suff. *Cromwell*, the King shall here of this thy dutie,
Whom I assure my selfe will well rewarde thee:
My Lord lets go vnto his Maiestie,
And show these writings which he longs to see.
[*Exit* Norffolke *and* Suffolke.

Enter Bedford *hastily.*

Bed. How now, whose this?
Cromwell, by my soule! welcome to England:
Thou once didst saue my life, didst not *Cromwell*?
Crom. If I did so, 'tis greater glorie for me,
That you remember it, then of my selfe
Vainelie to report it.
Bed. Well, *Cromwell*, now is the time,
I shall commend thee to my Soueraigne:
Cheere vp thy selfe, for I will raise thy state.
A *Russell* yet was neuer found ingrate. [*Exit.*
Hales. O how vncertaine is the wheele of state.
Who latelie greater then the Cardinall,
For feare, and loue? and now who lower lies?
Gaye honours are but Fortunes flatteries,
And whom this day pride and promotion swels,
To morrow enuie and ambition quels.
More. Who sees the Cob-web intangle the poore Flie,
May boldlie say the wretches death is nigh.

100 thou maist shut *Q 2, etc.*: or shut vp *Q 1*   101 hadst *Q 2, etc.*: haddest hadst *Q 1*   101 ff. *End Qq, Ff* me, me, thine, spell : *corr. M*   *S. D.* The Musick . . go in *after* Enter Chorus *Qq, Ff*   Act IV. *add. M*   1 doth] do *F 2*   10 is] are *F 2*   13 looks *M*   Scene I. *etc. add. M*   4 concern *F 2*   the present state *S*   13 Yet may my *M*   15–16 *One line Qq*: *Prose, given to* Suff. *Ff*   17–19 *End* writings, unto, Norfolk *M*   17 vpon] on *M*   27 Who *M*   30 *Ends* Cromwell *Qq, Ff*: soul *M*   31 my] by *Q 1*   33–5 *Two lines Qq, F 1, div. after* remember it   34 of] for *Q 2, etc.*   46 tangle *M*

Gard. I knew his state and proud ambition
Was too too violent to last ouer-long.
Hales. Who soares too neare the sunne with golden winges,
Meàltes them, to ruine his owne fortune bringes.

Enter the Duke of Suffolke.

Suf. *Cromwell,* kneele downe in king *Henries* name.—
Arise sir *Thomas Cromwell*; thus beginnes thy fame.

Enter the Duke of Norffolke.

Norf. *Cromwell*, the maiestie of England,
For the good liking he conceiues of thee,
Makes thee maister of the iewell house,
Chiefe Secretarie to himselfe, and with all,
Creates thee one of his highnesse priuie Counsell.

Enter the Earle *of* Bedforde.

Bed. Where is sir *Thomas Cromwell*? is he knighted?
Suf. He is, my Lorde.
Bed. Then to adde honour to his name,
The King creates him Lord keeper of
His priuie Seale, and maister of the Roules,
Which you sir *Christopher* do now enioy;
The King determines higher place for you.
Crom. My Lords,
These honors are too high for my desert.
More. O content thee, man; who would not choose it?
Yet thou art wise in seeming to refuse it.
Gard. Heres honors, titles, and promotions:
I feare this climing will haue a sudden fall.
Norff. Then come, my Lords; lets altogether bring
This new made Counseller to Englands King.
[*Exit all but* Gardiner.
Gard. But *Gardiner* meanes his glorie shall be dimde.
Shall *Cromwell* liue a greater man then I?
My enuie with his honour now is bred;
I hope to shorten *Cromwell* by the head. [*Exit.*

⟨Scene II. *London. A street before Cromwell's House.*⟩

Enter Friskiball *very poore.*

Fris. O *Friskiball,* what shall become of thee?
Where shalt thou go, or which way shalt thou turne?
Fortune, that turnes her too vnconstant wheele,
Hath turn'd thy wealth and riches in the Sea.
All parts abroade where euer I haue beene
Growes wearie of me, and denies me succour;
My debters, they that should releeue my want,
Forsweares my monie, saies they owe me none:
They know my state too meane to beare out law,
And here in London, where I oft haue beene,
And haue done good to manie a wretched man,
⟨I⟩ Am now most wretched here, dispisd my selfe.
In vaine it is, more of their hearts to trie;
Be patient, therefore, laye thee downe and die.
[*He lies downe.*

Enter good man Seely, *and his wife* Ioane.

Seely. Come, *Ioane,* come; lets see what heele doe for vs now. Iwis we haue done for him, when many a time and often he might haue gone a hungrie to bed.

Wife. Alas, man, now he is made a Lord, heele neuer looke vpon vs; heele fullfill the old Prouerbe: Set Beggers a horse-backe, and theile ride.—A, welliday for my Cowe! such as he hath made vs come behinde hand: we had neuer pawnd our Cowe els to pay our rent.

Seely. Well, *Ioane,* heele come this waye: and by Gods dickers, ile tell him roundlie of it, and if hee were tenne Lordes: a shall knowe that I had not my Cheese and my Bacon for nothing.

Wife. Doe you remember, husband, how hee woulde mouch vp my Cheese cakes? he hath forgot this now, but weele remember him.

Seelie. I, we shall haue now three flappes with a Foxe taile: but, I faith, ile gibber a ioynte, but ile tell him his owne. Staye, who comes heere? O stand vppe; heere hee comes; stand vppe.

Enter Hodge *verie fine with a Tipstafe:* Cromwell, *the Mace caryed before him:* Norffolke, *and* Suffolke, *and attendants.*

Hod. Come, away with these beggars here; rise vp, sirra.
Come, out the good people: runne afore there, ho!
[Friskiball *riseth, and stands a farre off.*

Seelie. I, wee are kicked awaye, now wee come for our owne; the time hath beene he woulde a looked more friendlye vpon vs. And

48 know *Qq, Ff* 49 were *M* 54 the gracious majesty *M* 56 thee the master *M* 61–2 *End* honour to, keeper *M* 62 *Ends* Seale *Qq, Ff* 62 him] him the *M* 66–7 *One line Qq, Ff* Scene II. etc. *add. M*

4 Hath drown'd *S* 12 Am *Qq*: And *Ff*: I am *M* here] and *S* 32 but now weel *Q 2, etc.*

you, *Hodge,* we know you well inough, though you are so fine.

Cro. Come hether, sirrah.—Stay, what men are these?
My honest Host of Hounslow and his wife!
I owe thee mony, father, do I not?

Seelie. I, by the bodie of mee, dooest thou. Woulde thou wouldest paye me: good foure pound it is, I haue a the poste at home.

Cro. I know tis true. Sirra, giue him ten Angels:
And looke your wife and you do stay to dinner:
And while you liue, I freelie giue to you
Foure pound a yeare, for the foure pound I ought you.

Seelie. Art not changed, art ould *Tom* still! Now God blesse the good Lord *Tom.* Home, *Ioane,* home; ile dine with my Lorde *Tom* to day, and thou shalt come next weeke. Fetch my Cow; home, *Ioane,* home.

Wife. Now God blesse thee, my good Lorde *Tom;* Ile fetch my Cow presentlie. [*Exit Wife.*

Enter Gardiner.

Cro. Sirra, goe to yon stranger; tell him I
Desire him stay at dinner. I must speake
With him.

Gar. My Lorde of *Norffolke,* see you this same bubble,
That same puffe? but marke the end, my Lord,
Marke the ende.

Nor. I promise you, I like not somthing he hath done,
But let that passe; the King doth loue him well.

Cro. Go⟨o⟩d morrow to my Lord of *Winchester.*
I know you beare me hard about the Abbie landes.

Gar. Haue I not reason, when religion is wronged?
You had no colour for what you haue done.

Cro. Yes; the abolishing of Antichrist,
And of this Popish order from our Realme.
I am no enemy to religion,
But what is done, it is for Englands good.
What did they serue for but to feede a sort
Of lazie Abbotes and of full fed Fryers?
They neither plow, nor sowe, and yet they reape
The fat of all the Land, and sucke the poore:
Looke, what was theirs, is in King *Henries* handes;
His wealth before lay in the Abbie lands.

Gar. Indeede these things you haue aledged, my Lord,
When God doth know the infant yet vnborne
Will curse the time the Abbies were puld downe.
I pray, now where is hospitality?
Where now may poore distressed people go,
For to releeue their neede, or rest their bones,
When weary trauell doth oppresse their limmes?
And where religious men should take them in,
Shall now be kept backe with a Mastiue dogge,
And thousand thousand—

Nor. O, my Lord, no more: thinges past redresse
Tis bootelesse to complaine.

Cro. What, shall we to the Conuocation house?

Nor. Weele follow you, my Lord; praie, leade the way.

Enter Old Cromwell *like a Farmer.*

Old. Cro. How? one *Cromwell* made Lord Keeper since I left Putnay
And dwelt in Yorkeshire. I neuer hard better newes:
Ile see that *Cromwell,* or it shall goe hard.

Cro. My aged father! state set aside,
Father, on my knee I craue your blessing:
One of my seruantes go and haue him in;
At better leasure will we talke with him.

Old. Cro. Now if I die, how happy were the day!
To see this comfort raines forth showers of ioy.
[*Exit Olde Cromwell*

Nor. This dutie in him showes a kinde of grace.

Cro. Go on before, for time drawes on apace. [*Exit all but* Friskiball.

Fris. I wonder what this Lord would haue with me,
His man so stricktlie gaue me charge to stay:
I neuer did offend him to my knowledge.
Well, good or bad, I meane to bide it all;
Worse then I am now neuer can befall.

Enter Banister *and his wife.*

Ba. Come, wife, I take it be almost dinner time,
For maister *Newton,* and maister *Crosbie* sent
To me last night, they would come dine with me,
And take their bond in: I pray thee, hie thee home,
And see that all things be in readinesse.

50 hav't *M* 55 ff. *Verse Qq, Ff : corr. M* 56 thee, good *Ff, etc.* 62–4 *Two lines Qq, div. after* desire him : *corr. M* 63 at] to *Q 2, etc.* 66–7 *One line Q 1* 66 That same] That's a mere *S* 70 *Ends* know *M* 94 *Ends* more *M* 97 follow *Q 2, etc.* : fellow *Q 1* 98–100 *Prose M* 101 state then set *M* 102 on] upon *M* 114 be] to be *M* *Two lines M* 115 *Ends* to me *Qq, Ff* : *corr. M*

Mi. Ba. They shalbe welcome, husband; ile go before.—
But is not that man maister *Friskiball*?
[*She runnes and imbrases him.*
Ba. O heauens, it is kinde maister *Friskiball*!
Say sir, what hap hath brought you to this passe?
Fris. The same that brought you to your misery.
Ba. Why would you not acquaint me with your state?
Is *Banister* your poore friend quite forgot:
Whose goods, whose loue, whose life and all is yours?
Fri. I thought your vsage would be as the rest,
That had more kindnesse at my handes then you,
Yet looked asconce, when as they saw me poore.
Mi. Ba. If *Banister* should beare so bace a hart,
I neuer would looke my husband in the face,
But hate him as I would a Cockatrise.
Ba. And well thou mightest, should *Banister* deale so.
Since that I saw you, sir, my state is mended:
And for the thousand pound I owe to you,
I haue it ready for you, sir, at home;
And though I greeue your fortune is so bad,
Yet that my hap's to helpe you makes me glad.
And now, sir, will it please you walke with me?
Fris. Not yet I cannot, for the Lord Chancelour
Hath here commaunded me to waight on him,
For what I know not: pray God tis for my good.
Ba. Neuer make doubt of that; ile warrant you,
He is as kinde a noble gentleman
As euer did possesse the place he hath.
Mi. Ba. Sir, my brother is his steward; if you please,
Weale go along and beare you company:
I know we shall not want for welcome there.
Fris. With all my hart: but whats become of *Bagot*?
Ba. He is hanged, for buying iewels of the Kinges.
Fris. A iust reward for one so impious.
The time drawes on, sir; will you go along?
Ba. Ile follow you, kinde maister *Friskiball*.
[*Exit Omnes.*

⟨Scene III. *The same. Another street.*⟩

Enter two Marchants.

1. Now, maister *Crosbie*, I see you haue a care,
To keepe your word, in paiment of your monie.
2. By my faith, I haue reason vpon a bond;
Three thousand pound is too much to forfeit.
Yet I doubt not Maister *Banister*.
1. By my faith, your summe is more then mine,
And yet I am not much behinde you too,
Considering that to day I paid at court.
2. Masse, and well remembred,
Whats the reason the Lord *Cromwels* men
Weare such long skirts vpon their coates.
They reach almost downe to their verie ham.
1. I will resolue you, sir; and thus it is:
The Bishop of *Winchester*, that loues not *Cromwell*,
As great men are enuied, as well as lesse—
A while agoe there was a iarre betweene them,
And it was brought to my Lord *Cromwels* eare,
That Bishop *Gardiner* would sit on his skirt;
Vpon which word, he made his men long Blew coates,
And in the Court wore one of them himselfe:
And meeting with the Bishop, quoth he, 'My Lord,
Here's skirt enough now for your Grace to sit on;'
Which vexed the Bishop to the very hart.
This is the reason why they weare long coates.
2. Tis alwaies seene, and marke it for a rule,
That one great man will enuie still another:
But tis a thing that nothing concernes me.
What, shall we now to Maister *Banisters*?
1. I, come, weele pay him royally for our dinner. [*Exit.*

⟨Scene IV. *The same. A room in Cromwell's house.*⟩

Enter the Vsher *and the* Shewer, *the meate goes ouer the Stage.*

Vsher. Vncouer there, Gentlemen.

Enter Cromwell, Bedford, Suffolke, *Old* Cromwell, Friskiball, *goodman* Seelie, *and attendants.*

Crom. My noble Lordes of *Suffolke* and of *Bedford*,

125 quite *om.* *Q2*, *Ff*: then forgot *M* 130 should] would *F2*, *etc.* 142 tis . . my] it be for *Q2*, *etc.*

Scene III. *etc. add. M* *S. D.* Enter Newton and Crosby *M* 3 vpon] on *M* 4 is far too *M* 5 And yet *M* 6 faith, sir, your *M* 9–12 *Three lines M, div. after* reason, upon 10 the Lord] Lord *M* 12 almost *om.* *Q2*, *etc.* 18 skirts *Q2*, *etc.* 22 skirts *Ff*, *etc.* Scene IV. *etc. add. M*

Your honors welcome to poore *Cromwels* house.
Where is my father? nay, be couered, Father.
Although that duty to these noble men
Doth challenge it, yet ile make bolde with them.
Your head doth beare the callender of care.
What, *Cromwell* couered and his Father bare!
It must not be. Now, sir, to you. Is not
Your name *Friskiball* and a *Florentine*?

Fris. My name was *Friskiball*, till cruell fate
Did rob me of my name and of my state.

Crom. What fortune brought you to this countrie now?

Fri. All other parts hath left me succorlesse,
Saue onelie this. Because of debts I haue,
I hope to gaine for to releeue my want.

Crom. Did you not once, vpon your *Florence* bridge,
Helpe two distressed men, robd by the Bandetti?—
His name was *Cromwell*.

Fri. I neuer made my braine a calender
Of any good I did;
I alwaies lou'd this nation with my heart.

Crom. I am that *Cromwell* that you there releeued.
Sixteene Duckets you gaue me for to cloath me,
Sixteene to beare my charges by the way,
And sixteene more I had for my horse hier:
There be those seuerall summes iustlie returnd,
Yet with iniustice, seruing at my need,
And to repay them without interest.
Therefore receiue of me these foure seuerall bags;
In each of them there is foure hundred marke;
And bring me the names of all your debitors,
And if they will not see you paide, I will:
O God forbid, that I should see him fall,
That helpt me in my greatest need of all.
Here stands my Father that first gaue me life,
Alas, what dutie is too much for him?
This man in time of need did saue my life,
And therefore ⟨I⟩ cannot do too much for him.
By this old man I often times was fed,
Els might I haue gone supperlesse to bed.
Such kindnesse haue I had of these three men,
That *Cromwell* no way can repaie againe.
Now in to dinner, for we stay too long,
And to good stomacks is no greater wrong.

[*Exit omnes.*

⟨SCENE V. *The same. A room in the Bishop of Winchester's house.*⟩

Enter Gardiner *in his studie, and his man.*

Gard. Sirra, where be those men I causd to stay?

Ser. They do attend your pleasure, sir, within.

Gard. Bid them come hether, and stay you without:—
For by those men, the Foxe of this same land,
That makes a Goose of better then himselfe,
Weele worie him vnto his latest home,
Or *Gardiner* will faile in his intent.
As for the Dukes of *Suffolke* and of *Norffolke,*
Whom I haue sent for to come speake with me,
Howsoeuer outwardlie they shadow it,
Yet in their hearts I know they loue him not:
As for the Earle of *Bedford,* he is but one,
And dares not gaine-say what we do set downe.

Enter the two witnesses.

Now, my friends, you know I sau'd your liues,
When by the law you had deserued death,
And then you promised me vpon your othes,
To venture both your liues to do me good.

Both wit. We swore no more then that we will performe,

Gard. I take your words; and that which you must do
Is seruice for your God, and for your King:
To roote a rebell from this flourishing land,
One thats an enemie vnto the Church:
And therefore must you take your solemne oathes,
That you heard *Cromwell,* the Lord Chauncellor,
Did wish a dagger at King *Henries* hart.
Feare not to sweare it, for I hard him speake it;
Therefore weele shield you from insuing harmes.

2. *Wit.* If you will warrant vs the deed is good,
Weele vndertake it.

Gar. Kneele downe, and I wil here absolue you both.
This Crucifix I lay vpon your head,
And sprinckle holy-water on your browes.
The deed is meritorious that you do,

3 are welcome *M* 5 *Ends* challenge it *Qq, Ff*: *corr. M* 9 *Ends* to you *Qq, Ff*: *corr. M* 18 two] a *Q 2, etc.* men] man *Ff, etc.* Bandetto *Qq* 20–1 *One line Qq, F 1*: *div. after* brain *F 2* 28 with iniustice] it iniustice were that *Q 2, etc.* 29 And to *Q 1*: For to *Q 2, Ff*: to *M*: And I *conj. pr. ed.* them] thee *M* 30 these *om. M* foure *om. S* 32 me] to me *Q 2, etc.* debtors *Q 2, etc.* 39 And] I *M* I *add. pr. ed.*

Scene V. *etc. add. M* 6 Must woried be *Q 2, etc.* 14 my good friends *M* 20 you God *Q 1* 31 heads *Q 2, etc.*

And by it shall you purchase grace from heauen.
1. Now, sir, weele vndertake it, by our soules.
2. For *Cromwell* neuer loued none of our sort.
Gar. I know he doth not, and for both of you,
I will preferre you to some place of worth:
Now get you in, vntill I call for you,
For presentlie the Dukes meanes to be here.
[*Exit wit.*
Cromwell, sit fast, thy time's not long to raigne.
The Abbies that were puld downe by thy meanes
Is now a meane for me to pull thee downe:
Thy pride also thy owne head lights vpon,
For thou art he hath changd religion:—
But now no more, for here the Dukes are come.

Enter Suffolke, Norffolke, *and the Earle of* Bedford.

Suff. Goodden to my Lord Bishop.
Nor. How fares my Lord? what, are you all alone?
Gar. No, not alone, my Lords; my mind is troubled;
I know your honours muse wherefore I sent,
And in such hast. What, came you from the King?
Norff. We did, and left none but Lord *Cromwell* with him.
Gard. O, what a dangerous time is this we liue in!
Theres *Thomas Wolsay,* hees alreadie gone,
And *Thomas Moore,* he followed after him:
Another *Thomas* yet there doth remaine,
That is farre worsse then either of those twaine,
And if with speed, my Lords, we not pursue it,
I feare the King and all the land will rue it.
Bed. Another *Thomas*! pray God it be not *Cromwell.*
Gard. My Lord of *Bedford,* it is that traitor *Cromwell.*
Bed. Is *Cromwell* false? my hart will neuer thinke it.
Suff. My Lord of *Winchester,* what likelihood,
Or proofe haue you of this his treacherie?
Gar. My Lord, too much.—Call in the men within.

Enter witnesses.

These men, my Lord, vpon their othes affirme,
That they did here Lord *Cromwell* in his garden,
Wished a dagger sticking at the hart
Of our King *Henrie.* What is this but treason?
Bed. If it be so, my hart doth bleed with sorrow.
Suff. How say you friends? what, did you here these words?
1. wit. We did, and like your grace.
Norff. In what place was Lord *Cromwell* when he spake them?
2. wit. In his Garden, where we did attend a sute,
Which we had waited for two yeare and more.
Suff. How long ist since you heard him speake these words?
2. wit. Some halfe yeare since.
Bed. How chance that you conceald it all this time?
1. wit. His greatnesse made vs feare, that was the cause.
Gard. I, I, his greatnesse; thats the cause indeed;
And to make his treason here more manifest,
He calles his seruants to him round about,
Telles them of *Wolsayes* life, and of his fall,
Saies that himselfe hath manie enemies,
And giues to some of them a Parke or Manor,
To others Leases, Lands to other some:
What need he doe thus in his prime of life,
And if he were not fearfull of his death?
Suff. My Lord, these likelihoods are very great.
Bed. Pardon me, Lords, for I must needs depart;
Their proofes are great, but greater is my heart. [*Exit* Bedford.
Norff. My friends, take heed of that which you haue said.
Your soules must answer what your tongues reports:
Therefore, take heed, be warie what you doe.
2. wit. My Lord, we speake no more but truth.
Norff. Let them
Depart.—My Lord of *Winchester,* let these men
Be close kept vntill the day of triall.
Gar. They shall, my Lord: hoe, take in these two men. [*Exit witnesses.*
My Lords, if *Cromwell* haue a publike triall,
That which we do is voide by his deniall:
You know the king will credit none but him.
Nor. Tis true, he rules the King euen as he pleases.
Suff. How shall we do for to attache him, then?

44 also *Q2, etc.* : vpon *Q1*   47 Good euen *Q2, etc.*   68 Wishing *M*   87 thus] this *S*   95–8 *End* truth, Winchester, kept, trial *Qq, Ff*: *corr. M*   96 them] him *conj. M*   97 let] and let *M*

Gard. Marie, my Lords, thus: by an Acte he made himselfe,
With an intent to intrap some of our liues,
And this it is: If any Councellor
Be conuicted of high treason, he shall
Be executed without a publike triall.
This Act, my Lords, he causd the King to make.
Suff. A did indeed, and I remember it,
And now it is like to fall vpon himselfe.
Nor. Let vs not slack it, tis for Englands good.
We must be warie, els heele go beyond vs.
Gar. Well hath your Grace said, my Lord of *Norffolke*;
Therefore let vs presently to *Lambeth*.
Thether comes *Cromwell* from the Court to night.
Let vs arest him, send him to the Tower,
And in the morning, cut off the traitors head.
Norf. Come, then, about it, let vs guard the towne.
This is the day that *Cromwell* must go downe.
Gard. Along, my Lords.—Well, *Cromwell* is halfe dead;
He shaked my hart, but I will shaue his head.
[*Exeunt.*

⟨Act V. Scene I. *A street in London.*⟩

Enter Bedford *solus.*

Bed. My soule is like a water troubled,
And *Gardiner* is the man that makes it so.
O, *Cromwell,* I do feare thy end is neare:
Yet Ile preuent their malice if I can.
And in good time, see where the man doth come,
Who little knowes how neares his day of dome.

Enter Cromwell *with his traine.* Bedford *makes as though he would speake to him: he goes on.*

Cro. Your well encountered, my good Lord of *Bedford.*
I see your honour is adressed to talke;
Pray pardon me, I am sent for to the king,
And do not know the businesse yet my selfe.
So fare you well, for I must needes be gone.
[*Exit all the traine.*
Bed. You must; well, what remedie?
I feare too soone you must be gone indeed.
The king hath businesse, but little doest thou know,
Whose busie for thy life: thou thinkes not so.

Enter Cromwell *and the traine agayne.*

Crom. The second time wel met, my Lord of *Bedford*;
I am very sory that my hast is such.
Lord *Marques Dorset* beeing sicke to death,
I must receaue of him the priuie seale.
At Lambeth, soone, my Lord, weele talke our fill.
[*Exit the traine.*
Bed. How smooth and easie is the way to death!

Enter a seruant.

Mes. My Lord, the dukes of *Norfolke* and of *Suffolke,*
Accompanied with the Bishop of Winchester,
Intreates you to come presently to Lambeth,
On earnest matters that concernes the state.
Bed. To Lambeth! so: goe fetch me pen and inke.
I and Lord *Cromwell* there shall talke enough;
I, and our last, I feare, and if he come.
[*He writes a letter.*
Heare, take this letter, and beare it to Lord *Cromwell.*
Bid him read it; say it concernes him neare:
Away, begone, make all the hast you can.
To Lambeth do I goe a woefull man. [*Exit.*

⟨Scene II. *A street near the Thames.*⟩

Enter Cromwell *and his traine.*

Crom. Is the Barge readie? I will straight to Lambeth,
And if this one dayes businesse once were past,
I'de take my ease to morrow after trouble.—
How now, my friend, wouldst thou speake with me?
[*The Messenger brings him the letter; he puts it in his pocket.*
Mes. Sir, heares a letter from my Lord of *Bedford.*
Crom. O good, my friend, commend me to thy Lord.
Hould, take those Angels; drinke them for thy paynes.
Mes. He doth desire your grace to reade it,
Because he sayes it doth concerne you neare.
Crom. Bid him assure himselfe of that. Farewell.
To morrow, tell him, shall he heare from me.—
Set on before there, and away to Lambeth.
[*Exeunt omnes.*

108 *Ends* treason *Qq, Ff*: *corr. M* 115 my good lord *M* 116 vs] us go *M* 123 shaue] shake *conj. M* Act V. *etc. add. M* 8 *om. Ff, R*

Scene II. *etc. add. M*

⟨SCENE III. *Lambeth.*⟩

Enter Winchester, Suffolke, Norfolke, Bedford, *Sargiant at armes, the Harauld, and halberts.*

Gar. Halberts, stand close vnto the water-side;
Sargiant at armes, be bould in your office;
Harrauld, deliuer your proclamation.

Ha. This is to giue notice to all the kings subiects: The late Lord Cromwell, Lord Chancellor of England, Vicor generall ouer the realme, him to hould and esteeme as a traytor agaynst the Crowne and dignitie of England: So God saue the king.

Gar. Amen.

Bed. Amen,—and roote thee from the land,
For whilst thou liuest truth cannot stand.

Nor. Make a lane there, the traitors at hand.
Keepe backe *Cromwels* men;
Drowne them if they come on.—Sargiant, your office.

Enter Cromwell, *they make a lane with their Halbertes.*

Cro. What meanes my Lord of *Norfolke* by these wordes?
Sirs, come along.

Gar. Kill them, if they come on.

Sar. Lord *Cromwell,* in king *Henries* name,
I do arrest your honour of high treason.

Crom. Sargiant, me of treason?
[Cromwels *men offer to drawe.*

Suf. Kill them, if they draw a sworde.

Crom. Hould; I charge you, as you loue me, draw not a sworde.
Who dares accuse *Cromwell* of treason now?

Gar. This is no place to recken vp your crime;
Your Doue-like lookes were viewed with serpents eyes.

Crom. With serpents eyes, indeed, by thine they were;
But *Gardiner* do thy woorst, I feare thee not.
My fayth, compared with thine, as much shall passe,
As doth the Diamond excell the glasse.
Attached of treason, no accusers by!
Indeede, what tongue dares speake so foule a lie?

Nor. My Lord, my Lord, matters are too well knowne,
And it is time the king had note thereof.

Crom. The king! let me goe to him face to face;
No better triall I desire then that:
Let him but say that *Cromwels* fayth was fayned,
Then let my honour and my name be stayned.
If euer my hart agaynst my king was set,
O let my soule in Iudgement aunswere it:
Then, if my faythes confirmed with his reason,
Gaynst whom hath *Cromwell,* then, committed treason?

Suf. My Lord, your matter shall be tried;
Meane time, with patience content your selfe.

Cro. Perforce I must with patience be content.
O deare friend *Bedford,* doest thou stand so neare?
Cromwell reioyceth one friend sheds a teare.
And whether ist? which way must *Cromwell* now?

Gar. My Lord, you must vnto the tower. Lieutenant,
Take him to your charge.

Cro. Well, where you please; yet before I part,
Let me conferre a little with my men.

Gar. As you goe by water, so you shall.

Cro. I haue some businesse present to impart.

Nor. You may not stay. Lieutenant, take your charge.

Cro. Well, well, my Lord, you second *Gardiners* text.
Norfolke, farewell; thy turne wilbe the next.
[*Exit* Cromwell *and the Lieutenant.*

Gar. His guiltie conscience makes him raue, my Lord.

Nor. I, let him talke; his time is short enough.

Gar. My Lord of *Bedford,* come; you weepe for him,
That would not shed halfe a teare for you.

Bed. It grieues me for to see his sudden fall.

Gar. Such successe wish I to traitours still.
[*Exeunt.*

⟨SCENE IV. *London. A street.*⟩

Enter two Citizens.

1. Why, can this newes be true? ist possible?
The great Lord *Cromwell* arreasted vpon treason!

Scene III. *etc. add. M* 2 be you bold *M* 4–9 *Verse in Qq, Ff: corr. M* 12 the truth *M* 14 *Ends* come on *M* 19 Lord Thomas Cromwell *M* 49 *Ends* tower *Qq, Ff: corr. M* 50 to] unto *M* 51 yet] but yet *M* 53 Ay, as *M* 61 halfe *om. Ff, R*: even half *M* 63 to] vnto *Q 2, etc.* Scene IV. *etc. add. M*

I hardly will beleeue it can be so.
2. It is too true, sir; would it were otherwise,
Condition I spent halfe the wealth I had.
I was at *Lambeth,* saw him there arrested,
And afterward committed to the Tower.
1. What, wast for treason that he was committed?
2. Kinde, noble Gentleman! I may rue the time.
All that I haue, I did inioy by him,
And if he die, then all my state is gone.
1. It may be doubted that he shall not die,
Because the King did fauour him so much.
2. O sir, you are deceiued in thinking so.
The grace and fauour he had with the king
Hath causde him haue so manie enemies:
He that in court secure will keepe himselfe,
Must not be great, for then he is enuied at.
The Shrub is safe, when as the Cedar shakes;
For where the King doth loue aboue compare,
Of others they as much more enuied are.
1. Tis pittie that this noble man should fall,
He did so many charitable deeds.
2. Tis true, and yet you see in each estate,
Theres none so good, but some one doth him hate.
And they before would smile him in the face,
Will be the formost to do him disgrace:
What, will you go along vnto the Court?
1. I care not if I do, and here the newes,
How men will iudge what shall become of him.
2. Some will speake hardly, some will speake in pitie.
Go you to the Court, Ile vnto the Citie;
There I am sure to here more newes then you.
1. Why, then, soone will we meet againe. [*Exit.*

⟨SCENE V. *A room in the Tower.*⟩

Enter Cromwell *in the Tower.*

Crom. Now, *Cromwell,* hast thou time to meditate,
And thinke vpon thy state, and of the time.
Thy honours came vnsought, I, and vnlooked for;
Thy fall as sudden, and vnlooked for to.
What glorie was in England that I had not?
Who in this land commanded more then *Cromwell*?
Except the King who greater then my selfe?
But now I see, what after ages shall:
The greater men, more sudden is their fall.
And now I do remember the Earle of *Bedford*
Was very desirous for to speake to me,
And afterward sent to me a letter,
The which I thinke I haue still in my pocket.
Now may I read it, for I now haue leasure,
And this I take it is. [*He reades the Letter.*
My Lord, come not this night to Lambeth,
For if you do, your state is ouerthrowne.
And much I doubt your life, and if you come:
Then if you loue your selfe, stay where you are.
O God! had I but read this letter,
Then had I beene free from the Lions paw;
Deferring this to read vntill to morrow,
I spurnd at ioy, and did imbrace my sorrow.

Enter the Leiutenant of the Tower and officers.

Now, maister *Lieutenant,* when's this day of death?
Lieu. Alas, my Lord, would I might neuer see it.
Here are the Dukes of *Suffolke* and of *Norffolke,*
Winchester, Bedford, and sir *Richard Ratcliffe,*
With others, but why they come I know not.
Crom. No matter wherefore, *Cromwell* is prepard;
For *Gardiner* has my state and life insnard.
Bid them come in, or you shall do them wrong,
For here stands he, whom some thinkes liues too long.
Learning killes learning, and insteed of Inck
To dip his Pen, *Cromwels* heart blood doth drinke.

Enter all the Nobles.

Norf. Good morrow, *Cromwell.* What, alone, so sad?
Crom. One good among you, none of you are bad.—
For my part, it best fits me be alone;
Sadnesse with me, not I with any one.
What, is the king acquainted with my cause?
Norf. We haue, and he hath answered vs, my Lord.
Cro. How, shall I come to speake with him my selfe?
Gard. The King is so aduertised of your guilt,
He will by no meanes admit you to his presence.
Cro. No way admit me? am I so soone forgot?
Did he but yesterday imbrace my neck,
And said that *Cromwell* was euen halfe himselfe,
And is his Princely eares so much bewitched

5 had] haue *Q 2, etc.* 12 doubted] hoped *Q 2, etc.* 32 vnto] go into *Q 2, etc.* 34 again : adieu *St.* Scene V. *etc. add. M* 9 men *Ff*: man *Qq* 12 to] vnto *Q 2, etc.* 20 O God, O God! *M* 28 others] others still *S* 40 We haue] He is *M*

With scandolous ignomie, and slanderous speeches,
That now he dooth denie to looke on me?
Well, my Lord of *Winchester*, no doubt but you
Are much in fauour with his Maiestie:
Will you beare a letter from me to his grace?
Gard. Pardon me, ile beare no traitors letters.
Crom. Ha! Will you do this kindnesse then? Tell him
By word of mouth, what I shall say to you?
Gard. That will I.
Crom. But, on your honour, will you?
Gard. I, on my honor.
Crom. Beare witnesse, Lords.—Tell him when he hath knowne you,
And tried your faith but halfe so much as mine,
Heele finde you to be the falsest harted man
In England. Pray, tell him this.
Bed. Be patient, good my Lord, in these extreames.
Crom. My kinde and honorable Lord of *Bedford,*
I know your honor alwaies loued me well;
But, pardon me, this still shall be my theame;
Gardiner is the cause makes *Cromwell* so extreame.
Sir *Ralphe Sadler,* pray, a word with you:
You were my man, and all that you possesse
Came by my meanes; to requite all this,
Will you take this letter here of me,
And giue it with your owne hands to the king?
Sad. I kisse your hand, and neuer will I rest,
Eare to the king this be deliuered. [*Exit* Sadler.
Crom. Why yet *Cromwell* hath one friend in store.
Gard. But all the hast he makes shall be but vaine.—
Heres a discharge for your prisoner,
To see him executed presentlie.—
My Lord, you here the tenor of your life.
Crom. I doe imbrace it, welcome my last date,
And of this glistering world I take last leaue:
And, noble Lords, I take my leaue of you.—
As willinglie I goe to meete with death,
As *Gardiner* did pronounce it with his breath:
From treason is my hart as white as Snowe,
My death onlie procured by my foe.
I pray, commend me to my Soueraigne king,
And tell him in what sort his *Cromwell* died,
To loose his head before his cause were tride:
But let his Grace, when he shall here my name,
Say onely this: *Gardiner* procured the same.

Enter young Cromwell.

Lieu. Here is your sonne, come to take his leaue.
Crom. To take his leaue! Come hether, *Harry Cromwell.*
Marke, boye, the last words that I speake to thee.
Flatter not Fortune, neither fawne vpon her;
Gape not for state, yet loose no sparke of honor;
Ambition, like the plague see thou eschew it;
I die for treason, boy, and neuer knew it.
Yet let thy faith as spotlesse be as mine,
And *Cromwels* vertues in thy face shall shine.
Come, goe along and see me leaue my breath,
And Ile leaue thee vpon the floure of death.
Son. O, father, I shall die to see that wound;
Your blood being spilt will make my hart to sound.
Cro. How, boy, not looke vpon the Axe!
How shall I do then to haue my head stroke off?
Come on, my childe, and see the end of all,
And after say that *Gardiner* was my fall.
Gar. My Lord, you speake it of an enuious hart;
I haue done no more then lawe and equitie.
Bed. O, good my Lord of *Winchester,* forbeare;
It would a better seemed you to beene absent,
Then with your wordes disturbe a dying man.
Cro. Who me, my Lord? no, he disturbes not me.
My minde he stirres not, though his mightie shocke
Hath brought mo peeres heads downe to the blocke.
Farewell, my boy! all *Cromwell* can bequeath,
My hartie blessing; so I take my leaue.
Hang. I am your deaths man; pray, my Lord, forgiue me.
Crom. Euen with my soule. Why, man, thou art my Doctor,
And bringes me precious Phisicke for my soule.—
My Lord of *Bedford,* I desire of you,
Before my death, a corporall imbrace.
[Bedford *comes to him,* Cromwell *imbraces him.*
Farewell, great Lord; my loue I do commend,
My hart to you; my soule to heauen I send.
This is my ioy that, eare my bodie fleete,

54 *Ends* then *Qq, Ff*: *corr. M* 59 *Two lines Qq, Ff, div. after* Lords 68 I pray *M* 70 to] sir, to *M* 71 Say will *M* 75 Why then yet *M* 77 for] sir, for *S* 86 procured only *M*

92 son, sir, come *M* 105 not dare to look *M* 112 a] have *M*: *om. Q2, Ff* beene] have been *M* 116 to] unto *M*

Your honourd armes is my true winding sheete.
Farewell, deare *Bedford*; my peace is made in heauen.
Thus falles great *Cromwell* a poore ell in length,
To rise to vnmeasured height, winged with new strength,
The land of Wormes, which dying men discouer,
My soule is shrinde with heauens celestiall couer.

[*Exit* Cromwell *and the officers, and others.*

Bed. Well, farewell, *Cromwell,* the trewest friend,
That euer *Bedford* shall possesse agayne.—
Well, Lordes, I feare, when this man is deade,
Youle wish in vayne that *Cromwell* had a head.

Enter one with Cromwels *head.*

Offi. Heare is the head of the deceased *Cromwell.*

Bed. Pray thee, goe hence, and beare his heade away
Vnto his bodie; inter them both in clay.

Enter sir Raulphe Sadler.

Sad. Ho now, my Lordes: what, is Lord *Cromwell* dead?

Bed. Lord *Cromwels* body now doth want a heade.

Sad. O God! a little speede had saued his life.
Here is a kinde repriue come from the king,
To bring him straight vnto his maiestie.

Suf. I, I, sir *Raulph,* repriues comes now too late.

Gar. My conscience now telles me this deede was ill:
Would Christ that *Cromwell* were aliue againe.

Nor. Come, let vs to the king, whom well I know,
Will grieue for *Cromwell,* that his death was so. [*Exeunt omnes.*

FINIS.

131 The *Qq, etc.*: Hail *conj. St.* 133 the] sure the *M* 135 that when *M*

148 whom] who *M*

THE LONDON Prodigall.

As it was plaide by the Kings Maie-
ſties ſeruants.

By *VVilliam Shakeſpeare,*

LONDON.

Printed by T. C. for *Nathaniel Butter*, and
are to be ſold neere *S* *Auſtins* gate,
at the ſigne of the pyde Bull.
1605.

Q	=	Quarto of 1605
F 1	=	(Third) Folio Shakespeare, 1664
F 2	=	(Fourth) ,, ,, 1685
R	=	Rowe, 1709
Pope	=	supplementary volume to Pope's Shakespeare, 1728
M	=	Malone, 1780
St.	=	Steevens, ibid.
Th.	=	Theobald, ibid.
S	=	Simms, 1848
T	=	Tyrrell, 1851
Haz.	=	Hazlitt, 1852
Molt.	=	Moltke, 1869
pr. ed.	=	present editor

THE LONDON PRODIGALL

⟨The Actors Names in the *London Prodigal.*

M. Flowerdale ⟨Senior⟩,[2] *a Merchant trading at* Venice.
Matth. Flowerdale, *his* Prodigal Son.
M. Flowerdale, ⟨Junior⟩,[3] *Brother to the Merchant.*
Sir Lancelot Spurcock, *of Lewsome in Kent.*
Frances. / Luce. / Delia. } *Daughters to Sir* Lancelot Spurcock.
Daffidill. / Hartichoak. } *Servants to Sir* Lance. Spurcock.

The Scene *London* ⟨*and the Parts adjacent*⟩.[1]

Sir Arthur Greenshood, *a Commander.* / Oliver *a Devonshire*[4] *Clothier.* } *In love with* Luce.
Weathercock, *a Parasite to Sir* Lance. Spurcock.
Tom Civet, *in love with* Frances.
Dick *and* Raph, *two cheating Gamesters.*
Ruffin, a Pander to Mistris Apricock *a Bawd.*
Sheriff and Officers.
A Citizen and his wife.
Drawers.⟩[5]

⟨ACT I. SCENE I. *London. A room in Flowerdale Junior's house.*⟩

Enter old Flowerdale *and his brother.*

Fath. Brother, from *Venice,* being thus disguisde,
I come to proue the humours of my sonne.
How hath he borne himselfe since my departure,
I leauing you his patrone and his guide?

Vnck. Ifaith, brother, so, as you will grieue to heare,
And I almost ashamde to report it.

Fath. Why, how ist, brother? what, doth he spend beyond the allowance I left him?

Vnck. How! beyond that? and farre more: why, your exibition is nothing. Hee hath spent that, and since hath borrowed; protested with oathes, alledged kindred to wring mony from me,—by the loue I bore his father, by the fortunes might fall vpon himself, to furnish his wants: that done, I haue had since his bond, his friend and friends bond. Altho I knowe that hee spends is yours; yet it grieues me to see the vnbridled wildnes that raines ouer him.

Fath. Brother, what is the manner of his life? howe is the name of his offences? If they do not rellish altogether of damnation, his youth may priuiledge his wantonnesse: I my selfe ranne an vnbrideled course till thirtie, nay, almost till fortie;—well, you see how I am: for vice, once looked into with the eies of discretion, and well balanced with the waites of reason, the course past seemes so abhominable, that the Landlord of himselfe, which is the heart of his body, will rather intombe himself in the earth, or seek a new Tenant to remaine in him:—which once settled, how much better are they that in their youth haue knowne all these vices, and left it, then those that knewe little, and in their age runnes into it? Beleeue me, brother, they that dye most vertuous hath in their youth liued most vicious, and none knowes the danger of the fire more then he that falles into it. But say, how is the course of his life? lets heare his particulars.

Vnck. Why, Ile tell you, brother; hee is a continual swearer, and a breaker of his oathes, which is bad.

Fath. I grant indeed to sweare is bad, but not in keeping those oathes is better: for who will set by a bad thing? Nay, by my faith, I hold this rather a vertue then a vice. Well, I pray, proceede.

Vnck. He is a mighty brawler, and comes commonly by the worst.

Fath. By my faith, this is none of the worst neither, for if he brawle and be beaten for it, it wil in time make him shunne it: For what brings man or child more to vertue then correction? What raignes ouer him else?

Vnck. He is a great drinker, and one that will forget himselfe.

Fath. O best of all! vice should be forgotten: let him drink on, so he drinke not churches. Nay, and this be the worst, I hold it rather a happines in him, then any iniquity. Hath he any more attendants?

Vnck. Brother, he is one that will borrow of any man.

Fath. Why, you see, so doth the sea: it borrowes of all the smal currents in the world, to encrease himselfe.

[1] and . . adjacent *add. R* [2], [3] *Add. M* [4] Cornish *Q, Ff*: *corr. M* [5] *Dram. Pers. add. F 1* Act I. *etc. add. M* 22 damdation *Q*

35 it] 'em *R* 36 run *F 2, etc.* it] 'em *R* 45 *Prefix* Vnck. *Q* 46 not in] in not *conj. M*: the not *Haz.* 47–70 Nay . . son *Verse Q, F 1* 62 a *om. Ff*

Vnck. I, but the sea paies it againe, and so will neuer your son.

Fath. No more would the sea neither, if it were as dry as my sonne.

Vnck. Then, brother, I see you rather like these vices in your sonne, then any way condemne them.

Fath. Nay, mistake me not, brother, for tho I slur them ouer now, as things slight and nothing, his crimes being in the budde, it would gall my heart, they should euer raigne in him.

Flow. Ho! whoes within? ho!

[*Flowerdale knockes within.*

Vnck. That's your sonne, hee is come to borrowe more money.

Fath. For Godsake giue it out I am dead; see how hele take it. Say I haue brought you newes from his father. I haue here drawne a formall will, as it were from my selfe, which Ile deliuer him.

Vnck. Goe too, brother, no more: I will.

Flow. Vnckle, where are you, Vnckle?

[*within.*

Vnck. Let my cousen in there.

Fath. I am a Sayler come from *Venice*, and my name is *Christopher*.

Enter Flowerdale.

Flow. By the Lord, in truth, Vnckle—

Vnck. In truth would a seru'd, cousen, without the Lord.

Flow. By your leaue, Vnckle, the Lord is the Lord of truth. A couple of rascalles at the gate set vpon me for my purse.

Vnck. You neuer come, but you bring a brawle in your mouth.

Flow. By my truth, Vnckle, you must needes lend me tenne pound.

Vnck. Giue my cousen some small beere here.

Flow. Nay, looke you, you turne it to a iest now: by this light, I should ryde to *Croydon* fayre, to meete syr *Lancelot Spurrock*. I should haue his daughter *Luce*, and for scuruy tenne pound, a man shal loose nine hundred three-score and odde pounds, and a daily friend beside. By this hande, Vnckle, tis true.

Vnck. Why, any thing is true for ought I know.

Flow. To see now! why, you shall haue my bond, Vnckle, or *Tom Whites*, *Iames Brocks*, or *Nick Halls*: as good rapyer and dagger men, as any be in *England*. Lets be dambn'd if wee doe not pay you: the worst of vs all will not damne our selues for ten pound. A poxe of ten pound!

Vnck. Cousen, this is not the first time I haue beleeu'd you.

Flow. Why, trust me now, you know not what may fall. If one thing were but true, I would not greatly care, I should not neede ten pound, but when a man cannot be beleeued, —ther's it.

Vnck. Why, what is it, cousen?

Flow. Mary, this, Vnckle: can you tell me if the Katern-hue be come home or no?

Vnck. I, mary, ist.

Flow. By God I thanke you for that newes. What, ist in the poole, can you tell?

Vnck. It is; what of that?

Flow. What? why then I haue sixe peeces of vellet sent me; Ile giue you a peece, Vnckle: for thus said the letter,—a peece of Ashcolour, a three pilde black, a colour de roy, a crimson, a sad greene, and a purple: yes, yfaith.

Vnck. From whom should you receiue this?

Flow. From who? why, from my father; with commendations to you, Vnckle, and thus he writes: I know, saith he, thou hast much troubled thy kinde Vnckle, whom God-willing at my returne I will see amply satisfied. Amply, I remember was the very word, so God helpe me.

Vnck. Haue you the letter here?

Flow. Yes, I haue the letter here, here is the letter: no, yes, no;—let me see, what breechs wore I a Satterday? let me see: a Tuesday my Calymanka; a Wednesday my peach colour Sattin; a Thursday my Vellure; a Friday my Callymanka againe; a Satterday —let me see—a Satterday,—for in those breeches I wore a Satterday is the letter: O, my ryding breeches, Vnckle, those that you thought had bene vellet; in those very breeches is the letter.

Vnck. When should it be dated?

Flow. Mary, *Decimo tertio septembris*—no, no—*decimo tertio Octobris*; I, *Octobris*, so it is.

Vnck. *Decimo tertio Octobris*! and here receiue I a letter that your father dyed in *Iune*: how say you, *Kester*?

Fath. Yes, truly, syr, your father is dead, these hands of mine holpe to winde him.

Flow. Dead?

Fath. I, syr, dead.

73–80 *Verse Q, F 1*   84–8 *Verse Q, Ff*   97–9, 106–10 Nay . . scuruy *Verse Q, F 1*   125–7 Why . . care *Verse Q, F 1*   132 Catherine and Hugh *M*   140 colourde deroy *Q* : *corr. M*   144 whom *M*   164–5 Didicimo tersios . . trydisimo tersios *Q* : *corr. M*   166 Dicditimo tersios *Q*

Flow. Sblood, how should my father come dead?

Fath. Yfaith, syr, according to the old Prouerbe:
The childe was borne and cryed, became man,
After fell sicke, and dyed.

Vnck. Nay, cousen, doe not take it so heauily.

Flow. Nay, I cannot weepe you extempory: mary, some two or three dayes hence, I shall weep without any stintance. But I hope he dyed in good memory.

Fath. Very well, syr, and set downe euery thing in good order; and the Katherine and Hue you talkt of, I came ouer in: and I saw all the billes of lading, and the vellet that you talkt of, there is no such aboord.

Flow. By God, I assure you, then, there is knauery abroad.

Fath. Ile be sworne of that: ther's knauery abroad,
Altho there were neuer a peece of vellet in *Venice.*

Flow. I hope he dyed in good estate.

Fath. To the report of the world he did, and made his will,
Of which I am an vnworthy bearer.

Flow. His will! haue you his will?

Fath. Yes, syr, and in the presence of your Vnckle
I was willed to deliuer it.

Vnck. I hope, cousen, now God hath blessed you with wealth, you will not be vnmindfull of me.

Flow. Ile doe reason, Vnckle, yet, yfaith, I take the deniall of this tenne pound very hardly.

Vnck. Nay, I denyde you not.

Flow. By God, you denide me directly.

Vnck. Ile be iudge⟨d⟩ by this good fellowe.

Fath. Not directly, syr.

Flow. Why, he said he would lend me none, and that had wont to be a direct denyall, if the old phrase holde. Well, Vnckle, come, weele fall to the Legasies: ⟨*reads*⟩ 'In the name of God, Amen. Item, I bequeath to my brother *Flowerdale* three hundred pounds, to pay such triu⟨i⟩all debts as I owe in *London.* Item, to my sonne *Mat Flowerdale*, I bequeath two bayle of false dyce; *Videllicet*, high men and loe men, fullomes, stop cater traies, and other bones of function.' Sblood, what doth he meane by this?

Vnck. Proceede, cousen.

Flow. "These precepts I leaue him: let him borrow of his oath, for of his word no body will trust him. Let him by no meanes marry an honest woman, for the other will keepe her selfe. Let him steale as much as he can, that a guilty conscience may bring him to his destinate repentance."—I thinke he meanes hanging. And this were his last will and Testament, the Diuell stood laughing at his beddes feete while he made it. Sblood, what, doth hee thinke to fop of his posteritie with Paradoxes?

Fath. This he made, syr, with his owne hands.

Flow. I, well; nay, come, good Vnckle, let me haue this ten pound. Imagine you haue lost it, or ⟨been⟩ robd of it, or misreckond your selfe so much: any way to make it come easily off, good Vnckle.

Vnck. Not a penny.

Fath. Yfaith, lend it him, syr. I my selfe haue an estate in the Citie worth twenty pound: all that ile ingage for him; he saith it concernes him in a marriage.

Flow. I, marry, doth it. This is a fellow of some sense, this: Come, good Vnckle.

Vnck. Will you giue your word for it, *Kester*?

Fath. I will, syr, willingly.

Vnck. Well, cousen, come to me some hower hence, you shall haue it readie.

Flow. Shall I not faile?

Vnck. You shall not, come or send.

Flow. Nay, ile come my selfe.

Fath. By my troath, would I were your worships man.

Flow. What, wouldst thou serue?

Fath. Very willingly, syr.

Flow. Why, ile tell thee what thou shalt doe: thou saith thou hast twentie pound; goe into *Burchin Lane*, put thy selfe into cloathes; thou shalt ride with me to *Croyden* fayre.

Fath. I thanke you, syr; I will attend you.

Flow. Well, Vnckle, you will not faile me an hower hence?

Vnck. I will not, cousen.

Flow. Whats thy name? *Kester*?

Fath. I, syr.

Flow. Well, prouide thy selfe: Vnckle, farewell till anon. [*Exit Flowerdale.*

180 cannon *Q* 207 judg'd *Ff*: iudge *Q* good-fellowe *Q* *S. D.* reads *add. M* 218 Videlliced *Q*

221 *Prefix* Flow. *repeated before this line Q, Ff* 223-9 These . . repentance *Verse Q, F 1* 233 fob *M*: lop *Walker* 239 been robd *pr. ed.*: robd *Q, Ff*: were robb'd *M* 252 some] an *R* 262 saist *Ff, etc.*

Vnck. Brother, how doe you like your sonne?
Fath. Yfaith, brother, like a mad vnbridled colt,
Or as a Hawke, that neuer stoop'd to lure:
The one must be tamde with an yron byt,
The other must be watched, or still she is wilde.
Such is my sonne; awhile let him be so:
For counsell still is follies deadly foe.
Ile serue his youth, for youth must haue his course,
For being restrainde, it makes him ten times worse:
His pride, his ryot, all that may be named,
Time may recall, and all his madnesse tamed.
⟨*Exeunt.*⟩

⟨Scene II. *The high street in Croydon. An inn appearing, with an open drinking booth before it.*⟩

Enter syr *Launcelot*, Maister *Weathercocke*, *Daffidill, Artichoake, Luce, and Francke.*

Lance. Syrrha *Artichoake*, get you home before,
And as you proued your selfe a calfe in bying,
Driue home your fellow calfes that you haue bought.
Arti. Yes, forsooth; shall not my fellow *Daffidill* goe along with me?
Lance. No, syr, no; I must haue one to waite on me.
Arty. Daffidill, farewell, good fellow *Daffidill*.
You may see, mistresse, I am set vp by the halues:
In steed of waiting on you, I am sent to driue home calues.
Lance. Yfaith, *Francke*, I must turne away this *Daffidill*,
Hees growne a very foolish sawcie fellow.
Fran. Indeed law, father, he was so since I had him:
Before he was wise enough for a foolish seruing-man.
Wea. But what say you to me, syr *Lancelot*?
Lance. O, about my daughters? wel, I will goe forward.
Heers two of them, God saue them: but the third,
O shees a stranger in her course of life.
Shee hath refused you, Maister *Weathercocke*.
Wea. I, by the Rood, syr *Lancelot*, that she hath,
But had she tride me,
She should a found a man of me indeed.
Lance. Nay be not angry, syr, at her deniall.
Shee hath refus'de seauen of the worshipfulst
And worthyest hous-keepers this day in *Kent*:
Indeed she will not marry, I suppose.
Wea. The more foole she.
Lance. What, is it folly to loue Chastitie?
Wea. No, mistake me not, syr *Lancelot*,
But tis an old prouerbe, and you know it well,
That women dying maides lead apes in hell.
Lance. Thats a foolish prouerbe, and a false.
Wea. By the masse I thinke it be, and therefore let it goe:
But who shall marry with mistresse *Frances*?
Fran. By my troath, they are talking of marrying me, sister.
Luce. Peace, let them talke:
Fooles may haue leaue to prattle as they walke.
Daff. Sentesses still, sweet mistresse;
You haue a wit, and it were your Alliblaster.
Luce. Yfaith, and thy tongue trips trenchmore.
Lance. No, of my knight-hood, not a shuter yet:
Alas, God helpe her, sillie girle, a foole, a verie foole:
But thers the other black-browes, a shroad girle,
Shee hath wit at will, and shuters two or three:
Syr *Arthur Greene-sheld* one, a gallant knight,
A valiant Souldier, but his power but poore.
Then thers yong *Oliuer*, the *Deuen-shyre* lad,
A wary fellow, marry, full of wit,
And rich by the rood; but thers a third all aire,
Light as a feather, changing as the wind:
Young *Flowerdale*.
Wea. O hee, syr, hees a desperate dick indeed.
Barre him your house.
Lance. Fye, not so, hees of good parentage.
Wea. By my faie and so he is, and a proper man.
Lance. I, proper enough, had he good qualities.
Wea. I, marrie, thers the point, syr *Lancelot*,
For thers an old saying:
Be he rich, or be he poore,
Be he hye, or be he lowe:
Be he borne in barne or hall,
Tis maners makes the man and all.
Lance. You are in the right, maister *Weathercock*.

S. D. Exeunt *add. R* Scene II. *etc. add. M* 19–20 *One line Q, Ff* 22–3 *Prose Q* : *corr. M* 26 Charitie *Q* : *corr. R* 27 No, no *M* 36 Sentences *R, etc.* 48–9 *One line Q* : *corr. F 2* 52 Fie, sir *M* 57 poore] poe *conj. M*

Enter Mounsier Ciuet.

Ciuet. Soule, I thinke I am sure crossed, or witcht with an owle. I haue hanted them, Inne after Inne, booth after booth, yet cannot finde them: ha, yonder they are; thats she. I hope to God tis shee! nay, I know tis shee now, for she treades her shooe a little awry.

Lance. Where is this Inne? we are past it, *Daffidill.*

Daffidill. The good signe is heere, syr, but the back gate is before.

Ciuet. Saue you, syr. I pray, may I borrow a peece of a word with you?

Daff. No peeces, syr.

Ciu. Why, then, the whole. I pray, syr, what may yonder gentlewomen be?

Daff. They may be Ladies, syr, if the destinies and mortalitie worke.

Ciu. Whats her name, syr?

Daff. Mistresse *Frances Spurcocke,* syr *Lancelots Spurcockes* daughter.

Ciu. Is she a maid, syr?

Daff. You may aske *Pluto,* and dame *Proserpine* that: I would be loth to be ridelled, syr.

Ciu. Is she married, I meane, syr?

Daff. The Fates knowes not yet what shoemaker shall make her wedding shooes.

Ciu. I pray, where Inne you syr? I would be very glad to bestowe the wine of that gentlewoman.

Daff. At the *George,* syr.

Ciu. God saue you, syr.

Daff. I pray your name, syr?

Ciu. My name is maister *Ciuet,* syr.

Daff. A sweet name. God be with you, good maister *Ciuet.* [*Exit Ciuet.*

Lance. A, haue we spide you, stout *S. George*?
For all your dragon, you had best selles good wine,
That needs no yuie-bush: well, weele not sit by it,
As you do on your horse. This roome shall serue:—
Drawer, let me haue sacke for vs old men:
For these girles and knaues small wines are best.
A pinte of sacke, no more.

Draw. A quart of sack in the three Tunnes.

Lance. A pinte, draw but a pinte.—*Daffidill,* call for wine to make your selues drinke.

Fran. And a cup of small beere, and a cake, good *Daffidill.*

Enter yong Flowerdale.

Flow. How now? fye, sit in the open roome? now, good syr *Lancelot,* & my kind friend worshipfull Maister *Weathercock!* What, at your pinte? a quart for shame.

Lance. Nay, Royster, by your leaue we will away.

Flow. Come, giues some Musicke, weele goe dance. Begone, syr *Lancelot*? what, and fayre day too?

Luce. Twere fowly done, to dance within the fayre.

Flow. Nay, if you say so, fairest of all faires, then ile not dance. A poxe vpon my tayler, he hath spoyled me a peach colour satten shute, cut vpon cloath of siluer, but if euer the Rascall serue me such an other tricke, Ile giue him leaue, yfaith, to put me in the calender of fooles: and you, and you, syr *Lancelot* and Maister *Weathercock.* My goldsmyth too, on tother side—I bespoke thee, *Luce,* a carkenet of gold, and thought thou shouldst a had it for a fayring, and the Rogue puts me in rerages for Oryant Pearle: but thou shalt haue it by sunday night, wench.

Enter the Drawer.

Draw. Syr, here is one hath sent you a pottle of rennish wine, brewed with Rosewater.

Flow. To me?

Draw. No, syr, to the knight; and desires his more acquaintance.

Lance. To me? whats he that proues so kind?

Daff. I haue a tricke to know his name, syr. He hath a moneths mind here to mistresse *Frances,* his name is maister *Ciuet.*

Lance. Call him in, *Daffidill.*

Flow. O I know him, syr, he is a foole,
But reasonable rich; his father was one of these lease-mongers, these corne-mongers, these mony-mongers, but he neuer had the wit to be a whore-monger.

Enter maister Ciuet.

Lance. I promise you, syr, you are at too much charge.

Cyuet. The charge is small charge, syr; I thanke God my father left me wherewithall: if it please you, syr, I haue a great mind to this gentlewoman here, in the way of marriage.

Lance. I thanke you, syr: please you come to *Lewsome*

68 Iinne *Q*   71 black gate *Ff, R*   106-7 *Verse Q* : *corr. M*   119 *Prefix* Lance *Q, Ff* : *corr. M*   121-4 Nay . . shute *Verse Q, F 1*   148 corne-monger- *Q*   157-60 *Prose Q* : *corr. M*

To my poore house, you shall be kindly welcome:
I knewe your father, he was a wary husband.—
To paie here, Drawer.

Draw. All is paid, syr: this gentleman hath paid all.

Lance. Yfaith, you do vs wrong,
But we shall liue to make amends ere long:
Maister *Flowerdale*, is that your man?

Flow. Yes, faith, a good old knaue.

Lance. Nay, then I thinke
You will turne wise, now you take such a seruant:
Come, youle ride with vs to *Lewsome;* lets away.
Tis scarce two howres to the end of day.

[*Exit Omnes.*

⟨ACT II. SCENE I. *A road near Sir Lancelot Spurcock's house, in Kent.*⟩

Enter syr Arthur Green-shood, Olyuer, *Lieutennant and Souldiers.*

Aur. Lieuftenant, leade your Souldiers to the ships.
There let them haue their coates, at their arriuall
They shall haue pay: farewell, looke to your charge.

Sol. I, we are now sent away, and cannot so much as speake with our friends.

Oly. No, man; what, ere you vsed a zutch a fashion, thicke you cannot take your leaue of your vreens?

Aur. Fellow, no more. Lieuftenant, lead them off.

Sol. Well, if I haue not my pay and my cloathes, Ile venture a running away tho I hang fort.

Aur. Away, surrha, charme your tongue.

[*Exit Souldiers.*

Oly. Bin you a presser, syr?

Aur. I am a commander, syr, vnder the King.

Oly. Sfoot, man, and you bee nere zutch a commander, shud a spoke with my vreens before I chid agone, so shud.

Aur. Content your selfe, man, my authority will stretch to presse so good a man as you.

Oly. Presse me? I deuye ⟨ye⟩, presse scoundrells, and thy messels: Presse me! chee scornes thee, yfaith: For seest thee, heres a worshipfull knight knowes cham not to be pressed by thee.

Enter syr Lancelet, Weathercocke, yong Flowerdale, old Flowerdale, Luce, Franck.

Lance. Syr *Arthur*, welcome to *Lewsome*, welcome by my troath. Whats the matter, man? why are you vext?

Oly. Why, man, he would presse me.

Lance. O Fie, syr *Arthur*, presse him? he is ⟨a⟩ man of reckoning.

Wea. I, that he is, syr *Arthur*, he hath the nobles,
The golden ruddockes he.

Ar. The fitter for the warres: and were he not
In fauour with your worships, he should see,
That I haue power to presse so good as he.

Oly. Chill stand to the triall, so chill.

Flow. I, marry, shall he, presse-cloath and karsie, white pot and drowsen broath: tut, tut, he cannot.

Oly. Well, syr, tho you see vlouten cloath and karsie, chee a zeene zutch a karsie coate weare out the towne sick a zilken Iacket, as thick a one you weare.

Flow. Well sed, vlitan vlattan.

Oly. A, and well sed, cocknell, and boe-bell too: what, doest thincke cham a vearde of thy zilken coate? nefer vere thee.

Lance. Nay, come, no more, be all louers and friends.

Wea. I, tis best so, good maister *Olyuer.*

Flow. Is your name maister *Oliuer*, I pray you?

Oly. What tit and be tit, and grieue you.

Flow. No, but Ide gladly know if a man might not haue a foolish plot out of maister *Oliuer* to worke vpon.

Oly. Worke thy plots vpon me! stand a side:—worke thy foolish plots vpon me! chill so vse thee, thou weart neuer so vsed since thy dame bound thy head. Worke vpon me?

Flow. Let him come, let him come.

Oly. Zyrrha, zyrrha, if it were not vor shame, chee would a giuen thee zutch a whisterpoope vnder the eare, chee would a made thee a vanged an other at my feete: stand a side, let me loose, cham all of a vlaming fire-brand; Stand aside.

Flow. Well, I forbeare you for your friends sake.

Oly. A vig for all my vreens! doest thou tell me of my vreens?

166 *Ends* wise *Q* : *corr. M* Act II. *etc. add. M* S. D. Greenshield *M* 6-8 No man what ere . . vreens *Q* 11-13 *Verse Q, Ff* 15 Bin and you *Q* : *corr. Ff* 24 deuye ye *pr. ed.*: deuye *Q, etc.*

34 a *add. F1* 37 *Ends* fauour *Q* : *corr. M* 41-3 *Verse Q* : *corr. M* 51 coate, *Q* nefer *pr. ed.*: no fer *Q, Ff* no vear vor thee *M* 68 whister poope *Q, Ff*

Lance. No more, good maister *Oliuer*; no more,
Syr *Arthur*. And, maiden, here in the sight
Of all your shuters, euery man of worth,
Ile tell you whom I fainest would preferre
To the hard bargine of your marriage bed.—
Shall I be plaine among you, gentlemen?

Arth. I, syr, tis best.

Lance. Then, syr, first to you:—
I doe confesse you a most gallant knight,
A worthy souldier, and an honest man:
But honestie maintaines ⟨not⟩ a french-hood,
Goes very seldome in a chain of gold,
Keepes a small traine of seruants: hath fewe friendes.—
And for this wilde oates here, young *Flowerdale*,
I will not iudge: God can worke myracles,
But hee were better make a hundred new,
Then thee a thrifty and an honest one.

Wea. Beleeue me, he hath byt you there, he hath touched you to the quicke, that hath he.

Flow. Woodcocke a my side! why, maister *Weathercocke*, you know I am honest, howsoeuer trifles—

Wea. Now, by my troath, I knowe no otherwise.
O your old mother was a dame indeed:
Heauen hath her soule, and my wiues too, I trust:
And your good father, honest gentleman,
He is gone a Iourney, as I heare, far hence.

Flow. I, God be praised, he is far enough.
He is gone a pylgrimage to Paradice,
And left me to cut a caper against care.
Luce, looke on me that am as light as ayre.

Luce. Yfaith, I like not shadowes, bubbles, breath,
I hate a light a loue, as I hate death.

Lance. Gyrle, hold thee there: looke on this Deuen-shyre lad:
Fat, faire, and louely, both in purse and person.

Oly. Well syr, cham as the Lord hath made me. You know me well, yuine: cha haue three-score packe a karsay, and blackem hal, and chiefe credit beside, and my fortunes may be so good as an others, zoe it may.

Luce. ⟨*aside to Ar.*⟩ Tis you I loue, whatsoeuer others say.

Ar. Thanks, fayrest.

Flow. ⟨*aside to Fath.*⟩ What, wouldst thou haue me quarrell with him?

Fath. Doe but say he shall heare from you.

Lance. Yet, gentlemen, howsoeuer I preferre
This Deuen-shyre shuter, Ile enforce no loue;
My daughter shall haue liberty to choose
Whom she likes best; in your loue shute proceed:
Not all of you, but onely one must speed.

Wea. You haue sed well: indeed, right well.

[*Enter Artychoak.*

Arty. Mistresse, heeres one would speake with you. My fellow *Daffidill* hath him in the sellor already: he knowes him; he met him at *Croyden* fayre.

Lance. O, I remember, a little man.

Arty. I, a very little man.

Lance. And yet a proper man.

Arty. A very proper, very little man.

Lance. His name is Mounsier *Ciuet*.

Arty. The same, syr.

Lance. Come, Gentlemen, if other shuters come,
My foolish daughter will be fitted too:
But *Delia* my saint, no man dare moue.

[*Exeunt all but young* Flowerdale *and* Olyuer, *and old* Flowerdale.

Flow. Harke you, syr, a word.

Oly. What haan you to say to me now?

Flow. Ye shall heare from me, and that very shortly.

Oly. Is that all? vare thee well, chee vere thee not a vig. [*Exit Olyuer.*

Flow. What if ⟨he⟩ should come now? I am fairely drest.

Fath. I doe not meane that you shall meete with him,
But presently weele goe and draw a will:
Where weele set downe land that we neuer sawe,
And we will haue it of so large a summe,
Syr *Lancelot* shall intreat you take his daughter:
This being formed, giue it maister *Weathercocke*,
And make syr *Lancelots* daughter heire of all:
And make him sweare neuer to show the will
To any one, vntil that you be dead.
This done, the foolish changing *Weathercocke*
Will straight discourse vnto syr *Lancelot*
The forme and tenor of your Testament.
Nor stand to pause of it, be rulde by mee:
What will inshue, that shall you quickly see.

76-92 *Prose Q*: *corr. M* 82 *Prefix* Arty. *Q* 86 not *add. M* 93 byt] hit *Ff, etc.* 94-5 that he hath *Ff, etc.* 108 breath *M*: broath *Q* 114-15 at Blackem-Hall *M* 118 *Prefix* Lance. *Q*: *corr. M*

124-6 *Two lines Q, div.* shuter: *corr. M* 124 gentleman *Q, F 1* 144 *S. D.* Exeunt] Exit at *Q* 146 ha an *Q, Ff* you say *Ff* 149 he *add. F 2* now *R*: more *Q, Ff* 163 Nor] Ne'er *M*

Flow. Come, lets about it: if that a will, sweet *Kyt*,
Can get the wench, I shall renowne thy wit.
[*Exit omnes.*

⟨SCENE II. *A room in sir Lancelot's house.*⟩

Enter Daffidill.

Daff. Mistresse, still froward? No kind lookes
Vnto your *Daffidill*? now by the Gods—
Luce. Away, you foolish knaue, let my hand goe.
Daff. There is your hand, but this shall goe with me:
My heart is thine, this is my true loues fee.
Luce. Ile haue your coate stript ore your eares for this,
You sawcie rascall.
[*Enter Lancelot and Weathercocke*
Lance. How now, maid, what is the newes with you?
Luce. Your man is something sawcie.
[*Exit Luce.*
Lance. Goe too, syrrha, Ile talke with you anon.
Daff. Syr, I am a man to be-talked withall,
I am no horse, I tro:
I Know my strength, then no more then so.

Wea. A, by the matkins, good syr *Lancelot*, I saw him the other day hold vp the bucklers, like an *Hercules*. Ifaith, God a marcie, lad, I like thee well.

Lance. I, I like him well: go, syrrha, fetch me a cup of wine,
That ere I part with maister *Weathercocke*,
We may drinke downe our farewell in French wine.
Wea. I thanke you, syr, I thanke you, friendly knight.
Ile come and visit you, by the mouse-foot I will:
In the meane time, take heed of cutting *Flowerdale*.
He is a desperate dyck, I warrant you.

Lance. He is, he is: fill, *Daffidill*, fill me some wine. Ha, what weares he on his arme? My daughter *Luces* bracelet. I, tis the same.—Ha to you, maister *Weathercocke*.

Wea. I thanke you, syr: Here, *Daffidill*, an honest fellow and a tall thou art. Well, ile take my leaue, good knight, and hope to haue you and all your daughters at my poore house; in good sooth I must.

Lance. Thankes, maister *Weathercocke*, I shall be bold to trouble you, be sure.

Wea. And welcome hartily; farewell.
[*Exit Weathercocke.*

Lance. Syrrha, I saw my daughters wrong, and withall her bracelet on your arme: off with it, and with it my liuery too. Haue I care to see my daughter matched with men of worship, and are you growne so bold? Goe, syrrha, from my house, or ile whip you hence.

Daff. Ile not be whipped, syr, theres your liuery.
This is a seruingmans reward: what care I?
I haue meanes to trust too: I scorne seruice, I.
[*Exit Daffidill.*
Lance. I, a lusty knaue, but I must let him goe,
Our seruants must be taught what they should know. ⟨*Exit.*⟩

⟨SCENE III. *The same.*⟩

Enter syr Arthur and Luce.

Luce. Syr, as I am a maid, I doe affect
You aboue any shuter that I haue,
Altho that souldiers scarce knowes how to loue.
Ar. I am a souldier, and a gentleman,
Knowes what belonges to war, what to a lady:
What man offends me, that my sword shall right:
What woman loues me, I am her faithfull knight.
Luce. I neither doubt your vallour, nor your loue,
But there be some that bares a souldiers forme,
That sweares by him they neuer thinke vpon,
Goes swaggering vp and downe from house to house,
Crying God payes: and—
Ar. Ifaith, Lady, ile discry you such a man.
Of them there be many which you haue spoke off,
That beare the name and shape of souldiers,
Yet God knowes very seldome saw the war:
That haunt your Tauerns, and your ordinaries,
Your ale-houses sometimes, for all a-like
To vphold the brutish humour of their mindes,
Being marked downe, for the bondmen of dispare:
Their mirth begins in wine, but endes in blood,
Their drinke is cleare, but their conceits are mud.

Scene II. *etc. add. M* 1 *Ends* froward *Q, Ff* 1-2 *Prose M* 11-13 *Prose M* 14 A] Ay *R, etc.* makins *M* 18 I, I, like *Q, Ff*: Ay, Ay, like *R, etc.*

S. D. Exit Daffodil *follows* 43 *Q* *S. D.* Exit *add. M* Scene III. Another room in the same *M* 1-3 *Prose Q, Ff*: *corr. M* 8-12 *Prose Q, Ff*: *corr. M* 12 and] all *M*

Luce. Yet these are great gentlemen souldiers.

Ar. No, they are wretched slaues,
Whose desperate liues doth bring them time-lesse graues.

Luce. Both for your selfe, and for your forme of life,
If I may choose, ile be a souldiers wife.
⟨*Exeunt.*⟩

⟨SCENE IV. *The same.*⟩

Enter syr Lancelot and Oliuer.

Oli. And tyt trust to it, so then.

Lance. Ashure your selfe,
You shall be married with all speed we may:
One day shall serue for *Frances* and for *Luce.*

Oli. Why che wood vaine know the time, for prouiding wedding rayments.

Lance. Why, no more but this: first get your ashurance made, touching my daughters ioynter; that dispatched, we wil in two daies make prouision.

Oli. Why, man, chil haue the writings made by to-morrow.

Lance. To morrow be it then: lets meet at the kings head in fish street.

Oli. No, fie, man, no, lets meet at the Rose at *Temple-bar.*
That will be nearer your counsellor and mine.

Lance. At the Rose be it then, the hower nine:
He that comes last forfeits a pinte of wine.

Oli. A pinte is no payment, let it be a whole quart or nothing.

Enter Artichoake.

Arty. Maister, here is a man would speake with maister *Oliuer*: he comes from young maister *Flowerdale.*

Oli. Why, chillspeake with him, chill speake with him.

Lance. Nay, sonne *Oliuer*, ile shurely see what young *Flowerdale* hath sent to you. I pray God it be no quarrell.

Oly. Why, man, if he quarrell with me, chill giue him his hands full.

[*Enter old Flowerdale.*

Fath. God saue you, good syr *Lancelot.*

Lance. Welcome, honest friend.

Fath. To you and yours my maister wisheth health,
But vnto you, syr, this, and this he sendes:
There is the length, syr, of his rapier,
And in that paper shall you know his mind.

Oly. Here, chill meet him, my vreend, chill meet him.

Lance. Meet him! you shall not meet the Ruffin, fye.

Oly. And I doe not meete him, chill giue you leaue to call me cut; where ist, syrrha? where ist? where ist?

Fath. The letter showes both the time and place,
And if you be a man, then keepe your word,

Lance. Syr, he shal not keepe his word, he shal not meet.

Fath. Why, let him choose, heele be the better knowne
For a base rascall, and reputed so.

Oly. Zyrrha, zyrrha: and tweare not an old fellow, and sent after an arrant, chid giue thee something, but chud be no mony: But hold thee, for I see thou art somewhat testorne; holde thee, theres vortie shillings: bring thy maister a veeld, chil giue thee vortie more; looke thou bring him: chil mall him, tell him, chill mar his dauncing tressels, chil vse him, he was nere so vsed since his dam bound his head; chill make him for capyring any more, chy vor thee.

Fath. You seeme a man, stout and resolute,
And I will so report, what ere befall.

Lance. And fall out ill, ashure thy maister this,
Ile make him flye the land, or vse him worse.

Fath. My maister, syr, deserues not this of you,
And that youle shortly finde.

Lance. Thy maister is an vnthrift, you a knaue,
And ile attache you first, next clap him vp
Or haue him bound vnto his good behauiour.

Oly. I wood you were a sprite, if you do him any harme for this. And you doe, chill nere see you, nor any of yours, while chill haue eyes open: what, doe you thinke, chil be abaffelled vp and downe the towne for a messell and a scoundrel? no, chy vor you: zyrrha, chil come; zay no more, chil come, tell him.

Fath. Well, sir, my Maister deserues not this of you,
And that youle shortly finde. [*Exit.*

Lanc. No matter, he's an vnthrift; I defie him.
Now, gentle sonne, let me know the place.

Oly. No, chy vore you.

S. D. add. M Scene IV. Another room in the same *M* 25–7 *Verse Q*

57 make] mar *M* 59 man] man, sir *M* 73 vor] bor *Q, Ff* 78 *Prefix* Oly. *Q, etc.*: *corr. pr. ed.* 79 *Prefix* Lanc. *before this line Q, etc.* Now *Pope*: No *Q, Ff* 80 No *Pope*: Now *Q, Ff*

Lanc. Let me see the note.

Oly. Nay, chill watch you for zutch a tricke. But if che meet him, zoe, if not, zoe: chill make him knowe me, or chill know why I shall not, chill vare the worse.

Lanc. What, will you then neglect my daughters loue?
Venture your state and hers, for a loose brawle?

Oly. Why, man, chill not kill him; marry, chill veze him too, and againe; and zoe God be with you, vather. What, man, we shall me⟨e⟩t to morrow. [*Exit.*

Lanc. Who would a thought he had bin so desperate.
Come forth, my honest seruant *Artichoake.*

Enter Artic.

Arti. Now, what's the matter? some brawle toward, I warrant you.

Lanc. Goe get me thy sword bright scowred, thy buckler mended. O for that knaue, that Vyllaine *Daffidill* would haue done good seruice. But to thee.

Art. I, this is the trickes of all you gentlemen, when you stand in neede of a good fellow. *O for that Daffidill, O where is he?* but if you be angry, and it bee but for the wagging of a strawe, then: *out a doores with the knaue, turne the coate ouer his eares.* This is the humour of you all.

Lanc. O for that knaue, that lustie *Daffidill!*

Art. Why, there tis now: our yeares wages and our vailes will scarce pay for broken swords and bucklers that wee vse in our quarrels. But Ile not fight if *Daffidill* bee a tother side, that's flat.

Lanc. Tis no such matter, man. Get weapons ready, and bee at London ere the breake of day: watch neere the lodging of the Deuon-shire Youth, but be vnseen: and as he goes out, as he willgoe out, and that very earely without doubt—

Art. What, would you haue me draw vpon him, as he goes in the streete?

Lanc. Not for a world, man: into the fields; for to the field he goes, there to meet the desperat *Flowerdale.* Take thou the part of *Olyuer* my sonne, for he shal be my son, and marry *Luce.* Doest vnderstand me, knaue?

Arty. I, syr, I doe vnderstand you, but my young mistresse might be better prouided in matching with my fellowe *Daffidill.*

Lance. No more; *Daffidill* is a knaue:
That *Daffidill* is a most notorious knaue. [*Exit* ⟨*Arti.*⟩.

Enter Weathercocke.

Maister *Weathercocke*, you come in happy time. The desperat *Flowerdale* hath writ a challenge: And who thinke you must answere it, but the Deuenshyre man, my sonne *Oliuer*?

Wea. Mary, I am sory for it, good syr *Lancelot*,
But if you will be ruled by me, weele stay the furie.

Lance. As how, I pray?

Wea. Marry, ile tell you: by promising yong *Flowerdale* the red lipped *Luce.*

Lance. Ile rather follow her vnto her graue.

Wea. I, syr *Lancelot*, I would haue thought so too, but you and I haue bene deceiued in him: come read this will, or deed, or what you call it, I know not. Come, come, your spectacles I pray.

Lance. Nay, I thanke God, I see very well.

Wea. Marry, God blesse your eyes, mine hath bene dim almost this thirtie yeares.

Lance. Ha, what is this? what is this?

Wea. Nay, there is true loue, indeede:
He gaue it to me but this very morne,
And bid me keepe it vnseene from any one.
Good youth, to see how men may be deceiued!

Lance. Passion of me, what a wretch am I
To hate this louing youth: he hath made me,
Together with my *Luce* hee loues so deare,
Executors of all his wealth.

Wea. All, all, good man; he hath giuen you all.

Lance. Three ships now in the straits & homeward bound,
Two Lordships of two hundred pound a yeare,
The one in *Wales*, the other in *Gloster*-shyre:
Debts and accounts are thirtie thousand pound;
Plate, mony, Iewels, 16. thousand more;
Two housen furnished well in *Cole-man* street:
Beside whatsoeuer his Vnckle leaues to him,
Being of great demeanes and wealth at *Peckham.*

Wea. How like you this, good knight? how like you this?

Lance. I haue done him wrong, but now ile make amends.
The Deuen-shyre man shall whistle for a wife:

114-19 *Verse M, div. after* ready, day, youth, out, doubt 120-1 *Verse Q* 122-7 *Verse Q, etc.*

132 *S.D.* Arti. *add. R* 139 the] their *M* 145-9 *Verse M* 152 haue *F2, etc.* 154-61 *Prose Q, Ff: corr. M* 170 domains *M*

He marrie *Luce*! *Luce* shall be *Flowerdales*.

Wea. Why, that is friendly said.
Lets ride to *London* and preuent their match,
By promising your daughter to that louely lad.

Lance. Weele ride to *London*:—or it shall not need,
Weele crosse to *Dedfort-strand*, and take a boat.
Where be these knaues? what, *Artichoake*? what, *Fop*?

Enter Artichoake.

Arty. Heere be the very knaues, but not the merry knaues.

Lance. Here, take my cloake, ile haue a walke to *Dedford*.

Arty. Syr, wee haue bin scouring of our swords and bucklers for your defence.

Lance. Defence me no defence! let your swords rust, ile haue no fighting: I, let blowes alone; bid *Delia* see all things be in readinesse against the wedding. Weele haue two at once, and that will saue charges, maister *Weathercocke*.

Arty. Well, we will doe it, syr. [*Exit Omnes.*

⟨Act III. Scene I. *A walk before sir Lancelot's house.*⟩

Enter Ciuet, Francke, and Delia.

Ciu. By my truth, this is good lucke, I thanke God for this. In good sooth, I haue euen my harts desire: sister *Delia*, now I may boldly call you so, for your father hath franck and freely giuen me his daughter *Francke*.

Fran. I, by my troth, *Tom*; thou hast my good will too, for I thanke God I longed for a husband, and, would I might neuer stir, for one his name was *Tom*.

Delia. Why, sister, now you haue your wish.

Ciu. You say very true, sister *Delia*: and I prethee call me nothing but *Tom* and ile call thee sweetheart, and *Franck*: will it not doe well, sister *Delia*?

Delia. It will doe very well with both of you.

Fran. But, *Tom*, must I goe as I doe now when I am married?

Ciu. No, *Francke*, ile haue thee goe like a Citizen
In a garded gowne, and a French-hood.

Fran. By my troth, that will be excellent indeed.

Delia. Brother, maintaine your wife to your estate:
Apparell you your selfe like to your father,
And let her goe like to your ancient mother.
He sparing got his wealth, left it to you;
Brother, take heed of pride, ⟨it⟩ soone bids thrift adue.

Ciu. So as my father and my mother went! thats a iest indeed: why she went in a fringed gowne, a single ruffe, and a white cap; and my father in a mocado coat, a paire of red satten sleeues, and a canuis backe.

Delia. And yet his wealth was all as much as yours.

Ciu. My estate, my estate, I thank God, is fortie pound a yere, in good leases and tenements, besides twenty marke a yeare at cuckoldes-hauen, and that comes to vs all by inheritance.

Delia. That may, indeed, tis very fitly plyed.
I know not how it comes, but so it falles out,
That those whose fathers haue died wonderous rich,
And tooke no pleasure but to gather wealth,
Thinking of little that they leaue behind
For them, they hope, will be of their like minde,—
But ⟨it⟩ falles out contrary: forty yeares sparing
Is scarce three seuen yeares spending,—neuer caring
What will inshue, when all their coyne is gone,
And all too late, then thrift is thought vpon:
Oft haue I heard, that pride and ryot kist,
And then repentance cryes, 'for had I wist.'

Ciu. You say well, sister *Delia*, you say well: but I meane to liue within my boundes: for looke you, I haue set downe my rest thus farre, but to maintaine my wife in her french-hood, and her coach, keepe a couple of geldings, and a brace of gray hounds, and this is all ile doe.

Delia. And youle do this with fortie pound a yeare?

Ciu. I, and a better penny, sister.

Fran. Sister, you forget that at couckolds-hauen.

Ciu. By my troath, well remembred, *Francke*;
Ile giue thee that to buy thee pinnes.

Delia. Keepe you the rest for points:—alas the day,

175-7 *Prose Q, Ff*: *div. after* London, promising *M* 176 And straight prevent *M* 179 Deptford-strand *M* 182 Deptford *M* Act III. *etc. add. M* 9 his] whose *M*

26 it soon *M*: some *Q, Ff* take heed; pride soon *Haz.* 44 it *add. M*

Fooles shall haue wealth, tho all the world
say nay:
Come, brother, will you in?. dinner staies for
vs.

Ciu. I, good sister, with all my heart.

Fran. I, by my troath, *Tom*, for I haue a good stomacke.

Ciu. And I the like, sweet *Francke*. No, sister, doe not thinke ile goe beyond my boundes.

Delia. God grant you may not.

[*Exit Omnes.*

⟨Scene II. *London. The street before young Flowerdale's house.*⟩

Enter young Flowerdale and his father, with foyles in their handes.

Flow. Syrrha *Kyt*, tarrie thou there, I haue spied syr *Lancelot*, and old *Weathercocke* comming this way; they are hard at hand. I will by no meanes be spoken withall.

Fath. Ile warrant you; goe, get you in.

Enter Lancelot and Weathercocke.

Lance. Now, my honest friend, thou doest belong to maister *Flowerdale*?

Fath. I doe, syr.

Lance. Is he within, my good fellow?

Fath. No, syr, he is not within.

Lance. I prethee, if he be within, let me speake with him.

Fath. Syr, to tell you true, my maister is within, but indeed would not be spoke withall: there be some tearmes that stands vpon his reputation, therefore he will not admit any conference till he hath shooke them off.

Lance. I prethee tell him his verie good friend, syr *Lancelot Spurcocke*, intreates to speake with him.

Fath. By my troath, syr, if you come to take vp the matter betweene my maister and the Deuen-shyre man, you doe but beguile your hopes, and loose your labour.

Lance. Honest friend, I haue not any such thing to him; I come to speake with him about other matters.

Fath. For my maister, syr, hath set down his resolution, either to redeeme his honour, or leaue his life behind him.

Lance. My friend, I doe not know any quarrell, touching thy maister or any other person: my businesse is of a different nature to him, and I prethee so tell him.

Fath. For howsoeuer the Deuenshire man is, my maisters mind is bloody: thats a round O,
And therefore, syr, intreatie is but vaine:

Lance. I haue no such thing to him, I tell
thee once againe.

Fath. I will then so signifie to him.

[*Exit Father.*

Lance. A, syrrha, I see this matter is hotly
carried,
But ile labour to disswade him from it.—

Enter Flowerdale.

Good morrow, maister *Flowerdale*.

Flow. Good morrow, good syr *Lancelot*; good morrowe, maister *Weathercocke*. By my troath, gentlemen, I haue bene a reading ouer *Nick Matchiuill*; I find him good to be known, not to be followed: a pestilent humane fellow. I haue made certaine anatations of him such as they be.—And how ist syr *Lancelot*? ha? how ist? A mad world, men cannot liue quiet in it.

Lance. Maister *Flowerdale*, I doe vnderstand there is
Some iarre betweene the Deuen-shyre man
and you.

Fath. They, syr? they are good friends as
can be.

Flow. Who? maister *Oliuer* and I? as good
friends as can be.

Lance. It is a kind of safetie in you to denie it, and a generous silence, which too few are indued withall: But, syr, such a thing I heare, and I could wish it otherwise.

Flow. No such thing, syr *Lancelot*, a my reputation, as I am an honest man.

Lance. Now I doe beleeue you, then, if you
doe
Ingage your reputation there is none.

Flow. Nay, I doe not ingage my reputation there is not. You shall not bind me to any condition of hardnesse: but if there be any thing betweene vs, then there is; if there be not, then there is not: be or be not, all is one.

Lance. I doe perceiue by this, that there is something betweene you, and I am very sorie for it.

Flow. You may be deceiued, syr *Lancelot*. The *Italian* hath a pretie saying, *Questo*— I haue forgot it too, tis out of my head, but in my translation, ift hold, thus: ⟨If⟩ thou hast a friend, keepe him; if a foe, trip him.

Lance. Come, I doe see by this there is somewhat betweene you, and, before God, I could wish it other wise.

69–71 *Verse Q, Ff* Scene II. *etc. add. M* 28–30 *Verse Q, Ff*

37 intreaties is *F 1*: intreaties are *F 2* 43–51 *Verse Q, Ff* 52–3 *Div. after* iarre *Q, F 1*: *Prose F 2* 56–122 brawle *Verse Q, F 1* 60 a] at *R*: on *M* 64–8 *Verse Q, Ff* 65 is none *Molt.* 75 If *add. M*

Flow. Well what is betweene vs can hardly be altered. Syr *Lancelot*, I am to ride forth to morrow. That way which I must ride, no man must denie me the Sunne; I would not by any particular man be denied common and generall passage. If any one saith, *Flowerdale, thou passest not this way:* my answere is, I must either on or returne, but returne is not my word, I must on: if I cannot, then, make my way, nature hath done the last for me, and thers the fine.

Lance. Maister *Flowerdale*, euery man hath one tongue, and two eares: nature, in her building, is a most curious worke-maister.

Flow. That is as much ⟨as⟩ to say, a man should heare more then he should speake.

Lance. You say true, and indeed I haue heard more then at this time I will speake.

Flow. You say well.

Lance. Slanders are more common then troathes, maister *Flowerdale*: but proofe is the rule for both.

Flow. You say true; what doe you call him hath it there in his third canton.

Lance. I haue heard you haue bin wild: I haue beleeued it.

Flow. Twas fit, twas necessarie.

Lance. But I haue seene somewhat of late in you, that hath confirmed in me an opinion of goodnesse toward you.

Flow. Yfaith, syr, I am shure I neuer did you harme: some good I haue done, either to you or yours, I am shure you know not; neither is it my will you should.

Lance. I, your will, syr.

Flow. I, my will, syr? sfoot, doe you know ought of my will? Begod, and you doe, syr, I am abused.

Lance. Goe, maister *Flowerdale*; what I know, I know: and know you thus much out of my knowledge, that I truly loue you. For my daughter, she's yours. And if you like a marriage better then a brawle, all quirks of reputation set aside, goe with me presently: And where you should fight a bloodie battle, you shall be married to a louely Ladie.

Flow. Nay but, syr *Lancelot*—

Lance. If you will not imbrace my offer, yet ashure your self thus much, I will haue order to hinder your incounter.

Flow. Nay, but heare me, syr *Lancelot*.

Lance. Nay, stand not you vpon imputatiue honour. Tis meerely vnsound, vnprofitable, and idle inferences: your busines is to wedde my daughter, therefore giue me your present word to doe it. Ile goe and prouide the maid, therefore giue mee your present resolution, either now or neuer.

Flow. Will you so put me too it?

Lance. I, afore God, either take me now, or take me neuer. Else what I thought should be our match, shal be our parting; so fare you well for euer.

Flow. Stay: fall out what may fall, my loue is aboue all: I will come.

Lance. I expect you, and so fare you well.
[*Exit syr Lancelot.*

Fath. Now, syr, how shall we doe for wedding apparell?

Flow. By the masse, thats true: now helpe, *Kyt*;
The marriage ended, weele make amendes for all.

Fath. Well, no more, prepare you for your bride,
We will not want for cloathes, what so ere betide.

Flow. And thou shalt see, when once I haue my dower,
In mirth weele spend full many a merry hower:
As for this wench I not regard a pin,
It is her gold must bring my pleasures in.
⟨*Exit.*⟩

Fath. Ist possible, he hath his second liuing,
Forsaking God, himselfe to the diuel giuing?
But that I knew his mother firme and chast,
My heart would say my hed she had disgrast:
Else would I sweare he neuer was my sonne,
But her faire mind so fowle a deed did shun.

Enter Vnckle.

Vnck. How now, brother, how doe you find your sonne?

Fath. O brother, heedlesse as a libertine,
Euen growne a maister in the schoole of vice,
One that doth nothing but inuent desceit:
For all the day he humours vp and downe,
How he the next day might deceiue his friend.
He thinkes of nothing but the present time:
For one groat readie downe, heele pay a shilling,
But then the lender must needes stay for it.
When I was young, I had the scope of youth,
Both wild, and wanton, carelesse and desperate:
But such mad straines as hee's possest withall,
I thought it wonder for to dreame vpon.

94 as *add.* F 2   121 She's *Ff*: She *Q*   133 idle: Inferences *Q*

139 *Prefix* Luce *Q, Ff*   149 Well, well *M*   150 whate'er *M*   S. D. *add. M*   159, 160 *trs. S*   166 may *Haz.*

Vnck. I told you so, but you would not beleeue it.
Fath. Well, I haue found it, but one thing comforts me:
Brother, to morrow hee's to be married
To beautious *Luce*, syr *Lancelot Spurcocks* daughter.
Vnck. Ist possible?
Fath. Tis true, and thus I meane to curbe him.
This day, brother, I will you shall arrest him:
If any thing will tame him, it must be that,
For he is ranck in mischiefe, chained to a life,
That will increase his shame, and kill his wife.
Vnck. What, arrest him on his wedding day?
That were vnchristian, and an vnhumane part:
How many couple euen for that very day
Hath purchast 7 yeares sorrow afterward?
Forbeare him then to day, doe it to morrow,
And this day mingle not his ioy with sorrow.
Fath. Brother, ile haue it done this very day,
And in the viewe of all, as he comes from Church:
Doe but obserue the course that he will take.
Vpon my life he will forsweare the debt:
And for weele haue the summe shall not be slight,
Say that he owes you neere three thousand pound:
Good brother, let ⟨it⟩ be done immediately.
Vnck. Well, seeing you will haue it so,
Brother, ile doot, and straite prouide the Sheriffe.
Fath. So, brother, by this meanes shall we perceiue
What syr *Lancelot* in this pinch will do:
And how his wife doth stand affected too him—
Her loue will then be tried to the vttermost—
And all the rest of them. Brother, what I will doo,
Shall harme him much, and much auaile him too. [*Exit.*

⟨SCENE III. *A high road near London.*

Enter Oliver; afterwards sir Arthur Greenshield.⟩

Oly. Cham ashured thick be the place, that the scoundrell appointed to meet me: if a come, zo: if a come not, zo. And che war avise, he should make a coystrell an vs, ched vese him, and che vang him in hand; che would hoyst him, and giue it him too and againe, zo chud: Who bin a there? syr *Arthur*! chil staie aside.

Ar. I haue dogd the Deuen-shyre man into the field,
For feare of any harme that should befall him:
I had an inckling of that yesternight,
That *Flowerdale* and he should meet this morning:
Tho, of my soule, *Oliuer* feares him not,
Yet for ide see faire play on either side,
Made me to come, to see their valours tride.
God morrow to maister *Oliuer*.
Oli. God an good morrow.
Ar. What, maister *Oliuer*, are you angry?
Oli. Why an it be, tyt and greeuen you?
Ar. Not me at all, syr, but I imagine by
Your being here thus armed, you stay for some
That you should fight withall.
Oli. Why, and he doe, che would not dezire you to take his part.
Ar. No, by my troath, I thinke you need it not,
For he you looke for, I thinke meanes not to come.
Oli. No, & che war ashure a that, ched avese him in another place.
[*Enter Daffidill.*
Daff. O syr *Arthur*, maister *Oliuer*, aye me!
Your loue, and yours, and mine, sweet mistresse *Luce*,
This morne is married to young *Flowerdale.*
Ar. Married to *Flowerdale*! tis impossible.
Oli. Married, man, che hope thou doest but iest,
To make an a volowten meryment of it.
Daf. O, tis too true. Here comes his Vncle.

Enter Flowerdale ⟨Junior⟩, Sheriffe, Officers.

Vncle. God morrow, sir *Arthur*, good morrow, M⟨aister⟩ *Oliuer*.
Oly. God and good morne, M⟨aister⟩ *Flowerdale.* I pray you tellen vs,
Is your scoundrell kinsman married?
Vncle. M⟨aister⟩ *Oliuer*, call him what you will, but hee is maryed to sir *Launcelots* daughter here.
Arth. Vnto her?

177 Lancelots Spurcocks *Q*   180 This] That *Haz.* Brother, that day *Molt.*   185 were] were an *M*   and an] and *M*   188 him] it *R*   189 this] that *Haz.*   190 this] the *Haz.*   196 it *add. F1*   Scene III. *etc. add. M*   1-8 *Verse Q, Ff*

5 ched vang *M*   20-2 *Dir. after* imagine armed *Q, Ff*   32 make a vlowten *M*   37 *Prefix* Vncle *M* : Arth. *Q, Ff*   40 *Prefix* Arth. *M* : Vncle *Q, Ff*   Vnto *M* : Sir Arthur, vnto *Q, Ff*

Oly. I, ha the olde yellow zarued me thick tricke?
Why, man, he was a promise, chil chud a had her.
Is a zitch a voxe? chill looke to his water, che vor him.

Vncle. The musicke playes, they are comming from the Church. Sheriffe, doe your Office: fellowes, stand stoutly too it.

Enter all to the Wedding.

Oly. God giue you ioy, as the old zaid Prouerbe is, and some zorrow among. You met vs well, did you not?

Lance. Nay, be not angry, sir, the fault is in me. I haue done all the wrong, kept him from comming to the field to you, as I might, sir, for I am a Iustice, and sworne to keepe the peace.

Wea. I, marry, is he, sir, a very Iustice, and sworne to keepe the peace: you must not disturbe the weddings.

Lanc. Nay, neuer frowne nor storme, sir; if you doe,
Ile haue an order taken for you.

Oly. Well, Well, chill be quiet.

Wea. M⟨aister⟩ *Flowerdale*! sir *Lancelot*, looke you who here is. M⟨aister⟩ *Flowerdale*.

Lanc. M⟨aister⟩ *Flowerdale*, welcome with all my heart.

Flow. Vncle, this is she, yfaith: Maister Vnder-sheriffe,
Arrest me? at whose sute? draw, *Kit*.

Vnc. At my sute, sir.

Lance. Why, whats the matter M⟨aister⟩ *Flowerdale*?

Vnc. This is the matter, sir: this vnthrift here hath cozened you, and hath had of me, in seuerall summes, three thousand pound.

Flow. Why, Vncle, Vncle.

Vnck. Cousen, cousen, you haue vnckled me, and if you be not staid, youle proue a cousoner vnto all that know you.

Lance. Why, syr, suppose he be to you in debt
Ten thousand pound, his state to me appeare⟨s⟩,
To be at least three thousand by the yeare.

Vnck. O syr, I was too late informed of that plot,
How that he went about to cousen you:
And formde a will, and sent it
To your good friend there, maister *Weather-cocke*,
In which was nothing true, but brags and lyes.

Lance. Ha, hath he not such Lordships, landes, and shippes?

Vnck. Not worth a groat, not worth a halfepenie, he.

Lance. I pray, tell vs true, be plaine, young *Flowerdale*?

Flow. My vnckle here's mad, and disposed to do me wrong, but heer's my man, an honest fellow, by the lord, and of good credit, knowes all is true.

Fath. Not I, syr.
I am too old to lye, I rather know
You forgde a will, where euery line you writ,
You studied where to coate your landes might lye.

Wea. And I prethee, where be they, honest friend?

Fath. Yfaith, no where, syr, for he hath none at all,

Wea. Benedicitie, we are ore wretched, I beleeue.

Lance. I am cousend, and my hopefulst child vndone.

Flow. You are not cousend, nor is she vndone. They slaunder me, by this light they slander me: Looke you, my vnckle heres an vsurer, and would vndoe me, but ile stand in law; do you but baile me, you shal do no more: you, brother *Ciuet*, and maister *Weather-cocke*, doe but baile me, and let me haue my marriage mony paid me, and weele ride downe, and there your owne eyes shall see, how my poore tenants there wil welcome me. You shall but baile me, you shall doe no more, and, you greedy gnat, their baile will serue.

Vnck. I, syr, ile aske no better baile.

Lance. No, syr, you shall not take my baile, nor his,
Nor my sonne *Ciuets*; ile not be cheated, I.
Shreeue, take your prisoner, ile not deale with him:
Let's Vncle make false dice with his false bones,
I will not haue to doe with him: mocked, guld, & wrongd!
Come, Girle, though it be late, it falls out well,
Thou shalt not liue with him in beggers hell.

Luc. He is my husband, & hie heauen doth know,
With what vnwillingnesse I went to Church,
But you inforced me, you compelled me too it:

42 chil] ? che· 55, 61 Wea. *Ff*: Whe. *Q* 70-2 *Verse Q, Ff* 78 appeare *Q*: appears *Ff* 82, 83 *End* good, was *Q, Ff*

91 here's] here *Q* 91-4 *Verse Q, Ff* 98 quote *F 2, etc.* 99 they *M*: thy *Q, Ff* 100 friends *Q, Ff* 103 ore reached *Ff* 107-18 *Verse Q, etc.* 118 you] you, you *conj. St.* gnats *St.* 123 Let's] Let his *M*

The holy Church-man pronounced these words but now:
I must not leaue my husband in distresse.
Now I must comfort him, not goe with you.
Lanc. Comfort a cozoner? on my curse, forsake him.
Luce. This day you caused me on your curse to take him:
Doe not, I pray, my greiued soule oppresse,
God knowes my heart doth bleed at his distresse.
Lanc. O M⟨aiȝter⟩ *Weathercock*,
I must confesse I forced her to this match,
Led with opinion his false will was true.
Wea. A, he hath ouer-reached me too.
Lanc. She might haue liued like *Delia*, in a happie Virgins state.
Delia. Father, be patient, sorrow comes too late.
Lance. And on her knees she begd & did entreat,
If she must needes taste a sad marriage life,
She craued to be sir *Arthur Greene-sheilds* wife.
Ar. You haue done her & me the greater wrong.
Lanc. O, take her yet.
Arthur. Not I.
Lanc. Or, M⟨aister⟩ *Oliuer*, accept my child,
And halfe my wealth is yours.
Oly. No, sir, chil breake no Lawes.
Luce. Neuer feare, she will not trouble you.
Delia. Yet, sister, in this passion,
Doe not runne headlong to confusion.
You may affect him, though not follow him.
Frank. Doe, sister; hang him, let him goe.
Wea. Doe, faith, Mistresse *Luce*, leaue him.
Luc. You are three grosse fooles, let me alone.
I sweare ile liue with him in all ⟨his⟩ mone.
Oly. But an he haue his legges at libertie,
Cham averd hee will neuer liue with you.
Art. I, but hee is now in hucksters handling for running away.
Lanc. Huswife, you heare how you and I am wrongd,
And if you will redresse it yet you may:
But if you stand on tearmes to follow him,
Neuer come neere my sight nor looke on me,
Call me not father, looke not for a groat,
For all thy portion I wil this day giue
Vnto thy syster *Frances*.
Fran. How say you to that, *Tom*, I shall haue a good deale. Besides ile be a good wife: and a good wife is a good thing, I can tell.
Ciu. Peace *Franck*, I would be sorry to see thy sister cast away, as I am a Gentleman.
Lance. What, are you yet resolued?
Luc. Yes, I am resolued.
Lanc. Come then, away; or now, or neuer, come.
Luc. This way I turne, goe you vnto your feast,
And I to weepe, that am with griefe opprest.
Lanc. For euer flie my sight: come, gentlemen,
Lets in, ile helpe you to far better wiues then her.
Delia, vpon my blessing talke not too her.
Bace Baggage, in such hast to beggery?
Vnc. Sheriffe, take your prisoner to your charge.
Flo. Vncle, be-god you haue vsd me very hardly,
By my troth, vpon my wedding day.
[*Exit all ⟨but Luce,⟩ yong Flowerdale, his father, Vncle, Sheriffe, and Officers.*
Luc. O M⟨aister⟩ *Flowerdale*, but heare me speake;
Stay but a little while, good M⟨aister⟩ Sheriffe,
If not for him, for my sake pittie him:
Good syr, stop not your eares at my complaint,
My voyce growes weake, for womens words are faint.
Flow. Looke you, Vncle, she kneeles to you.
Vnc. Faire maid, for you, I loue you with my heart,
And greeue, sweet soule, thy fortune is so bad,
That thou shouldst match with such a graceless Youth.
Go to thy father, thinke not vpon him,
Whom hell hath marked to be the sonne of shame.
Luc. Impute his wildnesse, syr, vnto his youth,
And thinke that now is the time he doth repent:
Alas, what good or gayne can you receiue,
To imprison him that nothing hath to pay?
And where nought is, the king doth lose his due:
O, pittie him, as God shall pittie you.
Vnc. Ladie, I know his humours all too well,
And nothing in the world can doe him good,
But miserie it selfe to chaine him with.

130 Church-man] church *Haz.* 137–8 *One line Q, F 1* 150 except *Q* 154–6 *Prose Q, Ff* 159 let] pray let *M* 160 his *add. R* 164 am] are *R* 171–6 *Verse Q, Ff* 187–8 *Prose M* *S. D.* all: yong *Q, Ff*: all but Luce, young *R*

Luc. Say that your debts were paid, then is he free?
Vnc. I, virgin, that being answered, I haue done,
But to him that is all as impossible,
As I to scale the hye Piramydies.
Sheriffe, take your prisoner: Maiden, fare thee well.
Luc. O goe not yet, good M⟨aister⟩ *Flowerdale*:
Take my word for the debt, my word, my bond.
Flow. I, by God, *Vncle*, and my bond too.
Luc. Alas, I nere ought nothing but I paid it,
And I can worke; alas, he can doe nothing:
I haue some friends perhaps will pittie me,
His chiefest friends doe seeke his miserie.
All that I can or beg, get, or receiue,
Shall be for you: O doe not turne away;
Me thinkes, within, a face so reuerent,
So well experienced in this tottering world,
Should haue some feeling of a maidens griefe:
For my sake, his fathers, and your brothers sake,
I, for your soules sake that doth hope for ioy,
Pittie my state: do not two soules destroy.
Vnc. Faire maid, stand vp; not in regard of him,
But in pittie of thy haplesse choise,
I doe release him. M⟨aister⟩ Sheriffe, I thanke you:
And, officers, there is for you to drinke.
Here, maide, take this monie; there is a 100 Angels:
And for I will be sure he shall not haue it,
Here, *Kester*, take it you, and vse it sparingly,
But let not her haue any want at all.
Dry your eyes, Neece, doe not too much lament
For him, whose life hath beene in ryot spent:
If well he vseth thee, he gets him friends,
If ill, a shamefull end on him depends.
[*Exit Vncle.*

Flow. A plague goe with you for an old fornicator. Come, *Kyt*, the monie; come, honest *Kyt*.

Fath. Nay, by my faith, sir, you shall pardon me.

Flow. And why, sir, pardon you? giue me the mony, you old Rascall, or I shall make you.

Luc. Pray, hold your hands: giue it him, honest friend.

Fath. If you be so content, with all my heart.

Flow. Content, syr: sblood, shee shall be content, whether she will or no. A rattle baby come to follow me! Goe, get you gone to the greasie chuffe your father, bring me your dowrie, or neuer looke on me.

Fath. Syr, she hath forsooke her father and all her friends for you.

Flow. Hang thee, her friends and father altogether.

Fath. Yet part with something to prouide her lodging.

Flo. Yes, I meane to part with her and you, but if I part with one Angel, hang me at a poste. Ile rather throwe them at a cast at Dice, as I haue done a thousand of their fellowes.

Fath. Nay, then, I will be plaine, degenerate boy.
Thou hadst a Father would haue beene a shamed.
Flow. My father was an Asse, an old Asse.
Fath. Thy father? proud, lycentious villaine!
What, are you at your foyles? ile foyle with you.
Luc. Good sir, forbeare him.
Fath. Did not this whining woman hang on me,
Ide teach thee what it was to abuse thy father:
Goe! hang, beg, starue, dice, game, that when all is gone,
Thou maist after dispaire and hang thy selfe.
Luce. O, doe not curse him.
Fath. I doe not curse him, and to pray for him were vaine;
It greeues me that he beares his fathers name.

Flow. Well, you old rascall, I shall meet with you. Syrrha, get you gone; I will not strip the liuery ouer your eares, because you paid for it: but do not vse my name, syrrha, doe you heare? looke you doe not vse my name, you were best.

Fath. Pay me the twentie pound, then, that I lent you,
Or giue me securitie, when I may haue it.

Flow. Ile pay thee not a penny, and for securitie, ile giue thee none. Minckins, looke you doe not follow me, looke you doe not: If you doe, begger, I shall slit your nose.

Luce. Alas, what shall I doe?

209 debt *M* 223 within a *Q*, *Ff*: that one with *S* reverend *R*, *etc.* 225 haue] live *conj. St.* 238 royot *Q* 241–3, 246–8 *Verse Q*, *Ff* 247 shall] will *R*

253–7 *Verse Q*, *Ff* 266 cast of *F 2*, *etc.* 272 proud] thou proud *M* 281 Fathers *Ff*: father *Q* 282–7 *Verse Q*, *Ff* 290–3 *Verse Q*, *etc.*

Flow. Why, turne whore, thats a good trade,
And so perhaps ile see thee now and then. [*Exit Flowerdale.*

Luce. Alas the day that euer I was borne.

Fath. Sweete mistresse, doe not weepe, ile sticke to you.

Luce. Alas, my friend, I know not what to do.
My father and my friends, they haue despised me:
And I, a wretched maid, thus cast away,
Knowes neither where to goe, nor what to say.

Fath. It grieues me at the soule, to see her teares
Thus staine the crimson roses of her cheekes.—
Lady, take comfort, doe not mourne in vaine.
I haue a little liuing in this towne,
The which I thinke comes to a hundred pound,
All that and more shall be at your dispose.
Ile straite goe helpe you to some strange disguise,
And place you in a seruice in this towne,
Where you shal know all, yet your selfe vnknowne:
Come, greeue no more, where no helpe can be had,
Weepe not for him that is more worse then bad.

Luce. I thanke you, syr. ⟨*Exeunt.*⟩

⟨ACT IV. SCENE I. *A room in Sir Lancelot Spurcock's house in Kent.*⟩

Enter syr Lancelot, maister Weathercocke and them.

Oli. Well, cha a bin zerued many a sluttish tricke, but such a lerripoope as thick ych was nere a sarued.

Lance. Son *Ciuet*, daughter *Frances*, beare with me,
You see how I am pressed downe with inward griefe,
About that lucklesse gyrle, your sister *Luce*:
But tis fallen out with me,
As with many families beside,
They are most vnhappie, that are most beloued.

Ciu. Father, tis so, tis euen fallen out so, but what remedie? set hand to your heart, and let it passe. Here is your daughter *Frances* and I, and weele not say, weele bring forth as wittie children, but as prettie children as euer she was: tho she had the pricke and praise for a prettie wench. But, father, done is the mouse: youle come?

Lance. I, sonne *Ciuet*, ile come.

Ciu. And you, maister *Oliuer*?

Oli. I, for che a vext out this veast, chill see if a gan make a better veast there.

Ciu. And you, syr *Arthur*?

Ar. I, syr, although my heart be full,
Ile be a partner at your wedding feast.

Ciu. And welcome all indeed, and welcome: come, *Francke* are you readie?

Fran. Ieshue, how hastie these husbands are. I pray, father, pray to God to blesse me.

Lance. God blesse thee, and I doe: God make thee wise,
Send you both ioy: I wish it with wet eyes.

Fran. But, Father, shall not my sister *Delia* goe along with vs? She is excellent good at cookery and such things.

Lance. Yes, mary, shall she: *Delia*, make you ready.

Deli. I am ready, syr. I will first goe to *Greene-witch*, from thence to my cousen *Chesterfeelds*, and so to *London.*

Ciu. It shall suffice, good sister Delia, it shall suffice, but faile vs not, good sister; giue order to cookes, and others, for I would not haue my sweet *Francke* to soyle her fingers.

Fran. No, by my troath, not I: a gentlewoman, and a married gentlewoman too, to be companions to cookes and kitchin-boyes! not I, yfaith: I scorne that.

Ciu. Why, I doe not meane thou shalt, sweete heart; thou seest I doe not goe about it: well farewell too you. Gods pitty, M⟨aister⟩ *Weathercocke*, we shal haue your company too?

Wea. With all my heart, for I loue good cheare.

Ciu. Well, God be with you all. Come, *Francke.*

Fran. God be with you, father, God be with you, syr *Arthur*, Maister *Oliuer*, and maister *Weathercocke*, sister, God be with you all: God be with you, father, God be with you euery one.

⟨*Exeunt Civet and Frances.*⟩

Wea. Why, how now, syr *Arthur*? all a mort? maister *Oliuer*, how now man?
Cheerely, syr *Lancelot*, and merily say,
Who can hold that will away?

Lance. I, shee is gone indeed, poore girle, vndone,
But when theyle be selfewilled, children must smart.

302 Know *M* *S. D. add. R* Act IV. *etc. add. M* 7–8 *One line Q, Ff*: *div. after* out *M* 10–17 *Verse Q, etc., seven lines Q, Ff*: *eight lines M*

31–51 *Verse Q, Ff* 45 companion *F 2, etc.* 49 too: You *Q, Ff* *S. D. add. M*

Ar. But, syr, that she is wronged, you are the chiefest cause,
Therefore tis reason, you redresse her wrong.

Wea. Indeed you must, syr *Lancelot*, you must.

Lance. Must? who can compell me, maister *Weathercock*?
I hope I may doe what I list.

Wea. I grant you may, you may doe what you list.

Oli. Nay, but and you be well euisen, it were not good by this vrampolnesse, and vrowardnesse, to cast away as pretty a dowsabell, as ani chould chance to see in a Sommers day. Chil tell you what chall doe. Chil goe spye vp and downe the towne, and see if I can heare any tale or tydings of her, and take her away from thick a messell, vor cham ashured, heele but bring her to the spoile. And so var you well; we shall meete at your sonne *Ciuets*.

Lance. I thanke you, syr, I take it very kindly.

Arth. To find her out, ile spend my dearest blood:
So well I loued her, to affect her good.

[*Exit both.*

Lance. O maister *Weathercocke*,
What hap had I, to force my daughter
From maister *Oliuer*, and this good knight
To one that hath no goodnesse in his thought?

Wea. Ill lucke, but what remedie?

Lance. Yes, I haue almost deuised a remedy:
Young *Flowerdale* is shure a prisoner.

Wea. Shure, nothing more shure.

Lance. And yet perhaps his Vnckle hath released him.

Wea. It may be very like, no doubt he hath.

Lance. Well, if he be in prison, ile haue warrants
To tache my daughter till the lawe be tried,
For I will shue him vpon couzonage.

Wea. Mary, may you, and ouerthrow him too.

Lance. Nay, thats not so, I may chance be scoft,
And sentence past with him.

Wea. Beleeue me, so he may, therefore take heede.

Lance. Well howsoeuer, yet I will haue warrants;
In prison, or at libertie, alls one:
You will helpe to serue them, maister *Weathercocke*?

[*Exit Omnes.*

⟨SCENE II. *A street in London.*⟩

Enter Flowerdale.

Flow. A plague of the diuell! the diuell take the dyce! The dyce, and the diuell, and his damme goe together. Of all my hundred golden angels, I haue not left me one denier: A poxe of *come a fiue*, what shall I doe? I can borrow no more of my credit: there's not any of my acquaintance, man, nor boy, but I haue borrowed more or lesse off: I would I knewe where to take a good purse, and goe cleare away; by this light, ile venture for it. Gods lid, my sister *Delia*! Ile rob her, by this hand.

Enter Delia, and Artichoake.

Deli. I prethee, *Artichoake*, goe not so fast:
The weather is hot, and I am something wearie.

Arti. Nay, I warrant you, mistresse *Delia*, ile not tire you with leading; weele goe an extreame moderate pace.

Flow. Stand, deliuer your purse.

Arti. O lord, theeues, theeues!

[*Exit Artichoake.*

Flow. Come, come, your purse, ladie, your purse.

Deli. That voice I haue heard often before this time.
What, brother *Flowerdale* become a theefe?

Flow. I, a plague ont, I thanke your father.
But, sister, come, your mony, come! What,
The world must find me, I am borne to liue,
Tis not a sinne to steale, when none will giue.

Deli. O God, is all grace banisht from thy heart?
Thinke of the shame that doth attend this fact.

Flow. Shame me no shames; come, giue me your purse.
Ile bind you, sister, least I faire the worse.

Deli. No, bind me not: hold, there is all I haue,
And would that mony would redeeme thy shame.

Enter Oliuer, syr Arthur, and Artichoake.

Arti. Theeues, theeues, theeues!

Oli. Theeues? where, man? why, how now mistresse *Delia*?
Ha you a liked to bin a robbed?

71 avisen *M*   71–81 *Verse Q, Ff*   74 ani *pr. ed.*: am *Q, Ff*: an *M*   77 dydings *Q*: tidings *Ff, etc.*   83 *Prefix* Arty *Q*: Arti *Ff*   84 *S. D. follows* 83 *Q, Ff*   85–8 *Div.* I, Oliver, goodness *M*   101 he] it *M*

Scene II. *etc. add. M*   23 *Ends* come *Q, Ff*

Delia. No, maister *Oliuer*; tis maister *Flowerdale*, hee did but iest with me.

Oli. How, *Flowerdale*, that scoundrell? sirrha, you meten vs well: vang thee that.

Flow. Well, sir, ile not meddle with you, because I haue a charge.

Deli. Here, brother *Flowerdale*, ile lend you this same mony.

Flow. I thanke you, sister.

Oli. I wad you were ysplit, and you let the mezell haue a penny. But since you cannot keepe it, chil keepe it my selfe.

Ar. Tis pittie to releeue him in this sort,
Who makes a triumphant life his daily sport.

Delia. Brother, you see how all men censure you,
Farewell, and I pray God amend your life.

Oly. Come, chill bring you along, and you safe enough from twentie such scoundrells as thick a one is. Farewell and be hanged, zyrrha, as I thinke so thou wilt be shortly. Come, syr *Arthur*.

[*Exit all but Flowerdale.*

Flow. A plague goe with you for a karsie rascall.
This Deuenshyre man, I think, is made all of porke,
His hands made onely for to heaue vp packs:
His hart as fat and big as his face;
As differing far from all braue gallant minds
As I to serue the hogges, and drinke with hindes,
As I am very neere now. Well, what remedie?
When mony, meanes, and friends doe growe so small,
Then farewell life, and ther's an end of all.

[*Exit.*

⟨SCENE III. *Another street. Before Civet's house.*⟩

Enter Father, Luce like a Dutch Frow, Ciuet, and his wife mistresse Frances.

Ciu. By my troath, god a mercie for this, good *Christopher*, I thanke thee for my maide, I like her very well. How doest thou like her, *Frances*?

Fran. In good sadnesse, *Tom*, very well, excellent well; she speakes so prettily.—I pray whats your name?

Luce. My name, forsooth, be called *Tanikin*.

Fran. By my troath, a fine name. O *Tanikin*, you are excellent for dressing ones head a newe fashion.

Luce. Me sall doe euery ting about da head.

Ciu. What countriwoman is she, *Kester*?

Fath. A dutch woman, sir.

Ciu. Why then she is outlandish, is she not?

Fath. I, Syr, she is.

Fran. O, then, thou canst tell how to helpe mee to cheekes and eares?

Luce. Yes, mistresse, verie vell.

Fath. Cheekes and eares! why, mistresse *Frances*, want you cheekes and eares? me thinkes you haue very faire ones.

Fran. Thou art a foole indeed. *Tom*, thou knowest what I meane.

Ciu. I, I, *Kester*, tis such as they weare a their heads. I prethee, *Kit*, haue her in, and shewe her my house.

Fath. I will, sir. Come, *Tanikin*.

Fran. O *Tom*, you haue not bussed me to day, *Tom*.

Ciu. No, *Frances*, we must not kisse afore folkes. God saue me, *Francke*,

Enter Delia, and Artichoake.

See yonder my sister *Delia* is come. Welcome, good sister.

Fran. Welcome, good sister, how do you like the tier of my head?

Delia. Very well, sister.

Ciu. I am glad you're come, sister *Delia*, to giue order for supper; they will be here soone.

Arty. I, but if good luck had not serued, she had not bin here now: filching *Flowerdale* had like to peppord vs; but for maister *Oliuer*, we had bin robbed.

Deli. Peace, syrrha, no more.

Fath. Robbed! by whom?

Arty. Marry, by none but by *Flowerdale*; he is turned theefe.

Ciu. By my faith, but that is not well; but God be praised for your escape. Will you draw neere, sister?

Fath. Syrrha, come hither. Would *Flowerdale*, hee that was my maister, a robbed you? I prethee, tell me true.

Arty. Yes, yfaith, euen that *Flowerdale*, that was thy maister.

Fath. Hold thee, there is a French crowne, and speake no more of this.

Arty. Not I, not a word.—Now do I smell knauerie:
In euery purse *Flowerdale* takes, he is halfe:
And giues me this to keepe counsell.—No, not a word I.

48 trompant *conj. M* 49 consure *Q* 64 *S. D.* Exit omnes *Q* Scene III. *etc. add. M* 1–7 *Verse Q, F 1* 11 one *Q, F 1*

34 save my *Ff* 40–6 *Verse Q, Ff* 45 to have pepper'd *M* 63 No *om. Ff, etc.*

Fath. Why, God a mercy.

Fran. Sister, looke here, I haue a new Dutch maid, and she speakes so fine, it would doe your heart good.

Ciu. How doe you like her, sister?

Deli. I like your maide well.

Ciu. Well, deare sister, will you draw neere, and giue directions for supper? guests will be here presently.

Delia. Yes, brother; leade the way; ile follow you.

[*Exit all but Delia and Luce.*

Harke you, Dutch frowe, a word.

Luce. Vat is your vill wit me?

Deli. Sister *Luce*, tis not your broken language,
Nor this same habit, can disguise your face
From I that know you: pray tell me, what meanes this?

Luce. Sister, I see you know me; yet be secret.
This borrowed shape, that I haue tane vpon me,
Is but to keepe my selfe a space vnknowne,
Both from my father, and my neerest friendes,
Vntill I see how time will bring to passe
The desperate course of maister *Flowerdale*.

Deli. O hee is worse then bad, I prethee leaue him,
And let not once thy heart to thinke on him.

Luce. Do not perswade me once to such a thought.
Imagine yet, that he is worse then naught:
Yet one houers time may all that ill vndo,
That all his former life did run into.
Therefore kind sister doe not disclose my estate:
If ere his heart doth turne, tis nere too late.

Dely. Well, seeing no counsell can remoue your mind,
Ile not disclose you that art wilfull blinde.

Luc. *Delia*, I thank you. I now must please her eies,
My sister *Frances*, neither faire nor wise.

[*Exit Omnes.*

⟨ACT V. SCENE I. *Scene before Civet's house.*⟩

Enter Flowerdale solus.

Flo. On goes he that knowes no end of his iourney. I haue passed the very vtmost bounds of shifting, I haue no course now but to hang my selfe: I haue liued since yesterday two a clocke of a spice-cake I had at a buriall: and for drinke, I got it at an Ale-house among Porters, such as will beare out a man, if he haue no mony indeed—I meane out of their companyes, for they are men of good carriage. Who comes heere? The two Conycatchers, that woon all my mony of me. Ile trie if thayle lend me any.

Enter Dicke and Rafe.

What, M⟨aister⟩ *Richard*, how doe you? How doest thou, *Rafe*? By God, gentlemen, the world growes bare with me: will you do as much as lend me an Angel betweene you both. You know you won a hundred of me the other day.

Rafe. How, an Angel? God damb vs, if we lost not euery peny, within an houre after thou wert gone.

Flow. I prethy lend me so much as will pay for my supper. Ile pay you againe, as I am a Gentleman.

Rafe. I faith, we haue not a farthing, not a myte:
I wonder at it, M⟨aister⟩ *Flowerdale*,
You will so carelesly vndo your selfe.
Why, you will loose more mony in an houre,
Then any honest man spend in a yeare.
For shame, betake you to some honest Trade,
And liue not thus so like a Vagabond.

[*Exit both.*

Flow. A Vagabond, indeed! more villaines you:
They gaue me counsell that first cozend me:
Those Diuels first brought me to this I am,
And being thus, the first that doe me wrong.
Well, yet I haue one friend left in store:
Not farre from hence there dwels a Cokatryce,
One that I first put in a satten gowne,
And not a tooth that dwells within her head,
But stands me at the least in 20. pound:
Her will I visite now my coyne is gone,
And, as I take it, heere dwelles the Gentlewoman.
What ho, is Mist⟨r⟩esse *Apricocke* within?

Enter Ruffyn.

Ruff. What sawsie Rascall is that which knocks so bold?
O, is it you? old spend-thrift, are you here?
One that is turned Cozoner about the towne:
My Mistresse saw you, and sends this word by me:
Either be packing quickly from the doore,

71 guests *F 2, etc.*: guesse *Q, F 1* 89 hour's *M*: houers *Q, Ff*: good *R* Act V. *etc. add. M* 1–24 *Verse Q, Ff*

5 of] on *M* 25 haue] haue haue *Q* 29 spends *Ff, etc.* 36 firiend *Q* left me in *M* 39 dwell *Q* 42 Gentlewomen *Q*

Or you shall haue such a greeting sent you strait,
As you will little like on: you had best be gone.

Flow. Why so, this is as it should be: being poore,
Thus art thou serued by a vile painted whoore.
Well, since thy damned crew doe so abuse thee,
Ile try of honest men, how they will vse mee.

Enter an auncient Citizen.

Sir, I beseech you to take compassion of a man, one whose Fortunes haue beene better then at this instant they seeme to bee: but if I might craue of you some such little portion, as would bring mee to my friends, I should rest thankfull, vntill I had requited so great a curtesie.

Citizen. Fie, fie, yong man, this course is very bad,
Too many such haue wee about this Cittie,
Yet for I haue not seene you in this sort,
Nor noted you to be a common begger:
Hold, theres an Angel, to beare your charges downe.
Goe to your freinds, do not on this depend:
Such bad beginnings oft haue worser ends. [*Exit Citt.*

Flow. Worser endes: nay, if it fall out no worse then in old angels I care not. Nay, now I haue had such a fortunate beginning, Ile not let a sixepennie-purse escape me. By the Masse, here comes another.

Enter a Citizens wife with a torch before her.

God blesse you, faire Mistresse. Now would it please you, gentlewoman, to looke into the wants of a poore Gentle-man, a yonger brother, I doubt not but God will treble restore it backe againe: one that neuer before this time demanded pennie, halfpenie, nor farthing.

Citiz. Wife. Stay, *Alexander.* Now, by my troth, a very proper man, and tis great pittie: hold, my friend, theres all the monie I haue about me, a couple of shillings, and God blesse thee.

Flow. Now God thanke you, sweete Lady: if you haue any friend, or Garden-house, where you may imploy a poore gentleman as your friend, I am yours to command in all secret seruice.

Citiz. I thanke you, good friend. I prethy let me see that againe I gaue thee: there is one of them a brasse shilling; giue me them, and here is halfe a crowne in gold. [*He giues it her.*] Nowe, out vpon thee, Rascall! secret seruice! what doest thou make of mee? it were a good deede to haue thee whipt. Now I haue my money againe, ile see thee hanged before I giue thee a pennie. Secret seruice! On, good *Alexander.* [*Exit both.*

Flow. This is villanous lucke. I perceiue dishonestie will not thriue: here comes more. God forgiue mee, Sir *Arthur*, and M⟨aister⟩ *Oliuer*: afore God, Ile speake to them.

Enter Sir Arthur, and M. Oliuer.

God saue you, Sir *Arthur*: God saue you, M⟨aister⟩ *Oliuer.*

Oli. Byn you there, zyrrha? come, will you ytaken your selfe to your tooles, Coystrell?

Flow. Nay, M⟨aister⟩ *Oliuer*, Ile not fight with you.
Alas, sir, you know it was not my dooings,
It was onely a plot to get Sir *Lancelots* daughter:
By God, I neuer meant you harme.

Oli. And whore is the Gentle-woman thy wife, Mezell? Whore is shee, Zyrrha, ha?

Flow. By my troth, M⟨aister⟩ *Oliuer*, sicke, very sicke; and God is my Iudge, I know not what meanes to make for her, good Gentle-woman.

Oli. Tell me true, is she sicke? tell me true, itch vise thee.

Flow. Yes, faith, I tell you true: M⟨aister⟩ *Oliuer*, if you would doe mee the small kindnesse, but to lend me fortie shillings: so God helpe me, I will pay you so soone as my abilitie shall make me able, as I am a gentleman.

Oli. Well, thou zaist thy wife is zicke: hold, thers vortie shillings; giue it to thy wife. Looke thon giue it her, or I shall zo veze thee, thou wert not so vezed this zeuen yeare; looke too it.

Art. Yfaith, M⟨aister⟩ *Oliuer*, it is in vaine
To giue to him that neuer thinkes of her.

Oli. Well, would che could yuind it.

Flow. I tell you true, sir *Arthur*, as I am a gentleman.

Oli. Well fare you well, zyrrah: come, sir *Arthur.* [*Exit both.*

Flow. By the Lord, this is excellent.
Fiue golden Angels compast in an houre!
If this trade hold, ile neuer seeke a new.
Welcome, sweet gold: and beggery, adue.

Enter Vnckle and Father.

Vnc. See, *Kester*, if you can find the house.

53 thee] me *S* 58 some such *pr. ed.*: so much *Q, Ff*: some *R* 66 *Ends* charges *Q, Ff* 68 end *M* 69 end *M*

127 giued *Q* 136 farewell *Ff, etc.*

Flow. Whose here? my Vnckle, and my man *Kester*? By the masse, tis they. How doe you, Vnckle, how dost thou, *Kester*? By my troath, Vnckle, you must needes lend me some mony: the poore gentlewoman my wife, so God helpe me, is verie sicke. I was robde of the hundred angels you gaue me; they are gone.

Vnc. I, they are gone indeed; come, *Kester*, away.

Flow. Nay, Vnckle, do you heare? good Vnckle.

Vnc. Out, hypocrite, I will not heare thee speake;
Come, leaue him, *Kester*.

Flow. *Kester*, honest *Kester*.

Fath. Syr, I haue nought to say to you. Open the doore, Tanikin: thou hadst best lockt fast, for theres a false knaue without.

Flow. You are an old lying Rascall, so you are. [*Exit both.*

Enter Luce.

Luce. Vat is de matter? Vat be you, yonker?

Flow. By this light, a Dutch Froe: they say they are calde kind. By this light, ile try her.

Luce. Vat bin you, yonker? why doe you not speake?

Flow. By my troath, sweet heart, a poore gentleman that would desire of you, if it stand with your liking, the bountie of your purse.

Enter father.

Luce. O here, God, so young an armine.

Flow. Armine, sweet-heart? I know not what you meane by that, but I am almost a begger.

Luce. Are you not a married man? vere bin your vife? Here is all I haue: take dis.

Flow. What, gold, young Froe? this is braue.

Fath.—If he haue any grace, heele now repent.

Luce. Why speake you not? were be your vife?

Flow. Dead, dead, shees dead; tis she hath vndone me: spent me all I had, and kept rascalls vnder mine nose to braue me.

Luce. Did you vse her vell?

Flow. Vse her? theres neuer a gentlewoman in *England* could be better vsed then I did her. I could but Coatch her; her diet stood me in fortie pound a moneth, but shee is dead and in her graue my cares are buried.

Luce. Indeed, dat vas not scone.

Fath. —He is turned more diuell then he was before.

Flow. Thou doest belong to maister *Ciuet* here, doest thou not?

Luce. Yes me doe.

Flow. Why, theres it: theres not a handfull of plate but belongs to me, Gods my Iudge: if I had but such a wench as thou art, theres neuer a man in *England* would make more of her, then I would doe, so she had any stocke.

They call within: O, why, *Tanikin*.

Luce. Stay, one doth call; I shall come by and by againe.

Flow. By this hand, this Dutch wench is in loue with me. Were it not admirall to make her steale all *Ciuets* Plate, and runne away.

Fath. Twere beastly. O maister *Flowerdale*,
Haue you no feare of God, nor conscience?
What doe you meane by this vilde course you take?

Flow. What doe I meane? why, to liue, that I meane.

Fath. To liue in this sort? fie vpon the course:
Your life doth show, you are a verie coward.

Flow. A coward? I pray, in what?

Fath. Why, you will borrow sixpence of a boy.

Flow. Snailes, is there such cowardice in that? I dare borrow it of a man, I, and of the tallest man in *England*, if he will lend it me. Let me borrowe it how I can, and let them come by it how they dare. And it is well knowne, I might a rid out a hundred times if I would: so I might.

Fath. It was not want of will, but cowardice.
There is none that lends to you, but know they gaine:
And what is that but onely stealth in you?
Delia might hang you now, did not her heart
Take pittie of you for her sisters sake.
Goe, get you hence, least, lingering where you stay,
You fall into their hands you looke not for.

Flow. Ile tarie here, till the Dutch Froe comes, if all the diuels in hell were here. [*Exit Father.*

143–50, 158–62 *Verse Q, Ff* 159 Tanikin *pr. ed.*: to my kin *Q, Ff*: to me, 'Kin *M*

195 shoen *Haz.* 201–5 *Verse Q, Ff* 203 but *om. Ff, etc.* 210 admirable *R, etc.* 209–11, 220–8 *Verse Q, Ff* 226 kowne *Q* 234 where *pr. ed.*: here *Q, Ff, etc.* your stay *M*

Enter syr Lancelot, maister Weathercocke, and Artichoake.

Lance. Where is the doore? are we not past it, *Artichoake*?

Arty. Bith masse, heres one; ile aske him. Doe you heare, sir? What, are you so proud? doe you heare? which is the way to maister *Ciuets* house? what will you not speake? O me, this is filching *Flowerdale*.

Lance. O wonderfull, is this leaude villaine here?
O you cheating Roague, you cut-purse conicatcher,
What ditch, you villaine, is my daughters graue?
A cozening rascall, that must make a will,
Take on him that strict habit—very that,
When he should turne to angell—a dying grace.
Ile father in lawe you, syr, ile make a will!
Speake, villaine, wheres my daughter?
Poysoned, I warrant you, or knockéd a the head
And to abuse good maister *Weathercocke*,
With his fordged will, and maister *Weathercocke*
To make my grounded resolution,
Then to abuse the Deuenshyre gentleman:
Goe, away with him to prison.

Flow. Wherefore to prison? syr, I will not goe.

Enter maister Ciuet, his wife, Oliuer, syr Arthur, Father, and Vnckle, Delia.

Lance. O heeres his Vnckle! welcome, gentlemen, welcome all. Such a cozoner, gentlemen, a murderer too, for any thing I know: my daughter is missing: hath bin looked for, cannot be found. A vild vpon thee.

Vnc. He is my kinsman, altho his life be vilde;
Therefore, in Gods name, doe with him what you will.

Lance. Marrie, to prison.

Flow. Wherefore to prison? snick vp, I owe you nothing.

Lance. Bring forth my daughter then: away with him.

Flow. Goe seeke your daughter; what doe you lay to my charge.

Lance. Suspition of murder: goe, away with him.

Flow. Murder, you dogs? I murder your daughter!
Come, Vnckle, I know youle baile me.

Vnc. Not I, were there no more, then I the Iaylor, thou the prisoner.

Lance. Goe; away with him.

Enter Luce like a Frowe.

Luce. O my life, here; where will you ha de man?
Vat ha de younker done?

Wea. Woman, he hath kild his wife.

Luce. His vife: dat is not good, dat is not seene.

Lance. Hang not vpon him, huswife; if you doe, ile lay you by him.

Luce. Haue me no oder way dan you haue him:
He tell me dat he loue me hartily.

Fran. Lead away my maide to prison! why, *Tom*, will you suffer that?

Ciu. No, by your leaue, father, she is no vagrant: she is my wiues chamber maid, & as true as the skin between any mans browes here.

Lance. Goe too, you're both fooles:
Sonne *Ciuet*, of my life, this is a plot,
Some stragling counterfait preferd to you,
No doubt to rob you of your plate and Iewels.
Ile haue you led away to prison, trull.

Luce. I am no trull, neither outlandish Frowe.
Nor he, nor I shall to the prison goe:
Know you me now? nay, neuer stand amazed.
Father, I know I haue offended you,
And tho that dutie wills me bend my knees
To you in dutie and obedience:
Yet this wayes doe I turne, and to him yeeld
My loue, my dutie and my humblenesse.

Lanc. Bastard in nature! kneele to such a slaue?

Luce. O M⟨aister⟩ *Flowerdale*, if too much griefe
Haue not stopt vp the orgens of your voyce,
Then speake to her that is thy faithfull wife:
Or doth contempt of me thus tye thy tongue?
Turne not away, I am no Æthyope,
No wanton *Cressed*, nor a changing *Hellen*:
But rather one made wretched by thy losse.
What, turnst thou still from me? O then
I gesse thee wofulst among haplesse men.

Flow. I am, indeed, wife, wonder among wiues!
Thy chastitie and vertue hath infused
Another soule in mee, red with defame,

238 *Prefix* Luce *Q* 240 Bith] By th' *Ff* 245 lewde *Ff* 249 a strict habit, feigning that *Haz.* 256 make] shake *conj. M* 257 gentlemen *Q, F1* 261 *Prefix* Luce *Q* 261–5 *Verse Q* 277 you dogs *pr. ed.*: your dogs *Q, etc.*

282 here *om. Ff*: hear *M* 286 shoen *Haz.* 289 oder . . dan *M*: and or . . doe *Q, Ff* leave him *R* 297 *Ends* Ciuet *Q, Ff* 308 way *M*

For in my blushing cheekes is seene my shame.

Lanc. Out, Hypocrite. I charge thee, trust him not.

Luce. Not trust him? by ⟨the⟩ hopes ⟨of⟩ after blisse,
I know no sorrow can be compar'd to his.

Lan. Well, since thou weart ordain'd to beggery,
Follow thy fortune; I defie thee, I.

Oly. Ywood che were so well ydoussed as was euer white cloth in a tocking mill, and che ha not made me weepe.

Fath. If he hath any grace, heele now repent.

Art. It moues my heart.

Wea. By my troth, I must weepe, I can not chuse.

Vncle. None but a beast would such a maide misuse.

Flow. Content thy selfe, I hope to win his fauour,
And to redeeme my reputation lost:
And, Gentlemen, beleeue me, I beseech you:
I hope your eyes shall behold such change,
As shall deceiue your expectation.

Oly. I would che were ysplit now, but che beleeue him.

Lance. How, beleeue him?

Wea. By the mackins, I doe.

Lance. What, doe you thinke that ere he will haue grace?

Wea. By my faith, it will goe hard.

Oly. Well, che vor ye, he is changed: and M⟨aister⟩ *Flowerdale*, in hope you been so, hold, theres vortie pound toward your zetting vp: what, bee not ashamed; vang it, man, vang it: bee a good husband, louen your wife: and you shall not want for vortie more, I che vor thee.

Arth. My meanes are little, but if youle follow me,
I will instruct you in my ablest power:
But to your wife I giue this Diamond,
And proue true Dimond faire in all your life.

Flow. Thankes, good sir *Arthur*, M⟨aister⟩ *Oliuer*,
You being my enemie, and growne so kind,
Bindes mee in all indeuour to restore—

Oly. What! restore me no restorings, man. I haue vortie pound more for *Luce*; here, vang it: Zouth, chil devie *London* els. What, do not thinke me a Mezel or a Scondrell to throw away my money: che haue a hundred pound more to pace of any good spotation: I hope your vader and your vncle here wil vollow my zamples.

Vncle. You haue gest right of me; if he leaue of this course of life, he shall be mine heire.

Lan. But he shall neuer get a groat of me:
A Cozoner, a deceiuer, one that kild
His painefull father, honest Gentleman
That passed the fearefull danger of the sea,
To get him liuing and maintaine him braue.

Wea. What, hath he kild his father?

Lance. I, sir, with conceit of his vild courses.

Fath. Sir, you are misinformed.

Lanc. Why, thou old knaue, thou toldst me so thy selfe.

Fa. I wrong'd him then: and toward my M⟨aisters⟩ stock,
Thers 20 Nobles for to make amends.

Flo. No, *Kester*, I haue troubled thee, and wrong'd thee more.
What thou in loue giues, I in loue restore.

Fra. Ha, ha, sister, there you playd bo-peepe with *Tom.* What shall I giue her toward houshold? Sister *Delia*, shall I giue her my Fanne?

Del. You were best aske your husband.

Fran. Shal I, *Tom?*

Ciuet. I, do, *Franck*; ile by thee a new one, with a longer handle.

Franck. A russet one, *Tom.*

Ciuit. I, with russet feathers.

Fran. Here, sister, theres my Fanne toward houshold, to keepe you warme.

Luce. I thanke you, sister.

Wea. Why this is well, and toward faire *Luces* stocke, heres fortie shillings: and fortie good shillings more, Ile giue her, marrie. Come, sir *Lancelot*, I must haue you friends.

Lance. Not I, all this is counterfeit;
He will consume it, were it a Million.

Fath. Sir, what is your daughters dower worth?

Lance. Had she been married to an honest man,
It had beene better then a thousand pound.

Fath. Pay it him, and ile giue you my bond,
To make her ioynter better worth then three.

Lance. Your bond, sir? why, what are you?

Fath. One whose word in *London*, tho I say it,
Will passe there for as much as yours.

325 the *add. Ff* of *add. R* 331 che] chea *Q*
353 louen to your *Ff, etc.*
369 vader *Percy* : vnder *Q, Ff* 385 wrong *Q*
387–90 *Verse Q* : *corr. M* 395 Tom] Francke *Q*
400–3 *Verse M* : *div. after* stock, more, Lancelot 409 him] to him *M*

Lanc. Weart not thou late that vnthrifts seruing-man?
Fath. Looke on me better, now my scarre is off.
Nere muse, man, at this metamorphosie.
Lance. M⟨aister⟩ *Flowerdale*!
Flow. My father! O, I shame to looke on him.
Pardon, deare father, the follyes that are past.
Fa. Sonne, sonne, I doe, and ioy at this thy change,
And applaud thy fortune in this vertuous maide,
Whom heauen hath sent to thee to saue thy soule.
Luc. This addeth ioy to ioy, hie heauen be prais'd.
Wea. M⟨aister⟩ *Flowerdale*!
Welcome from death, good M⟨aister⟩ *Flowerdale.*
Twas sed so here, twas sed so here, good faith.
Fath. I caused that rumour to be spred my selfe,
Because ide see the humours of my sonne,
Which to relate the circumstance is needlesse:
And, sirra, see you runne no more into
That same disease:
For he thats once cured of that maladie,
Of Ryot, Swearing, Drunkennes, and Pride,
And falles againe into the like distresse,
That feuor is deadly, doth till death indure:
Such men die mad as of a callenture.
Flow. Heauen helping me, ile hate the course as hell.
Vnc. Say it and do it, Cozen, all is well.
Lanc. Wel, being in hope youle proue an honest man,
I take you to my fauour. Brother *Flowerdale,*
Welcome with all my heart: I see your care
Hath brought these acts to this conclusion,
And I am glad of it: come, lets in and feast.
Oly. Nay, zoft you awhile: you promised to make Sir *Arthur* and me amends. Here is your wisest daughter; see which ans sheele haue.
Lanc. A Gods name, you haue my good will, get hers.
Oly. How say you then, Damsell, tyters hate?
Delia. I, sir, am yours.
Oly. Why, then, send for a Vicar, and chil haue it dispatched in a trice, so chill.
Delia. Pardon me, sir, I meane I am yours,
In loue, in dutie, and affection,
But not to loue as wife: shall neere be said,
Delya was buried married, but a mayd.
Arth. Doe not condemne your selfe for euer,
Vertuous faire, you were borne to loue.
Oly. Why, you say true, sir *Arthur*, she was ybere to it so well as her mother: but I pray you shew vs some zamples or reasons why you will not marry?
Deli. Not that I doe condemne a married life,
For tis no doubt a sanctimonious thing:
But for the care and crosses of a wife,
The trouble in this world that children bring;
My vow is in heauen in earth to liue alone,
Husbands, howsoeuer good, I will haue none.
Oly. Why, then che will liue Batcheller too. Che zet not a vig by a wife, if a wife zet not a vig by me. Come, shalls go to dinner?
Fa. To morrow I craue your companies in *Mark-lane*:
To night weele frolike in M⟨aister⟩ *Ciuites* house,
And to each health drinke downe a full carouse.

FINIS.

424–5 *One line Q, etc.* 430–1 *One line Q, Ff*: *div. after* see *M* 440 fauour brother *Q*: *corr. Ff*

444–7 *Verse Q, Ff* 446 ans] on us *M* 449 tyters hate *om. R, etc.* 453 I] that I *M* 455 it shall *M* 457–8 *Prose M* 459–62 *Verse Q, Ff* 460 ybore *Ff, etc.* 467 on earth *M* 469–71 *Verse Q, Ff* 469 che will *M*: chil will *Q*: chill *Ff* a Batchelor *Ff, etc.*

THE PVRITAINE

Or

THE VVIDDOVV

of Watling-ſtreete.

Acted by the Children of Paules.

Written by W. S.

Imprinted at London by G. ELD.
1607.

Q	=	Quarto of 1607
F 1	=	(Third) Folio Shakespeare, 1664
F 2	=	(Fourth) ,, ,, 1685
R	=	Rowe, 1709
Pope	=	Supplement to Pope's Shakespeare, 1728
M	=	Malone, 1780
St.	=	Steevens, ibid.
Th.	=	Theobald, ibid.
S	=	Simms, 1848
T	=	Tyrrell, 1851
Haz.	=	Hazlitt, 1852
pr. ed.	=	present editor

THE PVRITAINE WIDDOW

⟨The
Actors
Names
In the *Play* Intituled
The Puritan Widow.

The Scene *London*.

Lady Plus, a Citizens Widow.
Frances }
Moll } *her two Daughters.*
Sir Godfrey, Brother-in-Law to the Widow Plus.
Master Edmond, Son to the Widow Plus.
George Pye-boord, a Schollar and a Citizen.
Peter Skirmish, an old Soldier.
Captain Idle, a Highway-man.
Corporall Oath, a vain-glorious Fellow.
Nicholas St. Antlings }
Simon St. Mary Overies } *Serving-men to the Lady Plus.*
Frailty }
Sir Oliver Muck-hill, a Suiter to the Lady Plus.
Sir Iohn Penny-Dub, a Suiter to Moll.
Sir Andrew Tipstaffe, a Suiter to Frances.
The Sheriffe of London.
Puttock }
Ravenshaw } *Two of the Sheriffs Serjeants.*
Dogson, a Yeoman.
A Noble-man.
A Gentleman Citizen.
Officers.⟩ [1]

ACTVS PRIMVS.

⟨Scene I. *A Garden behind the widow's house.*⟩

Enter the Lady Widdow-Plus, *her two Daughters* Franke *and* Moll, *her husbands Brother an old Knight* Sir Godfrey, *with her Sonne and heyre Maister* Edmond, *all in moorning apparell,* Edmond *in a Cypresse Hatte. The Widdow wringing her hands, and bursting out into passion, as newly come from the Buriall of her husband.*

Widow. Oh, that euer I was borne, that euer I was borne!

Sir Godfrey. Nay, good Sister, deare sister, sweete sister, bee of good comfort; shew your selfe a woman, now or neuer.

Wid. Oh, I haue lost the deerest man, I haue buried the sweetest husband that euer lay by woman.

Sir God. Nay, giue him his due, hee was indeed an honest, vertuous, discreet, wise man,—hee was my Brother, as right as right.

Wid. O, I shall neuer forget him, neuer forget him; hee was a man so well giuen to a woman—oh!

Sir Godf. Nay, but, kinde Sister, I could weepe as much as any woman, but, alas, our teares cannot call him againe: me thinkes you are well read, Sister, and know that death is as common as *Homo,* a common name to all men:—a man shall bee taken when hee's making water.—Nay, did not the learned Parson, Maister *Pigman,* tell vs een now, that all Flesh is fraile, wee are borne to dye, Man ha's but a time: with such like deepe and profound perswasions, as hee is a rare fellow, you know, and an excellent Reader: and for example, (as there are examples aboundance,) did not Sir *Humfrey Bubble* dye tother day? There's a lustie Widdow; why, shee cryed not aboue halfe an houre—for shame, for shame! then followed him old Maister *Fulsome,* the Vsurer: there's a wise Widdow; why, shee cryed nere a whitte at all.

Wid. O, rancke not mee with those wicked women: I had a Husband out-shinde 'em all.

Syr Godf. I, that he did, Ifaith: he out-shind 'em all.

Widd. Doost thou stand there and see vs all weepe, and not once shed a teare for thy fathers death? oh, thou vngratious sonne and heyre, thou!

Edm. Troth, Mother, I should not weepe, I'me sure; I am past a childe, I hope, to make all my old Schoole fellowes laughe at me; I should bee mockt, so I should. Pray, let one of my Sisters weepe for mee. Ile laughe as much for her another time.

Widd. Oh, thou past-Grace, thou! out of my sight, thou gracelesse impe, thou grieuest mee more then the death of thy Father! oh, thou stubborne onely sonne! hadst thou such an honest man to thy Father—that would deceaue all the world to get riches for thee—and canst thou not afforde a little salt water? he that so wisely did quite ouer-throw the right heyre of those lands, which now you respect not: vp euery morning betwixt foure and fiue; so duely at Westminster Hall euery Tearme-Time, with all his Cardes and writings, for thee, thou wicked *Absolon*—oh, deare husband!

[1] *Dram. Pers. add. F1* Scene I. *etc. add. M* 10 wise-man *Q*

59 Cardes] charts *conj. M*

Edm. Weep, quotha? I protest I am glad hee's Churched; for now hee's gone, I shall spend in quiet.

Fran. Deere mother, pray cease; halfe your Teares suffize.
Tis time for you to take truce with youre eyes;
Let me weepe now.

Widd. Oh, such a deere knight! such a sweete husband haue I lost, haue I lost!—If Blessed bee the coarse the raine raynes vpon, he had it powring downe.

Syr Godf. Sister, be of good cheere, wee are all mortall our selues. I come vppon you freshly. I neare speake without comfort, heere me what I shall say:—my brother ha's left you wellthy, y'are rich.

Widd. Oh!

Syr Godf. I say y'ar rich: you are also faire.

Widd. Oh!

Sir Godf. Goe too, y'are faire, you cannot smother it; beauty will come to light; nor are your yeares so farre enter'd with you, but that you will bee sought after, and may very well answere another husband; the world is full of fine Gallants, choyse enow, Sister,—for what should wee doe with all our Knights, I pray, but to marry riche widdowes, wealthy Cittizens widdowes, lusty faire-browd Ladies? go too, bee of good comfort, I say: leaue snobbing and weeping—Yet my Brother was a kinde hearted man—I would not haue the Elfe see mee now! —Come, pluck vp a womans heart—here stands your Daughters, who be well estated, and at maturity will also bee enquir'd after with good husbands, so all these teares shall bee soone dryed vp and a better world then euer—What, Woman? you must not weepe still; hee's dead, hee's buried—yet I cannot chuse but weepe for him!

Wid. Marry againe! no! let me be buried quick then!
And that same part of Quire whereon I tread
To such intent, O may it be my graue;
And that the Priest may turne his wedding praiers,
E'en with a breath, to funerall dust and ashes!
Oh, out of a million of millions, I should nere finde such a husband; hee was vnmatchable,—vnmatchable! nothing was to hot, nor to deere for mee, I could not speake of that one thing, that I had not: beside I had keyes of all, kept all, receiu'd all, had money in my purse, spent what I would, went abroad when I would, came home when I would, and did all what I would. Oh, my sweete husband! I shall neuer haue the like.

Sir Godf. Sister, nere say so; hee was an honest brother of mine, and so, and you may light vpon one as honest againe, or one as honest againe may light vpon you: that's the properer phrase, indeed.

Wid. Neuer! oh, if you loue me, vrge it not. ⟨*Kneels.*⟩
Oh may I be the by-word of the world,
The common talke at Table in the mouth
Of euery Groome and Wayter, if e're more
I entertaine the carnall suite of Man!

Mol. I must kneele downe for fashion too.

Franck. And I, whom neuer man as yet hath scalde,
Ee'n in this depth of generall sorrow, vowe
Neuer to marry, to sustaine such losse
As a deere husband seemes to be, once dead.

Mol. I lou'd my father well, too; but to say,
Nay, vow, I would not marry for his death—
Sure, I should speake false Lattin, should I not?
Ide as soone vow neuer to come in Bed.
Tut! Women must liue by th' quick, and not by th' dead.

Wid. Deare Copie of my husband, oh let me kisse thee.
How like him is this Model! this briefe Picture
[*Drawing out her husbands Picture.*
Quickens my teares: my sorrowes are renew'd
At this fresh sight.

Sir Godf. Sister—

Wid. Away,
All honesty with him is turn'd to clay.
Oh my sweete husband, oh——

Franck. My deere father!
[*Exeunt mother and daughters.*

Mol. Heres a puling, indeede! I thinke my Mother weepes for all the women that euer buried husbands; for if from time to time all the Widdowers teares in England had beene bottled vp, I do not thinke all would haue fild a three-halfe-penny Bottle. Alasse, a small matter bucks a hand-kercher,—and somtimes the spittle stands to nie Saint *Thomas* a Watrings. Well, I can mourne in good sober sort as well as another; but where I spend one teare for a dead Father, I could giue twenty kisses for a quick husband. [*Exit Moll.*

Sir Godf. Well, go thy waies, old *Sir Godfrey,* and thou maist be proud on't, thou hast a kinde louing sister-in-lawe; how constant! how passionate! how full of Aprill the poore

75 has *Ff, etc.* 101 o' the choir *M* 107 too hot *M* : so hot *Q, Ff* : too good *conj. S*

S. D. Kneels *add. R after* 124 131 vow.. his *Ff, etc.*: now.. her *Q* 136 this.. this *M* : their.. their *Q, Ff* 138 this *M* : their *Q, Ff* 147 widows' *conj. St.*

soules eyes are! Well, I would my Brother knew on't, he should then know what a kinde wife hee had left behinde him: truth, and twere not for shame that the Neighbours at th' next garden should heare me, betweene ioye and griefe I should e'en cry out-right!

[*Exit Sir Godfrey*.

Edmond. So, a faire riddance! My fathers layde in dust; his Coffin and he is like a whole-meate-pye, and the wormes will cut him vp shortlie. Farewell, old Dad, farewell. Ile be curb'd in no more. I perceiue a sonne and heire may quickly be made a foole, and he will be one, but Ile take another order.—Now she would haue me weepe for him, for-sooth, and why? because he cozn'd the right heire, beeing a foole, and bestow'd those Lands vpon me his eldest Son; and therefore I must weepe for him, ha, ha. Why, al the world knowes, as long as twas his pleasure to get me, twas his duety to get for me: I know the law in that point; no Atturney can gull me. Well, my Vncle is an olde Asse, and an Admirable Cockscombe. Ile rule the Roast my selfe. Ile be kept vnder no more; I know what I may do well inough by my Fathers Copy: the Lawe's in mine owne hands now: nay, now I know my strength, Ile be strong inough for my Mother, I warrant you. [*Exit*.

⟨Scene II. *A street.*⟩

Enter George Py-bord, *a scholler and a Cittizen, and vnto him an old souldier,* Peter Skirmish.

Pye. What's to be done now, old Lad of War? thou that wert wont to be as hot as a turn-spit, as nimble as a fencer, & as lowzy as a schoole-maister; now thou art put to silence like a Sectarie.—War sitts now like a Iustice of peace, and does nothing. Where be your Muskets, Caleiuers and Hotshots? in *Long-lane,* at Pawne, at Pawne.—Now keies are your onely Guns, Key-guns, Key-guns, & Bawdes the Gunners, who are your centinells in peace, and stand ready charg'd to giue warning, with hems, hums, & pockey-coffs; only your Chambers are licenc'st to play vpon you, and Drabs enow to giue fire to 'em.

Skir. Well, I cannot tell, but I am sure it goes wrong with me, for since the cessure of the wars, I haue spent aboue a hundred crownes out a purse. I haue beene a souldier any time this forty yeares, and now I perceiue an olde souldier and an olde Courtier haue both one destinie, and in the end turne both into hob-nayles.

Pie. Prety mistery for a begger, for indeed a hob-naile is the true embleme of a beggers shoo-soale.

Skir. I will not say but that warre is a bloud-sucker, and so; but, in my conscience, (as there is no souldier but has a peice of one, tho it bee full of holes like a shot Antient; no matter, twill serue to sweare by) in my conscience, I thinke some kinde of Peace has more hidden oppressions, and violent heady sinnes, (tho looking of a gentle nature) then a profest warre.

Pye. Troth, and for mine owne part, I am a poore Gentleman, & a Scholler: I haue beene matriculated in the Vniuersitie, wore out sixe Gownes there, seene some fooles, and some Schollers, some of the Citty, and some of the Countrie, kept order, went bare-headed ouer the Quadrangle, eate my Commons with a good stomacke, and Battled with Discretion; at last, hauing done many slights and trickes to maintaine my witte in vse (as my braine would neuer endure mee to bee idle,) I was expeld the Vniuersitie, onely for stealing a Cheese out of *Iesus* Colledge.

Skir. Ist possible?

Pye. Oh! there was one *Welshman* (God forgiue him) pursued it hard; and neuer left, till I turnde my staffe toward *London,* where when I came, all my friends were pitt-hold, gone to *Graues,* (as indeed there was but a few left before.) Then was I turnde to my wittes, to shift in the world, to towre among Sonnes and Heyres, and Fooles, and Gulls, and Ladyes eldest Sonnes, to worke vpon nothing, to feede out of Flint, and euer since has my belly beene much beholding to my braine. But, now, to returne to you, old *Skirmish*: I say as you say, and for my part wish a Turbulency in the world, for I haue nothing to loose but my wittes, and I thinke they are as mad as they will be: and to strengthen your Argument the more, I say an honest warre is better then a bawdy peace, as touching my profession. The multiplicitie of Schollers, hatcht and nourisht in the idle Calmes of peace, makes 'em like Fishes one deuoure another; and the communitie of Learning has so plaide vpon affections, and thereby almost Religion is come about to Phantasie, and discredited by being too much spoken off—in so many & meane mouths, I my selfe, being a Scholler and a Graduate, haue no other comfort by

164 betwixt *Ff*　Scene II. *etc. add. M*　18 of purse *F2*　31 ha's *Q*　62 nothing in the world but *Ff*　70 ha's *Q*　71 that thereby *M*

my learning, but the Affection of my words, to know how Scholler-like to name what I want, & can call my selfe a Begger both in Greeke and Lattin: and therfore, not to cogg with Peace, Ile not be afraide to say, 'tis a great Breeder, but a barren Nourisher: a great getter of Children, which must either be Theeues or Rich-men, Knaues or Beggers.

Skirmish. Well, would I had beene borne a Knaue then, when I was borne a Begger; for if the truth were knowne, I thinke I was begot when my Father had neuer a penny in his purse.

Pye. Puh, faint not, old *Skirmish*; let this warrant thee, *Facilis Descensus Auerni*, 'tis an easie iourney to a Knaue; thou maist bee a Knaue when thou wilt; and Peace is a good Madam to all other professions, and an arrant Drabbe to vs, let vs handle her accordingly, and by our wittes thriue in despight of her; for since the lawe liues by quarrells, the Courtier by smooth God-morrowes; and euery profession makes it selfe greater by imperfections, why not wee then by shiftes, wiles, and forgeries? and seeing our braines are our onely Patrimonies, let's spend with iudgment, not like a desperate sonne and heire, but like a sober and discreete Templer,—one that will neuer marche beyond the bounds of his allowance. And for our thriuing meanes, thus: I my selfe will put on the Deceit of a Fortune-teller.

Skirm. A Fortune-teller? Very proper.

Pye. And you of a figure-caster, or a Coniurer.

Skir. A Coniurer?

Pye. Let me alone; Ile instruct you, and teach you to deceiue all eyes, but the Diuels.

Skir. Oh I, for I would not deceiue him, and I could choose, of all others.

Pye. Feare not, I warrant you; and so by those meanes wee shall helpe one another to Patients, as the condition of the age affoords creatures enow for cunning to worke vpon.

Skir. Oh wondrous! new fooles and fresh Asses.

Pye. Oh, fit, fit! excellent.

Skir. What, in the name of Coniuring?

Pye-boord. My memorie greetes mee happily with an admirable subiect to graze vpon: The Lady-Widdow, who of late I sawe weeping in her Garden for the death of her Husband; sure she'as but a watrish soule, and halfe on't by this time is dropt out of her Eyes: deuice well managde may doe good vppon her: it stands firme, my first practise shall bee there.

Skir. You haue my voyce, *George.*

Pye-boord. Sh'as a gray Gull to her Brother, a foole to her onely sonne, and an Ape to her yongest Daughter.—I ouerheard 'em seuerally, and from their words Ile deriue my deuice; and thou, old *Peter Skirmish,* shall be my second in all slights.

Skir. Nere doubt mee, *George Pye-boord,*—onely you must teach me to coniure.

Enter Captaine Idle, *pinioned, & with a guarde of Officers passeth ouer the Stage.*

Pye. Puh, Ile perfect thee, *Peter.*—How now? what's hee?

Skir. Oh *George*! this sight kils me. Tis my sworne Brother, Captaine *Idle.*

Pye. Captaine *Idle!*

Skir. Apprehended for some fellonious act or other. Hee has started out, h'as made a Night on't, lackt siluer. I cannot but commend his resolution; he would not pawne his Buffe-Ierkin. I would eyther some of vs were employde, or might pitch our Tents at Vsurers doores, to kill the slaues as they peepe out at the Wicket.

Pye. Indeed, those are our ancient Enimies; they keepe our moneyin their hands, and make vs to bee hangd for robbing of 'em. But, come, letts follow after to the Prison, and know the Nature of his offence; and what we can steed him in, hee shall be sure of; and Ile vphold it still, that a charitable Knaue is better then a soothing Puritaine. [*Exeunt.*

⟨Scene III. *A street.*⟩

Enter at one doore Corporall Oth, *a Vaine-glorious fellow; and at the other, three of the Widdow Puritaines Seruingmen,* Nicholas Saint-Tantlings, Simon Saint-Mary-Oueries, *and* Frailtie, *in black scuruie mourning coates, and Bookes at their Girdles, as comming from Church. They meete.*

Nich. What, Corporall *Oth*? I am sorry we haue met with you, next our hearts; you are the man that we are forbidden to keepe company withall. Wee must not sweare I can tell you, and you haue the name for swearing.

Sim. I, Corporall *Oth,* I would you would do so much as forsake vs, sir; we cannot abide you, wee must not be seene in your company.

76 Affliction *Q* 94 us. Let *M* 100 the onely *Ff* 108 A Fortune-teller *add. to line* 107 *Q*, *Ff*: *corr. M* 109 of *om. Ff, etc.* 117 those] these *Ff* 128 she'as] she's *Ff*: she has *M* on't] of't *M*

136 drive *Ff* Scene III. *etc. add. M*

Frail. There is none of vs, I can tell you, but shall be soundly whipt for swearing.

Corp. Why, how now, we three? Puritanicall Scrape-shoes, Flesh a good Fridayes! a hand.

All. Oh!

Corp. Why, *Nicholas Saint-Tantlings, Simon Saint Mary Oueries,* ha's the De'ele possest you, that you sweare no better? you halfe-Christned *Katomites,* you vngod-motherd Varlets, do's the first lesson teach you to bee proud, and the second to bee Cocks-combes? proud Cocks-combes! not once to doe dutie to a man of Marke!

Frail. A man of Marke, quatha! I doe not thinke he can shew a Beggers Noble.

Corpo. A Corporall, a Commander, one of spirit, that is able to blowe you vp all drye with your Bookes at your Girdles.

Simon. Wee are not taught to beleeue that, sir, for we know the breath of man is weake.

[*Corporall breaths vpon* Frailtie.

Frail. Foh, you lie, *Nicholas*; for here's one strong inough. Blowe vs vp, quatha: hee may well blow me aboue twelue-score off an him. I warrant, if the winde stood right, a man might smell him from the top of Newgate, to the Leades of Ludgate.

Corp. Sirrah, thou Hollow-Booke of Waxe-candle—

Nicho. I, you may say what you will, so you sweare not.

Corp. I sweare by the——

Nicho. Hold, hold, good Corporall *Oth*; for if you sweare once, wee shall all fall downe in a sowne presently.

Corp. I must and will sweare: you quiuering Cocks-combes, my Captaine is imprisoned, and by *Vulcans* Lether Cod-piece point——

Nich. O *Simon,* what an oth was there.

Frail. If hee should chance to breake it, the poore mans Breeches would fall downe about his heeles, for *Venus* allowes him but one point to his hose.

Corpor. With these my Bullye-Feete I will thumpe ope the Prison doores, and braine the Keeper with the begging Boxe, but Ile see my honest sweete Captaine *Idle* at libertie.

Nich. How, Captaine *Ydle*? my olde Aunts sonne, my deere Kinsman, in Capadochio?

Cor. I, thou Church-peeling, thou Holy-paring, religious outside, thou! if thou hadst any grace in thee, thou would'st visit him, releiue him, sweare to get him out.

Nicho. Assure you, Corporall, indeed-la, tis the first time I heard on't.

Cor. Why do't now, then, *Marmaset*: bring forth thy yearly-wages, let not a Commander perish!

Simon. But, if hee bee one of the wicked, hee shall perish.

Nich. Well, Corporall, Ile e'en along with you, to visit my Kinsman: if I can do him any good, I will,—but I haue nothing for him. *Simon* Saint *Mary Oueris* and *Fraylty*, pray make a lie for me to the Knight my Maister, old *Sir Godfrey.*

Cor. A lie? may you lie then?

Fray. O, I, we may lie, but we must not sweare.

Sim. True, wee may lie with our Neighbors wife, but wee must not sweare we did so.

Cor. Oh, an excellent Tag of religion!

Nic. Oh *Simon,* I haue thought vpon a sound excuse; it will go currant: say that I am gon to a Fast.

Sim. To a Fast? very good.

Nic. I, to a Fast, say, with Maister *Ful-bellie* the Minister.

Sim. Maister *Ful-bellie*? an honest man: he feedes the flock well, for he's an excellent feeder. [*Exit Corporal, Nicholas.*

Fray. O, I, I haue seene him eate vp a whole Pigge, and afterward falle to the pettitoes.

[*Exit Simon and Fraylty.*

⟨Scene IV.⟩

The Prison, Marshalsea.

Enter Captaine Ydle *at one dore, and* ⟨*later* Pyeboard *and*⟩ *old souldier at the other.* George Py-boord, *speaking within.*

Pye. Pray turne the key.

Sker. Turne the key, I pray.

Cap. Who should those be? I almost know their voyces.— O my friends! [*Entring.* Ya're welcome to a smelling Roome here. You newly tooke leaue of the ayre; ist not a strange sauour?

Pie. As all prisons haue: smells of sundry wretches,
Who, tho departed, leaue their sents behind 'em.
By Gold, Captaine, I am sincerely sory for thee.

Cap. By my troth, *George,* I thanke thee; but pish,—what must be, must bee.

Skir. Captaine, what doe you lie in for? ist great? what's your offence?

Cap. Faith, my offence is ordinarie,—com-

25 dryе] three *M* 42 swoon *F2, etc.* 51 -Feete] -Fleet *F2*

75 me must *Q* 89 vp *om. F2, etc.* 90 falls *Q*: fall *Ff, etc.* Scene IV. *add. M* 7 ist] has it *M*

mon: A Hie-waye; and I feare mee my penaltie will be ordinarie and common too: a halter.

Pie. Nay, prophecy not so ill; it shall go heard,
But Ile shift for thy life.

Cap. Whether I liue or die, thou'art an honest *George*. Ile tell you—siluer flou'd not with mee, as it had done, (for now the tide runnes to Bawdes and flatterers.) I had a start out, and by chaunce set vpon a fat steward, thinking his purse had beene as pursey as his bodie; and the slaue had about him but the poore purchase of tenne groates: notwithstanding, beeing descryed, pursued, and taken, I know the Law is so grim, in respect of many desprate, vnsetled souldiours, that I feare mee I shall daunce after their pipe for't.

Skir. I am twice sory for you, *Captaine*: first that your purchase was so small, and now that your danger is so great.

Cap. Push, the worst is but death,—ha you a pipe of Tobacco about you?

Skir. I thinke I haue there abouts about me. [*Cap. blowes a pipe.*

Cap. Her's a cleane Gentleman too, to receiue.

Pie. Well, I must cast about some happy slight.
Worke braine, that euer didst thy Maister right!

Cor. Keeper! let the key be turn'd! [*Corporall and Nicholas within.*

Nic. I, I pray, Maister keeper, giues a cast of your office.

Cap. How now? more Visitants?—what, Corporal *Oth*?

Pie. Skir. Corporal?

Cor. In prison, honest Captaine? this must not be.

Nic. How do you, Captaine Kinsman?

Cap. Good Cocks-combe! what makes that pure, starch'd foole here?

Nic. You see, Kinsman, I am som-what bould to call in, and see how you do. I heard you were safe inough, and I was very glad on't that it was no worse.

Cap. This is a double torture now,—this foole by'th booke
Do's vexe me more then my imprisonment.
What meant you, Corporall, to hooke him hither?

Cor. Who, he? he shall releiue thee, and supply thee;
Ile make him doo't.

37 Pish *M* 59-61 *Prose Ff, etc.* 60 Do's] doth *Ff, etc.*

Cap. ⟨*aside, to Oath*⟩ Fie, what vaine breath you spend! hee supply? Ile sooner expect mercy from a Vsurer when my bonds forfetted, sooner kindnesse from a Lawier when my mony's spent: nay, sooner charity from the deuill, then good from a Puritaine! Ile looke for releife from him, when Lucifer is restor'd to his bloud, and in Heauen againe!

Nic. I warrant, my Kinsman's talking of me, for my left eare burnes most tyrannically.

Pie. Captaine *Ydle,* what's he there? hee lookes like a Monkey vpward, and a Crane downe-ward.

Cap. Pshaw, a foolish Cozen of mine; I must thanke God for him.

Pie. Why, the better subiect to worke a scape vpon; thou shalt e'en change clothes with him, and leaue him here, and so—

Cap. Push, I publish't him e'en now to my Corporall: hee will be damn'd, ere hee do me so much good; why, I know a more proper, a more handsome deuice then that, if the slaue would be sociable. Now, goodman *Fleere-face*?

Nic. Oh, my Cozen begins to speake to me now: I shall bee acquainted with him againe, I hope.

Skirmish. Looke what ridiculous Raptures take hold of his wrinckles.

Pye. Then, what say you to this deuice? a happy one, Captaine?

Capt. Speake lowe, *George*; Prison Rattes haue wider eares then those in Malt-lofts.

Nic. Cozen, if it lay in my power, as they say—to—do—

Cap. Twould do me an exceeding pleasure, indeed, that, but nere talke forder on't: the foole will be hang'd, ere he do't. ⟨*To the Corporal.*⟩

Cor. Pax, Ile thump 'im to't.

Pie. Why, doe but trie the Fopster, and breake it to him bluntly.

Cap. And so my disgrace will dwell in his Iawes, and the slaue slauer out our purpose to his Maister, for would I were but as sure on't as I am sure he will deny to do't.

Nic. I would bee heartily glad, Cozen, if any of my friendships, as they say, might—stand—ah—

Pie. Why, you see he offers his friend-ship foolishly to you alreadie.

Captain. I, that's the hell on't, I would hee would offer it wisely.

Nich. Verily, and indeed la, Couzen—

Cap. I haue tooke note of thy fleeres a good while: if thou art minded to do mee good—as

100 but *om. Ff* 101 *S. D. add. M* 102 'im] 'em *Q*

thou gapst vpon me comfortably, and giu'st me charitable faces, which indeede is but a fashion in you all that are Puritaines—wilt soone at night steale me thy Maisters chaine?

Nich. Oh, I shall sowne!

Pie. Corporal, he starts already.

Cap. I know it to be worth three hundred Crownes, & with the halfe of that I can buy my life at a Brokers, at second hand, which now lies in pawne to th' Lawe: if this thou refuse to do, being easie and nothing dangerous, in that thou art held in good opinion of thy Maister, why tis a palpable Argument thou holdst my life at no price, and these thy broken & vnioynted offers are but only created in thy lip, now borne, and now buried, foolish breath onlie. What, woult do't? shall I looke for happinesse in thy answere?

Nic. Steale my Maisters chaine, quo'the? no, it shal nere bee sayd, that *Nicholas* Saint Tantlings committed Bird-lime!

Cap. Nay, I told you as much; did I not? tho he be a Puritaine, yet he will be a true man.

Nich. Why, Couzen, you know tis written, *thou shalt not steale.*

Cap. Why, and foole, *thou shalt loue thy Neighbour,* and helpe him in extremities.

Nich. Masse, I thinke it bee, indeede: in what Chapter's that, Couzen?

Cap. Why, in the first of Charity, the 2. verse.

Nich. The first of Charity, quatha! that's a good iest; there's no such Chapter in my booke!

Cap. No, I knew twas torne out of thy Booke, & that makes so little in thy heart.

Pie. Come, let me tell you, ya're too vnkinde a Kinsman, yfaith; the Captaine louing you so deerely, I, like the Pomwater of his eye, and you to be so vncomfortable: fie, fie.

Nic. Pray, do not wish me to bee hangd: any thing else that I can do, had it beene to rob, I would ha don't; but I must not steale: that's the word, the literall, *thou shalt not steale;* and would you wish me to steale, then?

Pie. No, faith, that were to much, to speake truth: why, woult thou nim it from him?

Nich. That I will!

Pie. Why, ynough, bullie; hee shall bee content with that, or he shall ha none; let mee alone with him now! Captaine, I ha dealt with your Kins-man in a Corner; a good, kinde-naturde fellow, mee thinkes: goe too, you shall not haue all your owne asking, you shall bate somewhat on't: he is not contented absolutely, as you would say, to steale the chaine from him,—but to do you a pleasure, he will nim it from him.

Nich. I, that I will, Couzen.

Cap. Well, seeing he will doe no more, as far as I see, I must bee contented with that.

Cor. Here's no notable gullery!

Pie. Nay, Ile come neerer to you, Gentleman: because weele haue onely but a helpe and a mirth on't, the knight shall not loose his chaine neither, but ⟨it shall⟩ be only laide out of the way some one or two daies.

Nich. I, that would be good indeed, Kinsman.

Pie. For I haue a farder reach to profit vs better by the missing on't onelie, then if wee had it out-right, as my discourse shall make it knowne too you.—When thou hast the chaine, do but conuay it out at back-dore into the Garden, and there hang it close in the Rosemary banck but for a small season; and by that harmlesse deuise, I know how to winde Captaine *Ydle* out of prison: the Knight thy Maister shall get his pardon and release him, & he satisfie thy Maister with his own chaine, & wondrous thankes on both hands.

Nich. That were rare indeed, la: pray, let me know how.

Pie. Nay, tis very necessary thou shouldst know, because thou must be imploide as an Actor.

Nich. An Actor? O no, that's a Plaier; and our Parson railes againe Plaiers mightily, I can tell you, because they brought him drunck vpp'oth Stage once,—as hee will bee horribly druncke.

Cor. Masse, I cannot blame him then, poore Church-spout.

Pie. Why, as an Intermedler, then?

Nich. I, that, that.

Pie. Giue me Audience, then: when the old Knight thy Maister has ragde his fill for the losse of the chaine, tell him thou hast a Kinsman in prison, of such exquisit Art, that the diuill himselfe is french Lackey to him, and runnes bare-headed by his horse-bellie (when hee has one) whome hee will cause with most *Yrish* Dexterity to fetch his chaine, tho twere hid vnder a mine of sea-cole, and nere make Spade or Pickaxe his instruments: tell him but this, with farder instruc-

154 know *Ff* 155 makes it so *R, etc.* 169 shall] will *Ff, etc.*

186 it shall *add. M* 191 on't] of't *M* 194 at] at a *Ff, etc.* 208 against *Ff, etc.* 210 upo'th' *Ff* 217 radge *Q*: rag'd *Ff*

tions thou shalt receiue from mee, and thou shoust thy selfe a Kinsman indeed.

Cor. A dainty Bullie.

Skir. An honest Booke-keeper.

Cap. And my three times thrice hunnie Couzen.

Nich. Nay, grace of God, Ile robbe him on't suddainlie, and hang it in the Rosemary banck; but I beare that minde, Couzen, I would not steale any thing, mee thinkes, for mine owne Father.

Skir. He beares a good minde in that, Captaine!

Pie. Why, well sayde; he begins to be an honest fellow, faith.

Cor. In troth, he does.

Nich. You see, Couzen, I am willing to do you any kindnesse, alwaies sauing my selfe harmelesse. [*Exit Nicholas.*

Captaine. Why, I thanke thee; fare thee well, I shall requite it.

Cor. Twill bee good for thee, Captaine, that thou hast such an egregious Asse to thy Coozen.

Cap. I, is hee not a fine foole, Corporall? But, *George,* thou talkst of Art and Coniuring; How shall that bee?

Pib. Puh, bee't not in your care;
Leaue that to me and my directions.
Well, Captaine, doubt not thy deliuerie now,
E'en with the vantage, man, to gaine by prison,
As my thoughts prompt me: hold on, braine and plot!
I ayme at many cunning far euents,
All which I doubt not but to hit at length.
Ile to the Widdow with a quaint assault.
Captaine, be merry.

Capt. Who, I? Kerrie, merry, Buffe-Ierkin.

Pye. Oh, I am happy in more slights, and one will knit strong in another.—Corporall *Oth.*

Corp. Hoh, Bully?

Pye. And thou, old *Peter Skirmish*; I haue a necessary taske for you both.

Skir. Lay't vpon, *George Pye-boord.*

Corp. What ere it bee, weele manage it.

Pye. I would haue you two maintaine a quarrell before the Lady Widdowes doore, and drawe your swords i'th edge of the Euening; clash a little, clash, clash.

Corp. Fuh!
Let vs alone to make our Blades ring noone,
Tho it be after Supper.

Pye. ⟨I⟩ Know you can. And out of that false fire, I doubt not but to raise strange beleefe—And, Captaine, to countenance my deuice the better, and grace my words to the Widdow, I haue a good plaine Sattin sute, that I had of a yong Reueller t'other night: for words passe not regarded now a dayes, vnlesse they come from a good suite of cloaths, which the Fates and my wittes haue bestowed vpon me. Well, Captaine *Idle,* if I did not highly loue thee, I would nere bee seene within twelue score of a prison, for I protest at this instant, I walke in great danger of small debts; I owe money to seuerall Hostisses, and you know such Iills will quickly be vpon a mans Iack.

Capt. True, *George.*

Pye. Fare thee well, Captaine. Come, Corporall and Ancient! thou shalt heare more newes next time we greete thee.

Corp. More newes! I, by yon Beare at Bridge-Foote in heauen shalt thou.

[*Exeunt ⟨Pyeboard, Skirmish, and Oath.⟩*

Capt. Inough: my friends, farewell.
This prison shewes as if Ghosts did part in Hell.

⟨Act II.⟩

⟨Scene I. *A room in the widow's house.*⟩

Enter Moll *yongest Daughter to the Widdow: alone.*

Moll. Not *Marry*? forsweare Marriage? why, all women know 'tis as honorable a thing as to lye with a man; and I to spight my Sisters vowe the more, haue entertainde a suter already, a fine gallant Knight of the last Fether: hee sayes he will Coach mee too, and well appoint mee, allow mee money to Dice with-all, and many such pleasing protestations hee sticks vpon my lips; indeed, his short-winded Father ith' Countrie is wondrous wealthy, a most abhominable Farmer, and therefore hee may doote in time: troth, Ile venture vpon him. Women are not without wayes enow to helpe them-selues: if he proue wise and good as his word, why, I shall loue him, and vse him kindly: and if hee prooue an Asse, why, in a quarter of an houres warning I can transforme him into an Oxe;—there comes in my Reliefe agen.

Enter Frailtie.

Frail. O, Mistresse *Moll,* Mistresse *Moll.*

Moll. How now? what's the newes?

247 *S. D.* Exit Nich. *repeated Q* 254 *Prefix* Peb *Q* 270 it upon us *M*

279 I *add. F1* 300 in heauen] in the even *conj. M* 302 if *om. M* Act II. *add. R* Scene I. *etc. add. M* 12 doote] dote *Ff*: do it *M*

Frail. The Knight your suter, sir *Iohn Penny-Dub*—
Moll. Sir *Iohn Penny-Dub*? where? where?
Frail. Hee's walking in the Gallerie.
Moll. Has my Mother seene him yet?
Frail. O no, shee's—spitting in the Kitchin.
Moll. Direct him hether softly, good *Frailtie*,——
Ile meete him halfe way.

Frail. That's iust like running a Tilt; but I hope heele breake nothing this time. ⟨*Exit.*⟩

Enter Sir Iohn Penny-Dub.

Moll. 'Tis happinesse my Mother saw him not:
O welcome, good Sir *Iohn.*

Penny-dub. I thanke you, faith.—Nay, you must stand mee, till I kisse you: 'tis the fashion euery where, I-faith, and I came from Court enow.

Moll. Nay, the Fates forfend that I should anger the fashion!

Penny. Then, not forgetting the sweete of new ceremonies, I first fall back, then recouering my selfe, make my honour to your lip thus: and then accost it.

Moll. Trust me, very pritty, and mouing; y'are worthy on't, sir.

Kissing: Enter Widdow and Sir Godfr.

O, my Mother, my Mother! now shee's here, weele steale into the Gallery. [*Exeunt.*

Sir Godf. Nay, Sister, let Reason rule you, doe not play the foole; stand not in your owne light. You haue wealthy offers, large tendrings; doe not with-stand your good fortune: who comes a wooing to you, I pray? no small foole; a rich Knight ath Citty, Sir *Oliuer Muck-hill*—no small foole I can tell you: and furthermore, as I heard late by your Maide-seruants, (as your Maide-seruants will say to mee any thing, I thanke 'em) both your Daughters are not without Suters, I, and worthy ones too! one a Briske Courtier, Sir *Andrew Tip-staffe*, suter a farre off to your eldest Daughter, and the third a huge-welthie Farmers sonne, a fine young Countrie Knight, they call him Sir *Iohn Penny-Dub*: a good name, marry; hee may haue it coynde when hee lackes money. What blessings are these, Sister!

Wid. Tempt me not, Satan.

Sir Godf. Satan? doe I looke like Satan?
I hope the Deuill's not so old as I, I tro.

Wid. You wound my sences, Brother, when you name
A suter to me:—oh, I cannot abide it,
I take in poison, when I heare one nam'd.

Enter Simon.

How now, *Simon*? where's my sonne *Edmund*?

Sim. Verily Madame, hee is at vaine Exercise, dripping in the Tennis-court.

Wid. At Tennis-court? oh, now his father's gon, I shall haue no rule with him; oh, wicked *Edmond,* I might well compare this with the Prophecie in the Chronicle, tho farre inferior: as *Harry* of *Monmouth* woone all, and *Harry* of *Windsor* lost all; so *Edmund* of *Bristow,* that was the Father, got all, and *Edmond* of *London,* that's his sonne now, will spend all.

Sir Godf. Peace, Sister, weele haue him reformd, there's hope on him yet, tho it be but a little.

Enter Frailtie.

Frail. Forsooth, Madam, there are two or three Archers at doore would very gladly speake with your Ladyship.

Wid. Archers?

Sir Godf. Your husbands Fletcher, I warrant.

Wid. Oh!
Let them come neere, they bring home things of his.
Troth, I should ha forgot 'em. How now, Villaine?
Which be those Archers?

Enter the suters Sir Andrew Tipstaffe, *Sir* Oliuer Muck-hill, *and* Penny-dub.

Frail. Why, do you not see 'em before you? are not these Archers? what do you call 'em? Shooters: Shooters and Archers are all one, I hope.

Wid. Out, ignorant slaue.

Muck. Nay, pray be patient, Lady,
We come in way of honorable loue.

Tipst. Penny. Wee doe.

Muck. To you.

Tipst. Penny. And to your Daughters.

Widdow. O, why will you offer mee this Gentlemen? indeed I will not looke vppon you —when the Teares are scarce out of mine Eyes, not yet washt off from my Cheekes, and my deere husbands body scarce so colde as the Coffin, what reason haue you to offer it? I am not like some of your Widdowes that will burie one in the Euening, and bee sure to another ere morning. Pray, away; pray, take your answeres, good Knights, and you

25 Ha's *Q*   *S. D.* Exit *add. M*   36 e'now *F2*: euen now *M*   39 of] in *conj. St.*   44 on't] of it *M*   62 Penny-Dab *Q*

82 him] hem *Q*   83 on] of *M*   93 *Ends* now *Q*, *Ff*: *corr. M*   112 sure to have *M*

bee sweete Knights. I haue vow'd neuer to marry;—and so haue my daughters too!

Penny. I, two of you haue, but the thirds a good wench!

Muck. Lady, a shrewde answere, marry; the best is, tis but the first, and hee's a blunt wooer, that will leaue for one sharpe answere.

Tip. Where bee your daughters, Lady? I hope theile giue vs better encouragements.

Wid. Indeed, theyle answere you so; tak't a my word, theile giue you the very same answere *Verbatim,* truely la.

Penny. Mum: *Moll's* a good wench still, I know what shee'le doo.

Muck. Well, Lady, for this time weele take our leaues, hoping for better comfort.

Wid. O neuer, neuer! and I liue these thousand yeares! and you bee good Knights, doe not hope; twill bee all Vaine, Vayne,—looke you, put off all your suites, and you come to me againe.

⟨*Exeunt Sir John and Sir Andrew.*⟩

Fray. Put off all their suites, quatha? I, that's the best wooing of a Widdow, indeed, when a man's Nonsuted; that is, when he's a bed with her. [*Going out, Muckhill and sir Godfrey.*

Muck. Sir *Godfrey,* here's twenty Angells more: worke hard for me; there's life int yet. [*Exit Muckhill.*

Sir Godf. Feare not, Sir *Oliuer Muckhill,* Ile stick close for you; leaue all with me.

Enter George Py-boord, *the scholler.*

Pye. By your leaue, Ladie Widdow.

Wid. What, another suiter now?

Py. A suiter! no, I protest, Ladie, if you'de giue me your selfe, Ide not be troubled with you.

Wid. Say you so, Sir? then you're the better welcome, sir.

Pie. Nay, Heauen blesse mee from a Widdow, vnlesse I were sure to bury her speedily!

Wid. Good bluntnesse: well, your businesse, sir?

Pie. Very needfull; if you were in priuate once.

Wid. Needfull? brother, pray leaue vs; and you, sir.

Fray. I should laugh now, if this blunt fellow should put 'em all by side the stirrop, and vault into the saddle himselfe. I haue seene as mad a trick. [*Exit* Frailtie.

Enter Daughters.

Wid. Now Sir?—here's none but we—Daughters, forbeare.

Pyb. O no, pray, let 'em stay, for what I haue to speake importeth equally to them as to you.

Wid. Then you may stay.

Pyb. I pray bestow on me a serious eare,
For what I speake is full of weight and feare.

Wid. Feare?

Pyb. I, ift passe vnregarded, and vneffected; Else peace and ioy:—I pray, Attention. Widdowe, I haue beene a meere stranger for these parts that you liue in, nor did I euer know the Husband of you, and Father of them, but I truly know by certaine spirituall Intelligence, that he is in Purgatorie.

Wid. Purgatorie? tuh; that word deserues to bee spit vpon. I wonder that a man of sober toung, as you seeme to be, should haue the folly to beleeue there's such a place.

Pyb. Well, Lady, in cold bloud I speake it; I assure you that there is a Purgatory, in which place I know your husband to recide, and wherein he is like to remaine, till the dissolution of the world, till the last generall Bon-fire, when all the earth shall melt into nothing and the Seas scalde their finnie labourers: so long is his abidance, vnlesse you alter the propertie of your purpose, together with each of your Daughters theirs; that is, the purpose of single life in your selfe and your eldest Daughter, and the speedie determination of marriage in your youngest.

Moll. How knowes hee that? what, has some Deuill told him?

Wid. Strange he should know our thoughts:——Why, but, Daughter, haue you purposde speedy Marriage?

Pyb. You see she tels you I, for shee sayes nothing. Nay, giue me credit as you please. I am a stranger to you, and yet you see I know your determinations, which must come to mee Metaphisically, and by a super-naturall intelligence.

Wid. This puts Amazement on me.

Franck. Know our seacrets!

Mol. Ide thought to steale a marriage: would his tongue
Had dropt out when he blabt it!

Wid. But, sir, my husband was too honest a dealing man to be now in any purgatories—

Pie. O, Do not loade your conscience with vntruths;
Tis but meere folly now to guild him ore,
That has past but for Copper. Praises here
Cannot vnbinde him there: confesse but truth.

134 your] yours *Q* 135 *S. D. add. M*

166–7 as you *Ff* 196 ha's *Q* 201 for *om. Ff* 203 and and *Q* 209–10 *Prose M* 214 him *M*: hem *Q*: 'em *Ff*

I know he got his wealth with a hard gripe:
Oh hardly, hardly.

Wid. This is most strange of all: how knowes he that?

Pie. He would eate fooles and ignorant heires cleane vp;
And had his drinck from many a poore mans browe,
E'en as their labour brewde it.
He would scrape ritches to him most vniustly;
The very durt betweene his nailes was Il-got,
And not his owne,—oh, I groane to speake on't,
The thought makes me shudder—shudder!

Wid. It quakes me too, now I thinke on't. —Sir, I am much grieu'd, that you, a stranger, should so deeply wrong my dead husband!

Pie. Oh!

Wid. A man that would keepe Church so duly; rise early, before his seruants, and e'en for Religious hast, go vngarterd, vnbuttend, nay, sir Reuerence, vntrust, to Morning Prayer.

Pie. Oh, vff.

Wid. Dine quickly vpon hie-dayes, and when I had great guests, would e'en shame me and rize from the Table, to get a good seate at an after-noone Sermon.

Pie. There's the diuill, there's the diuill! true, hee thought it Sanctity ynough, if he had kild a man, so tad beene done in a Pue, or vndon his Neigh⟨b⟩our, so ta'd beene nere ynough to'th Preacher. Oh,—a Sermon's a fine short cloake of an houre long, and wil hide the vpper-part of a dissembler.—Church! I, he seem'd al Church, & his conscience was as hard as the Pulpit!

Wid. I can no more endure this.

Pie. Nor I, widdow, endure to flatter.

Wid. Is this all your businesse with me?

Pie. No, Lady, tis but the induction too'te.
You may beleiue my straines, I strike all true,
And if your conscience would leap vp to your tongue, your selfe would affirme it: and that you shall perceiue I knowe of things to come as well as I doe of what is present, a Brother of your husbands shall shortly haue a losse.

Wid. A losse; marry, heauen for-fend! *Sir Godfrey,* my brother?

Pie. Nay, keepe in your wonders, till I haue told you the fortunes of you all; which are more fearefull, if not happily preuented:—for your part & your daughters, if there be not once this day some bloud-shed before your dore, wheerof the humaine creature dies, two of you—the elder—shall run mad.

Mother and Franck. Oh!

Mol. That's not I yet!

Pie. And with most impudent prostitution show your naked bodies to the veiw of all beholders.

Wid. Our naked bodies? fie, for shame!

Pie. Attend mee: and your yonger daughter bee strocken dumbe.

Mol. Dumbe? out, alasse: tis the worst paine of all for a Woman. Ide rather bee madde, or runne naked, or any thing: dumbe?

Pie. Giue eare: ere the euening fall vpon Hill, Bogge, and Meadow, this my speech shal haue past probation, and then shal I be belieued accordingly.

Widdow. If this bee true, wee are all sham'de, all vndon.

Mol. Dumbe? Ile speake as much as euer I can possible before euening!

Pie. But if it so come to passe (as for your faire sakes I wish it may) that this presage of your strange fortunes be preuented by that accident of death and bloud-shedding which I before told you off: take heed vpon your liues that two of you, which haue vow'd neuer to marry, seeke you out husbands with all present speede, and you, the third, that haue such a desire to out-strip chastitie, looke you meddle not with a husband.

Moll. A double torment.

Pyb. The breach of this keepes your father in Purgatorie, and the punishments that shall follow you in this world would with horror kill the Eare should heare 'em related.

Wid. Marry? why I vowd neuer to marry.

Franke. And so did I.

Moll. And I vowde neuer to be such an Asse, but to marry: what a crosse Fortune's this!

Pyb. Ladies, tho I bee a Fortune-teller, I cannot better Fortunes; you haue 'em from me as they are reueald to me: I would they were to your tempers, and fellowes with your blouds, that's all the bitternesse I would you.

Widdow. Oh, 'tis a iust vengeance for my husbands hard purchases.

Pyb. I wish you to be-thinke your selues, and leaue 'em.

Wid. Ile to Sir *Godfrey,* my Brother, and acquaint him with these fearefull presages.

Franck. For, Mother, they portend losses to him.

Wid. Oh, I, they doe, they doe.

222–6 *End* scrape, dirt, own, me, shudder *M* 225 *Ends* oh, *Q, Ff* 237 guests *F2*: guesse *Q, F1* 242 tad] it had *M*

266–7 of you two the elder *Ff* eldest *R* 286 possibly *M* 293 you *om. Ff, etc.* 315 leaue m *Q*

If any happy issue crowne thy words,
I will reward thy cunning.

Pyb. 'Tis enough Lady; I wish no higher. [*Exit* ⟨Wid. *and* Fran.⟩

Mol. Dumbe! and not marry, worse!
Neither to speake, nor kisse, a double curse. [*Exit.*

Pyb. So all this comes well about yet. I play the Fortune-teller as well as if I had had a Witch to my Grannam: for by good happinesse, being in my Hostisses Garden, which neighbours the Orchard of the Widdow, I laid the hole of mine eare to a hole in the wall, and heard 'em make these vowes, & speake those words vpon which I wrought these aduantages; and to encourage my forgerie the more, I may now perceiue in 'em a naturall simplicitie which will easily swallow an abuse, if any couering be ouer it: and to confirme my former presage to the Widdow, I haue aduizde old *Peter Skirmish,* the Souldier, to hurt Corporall *Oth* vpon the Leg; and in that hurry Ile rush amongst 'em, and in stead of giuing the Corporal some Cordiall to comfort him, Ile power into his mouth a potion of a sleepy Nature, to make him seeme as dead; for the which the old souldier beeing apprehended, and ready to bee borne to execution, Ile step in, & take vpon me the cure of the dead man, vpon paine of dying the condemneds death: the Corporall will wake at his minute, when the sleepy force has wrought it selfe, and so shall I get my selfe into a most admired opinion, and vnder the pretext of that cunning, beguile as I see occasion: and if that foolish *Nicholas* Saint *Tantlings* keepe true time with the chaine, my plot will be sound, the Captaine deliuered, and my wits applauded among schollers and souldiers for euer. [*Exit Py-boord.*

⟨Scene II. *A Garden.*⟩

Enter Nicholas Saint Tantlings with the chaine.

Nic. Oh, I haue found an excellent aduantage to take away the chaine: my Maister put it off e'en now to say on a new Doublet, and I sneak't it away by little & little most Puritanically. Wee shal haue good sport anon when ha's mist it about my Cozen the Coniurer. The world shall see I'me an honest man of my word, for now I'me going to hang it betweene Heauen & Earth among the Rosemary branches. [*Exit Nich.*

Actus 3.

⟨Scene I. *The street before the Widow's house.*⟩

Enter Simon Saint Mary-Oueries and Frailty.

Frai. Sirrah *Simon Saint Mary-Oueries,* my Mistris sends away all her suiters and puts fleas in their eares.

Sim. Frailty, she dos like an honest, chast, and vertuous woman; for widdowes ought not to wallow in the puddle of iniquity.

Fra. Yet, *Simon,* many widdowes wil do't, what so comes on't.

Sim. True, *Frailtie,* their filthy flesh desires a Coniunction Copulatiue. What strangers are within, *Frailty*?

Frai. Ther's none, *Simon,* but Maister *Pilfer* the Tailer: he's aboue with *Sir Godfreie* praysing of a Doublet: and I must trudge anon to fetch Maister Suds, the Barber.

Simon. Maister Suds,—a good man; he washes the sinns of the Beard cleane.

Enter old Skirmish the souldier.

Skir. How now, creatures? whats a clock?

Frai. Why, do you take vs to be Iacke ath' Clock-house?

Skir. I say agen to you what's a clocke?

Sim. Truly la, wee goe by the clocke of our conscience: all worldly Clockes, we know, goe false, and are set by drunken Sextons.

Skir. Then what's a clock in your conscience?—oh, I must breake off, here comes the corporall—hum, hum!—what's a clock?

Enter Corporall.

Corp. A clock? why, past seuenteene.

Frai. Past seuenteene? nay, ha's met with his match now, Corporall *Oth* will fit him.

Skir. Thou doost not bawke or baffle me, doost thou? I am a Souldier —past seuenteene!

Corp. I, thou art not angry with the figures, art thou? I will prooue it vnto thee: 12. and 1. is thirteene, I hope, 2. foureteene, 3. fifteene, 4. sixteene, and 5. seauenteene; then past seauenteene: I will take the Dyals part in a iust cause.

Skir. I say 'tis but past fiue, then.

Corp. Ile sweare 'tis past seauenteene, then: doost thou not know numbers? canst thou not cast?

323 *S. D.* Wid. *etc. add. R* 357 amongst *F 2, etc.* Scene II. *etc. add. M* 6 ha's *Q*: has *F 1*: he has *F 2, etc.*

Scene I. *etc. add. M* 16 Sud's a *Ff* *S. D. follows* 18 *Q, Ff* soulders *Q*: *corr. F 2* 19–20 at 'h *Q*: at th' *Ff* Jacks o' the *M* 21, 25, 27 what is't o'clock *M*

Skir. Cast? dost thou speake of my casting ith' street? [*Draw.*

Corp. I, and in the Market place.

Sim, Clubs, clubs, clubs!

[Simon *runs in.*

Frail. I, I knew by their shuffling, Clubs would be Trumpe; masse, here's the Knaue, and hee can doe any good vppon 'em: Clubs, clubs, clubs!

Enter Py-boord.

Corp. O villaine, thou hast opend a vaine in my leg.

Pyb. How now! for shame, for shame; put vp, put vp.

Corp. By yon blew Welkin, 'twas out of my part, *George,* to bee hurt on the leg.

Enter Officers.

Pyb. Oh peace now—I haue a Cordiall here to comfort thee.

Offi. Downe with 'em, downe with em; lay hands vpon the villaine.

Skir. Lay hands on me?

Pyb. Ile not be seene among em now.

⟨*Exit Pyeboard.*⟩

Corp. Ime hurt, and had more need haue Surgeons
Lay hands vpon me then rough Officers.

Offi. Goe, carry him to be drest then.

⟨*Exeunt some of the Sheriffs Officers with Corporal Oath.*⟩

This mutinous Souldier shall along with me to prison.

Skir. To prison? where's *George*?

Offi. Away with him. [*Exeunt with* Skir.

⟨*Re-enter Pyeboard.*⟩

Pyb. So.
All lights as I would wish. The amazd widdow
Will plant me strongly now in her beleefe,
And wonder at the vertue of my words:
For the euent turnes those presages from em
Of being mad and dumbe, and begets ioy
Mingled with admiration. These emptie creatures,
Souldier and Corporall, were but ordaind
As instruments for me to worke vpon.
Now to my patient; here's his potion.

[*Exit* Pyboord.

⟨Scene II. *An apartment in the Widow's house.*⟩

Enter the Widdow with her two Daughters.

Wid. O wondrous happinesse, beyond our thoughts:
O luckie faire euent! I thinke our fortunes,
Were blest een in our Cradles: we are quitted
Of all those shamefull violent presages
By this rash bleeding chance. Goe, *Frailtie,* run, and know,
Whether he be yet liuing, or yet dead,
That here before my doore receiu'd his hurt.

Frail. Madam, hee was carryed to the superiour, but if he had no money when hee came there, I warrant hee's dead by this time.

[*Exit* Frailtie.

Franck. Sure, that man is a rare fortune-teller; neuer lookt vpon our hands, nor vpon any marke about vs: a wondrous fellow, surelie,

Moll. I am glad, I haue the vse of my tongue yet: tho of nothing else. I shall finde the way to marry too, I hope, shortly.

Wid. O where's my Brother, sir *Godfrey*? I would hee were here, that I might relate to him how prophetically the cunning Gentleman spoke in all things.

Enter Sir Godfrey *in a rage.*

Sir Godf. O my Chaine, my Chaine! I haue lost my Chaine. Where be these Villains, Varlets?

Wid. Oh! has lost his Chaine.

Sir Godf. My Chaine, my chaine!

Widdow. Brother, bee patient, heare mee speake: you know I told you that a cunning man told me that you should haue a losse, and he has prophicied so true.

Sir Godf. Out, he's a villaine, to prophecy of the losse of my chaine: twas worth aboue three hundred Crownes,—besides, twas my Fathers, my fathers fathers, my Grand-fathers huge grand-fathers. I had as lieue ha lost my Neck, as the chaine that hung about it. O, my chaine, my chaine!

Wid. Oh, brother, who can be against a misfortune! tis happy twas no more.

Sir Godf. No, more! O goodly godly sister, would you had me lost more? my best gowne, too, with the cloth of gold-lace? my holiday Gascoines, and my Ierkin set with pearle? no more!

Wid. Oh, Brother! you can reade—

52, 56, 64 *Prefix* Cap. *Q, Ff* 63 *S. D. add. M* 66 *S. D. add. M* after 68 70 hem *Q* *S. D.* Scene II. The same. Re-enter Pyeboard *M* 75 em] them *M*

Scene II. *etc.*] Scene III. *etc. M* 9 superiour] surgeon *conj. St.* 24 has *Q*: h'as *Ff*: he has *M* 34 lieve *Ff*: liue *Q* 40 had] (?) have had

Sir Godf. But I cannot reade where my chaine is.—What strangers haue beene here? you let in strangers, Theeues, and Catch-poles; how comes it gonne? there was none aboue with mee but my Taylor; and my Taylor will not—steale, I hope?

Mol. No, he's afrayde of a chaine!

Enter Fraylty.

Wid. How now, sirrah? the newes?

Fray. O Mistres, he may well be cald a Corporall now, for his corpes are as dead as a cold Capons.

Wid. More happinesse.

Sir Godf. Sirrah, what's this to my chaine? where's my chaine, knaue?

Fray. Your chaine, sir?

Sir Godf. My chaine is lost, villaine.

Fray. I would hee were hang'd in chaines that has it then for me. Alasse, sir, I saw none of your chaine, since you were hung with it your selfe.

Sir Godf. Out, varlet! it had full three thousand Lincks.
I haue oft told it ouer at my praiers:
Ouer and ouer, full three thousand Lincks.

Frayl. Had it so, sir: sure, it cannot be lost then; Ile put you in that comfort.

Sir Godf. Why, why?

Frayl. Why, if your chaine had so many Lincks, it cannot chuse but come to light.

Enter Nicholas.

Sir Godf. Delusion! now, long *Nicholas,* wheres my chaine?

Nich. Why, about your Neck, ist not, sir?

Sir Godf. About my neck, Varlet! My chaine is lost.
Tis stole away, Ime robd.

Wid. Nay, Brother, show your selfe a man.

Nic. I, if it be lost or stole, if he would be patient, Mistres, I could bring him to a Cunning Kinsman of mine that would fetcht againe with a Sesarara.

Sir Godf. Canst thou? I will be patient: say, where dwells he?

Nic. Marry, he dwels now, Sir, where he would not dwell, and he could choose: in the Marshalsea, sir; but hee's an exlent fellow if he were out; has trauyld all the world ore, he, and beene in the seauen and twenty Prouinces: why, he would make it be fetcht, Sir, if twere rid a thousand mile out of towne.

Sir Godf. An admirable fellow: what lies he for?

Nic. Why, hee did but rob a Steward of ten groats tother Night, as any man would ha done, and there he lies fort.

Sir Godf. Ile make his peace: a Trifle! Ile get his pardon,
Beside a bountifull reward. Ile about it.
But see the Clearkes, the Iustice will doe much.
I will about it straight: good sister, pardon me.
All will be well, I hope, and turne to good,
The name of Coniurer has laid my blood.
[*Exeunt.*

⟨Scene III. *A street.*⟩

Enter two seriants ⟨with Yeoman Dogson⟩ to arrest the Scholer, George Pyeboord.

Put. His Hostesse where he lies will trust him no longer: she has feed me to arest him; and if you will accompany me, because I know not of what Nature the Scholler is, whether desperate or swift, you shall share with me, Seriant *Rauen-shaw.* I haue the good Angell to arrest him.

Rauen. Troth, Ile take part with thee, then, Sariant, not for the sake of the mony so much, as for the hate I beare to a Scholler: why, Seriant, tis Naturall in vs, you know, to hate Scholers, naturall: besides, they will publish our imperfections, Knaueryes, and Conuayances vpon Scaffolds and Stages.

Put. I, and spightfully, to; troth, I haue wounderd how the slaues could see into our brests so much, when our doublets are buttond with Pewter.

Rauen. I, and so close without yeelding; oh, their parlous fellows, they will search more with their wits then a Cunstable with all his officers.

Put. Whist, whist, whist! Yeoman *Dogson* Yeoman *Dogson.*

Dog. Ha, what saies Sariant?

Put. Is he in the Pothecaryes shop stil?

Dog. I, I.

Put. Haue an eye, ⟨haue an⟩ eye.

Rauen. The best is, Sariant, if he be a true Scholler, he weares no weapon, I thinke.

Put. No, no, he weares no weapon.

Rauen. Masse, I am right glad of that: 'tas put me in better heart. Nay, if I clutch him once, let me alone to drage him if he be stiff-necked. I haue beene one of the sixe my selfe, that has dragd as tall men of their hands, when their weapons haue bin gone, as euer bastinadoed a Sariant—I haue done, I can tel you.

54 are] is *M* 87 has] ha's *Ff*

97 Besides *Ff, etc.* Scene III. *etc.*] Scene IV. *etc. M* S. D. with, *etc. add. Ff* 3 and *om. Ff* 12 besides] because *conj. M* 17 doublers *Q* 28 haue an *add. F1*

Dog. Sariant *Puttocke,* Sariant *Puttocke.*

Put. Hoh.

Dog. Hees comming out single.

Put. Peace, peace, bee not to greedy; let him play a little, let him play a litle: weele ierke him vp of a sudaine. I ha fisht in my time.

Rauen. I, and caught many a foole, Seriant.

Enter Pyeboord.

Pye. I parted now from *Nicholas*: the chaynes coucht,
And the old Knight has spent his rage vpont;
The widdowe holds me in great Admiration
For cunning Art: mongst ioyes I am 'een lost,
For my deuice can no way now be crost.
And now I must to prison to the captaine,
And there—

Put. I arrest you, sir.

Pye. Oh—I spoke truer then I was a ware, I must to prison indeed.

Put. They say your a scholler: nay, sir—Yeoman *Dogson,* haue care to his armes—youle rayle againe Sariants, and stage 'em! you tickle their vices!

Pye. Nay, vse me like a Gentleman, I'me little lesse.

Put. You a Gentleman? thats a good Iest, ifaith; can a Scholler be a Gentleman,—when a Gentleman will not be a Scholler? looke vpon your welthy Citizenes sonnes, whether they be Scholers or no, that are Gentlemen by their fathers trades: a Scholler a Gentleman!

Pye. Nay, let Fortune driue all her stings into me, she cannot hurt that in me: a Gentleman is *Accidens Inseperabile* to my bloud.

Rauen. A rablement, nay, you shall haue a bloudy rablement vpon you, I warrant you.

Put. Goe, Yeoman *Dogson,* before, and Enter the Action 'ith Counter.

Pie. Pray do not hand me Cruelly, Ile goe, [*Exet* Dogson.
Whether you please to haue me.

Put. Oh, hees tame; let him loose, seriant.

Pie. Pray, at whose sute is this?

Put. Why at your Hostisses suite where you lie, Mistres *Cunnyburrow,* for bed and boord, the somme foure pound fiue shillings and fiue pence.

Pie. I know the somme to true, yet I presumde
Vpon a farder daie; well, tis my starres
And I must beare it now, tho neuer harder.
I sweare now, my deuice is crost indeed.
Captaine must lie bite: this is Deceytes seed.

Put. Come, come away.

Pye. Pray, giue me so much time as to knit my garter, and Ile a way with you.

Put. Well, we must be paid for this waiting vpon you, this is no paynes to attend thus.

[⟨Pyboard⟩ *Making to tie his garter.*

Pye. I am now wretched, and miserable. I shall nere recouer of this disease: hot Yron gnaw their fists! they haue strucke a Feuer into my shoulder, which I shall nere shake out agen, I feare me, till with a true *Habeas Corpus* the Sexton remooue me. Oh, if I take prison once, I shall bee prest to death with Actions, but not so happy as speedilie; perhaps I may bee forty yeare a pressing, till I be a thin old man; that, looking through the grates, men may looke through me. All my meanes is confounded: what shall I doe? has my wits serued me so long, and now giue me the slippe (like a Traynd seruant) when I haue most need of 'em? no deuice to keepe my poore carcase fro these Puttocks?—yes, happines! haue I a paper about me now? yes, too! Ile trie it, it may hit: *Extremity is Touch-stone vnto wit.* I, I.

Put. Sfoot, how many yards are in thy Garters, that thou art so long a tying on them? come away, sir.

Pyb. Troth, Seriant, I protest, you could neuer ha tooke me at a worse time; for now at this instant I haue no lawfull picture about me.

Put. Slid, how shall we come by our fees then?

Rau. We must haue fees, Sirra.

Pib. I could ha wisht, ifaith, that you had tooke me halfe an hower hence for your owne sake; for I protest, if you had not crost me, I was going in great ioy to receiue fiue pound of a Gentleman, for the Deuice of a Maske here, drawne in this paper. But now, come, I must be contented: tis but so much lost, and answerable to the rest of my fortunes.

Put. Why, how far hence dwells that Gentleman?

Rau. I, well said, seriant, tis good to cast about for mony.

Put. Speake; if it be not far—

Pyb. We are but a little past it, the next street behind vs.

Put. Slid, we haue waited vpon you grieuously already: if youle say youle be liberall when you hate, giue vs double fees, and spend

53 *Ends* there *Q, Ff* 61 you'll *M* 72 is *om. Ff* 77–8 *Prose M* 82 Misters *Q* 88 sweare] fear *conj. M*

89 bite] by't *Ff, etc.* 106 have *M* wit *Q, Ff* 110 fro] from *Ff, etc.* 112 the touchstone *M* 121 we] me *Q* 141 hate] ha't *Ff*: have it *M*

vpon's, why weele show you that kindnes, and goe along with you to the Gentleman.

Rau. I, well said still, seriant, vrge that.

Pyb. Troth, if it will suffice, it shall be all among you; for my part ile not pocket a penny: my hostisse shall haue her foure pound fiue shillings, and bate me the fiue pence, and the other fifteene shillings Ile spend vpon you.

Rauinsh. Why, now thou art a good Scholler.

Put. An excellent Scholler, Ifaith; has proceeded very well alate; come, weele along with you.

[*Exeunt with him: passing in they knock at the doore with a Knocker withinside.*

⟨SCENE IV. *A gallery in a gentleman's house.*
Enter a Servant.⟩

Ser. Who knocks? whose at doore? we had need of a Porter.

Pyb. A few friends here:—pray, is the Gentleman your maister within?

Ser. Yes, is your businesse to him?

Pyb. I, he knows it, when he see's me: I pray you, haue you forgot mee?

Ser. I, by my troth, sir. Pray come neere; Ile in and tell him of you: please you to walke here in the Gallery till he comes.

Pyb. Wee will attend his worship.—Worship, I thinke, for so much the Posts at his doore should signifie, and the faire comming in, and the wicket; else I neither knew him nor his worship, but 'tis happinesse he is within doores, what so ere he bee: if he be not too much a formall Citizen, hee may doe me good.—Seriant and Yeoman, how doe you like this house? ist not most wholsomly plotted?

Rauen. Troth, prisoner, an exceeding fine house.

Pyb. Yet I wonder how hee should forget me,—for hee nere knew mee.—No matter, what is forgot in you will bee remembred in your Maister. A pritty comfortable roome this, me thinkes: You haue no such roomes in prison now?

Put. Oh, dog-holes toote.

Pyb. Dog-holes, indeed. I can tell you, I haue great hope to haue my Chamber here shortly, nay, and dyet too, for hee's the most free-hartedst Gentleman where he takes: you would little thinke it! and what a fine Gallery were here for mee to walke and study, and make verses.

Put. O, it stands very pleasantly for a Scholler.

Enter Gentleman.

Pyb. Looke what maps, and pictures, and deuices, and things: neatly, delicately—masse, here he comes: he should be a Gentleman; I like his Beard well.—All happinesse to your worship.

Gentle. You're kindly welcome, sir.

Put. A simple salutation.

Rauen. Masse, it seemes the Gentleman makes great account of him.

Pyb. I haue the thing here for you, sir.

Pyb. I beseech you conceale me, sir, Ime vndone else,—I haue the Maske here for you, sir, Looke you, sir.—I beseech your worship first to pardon my rudenesse, for my extreames makes mee boulder then I would bee. I am a poore Gentleman and a Scholler, and now most vnfortunately falne into the Fangs of vnmercifull officers, arrested for debt, which tho small, I am not able to compasse, by reason Ime destitute of lands, money, and friends; so that if I fall into the hungrie swallow of the prison, I am like vtterly to perish, and with fees and extortions be pincht cleane to the bone. Now, if euer pitty had interest in the bloud of a Gentleman, I beseech you vouchsafe but to fauour that meanes of my escape, which I haue already thought vpon.

Gent. Goe forward.

Put. I warrant he likes it rarely.

Pyb. In the plundge of my extremities, being giddy, and doubtfull what to doe, at last it was put into my labouring thoughts, to make happy vse of this paper; and to bleare their vnlettered eyes, I told them there was a Deuice for a Maske drawne int', and that (but for their interception,) I was going to a Gentleman to receiue my reward for't: they, greedy at this word, and hoping to make purchase of me, offered their attendance, to goe along with mee. My hap was to make bolde with your doore, Sir, which my thoughts showde mee the most fairest and comfortablest entrance, and I hope I haue happened right vpon vnderstanding and pitty: may it please your good Worship, then, but to vphold my Deuice, which is to let one of your men put me out at back-doore, and I shall bee bound to your worship for euer.

Gent. By my troth, an excellent deuice.

Puttock. An excellent deuice, hee sayes; hee likes it wonderfully.

Scene IV. *etc.*] Scene V. *etc.* *M*   24 you . . your] him . . his *conj.* *M*

47 *Prefix* Gent. *Ff*   54 Fangs *Q*: hands *Ff*   69–70 make a happy *Ff*, *etc.*   84 at] at a *Ff*, *etc.*

Gent. A my faith, I neuer heard a better.

Rauenshaw. Harke, hee sweares hee neuer heard a better, Serieant.

Put. O, there's no talke on't, hees an excellent Scholler, and especially for a Maske.

Gent. Giue me your Paper, your Deuice; I was neuer better pleasde in all my life: good witte, braue witte, finely rought! come in, sir, and receiue your money, sir.

Pyb. Ile follow your good Worship.— You heard how he likte it now?

Put. Puh, we know hee could not choose but like it: goe thy wayes; thou art a witty fine fellow, ifaith, thou shalt discourse it to vs at Tauerne anon, wilt thou?

Pyb. I, I, that I will. Looke, Seriants, here are Maps, and prittie toyes: be dooing in the meane time. I shall quickly haue told out the money, you know.

Put. Goe, goe, little villaine, fetch thy chinck. I begin to loue thee; Ile be drunke to night in thy company.

Pyb. ⟨*Aside*⟩ This Gentleman I may well call a part
Of my saluation, in these earthly euils,
For hee has sau'd mee from three hungrie Deuils. [*Exit* George.

Puttock. Sirrah Seriant, these Mappes are prittie painted things, but I could nere fancie 'em yet: mee thinkes they're too busie, and full of Circles and Coniurations; they say all the world's in one of them, but I could nere finde the Counter in the Poultrie.

Rauen. I thinke so: how could you finde it? for you know it stands behind the houses.

Dogson. Masse, thats true; then we must looke ath' back-side fort. Sfoote, here's nothing, all's bare.

Rauen. I warrant thee, that stands for the Counter, for you know theres a company of bare fellowes there.

Put. Faith, like enough, Seriant; I neuer markt so much before. Sirrah Seriant, and Yeoman, I should loue these Maps out a crye now, if wee could see men peepe out of doore in em: oh, wee might haue em in a morning to our Breake-fast so finely, and nere knocke our heeles to the ground a whole day for em.

Rauen. I, marry, sir, Ide buye one then my selfe. But this talke is by the way: where shall's sup to night? Fiue pound receiu'd! let's talke of that. I haue a trick worth all: you two shall beare him to 'th Tauerne, whilst I goe close with his Hostisse, and worke out of her. I know shee would bee glad of the summe to finger money, because shee knowes tis but a desperat debt, and full of hazard. What will you say, if I bring it to passe that the Hostisse shall bee contented with one halfe for all; and wee to share tother fifty-shillings, bullies?

Put. Why, I would call thee King of *Seriants,* and thou shouldst be Chronicled in the Counter booke for euer.

Ra. Well, put it to me, weele make a Night on't, yfaith.

Dog. Sfoote, I thinke he receiues more money, he staies so long.

Put. Hee tarries long, indeed: may be, I can tell you, vpon the good liking ont the Gentleman may proue more bountifull.

Ra. That would be rare; weele search him.

Put. Nay, be sure of it, weele search him! and make him light ynough.

Enter the Gentleman.

Ra. Oh, here comes the Gentleman. By your leaue, sir.

Gen. God you god den, sirs,—would you speake with me?

Put. No, not with your worship, sir; only wee are bould to stay for a friend of ours that went in with your worship.

Gen. Who? not the scholler?

Put. Yes, e'en he, and it please your worship.

Gen. Did he make you stay for him? hee did you wrong, then: why, I can assure you hees gon aboue an houre agoe.

Ra. How, sir?

Gent. I payd him his money, and my man told me he went out at back-dore.

Put. Back-dore?

Gen. Why, whats the matter?

Put. He was our prisoner, sir; we did arrest him.

Gen. What! he was not! you the Sheriffes Officers! You were to blame then. Why did you not make knowne to me as much? I could haue kept him for you: I protest he receiude all of me in *Brittaine* Gold of the last coyning.

Ra. Vengeance dog him with't!

Put. Sfoote, has he guld vs so?

Dog. Where shall wee sup now Serieants?

Put. Sup, *Simon,* now! eate Porridge for a month. Well, wee cannot impute it to any lacke of good-will in your Worship,—you did but as another would haue done: twas our hard fortunes to misse the purchase, but if

111 Gentlemen *Q* 130 out of cry *M* 135 then *om. Ff* 135–8 I . . that] *Verse Q, Ff* 146 fift-shillings *Q* *S. D.* Gentlemen *Q* 163 God] Give *S* 183–6 *Verse Q*

ere wee clutch him againe, the Counter shall charmę him.

Rauen. The hole shall rotte him.

Dog. Amen. [*Exeunt.*

Gent. So,
Vex out your Lungs without doores. I am proud,
It was my hap to helpe him; it fell fit.
He went not emptie neither for his wit.
Alasse, poore wretch, I could not blame his braine
To labour his deliuerie, to be free
From their vnpittying fangs—Ime glad it stood
Within my power to doe a Scholler good. [*Exit.*

⟨Scene V. *A room in the Marshalsea prison.*⟩

Enter in the Prison, meeting, George *and Captaine,* George *comming in muffled.*

Cap. How now, whose that? what are you?

Pyb. The same that I should be, Captaine.

Capt. *George Pye-boord,* honest *George*? why camst thou in halfe fac'd, muffled so?

Pyb. Oh, Captaine, I thought we should nere ha laught agen, neuer spent frolick houre agen.

Capt. Why? why?

Pyb. I comming to prepare thee, and with newes
As happy as thy quick deliuerie,
Was trac'd out by the sent, arrested, Captaine.

Capt. Arrested, *George*!

Pyb. Arrested: gesse, gesse; how many Dogges doe you thinke Ide vpon me?

Capt. Dogs? I say? I know not.

Pyb. Almost as many as *George Stone* the Beare:
Three at once, three at once.

Capt. How didst thou shake 'em of, then?

Pyb. The time is busie, and calls vpon our witts.
Let it suffice,
Here I stand safe, and scapt by miracle.
Some other houre shall tell thee, when weele steepe
Our eyes in laughter. Captaine, my deuice
Leanes to thy happinesse, for ere the day
Be spent toth' Girdle, thou shalt be set free.
The Corporal's in his first sleepe, the Chaine is mist,
Thy Kinsman has exprest thee, and the old Knight
With Palsey-hams now labours thy release:
What rests is all in thee, to Coniure, Captaine.

Capt. Coniure! sfoote, *George,* you know the deuill a coniuring I can coniure.

Pib. The Deuill of coniuring? nay, by my fay, Ide not haue thee do so much, Captaine, as the Deuill a coniuring: looke here, I ha brought thee a circle ready characterd and all.

Capt. Sfoote, *George,* art in thy right wittes? doost know what thou saist? why doost talke to a Captaine a coniuring? didst thou euer heare of a Captaine coniure in thy life? doost cal't a Circle? tis too wide a thing, me thinkes: had it beene a lesser Circle, then I knew what to haue done.

Pib. Why, euery foole knowes that, Captaine: nay, then, Ile not cogge with you, Captaine; if youle stay and hang the next Sessions, you may.

Capt. No, by my faith, *George*: come, come, lets to coniuring, lets to coniuring.

Pib. But if you looke to be releasd—as my wittes haue tooke paine to worke it, and all meanes wrought to farther it—besides to put crownes in your purse, to make you a man of better hopes, and whereas before you were a Captaine or poore Souldier, to make you now a Commander of rich fooles, (which is truly the onely best purchase peace can allow you) safer then High-wayes, Heath, or Cunny-groues, and yet a farre better bootie; for your greatest theeues are neuer hangd, neuer hangd, for, why, they're wise, and cheate within doores: and wee geld fooles of more money in one night, then your false tailde Gelding will purchase in a twelue-moneths running; which confirmes the olde Beldamssaying, hee's wisest, that keepes himselfe warmest; that is, hee that robs by a good fire—

Capt. Well opened, yfaith, *George*; thou hast puld that saying out of the huske.

Pib. Captaine *Idle,* tis no time now to delude or delay: the old Knight will be here suddenly. Ile perfect you, direct you, tell you the trick on't: tis nothing.

Capt. Sfoote, *George,* I know not what to say toot: coniure? I shall be hangd ere I coniure.

Pyb. Nay, tell not me of that, Captaine; youle nere coniure after your hangd, I warrant you. Looke you, sir, a parlous matter, sure! first, to spred your circle vpon the ground, then, with a little coniuring ceremonie, as Ile

Scene V. *etc.*] Scene VI. *etc. M* 19–20 *One line Q, Ff* 25 set *om. Ff, etc.* shalt sure be free *S*

32 of] a *M* 38 captain of *M* 40 me] my *Q* 47–8 let's to conjuring *once Ff, etc.* 54 of poor soldiers *conj. M* 57 Hig-wayes *Q* 60 for why? *Ff, etc.* 63 a *om. M* 71 tell] till *Q*

haue an Hackney-mans wand siluerd ore a purpose for you,—then arriuing in the circle, with a huge word, and a great trample, as for instance:—haue you neuer seene a stalking-stamping Player, that will raise a tempest with his toung, and thunder with his heeles?

Cap. O yes, yes, yes: often, often.

Pyb. Why, be like such a one, for any thing will bleare the old Knights eyes: for you must note that heele nere dare to venture into the roome, onely perhaps peepe fearefully through the Key hole, to see how the Play goes forward.

Capt. Well, I may goe about it when I will, but marke the end ont: I shall but shame my selfe, ifaith, *George*. Speake big words, and stampe and stare, and he looke in at Key-hole! why, the very thought of that would make me laugh out-right, and spoile all: nay, Ile tell thee, *George*, when I apprehend a thing once, I am of such a laxatiue laughter, that if the Deuill him-selfe stood by, I should laugh in his face.

Pyb. Puh, thats but the babe of a man, and may easily bee husht; as to thinke vpon some disaster, some sad misfortune, as the death of thy Father ithe Country!

Cap. Sfoote, that would be the more to driue me into such an extasie, that I should nere lin laughing.

Pib. Why, then, thinke vpon going to hanging else.

Cap. Masse, that's well remembred; now ile do well, I warrant thee, nere feare me now: but how shall I do, *George*, for boysterous words, and horrible names?

Pyb. Puh, any fustian inuocations, Captaine, will serue as well as the best, so you rant them out well; or you may goe to a Pothecaries shop, and take all the words from the Boxes.

Cap. Troth, and you say true, *George*; there's strange words enow to raise a hundred Quack-saluers, tho they be nere so poore when they begin. But here lyes the feare on't, how ⟨if⟩ in this false coniuration, a true Deuill should pop vp indeed?

Pyb. A true Deuill, Captaine? why there was nere such a one: nay, faith, hee that has this place is as false a Knaue as our last Church-warden.

Capt. Then hees false inough a conscience, ifaith, *George*.

The Crie at Marshalsea.

Crie prisoners. Good Gentlemen ouer the way, send your reliefe. Good Gentlemen ouer the way,—Good sir *Godfrey*!

Pyb. Hees come, hees come.

Nich. Maister, thats my Kinsman yonder in the Buff-Ierkin—Kinsman, thats my Maister yonder ith' Taffetie Hatt—pray salute him intirely! [*They salute: and* Py-boord *salutes Maister* Edmond.

Sir God. Now, my friend.

Pib. May I pertake your name, sir?

Edm. My name is Maister *Edmund.*

Pyb. Maister *Edmond*?—are you not a Welchman, sir?

Edm. A Welshman? why?

Pyb. Because Maister is your Christen name, and *Edmond* your sir name.

Edm. O no; I haue more names at home: Maister *Edmund Plus* is my full name at length.

Pyb. O, crie you mercy, sir. (*Whispering.*)

Cap. I vnderstand that you are my Kinsmans good Maister, and in regard of that, the best of my skill is at your seruice: but had you fortunde a meere stranger, and made no meanes to me by acquaintance, I should haue vtterly denyed to haue beene the man; both by reason of the Act past in Parliament against Coniurers and Witches, as also, because I would not haue my Arte vulgar, trite, and common.

Sir Godf. I much commend your care therein, good Captaine Coniurer, and that I will be sure to haue it priuate enough, you shall doote in my Sisters house,—mine owne house, I may call it, for both our charges therein are proportiond.

Capt. Very good, sir—what may I call your losse, sir?

Sir Godf. O you may call't a great losse, sir, a grieuous losse, sir; as goodly a Chaine of gold, tho I say it, that wore it: how saiest thou, *Nicholas*?

Nich. O 'twas as delicious a Chaine a Gold! Kinsman, you know,—

Sir God. You know? did you know't, Captaine?

Capt. Trust a foole with secrets!—Sir, hee may say I know: his meaning is, because my Arte is such, that by it I may gather a knowledge of all things.

Sir Godf. I, very true.

Capt. A pax of all fooles—the excuse stucke vpon my toung like Ship-pitch vpon a Mariners gowne, not to come off in hast—Ber-lady,

112 else *om. F2, etc.* 126 if *add. F2*

160 past in *Q*: of *Ff, etc.* 165 there *Ff, etc.* 173 sir *om. Ff, etc.* 176 of Gold *F2, etc.*

Knight, to loose such a faire Chaine a gold were a foule losse. Well, I can put you in this good comfort on't: if it bee betweene Heauen and Earth, Knight, Ile ha't for you.

Sir God. A wonderfull Coniurer!—O, I, tis betweene heauen and earth, I warrant you; it cannot goe out of the realme.—I know tis some-where aboue the earth.

Capt. I, nigher the earth then thou wotst on.

Sir Godf. For, first, my Chaine was rich, and no rich thing shall enter into heauen, you know.

Nich. And as for the Deuill, Maiṣter, he has no need on't, for you know he ha's a great chaine of his owne.

Sir Godf. Thou saiest true, *Nicholas,* but hee has put off that now; that lyes by him.

Capt. Faith, Knight, in few wordes, I presume so much vpon the power of my Art; that I could warrant your Chaine againe.

Sir Godf. O daintie Captaine!

Capt. Marry, it will cost me much sweate; I were better goe to sixteene whot-houses.

Sir Godf. I, good man, I warrant thee.

Capt. Beside great vexation of Kidney and Liuer.

Nich. O, twill tickle you here-abouts, Coozen, because you haue not beene vsde toot.

Sir Godf. No? haue you not beene vsd too't, Captaine?

Capt. Plague of all fooles still!—Indeed, Knight, I haue not vsde it a good while, and therefore twill straine me so much the more, you know.

Sir Godf. Oh, it will, it will.

Cap. What plunges hee puts me to! were not this Knight a foole, I had beene twice spoyld now; that Captaynes worse then accurst that has an asse to his Kinsman. Sfoote, I feare hee will driuell't out before I come toote. —Now, sir—to come to the poynt in deede—you see I sticke here in the iawe of the Marshalsea, and cannot doo't.

Sir Godf. Tut, tut, I ⟨k⟩now thy meaning; thou wouldst say thou'rt a prisoner. I tell thee thou'rt none.

Cap. How none? why, is not this the Marshialsea?

Sir Godf. Woult heare me speake? I hard
of thy rare cuniuring;
My chayne was lost; I sweate for thy release,
As thou shalt doe the like at home for me.
Keeper. [*Enter Keeper.*

Keep. Sir.

Sir Godf. Speake, is not this man free?

Keep. Yes, at his pleasure, sir, the fees dischargd.

Sir Godf. Goe, goe, Ile discharge them I.

Keep. I thanke your worship. [*Exet Keeper.*

Cap. Now, trust me, yar a deere Knight. Kindnes vnexpected! oh theirs nothing to a free Gentle man.—I will cuniure for you, sir, till Froath come through my Buffe-ierkin!

Sir Godf. Nay, then thou shalt not passe with so little a bounty, for at the first sight of my chaine agen, Forty fine Angells shall appeare vnto thee.

Cap. Twil be a glorious showe, ifaith, Knight, a very fine show; but are all these of your owne house? are you sure of that, sir?

Sir Godf. I, I—no, no, whats he younder, talking with my wild Nephew? pray heauen, he giue him good counsell.

Cap. Who, he? hee's a rare friend of mine, an admirable fellow, Knight, the finest fortune-teller.

Sir Godf. Oh, tis he indeed that came to my Lady sister, & foretold the losse of my chaine. I am not angry with him now, for I see twas my fortune to loose it.—By your leaue, M⟨aister⟩ Fortune-teller, I had a glimps on you at home at my Sisters the Widdowes, there you prouisied of the losse of a chaine:—simply tho I stand here, I was he that lost it.

Pie. Was it you, sir?

Edm. A my troth, Nunckle, hee's the rarest fellow: has told me my fortune so right; I find it so right to my nature.

Sir Godf. What ist? God send it a good one!

Edm. O, tis a passing good one, Nuncle: for he sayes I shall proue such an excelent gamster in my time, that I shall spend al faster then my father got it.

Sir Godf. There's a fortune, in deed!

Edm. Nay, it hits my humour so pat.

Sir Godf. I, that will be the end ont: will the Curse of the beggar preuaile so much, that the sonne shall consume that foolishlie, which the father got craftilie? I, I, I; twill, twill, twill.

Pie. Stay, stay, stay.

[Pyeboord *with an Almanack and the Captaine.*

Cap. Turne ouer, *George.*

Pie. *Iune—Iulie:* here, *Iulie;* thats this month. Sunday thirteene, yester day forteene, to day fifteene.

Cap. Looke quickly for the fifteene day:—if within the compasse of these two dayes there wouldbe some Boystrousstorme or other, it would be the best, Ide defer him off till then: some tempest, and it be thy will.

188 of Gold *F2, etc.* 195 aboue] about *Ff* 243 fee's *Q* 252 forty fiue *Ff* 292 fifteenth *M, etc.*

Pie. Heres the fifteene day—hot and fayre.

Cap. Puh, would t'ad beene hot and foule.

Pie. The sixteene day; thats to morrow: the morning for the most part faire and pleasant—

Cap. No lucke.

Pie. But about hye-none, lighning and thunder.

Cap. Lighning and thunder! admirable, best of all: Ile coniure to morrow iust at hie none, *George*.

Pye. Happen but true to morrow, Almanack, and ile giue thee leaue to lie all the yeare after.

Cap. Sir, I must craue your patience, to bestowe this day vpon me, that I may furnish my selfe strongly. I sent a spirit into Lanckishire tother day, to fetch backe a knaue Drouer, and I looke for his returne this euening. To morrow morning my friend here and I will come and breake-fast with you.

Sir Godf. Oh, you shall be both most welcome.

Cap. And about Noone, without fayle, I purpose to coniure.

Sir Godf. Mid noone will be a fine time for you.

Edm. Coniuring! do you meane to coniure at our house to morrow, sir?

Cap. Marry, do I, sir: tis my intent, yong Gentleman.

Edm. By my troth, Ile loue you while I liue fort. O rare, *Nicholas,* we shall haue coniuring to morrowe.

Nic. Puh! I, I could ha tould you of that.

Cap. Law, hee could ha told him of that! foole, cockscombe, could yee?

Edm. Do you heare me, sir? I desire more acquaintance on you: you shall earne some money of me, now I knowe you can coniure; but can you fetch any that is lost?

Capt. Oh, any thing thats lost.

Edm. Why, looke you, sir, I tel't you as a frend and a Coniurer, I should marry a Poticaries daughter, and twas told me she lost her maidenhead at Stonie-stratford; now if youle do but so much as coniure fort, and make all whole agen—

Cap. That I will, sir.

Edm. By my troth, I thanke you, la.

Cap. A litle merry with your sisters sonne, sir.

Sir Godf. Oh, a simple yong man, very simple: come, Captaine, and you, sir, weele een part with a gallon of wine till to morrow breake-fast.

Pie. Cap. Troth, agreed, sir.

Nic. Kinsman—Scholler?

Pye. Why, now thou art a good Knaue, worth a hundred Brownists.

Nic. Am I indeed, la? I thanke you truely, la. [*Exeunt.*

Actus. 4.

⟨Scene I. *An apartment in the Widow's house.*⟩

Enter Moll, *and Sir* Iohn Penny-dub.

Penne. But I hope you will not serue a Knight so, Gentlewoman, will you? to casheere him, and cast him off at your pleasure? what, do you thinke I was dubd for nothing? no, by my faith, Ladies daughter.

Moll. Pray, Sir *Iohn Pennydub,* let it be deferd awhile. I haue as bigge a heart to marry as you can haue; but as the Fortune-teler tolld me—

Penny. Pax a'th Fortune-teller! would *Derecke* had beene his fortune seauen yeare agoe, to crosse my loue thus! did hee know what case I was in? why, this is able to make a man drowne himselfe in's Fathers fish-pond.

Moll. And then hee told mee more-ouer, Sir *Iohn,* that the breach of it kept my Father in Purgatorie.

Penny. In Purgatorie? why let him purge out his heart there, what haue we to do with that? there's Phisitions enow there to cast his water: is that any matter to vs? how can hee hinder our loue? why, let him bee hangd now hee's dead!—Well, haue I rid poste day and night, to bring you merry newes of my fathers death, and now——

Moll. Thy Fathers death? is the old Farmer dead?

Penny. As dead as his Barne doore, *Moll.*

Moll. And you'le keepe your word with mee now, Sir *Iohn,* that I shall haue my Coach and my Coach-man?

Penny. I, faith.

Moll. And two white Horses with black Fethers to draw it?

Penny. Too.

Moll. A guarded Lackey to run befor't, and pyed liueries to come trashing after't.

Penny. Thou shalt, *Moll.*

Moll. And to let me haue money in my purse to go whether I will.

Penny. All this.

Moll. Then come what so ere comes on't, weele bee made sure together before the Maides a' the Kitchin. [*Exeunt*

352 *Prefix* Tip. Cap. *Q*

356 truely *Q*: heartily *Ff, etc.* Scene I. *etc. add. M* 7 as bigge *om. Ff* 44 i' the *M*

⟨SCENE II. *A room in the Widow's house, with a door at the side, leading to another apartment.*⟩

Enter Widdow, with her eldest Daughter Franck *and* Frailtie.

Wid. How now? where's my Brother, Sir *Godfrey*? went hee forth this morning?

Frail. O no, Madame, hee's aboue at breake-fast, with, sir reuerence, a Coniurer.

Wid. A Coniurer? what manner a fellow is he?

Frail. Oh, a wondrous rare fellow, Mistris, very strongly made vpward, for he goes in a Buff-ierkin: he sayes hee will fetch Sir *Godfreys* Chaine agen, if it hang betweene heauen and earth.

Wid. What, he will not? then hee's an exlent fellow, I warrant. How happy were that woman to be blest with such a Husband! a man a cunning! how do's hee looke, *Frailtie?* very swartlie, I warrant, with black beard, scorcht cheekes, and smokie eyebrowes.

Frail. Fooh, hee's neither smoake-dryed, nor scorcht, nor black, nor nothing. I tell you, Madame, hee lookes as faire to see to, as one of vs; I do not thinke but if you saw him once, youde take him to be a Christian.

Frank. So faire, and yet so cunning: that's to bee wonderd at, Mother.

Enter Sir Oliuer Muck-hill, *and Sir* Andrew Tip-staffe.

Muck. Blesse you, sweete Lady.

Tip. And you, faire Mistrisse.

[*Exit* Frailtie.

Wid. Coades? what doe you meane, Gentlemen? fie, did I not giue you your answeres?

Muck. Sweete Lady.

Wid. Well, I will not stick with you now for a kisse.
Daughter, kisse the Gentleman for once.

Frank. Yes, forsooth.

Tip. Ime proud of such a fauour.

Wid. Truly la, sir *Oliuer,* y'are much to blame to come agen, when you know my minde, so well deliuerd as a Widdow could deliuer a thing.

Muck. But I expect a farther comfort, Lady.

Wid. Why la you now, did I not desire you to put off your sute quite & cleane, when you came to me againe? how say you? did I not?

Muc. But the sincere loue which my heart beares you—

Wid. Go to, ile cut you off: & Sir *Oliuer,* to put you in comfort a farre off, my fortune is read me: I must marry againe.

Muck. O blest fortune!

Wid. But not as long as I can choose;—nay, Ile hold out well.

Muc. Yet are my hopes now fairer.

Enter Frailtie.

Frail. O Madam, Madam.

Wid. How now, what's the hast?

[*In her eare.*

Tipst. Faith, Mistrisse *Francis,* Ile maintaine you gallantly. Ile bring you to Court, weane you among the faire society of ladies, poore Kinswomen of mine, in cloth of siluer: beside, you shal haue your Monckie, your Parrat, your Muskat, & your pisse, pisse, pisse.

Frank. It will do very well.

Wid. What, dos he meane to coniure here then? how shal I do to bee rid of these Knights?—Please you, Gentlemen, to walke a while ith Garden: go gather a pinck, or a Iilly-flower.

Both. With all our hearts, Lady, and count vs fauourd. [*Exit. Within Sir Go.*

Si. Go. Step in, *Nicholas*; looke, is the coast cleare.

Nic. Oh, as cleare as a Cattes eye, sir.

Sir Go. Then enter, Captaine Coniurer:—now—how like you your Roome, sir?

Enter Sir Godf. Capt. Pyb. Edm. Nick.

Cap. O, wonderfull conuenient.

Edm. I can tell you, Captaine, simplie tho it lies here, tis the fayrest Roome in my Mothers house: as dainty a Roome to Coniure in, mee thinkes—why, you may bidde, I cannot tell how many diuills welcome in't; my Father has had twentie here at once!

Pie. What, diuills?

Edm. Diuills? no, Deputies, & the welthiest men he could get.

Sir God. Nay, put by your chattes now, fall to your businesse roundly: the feskewe of the Diall is vpon the Chrisse-crosse of Noone, but oh, heare mee, Captaine, a qualme comes ore my stomack.

Cap. Why, what's the matter, sir?

Sir Godf. Oh, how if the diuill should proue a knaue, and teare the hangings?

Cap. Fuh, I warrant you, Sir Godfrey.

Edm. I, Nuncle, or spit fire vpp'oth seeling!

Sir Godf. Very true, too, for tis but thin

Scene II. *etc. add. M* 15 a man cunning *Ff*: a cunning man *M* *S. D.* Sir Andrew Muck-hill *Ff* 30 now *om. Ff, etc.*

45 bears to you *Ff* 52 *om. Ff* 65 go *Q*: to *Ff, etc.* 70 Cattes *Q*: Carter's *Ff* 72 your] our *Ff* 79 here *Q*: in't *Ff, etc.*

playsterd, and twill quickly take hold a the laths, and if hee chance to spit downeward too, he will burne all the boords.

Cap. My life for yours, Sir Godfrey.

Sir Godf. My Sister is very curious & dainty ore this Roome, I can tell, and therefore if he must needes spit, I pray desire him to spit ith Chimney.

Pie. Why, assure you, Sir Godfrey, he shall not be brought vp with so little manners to spit and spaule a'th flower.

Sir Godf. Why, I thanke you, good Captaine; pray haue a care. I, fall to your Circle; weele not trouble you, I warrant you: come, weele in to the next Roome, & be cause weele be sure to keepe him out there, weele bar vp the dore with some of the Godlies zealous workes.

Edm. That will bee a fine deuice, Nuncle, and because the ground shall be as holy as the doore, Ile teare two or three rosaries in peices, and strew the leaues about the Chamber.

[*Thunders.*

Oh, the deuill already. [*runs in.*

Py. Sfoote, Captaine, speake somwhat for shame; it lightens & thunders before thou wilt begin: why, when?

Cap. Pray, peace, *George*,—thou'lt make mee laugh anon and spoile all.

Pie. Oh, now it begins agen: now, now, now, Captaine.

Cap. *Rumbos—ragdayon, pur, pur, colucundrion, Hois-Plois.*

Sir Godf. Oh admirable Coniurer! has fetcht Thunder already:

[*Sir Godfrey through the keyhole; within.*

Pie. Harke, harke! agen, Captaine!

Cap. *Beniamino,—gaspois—kay—gosgothoteron—vmbrois.*

Sir Godf. Oh, I would the deuill would come away quicklie, he has no conscience to put a man to such paine.

Pie. Agen!

Cap. *Flowste — Kakopumpos — dragone— Leloomenos—hodge—podge.*

Pie. Well sayd, Captaine.

Sir Godf. So long a comming? oh, would I had nere begun't now, for I feare mee these roaring tempests will destroy all the fruites of the earth, and tread vpon my corne—oh!—ith Country.

Cap. *Gog de gog, hobgoblin, hunoks, hounslow, hockley te coome parke.*

Wid. ⟨*at the door*⟩. O brother, brother, what a tempests ith Garden: sure there's some coniuration abroad.

Sir Godf. Tis at home, sister!

Pie. By and by, Ile step in, Captaine.

Cap. *Nunck—Nunck—Rip—Gascoynes, Ipis, Drip—Dropite.*

Sir God. Hee drippes and droppes, poore man! alasse, alasse.

Pie. Now I come.

Cap. *O Sulphure Sooteface—*

Pie. Arch-coniurer, what wouldst thou with me?

Sir Godf. O the diuill, sister, ith dyning Chamber! sing, Sister, I warrant you that will keepe him out: quickly, quickly, quickly.

[*goes in.*

Pie. So, so, so, Ile release thee: ynough, Captaine, ynough; allowe vs some time to laughe a little: they're shuddering and shaking by this time, as if an Earth-quake were in their kidneyes.

Cap. Sirrah *George,* how wast, how wast? did I doo't well ynough?

Pie. Woult beleeue mee, Captaine? better then any Coniurer, for here was no harme in this, and yet their horrible expectation satisfied well. You were much beholding to thunder & lightning at this time: it gracst you well I can tell you.

Cap. I must needes say so, *George.* Sirrah, if wee could ha conuoide hether cleanly a cracker or a fire-wheele t'ad beene admirable.

Pie. Blurt, blurt! theirs nothing remaines to put thee to paine now, Captaine.

Cap. Paine? I protest, *George,* my heeles are sorer, then a Whitson Morris-dancer.

Pie. All's past now,—onely to reueale that the chaines ith Garden where thou knowst it has laine these two daies.

Cap. But I feare that fox *Nicholas* has reueald it already.

Pie. Feare not, Captaine, you must put it to'th venture now. Nay, tis time: call vpon e'm, take pitty on e'm, for I beleeue some off 'em are in a pittifull case by this time.

Cap. Sir *Godfrey*? *Nicholas,* Kinsman— Sfoot, they'r fast at it still, *George.* Sir *Godfrey*!

Sir Godf. Oh, is that the diuils voyce? how comes he to know my name?

Cap. Feare not, Sir *Godfrey,* all's quieted.

Sir Godf. What, is he layd?

Cap. Layde; and has newly dropt your chaine ith Garden.

99 ore] of *M*   tell] tell you *Ff, etc.*   104 flower] floor *Qq, etc.*   114 leaues] pieces *M*   *S. D.* runs in *part of Edmond's speech Q*   144 at . . door *add. M*   174 convey'd *M*   180 dancer's *Ff, etc.*   194-5 *S. D.* Enter Sir Godfrey, The Widow, Frances, and Nicholas *M*

Sir Godf. Ith Garden! in our Garden?

Cap. Your Garden.

Sir Godf. O sweete Coniurer! where abouts there?

Cap. Looke well about a banck of Rosemary.

Sir Godf. Sister, the Rosemary banck! come, come, ther's my chaine, he saies.

Wid. Oh happinesse! run, run.

[*supposed to goe.*

Edm. Captaine Coniurer?

[*Edm. at keyhoole.*

Cap. Who? Maister *Edmond?*

Edm. I, Maister *Edmond*: may I come in safely, without danger, thinke you?

Cap. Fuh, long agoe: tis all as twas at first. Feare nothing, pray come neere—how now, man?

Edm. Oh this Roomes mightily hot, ifaith: slid, my shirt sticks to my Belly already. What a steame the Rogue has left behind him! foh, this roome must be ayrd, Gentlemen; it smells horribly of Brimstoone—lets open the windowes.

Pye. Faith, maister *Edmond*, tis but your conceite.

Edm. I would you could make me beleeue that, ifaith. Why, do you thinke I cannot smell his sauour from another? yet I take it kindly from you, because you would not put me in a feare, ifaith; a my troth, I shal loue you for this the longest day of my life.

Cap. Puh, tis nothing, sir: loue me when you see more.

Edm. Masse, now I remember, Ile looke whether he has singed the hangings or no.

Pye. Captaine, to entertaine a litle sport till they come, make him beleeue youle charme him inuisible: hes apt to admire any thing, you see. Let me alone to giue force too't.

Cap. Goe, retire to yonder end then.

Edm. I protest you are a rare fellowe, are you not?

Cap. O maister *Edmond*, you know but the least part of me yet: why, now at this instant I could but florish my wand thrice ore your head, and charme you inuisible.

Edm. What, you could not? make me walke inuisible, man! I should laugh at that, ifaith; troth, ile requite your kindnes and youle doo't, good Captaine coniurer.

Cap. Nay, I should hardly deny you such a small kindnesse, Master *Edmond Plus*: why, looke you, sir, tis no more but this and thus and agen, and now yar inuisible!

Edm. Am I, ifaith? who would thinke it?

Cap. You see the fortune-teller yonder at farder end ath chamber: goe toward him, do what you will with him; he shall nere finde you.

Edm. Say you so? ile trie that, ifaith,——

[*Iustles him.*

Pie. How now? Captaine, whose that iustled me?

Cap. Iustled you? I saw no body.

Edm. Ha, ha, ha!——say twas a spirit.

Cap. Shall I?—may be some spirit that haunts the circle.

[⟨*Edmond*⟩ *Puls him by the Nose.*

Pye. O my nose agen! pray coniure then, Captaine.

Edm. Troth, this is exlent; I may do any knauery now and neuer be seene,—and now I remember mee, Sir *Godfrey* my Vncle abusde me tother day, & told tales of me to my Mother —Troth, now Ime inuisible, ile hit him a sound wherrit ath' eare, when he comes out ath' garden.—I may be reuengd on him now finely.

Enter Sir Godfrey, Widdow, Franck, Nicholas *with the Chaine.*

Sir God. I haue my Chaine againe, my Chaine's found againe. O sweete Captaine, O admirable Coniurer. [Edm. *strikes him.* Oh! what meane you by that, Nephew?

Edm. Nephew? I hope you do not know mee, Vncle?

Wid. Why did you strike your Vncle, sir?

Edm. Why, Captaine, am I not inuisible?

Capt. A good iest, *George*!—not now you are not, Sir.
Why, did you not see me when I did vncharme you?

Edm. Not I by my troth, Captaine. Then pray you pardon mee, Vncle; I thought Ide beene inuisible when I struck you.

Sir Godf. So, you would doo't? go,—y'are a foolish Boy,
And were I not ore-come with greater ioy,
Ide make you taste correction.

Edm. Correction, push!—no, neither you nor my Mother shall thinke to whip me as you haue done.

Sir Godf. Captaine, my ioy is such, I know not how to thanke you: let me embrace you, hug you. O my sweete Chaine! Gladnesse 'een makes mee giddy. Rare man! twas as iust ith' Rosemarie banck, as if one should ha laide it there—oh cunning, cunning!

Wid. Well, seeing my fortune tels mee

212-13 *S. D.* Enter Edmond *M* 248-9 thus agen *Ff* 256 How] Hoe *Ff* 261 *S. D.* Puls . . Nose *after* 263 *Q* 293 hug you *om. Ff, etc.*

I must marry, let me marry a man of witte, a man of parts. Here's a worthy Captaine, and 'tis a fine Title truely la to bee a Captaines Wife. A Captaines Wife, it goes very finely; beside all the world knows that a worthy Captaine is a fitte Companion to any Lord, then why not a sweete bed-fellow for any Lady, —Ile haue it so——

Enter Frailtie.

Frail. O Mistris, Gentlemen, there's the brauest sight comming along this way.

Wid. What braue sight?

Frai. Oh, one going to burying, & another going to hanging.

Wid. A rufull sight.

Pyb. Sfoot, Captaine, Ile pawne my life the Corporals coffind, and old *Skirmish* the souldier going to execution, & 'tis now full about the time of his waking; hold out a little longer, sleepie potion, and we shall haue exlent admiration; for Ile take vpon me the cure of him.

⟨SCENE III. *The street before the Widow's house.*⟩

Enter the Coffin of the Corporall, the souldier bound, and lead by Officers, the Sheriffe there. ⟨*From the house,* Sir Godfrey, *the Widow,* Idle, Pyeboard, Edmond, Frailty, *and* Nicholas.⟩

Frail. Oh here they come, here they come!

Pyb. Now must I close secretly with the Souldier, preuent his impatience, or else all's discouered.

Wid. O lamentable seeing! these were those Brothers, that fought and bled before our doore.

Sir Godf. What, they were not, Sister?

Skirm. *George,* looke toote, Ile peach at Tyburne else.

Pyb. Mum,—Gentles all, vouchsafe mee audience, and you especially, Maister Shiriffe:
Yon man is bound to execution,
Because he wounded this that now lyes coffind?

Shir. True, true; he shall haue the law,—and I know the law.

Pyb. But vnder fauour, Maister Sheriffe, if this man had beene cured and safe agen, he should haue beene releasde then?

Shir. Why make you question of that, Sir?

Pyb. Then I release him freely, and will take vpon mee the death that he should dye, if within a little season, I do not cure him to his proper health agen.

Shir. How Sir? recouer a dead man?
That were most strange of all.

[Franke *comes to him.*

Frank. Sweete Sir, I loue you deerely, and could wish my best part yours,—oh do not vndertake such an impossible venture.

Pyb. Loue you me? then for your sweet sake Ile doo't:
Let me entreate the corps to be set downe.

Shir. Bearers, set downe the Coffin.—This were wonderfull, and worthy *Stoes* Chronicle.

Pyb. I pray bestow the freedome of the ayre vpon our wholsome Arte.—Masse, his cheekes begin to receiue naturall warmth: nay, good Corporall, wake betime, or I shall haue a longer sleepe then you.—Sfoote, if he should proue dead indeed now, he were fully reuengd vpon me for making a property on him, yet I had rather run vpon the Ropes, then haue the Rope like a Tetter run vpon mee. Oh—he stirs—hee stirs agen—looke, Gentlemen, he recouers, he starts, he rises.

Shir. Oh, oh, defend vs!—out, alasse.

Pyb. Nay, pray be still; youle make him more giddy else:—he knowes no body yet.

Corp. Zounes: where am I? couerd with Snow? I maruaile.

Pyb. Nay, I knew hee would sweare the first thing hee did, as soone as euer he came to his life agen.

Corp. Sfoote, Hostesse, some hotte Porridge,—oh, oh, lay on a dozen of Fagots in the Moone parler, there.

Pyb. Lady, you must needs take a little pitty of him, yfaith, and send him in to your Kitchin fire.

Wid. Oh, with all my heart, sir. *Nicholas* and *Frailtie,* helpe to beare him in.

Nich. Beare him in, quatha? pray call out the Maides, I shall nere haue the heart to doo't, indeed la.

Frai. Nor I neither, I cannot abide to handle a Ghost of all men.

Cor. Sbloud, let me see: where was I drunke last night, heh—

Wid. Oh, shall I bid you once agen take him away?

Frai. Why, we're as fearefull as you, I warrant you—oh—

Wid. Away, villaines; bid the Maides make him a Cawdle presently to settle his braine,—or a Posset of Sack; quickly, quickly.

[*Exeunt* ⟨Frailty *and* Nicholas⟩ *pushing in the corpes.*

314 full *om. Ff, etc.* 315 waking *Ff, etc.*: walking *Q* Scene III. *etc. add. M. No change of scene intended by author* *S. D.* From . . Nicholas *add. M*

33 were] is *Ff* 40 on] of *M* 48 where *Ff, etc.*: who *Q* 51, 52 euer, his *om. Ff* 74 *S. D.* Frailty, *etc. add. M*

Shir. Sir, what so ere you are, I do more then admire you.

Wid. O, I, if you knew all, Maister Shiriffe, as you shall doe, you would say then, that here were two of the rarest men within the walls of Christendome.

Shir. Two of 'em? O wonderfull. Officers, I discharge you, set him free, all's in tune.

Sir Godf. I, and a banquet ready by this time, Maister Sheriffe, to which I most cheerefully enuite you, and your late prisoner there. See you this goodly chaine, sir? mun, no more words, twas lost, and is found againe; come, my inestimable bullies, weele talke of your noble Acts in sparkling Charnico, and in stead of a Iester, weele ha the ghost ith white sheete sit at vpper end a'th Table.

Sheriff. Exlent merry, man, yfaith.

⟨*Exeunt all but Frances.*⟩

Franck Well, seeing I am enioynd to loue and marry,
My foolish vow thus I casheere to Ayre
Which first begot it.—Now, loue, play thy part;
The scholler reades his lecture in my heart.

⟨*Exit.*⟩

Actus 5.

SCEN. I. ⟨*The street before the Widow's house.*⟩

Enter in hast Maister Edmund *and* Frayltie.

Ed. This is the marriage morning for my mother & my sister.

Frail. O me, Maister *Edmund*; we shall ha rare doings.

Ed. Nay, go, *Frayltie*, runne to the Sexton; you know my mother wilbe married at Saint Antlings. Hie thee, tis past fiue; bid them open the Church dore; my sister is almost ready.

Fra. What, al ready, Maister *Edmond*?

Ed. Nay, go, hie thee: first run to the Sexton, and runne to the Clarke, and then run to Maister *Pigman* the Parson, and then run to the Millanor, and then run home agen.

Frail. Heer's run, run, run——

Ed. But harke, *Frailty.*

Fra. What, more yet?

Edm. Has the maides remembred to strew the way to the Church.

Frail. Fagh, an houre ago; I helpt 'em my selfe.

Ed. Away, away, away, away then.

Frail. Away, away, away then.

[*Exit* Frailty.

Edm. I shall haue a simple Father inlawe, a braue Captaine able to beate all our streete: Captaine *Idle.* Now my Ladie Mother wilbe fitted for a delicate name: my Ladie *Idle,* my Ladie *Idle,* the finest name that can be for a woman; and then the Scholler, Maister *Pieboord,* for my sister *Francis,* that wilbe Mistris *Francis Pie-boord.*—Mistris *Francis Pie-boord!* theill keepe a good table I warrant you. Now all the knights noses are put out of ioynt; they may go to a bone setters now.

Enter Captaine and Pie-boord.

Harke, harke! oh who comes here with two Torches before 'em? my sweete Captaine, and my fine Scholler! oh, how brauely they are shot vp in one night; they looke like fine Brittaines now, me thinkes. Heres a gallant chaunge, ifaith: slid, they haue hir'd men and all by the clock.

Cap. Maister *Edmund,* kinde, honest, dainty Maister *Edmond.*

Edm. Fogh, sweete Captaine Father inlaw, a rare perfume, ifayth.

Pie. What, are the Brides stirring? may wee steall vpon 'em, thinkst thou, Maister *Edmond*?

Edm. Faw, there e'en vpon reddines, I can assure you, for they were at there Torch e'en now: by the same token I tumbled downe the staires.

Pie. Alas, poore Maister *Edmond.*

Enter musitians.

Cap. O, the musitians! I pree the, Maister *Edmond,* call 'em in and licquour 'em a little.

Ed. That I will, sweete Captaine father in law, and make ech of them as drunck as a common fiddeler. [*Exeunt omnes.*

⟨SCENE II. *The same.*⟩

Enter Sir Iohn Penidub, *and* Moll *aboue lacing of her clothes.*

Pen. Whewh, Mistris Mol, Mistris Mol.

Mol. Who's there?

Pen. Tis I.

Mol. Who? Sir *Iohn Penidub*? O you'r an early cocke, ifayth: who would haue thought you to be so rare a stirrer?

Pen. Preethe, Mol, let me come vp.

Mol. No, by my faith, Sir Iohn, Ile keepe you downe, for you Knights are very dangerous if once you get aboue.

Pen. Ile not stay, ifaith.

Mol. Ifaith, you shall staie, for, Sir Iohn,

75 *Prefix* Skir. *Q* 91 at the upper *M* *S. D.* Exeunt . . Frances *M*: Exit *Q* *S. D.* Exit *add. M* *S. D.* The street . . house *add. M* 19 help *Q* 22 then *Q*: away then *Ff, etc.*

Scene II. *etc. add. M*

you must note the nature of the Climates: your Northen wench in her owne Countrie may well hold out till shee bee fifteene, but if she touch the South once, and come vp to *London*, here the Chimes go presently after twelue.

Pen. O th'art a mad wench, *Moll*, but I pree thee make hast, for the Priest is gone before.

Moll. Do you follow him, Ile not be long after. [*Exeunt.*

⟨Scene III. *A room in Sir* Oliver Muckhill's *house.*⟩

Enter Sir Oliuer Muck-hill, *Sir* Andrew Tipstaffe, *and old* Skirmish *talking.*

Muck. O monstrous, vn-heard of forgerie.

Tip. Knight, I neuer heard of such villany in our owne countrie in my life.

Muck. Why, 'tis impossible; dare you maintaine your words?

Skir. Dare wee? een to their wezen pipes. We know all their plots, they cannot squander with vs; they haue knauishly abusd vs, made onely properties on's to aduance their selues vpon our shoulders, but they shall rue their abuses. This morning they are to bee married.

Muck. Tis too true; yet if the Widdow be not too much besotted on slights and forgeries, the reuelation of their villanies will make 'em loathsome: and to that end, be it in priuate to you, I sent late last night to an honourable personage, to whom I am much indebted in kindnesse, as he is to me, and therefore presume vpon the paiment of his tongue, and that hee will lay out good words for me: and to speake truth, for such needfull occasions, I onely preserue him in bond, and some-times he may doe mee more good here in the Cittie by a free word of his mouth, then if hee had paide one halfe in hand, and tooke Doomesday for t'other.

Tip. In troth, Sir, without soothing bee it spoken, you haue publisht much iudgement in these few words.

Muck. For you know, what such a man vtters will be thought effectuall and to waighty purpose, and therefore into his mouth weel put the approoued theame of their forgeries.

Skir. And Ile maintaine it, Knight, if yeele be true.

Enter a seruant.

Muck. How now, fellow?

Seru. May it please you, Sir, my Lord is newly lighted from his Coache.

Muc. Is my Lord come already? his honnors early.
You see he loues me well: vp before seauen!
Trust me, I haue found him night capt at eleuen.
Ther's good hope yet; come, Ile relate all to him. [*Exeunt.*

⟨Scene IV. *A street; a church appearing.*⟩

Enter the two Bridegromes, Captaine and Scholler; after them, Sir Godfrey *and* Edmond, Widdow *changde in apparell, mistris* Francis *led betweene two Knights, Sir* Iohn Penny-dub *and* Moll: *there meetes them a Noble man, Sir* Oliuer Muckil, *and Sir* Andrew Tip-staffe.

Nob. By your leaue, Lady.

Wid. My Lord, your honour is most chastly welcome.

Nob. Madam, tho I came now from court, I come not to flatter you: vpon whom can I iustly cast this blot, but vpon your owne forehead, that know not inke from milke? such is the blind besotting in the state of an vnheaded woman thats a widdow. For it is the property of all you that are widdowes (a hand full excepted) to hate those that honestly and carefully loue you, to the maintenance of credit, state, and posterity, and strongly to doat on those, that only loue you to vndo you: who regard you least are best regarded, who hate you most are best beloued. And if there be but one man amongst tenne thousand millions of men that is accurst, disastrous, and euilly planeted, whome Fortune beates most, whome God hates most, and all Societies esteeme least, that man is suere to be a husband.—Such is the peeuish Moone that rules your bloods. An Impudent fellow best woes you, a flattering lip best wins you, or in a mirth who talkes roughliest is most sweetest; nor can you distinguish truth from forgeries, mistes from Simplisity: witnes those two deceitfull monsters that you haue entertaind for bride-groomes.

Wid. Deceitfull!

Pie. All will out.

Cap. Sfoote, who has blabd, *George*? that foolish *Nicholas?*

Nob. For what they haue besotted your easie blood withall weare nought but forgeries: the fortune telling for husbands, the con-

Scene III. *etc. add. M* 9 on's] of us *M* 35 yeele *pr. ed.* : sheele *Q*, *Ff*: you'll *Haz.*

40 seauen *Q* : heaven *Ff* 41 at a eleuen *Q* 42 Ile] Iee *Q* Scene IV. *etc. add. M* 11 handfull *F1* 23 you bloods *Q* 25 a *om. Ff*

iuring for the chaine *Sir Godfrey* heard the falshod of: al nothing but meere knauery, deceit, and coozenage.

Wid. O wonderfull! indeed I wondred that my husband with all his craft could not keepe himselfe out of purgatory.

Sir Godf. And I more wonder that my chaine should be gon and my Taylor had none of it.

Mol. And I wondred most of all that I should be tyed from marriage, hauing such a mind too't. Come, *S⟨ir⟩ Iohn Pennydub,* faire wether on our side; the moone has chaingd since yester night.

Pie. The Sting of euery euill is with-in mee.

Nob. And that you may perceaue I faine not with you, behould their fellow actor in those forgeries; who, full of Spleene and enuy at their so suddaine aduancements, reueled all there plot in anger.

Pie. Base Souldier, to reueall vs.

Wid. Ist possible wee should be blinded so, and our eys open?

Nob. Widdow, wil you now beleeue that false, which to soone you beleeued true?

Wid. O, to my shame I doe.

Sir Godf. But vnder fauour, my Lord, my chaine was truely lost and straingly found againe.

Nob. Resolue him of that, Souldier.

S⟨k⟩ir. In few words, Knight, then, thou wert the arch-gull of all.

Sir Godf. How, Sir?

Skir. Nay, ile proue it: for the chayne was but hid in the rosemary bancke all this while, and thou gotst him out of pryson to Coniure for it, who did it admirably fustianly; for indeed what neede any others when he knew where it was?

Sir Godf. O vilainy of vilanies! but how came my chaine there?

Skir. Wheres *truly la, in deed la,* he that will not sweare, but lie, he that will not steale, But rob: pure *Nicholas Saint Antlings?*

Sir Godf. O Villaine! one of our society,
Deemd alwaies holy, pure, religious.
A Puritan a theefe, when wast euer hard?
Sooner wee'll kill a man then Steale, thou knowst.
Out, slaue! Ile rend my lyon from thy back
With mine owne hands.

Nich. Deare Maister, oh.

Nob. Nay, Knight, dwell in patience. And now, widdow, being so neere the Church, twer great pitty, nay vncharity, to send you home againe without a husband: drawe nerer you of true worship, state and credit, that should not stand so farre of from a widdow, and suffer forged shapes to come betweene you. Not that in these I blemish the true Title of a Captaine, or blot the faire margent of a Scholler; For I honnor worthy and deseruing parts in the one, and cherrish fruitfull Vertues in the other. Come Lady, and you, Virgin; bestowe your eys and your purest affections vpon men of estimation both in Court and Citty, that hath long woed you, and both with there hearts and wealth sincearly loue you.

Sir Godf. Good Sister, doe: Sweet little *Franke,* these are men of reputation; you shalbe welcome at Court: a great creddit for a Cittizen, sweet Sister.

Nob. Come, her scilence doos consent too't.

Wid. I know not with what face—

Nob. Pah, pah! why, with your owne face; they desire no other.

Wid. Pardon me, worthy Sirs; I and my daughter haue wrongd your loues.

Muck. Tis easily pardon'd, Lady,
If you vouchsafe it now.

Wid. With all my soule.

Fran. And I with all my heart.

Moll. And I, Sir *Iohn,* with soule, heart, lights and all.

Sir Ioh. They are all mine, *Moll.*

Nob. Now, Lady,
What honest Spirit but will applaud your choyce,
And gladly furnish you with hand and voyce?
A happy change which makes een heauen reioyce.
Come, enter into your Ioyes, you shall not want
For fathers now; I doubt it not, beleeue me,
But that you shall haue hands inough to giue ⟨ye⟩. [*Exeunt omnes.*

Deus dedit his quoq⟨ue⟩ finem.

FINIS

37 heare *S* 43 wonder'd *M* 74 needed *Ff, etc.* other *M* 76 vilanies] villains *Ff* 91 near *Ff* 102 hath *Q*: have *Ff, etc.* 120 *Prefix* Sir Godf. *Ff* 125 into] in *Ff* 127 give ye *R*: giue *Q*: give me *Ff* 128 Deus, *etc. om. Ff, etc.*

A YORKSHIRE Tragedy

Not ſo New as Lamentable and true.

Acted by his Maieſties Players at the *Globe*.

VVritten by VV. Shakſpeare.

AT LONDON
Printed by *R. B.* for *Thomas Pauier* and are to bee ſold at his ſhop on Cornhill, neere to the exchange.
1608.

811663 U

Q 1	=	Quarto of 1608
Q 2	=	„ „ 1619
F 1	=	(Third) Folio Shakespeare, 1664
F 2	=	(Fourth) „ i685
R	=	Rowe, 1709
M	=	Malone, 1780
St.	=	Steevens, ibid.
Th.	=	Theobald, ibid.
Kn.	=	Knight, 1839-41
S	=	Simms, 1848
T	=	Tyrrell, 1851
Haz.	=	Hazlitt, 1852
Molt.	=	Moltke, 1869
Col.	=	Collier, 1878
pr. ed.	=	present editor

ALL'S ONE,

OR, ONE OF THE FOURE PLAIES IN ONE, CALLED

A YORK-SHIRE TRAGEDY

AS IT WAS PLAID BY THE KINGS MAIESTIES PLAIERS.

⟨Dramatis Personae.

Husband.
Master of a College.
Knight, a Justice of Peace.
Oliver, Ralph, Samuel } Serving-men.
Other Servants, and Officers.
Wife.
Maid-servant.
A little Boy.⟩[1]

⟨SCENE I. *A room in Calverly Hall.*⟩

Enter Oliuer *and* Ralph, *two seruingmen.*

Oliu. Sirrah *Raph*, my yong Mistrisse is in such a pittifull passionate humor for the long absence of her loue—

Raph. Why, can you blame her? why, apples hanging longer on the tree then when they are ripe makes so many fallings; viz., Madde wenches, because they are not gathered in time, are faine to drop of them selues, and then tis Common you know for euery man to take em vp.

Oliu. Mass, thou saiest true, Tis common indeede: but, sirah, is neither our young maister returned, nor our fellow Sam come from London?

Ralph. Neither of either, as the Puritan bawde saies. Slidd, I heare *Sam*: *Sam's* come, her's! Tarry! come, yfaith, now my nose itches for news.

Oliue. And so doe's mine elbowe.

[*Sam calls within.* Where are you there?]

Sam. Boy, look you walk my horse with discretion; I haue rid him simply. I warrand his skin sticks to his back with very heate: if a should catch cold & get the Cough of the Lunges I were well serued, were I not?

⟨*Enter Sam.*⟩ *Furnisht with things from London.*

What, Raph and Oliuer.

Am⟨bo⟩. Honest fellow *Sam*, welcome, yfaith! what tricks hast thou brought from London?

Sa. You see I am hangd after the truest fashion: three hats, and two glasses, bobbing vpon em, two rebato wyers vpon my brest, a capcase by my side, a brush at my back, an Almanack in my pocket, & three ballats in my Codpeece: naie, I am the true picture of a Common seruingman.

Oliuer Ile sweare thou art. Thou maist set vp when thou wilt. Ther's many a one begins with lesse, I can tel thee, that proues a rich man ere he dyes. But whats the news from London, *Sam?*

Ralph. I, thats well sed; whats the newes from London, Sirrah? My young mistresse keeps such a puling for hir loue.

Sam. Why, the more foole shee; I, the more ninny hammer shee.

Oli. Why, *Sam*, why?

Sam. Why, hees married to another Long agoe.

Ambo. Ifaith, ye Iest.

Sam. Why, did you not know that till now? why, hees married, beates his wife, and has two or three children by her: for you must note that any woman beares the more when she is beaten.

Raph. I, thats true, for shee beares the blowes.

Oliu. Sirrah Sam, I would not for two years wages, my yong mistres knew so much; sheed run vpon the lefte hand of her wit, and nere be her owne woman agen.

Sam. And I think she was blest in her Cradle, that he neuer came in her bed: why, hee has consumed al, pawnd his lands, and made his vniuersitie brother stand in waxe

[1] *Add. R* Scene I. *etc. add. M* *S. D.* and Raphe *Q 2* 6 viz.] so *Haz.* 8 drop off *M* 10 em] them *Q 2, etc.* 17 heere tarry *Q 2, Ff*: here he is; tarry *M* 25 *S. D.* Enter Sam *add. M* Furnisht, *etc. follows* 28 *Qq, Ff*

61 her] here *Q 1* 62–3 was . . that . . came] were . . had . . come *conj. Percy*

for him—Thers a fine phrase for a scriuener! puh, he owes more then his skins worth.

Oli. Is't possible?

Sa. Nay, Ile tell you moreouer, he calls his wife whore as familiarly as one would cal *Mal & Dol*, and his children bastards as naturally as can bee.—But what haue we heere? I thought twas somwhat puld downe my breeches: I quite forgot my two poting-sticks. These came from London; now any thing is good heer that comes from London.

Oli. I, farre fetcht you know.

Sam. But speak in your conscience, yfaith, haue not we as good potingsticks ith Cuntry as need to be put ith fire. The mind of a thing is all. The mind of a thing's all, and as thou saidst eene now, farre fetcht is the best thinges for Ladies.

Oliu. I, and for waiting gentle women to.

Sam. But, Ralph, what, is our beer sower this thunder?

Oli. No, no, it holds countenance yet.

Sam. Why, then, follow me; Ile teach you the finest humor to be drunk in. I learnd it at London last week.

Am⟨bo⟩. I faith, lets heare it, lets heare it.

Sam. The brauest humor! twold do a man good to bee drunck in't; they call it knighting in London, when they drink vpon their knees.

Am⟨bo⟩. Faith, that's excellent. Come, follow me: Ile giue you all the degrees ont in order. [*Exeunt.*

⟨Scene II. *Another apartment in the same.*⟩

Enter wife.

Wife. What will become of vs? all will awaie.
My husband neuer ceases in expence,
Both to consume his credit and his house;
And tis set downe by heauens iust decree,
That Ryotts child must needs be beggery.
Are these the vertues that his youth did promise?
Dice, and voluptuous meetings, midnight Reuels,
Taking his bed with surfetts: Ill beseeming
The auncient honor of his howse and name!
And this not all: but that which killes me most,
When he recounts his Losses and false fortunes,
The weaknes of his state soe much deiected,
Not as a man repentant but halfe madd,
His fortunes cannot answere his expence:
He sits and sullenly lockes vp his Armes,
Forgetting heauen looks downward, which makes him
Appeare soe dreadfull that he frights my heart,
Walks heauyly, as if his soule were earth:
Not penitent for those his sinnes are past,
But vext his mony cannot make them last:—
A fearefull melancholie, vngodly sorrow.
Oh yonder he comes, now in despight of ills
Ile speake to him, and I will heare him speake,
And do my best to driue it from his heart.

Enter Husband.

Hus. Poxe oth Last throw! it made
Fiue hundred Angels vanish from my sight.
Ime damnd, Ime damnd: the Angels haue forsook me.
Nay, tis certainely true: for he that has
No coyne is damnd in this world: hee's gon, hee's gon.

Wi. Deere husband.

Hus. Oh! most punishment of all, I haue a wife.

Wi. I doe intreat you as you loue your soule,
Tell me the cause of this your discontent.

Hus. A vengeance strip thee naked! thou art cause,
Effect, quality, property, thou, thou, thou! [*Exit.*

Wife. Bad, turnd to worse! both beggery of the soule,
As of the bodie. And so much vnlike
Him selfe at first, as if some vexed spirit
Had got his form vpon him.—
[*Enter Husband againe.*
He comes agen.
He saies I am the cause; I neuer yet
Spoke lesse then wordes of duty, and of loue.

Hus. If mariage be honourable, then Cuckolds are honourable, for they cannot be made without marriage. Foole! what meant I to marry to get beggars? now must my eldest sonne be a knaue or nothing; he cannot liue vppot'h foole, for he wil haue no land to maintaine him: that morgage sits like a snaffle vpon mine inheritance, and makes me chaw vpon Iron. My second sonne must be a promooter, and my third a theefe, or an vnderputter, a slaue pander.

73 somwhat *Q 1*: something *Q 2, etc.* 74, 79 poking sticks *R* 78–80 Sam. But speak . . fire *add. to Oliver's speech M, etc.* 91 Faith *Q 2* 96 ont *Q 1*: of it *Q 2, etc.* Scene II. *etc. add. M.*

14 *Placed after* 9 *Haz.* 25–7 *End* angels, damn'd, Nay it is *M* 28 *Ends* coyne *Qq, etc.*: *corr. pr. ed.* 36–40 *Six lines Qq, ending* worse, bodie, first, spirit, him, agen 37 As] And *M*

Oh beggery, beggery, to what base vses dost thou put a man! I think the Deuill scornes to be a bawde. He beares himselfe more proudly, has more care on's credit. Base, slauish, abiect, filthie pouertie!

Wi. Good sir, by all our vowes I doe beseech you,
Show me the true cause of your discontent.

Hus. Mony, mony, mony, and thou must supply me.

Wi. Alas, I am the lest cause of your discontent,
Yet what is mine, either in rings or Iewels,
Vse to your own desire, but I beseech you,
As y'are a gentleman by many bloods,
Though I my selfe be out of your respect,
Thinke on the state of these three louely boies
You haue bin father to.

Hu. Puh! Bastards, bastards, bastards; begot in tricks, begot in tricks.

Wi. Heauen knowes how those words wrong me, but I maie
Endure these griefes among a thousand more.
Oh, call to mind your lands already morgadge,
Your selfe woond into debts, your hopefull brother
At the vniuersitie in bonds for you,
Like to be ceasd vpon; And—

Hu. Ha done, thou harlot,
Whome, though for fashion sake I married,
I neuer could abide; thinkst thou thy wordes
Shall kill my pleasures? Fal of to thy friends,
Thou and thy bastards begg: I will not bate
A whit in humor! midnight, still I loue you,
And reuel in your Company. Curbd in,
Shall it be said in all societies,
That I broke custome, that I flagd in monie?
No, those thy iewels I will play as freely
As when my state was fullest.

Wi. Be it so.

H. Nay I protest, and take that for an earnest, [*spurns her*
I will for euer hould thee in contempt,
And neuer touch the sheets that couer thee,
But be diuorst in bed till thou consent,
Thy dowry shall be sold to giue new life
Vnto those pleasures which I most affect.

Wi. Sir, doe but turne a gentle eye on me,
And what the law shall giue me leaue to do
You shall command.

Hu. Look it be done: shal I want dust & like a slaue
Weare nothing in my pockets but my hands
To fil them vp with nailes?
[*holding his hands in his pockets.*
Oh much against my blood! Let it be done.
I was neuer made to be a looker on,
A bawde to dice; Ile shake the drabbs my selfe
And made em yeeld. I saie, look it be done.

Wi. I take my leaue: it shall. [*Exit.*

Hu. Speedily, speedily. I hate the very howre I chose a wife: a trouble, trouble! three children like three euils hang vpon me. Fie, fie, fie, strumpet & bastards, strumpet and bastards!

Enter three Gentlemen heering him.

1 *Gent.* Still doe those loathsome thoughts Iare on your tongue?
Your selfe to staine the honour of your wife,
Nobly discended! Those whom men call mad
Endanger others; but hee's more then mad
That wounds himselfe, whose owne wordes do proclaym
Scandalls vniust, to soile his better name:
It is not fit; I pray, forsake it.

2 *Gen.* Good sir, let modestie reproue you.

3 *Gen.* Let honest kindnes sway so much with you.

Hu. God den, I thanke you, sir, how do you? adeiue! Ime glad to see you. Farewel Instructions, Admonitions. [*Exeun⟨t⟩ Gent.*

Enter a seruant.

Hu. How now, sirra; what wud you?

Ser. Only to certifie you, sir, that my mistris was met by the way, by them who were sent for her vp to London by her honorable vnkle, your worships late gardian.

Hus. So, sir, then she is gon and so may you be: But let her looke that the thing be done she wots of: or hel wil stand more pleasant then her house at home.
⟨*Exit seruant.*⟩

Enter a Gentleman.

Gen. Well or ill met, I care not.

Hus. No, nor I.

Gen. I am come with confidence to chide you.

Hu. Who? me?
Chide me? Doo't finely then: let it not moue me,
For if thou chidst me angry, I shall strike.

57 on's *Q 1* : on his *Q 2, Ff* : of his *M* 65 you are *Q 2, etc.* 71 I maie *Q 1* : I'll *Q 2, Ff* 73 morgadge *Qq* : mortgag'd *Ff, etc.* 98, 99 *End* dust, pockets *M*
99 my bare hands *M* 106–10 *Verse M* 108 vpon] on *M* 128–31 *Verse M* 129 that *om. F 2, etc.* *S. D.* Exit seruant *add. Q 2* 135–7 *Prose Qq* : *corr. M*

Gen. Strike thine owne follies, for it is they deserue
To be wel beaten. We are now in priuate:
Ther's none but thou and I. Thou'rt fond & peeuish,
An vncleane ryoter: thy landes and Credit
Lie now both sick of a consumption.
I am sorry for thee: that man spends with shame
That with his ritches does consume his name:
And such art thou.
Hus. Peace.
Gent. No, thou shalt heare me further:
Thy fathers and forefathers worthy honors,
Which were our country monuments, our grace,
Follies in thee begin now to deface.
The spring time of thy youth did fairely promise
Such a most fruitfull summer to thy friends
It scarce can enter into mens beliefes,
Such dearth should hang on thee. Wee that see it,
Are sorry to beleeue it: in thy change,
This voice into all places wil be hurld:
Thou and the deuill has deceaued the world.
Hus. Ile not indure thee.
Gent. But of all the worst:
Thy vertuous wife, right honourably allied,
Thou hast proclaimed a strumpet.
Hus. Nay, then, I know thee.
Thou art her champion, thou, her priuat friend,
The partie you wot on.
Gent. Oh ignoble thought.
I am past my patient bloode: shall I stand idle
And see my reputation toucht to death?
Hu. Ta's galde you, this, has it?
Gent. No, monster, I will proue
My thoughts did only tend to vertuous loue.
⟨*Hus.*⟩ Loue of her vertues? there it goes.
Gent. Base spirit,
To laie thy hate vpon the fruitfull Honor
Of thine own bed.
[*They fight and the Husbands hurt.*
Hu. Oh!
Ge. Woult thou yeeld it yet?
Hu. Sir, Sir, I haue not done with you.
Gent. I hope nor nere shall doe.
[*Fight agen.*
Hu. Haue you got tricks? are you in cunning with me?
Gent. No, plaine and right.
He needs no cunning that for truth doth fight. [*Husband falls downe.*
Hu. Hard fortune, am I leueld with the ground?
Gent. Now, sir, you lie at mercy.
Hu. I, you slaue.
Ge. Alas, that hate should bring vs to our graue.
You see my sword's not thirsty for your life,
I am sorrier for your woonde then your selfe.
Y'are of a vertuous house, show vertuous deeds;
Tis not your honour, tis your folly bleedes;
Much good has bin expected in your life,
Cancell not all mens hopes: you haue a wife
Kind and obedient: heape not wrongfull shame
On her ⟨and⟩ your posterity, ⟨nor blame
Your overthrow;⟩ let only sin be sore,
And by this fall, rise neuer to fall more.
And so I leaue you. [*Exit.*
Hu. Has the dogg left me, then,
After his tooth hath left me? oh, my hart
Would faine leape after him. Reuenge, I saye,
Ime mad to be reueng'd. My strumpet wife,
It is thy quarrel that rips thus my flesh,
And makes my brest spit blood, but thou shalt bleed.
Vanquisht? got downe? vnable eene to speak?
Surely tis want of mony makes men weake.
I, twas that orethrew me; Id'e nere bin downe els. [*Exit.*

⟨SCENE III. *The same.*⟩

Enter wife in a riding suite with a seruingman.

Seru. Faith, mistris, If it might not bee presumtion
In me to tell you so, for his excuse
You had smal reason, knowing his abuse.
Wi. I grant I had; but, alasse,
Whie should our faults at home be spred abroad?
Tis griefe enough within dores. At first sight
Myne Vncle could run ore his prodigall life
As perfectly, as if his serious eye
Had nombred all his follies:
Knew of his morgadg'd lands, his friends in bonds,

138 *Ends* they *Qq*: *corr. M* follies *Q 2, etc.*: follie *Q 1* 144 does *Q 1*: doth *Q 2, etc.* 149 county's *Haz.* 154 on] upon *M* 169 will *om. Q 2, Ff* 171 *Prefix om. Q 1* 173 *Ends* fruitfull *Qq*

192–3 *The compositors appear to have corrupted two lines into one* and *add. Q 2* 193–4 nor .. overthrow *conj. pr. ed.* 198 left] gor'd *conj. St.* Scene III. Another room in the same *M* 1 might *Q 1*: may *Q 2, Ff*

Himselfe withered with debts: And in that minute
Had I added his vsage and vnkindnes,
Twould haue confounded euery thought of good:
Where now, fathering his ryots on his youth,
Which time and tame experience will shake off,
Gessing his kindnes to me (as I smoothd him
With all the skill I had) though his deserts
Are in forme vglier then an vnshapte Bear,
Hee's reddy to prefer him to some office
And place at Court, A good and sure reliefe
To al his stooping fortunes: twil be a meanes, I hope,
To make new league between vs, and redeeme
His vertues with his landes.

Ser. I should think so, mistris. If he should not now be kinde to you and loue you, and cherish you vp, I should thinke the deuill himselfe kept open house in him.

Wi. I doubt not but he will now: prethe, leaue me; I think I heare him comming.

Ser. I am gone. [*Exit.*

Wife. By this good meanes I shal preserue my lands,
And free my husband out of vserers hands:
Now ther is no neede of sale, my Vncle's kind,
I hope, if ought, this will content his minde.—
Here comes my husband. [*Enter Husband.*

Hu. Now, are you come? wher's the mony? lets see the mony Is the rubbish sold, those wiseakers your lands? why, when? the mony! where ist? powr't down, down with it, downe with it: I say powr't oth ground! lets see't, lets see't.

Wi. Good sir, keep but in patience and I hope
My words shall like you well: I bring you better
Comfort then the sale of my Dowrie.

Hu. Hah, whats that?

Wi. Pray, do not fright me, sir, but vouchsafe me hearing: my Vncle, glad of your kindnes to mee & milde vsage—for soe I made it to him—has in pitty of your declining fortunes, prouided a place for you at Court of worth & credit, which so much ouerioyd me—

Hu. Out on thee, filth! ouer and ouerioyd, [*spurns her*] when Ime in torments? Thou pollitick whore, subtiller then nine Deuils, was this thy iourney to Nuncke, to set downe the historie of me, of my state and fortunes? Shall I that Dedicated my selfe to pleasure, be nowe confind in seruice to crouch and stand like an old man ith hams, my hat off? I that neuer could abide to vncover my head ith Church? base slut! this fruite beares thy complaints.

Wife. Oh, heauen knowes
That my complaintes were praises, and best wordes
Of you and your estate: onely my friends
Knew of our morgagde Landes, and were possest
Of euery accident before I came.
If thou suspect it but a plot in me
To keepe my dowrie, or for mine owne good
Or my poore childrens: (though it sutes a mother
To show a naturall care in their reliefs)
Yet ile forget my selfe to calme your blood:
Consume it, as your pleasure counsels you,
And all I wishe eene Clemency affoords:
Giue mee but comely looks and modest wordes.

Hu. Money, whore, money, or Ile— ⟨*Draws his dagger.*⟩

Enters a seruant very hastily.

What the deuel? how now? thy hasty news? [*to his man.*

Se. Maie it please you, sir— [*Seruant in a feare.*

Hu. What? maie I not looke vpon my dagger? Speake villaine, or I will execute the pointe on thee: quick, short.

Ser. Why, sir, a gentleman from the Vniuersity staies below to speake with you.

Hu. From the Vniuersity? so! Vniuersity—
That long word runs through mee. [*Exit.*

Wi. Was euer wife so wretchedlie beset? [*Wif. alone.*
Had not this newes stept in-between, the point
Had offered violence vnto my brest.
That which some women call greate misery
Would show but little heere: would scarce be seene
Amongst my miseries. I maie Compare
For wretched fortunes with all wiues that are.
Nothing will please him, vntill all be nothing.
He calls it slauery to be preferd,
A place of credit a base seruitude.
What shall become of me, and my poore children,
Two here, and one at nurse, my prettie beggers?

14 on *Q 2, etc.*: one *Q 1* 17 had)] *Parenthesis continued to* Bear *M* 40 oth *Q 1*: on the *Q 2, etc.* 42-4 *Prose M* 49 has *Q 1*: hath *Q 2, etc.* 53 torment *Q 2, etc.* 56 of my *Q 1*: my *Q 2, etc.*

75 comely *Q 1*: pleasant *Q 2, etc.* 76 *S. D. add. Q 2* 85 *S. D.* Exit *Q 2, etc.*: Exeunt *Q 1* 88 vnto *Q 2, Ff*: to *Q 1* 91 Among *Q 2, etc.*

I see how ruine with a palsie hand
Begins to shake the auncient seat to dust:
The heauy weight of sorrow drawes my liddes
Ouer my dankishe eies: I can scarce see:
Thus griefe will laste; it wakes and sleeps with mee. ⟨*Exit.*⟩

⟨Scene IV. *Another apartment in the same.*⟩

Enter the Husband with the master of the Colledge.

Hu. Please you draw neer, sir, y'are exceeding welcome.

Ma. Thats my doubt; I fear, I come not to be welcome.

Hus. Yes, howsoeuer.

Ma. Tis not my fashion, Sir, to dwell in long circumstance, but to be plain, and effectuall; therefore, to the purpose. The cause of my setting forth was pittious and lamentable: that hopefull young gentleman, your brother, whose vertues we all loue deerelie, through your default and vnnaturall negligence, lies in bond executed for your debt, a prisoner, all his studies amazed, his hope strook dead, and the pride of his youth muffled in theis dark clowds of oppression.

Hus. Hum, vm, vm.

Mr. Oh, you haue kild the towardest hope of all our vniue⟨r⟩sitie: wherefore, without repentance and amends, expect pondorus and suddain Iudgements to fall grieuosly vpon you. Your brother, a man who profited in his diuine Imployments, mighte haue made ten thousand soules fit for heauen, now by your carelesse courses caste in prison, which you must answere for, and assure your spirit it wil come home at length.

Hu. Oh god! oh!

Mr. Wise men think ill of you, others speake ill of you, no man loues you, nay, euen those whome honesty condemnes, condemne you: and take this from the vertuous affection I beare your brother; neuer looke for prosperous hower, good thought, quiet sleepes, contented walkes, nor any thing that makes man perfect til you redeem him. What is your answer? how will you bestow him? vpon desperate miserye, or better hopes? I suffer, till I heare your answer.

Hu. Sir, you haue much wrought with mee. I feele you in my soule, you are your artes master. I neuer had sence til now; your sillables haue cleft me. Both for your words and pains I thank you: I cannot but acknowledge grieuous wronges done to my brother, mighty, mighty, mighty wrongs.—Within there!

Enter a seruingman.

Hu. Sir, Fil me a bowle of wine. Alas, poore brother,
Brus'd with an execution for my sake.
[*Exit seruant for wine.*

Mr. A bruse indeed makes many a mortall sore
Till the graue cure em.

Enter with wine.

Hu. Sir, I begin to you, y'aue chid your welcome.

Mr. I could haue wisht it better for your sake.
I pledge you, sir, to the kind man in prison.

Hu. Let it be soe. Now, Sir, if you so please [*Drink both.*
To spend but a fewe minuts in a walke
About my grounds below, my man heere shall
Attend you.
I doubt not but by that time to be furnisht
Of a sufficient answere, and therein
My brother fully satisfied.

Mr. Good sir, in that the Angells would be pleasd,
And the worlds murmures calmd, and I should saye
I set forth then vpon a lucky daie. [*Exit.*

Hu. Oh thou confused man! thy pleasant sins haue vndone thee, thy damnation has beggerd thee! That heauen should say we must not sin, and yet made women! giues our sences waie to finde pleasure, which being found confounds vs. Why shold we know those things so much misuse vs?—oh, would vertue had been forbidden! wee should then haue prooued all vertuous, for tis our bloude to loue what were forbidden. Had not drunkennes byn forbidden, what man wold haue been foole to a beast, and Zany to a swine, to show tricks in the mire? what is there in three dice to make a man draw thrice three thousand acres into the compasse of a round little table, & with the gentlemans

98 palsied *M* 99 the] this *conj. Percy* 102 Thus] This *conj. M* Exit *add. M* Scene IV. *etc. add. M* 17 Umph, umph, umph! *M* 23 and might *Q 2, etc.* 24 now] is now *M* 34 thoughts *F 2, etc.* sleep *F 2, etc.*

46 mighty, mighty, mighty, mighty, *Ff, etc.* *S. D.* sermiugman *Q 1* 48 Sir (*rom.*) Hu. (*ital.*) Fil (*rom.*) *Q 1*: Sir *om. Q 2, etc.* 50 *Ends* mortall *Q 1*: *corr. Q 2* 57–61 *Prose all edd.* 68 give *M* 74 were *Q 1*: we are *Q 2, etc.* 80 little round *Q 2, etc.*

palsy in the hand shake out his posteritie thieues or beggars? Tis done! I ha dont, yfaith: terrible, horrible misery.——How well was I left! very well, very wel. My Lands shewed like a full moone about mee, but nowe the moon's ith last quarter, wayning, waining: And I am mad to think that moone was mine; Mine and my fathers, and my forefathers—generations, generations: downe goes the howse of vs, down, downe it sincks. Now is the name a beggar, begs in me! that name, which hundreds of yeeres has made this shiere famous, in me, and my posterity, runs out.

In my seede fiue are made miserable besides my selfe: my ryot is now my brothers iaylor, my wiues sighing, my three boyes penurie, and mine own confusion.

[*Teares his haire.*

Why sit my haires vpon my cursed head?
Will not this poyson scatter them? oh my brother's
In execution among deuells that
Stretch him & make him giue. And I in want,
Not able for to lyue, nor to redeeme him.
Divines and dying men may talke of hell,
But in my heart her seuerall torments dwell.
Slauery and mysery! Who in this case
Would not take vp mony vpon his soule,
Pawn his saluation, liue at interest?
I, that did euer in aboundance dwell,
For me to want, exceeds the throwes of hel.

Enters his little sonne with a top and a scourge.

Son. What, aile you father? are you not well? I cannot scourge my top as long as you stand so: you take vp all the roome with your wide legs. Puh, you cannot make mee afeard with this; I feare no vizards, nor bug-beares.

Husb. takes vp the childe by the skirts of his long coate in one hand and drawes his dagger with th' other.

Hu. Vp, sir, for heer thou hast no inheritance left.

Sonne. Oh, what will you do, father? I am your white boie.

Hu. Thou shalt be my red boie: take that.

[*strikes him.*

Son. Oh, you hurt me, father.

Hu. My eldest beggar! thou shalt not liue to aske an vsurer bread, to crie at a great mans gate, or followe, good your honour, by a Couch; no, nor your brother; tis charity to braine you.

Son. How shall I learne now my heads broke?

Hu. Bleed, bleed rather then beg, beg!

[*stabs him.*

Be not thy names disgrace:
Spurne thou thy fortunes first if they be base:
Come view thy second brother.—Fates,
My childrens bloud
Shall spin into your faces, you shall see
How Confidently we scorne beggery!

[*Exit with his Sonne.*

⟨SCENE V. *A bed-room in the same.*⟩

Enter a maide with a child in her armes, the mother by her a sleepe.

M⟨aide⟩. Sleep, sweet babe; sorrow makes thy mother sleep:
It boades small good when heauines falls so deepe.
Hush, prettie boy, thy hopes might haue been better.
Tis lost at Dice what ancient honour won:
Hard when the father plaies awaie the Sonne!
No thing but misery serues in this house.
Ruine and desolation, oh!

Enter husband with the boie bleeding.

Hu. Whore, giue me that boy.

[*Striues with her for the child.*

M⟨aide⟩. Oh help, help! out alas, murder murder!

Hus. Are you gossiping, prating, sturdy queane?
Ile breake your clamor with your neck: down staires!
Tumble, tumble, headlong! [*Throws her down.*] So!
The surest waie to charme a womans tongue
Is break hir neck: a pollitician did it.

Son. Mother, mother; I am kild, mother.

W⟨ife⟩ wakes. Ha, whose that cride? oh me, my children!
Both, both, both; bloudy, bloudy.

[*catches vp the yongest.*

Hu. Strumpet, let go the boy, let go the beggar.

Wi. Oh my sweet husband!

101–2 *Lines end* make, lyue *Q 1*: stretch him, want *Q 2, Ff* 103 for to lyue] to relieve *S* 106–7 *End* mysery, vpon his *Q 1*: *corr. Q 2* 111 What aile *Qq, etc.* 115 afraid *Q 2, etc.* 123–7 *Verse M, div. after* beggar, bread, follow, brother

126 coach *Q 2, etc.* 130 *Ends* bleed *M* beg *once M* 133 brother's *M* 133–5 *Div. after* fates, faces, see *Qq* 133–4 *One line M* Scene V. *add. M* A . . same *add. pr. ed.* 6 serues] survives *conj. S* 10 you prating *M* *Ends* Ile *Q 1* 11 *Ends* neck *Q 2, Ff* 12 *Ends* headlong *Qq* *S. D.* W. wakes *after* 16 *Q 1*

Hus. Filth, harlot.
Wi. Oh what will you doe, deare husband?
Hus. Giue me the bastard.
Wi. Your owne sweet boy!
Hu. There are too many beggars.
Wi. Good my hus-band—
Hu. Doest thou preuent me still?
Wi. Oh god!
Hus. Haue at his hart!
[*Stabs at the child in hir armes.*
Wi. Oh my deare boy! [*gets it from hir.*
Hu. Brat, thou shalt not liue to shame thy howse!
Wi. Oh heauen!
[*shee's hurt and sinks downe.*
Hu. And perish! now begon:
Thers whores enow, and want wold make thee one.

Enter a lusty seruant.

Ser. Oh Sir, what deeds are these?
Hus. Base slaue, my vassail:
Comst thou between my fury to question me?
Ser. Were you the Deuil, I would hold you, sir.
Hu. Hould me? presumption! Ile vndoe thee for't.
Ser. Sbloud, you haue vndone vs all, sir.
Hu. Tug at thy master!
Ser. Tug at a Monster.
Hus. Haue I no power? shall my slaue fetter me?
Ser. Nay, then, the Deuil wrastles, I am thowne.
Hu. Oh, villane, now Ile tug thee, [*ouercomes him*] now Ile teare thee;
Set quick spurres to my vassaile, bruize him, trample him.
So! I think thou wilt not folow me in hast.
My horse stands reddy sadled. Away, away;
Now to my brat at nursse, my sucking begger.
Fates, Ile not leaue you one to trample on.

⟨Scene VI. *Court before the house.*⟩

The Master meets him.

Ma. How ist with you, sir? me thinks you looke
Of a distracted colour.
Hu. Who? I, sir? tis but your fancie.
Please you walke in, Sir, and Ile soone resolue you:
I want one small parte to make vp the som,
And then my brother shall rest satisfied.
Mr. I shall be glad to see it: sir, Ile attend you. [*Exeu*⟨*nt*⟩.

⟨Scene VII. *The same as Scene V.*⟩

Ser. Oh I am scarce able to heaue vp my selfe:
Ha's so bruizd me with his diuelish waight,
And torne my flesh with his bloud-hasty spurre.
A man before of easie constitution
Till now hells power supplied, to his soules wrong.
Oh, how damnation can make weake men strong.

Enter Master, and two seruants.

Ser. Oh, the most pitteous deed, sir, since you came.
Mr. A deadly greeting! has he somde vp theis
To satisfie his brother? heer's an other:
And by the bleeding infants, the dead mother.
Wi. Oh, oh.
Mr. Surgeons, Surgeons! she recouers life.
One of his men al faint and bloudied!
1 *Seru.* Follow, our murderous master has took horse
To kill his child at nurse: oh, follow quickly.
Mr. I am the readiest, it shal be my charge
To raise the towne vpon him.
[*Exit Mr. and seruants.*
1 *Ser.* Good sir, do follow him.
Wi. Oh my children.
1 *Ser.* How is it with my most afflicted Mistris?
Wi. Why do I now recouer? why half liue?
To see my children bleede before mine eies?
A sight able to kill a mothers brest
Without an executioner! what, art thou
Mangled too?
1 *Ser.* I, thinking to preuent what his quicke mischiefes
Had so soone acted, came and rusht vpon him.
We strugled, but a fowler strength then his
Ore threw me with his armes; then did he bruize me
And rent my flesh, and robd me of my haire,
Like a man mad in execution;
Made me vnfit to rise and follow him.
Wi. What is it has beguild him of all grace
And stole awaie humanity from his brest?
To slaie his children, purpose to kill his wife,
And spoile his saruants.

35 enough *M* 52–3 *Prose Qq* 56 trample one *Qq* Scene VI. *etc. add. M* *S. D.* Enter Husband; to him the Master of the College *M* 1–2 *Prose Qq, Ff*: *div. after* sir *M*

Scene VII. *add. M* The same, *etc. pr. ed.* 5 Hell *M* 8 hath *Q 2, etc.* 23 *Ends* without *M* 24–5 *One line Qq* 26–7 *Prose Qq* 35 purpose *M*: purpos'd *Qq, Ff*

Enters two seruants.

Ambo Sir, please you leaue this most accursed place,
A surgeon waites within.

Wi. Willing to leaue it!
Tis guiltie of sweete bloud, innocent bloud:
Murder has tooke this chamber with ful hands,
And wil nere out as long as the house stands.
[*Exeunt.*

⟨SCENE VIII. *A high road.*⟩

Enter Husband as being thrown off his horse, And falls.

Hu. Oh stumbling Iade, the spauin ouertake thee,
The fiftie diseases stop thee!
Oh, I am sorely bruisde; plague founder thee:
Thou runst at ease and pleasure. Hart of chance!
To Throw me now within a flight oth Towne,
In such plaine euen ground, sfot, a man
May dice vp on't, and throw awaie the Medowes.
Filthy beast.

Crie within. Follow, follow, follow.

Hus. Ha! I hear sounds of men, like hew and crie:
Vp, vp, and struggle to thy horse, make on;
Dispatch that little begger and all's done.

Kni. Heere, this waie, this waye!

Hus. At my backe? oh,
What fate haue I? my limbes deny mee go,
My will is bated: beggery claimes a parte.
Oh, could I here reach to the infants heart.

Enter M. of the Colledge, 3. Gentlemen, and others with Holberds.

[*Finde him.*

All. Heere, heere: yonder, yonder.

Mr. Vnnaturall, flintie, more then barbarous:
The Scithians or the marble hearted fates
Could not haue acted more remorselesse deeds
In their relentlesse natures, then these of thine:
Was this the answear I long waited on,
The satisfaction for thy prisoned brother?

Hus. Why, he can haue no more on's then our skins,
And some of em want but fleaing.

1. Gen. Great sinnes haue made him impudent.

Mr. H'as shed so much bloud that he cannot blush.

2. Ge. Away with him, bear him a long to the Iustices;
A gentleman of woorship dwels at hand;
There shall his deeds be blazd.

Hus. Why, all the better.
My glory tis to haue my action knowne:
I grieue for nothing, but I mist of one.

Mr. Ther's little of a father in that griefe:
Beare him away. [*Exeunt.*

⟨SCENE IX. *A room in the house of a Magistrate.*⟩

Enters a knight with two or three Gentlemen.

Knig. Endangered so his wife? murdered his children?

1 *Gen.* So the Cry comes.

Kni. I am sorry I ere knew him,
That euer he took life and naturall being
From such an honoured stock, and fair discent;
Til this black minut without staine or blemish.

1 *Gent.* Here come the men.

Enter the master of the colledge and the rest, with the prisoner.

Kni. The serpent of his house! Ime sorry
For this time that I am in place of iustice.

Mr. Please you, Sir.

Kni. Doe not repeate it twice I know too muche,
Would it had nere byn thought on:
Sir, I bleede for you.

1 *Gent.* Your fathers sorrows are aliue in me:
What made you shew such monstrous crueltie?

Hu. In a worde, Sir, I haue consumd all, plaid awaie long acre, and I thought it the charitablest deed I could doe to cussen beggery and knock my house oth head.

Kni. Oh, in a cooler bloud you will repent it.

Hus. I repent now, that ones left vnkild,
My brat at nurse. Oh, I would ful fain haue weand him.

Knigh. Well, I doe not think but in to morrowes iudgement
The terror will sit closer to your soule,

S. D. Enter a Servant *M* 37 Ambo sir (*ital.*) *Q 1*: Ambo *Q 2*: Both *Ff*: Serv. *M* you *Qq, Ff*: you to *M* Scene VIII. *etc. add. M* 4 hart, of *Q 1* 13 Kni. *Q 1*: Cry Within *Q 2, etc.* Here, here *M* 16 bated] barred *conj. St.* 20 or the *conj. St.*: in their *Qq, Ff*: even the *M* fates] feats *conj. Percy* 25 Why *om. Q 2, Ff* on's *Q 1*: of vs *Q 2, etc.*

29 a long *om. Q 2, etc.* Scene IX. *etc. add. M* 3 *Prefix* 1. Gent. *Q 2, etc.*: 4 Gen. *Q 1* comes *Q 1*: goes *Q 2, etc.* 8, 15 *Prefix* 4 Gent. *Q 1* 9, 10 *Prose Qq*: *corr. M* 17–20 *Verse Qq, Ff*

When the dread thought of death remembers you;
To further which, take this sad voice from me:
Neuer was act plaid more vnnaturally.
Hus. I thank you, Sir.
Kni. Goe, leade him to the Iayle:
Where iustice claimes all, there must pitty faile.
Hus. Come, come, awaie with me. [*Exit prisoner.*
Mr. Sir, you deserue the worship of your place.
Would all did so: in you the law is grace.
Kni. It is my wish it should be so.—Ruinous man,
The desolation of his howse, the blot
Vpon his predecessors honord name!
That man is neerest shame that is past shame. [*Exit.*

⟨SCENE X. *Before Calverly Hall.*⟩

Enter Husband with the officers, The Maister and gentlemen, as going by his house.

Hu. I am right against my howse, seat of my Ancestors: I heare my wif's aliue; but much endangered. Let me intreat to speak with her, before the prison gripe me.

Enter his wife, brought in a chaire.

Gent. See heer she comes of her selfe.
Wi. Oh my sweete Hus-band, my deere distressed husband,
Now in the hands of vnrelenting lawes!
My greatest sorrow, my extremest bleeding,
Now my soule bleeds.
Hu. How now? kind to me? did I not wound thee, left thee for dead?
Wife. Tut, farre greater wounds did my brest feele:
Vnkindnes strikes a deeper wound then steele;
You haue been still vnkinde to mee.
Hus. Faith, and so I thinke I haue:
I did my murthers roughly, out of hand,
Desperate and suddaine, but thou hast deuiz'd
A fine way now to kill me, thou hast giuen mine eies
Seauen woonds a peece; now glides the deuill from mee,
Departes at euery ioynt, heaues vp my nailes.
Oh catch him new torments, that were near inuented,
Binde him one thousand more, you blessed Angells,
In that pit bottomlesse; let him not rise
To make men act vnnaturall tragedies,
To spred into a father, and in furie,
Make him his childrens executioners:
Murder his wife, his seruants, and who not?
For that man's darke, where heauen is quite forgot.
Wi. Oh my repentant husband.
Hus. My deere soull, whom I too much haue wrongd,
For death I die, and for this haue I longd.
Wi. Thou sholdst not (be assurde) for these faults die,
If the law cold forgiue as soone as I.
Hus. What sight is yonder? [*Children laid out.*
Wi. Oh, our two bleeding boyes
Laid forth vpon the thresholde.
Hu. Heer's weight enough to make a heart-string crack.
Oh, were it lawfull that your prettie soules
Might looke from heauen into your fathers eyes,
Then should you see the penitent glasses melt,
And both your murthers shoote vpon my cheekes;
But you are playing in the Angells lappes,
And will not looke on me,
Who void of grace, kild you in beggery.
Oh that I might my wishes now attaine,
I should then wish you liuing were againe,
Though I did begge with you, which thing I feard:
Oh, twas the enemy my eyes so bleard.
Oh, would you could pray heauen me to forgiue,
That will vnto my end repentant liue.
Wi. It makes me eene forget all other sorrowes
And liue aparte with this.
⟨*Officer*⟩. Come will you goe?
Hus. Ile kisse the bloud I spilt and then I goe:
My soull is bloudied, well may my lippes be so.
Farewell, deere wife, now thou and I must parte,
I of thy wrongs repent me with my harte.
Wi. Oh staye, thou shalt not goe.
Hus. That's but in vaine, you see it must be so.
Farewell, ye bloudie ashes of my boyes!
My punishments are their eternall ioyes.
Let euery father looke into my deedes,
And then their heirs may prosper, while mine bleeds.

Scene X. *etc. add. M* 1–4 *Verse M, div. after* ancestors, endanger'd, before 6–7 *Prose Qq, Ff* 21 new *om. M, etc.* 26 executioners *Qq, Ff*: executioner *M, etc.* 30 O my *M* 35 *Ends* vpon *Q 1*: *corr. Q 2* 43 *Ends* grace *M* 52 live apart *St.*: leaue parte *Qq, Ff* 53 *Prefix* Officer *add. Q 2*

Wi. More wretched am I now in this distresse,
[*Exeunt Husband with holberds.*
Then former sorrows made me.
Mr. Oh kinde wife,
Be comforted. One ioy is yet vnmurdered:
You haue a boy at nursse; your ioy's in him.
Wi. Dearer then all is my poore husbands life:
Heauen giue my body strength, which yet is faint
With much expence of bloud, and I will kneele,
Sue for his life, nomber vp all my friends,
To plead for pardon ⟨for⟩ my deare husbands life.
Mr. Was it in man to woond so kinde a creature?
Ile euer praise a woman for thy sake.
I must returne with griefe; my answer's set:
I shall bring newes weies heauier then the debt.—
Two brothers: one in bond lies ouerthrowne,
This on a deadlier execution.

FINIS.

66 *Ends* comforted *Qq, Ff* 70 is yet *Ff, etc.*

73 for *add. Q 2*

THE MERRY DEVILL OF EDMONTON.

As it hath beene ſundry times Acted, by his Maieſties Seruants, at the Globe, on the banke-ſide.

LONDON
Printed by *Henry Ballard* for *Arthur Iohnſon*, dwelling at the ſigne of the white-horſe in Paules Church yard, ouer againſt the great North doore of Paules. 1608.

Q 1	=	Quarto of 1608
Q 2	=	" " 1612
Q 3	=	" " 1617
Q 4	=	" " 1626
Q 5	=	" " 1631
Q 6	=	" " 1655
Dod.	=	Dodsley's Old Plays, 1st ed., 1744
Reed	=	Reed's Dodsley, 1780
Col.	=	Collier's Dodsley, 1825
T	=	Tyrrell, 1851
Haz.	=	Hazlitt's Dodsley, 1874-6
WP	=	Warnke and Proescholdt, 1884
Walker	=	'Temple Dramatists' ed., 1897
Daniel	=	Mr. P. A. Daniel's conjectures
pr. ed.	=	present editor

THE MERRY DEVILL OF EDMONTON

⟨DRAMATIS PERSONAE.

Sir Arthur Clare.
Sir Richard Mounchensey
Sir Ralph Jerningham.
Henry Clare.
Raymond Mounchensey.
Frank Jerningham.
Sir John [*a Priest*].
Banks [*the Miller of Waltham*].
Smug [*the Smith of Edmonton*].
Bilbo.
[Blague *the*] Host.
Brian.
[Raph, *Brian's man.*]
[Friar Hildersham.]
[Benedick.]
[Chamberlaine.]
[Coreb, *a Spirit.*]
Fabel [*the Merry Devil*].
Lady Clare.
Millisent.
Abbess.
Sexton.
Nuns and Attendants.⟩[1]

The Prologue.

Your silence and attention, worthy friends,
That your free spirits may with more pleasing sense
Relish the life of this our actiue sceane:
To which intent, to calme this murmuring breath,
We ring this round with our inuoking spelles;
If that your listning eares be yet prepard
To entertayne the subiect of our play,
Lend vs your patience.
Tis Peter Fabell, a renowned Scholler,
Whose fame hath still beene hitherto forgot
By all the writers of this latter age.
In Middle-sex his birth and his abode,
Not full seauen mile from this great famous Citty,
That, for his fame in sleights and magicke won,
Was calde the merry Fiend of Edmonton.
If any heere make doubt of such a name,
In Edmonton yet fresh vnto this day,
Fixt in the wall of that old antient Church,
His monument remayneth to be seene;
His memory yet in the mouths of men,
That whilst he liude he could deceiue the Deuill.
Imagine now that whilst he is retirde
From Cambridge backe vnto his natiue home,
Suppose the silent, sable visagde night
Casts her blacke curtaine ouer all the World;
And whilst he sleepes within his silent bed,
Toylde with the studies of the passed day,
The very time and houre wherein that spirite
That many yeeres attended his commaund,
And often times twixt Cambridge and that towne
Had in a minute borne him through the ayre,
By composition twixt the fiend and him,
Comes now to claime the Scholler for his due.
[*Draw the Curtaines.*
Behold him heere, laide on his restlesse couch,
His fatall chime prepared at his head,
His chamber guarded with these sable slights,
And by him stands that Necromanticke chaire,
In which he makes his direfull inuocations,
And binds the fiends that shall obey his will.
Sit with a pleased eye, vntill you know
The Commicke end of our sad Tragique show.
[*Exit.*

⟨INDUCTION.⟩

The Chime goes, in which time Fabell is oft seene to stare about him, and hold vp his hands

Fa. What meanes the tolling of this fatall chime?
O, what a trembling horror strikes my hart!
My stiffned haire stands vpright on my head,
As doe the bristles of a porcupine.

Enter Coreb, a Spirit.

Co. Fabell, awake, or I will beare thee hence
Headlong to hell.
Fab. Ha, ha,
Why dost thou wake me? Coreb, is it thou?
Cor. Tis I.
Fa. I know thee well: I heare the watchfull dogs
With hollow howling tell of thy approch;
The lights burne dim, affrighted with thy presence;
And this distemperd and tempestuous night
Tells me the ayre is troubled with some Deuill.

[1] *Add. Dod. Words in square brackets from WP* 14 ssleights *Q 1* 24 visage *Q 3* *S. D. follows* 32 *Qq* 36 these] his *Q 5, 6* Induction *WP*: Scene I. *T Haz.* 5–6 *Prose Qq* 7–8 *Div. after* me *Qq*: *corr.* WP 5 or] for

Cor. Come, art thou ready?
Fab. Whither? or to what?
Cor. Why, Scholler, this the houre my date expires;
I must depart, and come to claime my due.
Fa. Hah, what is thy due?
Cor. Fabell, thy selfe.
Fab. O, let not darkenes heare thee speake that word,
Lest that with force it hurry hence amaine,
And leaue the world to looke vpon my woe:
Yet ouerwhelme me with this globe of earth,
And let a little sparrow with her bill
Take but so much as shee can beare away,
That, euery day thus losing of my load,
I may againe in time yet hope to rise.
Cor. Didst thou not write thy name in thine owne blood,
And drewst the formall deed twixt thee and mee,
And is it not recorded now in hell?
Fa. Why comst thou in this sterne and horred shape,
Not in familiar sort, as thou wast wont?
Cor. Because the date of thy command is out,
And I am master of thy skill and thee.
Fa. Coreb, thou angry and impatient spirit,
I haue earnest busines for a priuate friend;
Reserue me, spirit, vntill some further time.
Cor. I will not for the mines of all the earth.
Fa. Then let me rise, and ere I leaue the world,
Dispatch some busines that I haue to doe;
And in meane time repose thee in that chayre.
Cor. Fabell, I will. [*Sit downe.*
Fa. O, that this soule, that cost so great a price
As the deere pretious blood of her redeemer,
Inspirde with knowledge, should by that alone
Which makes a man so meane vnto the powers,
Euen lead him downe into the depth of hell,
When men in their owne pride striue to know more
Then man should know!
For this alone God cast the Angelles downe.
The infinity of Arts is like a sea,
Into which, when man will take in hand to saile
Further then reason, which should be his pilot,
Hath skill to guide him, losing once his compasse,
He falleth to such deepe and dangerous whirlepooles,
As he doth lose the very sight of heauen:
The more he striues to come to quiet harbor,
The further still he finds himselfe from land.
Man, striuing still to finde the depth of euill,
Seeking to be a God, becomes a Deuill.
Cor. Come, Fabell, hast thou done?
Fab. Yes, yes; come hither.
Cor. Fabell, I cannot.
Fab. Cannot? — What ailes your hollownes?
Cor. Good Fabell, helpe me.
Fab. Alas, where lies your griefe? some *Aqua-vitae*!
The Deuil's very sicke, I feare hee'le die,
For he lookes very ill.
Cor. Darst thou deride the minister of darkenes?
In Lucifers dread name Coreb coniures thee
To set him free.
Fab. I will not for the mines of all the earth,
Vnles thou giue me libertie to see
Seauen yeares more, before thou sease on mee.
Cor. Fabell, I giue it thee.
Fab. Sweare, damned fiend.
Cor. Vnbind me, and by hell I will not touch thee,
Till seauen yeares from this houre be full expirde.
Fab. Enough, come out.
Cor. A vengeance take thy art!
Liue and conuert all piety to euill:
Neuer did man thus ouer-reach the Deuill.
No time on earth like Phaetontique flames
Can haue perpetuall being. Ile returne
To my infernall mansion; but be sure,
Thy seauen yeeres done, noe tricke shall make me tarry,
But, Coreb, thou to hell shalt Fabell carry. [*Exit.*
Fab. Then thus betwixt vs two this variance ends,
Thou to thy fellow Fiends, I to my friends. [*Exit.*

⟨ACT I.

SCENE I. *The George Inn, Waltham.*⟩

Enter Sir Arthur Clare, Dorcas, his Lady, Milliscent, his daughter, yong Harry Clare; the men booted, the gentlewomen in cloakes and safeguardes. Blague, the merry host of the George, comes in with them.

Host. Welcome, good knight, to the George at Waltham, my free-hold, my tenements,

39 Ile dispatch *Q 2, 4–6* 42 great] dear *Dod.* 45 meane] near *Q 6*

58 finde] know *Q 3* 68 dread] great *Q 4* 72 yeares *Q 3, etc.*: fiends *Q 1, 2* 79 Phaetontique *Q 4–6*: Phaetentique *Q 1–3*: Phaetonic *Haz.*: Phlegethonic *conj. Nicholson* 84 between *Q 6* Act I. Scene I. *WP* The . . Waltham *pr. ed.*

goods & chattels. Madam, heer's a roome is the very *Homer* and *Iliads* of a lodging, it hath none of the foure elements in it; I built it out of the Center, and I drinke neere the lesse sacke. Welcome, my little wast of maiden-heads! What? I serue the good Duke of Norfolke.

Clare. God a mercie, my good host Blague: Thou hast a good seate here.

Host. Tis correspondent or so: there's not a Tartarian nor a Carrier shall breath vpon your geldings; they haue villanous rancke feete, the rogues, and they shall not sweat in my linnen. Knights and Lords too haue bene drunke in my house, I thanke the destinies.

Har. Pre' the, good sinful Inkeeper, wil that corruption, thine Ostler, looke well to my gelding. Hay, a poxe a these rushes!

Host. You Saint Dennis, your gelding shall walke without doores, and coole his feete for his masters sake. By the body of S. George, I haue an excellent intellect to go steale some venison: now, when wast thou in the forrest?

Har. Away, you stale messe of white-broth! Come hither, sister, let me helpe you.

Clare. Mine Host, is not Sir Richard Mounchensey come yet, according to our appointment, when we last dinde here?

Host. The knight's not yet apparent.— Marry, heere's a forerunner that summons a parle, and saith, heele be here top and top-gallant presently.

Clare. Tis well, good mine host; goe downe, and see breakfast be prouided.

Host. Knight, thy breath hath the force of a woman, it takes me downe; I am for the baser element of the kitchin: I retire like a valiant souldier, face pointe blanke to the foe-man, or, like a Courtier, that must not shew the Prince his posteriors; vanish to know my canuasadoes, and my interrogatories, for I serue the good Duke of Norfolke. [*Exit.*

Cla. How doth my Lady? are you not weary, Madam?
Come hither, I must talke in priuate with you;
My daughter Milliscent must not ouer-heare.

Mill. I, whispring; pray God it tend my good!
Strange feare assailes my heart, vsurps my blood.

Cla. You know our meeting with the knight Mounchensey
Is to assure our daughter to his heire.

Dor. Tis, without question.

Cla. Two tedious winters haue past ore, since first
These couple lou'd each other, and in passion
Glewd first their naked hands with youthfull moysture —
Iust so long, on my knowledge.

Dor. And what of this?

Cla. This morning should my daughter lose her name,
And to Mounchenseys house conuey our armes,
Quartered within his scutchion; th' affiance, made
Twixt him and her, this morning should be sealde.

Dor. I know it should.

Cla. But there are crosses, wife; heere's one in Waltham,
Another at the Abby, and the third
At Cheston; and tis ominous to passe
Any of these without a pater-noster.
Crosses of loue still thwart this marriage,
Whilst that we two, like spirits, walke in night
About those stony and hard hearted plots.

Mill. O God, what meanes my father?

Cla. For looke you, wife, the riotous old knight
Hath o'rerun his annual reuenue
In keeping iolly Christmas all the yeere:
The nostrilles of his chimny are still stuft
With smoake, more chargeable then Cane-tobacco;
His hawkes deuoure his fattest dogs, whilst simple,
His leanest curres eate him hounds carrion.
Besides, I heard of late, his yonger brother,
A Turky merchant, hath sure suck'de the knight
By meanes of some great losses on the sea,
That, you conceiue mee, before God all ⟨is⟩ naught,
His seate is weake: thus, each thing rightly scand,
You'le see a flight, wife, shortly of his land.

Mill. Treason to my hearts truest soueraigne:
How soone is loue smothered in foggy gaine!

3 is] in *Q 2, 4–6* 6–18 Center . . destinies] *Verse Qq* 21, 22 gelding *Q 4, etc.*: geldings *Q 1–3* 34 saith] faith *Q 3–6* 41 souldiers face *Q 1, 3* 42 the] his *Q 6* 43 I vanish *WP* 49 tend to my *Q 4–6* 55 These] This *Q 6* 68 sprites *Q 3* 76 dogs] hogs *Haz.* 76–7 Simple, his leanest cur *Haz.* 77 eats *Haz.* him] his *Q 4, etc.* 79 A *Dod.*: Or *Qq* sure] sore *Q 6* 81 is *add. Q 6* 82 state *conj. Walker*

Dor. But how shall we preuent this dangerous match?

Cla. I haue a plot, a tricke, and this it is —
Vnder this colour Ile breake off the match:
Ile tell the knight that now my minde is changd
For marrying of my daughter, for I intend
To send her vnto Cheston Nunry.

Mill. O me accurst!

Cla. There to become a most religious Nunne.

Mill. Ile first be buried quicke.

Clar. To spend her beauty in most priuate prayers.

Mill. Ile sooner be a sinner in forsaking
Mother and father.

Cla. How dost like my plot?

Dor. Exceeding well; but is it your intent
Shee shall continue there?

Cla. Continue there? Ha, ha, that were a iest!
You know a virgin may continue there
A twelue moneth and a day onely on triall.
There shall my daughter soiourne some three moneths,
And in meane time Ile compasse a faire match
Twixt youthfull Ierningham, the lusty heire
Of Sir Raph Ierningham, dwelling in the forest —
I thinke they'le both come hither with Mounchensey.

Dor. Your care argues the loue you beare our childe;
I will subscribe to any thing youle haue me.
[*Exeunt.*

Mill. You will subscribe to it! good, good, tis well;
Loue hath two chaires of state, heauen and hell.
My deere Mounchensey, thou my death shalt rue,
Ere to thy heart Milliscent proue vntrue.
[*Exit.*

⟨SCENE II. *The same.*⟩

Enter Blague.

Host. Ostlers, you knaues and commanders, take the horses of the knights and competitors: your honourable hulkes haue put into harborough, theile take in fresh water here, and I haue prouided cleane chamber-pots. *Via, they come!*

Enter Sir Richard Mounchensey, Sir Raph Ierningham, yong Franke Ierningham, Raymond Mounchensey, Peter Fabell, and Bilbo.

Host. The destinies be most neate Chamberlaines to these swaggering puritanes, knights of the subsidy.

Sir Moun. God a mercy, good mine host.

Sir Ier. Thankes, good host Blague.

Host. Roome for my case of pistolles, that haue Greeke and Latine bullets in them; let me cling to your flanks, my nimble Giberalters, and blow wind in your calues to make them swell bigger. Ha, Ile caper in mine owne fee-simple; away with puntillioes and Orthography! I serue the good Duke of Norfolke. Bilbo, *Titere tu, patulae recubans sub tegmine fagi.*

Bil. Truely, mine host, Bilbo, though he be somewhat out of fashion, will be your onely blade still. I haue a villanous sharp stomacke to slice a breakfast.

Host. Thou shalt haue it without any more discontinuance, releases, or atturnement. What! we know our termes of hunting and the sea-card.

Bil. And doe you serue the good duke of Norfolke still?

Host. Still, and still, and still, my souldier of S. Quintins: come, follow me; I haue Charles waine below in a but of sacke, t'will glister like your Crab-fish.

Bil. You haue fine Scholler-like tearmes; your Coopers Dixionary is your onely booke to study in a celler, a man shall finde very strange words in it. Come, my host, lets serue the good duke of Norfolke.

Host. And still, and still, and still, my boy, Ile serue the good duke of Norfolke.
⟨*Exeunt Host and Bilbo.*

Enter Sir Arthur Clare, Harry Clare and Milliscent.⟩

Ier. Good Sir Arthur Clare!

Clar. What Gentleman is that? I know him not.

Moun. Tis M⟨aister⟩ Fabell, Sir, a Cambridge scholler,
My sonnes deere friend.

Clar. Sir, I intreat you know me.

Fab. Command me, sir; I am affected to you
For your Mounchenseys sake.

109 *S. D. follows* 98 *Q 1–3* : *om. Q 4–6* Scene II. WP 6 Voyez *Dod.* 19–20 Titere . . fagi *given to Bilbo Q 4–6* 32 Quintus *Q 1, 3* 33 t'will] I will *Q 2, 4–6* *S. D.* Exeunt *etc. add. Col.*

Clar. Alas, for him,
I not respect whether he sinke or swim:
A word in priuate, Sir Raph Ierningham.

Ray. Me thinks your father looketh strangely on me:
Say, loue, why are you sad?

Mill. I am not, sweete;
Passion is strong, when woe with woe doth meete.

Clar. Shall's in to breakfast? after wee'l conclude
The cause of this our comming: in and feed,
And let that vsher a more serious deed.

Mill. Whilst you desire his griefe, my heart shall bleed.

Yong Ier. Raymond Mounchensey, come, be frolick, friend,
This is the day thou hast expected long.

Ray. Pray God, deere Ierningham, it proue so happy.

Ier. There's nought can alter it. Be merry, lad!

Fab. There's nought shall alter it. Be liuely, Raymond!
Stand any opposition gainst thy hope,
Art shall confront it with her largest scope.
[*Exeunt*

⟨Scene III. *The same.*⟩

Peter Fabell, solus.

Fab. Good old Mounchensey, is thy hap so ill,
That for thy bounty and thy royall parts
Thy kind alliance should be held in scorne,
And after all these promises by Clare
Refuse to giue his daughter to thy sonne,
Onely because thy Reuenues cannot reach
To make her dowage of so rich a ioynture
As can the heire of wealthy Ierningham?
And therefore is the false foxe now in hand
To strike a match betwixt her and th' other;
And the old gray-beards now are close together,
Plotting it in the garden. Is't euen so?
Raymond Mounchensey, boy, haue thou and I
Thus long at Cambridge read the liberall Arts,
The Metaphysickes, Magicke, and those parts
Of the most secret deepe philosophy?
Haue I so many melancholy nights
Watch'd on the top of Peter-house highest tower?
And come we backe vnto our natiue home,
For want of skill to lose the wench thou lou'st?
Weele first hang Enuill in such rings of miste
As neuer rose from any dampish fenne:
Ile make the brinde sea to rise at Ware,
And drowne the marshes vnto Stratford bridge;
Ile driue the Deere from Waltham in their walkes,
And scatter them like sheepe in euery field.
We may perhaps be crost, but, if we be,
He shall crosse the deuill, that but crosses me.

Enter Raymond and yong Ierning. ⟨*and young Clare.*⟩

But here comes Raymond, disconsolate & sad,
And heeres the gallant that must haue the wench.

⟨*Ier.*⟩ I pri'thee, Raymond, leaue these solemne dumps:
Reuiue thy spirits, thou that before hast beene
More watchfull then the day-proclayming cocke,
As sportiue as a Kid, as francke and merry
As mirth herselfe.
If ought in me may thy content procure,
It is thine owne, thou mayst thy selfe assure.

Ray. Ha, Ierningham, if any but thy selfe
Had spoke that word, it would haue come as cold
As the bleake Northerne winds vpon the face
Of winter.
From thee they haue some power vpon my blood;
Yet being from thee, had but that hollow sound
Come from the lips of any liuing man,
It might haue won the credite of mine eare;
From thee it cannot.

Ier. If I vnderstand thee, I am a villain:
What, dost thou speake in parables to thy friends?

Clar. Come, boy, and make me this same groning loue,
Troubled with stitches and the cough a'th lungs,
That wept his eyes out when he was a childe,
And euer since hath shot at hudman-blind,
Make him leape, caper, ierke, and laugh, and sing,
And play me horse-trickes;
Make Cupid wanton as his mothers doue:
But in this sort, boy, I would haue thee loue.

Fab. Why, how now, mad-cap? what, my lusty Franke,
So neere a wife, and will not tell your friend?
But you will to this geere in hugger-mugger;
Art thou turnde miser, Rascall, in thy loues?

51 sad] so sad *Q 3* Scene III. *WP* 4 by *Qq*: my *Haz.* 21 Enuill *Qq*: Enfield *Haz.* *S. D.* and young Clare *add. Q 6* 31 *Prefix add. Q 4* 40 wind *Q 3* 53 him *Daniel*: her *Qq*

Ier. Who, I? z'blood, what should all you see in me, that I should looke like a married man, ha? Am I balde? are my legs too little for my hose? If I feele any thing in my forehead, I am a villain: doe I weare a night-cap? doe I bend in the hams? What dost thou see in me, that I should be towards marriage, ha?

Cla. What, thou married? let me looke vpon thee, Rogue; who has giuen out this of thee? how camst thou into this ill name? what company hast thou bin in, Rascall?

Fab. You are the man, sir, must haue Millescent:
The match is making in the garden now;
Her ioynture is agreed on, and th' old men,
Your fathers, meane to lanch their busy bags;
But in meane time to thrust Mountchensey off,
For colour of this new intended match,
Faire Millescent to Cheston must be sent,
To take the approbation for a Nun.
Nere looke vpon me, lad, the match is done.

Ier. Raymond Mountchensey, now I touch thy griefe
With the true feeling of a zealous friend.
And as for faire and beauteous Millescent,
With my vaine breath I will not seeke to slubber
Her angell like perfections; but thou know'st
That Essex hath the Saint that I adore.
Where ere did we meete thee and wanton springs,
That like a wag thou hast not laught at me,
And with regardles iesting mockt my loue?
How many a sad and weary summer night
My sighs haue drunke the dew from off the earth,
⟨And⟩ I haue taught the Niting-gale to wake,
And from the meadowes spring the earely Larke
An houre before she should haue list to sing:
I haue loaded the poore minutes with my moanes,
That I haue made the heauy slow pasde houres
To hang like heauie clogs vpon the day.
But, deere Mounchensey, had not my affection
Seasde on the beauty of another dame,
Before I would wrong the chase, and ouergiue loue
Of one so worthy and so true a friend,
I will abiure both beauty and her sight,
And will in loue become a counterfeit.

Mount. Deere Ierningham, thou hast begot my life,
And from the mouth of hell, where now I sate,
I feele my spirit rebound against the stars:
Thou hast conquerd me, deere friend, in my free soule;
Their time nor death can by their power controule.

Fab. Franke Ierningham, thou art a gallant boy;
And were he not my pupill, I would say
He were as fine a metled gentleman,
Of as free spirit, and of as fine a temper
As is in England; and he is a man
That very richly may deserue thy loue.
But, noble Clare, this while of our discourse,
What may Mounchenseys honour to thy selfe
Exact vpon the measure of thy grace?

Clar. Raymond Mounchensey, I would haue thee know,
He does not breath this ayre,
Whose loue I cherish, and whose soule I loue
More then Mounchenseyes:
Nor euer in my life did see the man
Whom, for his wit and many vertuous parts,
I thinke more worthy of my sisters loue.
But since the matter growes vnto this passe,
I must not seeme to crosse my Fathers will;
But when thou list to visit her by night,
My horses sadled, and the stable doore
Stands ready for thee; vse them at thy pleasure.
In honest mariage wed her frankly, boy,
And if thou getst her, lad, God giue thee ioy!

Moun. Then, care, away! let fates my fall pretend,
Backt with the fauours of so true a friend!

Fab. Let vs alone, to bussell for the set;
For age and craft with wit and Art haue met.
Ile make my spirits to dance such nightly Iigs
Along the way twixt this and Totnam crosse,
The Carriers Iades shall cast their heauie packs,
And the strong hedges scarse shall keepe them in:
The Milke-maides Cuts shall turne the wenches off,
And lay the Dossers tumbling in the dust:
The franke and merry London prentises,
That come for creame and lusty country cheere,
Shall lose their way; and, scrambling in the ditches,
All night shall whoop and hollow, cry and call,

61-5 am *Verse Qq* 88-9 did . . That *Q 1, 3*: did'st meete me, but (that *Q 6*) we two were Iouiall, But *Q 2, 4-6* 88 and] ? in 93 And *om. Q 1, 3* 94 spring *Q 1, 3*: sprung *Q 2, 4-6* 95 list] rest *Q 1, 3* 101 I'de *Q 3* wrong *Q 2-6*: vnage *Q 1* ouergiue *Q 1, 3*: leaue *Q 2, 4-6*

109 Their (= There)] Neither *WP* nor *Q 3*: or *Q 1, 2, 4-6* 114 *om. Q 1* 129 horse is *Q 4, etc.* 133 Fate *Q 4, etc.* 136 haue] hath *Q 4-6* 137 Iigs *om. Q 3* 142 lay their *Q 4-6*

Yet none to other finde the way at all.

Mount. Pursue the proiect, scholler: what we can do
To helpe indeauour, ioyne our liues thereto!
⟨*Exeunt.*⟩

⟨ACT II.

SCENE I. *Waltham: The house of Banks.*⟩

Enter Banks, Sir Iohn and Smug.

Banks. Take me with you, good Sir Iohn! A plague on thee, Smug, and thou touchest liquor, thou art founderd straight. What, are your braines alwayes water-milles? must they euer runne round?

Smug. Banks, your ale is a Philistine fox; z'hart, theres fire i'th taile on't; you are a rogue to charge vs with Mugs i'th rereward. A plague of this winde; O, it tickles our Catastrophe.

Sir Io. Neighbour Banks of Waltham, and Goodman Smug, the honest Smith of Edmonton, as I dwell betwixt you both at Enfield, I know the taste of both your ale houses, they are good both, smart both. Hem, Grasse and hay! we are all mortall; let's liue till we die, and be merry; and theres an end.

Banks. Well said, sir Iohn, you are of the same humor still; and doth the water runne the same way still, boy?

Smug. Vulcan was a rogue to him; Sir Iohn, locke, lock, lock fast, sir Iohn; so, sir Iohn. Ile one of these yeares, when it shall please the Goddesses and the destinies, be drunke in your company; thats all now, and God send vs health: shall I sweare I loue you?

Sir Io. No oathes, no oaths, good neighbour Smug! Weel wet our lips together and hugge; Carrouse in priuate, and eleuate the hart, and the liuer and the lights,—and the lights, marke you me, within vs; for hem, Grasse and hay! we are all mortall, lets liue till we die, and be Merry, and thers an end.

Banks. But to our former motion about stealing some venison; whither goe we?

Sir Io. Into the forrest, neighbour Banks, into Brians walke, the madde keeper.

Smug. Z' blood! Ile tickle your keeper.

Banks. Yfaith, thou art alwayes drunke when we haue neede of thee.

Smug. Neede of mee? z' hart, you shall haue neede of mee alwayes while theres yron in an Anuill.

Banks. M⟨aister⟩ Parson, may the Smith goe, thinke you, being in this taking?

Smug. Go? Ile goe in spight of all the belles in Waltham.

Sir Io. The question is, good neighboure Banks — let mee see: the Moone shines to night, — ther's not a narrow bridge betwixt this and the forrest, — his braine will be setled ere night; he may go, he may go, neighbour Banks. Now we want none but the company of mine host Blague at the George at Waltham; if he were here, our Consort were full. Looke where comes my good host, the Duke of Norfolks man! and how? and how? a hem, grasse and hay! wee are not yet mortall; lets liue till we die, and be merry; and ther's an end.

Enter Host.

Host. Ha, my Castilian dialogues! and art thou in breath stil, boy? Miller, doth the match hold? Smith, I see by thy eyes thou hast bin reading little Geneua print: but wend we merrily to the forrest, to steale some of the kings Deere. Ile meet you at the time appointed: away, I haue Knights and Colonells at my house, & must tend the Hungarions. If we be scard in the forrest, weele meete in the Church-porch at Enfield; ist Correspondent?

Ban. Tis well; but how, if any of vs should be taken?

Smi. He shall haue ransome, by the Lord.

Host. Tush, the knaue keepers are my bosonians & my pensioners. Nine a clocke! be valiant, my little Gogmagogs; Ile fence with all the Iustices in Hartford shire. Ile haue a Bucke til I die; Ile slay a Doe while I liue; hold your bow straight and steady. I serue the good duke of Norfolke.

Smu. O rare! who, ho, ho, boy!

Sir Io. Peace, neighbor Smug. You see this is a Boore, a Boore of the country, an illiterate Boore, and yet the Cittizen of good fellowes: come, lets prouide; a hem, Grasse and hay! wee are not yet all mortall; weel liue till we die, and be merry, and theres an end. Come, Smug!

Smug. Good night, Waltham — who, ho, ho, boy! [*Exeunt.*

⟨SCENE II. *The George Inn.*⟩

Enter the Knights and Gentlemen from breakfast againe.

Old Moun. Nor I for thee, Clare, not of this.

147 Yet] And *Q 2, 4–6* *S.D.* Exeunt *add. Q 4* Act II. Scene I. *WP* 7 on't] out *Q 1–3* 28 and *Q 2, 4–6* : in *Q 1, 3* 27–33 *Verse Qq* 50 not a narrow] narrow a *conj. Daniel* 51 will] may *Q 2, 4–6* 54 of the George *Q 2, 4–6* 74 by my sword *Q 4–6* 84 is a *om. Q 2, 4–6* 86 prouide a hen *Qq* : *corr. Dod.* Scene II. *WP*

What? hast thou fed me all this while with shalles.
And com'st to tell me now, thou lik'st it not?
Cla. **I doe not hold thy offer competent;**
Nor doe I like th' assurance of thy Land,
The title is so brangled with thy debts.
Old Mo. **Too good for thee; and, knight, thou knowst it well,**
I fawnd not on thee for thy goods, not I;
Twas thine owne motion; that thy wife doth know.
Lad. **Husband, it was so; he lies not in that.**
Clar. **Hold thy chat, queane.**
Old Moun. **To which I hearkned willingly, and the rather,**
Because I was perswaded it proceeded
From loue thou bor'st to me and to my boy;
And gau'st him free accesse vnto thy house,
Where he hath not behaude him to thy childe,
But as befits a gentleman to doe:
Nor is my poore distressed state so low,
That Ile shut vp my doores, I warrant thee.
⟨*Cla.*⟩ **Let it suffice, Mountchensey, I mislike it;**
Nor thinke thy sonne a match fit for my childe.
⟨*Moun.*⟩ **I tell thee, Clare, his blood is good and cleere**
As the best drop that panteth in thy veines:
But for this maide, thy faire and vertuous childe,
She is no more disparagd by thy basenes
Then the most orient and the pretious iewell,
Which still retaines his lustre and his beauty,
Although a slaue were owner of the same.
Cla. **She is the last is left me to bestow,**
And her I meane to dedicate to God.
Mount. **You doe, sir?**
Cla. **Sir, sir, I doe, she is mine owne.**
Mount. **And pity she is so!**
Damnation dog thee and thy wretched pelfe! [*aside.*
Cla. **Not thou, Mountchensey, shalt bestow my childe.**
Mount. **Neither shouldst thou bestow her where thou mean'st.**
Cla. **What wilt thou doe?**
Moun. **No matter, let that bee;**
I wil doe that, perhaps, shall anger thee:
Thou hast wrongd my loue, and, by Gods blessed Angell,
Thou shalt well know it.
Cla. **Tut, braue not me.**
Moun. **Braue thee, base Churle! were't not for man-hood sake—**
I say no more, but that there be some by
Whose blood is hotter then ours is,
Which being stird might make vs both repent
This foolish meeting. But, Harry Clare,
Although thy father haue abused my friendship,
Yet I loue thee, I doe, my noble boy,
I doe, yfaith.
Lady. **I, doe, do!**
Fill all the world with talke of vs, man, man;
I neuer lookt for better at your hands.
Fab. **I hop'd your great experience and your yeeres**
Would haue prou'de patience rather to your soule,
Then with this frantique and vntamed passion
To whet their skeens; and, but for that
I hope their friendships are too well confirmd,
And their minds temperd with more kindly heat,
Then for their froward parents soares
That they should breake forth into publique brawles—
How ere the rough hand of th' vntoward world
Hath moulded your proceedings in this matter,
Yet I am sure the first intent was loue:
Then since the first spring was so sweet and warme,
Let it die gently; ne're kill it with a scorne.
Ray. **O thou base world, how leprous is that soule**
That is once lim'd in that polluted mudde!
Oh, sir Arthur, you haue startled his free actiue spirits
With a too sharpe spur for his minde to beare.
Haue patience, sir; the remedy to woe
Is to leaue what of force we must forgoe.
Mill. **And I must take a twelue moneths approbation,**
That in meane time this sole and priuate life
At the yeares end may fashion me a wife:
But, sweet Mounchensey, ere this yeare be done,
Thou'st be a frier, if that I be a Nun.
And, father, ere yong Ierninghams Ile bee,
I will turne mad to spight both him and thee.

5 Land *Q 4–6* : loue *Q 1–3* 20, 22 *Prefixes om. Q 1–3* 22 I *Q 4–6, etc.*: To *Q 1–3* 25 no *om. Q 2, 4, 5* 28 the owner *Q 3* *S. D.* aside *printed as part of* 33 *Q 1–3* 38 by a blessed *Q 4–6* 44 Harry *Q 6* : Raph *Q 1, 2* : Ralph *Q 3–5* 45 hath *Q 5, 6* 49–50 *One line Qq* 51 hop d *Q 4–6* : hope *Q 1–3* 54 for *om. Q 1–3* 57 froward *Q 1, 3* : forward *Q 2, 4–6* : soares *Q 1–3* : frowardnesse *Q 4–6* 69 what *Q 1–3* : that *Q 4–6*

Cla. Wife, come, to horse, and, huswife, make you ready;
For, if I liue, I sweare by this good light,
Ile see you lodgde in Chesson house to night. ⟨*Exeunt.*⟩
Moun. Raymond, away! Thou seest how matters fall.
Churle, hell consume thee, and thy pelfe, and all!
Fab. Now, M⟨aister⟩ Clare, you see how matters fadge;
Your Milliscent must needes be made a Nun.
Well, sir, we are the men must plie this match:
Hold you your peace, and be a looker on,
And send her vnto Chesson—where he will,
Ile send mee fellowes of a handful hie
Into the Cloysters where the Nuns frequent,
Shall make them skip like Does about the Dale,
And with the Lady prioresse of the house
To play at leape-froge, naked in their smockes,
Vntill the merry wenches at their masse
Cry teehee weehee;
And tickling these mad lasses in their flanckes,
They'll sprawle, and squeke, and pinch their fellow Nunnes.
Be liuely, boyes, before the wench we lose,
Ile make the Abbas weare the Cannons hose. [*Exeunt.*

⟨Scene III. *The same.*⟩

Enter Harry Clare, Francke Ierningham, Peter Fabell, and Milliscent.

Ha. Cla. Spight now hath done her worst; sister, be patient.
Ier. Forewarnd poore Raymonds company! O heauen!
When the composure of weake frailtie meete
Vpon this mart of durt, O, then weake loue
Must in hir owne vnhappines be silent,
And winck on all deformities.
Milli. Tis well:
Whers Raymond, brother? whers my deere Mounchensey?
Would wee might weepe together and then part;
Our sighing parle would much ease my heart.
Fab. Sweete beautie, fould your sorrowes in the thought
Of future reconcilement: let your teares
Shew you a woman; but be no farther spent
Then from the eyes; for, sweete, experience sayes
That loue is firme thats flattered with delayes.
Milli. Alas, sir, thinke you I shall ere be his?
Fab. As sure as parting smiles on future blisse.
Yond comes my friend: see, he hath doted
So long vpon your beautie, that your want
Will with a pale retirement wast his blood;
For in true loue Musicke doth sweetly dwell:
Seuerd, theese lesse worlds beare within them hell.

Enter Mounchensey.

Mount. Harry and Francke, you are enioynd to waine
Your friendship from mee; we must part: the breath
Of all aduised corruption—pardon mee!
Faith, I must say so;—you may thinke I loue you;
I breath not, rougher spight do seuer vs;
Weele meete by stealth, sweet friend,—by stealth, you twaine;
Kisses are sweetest got with strugling paine.
Ier. Our friendship dies not, Raymond.
Mount. Pardon mee:
I am busied; I haue lost my faculties,
And buried them in Milliscents cleere eyes.
Mill. Alas, sweete Loue, what shall become of me?
I must to Chesson to the Nunry,
I shall nere see thee more.
Moun. How, sweete?
Ile be thy votary, weele often meete:
This kisse diuides vs, and breathes soft adiew,—
This be a double charme to keepe both true.
Fab. Haue done: your fathers may chance spie your parting.
Refuse not you by any meanes, good sweetnes,
To goe vnto the Nunnery; farre from hence
Must wee beget your loues sweete happines.
You shall not stay there long; your harder bed
Shall be more soft when Nun and maide are dead.

Enter Bilbo.

Moun. Now, sirra, whats the matter?
Bil. Marry, you must to horse presently; that villanous olde gowty churle, Sir Arthur Clare, longs till he be at the Nunry.
Ha. Cla. How, sir?
⟨*Bil.*⟩ O, I cry you mercy, he is your father, sir, indeed; but I am sure that theres lesse

79 this night *Q 3* *S. D.* Exeunt *add. Q 4* 84 plie] pile *Q 3* 86 where] when *Haz.* 90 *Ends play Q 1–3* with *Daniel*: make *Qq* 91 her smock *Dod.* 95 They'll *Daniel*: Shall *Qq* Scene III. *WP* 2 O] to *Q 1–3*

16 panting *Q 1–3* 17 Yonder *Q 3* 22–4 *Prose Q1–5* 24 all *Qq*: ill *Haz.*: old *Daniel* 26 do *Qq*: to *Haz.*: doth *Daniel* 27 meet by steale *Q 1–3* friends *Q 6* 46 Arthur *T*: Richard *Qq* 49 Bil. *add. Q 6* 50 sir *om. Q 3*

affinitie betwixt your two natures then there is betweene a broker and a cutpurse.

Moun. Bring my gelding, sirra.

Bil. Well, nothing greeues me, but for the poore wench; she must now cry *vale* to Lobster pies, hartichokes, and all such meates of mortalitie; poore gentlewoman, the signe must not be in virgo any longer with her, and that me grieues full well.

Poore Milliscent
Must pray and repent:
O fatalle wonder!
Sheele now be no fatter,
Loue must not come at her,
Yet she shall be keept vnder. [*Exit.*

Ier. Farwell, deere Raymond.

Ha. Cla. Friend, adew.

Mill. Deere sweete,
No ioy enioyes my hearte till wee next meete. [*Exeunt.*

Fab. Well, Raymond, now the tide of discontent
Beats in thy face; but, er't be long, the wind
Shall turne the flood. Wee must to Waltham abby,
And as faire Milliscent in Cheston liues,
A most vnwilling Nun, so thou shalt there
Become a beardles Nouice; to what end,
Let time and future accidents declare:
Tast thou my sleights, thy loue ile onely share.

Moun. Turne frier? Come, my good Counsellor, lets goe,
Yet that disguise will hardly shrowd my woe. [*Exeunt.*

⟨ACT III.

SCENE I. *Cheston Priory.*⟩

Enter the Prioresse of Cheston, with a Nun or two, Sir Arthur Clare, Sir Raph Ierningham, Henry and Francke, the Lady, and Bilbo, with Millisent.

La. Cla. Madam,
The loue vnto this holy sisterhood,
And our confirmd opinion of your zeale
Hath truely wonne vs to bestow our Childe
Rather on this then any neighbouring Cell.

Pri. Ihesus daughter, Maries childe,
Holy matron, woman milde,
For thee a masse shall still be sayd,
Euery sister drop a bead;
And those againe succeeding them
For you shall sing a Requiem.

Frank. The wench is gone, Harry; she is no more a woman of this world: marke her well, shee lookes like a Nun already. What thinkst on her?

Har. By my faith, her face comes handsomly to 't. But peace, lets heare the rest.

Sir Ar. Madam, for a tweluemonths approbation,
Wee meane to make this triall of our childe.
Your care and our deere blessing in meane time
Wee pray may prosper this intended worke.

Pri. May your happy soule be blithe,
That so truely pay your tithe:
He who many children gaue,
Tis fit that he one child should haue.
Then, faire virgin, heare my spell,
For I must your duty tell.

Mill.—Good men and true, stand together, and heare your charge.

Pri. First, a mornings take your booke,
The glasse wherein your selfe must looke;
Your young thoughts, so proud and iolly,
Must be turnd to motions holy;
For your buske, attires, and toyes
Haue your thoughts on heauenly ioyes;
And for all your follies past
You must do penance, pray, and fast.

Bil.—Let her take heed of fasting; and if euer she hurt her selfe with praying, Ile nere trust beast.

Mill.—This goes hard, berladye!

Pri. You shall ring the sacring bell,
Keepe your howers, and tell your knell,
Rise at midnight to your mattens,
Read your Psalter, sing your lattins,
And when your blood shall kindle pleasure,
Scourge your selfe in plenteous measure.

Mil.—Worse and worse, by Saint Mary.

Fr.—Sirra Hal, how does she hold hir countenance? Wel, goe thy wayes, if euer thou proue a Nun, Ile build an Abby.

Har.—She may be a Nun; but if euer shee prooue an Anchoresse, Ile dig her graue with my nailes.

Fra.—To her againe, mother!

Har.—Hold thine owne, wench!

Prio. You must read the mornings masse,
You must creepe vnto the Crosse,
Put cold ashes on your head,
Haue a haire cloth for your bed.

Bil.—She had rather haue a man in her bed.

59 fall well *Q 2, 3*: farewell *Q 4-6* Act III. Scene I. *WP* 11 sing] riug *Q 1*: ring *Q 2*

42 sacring *Q 2-6*: sauing *Q 1* 43 tell] toll *Haz.* 57 morning *Q 2, etc.*

Prio. Bid your beads, and tell your needes,
Your holy Auies, and your Creedes;
Holy maide, this must be done,
Yf you meane to liue a Nun.
Mill.—The holy maide will be no Nun.
Sir Ar. Madam, we haue some busines of import,
And must be gone.
Wilt please you take my wife into your closet,
Who further will acquaint you with my mind;
And so, good madam, for this time adiew.
⟨*Exeunt women.*
Sir Ra. Well now, Francke Ierningham, how saiest thou?
To be breefe,—
What wilt thou say for all this, if we two,
Her father and my selfe, can bring about,
That we conuert this Nun to be a wife,
And thou the husband to this pretty Nun?
How then, my lad? ha, Francke, it may be done.
Har.—I, now it workes.
Fra. O God, sir, you amaze mee at your words;
Thinke with your selfe, sir, what a thing it were
To cause a recluse to remoue her vow:
A maymed, contrite, and repentant soule,
Euer mortified with fasting and with prayer,
Whose thoughts, euen as hir eyes, are fixd on heauen,
To drawe a virgin, thus deuour'd with zeale,
Backe to the world: O impious deede!
Nor by the Canon Law can it be done
Without a dispensation from the Church:
Besides, she is so prone vnto this life,
As sheele euen shreeke to heare a husband namde.
Bil.—I, a poore innocent shee! Well, heres no knauery; hee flowts the old fooles to their teeth.
Sir Raph. Boy, I am glad to heare
Thou mak'st such scruple of that conscience;
And in a man so young as is your selfe,
I promise you tis very seldome seene.
But Franke, this is a tricke, a meere deuise,
A sleight plotted betwixt her father and my selfe,
To thrust Mounchenseys nose besides the cushion;
That, being thus debard of all accesse,
Time yet may worke him from her thoughts,
And giue thee ample scope to thy desires.
Bil.—A plague on you both for a couple of Iewes!
Har.—How now, Franke, what say you to that?
Fran.—Let me alone, I warrant thee.—
Sir, assurde that this motion doth proceede
From your most kinde and fatherly affection,
I do dispose my liking to your pleasure:
But for it is a matter of such moment
As holy marriage, I must craue thus much,
To haue some conference with my ghostly father,
Frier Hildersham, here by, at Waltham Abby,
To be absolude of things that it is fit
None only but my confessor should know.
Sir Ra. With all my heart: he is a reuerend man;
And to morrow morning wee will meet all at the Abby,
Where by th' opinion of that reuerend man
Wee will proceede; I like it passing well.
Till then we part, boy; I, thinke of it; farewell!
A parents care no mortall tongue can tell.
[*Exeunt.*

⟨Scene II. *Before the Priory Gate.*⟩

Enter Sir Arthur Clare, and Raymond Mounchensey, like a Frier.

Sir Ar. Holy yong Nouice, I haue told you now
My full intent, and doe refer the rest
To your professed secrecy and care:
And see,
Our serious speech hath stolne vpon the way,
That we are come vnto the Abby gate.
Because I know Mountchensey is a foxe,
That craftily doth ouerlooke my doings,
Ile not be seene, not I. Tush, I haue done:
I had a daughter, but shee's now a Nun.
Farewell, deere sonne, farewell. [*Exit.*
Moun. Fare you well! — I, you haue done!
Your daughter, sir, shall not be long a Nun.
O my rare Tutor! neuer mortall braine
Plotted out such a masse of policie;
And my deere bosome is so great with laughter,
Begot by his simplicity and error,
My soule is fallen in labour with her ioy.
O my true friends, Franke Ierningham and Clare,
Did you now know but how this iest takes fire—

62 Bid *WP*: Bind *Qq* 72 Ierningham *Q 6*: Clare *Q 1-5* 74 Her *Q 6*: Thy *Q 1-5* 85 deuout *Q 4-6*

118 Sir Ra. *Q 6*: Sir Ar. *Q 1-5* 118-20 *Prose Qq* 120 opnion *Q 1* 122 I thinke *Qq* Scene II. *WP* 11 sonne *Q 1, 4-6*: onne *Q 2*: one *Q 3* 15 masse *Q 1-3*: plot *Q 4, 5*: piece *Q 6* 19 true *om. Q 5* 20 now *Q 1-4*: but *Q 5, 6*

That good sir Arthur, thinking me a nouice,
Hath euen powrd himselfe into my bosome,
O, you would vent your spleenes with tickling mirth!
But, Raymond, peace, and haue an eye about,
For feare perhaps some of the Nuns looke out.
Peace and charity within,
Neuer touch't with deadly sin;
I cast my holy water pure
On this wall and on this doore,
That from euill shall defend,
And keepe you from the vgly fiend:
Euill spirit, by night nor day,
Shall approach or come this way;
Elfe nor Fary, by this grace,
Day nor night shall haunt this place.
Holy maidens! [*Knocke.*

[*Answere within.*] Who's that which knocks? ha, who's there?

Mount. Gentle Nun, here is a Frier.

Enter Nun.

Nun. A Frier without, now Christ vs saue!
Holy man, what wouldst thou haue?

Mount. Holy mayde, I hither come
From Frier and father Hildersome,
By the fauour and the grace
Of the Prioresse of this place,
Amongst you all to visit one
That's come for approbation;
Before she was as now you are,
The daughter of Sir Arthur Clare,
But since she now became a Nun,
Call'd Milliscent of Edmunton.

Nun. Holy man, repose you there;
This newes Ile to our Abbas beare,
To tell her what a man is sent,
And your message and intent.

Mount. Benedicite.

Nun. Benedicite. [*Exit.*

Mount. Doe, my good plumpe wench; if all fall right,
Ile make your sister-hood one lesse by night.
Now happy fortune speede this merry drift,
I like a wench comes roundly to her shrift.

Enter Lady, Milliscent.

Lad. Haue Friers recourse then to the house of Nuns?

Mill. Madam, it is the order of this place,
When any virgin comes for approbation,—
Lest that for feare or such sinister practise
Shee should be forcde to vndergoe this vaile,
Which should proceed from conscience and deuotion,—
A visitor is sent from Waltham house,
To take the true confession of the maide.

Lady. Is that the order? I commend it well:
You to your shrift, Ile backe vnto the cell. [*Exit.*

Mount. Life of my soule! bright Angell!

Mill. What meanes the Frier?

Mount. O Milliscent, tis I.

Mill. My heart misgiues me; I should know that voyce.
You? who are you? The holy virgin blesse me!
Tell me your name: you shall, ere you confesse me.

Mount. Mountchensey, thy true friend.

Mill. My Raymond, my deere heart!
Sweete life, giue leaue to my distracted soule,
To wake a little from this swoone of ioy.
By what meanes camst thou to assume this shape?

Mount. By meanes of Peter Fabell, my kind Tutor,
Who in the habite of Frier Hildersham,
Franke Ierninghams old friend and confessor,
⟨Helped me to act the part of priestly nouice,⟩
Plotted by Franke, by Fabell and my selfe,
And so deliuered to Sir Arthur Clare,
Who brought me heere vnto the Abby gate,
To be his Nun-made daughters visitor.

Mill. You are all sweete traytors to my poore old father.
O my deere life! I was a dream't to night
That, as I was a praying in mine Psalter,
There came a spirit vnto me as I kneeld,
And by his strong perswasions tempted me
To leaue this Nunry; and me thought
He came in the most glorious Angell shape,
That mortall eye did euer looke vpon.
Ha, thou art sure that spirit, for theres no forme
Is in mine eye so glorious as thine owne.

Mount. O thou Idolatresse, that dost this worship
To him whose likenes is but praise of thee!
Thou bright vnsetting star, which through this vaile,
For very enuy, mak'st the Sun looke pale!

Mill. Well, visitor, lest that perhaps my mother
Should thinke the Frier too strickt in his decrees,
I this confesse to my sweet ghostly father:
If chast pure loue be sin, I must confesse,

22 Had *WP* 28 my *om. Q 4–6* pure *Q 6* : poore *Q 1–5* 36 Holy maidens knocke *printed as S. D. Qq* : *corr. Dod.* 53 her *om. Q 1, 2, 4–6* 64 or such *Q 1, 2, 4–6* : of some *Q 3* : or *Walker*

84 *A line here appears to have been lost* : Helped .. nouice *conj. pr. ed.* 85 Fabell] Harry *WP* 91 a *om. Q 2, etc.* mine *Q 1, 2, 4* : my *Q 3, 5, 6*

I haue offended three yeares now with thee.
Mount. But doe you yet repent you of the same?
Mill. Yfaith, I cannot.
Moun. Nor will I absolue thee
Of that sweete sin, though it be venial;
Yet haue the pennance of a thousand kisses,
And I enioyne you to this pilgrimage:
That in the euening you bestow your selfe
Heere in the walke neere to the willow ground,
Where Ile be ready both with men and horse
To waite your comming, and conuey you hence
Vnto a lodge I haue in Enfield chase.
No more replie, if that you yeeld consent —
I see more eyes vpon our stay are bent.
Mill. Sweete life, farewell! Tis done: let that suffice;
What my tongue failes, I send thee by mine eyes. [*Exit.*

Enter Fabell, Clare, and Ierningham.

Ier. Now, Visitor, how does this new made Nun?
Cla. Come, come, how does she, noble Capouchin?
Moun. She may be poore in spirit, but for the flesh,
Tis fatte and plumpe, boyes. Ah, rogues, there is
A company of girles would turne you all Friers.
Fab. But how, Mountchensey? how, lad, for the wench?
Moun. Sound, lads, yfaith; I thanke my holy habit,
I haue confest her, and the Lady Prioresse
Hath giuen me ghostly counsell with hir blessing.
And how say yee, boyes,
If I be chose the weekely visitor?

Cla. Z'blood, sheel haue nere a Nun vnbagd to sing masse then.

Ier. The Abbat of Waltham will haue as many Children to put to nurse as he has calues in the Marsh.

Moun. Well, to be breefe, the Nun will soone at night turne tippit; if I can but deuise to quit her cleanly of the Nunry, she is mine owne.

Fab. But, Sirra Raymond,
What newes of Peter Fabel at the house?
Moun. Tush, hees the onely man;
A Necromancer and a Coniurer
That workes for yong Mountchensey altogether;
And if it be not for Fryer Benedicke,
That he can crosse him by his learned skill,
The Wench is gone;
Fabell will fetch her out by very magicke.
Fab. Stands the winde there, boy? keepe them in that key.
The wench is ours before to-morrow day.
Well, Hal and Franke, as ye are gentlemen,
Sticke to vs close this once! You know your fathers
Haue men and horse lie ready still at Chesson,
To watch the coast be cleere, to scowt about,
& haue an eye vnto Mountchenseys walks:
Therfore you two may houer thereabouts,
And no man will suspect you for the matter;
Be ready but to take her at our hands,
Leaue vs to scamble for hir getting out.
Ier. Z'bloud, if al Herford-shire were at our heeles,
Weele carry her away in spight of them.
Cla. But whither, Raymond?
Moun. To Brians vpper lodge in Enfield Chase;
He is mine honest Friend and a tall keeper;
Ile send my man vnto him presently
T' acquant him with your comminge and intent.
Fab. Be breefe and secret.
Moun. Soon at night remember
You bring your horses to the willow ground.
Ier. Tis done; no more!
Cla. We will not faile the hower.
My life and fortune now lies in your power.
Fab. About our busines! Raymond, lets away!
Thinke of your hower; it drawes well of the day. [*Exit.*

⟨ACT IV.

Scene I. *Enfield Chase.*⟩

Enter Blague, Banks, Smug, and Sir Iohn.

Bla. Come, yee Hungarian pilchers, we are once more come vnder the *zona torrida* of the forrest. Lets be resolute, lets flie to and againe; and if the deuill come, weele put him to his Interrogatories, and not budge a foote. What? s'foote, ile put fire into you, yee shall all three serue the good Duke of Norfolke.

Smu. Mine host, my bully, my pretious consull, my noble Holefernes, I haue bin drunke i' thy house twenty times and ten,

124-6 *Two lines Qq, div. after* boyes : *corr. Col.* 128 Zounds *Q 4-6* 129-30 *Prose Q 1-5* 139 tippet *Col.*: lippit *Qq* can *om. Q 3* 142-50 *Prose Qq* : *corr. WP* 148 him by *om. Q 3* 153 Hal *pr. ed.*: Ra⟨l⟩ph *Q 1-5* : Harry *Q 6, etc.* 153-63 *Prose Qq* : *corr. Col.* 157 Mountchensey *Q 1* walke *Q 3* 160 our] your *Q 3* 165-8 *Prose Qq* : *corr. Col.* Act. IV. Scene I. *WP* 10 thy] th *Q 3*

all's one for that: I was last night in the third heauens, my braine was poore, it had yest in 't; but now I am a man of action; is 't not so, lad?

Banks. Why, now thou hast two of the liberall sciences about thee, wit and reason, thou maist serue the Duke of Europe.

Smu. I will serue the Duke of Christendom, and doe him more credit in his celler then all the plate in his buttery; is 't not so, lad?

Sir Ioh. Mine host and Smug, stand there; Banks, you and your horse keepe together; but lie close, shew no trickes, for feare of the keeper. If we be scard, weel meete in the Church-porch at Enfeild.

Smug. Content, sir Iohn.

Banks. Smug, dost not thou remember the tree thou felst out of last night?

Smug. Tush, and 't had bin as high as the Abby, I should nere haue hurt my selfe; I haue fallen into the riuer, comming home from Waltham, and scapt drowning.

Sir Io. Come, seuer, feare no sprits! weele haue a Bucke presently; we haue watched later then this for a Doe, mine Host.

Host. Thou speakst as true as veluet.

Sir Io. Why then, come! Grasse and hay, &c. [*Exeunt.*

Enter Clare, Ierningham and Milliscent.

Clar. Franke Ierningham!

Ier. Speake softly, rogue; how now?

Clar. S'foot, we shall lose our way, it's so darke; wherabouts are we?

Ier. Why, man, at Potters gate; the way lies right: harke! the clocke strikes at Enfeild; whats the houre?

Cla. Ten, the bell sayes.

Ier. A lies in's throate, it was but eight when we set out of Chesson. Sir Iohn and his Sexton are at ale to night, the clocke runs at random.

Cla. Nay, as sure as thou liu'st, the villanous vicar is abroad in the chase this darke night: the stone Priest steales more venison then halfe the country.

Ier. Milliscent, how dost thou?

Mill. Sir, very well.
I would to God we were at Brians lodge.

Cla. We shall anon; z'ounds, harke! What meanes this noyse?

Ier. Stay, I heare horsemen.

Cla. I heare footmen too.

Ier. Nay, then I haue it: we haue bin discouerd,
And we are followed by our fathers men.

Mill. Brother and friend, alas, what shall we doe?

Cla. Sister, speake softly, or we are descride.
They are hard vpon vs, what so ere they be;
Shadow your selfe behind this brake of ferne,
Weele get into the wood, and let them passe.

Enter Sir Iohn, Blague, Smug, and Banks, one after another.

Sir Io. Grasse and hay! wee are all mortall; the keepers abroad, and ther's an end.

Ban. Sir Iohn!

Sir Io. Neighbour Bankes, what newes?

Ban. Z'wounds, Sir Iohn, the keepers are abroad; I was hard by 'am.

Sir Io. Grasse and hay! wher's mine host Blague?

Bla. Here, Metrapolitane. The philistines are vpon vs, be silent; let vs serue the good Duke of Norfolke. But where is Smug?

Smu. Here; a poxe on yee all, dogs; I haue kild the greatest Bucke in Brians walke. Shift for your selues, all the keepers are vp: lets meete in Enfield church porch; away, we are all taken els. [*Exeunt.*

Enter Brian, with his man, and his hound.

Bri. Raph, hearst thou any stirring?

Raph. I heard one speake here hard by, in the bottome. Peace, Maister, speake low; zownes, if I did not heare a bow goe off, and the Bucke bray, I neuer heard deere in my life.

Bri. When went your fellows out into their walks?

Ra. An hower agoe.

Bri. S'life, is there stealers abroad, and they cannot heare
Of them: where the deuill are my men to night?
Sirra, goe vp the wind towards Buckleyes lodge.
Ile cast about the bottome with my hound,
And I will meete thee vnder Cony ocke.

Ra. I will, Sir.

Bri. How now? by the masse, my hound stayes vpon something; harke, harke, Bowman, harke, harke, there!

Mill. Brother, Franke Ierningham, brother Clare!

12 heauen *Q 4–6* it] i't *Q 1* 15 Banks] Bil⟨bo⟩ *Q 1–3* 20–1 so, lad *om. Q 3* 25 in] at *Q 3* 30 the *Q 1, 3* : an *Q 2, 4–6* 34 feare] care *Q 1* 44 Poiters *Q 2, 3–6* 50 at] at their *Q 4–6* 58 Zounds *Q 1–3* : nounes *Q 4–6*

88 zownes] nounes *Q 4–6* 93–7 *Prose Qq* 93 Bri. . . heare of *follows* 89 *Q 3*

Bri. Peace; thats a womans voyce! Stand! who's there? Stand, or Ile shoote.
Milli. O Lord! hold your hands, I meane no harme, sir.
Bri. Speake, who are you?
Milli. I am a maid, sir; who? M⟨aister⟩ Brian?
Bri. The very same; sure, I should know her voyce;
Mistris Milliscent?
Mill. I, it is I, sir.
Bri. God for his passion! what make you here alone?
I lookd for you at my lodge an hower agoe.
What meanes your company to leaue you thus?
Who brought you hither?
Mil. My brother, Sir, and M⟨aister⟩ Ierningham,
Who, hearing folks about vs in the Chase,
Feard it had bin sir Ralph and my father,
Who had pursude vs, thus dispearsed our selues,
Till they were past vs.
Bri. But where be they?
Mill. They be not farre off, here about the groue.

Enter Clare and Ierningham.

Cla. Be not afraid, man, I heard Brians tongue,
Thats certain.
Ier. Call softly for your sister.
Cla. Milliscent!
Mill. I, brother, heere.
Bri. M⟨aister⟩ Clare!
Cla. I told you it was Brian.
Bri. Whoes that? M⟨aister⟩ Ierningham: you are a couple of hot-shots; does a man commit his wench to you, to put her to grasse at this time of night?
Ier. We heard a noyse about her in the chase,
And fearing that our fathers had pursude vs,
Seuerd our selues.
Cla. Brian, how hapd'st thou on her?
Bri. Seeking for stealers are abroad to night,
My hound staied on her, and so found her out.
Cla. They were these stealers that affrighted vs;
I was hard vpon them, when they horst their Deere,
And I perceiue they tooke me for a keeper.
Bri. Which way tooke they?
Ier. Towards Enfeild.
Bri. A plague vpon 't, thats that damned Priest, & Blague of the George, he that serues the good Duke of Norfolke.

A noyse within: Follow, follow, follow.

Cla. Peace, thats my fathers voyce.
Bri. Z'ownds, you suspected them, and now they are heere indeed.
Mill. Alas, what shall we doe?
Bri. If you goe to the lodge, you are surely taken;
Strike downe the wood to Enfeild presently,
And if Mounchensey come, Ile send him t'yee.
Let mee alone to bussle with your father;
I warrant you that I will keepe them play
Till you haue quit the chase; away, away!
⟨*Exeunt all but Brian.*⟩
Whoes there?

Enter the Knights.

Sir Rap. In the kings name, pursue the Rauisher!
Bri. Stand, or Ile shoote.
Sir Ar. Whoes there?
Bri. I am the keeper that doe charge you stand;
You haue stollen my Deere.
Sir Ar. We stolne thy Deere? we do pursue a thiefe.
Bri. You are arrant theeues, and ye haue stolne my Deere.
Sir Rap. We are Knights; sir Arthur Clare, and sir Raph Ierningham.
Bri. The more your shame, that Knights should bee such thieues.
Sir Ar. Who, or what art thou?
Bri. My name is Brian, keeper of this walke.
Sir Ar. O Brian, a villain!
Thou hast receiued my daughter to thy lodge.
Bri. You haue stolne the best Deere in my walke to night. My Deere!
Sir Ar. My daughter!
Stop not my way!
Bri. What make you in my walke? you haue stolne the best Bucke in my walke to night.
Sir Ar. My daughter!
Bri. My Deere!
Sir Rap. Where is Mountchensey?
Bri. Wheres my Bucke?

112-20 *Prose Qq* 118 Ralph *Q 6*: Arthur *Q 1-5* 134 her (= here?) *Q 1-3*: vs *Q 4-6* 136 hapnedst *Q 2, 4-6* 144 that] the *Q 5, 6* 148 Z'ownds] Nownes *Q 4-6* you] you haue *Q 5, 6* 154 Fathers *Q 6* 155 them] him *Q 3* *S. D. add. WP* 172 Sir Ar. *Q 6*: Sir Rap. *Q 1-5*

Sir Ar. I will complaine me of thee to the King.

Bri. Ile complaine vnto the King you spoile his game:
Tis strange that men of your account and calling
Will offer it!
I tell you true, Sir Arthur and sir Raph,
That none but you haue onely spoild my game.

Sir Ar. I charge you, stop vs not!

Bri. I charge you both ye get out of my ground!
Is this a time for such as you,
Men of ⟨your⟩ place and of your grauity,
To be abroad a theeuing? tis a shame;
And, afore God, if I had shot at you,
I had serude you well enough. [*Exeunt.*

⟨SCENE II. *Enfield Churchyard.*⟩

Enter Banks the Miller, wet on his legs.

Ban. S'foote, heeres a darke night indeed! I thinke I haue bin in fifteene ditches betweene this and the forrest. Soft, heers Enfeilde Church: I am so wet with climing ouer into an orchard for to steale some filberts. Well, heere Ile sit in the Church porch, and wait for the rest of my consort.

Enter the Sexton.

Sex. Heeres a sky as blacke as Lucifer. God blesse vs! heere was goodman Theophilus buried; hee was the best Nutcraker that euer dwelt in Enfeild. Well, tis 9. a clock, tis time to ring curfew. Lord blesse vs, what a white thing is that in the Church porch! O Lorde, my legges are too weake for my body, my haire is too stiffe for my night-cap, my heart failes; this is the ghost of Theophilus. O Lord, it followes me! I cannot say my prayers, and one would giue me a thousand pound. Good spirit, I haue bowld and drunke and followed the hounds with you a thousand times, though I haue not the spirit now to deale with you. O Lord!

Enter Priest.

Prie. Grasse and hey, we are all mortall. Who's there?

Sex. We are grasse and hay indeede; I know you to bee Master Parson by your phrase.

Prie. Sexton!

Sex. I, Sir.

Prie. For mortalities sake, Whats the matter?

Sex. O Lord, I am a man of another element; Maister Theophilus Ghost is in the Church porch. There was a hundred Cats, all fire, dancing here euen now, and they are clombe vp to the top of the steeple; ile not into the bellfree for a world.

Prie. O good Salomon; I haue bin about a deede of darknes to night: O Lord, I saw fifteen spirits in the forrest, like white bulles; if I lye, I am an arrant theefe: mortalitie haunts vs—grasse and hay! the deuills at our heeles, and lets hence to the parsonage. [*Exeunt.*

[*The Miller comes out very softly.*

Mill. What noise was that? tis the watch, sure; that villanous vnlucky rogue, Smug, is taine, vpon my life; and then all our villeny comes out; I heard one cry, sure.

Enter Host Blague.

Host. If I go steale any more veneson, I am a Paradox: s'foot, I can scarce beare the sinne of my flesh in the day, tis so heauy; if I turne not honest, and serue the good Duke of Norfolke, as true mareterraneum skinker should doe, let me neuer looke higher then the element of a Constable.

Mill. By the Lord, there are some watchmen; I heare them name Maister Constable; I would to God my Mill were an Eunuch, and wanted her stones, so I were hence.

Host. Who's there?

Mille. Tis the Constable, by this light; Ile steale hence, and if I can meete mine host Blague, ile tell him how Smug is taine, and will him to looke to himselfe. [*Exit.*

Host. What the deuill is that white thing? this same is a Church-yard, and I haue heard that ghosts and villenous goblins haue beene seene here.

Enter Sexton and Priest.

Pri. Grasse and hay! O, that I could coniure! wee saw a spirite here in the Churchyeard; and in the fallow field ther's the deuill with a mans body vpon his backe in a white sheet.

Sex. It may be a womans body, Sir Iohn.

Pri. If shee be a woman, the sheets damne her; Lord blesse vs, what a night of mortalitie is this!

186-97 *Prose Qq* : *corr. WP* 194 your place *Q 3* : place *Q 1, 2, 4-6* your grauity *Q 1, 2, 4-6* : grauity *Q 3* Scene II. *add. WP* 1 darke] blacke *Q 3* 7 Consorts *Q 4-6* 13 a *om. Q 2, 3* 18 a *om. Q 3*

34 here *om. Q 2, 4-6* 37 good *Q 1-4* : goodman *Q 5, 6* 42 parsonages *Q 1-3* 45 villeny *Q 1-3* : knauerie *Q 4-6* 48 foot *Q 4-6* 51 as *Q 1-3* : as a *Q 4-6* 54 *Prefix* Milla *Q 1* Lord] masse *Q 4-6* 74 Lord *om. Q 4-6*

Host. Priest!

Pri. Mine host!

Host. Did you not see a spirit all in white crosse you at the stile?

Sex. O no, mine host; but there sate one in the porch; I haue not breath ynough left to blesse me from the Deuill.

Host. Whoes that?

Pri. The Sexton, almost frighted out of his wits. Did you see Banks or Smug?

Host. No, they are gone to Waltham, sure: I would faine hence; come, lets to my house: Ile nere serue the duke of Norfolk in this fashion againe whilst I breath. If the deuill be amongst vs, tis time to hoist saile, and cry roomer. Keepe together; Sexton, thou art secret, what? lets be comfortable one to another.

Pri. We are all mortall, mine host.

Host. True; and Ile serue God in the night hereafter afore the Duke of Norfolke. [*Exeunt.*

⟨ACT V.

SCENE I. *An Inn opposite the George, Waltham.*⟩

Enter Sir Arthur Clare and Sir Ralph Ierningham, trussing their points as new vp.

Sir Rap. Good morrow, gentle knight.
A happy day after your short nights rest.

Sir Ar. Ha, ha, sir Raph, stirring so soone indeed?
Birlady, sir, rest would haue done right well;
Our riding late last night has made mee drowsie.
Goe to, goe to, those dayes are gone with vs.

Sir Ra. Sir Arthur, Sir Arthur, care go with those dayes,
Let 'am euen goe together, let 'am goe!
Tis time, yfaith, that wee were in our graues,
When Children leaue obedience to their parents,
When there's no feare of God, no care, no dutie.
Well, well, nay, nay, it shall not doe, it shall not;
No, Mountchensey, thou'st heare on't, thou shalt,
Thou shalt, yfaith!
Ile hang thy Son, if there be law in England.
A mans Child rauisht from a Nunry!
This is rare!
Well, well, ther's one gone for Frier Hildersam.

Sir Ar. Nay, gentle Knight, do not vexe thus,
It will but hurt your health.
You cannot greeue more then I doe, but to what end? But harke you, Sir Raph, I was about to say somthing—it makes no matter. But hearke you in your eare: the Frier's a knaue; but God forgiue me, a man cannot tel neither; s'foot, I am so out of patience, I know not what to say.

Sir Ra. Ther's one went for the Frier an hower agoe. Comes he not yet? s'foot, if I do find knauery vnders cowle, ile tickle him, ile firke him. Here, here, hee's here, hee's here. Good morrow, Frier; good morrow, gentle Frier.

Enter Hildersham.

Sir Ar. Good morrow, father Hildersham, good morrow.

Hild. Good morrow, reuerend Knights, vnto you both.

Sir Ar. Father, how now? you heare how matters go;
I am vndone, my Childe is cast away.
You did your best, at least I thinke the best;
But we are all crost; flately, all is dasht.

Hild. Alas, good knights, how might the matter be?
Let mee vnderstand your greefe for Charity.

Sir Ar. Who does not vnderstand my griefes? Alas, alas!
And yet yee do not! Will the Church permit
A Nun in approbation of her habit
To be rauished?

Hild. A holy woman, benedicite!
Now God forfend that any should presume
To touch the sister of a holy house.

Sir Ar. Ihesus deliuer mee!

Sir Ra. Why, Millisent, the daughter of this Knight
Is out of Chesson taken the last night.

Hild. Was that faire maiden late become a Nun?

Sir Ra. Was she, quotha? Knauery, knauery, knauery; I smell it, I smell it, yfaith; is the wind in that dore? is it euen so? doost thou aske me that now?

Hild. It is the first time that I ere heard of it.

Sir Ar. That's very strange.

Sir Ra. Why, tell me, Frier, tell mee; thou art counted a holy man; doe not play the hypocrite with me, nor beare with mee. I

80 Sex. *Q 4–6* : Priest *Q 1–3*   Act V. Scene I. *WP*   *S. D.* Arthur . . Ralph *Q 6* : Raph . . Arthur *Q 1–5*   12 nay, nay *Q 1, 3* : nay *Q 2, 4–6*   14–15 *One line Qq*   17–18 *One line Qq*   29 foote *Q 4–6*   42 griefe *Q 3–6*   46–8 *Prose Q 1–5*   51 the *Q 1, 3* : this *Q 2, 4–6*   61 nor] now *conj. Col.*

cannot dissemble: did I ought but by thy own consent? by thy allowance? nay, further, by thy warrant?

Hild. Why, Reuerend knight—

Sir Ra. Vnreuerend Frier—

Hild. Nay, then giue me leaue, sir, to depart in quiet; I had hopd you had sent for mee to some other end.

Sir Ar. Nay, stay, good Frier; if any thing hath hapd
About this matter in thy loue to vs,
That thy strickt order cannot iustifie,
Admit it be so, we will couer it.
Take no care, man:
Disclayme not yet thy counsell and aduise,
The wisest man that is may be orereacht.

Hild. Sir Arthur, by my order and my faith,
I know not what you meane.

Sir Ra. By your order and your faith?
This is most strange of all: Why, tell mee, Frier,
Are not you Confessor to my Son Francke?

Hild. Yes, that I am.

Sir Ra. And did not this good knight here and my selfe
Confesse with you, being his ghostly Father,
To deale with him about th' unbanded marriage
Betwixt him and that faire young Millisent?

Hild. I neuer heard of any match intended.

Sir Ar. Did not we breake our minds that very time,
That our deuice of making her a Nun
Was but a colour and a very plotte
To put by young Mountchensey? Ist not true?

Hild. The more I striue to know what you should meane,
The lesse I vnderstand you.

Sir Rap. Did not you tell vs still how Peter Fabell
At length would crosse vs, if we tooke not heed?

Hild. I haue heard of one that is a great magician,
But hees about the Vniuersity.

Sir Rap. Did not you send your nouice Benedic
To perswade the girle to leaue Mountchenseys loue,
To crosse that Peter Fabell in his art,
And to that purpose made him visitor?

Hild. I neuer sent my nouice from the house,
Nor haue we made our visitation yet.

Sir Ar. Neuer sent him? Nay, did he not goe?
And did not I direct him to the house,
And conferre with him by the way? and did he not
Tell me what charge he had receiued from you,
Word by word, as I requested at your hands?

Hild. That you shall know; hee came along with me,
And stayes without. Come hither, Benedic!

Enter Benedic.

Yong Benedic, were you ere sent by me
To Chesson Nunnery for a visitor?

Ben. Neuer, sir, truely.

Sir Rap. Stranger then all the rest!

Sir Ar. Did not I direct you to the house? Confer with you
From Waltham Abby vnto Chesson wall?

Ben. I neuer saw you, sir, before this hower.

Sir Raph. The deuill thou didst not! Hoe, Chamberlen!

⟨*Enter Chamberlaine.*⟩

Chamb. Anon, anon.

Sir Ra. Call mine host Blague hither!

Cham. I will send one ouer to see if he be vp; I thinke he bee scarce stirring yet.

Sir Rap. Why, knaue, didst thou not tell me an hower ago, mine host was vp?

Cham. I, sir, my Master's vp.

Sir Ra. You knaue, is a vp, and is a not vp? Dost thou mocke mee?

Cham. I, sir, my M. is vp; but I thinke M. Blague indeed be not stirring.

Sir Rap. Why, who's thy Master? is not the Master of the house thy Master?

Cham. Yes, sir; but M. Blague dwells ouer the way.

Sir Ar. Is not this the George? Before God, theres some villany in this.

Cham. Sfoote, our signes remooud; this is strange! ⟨*Exeunt.*⟩

⟨Scene II. *The George Inn.*⟩

Enter Blague, trussing his points.

Bla. Chamberlen, speake vp to the new lodgings, bid Nell looke well to the bakt meats.

73 be] to be *Q 5, 6* 75 thy *Q 1–3*: my *Q 4–6* 79–81 *Two lines Qq*: *corr. WP* 79 Sir Ra. *Q 4–6*: Sir Ar. *Q 1–3* 85 unbanded] intended *WP* 89 of *Q 1, 3*: in *Q 2, 4–6* 94–5 *Prose Qq*: *corr. WP* 102 the *Q 1, 3*: my *Q 2, 4–6*

104–12 *Prose Q 1–5* 113–14 *Prefixes* Sir Rap., Sir Ar. *transposed Q 1–5* 114–15 *Three lines Qq, div. after* house, Abby: *corr. WP* *S. D. add. Q 4* 120 Cham. *Q 4, etc.*: Cla. *Q 1–3* one] once *Q 2* ouer] ouer sir *Q 4–6* 133 God] Ioue *Q 4–6* 135 Foote *Q 4–6* Exeunt *add. WP* Scene II. *WP* 1–6 *Verse Qq*: *corr. WP* 1 speake] speed *Haz.* 3 meat *Q 6*

⟨*Enter Sir Arthur and Sir Raph.*⟩

How now, my old Ienerts bauke my house, my castle? lie in Waltham all night, and not vnder the Canopie of your host Blagues house?

Sir Ar. Mine host, mine host, we lay all night at the George in Waltham; but whether the George be your fee-simple or no, tis a doubtfull question: looke vpon your signe.

Host. Body of Saint George, this is mine ouerthwart neighbour hath done this to seduce my blind customers. Ile tickle his Catastrophe for this; if I doe not indite him at next assisses for Burglary, let me die of the yellowes; for I see tis no boote in these dayes to serue the good Duke of Norfolke. The villanous world is turnd manger; one Iade deceiues another, and your Ostler playes his part commonly for the fourth share. Haue wee Comedies in hand, you whoreson, villanous male London letcher?

Sir Ar. Mine host, we haue had the moylingst night of it that euer we had in our liues.

Host. Ist certaine?

Sir Rap. We haue bin in the Forrest all night almost.

Host. S'foot, how did I misse you? hart, I was a stealing a Bucke there.

Sir Ar. A plague on you; we were stayed for you.

Host. Were you, my noble Romanes? Why, you shall share; the venison is a footing. *Sine Cerere & Baccho friget Venus*; That is, theres a good breakfast prouided for a marriage thats in my house this morning.

Sir Ar. A marriage, mine host?

Host. A coniunction copulatiue; a gallant match betweene your daughter and M. Raymond Mountchensey, yong Iuuentus.

Sir Ar. How?

Host. Tis firme, tis done. Weele shew you a president i'th ciuill law fort.

Sir Rap. How? married?

Host. Leaue trickes and admiration. Theres a cleanely paire of sheetes in the bed in Orchard chamber, and they shall lie there. What? Ile doe it; Ile serue the good Duke of Norfolke.

Sir Ar. Thou shalt repent this, Blague.

Sir Rap. If any law in England will make thee smart for this, expect it with all seuerity.

S. D. add. WP 4 jennet's back *Haz.* bauke *WP*: banke *Qq* house *St.*: horse *Qq* 10 doubtfull *om. Q 2, 4–6* 13–14 seduce . . for this *om. Q 5, 6* 29 Foote *Q 4–6* 30 a stealing *Q 1–3*: stealing of *Q 4–6* 39–72 *om. Walker* 47–8 bed in *Q 1*: bed on the *Q 2*: bed in the *Q 3–6* 49 I serue *Q 4–6*

Host. I renounce your defiance; if you parle so roughly, Ile barracado my gates against you. Stand faire, bully; Priest, come off from the rereward! What can you say now? Twas done in my house; I haue shelter i'th Court for't. D'yee see yon bay window? I serue the good duke of Norfolk, & tis his lodging. Storm, I care not, seruing the good Duke of Norfolk: thou art an actor in this, and thou shalt carry fire in thy face eternally.

Enter Smug, Mountchensey, Harry Clare, and Milliscent.

Smug. Fire, s'blood, theres no fire in England like your Trinidado sacke. Is any man heere humorous? We stole the venison, and weele iustifie it: say you now!

Host. In good sooth, Smug, theres more sacke on the fire, Smug.

Smu. I do not take any exceptions against your sacke; but if youle lend mee a picke staffe, ile cudgle them all hence, by this hand.

Host. I say thou shalt in to the Celler.

Sm. S'foot, mine Host, shalls not grapple? Pray, pray you; I could fight now for all the world like a Cockatrices ege; shals not serue the Duke of Norfolke? [*Exit.*

Host. In, skipper, in!

Sir Arth. Sirra, hath young Mountchensey married your sister?

Ha. Cla. Tis Certaine, Sir; her's the priest that coupled them, the parties ioyned, and the honest witnesse that cride Amen.

Mount. Sir Arthur Clare, my new created Father, I beseech you, heare mee.

Sir Ar. Sir, Sir, you are a foolish boy; you haue done that you cannot answere; I dare be bould to ceaze her from you; for shee's a profest Nun.

Mill. With pardon, sir, that name is quite vndone;
This true-loue knot cancelles both maid and Nun.
When first you told me I should act that part,
How cold and bloody it crept ore my hart!
To Chesson with a smiling brow I went;
But yet, deere sir, it was to this intent,
That my sweete Raymond might find better meanes
To steale me thence. In breefe, disguisd he came,
Like Nouice to old father Hildersham;
His tutor here did act that cunning part,

59 D'yee *Q 3*: Dee *Q 1*: Doe *Q 2*: Doe you *Q 4–6* yon *Q 3–6*: your *Q 1, 2* 64 s'blood] nouns *Q 4–6* 75 Pray] Pray you *Q 3* 84–5 *Verse WP* 88 her] on her *Q 5, 6*

And in our loue hath ioynd much wit to art.
Cla. Is't euen so?
Mill. With pardon therfore wee intreat your smiles;
Loue thwarted turnes itselfe to thousand wiles.
Cla. Young Maister Ierningham, were you an actor
In your owne loues abuse?
Ier. My thoughts, good sir,
Did labour seriously vnto this end,
To wrong my selfe, ere ide abuse my friend.

Host. He speakes like a Batchelor of musicke, all in Numbers. Knights, if I had knowne you would haue let this couy of Partridges sit thus long vpon their knees vnder my signe post, I would haue spred my dore with old Couerlids.

Sir Ar. Well, sir, for this your signe was remoued, was it?

Host. Faith, wee followed the directions of the deuill, Master Peter Fabell; and Smug, Lord blesse vs, could neuer stand vpright since.

Sir Ar. You, sir, twas you was his minister that married them?

Sir Io. Sir, to proue my selfe an honest man, being that I was last night in the forrest stealing Venison — now, sir, to haue you stand my friend, if that matter should bee calld in question, I married your daughter to this worthy gentleman.

Sir Ar. I may chaunce to requite you, and make your necke crack for't.

Sir Io. If you doe, I am as resolute as my Neighbour vicar of Waltham Abby; a hem, Grasse and hay, wee are all mortall; lets liue till we be hangd, mine host, and be merry, and theres an end.

⟨*Enter Fabel.*⟩

Fab. Now, knights, I enter; now my part begins.
To end this difference, know, at first I knew
What you intended, ere your loue tooke flight
From old Mountchensey; you, sir Arthur Clare,
Were minded to haue married this sweete beauty
To yong Franke Ierningham; to crosse which match,
I vsde some pretty sleights; but I protest
Such as but sate vpon the skirts of Art;
No coniurations, nor such weighty spells
As tie the soule to their performancy.
Theese for his loue, who once was my deere puple,
Haue I effected. Now, mee thinks, tis strange
That you, being old in wisedome, should thus knit
Your forehead on this match, since reason failes;
No law can curbe the louers rash attempt;
Yeares, in resisting this, are sadly spent.
Smile, then, vpon your daughter and kind sonne,
And let our toyle to future ages proue,
The deuill of Edmonton did good in Loue.
Sir Ar. Well, tis in vaine to crosse the prouidence:
Deere Sonne, I take thee vp into my hart;
Rise, daughter; this is a kind fathers part.

Host. Why, Sir Iohn, send for Spindles noyse presently: Ha, ert be night, Ile serue the good Duke of Norfolke.

Pri. Grasse and hay, mine Host, lets liue till we die, and be mery, and thers an end.

Sir Ar. What, is breakfast ready, mine Host?

Host. Tis, my little Hebrew.

Sir Ar. Sirra, ride strait to Chesson Nunry,
Fetch thence my Lady; the house, I know,
By this time misses their yong votary.
Come, knights, lets in!

Bil. I will to horse presentlye, sir. — A plague a my Lady, I shall misse a good breakfast. Smug, how chaunce you cut so plaguely behind, Smug?

Smu. Stand away; ile founder you else.

Bil. Farewell, Smug, thou art in another element.

Smu. I will be by and by; I will be Saint George againe.

Sir Ar. Take heed the fellow do not hurt himselfe.
Sir Rap. Did we not last night find two S. Georges here?
Fab. Yes, Knights, this martialist was one of them.
Cla. Then thus conclude your night of merriment! [*Exeunt Omnes.*

FINIS.

104-5 *Prose Q 1-5* 113 old *om. Q 4-6* 124 that] the *Q 4-6* 125 your] you *Q 1* 129-33 *Verse Qq* *S. D. om. Q 1-3* Fabel *Q 6* : Fabian *Q 4, 5*

156 Iohn *Haz.*: George *Qq* ? St. George : *cf. footnote to* 175 175 Saint *Q 4, etc.* : Sir *Q 1-3* 180 Y. Cla. *WP* (*wrong*)

A Pleaſant Commodie,

of faire *Em* the Millers daughter
of Manchester: VVith the loue of
William the Conqueror:

As it was ſundrie times publiquely acted in the
honourable citie of London, by the right honourable
the Lord Strange his ſeruaunts.

Imprinted at London for T. N. and I. VV.
and are to be ſolde in S. Dunſtones Church-
yarde in Fleete-ſtreete.

Q 1	= undated Quarto
Q 2	= Quarto of 1631
Chet.	= Chetwood, 1750
T	= Tyrrell, 1851
D	= Delius, 1874
Simp.	= Simpson, 1878
WP	= Warnke and Proescholdt, 1883
pr. ed.	= present editor

A PLEASANT COMMODIE OF

FAIRE EM

THE MILLERS DAVGHTER OF MANCHESTER

WITH THE LOVE OF WILLIAM THE CONQVEROVR

⟨Dramatis Personae.

WILLIAM *the Conqueror.*
ZWENO, *King of* Denmark.
Duke DIROT.
Marquis of Lubeck.
MOUNTNEY.
MANVILLE.
ROZILIO.
DIMARCH.
Danish *Embassador.*
The Miller of Manchester.
TROTTER, *his Man.*
Citizen of Chester.

BLANCH, *Princess of* Denmark.
MARIANA, *Princess of* Suethia.
Fair EM, *the Miller's Daughter.*
ELINER, *the Citizen's Daughter.*
English *and* Danish *Nobles.*
Soldiers, Countrymen, and Attendants.⟩ [1]

Actus Primus. Scaena Prima.

⟨*Windsor. A State Apartment.*⟩

Enter William the Conqueror; Marques Lubeck, with a picture; Mountney; Manuile; Valingford; and Duke Dirot.

Marques. What meanes faire Britaines mighty Conqueror
So suddenly to cast away his staffe,
And all in passion to forsake the tylt?

D. Dirot. My Lord, this triumph we solemnise here
Is of meere loue to your increasing ioyes,
Only expecting cheerefull lookes for all;
What sudden pangs than moues your maiestie
To dimme the brightnes of the day with frownes?

W. Conqueror. Ah, good my Lords, misconster not the cause;
At least, suspect not my displeased browes:
I amorously do beare to your intent,
For thanks and all that you can wish I yeeld.
But that which makes me blush and shame to tell
Is cause why thus I turne my conquering eyes
To cowardes lookes and beaten fantasies.

Mountney. Since wee are giltlesse, wee the lesse dismay
To see this sudden change possesse your cheere,
For if it issue from your owne conceits
Bred by suggestion of some enuious thoughts,
Your highnes wisdome may suppresse it straight.
Yet tell vs, good my Lord, what thought it is
That thus bereaues you of your late content,
That in aduise we may assist your grace,
Or bend our forces to reuiue your spirits.

W. Con. Ah, Marques Lubeck, in thy power it lyes
To rid my bosome of these thraled dumps:
And therefore, good my Lords, forbeare a while
That we may parley of these priuate cares,
Whose strength subdues me more than all the world.

Valingford. We goe and wishe thee priuate conference
Publicke affectes in this accustomed peace.

[*Exit all but* William *and the* Marques.

William. Now, Marques, must a Conquerer at armes
Disclose himselfe thrald to vnarmed thoughts,
And, threatned of a shaddowe, yeeld to lust.
No sooner had my sparkeling eyes beheld
The flames of beautie blasing on this peece,
But sodenly a sence of myracle,
Imagined on thy louely Maistres face,
Made me abandon bodily regarde,
And cast all pleasures on my woonded soule:
Then, gentle Marques, tell me what she is,
That thus thou honourest on thy warlike shield;
And if thy loue and interest be such
As iustly may giue place to myne,
That if it be, my soule with honors wings
May fly into the bosome of my deere;

[1] *Add. Chet.* *S. D.* Windsor . . Apartment *add. pr. ed.* 15 coward *D*

30 thee (=the) *Qq*: this *D*: the *conj. Simp.* 31 effects *D*

Yf not, close them, and stoope into my graue!
Marques. Yf this be all, renowned Conquerer,
Aduance your drooping spirites, and reuiue
The wonted courage of your Conquering minde;
For this faire picture painted on my shield
Is the true counterfeit of louelie Blaunch,
Princes and daughter to the King of Danes,
Whose beautie and excesse of ornamentes
Deserues another manner of defence,
Pompe and high person to attend her state
Then Marques Lubeck any way presents.
Therefore her vertues I resigne to thee,
Alreadie shrinde in thy religious brest,
To be aduaunced and honoured to the full;
Nor beare I this an argument of loue,
But to renowne faire Blaunch, my Soueraignes child
In euerie place where I by armes may do it.
William. Ah, Marques, thy wordes bring heauen vnto my soule,
And had I heauen to giue for thy reward,
Thou shouldst be thronde in no vnworthie place.
But let my vttermost wealth suffice thy worth,
Which here I vowe; and to aspire the blisse
That hangs on quicke atchiuement of my loue,
Thy selfe and I will traueile in disguise,
To bring this Ladie to our Brittaine Court.
Marques. Let William but bethinke what may auayle,
And let me die if I denie my ayde.
William. Then thus: The Duke Dirot, and Therle Dima⟨r⟩ch,
Will I leaue substitutes to rule my Realme,
While mightie loue forbids my being here;
And in the name of Sir Robert of Windsor
Will goe with thee vnto the Danish Court.
Keepe Williams secretes, Marques, if thou loue him.
Bright Blaunch, I come! sweete fortune, fauour me,
And I will laud thy name eternally.
[*Exeunt.*

⟨SCENE II.⟩

⟨*Manchester. The Interior of a Mill.*⟩

Enter the Miller *and* Em, *his daughter.*

Miller. Come, daughter, we must learne to shake of pomp,
To leaue the state that earst beseemd a Knight
And gentleman of no meane discent,
To vndertake this homelie millers trade:
Thus must we maske to saue our wretched liues,
Threatned by Conquest of this haplesse Yle,
Whose sad inuasions by the Conqueror
Haue made a number such as we subiect
Their gentle neckes vnto their stubborne yoke
Of drudging labour and base pesantrie.
Sir Thomas Godard now old Goddard is,
Goddard the miller of faire Manchester.
Why should not I content me with this state,
As good Sir Edmund Trofferd did the flaile?
And thou, sweete Em, must stoope to high estate
To ioyne with mine that thus we may protect
Our harmles liues, which, ledd in greater port,
Would be an enuious obiect to our foes,
That seeke to roote all Britaines Gentrie
From bearing countenance against their tyrannie.
Em. Good Father, let my full resolued thoughts
With setled patiens to support this chaunce
Be some poore comfort to your aged soule;
For therein restes the height of my estate,
That you are pleased with this deiection,
And that all toyles my hands may vndertake
May serue to worke your worthines content.
Miller. Thankes, my deere Daughter. These thy plesant words
Transferre my soule into a second heauen:
And in thy setled minde my ioyes consist,
My state reuyued, and I in former plight.
Although our outward pomp be thus abased,
And thralde to drudging, staylesse of the world,
Let vs retaine those honorable mindes
That lately gouerned our superior state,
Wherein true gentrie is the only meane
That makes vs differ from base millers borne.
Though we expect no knightly delicates,
Nor thirst in soule for former soueraintie,
Yet may our myndes as highly scorne to stoope
To base desires of vulgars worldlynes,
As if we were in our presedent way.
And, louely daughter, since thy youthfull yeares
Must needes admit as yong affections,
And that sweete loue vnpartiall perceiues
Her daintie subiects through euery part,
In chiefe receiue these lessons from my lippes,
The true discouerers of a Virgins due,
Now requisite, now that I know thy mynde
Somthing enclynde to fauour Manuils sute,
A gentleman, thy Louer in protest;
And that thou maist not be by loue deceiued,
But trye his meaning fit for thy desert,

74 th'erle Demarch *WP* Scene II. *add. T* *S. D.* Manchester . . Mill *add. pr. ed.* 3 no] not a *conj. Simp.* 9 their] the *D* 15 to high *Qq*: from high *T*: thy high *D*: to like *Simp.* 35 Thar *Q 1* 41 vulgar *Chet.* 44 as] of *Chet.*

In pursuite of all amorous desires,
Regard thine honour. Let not vehement sighes,
Nor earnest vowes importing feruent loue,
Render thee subiect to the wrath of lust:
For that, transformed to form of sweete delight,
Will bring thy bodie and thy soule to shame.
Chaste thoughts and modest conuersations,
Of proofe to keepe out all inchaunting vowes,
Vaine sighes, forst teares, and pittifull aspectes,
Are they that make deformed Ladies faire,
Poore ritch: and such intycing men,
That seeke of all but onely present grace,
Shall in perseuerance of a Virgins due
Prefer the most refusers to the choyce
Of such a soule as yeelded what they thought.
But hoe: where is Trotter?

[*Here enters* Trotter, *the Millers man, to them: And they within call to him for their gryste.*

Trotter. Wheres Trotter? why, Trotter is here. Yfaith, you and your daughter go vp and downe weeping and wamenting, and keeping of a wamentation, as who should saye, the Mill would go with your wamenting.

Miller. How now, Trotter? why complainest thou so?

Trotter. Why, yonder is a company of yong men and maydes, keepe such a styr for their grist, that they would haue it before my stones be readie to grinde it. But, yfaith, I would I coulde breake winde enough backward: you should not tarrie for your gryst, I warrant you.

Miller. Content thee, Trotter, I will go pacifie them.

Trotter. Iwis you will when I cannot. Why, looke, you haue a Mill—Why, whats your Mill without mee? Or rather, Mistres, what were I without you?

[*Here he taketh* Em *about the neck.*

Em. Nay, Trotter, if you fall achyding, I will giue you ouer.

Trotter. I chyde you, dame, to amend you. You are too fyne to be a Millers daughter; for if you should but stoope to take vp the tole dish, you will haue the crampe in your finger at least ten weekes after.

Miller. Ah, well said, Trotter; teach her to plaie the good huswife, and thou shalt haue her to thy wife, if thou canst get her good will.

Trotter. Ah, words wherein I see Matrimonie come loaden with kisses to salute me! Now let me alone to pick the Mill, to fill the hopper, to take the tole, to mend the sayles, yea, and to make the mill to goe with the verie force of my loue.

[*Here they must call for their gryst within.*

Trotter. I come, I come; yfaith, now you shall haue your gryst, or else Trotter will trot and amble himselfe to death.

[*They call him againe. Exit.*

⟨Scene III.

The Danish Court.⟩

Enter king of Denmarke, *with some attendants,* Blanch *his daughter,* Mariana, Marques Lubeck, William *disguised.*

King of Denmarke. Lord Marques *Lubecke,* welcome home.
Welcome, braue Knight, vnto the *Denmarke* King,
For Williams sake, the noble *Norman* Duke,
So famous for his fortunes and successe,
That graceth him with name of Conqueror:
Right double welcome must thou be to vs.

Rob. Windsor. And to my Lord the king shall I recount
Your graces courteous entertainment,
That for his sake vouchsafe to honor me,
A simple Knight attendant on his grace.

King Den. But saie, Sir Knight, what may I call your name?

Robert Windsor. Robert Windsor, and like your Maiestie.

King Den. I tell thee, *Robert,* I so admire the man
As that I count it haynous guilt in him
That honors not Duke *William* with his heart.
Blanch, bid this straunger welcome, good my gyrle.

Blanch. Sir,
Should I neglect your highnes charge herein,
It might be thought of base discourtesie.
Welcome, Sir Knight, to Denmarke, hartelie.

Ro. Winds. Thanks, gentle Ladie. Lord Marques, what is shee?

Lubeck. That same is Blanch, daughter to the King,
The substance of the shadow that you saw.

Rob. Windsor. May this be shee, for whome I crost the Seas?
I am ashamde to think I was so fond.
In whom thers nothing that contents my mynd:
Ill head, worse featurde, vncomly, nothing courtly;

58 form of *conj. Simp.*: former *Qq*   64 ritch *pr. ed.*: wretch *Qq, etc.*: ones rich *conj. Simp.*   68 thought] sought *conj. Simp.*   70–4 *Printed as verse in Qq, the lines ending* here, weeping, wamentation, wamenting   77–82 *Verse in Q 1: so lines* 85–8, 91–5, 99–107 *in Qq*   88 *S. D. printed on margin and partly missing Qq*

Scene III, *etc. add. T*   17–18 *One line Qq*

Swart and ill fauoured, a Colliers sanguin skinne.
I neuer sawe a harder fauourd slut.
Loue her? for what? I can no whit abide her.

King of Denmark. *Mariana,* I haue this day receiued letters
From *Swethia,* that lets me vnderstand
Your raunsome is collecting there with speede,
And shortly shalbe hither sent to vs.

Mariana. Not that I finde occasion of mislike
My entertainment in your graces court,
But that I long to see my natiue home—

King Den. And reason haue you, Madam, for the same.
Lord *Marques,* I commit vnto your charge
The entertainement of Sir *Robert* here;
Let him remaine with you within the Court,
In solace and disport to spend the time.

Robert Wind. I thank your highnes, whose bounden I remaine.

[*Exit king of Denmarke.*

Blanch speaketh this secretly at one end of the stage. Vnhappie Blanch, what strange effects are these
That workes within my thoughts confusedly?
That still, me thinks, affection drawes me on,
To take, to like, nay more, to loue this Knight?

Robert Wind. A modest countenance; no heauie sullen looke;
Not verie fayer, but ritchly deckt with fauour;
A sweete face, an exceding daintie hand;
A bodie were it framed of wax
By all the cunning artists of the world,
It could not better be proportioned.

Lubeck. How now, Sir *Robert*? in a studie, man?
Here is no tyme for contemplation.

Robert Windsor. My Lord, there is a certaine odd conceite,
Which on the sudden greatly troubles me.

Lubeck. How like you *Blaunch*? I partly do perceiue
The little boy hath played the wagg with you.

Sir Robert. The more I looke the more I loue to looke.
Who seyes that Mariana is not faire?
Ile gage my gauntlet gainst the enuious man
That dares auowe there liueth her compare.

Lubeck. Sir *Robert,* you mistake your counterfeit.
This is the Ladie which you came to see.

Sir Robert. Yea, my Lord: Shee is counterfait in deede,
For there is the substance that best contents me.

Lubek. That is my loue. Sir *Robert,* you do wrong me.

Robert. The better for you, sir, she is your Loue—
As for the wrong, I see not how it growes.

Lubeck. In seeking that which is anothers right.

Robert. As who should saie your loue were priuileged,
That none might looke vpon her but your selfe.

Lubeck. These iarres becomes not our familiaritie,
Nor will I stand on termes to moue your patience.

Robert. Why, my Lord, am
Not I of flesh and bloud as well as you?
Then giue me leaue to loue as well as you.

Lubeck. To Loue, Sir Robert? but whome? not she I Loue?
Nor stands it with the honor of my state
To brooke corriuals with me in my loue.

Robert. So, Sir, we are thorough for that L⟨ady⟩.
Ladies, farewell. Lord *Marques,* will you go?
I will finde a time to speake with her, I trowe.

Lubeck. With all my heart. Come, Ladies, wil you walk? [*Exit.*

⟨SCENE IV.

The English Court.⟩

Enter Manuile alone, disguised.

Manuile. Ah, *Em*! the subiect of my restlesse thoughts,
The Anuyle whereupon my heart doth be
Framing thy state to thy desert—
Full yll this life becomes thy heauenly looke,
Wherein sweete loue and vertue sits enthroned.
Bad world, where riches is esteemd aboue them both,
In whose base eyes nought else is bountifull!
A Millers daughter, sayes the multitude,
Should not be loued of a Gentleman.
But let them breath their soules into the ayre,
Yet will I still affect thee as my selfe,
So thou be constant in thy plighted vowe.
But here comes one—I wil listen to his talke.

[*Manuile staies, hiding himselfe.*

[*Enter Valingford at another dore, disguised.*

Valingford. Goe, *William Conqueror,* and seeke thy loue.

35 to mislike 43 hightnes *Q 1* *S. D. after* 42 *Q q*

67 best contents me] contents me best *WP* 76–7 *One line Qq* Scene IV. *etc. add.* T 13 *S. D. incomplete in Q 1 because printed too near the margin of the page: Copy in Bodl. contains only* Man . . hidin . . selfe

Seeke thou a mynion in a forren land,
Whilest I drawe back and court my loue at home.
The millers daughter of faire Manchester
Hath bound my feete to this delightsome soyle,
And from her eyes do dart such golden beames
That holdes my harte in her subiection.

Manuile. He ruminates on my beloued choyce:
God graunt he come not to preuent my hope.
But heres another, him yle listen to.

[*Enter Mountney, disguised, at another dore.*

L. Mountney. Nature vniust, in vtterance of thy arte,
To grace a pesant with a Princes fame!
Pesant am I, so to misterme my loue:
Although a millers daughter by her birth,
Yet may her beautie and her vertues well suffice
To hyde the blemish of her birth in hell,
Where neither enuious eyes nor thought can perce,
But endlesse darknesse euer smother it.
Goe, *William Conqueror,* and seeke thy loue,
Whilest I drawe back and court mine owne the while,
Decking her bodie with such costly robes
As may become her beauties worthynes;
That so thy labors may be laughed to scorne,
And she thou seekest in forraine regions
Be darkened and eclipst when she arriues
By one that I haue chosen neerer home.

Manuile. What! comes he to, to intercept my loue?
Then hye thee *Manuile* to forestall such foes.
[*Exit Manuile.*

Mountney. What now, Lord *Valingford,* are you behind?
The king had chosen you to goe with him.

Valingford. So chose he you, therefore I marueile much
That both of vs should linger in this sort.
What may the king imagine of our staye?

Mountney. The king may iustly think we are to blame:
But I immagined I might well be spared,
And that no other man had borne my mind.

Valingford. The like did I: in frendship then resolue
What is the cause of your vnlookt for stay?

Mountney. Lord Valingford, I tell thee as a friend,
Loue is the cause why I haue stayed behind.

Valinford. Loue, my Lord? of whome?

Mountney. Em, the millers daughter of Manchester.

Valingford. But may this be?

Mountney. Why not, my Lord? I hope full well you know
That loue respectes no difference of state,
So beautie serue to stirr affection.

Valingford. But this it is that makes me wonder most:
That you and I should be of one conseite
In such a straunge vnlikly passion.

Mountney. But is that true? My Lord, I hope you do but iest.

Valingford. I would I did; then were my griefe the lesse.

Mountney. Nay, neuer grieue; for if the cause be such
To ioyne our thoughts in such a Simpathy,
All enuie set asyde, let vs agree
To yeeld to eythers fortune in this choyce.

Valingford. Content, say I: and what so ere befall,
Shake hands, my Lord, and fortune thriue at all.
[*Exeunt.*

⟨ACT II.

Scene I. *Manchester. The Mill.*⟩

Enter Em *and* Trotter, *the Millers man, with a kerchife on his head, and an Vrinall in his hand.*

Em. *Trotter,* where haue you beene?

Trotter. Where haue I bene? why, what signifies this?

Em. A kerchiefe, doth it not?

Trotter. What call you this, I praye?

Em. I saie it is an Vrinall.

Trotter. Then this is mystically to giue you to vnderstand, I haue beene at the Phismicaries house.

Em. How long hast thou beene sicke?

Trotter. Yfaith, euen as long as I haue not beene halfe well, and that hath beene a long time.

Em. A loytering time, I rather immagine.

Trot. It may be so: but the Phismicary tels me that you can help me.

Em. Why, any thing I can do for recouerie of thy health be right well assured of.

Trot. Then giue me your hand.

Em. To what end?

Trotter. That the ending of an old indenture is the beginning of a new bargaine.

Em. What bargaine?

55 Of Em *WP* 70 o'er all *conj. Simp.* Act II, Scene I. *D*: Scene V. *T*

Trot. That you promised to do any thing to recouer my helth.

Em. On that condition I giue thee my hand.

Trot. Ah, sweete *Em*!

[*Here he offers to kisse her.*

Em. How now, *Trotter*! your maisters daughter?

Trot. Yfaith, I aime at the fairest.
Ah, *Em*, sweet *Em*!
Fresh as the flowre,
That hath poure
To wound my harte,
And ease my smart,
Of me, poore theefe,
In prisón bounde—

Em. So all your ryme
Lies on the grounde.
But what meanes this?

Trot. Ah, marke the deuise—
For thee, my loue,
Full sicke I was,
In hazard of my life.
Thy promise was
To make me whole,
And for to be my wife.
Let me inioye
My loue, my deere,
And thou possesse
Thy *Trotter* here.

Em. But I meant no such matter.

Trot. Yes, woos, but you did. Ile goe to our Parson, Sir John, and he shall mumble vp the marriage out of hand.

Em. But here comes one that will forbid the Banes. [*Here enters Manuile to them.*

Trotter. Ah, Sir, you come too late.

Manuile. What remedie, *Trotter*?

Em. Goe, *Trotter*, my father calles.

Trotter. Would you haue me goe in, and leaue you two here?

Em. Why, darest thou not trust me?

Trotter. Yes, faith, euen as long as I see you.

Em. Goe thy waies, I praye thee hartely.

Trotter. That same word (hartely) is of great force. I will goe. But I praye, sir, beware you come not too neere the wench.

[*Exit Trotter.*

Manuile. I am greatly beholding to you.
Ah, Maistres, somtime I might haue said, my loue,
But time and fortune hath bereued me of that,
And I, an abiect in those gratious eyes,
That with remorse earst sawe into my griefe,
May sit and sigh the sorowes of my heart.

Em. In deede my *Manuile* hath some cause to doubt,
When such a Swaine is riuall in his loue!

Manuile. Ah, *Em*, were he the man that causeth this mistrust,
I should esteeme of thee as at the first.

Em. But is my loue in earnest all this while?

Manuile. Beleeue me, *Em*, it is not time to iest,
When others ioyes, what lately I possest.

Em. If touching loue my *Manuile* charge me thus,
Vnkindly must I take it at his handes,
For that my conscience cleeres me of offence.

Manuile. Ah, impudent and shamelesse in thy ill,
That with thy cunning and defraudfull toung
Seekes to delude the honest meaning minde!
Was neuer heard in *Manchester* before
Of truer loue then hath beene betwixte vs twaine:
And for my parte how I haue hazarded
Displeasure of my father and my freindes,
Thy selfe can witnes. Yet notwithstanding this,
Two gentlemen attending on *Duke William*,
Mountney and *Valingford*, as I heard them named,
Oft times resort to see and to be seene
Walking the streete fast by thy fathers dore,
Whose glauncing eyes vp to the windowes cast
Giues testies of their Maisters amorous hart.
This, *Em*, is noted and too much talked on,
Some see it without mistrust of ill—
Others there are that, scorning, grynne thereat,
And saith, 'There goes the millers daughters wooers'.
Ah me, whome chiefely and most of all it doth concerne,
To spend my time in griefe and vexe my soule,
To thinke my loue should be rewarded thus,
And for thy sake abhore all womenkind!

Em. May not a maide looke vpon a man
Without suspitious iudgement of the world?

Manuile. If sight do moue offence, it is the better not to see.
But thou didst more, vnconstant as thou art,
For with them thou hadst talke and conference.

31–40 *Six lines Qq, ending* fairest, flowre, harte, theefe, bound, ground 34 the power *Simp.* : the poure *WP* 43–52 *Four lines Qq, ending* life, wife, deere, here 50 Thy loue *WP*

74 I am *Qq* : I, an *Simp.* 89 seekese *Q 1* 91 true louer *Q 1* 95 genlemen *Q 1* 111 it is the] 'tis *conj. Simp.* : 'tis th' *WP*

Em. May not a maide talke with a man without mistrust?
Manuile. Not with such men suspected amorous.
Em. I grieue to see my *Manuiles* ielosie.
Manuile. Ah, *Em*, faithfull loue is full of ielosie.
So did I loue thee true and faithfully,
For which I am rewarded most vnthankfully.
[*Exit in a rage. Manet Em.*
⟨*Em.*⟩ And so awaie? What, in displeasure gone,
And left me such a bitter sweete to gnawe vpon?
Ah, *Manuile*, little wottest thou
How neere this parting goeth to my heart.
Vncourteous loue, whose followers reapes reward
Of hate, disdaine, reproach and infamie,
The fruit of frantike, bedlome ielozie!
[*Here enter Mountney to Em.*
But here comes one of these suspitious men:
Witnes, my God, without desert of me,
For onely *Manuile*, honor I in harte,
Nor shall vnkindnes cause me from him to starte.
Mountney. For this good fortune, Venus, be thou blest,
To meete my loue, the mistres of my heart,
Where time and place giues oportunitie
At full to let her vnderstand my loue.
[*He turnes to Em & offers to take her by the hand, & shee goes from him.*
Faire mistres, since my fortune sorts so well,
Heare you a word. What meaneth this?
Nay, stay, faire *Em*.
Em. I am going homewards, syr.
Mountney. Yet stay, sweete loue, to whom I must disclose
The hidden secrets of a louers thoughts,
Not doubting but to finde such kinde remorse
As naturally you are enclyned to.
Em. The Gentle-man, your friend, Syr,
I haue not seene him this foure dayes at the least.
Mountney. Whats that to me?
I speak not, sweete, in person of my friend,
But for my selfe, whom, if that loue deserue
To haue regard, being honourable loue,
Not base affects of loose lasciuious loue,
Whome youthfull wantons play and dally with,
But that vnites in honourable bands of holy rytes,
And knits the sacred knot that Gods—
[*Here Em cuts him off.*
Em. What meane you, sir, to keepe me here so long?
I cannot vnderstand you by your sygnes;
You keepe a pratling with your lippes,
But neuer a word you speake that I can heare.
Mountney. What, is shee deafe? a great impediment.
Yet remedies there are for such defects.
Sweete *Em*, it is no little griefe to mee,
To see, where nature in her pryde of art
Hath wrought perfections ritch and admirable—
Em. Speake you to mee, Sir?
Mountney. To thee, my onely ioy.
Em. I cannot heare you.
Mountney. Oh, plague of Fortune! Oh, hell without compare!
What bootes it vs to gaze and not enioy?
Em. Fare you well, Sir.
[*Exit Em. Manet Mountney.*
Mountney. Fare well, my loue. Nay, farewell life and all!
Could I procure redresse for this infirmitie,
It might be meanes shee would regard my sute.
I am acquainted with the Kings Phisitions,
Amongst the which theres one mine honest friend,
Seignior Alberto, a verie learned man.
His iudgement will I haue to help this ill.
Ah, *Em*, faire *Em*, if Art can make thee whole,
Ile buy that sence for thee, although it cost mee deere.
But, *Mountney*, stay: this may be but deceit,
A matter fained onely to delude thee,
And, not vnlike, perhaps by *Valingford*.
He loues faire *Em* as well as I—
As well as I? ah, no, not halfe so well.
Put case: yet may he be thine enimie,
And giue her counsell to dissemble thus.
Ile try the euent and if it fall out so,
Frindship, farewell: Loue makes me now a foe.
[*Exit Mountney.*

⟨SCENE II.

An Ante-Chamber at the Danish Court.⟩

Enter Marques Lubeck and Mariana.

Mariana. Trust me, my Lord, I am sorie for your hurt.
Lubeck. Gramercie, Madam; but it is not great:
Onely a thrust, prickt with a Rapiers point.
Mariana. How grew the quarrel, my Lord?
Lubeck. Sweet Ladie, for thy sake. There

120 *Prefix om. Qq*   144–5 *One line Q 1*   150 honourable *om. WP*

172 haue] crave *conj. Simp.*   Scene II. *D*: Act II. Scene I. *T*   5–22 *Verse Qq*

was this last night two maskes in one company, my selfe the formost. The other strangers were: amongst the which, when the Musick began to sound the Measures, eche Masker made choice of his Ladie; and one, more forward than the rest, stept towards thee, which I perceiuing, thrust him aside, and tooke thee my selfe. But this was taken in so ill parte that at my comming out of the court gate, with iustling togither, it was my chaunce to be thrust into the arme. The doer thereof, because he was the originall cause of the disorder at that inconuenient time, was presently committed, and is this morning sent for to aunswer the matter. And I think here he comes.

[*Here enters Sir* Robert of Windsor *with a Gaylor.*

What, Sir *Robert* of *Windsor,* how now?

Sir Robert. Yfaith, my Lord, a prisoner: but what ayles your arme?

Lubeck. Hurte the last night by mischaunce.

Sir Robert. What, not in the maske at the Court gate?

Lubeck. Yes, trust me, there.

Sir Rob. Why then, my Lorde, I thank you for my nights lodging.

Lubeck. And I you for my hurt, if it were so. Keeper, awaie, I discharge you of your prisoner. [*Exit the Keeper.*

Sir Robert. Lord *Marques,* you offerd me disgrace to shoulder me.

Lubeck. Sir, I knew you not, and therefore you must pardon me, and the rather it might be alleaged to me of meare simplisitie to see another daunce with my Maistris, disguysed, and I my selfe in presence. But seeing it was our happs to damnifie each other vnwillingly, let vs be content with our harmes, and laye the fault where it was, and so become friendes.

Sir Robert. Yfaith, I am content with my nights lodging, if you be content with your hurt.

Lubeck. Not content that I haue it, but content to forget how I came by it.

Sir Robert. My Lord, here comes Ladie *Blaunch,* lets away. [*Enter Blaunch.*

Lubeck. With good will. Ladie, you will staie? [*Exit Lubeck and Sir Robert.*

Mariana. Madam—

Blaunch. Mariana, as I am grieued with thy presence: so am I not offended for thy absence; and were it not a breach to modestie, thou shouldest know before I left thee.

Mariana. How neare is this humor to madnesse! If you hould on as you begyn, you are in a pretie waie to scoulding.

Blaunch. To scoulding, huswife?

Mariana. Maddam, here comes one.

[*Here enters one with a letter.*

Blaunch. There doth in deed. Fellow, wouldest thou haue any thing with any bodie here?

Messenger. I haue a letter to deliuer to the Ladie *Mariana.*

Blaunch. Giue it me.

Messen. There must none but shee haue it.

Blaunch snatcheth the letter from him. Et exit messenger. Go to, foolish fellow. And therefore, to ease the anger I sustaine, Ile be so bolde to open it. Whats here? Sir *Robert* greets you well? You, Maistries, his loue, his life? Oh amorous man, how he entertaines his new Maistres; and bestowes on Lubeck, his od friend, a horne night capp to keepe in his witt.

Mariana. Maddam, though you haue discourteously redd my letter, yet I praye you giue it me.

Blaunch. Then take it: there, and there, and there! [*She teares it. Et exit Blaunch.*

Mariana. How farr doth this differ from modestie! Yet will I gather vp the peeces, which happelie may shew to me the intent thereof, though not the meaning.

[*She gathers vpp the peeces and ioynes them.*

'Your seruant and loue, sir *Robert* of *Windsor, Alias William* the *Conqueror,* wisheth long health and happinesse'. Is this *William* the *Conqueror,* shrouded vnder the name of sir *Robert* of *Windsor?* Were he the Monarch of the world he should not disposesse *Lubeck* of his Loue. Therefore I will to the Court, and there, if I can, close to be friendes with Ladie *Blaunch;* and thereby keepe *Lubeck,* my Loue, for my selfe, and further the Ladie *Blaunch* in her sute, as much as I may. [*Exit.*

⟨Scene III.

Manchester. The Mill.⟩

Enter Em sola.

Em. Ielosie, that sharpes the louers sight,
And makes him conceiue and conster his intent,
Hath so bewitched my louely *Manuils* sences
That he misdoubts his *Em,* that loues his soule;

21 *S.D. Partly wanting Qq* 31-49 *Verse Qq* 60 If yon *Q 1* 71-98 *Verse Qq* 74 Your Maistries *Qq* 77 old *Chet.* 88 *Q 1 repeats the prefix* Mariana *before this line* 89 Alius *Qq* Scene III. *D*: Scene II. *T* *S.D.* solus *Qq*

He doth suspect corriuals in his loue,
Which, how vntrue it is, be iudge, my God!
But now no more—Here commeth *Valingford;*
Shift him off now, as thou hast done the other.

Enter Valingford.

Valingf. See how Fortune presents me with the hope I lookt for. Faire Em!

Em. Who is that?

Valingf. I am *Valingford,* thy loue and friend.

Em. I cry you mercie, Sir; I thought so by your speach.

Valingf. What ayleth thy eyes?

Em. Oh blinde, Sir, blinde, striken blind, by mishap, on a sudden.

Valingf. But is it possible you should be taken on such a suddain? Infortunate *Valingford,* to be thus crost in thy loue! Faire *Em,* I am not a little sorie to see this thy hard hap. Yet neuerthelesse, I am acquainted with a learned Phisitian that will do any thing for thee at my request. To him will I resort, and enquire his iudgement, as concerning the recouerie of so excellent a sence.

Em. Oh Lord, Sir: and of all things I cannot abide Phisicke, the verie name thereof to me is odious.

Valingford. No? not the thing will doe thee so much good? Sweete *Em,* hether I came to parley of loue, hoping to haue found thee in thy woonted prosperitie; and haue the gods so vnmercifully thwarted my expectation, by dealing so sinisterly with thee, sweete *Em*?

Em. Good sir, no more, it fits not me
To haue respect to such vaine fantasies
As idle loue presentes my eares withall.
More reason I should ghostlie giue my selfe
To sacred prayers for this my former sinne,
For which this plague is iustly fallen vpon me,
Then to harken to the vanities of loue.

Valingford. Yet, sweet *Em,*
Accept this iewell at my hand, which I
Bestowe on thee in token of my loue.

Em. A iewell, sir! what pleasure can I haue
In iewels, treasure, or any worldly thing
That want my sight that should deserne thereof?
Ah, sir, I must leaue you:
The paine of mine eyes is so extreame,
I cannot long staie in a place. I take my leaue. [*Exit Em.*

Valingford. Zoundes, what a crosse is this to my conceite! But, *Valingford,* serch the depth of this deuise. Why may not this be fained subteltie, by *Mountneies* inuention, to the intent that I seeing such occasion should leaue off my sute and not any more persiste to solicite her of loue? Ile trie the euent; if I can by any meanes perceaue the effect of this deceyte to be procured by his meanes, freind *Mountney,* the one of vs is like to repent our bargeine. [*Exit.*

⟨ACT III.

Scene I. *The Danish Court.*⟩

Enter Mariana and Marques Lubeck.

Lubeck. Ladie,
Since that occasion, forward in our good,
Presenteth place and opportunitie,
Let me intreat your woonted kind consent
And freindly furtherance in a suite I haue.

Mariana. My Lord, you know you neede not to intreat,
But may commaund *Mariana* to her power,
Be it no impeachment to my honest fame.

Lubeck. Free are my thoughts from such base villanie
As may in question, Ladie, call your name:
Yet is the matter of such consequence,
Standing vpon my honorable credit,
To be effected with such zeale and secresie
As, should I speake and faile my expectation,
It would redound greatly to my preiudice.

Mariana. My Lord, wherein hath *Mariana* giuen you
Occasion that you should mistrust, or else
Be ielous of my secrecie?

Lubeck. *Mariana,* do not misconster of me:
I not mistrust thee, nor thy secresie;
Nor let my loue misconster my intente,
Nor think thereof but well and honorable.
Thus stands the case:
Thou knowest from England hether came with me
Robert of Windsor, a noble man at Armes,
Lustie and valiant, in spring time of his yeares:
No maruell then though he proue amorous.

Mariana. True, my Lord, he came to see faire *Blanch.*

Lubeck. No, *Mariana,* that is not it. His loue to *Blanch*
Was then extinct, when first he sawe thy face.
'Tis thee he loues; yea, thou art onely shee
That is maistres and commaunder of his thoughts.

16 thine *Q 2*   19–36 *Verse Qq*   44–6 *Two lines Qq, ending* hand, loue   53–63 *Verse Qq*

Act III, Scene I. *D*: Scene III. *T*   1–2 *One line Qq*: *div. D*   15 I would *Q 1*   16–18 *Two lines Qq, div. after* occasion: *div. after* Mariana, mistrust *D*   29–30 *Three lines Qq, ending* it, extinct, face   29 not] non *Q 1*   Blnnch *Q 1*

Mariana. Well, well, my Lord, I like you, for such driftes
Put silly Ladies often to their shiftes.
Oft haue I heard you saye you loued me well,
Yea, sworne the same, and I beleeued you to.
Can this be found an action of good faith
Thus to dissemble where you found true loue?
Lubeck. *Mariana,* I not dissemble, on mine honour,
Nor failes my faith to thee. But for my friend,
For princely William, by whom thou shalt possesse
The tytle of estate and Maiestie,
Fitting thy loue, and vertues of thy minde—
For him I speake, for him do I intreat,
And with thy fauour fully do resigne
To him the claime and interest of my loue.
Sweete *Mariana,* then, denie mee not:
Loue William, loue my friend, and honour mee,
Who els is cleane dishonored by thy meanes.
Mariana. Borne to mishap, my selfe am onely shee
On whome the Sunne of Fortune neuer shyned:
But Planets rulde by retrogard aspect
Foretolde mine yll in my natiuitie.
Lubeck. Sweete Ladie, seace, let my intreatie serue
To pacifie the passion of thy griefe,
Which, well I know, proceedes of ardent loue.
Mariana. But Lubeck now regardes not *Mariana.*
Lubeck. Euen as my life, so loue I *Mariana.*
Mariana. Why do you poste mee to another then?
Lubeck. He is my friend, and I do loue the man.
Mariana. Then will *Duke William* robb me of my Loue?
Lubeck. No, as his life *Mariana* he doth loue.
Mariana. Speake for your selfe, my Lord, let him alone.
Lubeck. So do I, Madam, for he and I am one.
Mariana. Then louing you I do content you both.
Lubeck. In louing him, you shall content vs both:
Me, for I craue that fauour at your handes,
He, for ⟨he⟩ hopes that comfort at your hands.
Mariana. Leaue of, my Lord, here comes the Ladie *Blaunch.*

Enter Blaunch to them.

Lubeck. Hard hap to breake vs of our talke so soone!
Sweet *Mariana,* doe remember me.
[*Exit Lubeck.*

Mariana. Thy *Mariana* cannot chuse but remember thee.

Blaunch. Mariana, well met. You are verie forward in your Loue?

Mariana. Madam, be it in secret spoken to your selfe, if you wil but follow the complot I haue inuented, you will not think me so forward as your selfe shall proue fortunate.

Blaunch. As how?

Mariana. Madam, as thus: It is not vnknowen to you that *Sir Robert* of *Windsor,* a man that you do not little esteeme, hath long importuned me of Loue; but rather then I will be found false or vniust to the *Marques Lubeck,* I will, as did the constant ladie *Penelope,* vndertake to effect some great taske.

Blaunch. What of all this?

Mariana. The next tyme that *Sir Robert* shall come in his woonted sort to solicit me with Loue, I will seeme to agree and like of any thing that the Knight shal demaund, so far foorth as it be no impeachment to my chastitie: And, to conclude, poynt some place for to meete the man, for my conueiance from the *Denmarke* Court: which determined vpon, he will appoynt some certaine time for our departure: whereof you hauing intelligence, you may soone set downe a plot to were the English Crowne, and than—

Blanch. What then?

Mariana. If Sir *Robert* proue a King and you his Queene, how than?

Blanch. Were I assured of the one, as I am perswaded of the other, there were some possibilitie in it. But here comes the man.

Mariana. Madam, begon, and you shall see I will worke to your desire and my content.
[*Exit Blanch.*

⟨*Enter* W. Conqueror.⟩

William Con. Ladie, this is well and happelie met.
Fortune hetherto hath beene my foe,
And though I haue oft sought to speake with you,
Yet still I haue beene crost with sinister happs.
I cannot, Madame, tell a louing tale
Or court my Maistres with fabulous discourses,
That am a souldier sworne to followe armes:

42 and estate of *D* he *add. T* 68 Him, for he hopes *Simp.*

76–106 *Verse Qq* 100, 103 then *Q 2* 108 *S. D.* Enter, *etc. om. Qq* 109 Sweet Lady *WP* 110 For Fortune *Simp.* 114 discoursies *Q 1*

But this I bluntly let you vnderstand,
I honor you with such religious Zeale
As may become an honorable minde.
Nor may I make my loue the seege of Troye,
That am a straunger in this Countrie.
First, what I am I know you are resolued,
For that my friend hath let you that to vnderstand,
The *Marques Lubeck,* to whome I am so bound
That whilest I liue I count me onely his.

Mariana. Surely you are beholding to the *Marques,*
For he hath beene an earnest spokes-man in your cause.

William. And yealdes my Ladie, then, at his request,
To grace Duke *William* with her gratious loue?

Mariana. My Lord, I am a prisoner,
And hard it were to get me from the Courte.

William. An easie matter to get you from the Court,
If case that you will thereto giue consent.

Mariana. Put case I should, how would you vse me than?

William. Not otherwise but well and honorably.
I haue at Sea a shipp that doth attend,
Which shall foorthwith conducte vs into England,
Where when we are, I straight will marrie thee.
We may not stay deliberating long,
Least that suspition, enuious of our weale,
Set in a foote to hinder our pretence.

Mariana. But this I think were most conuenient,
To maske my face, the better to scape vnknowen.

William. A good deuise: till then, Farwell, faire loue.

Mariana. But this I must intreat your grace,
You would not seeke by lust vnlawfully
To wrong my chast determinations.

William. I hold that man most shameles in his sinne
That seekes to wrong an honest Ladies name
Whome he thinkes worthie of his mariage bed.

Mariana. In hope your othe is true,
I leaue your grace till the appoynted tyme.
[*Exit Mariana.*

William. O happie *William,* blessed in thy loue,
Most fortunate in *Marianaes* loue!
Well, *Lubeck,* well, this courtesie of thine
I will requite, if God permit me life. [*Exit.*

⟨Scene II.

Manchester. Near the Mill.⟩

Enter Valingford and Mountney at two sundrie dores, looking angerly each on other with Rapiers drauen.

Mountney. Valingford, so hardlie I disgest
An iniurie thou hast profered me,
As, were ⟨it⟩ not that I detest to doe
What stands not with the honor of my name,
Thy death should paie thy ransome of thy fault.

Valingford. And, *Mountney,* had not my reuenging wrath,
Incenst with more than ordinarie loue,
Beene loth for to depriue thee of thy life,
Thou hadst not liude to braue me as thou doest.
Wretch as thou arte,
Wherein hath *Valingford* offended thee?
That honourable bond which late we did
Confirme in presence of the Gods,
When with the Conqueror we arriued here,
For my part hath beene kept inuiolably,
Till now too much abused by thy villanie,
I am inforced to cancell all those bands,
By hating him which I so well did loue.

Mountney. Subtil thou art, and cunning in thy frawd,
That, giuing me occasion of offence,
Thou pickst a quarrell to excuse thy shame.
Why, *Valingford,* was it not enough for thee
To be a ryuall twixt me and my loue,
But counsell her, to my no small disgrace,
That, when I came to talke with her of loue,
She should seeme deafe, as fayning not to heare?

Valingford. But hath shee, *Mountney,* vsed thee as thou sayest?

Mountney. Thou knowest too well shee hath:
Wherein thou couldest not do me greater iniurie.

Valingford. Then I perceiue we are deluded both.
For when I offered many gifts of Gold,
And Iewels to entreat for loue,
Shee hath refused them with a coy disdaine,
Alledging that shee could not see the Sunne.
The same coniectured I to be thy drift,

122 you t' vnderstand *Simp.* 129-30 *Div. after* were *Qq*: *three lines WP, ending* Lord, were, Court 133 then *Q 2*

Scene II. *D* Manchester *etc. pr. ed.*: England. Country near the Court *T* 1-4 *Three lines Qq, ending* iniurie, stands, name 3 were it *D*: were *Q 1*: wer't *Q 2* 5 thy ransome] the ransom *T* 8 loth *pr. ed.*: such *Qq, etc.* 9-10 *One line Qq*: *div. D* 12 *Line ends* confirme *Qq*: *corr. D* 31-3 *Two lines Qq, div.* after Iewels: *corr. D*

That fayning so shee might be ridd of mee.
Mountney. The like did I by thee. But are not these
Naturall impediments?
Valingford. In my coniecture merely counterfeit:
Therefore lets ioyne hands in frindship once againe,
Since that the iarre grewe only by coniecture.
Mountney. With all my heart: Yet lets trye the truth hereof.
Valingf. With right good will. We wil straight vnto her father,
And there to learne whither it be so or no.
[*Exeunt.*

⟨Scene III.

Outside the Danish Palace.⟩

Enter William and Blanch disguised, with a maske ouer her face.

William. Come on, my loue, the comfort of my life.
Disguised thus we may remaine vnknowen,
And get we once to Seas, I force not then,
We quickly shall attaine the English shore.
Blaunch. But this I vrge you with your former oath:
You shall not seeke to violate mine honour,
Vntill our marriage rights be all performed.
William. Mariana, here I sweare to thee by heauen,
And by the honour that I beare to Armes,
Neuer to seeke or craue at hands of thee
The spoyle of honourable chastitie,
Vntill we do attaine the English coast,
Where thou shalt be my right espoused Queene.
Blanch. In hope your oath proceedeth from your heart,
Let's leaue the Court, and betake vs to his power
That gouernes all things to his mightie will,
And will reward the iust with endlesse ioye,
And plague the bad with most extreame annoy.
William. Lady, as little tarriance as wee may,
Lest some misfortune happen by the way.
[*Exit Blanch & William.*

⟨Scene IV.

Manchester. The Mill.⟩

Enter the Miller, his man Trotter, & Manuile.

Miller. I tell you, sir, it is no little greefe to mee, you should so hardly conseit of my daughter, whose honest report, though I saie it, was neuer blotted with any title of defamation.

Manuile. Father Miller, the repaire of those gentlemen to your house hath giuen me great occasion to mislike.

Miller. As for those gentlemen, I neuer saw in them any euill intreatie. But should they haue profered it, her chaste minde hath proofe enough to preuent it.

Trotter. Those gentlemen are as honest as euer I sawe: For yfaith one of them gaue me six pence to fetch a quart of Seck.—See, maister, here they come.

Enter Mountney and Valingford.

Miller. Trotter, call *Em.* Now they are here together, Ile haue this matter throughly debated. [*Exit Trotter.*

Mountney. Father, well met. We are come to conferre with you.

Manuile. Nay, with his daughter rather.

Valingford. Thus it is, father, we are come to craue your frindship in a matter.

Miller. Gentlemen, as you are straungers to me, yet by the waie of courtesie you shall demaund any reasonable thing at my hands.

Manuile. What, is the matter so forward they came to craue his good will?

Valinford. It is giuen vs to vnderstand that your daughter is sodenly become both blind and deafe.

Miller. Marie, God forbid! I haue sent for her. In deed, she hath kept her chamber this three daies. It were no litle griefe to me if it should be so.

Manuile. This is Gods iudgement for her trecherie.

Enter Trotter, leading Em.

Miller. Gentlemen, I feare your wordes are too true. See where Trotter comes leading of her.—What ayles my Em? Not blind, I hope?

Em. ⟨*Aside*⟩ *Mountney* and *Valingford* both together! And *Manuile,* to whom I haue faithfullie vowed my loue! Now, Em, suddenly helpe thy selfe.

Mountney. This is no desembling, *Valingford.*

Valingford. If it be, it is cunningly contriued of all sides.

Em. ⟨*Aside to* Trotter⟩ *Trotter,* lend me thy hand, and as thou louest me, keepe my

37–8 *One line Qq*: *div. D* 42 thereof *Q 2* Scene III. *D* Outside . . Palace *pr. ed.* Scene IV. *add. D* 1–94 *Verse Qq*

29 came *Q 1*: como *Q 2*, *etc.* 40 two true *Qq* *S. D.* Aside *add. T* 49 If ir be *Q 1* 51 *S. D. add. WP*

counsell, and iustifie what so euer I saie and Ile largely requite thee.

Trotter. Ah, thats as much as to saie you would tell a monstrous, terrible, horrible, outragious lie, and I shall sooth it—no, berladie!

Em. My present extremitie wills me,—if thou loue me, *Trotter.*

Trotter. That same word loue makes me to doe any thing.

Em. *Trotter,* wheres my father?

Trotter. Why, what a blynd dunce are you, can you not see? He standeth right before you. [*He thrusts Em vpon her father.*

Em. Is this my father?—Good father, giue me leaue to sit where I may not be disturbed, sith God hath visited me both of my sight and hearing.

Miller. Tell me, sweete Em, how came this blindnes? Thy eyes are louely to looke on, and yet haue they lost the benefit of their sight. What a griefe is this to thy poore father!

Em. Good father, let me not stand as an open gazing stock to euerie one, but in a place alone, as fits a creature so miserable.

Miller. *Trotter,* lead her in, the vtter ouerthrowe of poore *Goddardes* ioy and onely solace. [*Exit the Miller, Trotter and Em.*

Manuile. Both blind and deafe! Then is she no wife for me; and glad am I so good occasion is hapned: Now will I awaie to *Chester,* and leaue these gentlemen to their blind fortune. [*Exit Manuile.*

Mountney. Since fortune hath thus spitefully crost our hope, let vs leaue this quest and harken after our King, who is at this daie landed at *Lirpoole.* [*Exit Mountney.*

Valingford. Goe, my Lord, Ile follow you.—Well, now *Mountney* is gone, Ile staie behind to solicit my loue; for I imagine that I shall find this but a fained inuention, thereby to haue vs leaue off our sutes.

⟨*Exit Valingford.*⟩

⟨SCENE V.

The Danish Court.⟩

Enter Marques Lubeck and the King of Denmark, angerly with some attendants.

Zweno K. Well, *Lubeck,* well, it is not possible
But you must be concenting to this acte?
Is this the man so highly you extold?
And playe a parte so hatefull with his friend?
Since first he came with thee into the court,
What entertainement and what countenance
He hath receiued, none better knowes than thou.
In recompence whereof, he quites me well
To steale awaie faire *Mariana* my prisoner,
Whose raunsome being lately greed vpon,
I am deluded of by this escape.
Besides, I know not how to answere it,
When shee shal be demaunded home to Swethia.

Lubeck. My gracious Lord, coniecture not, I pray,
Worser of Lubeck than he doth deserue:
Your highnes knowes *Mariana* was my loue,
Sole paragon and mistres of my thoughts.
Is it likely I should know of her departure,
Wherein there is no man iniured more than I?

Zweno. That carries reason, *Marques,* I confesse.
Call foorth my daughter. Yet I am perswaded
That shee, poore soule, suspected not her going:
For as I heare, shee likewise loued the man,
Which he, to blame, did not at all regard.

⟨*Enter* Rocilio *and* Mariana.⟩

Rocilio. My Lord, here is the Princesse *Mariana*;
It is your daughter is conueyed away.

Zweno. What, my daughter gone?
Now, Marques, your villanie breakes foorth.
This match is of your making, gentle sir,
And you shall dearly know the price thereof.

Lubeck. Knew I thereof, or that there was intent
In Robert thus to steale your highnes daughter,
Let heauens in Iustice presently confound me.

Zweno. Not all the protestations thou canst vse
Shall saue thy life. Away with him to prison!
And, minion, otherwise it cannot be
But you are an agent in this trecherie.
I will reuenge it throughly on you both.
Away with her to prison! Heres stuffe in deede!
My daughter stolen away!—
It booteth not thus to disturbe my selfe,
But presently to send to English William,
To send me that proud knight of Windsor hither,
Here in my Court to suffer for his shame,
Or at my pleasure to be punished there,
Withall that *Blanch* be sent me home againe,

65 *S.D. after 62 Qq* 84 Chester *D*: Manchester *Qq* 87 quest *T*: guest *Qq* 88 harken] ? hasten *S. D. add. D* Scene V. *add. D* The Court *T*

S. D. add. D 24 *Prefix* Rocilia *Qq*

Or I shall fetch her vnto *Windsors* coste,
Yea, and *Williams* too, if he denie her mee.
[*Exit Zweno* ⟨*and the rest.*⟩

⟨SCENE VI.

England. Camp of the Earl Demarch.⟩

Enter William, taken with souldiers.

William. Could any crosse, could any plague be worse?
Could heauen or hell, did both conspire in one
To afflict my soule, inuent a greater scourge
Then presently I am tormented with?
Ah, *Mariana,* cause of my lament,
Ioy of my hart, and comfort of my life!
For tho I breath my sorrowes in the ayre
And tyre my selfe, or silently I sigh,
My sorrowes afflictes my soule with equall passion.

Souldier. Go to, sirha, put vp, it is to small purpose.

William. Hence, villaines, hence! dare you lay your hands
Vpon your Soueraigne?

Souldier. Well, sir, we will deale for that.
But here comes one will remedie all this.

Enter Demarch.

My Lord, watching this night in the campe,
We tooke this man, and know not what he is:
And in his companie was a gallant dame,
A woman faire in outward shewe shee seemde,
But that her face was maskte, we could not see
The grace and fauour of her countenance.

Demarch. Tell me, good fellow, of whence and what thou art.

Souldier. Why do you not answere my Lord?
He takes scorne to answer.

Demarch. And takest thou scorne to aunswer my demaund?
Thy proud behauiour verie well deserues
This misdemeanour at the worst be construed.
Why doest thou neither know, nor hast thou heard,
That in the absence of the Saxon Duke
Demarch is his especiall Substitute
To punish those that shall offend the lawes?

William. In knowing this, I know thou art a traytor;
A rebell, and mutenous conspirator.
Why, *Demarch,* knowest thou who I am?

Demarch. Pardon, my dread Lord, the error of my sence,
And misdemeaner to your princely excellencie.

Willi. Why, *Demarch,*
What is the cause my subiects are in armes?

Demarch. Free are my thoughts, my dread and gratious Lord,
From treason to your state and common weale;
Only reuengement of a priuate grudge
By Lord *Dirot* lately profered me,
That standes not with the honor of my name,
Is cause I haue assembled for my guard
Some men in armes that may withstand his force,
Whose setled malice aymeth at my life.

William. Where is Lord *Dirot*?

Demarch. In armes, my gratious Lord,
Not past two miles from hence, as credibly
I am assertained.

William. Well, come, let vs goe.
I feare I shall find traytors of you both.
[*Exit.*

⟨ACT IV.

SCENE I.⟩

⟨*Chester. Before the Citizen's House.*⟩

Enter the Citizen of Chester, and his daughter Elner, and Manuile.

Citizen. In deed, sir, it would do verie well if you could intreat your father to come hither: but if you thinke it be too farr, I care not much to take horse and ride to Manchester. I am sure my daughter is content with either. How saiest thou, *Elner,* art thou not?

Elner. As you shall think best I must be contented.

Manuile. Well, *Elner,* farwell. Onely thus much, I pray: make all things in a readines, either to serue here, or to carry thither with vs.

Citizen. As for that, sir, take you no care; and so I betake you to your iournie.
⟨*Exit Manuile.*⟩

Enter Valingford.

But soft, what gentleman is this?

Valingf. God speed, sir. Might a man craue a word or two with you?

Citizen. God forbid els, sir; I praye you speake your pleasure.

Valingford. The gentleman that parted from you, was he not of Manchester, his father lyuing there of good account?

Citizen. Yes, mary is he, sir. Why doe you

Scene VI, *D*: Act III. Scene I. *T* England *etc.* *add. T* 2 hell? Did *Q 1* 7 tho *pr. ed.*: thee *Qq*: whether *conj. Simp.* 8 or *conj. Simp.*: for *Qq* 9 me soule *Q 1* 15 *Prefix* Souldier *repeated Qq*

46–9 *Six lines Qq, ending* Dirot, Lord, hence, assertained, go, both. Act IV. Scene I. *add. D* *S. D.* Chester *T*: Manchester *Qq* 1–65 *Verse Qq* *S. D.* *add. T*

aske? Belike you haue had some acquaintance with him.

Valingford. I haue been acquainted in times past, but, through his double dealing, I am growen werie of his companie. For, be it spoken to you, he hath beene acquainted with a poore millers daughter, and diuers tymes hath promist her mariage. But what with his delayes and floutes he hath brought her into such a taking that I feare me it will cost her her life.

Citizen. To be playne with you, sir, his father and I haue beene of old acquaintance, and a motion was made betweene my daughter and his sonne, which is now throughly agreed vpon, saue onely the place appoynted for the mariage, whether it shall be kept here or at Manchester; and for no other occasion he is now ridden.

Elner. What hath he done to you, that you should speake so ill of the man?

Valingford. Oh, gentlewoman, I crie you mercie: he is your husband that shalbe.

Elner. If I knew this to be true, he should not be my husband were he neuer so good: And therefore, good father, I would desire you to take the paines to beare this gentleman companie to Manchester, to know whether this be true or no.

Citizen. Now trust me, gentleman, he deales with me verie hardly, knowing how well I ment to him; but I care not much to ride to Manchester, to know whether his fathers will be he should deale with me so badlie. Will it please you, sir, to goe in? We will presently take horse & awaie.

Valingford. If it please you to go in, Ile followe you presently.

[*Exit Elner and her father.*

Now shall I be reuenged on *Manuile,* and by this meanes get *Em* to my wife; and therefore I will strayght to her fathers and informe them both of all that is hapned. [*Exit.*

⟨Scene II.

The English Court.⟩

Enter William, the Ambassador of Denmarke, Demarch, and other attendants.

William. What newes with the Denmark Embassador?

Embassador. Mary, thus:
The King of Denmark and my Soueraine
Doth send to know of thee what is the cause
That iniuriously, against the law of armes,
Thou hast stolen awaie his onely daughter Blaunch,
The onely staie and comfort of his life.
Therefore by me
He willeth thee to send his daughter *Blaunch,*
Or else foorthwith he will leuy such an hoste,
As soone shall fetch her in dispite of thee.

William. *Embassador,* this answer I retorne thy King.
He willeth me to send his daughter *Blaunch,*
Saying, I conuaid her from the Danish court,
That neuer yet did once as think thereof.
As for his menacing and daunting threats,
I nill regard him nor his Danish power;
For if he come to fetch her foorth my Realme
I will prouide him such a banquet here,
That he shall haue small cause to giue me thanks.

Embassador. Is this your answer, then?

William. It is; and so begone.

Embassador. I goe; but to your cost.

[*Exit Ambassador.*

William. *Demarch,* our subiects, earst leuied in ciuill broyles,
Muster foorthwith, for to defend the Realme.
In hope whereof, that we shall find you true,
We freely pardon this thy late offence.

Demarch. Most humble thanks I render to your grace. [*Exeunt.*

⟨Scene III.

Manchester. The Mill.⟩

Enter the Miller and Valingford.

Miller. Alas, gentleman, why should you trouble your self so much, considering the imperfections of my daughter, which is able to with-drawe the loue of any man from her, as alreadie it hath done in her first choyce. Maister *Manuile* hath forsaken her, and at Chester shalbe maried to a mans daughter of no little wealth. But if my daughter knew so much, it would goe verie neere her heart, I feare me.

Valing. Father miller, such is the entyre affection to your daughter, as no misfortune whatsoeuer can alter. My fellow *Mountney,* thou seeste, gaue quicly ouer; but I, by reason of my good meaning, am not so soone to be changed, although I am borne off with scornes and deniall.

Enter Em to them.

Miller. Trust me, sir, I know not what to saie. My daughter is not to be compelled by

37 beteewene *Q 1* Scene II. *add. D* 2-3 *One line Qq* : *div. Elze*

8-9 *One line Qq* 24 *Two lines D, div. after* Demarch 25 Musterd *Qq* Scene III. *add. D* *S. D.* Millier *Q 1* 1-119 *Verse Qq*

me; but here she comes her self: speake to her and spare not, for I neuer was troubled with loue matters so much before.

Em. ⟨*Aside*⟩ Good Lord! shall I neuer be rid of this importunate man? Now must I dissemble blyndnes againe. Once more for thy sake, *Manuile,* thus am I inforced, because I shall complete my full resolued mynde to thee. Father, where are you?

Miller. Here, sweete *Em.* Answer this gentleman, that would so fayne enioye thy loue.

Em. Where are you, sir? wil you neuer leaue this idle and vaine pursuite of loue? Is not England stord enough to content you, but you must still trouble the poore contemptible mayd of Manchester?

Valing. None can content me but the fayre maide of Manchester.

Em. I perceiue loue is vainly described, that, being blynd himselfe, would haue you likewise troubled with a blinde wife, hauing the benefite of your eyes. But neither follow him so much in follie, but loue one in whome you may better delight.

Valingford. Father Miller, thy daughter shall haue honor by graunting mee her loue. I am a Gentleman of king Williams Court, and no meane man in king Williams fauour.

Em. If you be a Lorde, syr, as you saye, you offer both your selfe and mee great wrong: yours, as apparant, in limitting your loue so vnorderly, for which you rashly endure reprochement; mine, as open and euident, when, being shut from the vanities of this world, you would haue me as an open gazing stock to all the world; for lust, not loue, leades you into this error. But from the one I will keepe me as well as I can, and yeeld the other to none but to my father, as I am bound by duetie.

Valingford. Why, faire *Em, Manuile* hath forsaken thee, and must at Chester be married: which if I speake otherwise than true, let thy father speake what credibly he hath heard.

Em. But can it be Manuile will deale so vnkindly to reward my iustice with such monstrous vngentlenes? Haue I dissembled for thy sake, and doest thou now thus requite it? In deede these many daies I haue not seene him, which hath made me marueile at his long absence. But, father, are you assured of the wordes he spake were concerning *Manuile*?

Miller. In sooth, daughter, now it is foorth I must needes confirme it: Maister *Manuile* hath forsaken thee, and at Chester must be married to a mans daughter of no little wealth. His owne father procures it, and therefore I dare credit it; and do thou beleeue it, for trust mee, daughter, it is so.

Em. Then, good father, pardon the iniurie that I haue don to you, onely causing your griefe, by ouer-fond affecting a man so trothlesse. And you likewise, sir, I pray holde me excused, as I hope this cause will allow sufficiently for mee: My loue to *Manuile,* thinking he would requite it, hath made me double with my father and you, and many more besides, which I will no longer hyde from you. That inticing speeches should not beguile mee, I haue made my selfe deafe to any but to him; and lest any mans person should please mee more than his, I haue dissembled the want of my sight: Both which shaddowes of my irreuocable affections I haue not sparde to confirme before him, my father, and all other amorous soliciters—wherewith not made acquainted, I perceiue my true intent hath wrought mine owne sorrow, and seeking by loue to be regarded, am cut of with contempt, and dispised.

Miller. Tell me, sweet *Em,* hast thou but fained all this while for his loue, that hath so descourteously forsaken thee?

Em. Credit me, father, I haue told you the troth; wherewith I desire you and Lord *Valingford* not to be displeased. For ought else I shall saie, let my present griefe hold me excused. But, may I liue to see that vngratfull man iustly rewarded for his trecherie, poore *Em* woulde think her selfe not a little happie. Fauour my departing at this instant; for my troubled thought desires to meditate alone in silence. [*Exit Em.*

Valingf. Will not *Em* shew one chereful looke on *Valingford*?

Miller. Alas, sir, blame her not; you see she hath good cause, being so handled by this gentleman: And so Ile leaue you, and go comfort my poore wench as well as I may. [*Exit the Miller.*

Valingford. Farewell, good father.

[*Exit Valingford.*

⟨ACT V.

Scene I.⟩

⟨*Open country in England.*⟩

Enter Zweno, king of Denmarke, with Rosilio and other attendants.

Zweno. *Rosilio,* is this the place whereas the Duke *William* should meete mee?

23 Aside *add. D* 33 enought *Q 1* 70 of *Qq*: *om. T*: if *D* *Chet. inserts* true *after* were 104 yon *Q 1* Act V. Scene I. *add. D*: Act III. Scene V. *T* 1–2 *Verse D, div. after* whereas

Rosilio. It is, and like your grace.
Zweno. Goe, captaine! Away, regard the charge I gaue:
See all our men be martialed for the fight.
Dispose the Wardes as lately was deuised;
And let the prisoners vnder seuerall gardes
Be kept apart, vntill you heare from vs.
Let this suffise, you know my resolution.
If William, Duke of Saxons, be the man,
That by his answere sent vs, he would seem,
Not words, but wounds: not parleis, but alarmes,
Must be descider of this controuersie.
Rosilio, stay with mee; the rest begone.
[*Exeunt.*

Enter William, and Demarch with other attendants.

William. All but *Demarch* go shroud you out of sight;
For I will goe parley with the Prince my selfe.
Demarch. Should *Zweno* by this parley call you foorth,
Vpon intent iniuriously to deale,
This offereth too much oportunitie.
William. No, no, *Demarch,*
That were a breach against the law of Armes:
Therefore begon, and leaue vs here alone.
[*Exeunt.*
I see that *Zweno* is maister of his worde.
Zweno, William of Saxonie greeteth thee,
Either well or yll, according to thy intent.
If well thou wish to him and Saxonie,
He bids thee frindly welcome as he can.
If yll thou wish to him and Saxanie,
He must withstand thy mallice as he may.
Zweno. William,
For other name and title giue I none
To him, who, were he worthie of those honours
That Fortune and his predecessors left,
I ought, by right and humaine courtesie,
To grace his style with Duke of Saxonie;
But, for I finde a base, degenerate mynde,
I frame my speech according to the man,
And not the state that he vnworthie holdes.
William. Herein, *Zweno,* dost thou abase thy state,
To breake the peace which by our auncesters
Hath heretofore bene honourably kept.
Zweno. And should that peace for euer haue been kept,
Had not thy selfe beene author of the breach:
Nor stands it with the honor of my state,
Or nature of a father to his childe,
That I should so be robbed of my daughter,
And not vnto the vtmost of my power
Reuenge so intollerable an iniurie.
William. Is this the colour of your quarrell, *Zweno?*
I.well perceiue the wisest men may erre.
And thinke you I conueyed away your daughter *Blanch?*
Zweno. Art thou so impudent to denye thou didst,
When that the proofe thereof is manifest?
William. What proofe is there?
Zweno. Thine owne confession is sufficient proofe.
William. Did I confesse I stole your daughter *Blanch?*
Zweno. Thou didst confesse thou hadst a Ladie hence.
William. I haue, and do.
Zweno. Why, that was *Blanch,* my daughter.
William. Nay, that was *Mariana,*
Who wrongfully thou detainest prisoner.
Zweno. Shamelesse persisting in thy ill!
Thou doest mayntaine a manifest vntrothe,
As shee shall iustifie vnto thy teethe.
Rosilio, fetch her and the *Marques* hether.
[*Exit Rosilio for Mariana.*
William. It cannot be I should be so deceiued.
Demarch. I heard this night among the souldiers
That in their watch they tooke a pensiue Ladie,
Who, at the appoyntment of the Lord *Dirot,*
Is yet in keeping. What she is I know not:
Onely thus much I ouer-hard by chance.
William. And what of this?
Demarch. It may be *Blaunch,* the King of Denmarkes daughter.
William. It may be so: but on my lyfe it is not;
Yet, *Demarch,* goe, and fetch her strayght.
⟨*Exit* Demarch.⟩

Enter Rosilio with the Marques.

Rosilio. Pleaseth your highnes, here is the *Marques* and *Mariana.*
Zweno. See here, *Duke William,* your competitors,
That were consenting to my daughters scape.
Let them resolue you of the trueth herein.
And here I vowe and solemly protest,
That in thy presence they shall lose their heds,

10 Saxons *pr. ed.*: Saxon *Qq* : Saxonie *WP* 11 seem *conj. Simp.* : send *Qq* 20–2 *Div. after* breach, begon *Qq* : *corr. D* 30–1 *One line Qq* : *div. WP* 35 style his grace the *Simp.*: grace his style the *WP*

58 danghter *Q 1* 68–9 *Div. after* keeping *Qq* : *corr. D* S. D. *add. Elze* 78 resolut . . hereing *Q 1* : *corr. Q 2*

Vnlesse I here where as my daughter is.

William. Oh, *Marques Lubeck,* how it grieueth me,
That for my sake thou shouldest indure these bondes,
Be iudge my soule that feeles the martirdome!

Marques. Duke *William,* you know it is for your cause,
It pleaseth thus the King to misconceiue of me,
And for his pleasure doth me iniurie.

Enter Demarch with the Ladie Blaunch.

Demarch. May it please your highnes,
Here is the Ladie whom you sent me for.

William. Awaie, *Demarch*! what tellest thou me of Ladies?
I so detest the dealing of their sex,
As that I count a louers state to be
The base and vildest slauerie in the world.

Demarch. What humors are these? Heres a straunge alteration!

Zweno. See, Duke *William,* is this *Blaunch* or no?
You know her if you see her, I am sure.

William. *Zweno,* I was deceiued, yea vtterly deceiued;
Yet this is shee: this same is Ladie *Blaunch.*
And for mine error, here I am content
To do whatsoeuer *Zweno* shall set downe.
Ah, cruell *Mariana,* thus to vse
The man which loued and honored thee with his heart!

Mariana. When first I came into your highnes court,
And William often importing me of loue,
I did deuise, to ease the griefe your daughter did sustain,
Shee should meete Sir *William* masked, as I it were.
This put in proofe did take so good effect,
As yet it seemes his grace is not resolued,
But it was I which he conueid awaie.

William. May this be true? It cannot be but true.
Was it Ladie *Blaunch* which I conueid awaie?
Vnconstant *Mariana,* thus to deale
With him which ment to thee nought but faith!

Blaunch. Pardon, deere father, my follyes that are past,
Wherein I haue neglected my dutie,
Which I in reuerence ought to shew your grace;
For, led by loue, I thus haue gone astray,
And now repent the errors I was in.

Zweno. Stand vp, deare daughter: though thy fault deserues
For to be punisht in the extremest sort,
Yet loue, that couers multitude of sinns,
Makes loue in parents winke at childrens faults.
Sufficeth, *Blaunch,* thy father loues thee so,
Thy follies past he knowes, but will not know.
And here, Duke *William,* take my daughter to thy wife,
For well I am assured she loues thee well.

William. A proper coniun⟨c⟩tion! as who should saie,
Lately come out of the fyer,
I would goe thrust my selfe into the flame.
Let Maistres nice goe Saint it where she list,
And coyly quaint it with dissembling face.
I hold in scorne the fooleries that they vse:
I being free, will neuer subiect my selfe
To any such as shee is vnderneth the Sunne.

Zweno. Refusest thou to take my daughter to thy wife?
I tel thee, Duke, this rash deniall may bring
More mischiefe on thee then thou canst avoide.

William. Conseit hath wrought such generall dislike,
Through the false dealing of *Mariana,*
That vtterly I doe abhore their sex.
They are all disloyall, vnconstant, all vniust:
Who tryes as I haue tryed, and findes as I haue founde,
Will saie thers no such creatures on the ground.

Blanch. Vnconstant Knight, though some deserue no trust,
Thers others faithfull, louing, loyall, & iust.

Enter to them Valingford with Em and the Miller, and Mountney, and Manuile, and Elner.

Willi. How now, Lord *Valingford,* what makes these women here?

Valing. Here be two women, may it please your grace,
That are contracted to one man, and are
In strife whether shall haue him to their husband.

William. Stand foorth, women, and saie,
To whether of you did he first giue his faith.

Em. To me, forsooth.

Elner. To me, my gratious Lord.

William. Speak, *Manuile*: to whether didst thou giue thy faith?

88 hightnes *Q 1* 92 *Ends* base *Qq* 97 *WP set* Zweno *in a line by itself* 104 oft importuning *conj.* *Elze* 112–13 *Dir.* Mariana *Qq* : *corr. D* 115 my *Q 2* : me *Q 1* : thus my *D*

136 *Ends* deniall *Qq* : *corr. D* 142 *Two lines Qq, div. after* tryed 148 *Line ends* man *Qq*

Manuile. To saie the troth, this maide had first my loue.
Elner. Yea, *Manuile,* but there was no witnesse by.
Em. Thy conscience, Manuile, is a hundred witnesses.
Elner. Shee hath stolne a conscience to serue her owne turne; but you are deceiued, yfaith, he will none of you.
Manuile. In deede, dred Lord, so deere I held her loue
As in the same I put my whole delight;
But some impediments, which at that instant hapned,
Made me forsake her quite;
For which I had her fathers franke consent.
William. What were the impediments?
Manuile. Why, shee could neither heare nor see.
William. Now shee doth both. Mayden, how were you cured?
Em. Pardon, my Lord, Ile tell your grace the troth,
Be it not imputed to mee as discredite.
I loued this *Manuile* so much, that still my thought,
When he was absent, did present to mee
The forme and feature of that countenance
Which I did shrine an ydoll in mine heart.
And neuer could I see a man, methought,
That equald *Manuile* in my partiall eye.
Nor was there any loue betweene vs lost,
But that I held the same in high regard,
Vntill repaire of some vnto our house,
Of whome my *Manuile* grewe thus iealous
As if he tooke exception I vouchsafed
To heare them speake, or saw them when they came:
On which I straight tooke order with my selfe,
To voide the scrupule of his conscience,
By counterfaiting that I neither sawe nor heard,
Any wayes to rid my hands of them.
All this I did to keepe my *Manuiles* loue,
Which he vnkindly seekes for to rewarde.
Manuile. And did my *Em,* to keepe her faith with mee,
Dissemble that shee neither heard nor sawe?
Pardon me, sweet *Em,* for I am onely thine.
Em. Lay off thy hands, disloyall as thou art!
Nor shalt thou haue possession of my loue,
That canst so finely shift thy matters off.
Put case I had beene blinde, and could not see—
As often times such visitations falles
That pleaseth God, which all things doth dispose—
Shouldest thou forsake mee in regard of that?
I tell thee *Manuile,* hadst thou beene blinde,
Or deafe, or dumbe, or else what impediments might
Befall to man, *Em* would haue loued and kept,
And honoured thee: yea begde, if wealth had faylde,
For thy releefe.
Manuile. Forgiue mee, sweete *Em.*
Em. I do forgiue thee, with my heart,
And will forget thee too, if case I can:
But neuer speake to mee, nor seeme to know mee.
Manuile. Then farewell, frost! Well fare a wench that will!
Now, *Elner,* I am thine owne, my gyrle.
Elner. Mine, *Manuile*? thou neuer shalt be myne.
I so detest thy villanie,
That whilest I liue I will abhor thy company.
Manuile. Is it come to this? Of late I had choyce of twaine,
On either side, to haue me to her husband,
And now am vtterly reiected of them both.
Valingford. My Lord, this gentleman, when time was,
Stood some-thing in our light,
And now I thinke it not amisse
To laugh at him that sometime scorned at vs.
Mountney. Content my Lord, inuent the forme.
Valingford. Then thus.—
William. I see that women are not generall euils,
Blanch is faire: Methinkes I see in her
A modest countenance, a heauenly blush.
Zweno, receiue a reconciled foe,
Not as thy friend, but as thy sonne in law,
If so that thou be thus content.
Zweno. I ioy to see your grace so tractable.
Here, take my daughter *Blanch*;
And after my desease the Denmark crowne.
William. Now, sir, how stands the case with you?
Manuile. I partly am perswaded as your grace is,
My lord, he is best at ease that medleth least.
Valingford. Sir, may a man
Be so bolde as to craue a word with you?

158–60 *Verse Qq, div. after* turne 171 me thought *Qq*

200 *Ends* impediments *Qq* 208 *Two lines Qq, div. after* frost farewell a wench *WP* 221–78 *Elze proposes the following plausible alteration in the succession of lines*: 221, 234–54, 231–3, 222–30, 255–78 234 *Ends* bolde *Qq*

Manuile. Yea, two or three: what are they?
Valingford. I say, this maide will haue thee to her husband.
Mountney. And I say this: and therof will I lay
An hundred pound.
Valingf. And I say this: whereon I will lay as much.
Manuile. And I say neither: what say you to that?
Mountney. If that be true, then are we both deceiued.
Manuile. Why, it is true, and you are both deceiued.
Marques. In mine eyes this is the proprest wench;
Might I aduise thee, take her vnto thy wife.
Zweno. It seemes to me, shee hath refused him.
Marques. Why, theres the spite.
Zweno. If one refuse him, yet may he haue the other.
Marques. He will aske but her good will, and all her friends.
Zweno. Might I aduise thee, let them both alone.
Manuile. Yea, thats the course, and thereon wil I stand.
Such idle loue hencefoorth I will detest.
Valingford. The Foxe will eat no grapes, and why?
Mountney. I know full well, because they hang too hye.
William. And may it be a Millers daughter by her birth?
I cannot thinke but shee is better borne.

238-9 *One line Qq*

Valingford. Sir *Thomas Goddard* hight this reuerent man
Famed for his vertues, and his good successe:
Whose fame hath beene renowmed through the world.
William. Sir *Thomas Goddard,* welcome to thy Prince;
And, faire *Em,* frolike with thy good father;
As glad am I to finde Sir *Thomas Goddard,*
As good Sir *Edmund Treford,* on the plaines:
He like a sheepheard, and thou our countrie Miller.
Miller. And longer let not *Goddard* liue a day
Then he in honour loues his soueraigne.
William. But say, Sir *Thomas,* shall I giue thy daughter?
Miller. *Goddard,* and all that he hath,
Doth rest at the pleasure of your Maiestie.
William. And what sayes *Em* to louely *Valingford*?
It seemde he loued you well, that for your sake
Durst leaue his King.
Em. *Em* restes at the pleasure of your highnes:
And would I were a wife for his desert.
William. Then here, Lord *Valingford,* receiue faire *Em.*
Here take her, make her thy espoused wife.
Then goe we in, that preparation may be made,
To see these nuptials solemly performed.
[*Exeunt all. Sound drummes and Trumpets.*

FINIS

263 Sir Thomas *WP* 268 Sir Thomas Goddard *Simp.* 271-2 *Div. after* well *Qq* 275 *Two lines Qq, div. after* Valingford

THE TWO NOBLE KINSMEN:

Presented at the Blackfriers by the Kings Maieſties ſervants, with great applauſe:

Written by the memorable Worthies of their time;

{Mr. *John Fletcher*, and} Gent.
{Mr. *William Shakſpeare.*}

Printed at *London* by *Tho. Cotes*, for *Iohn Waterſon*: and are to be ſold at the ſigne of the *Crowne* in *Pauls* Church-yard. 1634.

Q	=	Quarto of 1634
F	=	(Second) Folio Beaumont and Fletcher, 1679
Tonson	=	Tonson's ed., 1711
Sew.	=	Seward, 1750
Sy.	=	Sympson, ibid.
Th.	=	Theobald, ibid.
Heath	=	H.'s MS. notes, quoted by Dyce
Colman	=	Colman's ed., 1778
Mason	=	M.'s comments, 1798
Weber	=	W.'s ed., 1812
Kn.	=	Knight, 1839–41 (and later edd.)
Dyce	=	Dyce's edition, 1846 (and later edd.)
S	=	Simms, 1848
T	=	Tyrrell, 1851
Walker	=	W.'s Critical Exam., 1860
Sk.	=	Skeat, 1875
Litt.	=	Littledale, 1876
Col.	=	Collier, 1878
Herford	=	'Temple Dramatists' ed., 1897
Daniel	=	Mr. P. A. Daniel's conjectures
pr. ed.	=	present editor

THE TWO NOBLE KINSMEN

⟨The Persons represented in the Play.

Hymen,
Theseus,
Hippolita, } *Bride and Sister to* Theseus [1]
Emelia, }
Nymphs,
Three Queens,
Three valiant Knights,
Palamon } *The two Noble Kinsmen, in love*
Arcite } *with fair* Emelia
Perithous,
Jaylor,
His Daughter, *in love with* Palamon
Countreymen,
Wenches,
A Taborer,
Gerrold, A Schoolmaster.⟩ [2]

PROLOGVE.

[Florish.]

New Playes, and Maydenheads, are neare a kin,
Much follow'd both, for both much mony g'yn,
If they stand sound, and well: And a good Play
(Whose modest Sceanes blush on his marriage day,
And shake to loose his honour) is like hir
That after holy Tye and first nights stir
Yet still is Modestie, and still retaines
More of the maid to sight, than Husbands paines;
We pray our Play may be so; For I am sure
It has a noble Breeder, and a pure,
A learned, and a Poet never went
More famous yet twixt Po and silver Trent:
Chaucer (of all admir'd) the Story gives,
There constant to Eternity it lives.
If we let fall the Noblenesse of this,
And the first sound this child heare, be a hisse,
How will it shake the bones of that good man,
And make him cry from under ground, 'O fan
From me the witles chaffe of such a wrighter
That blastes my Bayes, and my fam'd workes makes lighter
Then Robin Hood!' This is the feare we bring;
For to say Truth, it were an endlesse thing,
And too ambitious, to aspire to him,
Weake as we are, and almost breathlesse swim
In this deepe water. Do but you hold out
Your helping hands, and we shall take about,
And something doe to save us: You shall heare
Sceanes, though below his Art, may yet appeare
Worth two houres travell. To his bones sweet sleepe:
Content to you. If this play doe not keepe
A little dull time from us, we perceave
Our losses fall so thicke, we must needs leave.
[Florish.]

[1] Bride and Sister to] Sisters to *F* [2] *Add. F*

Actus Primus.

⟨SCENE I. *Athens. Before a temple.*⟩

Enter Hymen *with a Torch burning: a Boy, in a white Robe before singing, and strewing Flowres: After* Hymen, *a Nimph, encompast in her Tresses, bearing a wheaten Garland. Then* Theseus *betweene two other Nimphs with wheaten Chaplets on their heades. Then* Hipolita *the Bride, lead by* Pirithous, *and another holding a Garland over her head (her Tresses likewise hanging.) After her* Emilia *holding up her Traine.* ⟨Artesius *and Attendants.*⟩

The Song, *Musike.*

Roses their sharpe spines being gon,
Not royall in their smels alone,
But in their hew.
Maiden Pinckes, of odour faint,
Dazies smel-lesse, yet most quaint
And sweet Time true.

Prim-rose first borne child of Ver,
Merry Spring times Herbinger,
With her bels dimme.
Oxlips, in their Cradles growing,
Mary-golds, on death beds blowing,
Larkes-heeles trymme.

All deere natures children sweete,
Ly fore Bride and Bridegroomes feete, [Strew Flowers.
Blessing their sence.
Not an angle of the aire,
Bird melodious, or bird faire,
Is absent hence.

The Crow, the slaundrous Cuckoe, nor
The boding Raven, nor Chough hore
Nor chattring Pie,

Scene I. *etc. Dyce* *S. D.* led by Pirithous] lead by Theseus *Q, F* *S. D.* Artesius *etc. add. Dyce* 9 her bels *Q* : hair-bells *Sk.* 16 Angel *F, etc.* 18 Is *Q, F* : Be *Sew.* 20 Chough hore *Sew.* : Clough hee *Q, F*

May on our Bridehouse pearch or sing,
Or with them any discord bring,
But from it fly.

Enter 3. *Queenes in Blacke, with vailes staind, with imperiall Crownes. The* 1. *Queene fals downe at the foote of Theseus; The* 2. *fals downe at the foote of Hypolita. The* 3. *before Emilia.*

1. *Qu.* For pitties sake and true gentilities,
Heare, and respect me.
2. *Qu.* For your Mothers sake,
And as you wish your womb may thrive with faire ones,
Heare and respect me.
3. *Qu.* Now for the love of him whom *Iove* hath markd
The honour of your Bed, and for the sake
Of cleere virginity, be Advocate
For us, and our distresses. This good deede
Shall raze you out o'th Booke of Trespasses
All you are set downe there.
Theseus. Sad Lady, rise.
Hypol. Stand up.
Emil. No knees to me.
What woman I may steed that is distrest,
Does bind me to her.
Thes. What's your request? Deliver you for all.
1. *Qu.* We are 3. Queenes, whose Sover-aignes fel before
The wrath of cruell *Creon*; who endured
The Beakes of Ravens, Tallents of the Kights,
And pecks of Crowes, in the fowle feilds of Thebs.
He will not suffer us to burne their bones,
To urne their ashes, nor to take th' offence
Of mortall loathsomenes from the blest eye
Of holy *Phœbus*, but infects the windes
With stench of our slaine Lords. O pitty, Duke:
Thou purger of the earth, draw thy feard Sword
That does good turnes to'th world; give us the Bones
Of our dead Kings, that we may Chappell them;
And of thy boundles goodnes take some note
That for our crowned heades we have no roofe,
Save this which is the Lyons, and the Beares,
And vault to every thing.
Thes. Pray you, kneele not:
I was transported with your Speech, and suffer'd
Your knees to wrong themselves; I have heard the fortunes
Of your dead Lords, which gives me such lamenting
As wakes my vengeance, and revenge for'em.
King *Capaneus* was your Lord: the day
That he should marry you, at such a season,
As now it is with me, I met your Groome,
By *Marsis Altar*; you were that time faire,
Not *Iunos Mantle* fairer then your Tresses,
Nor in more bounty spread her. Your wheaten wreathe
Was then nor threashd, nor blasted; Fortune at you
Dimpled her Cheeke with smiles: *Hercules* our kinesman
(Then weaker than your eies) laide by his Club,
He tumbled downe upon his Nemean hide
And swore his sinews thawd: O greife, and time,
Fearefull consumers, you will all devoure.
1. *Qu.* O, I hope some God,
Some God hath put his mercy in your man-hood
Whereto heel infuse powre, and presse you forth
Our undertaker.
Thes. O no knees, none, Widdow,
Vnto the Helmeted Belona use them,
And pray for me your Souldier.
Troubled I am. [*turnes away.*
2. *Qu.* Honoured *Hypolita,*
Most dreaded *Amazonian*, that hast slaine
The Sith-tuskd Bore; that with thy Arme as strong
As it is white, wast neere to make the male
To thy Sex captive, but that this thy Lord,
Borne to uphold Creation in that honour
First nature stilde it in, shrunke thee into
The bownd thou wast ore-flowing, at once subduing
Thy force, and thy affection: Soldiresse
That equally canst poize sternenes with pitty,
Whom now I know hast much more power on him
Then ever he had on thee, who ow'st his strength
And his Love too, who is a Servant for
The Tenour of thy Speech: Deere Glasse of Ladies,
Bid him that we, whom flaming war doth scortch,
Vnder the shaddow of his Sword may coole us:
Require him he advance it ore our heades;
Speak't in a womans key: like such a woman

43 endure *Dyce, etc.*

68 her *om. Sew.* 72 Nenuan *Q, F* 93 Whom *Q*: Who *Dyce* 95 for] to *Sew.* 96 thy *Sew.*: the *Q, F*

As any of us three; weepe ere you faile;
Lend us a knee;
But touch the ground for us no longer time
Then a Doves motion, when the head's pluckt off:
Tell him if he i'th blood cizd field lay swolne,
Showing the Sun his Teeth, grinning at the Moone,
What you would doe.

Hip. Poore Lady, say no more:
I had as leife trace this good action with you
As that whereto I am going, and never yet
Went I so willing way. My Lord is taken
Hart deepe with your distresse: Let him consider:
Ile speake anon.

3. *Qu.* O my petition was [*kneele to Emilia.*
Set downe in yce, which by hot greefe uncandied
Melts into drops, so sorrow, wanting forme,
Is prest with deeper matter.

Emilia. Pray stand up,
Your greefe is written in your cheeke.

3. *Qu.* O woe,
You cannot reade it there, there through my teares—
Like wrinckled peobles in a glassie streame
You may behold 'em. Lady, Lady, alacke,
He that will all the Treasure know o'th earth
Must know the Center too; he that will fish
For my least minnow, let him lead his line
To catch one at my heart. O pardon me:
Extremity, that sharpens sundry wits,
Makes me a Foole.

Emili. Pray you say nothing, pray you:
Who cannot feele nor see the raine, being in't,
Knowes neither wet nor dry: if that you were
The ground-peece of some Painter, I would buy you
T'instruct me gainst a Capitall greefe indeed—
Such heart peirc'd demonstration; but, alas,
Being a naturall Sifter of our Sex
Your sorrow beates so ardently upon me,
That it shall make a counter reflect gainst
My Brothers heart, and warme it to some pitty,
Though it were made of stone: pray, have good comfort.

Thes. Forward to'th Temple, leave not out a Iot
O'th sacred Ceremony.

1. *Qu.* O, This Celebration
Will long last, and be more costly then
Your Suppliants war: Remember that your Fame
Knowles in the eare o'th world: what you doe quickly
Is not done rashly; your first thought is more
Then others laboured meditance: your premeditating
More then their actions: But, oh Iove! your actions,
Soone as they mooves, as Asprayes doe the fish,
Subdue before they touch: thinke, deere *Duke*, thinke
What beds our slaine Kings have.

2. *Qu.* What greifes our beds,
That our deere Lords have none.

3. *Qu.* None fit for 'th dead:
Those that with Cordes, Knives, drams precipitance,
Weary of this worlds light, have to themselves
Beene deathes most horrid Agents, humaine grace
Affords them dust and shaddow.

1. *Qu.* But our Lords
Ly blistring fore the visitating Sunne,
And were good Kings, when living.

Thes. It is true, and I will give you comfort,
To give your dead Lords graves: the which to doe,
Must make some worke with *Creon.*

1. *Qu.* And that worke presents it selfe to'th doing:
Now twill take forme, the heates are gone to morrow.
Then, booteles toyle must recompence it selfe
With it's owne sweat; Now he's secure,
Not dreames we stand before your puissance
Wrinching our holy begging in our eyes
To make petition cleere.

2. *Qu.* Now you may take him, drunke with his victory.

3. *Qu.* And his Army full of Bread, and sloth.

Thes. Artesius, that best knowest
How to draw out fit to this enterprise
The prim'st for this proceeding, and the number
To carry such a businesse, forth and levy
Our worthiest Instruments, whilst we despatch
This grand act of our life, this daring deede
Of Fate in wedlocke.

1. *Qu.* 'Dowagers, take hands;
Let us be Widdowes to our woes: delay
Commends us to a famishing hope.

101-2 *One line Q, F* 111 willing, way *Q, F* 121 here through *Sew.* 122 glassy *Sew.*: glasse *Q*: glass *F* 123 'em *Q, F*: it *Dyce* 144 long *Q, F*: longer *Sew.*

156 Drams, Precipitance *Sew.* 164 *Ends* graves *Q* 170 Not] Nor *Sew.* 182 Widdowes *Q*: wedded *conj. Sy.*

All. Farewell.
2. *Qu.* We come unseasonably: But when could greefe
Cull forth, as unpanged judgement can, fit'st time
For best solicitation.
Thes. Why, good Ladies,
This is a service, whereto I am going,
Greater then any was; it more imports me
Then all the actions that I have foregone,
Or futurely can cope.
1. *Qu.* The more proclaiming
Our suit shall be neglected: when her Armes
Able to locke *Iove* from a Synod, shall
By warranting Moone-light corslet thee, oh, when
Her twyning Cherries shall their sweetnes fall
Vpon thy tastefull lips, what wilt thou thinke
Of rotten Kings or blubberd Queenes, what care
For what thou feelst not? what thou feelst being able
To make *Mars* spurne his Drom. O, if thou couch
But one night with her, every howre in't will
Take hostage of thee for a hundred, and
Thou shalt remember nothing more then what
That Banket bids thee too.
Hip. Though much unlike ⟨*Kneeling.*⟩
You should be so transported, as much sorry
I should be such a Suitour; yet I thinke,
Did I not by th'abstayning of my joy,
Which breeds a deeper longing, cure their surfeit
That craves a present medcine, I should plucke
All Ladies scandall on me. Therefore, Sir,
As I shall here make tryall of my prayres,
Either presuming them to have some force,
Or sentencing for ay their vigour dombe:
Prorogue this busines we are going about, and hang
Your Sheild afore your Heart, about that necke
Which is my ffee, and which I freely lend
To doe these poore Queenes service.
All Queens. Oh helpe now,
Our Cause cries for your knee.
Emil. If you grant not ⟨*Kneeling.*⟩
My Sister her petition in that force,
With that Celerity and nature, which
Shee makes it in, from henceforth ile not dare
To aske you any thing, nor be so hardy
Ever to take a Husband.
Thes. Pray stand up.
I am entreating of my selfe to doe
That which you kneele to have me. *Pyrithous,*
Leade on the Bride; get you and pray the Gods
For successe, and returne; omit not any thing
In the pretended Celebration. Queenes,
Follow your Soldier. As before, hence you ⟨*to Artesius*⟩
And at the banckes of Aulis meete us with
The forces you can raise, where we shall finde
The moytie of a number, for a busines
More bigger look't. Since that our Theame is haste,
I stamp this kisse upon thy currant lippe;
Sweete, keepe it as my Token. Set you forward,
For I will see you gone.
[*Exeunt towards the Temple.*
Farewell, my beauteous Sister: *Pyrithous,*
Keepe the feast full, bate not an howre on't.
Pirithous. Sir,
Ile follow you at heeles; The Feasts solempnity
Shall want till your returne.
Thes. Cosen, I charge you
Boudge not from Athens; We shall be returning
Ere you can end this Feast, of which, I pray you,
Make no abatement; once more, farewell all.
1. *Qu.* Thus do'st thou still make good the tongue o'th world.
2. *Qu.* And earnst a Deity equal with Mars.
3. *Qu.* If not above him, for
Thou being but mortall makest affections bend
To Godlike honours; they themselves, some say,
Grone under such a Mastry.
Thes. As we are men,
Thus should we doe; being sensually subdude,
We loose our humane tytle. Good cheere, Ladies. [*Florish.*
Now turne we towards your Comforts.
[*Exeunt.*

Scæna 2. ⟨Thebs⟩.

Enter Palamon, and Arcite.

Arcite. Deere *Palamon,* deerer in love then Blood
And our prime Cosen, yet unhardned in
The Crimes of nature; Let us leave the Citty
Thebs, and the temptings in't, before we further

186 We] Ye *Herford* 191 was *Q, F*: war *Sew.* 198 twinning *Th.* 207 unlike *Q, F, etc.*: unliking *MS. correction in Lamb's copy of F* 207, 223 *S. D. add. Dyce*

235 *S. D. add. Dyce* 236 Aulis *Th.*: Anly *Q, F* 241 my] a *Herford* 242 *om. Herford* 247 want] wait *Sew.* *S. D.* Thebs *add. Sew.*

Sully our glosse of youth:
And here to keepe in abstinence we shame
As in Incontinence; for not to swim
I'th aide o'th Current were almost to sincke,
At least to frustrate striving, and to follow
The common Streame, twold bring us to an Edy
Where we should turne or drowne; if labour through,
Our gaine but life, and weakenes.
Pal. Your advice
Is cride up with example: what strange ruins
Since first we went to Schoole, may we perceive
Walking in Thebs? Skars, and bare weedes
The gaine o'th Martialist, who did propound
To his bold ends honour, and golden Ingots,
Which though he won, he had not, and now flurted
By peace for whom he fought: who then shall offer
To *Marsis* so scornd *Altar*? I doe bleede
When such I meete, and wish great *Iuno* would
Resume her ancient fit of *Ielouzie*
To get the Soldier worke, that peace might purge
For her repletion, and retaine anew
Her charitable heart now hard, and harsher
Then strife or war could be.
Arcite. Are you not out?
Meete you no ruine but the Soldier in
The Cranckes and turnes of Thebs? you did begin
As if you met decaies of many kindes:
Perceive you none, that doe arowse your pitty
But th'un-considerd Soldier?
Pal. Yes, I pitty
Decaies where ere I finde them, but such most
That, sweating in an honourable Toyle,
Are paide with yce to coole 'em.
Arcite. Tis not this
I did begin to speake of: This is vertue
Of no respect in Thebs; I spake of Thebs
How dangerous if we will keepe our Honours,
It is for our resyding, where every evill
Hath a good cullor; where eve'ry seeming good's
A certaine evill, where not to be ev'n Iumpe
As they are, here were to be strangers, and
Such things to be, meere Monsters.
Pal. Tis in our power,
(Vnlesse we feare that Apes can Tutor's) to
Be Masters of our manners: what neede I
Affect anothers gate, which is not catching
Where there is faith, or to be fond upon
Anothers way of speech, when by mine owne
I may be reasonably conceiv'd; sav'd too,
Speaking it truly? why am I bound
By any generous bond to follow him
Followes his Taylor, haply so long untill
The follow'd make pursuit? or let me know,
Why mine owne Barber is unblest, with him
My poore Chinne too, for tis not Cizard iust
To such a Favorites glasse: What Cannon is there
That does command my Rapier from my hip
To dangle't in my hand, or to go tip toe
Before the streete be foule? Either I am
The fore-horse in the Teame, or I am none
That draw i'th sequent trace: these poore sleight sores
Neede not a plantin; That which rips my bosome
Almost to'th heart's—
Arcite. Our Vncle *Creon.*
Pal. He,
A most unbounded Tyrant, whose successes
Makes heaven unfeard, and villany assured
Beyond its power there's nothing, almost puts
Faith in a feavour, and deifies alone
Voluble chance; who onely attributes
The faculties of other Instruments
To his owne Nerves and act; Commands men service,
And what they winne in't, boot and glory; on(e)
That feares not to do harm; good, dares not; Let
The blood of mine that's sibbe to him be suckt
From me with Leeches; Let them breake and fall
Off me with that corruption.
Arc. Cleere spirited Cozen,
Lets leave his Court, that we may nothing share
Of his lowd infamy: for our milke
Will relish of the pasture, and we must
Be vile or disobedient, not his kinesmen
In blood, unlesse in quality.
Pal. Nothing truer:
I thinke the Ecchoes of his shames have dea'ft
The eares of heav'nly Iustice: widdows cryes
Descend againe into their throates, and have not

Enter Valerius.

Due audience of the Gods.—*Valerius!*
Val. The King cals for you; yet be leaden footed,

8 aide] Head *conj. Th.* 25 retaine *Q, F*: reclaim *conj. Heath*: regain *conj. Sk.* 40 speak *Weber*

66 rips *Q*: tips *F* 73 feavour] Fear *conj. Th.* 77 boots and glories *Nicholson* on *Q, F*: one *Ingram*: too *Sew.*

Till his great rage be off him. *Phebus,* when
He broke his whipstocke and exclaimd against
The Horses of the Sun, but whisperd too
The lowdenesse of his Fury.
Pal. Small windes shake him:
But whats the matter?
Val. *Theseus* (who where he threates appals,) hath sent
Deadly defyance to him, and pronounces
Ruine to Thebs; who is at hand to seale
The promise of his wrath.
Arc. Let him approach;
But that we feare the Gods in him, he brings not
A jot of terrour to us; Yet what man
Thirds his owne worth (the case is each of ours)
When that his actions dregd with minde assurd
Tis bad he goes about?
Pal. Leave that unreasond.
Our services stand now for Thebs, not *Creon,*
Yet to be neutrall to him were dishonour;
Rebellious to oppose: therefore we must
With him stand to the mercy of our Fate,
Who hath bounded our last minute.
Arc. So we must.
Ist sed this warres a foote? or it shall be,
On faile of some condition?
Val. Tis in motion
The intelligence of state came in the instant
With the defier.
Pal. Lets to the king, who, were he
A quarter carrier of that honour which
His Enemy come in, the blood we venture
Should be as for our health, which were not spent,
Rather laide out for purchase: but, alas,
Our hands advanc'd before our hearts, what will
The fall o'th stroke doe damage?
Arci. Let th'event,
That never erring Arbitratour, tell us
When we know all our selves, and let us follow
The becking of our chance. [*Exeunt.*

Scæna 3. ⟨*Before the gates of Athens.*⟩

Enter Pirithous, Hipolita, Emilia.

Pir. No further.
Hip. Sir, farewell; repeat my wishes
To our great Lord, of whose succes I dare not
Make any timerous question; yet I wish him
Exces and overflow of power, and't might be,
To dure ill-dealing fortune: speede to him,
Store never hurtes good Gouernours.
Pir. Though I know
His Ocean needes not my poore drops, yet they
Must yeild their tribute there. My precious Maide,
Those best affections, that the heavens infuse
In their best temperd peices, keepe enthroand
In your deare heart.
Emil. Thanckes, Sir. Remember me
To our all royall Brother, for whose speede
The great Bellona ile sollicite; and
Since in our terrene State petitions are not
Without giftes understood, Ile offer to her
What I shall be advised she likes: our hearts
Are in his Army, in his Tent.
Hip. In's bosome:
We have bin Soldiers, and wee cannot weepe
When our Friends don their helmes, or put to sea,
Or tell of Babes broachd on the Launce, or women
That have sod their Infants in (and after eate them)
The brine, they wept at killing 'em; Then if
You stay to see of us such Spincsters, we
Should hold you here for ever.
Pir. Peace be to you,
As I pursue this war, which shall be then
Beyond further requiring. [*Exit Pir.*
Emil. How his longing
Followes his Friend! since his depart, his sportes
Though craving seriousnes, and skill, past slightly
His careles execution, where nor gaine
Made him regard, or losse consider; but
Playing one busines in his hand, another
Directing in his head, his minde, nurse equall
To these so diffring Twyns—have you observ'd him,
Since our great Lord departed?
Hip. With much labour,
And I did love him fort: they two have Cabind
In many as dangerous, as poore a Corner,
Perill and want contending; they have skift
Torrents whose roring tyranny and power
I'th least of these was dreadfull, and they have
Fought out together, where Deaths-selfe was lodgd,
Yet fate hath brought them off: Their knot of love,

124 come *Q*: came *F*: comes *Colman* *S. D.* Before *etc. add. Dyce*

6 dure *Q, F*: dare *conj. Sew.*: cure *conj. Sew.* 33 sportes] imports *conj. Coleridge* 37 one *Mason, Heath*: ore *Q*: o'er *F* 46 least . . was *Q, F*: best of Ships were *conj. Sew.* 47 Fought] Sought *conj. Litt.*

Tide, weau'd, intangled, with so true, so long,
And with a finger of so deepe a cunning,
May be outworne, never undone. I thinke
Theseus cannot be umpire to himselfe,
Cleaving his conscience into twaine and doing
Each side like Iustice, which he loves best.
Emil. Doubtlesse
There is a best, and reason has no manners
To say it is not you: I was acquainted
Once with a time, when I enjoyd a Play-fellow;
You were at wars, when she the grave enrichd,
Who made too proud the Bed, tooke leave o th Moone
(Which then lookt pale at parting) when our count
Was each eleven.
Hip. Twas *Flaui⟨n⟩a.*
Emil. Yes.
You talke of *Pirithous* and *Theseus* love;
Theirs has more ground, is more maturely seasond,
More buckled with strong Iudgement and their needes
The one of th'other may be said to water
[2. *Hearses ready with Palamon: and Arcite: the* 3. *Queenes. Theseus: and his Lordes ready.*
Their intertangled rootes of love; but I
And shee I sigh and spoke of were things innocent,
Lou'd for we did, and like the Elements
That know not what, nor why, yet doe effect
Rare issues by their operance, our soules
Did so to one another; what she lik'd,
Was then of me approov'd, what not, condemd,
No more arraignement; the flowre that I would plucke
And put betweene my breasts (then but beginning
To swell about the blossome) oh, she would long
Till shee had such another, and commit it
To the like innocent Cradle, where *Phenix* like
They dide in perfume: on my head no toy
But was her patterne; her affections (pretty,
Though, happely, her careles were) I followed
For my most serious decking; had mine eare
Stolne some new aire, or at adventure humd on
From musicall Coynadge, why it was a note
Whereon her spirits would sojourne (rather dwell on)
And sing it in her slumbers. This rehearsall
(Which ev'ry innocent wots well comes in
Like old importments bastard) has this end,
That the true love tweene Mayde, and mayde, may be
More then in sex idividuall.
Hip. Y'are out of breath
And this high speeded pace, is but to say
That you shall never like the Maide *Flavina*
Love any that's calld Man.
Emil. I am sure I shall not.
Hip. Now, alacke, weake Sister,
I must no more beleeve thee in this point
(Though in't I know thou dost beleeve thy selfe,)
Then I will trust a sickely appetite,
That loathes even as it longs; but, sure, my Sister,
If I were ripe for your perswasion, you
Have saide enough to shake me from the Arme
Of the all noble *Theseus*, for whose fortunes
I will now in, and kneele with great assurance,
That we, more then his *Pirothous*, possesse
The high throne in his heart.
Emil. I am not
Against your faith; yet I continew mine.
[*Exeunt. Cornets.*

Scæna 4. ⟨*A field before Thebes. Dead bodies lying on the ground.*⟩

A Battaile strooke within: Then a Retrait: Florish. Then Enter Theseus (victor), ⟨*Herald and* Attendants:⟩ *the three Queenes meete him, and fall on their faces before him.*

1. *Qu.* To thee no starre be darke.
2. *Qu.* Both heaven and earth
Friend thee for ever.
3. *Qu.* All the good that may
Be wishd upon thy head, I cry Amen too't.
Thes. Th'imparciall Gods, who from the mounted heavens
View us their mortall Heard, behold who erre,
And in their time chastice: goe and finde out
The bones of your dead Lords, and honour them

62 eleven *F, etc.*: a eleven *Q* 63 Flauia *Q*: Flavina *Sew.* *Cf.* l. 95 68 ff. *S. D.* 2 Hearses .. ready (*prompter's marginal note*) *after* l. 63 *T* 77 breasts (then *pr. ed.*: breasts, oh (then *Q, etc.* 78 blossome) oh, she *pr. ed.*: blossome) she *Q, etc.* 83 her *Q, F*: they *conj. Sy.*: hers *conj. Lamb* careles, were *Q, F*: careless wear *Colman*

85 on *Q, F*: one *conj. Sew.* 86 misicall *Q* 89 every innocent *Lamb*: fury-innocent *Q*: surely Innocence *Sy.* wots] wot I *Mason* 92 dividual *Sew.*: individuall *Q* 109 *Ends* faith *Q, F*: *corr. Dyce* *S. D.* A field *etc. add. Dyce* *S. D.* Herald *etc. add. Dyce*

With treble Ceremonie; rather then a gap
Should be in their deere rights, we would supply't.
But those we will depute, which shall invest
You in your dignities, and even each thing
Our hast does leave imperfect: So, adiew,
And heavens good eyes looke on you. What are those? [*Exeunt Queenes.*

Herald. Men of great quality, as may be judgd
By their appointment; Some of Thebs have told's
They are Sisters children, Nephewes to the King.

Thes. By'th Helme of Mars, I saw them in the war,
Like to a paire of Lions, smeard with prey,
Make lanes in troopes agast. I fixt my note
Constantly on them; for they were a marke
Worth a god's view: what prisoner was't that told me
When I enquired their names?

Herald. Wi' leave, they'r called *Arcite* and *Palamon.*

Thes. Tis right: those, those. They are not dead?

Her. Nor in a state of life: had they bin taken,
When their last hurts were given, twas possible
[3. *Hearses ready.*
They might have bin recovered; Yet they breathe
And haue the name of men.

Thes. Then like men use 'em.
The very lees of such (millions of rates)
Exceede the wine of others: all our Surgions
Convent in their behoofe; our richest balmes
Rather then niggard, waft: their lives concerne us
Much more then Thebs is worth: rather then have 'em
Freed of this plight, and in their morning state
(Sound and at liberty) I would 'em dead;
But forty thousand fold we had rather have 'em
Prisoners to us then death. Beare 'em speedily
From our kinde aire, to them unkinde, and minister
What man to man may doe—for our sake more,
Since I have knowne frights, fury, friends beheastes,
Loves provocations, zeale, a mistris Taske,
Desire of liberty, a feavour, madnes,
Hath set a marke which nature could not reach too
Without some imposition: sicknes in will
Or wrastling strength in reason. For our Love
And great *Appollos* mercy, all our best
Their best skill tender. Leade into the Citty,
Where having bound things scatterd, we will post [*Florish.*
To Athens for⟨e⟩ our Army [*Exeunt. Musicke.*

Scæna 5. ⟨*Another part of the same.*⟩

Enter the Queenes with the Hearses of their Knightes, in a Funerall Solempnity, &c.

Vrnes and odours bring away,
Vapours, sighes, darken the day;
Our dole more deadly lookes than dying;
Balmes, and Gummes, and heavy cheeres,
Sacred vials fill'd with teares,
And clamors through the wild ayre flying.

Come all sad and solempne Showes,
That are quick-eyd pleasures foes;
We convent nought else but woes.
We convent, &c.

3. *Qu.* This funeral path brings to your housholds grave:
Ioy ceaze on you againe: peace sleepe with him.

2. *Qu.* And this to yours.

1. *Qu.* Yours this way: Heavens lend
A thousand differing waies to one sure end.

3. *Qu.* This world's a Citty full of straying Streetes,
And Death's the market place, where each one meetes. [*Exeunt severally.*

Actus Secundus.

Scæna 1. ⟨*Athens. A garden, with a prison in the background.*⟩

Enter Iailor, and Wooer.

Iailor. I may depart with little, while I live; some thing I may cast to you, not much: Alas, the Prison I keepe, though it be for great ones, yet they seldome come; Before one *Salmon*, you shall take a number of Minnowes. I am given out to be better lyn'd then it can appeare to me report is a true Speaker: I would

11 Rites *Sew., etc.* supply't *F*: suppl' it *Q* 20 smeard] *some copies of Q* (*Dyce's, Colman's, Daniel's*) *read* succard 23 What was't that prisoner told *Dyce, etc.* 25 Wi' leave *Dyce*: We leave *Q, F*: With leave *Sew.*: We learn *conj. Heath*: We 'leave *Litt.*

43 fight's fury *Dyce* 43–4 friends, beheastes, Loves, provocations *Q, F* 44 zeal in a *Dyce* 52 for *Q, F*: 'fore *Sew.* *S. D.* Another *etc. add. Dyce* *S. D.* Athens *etc. add. Dyce* 1–68 *Verse Q, F*

I were really that I am deliverd to be. Marry, what I have (be it what it will) I will assure upon my daughter at the day of my death.

Wooer. Sir, I demaund no more then your owne offer, and I will estate your Daughter in what I have promised.

Iailor. Wel, we will talke more of this, when the solemnity is past. But have you a full promise of her? When that shall be seene, I tender my consent.

Enter Daughter.

Wooer. I have Sir; here shee comes.

Iailor. Your Friend and I have chanced to name you here, upon the old busines: But no more of that now; so soone as the Court hurry is over, we will have an end of it: I'th meane time looke tenderly to the two Prisoners. I can tell you they are princes.

Daug. These strewings are for their Chamber; tis pitty they are in prison, and twer pitty they should be out: I doe thinke they have patience to make any adversity asham'd; the prison it selfe is proud of 'em; and they have all the world in their Chamber.

Iailor. They are fam'd to be a paire of absolute men.

Daugh. By my troth, I think Fame but stammers 'em; they stand a greise above the reach of report.

Iai. I heard them reported in the Battaile to be the only doers.

Daugh. Nay, most likely, for they are noble suffrers; I mervaile how they would have lookd had they beene Victors, that with such a constant Nobility enforce a freedome out of Bondage, making misery their Mirth, and affliction a toy to jest at.

Iailor. Doe they so?

Daug. It seemes to me they have no more sence of their Captivity, then I of ruling Athens: they eate well, looke merrily, discourse of many things, but nothing of their owne restraint, and disasters: yet sometime a devided sigh, martyrd as 'twer i'th deliverance, will breake from one of them; when the other presently gives it so sweete a rebuke, that I could wish my selfe a Sigh to be so chid, or at least a Sigher to be comforted.

Wooer. I never saw 'em.

Iailor. The Duke himselfe came privately in the night,

Enter Palamon, and Arcite, above.

and so did they: what the reason of it is, I know not: Looke, yonder they are! that's *Arcite* lookes out.

Daugh. No, Sir, no, that's *Palamon: Arcite* is the lower of the twaine; you may perceive a part of him.

Iai. Goe too, leave your pointing; they would not make us their object; out of their sight.

Daugh. It is a holliday to looke on them: Lord, the diffrence of men! [*Exeunt.*

Scæna 2. ⟨*The prison*⟩ *Enter Palamon, and Arcite in prison.*

Pal. How doe you, Noble Cosen?
Arcite. How doe you, Sir?
Pal. Why strong inough to laugh at misery,
And beare the chance of warre, yet we are prisoners,
I feare, for ever, Cosen.
Arcite. I beleeve it,
And to that destiny have patiently
Laide up my houre to come.
Pal. Oh Cosen *Arcite*,
Where is Thebs now? where is our noble Country?
Where are our friends, and kindreds? never more
Must we behold those comforts, never see
The hardy youthes strive for the Games of honour
(Hung with the painted favours of their Ladies,
Like tallShips under saile) then start among'st 'em
And as an Eastwind leave 'em all behinde us,
Like lazy Clowdes, whilst *Palamon* and *Arcite*,
Even in the wagging of a wanton leg
Out-stript the peoples praises, won the Garlands,
Ere they have time to wish 'em ours. O never
Shall we two exercise, like Twyns of honour,
Our Armes againe, and feele our fyry horses
Like proud Seas under us: our good Swords now
(Better the red-eyd god of war nev'r wore)
Ravishd our sides, like age must run to rust,
And decke the Temples of those gods that hate us:
These hands shall never draw'em out like lightning,
To blast whole Armies more.
Arcite. No, *Palamon*,
Those hopes are Prisoners with us; here we are

S. D. after 16 *Q* 21 that. Now, *Q* : *corr. Dyce* 34 greise *Q* : grief *F* : Gree *conj. Sew.*

Scaena 2 *Dyce continues Scene I* *S. D.* The prison *add. pr. ed.* 19 ? Out-strip . . win 24 wore *Sew.* : were *Q, F* : ware *Dyce* 25 Ravish'd *Sew.* : Bravishd *Q, F*

And here the graces of our youthes must wither
Like a too-timely Spring; here age must finde us,
And, which is heaviest, *Palamon,* unmarried;
The sweete embraces of a loving wife,
Loden with kisses, armd with thousand Cupids
Shall never claspe our neckes, no issue know us,
No figures of our selves shall we ev'r see,
To glad our age, and like young Eagles teach 'em
Boldly to gaze against bright armes, and say:
'Remember what your fathers were, and conquer.'
The faire-eyd Maides, shall weepe our Banishments,
And in their Songs, curse ever-blinded fortune,
Till shee for shame see what a wrong she has done
To youth and nature. This is all our world;
We shall know nothing here but one another,
Heare nothing but the Clocke that tels our woes.
The Vine shall grow, but we shall never see it:
Sommer shall come, and with her all delights;
But dead-cold winter must inhabite here still.
Pal. Tis too true, *Arcite.* To our Theban houndes,
That shooke the aged Forrest with their ecchoes,
No more now must we halloa, no more shake
Our pointed Iavelyns, whilst the angry Swine
Flyes like a parthian quiver from our rages,
Strucke with our well-steeld Darts: All valiant uses
(The foode, and nourishment of noble mindes,)
In us two here shall perish; we shall die
(Which is the curse of honour) lastly
Children of greife, and Ignorance.
Arc. Yet, Cosen,
Even from the bottom of these miseries,
From all that fortune can inflict upon us,
I see two comforts rysing, two meere blessings,
If the gods please: to hold here a brave patience,
And the enjoying of our greefes together.
Whilst *Palamon* is with me, let me perish
If I thinke this our prison.
Pala. Certeinly,
Tis a maine goodnes, Cosen, that our fortunes
Were twyn'd together; tis most true, two soulos
Put in two noble Bodies—let 'em suffer
The gaule of hazard, so they grow together—
Will never sincke; they must not, say they could:
A willing man dies sleeping, and all's done.
Arc. Shall we make worthy uses of this place
That all men hate so much?
Pal. How, gentle Cosen?
Arc. Let's thinke this prison holy sanctuary,
To keepe us from corruption of worse men.
We are young and yet desire the waies of honour,
That liberty and common Conversation,
The poyson of pure spirits, might like women
Wooe us to wander from. What worthy blessing
Can be but our Imaginations
May make it ours? And heere being thus together,
We are an endles mine to one another;
We are one anothers wife, ever begetting
New birthes of love; we are father, friends, acquaintance;
We are, in one another, Families,
I am your heire, and you are mine: This place
Is our Inheritance, no hard Oppressour
Dare take this from us; here, with a little patience,
We shall live long, and loving: No surfeits seeke us:
The hand of war hurts none here, nor the Seas
Swallow their youth: were we at liberty,
A wife might part us lawfully, or busines;
Quarrels consume us, Envy of ill men
Grave our acquaintance; I might sicken, Cosen,
Where you should never know it, and so perish
Without your noble hand to close mine eies,
Or praiers to the gods: a thousand chaunces,
Were we from hence, would seaver us.
Pal. You have made me
(I thanke you, Cosen *Arcite*) almost wanton
With my Captivity: what a misery
It is to live abroade, and every where!
Tis like a Beast, me thinkes: I finde the Court here—
I am sure, a more content; and all those pleasures
That wooe the wils of men to vanity,
I see through now, and am sufficient
To tell the world, tis but a gaudy shaddow,
That old Time, as he passes by, takes with him.

58 lastly] lazily *Sew.* 64 please to hold's here: *conj. pr. ed.* 70 twinn'd *Sew.*

74 sseeping *Q* 98 Grave *Dyce*: Crave *Q, F*: Reave *Sew.*: Craze *Th.*: Carve *Sy.*: Raze *Heath*: Cleave *Mason*

What had we bin, old in the Court of *Creon*,
Where sin is Iustice, lust and ignorance
The vertues of the great ones! Cosen *Arcite*,
Had not the loving gods found this place for us,
We had died as they doe, ill old men, unwept,
And had their Epitaphes, the peoples Curses:
Shall I say more?
Arc. I would heare you still.
Pal. Ye shall.
Is there record of any two that lov'd
Better then we doe, *Arcite*?
Arc. Sure, there cannot.
Pal. I doe not thinke it possible our friendship
Should ever leave us.
Arc. Till our deathes it cannot;

Enter Emilia and her woman ⟨*below*⟩.

And after death our spirits shall be led
To those that love eternally. Speake on, Sir.
Emil. This garden has a world of pleasures in't.
What Flowre is this?
Wom. Tis calld Narcissus, Madam.
Emil. That was a faire Boy, certaine, but a foole,
To love himselfe; were there not maides enough?
Arc. Pray forward.
Pal. Yes.
Emil. Or were they all hard hearted?
Wom. They could not be to one so faire.
Emil. Thou wouldst not.
Wom. I thinke I should not, Madam.
Emil. That's a good wench:
But take heede to your kindnes though.
Wom. Why, Madam?
Emil. Men are mad things.
Arcite. Will ye goe forward, Cosen?
Emil. Canst not thou worke such flowers in silke, wench?
Wom. Yes.
Emil. Ile have a gowne full of 'em, and of these;
This is a pretty colour, wilt not doe
Rarely upon a Skirt, wench?
Wom. Deinty, Madam.
Arc. Cosen, Cosen, how doe you, Sir? Why, *Palamon*?
Pal. Never till now I was in prison, *Arcite*.
Arc. Why whats the matter, Man?
Pal. Behold, and wonder.
By heaven, shee is a Goddesse.
Arcite. Ha.
Pal. Doe reverence. She is a Goddesse, *Arcite*.
Emil. Of all Flowres, me thinkes a Rose is best.
Wom. Why, gentle Madam?
Emil. It is the very Embleme of a Maide.
For when the west wind courts her gently,
How modestly she blowes, and paints the Sun,
With her chaste blushes! When the North comes neere her,
Rude and impatient, then, like Chastity,
Shee lockes her beauties in her bud againe,
And leaves him to base briers.
Wom. Yet, good Madam,
Sometimes her modesty will blow so far
She fals for't: a Mayde,
If shee have any honour, would be loth
To take example by her.
Emil. Thou art wanton.
Arc. She is wondrous faire.
Pal. She is all the beauty extant.
Emil. The Sun grows high, lets walk in: keep these flowers;
Weele see how neere Art can come neere their colours.
I am wondrous merry hearted, I could laugh now.
Wom. I could lie downe, I am sure.
Emil. And take one with you?
Wom. That's as we bargaine, Madam.
Emil. Well, agree then.
[*Exeunt Emilia and woman.*
Pal. What thinke you of this beauty?
Arc. Tis a rare one.
Pal. Is't but a rare one?
Arc. Yes, a matchles beauty.
Pal. Might not a man well lose himselfe and love her?
Arc. I cannot tell what you have done, I have;
Beshrew mine eyes for't: now I feele my Shackles.
Pal. You love her, then?
Arc. Who would not?
Pal. And desire her?
Arc. Before my liberty.
Pal. I saw her first.
Arc. That's nothing.
Pal. But it shall be.
Arc. I saw her too.
Pal. Yes, but you must not love her.
Arc. I will not as you doe, to worship her,
As she is heavenly, and a blessed Goddes;
I love her as a woman, to enjoy her:
So both may love.
Pal. You shall not love at all.

127 *S. D.* below *add. Dyce* 130 *Prefix precedes* 131 *Q, F*

162 gentily *Sew.*

Arc. Not love at all!
Who shall deny me?
Pal. I, that first saw her; I, that tooke possession
First with mine eyes of all those beauties
In her reveald to mankinde: if thou lou'st her,
Or entertain'st a hope to blast my wishes,
Thou art a Traytour, *Arcite,* and a fellow
False as thy Title to her: friendship, blood,
And all the tyes betweene us I disclaime,
If thou once thinke upon her.
Arc. Yes, I love her,
And if the lives of all my name lay on it,
I must doe so; I love her with my soule:
If that will lose ye, farewell, *Palamon*;
I say againe, I love, and in loving her maintaine
I am as worthy and as free a lover,
And have as just a title to her beauty
As any *Palamon* or any living
That is a mans Sonne.
Pal. Have I cald thee friend?
Arc. Yes, and have found me so; why are you mov'd thus?
Let me deale coldly with you: am not I
Part of your blood, part of your soule? you have told me
That I was *Palamon,* and you were *Arcite.*
Pal. Yes.
Arc. Am not I liable to those affections,
Those joyes, greifes, angers, feares, my friend shall suffer?
Pal. Ye may be.
Arc. Why, then, would you deale so cunningly,
So strangely, so vnlike a noble kinesman,
To love alone? speake truely: doe you thinke me
Vnworthy of her sight?
Pal. No; but unjust,
If thou pursue that sight.
Arc. Because an other
First sees the Enemy, shall I stand still
And let mine honour downe, and never charge?
Pal. Yes, if he be but one.
Arc. But say that one
Had rather combat me?
Pal. Let that one say so,
And use thy freedome; els if thou pursuest her,
Be as that cursed man that hates his Country,
A branded villaine.
Arc. You are mad.
Pal. I must be,
Till thou art worthy, *Arcite*; it concernes me,
And in this madnes, if I hazard thee
And take thy life, I deale but truely.
Arc. Fie, Sir,
You play the Childe extreamely: I will love her,
I must, I ought to doe so, and I dare;
And all this justly.
Pal. O that now, that now
Thy false-selfe and thy friend had but this fortune,
To be one howre at liberty, and graspe
Our good Swords in our hands! I would quickly teach thee
What 'twer to filch affection from another:
Thou art baser in it then a Cutpurse;
Put but thy head out of this window more,
And as I have a soule, Ile naile thy life too't.
Arc. Thou dar'st not, foole, thou canst not, thou art feeble.
Put my head out? Ile throw my Body out,
And leape the garden, when I see her next

Enter Keeper.

And pitch between her armes to anger thee.
Pal. No more; the keeper's comming; I shall live
To knocke thy braines out with my Shackles.
Arc. Doe.
Keeper. By your leave, Gentlemen—
Pala. Now, honest keeper?
Keeper. Lord *Arcite,* you must presently to'th Duke;
The cause I know not yet.
Arc. I am ready, keeper.
Keeper. Prince *Palamon,* I must awhile bereave you
Of your faire Cosens Company.
[*Exeunt Arcite, and Keeper.*
Pal And me too,
Even when you please, of life. Why is he sent for?
It may be he shall marry her; he's goodly,
And like enough the Duke hath taken notice
Both of his blood and body: But his falsehood!
Why should a friend be treacherous? If that
Get him a wife so noble, and so faire,
Let honest men ne're love againe. Once more
I would but see this faire One. Blessed Garden,
And fruite, and flowers more blessed, that still blossom
As her bright eies shine on ye! would I were,
For all the fortune of my life hereafter,
Yon little Tree, yon blooming Apricocke;
How I would spread, and fling my wanton armes
In at her window; I would bring her fruite

207 *Ends* her *Sew.* 226 you blood *Q* 261 tw'er *Q*

Fit for the Gods to feed on: youth and pleasure
Still as she tasted should be doubled on her,
And if she be not heavenly, I would make her
So neere the Gods in nature, they should feare her,

Enter Keeper.

And then I am sure she would love me. How now, keeper,
Wher's *Arcite*?

Keeper. Banishd: Prince *Pirithous*
Obtained his liberty; but never more
Vpon his oth and life must he set foote
Vpon this Kingdome.

Pal. Hees a blessed man!
He shall see Thebs againe, and call to Armes
The bold yong men, that, when he bids 'em charge,
Fall on like fire: *Arcite* shall have a Fortune,
If he dare make himselfe a worthy Lover,
Yet in the Feild to strike a battle for her;
And if he lose her then, he's a cold Coward;
How bravely may he beare himselfe to win her
If he be noble *Arcite*—thousand waies.
Were I at liberty, I would doe things
Of such a vertuous greatnes, that this Lady,
This blushing virgine, should take manhood to her
And seeke to ravish me.

Keeper. My Lord for you
I have this charge too—

Pal. To discharge my life?

Keep. No, but from this place to remoove your Lordship:
The windowes are too open.

Pal. Devils take 'em,
That are so envious to me! pre'thee kill me.

Keep. And hang for't afterward.

Pal. By this good light,
Had I a sword I would kill thee.

Keep. Why, my Lord?

Pal. Thou bringst such pelting scuruy news continually
Thou art not worthy life. I will not goe.

Keep. Indeede, you must, my Lord.

Pal. May I see the garden?

Keep. Noe.

Pal. Then I am resolud, I will not goe.

Keep. I must constraine you then: and for you are dangerous,
Ile clap more yrons on you.

Pal. Doe, good keeper.
Ile shake 'em so, ye shall not sleepe;
Ile make ye a new Morrisse: must I goe?

Keep. There is no remedy.

Pal. Farewell, kinde window.
May rude winde never hurt thee. O, my Lady,
If ever thou hast felt what sorrow was,
Dreame how I suffer. Come; now bury me.
[*Exeunt Palamon, and Keeper.*

Scæna 3. ⟨*The country near Athens.*⟩

Enter Arcite.

Arcite. Banishd the kingdome? tis a benefit,
A mercy I must thanke 'em for, but banishd
The free enjoying of that face I die for,
Oh twas a studdied punishment, a death
Beyond Imagination: Such a vengeance
That, were I old and wicked, all my sins
Could never plucke upon me. *Palamon,*
Thou ha'st the Start now, thou shalt stay and see
Her bright eyes breake each morning gainst thy window,
And let in life into thee; thou shalt feede
Vpon the sweetenes of a noble beauty,
That nature nev'r exceeded, nor nev'r shall:
Good gods! what happines has *Palamon!*
Twenty to one, hee'le come to speake to her,
And if she be as gentle as she's faire,
I know she's his; he has a Tongue will tame
Tempests, and make the wild Rockes wanton.
Come what can come,
The worst is death; I will not leave the Kingdome.
I know mine owne is but a heape of ruins,
And no redresse there; if I goe, he has her.
I am resolu'd an other shape shall make me,
Or end my fortunes. Either way, I am happy:
Ile see her, and be neere her, or no more.

Enter 4. Country people, & one with a garlond before them.

1. My Masters, ile be there, that's certaine
2. And Ile be there.
3. And I.
4. Why, then, have with ye, Boyes; Tis but a chiding.
Let the plough play to day, ile tick'lt out
Of the Iades tailes to morrow.

1. I am sure
To have my wife as jealous as a Turkey:
But that's all one; ile goe through, let her mumble.

2. Clap her aboard to morrow night, and stoa her,
And all's made up againe.

3. I, doe but put a feskue in her fist, and you shall see her

319 life. *Q*

S. D. The . . Athens *add. Dyce*

Take a new lesson out, and be a good wench.
Doe we all hold against the Maying?
4. Hold? what should aile us?
3. *Arcas* will be there.
2. And *Sennois*.
And *Rycas*, and 3. better lads nev'r danc'd
Under green Tree. And yee know what wenches: ha?
But will the dainty Domine, the Schoolemaster,
Keep touch, doe you thinke? for he do's all, ye know.
3. Hee'l eate a hornebooke ere he faile: goe too, the matter's too farre driven betweene him and the Tanners daughter, to let slip now, and she must see the Duke, and she must daunce too.
4. Shall we be lusty?
2. All the Boyes in Athens blow wind i'th breech on's, and heere ile be and there ile be, for our Towne, and here againe, and there againe: ha, Boyes, heigh for the weavers.
1. This must be done i'th woods.
4. O, pardon me.
2. By any meanes, our thing of learning saies so:
Where he himselfe will edifie the Duke
Most parlously in our behalfes: hees excellent i'th woods;
Bring him to'th plaines, his learning makes no cry.
3. Weele see the sports, then; every man to's Tackle:
And, Sweete Companions, lets rehearse by any meanes,
Before the Ladies see us, and doe sweetly,
And God knows what May come on't.
4. Content; the sports once ended, wee'l performe.
Away, Boyes and hold.
Arc. By your leaves, honest friends: pray you, whither goe you?
4. Whither? why, what a question's that?
Arc. Yes, tis a question, to me that know not.
3. To the *Games*, my Friend.
2. Where were you bred, you know it not?
Arc. Not farre, Sir,
Are there such *Games* to day?
1. Yes, marry, are there:
And such as you neuer saw; The *Duke* himselfe
Will be in person there.
Arc. What pastimes are they?
2. Wrastling, and Running.—Tis a pretty Fellow.
3. Thou wilt not goe along?
Arc. Not yet, Sir.
4. Well, Sir,
Take your owne time: come, Boyes.
1. My minde misgives me;
This fellow has a veng'ance tricke o'th hip:
Marke how his Bodi's made for't
2. Ile be hangd, though,
If he dare venture; hang him, plumb porredge,
He wrastle? he rost eggs! Come, lets be gon, Lads. [*Exeunt* 4.
Arc. This is an offerd oportunity
I durst not wish for. Well I could have wrestled,
The best men calld it excellent, and run—
Swifter the winde upon a feild of Corne
(Curling the wealthy eares) never flew: Ile venture,
And in some poore disguize be there; who knowes
Whether my browes may not be girt with garlands?
And happines preferre me to a place,
Where I may ever dwell in sight of her.
[*Exit Arcite.*

Scæna 4. ⟨*Athens. A room in the prison.*⟩
Enter Iailors Daughter alone.

Daugh. Why should I love this Gentleman? Tis odds
He never will affect me; I am base,
My Father the meane Keeper of his Prison,
And he a prince: To marry him is hopelesse;
To be his whore is witles. Out upon't,
What pushes are we wenches driven to,
When fifteene once has found us! First, I saw him;
I (seeing) thought he was a goodly man;
He has as much to please a woman in him,
(If he please to bestow it so) as ever
These eyes yet lookt on. Next, I pittied him,
And so would any young wench, o' my Conscience,
That ever dream'd, or vow'd her Maydenhead
To a yong hansom Man; Then I lov'd him,
Extreamely lov'd him, infinitely lov'd him;
And yet he had a Cosen, faire as he too.
But in my heart was *Palamon*, and there,
Lord, what a coyle he keepes! To heare him
Sing in an evening, what a heaven it is!

42 *Ends* Tree *Q* 43 ye *Sew.*: yet *Q*, *F* 44 *Ends* touch *Q* 52-5 *Verse Sew., etc.* 58 says *Sew.*: sees *Q*, *F* 58-61 *Prose Q* 62-5 *Div. after* and, before, what *Q* 66 *Ends* Away *Q*

92 Well, I *Q*, *F* 94 the *Sew.*: then *Q*, *F* 95 never *Q*, *F*: near *Th.*: ever *Dyce* S. D. Athens, *etc. add. Dyce* 3 his *Q*, *F*: this *Sew.* 18 To heare *Q*, *F*: To sit and hear *Sew.*

And yet his Songs are sad ones. Fairer spoken
Was never Gentleman. When I come in
To bring him water in a morning, first
He bowes his noble body, then salutes me, thus:
'Faire, gentle Mayde, good morrow; may thy goodnes
Get thee a happy husband.' Once he kist me.
I lov'd my lips the better ten daies after.
Would he would doe so ev'ry day! He greives much,
And me as much to see his misery.
What should I doe, to make him know I love him?
For I would faine enjoy him. Say I ventur'd
To set him free? what saies the law then? Thus much
For Law, or kindred! I will doe it,
And this night, or to morrow, he shall love me. [*Exit.*

Scæna 5. ⟨*An open place in Athens.*⟩

Enter Theseus, Hipolita, Pirithous, Emilia: Arcite with a Garland, &c.

[*This short florish of Cornets and Showtes within.*

Thes. You have done worthily; I have not seene,
Since *Hercules*, a man of tougher synewes;
What ere you are, you run the best, and wrastle,
That these times can allow.
Arcite. I am proud to please you.
Thes. What Countrie bred you?
Arcite. This; but far off, Prince.
Thes. Are you a Gentleman?
Arcite. My father said so;
And to those gentle uses gave me life.
Thes. Are you his heire?
Arcite. His yongest, Sir.
Thes. Your Father
Sure is a happy Sire then: what prooves you?
Arcite. A little of all noble Quallities:
I could have kept a Hawke, and well have holloa'd
To a deepe crie of Dogges; I dare not praise
My feat in horsemanship, yet they that knew me
Would say it was my best peece: last, and greatest,
I would be thought a Souldier.
Thes. You are perfect.
Pirith. Vpon my soule, a proper man.
Emilia. He is so.
Per. How doe you like him, Ladie?
Hip. I admire him;
I have not seene so yong a man so noble
(If he say true,) of his sort.
Emil. Beleeve,
His mother was a wondrous handsome woman;
His face, me thinkes, goes that way.
Hyp. But his Body
And firie minde illustrate a brave Father.
Per. Marke how his vertue, like a hidden Sun,
Breakes through his baser garments.
Hyp. Hee's well got, sure.
Thes. What made you seeke this place, Sir?
Arc. Noble *Theseus*,
To purchase name, and doe my ablest service
To such a well-found wonder as thy worth,
For onely in thy Court, of all the world,
Dwells faire-eyd honor.
Per. All his words are worthy.
Thes. Sir, we are much endebted to your travell,
Nor shall you loose your wish: *Perithous*,
Dispose of this faire Gentleman.
Perith. Thankes, *Theseus*.
What ere you are y'ar mine, and I shall give you
To a most noble service, to this Lady,
This bright yong Virgin; pray, observe her goodnesse;
You have honourd hir faire birth-day with your vertues,
And as your due y'ar hirs: kisse her faire hand, Sir.
Arc. Sir, y'ar a noble Giver: dearest Bewtie,
Thus let me seale my vowd faith: when your Servant
(Your most unworthie Creature) but offends you,
Command him die, he shall.
Emil. That were too cruell.
If you deserve well, Sir, I shall soone see't:
Y'ar mine, and somewhat better than your rancke
Ile use you.
Per. Ile see you furnish'd, and because you say
You are a horseman, I must needs intreat you
This after noone to ride, but tis a rough one.
Arc. I like him better, Prince, I shall not then
Freeze in my Saddle.

32 doe it *Q*: do it, ay *Sew.* 33 or *Q*: and *Sew.* Scaena 4 *Q*: Scaena Secunda *F* *S. D.* An . . Athens *Litt.* 10 me *Q*: my *conj. Sew.* 14 proves *Q*: prove *Sew.*: profess *conj. Ingram*

40 Fo *Q* 58-9 *One line Q*

Thes. Sweet, you must be readie,
And you, *Emilia,* and you, Friend, and all,
To morrow by the Sun, to doe observance
To flowry May, in *Dians* wood: waite well, Sir,
Vpon your Mistris. *Emely,* I hope
He shall not goe a foote.
Emil. That were a shame, Sir,
While I have horses: take your choice, and what
You want at any time, let me but know it;
If you serve faithfully, I dare assure you
You'l finde a loving Mistris.
Arc. If I doe not,
Let me finde that my Father ever hated,
Disgrace and blowes.
Thes. Go, leade the way; you have won it:
It shall be so; you shall receave all dues
Fit for the honour you have won; Twer wrong else.
Sister, beshrew my heart, you have a Servant,
That, if I were a woman, would be Master,
But you are wise. [*Florish.*
Emil. I hope too wise for that, Sir.
[*Exeunt omnes.*

Scæna 6. ⟨*Before the prison.*⟩

Enter Iaylors Daughter alone.

Daughter. Let all the Dukes, and all the divells rore,
He is at liberty: I have venturd for him,
And out I have brought him to a little wood
A mile hence. I have sent him, where a Cedar,
Higher than all the rest, spreads like a plane
Fast by a Brooke, and there he shall keepe close,
Till I provide him Fyles and foode, for yet
His yron bracelets are not off. O Love,
What a stout hearted child thou art! My Father
Durst better have indur'd cold yron, than done it:
I love him beyond love and beyond reason,
Or wit, or safetie: I have made him know it.
I care not, I am desperate; If the law
Finde me, and then condemne me for't, some wenches,
Some honest harted Maides, will sing my Dirge,
And tell to memory my death was noble,
Dying almost a Martyr: That way he takes,
I purpose is my way too: Sure he cannot
Be so unmanly, as to leave me here;
If he doe, Maides will not so easily
Trust men againe: And yet he has not thank'd me
For what I have done: no not so much as kist me,
And that (me thinkes) is not so well; nor scarcely
Could I perswade him to become a Freeman,
He made such scruples of the wrong he did
To me, and to my Father. Yet I hope,
When he considers more, this love of mine
Will take more root within him: Let him doe
What he will with me, so he use me kindly;
For use me so he shall, or ile proclaime him,
And to his face, no man. Ile presently
Provide him necessaries, and packe my cloathes up,
And where there is a patch of ground Ile venture,
So hee be with me; By him, like a shadow,
Ile ever dwell; within this houre the whoobub
Will be all ore the prison: I am then
Kissing the man they looke for: farewell, Father;
Get many more such prisoners and such daughters,
And shortly you may keepe your selfe. Now to him!

Actus Tertius.

Scæna 1. ⟨*A forest near Athens.*⟩

Cornets in sundry places. Noise and hallowing as people a Maying.

Enter Arcite alone.

Arcite. The Duke has lost Hypolita; each tooke
A severall land. This is a solemne Right
They owe bloomd May, and the *Athenians* pay it
To'th heart of Ceremony. O Queene *Emilia,*
Fresher then May, sweeter
Then hir gold Buttons on the bowes, or all
Th' enamelld knackes o'th Meade or garden: yea,
We challenge too the bancke of any Nymph
That makes the streame seeme flowers; thou, o Iewell
O'th wood, o'th world, hast likewise blest a place
With thy sole presence: in thy rumination
That I, poore man, might eftsoones come betweene
And chop on some cold thought! thrice blessed chance,

S. D. Before . . prison *add. Dyce*

33 patch *Ingleby, Litt.*: path *Q, F* S. D. A forest *etc. add. Litt.* 2 land *Q ff.*: stand *conj. Heath*: laund *conj. Dyce* 10 place *Sew., etc.*: pace *Q, F*

To drop on such a Mistris, expectation
Most giltlesse on't! tell me, O Lady Fortune,
(Next after *Emely* my Soveraigne) how far
I may be prowd. She takes strong note of me,
Hath made me neere her; and this beuteous Morne
(The prim'st of all the yeare) presents me with
A brace of horses: two such Steeds might well
Be by a paire of Kings backt, in a Field
That their crownes titles tride. Alas, alas,
Poore Cosen *Palamon,* poore prisoner, thou
So little dream'st upon my fortune, that
Thou thinkst thy selfe the happier thing, to be
So neare *Emilia*; me thou deem'st at *Thebs,*
And therein wretched, although free. But if
Thou knew'st my Mistris breathd on me, and that
I ear'd her language, livde in her eye, O Coz,
What passion would enclose thee!

Enter Palamon as out of a Bush, with his Shackles: bends his fist at Arcite.

Palamon. Traytor kinseman,
Thou shouldst perceive my passion, if these signes
Of prisonment were off me, and this hand
But owner of a Sword: By all othes in one,
I and the iustice of my love would make thee
A confest Traytor. O thou most perfidious
That ever gently lookd; the voydest of honour,
That eu'r bore gentle Token; falsest Cosen
That ever blood made kin, call'st thou hir thine?
Ile prove it in my Shackles, with these hands,
Void of appointment, that thou ly'st, and art
A very theefe in love, a Chaffy Lord,
Nor worth the name of villaine: had I a Sword
And these house clogges away—

Arc. Deere Cosin *Palamon*—

Pal. Cosoner *Arcite,* give me language such
As thou hast shewd me feate.

Arc. Not finding in
The circuit of my breast any grosse stuffe
To forme me like your blazon, holds me to
This gentlenesse of answer; tis your passion
That thus mistakes, the which to you being enemy,
Cannot to me be kind: honor, and honestie
I cherish, and depend on, how so ev'r
You skip them in me, and with them, faire Coz,
Ile maintaine my proceedings; pray, be pleas'd
To shew in generous termes your griefes, since that
Your question's with your equall, who professes
To cleare his owne way with the minde and Sword
Of a true Gentleman.

Pal. That thou durst, *Arcite!*

Arc. My Coz, my Coz, you have beene well advertis'd
How much I dare, y'ave seene me use my Sword
Against th'advice of feare: sure, of another
You would not heare me doubted, but your silence
Should breake out, though i'th Sanctuary.

Pal. Sir,
I have seene you move in such a place, which well
Might justifie your manhood; you were calld
A good knight and a bold; But the whole weeke's not faire,
If any day it rayne: Their valiant temper
Men loose when they encline to trecherie,
And then they fight like coupelld Beares, would fly
Were they not tyde.

Arc. Kinsman, you might as well
Speake this and act it in your Glasse, as to
His eare which now disdaines you.

Pal. Come up to me,
Quit me of these cold Gyves, give me a Sword,
Though it be rustie, and the charity
Of one meale lend me; Come before me then,
A good Sword in thy hand, and doe but say
That *Emily* is thine: I will forgive
The trespasse thou hast done me, yea, my life,
If then thou carry't, and brave soules in shades
That have dyde manly, which will seeke of me
Some newes from earth, they shall get none but this,
That thou art brave and noble.

Arc. Be content:
Againe betake you to your hawthorne house;
With counsaile of the night, I will be here
With wholesome viands; these impediments
Will I file off; you shall have garments and
Perfumes to kill the smell o'th prison; after,
When you shall stretch your selfe and say but, '*Arcite,*
I am in plight,' there shall be at your choyce
Both Sword and Armour.

Pal. Oh you heavens, dares any
So noble beare a guilty busines! none
But onely *Arcite,* therefore none but *Arcite*
In this kinde is so bold.

37 voydes *Q, F* 43 Nor *Q, etc.*: Not *conj. Litt.*

68 well *om. Litt.* 73 coupel'd *F*: compelld *Q* 99 nobly *Sk.* busines] baseness *Dyce, ed. 1867*

Arc. Sweete *Palamon.*
Pal. I doe embrace you and your offer,—for
Your offer doo't I onely, Sir; your person,
Without hipocrisy I may not wish
[*Winde hornes of Cornets.*
More then my Swords edge ont.
Arc. You heare the Hornes;
Enter your Musite least this match between's
Be crost, er met: give me your hand; farewell.
Ile bring you every needfull thing: I pray you,
Take comfort and be strong.
Pal. Pray hold your promise;
And doe the deede with a bent brow: most certaine
You love me not, be rough with me, and powre
This oile out of your language; by this ayre,
I could for each word give a Cuffe, my stomach
Not reconcild by reason.
Arc. Plainely spoken,
Yet pardon me hard language: when I spur
[*Winde hornes.*
My horse, I chide him not; content and anger
In me have but one face. Harke, Sir, they call
The scatterd to the Banket; you must guesse
I have an office there.
Pal. Sir, your attendance
Cannot please heaven, and I know your office
Vnjustly is atcheev'd.
Arc. If a good title,
I am perswaded this question sicke between's
By bleeding must be cur'd. I am a Suitour,
That to your Sword you will bequeath this plea
And talke of it no more.
Pal. But this one word:
You are going now to gaze upon my Mistris,
For note you, mine she is—
Arc. Nay, then.
Pal. Nay, pray you,
You talke of feeding me to breed me strength:
You are going now to looke upon a Sun
That strengthens what it lookes on; there
You have a vantage ore me, but enjoy't till
I may enforce my remedy. Farewell.
[*Exeunt.*

Scæna 2. ⟨*Another Part of the forest.*⟩

Enter Iaylors daughter alone.

Daugh. He has mistooke the Brake I meant, is gone
After his fancy. Tis now welnigh morning;
No matter, would it were perpetuall night,
And darkenes Lord o'th world. Harke, tis a woolfe:
In me hath greife slaine feare, and but for one thing
I care for nothing, and that's *Palamon.*
I wreake not if the wolves would jaw me, so
He had this File: what if I hallowd for him?
I cannot hallow: if I whoop'd, what then?
If he not answeard, I should call a wolfe,
And doe him but that service. I have heard
Strange howles this live-long night, why may't not be
They have made prey of him? he has no weapons,
He cannot run, the Iengling of his Gives
Might call fell things to listen, who have in them
A sence to know a man unarmd, and can
Smell where resistance is. Ile set it downe
He's torne to peeces; they howld many together
And then they fed on him: So much for that,
Be bold to ring the Bell; how stand I then?
All's char'd when he is gone. No, no, I lye,
My Father's to be hang'd for his escape;
My selfe to beg, if I prizd life so much
As to deny my act, but that I would not,
Should I try death by dussons.—I am mop't,
Food tooke I none these two daies,
Sipt some water. I have not closd mine eyes
Save when my lids scowrd off their brine; alas,
Dissolue my life, Let not my sence unsettle,
Least I should drowne, or stab or hang my selfe.
O state of Nature, faile together in me,
Since thy best props are warpt! So, which way now?
The best way is the next way to a grave:
Each errant step beside is torment. Loe,
The Moone is down, the Cryckets chirpe, the Schreichowle
Calls in the dawne; all offices are done
Save what I faile in: But the point is this,
An end, and that is all. [*Exit.*

Scæna 3. ⟨*Same as Scene I.*⟩

Enter Arcite, with Meate, Wine, and Files.

Arc. I should be neere the place: hoa, Cosen *Palamon.* [*Enter Palamon.*
Pal. *Arcite?*

108 musite *Litt.*: musit *Knight*: Musicke *Q, F*: Muse quick *Sew.* 120 not *F, etc.*: nor *Q 1* 127 If *Q, F*: I've *Sew., etc.* 139 *Ends* have *Dyce, etc.* 140 enjoy it *Dyce, etc.* *S. D.* Another *etc. add. Dyce* 1 Brake *Th.*: Beake *Q*: Brook *Sy.*: Beck *Sew.*: Hawk *conj. Sew.*

7 wreake *Q*: reck *Sew., etc.* 19 fed *F, etc.*: feed *Q* 27 Sipt *Q*: only sipt *Sew.*: 'cept *conj. Sy.* 28 brine *Tonson*: bine *Q, F*

Arc. The same: I have brought you foode and files.
Come forth and feare not, here's no *Theseus.*
Pal. Nor none so honest, *Arcite.*
Arc. That's no matter,
Wee'l argue that hereafter: Come, take courage;
You shall not dye thus beastly: here, Sir, drinke;
I know you are faint: then ile talke further with you.
Pal. *Arcite,* thou mightst now poyson me.
Arc. I might,
But I must feare you first: Sit downe, and, good, now
No more of these vaine parlies; let us not,
Having our ancient reputation with us,
Make talke for Fooles and Cowards. To your health, &c.
Pal. Doe.
Arc. Pray, sit downe then; and let me entreate you,
By all the honesty and honour in you,
No mention of this woman: t'will disturbe us;
We shall have time enough.
Pal. Well, Sir, Ile pledge you.
Arc. Drinke a good hearty draught; it breeds good blood, man.
Doe not you feele it thaw you?
Pal. Stay, Ile tell you after a draught or two more.
Arc. Spare it not, the Duke has more, Cuz: Eate now.
Pal. Yes.
Arc. I am glad you have so good a stomach.
Pal. I am gladder I have so good meate too't.
Arc. Is't not mad lodging here in the wild woods, Cosen?
Pal. Yes, for them that have wilde Consciences.
Arc. How tasts your vittails? your hunger needs no sawce, I see.
Pal. Not much;
But if it did, yours is too tart, sweete Cosen: what is this?
Arc. Venison.
Pal. Tis a lusty meate:
Giue me more wine; here, *Arcite,* to the wenches
We have known in our daies. The Lord Stewards daughter,
Doe you remember her?
Arc. After you, Cuz.
Pal. She lov'd a black-haird man.
Arc. She did so; well, Sir.
Pal. And I have heard some call him *Arcite,* and—
Arc. Out with't, faith.
Pal. She met him in an Arbour:
What did she there, Cuz? play o'th virginals?
Arc. Something she did, Sir.
Pal. Made her groane a moneth for't, or 2. or 3. or 10.
Arc. The Marshals Sister
Had her share too, as I remember, Cosen,
Else there be tales abroade; you'l pledge her?
Pal. Yes.
Arc. A pretty broune wench t'is. There was a time
When yong men went a hunting, and a wood,
And a broade Beech: and thereby hangs a tale: —heigh ho!
Pal. For *Emily,* upon my life! Foole,
Away with this straind mirth; I say againe,
That sigh was breathd for *Emily*; base Cosen,
Dar'st thou breake first?
Arc. You are wide.
Pal. By heaven and earth, ther's nothing in thee honest.
Arc. Then Ile leave you: you are a Beast now.
Pal. As thou makst me, Traytour.
Arc. Ther's all things needfull, files and shirts, and perfumes:
Ile come againe some two howres hence, and bring
That that shall quiet all,
Pal. A Sword and Armour?
Arc. Feare me not; you are now too fowle; farewell.
Get off your Trinkets; you shall want nought.
Pal. Sir, ha—
Arc. Ile heare no more. [*Exit.*
Pal. If he keepe touch, he dies for't. [*Exit.*

Scæna 4. ⟨*Another part of the forest.*⟩
Enter Iaylors daughter.

Daugh. I am very cold, and all the Stars are out too,
The little Stars, and all, that looke like aglets:
The Sun has seene my Folly. *Palamon!*
Alas no; hees in heaven. Where am I now?
Yonder's the sea, and ther's a Ship; how't tumbles!
And ther's a Rocke lies watching under water;
Now, now, it beates upon it; now, now, now,
Ther's a leak sprung, a sound one, how they cry!

15 &c. *Q*: *S. D.* Drinks *Dyce* 30 them *F, etc.*: then *Q*

S. D. Another *etc. add. Dyce*

Spoon her before the winde, you'l loose all els:
Vp with a course or two, and take about, Boyes.
Good night, good night, y'ar gone.—I am very hungry.
Would I could finde a fine Frog; he would tell me
Newes from all parts o'th world, then would I make
A Carecke of a Cockle shell, and sayle
By east and North East to the King of *Pigmes*,
For he tels fortunes rarely. Now my Father,
Twenty to one, is trust up in a trice
To morrow morning; Ile say never a word.

[*Sing.*]

For ile cut my greene coat a foote above my knee,
And ile clip my yellow lockes an inch below mine eie.
hey, nonny, nonny, nonny,
He's buy me a white Cut, forth for to ride
And ile goe seeke him, throw the world that is so wide
hey nonny, nonny, nonny.

O for a pricke now like a Nightingale,
To put my breast against. I shall sleepe like a Top else. [*Exit.*

Scæna 5. ⟨*Another part of the forest.*⟩

Enter a Schoole master, 4. Countrymen, and Bavian. 2. or 3. wenches, with a Taborer.

Sch. Fy, fy, what tediosity, & disensanity is here among ye? have my Rudiments bin labourd so long with ye? milkd unto ye, and by a figure even the very plumbroth & marrow of my understanding laid upon ye? and do you still cry: where, and how, & wherfore? you most course freeze capacities, ye jane Iudgements, have I saide: thus let be, and there let be, and then let be, and no man understand mee? *Proh deum, medius fidius,* ye are all dunces! For why, here stand I, Here the Duke comes, there are you close in the Thicket; the Duke appeares, I meete him and unto him I utter learned things and many figures; he heares, and nods, and hums, and then cries: rare, and I goe forward; at length I fling my Cap up; marke there; then do you, as once did *Meleager* and the *Bore,* break comly out before him: like true lovers, cast your selves in a Body decently, and sweetly, by a figure trace and turne, Boyes.

9 Spoon *conj. Th.*: Vpon *Q*: Up with *Sew.*: Spoom *Weber*: Run *Sk.* 22 He s' *Sk.* 25 *Ends* breast *Q* Scæna 6 *Q* *S. D.* Another *etc. add. Dyce* *S. D.* Bavian *Sew.*: Baum *Q, F* 1–21 *Verse Sew., etc.* 7 jane *Dyce*: jave *Q, F*: sleave *Sew.*

1. And sweetly we will doe it Master *Gerrold.*

2. Draw up the Company. Where's the Taborour?

3. Why, *Timothy!*

Tab. Here, my mad boyes, have at ye.

Sch. But I say, where's their women?

4. Here's *Friz* and *Maudline.*

2. And little *Luce* with the white legs, and bouncing *Barbery.*

1. And freckeled *Nel,* that never faild her Master.

Sch. Wher be your Ribands, maids? swym with your Bodies
And carry it sweetly, and deliverly
And now and then a fauour, and a friske.

Nel. Let us alone, Sir.

Sch. Wher's the rest o'th Musicke?

3. Dispersd as you commanded.

Sch. Couple, then,
And see what's wanting; wher's the *Bavian?*
My friend, carry your taile without offence
Or scandall to the Ladies; and be sure
You tumble with audacity and manhood;
And when you barke, doe it with judgement.

Bau. Yes, Sir.

Sch. *Quo usque tandem?* Here is a woman wanting.

4. We may goe whistle: all the fat's i'th fire.

Sch. We have,
As learned Authours utter, washd a Tile,
We have beene *fatuus,* and laboured vainely.

2. This is that scornefull peece, that scurvy hilding,
That gave her promise faithfully, she would be here,
Cicely the Sempsters daughter:
The next gloves that I give her shall be dog skin;
Nay and she faile me once—you can tell, *Arcas,*
She swore by wine and bread, she would not breake.

Sch. An Eele and woman,
A learned Poet sayes, unles by'th taile
And with thy teeth thou hold, will either faile.
In manners this was false position

1. A fire ill take her; do's she flinch now?

3. What
Shall we determine, Sir?

Sch. Nothing.
Our busines is become a nullity;
Yea, and a woefull, and a pittious nullity.

49 *Ends* would 58 fire ill *Q*: wild-fire *conj. Dyce*: feril *Sew.*

4. Now when the credite of our Towne lay on it,
Now to be frampall, now to pisse o'th nettle!
Goe thy waies; ile remember thee, ile fit thee.

Enter Iaylors daughter.

Daughter. The George alow came from the South,
From the coast of Barbary a.
And there he met with brave gallants of war
By one, by two, by three, a.

Well haild, well haild, you jolly gallants,
And whither now are you bound a?
O let me have your company
[*Chaire and stooles out.*
Till ⟨*I*⟩ *come to the sound a.*

There was three fooles, fell out about an howlet:
The one sed it was an owle,
The other he sed nay,
The third he sed it was a hawke,
And her bels wer cut away.

3. Ther's a dainty mad woman M⟨aiste⟩r
Comes i'th Nick, as mad as a march hare:
If wee can get her daunce, wee are made againe:
I warrant her, shee'l doe the rarest gambols.
1. A mad woman? we are made, Boyes.
Sch. And are you mad, good woman?
Daugh. I would be sorry else;
Give me your hand.
Sch. Why?
Daugh. I can tell your fortune.
You are a foole: tell ten. I have pozd him: Buz!
Friend you must eate no whitebread; if you doe,
Your teeth will bleede extreamely. Shall we dance, ho?
I know you, y'ar a Tinker: Sirha Tinker,
Stop no more holes, but what you should.
Sch. Dij boni. A Tinker, Damzell?
Daug. Or a Conjurer:
Raise me a devill now, and let him play
Quipassa o'th bels and bones.
Sch. Goe, take her,
And fluently perswade her to a peace:
Et opus exegi, quod nec Iouis ira, nec ignis.
Strike up, and leade her in.
2. Come, Lasse, lets trip it.
Daugh. Ile leade. [*Winde Hornes:*
3. Doe, doe.
Sch. Perswasively, and cunningly: away, boyes,
[*Ex. all but Schoolemaster.*
I heare the hornes: give me some meditation,
And marke your Cue.—Pallas inspire me.

Enter Thes. Pir. Hip. Emil. Arcite, and traine.

Thes. This way the Stag tooke.
Sch. Stay, and edifie.
Thes. What have we here?
Per. Some Countrey sport, upon my life, Sir.
Thes. Well, Sir, goe forward, we will edifie.
Ladies, sit downe, wee'l stay it.
Sch. Thou, doughtie Duke, all haile: all haile, sweet Ladies.
Thes. This is a cold beginning.
Sch. If you but favour, our Country pastime made is.
We are a few of those collected here,
That ruder Tongues distinguish villager;
And to say veritie, and not to fable,
We are a merry rout, or else a rable,
Or company, or, by a figure, *Choris,*
That fore thy dignitie will dance a Morris.
And I, that am the rectifier of all,
By title Pedagogus, that let fall
The Birch upon the breeches of the small ones,
And humble with a Ferula the tall ones,
Doe here present this Machine, or this frame:
And daintie Duke, whose doughtie dismall fame
From *Dis* to *Dedalus,* from post to pillar,
Is blowne abroad, helpe me thy poore well willer,
And with thy twinckling eyes looke right and straight
Vpon this mighty *Morr*—of mickle waight;
Is now comes in, which being glewd together,
Makes *Morris,* and the cause that we came hether.
The body of our sport, of no small study,
I first appeare, though rude, and raw, and muddy,
To speake before thy noble grace this tenner:
At whose great feete I offer up my penner.
The next the Lord of May and Lady bright,
The Chambermaid and Servingman by night
That seeke out silent hanging: Then mine Host
And his fat Spowse, that welcomes to their cost
The gauled Traveller, and with a beckning
Informes the Tapster to inflame the reckning:
Then the beast eating Clowne, and next the foole,

67 alow *Q*: holla *Herford*: a hoy *conj. Daniel* 73–4 *One line Q* 74 I *add. Tonson* 80 Mr. *Q*: Magister *Sew.* 80–3 *Prose Q, F* 100 a peace *Q, F*: appease *conj. Reed*: a place *Mason*

113 *Prefix* Per. *Q, F* 143 welcome *Colman, etc* their] his *Walker* 146 beef-eating *Mason*

The *Bavian*, with long tayle and eke long toole,
Cum multis alijs that make a dance:
Say 'I,' and all shall presently advance.

Thes. I, I, by any meanes, deere Domine.

Per. Produce.

⟨*Sch.*⟩ *Intrate, filij;* Come forth, and foot it.—
[*Musicke, Dance. Knocke for Schoole.*

Enter the Dance.

Ladies, if we have beene merry,
And have pleasd yee with a derry,
And a derry, and a downe,
Say the Schoolemaster's no Clowne:
Duke, if we have pleasd thee too,
And have done as good Boyes should doe,
Give us but a tree or twaine
For a Maypole, and againe,
Ere another yeare run out,
Wee'l make thee laugh and all this rout.

Thes. Take 20., Domine; how does my sweet heart?

Hip. Never so pleasd, Sir.

Emil. Twas an excellent dance, and for a preface
I never heard a better.

Thes. Schoolemaster, I thanke you.—One see'em all rewarded.

Per. And heer's something to paint your Pole withall.

Thes. Now to our sports againe.

Sch. May the Stag thou huntst stand long,
And thy dogs be swift and strong:
May they kill him without lets,
And the Ladies eate his dowsets!
Come, we are all made. [*Winde Hornes.*
Dij Deæq⟨ue⟩ omnes, ye have danc'd rarely, wenches. [*Exeunt.*

Scæna 6. ⟨*Same as Scene III.*⟩

Enter Palamon from the Bush.

Pal. About this houre my Cosen gave his faith
To visit me againe, and with him bring
Two Swords, and two good Armors; if he faile,
He's neither man nor Souldier. When he left me,
I did not thinke a weeke could have restord
My lost strength to me, I was growne so low,
And Crest-falne with my wants: I thanke thee, *Arcite*,
Thou art yet a faire Foe; and I feele my selfe
With this refreshing, able once againe
To out dure danger: To delay it longer
Would make the world think, when it comes to hearing,
That I lay fatting like a Swine to fight,
And not a Souldier: Therefore, this blest morning
Shall be the last; and that Sword he refuses,
If it but hold, I kill him with; tis Iustice:
So love, and Fortune for me!—O, good morrow.

Enter Arcite with Armors and Swords.

Arc. Good morrow, noble kinesman.

Pal. I have put you to too much paines, Sir.

Arc. That too much, faire Cosen,
Is but a debt to honour, and my duty.

Pal. Would you were so in all, Sir; I could wish ye
As kinde a kinsman, as you force me finde
A beneficiall foe, that my embraces
Might thanke ye, not my blowes.

Arc. I shall thinke either, well done,
A noble recompence.

Pal. Then I shall quit you.

Arc. Defy me in these faire termes, and you show
More then a Mistris to me, no more anger
As you love any thing that's honourable:
We were not bred to talke, man; when we are arm'd
And both upon our guards, then let our fury,
Like meeting of two tides, fly strongly from us,
And then to whom the birthright of this Beauty
Truely pertaines (without obbraidings, scornes,
Dispisings of our persons, and such powtings,
Fitter for Girles and Schooleboyes) will be seene
And quickly, yours, or mine: wilt please you arme, Sir,
Or if you feele your selfe not fitting yet
And furnishd with your old strength, ile stay, Cosen,
And ev'ry day discourse you into health,
As I am spard: your person I am friends with,
And I could wish I had not saide I lov'd her,
Though I had dide; But loving such a Lady
And justifying my Love, I must not fly from't.

Pal. *Arcite*, thou art so brave an enemy,
That no man but thy Cosen's fit to kill thee:
I am well and lusty, choose your Armes.

Arc. Choose you, Sir.

Pal. Wilt thou exceede in all, or do'st thou doe it
To make me spare thee?

152 *Prefix* Ger ⟨= *Gerrold*⟩ *add. Dyce* 154 have *om. Sew.* ye *Sew.*: thee *Q* 157 thee *F, etc.*: three *Q* Scæna 7. *Q*

25 *Ends* either *Q*

Arc. If you thinke so, Cosen,
You are deceived, for as I am a Soldier,
I will not spare you.
Pal. That's well said.
Arc. You'l finde it.
Pal. Then, as I am an honest man and love
With all the justice of affection,
Ile pay thee soundly. This ile take.
Arc. That's mine, then;
Ile arme you first.
Pal. Do: pray thee, tell me, Cosen,
Where gotst thou this good Armour?
Arc. Tis the Dukes,
And to say true, I stole it; doe I pinch you?
Pal. Noe.
Arc. Is't not too heavie?
Pal. I have worne a lighter,
But I shall make it serve.
Arc. Ile buckl't close.
Pal. By any meanes.
Arc. You care not for a Grand guard?
Pal. No, no; wee'l use no horses: I perceave
You would faine be at that Fight.
Arc. I am indifferent.
Pal. Faith, so am I: good Cosen, thrust the buckle
Through far enough.
Arc. I warrant you.
Pal. My Caske now.
Arc. Will you fight bare-armd?
Pal. We shall be the nimbler.
Arc. But use your Gauntlets though; those are o'th least,
Prethee take mine, good Cosen.
Pal. Thanke you, *Arcite*.
How doe I looke? am I falne much away?
Arc. Faith, very little; love has usd you kindly.
Pal. Ile warrant thee, Ile strike home.
Arc. Doe, and spare not;
Ile give you cause, sweet Cosen.
Pal. Now to you, Sir:
Me thinkes this Armor's very like that, *Arcite*,
Thou wor'st that day the 3. Kings fell, but lighter.
Arc. That was a very good one; and that day,
I well remember, you outdid me, Cosen.
I never saw such valour: when you chargd
Vpon the left wing of the Enemie,
I spurd hard to come up, and under me
I had a right good horse.
Pal. You had indeede; a bright Bay, I remember.
Arc. Yes, but all
Was vainely labour'd in me; you outwent me,
Nor could my wishes reach you; yet a little
I did by imitation.
Pal. More by vertue;
You are modest, Cosen.
Arc. When I saw you charge first,
Me thought I heard a dreadfull clap of Thunder
Breake from the Troope.
Pal. But still before that flew
The lightning of your valour. Stay a little,
Is not this peece too streight?
Arc. No, no, tis well.
Pal. I would have nothing hurt thee but my Sword,
A bruise would be dishonour.
Arc. Now I am perfect.
Pal. Stand off, then.
Arc. Take my Sword, I hold it better.
Pal. I thanke ye: No, keepe it; your life lyes on it.
Here's one; if it but hold, I aske no more
For all my hopes: My Cause and honour guard me! [*They bow severall wayes: then advance and stand.*
Arc. And me my love! Is there ought else to say?
Pal. This onely, and no more: Thou art mine Aunts Son,
And that blood we desire to shed is mutuall;
In me, thine, and in thee, mine. My Sword
Is in my hand, and if thou killst me,
The gods and I forgive thee; If there be
A place prepar'd for those that sleepe in honour,
I wish his wearie soule that falls may win it:
Fight bravely, Cosen; give me thy noble hand.
Arc. Here, *Palamon*: This hand shall never more
Come neare thee with such friendship.
Pal. I commend thee.
Arc. If I fall, curse me, and say I was a coward,
For none but such dare die in these just Tryalls.
Once more farewell, my Cosen.
Pal. Farewell, *Arcite*. [*Fight.*
[*Hornes within: they stand.*
Arc. Loe, Cosen, loe, our Folly has undon us.
Pal. Why?
Arc. This is the Duke, a hunting as I told you.
If we be found, we are wretched. O retire
For honours sake, and safety presently
Into your Bush agen; Sir, we shall finde
Too many howres to dye in: gentle Cosen,

141 safety *Sew.*: safely *Q*

If you be seene you perish instantly
For breaking prison, and I, if you reveale me,
For my contempt. Then all the world will scorne us,
And say we had a noble difference,
But base disposers of it.
Pal. No, no, Cosen,
I will no more be hidden, nor put off
This great adventure to a second Tryall:
I know your cunning, and I know your cause;
He that faints now, shame take him: put thy selfe
Vpon thy present guard—
Arc. You are not mad?
Pal. Or I will make th'advantage of this howre
Mine owne, and what to come shall threaten me,
I feare lesse then my fortune: know, weake Cosen,
I love *Emilia,* and in that ile bury
Thee, and all crosses else.
Arc. Then, come what can come,
Thou shalt know, *Palamon,* I dare as well
Die, as discourse, or sleepe: Onely this feares me,
The law will have the honour of our ends.
Have at thy life.
Pal. Looke to thine owne well, *Arcite.*
[*Fight againe. Hornes.*

Enter Theseus, Hipolita, Emilia, Perithous and traine.

Theseus. What ignorant and mad malicious Traitors,
Are you, That gainst the tenor of my Lawes
Are making Battaile, thus like Knights appointed,
Without my leave, and Officers of Armes?
By *Castor,* both shall dye.
Pal. Hold thy word, *Theseus.*
We are certainly both Traitors, both despisers
Of thee and of thy goodnesse: I am *Palamon,*
That cannot love thee, he that broke thy Prison;
Thinke well what that deserves: and this is *Arcite,*
A bolder Traytor never trod thy ground,
A Falser neu'r seem'd friend: This is the man
Was begd and banish'd; this is he contemnes thee
And what thou dar'st doe, and in this disguise
Against thy owne Edict followes thy Sister,
That fortunate bright Star, the faire *Emilia,*
Whose servant, (if there be a right in seeing,
And first bequeathing of the soule to) justly
I am, and, which is more, dares thinke her his.
This treacherie, like a most trusty Lover,
I call'd him now to answer; if thou bee'st,
As thou art spoken, great and vertuous,
The true descider of all injuries,
Say, 'Fight againe,' and thou shalt see me, *Theseus,*
Doe such a Iustice, thou thy selfe wilt envie.
Then take my life; Ile wooe thee too't.
Per. O heaven,
What more then man is this!
Thes. I have sworne.
Arc. We seeke not
Thy breath of mercy, *Theseus.* Tis to me
A thing as soone to dye, as thee to say it,
And no more mov'd: where this man calls me Traitor,
Let me say thus much: if in love be Treason,
In service of so excellent a Beutie,
As I love most, and in that faith will perish,
As I have brought my life here to confirme it,
As I have serv'd her truest, worthiest,
As I dare kill this Cosen, that denies it,
So let me be most Traitor, and ye please me.
For scorning thy Edict, Duke, aske that Lady
Why she is faire, and why her eyes command me
Stay here to love her; and if she say 'Traytor,'
I am a villaine fit to lye unburied.
Pal. Thou shalt have pitty of us both, o *Theseus,*
If unto neither thou shew mercy; stop
(As thou art just) thy noble eare against us.
As thou art valiant, for thy Cosens soule
Whose 12. strong labours crowne his memory,
Lets die together, at one instant, Duke,
Onely a little let him fall before me,
That I may tell my Soule he shall not have her.
Thes. I grant your wish, for, to say true, your Cosen
Has ten times more offended; for I gave him
More mercy then you found, Sir, your offenses
Being no more then his. None here speake for 'em,
For, ere the Sun set, both shall sleepe for ever.
Hipol. Alas the pitty! now or never, Sister,
Speake, not to be denide; That face of yours
Will beare the curses else of after ages
For these lost Cosens.
Emil. In my face, deare Sister,
I finde no anger to 'em, nor no ruyn;
The misadventure of their owne eyes kill 'em;

181 thy own *Dyce*: this owne *Q*: this known *Sew.*: thine owne *Sk.*

230 kills *Sew.*

Yet that I will be woman, and have pitty,
My knees shall grow to'th ground but Ile get mercie.
Helpe me, deare Sister; in a deede so vertuous
The powers of all women will be with us.
Most royall Brother—

Hipol. Sir, by our tye of Marriage—

Emil. By your owne spotlesse honour—

Hip. By that faith,
That faire hand, and that honest heart you gave me.

Emil. By that you would have pitty in another,
By your owne vertues infinite.

Hip. By valour,
By all the chaste nights I have ever pleasd you.

Thes. These are strange Conjurings.

Per. Nay, then, Ile in too:
By all our friendship, Sir, by all our dangers,
By all you love most: warres and this sweet Lady.

Emil. By that you would have trembled to deny,
A blushing Maide.

Hip. By your owne eyes: By strength,
In which you swore I went beyond all women,
Almost all men, and yet I yeelded, *Theseus.*

Per. To crowne all this: By your most noble soule,
Which cannot want due mercie, I beg first.

Hip. Next, heare my prayers.

Emil. Last, let me intreate, Sir.

Per. For mercy.

Hip. Mercy.

Emil. Mercy on these Princes.

Thes. Ye make my faith reele: Say I felt
Compassion to'em both, how would you place it?

Emil. Vpon their lives: But with their banishments.

Thes. You are a right woman, Sister; you have pitty,
But want the vnderstanding where to use it.
If you desire their lives, invent a way
Safer then banishment: Can these two live
And have the agony of love about 'em,
And not kill one another? Every day
They'ld fight about you; howrely bring your honour
In publique question with their Swords. Be wise, then,
And here forget 'em; it concernes your credit
And my oth equally: I have said they die;
Better they fall by'th law, then one another.
Bow not my honor.

Emil. O my noble Brother,
That oth was rashly made, and in your anger,
Your reason will not hold it; if such vowes
Stand for expresse will, all the world must perish.
Beside, I have another oth gainst yours,
Of more authority, I am sure more love,
Not made in passion neither, but good heede.

Thes. What is it, Sister?

Per. Vrge it home, brave Lady.

Emil. That you would nev'r deny me any thing
Fit for my modest suit, and your free granting:
I tye you to your word now; if ye fall in't,
Thinke how you maime your honour,
(For now I am set a begging, Sir, I am deafe
To all but your compassion.) How, their lives
Might breed the ruine of my name, Opinion!
Shall any thing that loves me perish for me?
That were a cruell wisedome; doe men proyne
The straight yong Bowes that blush with thousand Blossoms,
Because they may be rotten? O Duke *Theseus,*
The goodly Mothers that have groand for these,
And all the longing Maides that ever lov'd,
If your vow stand, shall curse me and my Beauty,
And in their funerall songs for these two Cosens
Despise my crueltie, and cry woe worth me,
Till I am nothing but the scorne of women;
For heavens sake save their lives, and banish 'em.

Thes. On what conditions?

Emil. Sweare'em never more
To make me their Contention, or to know me,
To tread upon thy Dukedome; and to be,
Where ever they shall travel, ever strangers
To one another.

Pal. Ile be cut a peeces
Before I take this oth: forget I love her?
O all ye gods dispise me, then! Thy Banishment
I not mislike, so we may fairely carry
Our Swords and cause along: else, never trifle,
But take our lives, Duke: I must love and will,
And for that love must and dare kill this Cosen
On any peece the earth has.

Thes. Will you, *Arcite,*
Take these conditions?

Pal. He's a villaine, then.

Per. These are men.

Arcite. No, never, Duke: Tis worse to me than begging

286 fall *Q, F*: fail *Tonson* 290 name ; Opinion *Q* : Name—Opinion *Sew.* : names Opinion *Th.* 296 lo'vd them *Walker*

To take my life so basely; though I thinke
I never shall enjoy her, yet ile preserve
The honour of affection, and dye for her,
Make death a Devill.
Thes. What may be done? for now I feele compassion.
Per. Let it not fall agen, Sir.
Thes. Say, *Emilia,*
If one of them were dead, as one must, are you
Content to take th'other to your husband?
They cannot both enjoy you; They are Princes
As goodly as your owne eyes, and as noble
As ever fame yet spoke of; looke upon 'em,
And if you can love, end this difference.
I give consent; are you content too, Princes?
Both. With all our soules.
Thes. He that she refuses
Must dye, then.
Both. Any death thou canst invent, Duke.
Pal. If I fall from that mouth, I fall with favour,
And Lovers yet unborne shall blesse my ashes.
Arc. If she refuse me, yet my grave will wed me,
And Souldiers sing my Epitaph.
Thes. Make choice, then.
Emil. I cannot, Sir, they are both too excellent:
For me, a hayre shall never fall of these men.
Hip. What will become of 'em?
Thes. Thus I ordaine it;
And by mine honor, once againe, it stands,
Or both shall dye:—You shall both to your Countrey,
And each within this moneth, accompanied
With three faire Knights, appeare againe in this place,
In which Ile plant a Pyramid; and whether,
Before us that are here, can force his Cosen
By fayre and knightly strength to touch the Pillar,
He shall enjoy her: the other loose his head,
And all his friends; Nor shall he grudge to fall,
Nor thinke he dies with interest in this Lady:
Will this content yee?
Pal. Yes: here, Cosen *Arcite,*
I am friends againe, till that howre.
Arc. I embrace ye.
Thes. Are you content, Sister?
Emil. Yes, I must, Sir,
Els both miscarry.
Thes. Come, shake hands againe, then;
And take heede, as you are Gentlemen, this Quarrell
Sleepe till the howre prefixt; and hold your course.
Pal. We dare not faile thee, *Theseus.*
Thes. Come, Ile give ye
Now usage like to Princes, and to Friends:
When ye returne, who wins, Ile settle heere;
Who looses, yet Ile weepe upon his Beere.
[*Exeunt.*

Actus Quartus.

Scæna 1. ⟨*Athens. A room in the prison.*⟩

Enter Iailor and his friend.

Iailor. Heare you no more? was nothing saide of me
Concerning the escape of *Palamon*?
Good Sir, remember.
1. *Fr.* Nothing that I heard,
For I came home before the busines
Was fully ended: Yet I might perceive,
Ere I departed, a great likelihood
Of both their pardons: For *Hipolita,*
And faire-eyd *Emilie,* upon their knees
Begd with such hansom pitty, that the Duke
Me thought stood staggering, whether he should follow
His rash oth, or the sweet compassion
Of those two Ladies; and to second them,
That truely noble Prince *Perithous,*
Halfe his owne heart, set in too, that I hope
All shall be well: Neither heard I one question
Of your name or his scape.

Enter 2. Friend.

Iay. Pray heaven it hold so.
2. *Fr.* Be of good comfort, man; I bring you newes,
Good newes.
Iay. They are welcome,
2. *Fr.* *Palamon* has cleerd you,
And got your pardon, and discoverd how
And by whose meanes he escapt, which was your Daughters,
Whose pardon is procurd too; and the Prisoner,
Not to be held ungratefull to her goodnes,
Has given a summe of money to her Marriage,
A large one, ile assure you.
Iay. Ye are a good man
And ever bring good newes.
1. *Fr.* How was it ended?
2. *Fr.* Why, as it should be; they that nev'r begd
But they prevaild, had their suites fairely granted,
The prisoners have their lives.

331 as your *Q etc.*: in your *conj. Daniel* 344–5 too excellent For me *Q, F*

S. D. Athens . . *etc. add. Dyce* *S. D.* and First Friend *Dyce* 12 o'th *Q* 23 *Ends* discoverd *Q, F*

1. *Fr.* I knew t'would be so.
2. *Fr.* But there be new conditions, which you'l heare of
At better time.
Iay. I hope they are good.
2. *Fr.* They are honourable,
How good they'l prove, I know not.

Enter Wooer.

1. *Fr.* T'will be knowne.
Woo. Alas, Sir, wher's your Daughter?
Iay. Why doe you aske?
Woo. O, Sir, when did you see her?
2. *Fr.* How he lookes?
Iay. This morning.
Woo. Was she well? was she in health, Sir?
When did she sleepe?
1. *Fr.* These are strange Questions.
Iay. I doe not thinke she was very well, for now
You make me minde her, but this very day
I ask'd her questions, and she answered me
So farre from what she was, so childishly,
So sillily, as if she were a foole,
An Inocent, and I was very angry.
But what of her, Sir?
Woo. Nothing but my pitty;
But you must know it, and as good by me
As by an other that lesse loves her—
Iay. Well, Sir.
1. *Fr.* Not right?
2. *Fr.* Not well?——*Wooer,* No, Sir, not well.
Tis too true, she is mad.
1. *Fr.* It cannot be.
Woo. Beleeve, you'l finde it so.
Iay. I halfe suspected
What you ⟨have⟩ told me: the gods comfort her:
Either this was her love to *Palamon,*
Or feare of my miscarrying on his scape,
Or both.
Woo. Tis likely.
Iay. But why all this haste, Sir?
Woo. Ile tell you quickly. As I late was angling
In the great Lake that lies behind the Pallace,
From the far shore, thicke set with reedes and Sedges,
As patiently I was attending sport,
I heard a voyce, a shrill one, and attentive
I gave my eare, when I might well perceive
T'was one that sung, and by the smallnesse of it
A boy or woman. I then left my angle
To his owne skill, came neere, but yet perceivd not
Who made the sound, the rushes and the Reeds
Had so encompast it: I laide me downe
And listned to the words she sung, for then,
Through a small glade cut by the Fisher men,
I saw it was your Daughter.
Iay. Pray, goe on, Sir?
Woo. She sung much, but no sence; onely I heard her
Repeat this often: '*Palamon* is gone,
Is gone to'th wood to gather Mulberies;
Ile finde him out to morrow.'
1. *Fr.* Pretty soule.
Woo. 'His shackles will betray him, hee'l be taken,
And what shall I doe then? Ile bring a beavy,
A hundred blacke eyd Maides, that love as I doe,
With Chaplets on their heads of Daffadillies,
With cherry-lips, and cheekes of Damaske Roses,
And all wee'l daunce an Antique fore the Duke,
And beg his pardon.' Then she talk'd of you, Sir;
That you must loose your head to morrow morning,
And she must gather flowers to bury you,
And see the house made handsome: then she sung
Nothing but 'Willow, willow, willow,' and betweene
Ever was, '*Palamon,* faire *Palamon,*'
And '*Palamon* was a tall yong man.' The place
Was knee deepe where she sat; her careles Tresses
A wreathe of bull-rush rounded; about her stucke
Thousand fresh water flowers of severall cullors,
That me thought she appeard like the faire Nimph
That feedes the lake with waters, or as Iris
Newly dropt downe from heaven; Rings she made
Of rushes that grew by, and to 'em spoke
The prettiest posies: 'Thus our true love's tide,'
'This you may loose, not me,' and many a one:
And then she wept, and sung againe, and sigh'd,

63 *Prefix* Woo. *repeated before this line Q*   67 have *add. Sew.*   84 sung *F*: song *Q*   107 wreath *Sew.*: wreake *Q*: wreak *F*

And with the same breath smil'd, and kist her hand.
  2. *Fr.* Alas, what pitty it is!
  Wooer. I made in to her.
She saw me, and straight sought the flood; I sav'd her,
And set her safe to land: when presently
She slipt away, and to the Citty made,
With such a cry and swiftnes, that, beleeve me,
Shee left me farre behinde her; three or foure
I saw from farre off crosse her, one of 'em
I knew to be your brother; where she staid,
And fell, scarce to be got away: I left them with her,

Enter Brother, Daughter, and others.

And hether came to tell you. Here they are.
  Daugh. May you never more enjoy the light, &c.
Is not this a fine Song?
  Bro. O, a very fine one.
  Daugh. I can sing twenty more.
  Bro. I thinke you can.
  Daugh. Yes, truely, can I; I can sing the Broome,
And Bony Robin. Are not you a tailour?
  Bro. Yes.
  Daugh. Wher's my wedding Gowne?
  Bro. Ile bring it to morrow.
  Daugh. Doe, very rarely; I must be abroad else
To call the Maides, and pay the Minstrels,
For I must loose my Maydenhead by cock-light;
Twill never thrive else.
  O faire, oh sweete, &c. [*Singes.*
  Bro. You must ev'n take it patiently.
  Iay. Tis true.
  Daug. Good ev'n, good men; pray, did you ever heare
Of one yong *Palamon*?
  Iay. Yes, wench, we know him.
  Daugh. Is't not a fine yong Gentleman?
  Iay. Tis Love.
  Bro. By no meane crosse her; she is then distemperd
Far worse then now she showes.
  1. *Fr* Yes, he's a fine man.
  Daugh. O, is he so? you have a Sister?
  1. *Fr.* Yes.
  Daugh. But she shall never have him, tell her so,
For a tricke that I know; y'had best looke to her,
For if she see him once, she's gone, she's done,
And undon in an howre. All the young Maydes
Of our Towne are in love with him, but I laugh at 'em
And let 'em all alone; Is't not a wise course?
  1. *Fr.* Yes.
  Daugh. There is at least two hundred now with child by him—
There must be fowre; yet I keepe close for all this,
Close as a Cockle; and all these must be Boyes,
He has the tricke on't, and at ten yeares old
They must be all gelt for Musitians,
And sing the wars of *Theseus.*
  2. *Fr.* This is strange.
  Daugh. As ever you heard, but say nothing.
  1. *Fr.* No.
  Daugh. They come from all parts of the Dukedome to him;
Ile warrant ye, he had not so few last night
As twenty to dispatch: hee'l tickl't up
In two howres, if his hand be in.
  Iay. She's lost
Past all cure.
  Bro. Heaven forbid, man.
  Daugh. Come hither, you are a wise man.
  1. *Fr.* Do's she know him?
  2. *Fr.* No, would she did.
  Daugh. You are master of a Ship?
  Iay. Yes.
  Daugh. Wher's your Compasse?
  Iay. Heere.
  Daugh. Set it too'th North.
And now direct your course to'th wood, wher *Palamon*
Lyes longing for me; For the Tackling
Let me alone; Come, waygh, my hearts, cheerely!
  All. Owgh, owgh, owgh, tis up, the wind's faire,
Top the Bowling, out with the maine saile;
Wher's your Whistle, Master?
  Bro. Lets get her in.
  Iay. Vp to the top, Boy.
  Bro. Wher's the Pilot?
  1. *Fr.* Heere.
  Daugh. What ken'st thou?
  2. *Fr.* A faire wood.
  Daugh. Beare for it, master: take about! [*Singes.*
When Cinthia with her borrowed light, &c.
[*Exeunt.*

138 rarely *Q, F*: rearly *conj. Sy.*: early *Sew.* 149 Tis, Love *Q* 150 means *Colman* 151 For *Q, F*

180 *Prefix* 1. Fr. *Q* 189–91 *Div.* top-the, your *Q, F*

Scæna 2. ⟨*A Room in the Palace.*⟩

Enter Emilia alone, with 2. *Pictures*

Emilia. Yet I may binde those wounds up, that must open
And bleed to death for my sake else; Ile choose,
And end their strife: Two such yong hansom men
Shall never fall for me, their weeping Mothers,
Following the dead cold ashes of their Sonnes,
Shall never curse my cruelty. Good heaven,
What a sweet face has *Arcite!* if wise nature,
With all her best endowments, all those beuties
She sowes into the birthes of noble bodies,
Were here a mortall woman, and had in her
The coy denialls of yong Maydes, yet doubtles,
She would run mad for this man: what an eye,
Of what a fyry sparkle, and quick sweetnes,
Has this yong Prince! Here Love himselfe sits smyling,
Iust such another wanton *Ganimead*
Set Jove a fire with, and enforcd the god
Snatch up the goodly Boy, and set him by him
A shining constellation: What a brow,
Of what a spacious Majesty, he carries!
Arch'd like the great eyd *Iuno's*, but far sweeter,
Smoother then *Pelops* Shoulder! Fame and honour,
Me thinks, from hence, as from a Promontory
Pointed in heaven, should clap their wings, and sing
To all the under world the Loves and Fights
Of gods, and such men neere 'em. *Palamon*
Is but his foyle, to him a meere dull shadow:
Hee's swarth and meagre, of an eye as heavy
As if he had lost his mother; a still temper,
No stirring in him, no alacrity,
Of all this sprightly sharpenes not a smile;
Yet these that we count errours may become him:
Narcissus was a sad Boy, but a heavenly:—
Oh who can finde the bent of womans fancy?
I am a Foole, my reason is lost in me;
I have no choice, and I have ly'd so lewdly
That women ought to beate me. On my knees
I aske thy pardon, *Palamon*; thou art alone,
And only beutifull, and these the eyes,
These the bright lamps of beauty, that command
And threaten Love, and what yong Mayd dare crosse 'em?
What a bold gravity, and yet inviting,
Has this browne manly face! O Love, this only
From this howre is Complexion: Lye there, *Arcite*,
Thou art a changling to him, a meere Gipsey,
And this the noble Bodie. I am sotted,
Vtterly lost: My Virgins faith has fled me;
For if my brother but even now had ask'd me
Whether I lov'd, I had run mad for *Arcite*;
Now, if my Sister, More for *Palamon*.
Stand both together: Now, come aske me, Brother.—
Alas, I know not! Aske me now, sweet Sister;—
I may goe looke. What a meere child is *Fancie*,
That, having two faire gawdes of equall sweetnesse,
Cannot distinguish, but must crie for both.

Enter ⟨*a*⟩ *Gent*⟨*leman.*⟩

Emil. How now, Sir?
Gent. From the Noble Duke your Brother,
Madam, I bring you newes: The Knights are come.
Emil. To end the quarrell?
Gent. Yes.
Emil. Would I might end first:
What sinnes have I committed, chast *Diana*,
That my unspotted youth must now be soyld
With blood of *Princes*? and my Chastitie
Be made the Altar, where the lives of Lovers
(Two greater and two better never yet
Made mothers joy) must be the sacrifice
To my unhappy Beautie?

Enter Theseus, Hipolita, Perithous and attendants.

Theseus. Bring 'em in
Quickly, By any meanes; I long to see 'em.—
Your two contending Lovers are return'd,
And with them their faire Knights: Now, my faire Sister,
You must love one of them.
Emil. I had rather both,
So neither for my sake should fall untimely.

Enter Messenger. (*Curtis.*)

Thes. Who saw 'em?
Per. I, a while.
Gent. And I.

S. D. A Room *etc. add. T* 9 sowes *Q*: shews *F* 16 Jove *Sy.*: Love *Q, F* with *om. Sew.* 38 the *Q*: thy *F* 46 Virgin *Sew.* 52 may] must *conj. S* S. D. Enter Emil. and Gent. *Q, F* 68 *Ends* quickly *Q*: *corr. Dyce* 71 faire *Q*: sixe *conj. Walker* S. D. Messengers *Q*

Thes. From whence come you, Sir?
Mess. From the Knights.
Thes. Pray, speake,
You that have seene them, what they are.
Mess. I will, Sir,
And truly what I thinke: Six braver spirits
Then these they have brought, (if we judge by the outside)
I never saw, nor read of. He that stands
In the first place with *Arcite*, by his seeming,
Should be a stout man, by his face a Prince,
(His very lookes so say him) his complexion,
Nearer a browne, than blacke, sterne, and yet noble,
Which shewes him hardy, fearelesse, proud of dangers:
The circles of his eyes show fire within him,
And as a heated Lyon, so he lookes;
His haire hangs long behind him, blacke and shining
Like Ravens wings: his shoulders broad and strong,
Armd long and round, and on his Thigh a Sword
Hung by a curious Bauldricke, when he frownes
To seale his will with: better, o'my conscience
Was never Souldiers friend.
Thes. Thou ha'st well describde him.
Per. Yet a great deale short,
Me thinkes, of him that's first with *Palamon.*
Thes. Pray, speake him, friend.
Per. I ghesse he is a Prince too,
And, if it may be, greater; for his show
Has all the ornament of honour in't:
Hee's somewhat bigger, then the Knight he spoke of,
But of a face far sweeter; His complexion
Is (as a ripe grape) ruddy: he has felt,
Without doubt, what he fights for, and so apter
To make this cause his owne: In's face appeares
All the faire hopes of what he undertakes,
And when he's angry, then a setled valour
(Not tainted with extreames) runs through his body,
And guides his arme to brave things: Feare he cannot,
He shewes no such soft temper; his head's yellow,
Hard hayr'd, and curld, thicke twind like Ivy tods,
Not to undoe with thunder; In his face
The liverie of the warlike Maide appeares,
Pure red, and white, for yet no beard has blest him.
And in his rowling eyes sits victory,
As if she ever ment to court his valour:
His Nose stands high, a Character of honour.
His red lips, after fights, are fit for Ladies.
Emil. Must these men die too?
Per. When he speakes, his tongue
Sounds like a Trumpet; All his lyneaments
Are as a man would wish 'em, strong and cleane,
He weares a well-steeld Axe, the staffe of gold;
His age some five and twenty.
Mess. Ther's another,
A little man, but of a tough soule, seeming
As great as any: fairer promises
In such a Body yet I never look'd on.
Per. O, he that's freckle fac'd?
Mess. The same, my Lord;
Are they not sweet ones?
Per. Yes, they are well.
Mess. Me thinkes,
Being so few, and well disposd, they show
Great, and fine art in nature: he's white hair'd,
Not wanton white, but such a manly colour
Next to an aborne; tough, and nimble set,
Which showes an active soule; his armes are brawny,
Linde with strong sinewes: To the shoulder peece
Gently they swell, like women new conceav'd,
Which speakes him prone to labour, never fainting
Vnder the waight of Armes; stout harted, still,
But when he stirs, a Tiger; he's gray eyd,
Which yeelds compassion where he conquers: sharpe
To spy advantages, and where he finds 'em,
He's swift to make 'em his: He do's no wrongs,
Nor takes none; he's round fac'd, and when he smiles
He showes a Lover, when he frownes, a Souldier:
About his head he weares the winners oke,
And in it stucke the favour of his Lady:
His age, some six and thirtie. In his hand
He beares a charging Staffe, embost with silver.
Thes. Are they all thus?
Per. They are all the sonnes of honour.
Thes. Now, as I have a soule, I long to see'em.
Lady, you shall see men fight now.

84 these *Q* : those *F* 86 first *F, etc.* : fitst *Q* 91 fire *Heath, Dyce* : faire *Q* : far *Sew.* 95 Arms *Sew.* 116 tods *Litt.* : tops *Q, F*

121 court *conj. Dyce* : corect *Q* : crown *Sew.*

Hip. I wish it,
But not the cause, my Lord; They would show
Bravely about the Titles of two Kingdomes;
Tis pitty Love should be so tyrannous:
O' my soft harted Sister, what thinke you?
Weepe not, till they weepe blood, Wench; it must be.

Thes. You have steel'd 'em with your Beautie.—Honord Friend,
To you I give the Feild; pray, order it
Fitting the persons that must use it.

Per. Yes, Sir.

Thes. Come, Ile goe visit 'em: I cannot stay,
Their fame has fir'd me so; Till they appeare.
Good Friend, be royall.

Per. There shall want no bravery.

Emilia. Poore wench, goe weepe, for whosoever wins,
Looses a noble Cosen for thy sins. [*Exeunt.*

Scæna 3. (*A room in the prison.*)

Enter Iailor, Wooer, Doctor.

Doct. Her distraction is more at some time of the Moone, then at other some, is it not?

Iay. She is continually in a harmelesse distemper, sleepes little, altogether without appetite, save often drinking, dreaming of another world, and a better; and what broken peece of matter so'ere she's about, the name *Palamon* lardes it, that she farces ev'ry busines withall, fyts it to every question.—

Enter Daughter.

Looke where shee comes, you shall perceive her behaviour.

Daugh. I have forgot it quite; The burden on't, was *downe a, downe a*, and pend by no worse man, then *Giraldo, Emilias* Schoolemaster; he's as Fantasticall too, as ever he may goe upon's legs,—for in the next world will *Dido* see *Palamon*, and then will she be out of love with *Eneas*.

Doct. What stuff's here? pore soule!

Iay. Ev'n thus all day long.

Daugh. Now for this Charme, that I told you of: you must bring a peece of silver on the tip of your tongue, or no ferry: then, if it be your chance to come where the blessed spirits, as ther's a sight now—we maids that have our Lyvers perish'd, crakt to peeces with Love, we shall come there, and doe nothing all day long but picke flowers with Proserpine; then will I make *Palamon* a Nosegay; then let him marke me,—then—

Doct. How prettily she's amisse? note her a little further.

Dau. Faith, ile tell you, sometime we goe to Barly breake, we of the blessed; alas, tis a sore life they have i'th other place, such burning, frying, boyling, hissing, howling, chattring, cursing, oh they have shrowd measure! take heede; if one be mad, or hang or drowne themselves, thither they goe, *Iupiter* blesse vs, and there shall we be put in a Caldron of lead, and Vsurers grease, amongst a whole million of cutpurses, and there boyle like a Gamon of Bacon that will never be enough. [*Exit.*

Doct. How her braine coynes!

Daugh. Lords and Courtiers, that have got maids with Child, they are in this place: they shall stand in fire up to the Nav'le, and in yce up to'th hart, and there th'offending part burnes, and the deceaving part freezes; in troth, a very greevous punishment, as one would thinke, for such a Trifle; beleve me, one would marry a leaprous witch, to be rid on't, Ile assure you.

Doct. How she continues this fancie! Tis not an engraffed Madnesse, but a most thicke, and profound mellencholly.

Daugh. To heare there a proud Lady, and a proud Citty wiffe, howle together! I were a beast and il'd call it good sport: one cries, 'O this smoake!' another, 'this fire!' One cries, 'O, that ever I did it behind the arras!' and then howles; th'other curses a suing fellow and her garden house.
Sings] *I will be true, my stars, my fate, &c.*
[*Exit Daugh.*

Iay. What thinke you of her, Sir?

Doct. I thinke she has a perturbed minde, which I cannot minister to.

Iay. Alas, what then?

Doct. Vnderstand you, she ever affected any man, ere she beheld *Palamon*?

Iay. I was once, Sir, in great hope she had fixd her liking on this gentleman, my friend.

Woo. I did thinke so too, and would account I had a great pen-worth on't, to give halfe my state, that both she and I at this present stood unfainedly on the same tearmes.

Do. That intemprat surfeit of her eye hath distemperd the other sences: they may returne and settle againe to execute their

163 *Ends* bravely *Sew.* 164 about *Q, F*: Fighting about *Sew.* 167 blood; Wench *Q* *S. D.* A room *etc. add. Dyce* 1-44 *Verse Q, F*

35 i'th Thother *Q* 40 we *Q, etc.*: they *conj. Litt.* 61 another *Q*: th'other *Dyce* (*later edd.*) 62 behind] *The Bodleian copy of Q has* behold; *cf. note.* 70 *ff. Verse Q, F*

preordaind faculties, but they are now in a most extravagant vagary. This you must doe: Confine her to a place, where the light may rather seeme to steale in, then be permitted; take vpon you (yong Sir, her friend) the name of *Palamon*; say you come to eate with her, and to commune of Love; this will catch her attention, for this her minde beates upon; other objects that are inserted tweene her minde and eye become the prankes and friskins of her madnes; Sing to her such greene songs of Love, as she sayes *Palamon* hath sung in prison; Come to her, stucke in as sweet flowers as the season is mistres of, and thereto make an addition of som other compounded odours, which are grateful to the sence: all this shall become *Palamon*, for *Palamon* can sing, and *Palamon* is sweet, and ev'ry good thing: desire to eate with her, carve her, drinke to her, and still among, intermingle your petition of grace and acceptance into her favour: Learne what Maides have beene her companions and play-pheeres, and let them repaire to her with *Palamon* in their mouthes, and appeare with tokens, as if they suggested for him. It is a falsehood she is in, which is with falsehood to be combated. This may bring her to eate, to sleepe, and reduce what's now out of square in her, into their former law, and regiment; I have seene it approved, how many times I know not, but to make the number more, I have great hope in this. I will, betweene the passages of this project, come in with my applyance: Let us put it in execution, and hasten the successe, which, doubt not, will bring forth comfort. [*Florish. Exeunt.*

Actus Quintus

Scæna 1. ⟨*Before the Temples of Mars, Venus, and Diana.*⟩

Enter Thesius, Perithous, Hipolita, attendants.

Thes. Now let'em enter, and before the gods
Tender their holy prayers: Let the Temples
Burne bright with sacred fires, and the Altars
In hallowed clouds commend their swelling Incense
To those above us: Let no due be wanting;
[*Florish of Cornets.*
They have a noble worke in hand, will honour
The very powers that love 'em.

Enter Palamon and Arcite, and their Knights.

Per. Sir, they enter.
Thes. You valiant and strong harted Enemies,
You royall German foes, that this day come
To blow that furnesse out that flames betweene ye:
Lay by your anger for an houre, and dove-like,
Before the holy Altars of your helpers,
(The all feard gods) bow downe your stubborne bodies.
Your ire is more than mortall; So your helpe be,
And as the gods regard ye, fight with Iustice;
Ile leave you to your prayers, and betwixt ye
I part my wishes.
Per. Honour crowne the worthiest.
[*Exit Theseus, and his traine.*
Pal. The glasse is running now that cannot finish
Till one of us expire: Thinke you but thus,
That were there ought in me which strove to show
Mine enemy in this businesse, wer't one eye
Against another, Arme opprest by Arme,
I would destroy th'offender, Coz, I would,
Though parcell of my selfe: Then from this gather
How I should tender you.
Arc. I am in labour
To push your name, your auncient love, our kindred
Out of my memory; and i'th selfe same place
To seate something I would confound: So hoyst we
The sayles, that must these vessells port even where
The heavenly Lymiter pleases.
Pal. You speake well;
Before I turne, Let me embrace thee, Cosen:
This I shall never doe agen.
Arc. One farewell.
Pal. Why, let it be so: Farewell, Coz.
[*Exeunt Palamon and his Knights.*
Arc. Farewell, Sir.—
Knights, Kinsemen, Lovers, yea, my Sacrifices,
True worshippers of Mars, whose spirit in you
Expells the seedes of feare, and th'apprehension
Which still is farther off it, Goe with me
Before the god of our profession: There
Require of him the hearts of Lyons, and
The breath of Tigers, yea, the fearcenesse too,

91 friskings *Knight, Dyce.* 100 carve *F*: crave *Q*: carve for *Sew.* 110 Regimen *Sew.* *S. D.* Before *etc. add. Dyce* 4 smelling *conj. Th.*

11 furnesse *pr. ed.*: nearnesse *Q, etc.*: fiercenesse *conj. Ingleby* 32 part *Sew.* 43 father of *conj. Th.*

Yea, the speed also,—to goe on, I meane,
Else wish we to be Snayles: you know my prize
Must be drag'd out of blood; force and great feate
Must put my Garland on, where she stickes
The Queene of Flowers: our intercession then
Must be to him that makes the Campe a Cestron
Brymd with the blood of men: give me your aide
And bend your spirits towards him.
[*They kneele.*
Thou mighty one, that with thy power hast turnd
Greene Neptune into purple, ⟨whose Approach⟩
Comets prewarne, whose havocke in vaste Feild
Vnearthed skulls proclaime, whose breath blowes downe,
The teeming Ceres foyzon, who doth plucke
With hand armypotent from forth blew clowdes
The masond Turrets, that both mak'st and break'st
The stony girthes of Citties: me thy puple,
Yongest follower of thy Drom, instruct this day
With military skill, that to thy lawde
I may advance my Streamer, and by thee,
Be stil'd the Lord o'th day: give me, great Mars,
Some token of thy pleasure.
[*Here they fall on their faces as formerly, and there is heard clanging of Armor, with a short Thunder as the burst of a Battaile, whereupon they all rise and bow to the Altar.*
O Great Corrector of enormous times,
Shaker of ore-rank States, thou grand decider
Of dustie and old tytles, that healst with blood
The earth when it is sicke, and curst the world
O'th pluresie of people; I doe take
Thy signes auspiciously, and in thy name
To my designe march boldly. Let us goe.
[*Exeunt.*

Enter Palamon and his Knights, with the former observance.

Pal. Our stars must glister with new fire, or be
To daie extinct; our argument is love,
Which if the goddesse of it grant, she gives
Victory too: then blend your spirits with mine,
You, whose free noblenesse doe make my cause
Your personall hazard; to the goddesse *Venus*
Commend we our proceeding, and implore
Her power unto our partie.
[*Here they kneele as formerly.*
Haile, Soveraigne Queene of secrets, who hast power
To call the feircest Tyrant from his rage,
And weepe unto a Girle; that ha'st the might,
Even with an ey-glance, to choke *Marsis* Drom
And turne th'allarme to whispers; that canst make
A Criple florish with his Crutch, and cure him
Before *Apollo*; that may'st force the King
To be his subjects vassaile, and induce
Stale gravitie to daunce; the pould Bachelour—
Whose youth, like wonton Boyes through Bonfyres,
Have skipt thy flame—at seaventy thou canst catch
And make him, to the scorne of his hoarse throate,
Abuse yong laies of love: what godlike power
Hast thou not power upon? To *Phœbus* thou
Add'st flames hotter then his; the heavenly fyres
Did scortch his mortall Son, thine him; the huntresse
All moyst and cold, some say, began to throw
Her Bow away, and sigh. Take to thy grace
Me, thy vowd Souldier, who doe beare thy yoke
As t'wer a wreath of Roses, yet is heavier
Then Lead it selfe, stings more than Nettles.
I have never beene foule mouthd against thy law,
Nev'r reveald secret, for I knew none—would not,
Had I kend all that were; I never practised
Vpon mans wife, nor would the Libells reade
Of liberall wits; I never at great feastes
Sought to betray a Beautie, but have blush'd
At simpring Sirs that did; I have beene harsh
To large Confessors, and have hotly ask'd them
If they had Mothers: I had one, a woman,
And women t'wer they wrong'd. I knew a man

50 on *Q, etc.*: on me *conj. Litt.* stickes *Q*: will stick *Sew.* 54 *S. D.* They advance to the altar of Mars, and fall on their faces; then kneel *Dyce* 56 whose Approach *add. Sew.* 60 armipotent *Sew.*: armenypotent *Q* 63 Young *Sew.*

82 *S. D.* They advance to the altar of Venus, and fall on their faces; then kneel *Dyce.* 85 And *Q, F*: To *Sew.* unto *Q, F*: into *conj. Th.* 92 youth *Q*: Freaks of youth *Sew.*

Of eightie winters, this I told them, who
A Lasse of foureteene brided; twas thy power
To put life into dust; the aged Crampe
Had screw'd his square foote round,
The Gout had knit his fingers into knots,
Torturing Convulsions from his globie eyes,
Had almost drawne their spheeres, that what was life
In him seem'd torture: this Anatomie
Had by his yong faire pheare a Boy, and I
Beleev'd it was his, for she swore it was,
And who would not beleeve her? briefe, I am
To those that prate and have done no Companion;
To those that boast and have not a defyer;
To those that would and cannot a Rejoycer.
Yea, him I doe not love, that tells close offices
The fowlest way, nor names concealements in
The boldest language: such a one I am,
And vow that lover never yet made sigh
Truer then I. O, then, most soft, sweet goddesse,
Give me the victory of this question, which
Is true loves merit, and blesse me with a signe
Of thy great pleasure.

[*Here Musicke is heard, Doves are seene to flutter; they fall againe upon their faces, then on their knees.*

Pal. O thou, that from eleven to ninetie raign'st
In mortall bosomes, whose chase is this world,
And we in heards thy game: I give thee thankes
For this faire Token, which, being layd unto
Mine innocent true heart, armes in assurance [*They bow.*
My body to this businesse. Let us rise
And bow before the goddesse: Time comes on. [*Exeunt.*

[*Still Musicke of Records.*

Enter Emilia *in white, her haire about her shoulders, ⟨wearing⟩ a wheaten wreath: One in white holding up her traine, her haire stucke with flowers: One before her carrying a silver Hynde, in which is conveyd Incense and sweet odours, which being set upon the Altar ⟨of Diana⟩ her maides standing a loofe, she sets fire to it; then they curtsey and kneele.*

Emilia. O sacred, shadowie, cold and constant Queene,
Abandoner of Revells, mute, contemplative,
Sweet, solitary, white as chaste, and pure
As windefand Snow, who to thy femall knights
Alow'st no more blood than will make a blush,
Which is their orders robe: I heere, thy Priest,
Am humbled fore thine Altar; O vouchsafe,
With that thy rare greene eye, which never yet
Beheld thing maculate, looke on thy virgin;
And, sacred silver Mistris, lend thine eare
(Which nev'r heard scurrill terme, into whose port
Ne're entred wanton found,) to my petition
Seasond with holy feare: This is my last
Of vestall office; I am bride habited,
But mayden harted, a husband I have pointed,
But doe not know him; out of two I should
Choose one and pray for his successe, but I
Am guiltlesse of election: of mine eyes,
Were I to loose one, they are equall precious,
I could doombe neither, that which perish'd should
Goe too't unsentenc'd: Therefore, most modest Queene,
He of the two Pretenders, that best loves me
And has the truest title in't, Let him
Take off my wheaten Gerland, or else grant
The fyle and qualitie I hold, I may
Continue in thy Band.

[*Here the Hynde vanishes under the Altar: and in the place ascends a Rose Tree, having one Rose upon it.*

See what our Generall of Ebbs and Flowes
Out from the bowells of her holy Altar
With sacred act advances! But one Rose:
If well inspird, this Battaile shal confound
Both these brave Knights, and I, a virgin flowre
Must grow alone unpluck'd.

[*Here is heard a sodaine twang of Instruments, and the Rose fals from the Tree ⟨which vanishes under the altar.⟩*

The flowre is falne, the Tree descends: O, Mistris,
Thou here dischargest me; I shall be gather'd:
I thinke so, but I know not thine owne will;
Vnclaspe thy Misterie.—I hope she's pleas'd,
Her Signes were gratious. [*They curtsey and Exeunt.*

Scæna 2. ⟨*A darkened Room in the Prison.*⟩

Enter Doctor, Iaylor and Wooer, in habite of Palamon.

Doct. Has this advice I told you, done any good upon her?

122 pheare *Q*: Sphere *F* 126 defyer]desire *conj. S.* *S. D.* and wearing *add. Dyce* of Diana *add. Dyce*

150 greene *Q*: sheen *Sew.* 153 port *Q*, *etc.*: Porch *conj. Th.* 174 *S. D.* which . . altar *add. Dyce* *S. D.* A darkened *etc. add. T*

Wooer. O very much; The maids that kept her company
Have halfe perswaded her that I am *Palamon*;
Within this halfe houre she came smiling to me,
And asked me what I would eate, and when I would kisse her:
I told her presently, and kist her twice.
Doct. Twas well done; twentie times had bin far better,
For there the cure lies mainely.
Wooer. Then she told me
She would watch with me to night, for well she knew
What houre my fit would take me.
Doct. Let her doe so,
And when your fit comes, fit her home,
And presently.
Wooer. She would have me sing.
Doctor. You did so?
Wooer. No.
Doct. Twas very ill done, then;
You should observe her ev'ry way.
Wooer. Alas,
I have no voice, Sir, to confirme her that way.
Doctor. That's all one, if yee make a noyse;
If she intreate againe, doe any thing,—
Lye with her, if she aske you.
Iaylor. Hoa, there, *Doctor!*
Doctor. Yes, in the waie of cure.
Iaylor. But first, by your leave,
I'th way of honestie.
Doctor. That's but a nicenesse,
Nev'r cast your child away for honestie;
Cure her first this way, then if shee will be honest,
She has the path before her.
Iaylor. Thanke yee, *Doctor.*
Doctor. Pray, bring her in,
And let's see how shee is.
Iaylor. I will, and tell her
Her *Palamon* staies for her: But, *Doctor*,
Me thinkes you are i'th wrong still. [*Exit Iaylor.*
Doc. Goe, goe:
You Fathers are fine Fooles: her honesty?
And we should give her physicke till we finde that—
Wooer. Why, doe you thinke she is not honest, Sir?
Doctor. How old is she?
Wooer. She's eighteene.
Doctor. She may be,
But that's all one; tis nothing to our purpose.
What ere her Father saies, if you perceave
Her moode inclining that way that I spoke of,
Videlicet, the *way of flesh*—you have me?
Wooer. Yet, very well, Sir.
Doctor. Please her appetite,
And doe it home; it cures her, *ipso facto*,
The mellencholly humour that infects her.
Wooer. I am of your minde, *Doctor.*

Enter Iaylor, Daughter, Maide.

Docter. You'l finde it so; she comes, pray humour her.
Iaylor. Come, your Love *Palamon* staies for you, childe,
And has done this long houre, to visite you.
Daughter. I thanke him for his gentle patience;
He's a kind Gentleman, and I am much bound to him.
Did you nev'r see the horse he gave me?
Iaylor. Yes.
Daugh. How doe you like him?
Iaylor. He's a very faire one.
Daugh. You never saw him dance?
Iaylor. No.
Daugh. I have often.
He daunces very finely, very comely,
And for a Iigge, come cut and long taile to him,
He turnes ye like a Top.
Iaylor. That's fine, indeede.
Daugh. Hee'l dance the Morris twenty mile an houre,
And that will founder the best hobby-horse
(If I have any skill) in all the parish,
And gallops to the turne of *Light a' love*:
What thinke you of this horse?
Iaylor. Having these vertues,
I thinke he might be broght to play at Tennis.
Daugh. Alas, that's nothing.
Iaylor. Can he write and reade too?
Daugh. A very faire hand, and casts himselfe th'accounts
Of all his hay and provender: That Hostler
Must rise betime that cozens him. You know
The Chestnut Mare the Duke has?
Iaylor. Very well.
Daugh. She is horribly in love with him, poore beast,
But he is like his master, coy and scornefull.
Iaylor. What dowry has she?
Daugh. Some two hundred Bottles,
And twenty strike of Oates; but hee'l ne're have her;
He lispes in's neighing, able to entice
A Millars Mare: Hee'l be the death of her.

3-5 *End* this, what I, told her *Q*

50 Yet *Q*: Yes *F*, *etc.* 55 humour *Th.*: honour *Q*
74 turne *Q*: tune *Sew.*, *etc.*

Doctor. What stuffe she utters!
Iaylor. Make curtsie; here your love comes.
Wooer. Pretty soule,
How doe ye? that's a fine maide, ther's a curtsie!
Daugh. Yours to command ith way of honestie.
How far is't now to'th end o'th world, my Masters?
Doctor. Why, a daies Iorney, wench.
Daugh. Will you goe with me?
Wooer. What shall we doe there, wench?
Daugh. Why, play at stoole ball:
What is there else to doe?
Wooer. I am content,
If we shall keepe our wedding there.
Daugh. Tis true:
For there, I will assure you, we shall finde
Some blind Priest for the purpose, that will venture
To marry us, for here they are nice, and foolish;
Besides, my father must be hang'd to morrow
And that would be a blot i'th businesse.
Are not you *Palamon*?
Wooer. Doe not you know me?
Daugh. Yes, but you care not for me; I have nothing
But this pore petticoate, and too corse Smockes.
Wooer. That's all one; I will have you.
Daugh. Will you surely?
Wooer. Yes, by this faire hand, will I.
Daugh. Wee'l to bed, then.
Wooer. Ev'n when you will. ⟨*Kisses her.*⟩
Daugh. O Sir, you would faine be nibling.
Wooer. Why doe you rub my kisse off?
Daugh. Tis a sweet one,
And will perfume me finely against the wedding.
Is not this your Cosen *Arcite*?
Doctor. Yes, sweet heart,
And I am glad my Cosen *Palamon*
Has made so faire a choice.
Daugh. Doe you thinke hee'l have me?
Doctor. Yes, without doubt.
Daugh. Doe you thinke so too?
Iaylor. Yes.
Daugh. We shall have many children:—Lord, how y'ar growne!
My *Palamon*, I hope, will grow, too, finely,
Now he's at liberty: Alas, poore Chicken,
He was kept downe with hard meate and ill lodging,
But ile kisse him up againe.

Enter a Messenger.

Mess. What doe you here? you'l loose the noblest sight
That ev'r was seene.
Iaylor. Are they i'th Field?
Mess. They are.
You beare a charge there too.
Iaylor. Ile away straight.
I must ev'n leave you here.
Docter Nay, wee'l goe with you;
I will not loose the Fight.
Iaylor. How did you like her?
Doctor. Ile warrant you, within these 3. or 4. daies
Ile make her right againe. You must not from her,
But still preserve her in this way.
Wooer. I will.
Doc. Lets get her in.
Wooer. Come, sweete, wee'l goe to dinner;
And then weele play at Cardes.
Daugh. And shall we kisse too?
Wooer. A hundred times.
Daugh. And twenty.
Wooer. I, and twenty.
Daugh. And then wee'l sleepe together.
Doc. Take her offer.
Wooer. Yes, marry, will we.
Daugh. But you shall not hurt me.
Wooer. I will not, sweete.
Daugh. If you doe, Love, ile cry.
[*Florish. Exeunt*

Scæna 3. ⟨*A Place near the Lists.*⟩

Enter Theseus, Hipolita, Emilia, Perithous: and some Attendants, (*T. Tucke: Curtis.*)

Emil. Ile no step further.
Per. Will you loose this sight?
Emil. I had rather see a wren hawke at a fly
Then this decision; ev'ry blow that falls
Threats a brave life, each stroake laments
The place whereon it fals, and sounds more like
A Bell then blade: I will stay here;
It is enough my hearing shall be punishd
With what shall happen—gainst the which there is
No deaffing, but to heare—not taint mine eye
With dread sights, it may shun.
Pir. Sir, my good Lord,
Your Sister will no further.

119 *S. D. add. Dyce*

145 Fight *Q, F*: sight *Dyce* (*later edd.*), *Litt.* *S. D.* A Place *etc. add. T*: An Apartment in the Palace *Weber*: A part of the forest near the place appointed for the combat *Dyce* 9 happen, *Q* 10 heare ; *Q*

Thes. Oh, she must.
She shall see deeds of honour in their kinde,
Which sometime show well, pencild. Nature now
Shall make and act the Story, the beleife
Both seald with eye and eare; you must be present,
You are the victours meede, the price, and garlond
To crowne the Questions title.
Emil. Pardon me;
If I were there, I'ld winke.
Thes. You must be there;
This Tryall is as t'wer i'th night, and you
The onely star to shine.
Emil. I am extinct;
There is but envy in that light, which showes
The one the other: darkenes, which ever was
The dam of horrour, who do's stand accurst
Of many mortall Millions, may even now,
By casting her blacke mantle over both,
That neither coulde finde other, get her selfe
Some part of a good name, and many a murther
Set off wherto she's guilty.
Hip. You must goe.
Emil. In faith, I will not.
Thes. Why, the knights must kindle
Their valour at your eye: know, of this war
You are the Treasure, and must needes be by
To give the Service pay.
Emil. Sir, pardon me;
The tytle of a kingdome may be tride
Out of it selfe.
Thes. Well, well, then, at your pleasure;
Those that remaine with you could wish their office
To any of their Enemies.
Hip. Farewell, Sister;
I am like to know your husband fore your selfe
By some small start of time: he whom the gods
Doe of the two know best, I pray them he
Be made your Lot.
[*Exeunt Theseus, Hipolita, Perithous, &c.*
Emil. *Arcite* is gently visagd; yet his eye
Is like an Engyn bent, or a sharpe weapon
In a soft sheath; mercy and manly courage
Are bedfellowes in his visage. *Palamon*
Has a most menacing aspect: his brow
Is grav'd, and seemes to bury what it frownes on;
Yet sometime tis not so, but alters to
The quallity of his thoughts; long time his eye
Will dwell upon his object. Mellencholly
Becomes him nobly; So do's *Arcites* mirth,
But *Palamons* sadnes is a kinde of mirth,
So mingled, as if mirth did make him sad,
And sadnes, merry; those darker humours that
Sticke misbecomingly on others, on them
Live in faire dwelling.
[*Cornets. Trompets sound as to a charge.*
Harke, how yon spurs to spirit doe incite
The Princes to their proofe! *Arcite* may win me,
And yet may *Palamon* wound *Arcite* to
The spoyling of his figure. O, what pitty
Enough for such a chance; if I were by,
I might doe hurt, for they would glance their eies
Toward my Seat, and in that motion might
Omit a ward, or forfeit an offence
Which crav'd that very time: it is much better
I am not there; oh better never borne
Then minister to such harme. [*Cornets. A great cry and noice within, crying* '*a Palamon*'.] What is the chance?

Enter Servant.

Ser. The Crie's 'a *Palamon*'.
Emil. Then he has won! Twas ever likely;
He lookd all grace and successe, and he is
Doubtlesse the prim'st of men: I pre'thee, run
And tell me how it goes.
[*Showt, and Cornets: Crying,* '*a Palamon.*'
Ser. Still *Palamon*.
Emil. Run and enquire. Poore Servant, thou hast lost;
Vpon my right side still I wore thy picture,
Palamons on the left: why so, I know not;
I had no end in't else, chance would have it so.
On the sinister side the heart lyes; *Palamon*
Had the best boding chance. [*Another cry, and showt within, and Cornets.*] This burst of clamour
Is sure th'end o'th Combat.

Enter Servant.

Ser. They saide that *Palamon* had *Arcites* body
Within an inch o'th Pyramid, that the cry
Was generall 'a *Palamon*': But, anon,
Th'Assistants made a brave redemption, and

16 sometime *Q*: Time shall *Sew.* well pencild *Q*, *F* 20 questant's *Dyce* (*later edd.*) 29 dame *F*
65 them *Q*, *F*: him *Sew.*, *etc.* 66 in a fair *Sew.* 74 Defence *conj. Sy.* 77 *S. D. after* 75 *Q* 87 in't; else chance *Q*, *F*: in't; Chance *Sew.* else] 'less *conj. Sy.* 89 *S. D. after* 87 *Q*

The two bold Tytlers, at this instant are
Hand to hand at it.
Emil. Were they metamorphisd
Both into one! oh why? there were no woman
Worth so composd a Man: their single share,
Their noblenes peculier to them, gives
The prejudice of disparity, values shortnes,
[*Cornets. Cry within, Arcite, Arcite.*
To any Lady breathing——More exulting?
Palamon still?
Ser. Nay, now the sound is *Arcite.*
Emil. I pre'thee, lay attention to the Cry.
[*Cornets. A great showt and cry, 'Arcite, victory!'*
Set both thine eares to'th busines.
Ser. The cry is
'*Arcite*', and 'victory', harke: '*Arcite,* victory!'
The Combats consummation is proclaim'd
By the wind Instruments.
Emil. Halfe sights saw
That *Arcite* was no babe; god's lyd, his richnes
And costlines of spirit look't through him, it could
No more be hid in him then fire in flax,
Then humble banckes can goe to law with waters,
That drift windes force to raging: I did thinke
Good *Palamon* would miscarry; yet I knew not
Why I did thinke so; Our reasons are not prophets,
When oft our fancies are. They are comming off:
Alas, poore *Palamon!* [*Cornets.*

Enter Theseus, Hipolita, Pirithous, Arcite as victor, and attendants, &c.

Thes. Lo, where our Sister is in expectation,
Yet quaking, and unsetled.—Fairest *Emily,*
The gods by their divine arbitrament
Have given you this Knight; he is a good one
As ever strooke at head. Give me your hands;
Receive you her, you him; be plighted with
A love that growes, as you decay.
Arcite. Emily,
To buy you, I have lost what's deerest to me,
Save what is bought, and yet I purchase cheapely,
As I doe rate your value.
Thes. O loved Sister,
He speakes now of as brave a Knight as ere
Did spur a noble Steed: Surely, the gods
Would have him die a Batchelour, least his race
Should shew i'th world too godlike: His behaviour
So charmed me, that me thought *Alcides* was
To him a sow of lead: if I could praise
Each part of him to'th all I have spoke, your *Arcite*
Did not loose by't; For he that was thus good
Encountred yet his Better. I have heard
Two emulous Philomels beate the eare o'th night
With their contentious throates, now one the higher,
Anon the other, then againe the first,
And by and by out breasted, that the sence
Could not be judge betweene 'em: So it far'd
Good space betweene these kinesmen; till heavens did
Make hardly one the winner. Weare the Girlond
With joy that you have won: For the subdude,
Give them our present Iustice, since I know
Their lives but pinch 'em; Let it here be done.
The Sceane's not for our seeing, goe we hence,
Right joyfull, with some sorrow.—Arme your prize,
I know you will not loose her.—*Hipolita,*
I see one eye of yours conceives a teare
The which it will deliver. [*Florish.*
Emil. Is this wynning?
Oh all you heavenly powers, where is your mercy?
But that your wils have saide it must be so,
And charge me live to comfort this unfriended,
This miserable Prince, that cuts away
A life more worthy from him then all women,
I should, and would, die too.
Hip. Infinite pitty,
That fowre such eies should be so fixd on one
That two must needes be blinde fort.
Thes. So it is. [*Exeunt.*

Scæna 4. ⟨*The same; a Block prepared.*⟩

Enter Palamon and his Knightes pyniond: Iaylor, Executioner, &c. Gard.

Ther's many a man alive that hath out liv'd
The love o'th people; yea, i'th selfesame state
Stands many a Father with his childe; some comfort
We have by so considering: we expire
And not without mens pitty. To live still,
Have their good wishes; we prevent
The loathsome misery of age, beguile
The Gowt and Rheume, that in lag howres attend

95 Tyltlers *Tonson*: Tilters *Sew.* 100 *Om. F, Sew.*

139 to'th all *Q*: to thee. All *T* 158 your *F, etc.*: you *Q* *S. D.* The same *etc. add. Litt.*: The same part of the forest as in Act III, Scene VI. *Dyce*; An open place in the City with a Scaffold *Weber*

For grey approachers; we come towards the gods
Yong and unwapper'd, not halting under Crymes
Many and stale: that sure shall please the gods,
Sooner than such, to give us Nectar with 'em,
For we are more cleare Spirits. My deare kinsemen,
Whose lives (for this poore comfort) are laid downe,
You have sould 'em too too cheape.
1. K. What ending could be
Of more content? ore us the victors have
Fortune, whose title is as momentary,
As to us death is certaine: A graine of honour
They not ore'-weigh us.
2. K. Let us bid farewell;
And with our patience anger tottring Fortune,
Who at her certain'st reeles.
3. K. Come; who begins?
Pal. Ev'n he that led you to this Banket shall
Taste to you all.—Ah ha, my Friend, my Friend,
Your gentle daughter gave me freedome once;
You'l see't done now for ever: pray, how do'es she?
I heard she was not well; her kind of ill
Gave me some sorrow.
Iaylor. Sir, she's well restor'd,
And to be marryed shortly.
Pal. By my short life,
I am most glad on't; Tis the latest thing
I shall be glad of; pre'thee tell her so:
Commend me to her, and to peece her portion,
Tender her this. ⟨*Gives purse.*⟩
1. K. Nay lets be offerers all.
2. K. Is it a maide?
Pal. Verily, I thinke so,
A right good creature, more to me deserving
Then I can quight or speake of.
All K. Commend us to her.
[*They give their purses.*
Iaylor. The gods requight you all,
And make her thankefull.
Pal. Adiew; and let my life be now as short,
As my leave taking. [*Lies on the Blocke.*
1. K. Leade, couragious Cosin.
2. K. Wee'l follow cheerefully.
[*A great noise within crying, 'run, save, hold!'*

Enter in hast a Messenger.

Mess. Hold, hold! O hold, hold, hold!

Enter Pirithous in haste.

Pir. Hold! hoa! It is a cursed hast you made,
If you have done so quickly. Noble *Palamon,*
The gods will shew their glory in a life,
That thou art yet to leade.
Pal. Can that be,
When *Venus,* I have said, is false? How doe things fare?
Pir. Arise, great Sir, and give the tydings eare
That are most dearly sweet and bitter.
Pal. What
Hath wakt us from our dreame?
Pir. List then: your Cosen,
Mounted upon a Steed that *Emily*
Did first bestow on him, a blacke one, owing
Not a hayre worth of white—which some will say
Weakens his price, and many will not buy
His goodnesse with this note: Which superstition
Heere findes allowance—On this horse is *Arcite*
Trotting the stones of *Athens,* which the *Calkins*
Did rather tell then trample; for the horse
Would make his length a mile, if't pleas'd his Rider
To put pride in him: as he thus went counting
The flinty pavement, dancing, as t'wer, to'th Musicke
His owne hoofes made; (for as they say from iron
Came Musickes origen) what envious Flint,
Cold as old *Saturne,* and like him possest
With fire malevolent, darted a Sparke,
Or what feirce sulphur else, to this end made,
I comment not;—the hot horse, hot as fire,
Tooke Toy at this, and fell to what disorder
His power could give his will; bounds, comes on end,
Forgets schoole dooing, being therein traind,
And of kind mannadge; pig-like he whines
At the sharpe Rowell, which he freats at rather
Then any jot obaies; seekes all foule meanes
Of boystrous and rough Iadrie, to dis-seate
His Lord, that kept it bravely: when nought serv'd,
When neither Curb would cracke, girth breake nor diffring plunges
Dis-roote his Rider whence he grew, but that
He kept him tweene his legges, on his hind hoofes

10 unwapper'd *Q, F*: unwarp'd *Sew.*: unwappen'd *Kn.* *S. D.* Gives purse *add. Dyce* 49 *Prefix* 1. 2. K. *Q* 55 *Ends* when *Dyce* 58 dearly *Sew., etc.*: early *Q, F*: ? fearly

on end he stands,
That *Arcites* leggs, being higher then his head,
Seem'd with strange art to hang: His victors wreath
Even then fell off his head: and presently
Backeward the Iade comes ore, and his full poyze
Becomes the Riders loade: yet is he living,
But such a vessell tis, that floates but for
The surge that next approaches: he much desires
To have some speech with you: Loe he appeares.

Enter Theseus, Hipolita, Emilia, Arcite in a chaire.

Pal. O miserable end of our alliance!
The gods are mightie, *Arcite:* if thy heart,
Thy worthie, manly heart, be yet unbroken,
Give me thy last words; I am *Palamon,*
One that yet loves thee dying.
Arc. Take *Emilia*
And with her all the worlds joy: Reach thy hand:
Farewell: I have told my last houre. I was false,
Yet never treacherous: Forgive me, Cosen:—
One kisse from faire *Emilia*: Tis done:
Take her: I die.
Pal. Thy brave soule seeke *Elizium.*
Emil. Ile close thine eyes, Prince; blessed soules be with thee!
Thou art a right good man, and while I live,
This day I give to teares.
Pal. And I to honour.
Thes. In this place first you fought: ev'n very here
I sundred you: acknowledge to the gods
Our thankes that you are living.
His part is playd, and though it were too short,
He did it well: your day is lengthned, and
The blissefull dew of heaven do's arowze you.
The powerfull *Venus* well hath grac'd her Altar,
And given you your love: Our Master *Mars*
Hath vouch'd his Oracle, and to *Arcite* gave
The grace of the Contention: So the Deities
Have shewd due justice: Beare this hence.
Pal. O Cosen,
That we should things desire, which doe cost us
The losse of our desire! That nought could buy
Deare love, but losse of deare love!
Thes. Never Fortune
Did play a subtler Game: The conquerd triumphes,
The victor has the Losse: yet in the passage
The gods have beene most equall: *Palamon,*
Your kinseman hath confest the right o'th Lady
Did lye in you, for you first saw her, and
Even then proclaimd your fancie: He restord her
As your stolne Iewell, and desir'd your spirit
To send him hence forgiven; The gods my justice
Take from my hand, and they themselves become
The Executioners: Leade your Lady off;
And call your Lovers from the stage of death,
Whom I adopt my Frinds. A day or two
Let us looke sadly, and give grace unto
The Funerall of *Arcite*; in whose end
The visages of Bridegroomes weele put on
And smile with *Palamon*; for whom an houre,
But one houre, since, I was as dearely sorry,
As glad of *Arcite*: and am now as glad,
As for him sorry. O you heavenly Charmers,
What things you make of us! For what we lacke
We laugh, for what we have, are sorry: still
Are children in some kind. Let us be thankefull
For that which is, and with you leave dispute
That are above our question. Let's goe off,
And beare us like the time. [*Florish. Exeunt.*

EPILOGVE

I would now aske ye how ye like the Play,
But, as it is with Schoole Boyes, cannot say,
I am cruell fearefull: pray, yet stay a while,
And let me looke upon ye: No man smile?
Then it goes hard, I see; He that has
Lov'd a yong hansome wench, then, show his face—
Tis strange if none be heere—and if he will
Against his Conscience, let him hisse, and kill
Our Market: Tis in vaine, I see, to stay yee;
Have at the worst can come, then! Now what say ye?
And yet mistake me not: I am not bold;
We have no such cause. If the tale we have told
(For tis no other) any way content ye
(For to that honest purpose it was ment ye)
We have our end; and ye shall have ere long,
I dare say, many a better, to prolong
Your old loves to us: we, and all our might
Rest at your service. Gentlemen, good night.
[Florish.

FINIS

90 *So in Q: the first part of the line appears to have been lost* 92 victoros *Q* 100 gods *Q*: Cords *conj. Th.* 117 Our *Q, F*: Your *conj. Dyce* 123 Hath *pr. ed.*: Hast *Q, F*: Has *Sew.*

THE

BIRTH

OF

MERLIN:

OR,

The Childe hath found his Father.

As it hath been ſeveral times Acted with great Applauſe.

Written by *William Shakeſpear*, and *William Rowley*.

Placere cupio.

LONDON: Printed by *Tho. Johnſon* for *Francis Kirkman*, and *Henry Marſh*, and are to be ſold at the *Princes Arms* in *Chancery-Lane*. 1662.

Q	=	Quarto of 1662
T	=	Tyrrell, 1851
D	=	Delius, 1856
Molt.	=	Moltke, 1869
WP	=	Warnke and Proescholdt, 1887
pr. ed.	=	present editor

THE BIRTH OF MERLIN:

OR, THE CHILDE HATH FOUND HIS FATHER

Drammatis Personæ

The Scene *Brittain.*

Aurelius, King of *Brittain.*
Vortiger, King of ⟨*Welsh*⟩ *Brittain.*
Vter Pendragon the Prince, Brother to *Aurelius.*
Donobert, a Nobleman, and Father to *Constantia* and *Modestia.*
The Earl of *Gloster,* and Father to *Edwyn.*
Edoll, Earl of *Chester,* and General to King *Aurelius.*
Cador, Earl of *Cornwal,* and Suitor to *Constantia.*
Edwyn, Son to the Earl of *Gloster,* and Suitor to *Modestia.*
Toclio and *Oswald,* two Noblemen.
Merlin the Prophet.
Anselme the Hermit, after Bishop of *Winchester.*
Clown, brother to *Jone,* mother of *Merlin.*
Sir *Nichodemus Nothing,* a Courtier.
The Devil, father of *Merlin.*
Ostorius, the Saxon General.
Octa, a Saxon Nobleman.
Proximus, a Saxon Magician.
Two Bishops.
Two Saxon Lords.
Two of *Edols* Captains.
Two Gentlemen.
A little Antick Spirit.
Artesia, Sister to *Ostorius* the Saxon General.
Constantia and *Modestia* } Daughters to *Donobert.*
Jone Goe-too't, Mother of *Merlin.*
A Waiting-woman to *Artesia.*
Lucina, Queen of the Shades.

ACTUS I.

⟨SCENE I.

A Room in the Castle of Lord Donobert.⟩

Enter Donobert, Gloster, Cador, Edwin, Constantia, and Modestia.

Cador. You teach me language, sir, as one that knows
The Debt of Love I owe unto her Vertues;
Wherein like a true Courtier I have fed
My self with hope of fair Success, and now
Attend your wisht consent to my long Suit.
Dono. Believe me,. youthful Lord,
Time could not give an opportunity
More fitting your desires, always provided,
My Daughters love be suited with my Grant.
Cador. 'Tis the condition, sir, her Promise seal'd.
Dono. Ist so, *Constantia?*
Constan. I was content to give him words for oathes;
He swore so oft he lov'd me—
Dono. That thou believest him?
Const. He is a man, I hope.
Dono. That's in the trial, Girl.
Const. However, I am a woman, sir.
Dono. The Law's on thy side then: sha't have a Husband,
I, and a worthy one. Take her, brave *Cornwal,*
And make our happiness great as our wishes.
Cador. Sir, I thank you.
Glost. Double the fortunes of the day, my Lord,
And crown my wishes too: I have a son here,
Who in my absence would protest no less
Unto your other Daughter.
Dono. Ha, *Gloster,* is it so? what says Lord *Edwin?*
Will she protest as much to thee?
Edwin. Else must she want some of her Sisters faith, Sir.
Modesta. Of her credulity much rather, Sir:
My Lord, you are a Soldier, and methinks
The height of that Profession should diminish
All heat of Loves desires,
Being so late employ'd in blood and ruine.
Edwin. The more my Conscience tyes me to repair
The worlds losses in a new succession.
Modest. Necessity, it seems, ties your affections then,
And at that rate I would unwillingly
Be thrust upon you; a wife is a dish soon cloys, sir.
Edwin. Weak and diseased appetites it may.

The entire play, except the rhyming couplets, is printed as prose in Q: corr. D   Scene I. *etc. add. T*   2 her *WP*: their *Q*
20 your happiness *WP*

Modest. Most of your making have dull stomacks, sir.

Dono. If that be all, Girl, thou shalt quicken him;
Be kinde to him, *Modesta:* Noble *Edwin,*
Let it suffice, what's mine in her speaks yours;
For her consent, let your fair suit go on,
She is a woman, sir, and will be won.

Edwin. You give me comfort, sir.

Enter Toclio.

Dono. Now, *Toclio?*

Toclio. The King, my honor'd Lords, requires your presence,
And calls a Councel for return of answer
Unto the parling enemy, whose Embassadors
Are on the way to Court.

Dono. So suddenly?
Chester, it seems, has ply'd them hard at war,
They sue so fast for peace, which by my advice
They ne're shall have, unless they leave the Realm.
Come, noble *Gloster,* let's attend the King.
It lies, sir, in your Son to do me pleasure,
And save the charges of a Wedding Dinner;
If you'l make haste to end your Love affairs,
One cost may give discharge to both my cares. [*Exit Dono., Glost.*

Edwin. I'le do my best.

Cador. Now, *Toclio,* what stirring news at Court?

Toclio. Oh, my Lord, the Court's all fill'd with rumor, the City with news, and the Country with wonder, and all the bells i'th' Kingdom must proclaim it, we have a new Holyday a coming.

Consta. A holy-day! for whom? for thee?

Toclio. Me, Madam! 'sfoot! I'de be loath that any man should make a holy-day for me yet:
In brief, 'tis thus: there's here arriv'd at Court,
Sent by the Earl of *Chester* to the King,
A man of rare esteem for holyness,
A reverent hermit, that by miracle
Not onely saved our army,
But without aid of man o'rethrew
The pagan Host, and with such wonder, sir,
As might confirm a Kingdom to his faith.

Edwin. This is strange news, indeed; where is he?

Toclio. In conference with the King, that much respects him.

Modest. Trust me, I long to see him.

46 *S. D. after* 45 *Q*

Toclio. Faith, you will finde no great pleasure in him, for ought that I can see, Lady. They say he is half a Prophet too: would he could tell me any news of the lost Prince; there's twenty Talents offer'd to him that finds him.

Cador. Such news was breeding in the morning.

Toclio. And now it has birth and life, sir. If fortune bless me, I'le once more search those woods where then we lost him; I know not yet what fate may follow me. [*Exit.*

Cador. Fortune go with you, sir. Come, fair Mistriss,
Your Sister and Lord *Edwin* are in game,
And all their wits at stake to win the Set.

Consta. My sister has the hand yet; we had best leave them:
She will be out anon as well as I;
He wants but cunning to put in a Dye. [*Exit Cador, Constan.*

Edwin. You are a cunning Gamester, Madam.

Modest. It is a desperate Game, indeed, this Marriage,
Where there's no winning without loss to either.

Edwin. Why, what but your perfection, noble Lady,
Can bar the worthiness of this my suit?
If so you please I count my happiness
From difficult obtaining, you shall see
My duty and observance.

Modest. There shall be place to neither, noble sir;
I do beseech you, let this mild Reply
Give answer to your suit: for here I vow,
If e're I change my Virgin name, by you
It gains or looses.

Edwin. My wishes have their crown.

Modest. Let them confine you then,
As to my promise you give faith and credence.

Edwin. In your command my willing absence speaks it. [*Exit.*

Modest. Noble and vertuous: could I dream of Marriage,
I should affect thee, *Edwin.* Oh, my soul,
Here's something tells me that these best of creatures,
These models of the world, weak man and woman,
Should have their souls, their making, life, and being,
To some more excellent use: if what the sense
Calls pleasure were our ends, we might justly blame

Great natures wisdom, who rear'd a building
Of so much art and beauty to entertain
A guest so far incertain, so imperfect:
If onely speech distinguish us from beasts,
Who know no inequality of birth or place,
But still to fly from goodness: oh, how base
Were life at such a rate! No, no, that power
That gave to man his being, speech and wisdom,
Gave it for thankfulness. To him alone
That made me thus, may I whence truly know,
I'le pay to him, not man, the love I owe. [*Exit.*

⟨Scene II.

The British Court.⟩

Flourish Cornets. Enter Aurelius King of Brittain, Donobert, Gloster, Cador, Edwin, Toclio, Oswold, and Attendants.

Aurelius. No tiding of our brother yet? 'Tis strange,
So ne're the Court, and in our own Land too,
And yet no news of him: oh, this loss
Tempers the sweetness of our happy conquests
With much untimely sorrow.
Dono. Royal sir,
His safety being unquestion'd should to time
Leave the redress of sorrow: were he dead,
Or taken by the foe, our fatal loss
Had wanted no quick Herald to disclose it.
Aurelius. That hope alone sustains me,
Nor will we be so ingrateful unto heaven
To question what we fear with what we enjoy.
Is answer of our message yet return'd
From that religious man, the holy Hermit,
Sent by the Earl of *Chester* to confirm us
In that miraculous act? For 'twas no less:
Our Army being in rout, nay, quite o'rethrown,
As *Chester* writes, even then this holy man,
Arm'd with his cross and staff, went smiling on,
And boldly fronts the foe; at sight of whom
The *Saxons* stood amaz'd: for, to their seeming,
Above the Hermit's head appear'd such brightness,
Such clear and glorious beams, as if our men
March't all in fire; wherewith the *Pagans* fled,
And by our troops were all to death pursu'd.
Glost. 'Tis full of wonder, sir.
Aurel. Oh, *Gloster,* he's a jewel worth a Kingdom.
Where's *Oswold* with his answer?
Oswold. 'Tis here, my Royal Lord.
Aurel. In writing? will he not sit with us?
Oswo. His Orizons perform'd, he bad me say,
He would attend with all submission.
Aurel. Proceed to councel then; and let some give order,
The Embassadors being come to take our answer,
They have admittance. *Oswold, Toclio,*
Be it your charge!—⟨*Exeunt Os. and Toclio.*⟩
And now, my Lords, observe
The holy councel of this reverend Hermit:
[*reads*] *As you respect your safety, limit not*
That onely power that hath protected you;
Trust not an open enemy too far,
He's yet a looser, and knows you have won;
Mischiefs not ended are but then begun.
Anselme the Hermit.
Dono. Powerful and pithie, which my advice confirms:
No man leaves physick when his sickness slakes,
But doubles the receipts: the word of Peace
Seems fair to blood-shot eyes, but being appli'd
With such a medicine as blinds all the sight
Argues desire of Cure, but not of Art.
Aurel. You argue from defects; if both the name
And the condition of the Peace be one,
It is to be prefer'd, and in the offer,
Made by the *Saxon,* I see nought repugnant.
Glost. The time of Truce requir'd for thirty days
Carries suspicion in it, since half that space
Will serve to strength their weakned Regiment.
Cador. Who in less time will undertake to free
Our Country from them?
Edwin. Leave that unto our fortune.
Dono. Is not our bold and hopeful General
Still Master of the field, their Legions faln,
The rest intrencht for fear, half starv'd, and wounded,
And shall we now give o're our fair advantage?
'Fore heaven, my Lord, the danger is far more
In trusting to their words then to their weapons.

Enter Oswold.

Oswold. The Embassadors are come, sir.
Aurel. Conduct them in.
We are resolv'd, my Lords, since policy fail'd
In the beginning, it shall have no hand
In the conclusion.
That heavenly power that hath so well begun

130 thence *D* Scene II. *etc. add. T* 6 should] you should *WP* 22 Hermit *Q*

36 *S. D. add. T* 48 not of *Q*: not knowledge of *T* 55 regiments *T.* 56 Who] We *WP* 62 'Fore *T*: force *Q*

Their fatal overthrow, I know, can end it:
From which fair hope my self will give them answer.

Flourish Cornets. Enter Artesia with the Saxon Lords.

Dono. What's here? a woman Orator?
Aurel. Peace, *Donobert!*—Speak, what are you, Lady?
Artes. The sister of the *Saxon* General,
Warlike *Ostorius* the East *Anglese* King;
My name *Artesia,* who in terms of love
Brings peace and health to great *Aurelius,*
Wishing she may return as fair a present
As she makes tender of.
Aurel. The fairest present e're mine eyes were blest with!—
Command a chair there for this *Saxon* Beauty:—
Sit, Lady, we'l confer: your warlike brother
Sues for a peace, you say?
Artes. With endless love unto your State and Person.
Aurel. Ha's sent a moving Orator, believe me.—
What thinkst thou, *Donobert?*
Dono. Believe me, sir, were I but yong agen,
This gilded pill might take my stomack quickly.
Aurel. True, thou art old: how soon we do forget
Our own defects! Fair damsel,—oh, my tongue
Turns Traitor, and will betray my heart—sister to
Our enemy:—'sdeath, her beauty mazes me,
I cannot speak if I but look on her.—
What's that we did conclude?
Dono. This, Royal Lord—
Aurel. Pish, thou canst not utter it:—
Fair'st of creatures, tell the King your Brother,
That we, in love—ha!—and honor to our Country,
Command his Armies to depart our Realm.
But if you please, fair soul—Lord *Donobert,*
Deliver you our pleasure.
Dono. I shall, sir:
Lady, return, and certifie your brother—
Aurel. Thou art too blunt and rude! return so soon?
Fie, let her stay, and send some messenger
To certifie our pleasure.
Dono. What meanes your Grace?
Aurel. To give her time of rest to her long Journey;
We would not willingly be thought uncivil.
Artes. Great King of *Brittain,* let it not seem strange,
To embrace the Princely Offers of a friend,
Whose vertues with thine own, in fairest merit,
Both States in Peace and Love may now inherit.
Aurel. She speakes of Love agen:
Sure, 'tis my fear, she knows I do not hate her.
Artes. Be, then, thy self, most great *Aurelius,*
And let not envy nor a deeper sin
In these thy Councellors deprive thy goodness
Of that fair honor we in seeking peace
Give first to thee, who never use to sue
But force our wishes. Yet, if this seem light,
Oh, let my sex, though worthless your respect,
Take the report of thy humanity,
Whose mild and vertuous life loud fame displayes,
As being o'recome by one so worthy praise.
Aurel. She has an Angels tongue.—Speak still.
Dono. This flattery is gross, sir; hear no more on't.—
Lady, these childish complements are needless;
You have your answer, and believe it, Madam,
His Grace, though yong, doth wear within his breast
Too grave a Councellor to be seduc't
By smoothing flattery or oyly words.
Artes. I come not, sir, to wooe him.
Dono. 'Twere folly, if you should; you must not wed him.
⟨*Aur.*⟩ Shame take thy tongue! Being old and weak thy self,
Thou doat'st, and looking on thine own defects,
Speak'st what thou'dst wish in me. Do I command
The deeds of others, mine own act not free?
Be pleas'd to smile or frown, we respect neither:
My will and rule shall stand and fall together.
Most fair *Artesia,* see the King descends
To give thee welcome with these warlike *Saxons,*
And now on equal terms both sues and grants:
Instead of Truce, let a perpetual League
Seal our united bloods in holy marriage;
Send the East Angles King this happy news,
That thou with me hast made a League for ever,
And added to his state a friend and brother.
Speak, dearest Love, dare you confirm this Title?
Artes. I were no woman to deny a good

79 presence *T*

131 *Prefix add. T* Shame . . tongue *twice T* 146 a good *om. T*

So high and noble to my fame and Country.
Aurel. Live, then, a Queen in *Brittain.*
Glost. He meanes to marry her.
Dono. Death! he shall marry the devil first!
Marry a *Pagan,* an Idolater?
Cador. He has won her quickly.
Edwin. She was woo'd afore she came, sure,
Or came of purpose to conclude the Match.
Aurel. Who dares oppose our will? My Lord of *Gloster,*
Be you Embassador unto our Brother,
The Brother of our Queen *Artesia;*
Tell him for such our entertainment looks him,
Our marriage adding to the happiness
Of our intended joys; mans good or ill
In this like waves agree, come double still.

Enter Hermit.

Who's this? the Hermit? Welcome, my happiness!
Our Countries hope, most reverent holy man,
I wanted but thy blessing to make perfect
The infinite sum of my felicity.
Hermit. Alack, sweet Prince, that happiness is yonder,
Felicity and thou art far asunder;
This world can never give it.
Aurel. Thou art deceiv'd: see here what I have found,
Beauty, Alliance, Peace, and strength of Friends,
All in this all exceeding excellence:
The League's confirm'd.
Hermit. With whom, dear Lord?
Aurel. With the great Brother of this Beauteous woman,
The Royal *Saxon* King
Hermit. Oh, then I see,
And fear thou art too near thy misery.
What magick could so linck thee to this mischief?
By all the good that thou hast reapt by me,
Stand further from destruction.
Aurel. Speak as a man, and I shall hope to obey thee.
Hermit. Idolaters, get hence! fond King, let go:
Thou hug'st thy ruine and thy Countries woe.
Dono. Well spoke, old Father; too him, bait him soundly.
Now, by heavens blest Lady, I can scarce keep patience.
1. *Saxon Lord.* What devil is this?
2. *Saxon Lord.* That cursed Christian, by whose hellish charmes
Our army was o'rethrown.

147 noble a proposal to *T* 181 Idolatress *D*

Hermit. Why do you dally, sir? Oh, tempt not heaven;
Warm not a serpent in your naked bosom:
Discharge them from your Court.
Aurel. Thou speak'st like madness!
Command the frozen shepherd to the shade,
When he sits warm i'th' Sun; the fever sick
To add more heat unto his burning pain:
These may obey, 'tis less extremity
Then thou enjoynst to me. Cast but thine eye
Upon this beauty, do it, I'le forgive thee,
Though jealousie in others findes no pardon;
Then say thou dost not love; I shall then swear
Th'art immortal and no earthly man.
Oh, blame then my mortallity, not me.
Hermit. It is thy weakness brings thy misery,
Unhappy Prince.
Aurel. Be milder in thy doom.
Hermit. 'Tis you that must indure heavens doom, which faln
Remember's just.
Artes. Thou shalt not live to see it.—How fares my Lord?
If my poor presence breed dislike, great Prince,
I am no such neglected soul, will seek
To tie you to your word.
Aurel. My word, dear Love! may my Religion,
Crown, State, and Kingdom fail, when I fail thee.
Command Earl *Chester* to break up the camp
Without disturbance to our *Saxon* friends;
Send every hour swift posts to hasten on
The King her Brother, to conclude this League,
This endless happy Peace of Love and Marriage;
Till when provide for Revels, and give charge
That nought be wanting which ⟨may⟩ make our Triumphs
Sportful and free to all. If such fair blood
Ingender ill, man must not look for good.
[*Exit all but Hermit. Florish.*

Enter Modestia, reading in a book.

Modesta. How much the oft report of this blest *Hermit*
Hath won on my desires; I must behold him:
And sure this should be he. Oh, the world's folly,
Proud earth and dust, how low a price bears goodness!
All that should make man absolute shines in him.
Much reverent Sir, may I without offence
Give interruption to your holy thoughts?

198 love *D* : love me *Q* : love like me *T* 217 may make *D* : make *Q* : will make *T* 219 men *T*

Hermit. What would you, Lady?
Modest. That which till now ne're found a language in me:
I am in love.
Her. In Love? with what?
Modest. With vertue.
Her. There's no blame in that.
Modest. Nay, sir, with you, with your Religious Life,
Your Vertue, Goodness, if there be a name
To express affection greater, that,
That would I learn and utter: Reverent Sir,
If there be any thing to bar my suit,
Be charitable and expose it; your prayers
Are the same Orizons which I will number.
Holy Sir,
Keep not instruction back from willingness,
Possess me of that knowledge leads you on
To this humility; for well I know,
Were greatness good, you would not live so low.
Her. Are you a Virgin?
Modest. Yes, Sir.
Her. Your name?
Modest. *Modesta.*
Her. Your name and vertues meet, a Modest Virgin:
Live ever in the sanctimonious way
To Heaven and Happiness. There's goodness in you,
I must instruct you further. Come, look up,
Behold yon firmament: there sits a power,
Whose foot-stool is this earth. Oh, learn this lesson,
And practise it: he that will climb so high,
Must leave no joy beneath to move his eye. [*Exit.*
Modest. I apprehend you, sir: on Heaven I fix my love,
Earth gives us grief, our joys are all above;
For this was man in innocence naked born,
To show us wealth hinders our sweet return. [*Exit.*

ACTUS II.

⟨SCENE I.

A Forest.⟩

Enter Clown and his Sister great with childe.

Clown. Away, follow me no further, I am none of thy brother. What, with Childe? great with Childe, and knows not whose the Father on't! I am asham'd to call thee Sister.

Joan. Believe me, Brother, he was a Gentleman.

Clown. Nay, I believe that; he gives arms, and legs too, and has made you the Herald to blaze 'em: but, *Joan, Joan,* sister *Joan,* can you tell me his name that did it? how shall we call my Cousin, your bastard, when we have it?

Joan. Alas, I know not the Gentlemans name, Brother.
I met him in these woods the last great hunting;
He was so kinde and proffer'd me so much,
As I had not the heart to ask him more.

Clown. Not his name? why, this showes your Country breeding now; had you been brought up i'th' City, you'd have got a Father first, and the childe afterwards: hast thou no markes to know him by?

Joan. He had most rich Attire, a fair Hat and Feather, a gilt Sword, and most excellent Hangers.

Clown. Pox on his Hangers, would he had bin gelt for his labor.

Joan. Had you but heard him swear, you would have thought—

Clown. I, as you did; swearing and lying goes together still. Did his Oathes get you with Childe? we shall have a roaring Boy then, yfaith. Well, sister, I must leave you.

Joan. Dear Brother, stay, help me to finde him out,
I'le ask no further.

Clown. 'Sfoot, who should I finde? who should I ask for?

Joan. Alas, I know not, he uses in these woods,
And these are witness of his oathes and promise.

Clown. We are like to have a hot suit on't, when our best witness's but a Knight a'th' Post.

Joan. Do but enquire this Forrest, I'le go with you;
Some happy fate may guide us till we meet him.

Clown. Meet him? and what name shall we have for him, when we meet him? 'Sfoot, thou neither knowst him nor canst tell what to call him. Was ever man tyr'd with such a business, to have a sister got with childe, and know not who did it? Well, you shall see him, I'le do my best for you, Ile make Proclamation; if these Woods and Trees, as you say, will bear any witness, let them answer. Oh yes: If there be any man that wants a name will come in for conscience sake, and acknowledge himself to be a Whore-Master,

233 that *Q*: than that word *D* 254 leave *Q*: let *T* Exit *om. T* 258 Exeunt *T* Scene I. *etc. add. T* 3 know *T*

11 call] name *D* 45 weet *Q* 53 Oh yes *Q*: Oyes *D*

he shal have that laid to his charge in an hour, he shall not be rid on in an age; if he have Lands, he shall have an heir; if he have patience, he shall have a wife; if he have neither Lands nor patience, he shall have a whore. So ho, boy, so ho, so, so.

[*Within*] *Prince Vter.* So ho, boy, so ho, illo ho, illo ho.

Clown. Hark, hark, sister, there's one hollows to us; what a wicked world's this! a man cannot so soon name a whore, but a knave comes presently: and see where he is; stand close a while, sister.

Enter Prince Vter.

Prince. How like a voice that Eccho spake, but oh,
My thoughts are lost for ever in amazement.
Could I but meet a man to tell her beauties,
These trees would bend their tops to kiss the air
That from my lips should give her praises up.

Clown. He talks of a woman, sister.

Joan. This may be he, brother.

Clown. View him well; you see, he has a fair Sword, but his Hangers are faln.

Prince. Here did I see her first, here view her beauty:
Oh, had I known her name, I had been happy.

Clown. Sister, this is he, sure; he knows not thy name neither. A couple of wise fools yfaith, to get children, and know not one another.

Prince. You weeping leaves, upon whose tender cheeks
Doth stand a flood of tears at my complaint,
Who heard my vows and oathes—

Clown. Law, Law, he has been a great swearer too; tis he, sister.

Prince. For having overtook her;
As I have seen a forward blood-hound strip
The swifter of the cry, ready to seize
His wished hopes, upon the sudden view,
Struck with astonishment, at his arriv'd prey,
Instead of seizure stands at fearful bay;
Or like to *Marius* soldiers, who, o'retook,
The eye sight killing *Gorgon* at one look
Made everlasting stand: so fear'd my power,
Whose cloud aspir'd the Sun, dissolv'd a shower.
Pigmalion, then I tasted thy sad fate,
Whose Ivory picture and my fair were one:
Our dotage past imagination.
I saw and felt desire—

Clown. Pox a your fingering! did he feel, sister?

Prince. But enjoy'd not.
Oh fate, thou hadst thy days and nights to feed
On calm affection; one poor sight was all,
Converts my pleasure to perpetual thrall:
Imbracing thine, thou lostest breath and desire,
So I, relating mine, will here expire.
For here I vow to you mournful plants,
Who were the first made happy by her fame,
Never to part hence, till I know her name.

Clown. Give me thy hand, sister, *The Childe has found his Father.* This is he, sure; as I am a man, had I been a woman, these kinde words would have won me, I should have had a great belly too, that's certain. Well, I'le speak to him.—Most honest and fleshly minded Gentleman, give me your hand, sir.

Prince. Ha, what art thou, that thus rude and boldly darest
Take notice of a wretch so much ally'd
To misery as I am?

Clown. Nay, Sir, for our aliance, I shall be found to be a poor brother in Law of your worships: the Gentlewoman you spake on is my sister: you see what a clew she spreads; her name is *Joan Go-too't.* I am her elder, but she has been at it before me; 'tis a womans fault.—Pox a this bashfulness! come forward, *Jug,* prethee, speak to him.

Prince. Have you e're seen me, Lady?

Clown. Seen ye? ha, ha! It seems she has felt you too: here's a yong *Go-too't* a coming, sir; she is my sister; we all love to *Go-too't,* as well as your worship. She's a Maid yet, but you may make her a wife, when you please, sir.

Prince. I am amaz'd with wonder: Tell me, woman,
What sin have you committed worthy this?

Joan. Do you not know me, sir?

Prince. Know thee! as I do thunder, hell, and mischief;
Witch, scullion, hag!

Clown. I see he will marry her; he speaks so like a husband.

Prince. Death! I will cut their tongues out for this blasphemy.
Strumpet, villain, where have you ever seen me?

Clown. Speak for your self, with a pox to ye.

Prince. Slaves, Ile make you curse your selves for this temptation.

62 boy *T*: by *Q*   74 talk's *Q*   77 Hanger's *Q*   86 Who?] And *Q*: You *D*   91 swiftest *WP*   93 astonishment *Q*   95 whom *D*

103 not *T, etc.*: now *Q*   105 On *D*: Or *Q*   109 you *Q*: you, ye *T*   134 a] scarce a *conj. T*   137 you *Q*: I *conj. T*   140 scullion *D*: stallion *Q*

Joan. Oh, sir, if ever you did speak to me,
It was in smoother phrase, in fairer language.

Prince. Lightning consume me, if I ever saw thee.
My rage o'reflowes my blood, all patience flies me. [*Beats her.*]

Clown. Hold, I beseech you, sir, I have nothing to say to you.

Joan. Help, help! murder, murder!

Enter Toclio and Oswold.

Toclio. Make haste, Sir, this way the sound came, it was a ⟨th'⟩ wood.

Oswold. See where she is, and the Prince, the price of all our wishes.

Clown. The Prince, say ye? ha's made a poor Subject of me, I am sure.

Toclio. Sweet Prince, noble *Vter,* speak, how fare you, sir?

Oswold. Dear sir, recal your self; your fearful absence
Hath won too much already on the grief
Of our sad King, from whom our laboring search
Hath had this fair success in meeting you.

Toclio. His silence and his looks argue distraction.

Clown. Nay, he's mad, sure, he will not acknowledge my sister, nor the childe neither.

Oswold. Let us entreat your Grace along with us;
Your sight will bring new life to the King your Brother.

Toclio. Will you go, sir?

Prince. Yes, any whether; guide me, all's hell I see;
Man may change air, but not his misery.
[*Exit Prince, Toclio.*

Joan. Lend me one word with you, sir.

Clown. Well said, sister, he has a Feather, and fair Hangers too, this may be he.

Oswold. What would you, fair one?

Joan. Sure, I have seen you in these woods e're this.

Oswold. Trust me, never; I never saw this place,
Till at this time my friend conducted me.

Joan. The more's my sorrow then.

Oswold. Would I could comfort you.
I am a Bachelor, but it seems you have
A husband, you have been fouly o'reshot else.

Clown. A womans fault, we are all subject to go to't, sir.

Enter Toclio.

Toclio. *Oswold,* away; the Prince will not stir a foot without you.

Oswold. I am coming. Farewel, woman.

Toclio. Prithee, make haste. ⟨*Exit Oswold.*⟩

Joan. Good sir, but one word with you, e're you leave us.

Toclio. With me, fair soul?

Clown. Shee'l have a fling at him too; the Childe must have a Father.

Joan. Have you ne'er seen me, sir?

Toclio. Seen thee? 'Sfoot, I have seen many fair faces in my time: prithee, look up, and do not weep so. Sure, pretty wanton, I have seen this face before.

Joan. It is enough, though you ne're see me more. [*sinks down.*

Toclio. 'Sfoot, she's faln: this place is inchanted, sure; look to the woman, fellow. [*Exit.*

Clown. Oh, she's dead, she's dead! As you are a man, stay and help, sir.—*Joan, Joan,* sister *Joan,* why, *Joan Go too't,* I say; will you cast away your self, and your childe, and me too? what do you mean, sister?

Joan. Oh, give me pardon, sir; 'twas too much joy
Opprest my loving thoughts; I know you were
Too noble to deny me—ha! Where is he?

Clown. Who, the Gentleman? he's gone, sister.

Joan. Oh! I am undone, then! Run, tell him I did
But faint for joy; dear brother, haste; why dost thou stay?
Oh, never cease, till he give answer to thee.

Clown. He: which he? what do you call him, tro?

Joan. Unnatural brother,
Shew me the path he took; why dost thou dally?
Speak, oh, which way went he?

Clown. This way, that way, through the bushes there.

Joan. Were it through fire,
The Journey's easie, winged with sweet desire.
[*Exit.*

Clown. Hey day, there's some hope of this yet. Ile follow her for kindreds sake; if she miss of her purpose now, she'l challenge all she findes, I see; for if ever we meet with a two-leg'd creature in the whole Kingdom, the Childe shall have a Father, that's certain. [*Exit.*

⟨Scene II.

An Ante-chamber at the British Court.⟩

Loud Musick. Enter two with the Sword and Mace, Cador, Edwin, two Bishops, Aurelius, Ostorius, leading Artesia

156 a *Q* : i'th' *D* 180 *Prefix* Clown *Q*

192 *S. D. add. WP* 203 you *T, etc.* : your *Q 1* 213 thought *D* Scene II. *etc. add. T*

Crown'd, Constancia, Modestia, Octa, Proximus a Magician, Donobert, Gloster, Oswold, Toclio; all pass over the Stage. Manet Donobert, Gloster, Edwin, Cador.

Dono. Come, *Gloster,* I do not like this hasty Marriage.
Gloster. She was quickly wooed and won: not six days since
Arrived an enemy to sue for Peace,
And now crown'd Queen of *Brittain;* this is strange.
Dono. Her brother too made as quick speed in coming,
Leaving his *Saxons* and his starved Troops,
To take the advantage, whilst 'twas offer'd.
'Fore heaven, I fear the King's too credulous;
Our Army is discharg'd too.
Gloster. Yes, and our General commanded home.
Son *Edwin,* have you seen him since?
Edwin. He's come to Court, but will not view the presence,
Nor speak unto the King; he's so discontent
At this so strange aliance with the *Saxon,*
As nothing can perswade his patience.
Cador. You know his humor will indure no check,
No, if the King oppose it:
All crosses feeds both his spleen and his impatience;
Those affections are in him like powder,
Apt to inflame with every little spark,
And blow up all his reason.
Gloster. *Edol* of *Chester* is a noble Soldier.
Dono. So is he, by the Rood, ever most faithful
To the King and Kingdom, how e're his passions guide him.

Enter Edoll *with Captains.*

Cador. See where he comes, my Lord.
Omnes. Welcome to Court, brave Earl.
Edol. Do not deceive me by your flatteries:
Is not the Saxon here? the League confirm'd?
The Marriage ratifi'd? the Court divided
With Pagan Infidels, the least part Christians,
At least in their Commands? Oh, the gods!
It is a thought that takes away my sleep,
And dulls my senses so I scarcely know you:
Prepare my horses, 'Ile away to *Chester.*
Capt. What shall we do with our Companies, my Lord?
Edol. Keep them at home to increase Cuckolds,
And get some Cases for your Captainships;
Smooth up your brows, the wars has spoil'd your faces,
And few will now regard you.
Dono. Preserve your patience, Sir.
Edol. Preserve your Honors, Lords, your Countries Safety,
Your Lives and Lands from strangers. What black devil
Could so bewitch the King, so to discharge
A Royal Army in the height of conquest,
Nay, even already made victorious,
To give such credit to an enemy,
A starved foe, a stragling fugitive,
Beaten beneath our feet, so low dejected,
So servile, and so base, as hope of life
Had won them all to leave the Land for ever?
Dono. It was the Kings will.
Edol. It was your want of wisdom,
That should have laid before his tender youth
The dangers of a State, where forain Powers
Bandy for Soveraignty with Lawful Kings;
Who being setled once, to assure themselves,
Will never fail to seek the blood and life
Of all competitors.
Dono. Your words sound well, my Lord, and point at safety,
Both for the Realm and us; but why did you,
Within whose power it lay, as General,
With full Commission to dispose the war,
Lend ear to parly with the weakned foe?
Edol. Oh the good Gods!
Cador. And on that parly came this Embassie.
Edol. You will hear me?
Edwin. Your letters did declare it to the King,
Both of the Peace, and all Conditions
Brought by this *Saxon* Lady, whose fond love
Has thus bewitched him.
Edol. I will curse you all as black as hell,
Unless you hear me; your gross mistake would make
Wisdom her self run madding through the streets,
And quarrel with her shadow. Death!
Why kill'd ye not that woman?
Dono. Glost. Oh, my Lord!
Edol. The great devil take me quick, had I been by,
And all the women of the world were barren,
She should have died, e're he had married her
On these conditions.
Cador. It is not reason that directs you thus.
Edol. Then have I none, for all I have directs me.

17 No] Not even *conj. WP* 18 both *Q* : but *D*
36 Cuckolds with *conj. WP*
48 low *T, etc.* : love *Q* 75 ye *Q* : you *D*

Never was man so palpably abus'd,
So basely marted, bought and sold to scorn.
My Honor, Fame, and hopeful Victories,
The loss of Time, Expences, Blood, and Fortunes,
All vanisht into nothing.

Edwin. This rage is vain, my Lord:
What the King does nor they nor you can help.

Edol. My Sword must fail me then.

Cador. 'Gainst whom will you expose it?

Edol. What's that to you? 'gainst all the devils in hell,
To guard my country.

Edwin. These are airy words.

Edol. Sir, you tread too hard upon my patience.

Edwin. I speak the duty of a Subjects faith,
And say agen, had you been here in presence,
What the King did, you had not dar'd to cross it.

Edol. I will trample on his Life and Soul that says it.

Cador. My Lord!

Edwin. Come, come.

Edol. Now, before heaven—

Cador. Dear sir!

Edol. Not dare? thou liest beneath thy lungs.

Gloster. No more, son Edwin.

Edwin. I have done, sir; I take my leave.

Edol. But thou shalt not, you shall take no leave of me, Sir.

Dono. For wisdoms sake, my Lord —

Edol. Sir, I'le leave him, and you, and all of you,
The Court and King, and let my Sword and friends
Shuffle for *Edols* safety: stay you here,
And hug the *Saxons*, till they cut your throats,
Or bring the Land to servile slavery.
Such yokes of baseness *Chester* must not suffer.
Go, and repent betimes these foul misdeeds,
For in this League all our whole Kingdom bleeds,
Which Ile prevent, or perish. [*Exit Edol, Capt.*

Glost. See how his rage transports him!

Cador. These passions set apart, a braver soldier
Breathes not i'th' world this day.

Dono. I wish his own worth do not court his ruine.
The King must Rule, and we must learn to obay,
True vertue still directs the noble way.

90 expose *Q* : oppose *D* 95 you *T*, *etc.* : your *Q* 102 shall not *Q* 112 *S. D. after* 113 *Q*

⟨SCENE III.

Hall of state in the Palace.⟩

Loud Musick. Enter Aurelius, Artesia, Ostorius, Octa, Proximus, Toclio, Oswold, Hermit.

Aurel. Why is the Court so dull? me thinks, each room
And angle of our Palace should appear
Stuck full of objects fit for mirth and triumphs,
To show our high content. *Oswold*, fill wine!
Must we begin the Revels? Be it so, then!
Reach me the cup: Ile now begin a Health
To our lov'd Queen, the bright *Artesia*,
The Royal *Saxon* King, our warlike brother.
Go and command all the whole Court to pledge it.
Fill to the Hermit there! Most reverent *Anselme*,
Wee'l do thee Honor first, to pledge my Queen.

Her. I drink no healths, great King, and if I did,
I would be loath to part with health to those
That have no power to give it back agen.

Aurel. Mistake not, it is the argument of Love
And Duty to our Queen and us.

Artes. But he ows none, it seems.

Her. I do to vertue, Madam: temperate minds
Covets that health to drink, which nature gives
In every spring to man; he that doth hold
His body but a Tenement at will,
Bestows no cost, but to repair what's ill:
Yet if your healths or heat of Wine, fair Princes,
Could this old frame or these cras'd limbes restore,
Or keep out death or sickness, then fill more,
I'le make fresh way for appetite; if no,
On such a prodigal who would wealth bestow?

Ostorius. He speaks not like a guest to grace a wedding.

Enter Toclio.

Artes. No, sir, but like an envious imposter.

Octa. A Christian slave, a Cinick.

Ostor. What vertue could decline your Kingly spirit
To such respect of him whose magick spells
Met with your vanquisht Troops, and turn'd your Arms
To that necessity of fight, which, thro dispair

Scene III. *etc. add. T* *Scene II continued D* 8 and the *T* 34 which] when *D* through *WP*: the *Q* : but for the *T*

Of any hope to stand but by his charms,
Had been defeated in a bloody conquest?
Octa. 'Twas magick, hellbred magick did it, sir,
And that's a course, my Lord, which we esteem
In all our *Saxon* Wars unto the last
And lowest ebbe of servile treachery.
Aurel. Sure, you are deceiv'd, it was the hand of heaven
That in his vertue gave us victory.
Is there a power in man that can strike fear
Thorough a general camp, or create spirits
In recreant bosoms above present sense?
Ostor. To blind the sense there may, with apparition
Of well arm'd troops within themselves are air,
Form'd into humane shapes, and such that day
Were by that Sorcerer rais'd to cross our fortunes.
Aurel. There is a law tells us that words want force
To make deeds void; examples must be shown
By instances alike, e're I believe it.
Ostor. 'Tis easily perform'd, believe me, sir:
Propose your own desires, and give but way
To what our Magick here shall straight perform,
And then let his or our deserts be censur'd.
Aurel. We could not wish a greater happiness
Then what this satisfaction brings with it.
Let him proceed, fair brother.
Ostor. He shall, sir.
Come, learned *Proximus,* this task be thine:
Let thy great charms confound the opinion
This Christian by his spells hath falsly won.
Prox. Great King, propound your wishes, then:
What persons, of what State, what numbers, or how arm'd,
Please your own thoughts; they shall appear before you.
Aurel. Strange art! What thinkst thou, reverent *Hermit?*
Her. Let him go on, sir.
Aurel. Wilt thou behold his cunning?
Her. Right gladly, sir; it will be my joy to tell,
That I was here to laugh at him and hell.
Aurel. I like thy confidence.
Artes. His sawcy impudence! Proceed to th'trial.
Prox. Speak your desires my Lord, and be it place't
In any angle underneath the Moon,
The center of the Earth, the Sea, the Air,
The region of the fire, nay, hell it self,
And I'le present it.
Aurel. Wee'l have no sight so fearful, onely this:
If all thy art can reach it, show me here
The two great Champions of the *Trojan* War,
Achilles and brave *Hector,* our great Ancestor,
Both in their warlike habits, Armor, Shields,
And Weapons then in use for fight.
Prox. 'Tis done, my Lord, command a halt and silence,
As each man will respect his life or danger.
Armel, Plesgeth!

Enter Spirits.

Spirits. Quid vis?
Prox. Attend me.
Aurel. The Apparition comes; on our displeasure,
Let all keep place and silence.
[*Within Drums beat Marches.*

Enter Proximus, *bringing in* Hector, *attir'd and arm'd after the Trojan manner, with Target, Sword, and Battel-ax, a Trumpet before him, and a Spirit in flame colours with a Torch; at the other door* Achilles *with his Spear and Falchon, a Trumpet, and a Spirit in black before him; Trumpets sound alarm, and they manage their weapons to begin the Fight: and after some Charges, the Hermit steps between them, at which seeming amaz'd the spirits tremble. Thunder within.*

Prox. What means this stay, bright *Armel, Plesgeth?*
Why fear you and fall back?
Renew the Alarms, and enforce the Combat,
Or hell or darkness circles you for ever.
Arm. We dare not.
Prox. Ha!
Plesgeth. Our charms are all dissolv'd: *Armel,* away!
'Tis worse then hell to us, whilest here we stay. [*Exit all.*
Her. What! at a Non-plus, sir? command them back, for shame.
Prox. What power o're-aws my Spells? Return, you Hell-hounds!
Armel, Plesgeth, double damnation seize you!
By all the Infernal powers, the prince of devils
Is in this Hermits habit: what else could force
My Spirits quake or tremble thus?
Her. Weak argument to hide your want of skill:

47 within *Q* (=*which within*): which in *T*

S. D. Enter Spirit *Q*   *S. D.* tremble] and tremble *Q*

Does the devil fear the devil, or war with hell?
They have not been acquainted long, it seems.
Know, mis-believing Pagan, even that Power,
That overthrew your Forces, still lets you see,
He onely can controul both hell and thee.
Prox. Disgrace and mischief! Ile enforce new charms,
New spells, and spirits rais'd from the low Abyss
Of hells unbottom'd depths.
Aurel. We have enough, sir;
Give o're your charms, wee'l finde some other time
To praise your Art. I dare not but acknowledge
That heavenly Power my heart stands witness to:
Be not dismaid, my Lords, at this disaster,
Nor thou, my fairest Queen: we'l change the Scene
To some more pleasing sports. Lead to your Chamber.
How 'ere in this thy pleasures finde a cross,
Our joy's too fixed here to suffer loss.
Toclio. Which I shall adde to, sir, with news I bring:
The Prince, your Brother, lives.
Aurel. Ha!
Toclio. And comes to grace this high and heaven-knit Marriage.
Aurel. Why dost thou flatter me, to make me think
Such happiness attends me?

Enter Prince Uter and Oswold.

Toclio. His presence speaks my truth, sir.
Dono. Force me, 'tis he: look, *Gloster.*
Glost. A blessing beyond hope, sir.
Aurel. Ha! 'tis he: welcome, my second Comfort.
Artesia, Dearest Love, it is my Brother,
My Princely Brother, all my Kingdoms hope:
Oh, give him welcome, as thou lov'st my health.
Artes. You have so free a welcome, sir, from me,
As this your presence has such power, I swear,
O're me, a stranger, that I must forget
My Countrey, Name, and Friends, and count this place
My Joy and Birth-right.
Prince. 'Tis she! 'tis she, I swear! oh, ye good gods, 'tis she!
That face within those woods where first I saw her,
Captived my senses, and thus many moneths
Bar'd me from all society of men.
How came she to this place,
Brother *Aurelius?* Speak that Angels name,
Her heaven-blest name, oh, speak it quickly, Sir.
Aurel. It is *Artesia,* the Royal Saxon Princess.
Prince. A woman, and no Deity, no feigned shape,
To mock the reason of admiring sense,
On whom a hope as low as mine may live,
Love, and enjoy, dear Brother, may it not?
Aurel. She is all the Good or Vertue thou canst name,
My Wife, my Queen.
Prince. Ha! your wife!
Artes. Which you shall finde, sir, if that time and fortune
May make my love but worthy of your tryal.
Prince. Oh!
Aurel. What troubles you, dear Brother?
Why with so strange and fixt an eye dost thou
Behold my Joys?
Artes. You are not well, sir.
Prince. Yes, yes. — Oh, you immortal powers,
Why has poor man so many entrances
For sorrow to creep in at, when our sense
Is much too weak to hold his happiness?
Oh, say, I was born deaf: and let your silence
Confirm in me the knowing my defect;
At least be charitable to conceal my sin,
For hearing is no less in me, dear Brother.
Aurel. No more!
I see thou art a Rival in the Joys
Of my high Bliss. Come, my *Artesia;*
The Day's most prais'd when 'tis ecclipst by Night,
Great Good must have as great Ill opposite.
Prince. Stay, hear but a word; yet now I think on't,
This is your Wedding-night, and were it mine,
I should be angry with least loss of time.
Artes. Envy speaks no such words, has no such looks.
Prince. Sweet rest unto you both.
Aurel. Lights to our Nuptial Chamber.
Artes. Could you speak so,
I would not fear how much my grief did grow.
Aurel. Lights to our Chamber; on, on, set on! [*Exeunt. Manet Prince.*
Prince. 'Could you speak so,
I would not fear how much my griefs did grow.'
Those were her very words; sure, I am waking:
She wrung me by the hand, and spake them to me

119 your *Q*: our *WP* 120 Force *Q*: 'Fore *T, etc.*

184 grief *D, etc.*

With a most passionate affection.
Perhaps she loves, and now repents her choice,
In marriage with my brother. Oh, fond man,
How darest thou trust thy Traitors thoughts, thus to
Betray thy self? 'twas but a waking dream
Wherein thou madest thy wishes speak, not her,
In which thy foolish hopes strives to prolong
A wretched being. So sickly children play
With health lov'd toys, which for a time delay,
But do not cure the fit. Be, then, a man,
Meet that destruction which thou canst not flie.
From not to live, make it thy best to die,
And call her now, whom thou didst hope to wed,
Thy brothers wife: thou art too nere a kin,
And such an act above all name's a sin
Not to be blotted out; heaven pardon me!
She's banisht from my bosom now for ever.
To lowest ebbes men justly hope a flood;
When vice grows barren, all desires are good.

Enter Waiting Gentlewoman with a Jewel.

Gent. The noble Prince, I take it, sir?
Prince. You speak me what I should be, Lady.
Gent. Know, by that name, sir, Queen *Artesia* greets you.
Prince. Alas, good vertue, how is she mistaken!
Gent. Commending her affection in this Jewel, sir.
Prince. She binds my service to her: ha! a Jewel; 'tis
A fair one, trust me, and methinks, it much
Resembles something I have seen with her.
Gen. It is an artificial crab, Sir.
Prince. A creature that goes backward.
Gent. True, from the way it looks.
Prince. There is no moral in it aludes to her self?
Gent. 'Tis your construction gives you that, sir;
She's a woman.
Prince. And, like this, may use her legs and eyes
Two several ways.
Gent. Just like the Sea-crab,
Which on the Mussel prayes, whilst he bills at a stone.
Prince. Pretty in troth. Prithee, tell me, art thou honest?
Gent. I hope I seem no other, sir.
Prince. And those that seem so are sometimes bad enough.
Gent. If they will accuse themselves for want of witness,
Let them, I am not so foolish.
Prince. I see th'art wise.
Come, speak me truly: what is the greatest sin?
Gent. That which man never acted; what has been done
Is as the least, common to all as one.
Prince. Dost think thy Lady is of thy opinion?
Gent. She's a bad Scholar else; I have brought her up,
And she dares owe me still.
Prince. I, 'tis a fault in greatness, they dare owe
Many, e're they pay one. But darest thou
Expose thy scholar to my examining?
Gent. Yes, in good troth, sir, and pray put her to't too;
'Tis a hard lesson, if she answer it not.
Prince. Thou know'st the hardest?
Gent. As far as a woman may, sir.
Prince. I commend thy plainness.
When wilt thou bring me to thy Lady?
Gent. Next opportunity I attend you, sir.
Prince. Thanks, take this, and commend me to her.
Gent. Think of your Sea-crab, sir, I pray. [*Exit.*
Prince. Oh, by any means, Lady.—
What should all this tend to?
If it be Love or Lust that thus incites her,
The sin is horrid and incestuous;
If to betray my life, what hopes she by it?
Yes, it may be a practice 'twixt themselves,
To expel the *Brittains* and ensure the State
Through our destructions; all this may be
Valid, with a deeper reach in villany
Then all my thoughts can guess at; — however,
I will confer with her, and if I finde
Lust hath given Life to Envy in her minde,
I may prevent the danger: so men wise
By the same step by which they fell, may rise.
Vices are Vertues, if so thought and seen,
And Trees with foulest roots branch soonest green. [*Exit.*

ACT 3.

SCENE I.

⟨Before the Palace of King Aurelius.⟩

Enter Clown and his Sister.

Clown. Come, sister, thou that art all fool, all mad-woman.

190 traitorous *T*, *etc.* 198 best *Q* : hest *D* 200 ne're *Q*

254 Valid *Q* : Veil'd *D* *S. D.* Before *etc.* *add.* *T* 1 that *om.* *T*

Joan. Prithee, have patience, we are now at Court.

Clown. At Court! ha, ha, that proves thy madness: was there ever any woman in thy taking travel'd to Court for a husband? 'Slid, 'tis enough for them to get children, and the City to keep 'em, and the Countrey to finde Nurses: every thing must be done in his due place, sister.

Joan. Be but content a while; for, sure, I know
This Journey will be happy. Oh, dear brother,
This night my sweet Friend came to comfort me;
I saw him and embrac't him in mine arms.

Clown. Why did you not hold him, and call me to help you?

Joan. Alas, I thought I had been with him still,
But when I wak't —

Clown. Ah! pox of all Loger-heads, then you were but in a Dream all this while, and we may still go look him. Well, since we are come to Court, cast your Cats eyes about you, and either finde him out you dreamt on, or some other, for Ile trouble my self no further.

Ent⟨er⟩ Dono⟨bert⟩, Cador, Edw⟨in⟩ & Toclio.

See, see, here comes more Courtiers; look about you; come, pray, view 'em all well; the old man has none of the marks about him, the other have both Swords and Feathers: what thinkest thou of that tall yong Gentleman?

Joan. He much resembles him; but, sure, my friend,
Brother, was not so high of stature.

Clown. Oh, beast, wast thou got a childe with a short thing too?

Dono. Come, come, Ile hear no more on't: Go, Lord *Edwin,*
Tell her, this day her sister shall be married
To *Cador,* Earl of *Cornwal;* so shall she
To thee, brave *Edwin,* if she'l have my blessing.

Edwin. She is addicted to a single Life,
She will not hear of Marriage.

Dono. Tush, fear it not: go you from me to her,
Use your best skill, my Lord, and if you fail,
I have a trick shall do it: haste, haste about it.

Edwin. Sir, I am gone;
My hope is in your help more then my own.

Dono. And worthy *Toclio,* to your care I must
Commend this business
For Lights and Musick, and what else is needful.

Toclio. I shall, my Lord.

Clown. We would intreat a word, sir. Come forward, sister. [*Ex. Dono., Toc., Cador.*

Edwin. What lackst thou, fellow?

Clown. I lack a father for a childe, sir.

Edwin. How! a God-father?

Clown. No, sir, we mean the own father: it may be you, sir, for any thing we know; I think the childe is like you.

Edwin. Like me! prithee, where is it?

Clown. Nay, 'tis not born yet, sir, 'tis forth coming, you see; the childe must have a father: what do you think of my sister?

Edwin. Why, I think if she ne're had husband, she's a whore, and thou a fool. Farewell. [*Exit.*

Clown. I thank you, sir. Well, pull up thy heart, sister; if there be any Law i'th' Court, this fellow shall father it, 'cause he uses me so scurvily. There's a great Wedding towards, they say; we'l amongst them for a husband for thee.

Enter Sir Nicodemus *with a Letter.*

If we miss there, Ile have another bout with him that abus'd me. See! look, there comes another Hat and Feather, this should be a close Letcher, he's reading of a Love-letter.

Sir Nic. Earl *Cador's* Marriage, and a Masque to grace it.
So, so.
This night shall make me famous for Presentments.—
How now, what are you?

Clown. A couple of *Great Brittains* you may see by our bellies, sir.

Sir Nic. And what of this, sir?

Clown. Why, thus the matter stands, sir: There's one of your Courtiers Hunting Nags has made a Gap through another mans Inclosure. Now, sir, here's the question, who should be at charge of a Fur-bush to stop it?

Sir Nic. Ha, ha, this is out of my element: the Law must end it.

Clown. Your Worship says well; for, surely, I think some Lawyer had a hand in the business, we have such a troublesom Issue.

Sir Nic. But what's thy business with me now?

Clown. Nay, sir, the business is done already, you may see by my sisters belly.

Sir Nic. Oh, now I finde thee: this Gentlewoman, it seems, has been humbled.

Clown. As low as the ground would give her leave, sir, and your Worship knows this:

20 A pox *T*, *etc.* 22 look for him *T* 29 both *Q*: but *D* 33 got a *Q*: got with *T*

though there be many fathers without children, yet to have a childe without a father were most unnatural.

Sir Nic. That s true, ifaith, I never heard of a childe yet that e're begot his father.

Clown. Why, true, you say wisely, sir.

Sir Nic. And therefore I conclude, that he that got the childe is without all question the father of it.

Clown. I, now you come to the matter, sir; and our suit is to your Worship for the discovery of this father.

Sir Nic. Why, lives he in the Court here?

Joan. Yes, sir, and I desire but Marriage.

Sir Nic. And does the knave refuse it? Come, come, be merry, wench; he shall marry thee, and keep the childe too, if my Knighthood can do any thing. I am bound by mine Orders to help distressed Ladies, and can there be a greater injury to a woman with childe, then to lack a father for't? I am asham'd of your simpleness: Come, come, give me a Courtiers Fee for my pains, and Ile be thy Advocate my self, and justice shall be found; nay, Ile sue the Law for it; but give me my Fee first.

Clown. If all the money I have i'th world will do it, you shall have it, sir.

Sir Nic. An Angel does it.

Clown. Nay, there's two, for your better eye sight, sir.

Sir Nic. Why, well said! Give me thy hand, wench, Ile teach thee a trick for all this, shall get a father for thy childe presently, and this it is, mark now: You meet a man, as you meet me now, thou claimest Marriage of me, and layest the childe to my charge; I deny it: push, that's nothing, hold thy Claim fast, thy words carries it, and no Law can withstand it.

Clown. Ist possible?

Sir Nic. Past all opposition; her own word carries it: let her challenge any man, the childe shall call him Father; there's a trick for your money now.

Clown. Troth, Sir, we thank you, we'l make use of your trick, and go no further to seek the childe a Father, for we challenge you, Sir: sister, lay it to him, he shall marry thee, I shall have a worshipful old man to my brother.

Sir Nic. Ha, ha, I like thy pleasantness.

Joan. Nay, indeed, Sir, I do challenge you.

Clown. You think we jest, sir?

Sir Nic. I, by my troth, do I. I like thy wit, yfaith: thou shalt live at Court with me; didst never here of *Nicodemus Nothing?* I am the man.

Clown. Nothing? 'slid, we are out agen: thou wast never got with childe with nothing, sure.

Joan. I know not what to say.

Sir Nic. Never grieve, wench, show me the man, and process shall fly out.

Clown. 'Tis enough for us to finde the children, we look that you should finde the Father, and therefore either do us justice, or we'l stand to our first challenge.

Sir Nic. Would you have justice without an Adversary? unless you can show me the man, I can do you no good in it.

Clown. Why, then I hope you'l do us no harm, sir; you'l restore my money.

Sir Nic. What, my Fee? marry, Law forbid it!
Finde out the party, and you shall have justice,
Your fault clos'd up, and all shall be amended,
The Childe, his Father, and the Law ⟨def-⟩ended. [*Exit.*

Clown. Well, he has deserv'd his Fee, indeed, for he has brought our suit to a quick end, I promise you, and yet the Childe has never a Father; nor we have no more mony to seek after him. A shame of all lecherous placcats! now you look like a Cat had newly kitten'd; what will you do now, tro? Follow me no further, lest I beat your brains out.

Joan. Impose upon me any punishment,
Rather then leave me now.

Clown. Well, I think I am bewitcht with thee; I cannot finde in my heart to forsake her. There was never sister would have abus'd a poor brother as thou hast done; I am even pin'd away with fretting, there's nothing but flesh and bones about me. Well, and I had my money agen, it were some comfort. Hark, sister, [*Thunder*] does it not thunder?

Joan. Oh yes, most fearfully: What shall we do, brother?

Clown. Marry, e'ene get some shelter, e're the storm catch us: away, let's away, I prithee.

Enter the Devil in mans habit, richly attir'd, his feet and his head horrid.

Joan. Ha, 'tis he! Stay, brother, dear brother, stay.

Clown. What's the matter now?

Joan. My love, my friend is come; yonder he goes.

121 your *om. D*   130 eye *om T.*   136 push] pish *T, etc.*   137 word *D*   146 the childe *om. T*

168 do you *Q*: do *T*   172–3 Finde . . clos'd up *om. D*   174 child find his *D*   Law] Law-suit *WP*   defended *pr. ed.*: ended *Q, etc.*   178 we have no *Q*: have we *T*: we have on *D*   185 bewitch *Q*

Clown. Where, where? show me where;
I'le stop him, if the devil be not in him.
Joan. Look there, look yonder!
Oh, dear friend, pity my distress,
For heaven and goodness, do but speak to me.
Devil. She calls me, and yet drives me headlong from her.
Poor mortal, thou and I are much uneven,
Thou must not speak of goodness nor of heaven,
If I confer with thee; but be of comfort:
Whilst men do breath, and *Brittains* name be known,
The fatal fruit thou bear'st within thy womb
Shall here be famous till the day of doom.
Clown. 'Slid, who's that talks so? I can see no body.
Joan. Then art thou blind or mad. See where he goes,
And beckons me to come; oh, lead me forth,
I'le follow thee in spight of fear or death. [*Exit.*
Clown. Oh brave! she'l run to the devil for a husband; she's stark mad, sure, and talks to a shaddow, for I could see no substance: well, I'le after her; the childe was got by chance, and the father must be found at all adventure. [*Exit.*

⟨Scene II.

The Porch of a Church.⟩

Enter Hermit, Modesta, and Edwin.

Modesta. Oh, reverent sir, by you my heart hath reacht
At the large hopes of holy Piety,
And for this I craved your company,
Here in your sight religiously to vow
My chaste thoughts up to heaven, and make you now
The witness of my faith.
Her. Angels assist thy hopes.
Edwin. What meanes my Love? thou art my promis'd wife.
Modest. To part with willingly what friends and life
Can make no good assurance of.
Edwin. Oh, finde remorse, fair soul, to love and merit,
And yet recant thy vow.
Modest. Never:
This world and I are parted now for ever.
Her. To finde the way to bliss, oh, happy woman,
Th'ast learn'd the hardest Lesson well, I see.
Now show thy fortitude and constancy:
Let these thy friends thy sad departure weep,
Thou shalt but loose the wealth thou could'st not keep.
My contemplation calls me, I must leave ye.
Edwin. O, reverent Sir, perswade not her to leave me.
Her. My Lord, I do not, nor to cease to love ye;
I onely pray her faith may fixed stand;
Marriage was blest, I know, with heavens own hand. [*Exit.*
Edwin. You hear him, Lady, 'tis not a virgins state,
But sanctity of life, must make you happy.
Modest. Good sir, you say you love me; gentle *Edwin,*
Even by that love I do beseech you, leave me.
Edwin. Think of your fathers tears, your weeping friends,
Whom cruel grief makes pale and bloodless for you.
Modest. Would I were dead to all.
Edwin. Why do you weep?
Modest. Oh, who would live to see
How men with care and cost seek misery?
Edwin. Why do you seek it then? What joy, what pleasure
Can give you comfort in a single life?
Modest. The contemplation of a happy death,
Which is to me so pleasing that I think
No torture could divert me: What's this world,
Wherein you'd have me walk, but a sad passage
To a dread Judgement-Seat, from whence even now
We are but bail'd, upon our good abearing,
Till that great Sessions come, when Death, the Cryer,
Will surely summon us and all to appear,
To plead us guilty or our bail to clear?
What musick's this? [*Soft Musick.*

Enter two Bishops, Donobert, Gloster, Cador, Constancia, Oswold, Toclio.

Edwin. Oh, now resolve, and think upon my love!
This sounds the Marriage of your beauteous sister,
Vertuous *Constancia,* with the noble *Cador.*
Look, and behold this pleasure.
Modest. Cover me with night,
It is a vanity not worth the sight.
Dono. See, see, she's yonder.
Pass on, son *Cador,* Daughter *Constancia,*
I beseech you all, unless she first move speech,
Salute her not.—*Edwin,* what good success?

209 fruit] print *D* Scene II. *etc. add. T* 3 I] have I *D*

S. D. Bishops, Edwin, Donobert *Q*

Edwin. Nothing as yet, unless this object take her.
Dono. See, see, her eye is fixt upon her sister;
Seem careless all, and take no notice of her: —
On afore there; come, my *Constancia.*
Modest. Not speak to me, nor dain to cast an eye,
To look on my despised poverty?
I must be more charitable;—pray, stay, Lady,
Are not you she whom I did once call sister?
Constan. I did acknowledge such a name to one,
Whilst she was worthy of it, in whose folly,
Since you neglect your fame and friends together,
In you I drown'd a sisters name for ever.
Modest. Your looks did speak no less.
Glost. It now begins to work, this sight has moved her.
Dono. I knew this trick would take, or nothing.
Modest. Though you disdain in me a sisters name,
Yet charity, me thinks, should be so strong
To instruct e're you reject. I am a wretch,
Even follies instance, who perhaps have er'd,
Not having known the goodness bears so high
And fair a show in you; which being exprest,
I may recant this low despised life,
And please those friends whom I mov'd to grief.
Cador. She is coming, yfaith; be merry, *Edwin.*
Consta. Since you desire instruction, you shall have it.
What ist should make you thus desire to live
Vow'd to a single life?
Modest. Because I know I cannot flie from death.
Oh, my good sister, I beseech you, hear me:
This world is but a Masque, catching weak eyes
With what is not our selves but our disguise,
A Vizard that falls off, the Dance being done,
And leaves Deaths Glass for all to look upon;
Our best happiness here lasts but a night,
Whose burning Tapers makes false Ware seem right.
Who knows not this, and will not now provide
Some better shift before his shame be spy'd,
And knowing this vain world at last will leave him,
Shake off these robes that help but to deceive him?
Const. Her words are powerful, I am amaz'd to hear her!
Dono. Her soul's inchanted with infected Spells.
Leave her, best Girl; for now in thee
Ile seek the fruits of Age, Posterity.—
Out o' my sight! sure, I was half asleep
Or drunk, when I begot thee.
Const. Good sir, forbear. What say you to that, sister?
The joy of children, a blest Mothers Name!
Oh, who without much grief can loose such Fame?
Modest. Who can enjoy it without sorrow rather?
And that most certain where the joy's unsure,
Seeing the fruit that we beget endure
So many miseries, that oft we pray
The Heavens to shut up their afflicted day;
At best we do but bring forth Heirs to die,
And fill the Coffins of our enemy.
Const. Oh, my soul!
Dono. Hear her no more, *Constancia,*
She's sure bewitcht with Error; leave her, Girl.
Const. Then must I leave all goodness, sir: away,
Stand off, I say.
Dono. How's this?
Const. I have no father, friend, no husband now;
All are but borrowed robes, in which we masque
To waste and spend the time, when all our Life
Is but one good betwixt two Ague-days,
Which from the first e're we have time to praise,
A second Fever takes us: Oh, my best sister,
My souls eternal friend, forgive the rashness
Of my distemper'd tongue; for how could she,
Knew not her self, know thy felicity,
From which worlds cannot how remove me?
Dono. Art thou mad too, fond woman? what's thy meaning?
Const. To seek eternal happiness in heaven,
Which all this world affords not.
Cador. Think of thy Vow, thou art my promis'd Wife.
Const. Pray, trouble me no further.
Omnes. Strange alteration!
Cador. Why do you stand at gaze, you sacred Priests?
You holy men, be equal to the Gods,
And consummate my Marriage with this woman.
Bishop. Her self gives barr, my Lord, to your desires

70 knew *T*: know *Q* 78 mov'd *Q*: have mov'd *D*

And our performance; 'tis against the Law
And Orders of the Church to force a Marriage.
Cador. How am I wrong'd! Was this your trick, my Lord?
Dono. I am abus'd past sufferance;
Grief and amazement strive which Sense of mine
Shall loose her being first. Yet let me call thee Daughter.
Cador. Me, Wife.
Const. Your words are air, you speak of want to wealth,
And wish her sickness, newly rais'd to health.
Dono. Bewitched Girls, tempt not an old mans fury,
That hath no strength to uphold his feeble age,
But what your sights give life to: oh, beware,
And do not make me curse you.
[*Kneel.*] *Modest.* Dear father,
Here at your feet we kneel, grant us but this,
That, in your sight and hearing, the good Hermit
May plead our Cause; which, if it shall not give
Such satisfaction as your Age desires,
We will submit to you.
Const. You gave us life;
Save not our bodies, but our souls, from death.
Dono. This gives some comfort yet: Rise with my blessings. —
Have patience, noble *Cador,* worthy *Edwin;*
Send for the Hermit that we may confer.
For, sure, Religion tyes you not to leave
Your careful Father thus; if so it be,
Take you content, and give all grief to me.
[*Exeunt.*

⟨SCENE III.

A cave in the Forest.⟩

Thunder and Lightning; Enter Devil.

Devil. Mix light and darkness; earth and heaven dissolve,
Be of one piece agen, and turn to *Chaos;*
Break all your works, you powers, and spoil the world,
Or, if you will maintain earth still, give way
And life to this abortive birth now coming,
Whose fame shall add unto your Oracles.
Lucina, Hecate, dreadful Queen of Night,
Bright *Proserpine,* be pleas'd for *Ceres* love,
From *Stigian* darkness summon up the Fates,
And in a moment bring them quickly hither,
Lest death do vent her birth and her together.
[*Thunder.*
Assist, you spirits of infernal deeps,
Squint ey'd *Erictho,* midnight *Incubus,*
Rise, rise to aid this birth prodigious.

Enter Lucina and the three Fates.

Thanks, *Hecate;* hail, sister to the Gods!
There lies your way, haste with the Fates, and help,
Give quick dispatch unto her laboring throws,
To bring this mixture of infernal seed
To humane being; [*Exit Fates.*
And to beguil her pains, till back you come,
Anticks shall dance and Musick fill the room. —
[*Dance.*
Devil. Thanks, Queen of Shades.
Lucina. Farewel, great servant to th'infernal King.
In honor of this childe, the Fates shall bring
All their assisting powers of Knowledge, Arts,
Learning, Wisdom, all the hidden parts
Of all-admiring Prophecy, to fore-see
The event of times to come: his Art shall stand
A wall of brass to guard the *Brittain* Land.
Even from this minute, all his Arts appears
Manlike in Judgement, Person, State, and years.
Upon his brest the Fates have fixt his name,
And since his birth place was this forrest here,
They now have nam'd him *Merlin Silvester.*
Devil. And *Merlins* name in *Brittany* shall live,
Whilst men inhabit here or Fates can give
Power to amazing wonder; envy shall weep,
And mischief sit and shake her ebbone wings,
Whilst all the world of *Merlins* magick sings.
[*Exit.*

⟨SCENE IV.

The Forest.⟩

Enter Clown.

Clown. Well, I wonder how my poor sister does, after all this thundering; I think she's dead, for I can hear no tidings of her. Those woods yields small comfort for her; I could meet nothing but a swinherds wife, keeping hogs by the Forestside, but neither she nor none of her sowes would stir a foot to help us; indeed, I think she durst not trust her self amongst the trees with me, for I must needs confess I offer'd some kindness to her. Well, I would fain know what's become of my sister: if she have brought me a yong Cousin, his face may be a picture to finde his Father by. So oh! sister *Joan, Joan Go-too't,* where art thou?

148 *S. D.* Kneel *printed as part of text Q* 160 you *Q*: your *WP* Scene III. *etc. add. T*

14 *S. D. after* 13 *Q* 26 Learning, and wisdom *D* 35 Britany *D*: Brittain *Q* Scene IV. *etc. add. T*

(*Within*) *Joan.* Here, here, brother, stay but a while, I come to thee.

Clown. O brave! she's alive still, I know her voice; she speaks, and speaks cherfully, methinks. How now, what Moon-calf has she got with her?

Enter Joan and Merlin with a Book.

Joan. Come, my dear *Merlin,* why dost thou fix thine eye
So deeply on that book?

Merlin. To sound the depth
Of Arts, of Learning, Wisdom, Knowledge.

Joan. Oh, my dear, dear son,
Those studies fits thee when thou art a man.

Merlin. Why, mother, I can be but half a man at best,
And that is your mortality; the rest
In me is spirit; 'tis not meat, nor time,
That gives this growth and bigness; no, my years
Shall be more strange then yet my birth appears.
Look, mother, there's my Uncle.

Joan. How doest thou know him, son? thou never saw'st him.

Merlin. Yet I know him, and know the pains he has taken for ye, to finde out my Father.—Give me your hand, good Uncle.

Clown. Ha, ha, I'de laugh at that, yfaith. Do you know me, sir?

Merlin. Yes, by the same token that even now you kist the swinherds-wife i'th' woods, and would have done more, if she would have let you, Uncle.

Clown. A witch, a witch, a witch, sister: rid him out of your company, he is either a witch or a conjurer; he could never have known this else.

Joan. Pray, love him, brother, he is my son.

Clown. Ha, ha, this is worse then all the rest, yfaith; by his beard he is more like your husband. Let me see, is your great belly gone?

Joan. Yes, and this the happy fruit.

Clown. What, this Hartichoke? A Childe born with a beard on his face?

Merlin. Yes, and strong legs to go, and teeth to eat.

Clown. You can nurse up your self, then? There's some charges sav'd for Soap and Caudle. 'Slid, I have heard of some that has been born with teeth, but never none with such a talking tongue before.

Joan. Come, come, you must use him kindly, brother;
Did you but know his worth, you would make much of him.

Clown. Make much of a Moncky? This is worse then *Tom Thumb,* that let a fart in his Mothers belly; a Childe to speak, eat, and go the first hour of his birth; nay, such a Baby as had need of a Barber before he was born too; why, sister, this is monstrous, and shames all our kindred.

Joan. That thus 'gainst nature and our common births
He comes thus furnisht to salute the world,
Is power of Fates, and gift of his great father.

Clown. Why, of what profession is your father, sir?

Merlin. He keeps a Hot-house i'th' Low Countries; will you see him, sir?

Clown. See him? why, sister, has the childe found his father?

Mer. Yes, and Ile fetch him, Uncle. [*Exit.*

Clown. Do not Uncle me, till I know your kindred: for my conscience, some Baboon begot thee.—Surely, thou art horribly deceived, sister, this Urchin cannot be of thy breeding; I shall be asham'd to call him cousin, though his father be a Gentleman.

Enter Merlin and Devil.

Merlin. Now, my kinde Uncle, see:
The Childe has found his Father, this is he.

Clown. The devil it is; ha, ha, is this your sweet-heart, sister? have we run through the Countrey, haunted the City, and examin'd the Court to finde out a Gallant with a Hat and Feather, and a silken Sword, and golden Hangers, and do you now bring me to a Raga-muffin with a face like a Frying-pan?

Joan. Fie, brother, you mistake, behold him better.

Clown. How's this? do you juggle with me, or are mine eyes matches? Hat and Feather, Sword, and Hangers, and all! this is a Gallant indeed, sister; this has all the marks of him we look for.

Devil. And you have found him now, sir:
Give me your hand, I now must call you brother.

Clown. Not till you have married my sister, for all this while she's but your whore, sir.

Devil. Thou art too plain, Ile satisfie that wrong
To her, and thee, and all, with liberal hand:
Come, why art thou fearful?

Clown. Nay, I am not afraid, and you were the devil, sir.

35 Yet *Q* : Yes *D* 59 caudle *D* : Candle *Q* 82 for *Q* : fore *T*

Devil. Thou needst not; keep with thy sister still,
And Ile supply your wants, you shall lack nothing
That gold and wealth can purchase.

Clown. Thank you, brother: we have gone many a weary step to finde you; you may be a husband for a Lady, for you are far fetcht and dear bought, I assure you. Pray, how should I call your son, my cousin here?

Devil. His name is *Merlin.*

Clown. Merlin? Your hand, cousin *Merlin;* for your fathers sake I accept you to my kindred: if you grow in all things as your Beard does, you will be talkt on. By your Mothers side, cousin, you come of the *Go-too'ts, Suffolk* bred, but our standing house is at *Hocklye i'th' Hole,* and *Layton-buzzard.* For your father, no doubt you may from him claim Titles of Worship, but I cannot describe it; I think his Ancestors came first from *Hell-bree* in *Wales,* cousin.

Devil. No matter whence we do derive our Name:
All *Brittany* shall ring of *Merlin's* fame,
And wonder at his acts. Go hence to *Wales,*
There live a while; there *Vortiger* the King
Builds Castles and strong Holds, which cannot stand,
Unless supported by yong *Merlins* hand.
There shall thy fame begin: Wars are a breeding;
The Saxons practise Treason, yet unseen,
Which shortly shall break out.—Fair Love, farewel;
Dear son and brother, here must I leave you all,
Yet still I will be near at *Merlins* call. [*Exit.*

Merl. Will you go, Uncle?

Clown. Yes, Ile follow you, cousin.—Well, I do most horribly begin to suspect my kindred; this brother in law of mine is the Devil, sure, and though he hide his horns with his Hat and Feather, I spi'd his cloven foot for all his cunning. [*Exit.*

⟨SCENE V.

The British Court.⟩

Enter Ostorius, Octa, and Proximus.

Ostor. Come, come, time calls our close Complots to action.
Go, *Proximus* with winged speed flie hence,
Hye thee to *Wales:* salute great *Vortiger*
With these our Letters; bid the King to arms,
Tell him we have new friends, more Forces landed
In *Norfolk* and *Northumberland;* bid him
Make haste to meet us; if he keep his word,
Wee'l part the Realm between us.

Octa. Bend all thine Art to quit that late disgrace
The Christian Hermit gave thee; make thy revenge
Both sure and home.

Prox. That thought, sir, spurs me on,
Till I have wrought their swift destruction. [*Exit.*

Ostor. Go, then, and prosper. *Octa,* be vigilant:
Speak, are the Forts possest? the Guards made sure?
Revolve, I pray, on how large consequence
The bare event and sequel of our hopes
Joyntly consists, that have embark't our lives
Upon the hazzard of the least miscarriage.

Octa. All's sure: the Queen your sister hath contrived
The cunning Plot so sure, as at an instant
The Brothers shall be both surpriz'd and taken.

Ostor. And both shall die; yet one a while must live,
Till we by him have gather'd strength and power
To meet bold *Edol,* their stern General,
That now, contrary to the Kings command,
Hath re-united all his cashier'd Troops,
And this way beats his drums to threaten us.

Octa. Then our Plot's discover'd.

Ostor. Come, th'art a fool, his Army and his life
Is given unto us: where is the Queen my sister?

Octa. In conference with the Prince.

Ostor. Bring the Guards nearer, all is fair and good;
Their Conference, I hope, shall end in blood. [*Exeunt.*

⟨SCENE VI.

A Room in the Palace.⟩

Enter Prince and Artesia.

Artes. Come, come, you do but flatter;
What you term Love is but a Dream of blood,
Wakes with enjoying, and with open eyes
Forgot, contemn'd, and lost.

Prince. I must be wary, her words are dangerous.—
True, we'l speak of Love no more, then.

Artes. Nay, if you will, you may;
'Tis but in jest, and yet so children play
With fiery flames, and covet what is bright,
But, feeling his effects, abhor the light.

Scene V. *etc. add. T*

Scene VI. *D: Scene V continued T* A Room, *etc. add. WP*

Pleasure is like a Building, the more high,
The narrower still it grows; Cedars do dye
Soonest at top.
Prince. How does your instance suit?
Artes. From Art and Nature to make sure the root,
And lay a fast foundation, e're I try
The incertain Changes of a wavering Skie.
Make your example thus.—You have a kiss,—
Was it not pleasing?
Prince. Above all name to express it.
Artes. Yet now the pleasure's gone,
And you have lost your joys possession.
Prince. Yet when you please, this flood may ebb again.
Artes. But where it never ebbs, there runs the main.
Prince. Who can attain such hopes?
Artes. Ile show the way to it, give you
A taste once more of what you may enjoy. [*Kiss.*
Prince. Impudent whore!—
I were more false than Atheism can be,
Should I not call this high felicity.
Artes. If I should trust your faith, alas, I fear,
You soon would change belief.
Prince. I would covet Martyrdom to make't confirm'd.
Artes. Give me your hand on that you'l keep your word?
Prince. I will.
Artes. Enough: Help, husband, king *Aurelius,* help!
Rescue betraid *Artesia!*
Prince. Nay, then 'tis I that am betraid, I see;
Yet with thy blood Ile end thy Treachery.
Artes. How now! what troubles you? Is this you, sir,
That but even now would suffer Martyrdom
To win your hopes, and is there now such terror
In names of men to fright you? nay, then I see
What mettle you are made on.
Prince. Ha! was it but tryal? then I ask your pardon:
What a dull slave was I to be so fearful!—
Ile trust her now no more, yet try the utmost.—
I am resolved, no brother, no man breathing,
Were he my bloods begetter, should withhold
Me from your love; I'd leap into his bosom,
And from his brest pull forth that happiness
Heaven had reserved in you for my enjoying.
Artes. I, now you speak a Lover like a Prince!—
Treason, treason!
Prince. Agen?
Artes. Help, Saxon Princes: Treason!

Enter Ostorius, Octa &c.

Ostor. Rescue the Queen: strike down the Villain.

Enter Edoll, Aurelius, Donobert, Cador, Edwin, Toclio, Oswold, at the other Door.

Edol. Call in the Guards: the Prince in danger!
Fall back, dear Sir, my brest shall buckler you.
Aurel. Beat down their weapons!
Edol. Slave, wert thou made of brass, my sword shall bite thee.
Aurel. Withdraw, on pain of death: where is the Traitor?
Artes. Oh, save your life, my Lord; let it suffice,
My beauty forc't mine own captivity.
Aurel. Who did attempt to wrong thee?
Prince. Hear me, Sir.
Aurel. Oh, my sad soul! was't thou?
Artes. Oh, do not stand to speak; one minutes stay
Prevents a second speech for ever.
Aurel. Make our Guards strong:
My dear *Artesia,* let us know thy wrongs
And our own dangers.
Artes. The Prince your brother, with these Brittain Lords,
Have all agreed to take me hence by force
And marry me to him.
Prince. The Devil shall wed thee first:
Thy baseness and thy lust confound and rot thee!
Artes. He courted me even now, and in mine ear
Sham'd not to plead his most dishonest love,
And their attempts to seize your sacred person,
Either to shut you up within some prison,
Or, which is worse, I fear, to murther you.
Omnes Brittains. 'Tis all as false as hell.
Edol. And as foul as she is.
Artes. You know me, Sir?
Edol. Yes, Deadly Sin, we know you,
And shall discover all your villany.
Aurel. *Chester,* forbear!
Ostor. Their treasons, sir, are plain:
Why are their Souldiers lodg'd so near the Court?
Octa. Nay, why came he in arms so suddenly?

14 instance *T*, *etc.*: instanced *Q* 25 you *WP*: me *Q*

66 stand *Q*: stay *T* 81 all as *om. T*

Edol. You fleering Anticks, do not wake my fury.
Octa. Fury!
Edol. Ratsbane, do not urge me.
Artes. Good sir, keep farther from them.
Prince Oh, my sick heart!
She is a witch by nature, devil by art.
Aurel. Bite thine own slanderous tongue; 'tis thou art false.
I have observ'd your passions long ere this.
Ostor. Stand on your guard, my Lord, we are your friends,
And all our Force is yours.
Edol. To spoil and rob the Kingdom.
Aurel. Sir, be silent.
Edol. Silent! how long? till Doomsday? shall I stand by,
And hear mine Honor blasted with foul Treason,
The State half lost, and your life endanger'd,
Yet be silent?
Artes. Yes, my blunt Lord, unless you speak your Treasons.
Sir, let your Guards, as Traitors, seize them all,
And then let tortures and devulsive racks
Force a Confession from them.
Edol. Wilde-fire and Brimstone eat thee! Hear me, sir.
Aurel. Sir, Ile not hear you.
Edol. But you shall. Not hear me!
Were the worlds Monarch, *Cesar,* living, he
Should hear me.
I tell you, Sir, these serpents have betraid
Your Life and Kingdom: does not every day
Bring tidings of more swarms of lowsie slaves,
The offal fugitives of barren *Germany,*
That land upon our Coasts, and by our neglect
Settle in *Norfolk* and *Northumberland?*
Ostor. They come as Aids and Safeguards to the King.
Octa. Has he not need, when *Vortiger's* in arms,
And you raise Powers, 'tis thought, to joyn with him?
Edol. Peace, you pernicious Rat.
Dono. Prithee, forbear.
Edol. Away! suffer a gilded rascal,
A low-bred despicable creeper, an insulting Toad,
To spit his poison'd venome in my face!
Octa. Sir, sir!
Edol. Do not reply, you Cur; for, by the Gods,
Tho' the Kings presence guard thee, I shall break all patience,
And, like a Lion rous'd to spoil, shall run
Foul-mouth'd upon thee, and devour thee quick.—
Speak, sir: will you forsake these scorpions,
Or stay till they have stung you to the heart?
Aurel. Y'are traitors all. This is our wife, our Queen:
Brother *Ostorius,* troop your *Saxons* up,
We'l hence to *Winchester,* ⟨and⟩ raise more powers,
To man with strength the Castle *Camilot.*—
Go hence, false men, joyn you with *Vortiger,*
The murderer of our brother *Constantine:*
We'l hunt both him and you with dreadful vengance.
Since *Brittain* fails, we'l trust to forrain friends,
And guard our person from your traitorous ends.
[*Exeunt Aurel., Ostor., Octa, Artes., Toc., Osw.*
Edwin. He's sure bewitcht.
Glost. What counsel now for safety?
Dono. Onely this, sir: with all the speed we can,
Preserve the person of the King and Kingdom.
Cador. Which to effect, 'tis best march hence to *Wales,*
And set on *Vortiger* before he joyn
His Forces with the *Saxons.*
Edwin. On, then, with speed for *Wales* and *Vortiger!*
That tempest once o'reblown, we come, *Ostorius,*
To meet thy traiterous *Saxons,* thee and them,
That with advantage thus have won the King,
To back your factions and to work our ruines.
This, by the Gods and my good Sword, I'le set
In bloody lines upon thy Burgonet. [*Exeunt.*

ACT 4.

Scene I.

⟨*Before a Ruined Castle in Wales.*⟩

Enter Clown, Merlin, and a little antick Spirit.

Mer. How now, Uncle? why do you search your pockets so? Do you miss any thing?

Clown. Ha! Cousin *Merlin,* I hope your beard does not overgrow your honesty; I pray, remember, you are made up of sisters thread; I am your mothers brother, whosoever was your father.

102–3 *One line D* 102 and *om. WP* 103 Yet] And yet *WP* 114 slaves] knaves *T* 116 and] and have *T* 117 Settle *pr. ed.*: Settled *Q, etc.*

134 and *add. Molt., WP* 141 bewitch *Q* *S. D.* Before *etc. add. T* 5 of] of my *D*

Merlin. Why, wherein can you task my duty, Uncle?

Clown. Your self or your page it must be, I have kept no other company, since your mother bound your head to my Protectorship; I do feel a fault of one side; either it was that Sparrowhawk, or a Cast of *Merlins,* for I finde a Covy of Cardecu's sprung out of my pocket.

Merlin. Why, do you want any money, Uncle? Sirrah, had you any from him?

Clown. Deny it not, for my pockets are witness against you.

Spirit. Yes, I had, to teach you better wit to look to it.

Clown. Pray, use your fingers better, and my wit may serve as it is, sir.

Merlin. Well, restore it.

Spirit. There it is.

Clown. I, there's some honesty in this; 'twas a token from your invisible Father, Cousin, which I would not have to go invisibly from me agen.

Mer. Well, you are sure you have it now, Uncle?

Clown. Yes, and mean to keep it now from your pages filching fingers too.

Spirit. If you have it so sure, pray show it me agen.

Clown. Yes, my little juggler, I dare show it. Ha, cleanly conveyance agen! ye have no invisible fingers, have ye? 'Tis gone, certainly.

Spirit. Why, sir, I toucht you not.

Mer. Why, look you, Uncle, I have it now: how ill do you look to it! here, keep it safer.

Clown. Ha, ha, this is fine, yfaith. I must keep some other company, if you have these slights of hand.

Merlin. Come, come, Uncle, 'tis all my Art, which shall not offend you, sir, onely I give you a taste of it to show you sport.

Clown. Oh, but 'tis ill jesting with a mans pocket, tho'. But I am glad to see you cunning, Cousin, for now will I warrant thee a living till thou diest. You have heard the news in *Wales* here?

Mer. Uncle, let me prevent your care and counsel,
'Twill give you better knowledge of my cunning.
You would prefer me now, in hope of gain,
To *Vortiger*, King of the Welch *Brittains,*
To whom are all the Artists summon'd now,
That seeks the secrets of futurity:
The Bards, the Druids, Wizards, Conjurers,
Not an Auraspex with his whisling spells,
No Capnomanster with his musty fumes,
No Witch or Juggler, but is thither sent,
To calculate the strange and fear'd event
Of his prodigious Castle, now in building,
Where all the labors of the painful day
Are ruin'd still i'th' night, and to this place
You would have me go.

Clown. Well, if thy mother were not my sister, I would say she was a witch that begot thee; but this is thy father, not thy mother wit. Thou hast taken my tale into thy mouth, and spake my thoughts before me; therefore away, shuffle thy self amongst the Conjurers, and be a made man before thou comest to age.

Mer. Nay, but stay, Uncle, you overslip my dangers:
The Prophecies and all the cunning Wizards
Have certifi'd the King that this his Castle
Can never stand, till the foundation's laid
With Mortar temper'd with the fatal blood
Of such a childe whose father was no mortal.

Clown. What's this to thee? If the devil were thy father, was not thy mother born at *Carmarden?* Diggon for that, then; and then it must be a childes blood, and who will take thee for a childe with such a beard of thy face? Is there not diggon for that too, Cousin?

Merlin. I must not go: lend me your ear a while,
I'le give you reasons to the contrary.

Enter two Gentlemen.

1. *Gentle.* Sure, this is an endless piece of work the King has sent us about!

2. *Gentle.* Kings may do it, man; the like has been done to finde out the Unicorn.

1. *Gentle.* Which will be sooner found, I think, then this fiend begotten childe we seek for.

2. *Gentle.* Pox of those Conjurers that would speak of such a one, and yet all their cunning could not tell us where to finde him.

1. *Gentle.* In *Wales* they say assuredly he lives; come, let's enquire further.

Mer. Uncle, your perswasions must not prevail with me: I know mine enemies better then you do.

Clown. I say, th'art a bastard then, if thou disobey thine Uncle: was not *Joan Go-too't,* thy mother, my sister? If the devil were thy father, what kin art thou to any man alive

15 Covy] *Some copies of Q appear to read* Cony 50 you *Q*: your *D*, *etc.*

61 Aurasper *Q*: Aruspex *T*, *etc.* 62 Capuomanster *Q*: Capnomancer *T*, *etc.* 65 his] this *T* 71 thee *T*, *etc.*: this *Q* 73 spoke my words *D* 100 say] said *T*

but Bailys and Brokers? and they are but brothers in Law to thee neither.

1. *Gentle.* How's this? I think we shall speed here.

2. *Gentle.* I, and unlook't for too: go ne're and listen to them.

Clown. Hast thou a beard to hide it? wil't thou show thy self a childe? wil't thou have more hair then wit? Wil't thou deny thy mother, because no body knows thy father? Or shall thine Uncle be an ass?

1. *Gentle.* Bless ye, friend: pray, what call you this small Gentlemans name?

Clown. Small, sir? a small man may be a great Gentleman; his father may be of an ancient house, for ought we know, sir.

2. *Gentle.* Why? do you not know his father?

Clown. No, nor you neither, I think, unless the devil be in ye.

1. *Gentle.* What is his name, sir?

Clown. His name is my Cousin, sir, his education is my sisters son, but his maners are his own.

Merlin. Why ask ye, Gentlemen? my name is *Merlin.*

Clown. Yes, and a Goshawk was his father, for ought we know; for I am sure his mother was a Wind-sucker.

2. *Gentle.* He has a mother, then?

Clown. As sure as I have a sister, sir.

1. *Gentle.* But his father you leave doubtful.

Clown. Well, Sir, as wise men as you doubt whether he had a father or no?

1. *Gentle.* Sure, this is he we seek for.

2. *Gent.* I think no less: and, sir, we let you know
The King hath sent for you.

Clown. The more childe he; and he had bin rul'd by me,
He should have gone before he was sent for.

1. *Gent.* May we not see his mother?

Clown. Yes, and feel her too, if you anger her; a devilish thing, I can tell ye, she has been. Ile go fetch her to ye. [*Exit.*

2. *Gent.* Sir, it were fit you did resolve for speed,
You must unto the King.

Mer. My Service, sir,
Shall need no strict command, it shall obey
Most peaceably; but needless 'tis to fetch
What is brought home: my journey may be staid,
The King is coming hither
With the same quest you bore before him; hark,
This drum will tell ye.
[*Within Drums beat a low March.*

1. *Gent.* This is some cunning indeed, sir.

Florish. Enter Vortiger, reading a letter, Proximus, with Drum and Soldiers, &c.

Vorti. Still in our eye your message, *Proximus,*
We keep to spur our speed:
Ostorius and *Octa* we shall salute
With succor against Prince *Vter* and *Aurelius,*
Whom now we hear incamps at *Winchester.*
There's nothing interrupts our way so much
As doth the erection of this fatal Castle,
That spite of all our Art and daily labor,
The night still ruines.

Prox. As erst I did affirm, still I maintain,
The fiend begotten childe must be found out,
Whose blood gives strength to the foundation;
It cannot stand else.

Enter Clown and Joan, Merlin.

Vorti. Ha! Is't so?
Then, *Proximus,* by this intelligence
He should be found: speak, is this he you tell of?

Clown. Yes, Sir, and I his Uncle, and she his mother.

Vorti. And who is his father?

Clown. Why, she, his mother, can best tell you that, and yet I think the childe be wise enough, for he has found his father.

Vort. Woman, is this thy son?

Joan. It is, my Lord.

Vor. What was his father? Or where lives he?

Merl. Mother, speak freely and unastonisht;
That which you dar'd to act, dread not to name.

Joan. In which I shall betray my sin and shame.
But since it must be so, then know, great King,
All that my self yet knows of him is this:
In pride of blood and beauty I did live,
My glass the Altar was, my face the Idol;
Such was my peevish love unto my self,
That I did hate all other; such disdain
Was in my scornful eye that I suppos'd
No mortal creature worthy to enjoy me.
Thus with the Peacock I beheld my train,
But never saw the blackness of my feet;
Oft have I chid the winds for breathing on me,
And curst the Sun, fearing to blast my beauty.
In midst of this most leaprous disease,
A seeming fair yong man appear'd unto me,

115-16 Wilt then show *D*

164 encamp'd *D* 166 fatal *Q*: famous *T* 172 *S. D.* Joan, joining Merlin *WP*

In all things suiting my aspiring pride,
And with him brought along a conquering power,
To which my frailty yielded; from whose embraces
This issue came; what more he is, I know not.

Vorti. Some *Incubus* or Spirit of the night
Begot him then, for, sure, no mortal did it.

Mer. No matter who, my Lord; leave further quest,
Since 'tis as hurtful as unnecessary
More to enquire: Go to the cause, my Lord,
Why you have sought me thus?

Vorti. I doubt not but thou knowst; yet, to be plain,
I sought thee for thy blood.

Mer. By whose direction?

Prox. By mine;
My Art infalable instructed me,
Upon thy blood must the foundation rise
Of the Kings building; it cannot stand else.

Mer. Hast thou such leisure to enquire my Fate,
And let thine own hang careless over thee?
Knowst thou what pendelous mischief roofs thy head,
How fatal, and how sudden?

Prox. Pish!
Bearded abortive, thou foretel my danger!
My Lord, he trifles to delay his own.

Mer. No, I yield my self: and here before the King
Make good thine Augury, as I shall mine.
If thy fate fall not, thou hast spoke all truth,
And let my blood satisfie the Kings desires:
If thou thy self wilt write thine Epitaph,
Dispatch it quickly, there's not a minutes time
'Twixt thee and thy death.

Prox. Ha, ha, ha!

[*A stone falls and kills Proximus.*

Mer. I, so thou mayest die laughing.

Vorti. Ha! This is above admiration: look, is he dead?

Clown. Yes, sir, here's brains to make morter on, if you'l use them. Cousin *Merlin,* there's no more of this stone fruit ready to fall, is there? I pray, give your Uncle a little fair warning.

Mer. Remove that shape of death. And now, my Lord,
For clear satisfaction of your doubts,
Merlin will show the fatal cause that keeps
Your Castle down and hinders your proceedings.
Stand there, and by an apparition see
The labor and end of all your destiny.
Mother and Uncle, you must be absent.

Clown. Is your father coming, Cousin?

Mer. Nay, you must be gone.

Joan. Come, you'l offend him, brother.

Clown. I would fain see my Brother i'law; if you were married, I might lawfully call him so. ⟨*Exeunt Joan and Clown.*⟩ *Merlin strikes his wand. Thunder and Lightning; two Dragons appear, a White and a Red; they fight a while, and pause.*

Vor. What means this stay?

Mer. Be not amaz'd, my Lord, for on the victory,
Of loss or gain, as these two Champions ends,
Your fate, your life, and kingdom all depends;
Therefore observe it well.

Vor. I shall: heaven be auspicious to us.

[*Thunder: The two Dragons fight agen, and the White Dragon drives off the Red.*

Vor. The conquest is on the white Dragons part.
Now, *Merlin,* faithfully expound the meaning.

Mer. Your Grace must then not be offended with me.

Vor. It is the weakest part I found in thee,
To doubt of me so slightly. Shall I blame
My prophet that foretells me of my dangers?
Thy cunning I approve most excellent.

Mer. Then know, my Lord, there is a dampish Cave,
The nightly habitation of these Dragons,
Vaulted beneath where you would build your Castle,
Whose enmity and nightly combats there
Maintain a constant ruine of your labors.
To make it more plain, the Dragons, then,
Your self betoken and the *Saxon* King;
The vanquisht Red is, sir, your dreadful Emblem.

Vort. Oh, my fate!

Mer. Nay, you must hear with patience, Royal sir.
You slew the lawful King *Constantius:*
'Twas a red deed, your Crown his blood did cement.
The English *Saxon,* first brought in by you
For aid against *Constantius* brethren,

211 doubt not *Q*: have no doubt *D* 230 time *Q*: space *T* 231 Betwixt *WP* *S. D. after* 231 *Q* 242-3 *End* show, down *D*: *corr. pr. ed.*

244 your Castle *T, etc.*: your fatal Castle *Q* 246 and the end *WP* *S. D.* Exeunt . . Clown *add. T* 254 stay] play *conj. Elze* 263 Is it *D* found] have found *T* 271 our labour *T*

Is the white horror who now, knit together,
Have driven and shut you up in these wilde mountains;
And though they now seek to unite with friendship,
It is to wound your bosom, not embrace it,
And with an utter extirpation
To rout the *Brittains* out, and plant the English.
Seek for your safety, Sir, and spend no time
To build the⟨e⟩ airy Castles; for Prince *Vter,*
Armed with vengeance for his brothers blood,
Is hard upon you. If you mistrust me,
And to my words crave witness, sir, then know,
Here comes a messenger to tell you so.
[*Exit Mer.*

Enter Messenger.

Messen. My Lord! Prince *Vter!*
Vort. And who else, sir?
Messen. *Edol,* the great General.
Vort. The great Devil! they are coming to meet us?
Messen. With a full power, my Lord.
Vort. With a full vengeance,
They mean to meet us; so! we are ready
To their confront. At full march, double footing,
We'l loose no ground, nor shall their numbers fright us:
If it be Fate, it cannot be withstood;
We got our Crown so, be it lost in blood.
[*Exeunt.*

⟨SCENE II.

Open Country in Wales.⟩

Enter Prince Vter, Edol, Cador, Edwin, Toclio, with Drum and Soldiers.

Prince. Stay, and advice; hold, drum!
Edol. Beat, slave! why do you pause?
Why make a stand? where are our enemies?
Or do you mean we fight amongst our selves?
Prince. Nay, noble *Edol,*
Let us here take counsel, it cannot hurt,
It is the surest Garison to safety.
Edol. Fie on such slow delays! so fearful men,
That are to pass over a flowing river,
Stand on the bank to parly of the danger,
Till the tide rise, and then be swallowed.
Is not the King in field?
Cador. Proud *Vortiger,* the Trator, is in field.
Edwin. The Murderer and Usurper.
Edol. Let him be the devil, so I may fight with him.
For heavens love, sir, march on! Oh, my patience!
Will you delay, untill the *Saxons* come
To aid his party? [*A Tucket.*
Prince. There's no such fear: prithee, be calm a while.
Hark! it seems by this, he comes or sends to us.
Edol. If it be for parly, I will drown the summons,
If all our drums and hoarseness choke me not.

Enter Captain.

Prince. Nay, prithee, hear.—From whence art thou?
Cap. From the King *Vortiger,*
Edol. Traitor, there's none such: Alarum, drum; strike, slave,
Or, by mine honor, I will break thy head,
And beat thy drums heads both about thine ears.
Prince. Hold, noble *Edol,*
Let's hear what Articles he can inforce.
Edol. What articles or what conditions
Can you expect to value half your wrong,
Unless he kill himself by thousand tortures,
And send his carcase to appease your vengeance
For the foul murder of *Constantius,*
And that's not a tenth part neither.
Prince. 'Tis true,
My brothers blood is crying to me now;
I do applaud thy counsel: hence, be gone!—
[*Exit Capt.*
We'l hear no parly now but by our swords.
Edol. And those shall speak home in death killing words:
Alarum to the fight; sound, sound the Alarum. [*Exeunt.*

⟨SCENE III.

A Field of Battle.⟩

Alarum. Enter Edol, driving all Vortigers Force before him, then Exit. Enter Prince Vter pursuing Vortiger.

Vort. Dost follow me?
Prince. Yes, to thy death I will.
Vort. Stay, be advis'd;
I would not be the onely fall of Princes,
I slew thy brother.

289 To rout *Q*: Drive *T* 288 thee *pr. ed.*: the *Q, etc.* 291 craves *Q* 299 confront as full *Q*: *corr. D* Scene II. *etc. add. T* 11 then *Q*: they *T*

16–17 *End* on, delay *WP*: *corr. pr. ed.* 22 me *repeated Q* 27 drums heads *Q*: drumsticks *D* 38 appaud *Q* thy] your *T* counsels *D* Scene III. *etc. add. T* 1 thy *Q*: the *T* 3 I *Q*: It *D*

Prince. Thou didst, black Traitor,
And in that vengeance I pursue thee.
Vort. Take mercy for thy self, and flie my sword,
Save thine own life as satisfaction,
Which here I give thee for thy brothers death.
Prince. Give what's thine own: a Traitors heart and head,
That 's all thou art right Lord of. The Kingdom
Which thou usurp'st, thou most unhappy Tyrant,
Is leaving thee; the Saxons which thou broughtst
To back thy usurpations, are grown great,
And where they seat themselves, do hourly seek
To blot the Records of old *Brute* and *Brittains*
From memory of men, calling themselves
Hingest-men, and *Hingest-land,* that no more
The *Brittain* name be known: all this by thee,
Thou base destroyer of thy Native Countrey.

Enter Edol.

Edol. What, stand you talking? [*Fight.*
Prince. Hold, *Edol.*
Ed. Hold out, my sword,
And listen not to King or Princes word;
There's work enough abroad, this task is mine. [*Alarum.*
Prince. Prosper thy Valour, as thy Vertues shine. [*Exeunt.*

⟨SCENE IV.

Another Part of the Field of Battle.⟩

Enter Cador and Edwin.

Cador. Bright Victory her self fights on our part,
And, buckled in a golden Beaver, rides
Triumphantly before us.
Edw. Justice is with her,
Who ever takes the true and rightful cause.
Let us not lag behinde them.

Enter Prince.

Cador. Here comes the Prince. How goes our fortunes, Sir?
Prince. Hopeful and fair, brave *Cador.*
Proud *Vortiger,* beat down by *Edols* sword,
Was rescu'd by the following multitudes,
And now for safety's fled unto a Castle
Here standing on the hill: but I have sent
A cry of hounds as violent as hunger,
To break his stony walls; or, if they fail,
We'l send in wilde fire to dislodge him thence,
Or burn them all with flaming violence. [*Exeunt.*

⟨SCENE V.

Another Part of the Field.⟩

Blazing Star appears.

Florish Tromp. Enter Prince Vter, Edol, Cador, Edwin, Toclio, with Drum and Soldiers.

Prin. Look, *Edol:*
Still this fiery exalation shoots
His frightful horrors on th'amazed world;
See, in the beam that's 'bout his flaming ring,
A Dragons head appears, from out whose mouth
Two flaming flakes of fire stretch East and West.
Edol. And see, from forth the body of the Star
Seven smaller blazing streams directly point
On this affrighted kingdom.
Cador. 'Tis a dreadful Meteor.
Edwin. And doth portend strange fears.
Prince. This is no Crown of Peace; this angry fire
Hath something more to burn then *Vortiger;*
If it alone were pointed at his fall,
It would pull in his blasing Piramids
And be appeas'd, for *Vortiger* is dead.
Edol. These never come without their large effects.
Prince. The will of heaven be done! our sorrow's this,
We want a mistick *Pithon* to expound
This fiery Oracle.
Cador. Oh no, my Lord,
You have the best that ever *Brittain* bred;
And durst I prophecy of your Prophet, sir,
None like him shall succeed him.
Prince. You mean *Merlin?*
Cador. True, sir, wonderous *Merlin;*
He met us in the way, and did foretell
The fortunes of this day successful to us.
Edwin. He's sure about the Camp; send for him, sir.
Cador. He told the bloody *Vortiger* his fate,
And truely too, and if I could give faith
To any Wizards skill, it should be *Merlin.*

5 *Ends* didst *WP*   7 flie] flee *T*   18 and Brittain Hingest-land *WP*   21 *S. D.* Fight *printed as part of Edol's speech D*   Scene IV. *D*: *no new scene T*   Another *etc. add. WP*

Scene V] Scene IV *etc. T*   *S. D.* with *repeated Q*   1-2 *One line D*: *corr. Elze*   4 that's *T*: that *Q*   6 flakes *Q*: snakes *T*   15 his *Q*: its *T*

Enter Merlin and Clown.

Cador. And see, my Lord, as if to satisfie
Your Highness pleasure, *Merlin* is come.
Prince. See,
The Comet's in his eye, disturb him not.
Edol. With what a piercing judgement he beholds it!
Mer. Whither will Heaven and Fate translate this Kingdom?
What revolutions, rise and fall of Nations
Is figur'd yonder in that Star, that sings
The change of *Brittians* State and death of Kings?
Ha! He's dead already; how swiftly mischief creeps!
Thy fatal end, sweet Prince, even *Merlin* weeps.
Prince. He does foresee some evil, his action shows it,
For, e're he does expound, he weeps the story.
Edol. There's another weeps too. Sirrah, dost thou understand what thou lamentst for?
Clown. No, sir, I am his Uncle, and weep because my Cousin weeps; flesh and blood cannot forbear.
Prince. Gentle *Merlin,* speak thy prophetick knowledge
In explanation of this fiery horror,
From which we gather from thy mournful tears
Much sorrow and disaster in it.
Mer. 'Tis true,
Fair Prince, but you must hear the rest with patience.
Prince. I vow I will, tho' it portend my ruine.
Mer. There's no such fear.
This brought the fiery fall of *Vortiger,*
And yet not him alone: this day is faln
A King more good, the glory of our Land,
The milde and gentle, sweet *Aurelius.*
Prince. Our brother!
Edwin. Forefend it heaven!
Mer. He at his Palace Royal, sir,
At *Winchester,* this day is dead and poison'd.
Cador. By whom? Or what means, *Merlin?*
Mer. By the Traiterous Saxons.
Edol. I ever fear'd as much: that devil *Ostorius*
And the damn'd witch *Artesia,* sure, has done it.
Prince. Poison'd! oh, look further, gentle *Merlin,*
Behold the Star agen, and do but finde
Revenge for me, though it cost thousand lives,
And mine the foremost.
Mer. Comfort your self, the heavens have given it fully:
All the portentious ills to you is told.
Now hear a happy story, sir, from me
To you and to your fair posterity.
Clown. Me thinks, I see something like a peel'd Onion; it makes me weep agen.
Mer. Be silent, Uncle, you'l be forc't else.
Clown. Can you not finde in the Star, Cousin, whether I can hold my tongue or no?
Edol. Yes, I must cut it out.
Clown. Phu, you speak without book, sir, my Cousin *Merlin* knows.
Mer. True, I must tie it up. Now speak your pleasure, Uncle.
Clown. Hum, hum, hum, hum.
Mer. So, so.—
Now observe, my Lord, and there behold,
Above yon flame-hair'd beam that upward shoots,
Appears a Dragons head, out of whose mouth
Two streaming lights point their flame-feather'd darts
Contrary ways, yet both shall have their aims:
Again behold, from the ignifirent body
Seven splendant and illustrious rays are spred,
All speaking Heralds to this *Brittain* Isle,
And thus they are expounded: The Dragons head
Is the Herogliphick that figures out
Your Princely self, that here must reign a King;
Those by-form'd fires that from the Dragons mouth
Shoot East and West, emblem two Royal babes,
Which shall proceed from you, a son and daughter.
Her pointed constellation, Northwest bending,
Crowns Her a Queen in *Ireland,* of whom first springs
That Kingdoms Title to the *Brittain* Kings.
Clown. Hum, hum, hum.
Mer. But of your Son thus Fate and *Merlin* tells:
All after times shall fill their Chronicles
With fame of his renown, whose warlike sword
Shall pass through fertile *France* and *Germany;*
Nor shall his conquering foot be forc't to stand,
Till *Romes* Imperial Wreath hath crown'd his Fame

32–3 *Three lines D, div. after* Lord, pleasure: *corr. pr. ed.* 40 State *Q*: fate *T* 52 By which *Molt.* 56 *Prefix* Mer *Q* 59 him] his *conj. Elze* 66 what] by what *T*

79 Oinon *Q* 84 Phu *Q*: O, ha *D* 95 ignifirent *Q*: ignisirent *T*: igniferous *D* 104 bending *Q*: tending *D* 112 conquering *T, etc.*: conjuring *Q*

With Monarch of the West, from whose seven hills,
With Conquest and contributory Kings,
He back returns to inlarge the *Brittain* bounds,
His Heraldry adorn'd with thirteen Crowns.
Clown. Hum, hum, hum.
Mer. He to the world shall add another Worthy,
And, as a Loadstone, for his prowess draw
A train of Marshal Lovers to his Court:
It shall be then the best of Knight-hoods honor,
At *Winchester* to fill his Castle Hall,
And at his Royal Table sit and feast
In warlike orders, all their arms round hurl'd,
As if they meant to circumscribe the world.
[*he touches the Clowns mouth with his wand.*
Clown. Hum, hum, hum: oh, that I could speak a little!
Mer. I know your mind, Uncle; agen be silent. [*strikes agen.*
Prince. Thou speakst of wonders, *Merlin;* prithee, go on,
Declare at full this Constellation.
Mer. Those seven beams pointing downward, sir, betoken
The troubles of this Land, which then shall meet
With other Fate: War and Dissension strives
To make division, till seven Kings agree
To draw this Kingdom to a Hepterchy.
Prince. Thine art hath made such proof that we believe
Thy words authentical: be ever neer us,
My Prophet and the Guide of all my actions.
Mer. My service shall be faithful to your person,
And all my studies for my Countries safety.
Clown. Hum, hum, hum.
Mer. Come, you are releast, sir.
Clown. Cousin, pray, help me to my tongue agen; you do not mean I shall be dumb still, I hope?
Mer. Why, hast thou not thy tongue?
Clown. Ha! yes, I feel it now, I was so long dumb, I could not well tell whether I spake or no.
Prince. Is't thy advice we presently pursue
The bloody *Saxons,* that have slain my brother?
Mer. With your best speed, my Lord;
Prosperity will keep you company.
Cador. Take, then, your Title with you, Royal Prince,
'Twill adde unto our strength: *Long live King Uter!*
Edol. Put the Addition to't that Heaven hath given you:
The Dragon is your Emblem, bear it bravely,
And so live long and ever happy, styl'd
Vter-Pendragon, lawful King of *Brittain.*
Prince. Thanks, *Edol,* we imbrace the name and title,
And in our Sheild and Standard shall the figure
Of a Red Dragon still be born before us,
To fright the bloody Saxons. Oh, my *Aurelius,*
Sweet rest thy soul; let thy disturbed spirit
Expect revenge; think what it would, it hath:
The Dragon's coming in his fiery wrath.
[*Exeunt.*

ACT 5.

Scene I.

⟨*A barren Waste, a huge Rock appearing.*⟩
Thunder, then Musick.

Enter Joan fearfully, the Devil following her.

Joan. Hence, thou black horror! is thy lustful fire
Kindled agen? Not thy loud throated thunder
Nor thy adulterate infernal Musick
Shall e're bewitch me more: oh, too too much
Is past already.
Devil. Why dost thou fly me?
I come a Lover to thee, to imbrace
And gently twine thy body in mine arms.
Joan. Out, thou Hell-hound!
Devil. What hound so e're I be,
Fawning and sporting as I would with thee,
Why should I not be stroakt and plaid withal?
Will't thou not thank the Lion might devour thee,
If he shall let thee pass?
Joan. Yes, thou art he;
Free me, and Ile thank thee.
Devil. Why, whither wouldst?
I am at home with thee, thou art mine own,
Have we not charge of family together?
Where is your son?
Joan. Oh, darkness cover me!
Devil. There is a pride which thou hast won by me,
The mother of a fame, shall never die.
Kings shall have need of written Chronicles
To keep their names alive, but *Merlin* none;
Ages to ages shall like *Sabalists*
Report the wonders of his name and glory,
While there are tongues and times to tell his story.
Joan. Oh, rot my memory before my flesh,

153 you *Q*: your *T*

158 live long *T*: long live *Q*   *S. D.* A barren *etc. add. T*   23 Sabalists *Q*: satellites *D*

Let him be called some hell or earth-bred monster,
That ne're had hapless woman for a mother!
Sweet death, deliver me! Hence from my sight:
Why shouldst thou now appear? I had no pride
Nor lustful thought about me, to conjure
And call thee to my ruine, when as at first
Thy cursed person became visible.

Devil. I am the same I was.

Joan. But I am chang'd.

Devil. Agen Ile change thee to the same thou wert,
To quench my lust.—Come forth, by thunder led,
My Coajutors in the spoils of mortals. [*Thunder.*

Enter Spirit.

Claspe in your Ebon arms that prize of mine,
Mount her as high as palled *Hecate;*
And on this rock Ile stand to cast up fumes
And darkness o're the blew fac'd firmament:
From *Brittain* and from *Merlin* Ile remove her.
They ne're shall meet agen.

Joan. Help me some saving hand,
If not too late, I cry: let mercy come!

Enter Merlin.

Mer. Stay, you black slaves of night, let loose your hold,
Set her down safe, or by th'infernal Stix,
Ile binde you up with exorcisms so strong,
That all the black pentagoron of hell
Shall ne're release you. Save your selves and vanish! [*Exit Spirit.*

Devil. Ha! What's he?

Mer. *The Childe has found his Father.* Do you not know me?

Devil. *Merlin!*

Joan. Oh, help me, gentle son.

Mer. Fear not, they shall not hurt you.

Devil. Relievest thou her to disobey thy father?

Mer. Obedience is no lesson in your school;
Nature and kind to her commands my duty;
The part that you begot was against kinde,
So all I ow to you is to be unkind.

Devil. Ile blast thee, slave, to death, and on this rock
Stick thee ⟨as⟩ an eternal Monument.

Mer. Ha, ha, thy powers too weak; what art thou, devil,
But an inferior lustful *Incubus,*
Taking advantage of the wanton flesh,
Wherewith thou dost beguile the ignorant?
Put off the form of thy humanity,
And cral upon thy speckled belly, serpent,
Or Ile unclasp the jaws of *Achoron,*
And fix thee ever in the local fire.

Devil. Traitor to hell! curse that I e're begot thee!

Mer. Thou didst beget thy scourge: storm not, nor stir;
The power of *Merlins* Art is all confirm'd
In the Fates decretals. Ile ransack hell,
And make thy masters bow unto my spells.
Thou first shall taste it.—

[*Thunder and Lightning in the Rock.*

Tenibrarum princeps, devitiarum & infirorum Deus, hunc Incubum in ignis eterni abisum accipite, aut in hoc carcere tenebroso in sempeternum astringere mando.

[*the Rock incloses him.*

So! there beget earthquakes or some noisom damps,
For never shalt thou touch a woman more.—
How chear you, mother?

Joan. Oh, now my son is my deliverer,
Yet I must name him with my deepest sorrow.

[*Alarum afar off.*

Mer. Take comfort now: past times are ne're recal'd;
I did foresee your mischief, and prevent it.
Hark, how the sounds of war now call me hence
To aid *Pendragon* that in battail stands
Against the Saxons, from whose aid
Merlin must not be absent. Leave this soyl,
And Ile conduct you to a place retir'd,
Which I by art have rais'd, call'd *Merlins Bower.*
There shall you dwell with solitary sighs,
With grones and passions your companions,
To weep away this flesh you have offended with,
And leave all bare unto your aierial soul:
And when you die, I will erect a Monument
Upon the verdant Plains of *Salisbury,*
No King shall have so high a sepulchre,
With pendulous stones that I will hang by art,
Where neither Lime nor Morter shalbe us'd,
A dark *Enigma* to the memory,
For none shall have the power to number them,—
A place that I will hollow for your rest,

28 a] his *T* 36 quench to *Q* *S. D.* Spirits *D, etc.* 50 your] you *Q* *S. D.* Exeunt Spirits *D, etc.* 62 an *Q* : as an *D*

75 master *T* spell *D* 76 shalt *T, etc.* 77 princeps *conj. Elze* : precis *Q* 81 some *om. D* 103 the *Q* : thy *T* : men's *conj. WP* 105 hollow *Q* : hallow *T, etc.*

Where no Night-hag shall walk, nor Ware-wolf tread,
Where *Merlins* Mother shall be sepulcher'd.
[*Exeunt.*

⟨Scene II.
The British Camp.⟩

Enter Donobert, Gloster, and Hermit.

Dono. Sincerely, *Gloster,* I have told you all:
My Daughters are both vow'd to Single Life,
And this day gone unto the Nunnery,
Though I begot them to another end,
And fairly promis'd them in Marriage,
One to Earl *Cador,* t'other to your son,
My worthy friend, the Earl of *Gloster*.
Those lost, I am lost: they are lost, all's lost.
Answer me this, then: Ist a sin to marry?

Hermit. Oh no, my Lord.

Dono. Go to, then, Ile go no further with you;
I perswade you to no ill; perswade you, then,
That I perswade you well.

Gloster. 'Twill be a good Office in you, sir.

Enter Cador and Edwin.

Dono. Which since they thus neglect,
My memory shall lose them now for ever.—
See, see, the Noble Lords, their promis'd Husbands!
Had Fate so pleas'd, you might have call'd me Father.

Edwin. Those hopes are past, my Lord; for even this minute
We saw them both enter the Monastery,
Secluded from the world and men for ever.

Cador. 'Tis both our griefs we cannot, Sir:
But from the King take you the Times joy from us:
The Saxon King *Ostorius* slain and *Octa* fled,
That Woman-fury, Queen *Artesia,*
Is fast in hold, and forc't to re-deliver
London and *Winchester* (which she had fortifi'd)
To Princely *Vter,* lately styl'd *Pendragon,*
Who now triumphantly is marching hither
To be invested with the *Brittain* Crown.

Dono. The joy of this shall banish from my breast
All thought that I was Father to two Children,
Two stubborn Daughters, that have left me thus.
Let my old arms embrace, and call you Sons,
For, by the Honor of my Fathers House,
I'le part my estate most equally betwixt you.

Edwin, Cador. Sir y'are most noble!

Flor. Tromp. Enter Edol with Drum and Colours, Oswold bearing the Standard, Toclio the Sheild, with the Red Dragon pictur'd in'em, two Bishops with the Crown, Prince Vter, Merlin, Artesia bound, Guard, and Clown.

Prince. Set up our Sheild and Standard, noble Soldiers.
We have firm hope that, tho' our Dragon sleep,
Merlin will us and our fair Kingdom keep.

Clown. As his Uncle lives, I warrant you.

Glost. Happy Restorer of the *Brittains* fame,
Uprising Sun, let us salute thy glory:
Ride in a day perpetual about us,
And no night be in thy thrones zodiack.
Why do we stay to binde those Princely browes
With this Imperial Honor?

Prince. Stay, noble *Gloster:*
That monster first must be expel'd our eye,
Or we shall take no joy in it.

Dono. If that be hindrance, give her quick Judgement,
And send her hence to death; she has long deserv'd it.

Edol. Let my Sentence stand for all: take her hence,
And stake her carcase in the burning Sun,
Till it be parcht and dry, and then fley off
Her wicked skin, and stuff the pelt with straw
To be shown up and down at Fairs and Markets:
Two pence a piece to see so foul a Monster
Will be a fair Monopoly, and worth the begging.

Artes. Ha, ha, ha!

Edol. Dost laugh, *Erictho?*

Artes. Yes, at thy poor invention.
Is there no better torture-monger?

Dono. Burn her to dust.

Artes. That's a *Phœnix* death, and glorious.

Edol. I, that's to good for her.

Prince. Alive she shall be buried, circled in a wall.
Thou murdress of a King, there starve to death.

Artes. Then Ile starve death when he comes for his prey,
And i'th' mean time Ile live upon your curses.

Edol. I, 'tis diet good enough; away with her.

Scene II. *etc. add. T*   3 unto] into *T*   19 even *Q*: ever *T*   23 you the] the *conj. WP*   30 British *T*

39 firm *Q*: fair *T*   58 will *Q*: 'Twill *WP*   and ... begging *om. T*   69 'tis diet *Q*: it is *D*

Artes. With joy, my best of wishes is before;
Thy brother's poison'd, but I wanted more. [*Exit.*

Prince. Why does our Prophet *Merlin* stand apart,
Sadly observing these our Ceremonies,
And not applaud our joys with thy hid knowledge?
Let thy divining Art now satisfie
Some part of my desires; for well I know,
'Tis in thy power to show the full event,
That shall both end our Reign and Chronicle.
Speak, learned *Merlin,* and resolve my fears,
Whether by war we shal expel the Saxons,
Or govern what we hold with beauteous peace
In *Wales* and *Brittain?*

Mer. Long happiness attend *Pendragons* Reign!
What Heaven decrees, fate hath no power to alter:
The Saxons, sir, will keep the ground they have,
And by supplying numbers still increase,
Till *Brittain* be no more. So please your Grace,
I will in visible apparitions
Present you Prophecies which shall concern
Succeeding Princes which my Art shall raise,
Till men shall call these times the latter days.

Prince. Do it, my *Merlin,*
And Crown me with much joy and wonder.

Merlin strikes. Hoeboys. Enter a King in Armour, his Sheild quarter'd with thirteen Crowns. At the other door enter divers Princes who present their Crowns to him at his feet, and do him homage; then enters Death and strikes him; he, growing sick, Crowns Constantine. Exeunt.

Mer. This King, my Lord, presents your Royal Son,
Who in his prime of years shall be so fortunate,
That thirteen several Princes shall present
Their several Crowns unto him, and all Kings else
Shall so admire his fame and victories,
That they shall all be glad,
Either through fear or love, to do him homage;
But death (who neither favors the weak nor valliant)
In the middest of all his glories soon shall seize him,
Scarcely permitting him to appoint one
In all his purchased Kingdoms to succeed him.

Prince. Thanks to our Prophet
For this so wish'd for satisfaction;
And hereby now we learn that always Fate
Must be observ'd, what ever that decree:
All future times shall still record this Story,
Of *Merlin's* learned worth and *Arthur's* glory. [*Exeunt Omnes.*

FINIS.

86 incease *Q*

97 to him *T* 101 favours neither *T*

⟨SIR THOMAS MORE

AN ANONYMOUS PLAY OF THE SIXTEENTH CENTURY
ASCRIBED IN PART TO SHAKESPEARE.

FIRST PRINTED IN 1844

AND HERE RE-EDITED FROM THE HARLEIAN MS. 7368 IN THE
BRITISH MUSEUM⟩

MS.	= Manuscript, Harley 7368
Dyce	= Dyce's edition, 1844
Spedding	= conjectures in *Reviews and Discussions,* 1879
H	= Hopkinson, 1902
pr. ed.	= present editor

⟨SIR THOMAS MORE⟩[1]

⟨Dramatis Personæ.

Earl of Shrewsbury.
Earl of Surrey.
Sir Thomas Palmer.
Sir Roger Cholmley.
Sir John Munday.
Sir Thomas More.
Lord Mayor.
Aldermen.
Suresby, a Justice.
Other Justices.
Sheriffs.
Recorder.
Sergeant at Arms.
Clerk of the Council.
Erasmus.
Bishop of Rochester.
Roper, son-in-law to More.
John Lincoln, a broker.
George Betts.
His brother (the 'Clown').
Williamson, a carpenter.
Sherwin, a goldsmith.
Francis de Barde, } Lombards.
Caveler, } Lombards.
Lifter, a cut-purse.
Smart, plaintiff against him.

Harry, } Prentices.
Robin, } Prentices.
Kit, and others, } Prentices.
Morris.
Faulkner, his servant.
Players.
Gough, } Belonging to More's household.
Catesby, }
Randall, }
Butler, }
Brewer, }
Porter, }
Horsekeeper, }
Crofts.
Downes.
Lieutenant, } of the Tower.
Warders, } of the Tower.
Gentleman Porter, } of the Tower.
Hangman.
Lords, Gentlemen, Officers, Messengers, Guard, Attendants.

Lady More.
Lady Mayoress.
Mistress Roper, daughter to More.
Another daughter to More.
Doll, wife to Williamson.
A Poor Woman.
Ladies.⟩[2]

⟨ACT I.

Scene I.—London. A Street.⟩

Enter, at one end, Iohn Lincolne, *with* ⟨*the two* Bettses⟩ *together; at the other end, enters* Fraunces de ⟨Barde, *and* Doll⟩ *a lustie woman, he haling her by the arme.*

Doll. Whether wilt thou hale me?

Bard. Whether I please; thou art my prize, and I pleade purchase of thee.

Doll. Purchase of me! away, ye rascall! I am an honest plaine carpenters wife, and thoughe I haue no beautie to like a husband, yet whatsoeuer is mine scornes to stoupe to a straunger: hand off, then, when I bid thee!

Bard. Goe with me quietly, or Ile compell thee.

Doll. Compell me, ye dogges face! thou thinkst thou hast the goldsmiths wife in hand, whom thou enticedst from her husband with all his plate, and when thou turndst her home to him againe, madste him, like an asse, pay for his wifes boorde.

Bard. So will I make thy husband too, if please me.

Enter Caueler *with a paire of dooues;* Williamson *the carpenter, and* Sherwin *following him.*

Doll. Heere he comes himselfe; tell him so, if thou darste.

Caue. Followe me no further; I say thou shalt not haue them.

Wil. I bought them in Cheapeside, and paide my monie for them.

Sher. He did, sir, indeed; and you offer

[1] Sir Thomas More] *The name of the play is not given in the MS.* [2] *Add. Dyce* Act I. Scene I. *Acts and scenes first indicated H* S. D. *Bracketed words add. Dyce*

S. D. follows 20 in Dyce

him wrong, bothe to take them from him, and not restore him his monie neither.

Caue. If he paid for them, let it suffise that I possesse them: beefe and brewes may serue such hindes; are piggions meate for a coorse carpenter?

Lin. It is hard when Englishmens pacience must be thus jetted on by straungers, and they not dare to reuendge their owne wrongs.

Geo. Lincolne, lets beate them downe, and beare no more of these abuses.

Lin. We may not, Betts: be pacient, and heare more.

Doll. How now, husband! what, one straunger take thy food from thee, and another thy wife! bir-Lady, flesh and blood, I thinke, can hardly brooke that.

Lin. Will this geere neuer be otherwise? must these wrongs be thus endured?

Geo. Let vs step in, and help to reuendge their iniurie.

Bard. What art thou that talkest of reuendge? my lord ambassadour shall once more make your Maior haue a check, if he punishe thee not for this saucie presumption.

Will. Indeed, my lord Maior, on the ambassadours complainte, sent me to Newgate one day, because (against my will) I tooke the wall of a straunger: you may doo any thing; the goldsmith's wife and mine now must be at your comaundment.

Geo. The more pacient fooles are ye bothe, to suffer it.

Bard. Suffer it! mend it thou or he, if ye can or dare. I tell thee, fellowe, and she were the Maior of Londons wife, had I her once in my possession, I would keep her in spite of him that durst say nay.

Geo. I tell the, Lombard, these wordes should cost thy best cappe, were I not curbd by dutie and obedience: the Maior of Londons wife! Oh God, shall it be thus?

Doll. Why, Bettes, am not I as deare to my husband as my lord Maiors wife to him? and wilt thou so neglectly suffer thine owne shame? —Hands off, proude stranger! or, ⟨by⟩ him that bought me, if mens milkie harts dare not strike a straunger, yet women will beate them downe, ere they beare these abuses.

Bard. Mistresse, I say you shall along with me.

Doll. Touche not Doll Williamson, least she lay thee along on Gods deare earthe.—And you, sir (*To* Caueler), that allow such coorse cates to carpenters, whilste pidgions, which they pay for, must serue your daintie

71 by *add. Dyce*

appetite, deliuer them back to my husband again, or Ile call so many women to myne assistaunce as weele not leaue one inche vntorne of thee: if our husbands must be brideled by lawe, and forced to beare your wrongs, their wiues will be a little lawelesse, and soundly beate ye.

Caue. Come away, De Bard, and let vs goe complaine to my lord ambassadour. [*Ex. Ambo.*

Doll. I, goe, and send him among vs, and weele giue him his welcome too.—I am ashamed that freeborne Englishmen, hauing beatten straungers within their owne homes, should thus be brau'de and abusde by them at home.

Sher. It is not our lack of courage in the cause, but the strict obedience that we are bound too. I am the goldsmith whose wrongs you talkte of; but how to redresse yours or mine owne is a matter beyond all our abilities.

Lin. Not so, not so, my good freends: I, though a meane man, a broaker by profession, and namd Iohn Lincolne, haue long time winckt at these vilde ennormitees with mighty impacience, and, as these two bretheren heere (Betses by name) can witnesse, with losse of mine owne liffe would gladly remedie them.

Geo. And he is in a good forwardnesse, I tell ye, if all hit right.

Doll. As how, I prethee? tell it to Doll Williamson.

Lin. You knowe the Spittle sermons begin the next weeke: I haue drawne a ⟨bill⟩ of our wrongs and the straungers insolencies.

Geo. Which he meanes the preachers shall there openly publishe in the pulpit.

Wil. Oh, but that they would! yfaith, it would tickle our straungers thorowly.

Doll. I, and if you men durst not vndertake it, before God, we women ⟨would. Take⟩ an honest woman from her husband! why, it is intollerable.

Sher. But how finde ye the preachers affected to ⟨our proceeding⟩?

Lin. Master Doctor Standish ⟨hath answered that it becomes not him to move any such thing in his sermon, and tells us we must move the Mayor and aldermen to⟩ ⟨re⟩forme it, and doubts not but happie successe will ensu⟨e on statement of⟩ our wrongs. You shall perceiue ther's no hurt in the bill: heer's a copie of it; I pray ye, heare it.

114 bill *add. Dyce* 121 would. Take *add. Dyce* 125 our proceeding *add. Dyce* 126–9 hath . . alder-men to *add. H*: *MS. illegible* 129 reforme *Dyce* 131 ensue on statement of *pr. ed.*: ensure redress of *H*: *MS. illegible*

All. With all our harts; for Gods sake, read it.

Lin. ⟨*reads.*⟩ *To you all, the worshipfull lords and maisters of this cittie, that will take compassion ouer the poore people your neighbours, and also of the greate importable hurts, losses, and hinderaunces, wherof proceedeth extreame pouertie to all the kings subiects that inhabite within this cittie and subburbs of the same: ffor so it is that aliens and straungers eate the bread from the fatherlesse children, and take the liuing from all the artificers and the entercourse from all merchants, wherby pouertie is so much encreased, that euery man bewayleth the miserie of other; for craftsmen be brought to beggerie, and merchants to needines: wherfore, the premisses considered, the redresse must be of the commons knit and vnited to one parte: and as the hurt and damage greeueth all men, so must all men see to their willing power for remedie, and not suffer the sayde aliens in their wealth, and the naturall borne men of this region to come to confusion.*

Doll. Before God, tis excellent; and Ile maintaine the suite to be honest.

Sher. Well, say tis read, what is your further meaning in the matter?

Geo. What! marie, list to me. No doubt but this will store vs with freends enow, whose names we will closely keepe in writing; and on May day next in the morning weele goe foorthe a Maying, but make it the wurst May day for the straungers that euer they sawe. How say ye? doo ye subscribe, or are ye faint-harted reuolters?

Doll. Holde thee, George Bettes, ther's my hand and my hart: by the Lord, Ile make a captaine among ye, and doo somewhat to be talke of for euer after.

Wil. My maisters, ere we parte, lets freendly goe and drinke together, and sweare true secrecie vppon our liues.

Geo. There spake an angell. Come, let vs along, then. [*Exeunt.*

⟨SCENE II.—London. *The Sessions House.*⟩

An arras is drawne, and behinde it (as in sessions) sit the L..Maior, Iustice Suresbie, *and other Justices; Sheriffe* Moore *and the other Sherife sitting by.* Smart *is the plaintife,* Lifter *the prisoner at the barre.* ⟨*Recorder, Officers.*⟩

L. Mai. Hauing dispachte our weightier businesses,
We may giue eare to pettie fellonies.
M⟨aiste⟩r Sheriffe Moore, what is this fellowe?

Moore. My lord, he stands indited for a pursse;
He hath bin tryed, the jurie is together.

Mai. Who sent him in?

Sure. That did I, my lord:
Had he had right, he had bin hangd ere this;
The only captayne of the cutpursse crewe.

L. Mai. What is his name?

Sure. As his profession is, Lifter, my lord,
One that can lift a purse right cunningly.

L. Mai. And is that he accuses him?

Sure. The same, my lord, whom, by your honors leaue,
I must say somewhat too, because I finde
In some respectes he is well woorthie blame.

L. Mai. Good M⟨aiste⟩r Justice Suresbie, speake your minde;
We are well pleasde to giue you audience.

Sure. Heare me, Smart; thou art a foolish fellowe:
If Lifter be conuicted by the lawe,
As I see not how the jurie can acquit him,
Ile stand too't thou art guiltie of his death.

Moore. My lord, thats woorthe the hearing.

L. Mai. Listen, then, good Maister Moore.

Sure. I tell thee plaine, it is a shame for thee,
With such a sum to tempte necessitie;
No lesse then ten poundes, sir, will serue your turne,
To carie in your pursse about with ye,
To crake and brag in tauernes of your monie:
I promise ye, a man that goes abroade
With an intent of trueth, meeting such a bootie,
May be prouokte to that he neuer meante.
What makes so many pilferers and fellons,
But such fond baites that foolish people lay
To tempt the needie miserable wretche?
Ten poundes, odd monie; this is a prettie sum
To beare about, which were more safe at home.
Fore God, twere well to fine ye as much more
[*Lord Maior and* Moore *whisper.*
To the releefe of the po⟨ore pri⟩soners,
To teache ye be ⟨more careful of⟩ your owne,
⟨In sooth, I say ye were but⟩ rightlie seru'de.
⟨If ye had lost as much as twice ten pounds.⟩

Moore. Good my lord, soothe a ⟨point or two⟩ for once,
Only to trye conclusions in this case.

L. Maior. Content, good M⟨aiste⟩r Moore: weele rise awhile,
And, till the jurie can returne their verdict,
Walke in the garden.—How saye ye, Justices?

Scene II. *etc. add. H*   *S. D.* Recorder *etc. add. Dyce.*   39 po⟨ore pri⟩soners *Dyce*   40–3 *Bracketed words add. H*: *MS. illegible*

All. We like it well, my lord; weele follow ye. [*Ex. L. Maior and Iustices.*
Moore Nay, plaintife, goe you too;—and, officers, [*Ex.* Smart.
Stand you aside, and leaue the prisoner
To me awhile.—Lifter, come hether.
Lift. What is your woorships pleasure?
Moore. Sirra, you knowe that you are knowne to me,
And I haue often sau'de ye from this place,
Since first I came in office: thou seest beside,
That Justice Suresbie is thy heauie freend,
By all the blame that he pretends to Smarte,
For tempting thee with such a summe of monie.
I tell thee what; deuise me but a meanes
To pick or cutt his pursse, and, on my credit,
And as I am a Christian and a man,
I will procure thy pardon for that jeast.
Lift. Good M⟨aiste⟩r Shreeue, seeke not my ouerthrowe:
You knowe, sir, I haue manie heauie freends,
And more endictments like to come vppon me.
You are too deepe for me to deale withall;
You are knowne to be one of the wisest men
That is in England: I pray ye, M⟨aiste⟩r Sheriffe,
Goe not aboute to vndermine my life.
Moore. Lifter, I am true subiect to my king;
Thou much mistakste me: and, for thou shalt not thinke
I meane by this to hurt thy life at all,
I will maintaine the act when thou hast doone it.
Thou knowest there are such matters in my hands,
As if I pleasde to giue them to the jurie,
I should not need this way to circumuent thee.
All that I aime at is a merrie iest:
Performe it, Lifter, and expect my best.
Lift. I thanke your woorship: God preserue your life!
But Master Justice Suresbie is gon in;
I knowe not how to come neere where he is.
Moore. Let me alone for that; Ile be thy setter;
Ile send him hether to thee presently,
Vnder the couller of thine owne request,
Of priuate matters to acquainte him with.
Lift. If ye doo so, sir, then let me alone;
Fortie to one but then his pursse is gon.
Moore. Well said: but see that thou diminish not
One penie of the monie, but giue it me;
It is the cunning act that credits thee.
Lift. I will, good Master Sheriffe, I assure ye. [*Ex.* Moore.
I see the purpose of this gentleman
Is but to check the follie of the Justice,
For blaming others in a desperate case,
Wherin himselfe may fall as soone as any.
To saue my life, it is a good aduenter:
Silence there, hoe! now dooth the Justice enter.

Ent. Iust. Suresbie.

Sure. Now, sirra, now, what is your will with me?
Wilt thou discharge thy conscience like an honest man?
What sayst to me, sirra? be breefe, be breef.
Lift. As breefe, sir, as I can.—
If ye stand fayre, I will be breefe annon. [*Aside.*
Sure. Speake out, and mumble not; what saist thou, sirra?
Lift. Sir, I am chargde, as God shall be my comforte,
With more then's true.
Sure. Sir, sir, ye are indeed, with more then's true,
For you are flatly chargde with fellonie;
You'r chargde with more then trueth, and that is theft;
More then a true man should be chargde withall;
Thou art a varlet, that's no more then true.
Trifle not with me; doo not, doo not, sirra;
Confesse but what thou knowest, I aske no more.
Lift, There be, sir, there be, ift shall please your woorship——
Sure. There be, varlet! what be there? tell me what there be.
Come off or on: there be! what be there, knaue?
Lift. There be, sir, diuers very cunning fellowes,
That, while you stand and looke them in the face,
Will haue your pursse.
Sure. Th'art an honest knaue:
Tell me what are they? where they may be caught?
I, those are they I looke for.
Lift. You talke of me, sir;
Alas, I am a punie! ther's one indeed
Goes by my name, he puts downe all for pursses;
⟨He'll steal your worship's purse under your nose.
Sure. Ha, ha! Art thou so sure, varlet? Well, well,

51 *Hopkinson inserts S. D.* Exeunt Officers *after* awhile 67-9 *Lines divided in MS. after* England, aboute

125-7 *Bracketed words add. H: MS. illegible*

Be⟩ as familiare as thou wilt, my knaue;
Tis this I long to knowe.
Lift. And you shall haue your longing ere ye goe.—
This fellowe, sir, perhaps will meete ye thus,
Or thus, or thus, and in kinde complement
Pretend acquaintaunce, somewhat doubtfully;
And these embraces serue——
Sure. I, marie, Lifter, wherfore serue they? [*Shrugging gladly.*
Lift. Only to feele
Whether you goe full vnder saile or no,
Or that your lading be aboord your barke.
Sure. In playner English, Lifter, if my pursse
Be storde or no?
Lift. Ye haue it, sir.
Sure. Excellent, excellent.
Lift. Then, sir, you cannot but for manners sake
Walke on with him; for he will walke your way,
Alleadging either you haue much forgot him,
Or he mistakes you.
Sure. But in this time has he my pursse or no?
Lift. Not yet, sir, fye!—no, nor I haue not yours.— ⟨*Aside.*⟩

Ent. Lord Maior, &c.

But now we must forbeare; my lords returne.
Sure. A murren on't!—Lifter, weele more annon:
I, thou sayst true, there are shrewde knaues indeed; [*He sits downe.*
But let them gull me, widgen me, rooke me, foppe me!
Yfaith, yfaith, they are too short for me.
Knaues and fooles meete when pursses goe;
Wise men looke to their pursses well enough.
Moore. Lifter, is it doone?
Lift. Doone, M⟨aiste⟩r Shreeue; and there it is. ⟨*Aside.*⟩
Moore. Then builde vppon my woord, Ile saue thy life. ⟨*Aside.*⟩
Recor. Lifter, stand to the barre:
The jurie haue returnd thee guiltie; thou must dye,
According to the custome.—Looke to it, M⟨aiste⟩r Shreeue.
L. Maior. Then, gentlemen, as you are wunt to doo,
Because as yet we haue no buriall place,
What charitie your meaning's to bestowe
Toward buriall of the prisoners now condemnde,
Let it be giuen. There is first for me.
Recor. And thers for me.
Another. And me.
Sure. Bodie of me, my pursse is gon!
Moore. Gon, sir! what, heere! how can that be?
L. Maior. Against all reason, sitting on the benche.
Sure. Lifter, I talkte with you; you haue not lifted me? ha!
Lift. Suspect ye me, sir? Oh, what a world is this!
Moore. But heare ye, M⟨aiste⟩r Suresbie; are ye sure
Ye had a pursse about ye?
Sure. Sure, M⟨aiste⟩r Shreeue! as sure as you are there,
And in it seauen poundes, odd monie, on my faith.
Moore. Seauen poundes, odd monie! what, were you so madd,
Beeing a wise man and a magistrate,
To trust your pursse with such a liberall sum?
Seauen poundes, odd monie! fore God, it is a shame,
With such a summe to tempt necessitie:
I promise ye, a man that goes abroade
With an intent of trueth, meeting such a bootie,
May be wrought to that he neuer thought.
What makes so many pilferers and fellons,
But these fond baites that foolish people lay
To tempte the needie miserable wretche?
Should he be taken now that has your pursse,
Ide stand too't, you are guiltie of his death;
For, questionlesse, he would be cast by lawe.
Twere a good deed to fine ye as much more,
To the releefe of the poore prisoners,
To teache ye lock your monie vp at home.
Sure. Well, M⟨aiste⟩r Moore, you are a merie man;
I finde ye, sir, I finde ye well enough.
Moore. Nay, ye shall see, sir, trusting thus your monie,
And Lifter here in triall for like case,
But that the poore man is a prisoner,
It would be now suspected that he had it.
Thus may ye see what mischeefe often comes
By the fond cariage of such needlesse summes.
L. Maior. Beleeue me, M⟨aiste⟩r Suresbie, this is straunge,
You, beeing a man so setled in assuraunce,
Will fall in that which you condemnd in other.
Moore. Well, M⟨aiste⟩r Suresbie, theres your pursse agayne,

138–9 *One line in MS.*   *S. D. follows* 148 *Dyce*

And all your monie: feare nothing of Moore;
Wisedome still ⟨keeps the mean and locks⟩ the doore.

⟨Scene III.—London. A state apartment.⟩

Enter the Earles of Shrewesburie *and* Surrie, *Sir* Thomas Palmer, *and Sir* Roger Cholmeley.

Shrew. My lord of Surrey, and Sir Thomas Palmer,
Might I with pacience tempte your graue aduise,
I tell ye true, that in these daungerous times
I doo not like this frowning vulgare brow:
My searching eye did neuer entertaine
A more distracted countenaunce of greefe
Then I haue late obseru'de
In the displeased commons of the cittie.

Sur. Tis straunge that from his princely clemencie,
So well a tempred mercie and a grace,
To all the aliens in this fruitefull land,
That this highe-creasted insolence should spring
From them that breathe from his maiestick bountie,
That, fatned with the trafficque of our countrey,
Alreadie leape into his subiects face.

Pal. Yet Sherwin, hindred to commence his suite
Against De Bard by the ambassadour,
By supplication made vnto the king,
Who hauing first entic'de away his wife,
And gott his plate, neere woorth foure hundred pound,
To greeue some wronged cittizens that found
This vile disgrace oft cast into their teeth,
Of late sues Sherwin, and arrested him
For monie for the boording of his wife.

Sur. The more knaue Bard, that, vsing Sherwins goods,
Dooth aske him interest for the occupation.
I like not that, my lord of Shrewesburie:
Hees ill bested that lends a well pac'de horsse
Vnto a man that will not finde him meate.

Cholme. My lord of Surrey will be pleasant still.

Pal. I, beeing then imployed by your honors
To stay the broyle that fell about the same,
Wher by perswasion I enforc'de the wrongs,
And vrgde the greefe of the displeased cittie,
He answerd me, and with a sollemne oathe,
That, if he had the Maior of Londons wife,
He would keepe her in despight of any Englishe.

Sur. Tis good, Sir Thomas, then, for you and me;
Your wife is dead, and I a batcheler:
If no man can possesse his wife alone,
I am glad, Sir Thomas Palmer, I haue none.

Cholme. If a take my wife, a shall finde her meate.

Sur. And reason good, Sir Roger Cholmeley, too.
If these hott Frenchemen needsly will haue sporte,
They should in kindnesse yet deffraye the charge:
Tis hard when men possesse our wiues in quiet,
And yet leaue vs in, to discharge their diett.

Shrew. My lord, our catours shall not vse the markett
For our prouision, but some straunger now
Will take the vittailes from him he hath bought:
A carpenter, as I was late enformde,
Who hauing bought a paire of dooues in Cheape,
Immediatly a Frencheman tooke them from him,
And beat the poore man for resisting him;
And when the fellowe did complaine his wrongs,
He was seuerely punish'de for his labour.

Sur. But if the Englishe blood be once but vp,
As I perceiue theire harts alreadie full,
I feare me much, before their spleenes be coolde,
Some of these saucie aliens for their pride
Will pay for't soundly, wheresoere it lights:
This tyde of rage that with the eddie striues,
I feare me much, will drowne too manie liues.

Cholme. Now, afore God, your honors, pardon me:
Men of your place and greatnesse are to blame.
I tell ye true, my lords, in that his maiestie
Is not informed of this base abuse
And dayly wrongs are offered to his subiects;
For, if he were, I knowe his gracious wisedome
Would soone redresse it.

Enter a Messenger.

Shrew. Sirra, what newes?

Cholme. None good, I feare.

Mess. My lord, ill newes; and wurse, I feare, will followe,

207 *Bracketed words add. H* Scene III. *H* 1 ff. *Beside these lines is written* Mend y[t] *(by Tylney)*

37 Englishe] *Tylney has deleted this word, substituting* man 49 straunger] *Tylney has substituted* Lombard 53 Frencheman] Lombard *Tylney* 57–63 *Cross marks on margin of MS. indicate Tylney's disapproval*

If speedily it be not lookte vnto:
The cittie is in an vproare, and the Maior
Is threatned, if he come out of his house.
A number poore artifi⟨cers⟩ ⟨are up
In arms and threaten to avenge their wrongs.

Chol. We⟩ fearde what this would come vnto:
This followes on the doctors publishing
The bill of wrongs in publique at the Spittle.

Shrew. That Doctor Beale may chaunce beshrewe himselfe
For reading of the bill.

Pal. Let vs goe gather forces to the Maior,
For quick suppressing this rebellious route.

Sur. Now I bethinke myselfe of Maister Moore,
One of the sheriffes, a wise and learned gentleman,
And in especiall fauour with the people:
He, backt with other graue and sober men,
May by his gentle and perswasiue speeche
Perhaps preuaile more then we can with power.

Shrew. Beleeue me, but your honor well aduises:
Let vs make haste; for I doo greatly feare
Some to their graues this mornings woorke will beare. [*Exeunt.*

⟨ACT II.

Scene I.—Cheapside.⟩

Enter three or foure Prentises of trades, with a paire of cudgelles.

Harry. Come, lay downe the cudgelles. Hoh, Robin, you met vs well at Bunhill, to haue you with vs a Mayng this morning!

Robin. Faith, Harrie, the head drawer at the Miter by the great Conduite calld me vp, and we went to breakefast into St. Annes lane. But come, who beginnes? in good faith, I am cleane out of practise. When wast at Garrets schoole, Harrie?

Har. Not this great while, neuer since I brake his vshers head, when he plaid his schollers prize at the Starre in Bread-streete. I vse all to George Philpots at Dowgate; hees the best backswordeman in England.

Kit. Bate me an ace of that, quoth Bolton.

Har. Ile not bate ye a pinne on't, sir; for, by this cudgell, tis true.

Kit. I will cudgell that oppinion out of ye: did you breake an vshers head, sir?

Har. I, marie, did I, sir.

Kit. I am very glad on't: you shall breake mine too, and ye can.

Har. Sirra, I prethee, what art thou?

Kit. Why, I am a prentise as thou art; seest thou now? Ile play with thee at blunt heere in Cheapeside, and when thou hast doone, if thou beest angrie, Ile fight with thee at ⟨sharpe⟩ in Moore feildes. I haue a swoord to serue my turne in a fauor . . .
come Julie, to serue . . . .

⟨Scene II.—Saint Martins-le-Grand.⟩

Enter Lincolne, ⟨*two*⟩ Betses, Williamson, Sherwin, *and other, armed;* Doll *in a shirt of maile, a headpiece, sword, and buckler; a crewe attending.*

Clo. Come, come; wele tickle ther turnips, wele butter ther boxes. Shall strangers rule the roste? yes; but wele baste the roste. Come, come; a flawnt, a flaunte!

George. Brother, giue place, and heare Iohn Lincolne speake.

Clo. I, Lincolne my leder,
And Doll my true breder,
With the rest of our crue,
Shall ran tan tarra ran;
Doo all they what they can.
Shall we be bobd, braude? no:
Shall we be hellde vnder? no;
We ar freborne,
And doo take skorne
To be vsde soe.

Doll. Pease theare, I saye! heare Captaine Lincolne speake; Kepe silens, till we know his minde at large.

Clo. Then largelye dilliuer; speake, bullie: and he that presumes to interrupte the in thie orratione, this for him.

Lincol. Then, gallant bloods, you whoes fre sowles doo skorne
To beare the inforsed wrongs of aliens,
Ad rage to ressolutione, fier the howses
Of theis audatious strangers. This is St. Martins,
And yonder dwells Mutas, a welthy Piccardye,
At the Greene Gate,
De Bard, Peter Van Hollocke, Adrian Martine,
With many more outlandishe fugetiues.
Shall theis enioy more priueledge then wee
In our owne cuntry? lets, then, become ther slaues.

77 number of poor *H* artifi⟨cers⟩ *Dyce* 77–9 are In arms . . We *add. H* 94 *After this the MS. has the first sketch of Act II, Scene II, which was later elaborated* Act II. *etc. add. H*

28 sharpe *add. Dyce* 29–30 *MS. illegible* 30 *These lines are followed in MS. by the later draft of IV. v. 68 ff. See Appendix*, p. 419–20 Scene II. *etc. add. N* *S. D. from first sketch : omitted in revised version* 3 baste yt the roste *MS.* 27 Piccarde *in first sketch of the scene* 32 then] *from first sketch : omitted in revised version*

Since justis kepes not them in greater awe,
Wele be ourselues roughe ministers at lawe.

Clo. Vse no more swords, nor no more words, but fier the houses; braue captaine curragious, fier me ther houses.

Doll. I, for we maye as well make bonefiers on Maye daye as at midsommer: wele alter the daye in the callinder, and sett itt downe in flaming letters.

Sher. Staye!
No, that wold much indanger the hole cittie,
Whertoo I wold not the least preiudice.

Doll. No, nor I nether; so maie mine owne howse be burnd for companye. Ile tell ye what; wele drag the strangers into More feldes, and theare bumbaste them till they stinke againe.

Clo. And thats soone doone; for they smell for feare allredye.

Geor. Let some of vs enter the strangers houses,
And, if we finde them theare, then bringe them forthe.

Doll. But if ye bringe them forthe eare ye finde them, Ile neare alowe of thatt.

Clo. Now, Marsse, for thie honner,
Dutch or Frenshe,
So yt be a wenshe,
Ile vppon hir. [*Ex. some and* Sher.

Willia. Now, lads, sure shall we labor in our saftie.
I heare the Maire hath gatherd men in armes,
And that Shreue More an hower agoe risseude
Some of the Privye Cownsell in at Ludgate:
Forse now must make our pease, or eles we fall;
Twill soone be knowne we ar the principall.

Doll. And what of that? if thou beest afraide, husband, go home againe, and hide thy hed; for, by the Lord, Ile haue a lyttill sporte, now we ar att ytt.

Geor. Lets stand vppon our swerds, and, if they come,
Resseaue them as they weare our ennemyes.

En. Sher. *and the rest.*

Clo. A purchase, a purchase! we haue fownd, we ha fownde——

Doll. What?

Clo. Nothinge; nott a Frenshe Fleming nor a Fleming Frenshe to be fownde; but all fled, in plaine Inglishe.

Linco. How now! haue you fownd any?

Sher. No, not one; theyre all fled.

Lincol. Then fier the houses, that, the Maier beinge busye
Aboute the quenshinge of them, we mayeskape;
Burne downe ther kennells: let vs straite awaye,
Leaste this daye proue to vs an ill Maye daye.

Clo. Fier, fier! ile be the firste:
If hanging come, tis welcome; thats the worste. [*exeunt.*

⟨SCENE III.—The Guildhall.⟩

Enter at on dore S⟨i⟩r Thomas Moore *and Lord Maire; att an other doore Sir* Iohn Munday *hurt.*

L. Maior. What, Sir Iohn Munday, are you hurt?

Sir Iohn. A little knock, my lord. Ther was even now
A sort of prentises playing at cudgells;
I did comaund them to ther m⟨aisters'⟩ howses;
But one of them, backt by the other crew,
Wounded me in the forhead with his cudgill;
And now, I feare me, they are gon to joine
With Lincolne, Sherwine, and ther dangerous traine.

Moore. The captaines of this insurection
Have tane themselves to armes, and cam but now
To both the Counters, wher they haue releast
Sundrie indetted prisoners, and from thence
I heere that they are gonn into St. Martins,
Wher they intend to offer violence
To the amazed Lombards: therfore, my lord,
If we expect the saftie of the cittie,
Tis time that force or parley doe encownter
With thes displeased men.

Enter a Messenger.

L. Maior. How now! what newes?

Mess. My lord, the rebells haue broake open Newegate,
From whence they haue deliuerd manie prisoners,
Both fellons and notorious murderers,
That desperatlie cleaue to ther lawles traine.

L. Maior. Vpp with the drawbridge, gather som forces
To Cornhill and Cheapside:—and, gentlemen,

36-7 *All.* Fire the houses, fire the houses *first sketch* 42-3 *One line in MS.* 43 No, that] that *first sketch* 47 into] out into *first sketch* 54 But if] If *first sketch* eare] before *first sketch* 56-9 *Not in first sketch* 59 *S. D. from first sketch where it follows* 52 60 sure] how *first sketch* 69 we ar] I am *first sketch* 70 swerds] guarde *first sketch* 71 *S. D. from first sketch*

79 No, not] Not *first sketch* theyre all] th are *first sketch* 83 Leaste] Least that *first sketch* 84-5 *Not in first sketch* 85 exeunt *first sketch* : Manett Clowne *revised version, in different handwriting and certainly wrong* Scene III. *etc. add. H.*

If dilligence be vsde one every side,
A quiet ebb will follow this rough tide.

Enter Shrowsberie, Surrie, Palmer, Cholmley.

Shro. Lord Maior, his maiestie, receauing notice
Of this most dangerous insurection,
Hath sent my lord of Surry and myself,
Sir Thomas Palmer and our followers,
To add vnto your forces our best meanes
For pacifying of this mutinie.
In Gods name, then, sett one with happie speed!
The king laments, if one true subiect bleede.

Surr. I heere they meane to fier the Lumbards howses:
Oh power, what art thou in a madmans eies!
Thou makst the plodding iddiott bloudy-wise.

Moore. My lords, I dowt not but we shall appease
With a calm breath this flux of discontent:
To call them to a parley, questionles——

Palme. May fall out good: tis well said, M⟨aiste⟩r Moore.

Moor. Letts to thes simple men; for many sweat
Vnder this act, that knowes not the lawes debtt
Which hangs vppon ther lives; for sillie men
Plodd on they know not how, like a fooles penn,
That, ending, showes not any sentence writt,
Linckt but to common reason or sleightest witt:
Thes follow for no harme; but yett incurr
Self penaltie with those that raisd this stirr.
A Gods name, one, to calme our priuat foes
With breath of gravitie, not dangerous blowes!

[*Exeunt.*

⟨Scene IV.—Saint Martin's Gate.⟩

Enter Lincoln, Doll, *Clown,* Georg Betts, Williamson, *others; and a Sergaunt at armes.*

Lincolne. Peace, heare me: he that will not see a red hearing at a Herry grote, butter at alevenpence a pounde, meale at nyne shillings a bushell, and beeff at fower nobles a stone, lyst to me.

Geo. Bett. Yt will come to that passe, yf straingers be sufferd. Mark him.

Linco. Our countrie is a great eating country; argo, they eate more in our countrey then they do in their owne.

Betts. Clow. By a halfpenny loff, a day, troy waight.

Linc. They bring in straing rootes, which is meerly to the vndoing of poor prentizes; for whats a sorry parsnyp to a good hart?

William. Trash, trash; they breed sore eyes, and tis enough to infect the cytty with the palsey.

Lin. Nay, yt has infected yt with the palsey; for theise basterds of dung, as you knowe they growe in dung, haue infected vs, and yt is our infeccion will make the cytty shake, which partly coms through the eating of parsnyps.

Clown. Betts. Trewe; and pumpions togeather.

Seriant. What say ye to the mercy of the king?
Do ye refuse yt?

Lin. You would haue vs vppon thipp, woold you? no, marry, do we not; we accept of the kings mercy, but wee will showe no mercy vppon the straungers.

Seriaunt. You are the simplest things that euer stood
In such a question.

Lin. How say ye now, prentisses? prentisses symple! downe with him!

All. Prentisses symple! prentisses symple!

Enter the L. Maier, Surrey, Shrewsbury, ⟨More.⟩

Maior. Hold! in the kinges name, hold!

Surrey. Frendes, masters, countrymen——

Mayer. Peace, how, peace! I charg you, keep the peace!

Shro. My maisters, countrymen——

Williamson. The noble earle of Shrowsbury, letts hear him.

Ge. Betts. Weele heare the earle of Surrey.

Linc. The earle of Shrewsbury.

Betts. Weele heare both.

All. Both, both, both, both!

Linc. Peace, I say, peace! ar you men of wisdome, or what ar you?

Surr. What you will haue them; but not men of wisdome.

All. Weele not heare my lord of Surrey; no, no, no, no, no! Shrewsbury, Shrewsbury!

Moor. Whiles they ar ore the banck of their obedyence,
Thus will they bere downe all things.

Linc. Shreiff Moor speakes: shall we heare Shreef Moor speake?

Doll. Letts heare him: a keepes a plenty-

32 your forces *Dyce*: our forces *MS.* 37 thou *Dyce*: then *MS.* 43 thes] the *Dyce* Scene IV. *etc. add. H.*

37 *S. D.* More *add. pr. ed.*: Palmer, Cholmeley, and More *add. H*

full shrevaltry, and a made my brother Arther Watchins Seriant Safes yeoman: lets heare Shreeue Moore.

All. Shreiue Moor, Moor, More, Shreue Moore!

Moor. Even by the rule you haue among yoursealues,
Comand still audience.

All. Surrey, Sury!

All. Moor, Moor!

Lincolne. } *Betts.* } Peace, peace, scilens, peace.

Moor. You that haue voyce and credyt with the number,
Comaund them to a stilnes.

Lincolne. A plaigue on them, they will not hold their peace; the deule cannot rule them.

Moore. Then what a rough and ryotous charge haue you,
To leade those that the deule cannot rule?——
Good masters, heare me speake.

Doll. I, byth mas, will we, Moor: thart a good howskeeper, and I thanck thy good worship for my brother Arthur Watchins.

All. Peace, peace.

Moor. Look, what you do offend you cry vppon,
That is, the peace: not ⟨one⟩ of you heare present,
Had there such fellowes lyvd when you wer babes,
That coold haue topt the peace, as nowe you woold,
The peace wherin you haue till nowe growne vp
Had bin tane from you, and the bloody tymes
Coold not haue brought you to the state of men.
Alas, poor things, what is yt you haue gott,
Although we graunt you geat the thing you seeke?

Bett. Marry, the remouing of the straingers, which cannot choose but much advauntage the poor handycrafts of the cytty.

Moor. Graunt them remoued, and graunt that this your noyce
Hath chidd downe all the maiestie of Ingland;
Ymagin that you see the wretched straingers,
Their babyes at their backes and their poor lugage,
Plodding tooth ports and costes for transportacion,
And that you sytt as kinges in your desyres,
Aucthoryty quyte sylenct by your braule,
And you in ruff of your opynions clothd;
What had you gott? I'le tell you: you had taught
How insolence and strong hand shoold preuayle,
How ordere shoold be quelld; and by this patterne
Not on of you shoold lyue an aged man,
For other ruffians, as their fancies wrought,
With sealf same hand, sealf reasons, and sealf right,
Woold shark on you, and men lyke rauenous fishes
Woold feed on on another.

Doll. Before God, thats as trewe as the Gospell.

Lincoln. Nay, this ⟨is⟩ a sound fellowe, I tell you: lets mark him.

Moor. Let me sett vp before your thoughts, good freindes,
On supposytion; which if you will marke,
You shall perceaue howe horrible a shape
Your ynnouation beres: first, tis a sinn
Which oft thappostle did forwarne vs of,
Vrging obedience to authority;
And twere no error, yf I told you all,
You wer in armes gainst your ⟨God himself⟩

All. Marry, God forbid that!

Moo. Nay, certainly you are;
For to the king God hath his offyce lent
Of dread, of justyce, power and comaund,
Hath bid him rule, and willd you to obay;
And, to add ampler maiestie to this,
He hath not only lent the king his figure,
His throne and sword, but gyuen him his owne name,
Calls him a god on earth. What do you, then,
Rysing gainst him that God himsealf enstalls,
But ryse gainst God? what do you to your sowles
In doing this? O, desperat as you are,
Wash your foule mynds with teares, and those same handes,
That you lyke rebells lyft against the peace,
Lift vp for peace, and your vnreuerent knees,
Make them your feet to kneele to be forgyuen!
Tell me but this; what rebell captaine,
As mutynies ar incident, by his name
Can still the rout? who will obay a traytor?
Or howe can well that proclamation sounde,
When ther is no adicion but a rebell
To quallyfy a rebell? Youle put downe straingers,
Kill them, cutt their throts, possesse their howses,
And leade the ma⟨ies⟩tie of lawe in liom,

81 one *H*: *MS. illegible* 83 topt] kept *Spedding. The word is indistinct, but Dr. Furnivall and Mr. Herbert of the British Museum favour Dyce's reading.* 111 is *add. Dyce* 119 God himself *conj. Spedding*: sovereign *Dyce* 135–6 *Deletion in MS. Cf. Introduction.* 138 *Deletion after* obay *in MS.*

To slipp him lyke a hound. Say nowe the king
(As he is clement, yf thoffendor moorne)
Shoold so much com to short of your great trespas
As but to banysh you, whether woold you go?
What country, by the nature of your error,
Shoold geue you harber? go you to Fraunce or Flanders,
To any Jarman prouince, to Spaine or Portigall,
Nay, any where that not adheres to Ingland,—
Why, you must needes be straingers: woold you be pleasd
To find a nation of such barbarous temper,
That, breaking out in hiddious violence,
Woold not afoord you an abode on earth,
Whett their detested knyues against your throtes,
Spurne you lyke dogges, and lyke as yf that God
Owed not nor made not you, nor that the elamentes
Wer not all appropriat to your comfortes,
But charterd vnto them, what woold you thinck
To be thus vsd? this is the straingers case;
And this your momtanish inhumanytye.

All. Fayth, a saies trewe: letts do as we may be doon by.

Linco. Weele be ruld by you, Maister Moor, yf youle stand our freind to procure our pardon.

Moor. Submyt you to theise noble gentlemen,
Entreate their mediation to the kinge,
Geue vp yoursealfe to forme, obay the maiestrate,
And thers no doubt but mercy maie be found,
Yf you so seek.
To persist in it is present death: but, if you yeeld yourselues, no doubt what punishment you in simplicitie haue incurred, his highnesse in mercie will moste graciously pardon.

All. We yeeld, and desire his highnesse mercie. [*They lay by their weapons.*

Moore. No doubt his maiestie will graunt it you:
But you must yeeld to goe to seuerall prisons,
Till that his highnesse will be further knowne.

All. Moste willingly; whether you will haue vs.

Shrew. Lord Maior, let them be sent to seuerall prisons,
And there, in any case, be well intreated.—
My lord of Surrie, please you to take horsse,
And ride to Cheapeside, where the aldermen
Are with their seuerall companies in armes;
Will them to goe vnto their seuerall wardes,
Bothe for the stay of further mutinie,
And for the apprehending of such persons
As shall contend.

Sur. I goe, my noble lord. [*Ex.* Sur.

Shrew. Weele straite goe tell his highnesse these good newes;
Withall, Shreeue Moore, Ile tell him how your breath
Hath ransomde many a subiect from sad death.
[*Ex.* Shrew. *and* Cholm.

L. Maior. Lincolne and Sherwine, you shall bothe to Newgate;
The rest vnto the Counters.

Pal. Goe guarde them hence: a little breath well spent
Cheates expectation in his fairst euent.

Doll. Well, Sheriffe Moore, thou hast doone more with thy good woordes then all they could with their weapons: giue me thy hand; keepe thy promise now for the kings pardon, or, by the Lord, Ile call thee a plaine coniecatcher.

Lin. Farewell, Shreeue Moore; and as we yeeld by thee,
So make our peace; then thou dealst honestly.

Clo. Ay, and saue vs from the gallowes, eles a deules debble honnestlye!
[*They are led away.*

L. Maior. Maister Shreeue Moore, you haue preseru'de the cittie
From a moste daungerous fierce commotion;
For, if this limbe of riot heere in St. Martins
Had ioind with other braunches of the cittie
That did begin to kindle, twould haue bred
Great rage; that rage much murder would haue fed.
Not steele, but eloquence hath wrought this good:
You haue redeemde vs from much threatned blood.

Moore. My lord and bretheren, what I heere haue spoke,
My countries looue, and next the citties care,
Enioynde me to; which since it thus preuailes,
Thinke, God hath made weake Moore his instrument
To thwart seditions violent intent.
I thinke twere best, my lord, some two houres hence
We meete at the Guildehall, and there determine
That thorow euery warde the watche be clad

144 *Deletion after* hound *in MS.* 151 *Deletion after* where *in MS.* 159 all] alike *conj.* *Spedding* *Deletion after* to *in MS.* 162 momtanish] mountanish *Dyce* 173 *With this line the handwriting of MS. changes*

209–10 *Add. in different hand on margin of MS.*

In armour, but especially prouide
That at the cittie gates selected men,
Substantiall cittizens, doo warde to night,
For feare of further mischeife.
L. Maior. It shall be so:
But yond me thinks my lord of Shrewesburie.

Ent. Shrew.

Shrew. My lord, his maiestie sends loouing thankes
To you, your bretheren, and his faithfull subiects,
Your carefull cittizens.—But, M⟨aiste⟩r Moore, to you
A rougher, yet as kinde, a salutation:
Your name is yet too short; nay, you must kneele;
A knights creation is thys knightly steele.
Rise vp, Sir Thomas Moore.
Moore. I thanke his highnesse for thus honoring me.
Shrew. This is but first taste of his princely fauour;
For it hath pleased his high maiestie
(Noating your wisedome and deseruing meritt)
To put this staffe of honor in your hand,
For he hath chose you of his Priuie Councell.
Moore. My lord, for to denye my soueraignes bountie
Were to drop precious stones into the heapes
Whence first they came;
To vrdge my imperfections in excuse,
Were all as stale as custome: no, my lord,
My seruice is my kings; good reason why,—
Since life or death hangs on our soueraignes eye.
L. Maior. His maiestie hath honord much the cittie
In this his princely choise.
Moore. My lord and bretheren,
Though I departe for ⟨court⟩ my looue shall rest
⟨With you, as heretofore, a faithful guest.⟩
I now must sleepe in courte, sounde sleepes forbeare;
The chamberlain to state is publique care:
Yet, in this rising of my priuate blood,
My studious thoughts shall tend the citties good.

Ent. Croftes.

Shrew. How now, Croftes! what newes?
Croftes. My lord, his highnesse sends expresse commaunde
That a record be entred of this riott,
And that the cheefe and capitall offendours
Be theron straite arraignde, for himselfe intends
To sit in person on the rest to morrowe
At Westminster.
Shrew. Lord Maior, you heare your charge.—
Come, good Sir Thomas Moore, to court let's hye;
You are th' appeaser of this mutinie.
Moore. My lord, farewell: new dayes begets new tides;
Life whirles bout fate, then to a graue it slydes. [*Exeunt seuerally*

256-7 *Bracketed words add. H: MS. illegible*

⟨ACT III.

SCENE I.—Cheapside.⟩

Enter M⟨aiste⟩r Sheriffe, and meete a Messenger.

Sheriff. Messenger, what newes?
Mess. Is execution yet performde?
Sheriff. Not yet; the cartes stand readie at the stayres,
And they shall presently away to Tibourne.
Messe. Stay, M⟨aiste⟩r Shreeue; it is the councelles pleasure,
For more example in so bad a case,
A jibbit be erected in Cheapside,
Hard by the Standerd; whether you must bring
Lincolne and those that were the cheefe with him, [*Ent. Officers.*
To suffer death, and that immediatly.
Sheriff. It shalbe doone, sir [*Ex. Mess.*].
—Officers, be speedie;
Call for a jibbit, see it be erected;
Others make haste to Newgate, bid them bring
The prisoners hether, for they here must dye:
Away, I say, and see no time be slackt.
Off. We goe, sir.
[*Ex. some seuerally; others set vp the jibbit.*
Sheriff. Thats well said, fellowes; now you doo your dutie.—
God for his pittie help these troublous times!
The streetes stopte vp with gazing multitudes:
Commaund our armed officers with halberds
Make way for entraunce of the prisoners;
Let proclamation once againe be made,
That euery housholder, on paine of deathe,
Keep in his prentises, and euery man
Stand with a weapon readie at his doore,
As he will answere to the contrary.
Off. Ile see it doone, sir. [*Exit.*

Enter another Officer.

Sheriffe. Bring them away to execution:
The writt is come abooue two houres since;
The cittie will be fynde for this neglect.

Act III. *etc. add. H*

Off. Thers such a presse and multitude at Newgate,
They cannot bring the cartes onto the stayres,
To take the prisoners in.
Sheriff. Then let them come on foote;
We may not dally time with great commaund.
Off. Some of the benche, sir, thinke it very fit
That stay be made, and giue it out abroade
The execution is deferd till morning,
And, when the streetes shall be a little cleerd,
To chaine them vp, and suddenly dispatch it.
Sheriff. Stay; in meane time me thinkes they come along:
See, they are comming. So, tis very well:

The prisoners are brought in, well guarded.

Bring Lincolne there the first vnto the tree.
Clo. I, for I cry lug, sir.
Lin. I knewe the first, sir, did belong to me:
This the olde prouerbe now compleate dooth make,
That Lincolne should be hangd for Londons sake. [*He goes vp.*
A Gods name, let vs to woorke. Fellowe, dispatche:
I was the formoste man in this rebellion,
And I the formoste that must dye for it.
Doll. Brauely, Iohn Lincolne, let thy death expresse,
That, as thou liu'dst a man, thou dyedst no lesse.
Lin. Doll Williamson, thine eyes shall witnesse it.—
Then to all you that come to viewe mine end
I must confesse, I had no ill intent,
But against such as wrongd vs ouer much:
And now I can perceiue it was not fit
That priuate men should carue out their redresse,
Which way they list; no, learne it now by me,—
Obedience is the best in eche degree:
And asking mercie meekely of my king,
I paciently submit me to the lawe;
But God forgiue them that were cause of it!
And, as a Christian, truely from my hart
I likewise craue they would forgiue me too
⟨As freely as I do forgive their wrong⟩
That others by example of the same
Hencefoorth be warned to attempt the like
Gainst any alien that repaireth hether.
Fare ye well, all: the next time that we meete,
I trust in heauen we shall eche other greete.
[*He leapes off.*
Doll. Farewell, Iohn Lincolne: say all what they can,
Thou liu'dst a good fellowe, and dyedst an honest man.
Clo. Wold I weare so farre on my jurney! the first stretche is the werste, me thinks.
Sheriff. Bring Williamson there forwarde.
Doll. Good M⟨aiste⟩r Shreeue, I haue an earnest suite,
And, as you are a man, deny't me not.
Sheriff. Woman, what is it? be it in my power,
Thou shalt obtayne it.
Doll. Let me dye next, sir; that is all I craue:
You knowe not what a comforte you shall bring
To my poore hart, to dye before my husband.
Sheriff. Bring her to death; she shall haue her desire.
Clo. Sir, and I haue a suite to you too.
Sher. What is ytt?
Clo. That, as you haue hangd Lincolne first, and will hange hir nexte, so you will nott hange me at all.
Sher. Naye, you set ope the Counter gates, and you must hange ⟨for⟩ the foly.
Clo. Well, then, so much for it!
Doll. Sir, your free bountie much contents my minde.
Commend me to that good shreeue M⟨aiste⟩r Moore,
And tell him, had't not bin for his perswasion,
Iohn Lincolne had not hung heere as he does:
We would first haue lockt ⟨vs⟩ vp in Leadenhall,
And there bin burnt to ashes with the roofe.
Sheriff. Woman, what Master Moore did was a subiects dutie,
And hath so pleasde our gracious lord the king,
That he is hence remoou'de to higher place,
And made of councell to his maiestie.
Doll. Well is he woorthie of it, by my troth,
An honest, wise, well spoken gentleman;
Yet would I praise his honestie much more,
If he had kept his woord, and sau'de our liues:
But let that passe; men are but men, and so
Woords are but wordes, and paies not what men owe.—
You, husband, since perhaps the world may say
That through my meanes thou comste thus to thy end,
Heere I beginne this cuppe of death to thee,
Because thou shalt be sure to taste no wursse
Then I haue taken that must goe before thee.
What though I be a woman? thats no matter;
I doo owe God a death, and I must pay him.

44 *Add. in different hand on margin of MS.* 66 *Add. H* : *MS. illegible* 68 warned to] warned not to *H*

92 for *add. Dyce* 98 haue lockt vs *pr. ed.* : haue bin lockt *Dyce* : haue lockt *MS.*

Husband, giue me thy hand; be not dismayed;
This charre beeing charde, then all our debt is payd.
Only two little babes we leaue behinde vs,
And all I can bequeathe them at this time
Is but the looue of some good honest freend,
To bring them vp in charitable sorte:
What, maisters! he goes vpright that neuer haltes,
And they may liue to mend their parents faultes.

Will. Why, well sayd, wife; yfaith, thou cheerst my hart:
Giue me thy hand; lets kisse, and so lets part.
[*He kisses her on the ladder.*

Doll. The next kisse, Williamson, shalbe in heauen.—
Now cheerely, lads! George Bets, a hand with thee;
And thine too, Rafe; and thine, good honest Sherwin.
Now let me tell the women of this towne,
No straunger yet brought Doll to lying downe:
So long as I an Englishman can see,
Nor Frenche nor Dutche shall get a kisse of me;
And when that I am dead, for me yet say,
I dyed in scorne to be a straungers preye.
[*A great shout and noise.*

⟨*Cry*⟩ *within.* Pardon, pardon, pardon, pardon!
Roome for the Erle of Surrey, roome there, roome!

Enter Surrey.

Sur. Saue the mans life, if it be possible.

Sheriff. It is too late, my lord; hees dead alreadie.

Sur. I tell ye, M⟨aiste⟩r Sheriffe, you are too forwarde,
To make such haste with men vnto their death;
I thinke your paines will merit little thankes,
Since that his highnesse is so mercifull
As not to spill the blood of any subiect.

Sheriff. My noble lord, would we so much had knowen!
The Councelles warrant hastened our dispatche;
It had not else bin doone so suddenly.

Sur. Sir Thomas Moore humbly vppon his knee
Did begge the liues of all, since on his woord
They did so gently yeeld: the king hath graunted it,
And made him Lord High Chauncellour of England,
According as he woorthily deserues.
Since Lincolnes life cannot be had againe,
Then for the rest, from my dread soueraignes lippes,
I heere pronounce free pardon for them all.

All. God saue the king, God saue the king!
My good Lord Chauncellour, and the Earle of Surrey! [*Flinging vp cappes.*

Doll. And Doll desires it from her very hart,
Moores name may liue for this right noble part;
And whensoere we talke of ill May daie,
Praise Moore . . . .

Sur. In hope his highnesse clemencie and mercie,
Which in the armes of milde and meeke compassion
Would rather clip you, as the loouing nursse
Oft dooth the waywarde infant, then to leaue you
To the sharp rodd of justice, so to drawe you
To shun such lewde assemblies as beget
Vnlawfull riots and such trayterous acts,
That, striking with the hand of priuate hate,
Maime your deare countrie with a publique wounde:—
Oh God, that Mercie, whose maiestick browe
Should be vnwrinckled, and that awefull Justice,
Which looketh through a vaile of sufferaunce
Vppon the frailtie of the multitude,
Should with the clamours of outragious wrongs
Be stird and wakened thus to punishment!—
But your deserued death he dooth forgiue:
Who giues you life, pray all he long may liue.

All. God saue the king, God saue the king!
My good Lord Chauncellour, and the Earle of Surrey! [*Exeunt.*

⟨SCENE II.—Chelsea. A Room in More's House.⟩

A table beeing couered with a greene carpet, a state cushion on it, and the Pursse and Mace lying thereon, enter Sir Thomas Moore.

Moore. It is in Heauen that I am thus and thus;
And that which we prophanlie terme our fortuns
Is the provision of the power aboue,
Fitted and shapte just to that strength of nature
Which we are borne ⟨withal⟩. Good God, good God,

137 *S. D. follows* 135 *in MS.*

161 *End of line illegible* Scene II. *etc. add.* H
5 withal *add.* Dyce

That I from such an humble bench of birth
Should stepp as twere vp to my countries head,
And give the law out ther! I, in my fathers life,
To take prerogative and tyth of knees
From elder kinsmen, and him bynd by my place
To give the smooth and dexter way to me
That owe it him by nature! Sure, thes things,
Not phisickt by respecte, might turne our bloud
To much corruption: but, Moore, the more thou hast,
Ether of honor, office, wealth, and calling,
Which might accite thee to embrace and hugg them,
The more doe thou in serpents natures thinke them;
Feare ther gay skinns with thought of ther sharpe state;
And lett this be thy maxime, to be greate
Is when the thred of hayday is once spoun,
A bottom great woond vpp greatly vndonn.—
Com on, sir: are you redy?

⟨*Enter* Randall, *attyred like Sir* Thomas Moore.⟩

Randall. Yes, my lord, I stand but one a few points; I shall have donn presentlie. Before God, I have practised your lordshipps shift so well, that I thinke I shall grow prowd, my lord.

Moore. Tis fitt thou shouldst wax prowd, or ells thoult nere
Be neere allied to greatnes. Observe me, sirra.
The learned clarke Erasmus is arived
Within our English court: last night I heere
He feasted with our honord English poet,
The Earle of Surrey; and I learnd to day
The famous clarke of Rotherdam will visett
Sir Thomas Moore. Therfore, sir, take my seate;
You are Lord Chauncelor: dress your behaviour
According to my carriage; but beware
You talke not over much, for twill betray thee:
Who prates not much seemes wise; his witt few scan;
While the tongue blabs tales of the imperfitt man.
Ile see if greate Erasmus can distinguishe
Meritt and outward cerimony.

Rand. If I doe not deserve a share for playing of your lordship well, lett me be yeoman vsher to your sumpter, and be banisht from wearing of a gold chaine for ever.

Moore. Well, sir, Ile hide our motion: act my part
With a firme boldnes, and thou winst my hart.

Enter the Shreiue, with Fawkner *a ruffin, and Officers.*

How now! whats the matter?

Faulk. Tugg me not, Ime noe beare. Sbloud, if all the doggs in Paris Garden hung at my tale, Ide shake em of with this, that Ile appeere before noe king cristned but my good Lord Chauncelor.

Shre. Weele cristen you, sirra.—Bring him forward.

Moore. How now! what tumults make you?

Falk. The azurde heavens protect my noble Lord Chauncelor!

Moore. What fellowes this?

Shre. A ruffian, my lord, that hath sett half the cittie in an vpprore.

Falk. My lord——

Shre. Ther was a fray in Paternoster-row, and because they would not be parted, the street was choakt vpp with carts.

Fauk. My noble lord, Paniar Allies throat was open.

Moore. Sirra, hold your peace.

Fauk. Ile prove the street was not choakt, but is as well as ever it was since it was a streete.

Shreu. This fellow was a principall broacher of the broile.

Fawk. Sbloud, I brocht none; it was broacht and half ronn out, before I had a lick at it.

Shre. And would be brought before noe justice but your honor.

Fauk. I am haild, my noble lord.

Moore. No eare to choose for every triviall noice
But mine, and in so full a time? Away!
You wronge me, M⟨aiste⟩r Shreve: dispose of him
At your owne plesure; send the knave to Newgate.

Fauk. To Newgate! sbloud, Sir Thomas Moore, I appeale, I appeale from Newgate to any of the two worshippfull Counters.

Moore. Fellow, whose man are you, that are thus lustie?

Fauk. My names Jack Fawkner; I serve, next vnder God and my prince, M⟨aister⟩ Morris, secretary to my Lord of Winchester.

Moore. A fellow of your haire is very fitt
To be a secretaries follower!

Fauk. I hope so, my lord. The fray was

16 *Short word deleted after* might *in MS.* 23 ff. *For first draft of this passage see Appendix* p. 418

84 Sbloud *deleted in MS. before* To 91 ff. *For first draft of this passage see Appendix* pp. 418–9

betweene the Bishopps men of Eelie and Winchester; and I could not in honor but parte them. I thought it stood not with my reputation and degree to com to my questions and aunswers before a citty justice: I knew I should to the pott.

Moore. Thou hast byn ther, it seemes, to late allredie.

Fauk. I know your honor is wise and so forth; and I desire to be only cattachizd or examind by you, my noble Lord Chauncelor.

Moore. Sirra, sirra, you are a busie dangerous ruffian.

Fauk. Ruffian!

Moore. How long have you worne this haire?

Fauk. I have worne this haire ever since I was borne.

Moore. You know thats not my question, but how long
Hath this shagg fleece hung dangling on thy head?

Fauke. How long, my lord! why, somtimes thus long, somtimes lowere, as the Fates and humors please.

Moore. So quick, sir, with me, ha? I see, good fellow,
Thou lovest plaine dealing. Sirra, tell me now,
When were you last at barbars? how longe time
Have you vppon your head woorne this shagg haire?

Fauke. My lord, Jack Faukner tells noe Esops fables: troth, I was not at barbars this three yeires; I have not byn cutt nor will not be cutt, vppon a foolish vow, which, as the Destanies shall derect, I am sworne to keepe.

Moore. When comes that vow out?

Fauk. Why, when the humors are purgd, not theis three years.

Moore. Vowes are recorded in the court of Heaven,
For they are holly acts. Yong man, I charge thee
And doe advize thee, start not from that vow:
And, for I will be sure thou shalt not shreve,
Besides, because it is an odious sight
To see a man thus hairie, thou shalt lie
In Newgate till thy vow and thy three years
Be full expired.—Away with him!

Fauke. My lord——

Moor. Cut of this fleece, and lie ther but a moneth.

Fauk. Ile not loose a haire to be Lord Chauncelor of Europe.

Moore. To Newgate, then. Sirra, great sinns are brede
In all that body wher thers a foule head.
Away with him. [*Exeunt* ⟨*all except* Randall.⟩

Enter Surry, Erasmus, *and Attendants.*

Surry. Now, great Erasmus, you approch the presence
Of a most worthy learned gentleman:
This little ile holds not a trewer frend
Vnto the arts; nor doth his greatnes add
A fained florish to his worthie parts;
Hees great in studie; thats the statists grace,
That gaines more reverence then the outward place.

Erasmus. Report, my lord, hath crost the narrow seas,
And to the severall parts of Christendom
Hath borne the fame of your LordChauncelor:
I long to see him, whom with loving thoughts
I in my studie oft have visited.
Is that Sir Thomas Moore?

Surry. It is, Erasmus:
Now shall you view the honorablest scholler,
The most religious pollititian,
The worthiest counsailor that tends our state.
That study is the generall watch of England;
In it the princes saftie, and the peace
That shines vppon our comonwealth, are forgd
By loiall industrie.

Erasmus. I dowt him not
To be as neere the life of excellence
As you proclaime him, when his meanest servaunts
Are of some waight: you saw, my lord, his porter
Give entertainment to vs at the gate
In Latten good phrase; whats the m⟨aiste⟩r, then,
When such good parts shine in his meanest men?

Surry. His Lo⟨rdship⟩ hath som waightie busines;
For, see, as yett he takes noe notice of vs.

Erasmus. I thinke twere best I did my dutie to him
In a short Latin speech.—
Qui in celiberima patria natus est ett gloriosa, plus habet negotii ut in lucem veniat quam qui——

Rand. I prythee, good Erasmus, be covered. I have forsworne speaking of Lattin, ⟨else⟩, as I am true counsailor, Ide tickle you with

110-11 *Written as prose in MS.* 115-18 *Prose in MS.* 130 shreve] swerve *conj. Dyce*; shrive *H* 175 ut *Dyce*; et *MS.* 178 else *add. Dyce*

a speech. Nay, sitt, Erasmus;—sitt, good my Lord of Surry. Ile make my lady com to you annon, if she will, and give you entertainment.

Erasmus. Is this Sir Thomas Moore?

Surry. Oh good Erasmus, you must conceave his vaine:
Hees ever furnisht with thes conceits.

Rand. Yes, faith, my learned poet doth not lie for that matter: I am nether more nor less then mery Sir Thomas allwaies. Wilt supp with me? by God, I love a parlous wise fellow that smells of a pollititian better then a long progress.

Enter Sir Thomas Moore.

Surry. We are deluded; this is not his lordshipp.

Rand. I pray you, Erasmus, how longe will the Holland cheese in your countrie keepe without maggetts?

Moore. Foole, painted barbarisme, retire thyself
Into thy first creation! ⟨*Exit* Randal⟩.—Thus you see,
My loving learned frends, how far respecte
Waites often on the cerimonious traine
Of base illitterat welth, whilst men of schooles,
Shrowded in povertie, are counted fooles.
Pardon, thou reverent Germaine, I have mixt
So slight a jest to the faire entertainment
Of thy most worthy self; for know, Erasmus,
Mirth wrinckls vpp my face, and I still crave,
When that forsakes me I may hugg my grave.

Erasmus. Your honers mery humor is best phisick
Vnto your able boddy; for we learne
Wher mellancholly choaks the passages
Of bloud and breth, the errected spirit still
Lengthens our dayes with sportfull exercise:
Studie should be the saddest time of life,
The rest a sport exempt from thought of strife.

Moore. Erasmus preacheth gospell against phisicke,
My noble poet.

Surry. Oh, my Lord, you tax me
In that word poet of much idlenes:
It is a studie that makes poore our fate;
Poets were ever thought vnfitt for state.

Moore. O, give not vp faire poisie, sweet lord,
To such contempt! That I may speake my hart,
It is the sweetest heraldrie of art,
That setts a difference tweene the tough sharpe holly
And tender bay tree.

Surry. Yett, my lord,
It is become the very logic number
To all mechanick sciences.

Moore. Why, Ile show the reason:
This is noe age for poets; they should sing
To the lowd canon *heroica facta;*
Qui faciunt reges heroica carmina laudant:
And, as great subiects of ther pen decay,
Even so vnphisickt they doe melt away.

Enter M⟨aiste⟩r Morris.

Com, will your lordshipp in?—My deere Erasmus—
Ile heere you, M⟨aiste⟩r Moris, presentlie.——
My lord, I make you m⟨aiste⟩r of my howse:
Weele banquett heere with fresh and staid delights,
The Muses musick heer shall cheere our sprites;
The cates must be but meane wher scollers sitt,
For thar made all with courses of neate witt.

⟨*Exeunt* Surrey, Erasmus, *and Attendants.*⟩

How now, M⟨aiste⟩r Morris?

Moriss. I am a suter to your lordshipp in behalf of a servaunt of mine.

Moore. The fellow with long haire? good M⟨aister⟩ Moris,
Com to me three years hence, and then Ile heere you.

Moris. I vnderstand your honor: but the foolish knave has submitted himself to the mercy of a barber, and is without, redy to make a new vow before your lordshipp, heerafter to leve cavell.

Moore. Nay, then, letts talke with him: pray, call him in.

Enter Faukner *and Officers.*

Fauk. Bless your honor! a new man, my lord.

Moore. Why, sure, this ⟨is⟩ not he.

Fauk. And your lordshipp will, the barber shall give you a sample of my head: I am he in faith, my lord; I am *ipse.*

Moore. Why, now thy face is like an honest mans:
Thou hast plaid well at this new cutt, and wonn.

Fauk. No, my lord; lost all that ever God sent me.

Moore. God sent thee into the world as thou art now,

207-8 *Beside these lines on the margin of MS. is written* et tu Erasmus an Diabolus 216 noble *deleted in MS. before* Lord

254 is *add. Dyce* 255 *Word deleted in MS. after* will 260 god *deleted before* ever *in MS.*

With a short haire. How quickly are three years
Ronn out in Newgate!

Fauk. I think so, my lord; for ther was but a haires length betweene my going thether and so long time.

Moor. Because I see som grace in thee, goe free.—
Discharge him, fellowes.—Farewell, Master Moris.—
Thy head is for thy shoulders now more fitt;
Thou hast less haire vppon it, but more witt. [*Exit.*

Moris. Did not I tell thee allwaies of thes locks?

Fauk. And the locks were on againe, all the goldsmiths in Cheapside should not pick them open. Shart, if my haire stand not an end when I looke for my face in a glass, I am a polecatt. Heers a lowsie jest! but, if I notch not that rogue Tom barbar, that makes me looke thus like a Brownist, hange me! Ile be worss to the nitticall knave then ten tooth draweings. Heers a head, with a pox!

Morr. What ails thou? art thou mad now?

Faulk. Mad now! nayles, yf losse of hayre cannot mad a man, what can? I am deposde, my crowne is taken from me. Moore had bin better a scowred Moreditch than a notcht mee thus: does hee begin sheepesharing with Jack Faulkner?

Morr. Nay, and you feede this veyne, sir, fare you well.

Falk. Why, farewell, frost. Ile goe hang myselfe out for the Poll Head. Make a Sarcen of Jack?

Morr. Thou desperate knave! for that I see the divell
Wholy getts hold of thee——

Falk. The divells a dambd rascall.

Morr. I charge thee, wayte on mee no more; no more
Call mee thy m⟨aiste⟩r.

Falk. Why, then, a word, M⟨aiste⟩r Morris.

Morr. Ile heare no wordes, sir; fare you well.

Falk. Sbloud, farewell.

Morr. Why doest thou follow mee?

Falk. Because Ime an asse. Doe you sett your shavers vpon me, and then cast mee off? must I condole? haue the Fates playd the fooles? am I theire cutt? now the poore sconce is taken, must Jack march with bag and baggage? [*Weapes.*

Morr. You coxcomb!

Falk. Nay, you ha poacht mee; you ha given mee a hayre; its here, heare.

Morr. Away, you kynd asse! come, sir, dry your eyes:
Keepe your old place, and mend theis fooleryes.

Falk. I care not to bee tournd off, and twere a ladder, so it bee in my humor, or the Fates becon to mee. Nay, pray, sir, yf the Destinyes spin mee a fyne thred, Falkner flyes another pitch; and to avoyd the headach hereafter, before Ile bee a hayremonger, Ile bee a whoremonger. [*Exeunt.*

⟨Scene III.—Chelsea. Ante-chamber in More's House.⟩

Enter a Messenger to Moore.

Mess. (*T. Goedal*). My honorable lord, the Maior of London,
Accompanied with his lady and her traine,
Are coming hether, and are hard at hand,
To feast with you: a seriaunts come before,
To tell your lordshipp of ther neer aproche.

Moore. Why, this is cheerfull newes: frends goe and come:
Reverend Erasmus, whose delitious words
Express the very soule and life of witt,
Newlie toke sad leave of me, ⟨and⟩ with teares
Trubled the sillver channell of the Themes,
Which, glad of such a burden, prowdlie sweld
And one her bosom bore him toward the sea:
Hees gon to Roterdam; peace goe with him!
He left me heavy when he went from hence;
But this recomforts me; the kind Lo⟨rd⟩ Maior,
His bretheren aldermen, with ther faire wives,
Will feast this night with vs: why, so it shuld be;
Moores mery hart lives by good companie.—
Good gentlemen, be carefull; give great charge
Our diet be made daynty for the tast;
For, of all people that the earth affords,
The Londoners fare richest at ther bourds. ⟨*Exeunt.*⟩

⟨ACT IV.

Scene I.—Chelsea. A Room in More's House.⟩

Enter Sir Thomas Moore, *Master* Roper, *and Seruingmen setting stooles.*

Moore. Come, my good fellowes, stirre, be dilligent;
Sloth is an ydle fellowe, leaue him now;
The time requires your expeditious seruice.
Place me heere stooles, to set the ladyes on.—

283 *With this line a new handwriting begins in MS.* 293 for the *MS.*: of the *Dyce* 304 *Deletion in MS. after* follow

314 foole *deleted before* asse *in MS.* Scene III. *etc. add. H* 9 and *add. Dyce* 17 so it] soet *MS.* Act IV. *etc. add. H* 1 dilligent *MS.*: vigilent *H*

Sonne Roper, you haue giuen order for the banquet?
Ro. I haue, my lord, and euery thing is readie.

Enter his Lady.

Moore. Oh, welcome, wife! giue you direction
How women should be plac'de; you knowe it best.
For my Lord Maior, his bretheren, and the rest,
Let me alone; men best can order men.
La. I warrant ye, my lord, all shalbe well.
Ther's one without that stayes to speake with ye,
And bad me tell ye that he is a player.
Moore. A player, wife!—One of ye bid him come in. [*ex one.*
Nay, stirre there, fellowes; fye, ye are to slowe!
See that your lights be in a readines:
The banquet shalbe heere.—Gods me, madame,
Leaue my Lady Maioresse! bothe of vs from the boord!
And my sonne Roper too! what may our guests thinke?
La. My lord, they are risen, and sitting by the fire.
Moore. Why, yet goe you and keepe them companie;
It is not meete we should be absent bothe. [*ex. La.*

ent. Player.

Welcome, good freend; what is your will with me?
Player. My lord, my fellowes and myselfe
Are come to tender ye our willing seruice,
So please you to commaund vs.
Moore. What, for a play, you meane?
Whom doo ye serue?
Player. My Lord Cardinalles grace.
Moore. My Lord Cardinalls players! now, trust me, welcome:
You happen hether in a luckie time,
To pleasure me, and benefit yourselues.
The Maior of London and some aldermen,
His lady and their wiues, are my kinde guests
This night at supper: now, to haue a play
Before the banquet, will be excellent.—
How thinke you, sonne Roper?
Ro. Twill doo well, my lord,
And be right pleasing pastime to your guests.
Moore. I prethee, tell me, what playes haue ye?
Player. Diuers, my lord: *The Cradle of Securitie,*
Hit nayle o'th head, Impacient Pouertie,
The play of Foure Pees, Diues and Lazarus,
Lustie Juuentus, and *The Mariage of Witt and Wisedome.*
Moore. The Mariage of Witt and Wisedome! that, my lads;
Ile none but that; the theame is very good,
And may maintaine a liberall argument:
To marie wit to wisedome, asks some cunning;
Many haue witt, that may come short of wisedome.
Weele see how M⟨aiste⟩r poet playes his part,
And whether witt or wisedome grace his arte.—
Goe, make him drinke, and all his fellowes too.—
How manie are ye?
Player. Foure men and a boy, sir.
Moore. But one boy? then I see,
Ther's but fewe women in the play.
Player. Three, my lord; Dame Science, Lady Vanitie,
And Wisdome she herselfe.
Moore. And one boy play them all? bir lady, hees loden.
Well, my good fellowe, get ye straite together,
And make ye readie with what haste ye may.—
Prouide their supper gainste the play be doone,
Else shall we stay our guests heere ouer long.—
Make haste, I pray ye.
Player. We will, my lord. [*ex. Ser. & player.*
Moore. Where are the waytes? goe, bid them play,
To spend the time a while.

En. Lady.

How now, madame?
La. My lord, th'are coming hether.
Moore. Th'are welcome. Wife, Ile tell ye one thing;
Our sporte is somewhat mended; we shall haue
A play to night, *The Mariage of Witt and Wisedome,*
And acted by my good Lord Cardinalles players:
How like ye that, wife?
La. My lord, I like it well.
See, they are comming.

The waytes playes; enters Lord Maior, so many Aldermen as may, the Lady Maioresse in scarlet, with other Ladies and Sir Thomas Moores *Daughters; Seruauntes carying lighted torches by them.*

Moore. Once againe welcome, welcome, my good Lord Maior,
And bretheren all, for once I was your brother,

67 *S.D. follows* madame *in MS.*

And so am still in hart: it is not state
That can our looue from London seperate.
⟨True, vpstart fools, by sudden fortune tried,
Regard their former mates with⟩ naught but pride.
But they that cast an eye still whence they came,
Knowe how they rose, and how to vse the same.

L. Maior. My lord, you set a glosse on Londons fame,
And make it happie euer by your name.
Needs must we say, when we remember Moore,
Twas he that droue rebellion from our doore
With graue discretions milde and gentle breath,
Sheelding a many subiects liues from death.
Oh, how our cittie is by you renownde,
And with your vertues our endeauours crownde!

Moore No more, my good Lord Maior: but thanks to all,
That on so short a summons you would come
To visite him that holdes your kindnesse deere.—
Madame, you are not merie with my Lady Maioresse
And these fayre ladyes; pray ye, seate them all:—
And heere, my lord, let me appoint your place;—
The rest to seate themselues:—nay, Ile wearie ye;
You will not long in haste to visite me.

La. Good madame, sit; in sooth, you shall sit heere.

La. Mai. Good madame, pardon me; it may not be.

La. In troth, Ile haue it so: Ile sit heere by yee.—
Good ladyes, sit.—More stooles heere, hoe!

La. Mai. It is your fauour, madame, makes me thus
Presume abooue my merit.

La. When we come to you,
Then shall you rule vs as we rule you heere.
Now must I tell ye, madame, we haue a play,
To welcome ye withall; how good so ere,
That knowe not I; my lord will haue it so.

Moore. Wife, hope the best; I am sure theyle doo their best:
They that would better, comes not at their feaste.
My good Lord Cardinalles players, I thanke them for it,
Play vs a play, to lengthen out your welcome:
They say it is *The Mariage of Wit and Wisedome,*
A theame of some importe, how ere it prooue;
But, if arte faile, weele inche it out with looue.—

⟨Enter a Servant.⟩

What, are they readie?

Ser. My lord, one of the players craues to speake with you.

Moore. With me! where is he?

Enter Inclination *the Vise, readie.*

Incli. Heere, my lord.

Moore. How now! what's the matter?

Incli. We would desire your honor but to stay a little; one of my fellowes is but run to Oagles for a long beard for young Witt, and heele be heere presently.

Moore. A long beard for young Witt! why, man, he may be without a beard till he come to mariage, for witt goes not all by the hayre. When comes Witt in?

Incli. In the second scene, next to the Prologue, my lord.

Moore. Why, play on till that sceane come, and by that time Witts beard will be growne, or else the fellowe returned with it. And what part plaist thou?

Incli. Inclination the Vice, my lord.

Moore. Gramercies, now I may take the vice if I list: and wherfore hast thou that bridle in thy hand?

Incli. I must be bridled annon, my lord.

Moore. And thou beest not sadled too, it makes no matter, for then Witts inclination may gallop so fast, that he will outstrip Wisedome, and fall to follie.

Incli. Indeed, so he does to Lady Vanitie; but we haue no follie in our play.

Moore. Then ther's no witt in't, Ile be sworne: follie waites on witt, as the shaddowe on the bodie, and where witt is ripest there follie still is readiest. But beginne, I prethee: weele rather allowe a beardlesse Witt then Witt all bearde to haue no braine.

Incli. Nay, he has his apparell on too, my lord, and therfore he is the readier to enter.

Moore. Then, good Inclination, beginne at a venter.— [*Exit* ⟨Inclin.⟩
My Lord Maior,
Witt lacks a beard, or else they would beginne:

80-1 True . . mates with *pr. ed.* : Within this city I did long abide, And I regard it still with *conj. H*, *but this does not give the meaning* : *MS. illegible*

114 *Followed in MS. by the deleted line*: My good Lord Maior, and all my other freends 117 *S. D. add. H* 130 all] *lightly crossed out in MS. and perhaps to be omitted*

Ide lend him mine, but that it is too thinne.
Silence, they come.

The trompet soundes; enter the Prologue.

Pro. *Now, for as much as in these latter dayes,*
Throughout the whole world in euery land,
Vice doth encrease, and vertue decayes,
Iniquitie hauing the vpper hand;
We therfore intend, good gentle audience,
A prettie short enterlude to play at this present,
Desiring your leaue and quiet silence,
To shewe the same, as is meete and expedient.
It is called The Mariage of Witt and Wisedome,
A matter right pithie and pleasing to heare,
Wherof in breefe we will shewe the whole summe;
But I must be gon, for Witt dooth appeare.
[*Exit.*

Enter Witt *ruffling, and* Inclination the Vice.

Witt. *In an arbour greene, asleepe whereas I lay,*
The birdes sang sweetely in the midst of the day,
I dreamed fast of mirthe and play,—
In youth is pleasure, in youthe is pleasure.
Methought I walked still to and fro,
And from her companie I could not goe;
But when I waked, it was not so,—
In youth is pleasure, in youth is pleasure.
Therfore my hart is surely plight,
Of her alone to haue a sight,
Which is my ioy and harts delight,—
In youth is pleasure, in youth is pleasure.

Moore. Marke ye, my lord, this is Witt without a bearde: what will he be by that time he comes to the commoditie of a bearde?

Incli. *Oh, sir, the ground is the better on which she dooth goe;*
For she will make better cheere with a little she can get,
Then many a one can with a great banquet of meat.

Witt. *And is her name Wisedome?*

Incli. *I, sir, a wife moste fitt*
For you, my good maister, my daintie sweet Witt.

Witt. *To be in her companie my hart it is set:*
Therfore I prethee to let vs begon;
For vnto Wisedome Witt hath inclination.

Incli. *Oh, sir, she will come her selfe euen annon;*
For I tolde her before where we would stand,
And then she sayd she would beck vs with her hand.—
Back with these boyes and saucie great knaues!
[*Florishing his dagger.*
What, stand ye heere so bigge in your braues?
My dagger about your coxecombes shall walke,
If I may but so much as heare ye chat or talke.

Witt. *But will she take paines to come for vs hether?*

Incli. *I warrant ye; therfore you must be familiare with her:*
When she commeth in place,
You must her embrace
Somewhat hansomely,
Least she thinke it daunger,
Because you are a straunger,
To come in your companie.

Witt. *I warrant thee, Inclination, I will be busie:*
Oh, how Witt longs to be in Wisedomes companie!

Enter Lady Vanitie *singing, and beckning with her hand.*

Van. *Come hether, come hether, come hether, come:*
Such chere as I haue, thou shalt haue some.

Moore. This is Lady Vanitie, Ile holde my life:—
Beware, good Witt, you take not her to wife.

Incli. *What, vnknowne honestie? a woord in your eare.* [*She offers to depart.*
You shall not be gon as yet, I sweare:
Heer's none but your freends, you need not to fray;
This young gentleman looues ye, therfore you must stay.

Witt. *I trust in me she will thinke no daunger,*
For I looue well the companie of fayre women;
And though to you I am a straunger,
Yet Witt may pleasure you now and then.

Van. *Who, you? nay, you are such a holy man,*
That to touche one you dare not be bolde;
I thinke you would not kisse a young woman,
If one would giue ye twentie pound in golde.

Witt. *Yes, in good sadnesse, lady, that I would;*
I could finde in my hart to kisse you in your smock.

Van. *My back is broade enough to beare that mock;*
For it hath bin tolde me many a time
That you would be seene in no such companie as mine.

174 ff. *This interlude to line 243 is merely an adaptation of part of* Lusty Juventus   182 plight] pight *R*: pight *is the reading in* Lusty Juventus

208–9 *One line in MS.*   211–12 *One line in MS.*

Witt. *Not Witt in the companie of Lady Wisedome!*
Oh Joue, for what doo I hether come?

Incli. *Sir, she did this nothing else but to prooue*
Whether a little thing would you mooue
To be angrie and frett:
What, and if one sayd so?
Let such trifling matters g
And with a kinde kisse come out of her debt.—
Is Luggins come yet with the beard?

Enter an other Player.

Player. No, faith, he is not come: alas, what shall we doo?

Incli. Forsooth, we can goe no further till our fellowe Luggins come; for he plays Good Councell, and now he should enter, to admonishe Witt that this is Lady Vanitie, and not Lady Wisedome.

Moore. Nay, and it be no more but so, ye shall not tarie at a stand for that; weele not haue our play marde for lacke of a little good councell: till your fellowe come, Ile giue him the best councell that I can.—Pardon me, my Lord Maior; I loue to be merie.——
Oh . . Witt, thou art nowe on the bowe hand,
And blindely in thine owne oppinion doost stand.
I tell thee, this naughtie lewde Inclination
Does lead thee amisse in a very straunge fashion:
This is not Wisedome, but Lady Vanitie;
Therefore list to Good Councell, and be ruled by me.

Incli. In troth, my lord, it is as right to Lugginses part as can be.—Speake, Witt.

Moore. Nay, we will not haue our audience disappointed, if I can help it.

Witt. Art thou Good Councell, and wilt tell me so?
Wouldst thou haue Witt from Lady Wisedome to goe?
Thou art some deceiuer, I tell thee verily,
In saying that this is Lady Vanitie.

Moore. *Witt, iudge not things by the outwarde showe;*
The eye oft mistakes, right well you doo knowe:
Good Councell assures thee vppon his honestie,
That this is not Wisedome, but Lady Vanitie.

Enter Luggins *with the bearde.*

Incli. Oh, my lord, he is come; now we shall goe forwarde.

Moore. Art thou come? well, fellowe, I haue holpe to saue thine honestie a little. Now, if thou canst giue Witt any better councell then I haue doone, spare not: there I leaue him to thy mercie.
But by this time, I am sure, our banquet's readie:
My lord and ladyes, we will taste that first,
And then they shall begin the play againe,
Which through the fellowes absence, and by me,
Insted of helping, hath bin hindered.—
Prepare against we come.—Lights there, I say!—
Thus fooles oft times doo help to marre the play. [*exeunt.—ma. players.*

Witt. Fye, fellowe Luggins, you serue vs hansomely; doo ye not, thinke ye?

Lug. Why, Oagle was not within, and his wife would not let me haue the beard; and, by my troth, I ran so fast that I sweat againe.

Incli. Doo ye heare, fellowes? would not my lord make a rare player? oh, he would vpholde a companie beyond all hoe, better then Mason among the kings players! Did ye marke how extemprically he fell to the matter, and spake Lugginsses parte almoste as it is in the very booke set downe?

Witt. Peace; doo ye knowe what ye say? my lord a player! let vs not meddle with any such matters: yet I may be a little proude that my lord hath answerd me in my parte. But come, let vs goe, and be readie to begin the play againe.

Lug. I, thats the best, for now we lack nothing.

Enter a Servingman.

Man. Where be theis players?

All. Heere, sir.

Man. My lord is sent for to the courte,
And all the guests doo after supper parte;
And, for he will not troble you againe,
By me for your reward a sends 8 angills,
With many thanks. But supp before you goe:
Yt is his will you should be farely entreatid:
Follow, I praye ye.

Witt. This, Luggins, is your neclegens;
Wanting Witts beard brought things into dislike;
For otherwies the playe had bin all seene,
Wher now some curius cittisin disgraiste itt,
And discommendinge ytt, all is dismiste.

Vice. Fore God, a sayes true. But heare ye, sirs: 8 angells, ha! my lord wold neuer giues

312 *Two words deleted in MS. after* My lord 319 *After* Luggins, *the word* all *has been deleted in MS.* 322 cittisin] criticism *conj. H: several words deleted in MS.*

8 angells more or les for 12^{d}; other yt shold be 3^{l}, 5^{l}, or tenn li.; ther⟨s⟩ 20^{s} wantinge, sure.

Witt. Twenty to one, tis soe. I haue a tricke: my lord comes; stand aside.

Enter Moore, *with Attendants with Purss and Mace.*

Lord ⟨*Chan.*⟩ In haist to counsell! whats the busines now,
That all so late his highnes sends for me?—
What sekst thou, fellow?

Witt. Nay, nothinge: your lordship sent 8 angills by your man, and I haue lost too of them in the rishes.

Lord ⟨*Chan.*⟩ Wytt, looke to thatt:— 8 angells! I did send them tenn.—Who gaue yt them?

Man. I, my lord; I had no more aboute me;
But buy and buy they shall risseaue the rest.

Lord ⟨*Chan.*⟩ Well, Witt, twas wieslye donne; thou plaist Witt well endede,
Not to be thus disseaued of thy righte.—
Am I a man, by offis truely ordaind
Equally to deuide true righte his owne,
And shall I haue disseauers in my house?
Then what availes my bowntie, when such seruants
Disseaue the pore of what the M⟨aiste⟩r giues?
Goe one, and pull his cote ouer his eares:
Ther ar too manye such.—Giue them ther righte.—
Witt, let thie fellowes thanke the: twas well dunn;
Thou now disserueste to match with Ladye Wisdome. [*Exit* Moore *with Attend.*

Vice. God a mersye, Wytt!—Sir, you had a maister Sir Thomas More more; but now we shall haue more.

Lugg. God blesse him! I wold ther weare more of his minde! a loues our qualletie; and yit hees a larnid man, and knows what the world is.

Clo. Well, a kinde man, and more loving then many other: but I thinke we ha mett with the first . . .

Luggins. First serud his man that had our angills; and he maye chaunce dine with Duke Homphrye to morrow, beinge turnde awaye to daye. Come, lets goe.

Clo. And many such rewards wold make vs all ride, and horsse vs with the best nags in Smithfelde. ⟨*Exeunt.*⟩

330 ff. *For original draft of this passage see Appendix, p.* 419 337 gaue] gauie *MS.* 347 *Word deleted in MS. after* pore 360 *Deletion after* then

⟨Scene II.—Whitehall. The Council Chamber.⟩

Enter the Earles of Shrewesburie, Surrey, *Bishop of* Rochester, *and other Lordes, seuerally, dooing curtesie to eche other; Clark of the Councell waiting bareheaded.*

Sur. Good morrowe to my Lord of Shrewesburie.

Shrew. The like vnto the honourd Earle of Surrey.
Yond comes my Lord of Rochester.

Rochest. Good morrowe, my good lordes.

Sur. Clarke of the Councell, what time ist of day?

Clarke. Past eight of clock, my lord.

Shrew. I wunder that my good Lord Chauncellour
Dooth stay so long, considering ther's matters
Of high importaunce to be scand vppon.

Sur. Clarke of the Councell, certefie his lordship
The lordes expect him heere.

Rochest. It shall not need;
Yond comes his lordship.

Enter Sir Thomas Moore, *with Pursse and Mace borne before him.*

Moore. Good morrowe to this faire assemblye.
Come, my good lords, let 's sit. Oh serious square! [*They sit.*
Vppon this little borde is dayly scande
The health and preservation of the land;
We the phisitians that effect this good,
Now by choise diett, annon by letting blood;
Our toyle and carefull watching brings the king
In league with slumbers, to which peace dooth sing.—
Auoyde the roome there!—
What busines, lords, to day?

Shrew. This, my good lord;
About the entertainement of the emperour
Gainst the perfidious Frenche into our pay.

Sur. My lords, as tis the custome in this place
The youngest should speake first, so, if I chaunce
In this case to speake youngly, pardon me.
I will agree, Fraunce now hath her full strength,
As hauing newe recouered the pale blood
Which warre sluic'de foorth; and I consent to this,
That the coniunction of our Englishe forces
With armes of Germanie may sooner bring

Scene II. *etc. add. H* 26 *Deletion after* our

This prize of conquest in. But, then, my lordes,
As in the morrall hunting twixt the lyon
And other beastes, force ioynd ⟨with greed⟩
Frighted the weaker sharers from their partes;
So, if the empires soueraigne chaunce to put
His plea of partnership into warres courte,
Swoordes should discide the difference, and our blood
In priuate teares lament his entertainement.
Shrew. To doubt the wurst is still the wise mans sheeld,
That armes him safely: but the worlde knowes this,
The emperour is a man of royall faith;
His looue vnto our soueraigne brings him downe
From his emperiall seate, to marche in pay
Vnder our English flagge, and weare the crosse,
Like some high order, on his manly breast;
Thus seruing, hees not maister of himselfe,
But, like a collonell commaunding other,
Is by the generall ouer-awed himselfe.
Rochest. Yet, my good lord——
Shrew. Let me conclude my speeche.
As subiects share no portion in the conquest
Of their true soueraigne, other then the meritt
That from the soueraigne guerdons the true subiect;
So the good emperour, in a freendly league
Of amitie with England, will not soyle
His honor with the theft of Englishe spoyle.
Moore. There is no question but this entertainement
Will be moste honorable, moste commodious.
I haue oft heard good captaines wish to haue
Riche soldiours to attend them, such as would fight
Bothe for their liues and liuings; such a one
Is the good emperour: I would to God,
We had ten thousand of such able men!
Hah, then there would appeare no courte, no cittie,
But, where the warres were, they would pay themselues.
Then, to preuent in Frenche warres Englands losse,
Let Germaine flagges waue with our Englishe crosse.

Enter Sir Thomas Palmer.

Pal. My lordes, his maiestie hath sent by me
These articles enclos'de, first to be viewde,
And then to be subscribed to: I tender them
In that due reuerence which befitts this place.
[*With great reuerence.*
Moore. Subscribe these articles! stay, let vs pause;
Our conscience first shall parley with our lawes.—
My Lord of Rochester, viewe you the paper.
Rochest. Subscribe to these! now, good Sir Thomas Palmer,
Beseeche the king that he will pardon me:
My hart will check my hand whilste I doo write;
Subscribing so, I were an hipocrite.
Pal. Doo you refuse it, then, my lord?
Rochest. I doo, Sir Thomas.
Pal. Then heere I summon you foorthwith t'appeare
Before his maiestie, to answere there
This capitall contempt.
Rochest. I rise and parte,
In liew of this to tender him my hart.
[*He riseth.*
Pal. Wilt please your honor to subscribe, my lord?
Moore. Sir, tell his highnesse, I entreate
Some time for to bethinke me of this taske:
In the meane while I doo resigne mine office
Into my soueraignes hands.
Pal. Then, my lord,
Heare the prepared order from the king:
On your refusall, you shall straite departe
Vnto your house at Chelsey, till you knowe
Our soueraignes further pleasure.
Moore. Moste willingly I goe.—
My lordes, if you will visite me at Chelsey,
Weele goe a fishing, and with a cunning nett,
Not like weake filme, weele catche none but the great:
Farewell, my noble lordes. Why, this is right;
Good morrowe to the sunne, to state good night! [*ex.* Moore.
Pal. Will you subscribe, my lordes?
Sur. Instantly, good Sir Thomas,
Weele bring the writing vnto our soueraigne.
[*They write.*
Pal. My Lord of Rochester,
You must with me, to answere this contempt.
Roches. This is the wurst,
Who's freed from life is from all care exempt.
[*ex.* Ro. *and* Pal.
Sur. Now let vs ⟨hasten⟩ to our soueraigne.
Tis straunge that my Lord Chauncellour should refuse
The dutie that the lawe of God bequeathes
Vnto the king.
Shrew. Come, let vs in. No doubt

36 As *MS.*: Its *Dyce* 37 with greed *pr. ed.*: together *H*: *MS. illegible*

85 ff. *Cancelled by Tylney, who writes in margin* all altr'. 113 hasten *H*: *MS. illegible*

His minde will alter, and the bishops too:
Errour in learned heads hath much to doo.
⟨*Exeunt.*⟩

⟨Scene III.—Chelsea.⟩

Enter the Lady Moore, *her two Daughters, and M⟨aiste⟩r* Roper, *as walking.*

Ro. Madame, what ayles yee for to looke so sad?
Lady. Troth, sonne, I knowe not what; I am not sick,
And yet I am not well. I would be merie;
But somewhat lyes so heauie on my hart,
I cannot chuse but sigh. You are a scholler;
I pray ye, tell me, may one credit dreames?
Ro. Why ask you that, deare madame?
Lady. Because to night I had the straungest dreame
That ere my sleep was troubled with. Me thought twas night,
And that the king and queene went on the Themes
In bardges to heare musique: my lord and I
Were in a little boate me thought,—Lord, Lord,
What straunge things liue in slumbers!—and, beeing neere,
We grapled to the bardge that bare the king.
But after many pleasing voyces spent
In that still moouing musique house, me thought
The violence of the streame did seuer vs
Quite from the golden fleet, and hurried vs
Vnto the bridge, which with vnused horror
We entred at full tide: thence some slight shoote
Beeing caried by the waues, our boate stood still
Iust opposite the Tower, and there it turnde
And turnde about, as when a whirle-poole sucks
The circkled waters: me thought that we bothe cryed,
Till that we sunck; where arme in arme we dyed.
Ro. Giue no respect, deare madame, to fond dreames;
They are but slight illusions of the blood.
Lady. Tell me not all are so; for often dreames
Are true diuiners, either of good or ill:
I cannot be in quiet till I heare
How my lord fares.
Ro. (*aside.*) Nor I.—Come hether, wife:
I will not fright thy mother, to interprete
The nature of a dreame; but trust me, sweete,
This night I haue bin troubled with thy father
Beyond all thought.
Ro. Wife. Truely, and so haue I:
Methought I sawe him heere in Chelsey Churche,
Standing vppon the roodloft, now defac'de;
And whilste he kneeld and prayd before the ymage,
It fell with him into the vpper-quier,
Where my poore father lay all stainde in blood.
Ro. Our dreames all meet in one conclusion,
Fatall, I feare.
Lady. What's that you talke? I pray ye, let me knowe it.
Ro. Wife. Nothing, good mother.
Lady. This is your fashion still; I must knowe nothing.
Call Maister Catesbie; he shall straite to courte,
And see how my lord does: I shall not rest,
Vntill my hart leaue panting on his breast.

Enter Sir Thomas Moore *merily, Seruaunts attending.*

Daugh. See where my father comes, ioyfull and merie.
Moore. As seamen, hauing past a troubled storme,
Daunce on the pleasant shoare; so I—Oh, I could speake
Now like a poett! now, afore God, I am passing light!—
Wife, giue me kinde welcome: thou wast wunt to blame
My kissing when my beard was in the stubble;
But I haue bin trimde of late; I haue had
A smoothe courte shauing, in good faith, I haue.— [*Daughters kneele.*
God blesse ye!—Sonne Roper, giue me your hand.
Ro. Your honor's welcome home.
Moore. Honor! ha ha!—And how doost, wife?
Ro. He beares himselfe moste straungely.
Lady. Will your lordship in?
Moore. Lordship! no, wife, that's gon;
The ground was slight that we did leane vppon.
Lady. Lord, that your honor nere will leaue these jests!
In faith, it ill becomes yee.
Moore. Oh, good wife,
Honor and jests are bothe together fled;
The meriest councellour of England's dead.
Lady. Whose that, my lord?
Moore. Still lord! the Lord Chauncellour, wife.
Lady. Thats you.

Scene III. *etc. add.* H

Moore Certaine; but I haue chaungde my life.
Am I not leaner then I was before?
The fatt is gon; my title's only Moore.
Contented with one stile, Ile liue at rest:
They that haue many names are not still best.
I haue resignde mine office: count'st me not wise?
Lady. Oh God!
Moore. Come, breed not female children in your eyes:
The king will haue it so.
Lady. What's the offence?
Moore. Tush, let that passe; weele talke of that annon.
The king seemes a phisitian to my fate;
His princely minde would traine me back to state.
Ro. Then be his patient, my moste honord father.
Moore. Oh, sonne Roper,
Vbi turpis est medicina, sanari piget!—
No, wife, be merie;—and be merie, all:
You smilde at rising, weepe not at my fall.
Let's in, and heere ioy like to priuate freends,
Since dayes of pleasure haue repentant ends:
The light of greatnesse is with triumph borne;
It sets at midday oft with publique scorne.
[*Exeunt.*

⟨SCENE IV.—The Tower.⟩

Enter the Bishop of Rochester, Surrey, Shrewsbury, *Lieutenant of the Tower, and Warders with weapons.*

Rochest. Your kinde perswasions, honorable lords,
I can but thanke ye for; but in this brest
There liues a soule that aimes at higher things
Then temporarie pleasing earthly kings.
God blesse his highnesse euen with all my hart!—
We shall meete one day, though that now we part.
Sur. We not misdoubt, your wisedome can discerne
What best befits it; yet in looue and zeale
We could entreate, it might be otherwise.
Shrew. No doubt, your fatherhood will by yourselfe
Consider better of the present case,
And growe as great in fauour as before.
Rochest. For that, as pleaseth God. In my restrainte
From worldly causes, I shall better see
Into myselfe then at proude libertie:
The Tower and I will priuately conferre
Of things, wherin at freedome I may erre.
But I am troublesome vnto your honors,
And holde ye longer then becomes my dutie.—
M⟨aiste⟩r Lieutenant, I am now your charge;
And though you keep my bodie, yet my looue
Waites on my king and you, while Fisher liues.
Sur. Farewell, my Lord of Rochester; weele pray
For your release, and labour't as we may
Shrew. Therof assure yourselfe; so doo we leaue yee,
And to your happie priuate thoughts bequeath yee. [*ex. Lords.*
Rochest. Now, M⟨aiste⟩r Lieutenant, on; a Gods name, goe!
And with as glad a minde goe I with you
As euer trewant bad the schoole adiewe.
[*Exeunt.*

Scene IV. *add. H*

⟨SCENE V.—Chelsea. A Room in More's House.⟩

Enter Sir Thomas Moore, *his Lady, Daughters, M⟨aiste⟩r* Roper, *Gentlemen, and Seruaunts, as in his house at Chelsey.*

Moore. God morrowe, good sonne Roper.—
Sitt, good madame, [*Lowe stooles.*
Vppon an humble seate; the time so craues;
Rest your good hart on earth, the roofe of graues:
You see the floore of greatnesse is uneuen;
The cricket and high throane alike neere heauen.—
Now, daughters, you that like to braunches spred,
And giue best shaddowe to a priuate house,
Be comforted, my girles; your hopes stand faire:
Vertue breedes gentrie, she makes the best heire.
Both Daugh. God morrow to your honor.
Moore. Nay, good night rather;
Your honor's creast-falne with your happie father.
Ro. Oh, what formalitie, what square obseruaunce,
Liues in a little roome! heere publique care
Gagges not the eyes of slumber; heere fierce riott
Ruffles not proudely in a coate of trust,
Whilste, like a pawne at chesse, he keepes in ranck
With kings and mightie fellowes; yet indeed
Those men that stand on tiptoe smile to see
Him pawne his fortunes.
Moore. True, sonne, . . .

Scene V. *add. H* 21 *Several words have been lost. H supplies* you say well.

Nor does the wanton tongue heere skrewe itselfe
Into the eare, that like a vise drinkes vp
The yron instrument.
Lady. We are heere at peace.
Moore. Then peace, good wife.
Lady. For, keeping still in compasse, (a straunge poynte
In times newe nauigation) we haue sailde
Beyond our course.
Moore. Haue doone.
Lady. We are exilde the courte.
Moore. Still thou harpste on that:
Tis sinne for to deserue that banishment;
But he that nere knewe courte, courtes sweete content.
Lady. Oh, but, deare husband——
Moore. I will not heare thee, wife;
The winding laborinth of thy straunge discourse
Will nere haue end. Sit still; and, my good wife,
Entreate thy tongue be still; or, credit me,
Thou shalt not vnderstand a woord we speake;
Weele talke in Latine.
Humida vallis raros patitur fulminis ictus,
More rest enioyes the subiect meanely bred
Then he that beares the kingdome in his head.
Great men are still musitians, else the world lyes;
They learne lowe straines after the noates that rise.
Ro. Good sir, be still yourselfe, and but remember
How in this generall courte of short-liu'd pleasure,
The worlde, creation is the ample foode
That is digested in the mawe of tyme:
If man himselfe be subiect to such ruine,
How shall his garment, then, or the loose pointes
That tye respect vnto his awefull place,
Auoyde distruction? Moste honord father in lawe,
The blood you haue bequeath'de these seuerall hartes
To nourishe your posteritie, stands firme;
And, as with ioy you led vs first to rise,
So with like harts weele lock preferments eyes.
Moore. Close them not, then, with teares; for that ostent
Giues a wett signall of your discontent.
If you will share my fortunes, comfort then;
An hundred smiles for one sighe: what! we are men:
Resigne wett passion to these weaker eyes,
Which prooues their sexe, but grauntes ⟨it⟩ nere more wise.
Lets now suruaye our state. Heere sits my wife,
And deare esteemed issue; yonder stand
My loouing seruaunts: now the difference
Twixt those and these. Now you shall heare me speake
Like Moore in melanchollie. I conceiue that nature
Hath sundrie mettalles, out of which she frames
Vs mortalles, eche in valuation
Outprizing other: of the finest stuffe
The finest features come: the rest of earth,
Receiue base fortune euen before their birthe;
Hence slaues haue their creation; and I thinke
Nature prouides content for the base minde;
Vnder the whip, the burden, and the toyle,
Their lowe-wrought bodies drudge in pacience;
As for the prince in all his sweet-gorgde mawe,
And his ranck fleshe, that sinfully renewes
The noones excesse in the nights daungerous surfeits.
What meanes or miserie from our birth dooth flowe
Nature entitles to vs; that we owe:
But we, beeing subiect to the rack of hate,
Falling from happie life to bondage state,
Hauing seene better dayes, now know the lack
Of glorie that once rearde eche high-fed back.
But ⟨you⟩, that in your age did nere viewe better,
Challendge not fortune for your thriftlesse debter.
Catesbie. Sir, we haue seene farre better dayes then these.
Moore. I was the patrone of those dayes, and knowe
Those were but painted dayes, only for showe.
Then greeue not you to fall with him that gaue them:
Generosis seruis gloriosum mori.
Deare Gough, thou art my learned secretarie;
You, Master Catesbie, steward of my house;
The rest (like you) haue had fayre time to growe
In sun-shine of my fortunes. But I must tell ye,
Corruption is fled hence with eche mans office;
Bribes, that make open traffick twixt the soule
And netherland of hell, deliuer vp
Their guiltie homage to their second lordes.

57 And *Dyce*: As *MS.*

64 it *add. Dyce* 68–89 *This speech and all but the first three lines of More's next speech deleted in MS. For the revised version of this passage cf. Appendix, pp.* 419–20 94 *Deletion in MS. before* Generosis

Then, liuing thus vntainted, you are well:
Trueth is no pilot for the land of hell.

Enter a Seruaunt.

⟨*Ser.*⟩ My lord, there are new lighted at the gate
The Earles of Surrie ⟨and⟩ of Shrewesburie,
And they expect you in the inner courte.
Moore. Entreate their lordships come into the hall. ⟨*Exit Ser.*⟩
Lady. Oh, God, what newes with them?
Moore. Why, how now, wife!
They are but come to visite their olde freend.
Lady. Oh, God, I feare, I feare!
Moore. What shouldst thou feare, fond woman?
Justum, si fractus illabatur orbis, inpauidum ferient ruinæ.
Heere let me liue estraungde from great mens lookes;
They are like golden flyes on leaden hookes.

Enter the Earles, Downes *with his mace, and Attendants*

Shrew. Good morrowe, good Sir Thomas. [*Kinde salutations.*
Sur. Good day, good madame.
Moore. Welcome, my good lordes.
What ayles your lordships looke so melanchollie?
Oh, I knowe; you liue in courte, and the courte diett
Is only freend to phisick.
Sur. Oh, Sir Thomas,
Our woordes are now the kings, and our sad lookes
The interest of your looue! We are sent to you
From our milde soueraigne, once more to demaund
If youle subscribe vnto those articles
He sent ye th' other day: be well aduisde;
For, on mine honor, lord, graue Doctor Fisher
Bishop of Rochester, at the selfe same instant
Attachte with you, is sent vnto the Tower
For the like obstinacie: his maiestie
Hath only sent you prisoner to your house;
But, if you now refuse for to subscribe,
A stricter course will followe.
Lady. Oh, deare husband! [*Kneeling and weeping.*
Both Daugh. Deare father!
Moore. See, my lordes,
This partner and these subiects to my fleshe
Prooue rebelles to my conscience! But, my good lordes,
If I refuse, must I vnto the Tower?
Shrew. You must, my lord; heere is an officer
Readie for to arrest you of high treason.
Lady and Daugh. Oh, God, oh, God!
Ro. Be pacient, good madame.
Moore. I, Downes, ist thou? I once did saue thy life,
When else by cruell riottous assaulte
Thou hadst bin torne in pieces: thou art reseru'de
To be my sumner to yond spirituall courte.
Giue me thy hand; good fellowe, smooth thy face:
The diet that thou drinkst is spic'de with mace,
And I could nere abide it; twill not disgest,
Twill lye too heauie, man, on my weake brest.
Shrew. Be breefe, my lord, for we are limitted
Vnto an houre.
Moore. Vnto an houre! tis well:
The bell (earths thunder) soone shall toale my knell.
Lady. Deare loouing husband, if you respect not me,
Yet thinke vppon your daughters. [*Kneeling.*
Moore. Wife, stand vp; I haue bethought me,
And Ile now satisfye the kings good pleasure. [*Pondering to himselfe.*
Both Daugh. Oh, happie alteration!
Shrew. Come, then, subscribe, my lord.
Sur. I am right glad of this your fayre conuerssion.
Moore. Oh, pardon me!
I will subscribe to goe vnto the Tower
With all submissiue willingnes, and therto add
My bones to strengthen the foundation
Of Julius Cæsars pallace. Now, my lord,
Ile satisfye the king, euen with my blood;
Nor will I wrong your pacience.—Freend, doo thine office.
Dow. Sir Thomas Moore, Lord Chauncellour of England, I arrest you in the kings name of high treason.
Moore. Gramercies, freend.
To a great prison, to discharge the strife
Commenc'de twixte conscience and my frailer life,
Moore now must marche. Chelsey, adiewe, adiewe!
(Straunge farewell!) thou shalt nere more see Moore true,
For I shall nere see thee more.—Servauntes, farewell.——

106 and *add. Dyce*

157 *Drawn through with a pen in MS.* 163 subscribe *Dyce*: subscrible *MS.*

Wife, marre not thyne indifferent face; be wise:
Moores widd⟨ow's⟩ husband, he must make thee rise.—
Daughters, ... :—what's heere, what's heere?
Mine eye had almost parted with a teare.—
Deare sonne, possesse my vertue, that I nere gaue.—
Graue Moore thus lightly walkes to a quick graue.

Ro. *Curæ leues loquuntur, ingentes stupent.*

Moore. You that way in; minde you my course in prayer:
By water I to prison, to heauen through ayre.

[*Exeunt.*

⟨ACT V.

SCENE I.—The Tower Gate.⟩

Enter the Warders of the Tower, with halbards.

1. *Ward.* Hoe, make a guarde there!

2. M⟨aiste⟩r Lieutenant giues a straite commaund,
The people be auoyded from the bridge.

3. From whence is he committed, who can tell?

1. From Durham House, I heare.

2. The guarde were waiting there an houre agoe.

3. If he stay long, heele not get neere the wharffe,
Ther's such a croude of boates vppon the Thames.

2. Well, be it spoken without offence to any,
A wiser or more vertuous gentleman
Was neuer bred in England.

3. I thinke, the poore will burie him in teares:
I neuer heard a man, since I was borne,
So generally bewailde of euery one.

Enter a Poore Woman.

What meanes this woman?—Whether doost thou presse?

1. This woman will be trod to death annon.

2. What makest thou heere?

Wo. To speake with that good man, Sir Thomas Moore.

2. To speake with him! hees not Lord Chauncellour.

Wo. The more 's the pittie, sir, if it pleasde God.

2. Therfore, if thou hast a petition to deliuer,
Thou mayst keepe it now, for any thing I knowe.

Wo. I am a poore woman, and haue had (God knowes)
A suite this two yeare in the Chauncerie;
And he hath all the euidence I haue,
Which should I loose, I am vtterly vndoone.

2. Faith, and I feare thoult hardly come by am now:
I am sorie for thee, euen with all my hart.

Enter the Lords with Sir Thomas Moore, *and Attendants, and enter Lieutenant and Gentleman Porter.*

Woman, stand back, you must auoyde this place;
The lords must passe this way into the Tower.

Moore. I thanke your lordships for your paines thus farre
To my strong house.

Wo. Now, good Sir Thomas Moore, for Christes deare sake,
Deliuer me my writings back againe
That doo concerne my title.

Moore. What, my olde client, are thou got hether too?
Poore sillie wretche, I must confesse indeed,
I had such writings as concerne thee neere;
But the king has tane the matter into his owne hand;
He has all I had: then, woman, sue to him;
I cannot help thee; thou must beare with me.

Wo. Ah, gentle hart, my soule for thee is sad!
Farewell the best freend that the poore ere had.

[*exit woman.*

Gent. Por. Before you enter through the Towergate,
Your vpper garment, sir, belongs to me.

Moore. Sir, you shall haue it; there it is.

[*He giues him his cap.*

Gent. Por. The vpmoste on your back, sir; you mistake me.

Moore. Sir, now I understand ye very well:
But that you name my back,
Sure else my cap had bin the vppermoste.

Shrew. Farewell, kinde lord; God send vs merie meeting!

Moore. Amen, my lord.

Sur. Farewell, deare freend; I hope your safe returne.

Moore. My lord, and my deare fellowe in the Muses,
Farewell; farewell, moste noble poett.

182 widd⟨ow's⟩ *H* 183 *H supplies* be virtuous Act V. *etc. add. H* 5 1. *Dyce*: 2. *MS.* 16 1. *Dyce*: 2. *MS.*

54 moste. *deleted in MS. before* deare

Lieu. Adewe, moste honord lords. [*ex. Lords.*

Moore. Fayre prison, welcome; yet, methinkes,
For thy fayre building tis too foule a name.
Many a guiltie soule, and many an innocent,
Haue breathde their farewell to thy hollowe roomes.
I oft haue entred into thee this way;
Yet, I thanke God, nere with a clearer conscience
Then at this houre:
This is my comforte yet, how hard soere
My lodging prooue, the crye of the poore suter,
Fatherlesse orphane, or distressed widdowe,
Shall not disturbe me in my quiet sleepe.
On, then, a Gods name, to our closse aboade!
God is as strong heere as he is abroade. [*Exeunt.*

⟨SCENE II.—More's House.⟩

Enter Butler, Brewer, Porter, and Horssekeper seuerall wayes.

But. Robin brewer, how now, man! what cheere, what cheere?

Brew. Faith, Ned butler, sick of thy disease; and these our other fellowes heere, Rafe horssekeeper and Gyles porter, sad, sad; they say my lord goes to his triall to day.

Horss. To it, man! why, he is now at it, God send him well to speed!

Por. Amen; euen as I wishe to mine owne soule, so speed it with my honorable lord and maister, Sir Thomas Moore.

But. I cannot tell, I haue nothing to doo with matters abooue my capacitie; but, as God iudge me, if I might speake my minde, I thinke there liues not a more harmelesse gentleman in the vniuersall worlde.

Brew. Nor a wiser, nor a merier, nor an honester; goe too, Ile put that in vppon mine owne knowledge.

Por. Nay, and ye bate him his due of his housekeeping, hang ye all! ye haue many Lord Chauncellours comes in debt at the yeares end, and for very housekeeping.

Horsse. Well, he was too good a lord for vs, and therfore, I feare, God himselfe will take him: but Ile be hangd, if euer I haue such an other seruice.

Brew. Soft, man, we are not dischargde yet; my lord may come home againe, and all will be well.

But. I much mistrust it; when they goe to rayning once, ther's euer foule weather for a great while after. But soft; heere comes M⟨aiste⟩r Gough and Maister Catesbie: now we shall heare more.

Ent. Gough *and* Catesbie *with a paper.*

Horss. Before God, they are very sad; I doubt my lord is condemnde.

Por. God blesse his soule! and a figge then for all worldly condemnation.

Gough. Well said, Giles porter, I commend thee for it;
Twas spoken like a well affected seruaunte
Of him that was a kinde lord to vs all.

Cate. Which now no more he shall be; for, deare fellowes,
Now we are maisterlesse, though he may liue
So long as please the king: but lawe hath made him
A dead man to the world, and giuen the axe his head,
But his sweete soule to liue among the saintes.

Gough. Let vs entreate ye to goe call together
The rest of your sad fellowes (by the roule
Y'are iust seauen score), and tell them what ye heare
A vertuous honorable lord hath doone
Euen for the meanest follower that he had.
This writing found my ladie in his studie,
This instant morning, wherin is set downe
Eche seruaunts name, according to his place
And office in the house: on euery man
He franckly hath bestowne twentie nobles,
The best and wurst together, all alike,
Which M⟨aiste⟩r Catesbie heere foorth will pay ye.

Cate. Take it as it is meante, a kinde remembraunce
Of a farre kinder lord, with whose sad fall
He giues vp house and farewell to vs all:
Thus the fayre spreading oake falles not alone,
But all the neighbour plants and vnder-trees
Are crusht downe with his weight. No more of this:
Come, and receiue your due, and after goe
Fellow-like hence, copartners of one woe. [*Exeunt.*

⟨SCENE III.—The Tower.⟩

Enter Sir Thomas Moore, *the Lieutenant, and a Seruaunt attending, as in his chamber in the Tower.*

Moore. M⟨aiste⟩r Lieutenant, is the warrant come?
If it be so, a Gods name, let vs knowe it.

Lieu. My lord, it is.

Scene II. *add. H* 8 it *deleted after* send *in MS.*

Scene III. *add. H* 2 see *deleted in MS. before* knowe

Moore. Tis welcome, sir, to me with all my hart;
His blessed will be doone!
Lieu. Your wisedome, sir, hath bin so well approou'de,
And your fayre pacience in imprisonment
Hath euer shewne such constancie of minde
And Christian resolution in all troubles,
As warrante vs you are not vnpreparde.
Moore. No, M⟨aiste⟩r Lieutenant;
I thanke my God, I haue peace of conscience,
Though the world and I are at a little oddes:
But weele be euen now, I hope, ere long.
When is the execution of your warrant?
Lieu. To morrowe morning.
Moore. So, sir, I thanke ye;
I haue not liu'de so ill, I feare to dye.
M⟨aiste⟩r Lieutenant, I haue had a sore fitt of the stone to night; but the king hath sent me such a rare receipte, I thank him, as I shall not need to feare it much.
Lieu. In life and death still merie Sir Thomas Moore.
Moore. Sirra fellowe, reache me the vrinall:
[*Hee giues it him.*
Ha! let me see ⟨there's⟩ grauell in the water;
⟨And yet I see no grave danger in that⟩
The man were likely to liue long enoughe,
So pleasde the king.—Heere, fellowe, take it.
Ser. Shall I goe with it to the doctor, sir?
Moore. No, saue thy labour; weele cossen him of a fee:
Thou shalt see me take a dramme to morrowe morning,
Shall cure the stone, I warrant; doubt it not.—
M⟨aiste⟩r Lieutenant, what newes of my Lord of Rochester?
Lieu. Yesterday morning was he put to death.
Moore. The peace of soule sleepe with him!
He was a learned and a reuerend prelate,
And a riche man, beleeue me.
Lieu. If he were riche, what is Sir Thomas Moore,
That all this while hath bin Lord Chauncellour?
Moore. Say ye so, M⟨aiste⟩r Lieutenant? what doo you thinke
A man, that with my time had held my place,
Might purchase?
Lieu. Perhaps, my lord, two thousand pound a yeare.
Moore. M⟨aiste⟩r Lieutenant, I protest to you,
I neuer had the meanes in all my life
To purchase one poore hundred pound a yeare:
I thinke I am the poorest Chauncellour
That euer was in England, though I could wishe,
For credit of the place, that my estate were better.
Lieu. Its very straunge.
Moore. It will be found as true.
I thinke, sir, that with moste parte of my coyne
I haue purchased as straunge commodities
As euer you heard tell of in your life.
Lieu. Commodities, my lord!
Might I (without offence) enquire of them?
Moore. Croutches, M⟨aiste⟩r Lieutenant, and bare cloakes;
For halting soldiours and poore needie schollers
Haue had my gettings in the Chauncerie:
To thinke but what a cheate the crowne shall haue
By my attaindour! I prethee, if thou beest a gentleman,
Get but a copie of my inuentorie.
That parte of poett that was giuen me
Made me a very vnthrift;
For this is the disease attends vs all,
Poets were neuer thriftie, neuer shall.

Enter Lady Moore *mourning, Daughters,* *M⟨aiste⟩r* Roper.

Lieu. Oh, noble Moore!——
My lord, your wife, your sonne in lawe, and daughters.
Moore. Sonne Roper, welcome;—welcome, wife, and girles.
Why doo you weepe? because I liue at ease?
Did you not see, when I was Chauncellour,
I was so clogde with suters euery houre,
I could not sleepe, nor dine, nor suppe in quiet?
Heer's none of this; heere I can sit and talke
With my honest keeper halfe a day together,
Laugh and be merie: why, then, should you weepe?
Ro. These teares, my lord, for this your long restraint
Hope had dried vp, with comfort that we yet,
Although imprisond, might haue had your life.
Moore. To liue in prison, what a life were that!
The king (I thanke him) looues me more then so.
To morrowe I shall be at libertie
To goe euen whether I can,
After I haue dispachte my busines.
Lady. Ah, husband, husband, yet submit yourselfe!
Haue care of your poore wife and children.

25, 26 *Bracketed words add. H: MS. illegible* 39 *Word deleted in MS. before* Lord

Moore. Wife, so I haue; and I doo leaue you all
To his protection hath the power to keepe you
Safer then I can,—
The father of the widdowe and the orphane.
Ro. The world, my lord, hath euer held you wise;
And't shall be no distaste vnto your wisedome,
To yeeld to the oppinion of the state.
Moore. I haue deceiu'de myselfe, I must acknowledge;
And, as you say, sonne Roper, to confesse the same,
It will be no disparagement at all.
Lady. His highnesse shall be certefied therof [*Offering to departe.*
Immediatly.
Moore. Nay, heare me, wife; first let me tell ye how:
I thought to haue had a barber for my beard;
Now, I remember, that were labour lost,
The headsman now shall cut off head and all.
Ro. Wife. Father, his maiestie, vppon your meeke submission,
Will yet (they say) receiue you to his grace
In as great credit as you were before.
Moore. . . . .
Has appoynted me to doo a little busines.
If that were past, my girle, thou then shouldst see
What I would say to him about that matter;
But I shall be so busie vntill then,
I shall not tend it.
Daugh. Ah, my deare father!
Lady. Deare lord and husband!
Moore. Be comforted, good wife, to liue and looue my children;
For with thee leaue I all my care of them.—
Sonne Roper, for my sake that haue loou'de thee well,
And for her vertues sake, cherishe my childe.—
Girle, be not proude, but of thy husbands looue;
Euer retaine thy vertuous modestie;
That modestie is such a comely garment
As it is neuer out of fashion, sits as faire
Vppon the meaner woman as the empresse;
No stuffe that golde can buye is halfe so riche,
Nor ornament that so becomes a woman.
Liue all and looue together, and therby
You giue your father a riche obsequye.
Both Daugh. Your blessing, deare father.
Moore. I must be gon—God blesse you!—
To talke with God, who now dooth call.
Lady. A, my deare husband!
Moore. Sweet wife, good night, good night:
God send vs all his euerlasting light!
Ro. I thinke, before this houre,
More heauie harts nere parted in the Tower. [*Exeunt.*

⟨SCENE IV.—Tower Hill.⟩

Enter the Sheriffes of London and their Officers at one doore, the Warders with their halbards at another.

2 *Sher.* Officers, what time of day ist?
Offi. Almoste eight a clock.
2 *Sher.* We must make ⟨haste⟩ then, least we stay to long.
2 *Ward.* Good morrowe, M⟨aiste⟩r Shreeues of London; M⟨aiste⟩r Lieutenant
Willes ye repaire to the limits of the Tower,
There to receiue your prisoner.
1 *Sher.* Goe back, and tell his woorship we are readie.
2 *Sher.* Goe bid the officers make cleare the way,
There may be passage for the prisoner.

Enter Lieutenant and his Guarde, with Moore.

Moore. Yet, God be thanked, heer's a faire day toward,
To take our iourney in. M⟨aiste⟩r Lieutenant,
It were faire walking on the Tower leades.
Lieu. And so it might haue likte my soueraigne lord,
I would to God you might haue walkte there still! [*He weepes.*
Moore. Sir, we are walking to a better place.
Oh, sir, your kinde and loouing teares
Are like sweete odours to embalme your freend!
Thanke your good lady; since I was your guest,
She has made me a very wanton, in good sooth.
Lieu. Oh, I had hopte we should not yet haue parted!
Moore. But I must leaue ye for a little while:
Within an houre or two you may looke for me;
But there will be so many come to see me,
That I shall be so proude, I will not speake;
And, sure, my memorie is growne so ill,
I feare I shall forget my head behinde me.
Lieu. God and his blessed angelles be about ye!—

100 had *deleted before* thought *in MS.* 106 Nay, He, whom I've tried faithfully to serve, *add. H* : *MS. illegible* 121 fashion] fashis *MS.* sits *MS.* : fits *Dyce*

Scene IV. *etc. add. H* 3 haste *add. Dyce* 7 1 Sher. *add. Dyce* : 2 Sher. *MS.* 10 heer's *Dyce* : hee's *MS.*

Heere, M⟨aiste⟩r Shreeues, receiue your prisoner.

Moore. Good morrowe, M⟨aiste⟩r Shreeues of London, to ye bothe:
I thanke ye that ye will vouchsafe to meete me;
I see by this you haue not quite forgot
That I was in times past, as you are now,
A sheriffe of London.

2 *Sher.* Sir, then you knowe our dutie dooth require it.

Moore. I knowe it well, sir, else I would haue bin glad
You might haue sau'de a labour at this time.
Ah, M⟨aiste⟩r Sheriffe, you and I haue bin of olde acquaintaunce! you were a pacient auditor of mine, when I read the diuinitie lecture at St. Lauraunces.

2 *Sher.* Sir Thomas Moore, I haue heard you oft,
As many other did, to our great comforte.

Moore. Pray God, you may so now, with all my hart!
And, as I call to minde,
When I studyed the lawe in Lincolnes Inne,
I was of councell with ye in a cause.

2 *Sher.* I was about to say so, good Sir Thomas.

. . . .

Moore. Oh, is this the place?
I promise ye, it is a goodly scaffolde:
In sooth, I am come about a headlesse arrand,
For I haue not much to say, now I am heere.
Well, let's ascend, a Gods name:
In troth, me thinkes, your stayre is somewhat weake;
I prethee, honest freend, lend me thy hand
To help me vp; as for my comming downe,
Let me alone, Ile looke to that myselfe.

[*As he is going vp the stayres, enters the Earles of* Surrye *and* Shrewsburie.

My Lords of Surrey and of Shrewesburie, giue me your hands. Yet before we . . ye see, though it pleaseth the king to raise me thus high, yet I am not p⟨roud⟩, for the higher I mounte, the better I can see my freends about me. I am now ⟨on a⟩ farre voyage, and this straunge woodden horsse must beare me thether; yet ⟨I per⟩ceiue by your lookes you like my bargaine so ill, that ther's not one of ye all dare venter with me. Truely, heers a moste sweet gallerie; [*Walking*] I like the ayre of it better then my garden at Chelsey. By your pacience, good people, that haue prest thus into my bedchamber, if youle not trouble me, Ile take a sound sleepe heere.

Shrew. My lord, twere good you'ld publishe to the worlde
Your great offence vnto his maiestie.

Moore. My lord, Ile bequeathe this legacie to the hangman, [*Giues him his gowne*] and doo it instantly. I confesse, his maiestie hath bin euer good to me; and my offence to his highnesse makes me of a state pleader a stage player (though I am olde, and haue a bad voyce), to act this last sceane of my tragedie. Ile send him (for my trespasse) a reuerend head, somewhat balde; for it is not requisite any head should stand couerd to so high maiestie: if that content him not, because I thinke my bodie will then do me small pleasure, let him but burie it, and take it.

Sur. My lord, my lord, holde conference with your soule;
You see, my lord, the time of life is short.

Moore. I see it, my good lord; I dispatchte that busines the last night. I come hether only to be let blood; my doctor heere telles me it is good for the headache.

Hang. I beseeche ye, my lord, forgiue me!

Moore. Forgiue thee, honest fellowe! why?

Hang. For your death, my lord.

Moore. O, my death? I had rather it were in thy power to forgiue me, for thou hast the sharpest action against me; the lawe, my honest freend, lyes in thy hands now: hers thy fee [*His pursse*]; and, my good fellowe, let my suite be dispachte presently; for tis all one payne, to dye a lingering death, and to liue in the continuall mill of a lawe suite. But I can tell thee, my neck is so short, that, if thou shouldst behead an hundred noblemen like myselfe, thou wouldst nere get credit by it; therefore (looke ye, sir), doo it hansomely, or, of my woord, thou shalt neuer deale with me heerafter.

Hang. Ile take an order for that, my lord.

Moore. One thing more; take heed thou cutst not off my beard: oh, I forgot; execution past vppon that last night, and the bodie of it lies buried in the Tower.——Stay; ist not possible to make a scape from all this strong guarde? it is.
There is a thing within me, that will raise
And eleuate my better parte boue sight
Of these same weaker eyes: and, M⟨aiste⟩r Shreeues,
For all this troupe of steele that tends my death,

48 *MS. illegible*　59 mount *add. H*: *MS. illegible*　61 p⟨roud⟩ *Dyce*　63 on a *add. Dyce*　65 ⟨I per⟩ceive *Dyce*

79 highnesse *substituted for a deleted word, probably* maiestie　115 ff. *For earlier version of this passage cf. Appendix*

I shall breake from you, and flye vp to heauen.
Lets seeke the meanes for this.
Hang. My lord, I pray ye, put off your doublet.
Moore. Speake not so coldely to me; I am hoarse alreadie;
I would be lothe, good fellowe, to take more.
Point me the block; I nere was heere before.
Hang. To the easte side, my lord.
Moore. Then to the easte
We goe to sigh; that ore, to sleepe in rest.
Heere Moore forsakes all mirthe; good reason why;
The foole of fleshe must with her fraile life dye.
No eye salute my trunck with a sad teare:
Our birthe to heauen should be thus, voide of feare. [*Exit* ⟨*with Hangman, &c.*⟩
Sur. A very learned woorthie gentleman
Seales errour with his blood. Come, weele to courte.
Lets sadly hence to perfect vnknowne fates,
Whilste he tends prograce to the state of states.

FINIS.

APPENDIX TO SIR THOMAS MORE

FIRST DRAFT OF III. ii. 23 ff.

'This must be newe written.'[1]

A table beeing couered with a greene carpet, a state cushion on it, and the Pursse and Mace lying thereon, enter Sir Thomas Moore, and his man Randall with him, attyred like him.

Moore. Come on, sir: are you readie?

Ran. Yes, my lord, I stand but vppon a fewe pointes; I shall haue doone presently. Is it your honors pleasure that I should growe proude now?

Moore. I, I must haue thee proude, or else thou'lt nere
Be neere allyed to greatnesse. Obserue me, sir.
The learned clarke Erasmus is arriu'de
Within our Englishe courte: this day, I heare,
He feasteth with an Englishe honoured poett,
The Earle of Surrey; and I knowe this night
The famous clarke of Roterdame will visite
Sir Thomas Moore. Therfore, sir, acting parte,
There take my place, furnisht with pursse and mace:
Ile see if great Erasmus can distinguishe
Merit and outward ceremonie. Obserue me, sirra:
Ile be thy glasse, dresse thy behauiour
According to my cariage; but beware
Thou talke not ouermuch, for twill betray thee:
Who prates not oft seemes wise; his witt fewe scan,
Whilste the tounge blabs tales of th' imperfect man.

Ran. I conceiue your lordship, and haue learnde your shift
So well that I must needes be apprehensiue.
[*The waites playes within.*
Moore. This musique telles vs that the earle is come
With learnde Erasmus. Now, my Lord Chauncellour—
The rest is pasted over.

FIRST DRAFT OF III. ii. 91 ff.

Me thinkes this straunge and ruffinlike disguise
Fits not the follower of a secretarie.

Faulk. My lord, I weare my haire vppon a vow.

Shrew. But for no penaunce of your sinnes, I feare.
Sur. No, hees no haire-clothman, though he weare haire.
Moore. Faulkener, how long ist since you cutt your locks?
Faulk. Three yeares, my lord.
Moore. How long wilt be before your vow expire?

Faulk. As many yeares as since my haire was cut.

Moore. Sure, vowes are holy things, if they be made
To good intent; and, sir, you shall not say,
You were compelde by me to breake your vowe;
But till the expiration of the same,
Because I will not haue ye walke the streetes
For euery man to stand and wunder at,
I will committ ye prisoner vnto Newgate,

[1] This . . written *add. Tylney*

Except meane time your conscience giue you leaue
To dispense with the long vow that you haue made.—
Away with him!
Sur. A cell moste meete for such a votarie.
Faulk. Well, sir, and I may perhaps be bailde er't be long, and yet weare my haire.
[*They lead him out.*
Moore. And, M⟨aiste⟩r Sheriff of London,
Heere in his highnesse name we giue you charge
Continuall watche be kept throughout the cittie,
For the suppressing of these mutinies;
And, if hereafter any that belong
Either to my Lord of Winchester or Elie
Doo come into your cittie with a weapon,
Or abooue two of either faction
Shall be seene walking in the streetes together,
Or meete in tauerne or in ordinarie,
They be committed presently to prison.
Sur. And cause to be proclaimd about the cittie,
That no man whatsoeuer, that belongs
Either to my Lord of Winchester or Elie,
Doo walke without the liuerie of his lord,
Either in cloke or any other garment,
That notice may be taken of the offenders.

Enter M⟨aiste⟩r Morris, and ex. Sherif and the rest.

Moris. God saue your honor, my Lord Chauncellour!
Moor. Welcome, M⟨aiste⟩r Morris: what newes, sir?
Moris. I come moste humbly to entreate your honor
In the behalfe of a poore man of mine.
Moore. What! the votarie that will not cut his haire,
Vntill the expiration of his vow?
Moris. My lord, beeing sorie for his rude behauiour,
He hath cut his haire, and dooth conforme himselfe
. . . . in his attire.
The rest is pasted over.

FIRST DRAFT OF IV. i. 330 ff.

[*More.*] Lord Maier and ladies, and the rest, be patiente;
The state hathe sent, and I must nedes be gone:
But frollicque on.—Lead on theare.—What seekst thou, fellow?
[*Wit.*] Your lordship sent vs 8 angills by your man, and I haue loste one heare amongst the rishes.
[*More.*] 8 angills! whoo dilliuerd yt? I sent them ten.
[*S. Man.*] I, my lord, dilliuerd yt: anon they shall haue too more.
[*Wit.*] Thats more then we hard before, my lord.
[*More.*] Am I a man of righte and equetie,
Equallie to deuide true righte his owne,
And shall I haue diseauers in my house?—
Goe pull the cote ouer the varlets eares:
Ther ar too many suche; ile make them fuer by one.
Giue them ther dewe. Lead one, awaye.—
Come, fellowes, goe with me.

LATER DRAFT OF IV. v. 68 ff.

Moore. Now will I speake like man in melancholy;
For, if greefes power could with her sharpest darts
Pierce my firme bosome, heres sufficient cause
To take my farewell of mirths hurtles lawes.
Poore humbled lady, thou that wert of late
Placde with the noblest women of the land,
Invited to their angell companies,
Seeming a bright starre in the courtly sphere,
Why shouldst thou, like a widow, sit thus low,
And all thy faire consorts moove from the clowds
That ouerdreep thy beautie and thy worth?
Ile tell thee the true cause: the court, like Heauen,
Examines not the anger of the prince,
And being more fraile, composde of guilded earth,
Shines vpon them on whom the king doth shine,
Smiles if he smile, declines if he decline;
Yet, seeing both are mortall, court and king,
Shed not one teare for any earthly thing;
For, so God pardon me, in my saddest hower
Thou hast no more occasion to lament,
Nor these, nor those, my exile from the court,
No, nor this bodyes tortur, wert imposde,
(As commonly disgraces of great men
Are the forewarnings of a hastie death,)
Than to behold me after many a toyle
Honord with endlesse rest. Perchance the king,
Seeing the court is full of vanitie,

8 heaven of *deleted before* courtly 10 shun *deleted before* moove 13 kinge *deleted before* prince 15 king *substituted for original* prince 19 in *inserted above the line. The metre would be better without it.* 21 my mortall d *deleted after* these, nor 25 Beleeue me *deleted before* Than

Has pittie least our soules shuld be misled,
And sends vs to a life contemplatiue.
O happy banishment from worldly pride,
When soules by priuate life are sanctifide!
Wife. O, but I feare some plot against your life!
Moore. Why, then, tis thus; the king, of his high grace,
Seeing my faithfull seruice to his state,
Intends to send me to the King of Heauen
For a rich present; where my soule shall proue
A true remembrer of his majestie.
Come, prethee, mourne not: the worst chance is death,
And that brings endlesse joy for fickle breath.
Wife. Ah, but your children!
Moore. Tush, let them alone:
Say they be stript from this poore painted cloth,
This outside of the earth, left houselesse, bare,
They haue mindes instructed how to gather more;
Theres no man thats ingenuous can be poore:
And therefore doo not weep, my little ones,
Though you loose all the earth; keep your soules eeuen,
And you shall finde inheritance in heauen.
But for my seruants, theres my cheefest care.
Come hether, faithfull steward: be not greeude
That in thy person I discharge both thee
And all thy other fellow officers,
For my great master hath discharged mee.
If thou by seruing me hast sufferd losse,
Then benefit thyselfe by leauing mee.

36 if soules *deleted after* where 38 , since *deleted after* mourne 39 *An illegible word originally written for* brings 43 what have they *deleted before* left 47 all *deleted before* you 50 In you I *deleted before* Come 53 *After this line the following line has been deleted*: So for the rest my Gentlemen and y.

I hope thou hast not; for such times as theese
Bring gaine to officers, whoeuer leese:
Great lords haue onely name; but, in the fall,
Lord Spend-alls stuart's master, gathers all.
But I suspect not thee: admit thou hast,
Its good the seruants saue when masters wast.
But you, poore gentlemen, that had no place
T'inrich yourselues but by loathd briberie,
Which I abhord, and neuer found you loude,
Thinke, when an oake fals, vnderwood shrinkes downe,
And yet may liue, though brusd: I pray ye, striue
To shun my ruin; for the ax is set
Euen at my root, to fell me to the ground:
The best I can doo to prefer you all
With my meane store, expect; for Heauen can tell
That Moore loues all his followers more than well.

FIRST DRAFT OF V. iv. 115 ff.

Come, let's to the block.
Hang. My lord, I pray ye, put off your doublet.
Moore. No, my good freend, I haue a great colde alreadie, and I would be lothe to take more. Point me meete the block, for I was nere heere before.
Hang. To the easte side, my lord.
Moore. Then to the easte:
We goe to sighe; that ore, to sleep in rest.
No eye salute my trunck with a sad teare:
Our birth to heauen should be thus, voyde of feare. [*Exit.*

58 the] their *originally*: *last two letters deleted* 59 Sir [?] *deleted before* Lord 69 is [?] *deleted after all*

NOTES

ARDEN OF FEVERSHAM

ACT I

50. *as securely*: WP explain, 'as if thou wert quite secure,' which may be the meaning; but cf. *As vnsuspected*, II. ii. 212, and Abbott, *Shakespearian Grammar*, § 115.

60. *Ouidlike*: cf. Amor. Bk. I. 13. The Elegies of Ovid had been translated by Marlowe.

121. *thou wert* is here to be read as one syllable. Such slurring is very common in this play. Cf. in the first Act: *you are* 146; *here is* 148; *Ales* 206, 508, 577, 591; *leaue it* 247.

158. The pause in this line takes the place of one syllable. Cf. line 474, &c.

174. *Bolton*: this, according to Donne, is, 'Boughtón, looking down on Canterbury.' Jacob's conjecture *Bocton* may well be correct. This Boughton, or Bocton, is the *Boughton vnder Blee* mentioned by Chaucer at the beginning of the *Canon's Yeoman's Prologue*.

178. After this line Tyrrell inserts: *Scene II. Before Arden's House. Enter Alice from the House, meeting Mosbie.*

182. *daies*: adverbial genitive of time. So in *Troilus and Cressida*, IV. v. 12, *'Tis but early days.* Cf. N.E.D. s.v. *Day* 1. b, and Kellner, *Historical Outlines of English Syntax*, § 185.

226. *for* = 'to prevent'; cf. N.E.D. s. v. *For* 23. d.

244. A so-called nine-syllable line; the first foot consists of *Feare* alone. Cf. III. ii. 7, &c.

279. *makes*: this M.E. northern present plural in -s occurs repeatedly in Elizabethan literature. Cf. Abbott, *Sh. Gr.* §§ 332, 333.

313. *statute*: '37 Edward III. c. 9,' Bullen.

314. *that I doo*: for the very common omission of the relative in such cases cf. Kellner, l. c. § 109; Abbott, § 244.

361. After this line Tyrrell inserts: *Scene III. Room in Arden's House, as before. Enter* Arden, Franklin, Mosbie, Michael, *and* Alice.

384. *Methridate*: a general antidote against poison, &c. Cf. N.E.D. s. v. *Mithridate.*

427. *populos*: in the introduction to his edition of *The Birth of Merlin* (Vorrede xvii. note) Delius retracts his conjecture of *palpable* for *populos*, quoting Webster's *Appius and Virginia*, ed. Dyce, vol. ii, p. 261:

he I plead for
Has power to make your beauty populous.

524. *wager* seems to have here the meaning 'pay wages to'. *Wage* is frequently used in this sense.

539. Tyrrell begins Act II with this line.

545. *faire* is here to be pronounced in two syllables. Such lengthenings are very frequent with words containing liquids or nasals. Sometimes the difference in the number of syllables is indicated by the spelling, as in *coysterel*, III. ii. 59, beside *coistrell*, III. ii. 41.

ACT II

i. 58. *all to torne*: 'torn to pieces'. The O.E. prefix *to-* corresponds in such cases to *zer-* in N.H.G. *zerrissen*. Cf. Sweet, *New Eng. Grammar*, § 1579; Abbott, § 436.

66. *Tapsters head of the Lyon* = 'head of the tapster of the *Lion*'; cf. *Mucedorus the kings sonne of Valentia.* For the idiom see Kellner, § 469.

ii. 53. *ould*: great; cf. N.E.D. s. v. *Old* a. 6.

127. *what*: something; the O.E. indefinite *hwæt.*

200. Read: *choll'r makes me's drye's a dog.*

ACT III

i. 5. *cooch* = cause to germinate; cf. N.E.D. s. v. *Couch* v.[1] 5. This line, which has never been properly explained, appears to mean that scandal mongers nourish the unripe buds of dishonour, as fast as they appear, till they sprout and grow.

73. *bolstred*: 'propped up', hence 'erect'; cf. N.E.D. s. v. *Bolstered.*

ii. 19. *buges*: 'bugbears'; cf. N.E.D. s. v. *Bug* sb.[1]

47. *cockshut light*: 'twilight'; cf. N.E.D.

iii. 9. *whistely*: 'silently'; cf. Nares, *Glossary.*

13. *ill thewd*: 'evil-natured'. *Thews* referred originally to mental and moral qualities. Cf. Skeat, *Etymological Dict.* Nares quotes Spenser's 'rude, and thewed ill', *F. Q.* Bk. II. vi. 26.

46. *companye* is to be pronounced in two syllables.

iv. 21. *nor* = 'than'; cf. N.E.D. s. v. *Nor* conj.[2]

v. 17. *stary*: no satisfactory meaning or etymology for this word has been discovered, but the proposed emendation *stirry* is a very doubtful improvement.

24. *erre*: 'plough'; cf. N.E.D. s. v. *Ear* v.[1]

51. *pathaires*: '"Pathaire" I take to be some special form of "petarre", i.e. "petard", probably used in the metaphorical sense of passionate outburst.' Gollancz, *Lamb's Specimens*, I. i. 297. Cf. N.E.D. s. v. *Pathaire.* The proposed emendations of Delius have nothing to support them.

vi. 9. *dagge*: 'pistol'; cf. N.E.D. s. v. *Dag* sb.[2]

70. *brooke with*: 'agree with'; cf. N.E.D. s. v. *Brook* v. 3. b.

ACT IV

i. 3. *pace*: 'course', 'path'; cf. N.E.D. s. v. *Pace* sb.[1] 4. b.

61. *lordaine*: cf. N.E.D. s. v. *Lurdan.*

108. *can asunder*: some such word as *drive* is, of course, omitted. WP strangely regard *asunder* as a verb.

ACT V

i. 24. *natches of his tales*: 'notches off his tallies'. Without the tallies the clerk would be unable to reckon his accounts or recover his debts.

78. *arming*: cf. N.E.D. s. v. *Arming* 1. b.

86. *Patient*: cf. N.E.D. s. v. *Patient* vb.

243. *for*: cf. note to I. 226.

LOCRINE

ACT I

i. 29. *strangle*: there seems no need of emendation, though I have been unable to find unexceptionable authority for *strangle* in the sense of *struggle*.

80. *Ixions ouerdaring sonne* is, of course, Peirithous, the story of whose imprisonment in Hades is well known. There seems no reason, metrical or logical, for the word *his* in this line, and we should perhaps, like Malone, omit it altogether.

170. *America*: it is hardly necessary to remark on the anachronisms in which this play particularly abounds.

ii. 21. *Asse Tom*: Steevens suggests that *Acteon* is meant.

79. *pigsney*: 'darling'; cf. N.E.D. and *Roister Doister* (ed. Manly), I. iv. 42, III. iv. 32.

106. *capcase*: 'hand-bag'; cf. N.E.D.

ACT II

ii. 71. *gogs blew hood*: a euphemism, according to Malone, for *God's blood*.

iv. 1. *coronet*: 'company of cavalry'. The proper spelling is *cornet*. Cf. N.E.D. s. v. *Cornet* sb.[2] 4.

21. *wreake* = 'reck'.

v. The numbering of scenes in Q in the last part of this act is extraordinarily careless.

46–62. A striking illustration of the hold which the ideas of travel and exploration had on the Elizabethan imagination.

ACT III

i. 43–57. These three speeches are an instance of the tendency of the early dramatists to linger over one idea, giving it expression in several aspects from the mouths of different characters. It is a lyrical trait which finds its superlative illustration in the Lorenzo-Jessica speeches of *The Merchant of Venice* (v. i. 1–24).

54. Malone points out that Niobe was queen of Thebes, not Athens, and suggests *Amphion's*, but in this case the adjective *faire* would have little appositeness, while the small error in mythology is surely not too great for the author of *Locrine*.

iii. 5. *by my dorth* = 'by my troth'.

iv. 52. *detract*: 'avoid'; cf. N.E.D. s. v. *Detract* 7.

ACT IV

i. 28–43. An ebullition of national feeling inspired doubtless by the Armada. Cf. *Richard II*, II. i. 40 ff.

46–75. Five six-line stanzas, rhyming *a*, *b*, *a*, *b*, *c*, *c*. Tieck (*Alt-Eng. Theater*, vol. ii, Introduction) asserts that they are distinctly reminiscent of *Venus and Adonis*, and that they alone would prove the genuineness of the drama!

51. *platforme*: 'model'; cf. N.E.D. s. v. *Platform* sb. 3.

91–102. The lines form two almost regular stanzas such as those in ll. 46–75.

iv. 6. *pillowbeares*: 'pillow-cases'; cf. N.E.D. s. v. *Pillow-bere*.

ACT V

ii. 40. *reclaimes*: 'answer back'.

iv. 49. *feer*: 'mate'; cf. N.E.D. s. v. *Fere* sb.[1] 1.

236. *mastie*: 'mastiff'; cf. N.E.D.

269. *eight and thirtie yeares*: Elizabeth entered upon the thirty-eighth year of her reign in November 1595, the year in which *Locrine* was published. As the tragedy was registered, however, on July 20, 1594, we must assume either that the poet exaggerated the length of the reign by a couple of years or, as is more probable, that these concluding lines were added for some court performance in 1595. Cf. Introduction.

EDWARD III

ACT I

i. 98. *case*: 'skin'; cf. N.E.D. s. v. *Case* sb.[2] 4.

ii. 25. *Rods*: 'inroads'; cf. Schmidt, *Sh. Lex.* s. v. *Road*, 4.

29. *Iacks of Gymould mayle*: 'shirts of ringed mail'; cf. N.E.D. s. v. *Jack* sb.[2] 1. b and *Gimmal* 6.

123. *niggard*: 'supply sparingly'; cf. Schmidt s. v. *Niggard* v. 2.

125. *neare*: the old comparative. Cf. Sweet, *New Eng. Gram.*, § 1048.

131–4. For a parallel conceit cf. *Love's Labour's Lost*, I. i. 77 ff.

166. *host*: 'lodge'; cf. N.E.D. s. v. *Host* v.[2] 2.

ACT II

i. 4. *racke*: 'drive before the wind'; cf. N.E.D. s. v. *Rack* v.[1] 1.

57. *beauties Queene* is, of course, Venus, the idea being that the countess out-queens the goddess in her own dominion. WP's emendation is indefensible.

68. The editor of the Temple edition would substitute *Tokening* for *Talking*; certainly a very bad and needless alteration.

83. The relative *Which* is to be supplied before *Containes*. Cf. Abbott, *Sh. Gram.* § 244. Capell's bad emendation in 82, in which he has been followed by modern editors, is due to his failure to note the omission of the relative.

134. *Hers* = Her bewtie: *myne* = my affection. Cf. preceding line.

255–9. Cf. *Measure for Measure*, II. iv. 43–50.

303. *peise*: 'weigh down'; cf. N.E.D. s. v. *Peise* v. 4.

414. *inuierd*: 'environed', 'besieged'; cf. N.E.D. s. v. *Envire*.

426. *shame for shame*: the editor of the Temple edition proposes to read *shame for sin*, which, though plausible, is unnecessary.

439. *carrion . . . kisse*: cf. *good kissing carrion*, *Hamlet*, II. ii. 181.

451. It has often been pointed out that this is the last line of Shakespeare's 94th Sonnet. The only safe inference from the coincidence seems to be that the author of our play had seen the sonnets in MS. Cf. Meres' allusion to Shakespeare's 'sugred Sonnets among his private friends', *Palladis Tamia*, 1598.

ii. 50. *shipskin*: for the spelling *ship* = 'sheep', cf. *Mucedorus*, II. iv. 67, *shipstickes*.

68. *sweetest*: Swinburne conjectures *swift'st*.

82. *cloke it selfe on*: 'excuse itself with the pretence of'. Cf. N.E.D. s. v. *Cloak* v. 2.

92. The emendations of Capell seem inevitable.

99, 100. Capell's omission of *not* in 99 is hardly to be justified. There are really two questions loosely connected: 1. Shall not I, who go to conquer kings, subdue myself? 2. Shall I by failing to subdue myself be my enemies' friend?

102. *sweete*: 'sweeten'.

116. *rarieties*: rarities; cf. N.E.D. s. v. *Rariety*.

136. *I will* = that I will.

142. *louing*: 'beloved'; cf. Abbott, *Sh. Gr.* § 372.

147. A nine-syllable line, *So* forming the first foot; cf. III. iii. 137.

167. *packing*: 'deceptive', 'underhand'; cf. N.E.D. *Pack* v.[2] 1.

195–7. The allusion seems to be particularly to Shakespeare's poem. Heywood's play, *The Rape of Lucrece*, was first printed 1608.

ACT III

i. 52. *gaine*: the reading of Q 1 *game* can perhaps be justified; cf. N.E.D. s. v. *Game* sb. 7.

58. *Bayardlike*: *bayard* was originally a bay horse, then a slang term for any horse; cf. N.E.D.

77. *titely*: 'ably, adroitly, soundly'; cf. Schmidt, *Sh. Lex.* s. v. *Tightly*.

148, 149. *Admirall*: 'flagship'.

iii. 1. *guide*: 'guidance'; cf. N.E.D. s. v. *Guide* sb. 11.

38, 39. There is no need for Capell's sweeping change, which all succeeding editors have adopted. Some such verb as *were* or *stood* is to be supplied in 39. The punctuation is that of the present editor, as that of the Qq makes nonsense.

161. *resty*: 'stiff with too much rest'; cf. *Cymbeline*, III. vi. 34, and Schmidt, *Sh. Lex.*

224. *manage*: 'conduct', 'management'; cf. Schmidt.

v. 37. Capell's conjecture, *breathe* for *breaketh*, is clever but unnecessary. The meaning of the passage as it stands is that, if the prince escape after this seasoning of his courage, even a life as long as Nestor's will not cause him to outlive his fame. *That* is a conjunction, depending on *those* (= such) in 36.

58. The editor of the Temple edition would like to read *clang* or *clangour* for *charge*, and *sound* for *loud*, but the change is too sweeping, and the original is far from unintelligible, though a little obscure.

75. *Whose thousands*: Capell's emendation makes sense of the nonsense of the Qq, but is not thoroughly convincing.

82. *recorde*: 'call to mind'; cf. N.E.D. s. v. *Record* v. 4. This is somewhat nearer the 'ductus litterarum' of the Quarto reading than Capell's *remember*.

ACT IV

i. 14. *at*: the editor of the Temple edition quotes, in support of the Quarto reading *to*, *Antony and Cleopatra*, III. i. 35; but this is not a parallel case, for *to* follows *purposeth*, a verb implying motion.

16. *That*: the Quarto reading *Yet* may arise from *Yt* (= That) in the author's MS.

iv. 2. *to die*: the indefinite infinitive; cf. Abbott, *Sh. Gr.* § 356. The sense of the passage is: 'We have no comfort except that in dying we pay bitter earnest for a sweeter life to come.'

44, 45. *and . . . power*: 'and call it only a single whole'; this clause is parenthetical. Before *Easely* we must supply *is*.

75. *Bryttish*: 'relating to Brittany'.

99. *carping*: 'prating'; cf. N.E.D.

134. *inch-wise*: 'inch by inch'.

ix. 46. *Should*: 'Should she'. The subject, being easily understood, has been omitted. The Temple editor suggests that a line has been lost after 45.

ACT V

31. There is a break in the thought before this line. The idea is: What we assert is true, or may, &c.

97. *Brittaine*: 'Brittany'.

MUCEDORUS

Dramatis Personae. *Eight persons may easily play it.* From these words we may infer that the comedy was destined by the publishers particularly for companies of humble pretensions, such as that which performed it at Witney in 1653. Cf. Introduction.

Induction, 15. *Bellonas*: we should expect rather the name of Thalia, muse of comedy, but the error is doubtless that of the author.

54 ff. According to tradition, the accident at Witney occurred while these ominous words were being spoken. Cf. Introduction.

68. *I force it not*: 'I reck not of it'; cf. N.E.D. s. v. *Force* v.[1] 14.

79. *proue to*: 'turn to'. *their* refers to the actors; cf. l. 71.

ACT I

iv. 2. *as then*: 'then'; cf. N.E.D. s. v. *As* 34.

67, 68. *you know no bodie, and you knowe not mee*: a proverbial saying; cf. Heywood's play, *If you Know not Me, you Know Nobody*, 1605.

ACT II

i. 16. *alowe of*: 'approve of'; cf. N.E.D. s. v. *Allow* v. 2. b.

iv. 68. *shipstickes*: 'sheepsticks', 'hurdles'.

ACT III

i. 93. *No longer loue*: 'When I no longer love'.

iii. 49. *say*: 'essay', 'try'; cf. Abbott, *Sh. Gr.* § 460.

iv. 4. *a world*: 'a wonder'. Cf. *Much Ado*, III. v. 38; *Taming of the Shrew*, II. i. 305; and Schmidt, *Sh. Lex.*

ACT IV

i. 6. *are* agrees with the predicate *embers*.

8. *sight*: 'quality of being seen'.

25. *what*: 'that of which'.

iii. 2. The probable meaning of this difficult line is: 'I consider the gloomy character of the woods to be in keeping with Bremo's cruelty.' *like* is an adjective. The entire speech is an aside.

18, 19. *loue should limit life*, &c.: the meaning seems to be, 'Love should put an end to life rather than be made a murderer of the loved object.' *him selfe* refers to *loue*, personified in the beloved person.

87. *Waying*: 'considering', 'contrasting'. Tyrrell's explanation, *abandoning*, is obviously a guess.

99. *or fight or els*: 'either fight or else'.

ACT V

i. 170. The change of *it* to *her* is not necessary. The antecedent of *it* is *kingdome* in 169. Segasto is thinking rather of the kingdom he might have inherited through Amadine than of the lady herself.

172. *barnes doore* appears to have been used as an epithet for a lubberly, spiritless rustic; it is applied here, of course, to Segasto. Mouse's local pride is hurt that one born within his father's constabulary dominion should bear himself so meanly.

ii. 51. *farre*: 'far-fetched', 'remote'.

69. *his onely*: 'of him alone', *his* being here the true genitive singular of the personal pronoun.

98. *Prepared welcomes*: 'welcomes already prepared', alluding to the wish just expressed in 92, 93.

Epilogue. The two versions of the Epilogue with their fulsome praise of Elizabeth and James respectively furnish a somewhat melancholy illustration of the dependence of the players on court patronage. The later version is of particular interest as it shows that *Mucedorus* was presented as a peace offering after some other of the company's performances had incurred royal displeasure.

59, 60: an allusion to the fashion of afternoon representations.

SIR JOHN OLDCASTLE

Prologue, 6, 7. An allusion to Shakespeare's Falstaff, originally called Oldcastle. Malone thinks this play written after the representation of the first part of Henry IV and before that of the second part. That the slight sketch of Oldcastle-Falstaff in the *Famous Victories* is not meant is shown by direct references to Falstaff in III. iv.

ACT I

i. 9. *O yes*: 'Oyez', the customary cry to demand attention.

10. *Cossone*: 'gossoon'; N.E.D. records no instance of this word before 1684.

14. *pye Cosse plut*: 'by God's blood'.

127. *There be*: 'that there be'; cf. Abbott, *Sh. Gr.* § 311.

ii. 50. *remember*: 'remind'; cf. N.E.D. s. v. *Remember* v.[1] 7.

103. *brabling*: 'quarrelsome'; cf. N.E.D. s. v. *Brabbling*.

117. *the Arches*: the court of Arches, the seat of ecclesiastical justice, was so called from being held originally in the church Sancta Maria de Arcubus.

158. *rudduks*: literally 'robin redbreasts'; hence a cant term for golden coins. Cf. Nares s. v. *Ruddocks*.

161. *olde huddle and twang*: *huddle* is defined (N.E.D.) to be a 'miserly old person'; *twang* perhaps means a snivelling hypocrite. It appears not to be in the dictionaries.

iii. 12. *ceased*: 'assessed'; cf. Abbott, § 460, for the general principle of verbal abbreviation in Elizabethan English.

35. *Your backes*: the adornment of your backs; *the diuell and pride* is perhaps parenthetical.

ACT II

i. 31. *In good time*: à la bonne heure!

179. *by the macke*: an unmeaning exclamation suggested by *by Mary* or *by the Mass*. Cf. N.E.D. s. v. *Mack* sb.[2]

185. *ingle*: 'cajole'; cf. N.E.D.

188. *feak*: 'beat'. It is unnecessary to adopt the commoner *ferke* from Q 2; cf. N.E.D. s. v. *Feak* v.[1]

229. *lion of Cotswold*: 'ram', according to Steevens, the Cotswolds being famous for sheep raising. Malone conjectured improbably that the epithet refers to the Cotswold athletic games. Cf. *Roister Doister*, IV. vi. 39.

ii. 4. *God dild ye*: 'God ild (yield, reward) you'; cf. *Gammer Gurton's Needle*, V. ii. 62; *As You Like It*, III. iii. 81.

46. *Come to me there*: 'answer me that'.

118. *axetree*: *axletree* of Q 2, &c. is an unnecessary change, *axetree* being the native O.E. form. Cf. N.E.D.

iii. 40. *fact*: criminal act, as very often in Elizabethan English. Cf. N.E.D. s. v. *Fact* 1. c.

ACT III

i. 30. *Harry the first*: Malone, influenced perhaps by the obvious error of *first* for *fifth* in line 24, substitutes *Harry the fourth*, but this is hardly justifiable, for Cambridge is thinking rather of Henry Bolingbroke's relation to his son than of his place in the succession of English kings.

67. *absolute*: here used in its common sense of *perfect*.

68–71. The construction is very loose and elliptical, the subject changing in the course of the sentence from *life* to the general idea of Oldcastle's disgrace at court. There is doubtless no need to adopt Malone's emendation of *life* for *life's*, a change which after all does little to smoothe the syntax.

89. *Cowling*: Cobham's residence.

173. Scan *Who hath* as one syllable.

ii. 6. *Dunne is the mowse*: a very common saying not satisfactorily explained. Cf. *London Prodigal*, IV. i. 16, 17; *Romeo and Juliet*, I. iv. 40; and N.E.D. s. v. *Dun*. The meaning may be that the mouse's dun colour is not to be changed; that is, that present conditions cannot be helped.

15. *brave*: 'bravely attired'.

106. *boikin*: an affectionate diminutive of *boy*.

iii. 22, 23. *merely*: 'merrily'.

iv. 139. *bouer*: I have adopted Malone's conjecture for the *beuer* of Qq, Ff, because of the phrase *reuel in our bower*, v. ii. 56. Sir John is much given to repetition. *Bever*, which, as Steevens points out, means a luncheon before dinner, is quite possible. Cf. *Doctor Faustus*, sc. vi, speech of Gluttony; Ford, *Love's Sacrifice*, I. ii; and N.E.D. s. v. *Bever* sb. 3.

ACT IV

i. 43. *Passage*: Nares and N.E.D. quote as follows from Cotton, *Compl. Gamester*, 1680: 'Passage is a Game at dice to be played at but by two, and it is performed with three Dice. The Caster throws continually till he hath thrown Dubblets under ten, and then he is out and loseth; or Dubblets above ten, and then he *passeth* and wins.'

iii. Simms's insertion of scene v. i between IV. ii and IV. iii has at first sight much to recommend it, as it would save us a provoking and inartistic interruption of the catastrophe after it has already begun, and would make it possible to assume, as Malone and all modern editors do, that Cobham is present in the scene. The notes of time, however, make it quite impossible to place v. i before IV. iii, for in the former scene we are told of the king that 'this day . . . he will aboord . . . and set away for France' (ll. 14, 15), whereas in IV. iii we are told that he 'at Southampton doth repose this night' (l. 72).

30. *laid*: 'waylaid', 'watched'; cf. N.E.D. s. v. *Lay* v.[1] 18. c.

iii. 159. *the sickemans salue*: a devotional work by Thomas Becon, published 1561. Cf. *Eastward Hoe* (*Belles Lettres* ed.), V. ii. 72.

168. *Owleglass*: the adventures of the wandering clown known in Germany as *Till Eulenspiegel*.

169. *the Frier and the Boy*: an old ballad, from which Malone quotes extracts.

169. *Ellenor Rumming*: Skelton's poem 'The Tunnyng of Elynour Rummyng'.

172. *S. Margets ale*: 'water'. St. Margaret, Queen of Scotland 1069–93, was noted for her piety; she reformed the Lenten observances.

iv. 55. *for*: 'for fear of'.

ACT V

i. S. D. *A room in lord Cobham's house in Kent*: this indication of the place of the action is almost certainly wrong. There is nothing in the text to substantiate it, and the fact that the King is the same day to set sail for France combines with well-known historical fact to point to Southampton as the place of arrest of the conspirators. By no possibility could the journey from Cowling to Southampton be made before the close of the day.

15. *winds*: the reading of Q 1, *wind*, may be kept if we regard *The . . . faire* as an absolute construction: 'The wind being so fair'.

56, 57. We must understand these lines as an apostrophe to the absent Cobham.

ii. There can be no doubt of the correctness of Rowe's transposition of scenes ii–vii.

4. *nip the Boung*: cf. N.E.D. s. v. *Bung* sb.[2]

35. *is*: I's = I have.

41. *leufter*: perhaps a corruption of *lifter*, 'thief'; cf. N.E.D. and *James IV*, III. ii. 49.

iii. 31. *the three horse-loues*: the name of an

inn. Horses were formerly fed on loaves of coarse meal.

iv. 8. *passe*: 'care'; cf. N.E.D. s. v. *Pass* v. 23.

v. 12. *the sheeres*: the name of an inn.

vii. 37. *capons*: Percy's conjecture of *capuls* = 'horses' is unnecessary. The First Carrier in 1 *Henry IV*, II. i was carrying turkeys.

x. 83. *thicke*: 'thicket'.

125. *strouces*: the same word probably as *strossers* in *Henry V*, III. vii. 60. Loose Irish trousers. Cf. Nares s. v. *Strossers.*

LORD CROMWELL

ACT I

i. 7. *quile*: 'noise'; cf. N.E.D. s. v. *Coil* sb.[3] For the pronunciation cf. the seventeenth and eighteenth-century pronunciation of *boil, join.*

13. *strong Ale*: we have here a blending of two meanings of *Ale*; (*a*) the drink so called, and (*b*) the place where it is supplied. In III. i. 39 the word occurs in the latter sense alone. Cf. *Two Gentlemen of Verona*, II. v. 62, and N.E.D. s. v. *Ale* 2.

ii. 29. *walking*, according to Steevens, means no more than *moving*. There seems no need of emendation.

59. *He shall not here me*: Malone substituted *They* for *He*, and the alteration has been retained by subsequent editors. The reading of the Qq, however, seems clearly right. Old Cromwell is of two minds with regard to his hopeful son; his common sense bids him rebuke the latter's fantastic and impractical ambitions, even while the brilliance of the possibilities they suggest wrings from him against his better judgement the secret jubilations, which he is afraid to let Thomas perceive, lest his reckless imagination be further inflamed.

iii. 21. *day*: 'period'; cf. N.E.D. s. v. *Day* 11.

56. *be knowne thereof*: 'take cognizance of them' (i. e. his debts). Cf. N.E.D. s. v. *Known* 2, for the meaning *informed, aware of*. Malone quotes *Othello* (III. iii. 320), *Be not acknown on't.*

73–6. Lines 73–5 are omitted by the Ff, Rowe, and Pope. They were restored by Malone. Line 76 is omitted by all editions since the Qq, though it is indispensable to the sense, as Friskiball replies to it in 77. The state of the text shows clearly the carelessness with which all the editions of this play have been prepared. The cause of the omissions is easily seen. In F 1 the word *sell* (72) ends a page. In the bottom right-hand corner, as catch-word for the next page, *As* is indeed printed; so we should expect *As part to pay*, &c. to follow. The compositor's eye, however, has overlooked lines 73–6, beginning the next page with 77, which after 72 is obviously inappropriate. F 2 followed F 1 without referring to the Qq, and so the error was continued till Malone's casual collation of Q 2 (of the existence of Q 1 he knew only from hearsay) restored three of the four missing lines. That it should be left for the present edition to restore line 76, which common sense so obviously requires, is sufficient condemnation of Malone and his blind followers: Messrs. Simms, Tyrrell, Hazlitt, and Moltke.

97. *Portague*: a Portuguese coin worth from three to five pounds. As this sum seems rather great for Bagot's contempt in the light of his reference to *a score of crownes* (l. 107), Malone suggests that we substitute in 97 and 108 *cardecue* [quart d'ecu]. For *cardecue* cf. *Birth of Merlin*, IV. i. 15. There is no sufficient reason for the change; the poet, attracted by the sound of the word, may well have been ignorant or regardless of the precise value of a *Portague*. Cf. Nares, s. v. *Portague.*

ACT II

Chorus. 2. *Ledger*: 'commissioner' or 'agent'. Cf. N.E.D. s. v. *Ledger* 4.

ii. 40. *poyse*: 'weight'; cf. *peise* in *Edward III*, II. i. 303. The difference of diphthong depends on difference in the position of the accent in Old French; cf. *convoy* beside *convey*.

122. *race*: 'root'; cf. N.E.D. s. v. *Race* sb.[6]

iii. 105. *Stands*: 'If it stands'.

ACT III

i. 31. *it will be your owne another day*: 'you will have use for it hereafter'. Cf. *Athenaeum*, No. 2920, Oct. 13, 1883, p. 465, where parallels are quoted from *Love's Labour's Lost* (IV. i. 110), *The Tale of a Tub*, *The Witch*, and *Tu Quoque*.

77. *Florence*: the use of proper noun for adjective is very common. Cf. Abbott, *Sh. Gr.* § 22, *end*; and compare *Mantua port*, III. ii. 65.

iii. 12. *his*: 'its', referring to *trauell.* The observance of travel proves its value by producing a learned yet unaffected spirit.

52. *Ciuill*: 'Seville'.

84. *for*: 'because'; cf. N.E.D. s. v. *For* B. 1.

85. *that*, like French *que*, merely repeats the idea of the preceding conjunction *for*.

109. *leaue*: 'cease'; cf. N.E.D. s. v. *Leave* v.[1] 10. b.

ACT IV

ii. 16. *Iwis*: O.E., German *gewiss*, 'certainly'. Malone's *I wis* is due to misunderstanding.

34. *gibber*: N.E.D. quotes this single instance of the word, but does not hazard a definition. Cf. the common phrase *jeopard a joint*, 'risk a finger', which is probably what Seelie means.

78. *sort*: 'set'; cf. Nares.

iv. S. D. *Shewer*: cf. Nares, s. v. *Sewer*.

16. *I hope*: 'which I hope'.

29. *And to repay*: 'in case I should repay'; the so-called indefinite infinitive. Cf. Abbott, *Sh. Gr.* § 357.

ACT V

v. 33. *Learning* stands by personification for Gardiner; it is the subject of *doth drinke. learning*=Cromwell.

104. *sound*: 'swoon'; the d is parasitic, as in Mod. Eng. sound [Lat. *sonum*].

131, 132. As they stand these lines are hardly intelligible, nor has any convincing emendation been suggested. Perhaps we should insert a comma after *soule*, thus making it vocative, and regard *land* as subject of *is shrinde*.

148. *whom* is to be regarded as the subject of *Will grieue*. Two constructions have been confused. Cf. Abbott, *Sh. Gr.* § 410.

THE LONDON PRODIGAL

ACT I

i. 10. *exibition*: 'allowance'; cf. N.E.D. s. v. *Exhibition* sb. 2.

17. *that*: 'that which'.

45–6. The expression is clumsy but the meaning is fairly plain, and there seems no cause for emendation. 'I grant that it is bad to swear, but not that it is better to keep the oaths when sworn than to break them.'

63. *attendants*: 'attendant vices'.

132. *Katern-hue*: 'Katherine-Hugh'; cf. 185–6. *Katern* exactly represents the usual Elizabethan pronunciation of *Katherine*; cf. Sweet, *New Eng. Gram.* § 833.

164–6. The dates are absolute nonsense in Q, and I have not hesitated to adopt Malone's emendations. Percy suggests that the gibberish may have been meant to pass for Spanish.

168. *Kester*: an abbreviation of *Christopher*.

170. *winde*: enclose in his winding-sheet.

218–20. Cf. Malone's note with his quotation from *The English Rogue*, ed. 1680, p. 322. High fulloms were dice so loaded as generally to show the number four, five, or six, while low fulloms, or low men, showed one, two, or three. *Stop cater traies* (quatre-trois) Malone supposes to be dice stopping usually at three and four. Cf. *Merry Wives*, I. iii. 92–3, and N.E.D. s. v. *Fulham*.

233. *fop of*: 'fob off'; cf. N.E.D. s. v. *Fop*, v. 2.

ii. 7. *set vp by the halues*: apparently a proverbial saying.

37. *and*: 'as if'. *your* is ethical.

38. *trenchmore*: a dance; cf. Nares.

39. *shuter*: 'suitor'. The identity of pronunciation between this word and *shooter* is constant matter of joke; cf. *Puritan*, II. i. 97; *Love's Labour's Lost*, IV. i. 111–13.

77. *They may be Ladies*: i. e. by marrying knights; cf. *Eastward Hoe*, I. ii. 5.

105. *the three Tunnes*: one of the rooms in the inn.

132. *rerages*: the exact meaning is uncertain. The word may refer to old, unsaleable stock.

ACT II

i. 6–8. *zutch . . . vreens*: illustrations of the characteristic substitution of (voiced) z, v for (voiceless) s, f in the Southern dialects.

20. *chid*: I should; *ch* represents the Southern *ich*=I. So *cham, chill*; cf. Sweet, *New Eng. Gram.* § 1065.

36. *ruddockes*: cf. note to *Oldcastle*, I. ii. 158.

41–2. Sarcastic reference to the characteristic manufactures and dishes of Devonshire. Cf. Malone's note.

49. *cocknell*: 'cockney'; cf. N.E.D.

96. *Woodcocke*: 'dunce'; cf. Schmidt, *Sh. Lex.*, and Nares.

113. *yuine*: 'in fine'.

ii. 18. *I, I*: the first *I* is of course *Ay*.

23. *cutting*: 'swaggering'; cf. N.E.D.

iii. 5. *Knowes*: 'Who knows'.

iv. 41. *call me cut*: cf. Malone's note and N.E.D. s. v. *Cut* sb.[2] 2. a. The same expression occurs in *Twelfth Night*, II. iii. 203.

51. *testorne*: the apparent meaning is 'needy'; cf. *testern*=sixpence.

ACT III

i. 52. *set downe my rest*: 'firmly resolved', 'staked my last penny'. A gaming metaphor; cf. Schmidt, *Sh. Lex.* s. v. *Rest* [2].

ii. 36. *thats . . . O*: 'that's an absolute lie'. The words are an aside. Malone explains, 'That is a complete and absolute truth,' but Steevens's interpretation as given above seems undoubtedly the correct one.

90. *fine*: 'end'.

103. The reference, according to Steevens, is to the slandering of Una by Abessa in the third canto of the first book of the *Faerie Queene*, but this seems very doubtful.

155. *his second*: 'his match', 'one like him'.

165. *humours*: cf. N.E.D. s. v. *Humour*, v. 3.

iii. 32. *volowten*: 'flouting', according to Malone.

163. *in hucksters handling*: 'in great straits'; cf. N.E.D. s. v. *Huckster* sb. 3, and Greene's *Alphonsus*, I. i. 143.

221. *or . . . or*: 'either . . . or', as regularly in Milton.

ACT IV

i. 15. *pricke*: the mark at archery, and hence the prize.

16–17. *done is the mouse*: cf. *Oldcastle*, III. ii. 6.

ii. 48. *triumphant*: this word has not been satisfactorily explained. Steevens explains *triumphant life*—very improbably—as a life spent in looking for *triumphs* or trumps, while Malone would substitute for *triumphant trompant*, 'deceptive', a word which he coins from French *tromper*.

iii. 91. This line has been regarded as a sneer at Greene's *Never too Late*.

ACT V

i. 40. *stands . . . in*: 'costs'.

174. *armine*: 'a miserable creature'; cf. N.E.D. s. v. *Arming* sb.

249–50. *very that . . . angell* is parenthetic, explaining *habit*: just such a habit as would become him when he was about to turn to angel (die).

269. *snick vp*: cf. *Twelfth Night*, II. iii. 103, and Nares, s. v. *Sneck-up*.

THE PURITAN

It will be noted that the title of this play is given on the title-page as *The Puritaine or the Widdow of Watling-streete*, whereas the heading of the first page of text gives the abbreviated title *The Puritaine Widdow*. The inconsistency is of no importance except as explaining references to the play both as *The Puritan* and as *The Puritan Widow*.

ACT I

i. 89. *snobbing*: 'weeping'; the primary meaning of the verb seems to be *hiccup*. Cf. Stratmann, *M. E. Dict.* s. v. *Snobben*, and Wright, *Dial. Dict.*

107. *to hot, nor to deere*: a proverbial expression = 'too difficult of attainment'. Cf. notes of Malone and Steevens. Simms proposes the unnecessary emendation *good* for *hot*.

132. *speake false Lattin*: 'lie'.

136–8. Malone conjectures plausibly that the thrice repeated *their* of Q for *this*, which is almost certainly correct, is due to the use of an abbreviation in the MS. How common such abbreviations of familiar words were in Elizabethan cheirography is well known.

147. *Widdowers*: it would be convenient to take this word, as Malone suggests, in the sense of *widows*', but I have found no authority for such a use.

ii. 4, 5. *put to silence like a Sectarie*: a reference apparently to the silencing of the Puritans under the primacy of Archbishop Bancroft, appointed 1603.

29. *Antient*: 'ensign'; cf. N.E.D. s. v. *Ancient* sb.[2] 2.

41, 42. *Quadrangle, Battled*: Dr. Farmer pointed out that these terms are peculiar to Oxford. Peele, the probable original of Pye-board, was educated at Broadgates Hall, Oxford, and the author of this play was most likely a member of the same university.

46–9. *a Cheese out of Iesus Colledge . . . Welshman*: this is another indication that Pye-board is alluding to Oxford, for there is no connexion between Jesus College, Cambridge, and the Welsh.

92. *and Peace*: 'if Peace'; cf. Stratmann, *M. E. Dict.* s. v. *And* [2].

161 *soothing*: 'flattering', 'hypocritical'.

iii. 11. *we three*: Steevens refers to *Twelfth Night*, II. iii. 16, 17, 'How now, my hearts! Did you never see the picture of "we three"?' The picture represented two men in fools' coats, the spectator making the third.

25. *drye*: cf. *dry blows*, said of blows not drawing blood. N.E.D. s. v. *Dry* a. 12.

42. *sowne*: 'swoon'.

56. *Capadochio*: 'prison'. N.E.D. gives only this instance, but cf. Heywood, 1 *King Edward IV*, ed. 1874, p. 72: 'My son's in Dybell here, in *Caperdochy*, itha gaol.'

iv. 71. *bloud*: 'hereditary dignity'; cf. N.E.D. s. v. *Blood* 9.

158. *Pomwater*: 'apple'; cf. *Love's Labour's Lost*, IV. ii. 4.

159. *vncomfortable*: 'unconsoling'; cf. N.E.D. s. v. *Comfortable* 6.

299, 300. *Beare at Bridge-Foote*: a well-known inn by London Bridge; cf. Shirley, *Lady of Pleasure*, v. ii (*Mermaid* ed., p. 342); Middleton, *No Wit, no Help, etc.*, v. i. 267–8, and Bullen's note. There is no need of altering the words *in heauen*. The Corporal jocularly confuses in his oath the well-known tavern sign and the constellation of Ursa Major, calling the latter the Bear at Bridge-Foot of heaven.

ACT II

i. 36. *enow* seems to stand for *e'en now*.

97. Cf. note to *London Prodigal*, I. ii. 39.

112. *sure*: 'betrothed'. Cf. *As You Like It*, v. iv. 142.

201. *I*: 'Ay'.

234. *sir Reuerence*: 'save-reverence'; cf. Skeat, *Etymol. Dict.*, and IV. ii. 4.

237. The spelling *guesse* for *guests* is very common and doubtless represents the pronunciation.

357. Steevens has the following interesting note: 'Here is an odd agreement between a few circumstances in the present scene, and a few others in the last act of *Othello*. I shall only point them out, without any attempt to account for them. *Pyeboard* (Iago) advises *Skirmish* (Roderigo) to wound *Oath* (Cassio) In the confusion occasioned by this attempt, *Pyeboard* (Iago again) rushes among them, and instead of giving *Oath* (Cassio again) assistance, prepares somewhat to make him seem dead. Thus Iago wounds Cassio. The cut too is given on the *leg*; and *Pyeboard* takes on him the cure, as Iago comes out and proffers to bind up Cassio's wound. Query, which of these pieces was the elder?' The *Puritan* was entered on the Stationers' Register in 1607; there is no earlier reference to it, while *Othello* was acted before Lord Ellesmere and the Queen as early as 1602.

ii. 3. *say on*: assay or try on.

ACT III

i. 14. *praysing*: 'appraising'.
45. *casting*: 'vomiting'; cf. N.E.D. s. v. *Cast* v. 25.
ii. 9. *superiour*: Frailty must mean *surgeon.*
72. *Lincks*: a play, of course, on *link* = 'torch'.
81. *Sesarara*: according to Steevens, *Certiorari* is meant.
88. *seauen and twenty Prouinces*: this, Percy thinks, is a mistake for the seventeen provinces of the Low Countries.
iii. Steevens calls attention to the similarity of this scene to that in which Fang and Snare arrest Falstaff at the suit of his hostess. Cf. 2 *Henry IV*, II. i.
110. *Puttocks*: 'vultures'; cf. *Cymbeline*, I. i. 140; 2 *Henry VI*, III. ii. 191.
154. S. D. This stage direction is a good illustration of the simplicity of Elizabethan stage requirements. The author did not intend a change of scene.
iv. 12. *Posts*: symbols of civic authority.
116. *busie*: 'elaborate', 'intricate'; cf. N.E.D. s. v. *Busy* a. 8.
163. *god den*: 'good e'en'. Cf. *Love's Labour's Lost*, IV. i. 42; *Gammer Gurton's Needle*, IV. iii. 5; *Yorkshire Tragedy*, ii. 120; Tourneur, *Revenger's Tragedy*, IV. ii (*Mermaid* ed., p. 405).
190. *Sup, Simon, now*: an allusion, according to Steevens, to 'Simon of Southampton, alias Supbroth' in *Thomas of Reading, or the sixe worthie Yeomen of the West*, by Dekker.
197. *hole*: one of the worst rooms in the Woodstreet Counter; cf. *Eastward Hoe* (*Belles Lettres* ed., 1904), V. ii. 56.
v. 16, 17. *George Stone the Beare*: a famous bear at Paris Garden. Malone refers to *The Silent Woman* (III. i).
110. *lin*: cease; cf. N.E.D.
161, 162. *Act . . . Coniurers and Witches*: passed 1604.
271. *simply tho I stand here*: cf. IV. ii. 74, 75, and *Merry Wives*, I. i. 226.

ACT IV

i. 4. *dubd for nothing*: one of the innumerable references to King James's traffic in knighthoods. Cf. *Eastward Hoe* (*Belles Lettres* ed.), IV. i. 214.
11. *Derecke* was the hangman of the period. Steevens quotes several other contemporary references to him. Cf. Stat. Reg. (ed. Arber) ult. Mar. 1606.
36. *guarded Lackey*: one whose livery was adorned with guards or facings. Cf. N.E.D. s. v. *Guard* v. 7.
37. *trashing*: cf. *trace, Mucedorus*, IV. iii. 30, and *Cambises* (ed. Manly), 490.
iii. 41. *run vpon the Ropes*: take desperate risks; a metaphor from tight-rope walking.
90, 91. *ghost . . . Table*: an allusion, as Dr. Farmer pointed out, to Banquo's ghost at the banquet. Cf. *Macbeth*, III. iv.

ACT V

iii. 7. *squander*: cf. 'squandering glances', *As You Like It*, II. vii. 57.
iv. 27. *mistes*: 'deceits'; cf. N.E.D. s. v. *Mist* sb.[1] 2. b.

A YORKSHIRE TRAGEDY

i. This scene, which, as Steevens remarks, is not necessary to the plot, has given rise to much discussion. The circumstances to which the servants allude at the beginning are made clear by reference to *The Miseries of Enforced Marriage*, by George Wilkins. Mr. P. A. Daniel (*Athenaeum*, No. 2710, Oct. 4, 1879) first pointed out that the two plays treat of the same incidents, though the *Miseries* stops practically where our play begins. The *yong Mistresse* of line 1 is the Clare Harcop of Wilkins's drama. There is some difficulty as to the servants; they would appear to belong to the same household, and yet Ralph and Oliver seem to serve the *yong Mistresse*, while Sam is certainly in Calverley's employ. The truth probably is that the author of this hasty work had not imagined very consistently the details of Calverley's previous life.
32. *capcase*: cf. *Locrine*, I. ii. 106.
62, 63. Percy's emendations, quoted by Malone, are utterly unjustified.
74, 75. *potingsticks*: cf. Ford, *Love's Sacrifice*, IV. i. 15. The more usual spelling is *poking-stick*, as in Rowe and succeeding editors.
77, 82–3. A common proverb is alluded to. Steevens quotes from the *Stationers' Register*, 1566: 'a playe intituled Farre fetched and deare bowght ys good for ladies.'
78, 80. There is no sufficient reason for the alteration in the division of speeches introduced by Malone.
ii. 14. Some causal conjunction, such as *that* or *because*, is to be understood before *His*. Cf. Abbott, *Sh. Gr.* § 311. Hazlitt's indefensible displacement of the line is due to failure to grasp the meaning of the passage. Steevens had already suggested that lines 14 and 13 be transposed.
101. *blood*: 'nature'; cf. iv. 74 and N.E.D.
120. God den: cf. *Puritan*, III. iv. 163 and note.
149. *country* is, of course, used adjectivally. Cf. Abbott, *Sh. Gr.* § 22.
iii. 75. The substitution of *pleasant* for *comely* is probably the result of mere carelessness in the compositor of Q 2, who unintentionally substituted for one adjective a more familiar one with the same meaning.
iv. 120. *white boie*: a term of endearment. Cf. Ford, *'Tis Pity*, I. iv (*Mermaid* ed., p. 114).
125, 126. The meaning is: follow a coach, crying 'Good your Honour!' to the occupant.

v. 13, 14. The reference is to Leicester and Amy Robsart. Steevens quotes an apposite passage from *Leicester's Commonwealth* (1584, &c.).

viii. 16. *bated*: the meaning is probably not *abated* or *barred*, as Malone and Steevens respectively explain it, but *tormented*, as in bear-*baiting*. Cf. N.E.D. s. v. *Bait* v.[1] 4.

x. 22. *one thousand more*: *sc.* years. The reference, as Percy points out, is to *Revelation* xx. 2.

52. Some emendation is obviously required. Steevens suggests, as an alternative to the reading adopted in the text, *leave* (i. e. cease), *to part.*

THE MERRY DEVIL OF EDMONTON

Induction, 16. For the omission of *is* after *this* cf. Abbott, *Sh. Gr.* § 403.

45. Mr. P. A. Daniel is in favour of adopting Q 6's reading of *near* for *meane.* The change would certainly make the sense easier, but it is probably not absolutely necessary. The meaning of the line as it stands appears to be: 'which (knowledge) even when attained yet makes a man so mean in comparison with the higher powers'. Fabell laments that the soul should have to be sacrificed for the achievement of a power which when achieved is found to be relatively contemptible. For a different interpretation cf. WP.

79. *Phaetontique*: Walker reads *Phaetonic*, which he explains as relating to the sun-god, for whom *Phaethon* is an occasional epithet in Homer. Mr. Daniel informs me of Dr. Brinsley Nicholson's conjecture *Phlegethonic*, a reading which, though bold, has much to recommend it.

ACT I

i. 13. *Tartarian*: 'thief'; cf. *Nares.*

76, 77. These lines are doubtless the greatest crux in the play, the text of which abounds in obscurities. Fortunately, the general idea, Mounchensey's thriftlessness and extravagance, is clear. None of the suggested emendations improves the sense a whit, and it is at least possible that we have what the author wrote. If some satisfactory meaning for *simple* could be found, referring either to *hawkes* or *dogs*, all would be clear enough. *him* in 77 is, of course, the ethical dative, and the line means merely that the leanest and most worthless curs are fed on such meat as should be given only to valuable dogs.

81. *That*: 'so that'.

ii. 3. *your*: Lat. *iste*; cf. Abbott, *Sh. Gr.* § 221.

14. *Giberalters*: N.E.D. (s. v. *Gibraltar*) seems at last to have explained this puzzling word, which it defines as 'a Gibraltar monkey', quoting in addition to the present passage the following from Harvey, *Pierce's Super.* (1592), 158: 'Cumane Asse and foole, and dolt, and idiot, and *Gibaltar.*'

36. *Coopers Dixionary*: 'Thesaurus linguae Romanae et Britannicae'. Copies of editions of 1565, 1573, 1584 are in the Bodleian.

iii. 4. *by*: there is no cause for Hazlitt's emendation *my*, which rather increases the difficulty of the passage and can be explained only as an expression of 'contemptuous familiarity'. It is quite easy to supply *He should* before *Refuse* in the next line.

38–45. The passage is slightly obscure. The sense is: Offers of assistance from any but Jerningham would seem cold to Mounchensey, because of the inability of any one else to help him; yet he could believe in the sincerity of such offers from anybody except Jerningham, who is to profit by the injustice done him. *they* in 42 has the same antecedent as *that word* in 39; both refer to the whole of Jerningham's previous speech.

52. *hudman-blind*: 'blindman's-buff'. Cf. *Hamlet*, III. iv. 77, and N.E.D. s. v. *Hoodman-blind.*

53. *him*: *her Qq.* Mr. Daniel's emendation, which common sense appears to demand; but the change of gender can perhaps be adequately explained, as WP explain it, by the change of idea from Love personified, or Cupid, to love in the abstract.

59. *in hugger-mugger*: 'recklessly'. Cf. *Hamlet*, IV. v. 84; *Revenger's Tragedy*, V. i; *'Tis Pity*, III. i.

76. *busy bags*: Walker suspects a corruption.

141. *Cuts*: 'labouring horses'. Cf. 1 *Henry IV*, II. i. 6; *Twelfth Night*, II. iii. 206; *Merry Wives*, III. iv. 47; *Two Noble Kinsmen*, III. iv. 22; and N.E.D. s. v. *Cut* sb. 28.

142. *Dossers*: 'baskets'; cf. N.E.D. s. v. *Dosser* 2.

ACT II

i. 9, 10. *tickles . . . Catastrophe*: cf. V. ii. 13, 14; 2 *Henry IV*, II. i. 68.

50. *ther's not a narrow bridge*: Mr. Daniel has sent me the following note: 'I would read *there's narrow a bridge*: *never a*, *ne'er a*, a colloquialism to the present day. It takes the form of *narrow a*, *narro*, *narra*, *nary*, with or without the article. I have collected instances from Smollett, Fielding, Scott, and the *Referee* Newspaper of the present day.' Cf. N.E.D. s. v. *Nary.* There seems to be no special need for change, as the quarto reading makes perfect sense.

68. *Hungarions*: a quibble on *hungry ones*; cf. IV. i. 1.

75. *bosonians*: cf. 2 *Henry IV*, V. iii. 115; 2 *Henry VI*, IV. i. 134; and N.E.D. s. v. *Bezonian.*

85. *Cittizen*: Walker explains the word as 'fellow-citizen', but Sir John may mean 'paragon'.

ii. 11. *chat*: 'chatter'; cf. N.E.D. s. v. *Chat* sb.[1] 1.

54. *skeens*: Irish knives; cf. Nares, s. v. *Skain*.

57. *soares*: WP and Walker take the word as meaning 'soaring flights', but 'sore feelings' seems much more likely. The *frowardnesse* of Q 4–6 is evidently a mere gloss inspired by *froward* (*forward*) two words before, and inserted because *soares* was not intelligible to the editor or printer.

82. *fadge*: 'proceed'. Cf. *Love's Labour's Lost*, V. i. 158; *Twelfth Night*, II. ii. 34; and N.E.D. s. v. *Fadge* v. 4.

87. *handful*: 'palm', measure of four inches; cf. N.E.D.

90–5. Mr. Daniel's excellent emendations make sense of what is nonsense in all other editions. I should be glad to keep the text of the quartos and rearrange the order of lines as follows: 91, 90, 93, 94, 92, 95. In this way perfect sense would be restored, but the transposition is doubtless too arbitrary. Mr. Daniel remarks: 'My great difficulty with the passage is the two last lines (94, 95). I should like to strike them out altogether, they seem to me *de trop*; but as they must remain, I should be almost tempted to transpose them (always as altered) to a place between lines 91 and 92. The passage, I feel, *ought* to end with *teehee weehee*.'

iii. 3. *composure* is a collective noun = 'those composed', referring, of course, to the elder Clare and Jerningham.

17. The metre would be improved by the adoption of the *Yonder* of Q 3.

21. *lesse worlds*: well defined by Walker as 'the microcosms of the disunited youth and maid'.

23–6. A difficult passage. *the breath Of all aduised corruption*—that is, the voice, or command, of the personification of premeditated dishonesty—refers to old Clare and Jerningham. The sentence breaks off here, as the speaker turns to apologize to the sons: 'I must speak as I do of your fathers, and you may know I love you because I do not say that even greater malice (than "advised corruption") is the cause of our separation.' Mr. Daniel, changing *do* to *doth*, would regard the words *Pardon mee . . . spight* as parenthetical, and make *the breath* (23) subject of *doth seuer* (26).

ACT III

i. 28, 41, 48, 66. Mr. Daniel would transfer these speeches from Milliscent to Bilbo, but Milliscent's speech in 41 and the preceding speech of Bilbo (38–40) cannot belong to the same speaker, being separate comments, from different points of view, on what the prioress has just said (30–7).

100. *thrust . . . cushion*: 'disappoint'; cf. N.E.D. s. v. *Cushion* 10. c.

ii. 16. *deere*: 'inmost'.

84. This line has no authority, but it seems clear that some line or lines of similar meaning have been omitted by the quartos.

90. *a dream't*: Walker points out that this corresponds to the Chaucerian *a blakeberyed*, where the final dental indicates not the past participle, but an O.E. verbal substantive in *að*, the whole being a prepositional phrase. Cf. Skeat's note to *The Pardoneres Prologue*, 406 (Chaucer's *Man of Lawe*, &c., ed. Skeat, pp. 147, 148).

134. *vnbagd*: 'unpregnant'; cf. N.E.D. s. v. *Bag*.

139. *turne tippit*: 'change', used particularly of the change from unmarried to married state.

ACT IV

i. 54. *stone Priest*: cf. *Oldcastle*, II. i. 228.

ii. 51. *skinker*: 'tapster'; cf. Nares.

91. *roomer*: A nautical exclamation of doubtful meaning. Cf. Nares.

ACT V

ii. 4. WP's emendation *bauke* for *banke* seems absolutely certain.

41. *yong Iuuentus*: an allusion to the well-known moral interlude, 'Lusty Juventus.' Cf. *Sir Thomas More*, IV. i. 174 ff.

156. *Sir Iohn*: the quartos have *Sir George*, where *Sir* (*Sr.*) may well stand for *Saint* (*St.*) as in 175. It is possible, therefore, that the host is jocularly addressing Smug, who, as we learn below (179), had played the part of Saint George during the night.

157. *noyse*: 'band'; cf. 2 *Henry IV*, II. iv. 13, *Dutch Courtezan*, II. iii, and Nares.

178, 179. The author of the play appears to have made clumsy use of one of the incidents related in Antony Brewer's prose work, 'The Life and Death of the Merry-Deuill of Edmonton. With the pleasant pranks of Smug the Smith,' &c. One of the sections of this narrative (pp. 43–6) tells how Smug, chased by the keepers for deer stealing, escaped by climbing upon the sign of the White Horse Inn, thus converting it into the George and mystifying his pursuers, who thought they saw two George Inns, where there should have been but one. This is obviously what these lines allude to, but the object of the conspirators in the play was that the knights on their return should see only one Saint George—a false one—and so be decoyed into the wrong inn. What appears from lines 114–18 to have actually happened is that Smug removed the Saint George before Blague's inn altogether and then personated the saint by seating himself upon the sign of the horse before the inn opposite. Sir Ralph's allusion to two Saint Georges in 178 must, then, be a slip.

FAIR EM

ACT I

ii. 15. *to high estate*: the emendations of Delius and Simpson are tempting, but the reading of the Qq is quite possible if we take *to* as an adverb: 'thou must humble ⟨thy⟩ too high estate to join it with my present one (that of miller).'

33. *staylesse of the world*: occasionally throughout this insipid play we get, as here and in line 67 gleams of the imaginative brilliance which characterize the best Elizabethan poetry.

41. *vulgars*: 'the vulgar's,' a collective noun.

iii. 35. *mislike* is a noun; the object of *finde* is *entertainment*: 'not that I find my entertainment in your grace's court a matter for displeasure.' Tyrrell, Simpson, &c. fail to see the construction.

51. The editorial method of Tyrrell is illustrated by his interpolation of *graceful* before *body* to fill out the line. The eight-syllable verse is here a marked beauty. Such irregularities as to the number of feet are particularly common in *Faire Em.*

ACT II

i. 15. *Phismicary*: Trotter appears to have blended the two words *physician* and *apothecary.*

21, 22. 'That our old relation (servant and mistress) is to end, giving place to a new one (man and wife).'

74. *I, an*: the reading of Qq *I am* may be retained, if we place a semicolon at the end of 75 and supply *I* in 76 as subject of *May.* The emendation, however, is slight and makes the sense much easier.

91. *truer loue*: this, the reading of Q 2, is obviously right. The false reading of Q 1 is easily explainable: the compositor has by mistake added the *r* to the second instead of the first *ue.*

betwixte is to be read *'twixt.*

ii. 77. *od* (Q 2 *odde*): Chetwood's reading *old* may possibly be correct, as *l* could easily have been omitted by the compositor of Q 1, and Q 2—in case it was not printed from Q 1—could with equal ease have converted *l* of *olde* into *d.*

ACT III

i. 68. *He* for *Him* is, of course, extremely common in such cases, particularly after the like sounding correlative *Me* (67). The presence of *He* at the beginning of the line explains the omission of *he* in the Qq after *for*, whereas it is difficult to reconcile Simpson's *Him for he hopes* with the *He for hopes* of Qq.

119. *seege of Troye*: a metaphor from the long duration of the siege.

ii. 8. *loth*: all previous editors read *such* with Qq, but none attempts to explain the passage, which seems absolutely to require some such word as *loth.* In the Elizabethan hand *loth* and *such* look much alike.

iv. 84. *Chester*: Qq read *Manchester* both here and in IV. i, S. D., but this is an evident mistake. Cf. IV. i. 4, 51, 56, and IV. iii. 61.

vi. 7, 8. The text of Qq, retained without explanation by Tyrrell and Delius, makes nonsense. That which I have adopted is based, with the change of *whether* to *tho*, on Simpson's rendering. There is a not unusual ellipse after line 6, the idea being: 'I might as well give free expression to my sorrows, for though,' &c. There seem to be two other possible interpretations of these lines—the most obscure in the play. Both require a colon after *sigh* (8), line 9 being regarded as a general summing up, '⟨In either case,⟩ my sorrows,' &c.: (1) We may retain *thee* instead of *tho* in 7, leaving Simpson's *or* for *for* in 8. (2) We may keep the quarto reading throughout, inserting *thee* before *silently* in 8—an insertion which, however, spoils the metre.

49. *assertained* is to be accented on the second syllable.

ACT IV

i. 14. *betake*: commend, hand over. *Betake* in this sense is really a corruption for *beteach*; cf. both words in N.E.D.

iii. 70. It is barely possible to make sense of the passage as it stands in the Qq. Delius retains the *true* inserted by Chetwood after *were.*

ACT V

i. 10. *Saxons*: cf. *King of Danes*, I. i. 53.

11. *seem*: Qq's reading *send* is probably due to the preceding *sent.*

35. This is a characteristic Elizabethan expression which requires no emendation. 'To grace his style (name) with the title of Duke of Saxony.'

93. *base and vildest*: 'basest and vilest.'

104. *importing*: it is not necessary to read *importuning.* Cf. N.E.D. s. v. *Import* v. 3.

114. The same line with the trifling change of *my* to *the* occurs in *The London Prodigal*, V. i. 419. Such coincidences prove nothing as to authorship.

131. *quaint*: cf. N.E.D. s. v. *Quaint* v.[2] 2.

221 ff. Elze's rearrangement of the order of lines is rather plausible, but there seems no sufficient reason for so radical a change, and there is no sort of connexion between line 230 and 255 ff.

263. The author appears certainly to have written *Sir Edmund*, not *Sir Thomas.* Cf. I. ii. 14.

THE TWO NOBLE KINSMEN

Prologue, 13. *Chaucer . . . the Story gives*: in the *Knightes Tale.*

21. *Robin Hood*: the small merit of the tales concerning this worthy appears to have been

proverbial. Cf. *Piers Plowman*, B text, Passus, v. 402.

ACT I

i. 9. Skeat's emendation *hair-bells* was anticipated by a query of Simms: *Harebells*. There seems no need for the change.

16. *angle*: *Angel* F. The word is probably to be taken in its literal sense of 'messenger', meaning 'bird'. Theobald proposed *Augel* from Italian *augello*, a bird.

20. *Chough hore*: this reading, proposed by Seward, has been adopted by all editors, but is far from convincing. Charles Lamb wished to rhyme *Chough* and *Cuckoe*, deleting *nor* in 19 and ending 20 with *nor the Chough*, but this is too violent.

28. A characteristic Fletcherian line, though the scene as a whole is certainly not Fletcher's.

105. *blood cizd*: 'blood-covered'. Cf. *Hamlet*, ii. 493, 'o'er-sized with coagulate gore.'

121, 122. The meaning is a little obscure, the flow of the sentence being broken intentionally. The second *there* ought to be accompanied by a gesture toward the eyes; it is contrasted with the first *there*, which refers to *cheeke* in 119. After *teares* (121) there is a break, and the sentence is never finished; the antecedent of *'em* in 123 is 'eyes', suggested by *there*, as Monck Mason, I find, pointed out. The Queen's grief is to be read not in her cheek, but in her eyes, which through the flood of tears look wrinkled and hard like pebbles.

161. *visitating*: 'inspecting'. Simms is responsible for the foolish query *vegetating*.

164. *To give*: by giving; cf. Abbott, *Sh. Gr.* § 356.

183. *Widdowes*: this word has caused much trouble to commentators. It seems to be used rather carelessly by the author and to infer the idea of sorrow only, not separation. 'Let us live with our woes in widow-like grief.'

192. *foregone*: 'previously undergone' is Skeat's explanation and appears to be what is meant, though the dictionaries hardly sanction this usage. Cf. N.E.D. s. v. *Forego*.

195–206. These lines with their purely descriptive, non-dramatic lusciousness are not in Shakespeare's mature vein. For a speech in precisely the same tone cf. Massinger, *Duke of Milan*, I. iii. 40–52.

239. *More bigger look't*: 'of more apparent consequence'.

ii. 7–10. 'Not to swim in the direction of the current would be almost to sink altogether, at least to make our striving fruitless; while, on the other hand, to follow the stream would bring us to an eddy,' &c.

17. *Martialist*: cf. *Merry Devil of Edmonton*, v. ii. 179; *Edward III*, III. iii. 174. The word occurs in *Spanish Tragedy*, Prologue, 46, and twice in Beaumont and Fletcher.

25. *retaine*: 'take into service'; cf. *Henry VIII*, I. ii. 192, and Schmidt, *Sh. Lex.*

44. *Iumpe*: 'precisely'; cf. N.E.D. s. v. *Jump*, adv.

59. *for*: 'because'; cf. *Cromwell*, III. iii. 84.

77. *on*: 'one'. It is of some importance to note that certain copies of Q have a semicolon after *on*, while others have no punctuation at all. Cf. note to I. iv. 20.

107. *Thirds*: 'equals the third part of'.

127, 128. 'What damage may be done when our hands are advanced to strike before our hearts are in the cause;' *before* is temporal. Littledale explains *before* as 'further than', which gives the same general meaning.

iii. 30. *which* refers to *Peace* (29).

43, 44. 'In many a corner as dangerous as it was uncomfortable, where peril and want contended with each other.' Littledale thinks that 44 means 'clearly' 'contending against peril and want'.

46. *I'th least of these*: 'As regarded even the less terrible of the two qualities (tyranny and power).'

57. *you* is indefinite; it refers to the person reasoning.

68. S. D. The prompter's marginal memorandum of the persons and properties to be collected for Scene iv.

71. *Lou'd for we did*: 'Loved merely because we did love, without ulterior interest'.

77, 78. Littledale would like to regard the parenthesis as an unauthorized interpolation, but metre and sense are both satisfied by the easy supposition that *oh* was unintentionally misplaced by the compositor. In Q, &c. it stands in the middle of 77, immediately before the parenthesis, whereas its proper position seems to be in the middle of 78, immediately after the parenthesis.

82. *her affections*: 'what she affected'.

85. *on*: probably 'one', but it is possible to regard the word as an adverb depending on *humd*.

90. *Like old importments bastard*: 'like a feeble imitation of some threadbare homily.'

iv. 20. *smeard*: this is the reading of the Bodleian and British Museum copies of Q, but Mr. Daniel's copy reads *succard*. The latter, apparently, was a printer's error discovered and corrected after part of the edition had been printed. Littledale (Bibliography v.) notes six such differences, of which only this and that of I. ii. 77 are of practical consequence. Cf. also *Edward III*, I. ii. 28; *Birth of Merlin*, IV. i. 15 and IV. iii. 62 of this play, with note.

43 ff. These lines are to be taken in immediate connexion with *more* in 42. 'For my sake,' says Theseus, 'do even more than is humanly possible, for I have known mighty passions such as fright, fury, &c. to set and attain a mark which nature could not have reached except under abnormal circumstances.'

v. 9. *convent*: 'summon', 'call together'; cf. N.E.D. s. v. *Convent* v. 5, and *Twelfth Night*, v. i. 391.

ACT II

i. 1. *depart with*: 'give up'; cf. *King John*, II. i. 563; *Bartholomew Fair*, Induction (*Mermaid* ed., p. 10), and N.E.D. s. v. *Depart* 12. b.

6–7. 'I am reported to be in better circumstances than there seems to me any cause for rumour to assert.'

34. *greise*: 'step'; cf. Nares, s. v. *Grice*, and N.E.D. s. v. *Gree*, where the various spellings of the word are given.

ii. 63. *meere*: 'pure'; cf. N.E.D. s. v. *Mere* a.[2] 1. c.

64. The alteration suggested in the footnote would make the sense easier and would require the interpolation of only a single letter; *hold's* for *hold us* is, of course, common enough.

98. *Grave*: 'bury', 'put an end to'. This appears to be the best of the emendations. The original reading *Crave* is not impossible, but it makes the clause rather irrelevant: Arcite is thinking of the ways in which freedom might prove destructive to his friendship with Palamon, not of the danger of being envied by third parties.

110. *sufficient*: 'able'; cf. Schmidt, *Sh. Lex.*

162. *gently* is here trisyllabic. It is, of course, not necessary to adopt Seward's spelling *gentily*.

207. Q, F are right in ending this line with *beauties*, which is here to be pronounced in three syllables.

267. Most modern editors place the stage direction after 271, but it furnishes a good illustration as it stands of ancient theatrical arrangements. Our text is based on the prompter's stage copy, as we know from the S.D.D. to I. iii. 68, I. v. 28, &c. In the present case the Keeper is to start from behind the scenes at line 267; in 269 Palamon sees him advancing, and in 271 he is near enough to speak.

iii. 38. *against*: 'in regard to'; cf. N.E.D. s. v. *Against* 3.

54. *heigh for the weavers*: apparently an allusion to the psalm-singing propensities of the weavers, most of whom were Puritans. Cf. *Twelfth Night*, II. iii. 63; 1 *Henry IV*, II. iv. 148, 149.

v. 4. *allow*: 'praise'; cf. N.E.D.

67. *by the Sun*: 'by sunrise'.

vi. 39. *keepe your selfe*: 'have nobody to keep but yourself'.

ACT III

i. 46, 47. 'Give me language which accords with your actions towards me.'

108. *Musite*: cf. Nares, s. v. *Muse, Muset, or Musit.* The emendation seems inevitable unless some authority be found for Ingleby's suggestion that *musick* was an old form of *musit.*

127. 'Even granted that I have a good title to my present advantages.' The accent rests on *If.* Seward's emendation *I've* is without justification though it has been accepted by all previous editors.

ii. 7. The difference between the *wreake* of Q and the *reck* of Seward is a matter of spelling only.

21. *char'd*: 'done'; cf. *Sir Thomas More*, III. i. 118, and N.E.D. s. v. *Chare* v. 4. Simms conjectures *cleared* for *char'd*, which surely is no improvement.

27. There seems no reason to alter the text of Q. The various clauses are purposely joined to each other without connectives in order to indicate the wandering mind of the speaker. Seward and Dyce interpolate unnecessary words in order to fill out line 26.

iv. 9. *Spoon her*: 'let her spume, or sail'. Cf. Nares, s. v. *Spoom.* The proper reading is very doubtful. The reading of Q *Vpon* seems certainly wrong, the first two letters being taken from the line below. Herford has a note in defence of Skeat's emendation *Run*, but prints *Spoom* in his text.

v. S. D. *Bavian*: the reading of Q, F *Baum* is an obvious misprint, as we have *Bavian* in line 37. Cf. N.E.D. s. v. *Babion.*

7. *Jane*: 'jean'; cf. N.E.D. s. v. *Jean* 2. There can be little doubt that Dyce's emendation is right. Seward suggested *bays*, Knight and Simms *jape*, the latter adding the even worse conjecture *have.*

21. *trace*: cf. *Mucedorus*, IV. iii. 30; *Cambises*, l. 490 (ed. Manly), &c.

58. *fire ill*: explained by Littledale as meaning a particular disease.

67. *alow*: no very satisfactory interpretation of this word has been given. It is probably safest to regard it as a mere exclamation.

139. *penner*: 'case to hold pens'; cf. Nares. Littledale thinks that some document penned is meant.

vi. 240. *have pitty*: 'have pity on'.

290. *Opinion*: 'reputation'. The word stands in apposition with *name.* Littledale wishes to understand *Opinion* as 'notoriety' and quotes a not convincing passage from *Thierry and Theodoret* (II. ii). The exclamation refers, of course, to the words of Theseus, 268–72.

298. *worth*: 'befall'; cf. Skeat, *Etymol. Dict.* s. v. *Worth* (2).

324. *Make*: 'Though you make.' Simms, not understanding the construction, changes *dye* in 323 to *dying.*

331. The line makes good sense as it stands and should probably not be altered. Mr. Daniel, in addition to his change of *as your* to *in your*, proposes the further alteration to *in mine.*

ACT IV

i. 103. *Willow, willow, willow*: cf. *Othello*, IV. iii. 28–58, and Littledale's note to this line.

138. *rarely*: 'early'; cf. N.E.D. s. v. *Rearly*, which is the proper spelling.

ii. 14. *Here* refers to *eye* in 12. 'Eye' is also to be understood after *another* in 15.

74. S. D. *Curtis* was evidently the actor who took the messenger's part. The insertion of his

name is another proof that Q is printed from the prompter's copy. Cf. v. iii, S. D., and *Sir Thomas More*, III. iii. 1.

91. *friskins*: 'lively actions'. Cf. N.E.D. s. v. *Friskin* 1.

iii. 62. *behind*: here is another instance of variation among the different copies of the quarto, which Littledale has failed to observe. The British Museum copy and apparently most of the others (including Mr. Daniel's) read *behind*, which is obviously right, but the copy in the Bodleian has *behold*.

ACT V

i. 11. Littledale and Mr. Daniel are of opinion that the old reading *nearnesse* may be justified if taken in connexion with the words *German* (i. e. germane, near of kin) *foes* in the preceding line. I am unable to make sense of the passage, however, without some such emendation as that which I have ventured to introduce.

43. *it* refers to *feare*. Theobald's emendation, though adopted by Dyce and Skeat, seems unnecessary.

50, 51. *she* is apparently a personification of *force and great feate* in l. 49. *The Queene of Flowers* is Emilia. Simms reads *will stick* in 50.

52. *Cestron*: 'cistern'; cf. N.E.D. Simms misses the meaning and proposes *ceston*, 'a studded girdle,' referring to 'the ring or circle of spectators'!

85. *weepe unto a Girle*: Theobald's explanation of this difficult passage is perhaps the best: 'make him weep till he become girlishly weak.' There is no need of changing *unto* to *into*.

124. *briefe*: 'in brief'.

126. *defyer*: Simms's conjecture of *desire* betrays a total misunderstanding of the passage. *have done* in 125 means 'have really committed the sins they prate of.'

iii. 19. *price*: Littledale conjectures *prize*, but in Elizabethan language the two words are interchangeable.

101. *values shortnes*: I prefer to take *values* as a noun, the phrase being in apposition with *disparity*. Most editors regard *values* as a verb, but the explanation of the passage is then difficult.

iv. 10. *unwapper'd*: 'unwearied'; cf. Wright, *Dial. Dict.* s. v. *Wappered*.

58. *dearly* in the sense of 'intensely' is quite possible. Cf. *Merry Devil of Edmonton*, III. ii 16.

120. *arowze*: 'bedew'; cf. N.E.D. s. v. *Arrouse*.

THE BIRTH OF MERLIN

ACT I

i. 2. *her*: *their* is just possible, as Cador may mean courteously to include Donobert's other daughter.

35. *worlds*: two syllables.

43. *speaks yours*: 'declares itself in your favour'.

45. A common saying; cf. *Titus Andronicus*, II. i. 82, 83.

67–9. An allusion to the practice of declaring holidays in honour of the dead.

130. *may I whence truly know*: 'if I may keep in mind the true end of my creation.'

ii. 6, 7. 'The fact that his safety is unquestioned should make the healing of your grief a mere matter of time.' The *you* interpolated by WP is not needed.

55. *strength*: a verb.

56, 57. WP propose to give this speech to Aurelius.

87. *take my stomack*: 'excite my appetite'; not, as WP explain, 'take away my appetite.'

119–21. WP have probably found the correct interpretation of these lines. 120 should be regarded as parenthetical, and 121 taken in immediate connexion with *report of thy humanity* in 119. 'Let me because of my sex take back with me the news of your mercy (already a well-known attribute of yours) reporting that our conqueror is so worthy of praise.'

158. 'Tell him our prospective hospitality regards him as such (i. e. our brother).'

160, 161. The syntax is confused, but the meaning is: 'man's fortune, whether good or bad, resembles waves in this that it never comes singly'. Cf. *Hamlet*, IV. v. 78, 79, for the sense.

197. 'Though my jealousy will not pardon any one else for doing so.'

198. If the *me* of the quarto is to be retained after *love*, it must be understood as an 'ethical dative'. Cf. Abbott, *Sh. Gr.* § 220.

207. *will*: 'as will'.

ACT II

i. 40, 41. *Knight a'th Post*: said by WP to be a slang name for professional false witnesses.

53. *Oh yes*: 'Oyez'; cf. *Oldcastle*, I. i. 9, &c.

95–8. *who*, &c.: 'whom, once overtaken, the eyesight killing Gorgon with a single look made to stand still everlastingly: even so my might, abashed like a cloud which had aspired to cloak the sun, dissolved into a mere shower (of rain or tears).' WP try unsuccessfully to explain the allusions.

104. *thou*: the antecedent is *Pigmalion* in 99, *Oh fate* being a mere exclamation.

134. *a Maid*: Tyrrell proposed unnecessarily *scarce a maid*.

137. *you*: Tyrrell's conjecture of *I* may be correct and is adopted by WP, but the text has a satisfactory meaning as it stands.

157. *a* stands here apparently for *a'th*.

ii. 90. *expose*: 'unsheathe'.

iii. 34. The text of Q is obviously corrupt, and the most satisfactory emendation seems to be that of WP, which we have adopted. We must assume that the MS. had some such abbreviated form of *through* as *thro'* or *thr'*.

198. *best*: used substantively, 'best prospect.' This word seems genuine, but the line as a whole is certainly obscure and may be corrupt.

ACT III

i. 174. The line is certainly corrupt as it stands. I have no confidence in any of the emendations so far proposed.

209. *fruit*: D's reading *print* does not appear in his prefatory list of emendations and is probably only an uncorrected typographical error.

ii. 160. *you*, the quarto reading, is certainly correct, being contrasted with *me* at the end of the line.

iv. 117, 118. Cf. *Yorkshire Tragedy*, I. 82, 83.

vi. 3. 'Which wakes as soon as it has satisfied its desire and with open eyes is forgot,' &c.

14. *instance suit*: this emendation is claimed by Delius, but it had been silently introduced into the text by Tyrrell five years before.

83. *Deadly Sin*: a reminiscence of the moral interlude.

ACT IV

i. 14. *Cast*: the clown plays on two meanings of the word: (1) 'a number of birds' (N.E.D. s. v. 14), and (2) 'a trick' (N.E.D. s. v. 24).

15. *Covy*: WP give the quarto reading as *Cony*, but the Malone copy in the Bodleian certainly has *Covy*.

Cardecu: 'Quart d'ecu.'

257. *Of*: the modern English, as WP explain, would be *On*.

iii. 3. *fall*: 'cause of falling', 'slayer'; cf. N.E.D. s. v. *Fall* sb.[1] 17.

v. 79. *agen*: a mere intensive; cf. Abbott, *Sh. Gr.* § 27.

114. *With Monarch*: 'with the title of monarch'; cf. *Faire Em*, v. i. 35.

ACT V

i. 23. *Sabalists*: Delius quotes the quarto reading incorrectly as *Satalists* and conjectures *satellites*—a most feeble emendation. It is by no means certain that *Sabalists* is wrong, though no editor has been able to explain it. If we must have an emendation, I would suggest *Fabulists*, 'story tellers.' In case the author of the MS. from which Q was printed used a small initial the two words would have been almost identical in appearance.

77. *princeps*: WP retain the quarto reading *preçis*, which they explain as a cabalistic epithet of God. Du Cange, however, recognizes no such word.

ii. 12. *persuade you, then*: 'persuade yourselves (be convinced), then.'

30. *Brittain*: used as an adjective; cf. Abbott, *Sh. Gr.* § 22.

94. *presents*: 'represents'.

SIR THOMAS MORE

ACT I

i. 6. *like*: 'please'; cf. N.E.D. s. v. *Like* v.[1] 1.

33. *jetted on*: 'encroached upon'; cf. *Titus Andronicus*, II. i. 64; *Richard III*, II. iv. 51, and N.E.D. s. v. *Jet* v.[2] 1. b.

ii. 56, 64. *heauie friend*: 'enemy'; cf. N.E.D. s. v. *Heavy* a.[1] 22. b.

151. *foppe*: Hopkinson suggests *fob*, 'trick,' but *fop* is used in this sense. Cf. *London Prodigal*, I. i. 233.

154. *enough*: Hopkinson conjectures *enow* to rhyme with *goe* in 153.

iii. 16–24. The syntax is hopelessly confused, and the text, if not corrupt, must be the result of very careless work. The meaning, however, is clear.

ACT II

i. 15. A common proverb; cf. N.E.D. s. v. *Bate* v.[2] 6. d.

ii. Two draughts of this scene, varying in the details mentioned in the footnotes, have been preserved.

49. *againe*: 'again and again'; cf. *Birth of Merlin*, IV. v. 79, and Abbott, *Sh. Gr.* § 27.

iii. 3. *sort*: 'crowd'; cf. Webster, s. v. *Sort* n. 5.

37. *thou*: this is Dyce's emendation for *then* of the MS., but the latter is not impossible; after *art* in such sentences *thou* is frequently omitted. Cf. Abbott, *Sh. Gr.* § 241.

43. *thes*: the MS. reading. Dyce prints, apparently by mistake, *the*. Such inaccuracies in Dyce's edition are most rare.

iv. 1–172. These lines have been attributed with the greatest confidence to Shakespeare.

83. *topt*: Spedding thought that the word was *kept* in the MS., but Dyce's reading is probably correct.

119. *your*: after this word something has been lost in the MS. Spedding's conjecture fits the sense rather better than Dyce's.

159. *all*: Spedding's conjecture *alike* would somewhat improve sense and metre, but the MS. does not warrant the change.

162. *momtanish*: 'Mohammetanish'; as Mr. Fleay has pointed out, Dyce's change to *mountainish* is unjustifiable.

172. *seek*: with this word the so-called Shakespearean part of this scene ends. The rest is in a very different style and hand.

210. *debble*: cf. N.E.D. s. v. *Dibble* sb.

ACT III

i. 68. *warned to attempt*: 'warned about attempting'. *Warned* is disyllabic.

98. *haue lockt vs*: the MS. has simply *haue lockt*, with nothing to indicate an omission. The

reading of the text seems to suit the meaning better than Dyce's correction.

ii. 52. *cirstned*: 'christened'. The metathesis is common.

293. *Poll Head*: 'polled (bald) head', an inn sign.

iii. 1. Prefix, *T. Goedal*: these words are written in the MS. just under *Mess.*, showing that T. Goedal was to take the Messenger's part. For what is known of Thomas Goodall cf. Fleay, *History of the Stage*, pp. 84, 372.

ACT IV

i. 1. *dilligent*: there is no authority for Hopkinson's silent alteration *vigilent* (sic).

162–9. Taken from the Prologue to *The Disobedient Child.*

298. *Mason among the kings players*: nothing is known of such a player, nor were there any 'King's Players' in the time of Henry VIII. There may be a covert allusion to some member of the 'Queen's Players'.

363, 364. *dine with Duke Homphrye*: 'go without dinner'. Cf. N.E.D. s. v. *Dine* v. 1. b.

ii. 36. *morrall*: 'fabulous', relating to a moral or fable.

37. *with greed*: these words, like other such insertions where the MS. is illegible, have, of course, no authority, but they appear to come nearer to the sense of the passage than Hopkinson's meaningless *together*. Cf. IV. i. 80–1.

v. 68 ff. The revised version of this speech as given on pages 419–20 is considerably finer and should be introduced into the text, except for the difficulty of joining it to what precedes and follows.

ACT V

i. 27. *am*: 'em.

BIBLIOGRAPHY

I. Collections containing several apocryphal plays.
II. Lists of editions of each play.
III. Translations.
IV. General criticism.
V. Early Notices, Sources, Analogues, &c.
VI. Index to the bibliography of each play.

(Nos. I and III are arranged chronologically; Nos. IV, V, VI alphabetically. No. II alphabetically as regards plays and chronologically as regards editions.)

I. COLLECTIONS

1. *Mr. William Shakespear's Comedies, Histories, and Tragedies. Published according to the true Original Copies. The third Impression. And unto this Impression is added seven Playes, never before Printed in Folio. viz.* Pericles Prince of Tyre. The London Prodigall. The History of Thomas Ld. Cromwell. Sir John Oldcastle Lord Cobham. The Puritan Widow. A York-shire Tragedy. The Tragedy of Locrine. *London, Printed for P.C.* 1664. fol.
Reproduced in facsimile by Methuen & Co., London, 1905.

2. *Mr. William Shakespear's Comedies Histories, and Tragedies Published according to the true Original Copies. Unto which is added, Seven Plays, Never before* ⟨!⟩ *Printed in Folio: Viz.* Pericles Prince of Tyre. The London Prodigal. The history of Thomas, Lord Cromwell. Sir John Oldcastle Lord Cobham. The Puritan Widow. A Yorkshire Tragedy. The Tragedy of Locrine. *The Fourth Edition London, Printed for H. Herringman, E. Brewster, and R. Bentley, at the Anchor in the New Exchange, the Crane in St. Paul's Church-Yard, and in Russel-Street Covent-Garden.* 1685. fol.
Reproduced in facsimile by Methuen & Co., London, 1904.

3. *The Works of Mr. William Shakespear, in six volumes. Adorn'd with cuts. Revis'd and corrected, with an Account of the Life and Writings of the Author. By N. Rowe, Esq.*, 6 vol. *Jacob Tonson: London*, 1709. 8°. Volume vi contains the seven additional plays of the 3rd and 4th folios.
Second Edition. 9 vol. *Printed for J. Tonson, E. Curll, J. Pemberton, and K. Sanger: London*, 1714. 12°.
Volume viii contains the additional plays.

4. *The Works of Shakespear. In eight volumes. Collated and corrected by the former editions, by Mr. Pope. The second edition.* 9 vol. *J. Tonson: London*, 1728. 12°.
The supplementary ninth volume (1728) contains the additional plays. This volume does not bear Pope's name, and his connexion with it is conjectural.
⟨Another edition.⟩ *The Works of Shakespeare. In eight volumes* ⟨Pope's edition⟩. *Printed for J. Tonson and the rest of the Proprietors: London*, 1735. 12°.
The ninth volume of this edition, mentioned by Mr. Daniel as containing the seven additional plays, is not in the British Museum or the Bodleian catalogue.

5. ⟨Malone's⟩ *Supplement to the Edition of Shakespeare's Plays Published in* 1778 *By Samuel Johnson and George Steevens. In Two Volumes. Containing Additional Observations By Several of The Former Commentators: To Which are Subjoined The Genuine Poems of the same Author, and Seven Plays that have been Ascribed to him; With Notes By the Editor and Others* ⟨Motto⟩ *London, Printed for C. Bathurst* . . . 1780. 8°.
Volume ii contains the additional plays in the following order: Pericles; Locrine; Sir John Oldcastle; Lord Cromwell; London Prodigal; Puritan; Yorkshire Tragedy.
The notes are principally by Malone and Steevens.

6. *The Ancient British Drama. 3 Volumes. Printed for William Miller, By James Ballantyne & Co., London, Edinburgh,* 1810. 8°.
Vol. i includes THOMAS LORD CROMWELL, THE LONDON PRODIGAL, and A YORKSHIRE TRAGEDY; vol. ii, THE MERRY DEVIL OF EDMONTON.

7. *The Pictorial Edition of the Works of Shakspere, Edited by Charles Knight. London.* (1839–43). 8°.
(Vol. vii) *Doubtful Plays,* &c.
Contains TITUS ANDRONICUS, PERICLES, THE TWO NOBLE KINSMEN, A YORKSHIRE TRAGEDY.
Another edition, 1867. Doubtful plays in Vol. viii.

8. *A Supplement to the Plays of William Shakspeare: comprising the seven dramas, which have been ascribed to his pen, but which are not included with his writings in modern editions, namely:* THE TWO NOBLE KINSMEN; THE LONDON PRODIGAL; THOMAS, LORD CROMWELL; SIR JOHN OLDCASTLE; THE PURITAN, OR THE WIDOW OF WATLING STREET; THE (sic) YORKSHIRE TRAGEDY; THE TRAGEDY OF LOCRINE. *Edited with notes and an introduction to each play, by* W. G. SIMMS. *New York,* 1848, 8°.
Second edition. New York, 1855.

9. *The Doubtful Plays of Shakspeare; Being all the Dramas attributed to the Muse of the World's Great Poet; Revised from the Original Editions. Accompanied with Historical and Analytical Introductions to each Play, and Notes Critical and Explanatory: By* HENRY TYRRELL, *Esq.* (1851). *John Tallis & Co., London & N. Y.* 8°.
Contains: TITUS ANDRONICUS, PERICLES, A YORKSHIRE TRAGEDY, THE LONDON PRODIGAL, SIR JOHN OLDCASTLE, THOMAS LORD CROMWELL, THE PURITAN, LOCRINE, KING EDWARD III, THE MERRY DEVIL OF EDMONTON, FAIR EM, MUCEDORUS, ARDEN OF FEVERSHAM, THE BIRTH OF MERLIN, THE TWO NOBLE KINSMEN.
There is some doubt about the precise year of publication of this volume. It was brought out in connexion with an edition of Shakespeare, published 1851, but may have been a year or two later. The title page is not dated.

10. *The Supplementary Works of William Shakspeare, comprising his Poems and Doubtful Plays; with Glossarial and other Notes. A New Edition by* WILLIAM HAZLITT, *Esq. London,* 1852. 8°.
Contains: PERICLES, LOCRINE, SIR JOHN OLDCASTLE, THOMAS LORD CROMWELL, LONDON PRODIGAL, THE PURITAN, A YORKSHIRE TRAGEDY, TITUS ANDRONICUS.
The dramas in this book were reprinted in 1887 with the title: *The Doubtful Plays of William Shakspeare, with Glossarial and other Notes.* 8°.
Also in the *Excelsior Series.*

11. *Pseudo-Shakespere'sche Dramen. Herausgegeben von* NICOLAUS DELIUS. *Elberfeld,* 1854–74. 8°.
Published separately. EDWARD III, 1854; ARDEN OF FEVERSHAM, 1855; THE BIRTH OF MERLIN, 1856; MUCEDORUS, 1874; FAIR EM, 1874.

12. *Doubtful Plays of William Shakespeare. Leipzig,* 1869. 16°. *Edited by* MAX MOLTKE.
Vol. 1041 of the Tauchnitz Collection of British Authors, containing: KING EDWARD III, THOMAS LORD CROMWELL, LOCRINE, A YORKSHIRE TRAGEDY, THE LONDON PRODIGAL, THE BIRTH OF MERLIN.

13. *A Select Collection of Old Plays. Fourth edition (enlarged), edited by* W. C. HAZLITT. *In* 15 *Volumes. London,* 1874–6. 8°.
Vol. vii, MUCEDORUS; vol. x, THE MERRY DEVIL OF EDMONTON. Vol. ix contains WILY BEGUILED; vol. x, THE SECOND MAIDEN'S TRAGEDY; vol. xi, ALBUMAZAR. Of these plays only THE MERRY DEVIL OF EDMONTON and ALBUMAZAR are to be found in the earlier editions.

14. *The Leopold Shakspere. The Poet's Works, in Chronological Order, from the Text of Professor Delius, with* 'THE TWO NOBLE KINSMEN' *and* 'EDWARD III,' *and an Introduction by* F. J. FURNIVALL. *London,* &c. (1877). 8°.
Reprinted as *The Royal Shakspere* in 1898.

15. *The Plays and Poems of W. Shakespeare, with the purest text and briefest notes. Edited by* J. P. Collier. *Maidenhead* 1878. *Limited to 58 Copies.*

This edition, of which I have been unable to see a copy, includes: Edward III, The Two Noble Kinsmen, Mucedorus, and A Yorkshire Tragedy.

16. *The School of Shakespeare . . . Edited with Introductions and Notes . . . by* Richard Simpson. *In Two Volumes. London,* 1878.

Volume ii contains The Comedy of the Prodigal Son (pp. 90–123), A Warning for Fair Women (pp. 209–336), Faire Em (pp. 337–468).

17. *Pseudo-Shakespearian Plays. Edited by* Karl Warnke, *Ph.D. and* Ludwig Proescholdt, *Ph.D. Halle:* 1883–88. 8°.

Published separately. The Comedie of Faire Em, 1883; The Merry Devil of Edmonton, 1884; Edward III, 1886; The Birth of Merlin, 1887; Arden of Feversham, 1888.

18. *Old English Dramas Edited with Notes and Introductions by* T. Evan Jacob, *B.A. London; L. Reeve & Co.* 1889. *The Victoria Library II.*

This volume contains only The Life and Death of Thomas Lord Cromwell and The Birth of Merlin. The book has no textual or critical value.

19. *Shakespeare's Doubtful Plays. Edited, With an Introduction to Each Play, by* A. F. Hopkinson. *In Three Volumes. London,* 1891–5. 8°.

Separately paged and dated. Vol. i: Yorkshire Tragedy, 1891; Edward III, 1891; Merry Devil of Edmonton, 1891; Thomas Lord Cromwell, 1891. Vol. ii: Locrine, 1892; Birth of Merlin, 1892; Mucedorus, 1893; London Prodigal, 1893. Vol. iii: The Puritan, 1894; The Two Noble Kinsmen, 1894; Sir John Oldcastle, 1894; Fair Em, 1895.

II. EDITIONS OF EACH PLAY

(*a*) Arden of Feversham

1. *The Lamentable and True Tragedie of M. Arden of Feversham in Kent . . . Imprinted at London for Edward White . . .* 1592. 4°.

To be found in the Bodleian and in the Dyce Collection, South Kensington.

2. (Another edition with the same title) 1599. 4°.

The only known copy of this edition is in the Duke of Devonshire's Library. I have not been able to see the original, but its readings have been recorded by Warnke and Proescholdt.

3. (Another edition) *Printed by Eliz. Allde dwelling neere Christs-Church* 1633. 4°.

In the Bodleian and the British Museum.

4. *The Lamentable and True Tragedy of M. Arden, of Feversham, in Kent . . . With a Preface; in which some Reasons are offered in favour of its being the earliest dramatic Work of Shakespear now remaining; and a genuine Account given of the Murder . . .* ⟨By Edward Jacob⟩ *Reprinted verbatim* ⟨from the first quarto⟩ *Feversham,* 1770. 8°.

5. Tyrrell, H. *The Doubtful Plays of Shakspere.* 1851. 8°.

Pp. 373–410.

6. Delius, N., *Arden of Feversham. Ein Shakspere zugeschriebenes Drama. Elberfeld,* 1855.

Pseudo-Shakspere'sche Dramen II. 8°.

7. Bullen, A. H., *Arden of Feversham, a tragedy: reprinted from the edition of* 1592. *With an introduction by* A. H. B. *London,* 1887. 4°.

8. Warnke and Proescholdt, *Arden of Feversham. Revised and edited with Introduction and Notes. Halle,* 1888.

Pseudo-Shakespearian Plays V. 8°.

9. Bayne, Rev. Ronald, *Arden of Feversham. Edited with a Preface, Notes and Glossary. London,* 1897. 8°.

The Temple Dramatists.

(*b*) Birth of Merlin, The

1. *The Birth of Merlin: or, The Childe hath found his Father . . . Written by William Shakspear, and William Rowley . . . London, Printed by Tho. Iohnson for Francis Kirkman and Henry Marsh,* 1662.
The only early edition extant. Copies in the British Museum and the Bodleian.

2. Tyrrell, H., *The Doubtful Plays of Shakspere.* ⟨1851.⟩ 8°. Pp. 411–43.

3. Delius, N., *The Birth of Merlin. Ein Shakspere und Rowley zugeschriebenes Drama. Elberfeld,* 1856. 8°.
Pseudo-Shakspere'sche Dramen III.

4. Moltke, M., *Doubtful Plays of William Shakespeare. Leipzig,* 1869. 16°. Pp. 279–352.

5. Warnke and Proescholdt, *The Birth of Merlin. Revised and edited with Introduction and Notes. Halle,* 1887. 8°.
Pseudo-Shakespearian Plays IV.

6. Jacob, T. E., *Old English Dramas.* In the *Victoria Library.*

7. Hopkinson, A. F., *Shakespeare's Doubtful Plays, vol. ii. London,* 1892. 8°.

(*c*) Cromwell, Thomas Lord

1. *The True Chronicle Historie of the whole life and death of Thomas Lord Cromwell . . . Written by W. S. Imprinted at London for William Iones . . .* 1602. 4°.
In the Bodleian; very rare.

2. ⟨Another edition.⟩ *London; Printed by Thomas Snodham,* 1613. 4°.
In the British Museum and Bodleian.

3. The Third Folio of Shakespeare. London, 1664.

4. The Fourth Folio of Shakespeare. London, 1685.

5. Rowe's Shakespeare. Vol. vi. London, 1709. 8°.
Second edition. Vol. viii. London, 1714. 12°.

6. Pope's Shakespeare. Vol. ix. London, 1728. 12°.
Another edition. Vol. ix (?). London, 1735. 12°.

7. *The Life and Death of Thomas Lord Cromwell. A Tragedy. By Shakespear. R. Walker. Lond.* 1734. 12°.

8. ⟨Malone's⟩ *Supplement to Shakespeare, London,* 1780. Vol. ii, pp. 371–446.

9. *The Ancient British Drama. London, Edinburgh,* 1810. 8°. Vol. i.

10. Simms, W. G. *A Supplement to the Plays of William Shakspeare. New York,* 1848.
Second edition, 1855, pp. 67–85.

11. Tyrrell, H., *The Doubtful Plays of Shakspere. London,* 1851. 8°. Pp. 168–96.

12. Hazlitt, W. C., *The Supplementary Works of Shakespeare. London,* 1852. 8°. Pp. 165–205.
Another edition, 1887.

13. Moltke, M., *Doubtful Plays of William Shakespeare. Leipzig,* 1869. 16°. Pp. 77–130.

14. Jacob, T. E., *Old English Dramas. London,* 1889. In the *Victoria Library.*

15. Hopkinson, A. F., *Shakespeare's Doubtful Plays.* Vol. i. *London,* 1891. 8°.

(*d*) Edward III

1. *The Raigne of King Edward the Third:* ⟨Anon⟩ . . . *London, Printed for Cuthbert Burby.* 1596. 4°.
In the British Museum, the Bodleian, and Trinity College, Cambridge. The Bodleian copy is not complete.

2. ⟨Another edition⟩ *Imprinted at London by Simon Stafford, for Cuthbert Burby.* 1599.
In the British Museum and the Bodleian.

3. Capell, *Prolusions, or Select Pieces of Ancient Poetry. London*, 1760. 8°.

4. Tyrrell, *Doubtful Plays*, &c. *London*, 1851. 8°. Pp. 263–99.

5. Delius, *Edward III. Ein Shakspere zugeschriebenes Drama. Elberfeld*, 1854. 8°.
Pseudo-Shakspere'sche Dramen I.

6. Moltke, *Doubtful Plays*, &c. *Leipzig*, 1869. 16°. Pp. 1–76.

7. Furnivall, *Leopold Shakspere. London*, 1877. 8°. Pp. 1037–56.
Reprinted in the *Royal Shakspere*, 1898.

8. Collier, *Plays and Poems of W. Shakespeare. Maidenhead*, 1878.

9. Warnke and Proescholdt, *King Edward III. Revised and edited with Introduction and Notes. Halle*, 1886. 8°.
Pseudo-Shakespearian Plays III.

10. Hopkinson, *Shakespeare's Doubtful Plays.* Vol. i. *London*, 1891. 8°.

11. Donovan, Th., *English Historical Plays by Shakespeare, Marlowe, Peele, Heywood, Fletcher, and Ford, arranged for acting, as well as for reading.* In two volumes. London, 1896. 8°.
Edward III in vol. i. A garbled version.

12. Smith, G. C. Moore, *Edward the Third, Edited with a Preface, Notes and Glossary. London*, 1897. 8°.
The Temple Dramatists.

(*e*) Fair Em

1. *A Pleasant Commodie, of faire Em the Millers daughter of Manchester : With the Loue of William the Conqueror . . . Imprinted at London for T. N. and I. W. . . .* ⟨No date⟩. 4°.
The only known copy is in the Bodleian.

2. ⟨Another edition⟩ *London, printed for Iohn Wright*, 1631. 4°.
In the British Museum and the Bodleian.

---

3. Chetwood, W. R., *A Select Collection of Old Plays. Dublin*, 1750. 12°.
Contains untrustworthy reprints of six plays, of which Fair Em is the second.

4. Tyrrell, *Doubtful Plays*, &c. *London*, 1851. 8°. Pp. 324–47.

5. Delius, *Fair Em. Ein Shakspere zugeschriebenes Drama. Elberfeld*, 1874. 8°.
Pseudo-Shakspere'sche Dramen V.

6. Simpson, *School of Shakspere, London*, 1878. 8°. Vol. ii, pp. 337–468.

7. Warnke and Proescholdt, *The Comedie of Faire Em. Revised and edited with Introduction and Notes. Halle*, 1883. 8°.
Pseudo-Shakespearian Plays I.

8. Hopkinson, *Doubtful Plays of Shakespeare.* 8°. Vol. iii. *London*, 1895.

(*f*) Locrine

1. *The Lamentable Tragedie of Locrine, the eldest sonne of King Brutus . . . Newly set forth, ouerseene and corrected, by W. S. London. Printed by Thomas Creede*, 1595. 4°.
In the Bodleian and the British Museum.

---

2. The Third Folio of Shakespeare, London, 1664.

3. The Fourth Folio of Shakespeare, London, 1685.

4. Rowe's Shakespeare, vol. vi. London, 1709. 8°.
Second edition. Vol. viii. London, 1714. 12°.

5. Pope's Shakespeare. Vol. ix. London, 1728. 12°.
⟨Another edition⟩ vol. ix (?). London, 1735. 12°.

6. *The Tragedy of Locrine, the eldest son of King Brutus. By Mr. William Shakespear. J. Tonson. London*, 1734. 12°.

7. ⟨Another edition⟩ *By Shakespear. R. Walker : London*, 1734. 12°.

8. ⟨Malone's⟩ *Supplement to Shakespeare, London,* 1780. 8°. Vol. ii, pp. 187–264.

9. SIMMS, *Supplement to Shakspeare. New York,* 1848.
Second edition, 1855. Pp. 151–78.

10. TYRRELL, *Doubtful Plays,* &c. *London,* 1851. Pp. 232–62.

11. HAZLITT, *Supplementary Works of Shakespeare. London,* 1852. Pp. 57–104.
Second edition 1887.

12. MOLTKE, *Doubtful Plays of William Shakespeare. Leipzig,* 1869. Pp. 131–94.

13. HOPKINSON, *Shakespeare's Doubtful Plays.* Vol. ii. *London,* 1892.

(g) LONDON PRODIGAL, THE

1. *The London Prodigall . . . By William Shakespeare. London. Printed by T. C. for Nathaniel Butter . . .* 1605.
In the Bodleian.

---

2. The Third Folio of Shakespeare. London, 1664.

3. The Fourth Folio of Shakespeare. London, 1685.

4. *The London Prodigal, a comedy* ⟨Anonymous⟩. 1709. 8°.

5. Rowe's Shakespeare. Vol. vi. London, 1709. 8°.
Second edition. Vol. viii. London, 1714. 12°.

6. Pope's Shakespeare. Vol. ix. London, 1728. 12°.
Another edition. Vol. ix (?). London, 1735. 12°.

7. ⟨Another edition⟩ *By Mr. William Shakespear. J. Tonson. London,* 1734. 12°.

8. ⟨Another edition⟩ *By Shakespear. London. Printed by R. Walker . . .* 1734. 12°.

9. ⟨Malone's⟩ *Supplement to Shakespeare. London,* 1780. 8°. Vol. ii, pp. 447–529.

10. *The Ancient British Drama. London, Edinburgh,* 1810. 8°. Vol. i.

11. SIMMS, *Supplement to Shakspeare. New York,* 1848.
Second edition, 1855. Pp. 45–65.

12. TYRRELL, *Doubtful Plays,* &c. *London,* 1851. 8°. Pp. 97–127.

13. HAZLITT, W. C., *Supplementary Works of Shakespeare. London,* 1852. 8°. Pp. 206–48.
Second edition, 1887.

14. MOLTKE, *Doubtful Plays,* &c. *Leipzig,* 1869. 16°. Pp. 219–78.

15. HOPKINSON, *Shakespeare's Doubtful Plays.* Vol. ii. *London,* 1893. 8°.

(h) MERRY DEVIL OF EDMONTON, THE

1. *The Merry Deuill of Edmonton . . . London. Printed by Henry Ballard for Arthur Iohnson* . 1608. 4°.
In the library of Trinity College, Cambridge.

2. ⟨Another edition⟩ 1612. *Printed for Arthur Iohnson.* 4°.
In the library of Mr. A. H. Huth. I have not been able to see the unique copy of this edition, but its variant readings have been recorded by Warnke and Proescholdt.

3. ⟨Another edition⟩ 1617. *Printed for Arthur Iohnson.* 4°.
In the British Museum and the Bodleian.

4. ⟨Another edition⟩ 1626. *Printed for Francis Falkner.* 4°.
In the British Museum.

5. ⟨Another edition⟩ 1631. *Printed for Francis Falkner.* 4°.
In the British Museum and the Bodleian.

6. ⟨Another edition⟩ 1655. *Printed for W. Gilbertson.* 4°.
In the British Museum.

7. Dodsley's *Select Collection of Old Plays*, 1st ed. *London*, 1744. Vol. xi.

8. ⟨Reed's⟩ Dodsley *2nd ed. London*, 1780. 8°. Vol. v.

9. *The Ancient British Drama. Lond., Edin.*, 1810. 8°. Vol. ii.

10. ⟨Collier's⟩ Dodsley, *3rd ed. London*, 1825. Vol. v. 8°.

11. Tyrrell, *Doubtful Plays. London*, 1851. 8°. Pp. 300–23.

12. ⟨Hazlitt's⟩ Dodsley, *4th ed. London*, 1874–6. Vol. x. 8°.

13. Warnke and Proescholdt, *The Merry Devil of Edmonton. Revised and edited with Introduction and Notes. Halle*, 1884. 8°.
Pseudo-Shakespearian Plays II.

14. Hopkinson, *Shakespeare's Doubtful Plays.* Vol. i. *London*, 1891. 8°.

15. Walker, Hugh, *The Merry Devil of Edmonton. A Comedy. Edited with a Preface, Notes and Glossary. London*, 1897. 8°.
The Temple Dramatists.

(*i*) More, Sir Thomas

1. *MS. Harleian* 7368.
In the British Museum. The MS. bears neither title, date, nor the author's name.

2. Dyce, *Sir Thomas More. A Play; Now first printed. Edited by the Rev. Alexander Dyce. Printed for the Shakespeare Society*, 1844. 8°.

3. Hopkinson, *Sir Thomas More. Edited with an Introduction. For private circulation London*, 1902. 8°.

(*k*) Mucedorus

1. *A most pleasant Comedy of Mucedorus the king's sonne of Valentia and Amadine the king's daughter of Arragon, with the merie conceites of Mouse. Newly set foorth . . . London. Printed for William Iones* . . . 1598. 4°.
In the British Museum.

2. ⟨Another edition⟩ *Printed for William Iones.* 1606. 4°.
In the Dyce Collection, South Kensington.

3. ⟨Another edition⟩ *Amplified with new additions . . . Imprinted at London for William Iones* . . . 1610. 4°.
In the British Museum and Trinity College, Cambridge.

4. ⟨Another edition⟩ *Printed for William Iones.* 1611. 4°.
In the Bodleian.

5. ⟨Another edition⟩ *Printed for William Iones.* 1613. 4°.
In the British Museum.

6. ⟨Another edition⟩ *Printed for William Iones.* 1615. 4°.
In the British Museum and Trinity College, Cambridge.

7. ⟨Another edition⟩ *Printed for Iohn Wright.* 1618. 4°.
In Mr. Huth's Library. I have not seen this edition.

8. ⟨Another edition⟩ *Printed for Iohn Wright.* 1619. 4°.
In the British Museum and the Bodleian.

9. ⟨Another edition⟩ *Printed for Iohn Wright.* 1621. 4°.
In the Municipal Library of Danzig. I have not seen this edition. Warnke and Proescholdt record its variant readings.

10. ⟨Another edition⟩ *Printed for Iohn Wright.* 1626. 4°.
In the Dyce Collection.

11. ⟨Another edition⟩ *Printed for Iohn Wright.* 1631. 4°.
In the British Museum.

12. ⟨Another edition⟩ *Printed for Iohn Wright.* 1634. 4°.
In the British Museum.

13. ⟨Another edition⟩ *Printed for Iohn Wright.* 1639. 4°.
In Trinity College, Cambridge, Library.

14. ⟨Another edition⟩ *Printed for Francis Coles.* 1663. 4°.
In the Bodleian.

15. ⟨Another edition⟩ *Printed for Francis Coles.* 1668. 4°.
In British Museum, Bodleian, and Trinity College, Cambridge.

16. ⟨Another edition⟩ *Printed for Francis Coles.* (No date.) 4°.
In British Museum and Trinity College, Cambridge.

17. ⟨Another edition⟩
The only known copy, in Trinity College, Cambridge, has lost its title page.

---

18. Another edition published for subscribers by J. P. Collier, 1824.
This text claims for its original a quarto of 1609, which is probably fictitious. I have not been able to see a copy of this or of Collier's other edition (No. 22).

19. Tyrrell, *Doubtful Plays,* &c. *London,* 1851. 8°. Pp. 348–72.

20. ⟨Hazlitt, W. C.⟩ *A Select Collection of Old Plays.*
Fourth edition, London, 1874–6. 8°. Vol. vii.
The earlier editions of this collection (Dodsley's) did not include Mucedorus.

21. Delius, *Mucedorus. Ein Shakspere zugeschriebenes Drama. Elberfeld,* 1874. 8°. *Pseudo-Shakspere'sche Dramen IV.*

22. Collier, *Shakespeare's Plays and Poems. Maidenhead,* 1878.

23. Warnke and Proescholdt, *The Comedy of Mucedorus, revised and edited with Introduction and Notes. Halle,* 1878. 8°.

24. Hopkinson, *Shakespeare's Doubtful Plays.* Vol. ii. *London,* 1893. 8°.

(*l*) Oldcastle, Sir John

1. *The first part of the true and honorable historie, of the life of Sir John Old-castle, the good Lord Cobham* ⟨Anonymous⟩... *London. Printed by V. S. for Thomas Pauier* ... 1600. 4°.
In the Bodleian (Malone 768).

2. ⟨Another edition of the same year⟩ *Written by William Shakespeare. London, printed for T. P.* 1600. 4°.
In the Bodleian (Malone 222) and the British Museum.

---

3. The Third Folio of Shakespeare. London. 1664.

4. The Fourth Folio of Shakespeare. London. 1685.

5. Rowe's Shakespeare, vol. vi. London, 1709. 8°.
Second edition, vol. viii. London, 1714. 12°.

6. Pope's Shakespeare, vol. ix. London, 1728. 12°.
Another edition, vol. ix (?). London, 1735. 12°.

7. *The History of Sir John Oldcastle, the good Lord Cobham. By Mr. William Shakespear* ... *J. Tonson, London,* 1734. 8°.
In the British Museum.

8. ⟨Another edition⟩ *By Shakespear. London: Printed by R. Walker* ... 1734. 8°.
In the Bodleian.

9. ⟨Another impression ?⟩ *By Shakespeare.* ⟨London.⟩ 1735. 12°.
In the British Museum.

10. ⟨Malone's⟩ *Supplement to Shakespeare. London,* 1780. 8°. Vol. ii, pp. 265–370.

11. Simms, *Supplement to the Plays of William Shakspeare. New York,* 1848.
Second edition, 1855. Pp. 87–115.

12. Tyrrell, *Doubtful Plays. London,* 1851. 8°. Pp. 128–67.

13. HAZLITT, W. C., *Supplementary Works of Shakespeare. London*, 1852. 8°.
Pp. 105–64.
Reprinted 1887.

14. HOPKINSON, *Shakespeare's Doubtful Plays.* Vol. iii. *London*, 1894. 8°.

(*m*) THE PURITAN

1. *The Puritaine or the Widdow of Watling-streete. . . . Written by W. S. Imprinted at London by G. Eld*, 1607. 4°.
In the Bodleian and the British Museum.

---

2. The Third Folio of Shakespeare. London, 1664.

3. The Fourth Folio of Shakespeare. London, 1685.

4. Rowe's Shakespeare, vol. vi. *London*, 1709. 8°.
Second edition, vol. viii. *London*, 1714. 12°.

5. Pope's Shakespeare, vol. ix. *London*, 1728. 12°.
⟨Another edition⟩ vol. ix (?). *London*, 1735. 12°.

6. *The Puritan : or, the Widow of Watling-street. A Comedy. By Shakespear. London: Printed by R. Walker. . . .* 1734.
In the Bodleian ⟨Malone 935⟩; rare.

7. ⟨Another edition⟩ *By Mr. William Shakespear. J. Tonson : London*, 1734. 12°.
In the British Museum.

8. ⟨Malone's⟩ *Supplement to Shakespeare. London*, 1780. 8°. Vol. ii, pp. 531–627.

9. SIMMS, *Supplement to the Plays of William Shakespeare. New York*, 1848.
Second edition, 1855. Pp. 117–40.

10. TYRRELL, *Doubtful Plays*, &c. *London*, 1851. 8°. Pp. 197–231.

11. HAZLITT, W. C., *Supplementary Works of Shakespeare. London*, 1852. 8°.
Pp. 249–98.
Second edition, 1887.

12. HOPKINSON, *Shakespeare's Doubtful Plays*, vol. iii. *London*. 1895. 8°.

(*n*) TWO NOBLE KINSMEN, THE

1. *The Two Noble Kinsmen . . . Written by the memorable Worthies of their time Mr. John Fletcher, and Mr. William Shakspeare, Gent. Printed at London by Tho. Cotes, for John Waterson . . .* 1634. 4°.
In the Bodleian, British Museum, &c.

2. *Fifty Comedies and Tragedies. Written by Francis Beaumont and John Fletcher Gentlemen. All in One Volume . . . Printed by J. Macock, for John Martyn. . . .* 1679. Fol.
The second folio of Beaumont and Fletcher. THE TWO NOBLE KINSMEN is printed in the second part of the volume, pp. 425–49, with no mention of Shakespeare's authorship.

---

3. The Third Edition of Beaumont and Fletcher. *London* (*Tonson*), 1711. Volume x.

4. The Fourth Edition of Beaumont and Fletcher. London, 1750. Volume x. 8°.
Edited by Seward, Sympson & Theobald.

5. The Fifth Edition of Beaumont and Fletcher, *London*, 1778. 8°.
Edited by Colman.

6. *The Dramatic Works of Ben Jonson, and Beaumont and Fletcher . . . the latter from the text and with the notes of G. Coleman.* 1811. 8°.

7. *The Modern British Drama. London, Edinburgh*, 1811. 8°. Five vols.
Vol. i contains THE TWO NOBLE KINSMEN.

8. The Seventh Edition of Beaumont and Fletcher. *London*, 1812. 8°.
Edited by Weber.

9. Knight, *Pictorial Shakespeare. London*, 1839–43. 8°. Vol. vii, pp. 121–87.
Second edition, 1866, with improved text.

10. *Works of Beaumont and Fletcher. With an Introduction by* George Darley. *In Two Volumes. London*, 1839–40. Vol. ii. 8°.
Another edition, 1872. Vol. ii, pp. 553–80.

11. *Works of Beaumont and Fletcher; The Text formed from a New Collation of the Early Editions . . . by the* Rev. Alexander Dyce. Vol. xi. *London*, 1846. 8°.
Improved text.

12. Simms, *Supplement*, &c. *New York*, 1848. 8°.
Second edition, 1855. Pp. 13–44.

13. Tyrrell, *Doubtful Plays*, &c. *London*, 1851. 8°. Pp. 444–84.

14. Dyce, *Works of Shakespeare. 2nd Edition.* 1867. Vol. viii. Pp. 115–233.
Reprinted in the third edition, 1876.

15. Skeat, *The Two Noble Kinsmen. Cambridge*, 1875. 8°.

16. Littledale, *The Two Noble Kinsmen. Reprint of the First Quarto*, 1634, *with a Collation of the Second Edition, Folio*, 1679, *and Revised Text. Published for the New Shakspere Society. London.* 1876. 4°.
This is the standard edition.

17. Furnivall, *The Leopold Shakspere. London*, &c., 1877. 8°. Pp. 1010–36.
Reprinted as *The Royal Shakspere*, 1894–8.

18. Collier, *Shakespeare's Plays and Poems. Maidenhead*, 1878.
This edition I have not seen.

19. Fitzgibbon, H. M., *Famous Elizabethan Plays. Expurgated . . . London*, 1890. 8°.

20. Rolfe, W. J., *The Two Noble Kinsmen. Edited with notes. New York*, 1891. 8°.
The Friendly Edition.

21. Hudson, H. N., *The Two Noble Kinsmen, edited with notes. Edinburgh.* 8°.
The Windsor Shakespeare, published in America as the *Harvard Shakespeare.*

22. Hopkinson, *Shakespeare's Doubtful Plays.* Vol. iii. *London*, 1894. 8°.

23. Herford, *The Two Noble Kinsmen. Edited with a Preface, Notes, and Glossary. London*, 1897. 8°.
The Temple Dramatists.

(*o*) Yorkshire Tragedy, A

1. *A Yorkshire Tragedy. Not so New as Lamentable and true. Acted by his Maiesties Players at the Globe. Written by W. Shakspeare. At London. Printed by R. B. for Thomas Pauier* . . 1608.
In the Bodleian and the British Museum.

2. ⟨Another edition⟩ *Written by W. Shakespeare. Printed for T. P.*, 1619.
In the Bodleian and the British Museum.

3. Third Folio of Shakespeare. London, 1664.

4. Fourth Folio of Shakespeare. London, 1685.

5. Rowe's Shakespeare, vol. vi. *London*, 1709. 8°.
Second edition, vol. viii. *London*, 1714. 12°.

6. Pope's Shakespeare, vol. ix. *London*, 1728. 12°.
⟨Another edition⟩ vol. ix (?). *London*, 1735. 12°.

7. *A Yorkshire Tragedy . . . By Mr. William Shakespear . . . J. Tonson. London*, 1735.

8. ⟨Malone's⟩ *Supplement to Shakespeare. London*, 1780.
Vol. ii. Pp. 629–79.

9. *The Ancient British Drama. London, Edinburgh*, 1810. 8°. Vol. i.

10. Knight, *Pictorial Shakespeare. London*, 1839-43. 8°. Vol. vii. Pp. 239-55.

11. Simms, *Supplement to the Plays of W. Shakspeare. New York*, 1848. Second edition, 1855. Pp. 141-50.

12. Tyrrell, *Doubtful Plays*, &c. *London*, 1851. 8°. Pp. 81-96.

13. Hazlitt, W. C., *Supplementary Works*, &c. *London*, 1852. 8°. Pp. 299-317. Reprinted 1887.

14. Moltke, *Doubtful Plays*, &c. *Leipzig*, 1869. 16°. Pp. 195-218.

15. Collier, *Plays and Poems of Shakespeare. Maidenhead*, 1878. Very rare. I have not been able to see a copy.

16. Hopkinson, *Shakespeare's Doubtful Plays*. Vol. i. *London*, 1891. 8°.

III. TRANSLATIONS

1. Tieck, L., *Altenglisches Theater, oder Supplemente zum Shakespeare*. 2 Bde. *Berlin*, 1811. 8°.
Vol. i: German Translation of The Troublesome Reign of King John, George a Greene, Pericles. Vol. ii: Locrine, The Merry Devil of Edmonton, King Leir and his Daughters.

2. Tieck, L., *Shakespere's Vorschule. Leipzig*, 1823. 8°.
Translation of Arden of Feversham, Fair Em, The Birth of Merlin.

3. Döring, H. ⟨German translation of *Arden of Feversham*⟩, *Gotha*, 1833. 2nd edition, Erfurt, 1840.
Quoted by Warnke and Proescholdt: I have not seen a copy.

4. Tieck, L., *Vier Schauspiele von Shakspeare. Übersetzt von L. Tieck. Stuttgart und Tübingen*, 1836. 8°.
Translation of Edward III, Cromwell, Sir John Oldcastle, The London Prodigal (Der Londoner verlorne Sohn).

5. Ortlepp, Ernst, *Nachträge zu Shakspeare's Werken von Schlegel und Tieck*. 4 Bde. *Stuttgart*, 1840. 8°.
Contents: Vol. i, Der Londoner verlorne Sohn, Leben und Tod des Thomas Cromwell, Die Geburt des Merlin, Sir John Oldcastle, Ein Trauerspiel in Yorkshire; Vol. ii: Perikles Fürst von Tyrus, Eduard der Dritte, Der lustige Teufel von Edmonton, Lokrine; Vol. iii: Arden von Feversham, Vermischte Gedichte, &c.
These translations are based very largely on those of Tieck.

6. Hugo, François Victor ⟨French translation of pseudo-Shakespearean plays in supplement of⟩, *Oeuvres de William Shakespeare Traduits*, &c. Paris, 1859-67.

7. Moltke, M., *König Eduard der Dritte, Uebersetzt und mit einem Nachwort begleitet. Leipzig* (1875).
No. 65 of Reclam's *Universal-Bibliothek*.

8. Hagen, August, *Eduard der Dritte. Trauerspiel in fünf Aufzügen von William Shakespeare. Nach der Uebersetzung von Ludwig Tieck frei bearbeitet. Leipzig*, 1879.

9. Kuitert, G. B., *Meesterstukken onder Shakespeare's Pseudo-Drama's, vertaald en toegelicht door G. B. K. Leiden*, 1882.
Contains translation into Dutch of Arden of Feversham and A Yorkshire Tragedy, with commentary.

10. Mucedorus. *Übersetzt von L. Tieck*. 1893. 8°.
Discovered among Tieck's literary remains and published by Dr. J. Bolte.

IV. GENERAL CRITICISM

1. Baeske, Wilhelm. *Oldcastle-Falstaff in der Englischen Literatur bis zu Shakespeare. Berlin*, 1905.

2. Bayne, Rev. Ronald, Preface to *Arden of Feversham* in the *Temple Dramatists* Series. *London*, 1897.

3. BIERFREUND, DR. TH., *Palamon og Arcite. En Literaturhistorisk Undersøgeke som bidrag til Shakespearekritiken. København*, 1891.

4. BOAS, FREDERICK S., *The Works of Thomas Kyd, edited from the Original Texts with Introduction, Notes, and Facsimile. Oxford*, 1901.
Introduction, pp. lxxix, ff. (*Arden of Feversham*).

5. BOURGES, *Un drame du 16e siècle, Arden de Feversham.* In '*Parlement*', 28 Août, 1882. I have not seen this.

6. BOYLE, ROBERT, *Shakespeare und die beiden edlen Vettern. Eine metrisch-kritische Abhandlung. St. Petersburg*, 1880.

7. ——, *On Massinger and the Two Noble Kinsmen. Transactions New Shakspere Society*, 1880–5, pp. 371–99.

8. BROMILOW, A. H., *Arden of Feversham.*
Colburn's New Monthly Magazine 164 : 175.
I have not seen this.

9. BULLEN, A. H., *Arden of Feversham, London*, 1887.
Critical Introduction to the play.

10. ——, *The Works of Thomas Middleton. London*, 1885.
Introduction, pp. lxxxix–xc, for discussion of *The Puritan.*

11. CAPELL, EDWARD, *Prolusions, or Select Pieces of Ancient Poetry. London*, 1760.
Preface to *Edward III.*

12. CHASLES, PHILARET und F. GUIZOT, *William Shakespeare, sein Leben, seine Werke und seine Zeit. Leipzig.* 1855.
Pp. 336–43.
Summary of German opinion on the doubtful plays.

13. CLIFTON SHAKESPEARE SOCIETY. *Report of Meetings.*
January 23, 1886, *Locrine*; March 27, 1887, *The London Prodigal*; May 28, 1887, *Edward III.*

14. COLERIDGE, S. T., *Literary Remains. London*, 1836. Vol. ii, pp. 320–1.
The Two Noble Kinsmen.

15. COLLIER, J. PAYNE, *The History of English Dramatic Poetry to the Time of Shakespeare: and Annals of the Stage to the Restoration.* 3 vol. *London*, 1831.
Discussion of *A Yorkshire Tragedy* and *Arden of Feversham* in vol. iii, pp. 49–60, with other references.

16. ——, *King Edward III : A Historical Play by William Shakespeare. An Essay in Vindication of Shakespeare's Authorship of the Play. Maidenhead*, 1874.
Same article *Athenaeum*, No. 2422, p. 426, March 28, 1874.

17. COLLINS, J. CHURTON, *The Plays and Poems of Robert Greene, Edited with Introductions and Notes.* 2 volumes. *Oxford*, 1905. General Introduction, pp. 60–1, 64–7.
Mucedorus and *Locrine.*

18. CRAWFORD, CHARLES, *The Authorship of Arden of Feversham.* Jahrbuch der deutschen Shakespeare-Gesellschaft xxxix, pp. 74–86. Berlin, 1903.

19. ——, *Spenser, 'Locrine,' and 'Selimus'.* 9 Notes and Queries vii, pp. 61–3, 101–3, 142–4, 203–5, 261–3, 324–5, 384–6. 1901.

20. DANIEL, P. A. *Athenaeum*, No. 2710, October 4, 1879.
Note on '*Shakespeare's* (?) *Yorkshire Tragedy*, 1608'.

21. ——, *Athenaeum*, No. 3677, April 16, 1898.
Note on '*Locrine* and *Selimus*'.

22. DARLEY, G., *Works of Beaumont and Fletcher. London*, 1856. Introduction, p. xlii.
The Two Noble Kinsmen.

23. DELIUS, NICOLAUS, *Abhandlungen zu Shakspere. Neue Folge. Elberfeld,* 1888. Pp. 1-34: Die angebliche Shakspere-Fletcher'sche Autorschaft des Dramas *The Two Noble Kinsmen.*

24. —— *Pseudo-Shakespere'sche Dramen. Elberfeld,* 1854-74.
Vorreden to texts of *Edward III, Arden of Feversham, The Birth of Merlin, Mucedorus, Fair Em.*

25. DE QUINCEY, THOMAS, *Style and Rhetoric and other Papers.* Complete Works, vol. x. Edinburgh, 1862. P. 49, note. *The Two Noble Kinsmen.*

26. DONNE, C. E., *An Essay on the Tragedy of Arden of Feversham. London and Faversham,* 1873.

27. ELZE, KARL, *Notes on Elizabethan Dramatists. Halle,* 1880.
Brief mention and discussion of nine doubtful plays.

28. ——, *Nachträgliche Bemerkungen zu* ' MUCEDORUS ' *und* ' FAIR EM '. Jahrbuch der deutsch. Shakspere-Gesellschaft, xv, pp. 339-52. 1880.

29. ERBE, THEODOR, *Die Locrinesage und die Quellen des Pseudo-Shakespeareschen Locrine. Halle a. S.,* 1904.
FARMER. See MALONE.

30. FLEAY, FREDERICK GARD, *On the play called ' Edward the Third '. Academy,* April 25, 1874, pp. 462-3.

31. ——, *Mr. Hickson's Division of The Two Noble Kinsmen Confirmed by Metrical Tests.*
Transactions New Shakspere Society, 1874, pp. 61*-64*.

32. ——, *Shakespeare Manual. London,* 1876. Pp. 52, 56-7, 59, 172-4, 281-6, 303-6.

33. ——, *Chronicle History of the Life and Work of Wm. Shakespeare, Player, Poet, and Playmaker. London,* 1886, pp. 252-4, 282-3, 285-90, 291-6, 298-301, 302-5.

34. ——, *A Chronicle History of the London Stage* 1559-1642. *London,* 1890.

35. ——, *A Biographical Chronicle of the English Drama* 1559-1642. Two volumes. *London,* 1891.

36. FRIESEN, H. FREIHERR VON, *Flüchtige Bemerkungen über einige Stücke, welche Shakespeare zugeschrieben werden.* Jahrbuch d. deutsch. Sh.-Gesellschaft I, pp. 160-5. 1865.
Discusses *The Merry Devil of Edmonton* and *The Two Noble Kinsmen.*

37. ——, *Edward III. Angeblich ein Stück von Shakespeare.* Jahrbuch d. deutsch. Sh.-Gesellschaft II, pp. 64-89. 1867.

38. ——, *Zur Shakespeare-Literatur von* 1874. Jahrbuch d. deutsch. Sh.-Gesellschaft X, pp. 369-72. 1875.
Mucedorus and *Fair Em.*

39. FURNIVALL, FREDERICK J. *Transactions New Sh. Society* 1874, pp. 73-4.
Authenticity of *The Two Noble Kinsmen* defended.

40. ——, *Mr. Hickson's Division of* THE TWO NOBLE KINSMEN *confirmed by the Stopt-Line Test.* Transactions New Sh. Society 1874, pp. 64*-65*.

41. ——, *The Succession of Shakspere's Works and the Use of Metrical Tests in Settling It . . . being the Introduction to* PROF. GERVINUS'S ' *Commentaries on Shakspere*', *Translated by Miss Burnett. London,* 1874.
The Two Noble Kinsmen.

42. ——, *Forewords* (to Spalding's Letter on Shakespeare's Authorship of *The Two Noble Kinsmen*). New Sh. Society, 1876.
Shakespeare's Authorship denied.

43. ——, Introduction to the *Royal Shakspere,* 1894, pp. cviii-cxv.
Discussion of *The Two Noble Kinsmen, Edward III,* and *Sir Thomas More.* Revised from Introduction to the *Leopold Shakspere,* 1877.

44. ——, *Academy*, vol. xvii, p. 196, March 13, 1880.
A paragraph discussing the first attribution of *Edward III* to Shakespeare.

45. Greg, W. W., *On the Editions of 'Mucedorus'. A study of printers and compositors in the time of Shakespeare.* Jahrbuch d. deutsch. Sh.-Gesellschaft xl, pp. 95–107. 1904.

46. Halliwell-Phillips, J. O., *Outlines of the Life of Shakespeare.* 3rd Edition. *London,* 1883.
Oldcastle, pp. 162–3; *Yorkshire Tragedy,* 193–5; *The Two Noble Kinsmen,* 730–4.

47. Hazlitt, Wm., *Characters of Shakespear's Plays. London,* ed. 1906, pp. 256–62 (Doubtful Plays of Shakespear).
Essay on the Doubtful Plays.

48. ——, *Lectures on the Dramatic Literature of the Reign of Queen Elizabeth.* London, 1820.
Discussion of *The Merry Devil of Edmonton,* in Lecture V, near the end. (Ed. 1870, pp. 169–70.)

49. Herford, C. H., Preface to the Temple Edition of *The Two Noble Kinsmen,* London, 1897.

50. Hickson, Samuel, *The Shares of Shakspere and Fletcher in The Two Noble Kinsmen.* Westminster Review, xlvii, pp. 59–88. 1847. Reprinted in Transactions New Sh. Society, 1874, pp. 25*–61*.

51. Hopkinson, A. F., *Essays on Shakespeare's Doubtful Plays. London,* 1900.
Reprinted from his edition of the plays, 1891–5.

52. ——, Introduction to his edition of *Sir Thomas More.* For private circulation. London, 1902.

53. Horn, Franz, *Shakspeare's Schauspiele erläutert.* 5 Bde. *Leipzig,* 1823. Volume v, pp. 271–300.
Birth of Merlin, Fair Em, Merry Devil of Edmonton, George a Greene.

54. Knight, Charles, *Pictorial Edition of the Works of Shakespeare.* Supplementary (7th) volume. London, 1839–43.
Discussion of various doubtful plays.

55. Kuitert, G. B., *Meesterstukken onder Shakespeare's Pseudo-Drama's, vertaald en toegelicht door G. B. K. Leiden,* 1882.
Discussion of *Arden of Feversham* and *A Yorkshire Tragedy.*

56. Lamb, Charles, *Specimens of English Dramatic Poets who lived about the time of Shakespeare. With Notes.* Two vols. *London,* 1835. Vol. i, note p. 59.
The Merry Devil of Edmonton and *Two Noble Kinsmen.*

57. Leuschner, Bruno, *Über das Verhältnis von The Two Noble Kinsmen zu Chaucer's Knightes Tale.* Inaug. Diss. Halle a. S., 1903.

58. Liebau, Dr. Gustav, *König Eduard III. von England und die Gräfin von Salisbury, dargestellt in ihren Beziehungen nach Geschichte, Sage und Dichtung, unter eingehender Berücksichtigung des pseudo-shakespeare'schen Schauspiels, 'The Raigne of King Edward the Third.' Berlin.* 1900.

59. Littledale, Harold, Introduction to *The Two Noble Kinsmen,* Published for The New Shakspere Society. London, 1885.

60. Malone, Edmond, *Supplement to the Edition of Shakspeare's Plays Published in* 1778 . . . *London,* 1780.
Vol. ii. Notes by Malone, Steevens, Percy, &c., to *Pericles, Locrine, Oldcastle, Cromwell, The London Prodigal, The Puritan, A Yorkshire Tragedy.*

61. Margerison, Samuel, *The first volume of the Registers of the parish church of Calverley. Bradford,* 1880. 8°.
Records concerning characters in *A Yorkshire Tragedy.*

62. MASON, MONCK, *Comments*, &c., 1798.
The Two Noble Kinsmen.

63. MORGAN, A., *Pseudo-Shakespearean Plays.* The Catholic World, lv, 203 ff, 397 ff.
I have been unable to see these articles.
PERCY. See MALONE.

64. QUARTERLY REVIEW, 134, p. 249, 1873.
A brief anonymous discussion of *The Two Noble Kinsmen* in an article called *Chaucer and Shakespeare.*

65. RETROSPECTIVE REVIEW, *The Yorkshire Tragedy.* Vol. ix, pp. 238–50. 1824.
An anonymous criticism of the play.

66. ROLFE, W. J., Introduction to the *Friendly Edition* of *The Two Noble Kinsmen.* New York, 1891.

67. SACHS, R., *Die Shakespeare zugeschriebenen zweifelhaften Stücke.* Jahrbuch d. deutsch. Sh.-Gesellschaft xxvii, pp. 135–99. 1892.

68. SAINTSBURY, G., *A History of Elizabethan Literature.* London, 1887. Pp. 423–5.
List of doubtful plays with brief comments.

69. SARRAZIN, GREGOR, *Thomas Kyd und sein Kreis. Eine litterar-historische Untersuchung. Berlin,* 1892. 8°. Pp. 73, 74.
Discussion of the authorship of *Arden of Feversham.*

70. SCHICK, J., *The Spanish Tragedy . . . Edited with a Preface, Notes and Glossary. London,* 1898. 2nd Edition, 1907.
Discussion of the source of *Faire Em,* pp. xxv, xxvi.

71. SCHLEGEL, A. W., *A Course of Lectures on Dramatic Art and Literature. Translated from the original German by John Black.* In two volumes. 2nd Ed. London, 1840. Vol. ii, pp. 256–8.

72. SHELLEY, P. B., *Prose Works.* London, 1888. Vol. ii, p. 235.
Letter to Mrs. Shelley, discussing *The Two Noble Kinsmen.*

73. SIMPSON, RICHARD, *Are there any extant MS. in Shakespeare's Handwriting?* 4 Notes and Queries viii, pp. 1 ff. 1871.
Sir Thomas More.

74.——, *On some Plays Attributed to Shakespeare.* Transactions New Sh. Society, 1875–6, pp. 155 ff.
List of apocryphal plays with special discussion of *Mucedorus* and *Fair Em.*

75. ——, *Academy,* vol. ix, pp. 401–2. April 29, 1876.
A review of Delius's edition of *Mucedorus.*

76. ——, *The School of Shakespeare.* London, 1878. Vol. ii, pp. 237 ff.
Discussion of *Fair Em.*

77. SKEAT, REV. W. W., *The Two Noble Kinsmen.* Cambridge, 1875.
Introduction.

78. SMITH, G. C. MOORE, Preface to *Edward the Third* in the *Temple Dramatists* Series. London, 1897.

79. SOFFÉ, EMIL, *Ist Mucedorus ein Schauspiel Shakspere's? Brünn,* 1887 (Programme, 13 pp.).

80. S(PALDING), W., *A Letter on Shakespeare's Authorship of* THE TWO NOBLE KINSMEN . . . *Edinburgh,* 1833. 8°.
Reprinted by the New Shakspere Society, 1876.

81. ——, *Recent Shakspearian Literature.* Edinburgh Review lxxi, 1840, pp. 467–74.
Doubtful plays discussed.

82. SPEDDING, JAMES, *Shakespeare's Handwriting.* 4 Notes and Queries x, 227. September 21, 1872.
Sir Thomas More.

83. ——, *Reviews and Discussions, Literary, Political, and Historical, not relating to Bacon. London,* 1879. 8°.
'XV. On a Question concerning a Supposed Specimen of Shakespeare's Handwriting.' Criticism and conjectural emendations to the text of *Sir Thomas More.*

STEEVENS. See MALONE.

84. STREIT, WILLY, *The Life and Death of Thomas Lord Cromwell, eine literar-historische Untersuchung. Jena, Blankenhaim Thür,* 1904.
Dissertation.

85. SWINBURNE, A. C., *On the Historical Play of* KING EDWARD III. Gentleman's Magazine N. S. xxiii, pp. 170 ff., 330 ff.
Same article in *A Study of Shakespeare,* 3rd ed. London, 1895. With other matter.

86. SYMONDS, JOHN ADDINGTON, *Shakspere's Predecessors in the English Drama.* New edition, London, 1900. Pp. 296 ff., 332–4, 350–66.

87. TEETGEN, ALEXANDER, *Shakespeare's 'King Edward the Third', absurdly called, and scandalously treated as a 'Doubtful Play'; an Indignation Pamphlet . . . London,* 1875.

88. TIECK, L. Prefaces to his translations of the doubtful plays. 1811–36. Cf. III. 1, 2, 4.

89. TYRRELL, H., *The Doubtful Plays of Shakspere. London,* 1851.
Introductions to the text of the various plays.

90. ULRICI, DR. HERMANN, *Über Shakspere's dramatische Kunst und sein Verhältnis zu Calderon und Göthe.* Halle, 1839. Pp. 470–502.
Third edition, enlarged, translated by L. Dora Schmitz, London, 1876. Book vii, pp. 366–409.

91. VINCKE, GISBERT FREIHERR VON, *Die zweifelhaften Stücke Shakespeare's.* Jahrbuch d. deutsch. Sh.-Gesellschaft VIII, 368–76. 1873.

92. ——, *König Eduard III.—ein bühnenstück?* Jahrbuch d. deutsch. Sh.-Gesellschaft XIV, pp. 304–18. 1879.

93. WAGNER, WILHELM, *Ueber und zu Mucedorus.* Jahrbuch d. deutsch. Sh.-Gesellschaft XI, pp. 59–69. 1876.

94. ——, *Neue Conjecturen zum Mucedorus.*
Ibid. XIV, pp. 274–84. 1879.

95. WALKER, HUGH, Preface to *The Merry Devil of Edmonton* in the *Temple Dramatists* Series. London, 1897.

96. WALKER, SIDNEY, *Critical Examination of the Text of Shakespeare. London,* 1860.
The Two Noble Kinsmen.

97. WARD, A. W., *A History of English Dramatic Literature to the Death of Queen Anne.* 2nd edition. *London,* 1899. Vol. ii, pp. 209–45.
Discussion of the various doubtful plays.

98. WARNKE and PROESCHOLDT. Prefaces to editions of *Mucedorus, Fair Em, The Merry Devil of Edmonton, King Edward III, The Birth of Merlin,* and *Arden of Feversham.* Halle, 1878–88.

V. EARLY NOTICES, SOURCES, ANALOGUES, ETC.

(a) NOTICES IN CONTEMPORARY DOCUMENTS

1. *A Transcript of the Registers of the Company of Stationers of London,* 1554–1640. *By* EDWARD ARBER. Four volumes. *Privately Printed. London,* 1875–7.
Contains licensing notices of most of the plays.

2. *Extracts from the accounts of the Revels at Court, in the reign of Queen Elizabeth and James I.* Edited for the *Shakespeare Society* by PETER CUNNINGHAM. *London,* 1842.
Record of Court presentation of THE MERRY DEVIL OF EDMONTON (p. xlv) and other information.

3. *The Diary of Philip Henslowe from* 1591 *to* 1609. Edited for the *Shakespeare Society* by J. PAYNE COLLIER. *London*, 1845.
Record of the authors of THE FIRST PART OF SIR JOHN OLDCASTLE (p. 158, October 16, 1599) and other information.

(*b*) EARLY CATALOGUES OF PLAYS

1. *An exact and perfect Catalogue of all the Plaies that were ever printed ; together with all the Authors Names ; and what are Comedies, Histories, Interludes, Masks, Pastorels, Tragedies* . . . [Printed at the end of *The Old Law*, 1656].
This list assigns to Shakespeare : THE ARRAIGNMENT OF PARIS ; THE CHANCES ; CROMWELL'S HISTORIE ; HOFFMAN ; HIERONIMO, both parts ; JOHN K. OF ENGLAND, both parts ; LONDON PRODIGALL ; MERRY DIVELL OF EDMOND. ; MUCIDORUS ; PURITAN WIDOW ; PYROCLES PRINCE OF TYRE ; ROMAN ACTOR ; TWO NOBLE KINSMEN ; TAMING OF A SHREW ; TRICK TO CATCH THE OLD ONE ; YORKSHIRE TRAGEDIE.

2. *An exact and perfect Catalogue of all Playes that are Printed* . . . [Affixed to Th. Goff's *Careless Shepherdess*, 1656].
Assigns to Shakespeare, besides the usual doubtful plays, EDWARD II, EDWARD III, and EDWARD IV.

3. FRANCIS KIRKMAN, *A True, Perfect, and exact Catalogue of all the Comedies, Tragedies . . . that were ever yet printed and published, till this present year* 1661.
Assigns to Shakespeare : THE ARRAIGNMENT OF PARIS ; CROMWELL'S HISTORY ; JOHN KING OF ENGLAND [two parts, the old play] ; LEIR AND HIS DAUGHTERS [the old play] ; LONDON PRODIGAL ; MERRY DIVEL OF EDMONTON ; MUCIDORUS ; OLD CASTLES LIFE AND DEATH ; PURITAN WIDOW ; YORKSHIRE TRAGEDY.
2nd edition, 1671.

4. *An Exact Catalogue of All the Comedies, Tragedies, Tragi-Comedies, Opera's, Masks, Pastorals, and Interludes That were ever yet Printed and Published, till this present year* 1680. *Oxon, Printed by L. Lichfield, Printer to the University, for Nicholas Cox, Anno Dom.*, 1680.
Assigns to Shakespeare: ARRAIGNMENT OF PARIS ; BIRTH OF MERLIN (*Shakespear and Rowley*) ; CROMWEL'S HISTORY ; YORKSHIRE TRAGEDY.
Pages 6–14, C–W in the alphabetical list of plays, are missing from the Bodleian copy (Wood 26 C).

5. PHILLIPS, EDWARD, *Theatrum Poetarum, or a Compleat Collection of the Poets, Especially the most Eminent of all Ages . . . With some Observations and Reflections upon many of them, particularly those of our own Nation . . . London*, 1675.
Part II, p. 162, ascribes FAIR EMME to Robert Green. Part II, p. 228, ascribes THE PINNER OF WAKEFIELD to John Heywood (the writer of interludes).

6. LANGBAINE, GERARD, *A New Catalogue of English Plays . . . London, Printed for N. Cox* . . . 1688.
Assigns to Shakespeare : CROMWELL'S HISTORY ; JOHN K. OF ENGLAND, 2 pts. ; LOCRINE'S TRAGEDY ; LONDON PRODIGAL ; OLD-CASTLE ; PURITAN WIDOW ; YORKSHIRE TRAGEDY ; BIRTH OF MERLIN.

7. LANGBAINE–GILDON. *The Lives and Characters of the English Dramatick Poets. Also an Exact Account of all the Plays that were ever yet Printed in the English Tongue . . . with Remarks and Observations on most of the said Plays. First begun by Mr. Langbain, improv'd and continued down to this Time, by a Careful Hand* ⟨Ch. Gildon⟩. *London* ⟨1698⟩, pp. 126–9, 157, 159, 160, &c.
Ascribes to Shakespeare : ARRAIGNMENT OF PARIS ⟨on Kirkman's authority, but doubtingly⟩; YORKSHIRE TRAGEDY ; PURITAN ; OLDCASTLE ; LONDON PRODIGAL ; LOCRINE ; JOHN K. OF ENGLAND, HIS TROUBLESOME REIGN *in two parts ;* CROMWELL ; BIRTH OF MERLIN.
Many other catalogues repeat these attributions ; e. g.,

8. *A True and Exact Catalogue Of all the Plays That were ever yet Printed in the English Tongue. . . continued down to October*, 1713. *Printed for* W. MEARS *at the Lamb without Temple-bar*, 1713.

9. *A Compleat Catalogue Of all the Plays, &c. London: Printed for W. Mears . . .* 1719. Another edition 1726.

(*c*) WORKS CONTAINING SOURCES OF THE PLOT, ANALOGUES, ETC.

1. EVANS ⟨Thomas⟩, *Old Ballads, Historical and Narrative, with Some of Modern Date.* 2 vol. *London,* 1777. 8°.
Robin Hood and the pinder of Wakefield, i, 97–101. *King Edward III and the fair countess of Salisbury,* i, 270–6. *The story of Ill May-day* (Illustrating SIR THOMAS MORE), ii, 41–7. *The complaint and lamentation of mistresse Arden of Feversham.*

2. FOX, JOHN, *Acts and Monuments of Matters Most Special and Memorable, Happening in the Church . . .*
Containing the source of THOMAS LORD CROMWELL and perhaps of SIR JOHN OLDCASTLE.

3. GEOFFREY OF MONMOUTH'S *Histories of the Kings of Britain.* Translated by Sebastian Evans, LL.D., London, 1903.
Source of LOCRINE: Book II, ch. 1–5.
Source of THE BIRTH OF MERLIN: Book VI, ch. 17–19; Book VIII, ch. 10–15.

4. HALL, *Chronicle,* 1548, fol. lix (*b*).
Source of SIR THOMAS MORE.

5. HOLINSHED'S *Chronicles of England, Scotland, and Ireland.* In six volumes. London, 1808.
Source of ARDEN OF FEVERSHAM, iii, 1024–30.
Source of EDWARD III (in part) ii, 604 ff., and v, 376–8, 608. For detailed citation of the pertinent passages in Holinshed, cf. Warnke and Proescholdt's Introduction x–xxi.

6. PAINTER, WILLIAM, *The Palace of Pleasure. Done into English by* W., P. ed. Jacobs, 1890.
Novel Forty-six: *A King of England loved the daughter of one of his noble men, which was Countesse of Salesburie . . .*
The source, in part, of EDWARD III.

7. PEELE, GEORGE, *Merrie conceited Jests of George Peele, Gent. Sometimes Student in Oxford. . . . London,* 1607. [Reprinted Bullen, *Peele's Works,* ii.]
The second and eleventh jests (Bullen ii, pp. 379–83, 397–9) were used by the author of THE PURITAN.

8. ROXBURGHE BALLADS. *Ancient Songs and Ballads: Written on Various Subjects, and Printed between the years MDLX and MDCC. . . . Arranged and Bound in the Year* 1774.
Contains: *Complaint and lamentation of Mistresse Arden of Feversham . . .* [Reprinted by Evans] and *The Wandring Prince and Princess or Musidorus and Amadine . . .* Vol. ii, pp. 490–1.

9. STOW, JOHN. *Annales or a Generall Chronicle of England. Begun by* J. S. *Continued and Augmented . . . unto the end of this present yeare,* 1631. *By Edmund Howes.*
Account of Arden's murder, p. 605, anno 1551.
Account of the Calverly murders, anno 1605.

10. YVER, JAQUES. *Le Prin-Temps d'Yver: contenant cinq Histoires, Discovrves par cinq Iournees, en vne noble compagnie, au Chasteau du Prin-temps: Par Iaques Yver, seigneur de Plaisance & de la Bigottrie gentil-homme Poicteuin. Veu et corrigé de nouveau. A Roven, Chez Pierre Calles . . .* 1599.
This edition is in the Bodleian, but is certainly not the first. An English translation by H⟨enry⟩ W⟨otton⟩ appeared in 1578 with the title: *A Courtlie controuersie of Cupids Cautels: Conteyning fiue Tragicall Histories, very pithie, pleasant, pitiful, and profitable: Discoursed vppon wyth Argumentes of Loue, by three Gentlemen and two Gentlewomen, entermeddled with diuers delicate Sonets and Rithmes, exceeding delightfull to refresh the yrkesomnesse of tedious tyme. Translated out of French as neare as our English phrase will permit, by H. W., Gentleman. At London . . . Anno* 1578.
The William the Conqueror part of FAIR EM is taken, with considerable alterations, from the fourth tale in this book.

VI. INDEX TO THE BIBLIOGRAPHY OF EACH PLAY

www.ingramcontent.com/pod-product-compliance
Lightning Source LLC
Chambersburg PA
CBHW032031080426
42733CB00006B/53

* 9 7 8 0 9 7 4 7 6 2 3 2 6 *